NORTH CAROLINA 1810 CENSUS INDEX

Compiled by

Dora Wilson Smith

Heritage House
THOMSON, ILLINOIS 61285

Notice

In many older books, foxing (or discoloration) occurs and, in some instances, print lightens with wear and age. Reprinted books, such as this, often duplicate these flaws, notwithstanding efforts to reduce or eliminate them. The pages of this reprint have been digitally enhanced and, where possible, the flaws eliminated in order to provide clarity of content and a pleasant reading experience.

North Carolina 1810 Census Index

Copyright © 1977, Heritage House

Originally published
Thomson, Illinois
1977

Reprinted by:

Janaway Publishing, Inc.
732 Kelsey Ct.
Santa Maria, California 93454
(805) 925-1038
www.janawaygenealogy.com

2014

Library of Congress Catalog Card Number: 77-79657

ISBN: 978-1-59641-172-2

Reprinted with the kind permission of Pat Gooldy,
Ye Olde Genealogie Shoppe,
Indianapolis, Indiana

Made in the United States of America

PREFACE

On the last page of most counties the census taker has provided a variety of information. In some cases it is only the population total and the census taker's name. Others have provided manufacturing statistics. Daniel Gallent in Mecklenburg County noted that even though there were 12 stills producing 261,458 gallons of whiskey and brandy each year, it "don't more than half supply" their population of 14,270, an average comsumption of 23 gallons.

Some census takers requested additional payment because of hardships or unusual circumstances in enumerating the county. The standard salary was $1.00 for every 100 persons counted.

Ashe County - population, 3,094. Saml. Cox.

Beaufort County - population, 7,203. Wm. Vines, 10 November 1810.

Bertie County - population, 11,218. Blady Ashburn, 4 December 1810.

Bladen County - free col'd persons, 114; slaves 1,985; total population, 5,666. 63,066 yds. of woolen & cotton homespun average price 40 per yd. Robert Lytle.

Buncombe County - Gentlemen: The reason I beg leave to offer to you to be allowed an Extra Allowance for Taking the Census are as follow to wit-- 1st The great Extent of Territory which that county is composed of, 2nd The many Large mountains which Divide Small Settlements apart and the Dispersed situation of the Inhabitants in the mountains all of which has a tendency to make the Business Verry Tedious.
                              Phillip Brittain

Brunswick County - Fredk Sullivan.
    2 Rice pounding mills by water
    4 Rice picker machines by horses or oxen
    1 Cotton machine by water
    1 Still yealding 24 galls annually valued at $15,824.00
28,785 yds homespun Valued at 50 cts per yd   14,392.50
1,152 sides of leather valued at $1.50 per side   1,728.00

Burke County - population, 11,007. E. Sharp, 5 December 1810.
Number of looms worked and made use of
    542 No. of looms
77,025 No. of yards made of this quantity woolen
    7,700 yards at 100 cents per yard $ 7,700
    69,325 yards of this quantity cotton and linen at 50 cts   27,730
Number of stills worked and made use of
    100 No of stills
20,400 No. of gallons of spirits at 50 cents per gallon   10,200
Number of iron works
    6 No. of bloomeries & forges
234,800 Quantity of iron made at $6.25 per 100 lbs   15,260
25,200 Quantity of iron manufactured at 20 cents per lb   5,040
Number of tanners
    3 No. of taning yards
1,200 Quantity of hides tanned at $4.00 per hide   4,800

Cabarrus County - J. P. Young, 8 November 1810.
66 stills distilling 20,225 gallons
257 looms making 37,550 yds plain cloth, 2010 mixed
  2 tanyards tanning 800 hides
  1 hatter shop making 700 fine hats, 3000 corse

Camden County - William T. Perkins, 28 November 1810.
  420 Looms
  1,104 Linen, Woolen and Cotton Wheels

25,800 yds cotton & woolen at 75 cents per yd	$10,350
51,612 yds linen at 50 cents per yd	25,806
25,800 yds coarse linen at 20 cents per yd	12,900
1,227 hides at $4	4,908
13,126 gallons brandy at 75 cents per gall	9,844

Carteret County - Elijah Whitehurst.
  106 Indians not taxed
   11 Wind grist mills
    4 Saw Jins, 66 Saws
    4 Saw Mills
    2 Turpentine stills
   14 Blacksmith forges
  126 looms, 238 woolen wheels, 163 linnen wheels, (210 families) - 80,000 yards.

Chatham County - population, 12,980. Thos. Waddill, 21 December 1810.

Chowan County - population, 6,538. Edmund Hoskins, 13 February 1811.

Columbus County - population, 3,148. John White, 1 December 1810.

Cumberland County - population of Fayetteville - 1,992, population of remainder of county - 9,382. Cun. Buis, 10 January 1811.

Currituck County - population, 7,322. James Etheridge, 7 November 1810.

Edgecombe County - population, 12,433. Isaac Norfleet, 10 December 1810.

Franklin County - population 10,230. Will Brickell, 26 November 1810.
173,288 yards of Domestick Manufactures, rated at 33-1/2 cents p yard
  550 looms with three spinning machines at 40 spindles each
  100 stills
  29,725 spirits (brandy) in one year at 70 cents p g

Gentlemen--Although the district allotted to me be small and the total number of persons comparatively few, with others, yet to me was an arduous task, except out the County Town considerable scattered--and some weeks did not obtain more than twenty-five heads of families. I had also to combat and remove as much in my power the ignorant prejudices of people to obtain the knowledge wished by the General Government as to the Domestick Manufactures, looms, stills, spirits and I pray you to take into consideration these statements and make me that extra allowance you may be pleased to think my labour merits.

Gates County - population, 2,790. Joseph Reddick, Jr.

Granville County - population, 15,576. Willis Lewis.

Guilford County - Joseph Davis.

11 Taneries	24,775 leather	? 9,995
226 Distileries	68,978 gallons of spirits	36,167
2 Oil mills	1,600 gallons of oil	1,560
22 Spining Machines	529 spindles	
3 Fuling Mills	5,426 yards fulled	5,426
1103 Looms	3,148,487 yards woven	7,350
22 Jinneys		
8 Hatters	1,750 hats	4,350
5 ? smiths	690 barrels	83,475
1 Coppersmiths	66 stills	4,000
2 Powder mills	400 lbs powder	300

The manufacturing list consumed more of my time and was considerable more trouble than that of the sencus and I flatter myself that when the allowance is to be made I shall be sufficiently compensated for my trouble.

Halifax County - Rhesa Read, 26 December 1810.
$86,108 value of yards of woolen linen at 40 cts yd.
24,632 value of spirits distilled at 80 ct per gallon.

Haywood County - population - 384 families with 2,780 people.
Thomas D. Love, 6 November 1810.

Altho the number (of people) is small yet they are extended over a Large Scope of Territory, ... within which limits sundry settlements are formed which lye detached from the principal Settlements of said County, from twelve to fifteen and far as Eighteen Miles. Owing to the huge piles of mountains which are interspersed throughout the whole of this County, for Instance the settlements on the Caney Fork Tuckasigah river lyes from fifteen to eighteen miles from any other inhavitants and consists of only 8 or 10 families. The Settlement on Oconslusty lyes nearly the same distance from any other inhabitants and about 12 or 15 families. The Settlements on Fever Creek and the east fork of Pigeon also Lye very remote from the Body of the County, and under those circumstances I claim such additional allowance as may be covered by the Act of Congress.

In conformity with the request of Congress, I have collected the best information of the nature and extent of household manufactures, that the Nature of the case would admit. The request created jealousies in the minds of a Great Number of the people, Consequently no Great reliance can be placed on the same.

632	No. of Spining wheels	
153	No. of Flax Brakes	
286	No. of looms	
4,200	No. of yards of cotton & linen	$1,680
2,000	No. of yards of cotton & woolen	800
6,400	No. of yards of cotton	1,500
4,500	No. of yards of linen	1,500
21	No. of distilleries	
4,300	No. of gallons distilled	2,150
1	No. of tanneries	
220	No. of hides tanned	440
1	No. of Powder Mills	
200	Quantity of powder made	100

In making out the within list in Alphabetical order I had intended to leave a space between each letter, but having by some means Omited severall names, particularly of those under the letter of which is the cause of four or five names in that letter being so crowded, the thing being new to me, and the country a new one also. I have not been able to draw to my assistance the aid of any Experienced person, Therefore I hope any errors or want of accuracy will be overlooked.

Hertford County - population 6,052. Jas. Jones, 12 February 1811.

Hyde County - population 6,110. Thomas Jordan, 1 January 1811.

With regard to the several requisites respecting manufactories I having perfect knowledge of this county as it is the place of my nativity. Only observe that with very few exceptions every Household employs a common weaving loom, carder, and almost without exception every family tans their own leather which is consumed in the county, that no machines of a peculiar kind is used or belongs in the county, the materials for clothing is raised and consumed by the Inhabitants. The result of Inquiries respecting the Quantity is as Near as may be 26 yards for each person which would amount to 158,860 yards. Not a simgle machine point out in the instruction is used in this county.

Iredell County - population 10,972. (no signature)

Johnston County - Wm. W. Bryan, 7 January 1811.
73,187 yards of common cloth; value, 35 to 40 cents pr yard.
37,061 yards of cotton & wool mixed; value from 40 to 50 cents pr yard
   582 looms, with the necessary gear
     1 whiskey distillery averaging 175 barrels pr year; value from 80 to 100 cents pr gallon
     5 cotton gins
     1 set of iron works with 2 forges, at present out of repair and not used.

Jones County
   370 looms weaving 57,671 yards cloth worth 50 cents pr yd.
    16 Brandy stills distilling 1444 gals spirits worth 100 per gallon
     2 Turpentine stills distilling 5000 gals of spirits Turpentine per ann worth 200 cts per gal.

Martin County - population 5,987. John Smithwick.

Mecklenburg County - population 14,270. Daniel Gallent.
    62 Stills making yearly 261,458 gallons of whiskey and brandy and from the Best Information dont more than half supply the county.   at 75 cts $19,942
     5 Tanyards. With what the people doe themself Supplys the County in leather.   5,100
     7 Hatter Shops   4,450
    21 Water Mills & Manufactures 4057 berrels of flower worth about $5 p berrel   20,295
     2 fulling Mills & fulls about 700 yds.   700
     1 Oil Mill about 40 gallons of Oil worth 1 Doller p Gallon   40
    79 Blacksmith shops takes to doe the work of the county
191,264 yards of every kind of home made cloth average price 40 cents   76,505

103 Cotten Gins and picks as given in 3512 bags of cotton. Each bag about 250 wt and $25 a bag amounting to in dollars and all sent to market principally Charleston, S. Carolina   7,400
17 S----- presses to press cotten

Montgomery County - population 8,470. Edmund DeBerry, 15 November 1810.

Moore County - population 6,367. Archd. McNeill.

Nash County - population 7,282. Francis Drake.

Northampton County - population 13,082. Matthew S. Lockart, 25 December 1810.

Onslow County - population 6,669. Banester Lester, 3 January 1811.

Orange County - Charles Christmas and Hugh Mulhollan, 7 January 1811.

Pasquotank County - population, 7,674. Tho. Wooday.

Perquimans County - Josiah Townsend.
119 - free persons of colour
3916 - whole number of whites
4052 - total of all descriptions

Person County - population 6,676. Laurance Van Hook, 4 January 1811.

Randolph County - Michael Harvey, 15 November 1810.

Richmond County - population 6,695. J. McAlester, Jr.
```
    540 - No. of Weaving Looms
  1,220 - No. of Spinning Wheels
  2,185 - yards of woolen cloth at $2 p yd            $ 4,370
111,279 - yards of cotton cloth at 50 cts p yd         4,151.16
 13,111 - yards of mixed wool & cotton at 60 cts p yd  7,866.60
 13,491 - gallons of spirits at 1.00 p gal            13,491
      3 - No. of distilleries
     30 - No. of cotten picking machines.
```

Robeson County - population 7,528. Gilbert Sellers, 17 December 1810.
```
     2 - Tanneries valued at                    $ 3,000
     9 - Cotton Machines
   108 - Stills - 6,834 gallons valued at        5,467.20
 1,457 - Spinning wheels
   666 - Looms
 3,522 - Yds of wool valued at $1 per yd         3,522
42,824 - Yds of linen valued at 35 cts per yd   24,984.40
18,740 - Mixtures valued at 50 cts per yd        9,370
 1,133 - Flax valued at 50 cts per yd              566.50
```

Rutherford County - Leonard Daniel, December 1810.
```
2,263 - free white males under 10 years of age
  955 - of 10 and under 16
1,032 - of 16 and under 26
  984 - of 26 and under 45
  574 - of 45 and upwards
```

viii

```
 2,149 - free white females under 10 years of age
   891 - of 10 and under 16
 1,015 - of 16 and under 26
   910 - of 26 and under 45
   542 - of 45 and upwards

    62 - all other free persons (Indians excepted)
 1,744 - slaves
13,221 - of whom. 41 free whites, 3 free persons of color and 43
         slaves are residents of the town of Rutherford.
```

```
    1 - iron works consisting of a forge, one hammer, two
        blooming fires, a Rolling Mill, a Machine to cut
        Nails, an air furnace to heat the Iron to be Roled
        computed annually to manufacture 45 tons of Iron
        valued at $125 per ton amounting to $5624 exclusive
        of the profits arising from the Nail factory.
        Lately erected.                                           $ 5,625
    5 - public tan yards having tanned 3,360 hydes valued
        at $3 each Hyde                                            10,080
  236 - stills distilling 42,327 gallons at 50 cts                 21,313
    3 - Hatter shops manufacturing 500 hats at $4 each              2,000
   28 - Cotton Saw Gins having picked and cleaned and
        packed 105,350 weight of cotton fit for market
        at 12 cts.                                                  2,793
1,147 - looms having woven 139,611 yards of home spun
        woolen cotton and flaxen cloth including mixtures
        of either averaging 50 cts p yd                            69,305
```

The inhabitants being scattered over a county upwards of sixty miles in length and nearly thirty in width encompassing Enumerable Lofty Mountains amongst which are a part of the Blue Ridge, Sugar Loaf Mountain, Pacatel Mountain, Tryon Mountain, White Oak Mountain, Biggerstaff Mountain, Flin Hill Mountain, Cane Creek Mountain, and Broad River Mountain and to add to the difficulty a false report having by some means gone abroad that every species of Manufactories if given in were to be taxed which prevented a number of the good citizens from coming forward at public places and public times to make return of their families and even caused some to refuse to give in and others to Endeavor to avoid me and my assistant which rendered it very difficult for me to procure the numbers of their families.

Stokes County - Ge Tono, 24 December 1810.
Certifications are given by Justices of the Peace, Jest John, Jr. and Wm. Sobro, that copies of the census were posted at the tavern of Jeremiah Gibson in Germantown and at the tavern in Salem.

Surry County - Chas. Taliaferro.
```
    5 - Blumeryes annually making 156 tons of iron woth 120 p ton
  117 - Fixt Distilleryes annually making 41,025 gallons of spirits
        50 cts pr gallon
  904 - Looms annually weaving 142,206 yds of cotton and lining cloth
        including a mixture of each worth 50 cts p yd
    1 - Fuling mill annually fulling 1700 yds of cloth which he says
        is worth $1 p yd and further states that he believes that two
        thirds of the whole is made in this county
    1 - Powder Mill annually making 200 lbs powder worth 75 cents per
        pound.
```

2 - Tanneryes annually Taning 550 hides worth 2200 after tand and drest.
   4 - Jannyes 25 spindles Each
   8 - cotton Picking machines containing 255 saws in the whole
   1 - wash machine

Tyrrell County - Moses E. Cator.
22,346 - yards linen cloth
26,064 - yards cotton cloth
<u>10,114</u> - yards wollen cloth
58,524 - total yards at 50 cts per yard

   339 - looms
 1,614 - sides of leather at $2 each
 3,123 - Brandey distilled at 75 Cents p gallon
 1,000 - gallons of Wine at 85 cents per gallon
 6,500 - gallons of Hunney at 62-1/2 cents per gallon
     2 - Cotton machinery.

Note, the above cloth brandey etc. I took down from Every Seperate familey where I took their number or Censes which I Believe is as Correct as the people could Recolect. The Wine and Hunney I did not take in the above maner as I had taken a good many familyes before I made such inquiry for I had no Ideah of their being so much made in the County. But after I discovered that there was so much made, I used every Effort to ascertain the Quantity which I do believe the above is nearly Correct.

Warren County - Halcott Terrell, 26 November 1810. Total population, 11,004, free people of colour 231, slaves 6,282. Two copies of the census were put at the Court House and at George Nicholsons.

Washington County - population 3,464. James M. Count.

Wayne County - Philip Hooks, 1 September 1810.
 2,737 - free white males
 2,888 - free white females
   111 - free persons except Indians not taxes.
 2,753 - slaves

Wilkes County - population 9,054. R. Allen, 22 December 1810.

CENSUS INDEX INSTRUCTIONS

The purpose of the NORTH CAROLINA 1810 CENSUS INDEX is to put all the heads of families that were enumerated in North Carolina in one alphabetical sequence. The names were copied from the National Archives microfilm M 33-80, 81, 82, 83, 84, and 85.

The original census books were also used at the National Archives, Washington, D.C., to read the names that were illegible on the microfilmed copy. These books are closed to public inspection because of their fragile condition. On a few pages the last name at the bottom of the page has disappeared. We are grateful to James D. Walker of the National Archives for allowing us to use the original census books to prepare this index.

The information contained in this index includes:

1. The head of householder's name,
2. The abbreviated county of residence, and
3. The census page number where the name can be found.

A. Head of Householder's Name

The spelling of the names in the index is the same as on the original census to the best of our ability. Some surnames are listed under several spellings. No attempt has been made to cross-index the various spellings because of the volume.

The following hints should be kept in mind when trying to locate all the various spellings of a surname.

1. Substitution of vowels (Stansel and Stansul)
2. Substitution of consonants (Stancill and Stansil)
3. Dropping consonants (Stallings and Stallins)
4. Dropping vowels (Baily and Bailey, Sparks and Sparkes)
5. Double letters (Staling and Stalling)
6. Plural names (Spring and Springs)

B. County of Residence

Four counties are not included in this index. The census manuscripts for these counties are missing.

Craven
Greene
New Hanover
Wake

Each county's name has been abbreviated in the index. The following table gives the abbreviation and the full name of the county.

Ans	Anson	Fra	Franklin	Ons	Onslow
Ash	Ashe	Gat	Gates	Ora	Orange
Bft	Beaufort	Glf	Guilford	Pas	Pasquotank
Bla	Bladen	Grn	Granville	Prq	Perquimans
Brt	Bertie	Hal	Halifax	Per	Person
Bru	Brunswick	Hay	Haywood	Pit	Pitt
Bun	Buncombe	Hrt	Hertford	Ran	Randolph
Bur	Burke	Hyd	Hyde	Rch	Richmond
Cab	Cabarrus	Ire	Iredell	Rob	Robeson
Cam	Camden	Joh	Johnston	Roc	Rockingham
Car	Carteret	Jon	Jones	Row	Rowan
Cas	Caswell	Len	Lenoir	Rth	Rutherford
Cha	Chatham	Lnc	Lincoln	Sam	Sampson
Cho	Chowan	Mar	Martin	Sto	Stokes
Col	Columbus	Mec	Mecklenburg	Sur	Surry
Cum	Cumberland	Mon	Montgomery	Tyr	Tyrrell
Cur	Currituck	Mor	Moore	War	Warren
Cup	Duplin	Nor	Northampton	Wsh	Washington
Edg	Edgecome	Nsh	Nash	Way	Wayne
				Wil	Wilkes

C. <u>Census Page Number</u>

There are generally two numbers on each page of the 1810 North Carolina census. This index has used the stamped page number except in four instances when it was not available. The handwritten page numbers were used for:

       Nash County - pages 643 and 644
       Martin County - pages 445 and 446
       Orange County - pages 943 and 944
       Brunswick County - pages 226,228,230,232,234,236, 238, and 240.

The stamped page number refers to two frames on the microfilm -- the frame which shows the stamped number and the preceding frame.

D. Other Information

The census contains additional information not included in this index.

1. Free white males under 10 years of age
2. Free white males of 10 years and under 16
3. Free white males of 16 years and under 26
4. Free white males of 26 years and under 45
5. Free white males of 45 years and upwards
6. Free white females under 10 years of age
7. Free white females of 10 years and under 16
8. Free white females of 16 years and under 26
9. Free white females of 26 years and under 45
10. Free white females of 45 years and upwards
11. All other persons except Indians not taxed
12. Slaves

Name	Ref	Name	Ref	Name	Ref
Illegible	Mor- 68	Abernathy,John	Lnc-366	Acru,Isaac	War-176
Illegible	Tyr-207	Jones	Lnc-361	John	War-176
Illegible	Tyr-205	Joseph	Lnc-361	Joshua	War-176
Illegible	Ons-100	Lostrick	Fra- 97	Actor,Andrew	Roc- 21
Illebigle	Cab-143	Miles	Lnc-343	Adair,Ely	Rth- 84
Illegible	Cab-143	Miles	Lnc-361	Adam,Charles	Wil-276
-walton,-----	Bur-105	Miles	Lnc-366	Samuel	Mec- 24
---ane,-----	Tyr-205	Moses	Lnc-367	Adams,Abednego	Lnc-339
-rasdet,-----	But-106	Nathan	Lnc-347	Abednigo	Rth- 86
-regham,Wm	Lnc-333	Nathan	Lnc-375	Abednigo Jr	Rth- 86
-----,Abner	Mor- 65	Patter	Lnc-366	Abner	Pit-258
-----,Benjamin	Cha-189	Robert	Lnc-358	Abraham	Pit-258
-----,Elijah	Bur-104	Robert	Lnc-358	Abraham	Wil-270
-----,Jacob	Cha-196	Robert Jr	Lnc-361	Abram	Bft- 20
-----,John	Tyr-211	Robert Senr	Lnc-361	Absolem	Pit-250
-----,John	Lnc-329	Samuel	Lnc-358	Absalom	Rob-240
-----,John	Sto-121	Seth	Lnc-353	Allen	Joh-277
-----,Neill	Mor- 58	Shade	Lnc-361	Andrew	Ire-248
-----,Pheby	Ons-104	Smith	Rth- 84	Anna	Sto-106
-de--,Sarah	Lnc-342	Smith	Rth- 84	Anne	Sto-141
-----,Sarah	Bur-112	Turner	Lnc-326	Archabald	Pit-252
-----,Susana	Bur-105	Turner	Lnc-367	Benjamin	Hal- 95
		William	Lnc-361	Benjamin	Wil-260
Aaron,-----	Pas-180	William	Lnc-367	Bryan	Joh-276
Henry	Hal- 96	Williams	Lnc-375	Charles	Mec- 31
Abba,-----	Pas-180	Abington,Boules	Sto-123	Charles	Wil-267
Abbet,John	Rob-221	Bouls	Sto- 95	Charles Jr	Wil-267
Saml	Len-323	Hardymond	Nor- 59	Clabin	Joh-277
Thos	Len-315	Able,John	Bun- 89	Daniel	Ire-246
Abbitt,Jonathan	Bur-121	Thomas	Bun- 83	David	Bft- 30
Abbot,Benj	Ros- 39	Abrahams,Robert	Ons-102	David	Pit-251
Elizabeth	Ire-266	Abrams,Saml	Bft- 37	Densey	Mec- 29
Abbott,Absalom	Bur-120	William	Pit-250	Edney	Bft- 36
J	Cam-158	Absair,Josiah	Ans- 32	Elija	Row- 60
John	Ora-131	Abshear,William	Wil-260	Elisebeth	Cur- 81
Joseph	Bur-109	Absher,John	Wil-272	Elizabeth	Rob-241
Joseph	Sto-107	Ackins,Josiah	Bur-116	Enis	Ran-156
Joseph	Sto-142	Ackis,Henery	Cur- 79	Francis	Rth- 86
Abell,Jacob	Brt- 62	Thomas	Pas-180	Frederick	Nor- 59
Abernathy,Aaron	Lnc-364	Acklin,Isaac	Bft- 30	George	Sur-166
Battee	Lnc-361	James	Cur- 88	George	Ran-156
Battee Jr	Lnc-361	Joshua	Bft- 29	Henry	Wil-267
Bettee	Lnc-366	Mary	Bft- 30	Henry	Edg- 47
Buckner	Fra- 90	Saml	Bft- 29	Isaac	Row- 59
Buckner	Lnc-358	Ackling,Phillip	Cur- 88	J	Glf-184
Charles	Lnc-375	Acock,Henry	Ans- 23	Jacob	Ash- 6
David	Lnc-367	Acorn,Mrs.	Mec- 46	Jacob	Joh-288
David	Lnc-375	Acree,Edward	Brt- 57	Jacob	Wil-260
Harbert	Lnc-358	Henley	Brt- 55	Jacob	Row- 59
James	Bur-129	John Jnr	Brt- 55	Jacob	Row- 72
James	Lnc-366	John Senr	Brt- 55	James	Joh-276
James	Lnc-375	Leonard	Brt- 55	James	Wsh-226
James P	Lnc-366	Thos	Brt- 57	James	Pit-231
Jeremiah	Lnc-361	William	Row- 62	James	Edg- 7?
John	Fra- 93	Wm	Brt- 55	James	Ora-125
John	Lnc-358	Acres,Leroy	Ora-127	James	Sur-181
John	Lnc-361	Acru,Abraham	War-168	Jamis	Ire-248

-1-

Adams,Jamis	Ire-248	Adams,William	Edg- 54	Adkins,W		Bru-236
Jas	Lnc-335	Williams	Wil-266	W		Ash- 8
Jas S	Lnc-336	Wm	Row- 51	William		Rth- 84
Jerry	Mec- 41	Wm	Cur- 81	William		Edg- 60
Jesse	Pit-236	Wm	Bft- 31	Wm		Rob-219
Jessee	Nsh- 82	Wm H	Ora-126	Adkinson,Britain		Rch-202
Jno	Ora-125	Willoughby	Rob-236	John		Roc- 3
Jno	Ora-122	Adamson,John	Glf-155	John		Cha-197
Jno	Car-181	Adcock,Ethiache	Grn-130	Sarah		Rob-220
John	Rth- 85	George	Grn-138	Wm		Rob-238
John	Pit-252	Henry	Ans- 32	Adkison,Wm		Cab-140
John	Wil-274	James	Ran-156	Aegele,George		Row- 68
John	Wil-281	Jessy	Grn-136	George		Row- 68
John	Cum-263	Leonard	Ran-156	Philip		Row- 68
John	Pas-180	Sinson	Grn-136	Agetaul,William		Rth- 86
John	Sur-184	Susanna	Ans- 32	Agner,Daniel		Row- 79
John	Wil-271	Thos	Ans- 32	Elizabeth		Row- 79
John	Lnc-333	Wm	Grn-138	Margaret		Row- 78
John	Row- 39	Addams,Delilah	Rch-198	Peter		Row- 78
John	Row- 51	Elijah	Ans- 17	Ahart,Jacob		Cas- 47
Jonathan	Sur-184	Emanuel	Ans- 6	Ahorn,Lignal		Cas- 47
Joseph	Wsh-225	Hardy	Jon-292	Aiken,Joshua		Bur-129
Joseph	Car-181	Jacob	Ans- 7	Aikens,Jas		Cab-137
Joseph	Grn-136	Jno	Ans- 7	Aikin,John		Bur-129
Joshua	Ire-240	John	Hyd-220	Aimes,Edward		Mar- 7
Levi	Bft- 32	Levi	Ans- 30	Thomas		Mar- 6
Kinchen	Sam-159	Lucy	Rch-212	Ainsworth,Jas	Sr	Bur-116
Margaret	Wil-272	Micajah	Jon-292	Wm		Bur-116
Martha	Wsh-225	Owins	Jon-292	Airs,Derias		Len-318
Martin	Rth- 86	Tebetha	Rch-212	David Junr		Wsh-226
Matthew	Wil-281	Thos C	Ans- 6	David Senr		Wsh-225
Moses	Sur-171	William	Jon-292	Hosea		Wsh-226
Nancy	Bft- 19	Zach	Hyd-224	Isaac		Wsh-226
Nathan	Car-182	Addcock,Henry	Rth- 85	John		Wsh-224
Nimrod	Row- 58	Joshua	Cha-207	Nathan		Wsh-223
Peter	Grn-136	Adderson,M	Col- 20	Robert		Bun- 81
Peter	Pit-242	Thomas Junr	Ran-156	Thomas		Way-247
Philip	Wsh-224	Thomas Snr	Ran-156	Airy,John		Row- 85
Robert	Fra- 86	William	Ran-156	Akin,Godfrey		Grn-135
Saml	Grn-136	Addesholdt,George	Lnc-328	James		Glf-153
Saml	Mec- 31	Jacob	Lnc-328	John		Grn-135
Samuel	Rth- 86	Addeston,Jery	Mon- 50	Thomas		Grn-140
Samuel	Ran-156	Addington,John	Bun- 84	William		Glf-154
Simon	Cas- 47	William	Bun- 83	Wm		Grn-125
Sina	Edg- 71	Aden,---ael	Rth- 84	Akins,James		Cum-157
Summer	Pit-242	Aders,Elijah	Jon-292	Jno		Mec- 30
Thomas	Sto-101	Adie,Andrew	Wil-284	Sam		Bur-129
Thomas	Sto-132	Adkerson,Barbara	Hal- 96	Akurs,John		Bun- 97
Thomas	Pit-238	Joel	Hal- 96	Alay,Wiseman		Wil-263
Thomas	Wil-278	Jordan	Brt- 48	Albarty,Fredk		Sur-164
Thos	Cur- 87	William	Hal- 96	Jesse		Sur-184
William	Lnc-333	Adkins,C	Bru-228	Alberry,Ben		Bur-119
William	Glf-159	J	Ash- 7	Alberson,Arthur		Row- 83
William	Pit-242	John	Tyr-205	David		Dup- 27
William	Pit-242	R	Cam-163	Edward		Dup- 26
William	Wil-276	Sarah	Hal- 97	Elias		Glf-164
William	Ran-156	T	Bru-232	John		Ran-156

Alberson,Phineas	Glf-166	Alby,Joseph	Ire-243	Alexander,Benj	Cab-137
Samuel	Dup- 27	Thomas	Ire-266	Benjamin Senr	Cab-137
Samuel	Ran-156	Alcock,Shadrick	Tyr-211	Catey	Roc- 24
Sarah	Dup- 29	Alcut,S	Bru-238	Charles	Mec- 50
William	Dup- 26	Alden,Wm	Mon- 30	Charles	Mec- 47
Albert,Jamima	Pit-256	Alderdice,Alexr	Roc- 15	Charles I	Mec- 44
Richd	Bft- 34	Alderman,David Jr	Dup- 21	Cooley	Mec- 22
Solomon	Pit-256	David Sr	Dup- 23	Corn	Tyr-204
Albertson,Aaron	Prq-212	John Jr	Dup- 21	Daniel	Mec- 49
Aaron	Pas-180	John Sr	Dup- 21	Daniel	Ire-245
Benja Sr	Prq-212	Aldermon,Danl Jr	Dup- 17	Daniel	Bur-120
Benjamin	Prq-212	Daniel Sr	Dup- 17	Darcas	Mec- 49
Benjn	Row- 44	Alders,William	Roc- 28	David	Ire-247
Chalkly	Prq-212	Alderson,Simon	Htd-233	David	Bur-120
Francis	Prq-212	Tho Jun	Bft- 35	Eli	Mec- 53
Jesse	Row- 88	Tho Sen	Bft- 36	Eli	Cab-137
Joseph	Row- 44	Aldorson,Cath	Bft- 36	Elias	Mec- 39
Joseph	Prq-212	Aldred,James	Glf-153	Elias	Rth- 86
Joseph	Row- 88	Aldridge,Alsy	Cas- 47	Elijah	Mec- 22
Joshua	Prq-212	Ezekiel	Ran-156	Elijah	Roc- 35
Keziah	Prq-212	Isham	Per-126	Elijah	Roc- 9
Mary	Prq-212	Isaac	Ran-156	Elinor	Mec- 40
Nathan	Prq-212	Isaac	Rth- 85	Eliza	Bur-110
Sally	Pas-180	John	Ran-156	Elizabeth	War-171
Solomon	Pit-255	Jonathan	Roc- 8	Enoch	Wsh-218
Thoms	Prq-212	Molly	Per-126	Ezra	Mec- 49
William	Pas-180	Peter	Per-126	Francis	Rth- 85
Albes,Andrew	Cum-240	Winny	Dup- 13	Geo	Glf-155
Albright,-----	Ora-172	Aldrige,Aaron	Cha-203	Geo	Glf-172
Danl	Ora-120	Joseph	Sur-194	Geo	Cab-137
Danl	Ora-118	Mary	Sur-166	George	Mec- 49
G	Ora-121	Ruth	Sur-189	Gideon	Wsh-220
H	Ora-171	Alens,Richard	Cur- 87	Henry	Tyr-204
J	Ora-131	Alensthester,Wm	Glf-159	Hesekiah	Mec- 50
Jacob	Row- 69	Aler,Philip	Sto-114	Hezh	Cab-136
Jacob	Ora-172	Philip	Sto-104	Hezk	Tyr-204
Jacob	Ora-119	Philip	Sto-137	I B I	Mec- 38
John	Row- 71	Alexander,-----	Tyr-204	Isaac	Mec- 48
John	Ora-172	-----	Mec- 25	Isaac	Mec- 46
John	Row- 89	A	Glf-173	Isaac	Rth- 85
Jos	Ora-146	Abijah	Cab-136	Isaac Senr	Tyr-203
Ludwick	Ora-171	Abner	Mec- 49	Isaiah	Tyr-206
Michl	Row- 68	Abner	Tyr-206	J----	Tyr-208
Nancy	Prq-213	Abolen	Mec- 23	J	Glf-172
Peter	Row- 70	Abraham	Tyr-203	James	Mec- 22
Peter	Row- 69	Abram	Ire-249	James	Ire-246
Peter	Row- 68	Abram	Rth- 85	James	Bun- 83
W	Pas-180	Abrm	Cab-136	James	Ire-237
Albriton,Adam	Pit-235	Absalom	Mec- 49	James	Bur-109
Henry	Pit-242	Adam	Mec- 51	James	Row- 73
Joel	Pit-235	Alice	Mec- 49	Jas	Mec- 52
Jonathan	Pit-241	Allen	Ire-245	Jas	Mec- 51
Jonathan	Pit-234	Ambrose	Cab-136	Jas	Mec- 47
Luke	Pit-235	Amos	Mec- 24	Jas	Mec- 46
Samuel	Pit-240	Anthony	Tyr-212	Jas	Ora-131
Alburt,Mary	Ora-173	Anthony	Was-221	Jas	Ora-144
Alby,Benjamin	Ire-243	Armond	Tyr-212	Jas	Ora-172
Cramberry	Ire-266	Augustus	Mec- 50	Jediah	Mec- 26

-3-

Alexander,Jesse	Wil-260	Alexander,Thos	Mec- 40	Allen,Anne	War-167
Jesse Jr	Tyr-212	Tipple	Hrt-216	Anne	Roc- 32
Jessee Sr	Tyr-212	Tom	Ora-133	Apsabeth	Joh-290
Joab	Mec- 22	Uriah	Mec- 49	Arthur	Nor- 5?
Joal	Mec- 38	Will Jr	Bur-110	Ben	Pas-180
Joanh	Tyr-204	William	Ire-246	Benj	Lnc-264
Jno	Mec- 47	William	Bur-109	Benjamin	Nor- 59
John	Mec- 47	William	Bur-120	Benjamin	Roc- 27
John	Tyr-203	William	Wil-263	Benj	Ans- 17
John	Bun- 89	Wm	Mec- 38	Bethia	Roc- 27
John	Rth- 85	Wm	Mec- 39	Betsey	Nor- 59
John	War-175	Wm	Cab-144	Caleb	Ons-109
John	Lnc-334	Wm	Tyr-204	Champion	Grn-121
John Jun	Tyr-203	Wm B	Mec- 46	Charles	Rth- 85
Johnson	Glf-155	Willis	Wil-260	Charles	Rth- 85
Johnson	Glf-161	Zebulon	Mec- 50	Charles	War-169
Jonathan	Mec- 38	Zekiel	Mec- 39	Charles Senr	War-169
Jos	Glf-171	Zekiel	Mec- 39	Daniel	Bun- 82
Joseph	Bun- 74	Zekiel	Mec- 36	Daniel	Roc- 31
Joseph	Ire-246	Zenno	Mec- 25	Daniel (Coast)	Roc- 27
Joseph	Bur-129	Alexr, John Senr	Tyr-209	Darling	Ire-249
Joseph	Cab-138	Alford,Abram	Fra- 81	David	Wil-276
Joshua	Wsh-218	Benj	Way-254	David	Ans- 9
Josiah	Mec- 54	Elias	Rob-218	David Jr	Wil-276
Josiah	Mec- 48	Harren	Rob-232	Denny	Rth- 84
Kisander	Mec- 39	Isaac	Fra- 96	Drury	Ans- 22
Mary	Tyr-213	Jacob	Fra- 82	E	Bru-234
Mary	Med- 45	Jas	Rob-233	Eatheldred	Ans- 7
Matthew	Mec- 40	John	Hyd-227	Ed	Ora-136
Moses	Mec- 38	John	Fra- 82	Edmond	Ora-143
Moses	Cab-136	Kinchen	Fra- 81	Elender	Roc- 27
Mosses	Ire-246	Lemuel	Fra- 97	Eliza	Bft- 24
Natl	Cab-137	Mary	Rob-228	Elizabeth	Joh-290
Noble	Bur-108	Sion	Rob-228	Elizabeth	Sto-149
Ozne	Mec- 39	West	Way-254	Elizabeth	Sto-110
Ozwald	Mec- 39	William	Sto-135	Ezkl	Bla- 2
Ozwell	Mec- 54	William	Sto-102	Fredrick	Hyd-220
Parris	Mec- 24	Alfred,Jesse	Pit-247	Garland	Grn-143
Phineas	Mec- 36	Alger,Nathl	Ora-169	Geo of Twl	Ora-136
Phlexam	Mec- 22	Alice,Allen	Cha-201	Geo	Mon- 32
Robert	Lnc-368	John	Cha-200	Geo	Mon- 39
Robt J	Lnc-368	Nancy	Cha-200	Geo	Bun- 82
Ruben	Ire-246	Aliday,William	Glf-179	George	Roc- 34
Sample	Mec- 54	Aling,Kervis	Cur- 87	George	Bur-131
Saml	Bur-108	Alison,Robert Jr	Grn-128	George	Roc- 28
Samuel	Mec- 22	Allan,E W	Bla- 2	George	Mec- 39
Samuel	Ran-157	Henry	Cum-236	George	Bun- 73
Sarah	Roc- 35	John	Bla- 2	George	Ire-249
Sarah	Lnc-339	Joseph	Bla- 2	George	War-172
Silas	Mec- 50	Morgan	Bla- 2	Gideon	Joh-290
Stephen	Cab-136	William	Bla- 2	Gideon	Joh-287
Stephen	Cab-138	Alldridge,John	Ran-156	Gideon	Pit-257
Susanah	Mec- 39	Allen,Adneram	Bun- 79	Gideon	Wil-273
Thomas	Joh-287	Alex	Ora-115	Henry	Dup- 18
Thomas	Ran-156	Alexander	Cab-144	Hezekiah	Bun- 96
Thomas	Ran-157	Alexr	Cab-143	Hugh	Row- 73
Thos	Mec- 52	Andrew	Roc- 27	J	Bru-232
Thos	Ora-172	Annanias	Bur-112	Jacob	Rob-242

Name	Code	Name	Code	Name	Code	Name	Code
Allen,Jacob	Ans- 17	Allen,Reynold	Ire-244	Alley,Shade	Ire-257		
James	War-172	Richard	Sur-167	Allgood,Presley	Sur-190		
Jas	Mec- 37	Richard	Wil-168	William	Row- 62		
Jas	Ans- 5	Richard	Rth- 85	William	Sur-174		
Jeremiah	Nor- 59	Richd	Ans- 19	Allice,Allen	Mor- 66		
Jesse	Wil-268	Robert	Grn-121	Allin,Benj	Mon- 22		
Jesse	Sto-148	Robert	Ora-943	David	Per-142		
Jesse	Sto-111	Robert	Lnc-356	Drury	Per-142		
Jesse L	Mon- 41	Robt	Mec- 44	George	Gat-115		
Jno	Mec- 23	Robt	Mec- 36	Howard	Per-142		
John	Bun- 78	Roger	Pit-255	John	Per-135		
John	Lnc-356	Rubin	Row- 61	Nathaniel	Gat-114		
John	Lnc-364	S	Mon- 42	Shad	Glf-179		
John	Bun- 92	Sally	Pit-252	Stokes	Per-148		
John	Hyd-234	Sam	Ora-122	Thomas	Per-135		
John	Dup- 20	Sam	Mon- 32	William	Per-135		
John	Rth- 85	Sam Sen	Ora-130	William Esq	Per-135		
John	Rth- 85	Saml	Grn-121	Wm	Per-148		
John	Rth- 85	Samuel	Ran-157	Alling,John	Cur- 87		
John	Rth- 84	Samuel	Rth- 84	Thos	Cur- 86		
John	War-175	Samuel	Roc- 32	Allings,Thos	Cur- 87		
John	Fra- 93	Sarah	Hyd-234	Allison,Andrew	Mec- 36		
John	Cha-194	Shadrach Lew	Bun- 72	Antone	Lnc-367		
John	Cha-212	Shd	Glf-184	Ben	Bur-119		
John	Roc- 16	Solomon	Roc- 16	Benjamin	Bur-125		
John	Hal- 95	Tabitha	Nor- 59	Burch	Bur-110		
John	Mon- 32	Tho	Bft- 29	Francis	Bur-120		
John	Brt- 45	Thomas	Hal- 96	George	Bur-120		
John --- Taylor	Roc- 10	Thomas	Roc- 27	George	Bur-125		
John H	Ire-249	Thomas	Wil-261	H	Ora-153		
John Jr	Lnc-364	Thomas	Joh-277	Henry	Bur-118		
John Sen	Ora-134	Thomas	Rth- 84	Israel	Glf-156		
John Sr	Cha-194	Thos	Prq-212	James	Ora-126		
Jonathen	Ran-157	Thos	Ans- 17	James	Grn-130		
Jonathan	Wil-282	Thos	Mon- 40	Jeremiah	Row- 39		
Joseph	Bla- 5	Vincent	Lnc-364	John	Ora-111		
Joseph	Ran-156	Vincent	War-182	John	Glf-179		
Joseph	Wil-275	William	Pas-180	John	Ora-126		
Joseph	Rth- 84	William	Bun- 92	John	Rth- 85		
Joseph	Cha-194	William	Wsh-226	John	Cab-138		
Joseph	Len-316	William	Joh-276	Joseph	Ora-123		
Joseph	Mor- 57	William	War-183	Joseph	Ire-266		
Joseph	Row- 61	William	Rth- 85	Joseph Jr	Ora-127		
Joseph	Mon- 32	William	Wil-268	Posey	Bur-120		
Josiah	Ans- 6	William col	Fra-100	Richard	Bur-127		
Judith	Ans- 22	William	Cha-203	Richd	Bur-119		
Julas	Ans- 22	William M	Ire-249	Samuel	Glf-188		
Larkin	Rth- 86	Wm	Ora-144	Sarah	Cab-138		
Levisa	Roc- 27	Wm	Row- 61	Tho	Ora-126		
Martha	Len-316	Wm	Mon- 32	Thomas	Ire-237		
Mary	Wil-275	Wm	Cab-138	Thomas	Bur-125		
Micajah	Sto-149	Wm H	Ora-175	Thos	Cab-138		
Morseman	Pit-253	Zachariah	Hyd-224	William	Ire-262		
N	Col- 18	Allender,Elizth	Hal- 96	Wm	Ora-127		
Nathan	Mor- 67	Alley,Howel	Ire-257	Wm	Grn-130		
Paul	Rob-243	Leven	Sto- 94	Wm	Mec- 36		
Peter	Cha-212	Leven	Sto-123	Wm Charlotte	Mec- 24		
Reuben	Mon- 32	Richard	Fra- 91	Allisson,Andrew	Ire-242		

Name	Loc	Name	Loc	Name	Loc
Allisson,Anne	Ire-242	Alsobrook,James Jr	Hal- 96	Ambrose,David	Wsh-219
James	Ire-242	James Senr	Hal- 96	James	Wsh-219
Martha	Ire-237	Jesse	Ans- 11	James	Edg- 68
Martha	Ire-242	Jno	Ans- 11	Mary Ann	Wsh-219
Richard	Ire-237	Landon	Hal- 96	Micajah	Wsh-219
Theophilus	Ire-257	Leml	Ans- 19	Reuben	Ons-103
William	Ire-242	Marmaduke	Hal- 96	Shadrach	Ons- 97
Allman,Andrew	Mor- 59	Thomas	Edg- 59	Amburgy,John	Wil-268
Allmon,Edward	Rch-209	William	Hal- 95	Amburn,Aleana	Bur-130
Nathan	Joh-290	Willie	Hal- 95	J	Col- 18
Alloy,John H	Rth- 84	Willis	Ans- 11	Amciple,And	Glf-179
Alloway,John	Bun- 74	Alsobrooks,Partheny	Edg-64	Ames,Elijah	Pit-233
Allred,Elias	Ran-156	Alspach,Henry	Sto-135	John D	Nor- 59
James	Ran-156	Alspack,Henry	Sto-103	Lewis	Grn-119
Jesse	Ran-156	Alston,Elizabeth	War-170	William	Nor- 59
John Jr	Ran-156	George	Grn-119	Free Amey	Bft- 31
Joseph	Ran-156	Gideon	Hal- 95	Amick,David	Ran-156
Levi	Ran-156	Henry	Hal- 95	J	Glf-177
Samuel	Ran-156	James	Hal- 95	John Jnr	Ran-156
Thomas Jnr	Ran-156	John	Hal- 95	John Snr	Ran-156
William Jnr	Ran-156	John	War-174	Nicholas	Ran-156
William Snr	Ran-156	John	Ora-125	P	Glf-177
Allridge,Thomas	Ran-156	John J	Cha-211	Peter	Glf-177
Allston,Ann	Hrt-213	Joseph J	Hal- 95	Peter Jnr	Ran-156
F	Bru-228	Lucy	War-177	Peter	Ran-156
M	Col- 17	Mathias	Ora-171	Philip	Ran-156
Martha	War-177	Nicholas	War-178	Wm Sr	Grn-119
Allums,Charles	Mec- 50	Orson	Cha-203	Amis,John	Grn-145
Alman,Katy	Bur-131	Philip	Cha-189	Wm	Grn-145
Lewis	Bur-107	Phill	War-179	Wm Jr	Grn-124
Almon,John P H	Rch-201	Phill G	War-178	Ammons,Ephraim	Bun- 92
Matthew	Rch-203	Sally	War-180	Jesse	Way-235
Almond,Edmd	Mon- 47	Whitmill	War-183	John	Sam-152
Edmd	Mon- 38	William	Hal- 95	John	Bun- 93
Edwd	Mon- 38	William	War-183	John	Rob-219
Elisabeth	Mon- 48	Willis Junr	Hal- 95	Amons,Stepon	Rob-239
Martin	Mon- 49	Willis Senr	Hal- 95	Amorett,-----	Pas-180
Nathan	Mon- 49	Alstons,Thos Est	War-172	Amos,James	Hal- 96
Richd	Mon- 48	Altman,Joel	Way-250	John Junr	Roc- 24
Almonds,Edmd	Mon- 49	Altom,James	Lnc-339	John Junr	Roc- 23
Alnold,Meltire	Jon-292	Alue,And	Bur-104	Pleasant	Roc- 22
Alphen,Hezekiah	Gat-105	Alverson,Archd	Cas- 47	Ancil,Henry	Nor- 59
William	Dup- 25	Elisha	Cas- 47	Andas,Thomas	Sur-188
Alpheus,Sally	Cho-222	Mary	Cas- 47	Anders,Addam	Jon-292
Alphin,David	Jon-292	Alves,Walter	Ora-142	Adonijah	Jon-292
Thomas	Jon-292	Aluy,Elisha	Wil-261	Daniel	Jon-292
Alran,John	Bur-103	Alvy,Fielder	Wil-269	Elizabeth	Hrt-209
Alridge,Jno	Len-311	John	Wil-269	Francis	Jon-292
Thomas	Len-312	Amal,Moses	Joh-285	John	Fra- 81
Alsobrook,Benj	Hal- 96	Amason,Benjamin	Edg- 48	John Junr	Jon-292
Carter	Hal- 97	Eli	Edg- 48	Peter Senr	Jon-292
David	Hal- 95	Isaac	Edg- 49	Peter Junr	Jon-292
Drewry	Hal- 96	John	Edg- 49	Whitmal	Sam-152
Elizabeth	Hal- 95	Man	Edg- 49	Willm	Fra- 96
Howel	Hal- 95	William	Edg- 49	Willm Junr	Fra- 90
Hutson	Hal- 96	Ambers,Daniel	Jon-292	Anderson,Abel	Grn-148
Isham	Ans- 11	Ambrose,Daniel	Ons- 95	Andrew	Mor- 64

Name	Loc	Name	Loc	Name	Loc	Name	Loc
Anderson,Augustin	Grn-145	Anderson,Josiah	Bun- 78	Andres,Saml		Bla- 2
Benjamin	Rth- 85	Keneth	Ora-111	William		Car-179
Benjamin	War-168	Lettice	Ora-126	Andrew,B		Glf-173
Benjamin	Grn-140	Levi	Bun- 96	Caleb V		Pas-180
C	Col- 17	Lewis	Grn-148	Custis		Glf-154
Charles	Sto-144	Mary	Edg- 62	Elizabeth		Cab-144
Charles Jr	Row- 63	Miles	Way-250	Hugh		Ire-263
Churchwell	Nsh-644	Nathan	Bun- 86	James		Ons-101
David	Row- 70	Nelson	Row- 63	James		Ire-265
David	Cum-237	Nicholas	Mec- 45	Jas		Ora-171
David	Ora-176	Penelope	Edg- 62	John		Sur-193
Edmond	Pit-261	Peter	Grn-143	John		Sur-193
Eli Cook	Bun- 83	Quinton	Cas- 47	John		Bun -94
Elisabeth	Mar- 8	R	Ora-135	John Jn		Sur-193
Ely	Glf-180	Rachael	Ans- 15	Joseph		Sur-181
Frank	Fra-100	Rachal	Edg- 60	Luke		Glf-154
Geo	Bun- 92	Rachal	Edg- 62	Moses		Cab-138
Georg	Per-126	Redden	Ans- 19	Robert		Cha-195
George	Grn-143	Reddick	Fra- 90	Willm		Cab-143
George	Cum-257	Richard	Row- 68	Andrews,Abner		Ons- 99
George	Edg- 61	Robert	Bun- 94	Arden		Mar- 14
Gordon	Bun- 83	Robt	Ora-117	Asa		Ran-187
Henry	Bun- 79	Robt	Ora-161	Cullen, Est of		Edg- 55
Henry	Edg- 61	Robt	Ora-173	David		Sto-136
Isaac	Grn-143	Samuel	Wil-265	Drury		War-170
Isaac	Glf-169	Samuel	Rth- 84	Elizabeth		Edg- 63
Isaac	Row- 75	Sarah	Pit-256	Felson		Grn-127
Isam	Mar- 11	Stephen	Rth- 85	George		Row- 72
J	Glf-177	T	Bru-232	H		Ora-136
J	Bru-232	Tho	Ora-110	Harmon		Ran-156
J	Bru-232	Thomas	Grn-140	Henrietta		Ran-187
J Sr	Bru-226	Thomas	Row- 75	Henry		Lnc-353
Jacob	Grn-143	Thos	Row- 39	Henry		Ora-129
Jacob	Bru-228	Wallace	Bft- 26	Irvin		Cum-248
James	Bun- 84	William	Bun- 86	J		Mon- 34
James	Bun- 86	William	Bun- 89	James		Wil-273
James	Cum-265	William	Edg- 58	James		Row- 72
James	Edg- 58	William	Edg- 60	John		Row- 72
James	Per-135	William	Prq-212	L		Ora-136
James	Cum-252	William	Pit-248	Littleberry		War-177
James	Row- 68	William	Pit-262	M		Ora-136
James	Hal- 95	William	Cas- 47	Rebecca		Dup- 32
James Senr	Bun- 86	William	Mar- 12	Richard		Ran-156
Jane	Ora-123	William	Cum-252	Robert		Wil-284
Jno	Ora-123	William	Edg- 46	S		Ora-136
Jo	Ora-176	William	Glf-169	S		Mon- 35
Jo	Bft- 25	William	Row- 65	Sam		Ora-129
John	Bun- 86	William	Cur- 89	Saml		Ora-119
John	Cas- 47	William	Hal- 95	Samuel		Roc- 10
John	Pit-237	William Junr	Cum-249	Starling		Mon- 25
John	Rth- 84	Wm	Len-323	Thomas		Ran-156
John	Rth- 84	Wm	Grn-130	Thomas		Hal- 95
John	Grn-140	Winefred	Mar- 16	Thomas		Cha-199
John	Glf-158	Andleton,John	Edg- 64	W Sen		Ora-136
John	Bft- 38	Andres,Elisha	Bla- 2	Warren		Pit-245
John	Bft- 38	Evan	Bla- 13	Warren		Mar- 15
Jordan	Pit-238	Jas	Bla- 13	Whitdon		Edg- 54
Joseph	Row- 81	John Junr	Bla- 13	William		Pit-245

Name	Code	Name	Code	Name	Code
Andrews, William	Len-318	Applewhite, Jno	Rob-237	Armfield, Will	Glf-151
Wm	Ora-129	Jno	Ans- 23	Wm	Glf-161
Wm	Grn-132	John	Way-252	Armicy, John	Row- 58
Andrus, Alex	Mon- 23	Thomas	Hal- 95	Armistead, Ann C	Wsh-227
Anet, Pervey	Rob-239	Applin, William	Mar- 8	Anthony	Cha-198
Angel, Charles	Sto-140	Appling, Thomas	Grn-132	Carere	Cha-206
Charles	Sto-105	Arands, Frederick	Mec- 29	John	Wsh-228
Charles Jnr	Sto-140	Archbell, Jas	Bft- 32	Mary	Wsh-227
James	Bun- 78	John	Bft- 21	Stark	Brt- 43
John	Rth- 84	John B	Bft- 21	Armisted, Wistward	Cha-200
Joshua	Sur-193	Mary	Bft- 21	Armit, Hollis	Wsh-225
Josiah	Lnc-329	Archer, Armstrong	Hrt-215	Armour, Charles	Tyr-201
Laurance	Sto-147	Charles	Roc- 14	Arms, Robert	Wil-260
Laurance	Sto-105	D	Glf-162	Armstead, Sarah	Brt- 67
Peter	Hyd-232	Etheldred	Hrt-215	William	Ran-156
William	Bun- 76	J	Glf-162	Armstrong, Andrew	Wsh-224
Angell, Laurance	Sto-140	John	Glf-164	Ann	Ora-175
Angely, John	Bur-127	John	Hal- 96	Bennet	Tyr-211
Angle, Philip	Bun- 81	John	Hal- 96	Carnl	Bft- 28
Anglin, Nancy	Bun- 77	Jonathan	Edg- 68	Edwd	Dup- 10
Ansel, Henery	Cur- 90	Norfleet	Hal- 97	Elizebeth	Sur-186
James	Cur- 92	Penny	Hal- 97	Guy	Edg- 61
James	Cur- 90	Ralph	Hrt-215	Holaway	Tyr-212
John	Cur- 92	Reddick	Edg- 47	Isaac	Rch-199
Ansley, Joseph	Tyr-211	Simon	Hrt-215	James	Lnc-358
Joseph Jr	Tyr-210	Stephen	Mec- 52	James	Ora-123
Nathan	Tyr-210	Thomas	Nor- 59	James	Pit-263
Anstead, Joseph	War-173	William	Hrt-215	James	Dup- 11
Anthony, Danl	Lnc-335	Zachariah	Edg- 69	Janet	Cum-267
Darling	Lnc-336	Archibald, Moses	Cab-143	John	Lnc-367
George	Lnc-337	Samuel	Ire-242	John	Lnc-367
Jacb	Ora-144	William	Ire-242	John	Ire-266
James	Sur-169	Archy, Thomas	Cha-195	John	Bur-111
John	Rth- 86	Ardin, Richard	Sur-162	John	Roc- 12
John	Hal- 97	William	Sur-162	Joe	Ora-169
Obed	Glf-172	Arey, Abraham	Row- 79	Jos (Red)	Ora-164
Paul	Bur-116	Peter	Row- 78	Joseph	Edg- 45
Paul	Lnc-335	Argo, William Jnr	Ran-156	Mat	Lnc-367
Philip	Lnc-334	William Snr	Ran-156	Nancy	Sur-196
Thomas	Sur-194	Argoe, Isbel	Cha-204	Racl	Ora-159
William	Glf-186	Robert	Len-314	Richd	Ans- 6
Philip	Bur-102	Arinaton, Abner	Mor- 67	Robert	Lnc-367
Antwine, Dyanna	Jon-292	Arington, Frederic	Wsh-227	Robert	Hal- 97
Gashum	Jon-292	Jno	Ans- 29	Russell	Tyr-213
Apley, John	Lnc-335	Sion	Mor- 66	Squire	Tyr-206
Apperson, William	Sur-182	Arkill, Hannah	Prq-212	Tho	Ora-127
Apple, D	Glf-179	Arledge, Isaac	Ran-156	Thos	Sto-124
D Jr	Glf-179	Arling, Emma	Ire-251	Wesley	Sur-196
J	Glf-179	Arliss, Jno col	Rob-240	William	Cum-240
John	Glf-188	Arm, J	Ash- 13	William	Cum-266
Naomi	Glf-188	M	Ash- 4	William	Row- 75
T	Glf-176	Armfield, D	Glf-172	Wm	Cum-240
Applebee, Betsy	Pas-180	Isaac	Glf-182	Wm	Lnc-336
Applegate, Wm	Sur-204	Isaac	Glf-158	Wm	Ans- 6
Applewhite, Elisha	Way-252	Isaac	Glf-171	Wm Jr	Ora-162
Isaac	Way-252	Jas	Glf-169	Wm Sr	Ora-162
Henry	Hal- 95	Nathan	Glf-157	Arnal, Jacob	Sur-165
Jno	Rob-237	Sol	Glf-176	John	Ora-130

Name	Ref	Name	Ref	Name	Ref
Arnal,Thomas	Sur-167	Aronhart,Philip	Row- 67	Arundell,Willm	Fra- 95
Arnald,O	Bru-240	Philip	Row- 67	Arunt,John	Cha-191
Arnet,John	Mor- 69	William	Row- 89	Ary,Zachariah	Row- 85
Peter	Ans- 9	Arps,Valentine	Prq-212	Asbel,Christopher	Ran-156
Arnett,David	Mec- 46	William	Prq-212	Manuel	Ran-156
Deborah	Dup- 28	Arrawood,Benj	Lnc-356	William	Ran-157
John	Cas- 47	Loyd	Lnc-356	Asbell,Joseph	Brt- 61
John	Dup- 28	Arrendale,Wm	Len-312	Asbey,J	Bru-228
Joseph B	Cas- 47	Arrenton,Deborah	Prq-213	Asborn,Andrew	Sto- 98
Joseph L	Cas- 47	Ezekiel	Prq-212	Asbridge,Joseph	Roc- 20
Valentine	Sto-133	Nancy	Prq-212	Joseph	Roc- 11
Arney,Christian	Lnc-345	Thos	Prq-212	Asbury,Daniel	Lnc-358
Henry	Sto- 97	William	Prq-212	George L	Dup- 26
Henry	Sto-126	Arriman,Sam	Ora-121	Asby,B	Bru-226
Henry	Sto-130	Arrington,Abel	Ire-249	M	Bru-226
John	Lnc-345	Anne	War-167	Ash,Bales	Nor- 59
Arnnets,M	Glf-172	Arthur	Hal- 95	Jesse	Nor- 59
Arnold,Benj	Tyr-211	Carter	Nsh- 75	Ashbee,Nancey	Cur- 80
Benj	Way-244	Henry	Nsh- 75	Samuel	Cur- 83
Clement	Ran-156	James	Bun- 78	Solomon	Cur- 87
David	Hal- 97	James	War-173	William	Cur- 83
Elizabeth	Pit-232	John	Ire-249	Ashbraner,Danl	Bur-130
Henry	Pit-232	John	Nsh- 73	Ashburn,Baldy	Brt- 44
Hezekiah	Tyr-211	Joseph	Nsh- 75	Frederick	Sto-127
J	Col- 17	Joseph	Nsh- 76	John	Brt- 43
James	Pit-232	Peter	Nsh- 75	Mary	Brt- 45
John	Ora-116	Richd	Nsh- 75	Thomas	Brt- 47
John	Pit-263	Sion	Wil-278	Ashby,Cuddy	Sto-124
John	Gat-115	Timothy	Bun- 90	Hallifax	Sur-178
Joseph	Wsh-216	Willis	War-182	John	Sto-112
Joseph	Way-248	Wm	Nsh- 75	John	Sto-155
Levi	Ons- 98	Arriwood,James	Bun- 87	Ashcraft,Benjn	Ans- 11
Luke	Cas- 47	James	Wil-266	Thos	Ans- 13
Nathan	Way-244	Zachariah	Bun- 86	Wm	Ans- 11
Richard	Cas- 47	Arrwood,John	Bur-118	Ashe,Charles	Hal- 95
Richard	Fra- 84	Artes,Isom	Hrt-214	Christopher	Hal- 97
Richd	Brt- 64	Arthur,Elijah	Car-178	Elizabeth	Hal- 97
Robert	Ran-157	Gideon	Bup- 8	Elven	Hal- 96
Samuel	Sur-175	James	Cha-196	James	Lnc-353
Smith	Ran-156	John	Car-179	James	Hal- 96
Solomon	War-180	Louisa	Car-178	James	Hal- 97
Tho	Bft- 30	Rebecca	Car-178	Jesse	Lnc-378
Thomas	Pas-180	Richard	Car-178	Sarah	Hal- 97
Whillack	Ran-156	Seth	Car-178	Thomas Jr	Lnc-353
William	Way-248	Artis,Abraham	Hal- 96	Thomas Senr	Lnc-353
William	Wsh-220	Artist,Ann	Edg- 50	William	Sto- 97
William	Hyd-233	Champin	Edg- 49	Ashebraner,Barbara	Lnc-239
William	Pit-232	Delany	Edg- 50	Henry	Lnc-329
Arnt,Hannah	Lnc-343	George	Nor- 59	Ashbord,Dincy	Cas- 47
Aronhart,George	Row- 77	Lewis	Edg- 49	John	Sam-163
George	Row- 68	Mark	Sam-159	Street	Bla- 2
George	Row- 67	Richard	Edg- 49	William	Cas- 47
Jacob	Row- 67	William	Edg- 49	Willis	Cas- 47
John	Row- 77	Winny	Edg- 50	Ashley,Grant	Per-126
John	Row- 39	Zilpha	Edg- 49	Howel	Sur-194
Killian	Row- 77	Arthursy,Abraham	Hyd-225	J	Ash- 12
Peter	Row- 67	Arturs,Joseph	Ire-258	James	Cab-148
Philip	Row- 66	Arundell,Thomas	Fra- 90	Jeremiah	Prq-212

Name	Ref	Name	Ref	Name	Ref	Name	Ref
Ashley,Miles	Cho-227	Atkins,Daniel	Ora-165	Aulnutt,Jesse	Sur-195		
Robert	Ora-169	George	Roc- 26	Aultey,Kinch	Bft- 29		
Robert	Sur-194	Ica	Cum-258	Auntony,Harry	Ora-172		
William	Rob-218	James	Cum-256	Aurant,John	Lnc-352		
William	Hyd-231	Jas	Mon- 50	Aurent,Jacob	Lnc-353		
William Jr	Sur-194	John	Cum-252	John	Lnc-346		
Ashly,Joseph	Prq-212	John	Mon- 24	Ausben,Jesse	Ran-156		
William	Sur-169	John	Roc- 26	Ausbin,Jonathan	Ran-157		
Ashworth,John	Bun- 80	Marthey	Cas- 47	William	Ran-157		
Nancy	Bun- 89	Richd	Cum-252	Auscoat,Samuel	Cur- 85		
Askew,Aaron	Hrt-206	Robert B	Sur-173	Ausley,John	Cha-201		
Aaron	Brt- 52	William	Cas- 47	Aust,Frederick	Sto-129		
Asa	Hrt-216	William	Sur-173	Leonard	Sto-131		
Benj	Hrt-212	Atkinson,Aaron	Edg- 70	Austan,Bryan	Mon- 47		
David	Brt- 52	Allen	Pit-254	Austill,Isaac	Sur-167		
Enoch	Ons-105	Benjamin	Pit-249	Major	Sur-169		
Enos	Hrt-208	Benjamin	Cum-249	Malin	Sur-194		
Frederick	Ons- 98	Daniel	Cum-249	Austin,Benjamin	Bur-107		
George	Brt- 52	Elizabeth	Edg- 41	Benjamin Jr	Bur-106		
George	Hrt-216	Henry	Nsh- 89	Curnelous	Cur- 82		
James	Bur-121	Henry	Cum-249	Elijah	Bur-107		
Jara D	Hrt-215	James	Ora-119	Elijah	Bur-108		
Jas	Hrt-211	James	Ora-124	Hnery	Edg- 41		
Jeremiah	Hrt-208	John	Nsh- 72	Jacob	Ans- 8		
John	Brt- 62	John	Nsh- 77	James	Ans- 25		
John	Brt- 51	John	Per-135	Jno	Ans- 25		
John powder	Hrt-216	John	Joh-280	Jno	Ans- 26		
Josiah	Edg- 66	John	Cum-247	Nathan	Bur-107		
Moses	Mar- 15	Joseph	Way-252	Richd	Ans- 9		
Nathan	Ons-101	Newel	Ora-116	Samuel	Bur-106		
Noah	Hrt-208	Richard	Per-135	Samuel	Bur-107		
Shadrick	Hrt-206	Riden	Ora-123	Samuel	Bur-108		
Thos	Brt- 50	William	Roc- 13	Samuel	Row- 61		
William	Edg- 65	William	Roc- 29	Samuel	Row- 66		
Wm T	Hrt-206	Atkison,Jene	Mec- 37	Underdew	Hal- 96		
Asky,Benjamin	Jon-292	Attright,Wm	Glf-180	William	Sur-189		
Aspra,John F	Hyd-220	Attwell,Jas	Per-126	William	Bur-107		
Aspray,Benjamin	Mar- 5	Atwater,Falis	Bur-117	William	Row- 60		
Asque,Benjn	Fra- 79	M	Ora-144	Auston,Daniel	Cur- 83		
Charles	Fra- 95	Atwell,Eleph	Bla- 2	Green	Joh-275		
James	Fra- 77	J	Glf-176	Henry	Per-135		
Willm Senr	Fra- 80	John Jr	Cas- 47	John	Per-135		
Astin,John	Roc- 32	John Sr	Cas- 47	Sarey	Cur- 82		
Aston,Samuel	Ran-156	Lock	Cas- 47	Thos	Cur- 93		
Aswald,David	Rob-218	Shadrick	Glf-156	Thos	Cur- 82		
Aswell,Jas	Cho-228	John	Sur-172	Thos Jnr	Cur- 82		
Atchison,James	Row- 60	Thos Sen	Ora-136	Autary,William	Ons- 95		
John	Row- 59	Auberry,Thomas	Wil-270	Autery,Alexr	Mor- 61		
Ater,Matthew	Cha-203	Aughtry,Absalom	Sam-153	Elijah	Mor- 61		
Atha,Henson	Sur-190	Cornilius	Sam-153	Fedrick	Mor- 59		
Athia,Horatio	Sur-191	John	Sam-153	James	Mor- 61		
Atkee,Wm	Mec- 25	Newsam	Sam-153	Jas	Ans- 13		
Atkerson,Benj	Nsh- 80	Auglin,Caleb	Cas- 47	Jno	Ans- 10		
Elijah	Nsh- 80	Auld,Henry W	Cha-216	Polly	Mor- 61		
Henry	Nsh- 81	Jas S	Ans- 18	Reddin	Ans- 27		
James	Nsh- 91	Jno	Ans- 23	Wm	Mor- 61		
Atkin,Henry	Bur-115	Auldridge,Ben	Lnc-330	Avara,Lewis	Cum-248		
Atkins,Allen	Ora-167	Auldugar,Jesse	Rob-221	Avary,Johatahan	Cum-260		

-10-

Avary,Richd	Cum-262	Ayers,Robert	Wil-280	Bagby,Thomas	Hal- 99
Sarah	Cum-261	Samuel	Roc- 22	William	Sur-194
William R	Cum-263	Ayes,Noah	Rch-199	Bagee,Isham	Grn-121
William Senr	Cum-262	Ayres,James	Bun- 74	Baget,Andrew	Grn-141
Avent,Abner	Nsh- 76	Murphy	Sur-179	Bagett,John	Len-319
James	Cha-206	Ayrs,Thomas	Way-245	Baggan,Jesse	Ans- 15
Julian	Cha-206	Ayts,William	Way-244	Bagge,Charles	Sto-136
Nancy	Cha-206	Azment,Thos	Glf-151	Baggerty,Thomas	Row- 63
Wm	Cha-215			Bagget,Benton	Grn-138
Wm	Nsh- 75	B----,James	Jon-293	Granbary	Nsh- 75
Avera,Aventon	Joh-278	B----,Edward	Ran-159	James	Grn-141
David	Joh-278	B----,Eli	Ran-158	John	Grn-142
Eader	Joh-272	Ba----,Joshua	Ran-157	Zilpah	Cum-160
John	Joh-290	Ba----,William	Hal- 97	Baggett,Allen	Ans- 24
Thomas	Joh-272	Babb,Getho	Roc- 34	Asa	Ans- 21
Averett,Dempsy	Pit-257	John	Fra- 84	Avery	Mor- 67
Jas	Glf-176	Thomas	Fra- 94	Burrett	Hay-193
Sterling	Pit-257	Babbs,John	Gat-114	Josiah	Nor- 61
Averit,Abner	Jon-292	Baber,Benjamin	Rth- 87	Nathan	Nor- 60
Thos	Bla- 2	James	Rth- 86	Stephen	Ans- 24
Avert,Martin	Row- 48	John	Rth- 86	Baggit,Yiol	Mec- 50
Avery,Elizabeth	Bun- 90	Thomas	Rth- 88	Baggot,John	Sam-159
Frederick	Prq-213	William	Rth- 86	Josiah	Sam-160
Jacob	Lnc-329	Bace,Meredith	Grn-147	Baggs,Peter	Ora-121
John	Mon- 34	Bachan,Benj	Glf-166	Bagley,Elisha	Cha-192
John	Lnc-339	C Jr	Glf-166	George	Roc- 32
John	Lnc-329	Charles	Glf-166	Joab	Cha-201
Maightible	Bur-124	Nathal	Glf-166	John	Prq-214
Thos	Row- 43	Bachelor,William	Hal- 99	Joseph	Prq-213
William	Bla- 2	Wright W	Hal- 98	Josiah	Joh-284
Averytt,Daniel	Joh-276	Backley,James	Rth- 88	Nathan	Prq-213
Ellick Jr	Joh-290	Backus,Dotern	Brt- 51	Sarah	Prq-214
Simon	Joh-273	Thos	Cho-232	Thomas	Brt- 46
Avett,Thos	Ans- 16	Bacley,John	Rth- 87	Trotman	Gat-108
Thos	Ans- 12	Badden,Benjamin	Mec- 35	William	Prq-213
Avin,Peter	Cum-258	Jackson	Mec- 37	William Sr	Prq-214
Avington,Fanny	Cha-211	Jacob	Mec- 37	Bagly,Henry	Cha-197
Avins,Amos	Cha-197	Wm	Mec- 37	Milly	War-177
Avitt,Joseph	Ire-256	Baddon,Upton	Mec- 36	Bagwell,Drury	Rth- 89
Awatt,Mich	Bur-103	Baddy,James	Row- 77	Eli	Ire- 254
Awberry,Sarah	Sur-163	Badger,Hugh	Mec- 33	Levi	Ire-253
Axam,Mary	Ans- 26	Jas	Mec- 33	Lunsford	Rth- 86
Axton,Enoch	Roc- 7	Jno	Mec- 33	Nathaniel	Ire-247
Robert	Roc- 33	Badgers,Jno	Mec- 38	Thomas	Ire-249
Joseph	Sur-196	Badget,Bartley	Lnc-347	Bailey,Abner	Ora-126
Kinchen	Nsh- 78	Badgett,Abraham	Sur-171	Arnal	Joh-285
Aycock,Abner	War-167	James	Sur-170	Arthur	Joh-285
Amos	Mor- 65	Peeter	Per-128	Augustus	Rth- 89
Ephraim	Way-243	Ransom	Sur-171	Benjn	Pas-184
Henry	War-184	Thomas	Per-143	Brian	Hyd-233
James	Way-242	William	Cas- 48	Carr	Rth- 88
Jesse	Way-243	Wm	Per-143	Carr M	Rth- 89.
Simon	Way-254	Badham,Jno	Cho-226	Charles	Wil-262
Simon	Way-249	Miles	Wsh-227	Gabl	Pas-182
Aydelott,John	Roc- 21	Baety,Walter	Bun- 81	H	Ora-143
Aydetoll,John	Roc- 20	Bagby,David	Hal- 99	Henry	Bur-127
Aydlott,A	Cam-155	Edmon	Sur-193	Isom	Joh-285
H	Cam-155	John	Sur-169	James	Hyd-222

-11-

Name	Ref	Name	Ref	Name	Ref
Bailey,James	Nor- 61	Baines,John	Mar-445	Baker,Henry	Hrt-209
Jno	Ans- 23	Phillip	Cas- 48	Henry	Sto-108
Joel	Cho-224	Bainn,Lucretia	Hyd-226	Henry	Sto-108
John	Pas-182	Bains,Absalom	Fra- 96	Henry	Bft- 35
John	Lnc-333	George	Prq-214	Henry	Bur-126
John	Bur-130	Isaac	Mec- 53	Henry	Bur-107
John	Lnc-328	Isom	Row- 86	Henry Junr	Fra- 80
Joshua	Hyd-221	James	Cho-224	Henry Senr	Fra- 81
Josiah	Pas-182	Thornton	Cas- 48	Horatio	Row- 71
Martin	Rth- 89	Thos	Cho-224	Isaac	Bru-228
Margryt	Hyd-221	Wm	Cho-226	Isaac	Hrt-210
Mary	Hyd-221	Baird,Absalom	Bun- 98	Isaac	Ire-263
Matthew	Nor- 62	Adam	Lnc-331	Isaac	Sto-145
Richard	Hyd-222	B	Ash- 12	Isaac	Dup- 32
Robt	Pas-182	Bedunt	Bun- 93	J	Ash- 5
Salley	Rth- 89	John	Bun- 84	J	Ash- 8
Sally	Pas-182	John	Bur-113	J	Ash- 8
Samuel	Rth- 90	Phebe	Bun- 90	J C	Bru-228
Simon	Hyd-221	Richard	Bur-119	Jacob	Wil-260
Stephen	Mon- 18	Robert	Lnc-334	James	Gat-107
Sundia	Hyd-221	Saml	Mec- 51	James	Fra- 84
Thomas	Pas-182	W	Ash- 12	James (blk)	Fra- 89
Thomas	Pas-182	Will	Lnc-334	James	Edg- 51
William	Hyd-222	Wm	Mec- 51	Jas	Ora-123
William	Row- 64	Zebulon	Bun- 94	Jephtha	Mec- 35
Wm	Ans- 31	Baisden,James	Ons-101	Jerh	Brt- 43
Wm	Lnc-342	Jesse	Ons-104	Jesse	Pit-260
Bailiff,John	Cha-210	Jonah	Ons-104	Jno	Ans- 12
Bails,William	Cha-204	Baker,Alden	Mon- 22	Jno	Ans- 13
Baily,Aqnis	Ire-265	Allen	Bur-131	Jno	Ans- 24
Ansem	Bur-115	Allen	Nsh- 82	Job	Bla- 10
Benj	Mor- 67	Ama	Brt- 63	Joel	Bft- 24
David	Ire-265	Ann	Brt- 50	John	Cab-139
Francis	Lnc-275	Anna	Brt- 57	John	Bur-127
Jeremiah	Ran-157	Archd	Cum-260	John	Hal- 97
John	Ran-159	Archd	Cum-268	John	Mor- 67
John	Bur-127	Archd	Nsh- 81	John	Hyd-225
John	Ire-265	Aron	Mec- 37	John	Lnc-329
John	Lnc-375	Asa	Pit-260	John	Row- 71
John	Ons-101	Benj	Hrt-209	John	Mor- 69
John	Bur-115	Benjamin	Pit-260	John	Bun- 77
Martha	Lnc-355	Benjamin	Gat-107	John	Brt- 66
Miriam	Pas-183	Blake	War-168	John	Roc- 5
William	Bur-115	Blake	Gat-114	John	Ire-263
William	Ran-158	Bray	Gat-106	John	Cha-216
Bain,Archabald	Bun- 95	Claban	Hal- 98	John	Cum-266
G	Cam-162	Criteton	Bur-128	John	Lnc-353
Hugh Senr	Cum-267	Daniel Esq	Cum-251	John	Nsh- 81
Jean	Cum-256	David	Bur-114	John B	Gat-108
John	Cum-268	Dredd	Hrt-210	John R	Cum-269
John	Ran-157	Dugald	Cum-267	Jonathan	Mec- 37
Jonathan	Ran-157	Edward B	Brt- 44	Jonathan	Way-248
Lydia	Cur- 91	Elijah	Mec- 39	Jonathan	Joh-289
Peter	Cum-267	George	Mec- 37	Jonathan	Nsh- 87
Bainer,John	Bft- 25	George	Sur-176	Jordan	Hal- 97
Richd	Bft- 25	George	Bur-131	Jos	Bft- 36
Sarah	Bft- 25	George	Mec- 42	Jos	Ora-137
Baines,Edward	Ire-246	Hector	Rob-243	Joseph	Ora-130

Name	Loc	Name	Loc	Name	Loc
Baker,Joseph	Row- 71	Balam	Bru-232	Balentine,Peter	Cur- 90
Joseph	Mec- 42	Balance,P	Cam-155	Bales,Caleb	Glf-170
Joshua	Cab-136	Balcom,Britain	Sur-169	Jesse	Glf-163
Joushua	Cab-139	Balcomb,Hester	Dup- 17	John	Rth- 86
Juditha	Gat-116	Balcum,Ichabud	Joh-283	John	Glf-169
Larry	Brt- 63	Baldance,Jno	Pit-232	Nathan	Sur-186
Levy	Brt- 63	Wm	Pit-232	Thomas	Sur-186
M	Ash- 10	Baldaree,Richard	Pit-235	Balew,Stepen	Bur-104
Malcolm	Mor- 69	Balderee,William	Pit-235	Baley,Averytt	Joh-284
Martha	Cha-206	Baldin,E	Bru-234	Carr	Row- 58
Michael	Ans- 27	John	Lnc-333	Champion	Grn-121
Michal	Row- 69	Balding,Abner	Cha-213	Daniel	Joh-285
Moses	Edg- 44	Baldiy,William	Rth- 89	Henry	Per-126
Nancy	Bur-127	Baldridge,Alexr	Rth- 86	Israel	Grn-121
Nathan	Hal- 99	Alexander	Lnc-360	James	Roc- 3
Nathan	Ire-263	Danl	Ora-125	James	Sur-166
Nathan	Lnc-334	Danl Jun	Ora-173	Jeremiah	Grn-121
Neill	Rob-232	ohn	Rth- 86	Jessey	Joh-284
Penelope	Hrt-211	John	Rth- 88	John	Hrt-214
Peter	Mec- 44	Michael	Lnc-361	John	Row- 61
Phillip	Lnc-353	William	Rth- 86	John	Joh-286
Polley	Cur- 85	Baldtrip,John	Wil-262	John	Grn-121
R	Bla- 11	Baldwin,A	Ora-132	John	Joh-283
Richard	Hrt-213	C	Col- 17	John	Cha-208
Richard	Bur-127	C	Col- 17	Moses	Lnc-356
Richd	Brt- 63	Danl	Glf-163	Richard	Grn-121
S	Bru-226	E	Ash- 15	Sarah	Per-126
S	Ash- 12	Elisha	Bur-126	Thos	Cha-213
S	Ash- 8	J	Ash- 15	W	Ora-136
Salley	Hrt-211	J	Ash- 15	William	Bun- 81
Saml	Mec- 33	J	Ash- 4	William	Hrt-214
Saml	Bur-104	J	Col- 17	William	Joh-284
Samuel	Gat-114	J	Col- 17	Wm	Grn-124
Sarah	Wil-280	J	Col- 17	Balfour,Eliza	Row- 89
Sary	Hrt-208	J	Col- 17	William	Edg- 44
Shadrack	Hrt-208	J	Col- 20	Baling,Andrew	Wil-277
Silas	Lnc-340	J	Ash- 6	Benjn Jnr	Ran-158
Simmons J	Mar- 5	J	Ora-169	Charles	Ran-157
Susannah	Cum-258	Jesse	Glf-164	John	Ran-157
T	Col- 17	John	Glf-166	Justice	Wil-263
Thomas	Wil-267	John	Cha-213	William	Ran-157
Thomas	Bur-114	John	Ora-119	Ball,Benjamin	Ire-255
Uriah	Brt- 52	John	Glf-187	Cassey	Ran-158
William	Way-248	John Jr	Glf-166	Daniel	Bun- 90
William	Hyd-223	P	Col- 17	Daniel	War-170
William	Brt- 47	Robt	Ora-159	Darquis	Ons-103
William	Rth- 87	S	Ash- 10	David	Jon-293
William	Bur-115	Saml	Cha-199	David	Wil-267
Wm	Bru-228	Uriah	Glf-163	Elijah	Ons-103
Wm	Mon- 22	W	Col- 20	James	Ons- 97
Wm	Ans- 11	W	Ash- 8	Jarret	Row- 44
Wm	Nsh- 82	Wm	Cha-213	Jas	Bft- 27
Wm	Rob-231	Wm	Ora-126	Jay	Bun- 90
Winny	Brt- 63	Balenger,Mary	Joh-290	John	Wil-264
Z	Ash- 6	Balentine,Davies	Cur- 90	John	Bft- 27
Z W	Bft- 31	Joseph	Cur- 90	John	Jon-293
Zebadiah	Wil-265	Joseph	Cur- 90	Lewis	Bun- 81
Bakers,Simmons	Hal- 98	Linsay	Cur- 90	Morning	Nsh- 76

Name	Ref	Name	Ref	Name	Ref	Name	Ref
Ball,Moses	Jon-293	Ballard,Sarah	Row- 56	Baning,Francis	Bur-119		
Osborn	Grn-128	Shanrick	Rob-235	James	Bur-120		
Ozborn	Bun- 81	Silas	Mar- 8	Banker,Jacob	Mec- 29		
Samuel	Ire-263	Silas E	Mar- 14	Bankes,James	Cur- 91		
William	Wil-267	Thomas	Bun- 98	Thos	Cur- 90		
William	Row- 46	Thomas	Sur-162	Bankhead,Hugh	Bun- 80		
Wm	Row- 51	Thomas	Gat-109	Bankly,Wm	Per-126		
Wm	Nsh- 79	Thos	Glf-162	Banks,Brittain	Hrt-213		
Wm	Cha-201	W	Glf-162	George	Nor- 61		
Ballabaugh,Abram	Ran-159	W M	Ora-141	Gerard	Cum-260		
Ballad,Edward	War-171	Wiley	Lnc-364	Hennis	Sto-105		
Ballance,Aron	Hyd-228	William	Cas- 49	Hennis	Sto-139		
Caleb	Hyd-228	William	Rth- 90	Henry	Wil-283		
Caleb	Cur- 88	William	Rth- 90	Henry	Bft- 33		
Charles	Cur- 86	Wilson	Len-313	Isaac	Grn-128		
Demsey	Cur- 88	Wm	Glf-162	Jacob	Edg- 44		
James	Cur- 87	Wyatt	Ora-160	Jenny	Cho-222		
John	Cur- 88	Wyot	Cas- 49	Joel	Row- 65		
John	Hyd-231	Ballen,William Jr	Bur-111	John	Edg- 58		
Johuay	Cur- 82	Ballentine,Willeby	Nsh- 88	John	Sto-123		
Laban	Hyd-231	Ballew,Charles	Bur-119	John	Row- 64		
Levin	Cur- 88	Joseph	Bur-119	John	Bun- 80		
Morey	Cur- 91	M	Ash- 14	John	Wil-272		
Thos	Cur- 91	Robert Jr	Bur-129	John G	Wil-283		
Wallis	Cur- 82	Robert Snr	Bur-124	Jona	Pas-182		
Wm	Cur- 82	Tho	Bur-124	Joseph	Pas-183		
Ballard,Andr	Cas- 50	William	Bur-127	Joshua	Per-126		
Benjamin	Ire-257	Balley,W	Glf-178	Lettice	Cho-223		
Byrum	Sto-154	Ballinger,Jesse	Glf-163	Mary	Tyr-207		
Byrum	Sto-113	Jos	Glf-163	Nancy	Bft- 33		
Caleb	Way-233	H	Glf-163	Nathaniel	Bun- 87		
Daniel	Ons-100	Julian D	Prq-214	Omey	Nor- 62		
Easter	Row- 86	Balls,William	Edg- 65	Samuel	Sto-104		
Edward	Nsh- 80	Balthrop,Augustin	War-167	Samuel	Sto-109		
Edwin	Gat-109	Francis	War-171	Samuel	Sto-145		
Elias	Way-252	William	War-183	Samuel	Sto-138		
Elisha	Nor- 62	William	War-183	Solomon	Row- 65		
H	Mon- 35	Baly,Gabriel	Per-148	Tempy	Hal- 99		
J	Mon- 35	William	Bun- 94	Thomas	Edg- 57		
Hincher	Mon- 25	Bameycastle,John	Row- 60	Thomas	Pas-182		
James	Lnc-364	Bamsay,William	Wsh-227	W	Ash- 15		
James	Ons-107	Ban,Duncan Buie	Cum-270	Westley	Bun- 92		
Jas	Mor- 67	Banch,Edwd	Cha-213	Will C	Pas-183		
John	Cur- 91	Bandy,George	Lnc-347	William	Hyd-233		
John	Rth- 87	James	Edg- 59	William	Wil-253		
John	Ire-237	Thomas	Lnc-347	Bankston,Andrew	Mon- 50		
John	Ons-100	Bane,Alexr	Mec- 54	Banner,Benjamin Sr	Sto-126		
John	Rth- 90	Francis	Cha-201	Benjn	Sto- 96		
John	Mon- 25	Hugh	Mec- 44	Charles	Sto-125		
Joseph	Ons-104	Jno	Mec- 40	Charles	Sto- 95		
Kader	Gat-108	Matthew	Mec- 38	James	Sto-138		
Leary	Mar- 13	Robt	Mec- 40	Joseph	Sto-104		
Levi	Mor- 67	Banes,Henry	Nsh- 85	Joshua	Sto- 96		
Lott	Ons-101	Henry Sr	Nsh- 85	Joshua	Sto-125		
Mary	Way-235	Baney,Giden	Cur- 93	Banow,Polley	Glf-172		
N	Glf-162	John	Cur- 93	William	Glf-185		
Rebekah	Hal-100	Banfield,David	Rob-234	Banta,Mary	Cur- 85		
Reuben	Lnc-364	Bangor,John	Bur-116	Banter,Samuel	Row- 62		
S	Mon- 35	Banick,Jeremiah	Rth- 86	Banton,Ebbenazer	Ran-158		

Name	Ref	Name	Ref	Name	Ref
Baram,Thos	Cha-191	Barbers,Cullen	Wsh-226	Barfield,Lewis Jr	Dup- 28
Barath,Henry	Sto- 97	Barbary,Allen	Sam-152	Lewis Sr	Dup- 28
Barbarick,Leonard	Cab-142	Barbour,John	Wsh-228	Nathan	Ons-100
Barbee,Ann	Cha-200	Barby,Gray	Cha-190	Solomon	Way-247
B	Ora-141	James	Way-239	Thomas	Edg- 53
C	Ora-156	Barclift,Demsy	Prq-213	William	Edg- 54
Francis	Ora-116	J	Cam-160	Barge,Mrs. C.	Cum-240
Gray	Ora-116	J	Cam-153	L	Cum-237
J	Ora-141	J	Cam-159	G K	Cum-239
Joseph	Cha-211	John D	Prq-213	Barger,Geo H	Row- 67
Josiah	Cha-200	Joseph	Prq-213	Henry	Row- 67
Mark	Ora-170	N	Cam-156	Isaac	Lnc-375
Mordecai	Cha-200	Nancy	Prq-215	Jacob	Cab-140
Wm	Ora-116	Samn Jr	Prq-213	Jacob	Cab-144
Wm Jr	Ora-142	Samuel Sr	Prq-213	John	Cab-144
Barber,Absalam	Ons-102	Thos	Prq-213	John	Cab-140
Barbary	Row- 81	Barcly,Freddick	Ran-159	Simeon	Lnc-375
Benjamin	Rch-207	Barco,B	Cam-155	Barham,Charles	Sto-133
Burwell	Joh-275	D	Cam-159	Daniel	Sto-108
David	Row- 80	J	Cam-156	Daniel	Sto-143
Elias	Row- 74	L	Cam-156	Edmund	Sto-133
Eliza	Ons-103	Bard,Alexander	Ire-237	Hartwell	Sto-148
Elizabeth	Cha-213	James	Lnc-331	James	Sto-132
Elizebeth	Ans- 33	Barden,Arthur	Way-246	Littleton	Sto-133
Frederick	Brt- 45	James	Hrt-212	Nathan	Sto-127
Geo	Cha-216	John	Way-329	Nusom	Roc- 33
George	Joh-277	Mary	Mar- 16	Run	Glf-180
Isaac	Prq-214	William	Way-243	Thomas	Sto-147
Isaac	Ons- 97	Bardin,Richard	Hrt-212	Barickfriend,Geo	Cab-138
Jas	Ora-146	Bardon,Richard	Hrt-213	Baringer,Geo	Cab-145
Jno	Mon- 37	Bardus,John	Wil-284	Jacob	Cab-138
Jno	Ans- 9	Bare,Abraham	Gat-109	John	Cab-140
John	Lnc-335	H	Ash- 10	Mathias	Cab-146
John	Hal- 98	H	Ash- 6	Paul	Cab-146
John	Mon- 48	J	Ash- 10	Barington,Samuel	Mor- 64
John	Cab-141	Barefield,A	Col- 21	Barkeman,J	Glf-177
John	Ons-103	A	Col- 18	Barker,Ann	Pas-181
Jonathan	Row- 72	Abraham	Rob-238	Burnley	Cas- 49
M	Ora-140	Archd	Rob-240	Burwell	Ire-249
Matthew	Ora-167	Charles	Rob-240	Charles	Rob-243
Mitchell	Ons- 98	Depey	Rob-237	Daniel	Sur-184
Moses	Prq-213	J	Col- 20	David	Cas- 49
Mourning	Prq-214	Jesse	Rob-239	David	Bur-115
Owen	Joh-277	Levi	Rob-240	Elizabeth	Prq-214
Plyar	Joh-275	S	Col- 20	Fanny	Len-310
Prudence	Wsh-226	Willie	Rob-236	Geo	Bun- 90
Reuben	Joh-276	Willis	Rob-237	George	Cas- 49
Rhoda	Ans- 10	Barefoot,Cloah	Way-246	George M	Sur-185
Robert	Lnc-342	Elizabeth	Edg- 67	George W	Roc- 7
Robert	Lnc-330	J	Col- 17	Willum	Ire-249
Barber Shop	Bft- 36	Jack	Way-245	H. John	Cas- 48
Thomas	Joh-276	Noah	Joh-289	Hezekiah	Wil-258
Thomas	Ons-101	Stephen	Edg- 67	Hezekiah Jr	Wil-272
Travers	Roc- 12	Barfield,Blake	Way-247	Hinchen	Ire-249
William	Roc- 12	Ephraim	Edg- 54	Howel	Ire-249
William	Sur-194	Esther	Edg- 54	Howel	Ire-249
William Jr	Sur-194	Jas	Ans- 18	Howell	Nor- 62
Wm	Ora-160	John	Edg- 54	James	Roc- 14
Wm D	Brt- 45	Lewis	Dup- 15	Joannah	Nor- 62

-15-

Name	Loc	Name	Loc	Name	Loc
Barker,John	Prq-214	Barnard,Willowbey	Cur- 89	Barnes,John	Edg- 67
John	Prq-215	Barner,Martha	Sto-128	John Jr	Way-243
John	Roc- 22	Martha	Sto- 98	John Jr	Nor- 61
John	Nor- 61	Barnes,Abraham	Edg- 48	Joseph	Edg- 66
John	Ire-263	Agathy	Roc- 33	Joshua	Pit-260
John	Cas- 49	Archelus	Edg- 48	Joshua	Rob-237
John Jr	Cas- 48	Benja	Len-216	Josiah	Nor- 61
Joseph	Prq-214	Benjamin	Edg- 65	Josiah	Edg- 48
Lemon	Prq-214	Britain	Rob-236	Julon	Edg- 64
Leonard	Roc- 22	Britain Jnr	Rob-236	Malecha	Edg- 60
Robt	Cha-207	Brittain	Nsh- 89	Maradeth	Rob-237
Stephen	Cha-203	Britton	Edg- 65	Mary	Mar-445
Thomas	Bun- 90	Burwell	Edg- 64	McCollins	Nor- 61
Thomas	Sur-183	Charles	Edg- 61	Michael	Bur-127
Wilson	Prq-214	Chesley	Roc- 24	Miles	Nsh- 88
Barkers,Judith Negr	Hal- 99	David	Way-232	Morning	Edg- 49
Barkey,Robert	Lnc-364	David	Edg- 40	Nathaniel	Roc- 24
Barkley,Henry	Lnc-364	Drury	Way-246	Nathl	Roc- 22
James	Ire-249	Elias	Row- 52	Noah	Edg- 49
John	Nor- 61	Henery	Cur- 81	Reddick	Way-246
Mary	Row- 73	Henry	Nor- 61	Reddick	Edg- 65
Rhodes	Nor- 61	Jacob	Way-232	Richard	Gat-113
Barkly,James	Ire-252	Jacob	Rob-233	Richd	Row- 51
James	Ire-252	Jacob	Edg- 48	Rodom	Hal- 98
Ruth	Ire-251	Jacob	Way-245	Saml	Row- 51
Barks,Tamar	Sam-159	Jacob Sr	Way-254	Samuel	Roc- 21
Barksdale,Daniel	Edg- 57	James	Hal- 98	Samuel	Roc- 13
Sherod	Cum-253	James	Row- 51	Samuel	Ire-256
Barlee,Zadock	Cha-198	James	Roc- 20	Samuel	Nsh- 78
Barlow,Mrs.	Bru-236	James	Nsh- 78	Samuel Jr	Way-254
Benjamin	Edg- 63	James	Edg- 66	Samuel Sr	Way-254
David	Edg- 63	James	Edg- 48	Sarah	Edg- 49
John Jr	Wil-273	James	Bur-109	Simon	Way-254
John	Wil-274	James	Gat-108	Sollomon	Edg- 48
Marsh	Rob-228	James	Sto-156	Stephen	Edg- 65
Ralph	Rob-223	James	Edg- 65	Thos	Rob-237
Thos	Ora-117	James Jr	Edg- 63	William Sq A	Roc- 34
Thos	Ora-177	James Sen	Edg- 63	William	Roc- 35
Zac	Row- 59	Jas	Rob-239	William	Ire-263
Barmer,Grey	Nor- 61	Jas	Rob-238	William	Ire-249
John	Mon- 24	Jessee	Rob-237	William	Edg- 60
Jourden	Mon- 24	Jessee	Edg- 66	William Jr	Way-254
Barmes,Thomas	Gat-116	Jethro	Way-232	Willie	Edg- 64
Barmight,Nathan	Pas-183	Jethro	Rob-237	Wm, Capt.	Rob-238
Barnard,Agatha	Wsh-228	Jethrow	Edg- 64	Wm	Grn-138
Asa	Sto-149	Jno	Rob-237	Wm	Nsh- 79
Christopher	Ire-268	Jno	Rob-233	Barnet,Hannah	Ons-104
E	Glf-170	John	Way-246	James	Jon-293
F	Cam-159	John	Way-254	Jessee Jnr	Grn-141
J	Cam-155	John	Hal- 98	John Jr	Grn-145
Jessey	Cur- 86	John	Hal- 99	John Jr	Grn-147
Job	Bun- 94	John	Roc- 20	Thomas	Lnc-361
Joshuay	Cur- 81	John	Roc- 24	Thomas	Pas-184
Luke	Cur- 89	John	Wsh-218	Barnett, Mrs.	Mec- 37
Luke	Bun- 78	John	Nsh- 79	Able	Mec- 33
Peter	Cur- 89	John	Edg- 66	Abraham	Glf-157
Reuben	Ire-268	John	Edg- 65	Ann	Tyr-209
William	Sto-133	John	Bur-107	Asa	Sto-114

Barnett,Asa	Sto-111	Barnhill,Nathan	Pit-255	Barnwell,William	Cas- 49	
Eliz	Len-319	R	Ora-154	Baroth,Henry	Sto-126	
J	Glf-162	Robt	Mec- 39	John	Sto-103	
J	Glf-179	Samuel	Mar- 11	Barott,Aney	Cur- 86	
James	Per-136	William	Bun- 79	Barr,David	Mec- 40	
James	Tyr-209	William	Pit-254	James	Sto-116	
James	Grn-135	Wm	Ora-164	James	Sto-109	
Jas	Glf-157	Barnicastle,Beverly	Brt- 45	James	Sto-145	
Jessee	Ans- 14	Barnite,James	Tyr-209	James	Sto-156	
Jessey	Grn-135	Jonan	Tyr-209	John Senr	Row- 71	
Jno	Mec- 25	Slly	Tyr-209	Moses D	Lnc-331	
John	Grn-147	Barns,Absalom	Brt- 52	Robert	Roc- 19	
John	Per-127	Brinsley	Wil-277	William	Gat-115	
Joseph	Grn-135	Bursil	Ran-157	William	Rth- 88	
Matthew	Ans- 14	Charles	Hrt-212	William	Sto-132	
Matthew	Len-319	Conrad	Bur-105	William	Gat-109	
R	Tyr-209	Elijah	Wil-278	Wm	Row- 72	
Rebecca	Len-320	Elizabeth	Wil-278	Barradail,Jas	Brt- 62	
Reuben	Ire-269	Fanny	Rth- 90	Barrd,Adam	Lnc-331	
Robert	Hyd-223	George	Bun- 74	John	Lnc-331	
Robt	Mec- 35	Henry	Brt- 63	Barrem,Abraham	Row- 77	
Rosanah	Mec- 50	Isaac	Brt- 51	Barren,Phillip	Row- 38	
Sion	Mec- 38	James	Hrt-207	Barrenger,Peter	Row- 67	
Stephen	Tyr-205	Jesse	Wil-275	Barrens,L	Ora-139	
Thomas	Rth- 90	Jesse	Brt- 51	Barrenton,Isaac	Car-184	
Thos	Mec- 51	Jesse	Rch-203	John	Car-174	
William	Cas- 48	Jno	Mec- 50	Lemuel	Pas-183	
William	Sto-109	John	Wil-278	Barret,Nancy	Jon-294	
William	Ire-269	John	Wil-275	Sollomon	Mor- 56	
William	Rth- 89	John	Lnc-355	Barrett,Abner	Ire-270	
William	Sto-145	John	Cha-207	James	Nor- 62	
Wm	Mec- 27	John	Fra- 79	Mashack	Sto-124	
Wm	Grn-135	John Senr	Nor- 61	Riddick	Edg- 70	
Barney,Benjamin	Hyd-233	Jonathan	Cha-204	Thomas	Ans- 11	
Barnhart,Charles	Cab-141	Joshua	Hrt-212	William	Cha-197	
Charles	Cab-141	Joshua	Wil-278	Barrier,Henry	Row- 67	
Charles Senr	Cab-141	Nicholas	Bur-104	Nicholas	Row- 68	
Christr	Cab-140	Penny	Brt- 51	Barringer,Geo	Cab-140	
Geo	Cab-142	Prrain D	Nsh- 78	Henry	Ire-256	
H	Glf-177	Reuben	Wil-282	John	Cab-140	
Jacob	Cab-141	Reubin	Brt- 63	Mathias	Lnc-378	
John	Cab-141	Reubin	Brt- 51	Mattw	Cab-141	
John	Cab-141	Richard	Row- 86	Paul	Cab-140	
Mathew	Cab-141	Richard	Row- 83	Stophel	Cab-	
Mathias	Cab-140	Rubin	Tyr-212	Barrington,John	Jon-293	
Nancy	Cab-142	Solomon	Wil-278	Barrinow,Benj	Ons-104	
Paul	Cab-142	Thomas	Wil-285	Charles	Ons-104	
Phillip	Cab-142	Thomas	Tyr-205	Ephraim	Ons- 99	
Stophel	Cab-140	Wilby	Rob-239	James	Onc- 99	
Stophel	Cab-141	William	Pas-183	Risdon	Ons-101	
Barnhill,David	Mar- 13	William	Ons-101	Barris,Sarah	Jon-294	
George	Pit-254	Wm	Ans- 24	Barrock,Isaac	Len-320	
Henry	Pit-255	Wm	Brt- 51	Wm	Len-311	
J	Ora-155	Zacheus	Wil-278	Zach	Len-311	
James	Mar- 14	Barnswell,Thos	Cho-222	Barrod,Booz	Mar- 13	
James	Mar- 5	Barnwell,David	Cas- 49	Barron,Eliza	Bft- 24	
Jesse	Pit-254	Edwd	Cas- 48	Geo	Bft- 23	
John	Pit-254	Robt	Cas- 48	Isaiah	Bft- 27	

Name	Ref	Name	Ref	Name	Ref
Barron,James	Brt- 45	Bartlet,Edward	Pit-243	Basnett,Etenardry	Cur- 81
Jonathan	Row- 75	Elizabeth	War-171	Basnight,Joseph	Tyr-204
Moses	Sto- 50	Elizabeth	Hyd-225	Lemuel	Tyr-204
Barrot,Alce	Gat-109	John	Bun- 83	Basnite,Jos D	Tyr-204
Dominie	Mon- 25	John	Cur- 87	Wm	Tyr-204
Isom	Bun- 92	Saml	Ans- 25	Bason,Fredrick	Roc- 2
John	Per-134	Samuel	War-181	Jacob	Ora-163
John	Row- 66	Spears	War-181	Jas	Ora-123
John	Bun- 92	William	War-184	Jno	Ora-124
Miles	Bun- 78	Bartlett,Benj	Way-242	Jno Sen	Ora-136
Nathan	Mor- 58	Hartin	Cas- 49	Bass,Aaron	Cha-201
Ward	Bun- 92	Merrit	Way-242	Abraham	Way-246
William	Bun- 86	Samuel	Way-242	Absalom	Per-136
William	Ons-106	Sollomon	Edg- 54	Agtor	Nsh- 74
Wm	Mor- 63	Bartley,John	Lnc-336	Alexander	Way-234
Barrott,Henry	Sto-112	John	Lnc-340	Alexr	Sam-155
Wiley	Mor- 6	John	Row- 73	Aley	Way-236
Barrotts,Isaac	Row- 81	John	Rth- 90	Andrew	Dup- 14
Barrow,Ann	Hyd-220	Robert	Sur-171	Andrew	Sam-159
Bartholomew	Hal- 98	Sam	Ora-134	Ann	Nsh- 74
Benj	Ons- 98	Bartly,Catherin	Row- 72	Arthur	Way-243
Bennett	Edg- 40	James	Rth- 89	Arthur Jr	Way-243
Edmund	Nsh- 77	John	Glf-156	Benjamin	Rch-196
Elizth	Hyd-222	Barton,A	Ora-155	Bryan	Way-243
Eri	Prq-214	Aqulla	Cas- 49	Caleb	Sam-159
Fredrick	Hyd-220	Dorrel	Row- 59	Cason	Grn-143
George	Hyd-227	Elijah	Sur-163	Council	Nor- 62
Holly	War-172	Elisha	Cas- 49	Darling	Grn-143
James	Pit-235	Hudgins	Per-136	Deley	Grn-130
James	Hyd-222	Jas	Ora-161	Dempsey	Grn-143
James	Fra- 88	Jno	Ora-157	Demsy	Grn-119
Jesse	Hyd-220	John	Glf-189	Dennis	Nor- 62
John	Edg- 63	Lewis	Cas- 50	Drury	Nor- 62
John	Len-312	Lewis	Cas- 49	Edward	Sur-183
Joseph	Len-311	Tho	Ora-130	Elijah	Rob-237
Joseph	Prq-214	Tho	Ora-115	Ephraim	Way-246
Moes	Sto-110	William	Ran-159	Everit	Sam-157
Patience	Pit-239	Barvard,Zebulon	Bun- 79	Frederick	Ans- 21
Thomas	Hal- 98	Basar,William	Per-136	Fredrick	Sur-179
Barrows,Wm	Mon- 49	Basdel,Richd	Cas- 49	Henry	Ans- 21
Barrs,John	Len-316	Baseden,John	Dup- 31	Hosea	Way-254
John Senr	Len-312	Lyben	Dup- 12	Isaac	Hal- 97
Barrum,-----	Hrt-208	Mary	Dup- 21	Isaac	Sur-172
Barry,John	Lnc-336	William	Dup- 33	J	Cam-155
Barrycastle,John	Row- 54	Basel,Berneby	Ran-159	Jacob	Fra- 95
Barson,Asa	Cum-258	Basford,C	Bru-224	James	Nor- 62
Jno	Ora-143	W	Bru-224	Jeremiah	Way-254
Barsons,-----	Glf-157	Bashford,Jas	Ans- 33	Jessee	Nsh- 83
Barster,Henry	Mon- 43	Basil,Caleb	Cur- 92	Jethro	Nor- 62
Bartee,John	Pas-181	Basinger,Geo	Row- 39	Jethro	Way-254
Barten,William	Row- 83	Henry	Row- 88	Jethro	Nsh- 83
William	Ran-157	John	Row- 86	Joel	Sam-154
Barter,Hugh	Sto-127	Joseph	Row- 69	John	Brt- 64
John	Edg- 49	Basker,Robert	Ran-158	John	Way-238
Bartholomew,Jacob	Fra- 87	Basket,Pleasant	War-178	John	Way-254
John	Fra- 92	Baskin,John	Ran-157	John	Cum-250
Lewis	War-177	William	Ran-157	John	Nsh- 83
Bartick,James	Rch-200	Basnet,Archibell	Cur- 81	John	Nor- 62
Thomas	Rch-200	Willowbey	Cur- 81	Joseph	Pit-244

-18-

Name	Ref	Name	Ref	Name	Ref
Bass,Joseph	Mon- 26	Batchelor,William	Hal- 97	Battle,Isiah	Edg- 55
Joshua	Sam-163	Willm	Fra- 89	James	Edg- 62
Lindsey	Sam-159	Batcheltor,Stephen	Nsh- 81	James	Hrt-214
Macklin	Hal- 99	Bateman,Ann	Row- 76	James	Cum-257
Mary	Joh-288	Benjn	Tyr-211	Jeremiah	Edg- 40
Mary	Cum-238	Daniel	Wsh-218	Jethrow	Edg- 56
Moses	Ran-159	Ebenezer	Wsh-219	Joel	Edg- 62
Moses	Sur-191	Eliz M	Tyr-212	Jno	Ans- 18
Moses	Grn-143	Esaus	Cum-247	Josiah	Nsh- 77
Nathan	Grn-128	Evan	Wsh-219	Randolf	Cha-191
Needham	Way-236	Godfrey	Tyr-211	Thomas	Ons- 99
Owen	Ire-256	Isaac	Wsh-220	Battles,Wm	Nsh- 77
Rassey	Grn-119	Jacob	Roc- 27	Batton,J	Col- 18
Reese	Cum-266	James	Roc- 26	Josuah	Rch-197
Reuben	Glf-165	James	Cho-223	Batts,Bayley	Edg- 64
Rice	Rob-231	Jeremiah	Edg- 65	Hannah	Dup- 34
Richd	Ans- 25	Jesse	Wsh-217	Jesse	Dup- 35
Salley	Way-238	John	Tyr-211	John	Nor- 62
Salley	Grn-130	John	Cho-222	John	Edg- 64
Samuel	Hal- 97	Jonathan	Cum-262	Lewis	Nor- 63
Seth	Ora-157	Joseph	Tyr-211	Lucy	Edg- 63
Simon	Hal- 98	Lamuel	Prq-214	Priscilla	Dup- 35
Thomas	Brt- 64	Levi	Tyr-211	Sarah	Dup- 35
Thomas	Sto-147	Miles	Wsh-219	William	Edg- 63
Thomas	Way-235	Nancy	Prq-215	Baty,David	Sur-191
Thomas	Rch-196	Nathan	Tyr-211	Baucum,Bennet	Joh-274
Uriah Sr	Way-250	Rabeckah	Edg- 50	Baudeford,Wm	Rob-243
Uriah Jr	Way-248	Sarah	Tyr-212	Baugust,Henry	Wil-259
W	Cam-163	Stephen	Tyr-211	James	Wil-271
William	Cas- 49	Stephn	Tyr-210	Richard	Wil-259
William	Sam-155	Zilpha	Prq-214	Robert	Wil-259
William	Nor- 62	Batemon,John	Cas- 48	Baul,Joshuay	Cur- 86
Willis	Grn-119	Bates,---rdw	Cur- 90	Baulding,Eliza	Cas- 49
Bassell,Lewis	Sur-180	Elisha	Pit-242	Henry	Cas- 50
Basset,Lewis	Hrt-214	George	Sur-174	Luke	Cas- 49
Stephen	Cum-245	Jacob	Sur-190	Baull,Hosey	Cur- 86
Willie	Hrt-214	Jacob	Sur-177	William	Cur- 86
Bastin,John	Cas- 49	James	Grn-147	Baum,Aberaham Jr	Cur- 80
Thomas Jr	Cas- 49	James	Pit-242	Aberaham Sr	Cur- 80
Thomas Sr	Cas- 49	John	Wil-282	Daniel	Cur- 80
William	Cas- 49	John Estate	Grn-147	Ezra	Cur- 82
Baswood,Thos	Cur- 91	Matthias	Wil-280	John	Nor- 60
Batchedor,Benj	Hyd-222	Robert	Row- 56	Judey	Cur- 80
Batcheldor,John	Dup- 34	William	Roc- 14	Moses	Cur- 80
Richd	Dup- 35	Bathune,Angus	Mon- 30	Nancy	Rob-228
Batchellor,Brney	Nsh- 83	Jno	Mon- 30	Norris	Nor- 60
James	Nsh- 83	Neil	Mon- 30	P	Cam-153
John	Nsh- 83	Bator,John	Bur-129	Robert	Nor- 60
Joseph	Nsh- 83	Batter,Wm	Bur-130	Baunt,James	Row- 60
Saml	Nsh- 83	Battern,Meradeth	Rch-200	Baviar,Nathan	Bur-117
Willis	Nsh- 83	William	Rch-200	Baw,Isaiah H	Sto-153
Wilson	Nsh- 84	Battin,David	Hrt-214	Richard	Sto-154
Wm	Nsh- 83	J	Mon- 36	Bawldin,Aaron	Rch-200
Batchelor,Danil	Nsh- 80	M	Mon- 36	Jesse	Rch-198
John	Hal- 99	Battle,Alfred J	Edg- 55	John	Rch-201
Joseph	Nsh-	Demsey	Edg- 55	Moses	Rch-201
Reuben	Fra- 89	Elisha Sen	Edg- 61	Bawm,Lemuel	Ran-158
Right	Nsh- 84	Elisha Jr	Edg- 60	Baxley,Jacob	Rob-234
Solomon	Fra- 89	Isaac	Edg- 70	James	Rob-234

Name	Ref	Name	Ref	Name	Ref	Name	Ref
Baxley,Willis	Rob-227	Beacham,John	Rch-204	Beard,James	Cum-248		
Wm	Rob-234	Stephen	Row- 61	Jesse	Ran-159		
Baxly,Barnabas	Mec- 45	Zeblon	Cur- 87	John	Row- 90		
Baxter,Daniel	Mec- 35	Beachum,Sarah	Bft- 25	John Junr	Cum-249		
David	Row- 82	Beaders,Jane	Row- 56	Joseph	Cum-248		
James	Hal- 97	Beadle,Caleb	Pas-181	Lewis	Row- 89		
James	Row- 56	Beagles,Beasel	Mec- 35	Michl	Row- 88		
James	Row- 73	Beal,Daniel	Cha-214	Neill Senr	Cum-248		
James	War-175	Edmd	Pas-184	Nub	Bla- 8		
John	War-176	James O	Ire-242	R	Glf-167		
John	Cum-239	John	Joh-272	Richd	Glf-165		
John	Row- 66	Joseph	Row- 63	Robert	Ire-237		
Martha	Row- 86	Joshua	Cha-214	Thomas	Ire-242		
Martha	Row- 73	Rachel	Ire-242	William	Joh-288		
Nathaniel	War-178	Thomas	Ire-243	William	Cum-260		
Sarah	Lnc-337	Thos	Cha-214	William	Ire-242		
William	Rth- 87	Willis	Nor- 62	Wm	Glf-163		
Baxtor,Ilas	Cur- 88	Beale,Benjn	Lnc-339	Wm	Glf-162		
John	Cas- 48	Richd	Lnc-277	Beardin,Benj	Grn-143		
Joseph	Cur- 88	William	Lnc-361	Charles	Grn-143		
Joseph	Cur- 89	Bealer,Solomon	Pit-233	Bearding,John	Rth- 89		
Thomas	Cas- 48	Beales,Alex	Cur- 86	Bearmon,Abraham	Gat-113		
Thos	Cur- 89	Bealow,John F	Sto-145	Beas,John	War-175		
Bayer,Isaac	Sto-152	Beam,Christy	Lnc-335	Beasely,M	Col- 17		
John	Sto-151	Jacob	Cab-142	Beasley,A	Bru-240		
Bayett,George	Joh-285	John	Lnc-328	Barnet	War-168		
Joseph	Joh-283	John	Row- 78	Eliza	Cho-224		
Bayken,James	Edg- 58	Beaman,Abram	Mon- 34	Eliza	Cho-227		
Baykin,William	Way-253	Abram	Mon- 34	James	Bft- 23		
Bayley,Dorton	Gat-105	David	Mon- 34	James	War-173		
Jonathan	Edg- 63	Francis	Mon- 34	John	Cho-219		
Joseph	Edg- 49	Isaac	Mon- 34	John	War-176		
Levi	Bun- 92	Jacob	Mon- 34	Major	Wsh-227		
Susanna	Edg- 50	Beamguard,Philip	Pas-184	Oxd	Bru-240		
Bayly,William	Hrt-212	Bean,Benjamin	Row- 63	Pitts	War-179		
Bazel,William	Bur-106	Margaret	Cab-144	Polly	Wsh-227		
Bazemore,Bisha	Brt- 62	Mary	Row- 65	Robt	Cho-224		
Hezekiah	Brt- 64	Mathias	Cab-144	Sam	Ora-124		
James	Brt- 64	Nicholas	Sto-144	Thomas	War-181		
John	Brt- 64	Nicholas	Sto-108	William	Tyr-208		
Milly	Brt- 64	Thos	Ora-171	Beasly,Clary	Cha-201		
Penny	Brt- 64	William	Bun- 95	Fendal	Cha-200		
Rebecca	Brt- 64	Wm	Cab-138	Thos	Cha-201		
Turner	Brt- 64	Wm	Mon- 33	Beason,Joseph	Ire-269		
Bazwell,Samuel	Wil-268	Beann,Jeremiah	Bur-111	Richard	Sto-133		
Bazzel,Reubeon	Mec- 24	Jesse	Bur-111	Richard	Sto-101		
Beacey,Levern	Cas- 48	Johnston	Bur-107	William	Ire-269		
Beach,Abraham	Wil-279	Richard	Bur-111	William	Sto-133		
Benjamin	Mar- 11	Thomas	Bur-111	Beatty,James	Lnc-335		
Benjamin	Wil-284	William	Bur-122	Jas	Lnc-354		
Elijah	Bur-126	Beard,Alexr	Mor- 60	Moses	Bur-131		
Isaac	Bft- 28	Anthony	War-168	W H	Bla- 11		
Jedida	Bur-126	Benj	Glf-164	Beaty,David	Ire-240		
Job	Mar- 16	Benjamin	Cum-258	Ephraim	Ire-240		
Thos Junr	Mar- 16	Benjamin	War-168	Francis	Rth- 91		
Thos Senr	Mar- 16	Betty	Way-238	Francis	Mec- 37		
William	Wil-278	David	Ire-243	Isaac	Mec- 36		
Beacham,Alexr	Ans- 25	David	Glf-171	James	Rth- 91		
Henry	Rch-204	Geo	Glf-163	James	Lnc-367		

Name	Loc	Name	Loc	Name	Loc
Beaty,Jas	Mec- 35	Beck,John	Hay-193	Beeks,Ann	Bft- 24
Jno	Mec- 25	John	Row- 87	Beel,Benj	Cha-197
John	Ire-268	John	Dup- 12	John	Cha-191
John	Lnc-364	John	Bur-115	Thos Jr	Cha-198
Moses	Mec- 35	John G	Sto-146	Beeland,John	Edg- 43
Nathan	Mec- 39	Kelab	Sam-163	Beeles,John	Ran-159
Robert	Lnc-367	Michal	Row- 83	Beels,J	Cam-157
Saml	Mec- 38	Nathaniel	Sam-160	M	Cam-156
Thomas	Ire-240	Philip	Row- 63	S	Cam-156
Thos	Lnc-364	Samuel	Dup- 24	Z	Cam-156
Wallis	Rth- 90	Samuel	Row- 63	Beem,Elisabeth	Lnc-337
William	Lnc-364	Solomon	Sto-107	Beeman,Benja	Nor- 61
William	Row- 62	Solomon	Sto-143	James	Fra- 82
Wm	Mec- 38	William	Sto-131	Parkes	Ans- 19
Wm	Mec- 25	William	Sam-154	Thomas	Row- 63
Beaver,Christian	Row- 73	William	Sto-100	Been,Jesse	Mor- 54
David	Row- 70	Becker,John F	Sto-146	William	Row- 86
Devoll	Row- 73	Beckey	Cum-241	Beeson,B	Glf-163
George	Row- 72	Beckham,Jessee	War-173	E	Glf-163
Henry	Row- 66	John	Ire-249	Edward	Sur-173
Henry	Row- 71	Solomon	War-180	Isaac	Glf-170
Jacob	Row- 71	Solomon	War-180	Isaac	Glf-163
Jas	Mon- 45	Zachariah	War-184	John	Glf-165
Jere	Cas- 48	Becknal,H	Ash- 13	Nathl	Glf-163
Jesse	Cas- 48	Becknall,Benjamin	Wil-270	Richard	Sur-179
John	Row- 70	Randolph	Wil-264	Saml	Glf-165
Joshua	Cas- 48	Becknell,Rachel	Bur-124	Solomon	Rth- 89
Michl	Row- 66	Samuel	Wil-272	Beeton,Fredk E	Len-317
Michl	Row- 69	William	Bur-116	John	Jon-294
Nicholas	Row- 70	Becks,Thomas	Pas-181	John B	Len-318
Paul	Row- 67	Beckum,Simon	Ora-113	Mary	Jon-294
Peter	Row- 66	Beckwith,Amos	Nsh- 92	Beever,William	Sur-168
W	Ora-146	Burrel	Nsh- 74	Beezly,Benj	Ons-108
Wm	Mon- 45	Lyon	Nsh- 74	John	Ons-108
Beavis,Solomon	Cas- 50	Thos	Nsh- 74	Befel,Barbary	Row- 82
Beazley,Benj	Sto- 93	Bedford,James	Rth- 87	Begerly,Francis	Ire-266
Benjamin	Sto-122	John	Pit-247	Henry	Ire-268
Charles	Sto-108	Jonas	Rth- 89	Beggarly,Benjamin	Ire-243
Daniel	Rch-204	Raymond	Rth- 87	Benjamin	Ire-243
Edmund	Sto-122	Seth	Rth- 89	David	Ire-243
Edmund	Sto- 93	Stephen	Rth- 88	Thomas	Ire-243
Elizabeth	Sto- 93	Bedgood,Benja	Prq-215	Beggs,Jas	Cum-240
Jeremiah	Sto- 93	William	Prq-214	Beirley,Daniel	Row- 79
Jeremiah	Sto-121	Bediford,Stephen	Mec- 46	Jacob Jr	Row- 79
Robert	Sto-121	Bedsoe,Thos	Bla- 8	Joseph	Pas-181
Beazly,Charles	Sto-144	Thos	Bla- 9	Beker,Henry	Row- 83
Robert	Sto- 92	William	Bla- 9	Beladgey,Elisha	Tyr-208
Beccom,S	Ora-144	Beebe,Asa	Cum-246	Belandgey,Sally	Tyr-208
Beck,Abraham	Sto-132	Ned	Cum-246	Belch,Elisha	Hrt-210
Abraham	Sto-100	Samuel	Prq-214	Jesse	Brt- 51
Andrew	Ran-159	Beecham,Ann	Hyd-225	Lewis	Brt- 51
Danl	Bur-103	Samuel	Ire-263	Miles	Nor- 62
Eliza	Bur-11r	Beedle,David	Bur-106	Paul	Hrt-210
Eliza	Nsh- 90	Beek,David	Grn-125	Ryan	Brt- 51
Henry	Sto-132	Fedrick	Grn-125	Belcher,Beverly	Edg- 68
Henry	Sto-100	John	Cha-196	Belden,Simeon	Cum-239
James	Cha-190	Will Jr	Dup- 6	Belew,Abraham	Ans- 19
John	Row- 87	Will Sr	Dup- 6	Abraham	Ans- 12

-21-

Name	Code	Name	Code	Name	Code	Name	Code
Belflower,James	Mar- 5	Bell,James		Rth- 88	Bell,Noah		Hyd-233
Beliter,Jebediah	Sto-109	James		Cab-138	Noah		Edg- 62
Belk,Chamberlain	Lnc-329	James		Row- 73	Orsan Junr		Sam-156
Darling	Mec- 44	James		Mon- 21	Orsan Senr		Sam-156
Darling	Mec- 44	James		Lnc-336	Perney		Cur- 90
Geo	Mec- 22	James		Hal- 98	Persons		Edg- 63
James	Hay-193	James		Pit-255	R		Cam-157
Mary An	Mec- 44	James		Per-127	Reason W		Edg- 63
Patan	Lnc-364	James Senr		Car-181	Rebecca		Car-183
William	Rth- 89	Jas		Cab-138	Rebecca		Car-183
Bell,A	Cam-162	Jesse		War-174	Richard		Hyd-232
Abner Senr	Car-182	Jno		Mec- 24	Richd		Mon- 21
Abner Senr	Car-181	John		Cha-126	Robert		Cur- 89
Abram	Dup- 16	John		Ire-256	Robt		Ora-118
Abasalom	Car-181	John		Car-182	Robt		Glf-185
Andrew	Rth- 89	John		Mon- 21	Robt Senr		Sam-154
Archa	Ons-105	John		Lnc-333	S		Cam-159
Archd	Sam-157	John		Lnc-333	S Snr		Cam-152
Arthur	Hal- 98	John		Cur- 89	Saml		Hrt-209
Azel	Car-176	John		Glf-167	Saml		Bru-230
B	Cam-153	John		Pit-247	Saml		Hyd-232
Benj	Joh-278	John		Hyd-233	Samuel		Rob-234
Benj	Mon- 21	John		Hyd-232	Samuel		Bun- 75
Benjamin	Edg- 63	John Snr		Hyd-232	Sarah		Way-237
Benjamin	War-169	Jonathan		Hyd-230	Sarah		Car-182
Benjamin	Hal- 98	Jonathan		Hyd-230	Sarah		Edg- 64
Branson	Cur- 91	Jonathan		Hyd-233	Sephire		Car-176
Bursh H	Cur- 89	Joseph		Car-185	Solomon		Cho-222
Burwell	Pit-256	Joseph		Edg- 41	Starky		Pit-234
Caleb Senr	Car-183	Joseph		Mon- 21	Stephen		Car-183
Charles	War-169	Joseph C		Car-179	Susannah		Car-177
Daley	Cur- 89	Joseph Junr		Car-181	T		Glf-175
David	Joh-290	Joseph Senr		Car-182	T Esq		Cam-154
David	Car-181	Joshua		Hyd-232	Thomas		Ire-265
David	Mon- 21	Joshua		Hyd-232	Thomas		Bun- 81
David Senr	Car-183	Joshua		Edg- 54	Thomas		Car-182
Dinah	Bft- 32	Joshuay		Cur- 88	Thomas		Edg- 63
Duke	Cur- 90	Josiah		Car-182	Thomas		War-181
Ebenezer	Hyd-232	Josiah		Len-322	Thomas		Cas- 49
Eden	Ons-105	Josiah		Cur- 91	Thomas Jr		Ran-159
Edward	Car-181	Laban		Hyd-233	Thomas Jr		War-181
Enoch	Cha-190	Leasar		Bft- 38	Thomas A		Ons- 98
Etheldred	Joh-291	Littleton		Hyd-232	Thos		Lnc-340
Felix	Sam-163	Litteton		Hyd-232	Thos		Cha-216
Francis	Car-177	Lovett		Hyd-229	Thos		Lnc-364
Frederick	Edg- 63	Marmaduke		Edg- 59	Uriah		Hyd-231
George	Car-182	Martha		Dup- 19	Walter		Ire-266
George	Car-183	Mary		Car-171	Walter		Cab-138
H	Cam-157	Mary		Dup- 23	Watson		Hyd-233
Hannah	Ons-105	Methias		Cur- 91	Whitmill		Edg- 59
Horace	War-184	Miles		Car-180	William		Car-183
Horatio	Ire-265	Morris		Hyd-232	William		Car-169
J	Cam-152	Nancy		Edg- 60	William		War-184
J	Cam-154	Nancy		Per-143	William		Bur-127
J	Cam-155	Nathan		Car-183	William		Row- 73
J	Cam-159	Nathaniel		Car-183	William		Pit-247
J	Bru-230	Nathl		Ora-133	William		Ran-158
Jacob	War-175	Newel		Car-176	William		Ran-158
James	Lnc-364	Newel Senr		Car-181	William		Per-127

-22-

Bell,William Jnr	Ran-158	Beninger,Paul	Cab-145	Bennett,John	Sto-119
Willm C	Car-182	Benjamin	Pit-256	John	Bun- 72
Wm	Cab-138	Benjamin,Eliza	Bft- 39	John	Sto- 91
Zachariah	Bun- 94	Benjamon,Thos	Glf-188	Joseph	Ora-122
Zadoc	Hal- 98	Benlor,Jesse	Row- 80	Joshua	Ire-267
Bellak,John	Hay-193	Benn,George	Nor- 61	Judah	Bun- 76
Bellen,James	Tyr-204	Bennatt,Milner	Cas- 48	Richard	Bun- 76
Beller,Eli	Sto-151	Richard	Cas- 48	M	Glf-176
Rachel	Ire-245	Thomas	Cas- 48	Mark	Mon- 23
Belleter,Alexr	Sto- 98	Benneham,Ricd	Ora-159	Mary	Sto-131
Bellew,Jesse	Bun- 73	Bennet,Abm	Lnc-334	Mary	Sto-100
Joshua	Bur-129	Benj	Bur-110	Nevil	Ans- 5
Micajah	Bun- 74	Charles	War-169	Sampson	Sam-158
Belling,Martha	Wsh-219	Christen	Gat-107	Solomon	Mon- 33
Bells,Mary	Car-184	Geo	Lnc-377	Thomas	Ire-269
Bellune,D	Bru-238	George	Gat-111	Thomas	Ran-157
Belsiah,Thomas	Cas- 49	Henry	War-172	Thomas	Sto-156
Belter,Eli	Sto-109	Isham	War-173	Thomas Jr	Dup- 13
Belting,Anthony	Sto-126	John	Rch-196	William	Sto-156
Anthony	Sto- 96	John	Bun- 77	William	Bun- 72
John	Sto- 96	John Senr	Bun- 77	William	Way-235
John	Sto-125	Josiah	Bft- 33	William	Ran-158
Belton,James	Roc- 23	Josiah	Row- 63	Wm	Ans- 30
Susanna	Roc- 24	Lewis	Grn-148	Wm	Ans- 21
Belyew,Jno	Ans- 6	Mary	Roc- 31	Wm	Ans- 13
Beman,John	Sam-162	Moses	War-177	Benning,Jacob	Row- 71
John	Row- 63	Pilliman	Nsh- 92	Bennitt,Ann	Edg- 53
Sarah	Ran-158	Richard	Ire-249	James	Mar- 9
Bembery,Miles	Mar-446	Richard	War-179	James	Mar-445
Bembridge,Caleb	Wsh-224	Richard K	War-179	Joel	Mar-445
Ben,Taxes	Pas-183	Samuel	Rch-197	John	Mar- 11
Benbottom,Simon	Cha-207	Stephen	Bur-114	Luke	Mar- 10
Benbow,Benj	Glf-187	Thomas	War-181	Silas	Mar- 14
J	Glf-183	Thomas Sr	Dup- 13	Thomas	Mar- 9
Thos	Glf-156	Travers	Roc- 14	Thomas	Mar- 12
Benbury,Jos C	Cho-224	William	Bun- 81	William	Edg- 54
Mary	Cho-224	William	Bun- 77	Bennut,Charles	Cha-203
Bender,Brice Esqr	Ons-105	Wm	Rob-234	Benrow,Martha	Ora-163
Bryan	Ons- 99	Wm	Cha-190	Bensam,Samuel	Cur- 83
Daniel	Ons-103	Wm	Cha-198	Bensel,William	Wil-268
John	Ons- 97	Bennett,Ambrose	Cas- 48	Benson,Mrs. Ann	Brt- 48
John	Jon-293	Artixerxes	Ran-187	D	Bla- 13
Martin	Ons-104	As	Sto-133	Dred	Sam-157
Bendermas,Wm	Lnc-360	Benjamin	Sto-156	Eliza	Cho-223
Bener,James	Wil-285	Benjamin	Sto-114	Francis	Bla- 10
Beney,Elisha	Rob-227	Charles	Fra- 84	Jas	Bla- 11
Benfield,Henry	Lnc-352	Clary	Nor- 61	Jno	Moc- 53
George	Bur-105	Rody	Nor- 61	John	Bla- 13
John	Lnc-378	Davd	Bft- 32	John	Glf-166
John Senr	Lnc-353	Eliza	Way-239	R	Glf-169
Benge,James	Wil-269	Esther	Cho-222	Robt	Glf-163
Richard	Wil-261	H G	Cho-226	Tho	Bla- 11
Thomas	Sur-165	J	Bru-222	Thos	Cab-139
Thomas	Wil-269	Jacob	Mon- 23	U	Col- 19
Thomas Jr	Wil-264	James	Way-242	Wm	Glf-155
William	Wil-269	Jesse	Dup- 15	Wm	Bla- 11
Beninger,Arasmus	Cab-144	Jno	Ans- 24	Benston,John	Hyd-230
Martin	Cab-146	John	Bla- 6	Reuben	Hyd-230
		John	Nor- 62	Sarah	Hyd-230

-23-

Bent, James R	Cho-219	Berdew, Dennis	Way-248	Berry, Mathias	Lnc-364		
Benthall, Azel	Hrt-216	Berey, John	Cur- 87	R	Cam-157		
Lewis	Hrt-212	John	Cur- 90	Rhody	Ora-112		
Miles	Hrt-211	Samuel	Cur- 91	Richard	Mec- 46		
Benthel, Jacob	Car-182	William	Cur- 87	Robt	Ora-162		
Bentley, Jno	Ans- 18	Bergen, Benj Jr	Bur-110	Robt	Per-126		
John	Brt- 65	Berger, Coty	Row- 53	Thos	Per-126		
Thomas	Pit-258	Bergin, Ben Sr	Bur-124	S	Cam-160		
Bently, Benjamin	Ire-263	James	Bur-119	S	Cam-158		
Benjamin	Ire-263	Jesse	Bur-124	Simpson	Rth- 86		
James	Ire-263	John	Bur-124	Solomon	Hal- 99		
Squire	Ire-263	Minet	Bur-124	T	Cam-161		
Thomas	Pit-237	Beriman, William	Gat-107	William	Cas- 48		
Benton, A	Bru-224	Berings, James	Lnc-345	William	Fra-100		
Abraham	Gat-110	Bernard, Francis Esq	Wil-257	William	Lnc-330		
Alexr	Sam-159	S	Bru-234	William	Lnc-377		
Babel	Nor- 60	Uriah	Sur-168	Beryhill, Andrew	Mec- 36		
Burwill	Ans- 12	Bernit, Swan	Bun- 81	Jas M	Mec- 37		
Caąn	Pas-182	Bernston, Ruth	Cur- 92	Jno	Mec- 37		
Cathr	Bft- 20	Beroth, Henry	Sto-153	Saml	Mec- 36		
Charity	Edg- 58	Berrey, Ezekel	Hyd-230	Wm	Mec- 25		
D	Bru-222	John	Hyd-230	Berryman, Benjn	Row- 57		
David	Gat-108	Robert	Hyd-231	Jilson	Row- 57		
David	Dup- 17	William	Hyd-230	Mary	Prq-214		
Edmond	Ire-256	Wm G	Bun- 89	Steven	Mor- 64		
F	Bru-224	Berriman, Wm	Row- 58	Wm	Mor- 68		
Francis	Len-310	Berry, Abner	Lnc-367	Bery, Andrew	Mec- 46		
Henry	Fra- 92	B	Cam-154	Beseley, Bilsey	Cur- 92		
Henry H	Gat-115	B	Ora-141	Henery	Cur- 80		
J	Mon- 36	Buckner	Ons- 99	Henery	Cur- 92		
James	Edg- 57	C	Cam-158	Henery	Cur- 92		
James	Gat-110	David	Roc- 11	Jacob	Cur- 80		
James	Pas-182	David	Ora-173	John	Cur- 92		
Jas	Ans- 9	Elias	Bur-125	Lydia	Cur- 93		
Jesse B	Gat-115	Franklin	Bun- 94	Maleckey	Cur- 92		
Jethro	Gat-115	G	Mon- 34	Samuel	Cur- 92		
Job	Bru-224	Hannah	Ora-162	Stephen	Cur- 83		
Joel	Roc- 17	Hiram	Lnc-326	Taylor	Cur- 92		
John	Len-310	Hugh	Mec- 22	William	Cur- 92		
John T	Gat-108	Isaac	Roc- 11	Beshears, Martha	Wil-265		
Joseph	Cas- 49	J	Ora-146	Mary	Wil-265		
Joseph	Way-249	J	Cam-155	Beson, Isaac	Ran-158		
Joshua	Pas-183	J Snr	Cam-155	Richard	Ran-158		
Josiah	Gat-113	Jacob	Lnc-361	Richard Jnr	Ran-158		
Kedar	Sam-158	James	Jon-293	Saml	Ran-158		
Miriam	Pas-183	Jas	Bla- 9	Vestel	Ran-158		
Prudence	Sam-154	Jesse	Wil-266	William	Ran-158		
Sally	Pas-182	Jessee	Bur-129	William	Ran-159		
Sally	Pas-183	John	Fra-100	Besongs, William	Ran-158		
Sam	Ora-110	John	Roc- 10	Bess, Jacob	Lnc-368		
Saml	Bla- 12	John	Lnc-334	John	Lnc-368		
Seth	Gat-110	John	Cas- 48	Peter	Lnc-368		
Thomas	Pas-182	John Sen	Roc- 11	Best, Absolom	Dup- 10		
Wm	Ans- 19	Joseph	Bur-129	Anney	Cur- 82		
Benzun, Christian	Sto-112	L	Cam-162	Benjn	Dup- 10		
Beoth, Duncan	Roc- 19	Leond	Lnc-363	Benjn	Way-237		
Beowder, Telitha	Roc- 11	Lot	Bur-126	Boston	Lnc-335		
Berath, John	Sto-136	Margaret	Row- 81	Briant	Rob-220		
Berckfield, Elias	Sto-108	Mark	Ons- 98	Christian	Lnc-340		

-24-

Name	Ref	Name	Ref	Name	Ref
Best,Dred	Sam-159	Bevin,Josiah	Bla- 12	Bigham,Matthews	Mec- 36
Edman	Cur- 87	Thomas	Bla- 12	Robt	Mec- 26
Elias	Prq-214	Wm	Bla- 11	Robt Snr	Mec- 27
Fred	Lnc-336	Bevins,Thos	Ora-134	Saml	Lnc-337
Henry	Mar- 8	Bevion,Nathl	Ans- 24	Saml Junr	Lnc-337
Henry	Sam-159	Bewell,W	Glf-159	Thos	Mec- 28
Henry	Bft- 36	Bezzell,Asher	Way-240	Wm	Mec- 50
Henry	Hrt-215	David	Way-242	Wm	Mec- 28
Howell	Dup- 10	Hannah	Way-240	Bignall,Edward	War-170
J	Col- 20	Thomas	Way-240	Bigs,Andrew	Bur-118
Jno W	Hrt-211	Thomas Sr	Way-240	Willis	Bur-118
John	Dup- 9	William	Way-240	Bilberry,Duel	Edg- 60
John	Dup- 11	Bezzet,Joseph	Nsh- 91	E	Col- 19
Joseph	Cur- 83	Bias,John	Per-135	Nathaniel	Edg- 41
Kader	War-177	Bibb,Sally	Sur-193	Bilbery,J	Col- 19
Martin	Lnc-328	Bibby,Absolam col	Fra-100	Bilbo,J	Ora-141
Michael	Tyr-202	Solomon col	Fra-100	Jo	Ora-157
Nancy	Ons-106	Biby,John	Sto-149	Bilbro,Beryman	Nsh- 82
Redden	Dup- 11	William	Rth- 89	Biles,Alexr	Mon- 45
Sion	Rob-234	Bickedite,Amos	Ran-158	Anne	Row- 86
Theophilus	Way-251	Bicket,Jas	Mec- 31	Charles	Row- 75
Thomas	Edg- 53	John	Row- 74	Daniel	Row- 76
Thos	Cur- 87	Saml	Mec- 31	Isaac	Mon- 45
Thos	Hrt-216	Biddingfield,John	Joh-272	John	Row- 80
Will Junr	Cur- 83	Biddle,Elijah	Ons-104	Thos	Mon- 45
William	Edg- 54	Bierley,Martin	Row- 83	Bileter,Mark	Sto-151
Wm Senr	Cur- 83	Bierly,David	Row- 52	Zebediah	Sto-151
Bethal, John	Cum-252	Peter	Row- 80	Zebediah	Sto-112
Bethell,William	Roc- 16	Biffle, Jacob	Hay-193	Bilfore,Andrew	Ran-157
Bethone,David	Rob-225	John	Bun- 96	Billes,John	Cur- 82
Bethune,Alexr	Mor- 64	Bigalow,Roderick	War-179	Billeter,Zebediah	Sto-145
Caty	Mor- 63	Bigford,Saml	Bla- 9	Billings,Benjn	Row- 87
Colin	Cum-244	Bigger,Johnston	Cab-144	James	Wil-271
Malcom	Rch-192	Biggerstaff,Aaron	Rth- 88	Jasper	Wil-258
Bettas,Samuel	Roc- 6	Rebekah	Rth- 91	Jasper Jr	Wil-259
Bettorny,Wm	Nsh- 79	Samuel	Rth- 88	John	Row- 50
Betts,Abraham	Pas-184	Susannah	Rth- 91	Thomas	Wil-259
E	Bru-234	Biggott,John W	Rth- 89	Billingsbe,John	Rch-210
Betty,Benjamin	War-169	Biggs,Amariah	Wsh-220	Billingsley,B	Glf-159
Henry	War-172	Benjamin	Row- 82	Elias	Ans- 17
Bevaker,Thomas	Rob-220	Daniel	Mar- 7	Hezekiah	Ans- 12
Bevaul,Samuel	Tyr-205	James	Edg- 62	James	Mon- 26
Bevell,E	Glf-160	Jas	Rob-230	Jno B	Ans- 5
Hezekiah	Glf-182	Jas	Rob-230	John	Mon- 24
Thos	Glf-161	Jemimah	Mar- 11	Lias	Mon- 24
Bever,Benj	Bur-124	John	Wsh-220	Lias	Mon- 26
Hezekiah	Bur-118	John	Mar- 11	Thos	Ans- 23
J	Ora-154	John	Rob-230	Billington,Ezekl	Joh-277
William	Bur-124	Joseph	Mar- 11	Billiter,Alexr	Sto-128
Beveret,Jacob	Dup- 18	Kidar	Mar- 8	Billops,John	Edg- 72
Beverley,Jesse	Ans- 20	Michael	Rob-231	William	Edg- 71
Jno	Ans- 4	Reuben	Bft- 26	Bills,Daniel	Sur-164
Beverly,Benj	Hrt-206	Samuel	Rob-230	Daniel Jnr	Sur-172
John	Ran-158	William	Mar- 14	Gersham	Sur-164
Isaac	Cha-194	William	Mar- 15	William	Sur-173
William	Nor- 60	William	Mar- 10	Billups,Ann	Cho-223
Bevil,Clayton	Per-127	Bigham,Mrs.	Mec- 27	Langley	Prq-214
Beviley,Jacob	Row- 79	Hugh	Mec- 28	Mrs. S	Brt- 48
Bevill,E	Ora-148	John	Rth- 87	Binam,Wm	Cha-193

-25-

Name	Ref	Name	Ref	Name	Ref
Binckley,John	Dup- 17	Bird,Josiah	Nor- 62	Bissell,Purley	Wil-265
Bine,Neill	Rob-230	Mary	Hal- 99	Thos	Cho-219
Binford,James	Nor- 62	Michl	Row- 72	Bits,Liley	Gat-110
Joshua	Nor- 62	Peter	Row- 87	Bitticks,John	Sur-164
M. John	Nor- 62	Richard	Hal- 99	Bittle,Boston	Nor- 62
Micajah	Nor- 63	Susanna	Hal- 99	Elizebeth	Ans- 26
Bingham,Benjamin	Sur-174	Susanna	Row- 69	Jeremiah	Nor- 62
Christopher	Ran-157	Tho	Ora-170	Jesse	Ans- 29
Elijah	Ran-157	Thomas	Hay-193	John	Nor- 62
Hannah	Nsh- 90	Thos W	Mec- 40	John	Brt- 55
Martin	Ans- 11	Valentine	Row- 68	Bizzell,A	Col- 20
Michael	Ran-157	William	Cas- 49	Jesse	Way-239
Robert	Wil-282	Wm	Rob-242	Nancy	Way-239
Robt	Cha-215	Birk,Anderson	Cas- 48	Noah	Hrt-212
Thomas	Ran-157	Benjamin	Cas- 48	Bizzet,John	Nsh- 82
Thomas	Sur-185	James Jr	Cas- 49	Lodrick	Nsh- 91
Wm	Cha-193	James Senr	Cas- 48	Bizzle,Ann	Bla- 12
Binkley,John	Sur-175	Johnston	Cas- 48	Black, Mrs.	Cum-240
Binkly,Frederic	Sto-153	Matson	Cas- 49	Mrs.	Mec- 50
Peter	Sto-152	Thompson	Cas- 49	Adam	Row- 60
Peter Jnr	Sto-153	William	Lnc-341	Alexr	Cum-250
Binom,Rapley	Cha-205	Birrot,John	Nsh- 78	Angus	Rob-235
Binse,Catharine	Cab-146	Birum,Isaac	Cho-229	Archd	Cum-250
Binum,Gideon	Pit-260	Wm	Cho-227	Carolina	Car-184
Joseph	Pit-260	Wm Senr	Cho-228	Caty	Mor- 68
Tuner	Pit-260	Bisant,J	Bru-224	Caty	Mor- 60
Biram,Jas	Cho-228	Bishop,-----	Way-244	Daniel	Bun- 73
Birch,Charles	Sto-140	A	Glf-160	Daniel	Cum-250
Richd	Lnc-364	Abraham	Wil-276	Daniel	Cum-251
Birchfield.Robert	Bur-115	Ann	Cha-201	Danl	Row- 48
Bird,A	Col- 17	Arthur	Hal- 98	David	Ire-247
Abner	Mor- 63	Asa	Car-174	Dinah	Car-184
Andrew	Mon- 47	Benj	Mor- 67	Duncan	Cum-250
Baylor	Cas- 48	Benj	Cha-194	Duncan	Cum-256
Benj	Mon- 23	Bolen	Hal- 99	Duncan Junr	Cum-250
Benj	Mor- 63	Buckner	Ora-114	Elizabeth	Roc- 33
Benjamin	Bur-120	Greaer	Ons-108	Eph	Lnc-331
Bonney	Mec- 41	Hardemon	Edg- 63	F	Ash- 9
Christopher	Bun- 77	Henry	Ora-117	F	Bla- 10
David	Cha-193	James	Hal- 98	Frederick	Row- 61
David	Cas- 49	John	Hal- 98	Geo	Bun- 83
Edmond	Hal- 98	Markus	Hal- 97	Geo	Row- 59
Edward	Brt- 47	Moses	Brt- 56	George	Ran-157
Francis	Hay-193	Nancy	Edg- 72	Hammilton	Mec- 22
Geo	Bun- 78	Nathan	Glf-156	Henly	Mec- 45
Henry	Rob-242	Phillop	Grn-147	Hugh	Mor- 58
Isaac	Rob-240	Robert Jr	Dup- 32	Hugh	Rth- 86
Jacob	Cha-193	Robert Sr	Dup- 32	Hugh	Rth- 89
James	Cas- 49	Rogert	Wil-283	J	Ash- 7
Jas	Mec- 41	Samuel	Wil-283	Jacob	Row- 80
Jas	Mec- 46	Thomas	Joh-288	Jacob	Row- 80
Jesse	Hal- 99	William	Hyd-224	Jacob	Row- 60
Jesse	Cha-193	Willie	Hal- 98	Jacob	Sto-152
Joel	Rob-240	Bissell,Benjn	Cho-219	James	Bun- 87
Jno	Mec- 46	Charles	Cho-219	James	Lnc-364
John	Brt- 47	Hardy	Dup- 12	James	Rth- 87
John	Row- 69	James	Dup- 12	Jas	Mec- 41
Jonathan	Bur-120	Nancy	Dup- 13	Jas R	Ans- 5
Joseph	Sur-189	Nathl	Cho-219	Jane	Bur-131

Name	Location	Name	Location	Name	Location
Black,Jane	Row- 66	Blackburn,William	Sto- 96	Blackwell,William	Rth- 87
Jno	Mec- 22	William	Wil-271	William	Rch-200
Jno	Mec- 40	Younger	Sto-157	Wm	Grn-140
Jno	Mor- 61	Blackledge,Susinah	Hrt-213	Blackwilder,Caleb	Cab-140
John	Mor- 63	Blackley,Charles	Grn-128	Danl	Cab-140
John	Cab-148	Tiby	Grn-130	Isaac	Cab-140
John	Rch-213	Blackly,James	Lnc-364	Isaac	Cab-138
John	Cum-250	Blackman,Arthur	Joh-276	Jacob	Cab-140
John	Ire-257	Barnabas	Sam-160	Martin	Cab-140
John	Ire-252	Barzella	Joh-289	Blackwood,Gedeon	Lnc-334
Jos	Lnc-331	Cullen	Way-253	Jno	Ora-143
Joseph	Bun- 83	Edmon	Joh-282	John	Lnc-333
Joseph	Bun- 81	Elizab	Joh-290	John	Lnc-340
Joseph M	Rth- 90	J	Col- 21	John	Ora-114
Malcolm	Mor- 54	Joab	Sam-159	Joseph	Mec- 24
Malcolm	Mor- 60	Josiah	Sam-159	Richd	Ora-123
Malcom	Cum-243	Kedar	Sam-159	Saml	Lnc-330
Matthew	Bur-118	Sion	Rch-201	Wm	Ora-143
Mitchel	Roc- 16	William	Joh-277	Blades,Edwd	Row- 51
Moses	Rth- 89	William Junr	Sam-155	Tilman	Row- 87
Neill	Cum-247	William Senr	Sam-159	Blagg,John	Roc- 4
Ot	Lnc-364	Blackmon,Elizebeth	Sur-194	Blailock,Julius	Cha-190
Reuben	Bun- 75	Blacknell,John	Grn-130	Blair,Abner	Ran-159
Robert	Ire-257	Blackshear,Ezekiel	Jon-293	Enis	Ran-159
Rosanah	Mec- 33	James	Jon-293	George	Cho-219
Saml	Mec- 40	Blackstocks,William	Ire-244	George	Row- 49
Samuel	Cab-148	Blackston,Levi	Len-321	Hugh	Ran-159
Sarah	Car-184	Tho	Ora-118	Jacob	Wil-259
Thos	Mec- 45	Blackstone,Jesse	Pit-237	James	Bur-127
William	Lnc-356	James	Pit-238	James	Roc- 17
William	Ire-252	Blackwelder,Chs	Row- 71	James Junr	Bur-111
William Jr	Lnc-364	Blackwell,Abraham	Bla- 6	Jas	Mec- 44
William Senr	Lnc-364	Carter	Cas- 50	Jesse	Ran-158
Wm	Mec- 40	Charles	Rth- 87	John	Glf-165
Wm	Mec- 39	David	Sur-162	Saml	Mec- 22
Zekial	Mec- 38	David	Rth- 88	William	Prq-214
Blackadder,Chas	Cab-142	Pury	Rth- 90	Wm	Glf-184
Jacob	Cab-142	George	Bla- 9	Blaize,George	Row- 85
Blackburn,Allen	Wil-272	Joel	Rth- 89	Blak,Lucy	Per-126
B	Bla- 8	Joel	Rth- 87	Blake,Azariah	Tyr-207
Ben	Mec- 35	John	Rth- 89	Dempsey	Pit-256
Bryson	Sto-108	John	Rth- 90	F	Col- 18
Bryson	Sto-143	John	Row- 76	Fanny	Jon-293
E	Ash- 11	John Jr	Grn-132	Howel	Mon- 30
Enos	Sto-147	John Jr	Rth- 90	J	Cum-238
Hiram	Sam-164	John Senr	Grn-132	John	Per-127
Hugh	Mec- 37	Jos	Per-148	John	Sto-103
Hugh	Sto-152	Levi	Cas- 50	John	Sto-137
Hugh	Sto-143	P	Bla- 10	Joshua	Dup- 16
Jenny	Cho-223	Patience	Bla- 6	Josiah	Mon- 27
John	Roc- 20	Peter	Rth- 87	R	Mon- 27
John	Lnc-347	Pumphry	Grn-124	Richd	Ora-130
John Senr	Roc- 20	Pheubin	Bla- 5	Robert	Per-127
Lucy	Sto-125	Robert	Row- 89	Robert	Hal- 97
Martha	War-177	Robert	Cas- 48	Sam	Mon- 29
Samuel	Rth- 87	Samuel	Per-136	Samuel	Mon- 30
William	Sto-126	Thomas	Roc- 26	Thomas	Mon- 29
William	Hal- 98	Thos	Grn-146	Thomas	Mon- 30

Name	Ref	Name	Ref	Name	Ref
Blake,Thomas	Sto-136	Bland,Jemimah	Mar- 3	Bledsoe,Benjamin	Sur-175
Blakeney,Mary	Ans- 32	Joel	Rth- 88	Elizabeth	Rob-236
Blakley,Jas	Mec- 53	John	Cha-199	Miss Farny	Fra- 78
Thos	Mec- 53	John	Cha-196	Geo	Mon- 29
Blakney,Mary	Ans- 29	Theophilus	Pit-257	Isaac	Rob-238
Blalock,Charles	Cum-252	William Jr	Dup- 19	Isaac	Sur-175
D	Mon- 40	William Sr	Dup- 19	John	Way-250
David	Mon- 21	Wm	Cha-213	Larkin	Sur-164
David	Cha-191	Blaney,B	Bru-234	Rush	Fra- 86
David	Cha-211	Blanford,Mary	Edg- 67	Sarah	Sur-180
David	Grn-130	Mary	Edg- 67	Thos	Mon- 28
Giles	Mon- 38	Blango,Gabe	Bft- 30	Blelock,Wm	Mec- 27
H	Ora-134	Isaac	Bft- 31	Blesley,John	Row- 80
Hardy	Cum-257	Sall	Bft- 31	Blevins,E	Ash- 15
James	Per-127	Sarah	Bft- 31	J	Ash- 5
Jesse	Ora-114	Blankenship,Fora	Ire-262	J	Ash- 13
Jno	Ora-123	S	Ash- 4	N	Ash- 13
John	Cum-261	Samuel	Ire-249	W	Ash- 13
John	Lnc-361	Samuel	Ire-250	Blew,Barbary	Row- 88
John	Bur-115	Thomas	Ire-250	John	Row- 88
Meridy	Ora-127	Blankingship,Elijah	Rth- 89	Bleweitt,Elizebeth	Ans- 32
Milington	Per-135	Blankinship,Ashford	Rth- 86	Wm	Ans- 6
Milint Junr	Per-127	Bosley	Rth- 87	Bleze,Jas	Mec- 31
Richard	Bur-115	Elijah	Rth- 87	Bliss,Joseph	Cab-140
Thomas Junr	Per-136	Elisha	Rth- 88	Blissard,Hezekiah	Dup- 27
William	Cum-257	Blanks,Richard	Grn-132	John	Sup- 25
William	Lnc-360	Thos	Grn-143	Solomon	Dup- 26
Wm	Mon- 21	Blans,John	Pit-253	Blith,Saml	Mec- 31
Wm	Ora-126	Blanshet,Thos	Mec- 36	Blizard,Ezekiel	Cum-264
Zadock	Ran-157	Blanton,Archibald	Wil-283	Purnal	Sur-184
Blan,Jason	Mec- 37	Burrel	Rth- 86	Blocker,Mrs.	Cum-236
Blanchard,Amiriah	Gat-109	Burrell	Rth- 89	Mrs. P.	Cum-234
Benjamin	Gat-107	Cleyburn	Rth- 88	Bloodgood,Mary	Car-177
Demsey	Gat-111	Daniel	Rth- 91	Bloodworth,John D	Dup- 21
Elizabeth	Gat-112	James	Rth- 91	Bloomfield,Jas	Bft- 33
Febery	Gat-111	James	Dup- 18	Bloss,Penny	Hal- 99
Josiah	Prq-214	James	Dup- 20	Blount,Allen	Pit-258
Josiah	Nor- 60	Jeremiah	Rth- 87	Ann	Cho-219
Noah	Dup- 5	Jesse	Rth- 87	Annie	Dup- 5
Palitial	Gat-106	John	Rth- 90	Ben	Bft- 38
Reuben	Dup- 5	John Jr	Rth- 90	Benjamin	Wsh-225
Uriah	Dup- 6	Joshua	Dup- 17	Benjn	Sam-164
Uriah Sr	Dup- 7	Lewis	Rth- 91	Clemt H	Cho-224
William	Gat-106	Obediah	Rth- 89	Edmund	Wsh-225
Wm	Cho-229	Reuben	Rth- 91	Ezekiel	Wsh-225
Blanchd,Jerry	Dup- 7	Richd	Dup- 19	Hannah	Wsh-225
Blanchet,Alslam	Cum-252	Susanna	Rth- 91	Henry	Hyd-223
Benj	Way-250	William	Rth- 90	I G	Bft- 36
Edward	Cum-252	William	Rth- 87	J G	Hyd-230
Fed	Ora-171	Blanzet,Fanny	Pas-181	James	Wsh-224
Jesse	Way-238	Blare,John	Bur-103	James Junr	Wsh-223
Nancy	War-178	Blatchford,Rebecka	Pas-181	James Senr	Wsh-224
Bland,Benjn	Ran-158	Blaxter,Elisah	Ora-133	Jas	Bft- 28
Charles	Glf-156	Blaxton,Henry	Brt- 59	John	Cho-224
Elisabeth	Mar- 14	Richard	Edg- 62	John	Sam-164
G	Ora-144	Blaylock,Isham	Hay-193	John B	Cho-219
Jacob	Cha-210	Bledso,J	Ora-140	Joseph	Brt- 53
James	Cha-200	Bledsoe,Aaron	Fra- 79	Levi	Wsh-223

-28-

Name	Ref	Name	Ref	Name	Ref
Blount,Levi	Wsh-225	Blunt,Margaret	Rob-241	Boger,Daniel	Cab-141
Lucy	Bft- 26	Philip	Rob-234	Daniel	Row- 66
Mary	Cho-224	Reuben	Mec- 43	Jacob	Cab-145
Miles	Bft- 29	Rhoda	Pas-184	Jacob	Cab-146
Miles	Bft- 19	Salley	Hrt-214	Peter	Cab-145
N G	Len-323	Thomas	Wsh-228	Boggan,Abner	Ans- 9
Nathaniel	Pit-241	Blythe,Jessee	Bun- 89	Batts	Ans- 7
Needham	Dup- 5	Sion	Bun- 89	Chas	Ans- 10
Robert	Hal- 99	William	Bun- 89	James	Ans- 10
Salley	Bft- 37	Boan,David	Rch-206	Jane	Ans- 33
Samuel Esqr	Wsh-224	George	Rch-207	Jonathan	Ans- 5
Stephen	Mar- 8	Boasman,A	Bru-224	Pattrick	Ans- 5
Susan	Bft- 36	E	Bru-224	Peggy	Ans- 10
Thomas	Edg- 41	Boatwright,Ann	Bru-228	Richd	Ans- 5
Thomas	Was-182	Bobbet,Britton	Grn-121	Sol	Ans- 10
Thos	Pit-243	Harris	War-172	Boggs,Benjn	Ran-158
Wiley	Bft- 29	Henry	Mec- 50	Elisha	Ran-159
William	Prq-214	John	Grn-122	James	Lnc-335
Wm	Bft- 36	Sherwood	Hal-118	John	Ran-158
Blounts,I G Plantation		Bobbett,A	Ora-146	William	Lnc-337
See Tho Satterwaite		Drewry	Cha-211	Bogle,George	Ire-263
	Bft- 31	Bobbit,Arthur	War-167	James	Ora-115
Blow,Benj	Hrt-214	Drury Senr	War-170	Jane	Ire-263
Benjn	Ans- 16	James	War-173	Bogue,Elizabeth	Prq-214
John	Hrt-212	John	War-174	Icabud	Prq-213
Richd	Way-240	John	War-173	John	Brt- 45
Blue,Daniel	Mor- 55	Joshua	War-175	John	Prq-213
Daniel	Mor- 60	Lewis	War-177	Josiah	Prq-214
Daniel	Fra- 87	Stephen	War-180	Mary	Prq-214
Dugald	Rch-191	Solomon	Fra- 91	Meshack	Bur-131
Dugald Senr	Bla- 7	Turner	Fra- 91	Newby	Prq-214
Duncan	Bla- 7	Bobbitt,Willm	Fra- 91	Robert	Prq-213
Duncan	Cum-269	Bobet,John	Grn-122	Thos	Prq-214
Duncan	Rch-197	Boble,John	Bur-113	William	Prq-213
Duncan	Mor- 58	Bochtel,Andrew	Row- 70	Bogy,Alexander	Jon-294
James	Cum-264	Bock,James	Per-127	Bohanan,Thos	Per-132
Jno	Rob-231	Bockum,Jas	Ans- 14	Bohannan,Neal	Sur-165
John	Mor- 60	Josiah	Ans- 14	Bohannon,Benony	Cas- 48
John	Rch-193	Bocton,Edwin	Jon-294	Elliott	Sto- 94
John Junr	Bla- 7	Bodden,Lewis	Mec- 25	Francis	Sto- 94
John Senr	Bla- 7	Bodder,Henry	Row- 80	James	Sto- 93
Margaret	Cum-251	Boddie,George	Nsh- 74	James	Sto-122
Mary	Cum-270	Willie	Nor- 60	Bohnnon,Elliott	Sto-122
Peter	Mor- 58	Willis	Nor- 61	Francis	Sto-122
Stephen	Mec- 32	Wm	Nsh- 72	John	Sto-124
Thos	Mec- 32	Bodenhamer,Christopher		Boice,Jonathan	Gat-109
Blueford,William	Wil-264		Row- 46	Boid,John	Sur-177
Bluett,Thomas	Rch-210	Peter	Row- 43	John	Ran-158
Blume,David	Sto-144	Wm	Row- 38	Saml	Ran-159
Lewis	Sto-125	Bodenhammer,David	Row- 46	William	Ran-159
Lewis	Sto- 96	Geo	Row- 46	Boiles,Charles	Lnc-338
Mersa E	Sto-146	Jacob	Row- 46	Boils,John	Lnc-339
Blunt,Benja	Nsh- 75	John	Row- 46	Bolajack,John	Wil-280
Benjamin	Rob-230	John	Row- 46	Boland,Jas	Mec- 40
Fred	Pas-184	Wm	Row- 47	Bold,Mary	Cha-197
Jacob	Rob-241	Wm	Row- 46	Bolden,R	Ora-157
Jacob	Rob-234	Bodey,William	Cur- 89	Bolding,John	Ora-151
Jas	Mec- 43	Bodine,Gabriel	Ire-263	Bolds,Robt	Mor- 65
Jno	Rob-234	Bogal,Joseph	Ire-238	Boles,Abel	Sto- 44

-29-

Name	Ref	Name	Ref	Name	Ref	Name	Ref
Boles,Abel	Sto-156	Bond,John Sr	Cho-226	Bonnon,Ezekel	Grn-125		
Alexr	Sto-116	Joseph	Glf-163	Bony,David	Ons-107		
Alexr	Sto-156	Joseph	Sto-154	James	Dup- 20		
Alexr	Sto-156	Lewis	Cho-226	William	Dup- 22		
Alexander	Sto- 92	Lewis	Hal- 98	Boo,Elizabeth	Pit-240		
Alexander Jnr	Sto-120	Lewis	Brt- 59	Ellinor	Row- 67		
James	Sto-114	Mary	Mar- 16	Jacob	Row- 37		
James	Sto-116	Nathl	Cho-219	Book,John	Roc- 29		
James	Sto-156	Patton	Prq-214	Robert	Roc- 19		
James	Sto-156	Rachel	Bft- 33	Rhos	Sam-158		
Joseph	Sto-114	Richard	Gat-110	Booker,Daniel	Cum-257		
Joseph	Sto-156	Richard Junr	Gat-107	James	Grn-143		
Jourdin	Grn-142	Thomas	Gat-107	James	Cha-200		
William	Sto-116	Thomas	Sto-153	John	Cum-252		
William	Sto-156	Thomas	Sto-113	Naomi	Cha-195		
Bolick,Adam	Lnc-378	Thos	Brt- 59	W	Glf-179		
Adam Jr	Lnc-353	William	Gat-111	Wm	Glf-174		
Bastian	Lnc-378	Wm	Ora-112	Bookout,John	Ran-158		
Casper Jr	Lnc-398	Bonds,Jas	Mec- 29	Boom,Matthias	Hrt-214		
Casper Senr	Lnc-378	John	Nsh- 83	Boomer,Benjamin	Hyd-230		
Godfrey	Lnc-353	Lewis	Roc- 7	Mathew	Hyd-230		
Jacob	Lnc-378	Lewis	Fra- 92	Sarah	Hyd-226		
John	Lnc-378	Shesbrick	Mec- 29	Boon,Allen	Hrt-212		
Michael J P	Lnc-378	Bone,Archd	Cum-247	Benjamin	Nor- 62		
Bolijack,Samuel	Sur-183	David	Cum-248	Benja	Nsh- 74		
Bolile,Mary	Cum-238	John	Nsh- 82	Benjn	Fra- 94		
Bolin,James	Cum-263	Lewis	Ans- 28	Benja	Brt- 57		
Bolling,Mary	Mon- 40	Thomas	Cum-248	Betty	Nor- 61		
Wm	Mon- 40	Wiley	Nsh- 81	Bird	Hrt-212		
Bollinger,David	Bur-106	William	Ire-237	Bryant	Hrt-206		
Bolton,Abraham	Cum-269	William	Bur-129	Cader	Brt- 54		
Granften	Hrt-213	William	Gat-107	Daniel	Bur-127		
John	Nor- 61	Boner,Isaac	Sto- 98	Daniel	Joh-282		
Peter	Cum-269	Isaac	Sto-129	David	Nor- 62		
Boman,Amey	Wil-280	Joseph	Row- 56	Debbie	Nor- 60		
Peter	Wil-272	Joshua	Sto-146	Elias	Nsh- 75		
Samuel	Cas- 49	Joshua	Sto-112	Mrs. Elizh	Fra- 97		
Thomas	Cas- 48	Boney,Daniel	Dup- 23	Henry	Nor- 61		
Bond,Benjamin	Glf-187	Jacob	Dup- 23	Israel	Bur-128		
Betsey	Bft- 33	John	Dup- 36	J	Ash- 8		
Charles	Bun- 85	William	Cur- 92	J	Ash- 12		
Crispin	Len-321	Bonham,Ard	Lnc-336	J	Glf-178		
Edward	Sur-183	Bonner,Ann	Pit-247	J	Glf-174		
Edward	Sur-172	Edwd	Bft- 27	Jacob	Glf-180		
Elisha H	Gat-108	Mrs. Eliza	Brt- 46	James	Fra- 85		
Francis	Pit-232	George	Cho-223	James	Nor- 61		
George	Brt- 64	John	Edg- 41	James	Nor- 61		
Henry	Cho-219	John	Hyd-228	Jesse	Bur-128		
J	Ash- 3	L	Ash- 13	Jesse	Nor- 61		
James	Cho-226	Leah	Prq-214	Jessee	Nsh- 74		
James	Gat-114	Mary	Bft- 27	Jno	Ora-119		
John	Sur-190	Matthew	Glf-182	John	Row- 64		
John	Tyr-201	Nancy	Brt- 46	John	Cum-247		
John	Ons- 99	Preston	Edg- 70	John	Edg- 58		
John	Prq-214	Robt S	Bft- 37	John	Glf-167		
John	Brt- 57	Stapleton Junr	Mar- 12	John Jr	Nor- 62		
John	Brt- 59	Stapleton Senr	Mar- 12	John Senr	Nor- 61		
John Jnr	Cho-326	Thomas	Edg- 46	Jonathan	Bur-113		

-30-

Name	Loc	Name	Loc	Name	Loc
Boon,Joseph Jr	Joh-280	Borden,Joseph	Car-183	Boswell,Gustavus	Row- 63
Joseph Sr	Joh-280	Levi	Dup- 6	Hezekiah	Cas- 49
Joyner	Nor- 60	Wm	Car-180	Ichabod	Way-244
Judith	Hrt-216	Borders,Peter	Bun- 98	James	Per-148
Kinchen	Fra- 90	Boreland,Alex	Ora-168	James Senr	Per-136
Lewis	Fra- 98	Borner,Horatio	Sur-188	Jesse	Way-245
Lewis	Hal- 97	Bornor,James	Sur-188	John	Brt- 43
Mrs. Martha	Fra- 85	Borough,Bryan	Mor- 54	John	Grn-128
Patsay	Hrt-216	Boroughs,David	Pit-261	John	Way-246
Raford	Cha-216	Reuben	Ora-125	Joseph	Rth- 90
Raford	Nsh- 73	Borses,John	Mon- 50	Joseph	Grn-125
Mrs. Rebecca	Fra- 90	Bortis,Mary	Bft- 34	Joseph	Way-244
Rhodick	Hrt-216	Boschs,John	Cas- 67	S	Col- 21
Roselly	Nor- 62	Boseman,Elizabeth	Hal- 99	Simon	Way-243
Sarah	Brt- 57	James	Hal- 98	T	Col- 21
Stephen	Cum-235	Bosman,Button	Edg- 51	Thomas	Ora-165
Tho	Bur-130	Boss,Right	Row- 61	Thomas	Way-233
Thomas	Nor- 60	Bossell,Andw	Ora-121	Thomas	Way-232
Thomas	Nor- 62	Bost,Conrod	Bur-131	Thos	Prq-214
Thomas	Rob-229	Daniel	Cab-141	Thos	Brt- 59
Thomas	Edg- 44	Elias	Cab-141	W	Col- 20
William	Brt- 47	Elias	Lnc-378	William	Ora-162
William	Nor- 61	Geo	Cab-140	Wm	Brt- 60
William Senr	Nor- 61	Jacob	Cab-140	Bosworth,Jonathan	Mon- 40
Willis	Fra- 94	John	Cab-141	Botfoot,George	Row- 55
Boone,James	Len-314	John	Cab-144	Bothrop,Wm	Grn-134
Boos,John	Hyd-234	John	Lnc-378	Botkins,Jno	Mec- 47
Booth,Arkel	Nsh- 92	William	Lnc-378	Bottles,Chrsit	Bur-103
Elisabeth	Mar- 5	Wm	Cab-148	Bottoms,Anemenly	Edg- 41
George	Sto-127	Bosten,Jacob	Ire-246	Wm L	Nsh- 82
George	Sto-106	Bostian,Andrew	Row- 69	Botton,Matthew	War-178
George	Sto- 98	Andrew Jr	Row- 69	Botts,Bartholomy	Rth- 91
George	Sto-142	David	Row- 70	Bottums,Amos	Nsh- 81
Gray	Glf-189	Jacob	Row- 69	Brittain	Nsh- 80
James	Gat-106	James	Row- 70	John	Nsh- 81
James	Edg- 72	John	Row- 68	Bouge,Benj	Way-242
Jessee	Nsh- 92	John	Row- 69	Saml	Pas-182
Joel	Grn-147	Mattias	Row- 69	Boughnes,Rubin	Ora-143
Jno	Ora-156	Michal	Row- 70	Boulding,James	Cas- 48
John	Edg- 71	Philip	Row- 70	John	Cas- 48
Lewis	Edg- 65	Bostic,Charles	Rth- 88	Thomas	Cas- 48
M	Ora-156	Richard	Rth- 88	Boules,Barbara	Bft- 36
Mark	Ora-150	Bostick,Absalem	Sto-157	Boulton,Allen	Edg- 68
Zachariah	Gat-115	Charles	Dup- 20	Benjamin	Rch-197
Boothe,Andrew	Sur-187	Chesley	Rth- 91	Mary	Cas- 49
Clarissa	War-169	Fardinand	Sto- 94	Phebia	Cas- 49
Harper	Grn-147	Ferdinand	Sto-123	Richard	Edg- 69
J	Ora-141	Levi	Mor- 66	Boum,Wm	Ora-131
J	Ora-141	Levi	Mor- 60	Bounch,David	Prq-214
John	Ora-142	Saml	Dup- 9	Isaac	Prq-213
Morris	Sur-195	William	Rch-198	Nazareth	Prq-214
Moses	Cha-201	Boswel,John	Pas-182	Penelope	Prq-214
Prisl	Ora-117	Malachi	Pas-182	Bounds,George	Rch-194
Tapley	Ora-146	William	Pas-182	George	Rch-209
Zac	Row- 84	Boswell,Mrs.	Brt- 67	James Junr	Rch-209
Booty,Aner	Pit-240	Ben	Way-254	James Senr	Rch-209
Wm	Bft- 29	C	Col- 20	Jesse	Rch-209
Bord,Desey	Mon- 27	D	Col- 19	Jesse Junr	Rch-194
Borden,John	Rth- 90	George	Fra- 84	Jesse Senr	Rch-194

-31-

Name	Ref	Name	Ref	Name	Ref	Name	Ref
Bounds, Stephen	Rch-209	Bower, G		Ash- 5		Bowman, Henry	Lnc-378
Bourgosis, Gregory	Bft- 36	Henry		Row- 78		J H	Ora-135
Bourn, John	Sur-178	J		Ash- 3		Jacob	Bur-114
Bourras, John	Cha-191	John		Grn-149		John	Bur-131
Coushall, J	Cam-155	P		Ash- 13		John	Lnc-378
T	Cam-152	Bowers, Abraham		Pit-250		John	Ire-242
Boushell, R	Cam-154	Adam		Cab-143		John	Cas- 50
Bovey, Mathias	Lnc-378	Barney		Row- 40		John	Cas- 49
Bovinder, John	Sur-175	Bartholemew		Mar- 8		Mary	Rth- 88
Bow, Josiah H	Sto-112	Ben		Pit-233		R	Col- 17
Bowden, Baker	Way-235	Burton		Ora-150		Richard	Bur-129
Benjamin	Per-148	Caty		Row- 80		Richd	Glf-165
Bryan	Dup- 12	David		Lnc-359		Robert	Cas- 49
Jesse	Row- 59	Francis		Sur-165		Sherwood	Bur-125
Jno	Mec- 36	George		Row- 80		Vinson	Rth- 88
John	Fra- 90	Green		Ora-113		William Jr	Glf-188
John	Row- 62	James		Row- 75		Bowser, Mary	Cur- 80
Polly	Nor- 62	John		Pit-243		Sarey	Cur- 80
Bowsen, Will	Dup- 24	John		Row- 80		Bowshell, Thos	Bur-102
Willm	Fra- 95	John		Per-149		Bowson, Isaac	Wsh-220
Bowdin, Benjn	Dup- 14	Lemuel		Cas- 48		Bowzer, Charles	Hal- 98
Henry	Dup- 15	Lewelling		Mar- 8		Elizabeth	Hal- 99
James	Dup- 15	Rebecca		Nor- 61		Thomas	Hal- 98
Nicholas	Dup- 15	William		Pit-261		Box, Saml	Ora-114
Reddin	Dup- 16	Wm		Grn-130		Tho	Ora-129
Saml	Dup- 16	Wm		Nsh- 81		Boyan, Ephraim	Ora-171
Bowdown, John	War-175	Bowie, Ard		Bla- 12		Boyce, Abso	Cho-231
John	War-175	Bowin, Alexander		Rch-197		Dempsey	Brt- 49
John	Rch-200	Edwd		Dup- 17		Hardy	Brt- 58
P	Mon- 28	Frederick		Dup- 18		John	Prq-214
Bowe, H	Cum-241	John		Rch-199		Joseph	Way-245
Joshua	Pas-183	Mark		Dup- 19		Josiah	Hrt-216
Sarah	Pas-184	Sessions		Mar- 7		Josiah	Prq-214
Tully	Pas-183	Bowlan, Baxter		Ora-151		Miles	Hrt-216
Bowel, A	Cum-238	Bowland, Benj		Ora-151		Miles	Brt- 49
Austin	Rob-230	Bowles, Benj		Mon- 27		Mills	Nor- 61
Crecy	Hrt-209	William		Sto- 93		Moses	Prq-214
Louis	Rob-235	Bowling, Jarrott		Roc- 34		Sion	Nor- 61
Bowen, Ben	Bft- 33	Rodney		Roc- 13		W H	Hrt-208
Dindel	Dup- 27	Shewbd		Mon- 32		Boyd, Alexr	Cha-213
E	Glf-163	Bowls, Ar		Ora-154		Alexr	Mor- 64
Elijah	Dup- 27	D		Ora-153		Andrew	Roc- 29
Ezekiel	Roc- 4	J		Ora-154		Anna	Bft- 24
Hardy	Brt- 47	James of Wm		Ora-159		Anny	Grn-119
John	Bft- 22	John		Ire-270		Bythina	Bft- 23
Jos Jr	Per-127	Thos		Mec- 48		Coleman	Bft- 23
Joshua	Brt- 47	Wm		Ora-175		Edward	Lnc-368
Lucy	Len-319	Wm Sen		Ora-123		Fedk	Bft- 21
Luke	Cum-241	Bowly, John		Per-136		J	Glf-168
Polly	Dup- 22	Bowman, Andrew		Sto-158		J B	Bft- 24
Robert	Bft- 22	Archabald		Sto-112		James	Grn-140
Sarah	Len-319	Archablad		Sto-150		James	Glf-168
Thomas	Bft- 33	Daniel		Bur-131		James	Bun- 82
William	Prq-213	Daniel		Lnd-378		Jas	Mec- 41
Bowens, John Jnr	Pit-239	David		Bur-105		John	Bft- 20
Bower, A	Ash- 7	George		Sto-150		John	Bft- 24
Andrew	Row- 78	George		Sto-132		John	Lnc-368
Barnet	Lnc-353	Groves		Bur-129		John	Bur-107
Bathow	Lnc-352	H		Glf-177		John	Cha-189

Name	Loc	Name	Loc	Name	Loc
Boyd,John	Pas-183	Boyles,William	Sto-122	Bradaway,John	Lnc-361
Joseph	Ire-249	William	Sto-120	Bradberry,Aron	Way-253
Moses	Ire-248	William	Sto- 91	Eliza	Way-253
Patrick	Mec- 37	Boys,Patsey	Rth- 87	George	Way-253
Reding	Cha-189	Boyser,Isaac	Sto-143	James	Way-241
Richard	War-179	Boyt,Etheldred	Bat-113	John	Way-253
Robert	Ire-263	Periby	Mon- 37	Solomon	Way-253
Robert	Ire-249	Boyte,Amos	Way-253	Bradburn,Jno	But-108
Robt	Mec- 41	Burwell	Way-253	John	Bur-126
Tho	Bft- 21	Henry	Way-251	Thomas	Bur-105
Tho Esq	Bft- 21	Jacob B	Way-251	Bradbury,William	Roc- 26
Thos	Mec- 25	Joseph B	Way-251	Braddy,Elisha	Pit-249
Wm Esq	Bft- 20	Micajah	Way-252	Elisha	Edg- 52
Wm	Bft- 21	Moses	Way-251	Job	Edg- 62
Wm	Bru-222	Thomas	Way-253	John	Pit-249
Wm (B C)	Bft- 22	Bozdall,John	Cas- 49	Nathan	Pit-249
Boyed,Henry	Row- 87	Bozman,Benjamin	Rch-210	W	Bru-238
John	Pit-242	Biselon	Wsh-227	William	Pit-249
Joseph	Pit-243	James	Rch-197	William	Joh-281
Joseph	Pit-242	John	Brt- 48	Bradey,Eli	Ran-159
Robert	Pit-234	Joseph	Cho-219	Thos	Cur- 81
Sam	Pit-233	Levin Esqr	Wsh-225	Bradfield,Lewis	Roc- 2
William	Pit-242	Samuel	Rch-210	Bradford,Burnet	Bur-107
William	Pit-234	William	Rch-201	D W	Ora-155
Boyes,Jas	Mec- 50	Bozwell,Judith	Cas- 50	David	Ora-167
Jno	Mec- 33	Randsom	Cas- 49	David	Cab-138
Saml	Mec- 50	Brabel,William	Cur- 88	Edward	Cum-268
Boyet,Dolly	Dup- 11	Brabell,John	Cur- 88	Elizah	Grn-121
Ephraim	Ons-102	Tatum	Cur- 88	Ephm	Mon- 40
James	Dup- 24	Bracewell,Amy	Edg- 57	Eve	Grn-149
Jesse	Dup- 29	Archelas	Edg- 59	Henry	Hal- 98
John	Dup- 10	Bythal	Edg- 43	Jas	Cab-138
Jones	Dup- 30	Edermenton	Edg- 42	John	Bur-106
Mich	Dup- 7	Isaac	Edg- 43	John	Grn-130
Will	Dup- 11	Jacob	Edg- 47	John	Mon- 45
William	Ons- 99	James	Edg- 55	Saml	Ora-113
Boyete,Solomon	Mar- 8	James	Edg- 46	Tho Jr	Ora-165
Boyett,Absalom	Len-320	Reddick	Edg- 45	Tho Senr	Ora-165
Danl	Len-320	Sollomon	Edg- 46	William	Hal- 97
John	Sam-154	Zadock	Edg- 43	Wm	Grn-128
Boyken,Hardy	Nsh- 92	Brach,Burwell	Wil-274	Wm	Ora-170
Hardy	Nsh- 87	Raney	Wil-274	Bradham,John	Ons- 95
William	Hal- 97	Brachbeam,John	Cur- 82	Stephen	Ons- 95
Boykin,Arthur	Nor- 61	Brack,George	Ire-250	Bradick,Bill	Car-184
Edwards	Edg- 46	Samuel	War-181	Bradis,Michael	Roc- 13
John	Nor- 63	Bracken,H	Ora-155	Bradley,Ajy	Edg- 59
Lucy	Nor- 62	J	Ora-155	Ansalem	Rth- 86
Sterling	Nor- 62	William	Row- 65	Benjamin	Edg- 57
Thomas	Sam-156	Wm	Ora-155	Benjamin	War-168
Boyle,James	Rth- 86	Brackens,James	Bun- 85	Burwell	Edg- 59
John	Ora-168	Bracket,Thomas	Rth- 89	Coleman	Rth- 88
Boyles,Charles	Rth- 86	Brackin,Isaac	Ora-125	David	Row- 66
Daniel	Roc- 31	Isaac	Ora-135	David	Edg- 57
Elizabeth	Sto-127	Joseph	Cas- 48	Drewry	Hal- 98
Elizabeth	Sto- 97	Samuel	Cas- 48	Edward	Rth- 88
Hugh	Sto- 77	Brackins,John	Bun- 85	Elizabeth	Rth- 90
Jno	Ora-155	Brackun,William	Per-135	Henry	Edg- 57
Jno Sen	Ora-136	Bracy,Irby	Grn-141	Hugh	Rth- 91
R	Ora-153	Mary	Grn-143	Isaac	Rth- 90

Bradley,Isaiah	Cab-138	Bradshaw,John	Bur-103	Braley,James	Row- 73		
James	Edg- 59	John	Cab-148	John	Ire-240		
James	Hal- 98	John Jr	Lnc-377	John	Ire-240		
James	Hal- 97	John	Lnc-347	Neil	Ire-240		
James	Wil-276	John Senr	Lnc-377	Neil	Ire-240		
James	Rth- 86	Jonas	Lnc-377	Robert	Ire-240		
James	Rth- 91	Josiah	Lnc-377	Bramble,William	Cum-248		
Jesse	Ran-158	Obadiah	Hay-193	Bramly,Eli	Per-214		
Jessee	Nor- 62	Pride	Lnc-360	Bran,John	Per-127		
John	Hal- 97	Peaton	Mec- 29	Thomas	Per-126		
John	Wil-284	Ryas	Sam-158	Brance,Samuel	Row- 57		
John	Lnc-333	Seth	Bur-121	Train	Row- 57		
John	Rth- 86	Tho	Ora-115	Wm	Row- 57		
John	Rth- 88	Tho Jun	Ora-113	Branch,Anderson	Bur-109		
John	Rth- 87	Thos Jr	Ora-158	Arch	Dup- 26		
John Jr	Rth- 86	William	Bur-111	Benjamin	Cum-264		
Jonathan	Edg- 57	Wm	Ora-134	Boon	Nor- 62		
Jones	Rth- 88	Bradsher,Abner	Per-127	Bryan	Dup- 3		
Joseph	War-173	Jas	Per-128	Burwell	Dup- 14		
Joseph	Rth- 91	Moses	Per-128	Dred	Dup- 3		
Josiah	Car-173	Brady,Archibald	Ire-247	Mrs. Elizh	Fra- 93		
Ledbetter	Rth- 88	Basdel	Nsh- 76	Isacher	Prq-214		
Margaret	Bla- 9	Ben	Bft- 23	James	Pit-250		
N	Mon- 36	Ben	Bft- 33	James	Bur-109		
Peter	Cur- 79	Charles	Mor- 55	James	Nor- 61		
Richard	Edg- 57	George	Ire-248	James	Cum-265		
Richard	Rth- 90	Isaac Jr	Ran-159	Jesse	Dup- 30		
Richd	Dup- 5	Isaac Sr	Ran-159	Jesse	Dup- 3		
Sherwood	Rth- 91	James	Ran-159	Jesse	Cum-266		
Simeon	Dup- 13	James	Gat-112	John	Hal- 98		
Stephen	Edg- 57	James	Gat-115	John	Bur-109		
Terry	Rth- 90	James	Nsh- 77	Martha	Hal- 99		
Thomas	Edg- 55	John	Joh-281	Mary	Nor- 62		
Walton	Rth- 86	John	Gat-115	Matthew	Dup- 4		
Walton	Rth- 88	Luis	Ran-159	Moses	Rob-239		
William	Hal- 98	Maee	Bft- 24	Norman	Nor- 62		
William	Nor- 62	Mary	Bft- 24	Reuben	Dup- 26		
Wm	Bft- 27	Phorp	Bft- 23	Samuel	Hal- 99		
Willis	Edg- 62	Spencer	Ire-267	Stephen	Bur-121		
Bradly,Jas	Mec- 47	Susanna	Row- 66	Thomas	Nor- 62		
John	Pit-247	William	Bun- 83	William	Dup- 5		
Laurence	Bur-112	William	Nor- 62	William	Dup- 13		
Richd	Bur-112	Wm	Bft- 24	Wm S	Per-136		
Ussa	Hal- 99	Brag,Jesse	Car-172	Willis	Gat-108		
Bradnor,John B	War-173	Joseph	Car-172	Brand,James	Roc- 28		
Bradock,Jacob	Hyd-226	Bragdon,William	Sur-190	Mary	Roc- 30		
Bradon,James	Rth- 89	Bragg,Frances	Bft- 37	Brandle,Daniel	Sur-165		
Robert	Rth- 89	Hugh	Grn-130	George	Sur-165		
Bradshaw,Barnabas	Sam-158	Sol	Bft- 38	Brandon,George	Row- 63		
Benj	Lnc-366	Thomas	War-184	James	Row- 88		
Benjn	Dup- 18	Brahan,Thomas	Row- 65	John	Row- 64		
Christopher	Sam-158	Braik,George	Ire-249	John	Bun- 95		
David	Cab-143	Brake,Jacob	Edg- 61	John	Bur-125		
Eli	Cab-148	Jessee	Edg- 61	John Colo	Row- 68		
Ephraim	Sam-154	John	Edg- 55	Mattheq	Row- 68		
James	Hay-193	Nathan	Edg- 61	Thomas	Sto-103		
James	Cab-148	Sherwood	Edg- 60	Thomas	Sto-136		
Jesse	Sam-151	Braley,Hugh	Row- 71	Thomas	Lnc-338		
Jno	Bur-117	James	Ire-240	Thomas	Lnc-338		

-34-

Name	Ref	Name	Ref	Name	Ref
Brandy,Jim L	Pas-184	Brantly,Nancy	Hal- 97	Brawdway,Elizth	Row- 81
Branham,Benjn	Sto-107	Wm Sr	Cha-197	Brawley,Jos	Glf-175
Benjn	Sto-142	Branton,M	Col- 18	Brawly,Jas	Glf-175
Joel	Wil-274	Wm	Cha-109	Brawn,Joseph	Joh-291
John	Sto-120	Wm	Len-315	Brawn,Joseph	Joh-291
John	Sto- 91	Brasdel,David	Per-126	Richard	Joh-289
John	Sur-179	Brasel,Aaron	Rob-221	Stephen	Joh-290
Braning,James	Bur-125	Arathur	Rob-221	Brawton,Addam	Jon-293
Brank,Robert	Bun- 93	David	Rob-221	Braxton,John	Cha-210
Brann,Dickey	Grn-134	Braser,Harry	Ire-266	Thos	Cha-216
John	Grn-134	Brasfield,Jesse	Sur-171	William John	Len-215
Brannam,Christopher	Roc- 34	Wila	Sur-171	Bray,--uolis	Cur- 89
Brannock,Henry	Ora-162	Brashear,Eden	Hrt-335	Berry	Sur-164
Wm	Ora-162	Brashears,Thos	Ire-254	D Snr	Cam-165
Brannon,Becka	Joh-287	Brashee,Henry	Ire-246	D Jnr	Cam-155
Cader	Joh-287	Brasher,Asa	Roc- 5	David	Sur-164
Caron	Joh-287	Jesse	Glf-188	David Jn	Sur-172
John	Bun- 75	John	Per-136	H Jnr	Cam-160
William	Joh-291	Lemuel	Roc- 18	H Snr	Cam-153
Brannum,James	Glf-165	Z D	Glf-166	Hanon	Sur-173
Brans,Elizabeth	Nsh-643	Brasing,Andrew	Sto-146	Henry	Pas-181
Jacob	Nsh-643	Braskshire,Wm	Wil-273	Henry	Cha-193
Branson,Eli	Cha-203	Brass,John	Lnc-342	Henry J.	Cha-204
Henery	Cum-237	Brassfield,Silvy	Grn-130	James and Aul	Cur- 90
Henry	Sto-150	Brasswell,David	Hal- 98	James	Wil-274
John	Sto-110	Drewry	Hal- 98	James	Cha-207
John	Sto-150	Braswell,Baldy	Nsh- 74	Jesse	Pas-181
Joseph	Cha-195	Benj	Nsh- 82	Jesse	Cha-197
Levi	Ran-158	Blake	Roc- 20	Joseph	Sur-183
Levi	Glf-187	Brittain	Nsh- 73	Joseph	Dup- 8
Levi	Cha-212	Demsey	Nsh- 78	Matthias	Ran-159
William	Sto-150	Jacob	Nsh- 74	Nathan	Sur-176
Zachariah	Sto-144	Jacob	Joh-279	Richard	Sur-181
Zachariah	Sto-108	Jacob Jr	Nsh- 75	S	Cam-153
Branston,Wm	Cha-195	Jesse	Nsh- 73	Thos	Cur- 92
Brantley,Benj	Hrt-216	Marmaduke	Hal- 97	Thos	Cam-157
Blake	Cha-208	Naron	Nsh- 86	W	Cam-159
Edward	Hrt-208	Orrain	Nsh- 84	William	Sur-164
Elizabeth	Hal- 98	Polly	Nor- 61	Wm	Cha-197
James Jr	Nor- 62	Richd	Joh-278	Zack L	Cur- 89
James Senr	Nor- 63	Shadrick	Way-241	Brayboy,John	Bft- 32
John	Cha-216	Stephen	Way-241	Brayden,Henry	Cha-196
John	Edg- 48	William	Joh-277	Brazell,E	Glf-160
Joshua	Brt- 47	Wm	Nsh- 75	Jacob	Glf-159
Lewis	Hrt-216	Wilson	Nsh- 78	Jesse	Ans- 16
Robert	Hal- 98	Bratcher,Philip	Way-241	Brazer,Elijah	Cum-257
Samuel	Hal- 98	Sion	Way-247	Brazier,Elija	Row- 58
Sherward	Nsh- 91	Brattain,Robt	Glf-170	Isaac	Edg- 56
T	Col- 20	Bratten,Benjamin	Prq-214	James	Row- 58
Wm	Cha-213	Thos	Prq-214	William	Sur-191
Brantly,Mrs.	Fra- 79	William	Prq-214	Brazil,Robert	Bur-105
Bennet	Nsh- 82	Brattern,John	Ran-158	Brdley,Asa	Bun- 82
Edward	Cha-198	Brattin,Benjn	Ran-158	Breach,Wm	Grn-134
James	Cum-241	John	Ran-158	Breedlove,James	Rth- 87
Jesse	Bla- 11	William	Ran-158	John	War-173
John	Joh-280	Brau,William	Sur-176	Nancy	War-178
Joseph	Cha-189	Braughton,Jere	Cas- 48	Nathan	War-178
Joseph	Cha-206	Braveboy,Jacob	Cum-251	Newman	War-178
Mary	Cha-197	Braveboys,L	Cum-238	Sarah	Roc- 23

-35-

Breedlove,William	War-182	Brewer,Tho Esq	Qra-170	Bride,William	Ire-239		
Breece,Henderson	Ons-107	Will	Ora-131	Bridger,John	Ons-106		
Richard	Ons-107	William	Hal- 99	Robert	Ons-106		
Breeze,John	Ora-160	William	Ran-159	Bridgers,Benjn	Nor- 61		
Brenan,John	Pit-256	William	Nor- 62	David	Joh-280		
Brent,John	Roc- 2	William	Mar- 13	Elizth	Nsh- 74		
Thomas C	Roc- 2	Willis	Mor- 56	George	Way-233		
Brevard,Adam	Ire-240	Brain,Isaac	Rob-242	James	Nor- 61		
Alexr	Lnc-377	Jacob	Rob-241	James	Way-241		
Benjamin	Ire-240	John	Cum-265	John	Edg- 45		
Hamilton	Mec- 24	Joseph	Rob-242	Joseph	Nor- 61		
John	Ire-240	Thomas	Rob-243	Josiah	Hrt-207		
Robert	Ire-240	William	Cum-267	Judith	Nor- 61		
Brewer,Abel	Cha-210	Braint,Geo	Ans- 13	Micajah Esq	Fra- 83		
Abell	Cha-199	M	Cam-160	William	Edg- 65		
Ambrose	Mor- 62	Thomas	Grn-134	William	Nor- 61		
Annell	Cha-204	Thomas	Nsh- 84	Young	Joh-290		
Arthur	Pit-255	Briatts,Christ	Cas- 48	Bridges,Aaron	Rth- 87		
Christopher	Cha-213	Bricay,Christian	Sto-114	Aaron	Rth- 90		
Danl	Mor- 63	Brice,Alexr	Mor- 66	Aaron	Rth- 91		
Drury	Mor- 61	Daniel	Mor- 54	Amos	Fra- 84		
Ezekiel	Ora-130	Duncan	Cum-250	Amos	Fra- 90		
Fedrick	Mor- 58	Duncan	Mor- 57	Ben	Ora-131		
Gant	Ora-131	Duncan	Mor- 62	Benj	Cha-201		
Geo	Cha-196	Flora	Mor- 68	Benj Junr	Fra- 99		
Harmon	Mor- 59	Gilbert	Mor- 66	Benjn Senr	Fra- 88		
Henry	Mor- 59	Gilbt Mil	Mor- 66	Francis	Cha-190		
Henry	Ran-159	James	Nsh- 83	Isaac	Rth- 90		
Henry	Cha-196	John	Mor- 62	James	Bun- 88		
Henry	Sam-159	John	Dup- 32	James	Rth- 91		
Hinchan	Cha-206	Joseph	Dup- 18	James	Rth- 91		
Howel	Mor- 62	Mary	Mor- 60	James	Lnc-356		
Isaac	Mar- 12	Bricen,Robert	Ire-237	Jesse	Rth- 88		
J	Ora-157	Brickall,Thomas	Gat-107	Jessee	Bun- 90		
Jacob	Rob-204	Brickell,Benj Esq	Fra- 89	John	Grn-121		
James	Grn-143	Joseph	Pit-262	John	Rth- 90		
James	Mar- 6	Thomas N	Brt- 48	John	Rth- 88		
Jeremiah	Cha-204	William	Fra-100	John	Lnc-356		
Jesse	Way-248	Brickenhouse Hen S	Row- 60	Joseph	Cha-201		
Jesse	Hal- 99	Brickhous,Benj	Cur- 90	Joseph	Bun- 97		
John	Row- 56	Edwd	Cur- 85	Joseph	Cha-203		
John	Cha-209	Elishey	Cur- 85	Josiah	Fra- 87		
Jones	Cha-216	Hayes	Tyr-202	Misser	Rth- 90		
Lackfield	Ora-166	Simeon	Cur- 85	Moses	Rth- 90		
Lazerus	Pit-258	Brickhouse,John	Tyr-203	Salley	Lnc-355		
Macaijah	Mor- 58	Major	Tyr-206	Sampson	Rob-222		
Mark	Cha-198	Mathew Jr	Tyr-212	Samuel	Rth- 90		
Mary	Mar- 12	Math Sr	Tyr-206	Stephen	Grn-122		
Moses	Way-248	Peter	Tyr-206	Thomas	Rth- 90		
Nathan	Cha-204	Peter Jr	Tyr-212	William	Bun- 97		
Nathaniel	Cha-211	Sarah	Tyr-212	William	Rth- 89		
Nathl	Cha-215	Willm Jr	Tyr-212	William	Rth- 90		
Nicholas	Nor- 62	Wm Sen	Tyr-206	Willm	Fra- 86		
Nicolas	Cha-198	Brickle,Britain	Nor- 62	Wm	Cha-201		
Peter	Cha-198	John	Bft- 21	Bridgman,James	Hyd-230		
Rebeccah	Cha-213	Mary	Nor- 62	Thomas	Hyd-230		
Rebekah	Rth- 89	Mary	Hal- 99	Bridgmen,Polly	Ire-251		
Saml	Cha-192	Nancy	Hal- 97	Bridgmon,John	Sur-171		
Sollomon	Mor- 59	William	Hal- 97	Matthew	Sur-178		

-36-

Brigges,Samuel	Rth- 87	Brigs,Edward	Bun- 78	Brinkly,Mourning	Prq-214
Briggs,Benjamin	Sto-110	George	Grn-138	Nathaniel	Prq-214
Benjamin	Sto-149	Thomas	Row- 82	Nicey	Pit-240
Edward	Bun- 79	Briles,George	Row- 79	P Junior	Ora-137
Henry	Sto-130	Jacob	Ran-158	Peter	Ora-137
John	Sto-128	Briley,Benjamin	Pit-247	Robt	Ora-177
Howel	Grn-132	Geo	Ans- 33	Simon	Gat-109
Howell	Bur-122	Isaac	Pit-249	Willis	Gat-109
James	Ora-167	Jas	Ans- 23	Wm	Per-127
James	Row- 75	Jno	Ans- 33	Brinn,Mary	Edg- 59
Jesse	Sto- 97	Joseph	Pit-254	Brinsfield,J	Glf-178
Jesse	Sto-128	William	Pit-254	Brinson,Elizth	Ons-108
John	Sto- 98	William	Pit-254	Lott	Ons-104
John	Car-176	Brim,Conrad	Row- 75	Brintle,Jesse	Cas- 49
Josiah	Gat-106	Jacob	Lnc-345	Solomon	Cas- 49
Kader	Gat-110	John Jun	Roc- 4	William Jr	Cas- 50
Moses	Gat-109	Brimage,Elizth	Brt- 45	William Sr	Cas- 50
Richard	Gat-107	Brimer,Isaac	Lnc-332	Briscoe,Phillip	Rth- 90
Solomon	Gat-110	Saml	Lnc-332	Brisko,Eben	Gat-112
Thomas	Bun- 76	Brimm,John Senr	Roc- 17	Briscon,Hugh	Lnc-335
William	Sto-128	Rakins	Roc- 9	John	Lnc-335
William	Sto- 98	Rice	Roc- 9	Brisson,Anthony	Bla- 6
Bright,Aaron	Cur- 90	Brinager,A	Ash- 14	Brister,Warner	Nor- 61
Asa	Pas-183	J	Ash- 14	Wm	Ora-147
B	Col- 18	Brincefield,Thos	Cas- 48	Bristo,Ben Bo col	Rch-202
Ephraim	Pas-181	Brindle,Henry	Lnc-339	Twiman	Cum-251
Isaac	Cha-194	John	Lnc-337	Brit,Benj	Mor- 60
J	Col- 20	John	Lnc-337	Joel	Sam-154
Jabe-	Pas-182	John	Row- 56	Oliva	Mor- 60
James	Bur-119	Jos	Lnc-339	Rodger	Mor- 60
James	Sam-151	Brinegar,Paul	Sur-166	Britain,Aaron	Bur-104
James	Glf-152	Brinkey,S	Ora-146	Alsa	Bur-105
Jas	Len-323	Brinkle,Christian	Row- 88	Benj	Hrt-209
Jas Jr	Len-322	Christy	Lnc-337	Jessee	Nor- 61
Jas Senr	Len-322	Gasper	Row- 79	Michael	Hrt-210
Jervis	Cha-199	Brinkley,Abraham	Edg- 52	Nathan	Nor- 62
Jesse	Pas-181	Daniel	Row- 54	William	Sur-169
Jesse	Bur-117	Francis	Row- 54	Wm	Brt- 56
John	Bur-118	James	Gat-108	Brite,A	Cam-161
Joseph	Pas-183	James	Grn-141	C	Cam-163
Malachi	Pas-184	Jane	Hal- 98	Edwd	Cur- 91
Mary	Len-323	John	Row- 54	H	Cam-164
Nathan	Pas-182	John	Edg- 52	H Jnr	Cam-159
R	Col- 21	John	Gat-107	Henery	Cur- 91
Richard	Pas-183	Josiah	Hal- 97	Isah	Cur- 90
Rob	Bla- 11	Robert	Grn-143	J	Cam-164
S	Col- 20	Sarah	Edg- 51	J	Cam-164
Sally	Pas-182	Stephen	Row- 54	J	Cam-157
Simon	Cha-214	William	Gat-108	J	Cam-158
Solomon	Row- 47	Wm	Grn-141	Jonathan	Cur- 89
Timothy	Pas-184	Wm	Hal- 97	Lucy	Cur- 89
William	Bur-118	Brinkly,Cherry	Hal- 98	M	Cam-159
William	Pit-243	David	Gat-109	M	Cam-162
Willis	Pas-181	Elish	Gat-109	M	Cam-164
Brigman,Augusten	Rch-205	Henry	Gat-109	N	Cam-162
Josuah	Rch-205	James	Sto-140	R	Cam-164
Tebitha	Rch-209	James	Sto-105	R	Cam-164
Wm	Mec- 44	John	Pit-239	S	Cam-165
Brigmon,Solomon	Bun- 86	Josiah	Gat-110	S	Cam-165

Name	Ref	Name	Ref	Name	Ref
Brite,S	Cam-164	Brittle,Philip	Nor- 61	Brogden,John	Fra- 98
Sals	Cur- 90	Britton,John	Ons-106	Susanah	Mar-445
W	Cam-164	Saml	Glf-164	William	Wsh-225
W	Cam-165	Jos	Glf-166	Brogdon,Aaron	Brt- 59
Britian,Joh	Sur-168	Brittun,Arthur	Pit-235	Edward	Nsh- 74
Brition,James G	War-175	Brivard,Thomas	Bur-125	John	Way-238
Briton,John	Pit-261	Brnes,Edwin	Nsh- 79	Moses	Brt- 59
John	Nor- 62	Broach,James	Per-135	Thomas	Way-238
Mark	Bur-103	Broadaway,Jno	Ans- 9	Thos	Brt- 59
Philip	Bur-104	Broadfoot,Mrs.	Cum-239	Bromet,William	Cas- 48
Uriah	Pit-241	William	Cum-239	Bromlow,Mrs.	Mec- 41
Britt,Alexr	Rob-238	Broadstreet,Betty	Joh-282	David	Mec- 43
Benj	Hrt-212	Cloah	Way-245	Jno	Mec- 34
Benj	Hrt-213	Patty	Joh-287	Peter	Mec- 41
Benjamin Jnr	Rob-235	Broadway,Samuel	Rth- 88	Bromly,Thos	Mec- 47
Benjamin Snr	Rob-235	William	Ire-256	Bront,James Senr	Hal- 98
Britain	Rob-235	Broch,George	Cas- 48	Brook,Jesse Jr	Dup- 15
Burrel	Rob-235	Brock,Benjamin	Dup- 26	M	Cam-154
Culiver	Rch-208	Benjamin	Jon-294	Mary	Edg- 64
Cullin	Hrt-214	Christopher	Jon-294	Thos	Cha-197
David	Rch-208	David	Dup- 8	Brookcorn,Rob	Ora-126
Etheldred	Hrt-212	David	Dup- 14	Brookens,S	Ash- 14
Hardy	Hrt-208	David	Sur-180	Brookes,Jesse	Cur- 79
Henry	Way-237	Elias	Car-180	Marrey	Cur- 79
Henry	Roc- 13	Enoo	Row- 60	Brooks,Aaron	Ans- 20
James E	Hrt-212	George	Bun- 73	Aaron	Wil-260
Jas	Ans- 32	George Junr	Bun- 74	Abner	Cha-203
Jas Senr	Hrt-214	J	Cam-161	Absolam	Rob-237
Jesse	Way-249	Jessy	Jon-293	Andrew	Ora-112
Jno	Rob-233	John	Dup- 15	Ann	Pit-255
Joel	Hrt-212	John	Bft- 27	Arthur	Per-135
Jonathan	Joh-284	John	Jon-294	Arthur Junr	Per-135
Johnson	Joh-288	John	Dup- 32	B. William	Cas- 48
Kinchen	Way-249	John	Dup- 31	Bartley	Brt- 60
Kindred	Rob-235	Lawsn	Bft- 24	Charles	Cas- 48
Matthew	Hrt-212	Lewis	Dup- 32	Christopher	Fra- 77
Nathan	Rob-238	Major	Cas- 49	Christopr Junr	Fra- 77
Nathan	Rob-235	Martin	Jon-294	Daniel	Cho-222
Sarah	Brt- 60	Nathaniel	Row- 60	David	Per-127
Shaderick	Hrt-214	Obed	Dup- 30	David	Rth- 88
Silas	Hrt-208	Stephen	Dup- 32	David	Sto-147
Thos	Sam-154	Thomas	Bun- 73	Eaphraim	Ans- 18
Thos	Brt- 43	Thomas	Dup- 12	Elijah	Dup- 31
Thos	Hrt-208	William	Dup- 33	Elisa	Ora-111
William	Way-236	William	Sto-138	Ephram	Pit-251
William	Edg- 47	Brocket,Frederic	Jon-294	Fed	Bft- 38
William W	Hrt-213	John A	Pas-183	George	Gat-106
Wm	Rob-235	Brockett,D B	Cam-155	Humphrey	Sto-105
Wm D	Hrt-214	J	Cam-153	Humphrey	Sto-139
Wm Jnr	Rob-235	J	Cam-159	Humphry	Sto-114
Brittain,Benj	Bun- 97	R	Cam-155	Humphry	Sto-119
Benjn	Dup- 12	T R	Cam-157	Isaaih	Cha-203
James	Bun-	Brockwell,Edwd	Ora-151	Jacob	Joh-273
Daniel	Brt- 53	W	Ora-148	James	Wil-270
William	Hrt-209	Brodee,John	Grn-148	James	Pit-250
William	Bun- 89	Brodey,Marey	Cur- 91	James	Pit-251
Brittimem,Demsay	Hrt-215	Brodie,Charlott	Grn-132	James W C	Wil-281
Brittle,Martha	Nor- 61	John	War-174	James	Car-178
Micajah	Nor- 62	Brogden,David	Grn-125	James	Edg- 41

-38-

Name	Ref	Name	Ref	Name	Ref
Brooks,Jas	Ans- 30	Brooks,William Sr	Sto-139	Brothers,William	Gat-108
Jeremiah	Per-135	Wm	Ans- 31	Brotherton,Widow	Lnc-364
Jesse	Wsh-225	Wm	Ans- 25	George	Ire-262
Jesse	Sto-147	Wm	Mon- 47	James	Ire-262
Jno	Rob-232	Woody	Per-132	James	Lnc-361
Jno	Mon- 47	Brooksher,James	Ran-157	John	Ire-262
Jno Senr	Per-126	Manuel	Ran-157	Joseph	Lnc-361
Joab	Cha-201	Thomas	Ran-157	Thomas	Ire-263
Joel	Ran-159	Brookshere,James	Hay-193	Brougher,Geo	Lnc-364
John	Row- 46	Brookshire,Henry	Wil-278	John	Lnc-364
John	Pit-250	Thomas	Hay-193	Broughton,Jess	Bun- 92
John	Sto-101	Broom,Allen	Mec- 42	Job	Bun-. 92
John	Sto-104	Burrel	Mec- 42	William	Bun- 92
John	Wil-263	H----	Hal- 97	Woodard	Bun- 93
John	Bun- 79	Jacob	Mec- 42	Brount,James	Hal- 97
John	Bun- 73	James	Ran-157	Browder,Augustin	Roc- 15
John	Car-177	Jno	Mec- 42	Isham	Sur-179
John	Sto-133	John	Hal- 97	Isham	Roc- 15
John	Sto-139	Lucy	Hal- 99	Jeremiah	Roc- 17
John	Rth- 87	M	Ora-139	William	Glf-185
John Jnr	Pit-239	Melus	Ora-124	Browdiway,Joseph	Per-148
Jonathan	Cas- 48	Thomas	Fra- 80	Brower,Abraham	Ran-157
Jonathan	Dup- 34	Walker	Mec- 42	Adam	Ran-157
Joseph	Pit-263	William	Pit-239	Christen	Ran-157
Joseph	Dup- 24	Wm	Mec- 42	Jacob	Ran-157
Joseph J	Cha-215	Brosher,Anna	Pas-181	John Jnr	Ran-157
Larkin	Cha-207	Simons	Pas-181	John Snr	Ran-157
Lasken	Per-126	Brothers,Andrew	Pas-183	Nicholas	Ran-157
Maj	Ora-133	Benjn	Ran-159	Browing,Levy	Hal- 99
Mark	Cha-216	Briant	Pas-183	Brown	Mon- 51
Mary	Hyd-222	David	Pas-184	Mrs.	Mec- 50
Mordeca	Sto-105	Deba	Pas-183	A	Mon- 38
Mordia	Sto-139	Demsy	Pas-183	Aaron	Wil-262
Moses	Bur-120	Demsy	Pas-183	Abaham	Rob-230
Patience	Sam-152	Enoch	Pas-182	Abner	Mar- 14
Philip	Rch-201	Henry	Pas-183	Abraham	Row- 89
Rachael	Lnc-327	Jerry	Pas-184	Absalom	Hal- 97
Richd	Cha-207	John	Pas-182	Absalom	Hal- 97
Robert	Wil-270	John	Gat-109	Absolum	Lnc-351
Robert	Per-135	John Jnr	Pas-183	Adam	Mec- 50
Samuel	Ire-240	John Junr	Pas-183	Alexander	Rth- 89
Samuel	Ire-240	John Senr	Pas-183	Alexander	Roc- 17
Samuel	Bun- 73	Joseph	Pas-182	Alfred	Per-136
Samuel	Row- 81	Joseph	Pas-183	Alis	Sto-140
T	Ash- 5	Joshua	Pas-184	Andrew	Cha-210
Terry	Cha-194	Leml	Pas-183	Andrew	Ire-238
Thomas	Pit-250	M	Glf-177	Andrew	Bun- 74
Thomas	Cas- 48	Malc	Pas-183	Andw	Bft- 26
Thomas	Cas- 49	Miles	Pas-183	Angus	Rob-229
Walter	Sto-105	Miriam	Pas-183	Angus	Rob-228
William	Sto-139	Nancy	Pas-182	Archd	Cha-203
William	Pit-236	Nancy	Pas-182	Archd Senr	Cum-266
William	Sto-104	Nathanl	Ire-253	Archibald	War-167
William	Hyd-229	Rew	Pas-181	Archibald	Ire-240
William	Pit-250	Richard	Pas-182	Archibald	Wil-282
William	Sto-139	Richard Junr	Pas-183	Arther	Sam-157
William	Ora-166	Thomas	Pas-184	Asa	Edg- 72
William	Gat-112	Thomas	Pas-183	Athony	Per-127
William	Rth- 88	Will	Pas-183	B	Glf-175

Brown,B	Ash- 3	Brown,Francis	Rth- 90	Brown,James			Glf-162
B	Ash- 6	Freddrick	Ran-157	James	(Birle)		Wil-261
Barbary	Row- 79	Frederick	Roc- 17	James			Len-218
Barnett	Mon- 24	Geo	Cha-202	James			Bun- 96
Bartholomew	Edg- 58	Geo	Cab-142	James			Wsh-220
Basil	Row- 71	Geo	Mor- 67	James Esq			Wil-284
Benj	Hrt-215	George	Wil-264	James Jr			Cas- 49
Benj Senr	Hrt-213	George	Roc- 18	James Sr			Cas- 49
Benjamin	Pit-254	George	Ons- 98	Jas			Mec- 51
Benjamin	Wil-261	Green	Cas- 50	Jas			Glf-157
Benjaman	Mec- 37	H	Col- 19	Jas			Mec- 37
Benjamin	Nor- 62	H	Cam-157	Jas			Mec- 24
Benjamin	Ire-263	Henry	Sur-169	Jas			Bla- 3
Betsey	Cur- 86	Henry	Bur-114	Jannett			Brt- 51
Bond	Cas- 49	Henry	Mar- 15	Jean			Ran-157
Cannon	Row- 84	Henry	Wil-282	Jehu			Sto-106
Charles	Ons-100	Henry	Ran-159	Jennette			Rch-193
Charles	Bur-120	Henry	Row- 85	Jeremiah			Wil-275
Christen	Ran-158	Hubbard	Roc- 23	Jeremiah			Row- 89
D	Glf-174	Hugh	Rob-230	Jesse			Per-149
Dabney	Sur-181	Hugh	Lnc-338	Jesse			Way-254
Daniel	Bur-116	Hugh	Ran-157	Jesse			Way-254
Daniel	Row- 79	Isaac	Sto-137	Jesse			Hal- 99
Daniel	Wil-265	Isaac	Jon-294	Jesse			Mor- 60
Daniel	Mor- 65	Isaac	Ran-158	Jesse			Sto-106
Danl	Cha-202	Isaac	Pit-247	Jesse			Sur-170
David	Mec- 49	Isaac	Wsh-222	Jesse	B T		Sur-176
David	Row- 82	Isaac	Bur-104	Jesse			Sto-142
David	Ire-240	J	Ash- 12	Jesse			Cha-196
David	Wsh-226	J	Ash- 5	Jesse			Sur-190
David	Hal- 99	J	Bru-234	Jessee			Roc- 18
Dempsey	Len-321	Jacob	Row- 79	Jethro			Cas- 49
Drewry	Cha-210	Jacob	Ire-263	Joab			Way-240
Duncan	Mor- 60	Jacob Jn	Sur-172	Joel			Ran-159
Duncan	Rob-227	Jacob Jr	Dup- 32	Joel			Wil-265
E	Ash- 9	Jacob	Mar- 14	Jno Jnr			Row- 40
E	Cum-159	James	Gat-113	Jno			Mec- 52
Ebenezer	Cha-210	James	Sur-179	Jno			Mec- 51
Edward	Cas- 49	James	Sur-172	Jno			Mec- 51
Edward	Sam-161	James	Sur-166	Jno			Rob-229
Edward	Jon-294	James	Sto-142	John			Ora-166
Edwin	Wil-278	James	Jon-294	John			Ora-164
Eli	Bft- 26	James	Len-317	John			Edg- 68
Elias	Hal- 99	James	Mar- 14	John			Nsh- 84
Elijah	Cas- 48	James	Mar- 10	John			Sto-142
Elijah	Rob- 16	James	Sur-188	John			Sto-142
Elisha	Cum-257	James	Lnc-331	John			Sto-142
Elisha	Row- 74	James	Sto-107	John			Sto-138
Eliza	Way-240	James	Mon- 32	John			Len-317
Eliza	Bur-111	James	Row- 73	John			Cha-194
Elizabeth	Wil-269	James	Hrt-208	John			Ire-263
Elizabeth	Brt- 56	James	Bur-129	John			Mar- 9
Elizabeth	Hrt-209	James	Bur-131	John			Joh-283
Ellena	Row- 82	James	Ire-239	John			Sur-196
Ellis	Roc- 25	James Y R	Wil-284	John			Bla- 9
Ezekel	Row- 50	James	Pit-254	John			Sto-107
Ezekiel	Wil-260	James	Row- 88	John			Row- 71
Fanny	Bft- 27	James	Roc- 32	John			Row- 67
Francis	Hrt-215	James	Glf-163	John			Roc- 10

-40-

Brown,John		Roc- 25	Brown,Nancy	Ons-104	Brown,Thomas		Cha-196
John		Bur-124	Nathan	Wil-277	Thomas		Cas- 49
John		Bur-130	Nathan	Bft- 27	Thomas		Roc- 31
John		Cab-138	Nathaniel	Ire-246	Thomas		Wsh-227
John		Cas- 49	Nathl	Hyd-232	Thos		Cur- 83
John	L R	Wil-275	Nathl	War-178	Thos		Cha-205
John		Row- 54	Neill	Rob-244	Thos		Bur-104
John		Roc- 32	Neill Esq	Rob-226	Genl Thos		Bla- 9
John		Row- 57	Old	Pas-182	Thos F		Bla- 3
John		Ran-158	Paley	Cur- 90	V		Ash- 7
John		Ran-159	Patrick	Hrt-209	V. William		Cas- 49
John		Per-136	Peter	Row- 89	Valentine		Wil-264
John		Row- 86	Peter	Hal- 99	Vincent		Sto-101
John	R R	Wil-259	Peter son A	Row- 85	Vincent		Sto-132
John		Pas-181	Phebe	Lnc-346	W		Cam-155
John		Pas-183	Phebery	Hrt-208	Walter		Wil-263
John		Ora-126	Philip	Row- 88	William		Du- 17
John Esqr		Wil-274	Philip Jr	Row- 86	William		War-183
John Jn		Sur-172	Phillip Sr	Row- 86	William		War-182
John Srn		Sto-142	Polly	Row- 89	William		Rob-218
John W		Rth- 92	Rachel	Bla- 9	William		Ons- 96
Joseph		Brt- 65	Rebecca	Wil-265	William		Sto-138
Joseph		Wil-261	Reuben	Mar- 6	William		Len-318
Joseph		Cha-198	Reubin	Edg- 54	William		Bur-111
Joseph Jnr		Ran-157	Rich	Sto- 94	William		Ire-257
Joseph Snr		Ran-158	Rick	Sto-123	William		Ire-253
Joseph Jn		Sur-175	Robert	Ire-256	William		Ire-263
Joshua		Sur-196	Robert	Ire-255	William		Lnc-355
Joshua		Bur-130	Robert	Roc- 19	William		Mar- 11
Josiah		Cum-258	Robert	Cas- 48	William		Rch-212
Josiah		Sur-188	Robert	Bun- 97	William		Sur-190
Josiah		Per-136	Robt	Lnc-337	William		Sur-192
Josiah		Way-239	Robt	Sam-163	William		Row- 68
Josiah		Mec- 36	Rody	Jon-294	William		Hrt-208
Judah		Pas-181	S	Cam-157	William		Ire-240
Kelan		Way-239	Sam	Mon- 41	William		Ire-240
Lee		Way-240	Saml	Hrt-208	William		Ire-238
Leroy		Jon-293	Saml	Hrt-212	William		Cas- 49
Lewis		Hrt-215	Saml	Mec- 51	William	W C	Wil-277
Luke		Cur- 87	Saml	Sto-130	William		Hal- 97
M		Mon- 36	Saml Jnr	Ran-158	William		Ran-159
Mal		Rob-226	Saml	Bur-105	William		Per-135
Marlam		Hrt-210	Samuel	Sur-170	William		Row- 85
Martha		Wil-269	Samuel	Jon-294	William		Row- 87
Mary		Sto-119	Samuel	Gat-108	William		Bun- 74
Mary		Bun- 87	Samuel	Mon- 41	William	H C	Wil-264
Mary		Ire-240	Samuel	Hrt-215	William	M C	Wil-260
Mary		Grn-129	Samuel	Wil-276	William H		War-184
Mary		Nor- 63	Samuel	Ran-157	William Jr		Sur-171
Mary Ann		Lnc-338	Sarah	Wil-278	William R		Mar-446
Matthew		Glf-181	Sarah	Wil-275	Wm		Glf-175
Matthew		Cum-256	Sarah	Bur-130	Wm		Mec- 51
Michal		Row- 69	Sherod	Sam-152	Wm		Nsh- 74
Michael		Ran-157	Solomon	Cas- 49	Wm		Rob-236
Milly		Bft- 26	Thomas	Rth- 88	Wm		Rob-226
Moses		Row- 88	Thomas	Sur-192	Wm		Cha-196
Moses		Sur-173	Thomas	Sur-172	Wm		Cha-210
Mrs. N		Brt- 56	Thomas	Sur-172	Wm		Glf-154
Nancy		Row- 45	Thomas	Nsh- 82	Wm		Bft- 29

Name	Loc	Name	Loc	Name	Loc
Brown,Wm	Bla- 3	Bruce,Charles	Glf-171	Bryan,Bartrim	Mon- 31
Wm	Cha-214	Cornelious	Ons- 95	Benajah	Ons- 96
Wm	Cha-215	Cornelius	Joh-279	Benj	Way-241
Wm	Brt- 51	David	Wil-271	Benj	Ons-102
Wm	Glf-165	Dunning	Brt- 62	Bratly	Row- 62
Wm	Per-127	Elijah	Bun- 85	Brinson	Ons-100
Wm	Mec- 36	Geo	Bun- 95	Christopher	Jon-294
Wm	Mec- 29	James	Cas- 49	D	Col- 18
Wm	Ora-128	James	Bur-118	David	Ora-130
Wm	Ora-125	James	Car-182	David	Mec- 37
Willis	Gat-115	Joel	Ire-249	Delpha G	Wil-268
Winnefred	Mar- 3	John	Wil-281	Demsey	Edg- 59
Zachariah	Sto-125	John D	Sur-173	E	Col- 17
Browne,Abigail	Nor- 60	Joseph	Jon-294	Edward	Jon-294
Benjn	Dup- 8	Jourdan	Edg- 49	Elias	Ed- 57
Beverly	Nor- 61	Miles	Nor- 60	Eliz	Len-314
Jacob Jr	Dup- 31	Mordecai	Wil-280	Eliz	Brt- 57
Jesse	Dup- 31	Robert	Cas- 49	Elizabeth	Brt- 67
John	Dup- 32	William	Cas- 49	F	Ash- 14
John	Dup- 34	William	Cum-255	Hardy	Way-234
Peterson	Nor- 60	William	Hrt-208	Hardy	Jon-293
Sherrod	Dup- 33	Wm P	Car-184	Hardy	Joh-278
Stephen	Dup- 9	Brudford,Wm	Ora-133	Henry	Wil-266
Thomas	Grn-119	Bruer,Benjamin	Sur-194	Henry	Cab-146
Brownell,John	Wsh-226	James	Sur-195	James	Edg- 55
Browney,Hannah	Mar- 9	John	Sur-175	James B S	Bla- 5
Browning,Charles	Bur-115	Thomas	Row- 55	James C	Jon-293
David	Bur-113	Bruffitt,Auther	Bft- 33	James R	Jon-293
Edward	Pit-251	Bruice,Washington	Ire-249	Jas	Ora-173
J	Bru-230	Brumbelow,Jas	Ans- 24	Jas	Mec- 38
J	Ora-148	Brumble,J	Col- 17	Jason	Nor- 60
James	Cas- 50	Jilbert	Rob-233	Jesse	Mec- 41
Jno	Ora-154	Brumfield,Obadiah	Sto-103	Joel	Way-241
Jno	Ora-150	Obediah	Sto-136	John	Pit-258
John	Bur-113	Brumit,Nimrod	Grn-128	John	Pit-245
Martin	Cas- 48	Brummel,Jacob	Row- 46	John	Sam-152
Martin	Bur-113	Brummit,John	Grn-128	John	Bla- 3
Reubin	Cas- 50	Brumsey,John	Cur- 86	John Esq	Wil-258
Richd	Ora-121	William	Cur- 88	John A	Joh-274
Robert	Cas- 48	Bruner,Caty	Row- 78	John Jr	Joh-290
Thos	Bur-113	Jacob	Row- 78	John T	Dup- 15
Thos	Ora-149	Michael	Sto-103	Jonathan	Bla- 9
Thos	Ora-159	Brunt,John	Joh-288	Joseph	Jon-294
Will	Dup- 19	Richd	Way-248	Joseph H	Brt- 48
William	Pit-249	Bruton,James	Mon- 27	Larry	Joh-288
William	Cas- 48	Joseph Jr	Len-317	Lewis	Way-234
Brownrig,George	Edg- 64	Joseph Senr	Len-321	Lewis	Len-318
Brownrigg,Thos	Cho-227	Simon	Len-317	Lewis	Jon-293
Brownsen,J	Bru-236	Wm	Mon- 27	Lewis	Joh-286
Brubaker,David	Sur-183	Brutus	Pas-183	Margaret	Pit-249
Bruce,A B	Ora-110	Brutz,Christian	Sto-146	Mark	Bla- 6
Alexander	Cas- 49	Bruver,Elijah	Nor- 61	Martha	Nor- 60
Allen	Wil-262	Willis	Nor- 62	Mary	Bft- 36
Allen	Nor- 60	Bryan,Alfred	Sur-196	Milla	Ons-100
Archd	Cum-255	Allen	Nor- 60	Needham	Joh-275
Arnold	Ire-249	Ann	Sam-159	Nicholas	Hal- 97
Bailas	Bun- 83	Ann	Bla- 7	Nicholas	Dup- 20
Bennet	Hrt-213	Asey	Joh-289	P	Bla- 10
Cader	Brt- 62	Asy Jr	Joh-289	Phillip	Cha-201

Name	Ref	Name	Ref	Name	Ref
Bryan,R	Col- 20	Bryant,Samuel	Grn-132	Buchannan,Mary	Cha-206
Reuben	Sur-196	Silas	Edg- 59	Sarah	Cum-266
Robt	Way-236	Smith	Edg- 59	Thos	Lnc-331
Roundtree	Sam-158	Susanna	Sur-192	Buchannon,William	Sto-126
Stephen	Bla- 6	Temperance	Grn-145	Buchen,James	Per-136
Thomas	Ons- 98	Thomas	Pit-254	Buchermon,Andrew	Grn-121
Welthy	Ora-130	Thomas	Bur-112	James A	Grn-121
William	Hal- 98	Thomas	Sur-181	Thomas (moved)	Grn-121
William	Way-243	Timothy	Dup- 23	Buck,Aaron	Roc- 32
William	Way-234	Turner	Edg- 59	Apollus	Pit-242
William	Pit-245	William	Way-249	Benjamin	Row- 89
William	Pit-234	William	Mar- 5	Benjamin	Pit-243
William	Joh-286	William	Pit-254	Brian	Car-181
William	Joh-289	Wm	Glf-168	Charles	Row- 70
William	Joh-274	Wm	Nsh- 84	Edward	Rch-199
William W	Joh-281	Wm	Mec- 37	Eliza	Bft- 29
Wm	Bru-222	Wm	Cha-209	Hosea	Pit-243
Wm Jun	Bla- 4	Wm Jr	Cha-216	James	Bft- 29
Wright	Edg- 60	Wm Senr	Bla- 4	James	Pit-243
Bryans,Joseph Ner	Hal- 99	Bryon,Ann	Bla- 8	John	Row- 70
Bryant,Aaron Jr	Cha-208	Bryson,Hugh	Mec- 51	John	Pit-233
Aaron Sr	Cha-208	James	Bun- 74	Morgn	Bft- 38
Andrew	Fra- 93	James	Sur-160	Noah	Pit-243
Archd	Cah-205	James	Hay-193	Richd	Bft- 28
Benjamin	Bun- 89	John	Bun- 82	Sarah	Bft- 29
Drury	Edg- 60	John	Sur-161	Buckanan,Ben	Cha-195
Edward	Grn-127	Sally	Sur-162	Buckannan,Beo	Ans- 18
Elias	Mar- 4	William	Bun- 74	Buckham,George	Cur- 86
Fedrick	Pit-254	William Junr	Bun- 83	Buckhannan,Eliza	Cha-208
Fredrick	Pit-254	William Senr	Bun- 96	Buckhannon,Abner	Cha-193
Francis	Pit-254	Wm	Mec- 52	Duncan	Rch-193
Jacob	Cha-208	Bu-----, Edward	Ran-159	Jane	Rth- 88
James	Mar- 8	Bucey,William	Cas- 50	Jno	Ans- 31
Jeremiah	Cha-191	Bucham,Peter	Rob-226	John	Rch-192
Jerusha	Mar- 5	Buchan,Caty	Mor- 60	John	Rch-202
John	Wil-279	Buchanan,Andrew	Per-132	Joseph	Cha-193
John	Bur-105	Arthur	Per-132	Robt	Mec- 23
John	Bun- 96	Arthur	Bur-114	William	Sto-156
John	Bur-112	Arthur Senr	Bur-114	William	Rch-192
John	Row- 63	B. Jas	Per-132	William	Sto-114
John	Cha-203	Danl	Mor- 64	Wm	Ans- 10
John	Cas- 75	David	Per-126	Buckingham,J	Ora-133
John	Tyr-205	James	Bur-129	Levi	Glf-162
John	Row- 75	Jas	Per-132	Wm	Roc- 12
John Sr	Dup- 20	Jno	Per-132	Buckly,Randolph	Sur-161
Joseph	Mar- 8	John	Buf-129	Buckman,Samuel	Car-171
Lewis	Row- 57	Joseph	Cha-195	Buckner,Mr	Bun- 90
Lewis	Bun- 80	Joseph	Bur-113	Avery	Row- 65
Lewis	Mar- 14	Joseph	Bur-129	Benjamin	Row- 64
Lewis	Brt- 53	Mary	Bur-129	Edward	Cha-195
Martha	Bur-113	Samuel	War-180	Edwd	Row- 84
Mary	Mar- 5	William	Bur-114	Elisha	Cha-213
Michael	Mor- 57	Wm	Per-132	Geo	Bun- 90
Nancy	Tyr-211	Buchannan,Widow	Lnc-329	George	Cas- 49
Needham	Brt- 57	Alexr	Cum-266	James	Bur-113
Nicholas	Row- 81	David	Cas- 48	James	Bun- 90
Richard	Rth- 89	John	Cas- 48	Jesse	Cha-213
Robert	Wil-279	Joseph	Cum-247	Jessee	Bun- 92
Rowland	Grn-145	Maclain	Cum-247	John	Row- 83

-43-

Name	Ref	Name	Ref	Name	Ref
Buckner, John	Bur-128	Bullock, Balaam	Edg- 46	Bumpus, John	Hal- 97
Nathaniel	Cha-210	Doc Ben	Ora-160	Bunch, Abner	Cho-231
William	Cha-203	Celia	Edg- 60	D	Glf-165
Bucks, Francis	Car-181	Charles	Rob-238	Henry	Ora-170
Bucway, John	Cho-219	Charles	Grn-136	Jeremiah	Brt- 64
Bucy, Charles	Wil-265	David	Edg- 45	John	Cur- 92
Charles	Row- 66	David Jr	Edg- 46	John	Row- 65
Budd, John	Len-314	Edward	Glf-188	Jos	Cho-220
Thomas	Len-214	Edward	Grn-125	Micaj	Cho-226
Buddridg, Thomas	Per-148	Edwin	Edg- 42	Micajah	Brt- 65
Buff, Widow	Lnc-345	Elizabeth	Grn-119	Nehemiah	Brt- 65
John	Lnc-337	George	Grn-136	Solomon	Cho-227
Martin	Hay-193	Henry	Rob-239	William	Brt- 65
Buffoon, Matthew	Nor- 62	James	Mar- 16	Wm	Glf-166
William	Nor- 62	James	Grn-136	Bundan, Brury	Sto-113
Bufkin, Wm	Cho-228	James	Glf-185	Drury	Sto-154
Bug, William	Hay-193	James	War-173	Bunday, Abraham	Glf-164
Bugg, John	Rth- 89	Jeremiah	Grn-136	C	Glf-170
Buie, Archd G S	Cum-255	Joel	Rob-239	W	Glf-170
Daniel	Cum-246	John	Way-242	Bundle, Edward	Mec- 28
Daniel	Cum-254	Joshua	Grn-136	Bundran, Thomas	Sto-150
Duncan C	Cum-261	Joshua	Edg- 46	Bundrant, Francis	Roc- 25
John	Cum-270	Len	Glf-188	Richd	Roc- 24
John	Cum-254	Leonard	Grn-125	Bundy, Benja	Pas-182
John	Cum-246	Lucy	Edg- 43	Betsy	Pas-182
Malcolm Junr	Cum-254	Martha	Edg- 46	Caleb	Pas-182
Malcom Senr	Cum-254	Micajah	Grn-125	Christo	Pas-182
Margaret	Cum-246	Obediah	Mar- 13	David	Nsh- 89
Neill	Cum-246	John	Cho-219	Eliz	Pas-182
Neill Senr	Cum-251	Richard	Grn-136	George	Prq-213
Buis, Archd	Rob-224	Richard	Rob-239	Giddain	Ran-159
Jno	Rob-230	Richard	War-179	James	Pas-182
Jno	Rob-230	Saml (Entered)	Grn-137	John	Pas-182
John Junr	Row- 52	Saml	Grn-149	Jona	Pas-183
Mary	Rob-224	Thomas	Nor- 60	Josiah	Pit-259
Nancy	Rob-226	Thomas	Cum-265	Josiah	Prq-213
Buise, John Senr	Row- 88	Thos	Mar- 16	Moses	Ran-159
Buknal, Micajah	Sur-193	Wm	Grn-119	Nathan	Prq-213
Bull, Jacob	Per-127	Bulls, Barnaby	Joh-280	Reuben	Ran-157
Stephen	Hal- 97	William	Joh-280	Salley	Way-239
Bulla, John	Ran-158	Bulluck, John	Pit-247	Sally	Pas-182
Wester	Ran-158	Bully, William	Hal- 98	Samuel	Prq-213
Bullach, Allen	Mor- 57	Bumgardner, Elizth	Sto-144	Bunell, Edw	Cur- 89
Francis	Mor- 57	Bumgarner, J	Ash- 7	Maris	Cur- 90
Bullard, Ambrose	Cha-199	John	Lnc-347	Bunen, Elizabeth	Sto-100
Barton	Sam-153	L	Ash- 8	Bunker, A	Glf-164
Dempsey	Cum-263	Leonard	Wil-280	Obed	Glf-187
James	Cha-214	Lewis	Rth- 90	R	Glf-168
James	Rob-222	Thomas	Lnc-347	Reuben Jr	Glf-187
Nancy	Roc- 6	Bumpass, Elizabeth	Cum-259	Bunn, Benja	Nsh- 77
Robert	Rob-222	Gabriel	Per-126	Jno	Asn- 6
Sion	Rob-236	Jesse	Per-136	Mary	Nsh-643
Bullen, John	Mon- 43	Jno	Per-136	Tredmun	Nsh- 79
Joseph	Bur-104	John Esq	Per-136	Wiley	Nsh- 80
Bullin, George	Row- 88	Jno Senr	Per-127	Bunten, Jeremiah	Nsh- 80
Bullinger, Geo T	Lnc-378	Saml	Per-127	John	Edg- 70
Henry	Lnc-378	Saml	Per-126	Lydia	Way-254
Bullison, Benjamin	Wil-283	Samuel	Per-135	Wm	Nsh- 81
Peggy	Wil-283	Samuel Junr	Per-127	Bunting, David	Sam-163

-44-

Bunton,Abner Jnr	Ran-158	Burdoux,Isaiah	Cho-223	Burk,Mary		Nor- 61
Daniel	Edg- 54	Burfoot,A	Cam-156	Rebecca		Ons- 97
John	Wil-283	J	Cam-157	Samuel		Per-143
Robert	Row- 74	Burford,T Philip	Hay-193	Samuel		Per-127
Bunyard,E	Ash- 13	Burge,Alan	Sto- 92	Stillinder		Cha-211
J	Ash- 13	Alan	Sto-121	William		Hrt-208
J B	Ash- 4	Alexander	Sto-106	Wm		Mor- 65
Bunzen,Christian L	Sto-145	Alexr	Sto-141	Zinos		Cas- 49
Burbage,Geo C	Bft- 36	David	Rth- 88	Burke,Benjamin		Bun- 85
Hy	Bft- 24	John	Rth- 90	David		Bun- 85
Burch,Baylor	Per-127	John	Rth- 89	Nancy		Cho-223
Edmond	Per-148	John	Rth- 88	Patrick		Lnc-339
George	Sur-185	Woody	Rth- 86	Burket,C		Ash- 5
George	Cas- 48	Burger,Henry B	Fra- 90	C		Ash- 8
George	Cas- 48	Burges,A	Cam-161	Henry		Row- 54
Henry	Per-148	A	Cam-156	J		Ash- 8
Henry	Ora-150	Eli	Ran-157	Moses		Way-235
Henry	Ora-122	H	Cam-158	Nathaniel		Row- 56
Henry	Cas- 48	J	Cam-156	Reubin		Way-234
J	Bru-234	James	Ran-157	Burkets,Abraham		Row- 54
James	Sur-185	L	Cam-153	Burkett,Lemuel		Nor- 60
James	Per-135	Malachi	Cum-266	Burkhart,Daniel		Row- 85
John	Sur-179	Mary	Bur-103	John		Row- 83
John	Cas- 48	Mary	Cas- 48	Burkitt,William		Edg- 71
John	Cas- 48	N	Cam-157	Burklow,P		Cum-240
Joseph	Sur-181	N	Cam-156	Saml		Cum-240
Mary	Ora-167	S	Cam-156	Burks,John		Cha-210
Nicholas	Bur- 48	T Esq	Cam-159	Millender		Cha-202
Phillip	Per-126	William	Ran-157	Rebekah		Roc- 21
Robert	Sur-185	Wilson	Car-172	Burleson,Aron		Bur-113
Thomas	Per-148	Burgess,Dempsey	Hal- 97	Simon		Bur-113
Thomas	Wil-284	Draper	Mon- 47	Thos		Bur-113
Thomas	Cas- 48	Malachi	Nor- 61	Burleston,Jno		Mec- 32
Thomas C	Sur-175	Edward	Gat-115	Burley,George		Edg- 40
William	Cas- 49	Henry	Hal- 98	Burlingham,Capt Wm		Fra- 78
William	Roc- 30	John	War-173	Burlison,Edward		Bun- 94
William Esq	Sur-172	John	Cha-209	Isaac		Bun- 86
William S	Sur-179	John	Hal- 97	Isaac		Mon- 49
William Jn	Sur-184	Joshua	Mon- 47	Isaac		Mon- 49
Burcham,Henry	Sto-155	Judah	Wsh-225	Isaac		Mon- 50
James	Sur-186	Mary	Hyd-234	Burly,Davd		Row- 40
John	Sur-186	Nathaniel Jr	Nor- 61	Jacob		Row- 43
Reuben	Sur-186	Nathl	Nor- 60	Martin		Row- 41
Shubel	Sur-186	Salley	Hal- 98	Burmingham,Caleb		Ans- 26
Burchead,Eleazur	Mor- 57	William	Hal- 97	Jno		Ans- 26
Burchet,Martha	War-177	Burgis,Adam	Cur- 85	Joshua		Ans- 26
Theoderic	Rth- 91	Duncey	Cur- 86	Stephen		Ans- 12
Burchett,John	Wil-272	Rubin	Row- 66	Burn,Darius		Rch-203
Burchfell,William	Sur-172	Rubin	Row- 64	Frederick		Way-250
Burchfield,Adam	Wil-270	Thomas	Row- 61	John		Brt- 43
Elias	Sto-144	Burguin,George W B	Jon-293	Pharoah		Way-250
John	Wil-262	Burgus,Joseph	Mec- 40	William		Way-235
Burchifield,Abberilla		Burgwin,G W B	Ora-110	Burnam,William		Prq-213
	Bur-114	Burk,Casper	Row- 48	Burnap,Abraham		Ons-105
Burch,Richd	Cas- 49	Edwd	Row- 50	Ebenezer		Ons- 97
Burd,Andrew	Bur-130	Elizabeth	Cha-197	Isaac		Ons-105
Burwell	Grn-128	Henry	Row- 74	John		Ons-105
Burdale,Wm	Brt- 52	Joab	Cha-209	Burndsides,B		Ora-153
Burdoe,Jas	Bla- 11	John	Row- 74	J		Ora-155

-45-

Name	Loc	Name	Loc	Name	Loc
Burndaides,Robert	Ora-152	Burns,John Jr	Cha-108	Bursham,John	Pas-183
Burnet,Aron	Ora-133	John Younger	Cha-192	Burshal,Jezediah	Cha-202
Danl	Cha-196	Joseph	Ons- 95	Burt,Jesse	Hal- 98
Danl	Cha-196	Leard	Mec- 32	John	Cum-258
Frederick	Bun- 87	Levy	Rth-'87	John Junr	Hal- 99
James	Hal- 98	Mathew	Row- 42	John Senr	Hal- 99
John	Ons-108	Otway	Ons-105	Joseph	Hal- 99
Thomas	Ran-157	S	Ora-144	Richard	Hal- 98
William	Cum-268	Sanders	Mec- 42	William	Fra- 86
Wm	Bur-103	Thomas	Cha-189	William	War-183
Burnett,Caburn	Rth- 86	Wm	Cha-192	William Senr	Hal- 98
David	Fra- 90	Burnside,Benj	Ora-129	Wm Junr	Hal-'99
Eldridge	Rth- 89	James	Sur-183	Willie	Hal- 98
Isaac	Fra- 92	James	Ora-165	Young	Cum-257
Jesse	Rth- 88	John	Ora-943	Burthred,William	Pit-232
Jno	Mec- 44	Robt	Ora-943	Burtin,Martha	Hal- 98
Joseph	Rth- 88	Burows,Caley	Cur- 81	Thomas	Hal- 98
Joseph	Fra- 95	John	Cur- 82	Burtis,Hesekah	Per-127
Josiah	Cha-209	John	Cur- 81	Burton,A	Ash- 15
Martha	Ire-255	Rheubin	Cur- 82	Allan	War-168
Mary	Brt- 46	Robert	Cur- 82	Allen	Per-126
Matthew	Fra- 92	Burpo,Jacob	Ire-247	Allin	Cas- 48
Robert	Nor- 62	James	Ire-246	Bartlett	Cur- 89
S	Ora-172	Burrage,Wm	Row- 78	Cuthbert	Ora-115
Burney,Abell	Bla- 4	Burras,Thomas	Sur-163	David	Per-132
Robt	Glf-158	William	War-183	David	War-170
S	Glf-184	Burrass,C	Glf-174	Drury	Cas- 48
Simon	Bla- 4	Burrel,Walter	Bun- 85	Edward	Ire-262
Simon	Pit-237	Burris,Benoma	Ran-158	Frank	Grn-134
W	Col- 17	Daniel	Brt- 61	Henry	Cas- 48
Wm	Glf-158	Francis	Ons-106	Isaac	Row- 44
Burnham,B	Cam-163	Hardy F	Edg- 52	J	Ash- 10
E	Cam-164	Nathan	Hrt-206	James	Cas- 48
E	Cam-162	Burriss,James	Hrt-209	James	Grn-148
Edwd	Dup- 12	Burros,Jno	Cho-231	James M	Grn-137
Elijah	Dup- 12	Burroughs,Allen	Row- 82	Jane	Bun- 91
Joel	Dup- 13	James	Cas- 49	Jesse	Row- 44
Thomas	Pas-184	Jonathan	Row- 75	Jesse	Rth- 89
William	Dup- 13	Rosa	Cas- 48	John	Hal- 97
Burnitt,Eli	Mar- 4	Townsen	Row- 75	John	Cas- 48
James	Mar- 4	Burrow,D	Ora-121	John	Dup- 34
Silas	Mar- 4	E	Glf-155	Joshua	Row- 44
William	Mar- 3	Francis	War-171	Peter	Sto-140
Burns,Andw	Ora-142	Henry	Ran-158	Peter	Sto-106
Ann	Hay-193	Joans	Ran-157	R	Ash- 4
Bat	Dup- 12	R	Glf-176	Richd	Per-136
Benjamin	Rth- 91	Thos	Glf-180	Robert	Grn-134
Frederick	Ons- 97	William	War-183	Sally	Per-132
Jacob	Lnc-347	Burrows,Berneby	Ran-158	Samuel	Wil-263
James	Cha-189	Dobson	Ran-158	Thomas	Cas- 75
James	Sto-148	John	Grn-119	Thos	Per-132
James	Ons-102	Nancy	Ora-143	Thos	Glf-167
James	Cum-250	Peter	Mec- 34	Umphrey	Per-132
James	Sto-111	Solomon	Mon- 49	Watson	Dup- 9
James	Cab-143	Tafter	Mon- 49	Burtz,Elizabeth	Cum-246
John	Cha-189	Zecherias	Ora-143	Burwell,Spotswood	Grn-140
John	Ran-158	Burrus,Charles	Sur-179	Busby,E	Bla- 13
John	Bun- 96	George	Sur-163	Wm	Bla- 13
John	Dup- 14	Martin	Sur-162	Buse,Ignatius	Bur-118

-46-

Busely,Auston	Dup- 16	Butler,Jethro		Brt- 60	Butterton,Chas		Brt- 56
Bush,Bennatt	Cas- 49	John		Row- 65	Buttery,Abram		Cas- 48
Charity	Mec- 41	John		Bla- 5	Butterry,James		Mar- 11
Delilah	Cas- 49	John	(B S)	Bla- 6	Button,Wm		Glf-165
J	Glf-159	John		Brt- 63	Butts,Jesse		Hal- 99
J	Glf-159	John C F		Cum-248	Michael		Lnc-377
Jere	Cas- 49	John Junr		Sam-161	Willie		Hal- 99
John	Bur-126	Joseph		Cum-256	Wilson		Hal- 97
John	Dup- 9	Joseph		Bla- 6	Buzby,Jacob		Bun- 97
Lua	Bft- 38	Joshua		Mon- 34	Buzzel,John		Per-152
Margarett	Cas- 49	Larcy		Cum-249	John		Hrt-213
Michael	Ran-157	Magary		Grn-124	Byars,David		Rth- 87
Rachel	Len-316	Mary		Grn-143	David		Rth- 87
Richd	Cha-208	Moses		Glf-157	David		Rth- 87
William	Rth- 87	Polly		Mor- 60	David		Rth- 88
William	Dup- 9	Reuben		Grn-136	David		Rth- 89
Bushaw,Gigory	Hyd-233	Rhoda		Brt- 60	George		Rth- 87
Bushic,Consider	Len-317	Robert		Bla- 6	James		Rth- 89
Bushop,James	War-176	Robert		Sam-153	Nathan		Rth- 87
John	Hyd-225	Silus		Brt- 63	Nicholas		Grn-125
Busic,Mary	Jon-293	Silus		Brt- 53	Robert		Rth- 87
Busick,C	Glf-175	Sterling		Fra- 98	Stripling		Rth- 87
Geo B	Ora-162	T R		Cam-154	Wm		Grn-125
John	Ora-162	Thomas		Mon- 33	Byby,John		Bun- 90
William	Ora-162	Thomas		Dup- 35	Bycie,G		Mon- 42
Buskard,Jacob	Cab-140	Tobias		Bft- 26	Byden,Jacob		Nsh- 87
Buss,Mrs.	Cum-236	Travers		Sam-161	Byers,J		Lnc-378
Bussell,John	Wil-265	Will		Sam-162	Joseph		Ire-259
Busteral,Jonus	Mec- 25	William		Row- 65	Joseph		Ire-259
Bustian,Dorothy	Nor- 62	William		Ire-267	Joseph		Bun- 84
Busy,Charles	Ire-253	William		Edg- 59	Robert		Ire-246
Edward	Cas- 48	William		Prq-214	Robert		Ire-259
Butcher,James	Sur-178	William		Row- 55	Samuel		Bun- 73
Mary	Edg- 49	Wm		Mon- 27	Thos		Mec- 53
Bute,Jeremiah	Cur- 89	Wm		Grn-128	Thomas		Row- 83
Butkins,Wm	Mec- 47	Winefred		Brt- 53	William		Bun- 95
Butlar,Timothy	Sam-157	Winny		Brt- 63	Byler,Joseph		Bun- 94
Butler,Absalom	Ora-168	Zachariah		Cum-248	Bynam,A Francis		Nor- 62
Amelia R	Cum-248	Zachariah		Roc- 15	Hampton		Sur-165
Anthony	Pas-183	Butlor,J		Col- 19	Bynim,Upton		Mec- 28
Chas Junr	Sam-153	Butner,Adam		Sto-128	Bynum,Widow		Lnc-329
Charles Senr	Sam-153	David		Row- 79	Abram		Bft- 19
E	Mon- 37	David		Row- 86	Arthur		Lnc-377
Edward	Rch-211	Elizabeth		Sto-131	Beverly		Mec- 36
Elias	Mon- 32	Elizabeth		Sto-136	Cordall		Nor- 62
Eliza	Dup- 36	Elizabeth		Sto-103	Drewry		Nsh- 79
Gabriel	Sam-161	Harmon		Sto-131	Hampton		Sto-145
Hartwell	Sam-161	Jesse		Sto-143	James		Lnc-358
Henry	Bla- 5	John		Sto-131	Jas		Mec- 36
J	Mon- 36	John		Row- 79	Jas		Mec- 37
J	Glf-174	Sarah		Sto-154	John		Lnc-341
James	Mon- 33	Thomas		Sto-136	Luke		Cha-216
James	Mon- 29	Butt,Ambrose		Cas- 49	Mark		Cha-209
James	Rch-195	Bartlet		Pas-181	Martha		Cha-216
James	Car-181	David		Prq-214	Tapley		Ora-129
James	Dup- 16	Seth		Ans- 7	Troy		Lnc-377
James	Sam-162	Butter,Edwd		Per-136	Turner		Lnc-343
Jesse	Way-252	Butteral,William		Cum-253	Turner		Nor- 63
Jesse	Cum-251	Butterton,Mrs.		Brt- 49	Wm		Cha-216

Name	Loc	Name	Loc	Name	Loc
Byram, James	Cho-229	Cable, A Senr	Ora-145	Cail, Jacob	Edg- 50
Joel	Cho-229	Jas	Ora-145	John	Prq-215
Reuben	War-179	Peter	Cab-145	Nathaniel	Prq-215
Byrd, Catharine	Len-321	Cabness, John	Mor- 62	Robert	Prq-215
Caty	Nsh- 86	Caddell, John	Sto-150	Cain, A	Ora-139
Edward	Joh-275	Caddle, Peter	Row- 67	A	Glf-163
Edward	Mar- 12	Caddock, Eleazer	Tyr-206	Amos	Bla- 11
Elijah	Len-316	Cadle, Thomas	Sur-164	Andrew	Glf-186
Elisha	Len-319	Cadwell, Benjamin	Mor- 60	Chloe	Hal-110
George	Joh-277	Danl	Mor- 56	Daniel	Lnc-328
Isaac	Mar- 13	Jonathan	Mor- 57	Duncan	Nsh- 76
James	Nor- 62	Wm	Mor- 55	Elijah	Hal-110
John	Len-321	Cafer, Joel	Glf-160	Elisha	Mec- 35
John	Joh-277	Caffee, J	Glf-174	Frankey	Rch-211
John	Sam-154	Cafferty, Van	Ora-159	Hardy	Nsh- 84
Josha	Len-322	Caffey, Henry	Roc- 28	Hugh	Ora-160
Josha Senr	Len-319	John	Roc- 29	Hugh	Ora-165
Mrs. Kesian	Fra- 93	John	Hyd-231	James	Ora-151
L	Ora-155	Marget	Roc- 29	James	Nsh- 77
Leml	Len-317	Michael	Roc- 29	James	Bla- 11
M	Ora-155	Thomas	Roc- 28	James Junr	Bla- 6
Martin B	Wsh-223	Cafton, William	Cas- 51	Jas	Ans- 6
Michl	Dup- 4	Cagle, -----	Mon- 51	Jas	Ora-128
Miller	Len-313	Benj	Mon- 38	Jedediah	Glf-189
Nathan	Ans- 7	Caty	Mor- 60	Jeremiah	Hal-110
R	Ora-154	Caty	Mor- 59	John	Glf-164
Richd	Way-248	Charles	Mon- 46	John	Ora-166
Richard	Joh-277	Christopher	Mor- 59	John	Ora-151
Richard Jr	Joh-277	David	Mon- 46	Joseph	Bla- 7
Sarah	Dup- 4	Geo	Mon- 47	Levy	Hal-110
Sutton	Len-319	Geo	Mon- 46	Margret	Nsh- 77
Thomas	Len-321	George	Mor- 62	Robert	Hay-194
Thomas	Len-312	George	Mor- 59	S Senr	Bla- 13
Thomas	Sam-164	Henry	Mor- 60	Saml Jnr	Bla- 11
Wilie	Nsh- 92	Henry	Mor- 59	Thomas	Row- 62
William	Wil-271	Henry	Ran-160	U	Glf-176
William	Mar- 11	Jacob	Mor- 59	Will Sr	Ora-151
William	Sam-164	Jacob	Mon- 47	William	Hay-194
Wm	Len-319	Jacob	Bun- 96	William	Bun- 73
Byrne, Matthew	Bla- 6	John	Bun- 72	Wm	Bla- 6
Byrum, Abner	Brt- 60	John	Mor- 59	Wm Junr	Ora-110
James	Hrt-210	John	Mor- 62	Cains, J	Bru-232
John	Brt- 67	John	Bur-131	Caisey, Wm	Cur- 81
Thomas	Edg- 52	L	Mon- 48	Caisman, J	Glf-178
Wm	Brt- 67	Leonard	Lnc-352	Caison, Cannon	Sam-152
Bysinger, Henry	Lnc-347	Peter	Mor- 59	Hillory	Sam-162
Byson, James	Rth- 90	William	Ran-160	Jane	Sam-152
Peter	Roc- 26	Cahill, Richard	Car-177	Calae, Irena	Bft- 19
		Cahoon, Etheldred	Edg- 61	Calahan, Benj	Ire-262
C-----, John	Ran-160	James	Sur-194	James	Ire-262
C-----, John	Rch-191	Mary	Edg- 43	Caldeclaugh, Andrew	Row- 41
C-----, Judith	Sto- 93	William	Edg- 61	Caldwell, Widow	Mec- 38
Cabarrus, Anah	Cho-226	Cahran, John	Cab-143	Alexander	Hay-193
Cabble, Adam	Row- 39	John	Cab-143	Andrew	Ire-258
John	Row- 39	Robt	Cab-143	Andrew	Ire-243
Cabe, John	Ora-126	Robt Junr	Cab-144	Curtis	Rth- 94
W	Ora-138	Wm	Cab-143	Daniel	Mec- 39
Cabiness, George	Rth- 96	Caid, Waddle	Cum-265	Daniel	Bur-113
Cable, A Junr	Ora-145	Cail, Husly	Prq-215	David	Glf-156

-48-

Name	Loc	Name	Loc	Name	Loc
Caldwell,James	Lnc-346	Callicast,Beverly	Ran-160	Cammel,James	Bun- 91
James	Lnc-346	John	Ran-160	John	Rth- 94
James	Ire-257	Callicoat,Geo	Mon- 33	Camp,Aaron	Rth- 93
James	Ire-259	James	Mon- 32	Abner	Lnc-339
Jno	Len-312	Jno	Mon- 33	Cleyburn	Rth- 92
Jno	Mec- 38	Wm	Mon- 34	George Esq	Rth- 91
John	Sam-158	Callicost,Pleasnt	Mon- 22	John	Nor- 63
John	Lnc-346	Callins,Jas	Cab-136	Stephen	Rth- 95
John	Bur-122	Wm	Cab-137	William	Hal-100
John	Ire-243	Calloway,Charles	Bun- 79	William	Rth- 92
Rev. Jos	Ora-125	E	Ash- 10	Campaign,James	Pit-243
Richard	Sam-158	J	Ash- 10	Camparis,John	Bft- 37
Robt	Mec- 38	J	Ash- 3	Campbel,George	Roc- 12
Robt	Mec- 39	T	Ash- 3	James	Roc- 30
Rev. S C	Mec- 40	Callum,Willis	Brt- 56	William	Roc- 23
Samuel	Lnc-367	Calor,John	Sto- 99	Campbell,Alexr	Rob-220
Spencer	Rob-234	Calos,Jacob	Bun- 88	Alexr	Cum-238
Thomas	Hay-194	Calton,John	Per-138	Alexander	Cum-268
William	Lnc-355	Calun,David	Sto-123	Alexander	Rch-213
Wm	Mec- 47	Calvert,James	War-175	Alexr	Cum-259
Wm	Mec- 53	John	Row- 60	Alexr	Mor- 57
Cale,Dempsey	Brt- 50	Thomas	Fra- 79	Alexr	Rob-224
Elizth	Brt- 61	Calvet,Ruth	Ons-102	Alexr	Mor- 67
Job	Brt- 62	Stephen	Ons-101	Allen	Cum-242
Rachael	Brt- 61	William	Ons- 98	Andrew	Rth- 93
Caleb,Shadrack	Hal- 99	Calvin,William	Cum-243	Angus	Cum-242
Caler,Lewis	Row- 78	Cambell,John	Row- 68	Angus	Mor- 62
Calew,Martha	Hal-101	Mildred	Bft- 39	Angus	Rch-194
Calhoon,James	Glf-186	Ran	Bft- 29	Archabald	Sto-134
Robt	Glf-185	Sarah	Bft- 21	Archabald	Sto-102
Saml	Glf-186	Cambill,Wm	Bft- 20	Archd	Cum-254
Calico,Eli	Mor- 60	Cambirling,Aten	Bft- 36	Ard	Bla- 4
Calihan,Henry	Rth- 92	Cambel,James	Hal-101	Benj	Nor- 63
Caline,Tulley	Cur- 89	John	Hal-100	Ca Esq	Ora-111
Calison,Robert	Ire-267	John	Hal-101	Charles	Cab-137
Call,Daniel	Row- 57	Cameron,Absolam	Row- 37	Christian	Bla- 5
Daniel	Row- 61	Allen	Cum-255	Christian	Rch-204
Henry	Row- 62	Ann	Cum-255	Colin	Ire-244
John	Grn-130	Archd	Cum-267	D	Bla- 10
John	Row- 60	D	Ora-146	Danl	Rob-227
Jonathan	Ran-162	Daniel	Rch-197	Daniel	Rch-193
Joseph	Row- 61	Daniel	Cum-255	Daniel	Rch-213
Mack	Ran-159	Duncan	Rch-198	Daniel	Rch-213
Matthew	Ran-163	Effie	Rob-229	Daniel	Rch-212
Stephen	Ran-159	J A	Cum-239	Daniel	Lnc-346
Thomas	Wil-264	James	Cum-254	Daniel	Cum-269
William	Ran-160	John Esq	Cum-254	Daniel	Cum-243
Calladge,Elijah	Ans- 15	John	Cum-253	Daniel	Cum-256
Callahan,Edward	Roc- 8	John	Rch-193	Danl	Bla- 4
Ezekiel	Roc- 9	John	Rch-198	Danl	Mor- 68
Unity	Roc- 9	John Fork	Cum-255	Dugald	Cum-262
Calland,Jno	Mec- 46	Kenneth	Cum-254	Duncan	Cum-251
Callars,Right	Nsh- 81	Margaret	Rch-193	Duncan	Cum-237
Callaway,Catharine	Brt- 48	Margaret	Rch-206	Duncan	Mon- 25
Ferce	Sur-169	Murdock	Rch-193	Duncan	Rch-204
James	Sur-169	Norman	Cum-254	Eanes	Ire-243
Samuel	Sur-168	Stephen	Ora-132	Elisa	Ora-133
Callersat,William	Ran-162	Camles,Frederic	Wil-273	Elisha	Nor- 63
Calleway,Isaac	Mon- 45	Cammel,E-----	Bur-105	Eliza	Bur-122

Name	Ref	Name	Ref	Name	Ref	Name	Ref
Campbell,Elliner	Ire-243	Campbell,John	Mor- 67	Campble,Jno	Rob-244
Enass	Ire-243	John	Mor- 68	Jno	Rob-230
Finly	Ans- 27	John	Mor- 64	Campebell,S	Bru-236
Flora	Cum-245	Joseph	Lnc-368	Campeign,John	Rth- 94
G	Ora-148	Joseph	Ire-263	Campell,Norman	Rch-201
George	Sto-109	Lydia	Pit-236	Campen,Ben	Bft- 34
George	Mec- 40	Malcom	Ran-160	David	Bft- 34
George	Sto-150	Malcom	Cum-243	Jos	Bft- 33
George	Lnc-355	Margaret	Rch-213	Jos Jun	Bft- 34
Hugh	Rch-210	Margarett	Mec- 38	Jos 3rd	Bft- 34
Hugh	Ire-250	Margret	Rob-224	Camper,James	Hyd-225
Hugh	Cum-238	Marsden	Bru-222	Campin,James	Bft- 19
Isaac	Mec- 39	Mary	Bla- 10	Camplin,H	Glf-170
J	Bla- 12	Mary	Lnc-346	Hooper	Glf-184
J	Ash- 6	Mary	Cum-266	Jacob	Sto-139
J	Ora-156	Murdoch	Cum-252	Rebia	Glf-170
J	Ora-152	Nancy	Mor- 60	Campton,Keziah	Roc- 4
Jacob	Ora-174	Nancy	Rob-224	Camron,Alexr	Mor- 66
Jain	Roc- 17	Neal	Sam-153	Archd	Mor- 62
James	Cum-259	Neill	Bla- 12	Archd	Mor- 69
James	Ora-126	Neill	Cum-255	Hugh	Mor- 69
James	Ora-129	Neill	Cum-243	John	Mor- 57
James	Mar- 13	Peter	Wil-285	Phillip	Mor- 62
James	Ire-250	Pureshpull	Ire-254	Camwell,Micajah	Rth- 93
James	Bla- 3	Rachel	Len-319	Canaan,J	Bru-238
James	Cum-237	Rebekah	Roc- 18	Canada,Elizabeth	Jon-295
James	Row- 39	Ricd	Ora-133	Jesse	Sur-180
James	Ora-115	Richard	Pit-243	John	Ran-162
James	Hay-194	Richd	Ora-129	Canaday,Asa	Car-170
James	Pit-236	Robert	Rth- 95	Cornelius	Car-181
Jas (M)	Bla- 3	Robert	Rch-193	Elijah	Car-169
Jas	Ora-147	Robert	Ire-238	Elijah Junr	Car-184
Jane	Ire-262	Saml	Cum-240	Lewis	Car-180
Jno	Ans- 31	Saml	Mor- 61	Richard	Car-180
Jno	Mor- 61	Samuel	Rth- 91	Richard	Car-181
Jno	Mor- 61	Sarah	Len-322	Uriah	Car-180
John	Sto-121	Sarah	Len-312	Willet	Car-180
John	Way-245	Tho	Ora-117	Canady,Elizabeth	Car-171
John	Ran-160	Thomas	Rth- 95	John	Roc- 16
John	Ora-126	Thomas	Len-317	Polly	Joh-291
John	Cum-256	Vineard	Hyd-233	Solomon	Ons-101
John	Cum-254	William	Mar- 5	Canatzer,John	Row- 84
John	Ire-253	William	Ire-250	Candler,Zachariah	Bun- 89
John	Cum-259	William	Cum-259	Candy,Robt	Bft- 24
John	Bur-120	William	War-182	Cane,Absalom	Cha-216
John	Rth- 95	William	Rth- 91	James	Cum-238
John	Rth- 91	William	Sto-155	Jesse	Prq-215
John	Sto-144	William	Sto-113	Wm	Cha-216
John	Cum-243	Wm	Ora-133	Caneday,William	Lnc-355
John	Cum-243	Wm	Ora-168	Canley,Edmund	Wil-260
John	Cum-241	Wm	Ora-165	Canly,Larkin	Bur-106
John	Ire-269	Wm	Ora-114	Cannen,James	Cab-138
John	Sto-108	Wm	Mec- 36	John	Cab-139
John	Mor- 61	Wm	Mor- 67	Cannon,Abraham	Pit-237
John	Sto- 92	Campbill,Thomas	Cas- 52	Allen	Pit-238
John	Ran-162	Campble,Alexr	Rob-237	Caleb	Pit-237
John	Ora-168	Angus	Rob-244	Dennis	Dup- 5
John	Ora-165	Israel	Rob-243	Dennis	Pit-238
John	Mor- 54	Jno	Rob-238	Dennis Jr	Pit-236

Name	Ref	Name	Ref	Name	Ref
Cannon,Eliza	Way-238	Capell,John	Nor- 63	Cardwell,William	Sto- 92
Furneyfold	Pit-238	Ransom	Nor- 63	Wm	Grn-136
J	Col- 17	Rebecca	Nor- 64	Care,Joshua	Hrt-212
Jeremiah	Jon-294	Sterling	Nor- 63	Robert	Hrt-214
Joab	Mec- 47	Caperse,A	Glf-179	Carear,Geo	Mon-49
John	Lnc-360	Caple,Thomas	Rth- 95	Carelack,Jno	Mec- 44
Joseph	Prq-215	Thomas	Rth- 94	Careless,William	Nor- 63
M B	Cum-240	Caples,Caleb Senr	Cur- 93	Carell,Jno	Ans- 21
Mary	Way-178	Capps,Amos	Glf-188	Marey	Cur- 92
Micjah	Dup- 24	Amsley	Cur- 91	Carethers,David	Ire-240
Nancy	Len-314	Betsey	Cur- 93	Hugh	Ire-240
Palmer	Pit-251	Caleb	Cur- 93	Carfield,Mary	Row- 85
Radford	Pit-251	Cason	Ons-108	Cargill,Charles	Wil-271
Rebeca	Pit-263	Cason	Ora-119	James	Wil-263
Rebecca	Pit-236	Cilas	War-169	William	Wil-268
Samuel	Way-241	Francis	War-171	Carigen,Jas	Mec- 35
Samuel	Way-247	Gedion	Ons-102	Cariker,Jno	Ans- 22
Sarah	Pit-250	Hillary	War-172	Carinder,Daniel	Bun- 86
Susanna	Pit-236	Horatio	War-172	Carker,Andw	Cab-141
Thomas	War-182	John	War-174	R	Ora-155
Thomas	Pit-238	John	Cur- 90	Carl,Daniel	Cab-139
Wilie	Pit-251	Marmaduke	Hyd-223	Carless,Robt C D	Sur-160
Cannris,John	Glf-158	Matthew	War-177	Carlisle,J	Col- 19
Cannutt,Jacob	Glf-154	Moses	Cur- 88	James	Hal-102
Canon,William	Sur-174	Obediah	Cur- 91	John	Bla- 4
Canseller,Joseph	Rth- 95	Polly	War-178	Nathaniel	Hal-101
Cansellor,John	Rth- 93	Ruth	Hyd-221	R	Col- 18
Cansler,Phillip	Lnc-345	Thomas	Hyd-222	Robert	Hal-100
Canter,Erasmus	Row- 60	Thomas	Onc- 99	Robert	Edg- 53
James	Wil-272	William	Bun- 95	Saml	Len-312
Canthan,N	Mon- 40	William	War-182	Sanders	Rob-235
Cantrell,Aron	Roc- 10	Caps,Caleb	Mec- 55	Sarah	Hal-100
Jacob	Rth- 95	Calop	Tyr-213	W	Col- 18
Jacob	Roc- 11	Henry	Mec- 35	Wm	Rob-235
John	Rth- 96	Jno	Mec- 47	Carloss,Archilous	Cha-202
Josiah	Rth- 94	Thos	Mec- 28	Carlton,Capt Ambrose	
Peter	Bun- 86	Capshaw,James	Rth- 94		Wil-274
Robert	Roc- 6	Josiah	Rth- 93	David	Dup- 10
Samuel	Rth- 95	William	Rth- 94	Elijah	Sur-192
Cantril,Benjan	Cas- 51	Carall,Stephen	Ora-151	Fredrick	Sur-184
Isaac	Cas- 51	Caraway,Bedredin	Cum-266	Hardy	Dup- 18
William	Cas- 51	Charles S	Cum-260	Henry	Wil-274
Cantrill,Joseph	Bur-113	Carboy,William	Bur-112	Joel	Sur-165
Canup,Thomas	Lnc-375	Card,Richd	Cum-251	John	Sur-168
Canus,J	Col- 18	Samuel	Grn-132	John	Mor- 63
Canvill,Nancy	Len-323	Carden,Frederick	Sto-128	John Esqr	Wil-277
Capehart,Cullen	Brt- 43	Jas	Ora-150	L	Ora-156
John	Brt- 49	Jno	Ora-150	Lewis Esqr	Wil-274
Michl	Brt- 49	John	Sto-134	Lewis	Dup- 18
William	Brt- 48	Cardwell,Asa	Wil-267	Lewis Jr	Wil-274
Capeheart,George	Brt- 43	Daniel	Wil-280	Linsey	Sur-165
Thos	Bur-102	Joel	Roc- 22	Martha	Dup- 17
Capel,Charles	Rch-211	John	Sto- 93	Micajah	Sur-192
James	Rch-210	John	Sto-122	Peter	Dup- 17
Robinson	Ans- 26	Leonard	Grn-134	Shade	Dup- 24
Watson	Ans- 30	Peter	Wil-271	Thomas	Wil-274
William	Rch-210	Rebekah	Roc- 23	Thos	Ora-150
William C	Rch-201	Thomas	Sto-122	Carly,Henry	Bur-116
Capell,Charles	Nor- 63	Thomas	Sto- 93	Carmady,Elizabeth	Len-314

-51-

Carmalt,Pheby	Ons-105	Carpenter,John Senr	Lnc-327	Carraway,Richd	Way-251
Carmen,James	Pas-184	John Sen	Lnc-328	Snode B	Wsh-216
Carmer,James	Mar- 6	Jonas	Lnc-332	William	Sam-151
Carmical,A	Glf-177	Jonathan	Rth- 92	William	Mar- 13
William	Ran-161	Joseph	Rth- 93	Carrel,Anne	War-168
Carmicall,John	Bft- 28	Kinchen	Rth- 95	Dennis	Bun-.93
Carmichael,Archd	Rch-192	Lewis	Sur-180	Jas	Lnc-330
Daniel Junr	Rch-203	Ludwell	Ans- 25	Jas	Lnc-336
Danl Sr	Rch-203	M	Ash- 8	John	Bun- 78
Duncan	Rch-202	Mary	Nsh- 91	Joseph	Lnc-335
Duncan	Rch-192	Michl	Lnc-337	Nancy	Bun- 76
Gilbert	Cum-269	Peter	Lnc-330	Thomas	War-181
John	Rch-202	Peter	Lnc-332	William	Lnc-326
John Junr	Rch-202	Rheuben	Nsh- 91	Willis	Bun- 93
Carmicle,Hugh	Rob-228	Saml	Lnc-331	Carrell,Benjn	Joh-275
Lemuel	Sto- 96	Saml	Lnc-332	Isaac	Pit-251
Lemuel	Sto-125	Samuel	Cum-258	James	Joh-275
Starlin	Sur-187	Samuel Senr	Cum-258	John	Joh-276
Carmille,Archd	Sur-176	Simeon	Fra- 82	John	Pit-231
Carmon',Elijah	Cas- 51	Thomas	Lnc-330	John	Ire-246
Carmual,James	Glf-169	William	Sur-180	John	Rth- 92
Carnal,Archd	Per-136	Wm	Ans- 19	John	Rth- 93
Reuben	Wsh-227	Wm	Nsh- 91	Joshua	Pit-236
Carnel,Wm	Grn-144	Wm	Nsh- 79	Samuel	Ire-246
Carnell,John	Ora-134	Carr,Elias	Pit-260	Thomas	Pit-237
Carney,James	Hal-101	Elias	Fra- 86	William	War-182
John	Roc- 30	J	Ora-156	William	Joh-272
John	Roc- 28	James	Ora-130	William	Joh-275
Joshua	Cas- 51	John	Sto- 95	Carrigan,Jas	Cab-138
Josiah	Pit-237	John	Sto-123	John	Cab-138
Moses	Grn-142	John	Per-136	Mark	Cab-137
Rhobts	Per-127	John	Fra- 87	William	Ire-269
Thomas	Pit-235	John	Dup- 20	William	Ire-256
Stephen W	Hal-101	John F	Sto-157	Wm	Cab-138
William	Pit-245	Jonathan	Sam-150	Carriker,Geo	Ans- 8
Wm	Grn-142	Mary	Sam-150	Paul	Cab-141
Carnutt,W	Ash- 13	N	Glf-178	Carrill,Leah	Rth- 95
Carol,Lemuel	Ora-134	Patience	Sam-150	Carrington,Ben	Ora-166
Carother,Edmond	Mec- 51	Solomon	Pit-260	Ephm	Ora-142
Carpenter,Abm	Lnc-327	Theo	Sam-163	Geo	Ora-115
Alexr	Cha-199	Thomas	Sur-163	James	Ora-164
Benjn	Fra- 95	Turner	Sam-163	Jas Jr	Ora-135
Benjn	Fra- 82	William	Sto- 98	Jno	Ora-128
Daniel	Lnc-330	William	Dup- 23	N	Ora-146
David	Rth- 92	William	Bun- 97	Thomas	Ora-164
Fred	Lnc-328	William	Ran-162	Wm	Ora-159
Fred	Lnc-331	William	Sur-194	Wm	Ora-165
Guilford	Cha-200	William	Sto-128	Carriol,William	Row- 79
Henery	Lnc-332	Wm	Ans- 9	Carrione,Thomas	Hyd-230
Henry	Lnc-341	Carragan,John	Ora-127	Carriwon,Francis	Hyd-230
Henry	Lnc-320	Carral,Charles	Ons-105	Joseph	Hyd-230
Henry	Lnc-335	Carrall,John	Ora-124	Carrll,James	War-175
Henry	Lnc-345	Carraway,Archd	Ans- 17	Carrol,Alexr	Mor- 56
Isaac	Ans- 6	Bedreadon	Sam-163	Alexr	Cha-200
Jacob	Lnc-335	Bryan	Way-234	Benjamin	Roc- 14
Jacob	Bur-113	James	Way-237	Henry	Roc- 26
Jacob Esq	Lnc-327	James	Sam-159	Danl	Cha-197
John	Lnc-330	John	Way-236	J B	Mor- 57
John	Fra- 82	Joseph G	Mar- 12	James	Cha-214

Name	Ref	Name	Ref	Name	Ref
Carrol, Jesse	Mor- 57	Carson, Elizabeth	Lnc-330	Carter, Edward	Bun- 77
John	Mor- 56	Faney	Cur- 90	Edy	War-171
John	Bla- 8	Hugh	Row- 65	Elijah	Mon- 44
John	Grn-122	Jacob	Sto-113	Eliza	Rob-222
John Sen	Mor- 55	James	Bun- 94	Emanuel	Dup- 31
Manson	Sam-152	James	Lnc-333	Enoch	Hrt-215
N	Ora-148	James	Sto-109	Ephraim	Sur-193
Nathl	Lnc-315	Jason	Bur-120	Ezekiel	Ons-100
Nimrod	Ora-151	John	Cab-147	Francis	Hal-101
Owen	Bla- 6	John	Sto-113	Geo	Ora-133
Carroll,-----	Tyr-210	John	Bun- 92	George	Roc- 34
Arch	Ora-168	John	Bur-117	Gilbert	Rob-243
Ben	Ora-168	John	Fra- 78	Hannah	Car-182
Charles	Dup- 17	John (col)	Rth- 91	Hartwell	Roc- 26
Charles	Bur-107	John	Sto-153	Henchy	Mon- 28
Daniel	Cas- 52	Joseph	Rth- 92	Henry	Row- 55
Edmond	Sam-157	Michael	Sto-129	Henry	Mon- 50
Elisha	Dup- 17	Robert	Ire-270	Henry	Sam-163
George	Cas- 52	Robert	Ire-263	Henry	Sam-157
Hardy	Dup- 3	Robt	Ora-170	Henry	Len-311
James	Bur-111	Robt Eno	Ora-126	Isaac	Ora-129
Jas	Ora-152	Uriah	Sur-186	Isaac	Hrt-214
Jesse	Sam-163	Wallis	Rth- 92	Isaac	Edg- 51
John	Sam-163	William	Rth- 95	Isaac	Roc- 14
Joseph	Sam-163	Wm Charlotte	Mec- 25	J	Bla- 10
M	Ora-147	Carstarphen, Tho C	Hal-100	Jacob	Mon- 44
Milly	Wsh-224	Carsterphen, James	Hal-101	Jacob	Hal-100
Patsey	Cas- 52	Oxen D	Hal-101	Jacob Jr	Mon- 44
Sarah	Sam-156	Carswell, Jos	Glf-175	James	Brt- 43
Starling	Cas- 75	William	Sto-121	James	Hal-100
Stephen Senr	Wil-259	Carsy, Abram	Glf-170	James	Sto-105
Thos	Sam-163	Carter, Abraham	Cum-257	James	War-174
William	Bur-110	Abyram	Sur-193	James	Cha-202
Carron, Jas	Bft- 20	Alexander	Way-239	James	Len-320
John	Bft- 20	Alexander	Dup- 27	James	Sto-140
Sarah	Tyr-205	Alexandrew	Gat-112	James	Sur-178
Thomas	Tyr-205	Allen	Cha-193	James	Nsh- 88
Carrouth, Robert	Cum-268	Assention	Len-316	Jas	Ora-129
Carrow, Henry	Hyd-228	B	Cam-160	Jas	Rob-233
John	Hyd-227	Barnabas	Wil-268	Jas	Mon- 50
Carroway, Amirina	Hyd-230	Bartlett	Mon- 44	Jas	Asn- 29
Carowon, John	Hyd-229	Benjamin	Hal-100	Jesse	Hal-100
Carrowone, Green	Hyd-230	Benjamin	Sur-193	Jesse	Prq-215
Carruth, John	Lnc-339	Britain	Nor- 63	Jesse	Cas- 51
Carruthers, George	Prq-215	Britain	Cha-202	Jesse	Way-239
Carry, Angus	Mor- 55	Catharine	Cum-258	Jesse	War-176
Cullen	Hal-102	Charles	Hal-100	Jesse	Bla- 12
Carsen, Jacob	Sto-154	Charles	Gat-113	Jesse	Rth- 93
Carsey, Danl	Glf-170	Charles	Grn-149	Jesse	Cum-265
Danl	Ran-159	Charles	Nsh- 89	Jinny	Ons-105
John	Bun- 87	Clement	Sur-176	John	Joh-280
Carson, Widow	Cab-146	Clement	Mon- 45	John	Joh-278
Alexander	Fra- 88	D	Bla- 10	John	Mon- 44
Andrew	Ire-267	Daniel	Roc- 5	John	Roc- 11
Andrew	Ire-263	David	Roc- 10	John	Roc- 34
Baitor	Sto-113	David	Hyd-227	John	Hal-101
Bowetor	Sto-153	David	Fra- 88	John	Glf-183
Daniel	Rth- 95	Deonitia	Hal-101	John	Ons-100
David	Bun- 95	Drew	Hrt-214	John	Hyd-229

-53-

Carter,John	Cha-212	Carter,Thomas Senr	Roc- 34	Cartwright,John Jnr	Pas-185
John	Ire-248	Thos	Ora-121	John Senr	Pas-185
John	Cum-264	Thornton	Cha-193	M	Cam-158
John	Cha-191	Vicy	Mon- 44	M	Cam-161
John	Cha-194	Walker	Dup- 28	Ockaro	Pas-185
John	Rth- 93	Watt	Hal-100	S	Cam-159
John	Sur-191	Wilford	Roc- 33	Samuel	Hyd-225
John	Bla- 6	William	Pas-184	Sary	Hyd-226
John Junr	Hal-100	William	Pas-185	T	Cam-158
Johnson	Mon- 43	William	Per-136	T	Cam-156
Jonah	Hrt-214	William	Gat-107	W	Cam-155
Joseph	Cas- 51	William	Rth- 95	W	Cam-162
Joseph	Sur-167	William	Edg- 50	Caruth,Alexander	Rth- 94
Joshua	Mon- 44	Wm	Ora-112	Ephraim	Rth- 93
Joshua	Mon- 44	Wm	Cho-219	James	Rth- 94
Joshua	Sur-192	Wm	Cha-193	Robert	Rth- 94
Josiah	Sam-153	Wm	Ans- 27	Caruthers,James	Prq-215
Julius	Rth- 95	Wm	Nsh- 88	John	Cab-147
Labon	Mon- 44	Wm	Nsh- 86	Margaret	Cab-144
Landon	Sto-140	Wm Sen	Ora-129	Thos	Cab-139
Landon	Sto-105	Wilson W	Hal-100	Carval,Wm	Row- 49
Lewis	Hrt-212	Zach	Dup- 23	Carvan,Thos	Cur- 88
Mansfield	Hal- 99	Zachariah	Dup- 37	Carvender,Joseph	Pas-185
Manuel	Rob-231	Cartner,Jno	Mon- 39	Carveniss,George	Grn-136
Manuel	Rob-218	William	Row- 69	Carver,Benjamin	Per-127
Manuel	Dup- 28	Cartright,Benoni	Pas-185	Brazel	Cum-247
Margaret	Brt- 66	Betsy	Pas-184	Christopher	Bun- 82
Margaret	Len-320	Christo	Pas-185	David	Cum-248
Mary	Nsh- 82	Hezek	Pas-184	Elias	Pas-186
Mary	Len-320	Hezek	Pas-185	Elizabeth	Cum-248
Mary	Sur-192	Isaac	Pas-185	Evrigan	Pas-186
Matthew	Nsh- 88	James Senr	Pas-185	George	Sto-152
Melican	Rob-231	Jas	Pas-184	Hosea	Per-140
Moore	Nor- 63	Job	Pas-185	James	Pas-186
Moses	Sam-157	John	Pas-185	John	Mon- 39
N	Ash- 13	John	Cum-240	John	Per-136
Nathl	Ora-114	Joseph	Pas-184	Joseph	Per-139
Polly	Joh-274	Matthias	Pas-185	Joseph	Per-147
Rebecca	Nor- 63	Nancy	Pas-184	Losen	Per-136
Richard	Hal-100	Nancy	Pas-184	Mary	Cum-248
Sally	Bft- 35	Polly	Pas-184	Robert	Per-136
Saml	Mon- 44	Polly	Pas-186	Sampson	Cum-248
Saml	Glf-168	Thomas	Pas-186	William	Per-127
Saml	Cha-212	Thomas	Pas-185	William Junr	Cum-251
Samuel	Sur-193	Thos Son John	Pas-186	William Senr	Per-127
Samuel	Hal- 99	William	Pas-185	William Senr	Cum-248
Silas	Ons-102	Wm	Glf-179	Cary,Elisha	Per-128
Silas Junr	Ons- 99	Cartwright,B	Cam-156	John	Ons- 96
Solomon	Sur-167	C	Cam-156	Leaven	Grn-125
Stephen	Ran-160	D	Cam-162	Solomon	Jon-295
Stephen	Hyd-232	E	Cam-156	Thomas	Ons- 97
Sterling	War-180	E	Cam-156	William	Bur-110
Susanna	War-180	G	Cam-157	Casa,John	Way-235
Tho	Ora-117	J	Cam-160	Sarah	Way-235
Thomas	Roc- 10	J	Cam-157	William	Way-237
Thomas	Roc- 34	J	Cam-156	Casan,Benj Jr	Ran-160
Thomas	Nsh- 88	J	Cam-163	Edward	Wil-284
Thomas	Nsh- 92	J	Cam-163	Casaway,Susanna	Way-236
Thomas Jr	Nsh- 82	J	Cam-156	Case,free man of colour	
					Ran-187

-54-

Name	Ref	Name	Ref	Name	Ref
Case,Daniel	Bun- 72	Cashwell,Nevel	Bla- 8	Caster,Henry	Cab-143
Isaiah	Wil-280	Casick,Jed	Glf-154	Henry	Cab-142
Jessee	Bun- 95	Cask,John	Wil-262	Kindred	Gat-114
Job	Cur- 85	Caskeaden,George	Pas-184	Mial	Glf-160
John Junr	Bun- 73	Casle,Jas	Mon- 50	Castillo,Eliz	Row- 89
John Senr	Bun- 95	Thos	Mon- 49	Castilow,Jno D	Cho-226
Nancy	Wil-277	Casler,Cunrod	Lnc-345	Castlebury,D	Ora-141
Nathan	Wil-277	Stephen	Ran-162	S	Ora-141
Thomas	Bun- 73	Casner,John	Sto-134	Casway,Lemmon	Edg- 45
Casewell,Shine	Sam-157	John	Sto-134	Philip	Edg- 68
Casey,Caleb	Pas-185	Cason,Eliga	Cur- 92	Willie	Edg- 70
Enoch	Pas-184	James	Ons-108	Caswell,Dollam	Len-317
Geo	Glf-184	James	Pit-258	John	Bur-126
Isaac	Cur- 88	James	Pit-240	Saml	Brt- 49
Jemmiah	Rch-206	James	Pit-234	William	Pit-236
John	Pas-185	Jas	Mon- 44	Casy,David	Row- 63
Joseph	Pit-238	Jamima	Hrt-210	Samuel	Row- 63
Shadrach	Ons- 99	Jno	Ans- 17	Cate,B	Ora-152
William	Cur- 87	John	Cur- 92	Bard	Ora-126
Willis	Pas-184	Thomas	Pit-257	Chas	Ora-113
Willis	Pas-184	Thomas	Pit-245	Clary	Ora-164
Cash,Aron	Per-127	William	Pit-245	Davd	Ora-147
Bryant	Grn-125	Casons,Nathan	Hyd-227	David	Ora-126
Daniel	Per-127	Casort,Benjn	Per-128	Elisha	Ora-115
Ingoe D	Ans- 12	Elseth	Per-128	Jno Senr	Per-128
James	Grn-125	Jenny	Per-128	John	Ora-168
Jas	Ans- 18	William	Per-128	John Senr	Ora-165
Jno	Per-127	Casper,Adam	Row- 67	Jon M	Ora-113
Joel	Ire-241	Henry	Row- 81	Joshua	Per-127
John	Ire-266	Peter	Row- 67	Mathew	Per-127
Jonathan	Ire-243	Thos	Brt- 62	Moses	Ora-114
Jonathan	Ire-266	William	Brt- 62	Richd	Ora-147
Larkin	Wil-266	Cass,J	Glf-172	Richd Sr	Cha-209
Lewis	Wil-266	James	Sur-194	Robt Jr	Per-127
Mishal	Per-127	James	Ire-267	Sol	Ora-114
Moses	Per-127	Jonas	Glf-159	Solomon	Per-127
Peter Jr	Grn-125	Needham	Joh-280	Stephen	Ora-127
Peter Sr	Grn-125	Samuel	Ire-254	Rev. Tho	Ora-126
Polley	Grn-127	William	Joh-280	Tho	Ora-114
Richard	Ire-266	Wm	Glf-160	Tho P	Ora-114
Thomas	Grn-125	Cassada,James	Sur-165	Thos Son of J	Ora-136
Thomas	Rch-212	Cassay,Isaac	Ran-161	Thos of M	Ora-147
William	Ire-265	Casse,James	Bun- 95	Thos Preacher	Ora-136
William	Wil-266	Cassel,Samuel	Wil-277	Cater,John	Wil-284
William (L F)	Wil-281	Cassell,Ebenezer	Wil-280	Cates,Caleb	Cur- 83
Wm	Ans- 29	Casson,Daniel	Nsh- 83	R	Ora-138
Wm	Grn-125	Cast,James	Wil-270	Richard	Cas- 51
Cashans,D	Bru-224	John	Wil-272	Robert Senr	Per-136
Cashat,Jacob	Ran-160	Moses	Wil-258	Robt	Cha-211
John	Ran-160	Casteen,Jacob	Dup- 34	Sion	Lnc-377
Cashatt,Peter	Sto-112	Castellam,John	Brt- 43	Catha,Alexr	Mec- 37
Cashing,John	Lnc-360	Castellaw,Mrs.	Brt- 48	Alexr	Mec- 24
Cashon,Burrel	Mec- 51	Bartholomew	Brt- 45	Archibald	Mec- 24
Elsy	Ire-259	John	Brt- 48	Betey	Mec- 36
James	Ire-257	Casteller,Miles	Rth- 92	George	Mec- 36
Joel	Ire-256	Castephens,John	Sur-169	Henry	Mec- 36
Pleasant	Bur-119	John Jn	Sur-170	Jesse	Mec- 28
Thos	Mec- 52	Caster,Christina	Row- 70	Jno	Mec- 25
Cashwell,Jas	Bla- 8	Elizabeth	Gat-116	Cathcart,Jno	Mec- 36

Name	Ref	Name	Ref	Name	Ref
Cathe,Wm Esq	Per-136	Cauly,Mary	Len-319	Celia,Saml	Rob-237
Cathey,John	Glf-183	Thos	Len-319	Cellers,Rite	Nsh- 82
M	Glf-179	Cauper,Thos	Grn-124	Celliers,Thos	Ora-137
Cathron,James	Per-127	Causby,Ham	Glf-180	Thos Jnr	Ora-137
John Senr	Per-127	James	Glf-155	Cepple,John	Cab-145
Cathy,Archd	Lnc-368	William	Rth- 92	Kelion	Cab-146
Daniel	Hay-194	Causey,Greenberry	Pit-236	Peter	Cab-146
Ellison	Hay-194	Hubbard	Row- 71	Wm	Cab-145
George	Lnc-368	Causway,Mary	Bft- 36	Ceravan,James	Cum-240
George	Hay-194	Cauthan,Henry	War-172	Cerkin,Maddoc	Rth- 93
George	Hay-194	Vincent	War-182	Cernal,Hubbrd	Per-130
George Snr	Hay-194	Cauthorn,Dabney	Hal-100	Richard	Per-130
James	Ire-250	Cave,John	Sur-162	Cerney,Rhobarts	Per-143
James	Lnc-360	Cavenah,William	Dup- 33	Cerny,Moses	Per-128
James	Hay-194	Cavender,Henry	Cha-202	Certain,Leonard	Roc- 31
James	Hay-194	Cavendish,Geo	Cha-204	Thomas	Roc- 31
William	Hay-193	Cavenis,Bryant	Grn-122	Ceasar,free man of colour	
William Senr	Hay-194	John	Grn-122		Ran-187
Catlett,Clark	Grn-122	Caveniss,John	Grn-119	Cessna,John	Bun- 89
Catlin,James	Rth- 93	Cavin,John	Ire-239	Chadwell,George	Roc- 32
Caton,Charles	Row- 56	Robert	Ire-239	Chadwick,Barnabas	Car-177
Jesse	Bft- 33	Samuel	Ire-239	Bartholemew	Car-179
John	Cur- 91	William	Ire-239	Gees	Car-177
John	Row- 84	Cavinah,James	Dup- 22	Jacob	Bun- 88
Joshua	Row- 84	Cavins,Mathew	Cha-197	James	Car-178
Sol	Bft- 32	Cavley,Bartholomew	Len-315	Joseph	Car-184
Thomas B	War-182	Cavness,Ann	Ran-160	Martin	Car-177
Cator,Leven	Prq-215	Benjn	Ran-162	Melia	Car-170
Catrel,J	Col- 19	Frederick	Ran-162	Oliver	Car-177
J	Col- 18	George	Ran-161	Samuel	Car-177
Catrell,E	Col- 19	Henry Jr	Ran-160	Solomon	Car-178
S	Col- 19	Henry Jr	Ran-160	Thomas	Bun- 86
Catur,Moses E	Tyr-204	Henry Jr	Ran-161	Wheeler	Glf-164
Caude,Jesse	Wil-268	Mary	Ran-160	Chafers,Jordan	Wil-266
Caudle,Abner	Wil-259	Mary	Ran-161	Chaffin,Amos	Bur-110
Benjamin	Wil-259	Richard	Ran-161	Edwin	Sur-172
Benjamin Jnr	Wil-260	Robt	Ran-161	Gallant	Row- 62
Bledsoe	Cha-201	Walker	Ran-162	Jo	Row- 37
David	Wil-260	William	Ran-160	Nathan	Row- 59
David Jr	Wil-260	Cavondish,Richd	Cha-195	Nathan	Sur-176
Henry	Wil-260	Cawdle,Absolem	Ans- 25	Omega	Roc- 6
Isham	Cha-201	Cawley,Peter	Row- 68	Stanley	Row- 60
James	Cha-199	Cayson,J	Bru-238	Thomas	Row- 66
James Jnr	Wil-260	Cayton,Charity	Sto-114	Chairs,Benjn	Ans- 7
Jeremiah	Wil-262	James	Row- 76	Nathl	Ans- 33
Jesse	Cha-214	Cazan,David	Sto- 95	Vachael	Ans- 13
John	Cha-215	Cazee,John	Glf-188	Chalk,Pegga	Hrt-211
Jonathan	Joh-276	Cazort,Bubard	Grn-138	Richard	Pas-185
Lewis	Joh-276	James	Grn-138	William	Hrt-211
Moses	Sur-192	James	Grn-141	Challis,John	Roc- 14
Stephen (B Smith)	Wil-260	Reuben	Grn-149	Chalmers,Charles	Cum-240
Stephen Jr	Wil-272	Reubin	Grn-139	John P	Roc- 30
Caugan,James	Glf-155	Wm	Grn-138	Chamber,Samuel	Dup- 24
Caughanhour,Mary	Row- 76	Ceagle,David	Cab-148	Chamberlain,Elijah	Pit-256
Cauley,Roger	Len-317	Henry	Cab-147	Enoc	Row- 56
Caulk,D	Glf-160	Henry Junr	Cab-147	James	Pas-185
H	Glf-160	Cearson,Sam	Ora-151	John	Cas- 51
J	Glf-179	Celey,Wm	Nsh- 81	John	Cab-146
Levin	Glf-184	Celia,David	Rob-236	Rebeca	Pas-185

-56-

Chamberlin,J	Cam-161	Chambers,Wm	Hay-194	Chandler,Robert	Sto-138	
J	Cam-158	Wilson	Hay-194	Saml,free man of colour		
Levy	Brt- 64	Chamblis,James	Nsh- 76		Ran-187	
Nancy	Brt- 59	Chambless,Joel	Grn-136	Shad	Ora-149	
S	Cam-165	Chamblis,Wm	Nsh- 75	Stephen	Cas- 51	
Chamberling,H	Cam-162	Chamless,John	Bun- 72	Thos	Cur- 86	
H	Cam-161	Chamness,Edward	Ran-161	William	Cas- 51	
Chambers,Widow	Mec- 51	Joseph	Ran-161	William	Sur-186	
Absom	Dup- 10	Joshua	Cha-195	Wm,free man of colour		
Arthur	Ire-242	N-----	Ran-161		Ran-187	
Benajah	Ons- 97	Stephanos	Cha-203	Chandly,Timothy	Mon- 18	
Benjamin	Per-127	Wm	Cha-209	Chaney,Thomas	Bla- 7	
Betsy	Pas-186	Chamney,Claibern	Ans- 25	Chanler,John	Bun- 77	
Caleb	Hyd-220	Champel,John	Hrt-208	Richard	Bun- 88	
Daniel	Bun- 80	Champian,John	Cha-205	Robt	Ran-160	
Davison	Per-136	Champion,Abram	Dup- 23	Channon,C	Cam-162	
Edward	Row- 82	Elias	Cum-245	Chapel,Ambrde	Sur-166	
Edwd	Mon- 31	Isaac	Cum-262	George	Wil-268	
Edwd O	Per-136	James	Hal-101	Job	Hal-101	
Elihu	Hay-194	James	Cum-261	Rhody	Cur- 92	
Elisha	Bur-128	John	Cum-263	Chaplin,Elisha	Ran-160	
Elisha	Bur-128	John	Rth- 93	Sarah	Pas-214	
Francis	Ons- 97	John	Rth- 94	Chapman,Allen	Nor- 64	
H	Ash- 13	Nancy	Grn-149	Benjamin	Cum-249	
Henry	Cas- 51	Richard	Grn-122	Benjn	Row- 59	
Henry	Ire-242	Richard	Rth- 94	David	Cha-200	
James	Nsh- 76	Zacheus	Brt- 66	Edmund	Rth- 92	
James	Dup- 11	Champon,Jerry	Dup- 21	Eleanor	Cho-222	
James Jr	Dup- 11	Chance,Benj	Hyd-233	Erasmus	Row- 59	
Jasen	Wil-261	Benjamin	Hyd-229	George	Grn-140	
John	Bun- 89	Charrity	Ons-102	George	Lnc-339	
John	Wil-257	Henry	Pit-262	Jessee	Tyr-212	
John	Hyd-222	Jeremih	Hyd-225	John	Wil-275	
John	Ons- 97	John	Sam-152	John	Roc- 31	
John Sr	Dup- 12	John	Mon- 34	John	Cas- 51	
Joseph	Ire-237	Mary	Rch-206	John Jr	Wil-285	
Joseph	Hay-194	Nathan Senr	Sam-164	Moses	Rth- 93	
M	Glf-172	P	Glf-180	Moses	Rth- 93	
Margaret	Ire-238	Redding	Rch-194	Nichl	Lnc-339	
Margaret	Row- 86	Samuel	Rch-195	Robert	Rth- 92	
Margryt	Hyd-222	Sarah	Hyd-223	Samuel	Glf-188	
Mary	Wil-285	Thomas	Pit-261	Seth	Pit-237	
Moses	Per-138	Thomas E	Pit-261	Thomas	Roc- 16	
Nancy	Per-150	Warner	Rch-194	Thomas	Row- 59	
Nancy (H C)	Wil-265	Chancy,J	Col- 16	Thos	Cum-240	
Nancy (F C)	Wil-271	James	Row- 55	William	Cum-240	
Obedh	Tyr-208	Robert	Pas-186	William	Row- 84	
Philip	Hay-194	Chander,Mathew	Grn-125	William	Wil-275	
Sam	Ora-119	Chandler,Bengaman	Cur- 86	William	Wil-275	
Samuel	Wil-263	Daniel	Wil-270	Chapmon,Richd	Tyr-209	
Sarah	Ora-943	David	Grn-124	Chapn,Jemima	Tyr-209	
Sarah	Hyd-222	David Jn	Sur-166	Chappel,Abso	Cho-226	
Thomas	Roc- 15	David Sn	Sur-184	Ambrose	Glf-169	
Thomas	Row- 61	Jane	Grn-124	Amos	Cur-168	
Thomas J	Per-136	Joel	Wil-176	Caleb	Prq-215	
Thos	Cho-226	John	Grn-132	Elisha	Sur-167	
William	Ire-238	John	Bur-116	Elizabeth	Prq-216	
William	Wil-282	Josiah	Cas- 51	Gabriel	Prq-215	
Wm	Ora-114	Robert	Sto-104	James	Sur-167	

Name	Code	Name	Code	Name	Code
Chappel, Jas	Cho-228	Chasten, Richard	Dup- 22	Cheek, Robt Jr	Ora-136
Mary	Cho-228	William	Dup- 20	Cheeson, Shaderick	Hrt-208
Sarah	Prq-215	Chatham, Isaac	Glf-186	Cheetham, Hinchen	Ire-250
William	Prq-216	Chatwell, Joshua	Row- 83	James	Ire-250
Chappell,-----	Mon- 51	Chaulder, Peter	Rch-204	James	Ire-249
Christopher	Mon- 30	Chauncy, Miles	Bft- 27	Weet	Ire-250
Gideon	Prq-215	Saml	Bft- 25	William	Ora-162
James	Mon- 30	Saml Jun	Bft- 27	Wm	Ora-160
Henry	Prq-215	Chavas, Anthony	Grn-119	Cheetum, Caroline	Wil-266
John	Prq-215	Bartholomew	Hal-101	Cheeves, James	Fra- 81
Mallichi	Mar- 13	Charles	Grn-119	John	Cab-136
Mark	Prq-215	Evin	Grn-119	Cheiry, Samuel	Edg- 54
Parks	Mon- 31	Isaac	Grn-119	Chenault, Abner	Roc- 3
Rainer	Prq-215	Martha	Hal-101	Cheny, Eliza	Bft- 20
Rebekah	Roc- 14	Matthew	Hal-101	Lydia	Cur- 91
Rowland	Mon- 30	Robert	Hal-101	Chepon, Eli	Wsh-219
Saml	Grn-125	Sarah	Hal-101	William	Wsh-220
Samuel	Prq-215	Solomon	Hal-101	Cherry, Aaron	Edg- 72
Sarah	Prq-215	Thomas	Grn-124	Abner	Mar-446
Chapple, Isaac	Cho-229	William	Hal-101	David	Lnc-360
S	Ash- 14	Chavens, William	Bla- 9	Davis	Mar- 12
Chapting, Caleb	Cur- 84	Chavers, John	Cha-193	Elisabeth	Mar- 11
James	Cur- 84	Peter	Cha-194	Elizabeth	Brt- 64
John	Cur- 84	Washington	Cha-209	George	Pit-235
Spence	Cur- 84	Cahves, William	Cum-256	Henry	Bft- 26
Chales Negro	Way-235	Chavis, Burrell	Rth- 95	Hilory	Pit-241
Charles (sic)	Cum-236	Jesse	Grn-147	James	Mar- 5
E	Glf-170	John	Grn-124	Jesse	Mar-445
Elisha	Glf-164	Kinchin	Ora-127	Jesse	Mar- 14
Henry	Mec- 41	Chavius, J	Bru-232	Joel	Ans- 19
John	Sto-143	J	Bru-232	Joel	Mar-445
John	Way-244	R	Bru-232	John	Pit-235
John	Sto-108	Chavois, Joe	Rob-218	John	Bft- 27
Laven	Row- 49	Jno	Rob-222	John	Pit-251
Lavin	Row- 49	Chavos, John B	Cha-216	Jonathan Junr	Mar- 5
Leon	Glf-171	Chears, James	Bru-226	Jonathan Senr	Mar- 5
M	Ora-145	Lively	Rch-291	Joseph	Mar- 12
Nathanl	Row- 49	Cheatam, Christopher	Hrt-213	Josh	Brt- 27
Risdon	Row- 50	Godfrey	Cur- 81	Kinchen	Pit-247
Risdon	Glf-187	Wm B	Hrt-208	Laml	Bft- 26
Samuel	Ran-159	Cheek, Cylas	Mec- 33	Lamuel	Pit-235
William	Ran-160	Elisha	Cab-148	Lemuel	Dup- 13
Charlescraft, Charles		Hartwell	Ora-123	Levy	Edg- 71
	Ons-102	James	Sto-121	Levy Jr	Edg- 72
Ester	Ons- 95	James	Mor- 66	Luke	Edg- 70
Isaac	Ons- 95	James	Sto- 93	Moses	Bft- 27
Isaac Junr	Ons- 97	Jas	Ora-114	Nathan	Pit-241
Jaconiah	Ons- 99	Jas Jun	Ora-113	Obediah	Edg- 71
Charleston, Berthiah	Cho-224	Jas Jun	Ora-113	Redderick	Pit-245
Charton, Benjn	Dup- 20	Jesse	Mec- 28	Robert	Edg- 70
Chase, John	Way-249	Jno	Ora-147	Robert	Rth- 92
Vincent	Pas-184	Joab	Mor- 66	Robt	Lnc-337
Zimri	Glf-188	John	Mor- 56	Sarah	Dup- 13
Chasen, Joseph	Cum-265	John	War-173	Solomon Jnr	Brt- 58
Chason, Joseph	Cum-264	John	Sur-169	Solomon Senr	Brt- 53
Chastain, Abner	Hay-194	Mastin	Ora-112	Susanah	Brt- 63
Edward	Hay-194	Randol	Mor- 55	Will	Dup- 14
Elijah	Hay-193	Richd	Mor- 63	William	Pit-235
James	Bun- 85	Robert T	War-179	William	Lnc-363

Name	Ref	Name	Ref	Name	Ref
Cherry,Wm	Bft- 27	Chinn,Perry	Sur-171	Christian,Wm	Mon- 25
Willie	Edg- 70	Raleigh	Sur-178	Christie,Abeshal	Hal-100
Willie Sr	Edg- 71	Chinnus,B	Bru-238	Jesse	Hal-100
Willis	Edg- 52	Chinton,Alfred	Cho-219	Thomas	Hal-100
Cheshire,John	Cho-219	Chipley,William	Ire-262	William	Hal-100
John	Row- 37	Chipman,H	Glf-162	Christman,Daniel	Sto-146
Chesnut,Alexn	Ans- 24	John	Glf-166	Christmas,Cols C	Ora-172
Charles	Sam-159	Chirstian,Tho	Ora-118	Ricd	Ora-159
Hardy	Sam-152	Chisenhall,Burl	Ora-170	Thomas	War-182
Joshua Senr	Sam-157	Wm	Ora-167	Thos Jr	War-181
Chesnutt,Arther	Sam-162	Chisham,Wm	Mon- 24	William	Roc- 20
Jacob	Sam-152	Chisher,Elizabeth	Dup- 27	Christmus,James	Ora-122
John	Sam-152	Chisholm,A	Col- 17	Christopher,Ambrose	Rth- 94
John	Sam-163	Angus	Mon- 18	Ar	Ora-155
Joseph	Sam-152	Danl	Mon- 29	John	Roc- 29
Joshua Jr	Sam-157	Fendly	Cum-239	Joseph	Wsh-221
Saml	Sam-163	Gatewood	Rth- 94	R	Ora-155
Chessen,Tenneson	Wil-261	John	Mon- 29	Thomas	Lnc-352
Chesson,Elizabeth	Wsh-223	Chisnil,Peter	Cur- 89	William	Rth- 95
Chester,Bethian	Edg- 51	Chisolm,Alex	Rob-219	Christy,Andrew	Ire-258
Briton	Bur-129	Alexr	Rob-231	James	Ire-240
Saml	Bft- 31	Danl	Rob-231	Joseph	Ire-240
Tho	Bur-129	Jas	Rob-219	Joseph	Ire-238
Wm	Ans- 11	Jno	Rob-219	Chriswell,J	Ora-155
Chewning,Jno	Ans- 23	Chisshin,Nicholas	Bla- 7	Chrutchfield,Jno	Ora-130
Chickaster,Stephen	Rth- 94	Randolph	Bla- 6	Chumbers,Jas	Ora-152
Chickens,J	Col- 21	Richd	Bla- 7	Chumbley,Polley	Cas- 51
Child,Frances	Ora-110	Chisson,Charles	Wsh-223	Chumly,Elizabeth	Sur-193
James	Ora-110	Elizabeth	Wsh-221	Chun,Thomas	Row- 73
Saml	Ora-112	John	Wsh-224	Chunn,Berry	Rch-200
Sarah	Ans- 22	Joshua	Wsh-221	Samuel	Bun- 98
Childers,James	Ran-161	Chister,David	Lnc-375	Silvester	Rch-200
James	Ire-263	Chisum,Floyd	Cur- 89	Church,Aaron	Wil-281
John	Lnc-363	Chitham,William	Lnc-368	Allen	Brt- 55
Nicholas	Grn-132	Chittim,John	Lnc-336	Amos	Wil-281
Robert	Per-138	Chitty,Charles	Sto-136	E	Ash- 11
Robert	Lnd-358	John	Sto-100	Elijah	Wil-281
William	Lnc-333	John	Sto-131	Isaac	Sto-128
Childras,David	Sur-184	John	Sto-112	Jenny	Wil-281
Childress,Anne	War-168	John	Sto-153	Joel	Wil-281
Benjamin	Sto-126	Chitwood,,James	Rth- 93	John	Wil-283
Benjamin	Sto- 96	Choat,Sabret	Wil-259	John	Pit-247
Isam	Rth- 92	Chocthain,James	Grn-148	John	Bur-110
Jesse	Sto-114	Chopefelt,George	Lnc-329	John M	Lnc-352
Jesse	Sto-156	Choves,Fanus	Cha-205	Jonn M	Lnc-355
John	Rth- 93	Chrisman,Chalres	Sur-177	Joshua	Hay-194
Matthew	Sto-127	Henry	Glf-189	Nathaniel	Prq-215
Pleasant	Cas- 51	John	Glf-189	P	Ash- 11
Samuel	Bun- 75	Christ,Rudolf	Sto-146	Philip	Bur-121
William	Sto-127	Christenbery,Wm	Hal-101	Robert	Bur-121
William Jnr	Sto-120	Moses	Hal-101	William	Wil-251
William Snr	Sto- 97	Christian,J	Mon- 36	Churchal,Benjamin	Gat-107
Childs,Jas	Ans- 4	James	Nor- 63	Churchwell,Simon	Ans- 26
Sarah	Ans- 30	John	Mon- 23	Chyle,Jane	Ire-239
Chiles,Hezikiah	Cas- 51	John	Cha-192	Ciler,James	Bur-122
Chilton,James	Cas- 51	Marian	Cho-222	Cimmons,Andw	Cab-143
John	Cas- 51	Thos	Mon- 23	Hugh	Cab-143
Chiney,Wm	Mec- 43	Thos	Ora-150	Cimp,William	Cur- 87
Wm	Mec- 43	W	Mon- 35	Cinter,F	Cum-241

Cirkpatrick,C	Ora-171	Clark,Alexr	Mor- 68	Clark,Jane	Cha-205	
Cissel,Allin	Row- 45	Allen	Hrt-212	Jery	Bur-112	
Citizen,Isaac	Wsh-223	Amelia	Cum-247	Jesse	Mec- 25	
Isaac	Cho-225	Amelia	Brt- 64	Jesse	Glf-167	
Stephen	Cho-225	Anna	Glf-166	Jessy	Ora-161	
Civils,Betsy	Pas-186	Archd	Cum-255	Joanna	Bur-127	
Clabrooks,Moses	Row- 65	Archd McC	Cum-256	John	Bft- 34	
Clack,Eldrige	Hal-100	Archd	Mor- 60	John	Bur-107	
Henry	Grn-145	B	Col- 19	John	Cha-202	
Martin	Cas- 51	B	Ora-152	John	War-173	
Clagg,Thomas	Cho-202	Baptist	Ran-160	John	Ire-255	
Claggett,Henry	Ire-266	Barnet	Pas-184	John	Mar- 13	
Claghorn,Benjamin	Wsh-223	Benjaman	Mec- 47	John	Glf-174	
Claiborne,George	War-172	Benjamin	Hay-194	John	Glf-163	
Clake,Willie	Nor- 64	Betsey	Bft- 34	John	Hal-101	
Clall,Joseph	Glf-156	Caleb	Glf-182	John	Ran-161	
Clampet,Govia	Row- 81	Charles	Grn-145	John	Edg- 59	
Clampett,George	Sto-134	Clary	Sto-140	John B	Row- 63	
Richard	Sto-134	Cornelius	Lnc-363	John Junr	Cum-255	
Richard	Sto-102	Dagan	Ran-160	John M C	Cum-255	
William	Sto-102	Daniel	Bur-113	John Scotch	Cum-255	
William	Sto-134	Daniel McC	Cum-256	John Senr	Cum-254	
Clancy,Geo	Ora-110	Danl	Bla- 12	Jonas	Mec- 25	
Tho	Ora-111	Danl	Mor- 60	Jonathan	Glf-181	
Clant,Charles	Bun- 82	Danl	Ran-161	Joseph	Bur-107	
Clanton,Abraham	War-168	David	Cum-254	Joseph	Ans- 17	
Charles	Sur-192	David	Hal-101	Joseph	Glf-152	
Dudley	War-170	Eli	Joh-282	Joseph	Jon-294	
Edward	Sur-190	Ephraim	Pas-184	Joseph	Pas-186	
Edward	Ire-250	Ephraim	Pas-184	Joseph	Ora-169	
James	Ire-250	F	Glf-158	Joseph	Mec- 47	
Jeremiah	Hal-101	Francis	Ans- 32	Joseph	Row- 40	
Lucy	Ire-251	Francis	Cha-211	Keneth	Mor- 60	
Thomas	Sur-178	Francis	Sam-160	Kenneth	Brt- 43	
Clap,John	Glf-155	G	Glf-158	Lemuel	Wsh-220	
John Miller	Ora-145	George	Tyr-205	Lucinda	Roc- 34	
John Jr	Ran-160	George	Ran-162	M	Col- 18	
John Sr	Ran-160	Gilbert	Cum-255	Major J	Hyd-225	
John Jr	Ora-121	Goshen	Pas-186	Malcom	Cum-254	
Clapp,B	Ora-131	Hardy	Bla- 7	Malcom	Mor- 60	
C	Glf-177	Henry	Mar- 6	Margorett	Mec- 37	
Daniel	Glf-178	Henry	Bla- 5	Mary	Bur-122	
Danl	Glf-177	Henry	Per-136	Mary	Cum-263	
Felty	Glf-155	Henry	Hyd-225	Mary	Hyd-225	
Felty	Glf-177	Henry	Bft- 37	Matthew	Glf-187	
Geo	Glf-177	Hezekiah	Cha-201	Milly	Glf-186	
H	Glf-177	Isaac	Pas-186	Moses	Ire-250	
J Jr	Ora-131	Isaac	Len-215	Nathanl	Cha-214	
Jacob	Glf-189	J	Col- 19	Neill	Cum-253	
Jacob	Glf-178	Jack	Rch-203	Neill	Cum-255	
Jno	Ora-172	James	Bur-119	Neill	Bla- 12	
Jno Sen	Ora-132	James	Cha-202	Neven	Mon- 30	
John H	Ora-119	James	Mar- 16	Nicolas	Rch-208	
Tobiah	Glf-154	James	Glf-166	Patty	Cha-203	
W	Glf-177	James	Hrt-215	Rachel	Rch-208	
Clapton,Walter	Bun- 86	James	Edg- 62	Rew	Pas-184	
Clardy,M	Bla- 10	Jas	Mec- 35	Robert	Sur-166	
Penelope	Bla- 10	Jas	Mec- 35	Robert	Row- 61	
Clark,Alexr	Cum-253	Jas Enos	Ora-169	Robt	Ans- 29	

Name	Ref	Name	Ref	Name	Ref
Clark,S	Mon- 34	Clarke, Wm of	Ora-126	Clayton,Wm Senr	Per-128
Saml Snr	Ran-161	Wm	Cur- 79	Claywell,Peter	Ire-261
Samuel	Sto-140	Wm	Ora-161	Clearcum,Joseph	Ora-166
Samuel	Sur-193	Wm F R	Ora-127	Cleark,Benjamin	Bur-104
Samuel	Pit-248	Zachariah	Hay-194	Beverly	Bur-129
Samuel	Hyd-225	Clarkson,Sarey	Cur- 88	Cleasley,Jessey	Rob-227
Samuel	Sto-105	Clary,Daniel	Row- 88	Cleaves,Hosea	Hyd-232
Samuel Jr	Ran-161	David	Row- 77	John	Hal-100
Sarah	Cum-248	George	Ora-149	Sally	Nor- 63
Silas	Cha-191	Henry	Grn-148	William	Gat-114
T	Ora-169	James	Prq-215	Cleevis,George	Bru-224
Thomas	War-181	John	Prq-215	Cleghorn,James	Rth- 95
Thomas	Wil-265	John	Ire-269	James	Rth- 92
Thomas	Ran-161	Jordan	Prq-215	Clemant,John	Grn-138
Thos	Hrt-208	Lemuel	Hal-100	Saml	Grn-138
Timothy	Grn-147	Mary	Row- 88	Clemar,George	Lnc-341
Timothy	Grn-121	Clasby,Charles	Ire-268	John	Lnc-341
Vachel	Mon- 21	Clase,Thomas	Ran-161	Lewis	Lnc-341
William	War-182	Class,Thos	Ran-162	Clement,Isaac	Rth- 95
William	Lnc-352	Claton,Elliott	Hyd-226	Johnson	Sto- 92
William	Lnc-363	William	Per-127	Johnson	Sto-121
William	Hyd-233	Clator,Nimrod	Way-242	Mary	Grn-122
William	Edg- 59	Claud,Jacob	Ran-160	Peter	Sto-144
William	Hay-194	Claunich,Jeremia	Row- 57	Peter	Sto-108
William Jr	Ran-161	Clausell,John Lewis	Hyd-234	Wm	Grn-122
William Jr	Ran-160	Clauson,W	Ash- 11	Clements,William	Nor- 64
Wm	Bft- 38	Clauzon,John	Har-180	Clemmans,Widow	Lnc-329
Wm	Mec- 48	Clay,Doctor	Grn-145	Clemmon,Ezekel	Row- 56
Wm	Cho-221	Edwd Senr	Per-136	Clemmons,Andrew	Rth- 91
Wm	Cha-216	Isaac	Lnc-326	Cornelius	Rth- 92
Clarke,Alexander	Bur-122	Jeffrey	Hal-100	E Jr	Bru-226
Alexander	Lnc-358	Peter	Grn-143	Godfrey	Row- 80
Anthony	Lnc-337	Clayten,Britin	Sto-'99	Henry	Row- 65
Archd	Ora-127	Clayton,Britin	Sto-130	Isaac	Rth- 91
Arthur	Rth- 92	Charles	Bun- 92	Peter	Row- 56
Burton	Ora-116	Charles	Glf-181	Saml	Mon- 21
David	Lnc-358	Charity	Sto-157	Tm	Bru-226
George	Hay-194	David	Tyr-202	Clemmont,Laurence	Row- 65
Henry	Cur- 81	Eliza	Row- 49	Clemon,Thomas	Hal-100
James	Bur-119	George	Ire-255	Clemons,E	Bru-238
James	Ire-257	Henry	Hal-101	James	Glf-165
James	Rch-199	James	Cha-213	John	Rch-210
James	Lnc-328	James	Bun- 91	John	Row- 40
James Elder	Ora-176	John	Bun- 86	Vachel	Hrt-207
Jas	Ora-122	John	Tyr-209	William	Pit-261
John	Lnc-337	John	Per-127	Clempson,William	Cas- 51
John	Hay-194	John	Glf-158	Clendenen,Fisher	Ora-116
John	Rth- 94	John	Prq-215	Jas	Ora-114
John	Rch-195	Lambert	Bun- 84	Wm	Ora-114
John	Ons- 98	Molly	Per-140	Clendenin,Mary	Ora-121
John	Cur- 79	Richard	Pas-186	Clendenning,John	Cas- 51
John	Bun- 85	Richard	Per-140	Clenderson,Matthew	Ire-239
Neil	Cur-119	Richd	Per-130	Clenny,Saml	Joh-289
Nelly	Rth- 95	Richd B	Per-136	William	Sam-155
Osborn	Pit-236	Sarah	Hal-101	Wm	Ora-167
Sally	Rth- 93	Sudat	Tyr-207	Cleason,W S	Sam-157
William	Wsh-228	Thomas	Per-136	Clenton,Betsey	Ora-149
William	Bun- 93	Thomas	Mon- 47	Saml	Ora-150
William	Nor- 63	Thomas Jr	Per-136	Clerk,Eliza	Car-169

Name	Ref	Name	Ref	Name	Ref
Clerk,Jery	Bur-127	Clinton,Richard D	Sam-152	Clughan,Jas	Mec- 33
Clery,Richard	Ire-246	Robert	Rth- 93	Cluk,Geo	Cab-146
Cleveland,E	Ash- 3	Sam	Ora-158	Clure,Abraham	Sto-137
M	Ash- 5	Clip,Michl	Row- 64	Cluts,Barbary	Row- 68
Robert	Wil-280	Clipperd,Eliz	Lnc-346	Henry	Row- 68
Cliburn,Jno	Rob-235	Henry	Lnc-346	Jacob	Row- 67
Click,Nicholas	Row- 65	Clively,Jno	Per-127	Jacob	Row- 68
Nicholas Jnr	Row- 65	Clodfelter,Elias	Row- 42	John	Cab-145
Clide,R	Cum-240	George	Row- 72	Leonard	Cab-145
Clifford,John	Row- 63	George Jr	Row- 72	Tobias	Cab-141
Joseph	Row- 63	Jacob	Row- 42	Clutz,Jacob	Bur-126
Clifton,Cloyd	Nor- 63	John	Row- 49	Cluvis,J	Bru-224
David	Lnc-366	John	Row- 49	Saml	Bru-226
Gervas	Brt- 48	John	Row- 42	Clyfton,Dycy	Bla- 9
James	Lnc-360	Mary	Row- 42	Coaker,John	Nor- 63
Joel	Joh-275	Michl	Row- 49	Sally	Nor- 63
John	Fra- 93	Peter	Row- 79	Seegars	Nor- 63
Jonas	Nor- 63	Cloer,Michl	Lnc-377	Coakley,Ben	Bft- 37
Josh	Ora-143	Nicholas	Lnc-347	Plantation (13)	Bft- 24
Reuben	Wsh-216	Cloine,J	Ora-139	Coal,Charles	Nsh- 82
Robert	Wsh-220	Cloire,John	Bur-119	Levy	Ora-137
Sarah	Jon-294	Cloman,John	Edg- 53	Thomas	Rth- 93
Thomas	Wsh-217	Clonch,Jeremiah	Ans- 24	Coalburn,Revel	Cha-191
Willie	Fra- 93	Cloninger,Adam	Lnc-368	Coalman,A	Col- 18
Clik,Daniel	Row- 65	Adam	Lnc-366	D	Col- 19
Climer,C	Glf-176	David	Lnc-340	Eldred	Bru-230
D	Glf-176	John	Lnc-363	F	Col- 18
T	Glf-176	Phillip	Lnc-363	J	Col- 18
T	Glf-174	Michl	Lnc-363	Joseph	Cas- 51
Wm	Glf-176	Cloonse,Christian	Bur-111	L	Col- 18
Clinard,Danl	Row- 48	George	Bur-111	P	Col- 19
Danl	Row- 46	Clopton,Gery	Fra- 89	Coaly,Francis	Cha-197
Jacob	Row- 84	Peggy	Fra- 91	Coan,Benjamin	Nsh- 85
Peter	Row- 51	Close,John	Sto-149	Gilford	Nsh- 85
Peter	Row- 48	Clotfelter,George	Lnc-347	Gillan	Nsh- 85
Philip	Row- 50	Clotz,Henry	Mec- 45	James	Nsh- 85
Cline,Andrew	Lnc-347	Jeremiah	Mec- 45	Coart,Jesse	Pit-231
Charity	Lnc-347	Cloud,D	Ora-139	Coarts,George	Roc- 16
Daniel	Lnc-352	Danl	Ora-117	Coates,A	Cam-161
Daniel	Cab-142	George	Sto-122	John	Row- 52
David	Rth- 95	George	Sto-137	Tempy	Row- 52
David	Lnc-377	Isaac	Rth- 94	Thos	Row- 52
David	Cab-141	Isham	Roc- 24	Coatney,Emanuel	Ans- 19
Geo	Cab-142	Jeremiah	Sto-137	Mary	Ans- 19
Henry	Lnc-345	Jesse	Rth- 93	Stephen	Ans- 19
Henry	Cab-143	Joseph Jnr	Sto-121	Coats,Widow	Ire-250
Jacob	Lnc-377	Joseph Snr	Sto-122	Burrell	Sam-160
Jacob Senr	Lnc-377	Joseph Snr	Sto-137	Burweill	Joh-289
John	Lnc-347	Saml	Ora-127	Fanny	Wil-265
John	Lnc-377	Clough,William	Tyr-206	John	Joh-274
John Jr	Lnc-377	Clouse,John	Sto-135	Jordan	Sam-160
Michael	Lnc-377	Clowder,Charles D	Sto-112	Martha	Nor- 63
Michal	Row- 86	Charles G	Sto-114	William	Joh-274
Phillip	Lnc-346	Clows,John	Sto-136	Wm	Mor- 60
Stovel	Bur-130	Clubb,Daniel	Lnc-363	Cob,Benj	Nsh- 89
William	Lnc-377	George A	Lnc-366	Cobb,Widow	Lnc-366
Clingmon,Peter	Sur-174	George Jr	Lnc-366	Abe	Cas- 51
Clinton,Eliz	Ora-149	Hosjah	Bur-108	Archibald	Ire-253
Jno	Ora-149	John	Lnc-377	Benjn	Bur-130

Cobb,Betsy	Cas- 51	Cobble,George	Row- 81	Cockran,Abram	Mon- 27
Charles	Brt- 45	Michl	Row- 78	David	Mon- 27
Dawson	Edg- 43	Peter	Row- 77	Eli	Mec- 29
Eaton	Edg- 72	Coblar,Nicholas	Roc- 9	Eli	Mec- 30
Edward	Edg- 68	Thomas	Roc- 8	Jacob	Mon- 31
Edward	Edg- 42	Coble,David	Mon- 38	James Esq	Per-127
Eliz	Len-323	David	Glf-155	Jas	Mec- 30
Elizabeth	Brt- 61	David	Ora-133	Jas	Mec- 29
Grey	Sam-159	F	Glf-173	Moses	Mec- 30
Hardy	Mar-445	Geo	Ora-120	Robert	Rth- 91
Harmon	Pit-247	Geo	Glf-155	Robt	Mec- 29
Henry	Cas- 51	Geo Snr	Glf-173	Simeon	Per-150
Henry Jnr	Brt- 48	Henry	Glf-178	Thos	Mec- 29
Henry Senr	Brt- 48	Henry	Ora-133	Cockrel,Jonathan	Fra- 82
J	Glf-178	J of Shady	Ora-172	Cockrell,John	Joh-284
James	Brt- 48	Jacob	Glf-155	Saml	Joh-283
James	Brt- 45	John	Glf-155	Simon	Joh-284
James	Lnc-339	Jno	Ora-131	William	Joh-283
James	Sam-154	N	Glf-173	Cockron,Robert	Hal-101
James	Cas- 51	Nicholas	Glf-171	Cocks,Aaron	Bun- 75
James Senr	Brt- 53	P	Glf-173	B	Col- 19
Jesse	Fra- 89	Peter	Row- 38	G Charles	Cas- 51
Jno	Ans- 18	Vol	Glf-180	J	Col- 18
Jno P	Mon- 46	Coburn,Abner	Mar- 15	Jas	Mon- 45
John	Edg- 70	Elijah	Ans- 8	John	Bun- 81
John	Lnc-347	Griffen	Mar- 13	Moses	Mon- 50
John	Len-317	Hedley	Ans- 8	Nancy	Grn-138
John	Cas- 51	Jas	Ans- 24	Reubin	Cas- 51
John B	Way-232	Jesse	Mar- 8	Thos	Mon- 45
Jonas	Edg- 43	John	Mar- 10	Cody,Godfrey	Bun- 92
Joseph H	Brt- 48	John	Lnc-339	John	Roc- 28
Josiah	Edg- 70	Pheby	Ans- 24	Stephen	Bun- 92
Kinchen	Pit-247	William	Mar- 8	Coe,Elizabeth	Sur-189
Levy	Cas- 51	Cochram,James	Roc- 27	John	Glf-156
Martha	Nor- 63	William	Bun- 82	John	Sur-189
Martha	Pit-252	Cochran,Benj	Bur-118	Joseph	Glf-156
Mathew	Cas- 41	Jno	Ans- 18	Sarah	Glf-171
Moses	Pit-253	Thos	Cho-231	William	Sur-176
Nathan	Brt- 61	Wm	Ans- 16	Coertly,Margt	Bur-124
Ralph	Lnc-347	Cocke,Joseph	War-173	Cofer,George Z	Hal-101
Reddon	Sam-154	Cockerham,Daniel	Sur-174	James	Hal-100
Reuben	Pit-253	David	Sur-192	Coffan,Seth	Sto-148
Robert	Nor- 63	Humphrey	Wil-261	Coffe,James	Sto-124
Sally	Lnc-366	Moses	Sur-192	Coffee,Archelaus	Bur-128
Sampson	Edg- 59	Moses	Sur-163	Becom	Pit-253
Samuel	Cas- 51	Rebecca	Sur-193	Benjamin	Bur-131
Selah	Edg- 72	William	Sur-173	Eli Esqr	Wil-279
Shade	Lnc-368	William Sr	Sur-175	Elijah	Bur-128
Stephen	Edg- 69	Cocklereese,Wm	Ora-139	Eloisa	Bur-127
Stephen	Way-245	Cockley,Alexr	Grn-122	Hugh	Mec- 33
Thomas	Edg- 61	Cockman,Cathrine	Mor-59	James	Wil-274
Thos	Brt- 47	John	Mor- 57	James Jr	Wil-279
William	Lnc-366	Cockral,Joseph	Nsh- 81	Jesse	Bur-128
William	Pit-247	Nancy	Nsh- 88	Joel	Bur-110
William	Cas- 51	Nathan	Nsh- 86	John (Stetter)	Wil-279
Wm	Bur-130	Cockram,Henry	Rth- 95	John Senr	Wil-279
Cobbart,John	Hay-194	James	Rth- 91	Joseph	Brt- 46
Cobble,Adam	Row- 79	Miner	Rth- 92	Joseph	Bur-110
Adam	Row- 85	Thomas	Rth- 94	Levi	Wil-279

-63-

Name	Ref	Name	Ref	Name	Ref
Coffee,Lewis	Wil-279	Coggin (sic)	Mon- 51	Colclough,Sarah	War-181
Reuben	Bur-127	Burwell	Mon- 19	Colderon,Jacob	Row- 87
Reuben	Bur-128	Eli	Mon- 20	Coldiron,J	Ash- 8
S	Ash- 12	James	Fra- 98	Coldman,Charles	Edg- 66
Smith	Bur-128	John	Pit-247	John	Edg- 67
Thomas Senr	Wil-276	Matthew	Mon- 18	Robert	Edg- 66
W	Ash- 7	Moses	Cha-202	Thos	Ora-137
William	Bur-128	Nancy	Sam-159	Willie	Edg- 67
William	Wil-279	Repps	Ora-167	Coldwell,Allen	Roc- 10
William (Ripskin)	Wil-284	Robert	Fra- 94	Cole,Abram	Mor- 56
Coffer,Aaron	Sto-148	Robt	Cha-197	Alexr	Bur-113
Benjamin	Sto-148	Simon	Mon- 20	Andrew	Mor- 63
Henry	Mor- 64	Thomas	Rth- 94	David	Brt- 58
Jacob	Sto-147	William	Rth- 95	David	Bun- 96
James	Sto-111	Zacheriah	Pit-247	Fanney	Grn-132
James	Sto-148	Coghill,Frederick	War-171	Frank	Rch-211
James Jnr	Sto-148	Isrum	War-174	Geo	Cha-213
James Snr	Sto-111	Reuben	War-179	George	Rch-196
John	Roc- 6	Thos	Grn-134	Harberd	Mor- 63
Sarah	Sto-138	Zachariah	War-184	Henson	Roc- 11
Thomas	Sto-147	Cogshall,Tristram	Sur-196	Isaac	Cha-199
Coffey,Henry	Roc- 21	Cogshall,Peter	Sto-147	J	Glf-184
Reuben	Bur-103	Cogswell,William	Cur- 89	Jacob	Bft= 37
Thomas	Roc- 20	Cogwell,Mrs.	Grn-130	James	Row- 38
Coffield,Benj	Cho-226	Cohoon,Abel	Tyr-211	James	Rch-208
Benj	Brt- 56	Alexander	Hyd-228	James	Way-248
Benj	art- 43	Benjn	Tyr-208	James	Mor- 64
Fredk	Cho-224	Catharine	Tyr-201	James Jr	Way-248
Isaac	Brt- 59	David	Tyr-201	Jereh	Brt- 58
Jethro	Brt- 44	Ezekel	Hyd-230	Jeremiah	Hrt-211
Jno Jnr	Cho-230	Gidion	Tyr-201	Jesse	Rch-196
John	Cho-226	Cohoon,Jam of Jno	Tyr-208	Jesse	Cha-199
Mary	Cho-227	James	Tyr-202	Jessee	Bun- 90
Thomas	Mar- 15	John of Gn	Tyr-207	Job	Wil-267
Coffin,Aaron	Sto-111	John of Jr	Tyr-208	Jno	Mec- 45
Abel	Glf-165	Joseph	Tyr-201	John	Ora-115
Barnabas	Glf-187	Solomon	Ans- 16	John	Mor- 63
Elihu	Glf-163	Thulin	Tyr-207	John	Rch-211
Elisha	Glf-163	William	Tyr-207	John	Rch-197
Elizabeth	Glf-181	Willm of Jeal	Tyr-208	John	Ora-138
James	Glf-170	Cohorn,James	Per-136	John	Mec- 34
John	Ran-161	John Junr	Per-136	John	Mor- 55
Joseph	Glf-165	John	Ire-262	John	Mor- 64
L	Glf-184	William	Per-136	John CP	Rth- 95
Matthew	Glf-170	Cohran,Robt	Cab-138	Joseph	Mor- 64
Nathen	Ran-162	Coiles,Elizabeth	Cas- 52	Joshua	Hal-101
Thos	Glf-165	Nicholas	Cas- 52	Martha	Ora-129
Zacheus	Glf-185	Coin,Daniel	Row- 62	Mathew	Bun- 93
Cofield,Benjamin	Edg- 57	Peter	Bun- 83	Matthew	Rch-211
Benjamin Jr	Edg- 57	Coins,Ephraim	Bur-105	Merimon	Ora-151
David	Edg- 57	Coker,Brumble	Row- 62	Merrimon	Ora-943
Thomas	Edg- 46	Ephraim	Mon- 22	P	Cam-165
Cofn,Abraham	Roc- 32	James	Len-311	Pascal	Ran-161
Cogdall,Daniel	Sam-154	James Jr	Edg- 57	Peter	Rch-196
Cogdell,Lewis	Way-247	Nathaniel	Ans- 18	Peter H	Rch-207
Richd	Way-247	Thomas	Rth- 92	R	Glf-184
Richd	Bft- 19	William	Row- 62	Richd	Bft- 25
William	Bun- 82	Colamon,Jas	Mon- 50	Robert	Row- 63
William Senr	Bun- 82	Colclough,Benj	War-169	Robert	War-179

Cole,Robert Sr	Dup- 35	Coleson,William	Prq-215	Collier,Mark	Cas- 51
Sam Jr	Ora-151	Coletrain,Danl	Ran-161	Moses	Nor- 63
Samuel	Bun- 74	Jacob	Ran-161	Robert	Way-235
Silvy	Mor- 65	William	Ran-160	Samuel	Way-253
T	Cam-157	William	Ran-161	Sarah	Nor- 63
Thomas	Mor- 56	William	Ran-161	William	Nor- 63
Thomas	Cha-199	Coley,Mrs.	Fra- 79	Zach	Way-254
Thomas	Dup- 35	Charles	War-169	Collin,Henry	Cha-200
Thos	Ora-137	Claiborn	Fra- 92	Collings,Timothy	Mar- 4
William	Roc- 27	David	Grn-125	Collins,---ele	Wsh-221
William	Mar- 9	Francis	Hal-100	A	Ash- 12
William	Rch-200	Gabriel	Way-254	Abraham	Lnc-307
Wm	Grn-130	J	Mon- 38	Abram	Rth- 92
Wm	Ora-164	James	Hal-100	Abram M M	Rth- 95
Wm	Sam-151	Jesse	Mon- 41	Allen	Joh-282
Wm	Ora-124	Julius	Cha-205	Andw	Ora-143
Wm	Mor- 64	O	Col- 20	Anthony	Sto- 92
Wm Jnr	Cha-199	Richard	Hal-100	Anthony	Sto-121
Wm Sr	Cha-215	Robert	Hal-100	Benjamin	Rth- 94
Willis	Joh-289	Sarah	Mon- 38	Betsy	Pas-185
Coleman,Archd	Cas- 51	Susanna	Hal-100	Brice	Bur-108
Benj	Len-318	Theoderick	Hal- 99	Brier	Cas- 51
Beverly	Wil-269	W	Col- 21	Bryant	Grn-145
Carter	War-169	Washington	Mon- 38	Charles	Rch-210
Charles	Wil-272	Wm	Mon- 38	Daniel	Rch-206
Daniel	Cab-146	Colgohoon,Archd	Rch-203	Deal	Joh-282
Elijah	Way-246	Charles	Rch-192	E	Ash- 12
Honour	Way-247	Duncan	Rch-191	Edward	Sto- 94
Isaac	Pas-185	Duncan	Rch-191	Edward	Sto-122
Jacob	Cab-142	Effie	Rch-202	Elijah	Rch-206
Jacob	Cab-139	Mary	Rch-212	Elizabeth	Prq-215
Jacob	War-173	Colier,Henry	Glf-171	Enoch	Ora-116
James	Rch-207	Thomas	Grn-130	Enoch	Cas- 51
James	Hrt-213	Colins,Nancey	Cur- 89	Frederick	Prq-215
Jas	Ans- 5	Collan,Benjamin	Per-130	George	Way-235
Jno	Ans- 19	Collands,Benj Jr	Jon-294	Isaac	Rth- 93
John	Row- 71	Benjamin Senr	Jon-294	J	Ash- 9
John	Hal-100	Collans,Isaac	Jon-294	Jacob	Lnc-339
Mark	Hay-194	Solomon	Jon-294	James	Hal-100
Mary	Len-315	College,Henry	Cab-148	James	Cha-208
Nancy	Bft- 38	Collen,Wm	Mec- 31	James	Cha-203
Philip	Row- 71	Wm	Mec- 49	James	Cum-244
Robert	Roc- 8	Collet,Charles	Ran-162	James	Ora-122
Robert	Ire-254	Collett,Charles	Bur-111	James	Ora-129
Robert S	Roc- 8	Colley,John	Way-250	James	Fra- 94
Seth	Per-136	Colliar,Fredk	Ans- 27	James Senr	Fra-100
Thomas	Bur-125	Collier,Doctor	Fra- 84	Jane	Prq-215
Thos	Hrt-210	Drury	Lnc-366	Jean	Lnc-377
William	Roc- 8	Fred	Ora-130	Jeremiah	Sto- 93
William	Row- 70	Frederick	Nor- 64	Jeremiah	Sto-122
Wm	Rob-233	Harbert	Cha-215	Jerry	Rch-212
Colemon,John	Cas- 52	Henry	Mec- 32	Jesse	Wsh-224
Coles,Fanny	Grn-132	Henry	Fra- 91	Jilson	Sto-121
Joseph	Rth- 92	James	Lnc-339	Jno	Ora-111
Wm	Row- 51	James	Bur-126	Jno Enoch	Ora-176
Willis	Grn-130	Jessee	Nor- 64	John	Bur-113
Coleson,George	Roc- 24	Joseph	Way-253	John	Ora-116
Gilbert	Prq-215	Joseph	Cas- 51	John	Sto- 93
John	Roc- 25	Light	Lnc-331	John	Sto-121

Name	Ref	Name	Ref	Name	Ref
Collins,John	Lnc-377	Colvard,William	Wil-260	Conditt,Fielding	Fra- 97
John	Mar- 10	Colvarn,Berryman	Sur-189	Condon,John	Roc- 34
John	Rth- 95	Colvet,John	Jon-295	Condra,Sarah	Hyd-223
John	Rth- 96	Mary	Jon-295	Condrey,William	Rth- 94
John S	Jon-294	Colvil,Archd	Cum-245	Condry,Cleburn	Rth- 92
Jos	Cho-219	James	Cum-245	Dens	Bft- 19
Jos Junr	Lnc-330	Robert	Cum-257	John	Bft- 20
Joseph	Lnc-339	William	Cum-261	Wm	Bft- 20
Joseph	Ons-103	William	Cum-245	Cone,Elizabeth	Edg- 46
Kader	Cum-263	Colvin,Francis	Rob-230	Ephrim	Mar- 16
Lewis	Cab-148	Colvord,John	Sur-183	Jesse	Mar- 7
M	Cam-157	Colwell,Henry	Bun- 96	Jessee	Nor- 63
Martin	Lnc-339	J	Ash- 15	Jessee	Nor- 63
Mary	Lnc-339	Coly,Phillip	Dup- 7	John	Bft- 30
Merrel	Cum-263	Coman,Robt	Ans- 12	John	Mar- 11
Nichl	Nsh- 73	Comb,James	Ora-176	Levi	Mar- 16
Mordica	Row- 50	John	Ora-176	Neal	Mar- 7
Mourning	Mor- 60	Mary	Ora-176	Thomas	Brt- 57
Nancy	Nsh- 90	Combs,Bird	Sur-177	Conger,David	Hrt-210
Obediah	Sur-166	David	Brt- 64	Congleton,Allen	Pit-261
Patty	Joh-287	George	Wil-263	Danl	Bft- 25
Peter	Fra- 94	Hicks	Wil-264	James	Pit-262
Richard	Ons- 97	Hiram	Per-136	Jas	Bft- 25
Ruben	Ans- 11	James	Jon-295	Jane	Bft- 37
Sally	Hrt-209	John	Jon-294	John	Bft- 37
Saml	Lnc-327	John	Tyr-209	Mary	Bft- 25
Samuel	Lnc-339	Martha	Roc- 13	Mos	Bft- 25
Shadrack	Edg- 47	Peter	Wil-265	Congor,Eli	Mec- 53
Solomon	Nsh- 83	Polly	Nor- 63	Conklin,David	Bun- 92
T	Bru-226	Sarah	Len-316	Conlay,J	Ash- 14
T	Ash- 9	Thos	Tyr-209	Conley,Caleb	Ire-262
Watson	Rth- 93	William	Jon-294	Danl	Rob-226
Watson	Nsh- 83	William	Roc- 9	E	Ash- 14
William	Fra- 86	Wm	Tyr-204	Elizabeth	Rob-218
William	Sto- 93	Comer,Adam	Mor- 56	J	Ash- 14
William	Lnc-339	Amos	Ran-160	J	Ash- 14
William	Sto-121	John	Mor- 55	R	Ash- 14
William	Rth- 92	Nathanl	Cas- 51	W	Ash- 14
Wm	Grn-140	William	Ran-160	Conly,Duncan	Cum-268
Zach	Mon- 34	Comford, Old	Pas-186	John	Cum-245
Collum,Betty	Bla- 12	Commander,Lukes	Pas-185	Neill	Cum-256
Colman,J	Glf-178	Miles	Pas-185	William	Wil-279
P	Ash- 14	Polly	Pas-185	Conn,Mrs.	Fra- 87
Coloway,Thomas	Bun- 79	Polly	Pas-185	Connail,David	Bla- 9
Colquehoun,Archd	Sam-155	Thomas	Pas-185	Connalley,George	Cas- 51
Colquest,Ransom	Roc- 12	Commins,Jasper	Ire-255	Thomas	Cas- 51
Colquhoun,John	Cum-259	Common,William	Ran-160	Connally,John	Ora-130
Lauchlan	Cum-250	Compton,Aqullia	Cas- 51	Conneil,Arthur	Bla- 3
Malcom	Cum-267	Erasmus	Ora-118	Connel,Avery	War-167
Colquhour,John	Cum-251	J	Ora-148	Benjaman	Mec- 28
Colsey,John	Rth- 94	Levi	Ora-126	Connell,John	Sto-127
Colson,James Jnr	Hrt-211	Norris	Ora-118	Connelly,Anne	Len-312
James Snr	Hrt-211	William	Cas- 51	Bryant	Bur-109
John	Har-130	Wm	Ora-124	Cullen	Dup- 5
Thos	Ans- 12	Comstock,Job Esqr	Wsh-219	Cyrus P	Bur-125
Colter,Hanson	Ora-129	Conada,Mary	Hal-101	Hugh	Bur-121
Elijah	Cab-146	Conaly,Elizabeth	Glf-187	Jno	Mec- 53
Coltson,Susannah	Nor- 63	Conburns,Azariah	Mec- 44	John	Bur-121
Colvard,John	Hay-194	Conder,Peter	Cab-143	John	Bur-129

-66-

Connelly,John	Dup- 3	Conrad,Leonard	Sto-151	Cook,Isaac	Sur-193
Mary	Bur-121	Peter	Sto-130	Isaac	Glf-170
Owen	Dup- 4	Peter	Sto- 99	J	Glf-173
Polly	War-178	Conry,Peggy	Cho-223	Jacob	Row- 81
William	Bur-108	Consler,Lewis	Mec- 41	Jacob	Bur-130
Willm	Fra- 83	Constable,William	Bur-114	Jacob	Way-243
Wm	Bur-129	Constant (sic)	Lnc-327	James	Ora-125
Conner,Ann	Hyd-222	Consway,John	Cur- 84	James	Sto- 92
Cornelius	Lnc-358	Conway,Gunby	Ons-103	James	Sto-121
Crawford	Prq-215	James	Jon-294	James	Sam-157
Danniel	Dup- 28	Jas	Mec- 26	James	Rth- 91
Danniel	Edg- 71	John	Bur-127	Jas	Mec- 23
David	Mon- 20	Conyers,Ephraim	Fra- 90	Jas Junr	Bla- 5
Dorothy	Hal-102	J	Bru-234	Jas Jun	Ora-125
Edward	Len-318	Cood,Timothy	Ran-161	Jane	Row- 73
Ephraim	Jon-295	Coohoon,William	Hyd-228	Jesse	Glf-173
George	Rth- 95	Cook,Mrs.	Mec- 28	Jno	Ora-171
George	Car-183	A	Glf-165	Jno	Mec- 32
Henry	Ire-257	Aaron	Wil-261	Capt John	Fra- 84
Jacob	Hyd-222	Abraham	Cha-197	John	Fra- 84
James	Glf-187	Abraham	Lnc-375	John	Glf-185
Jas	Mec- 39	Abram	Ire-253	John	Nor- 63
Jas Esqr	Mec- 24	Allen	Ire-254	John	Hal-100
Jesse	Len-318	Alexdr	Row- 47	John	Ire-238
Joel	Nor- 63	Amey	Fra- 89	John	Hal-101
John	Jon-295	Archd	Ora-124	John	Cha-210
John Junr	Jon-295	Austin	Hal-100	John	Sto-136
John Senr	Jon-295	Benjn Junr	Fra- 94	John	Sto-154
Owins	Jon-295	Benj Senr	Fra- 96	John	Ire-256
Rebecah	Jon-295	Betsey	Sur-193	John	Ora-119
Ruth	Ans- 18	Blanton	Mon- 31	John	Bla- 7
Thomas	Brt- 63	Brittain	Pas-186	John	Cum-235
Thos	Lnc-342	Charity	Prq-215	John	Cum-236
William	Ran-162	Chas	Ans- 24	John	Glf-166
William	Roc- 29	Chiner B	Sto-147	John	Way-242
William	Lnc-342	Christopher	Nor- 63	John Jr	Glf-185
William H	Jon-294	Clabourn	Grn-130	John Junr	Cum-251
Wm	Brt- 54	Cornelius	Roc- 4	John Sr	Sto-154
Connerly,William	Jon-295	Cornelius	Cha-204	John Senr	Cum-251
Conners,Darby	Bur-116	Cornelius	Glf-185	John Sr	Sto-113
Connerway,Wm	Hal-102	David	Ire-240	Jonathan	Ora-159
Connery,Tho	Bft- 27	David	Ora-124	Capt. Jones	Fra- 83
Connor,Andrew	Roc- 2	Diana	Bur-109	Jordan	Fra- 86
Cornelius	Roc- 34	E	Ora-139	Joseph	Glf-187
John	Ran-161	Ed	Ora-124	Joseph	Fra- 84
Michel	Rob-242	Edmund	Cum-249	Keziah	Sur-193
Conoway,Robert	Cas- 51	Elisha	Lnc-363	Lazarus	Hrt-211
Conrad,Daniel	Lnc-340	Eliza	Brt- 49	Lee	Nor- 64
Daniel	Sto-151	Mrs. Elizah	Fra- 96	Lucy	Fra- 97
Henry	Row- 41	Feby	Ans- 14	Marium	Way-243
Jacob	Sto-119	Geo	Row- 56	Martha	Hal-117
Jacob	Sto-143	Geo	Glf- 166	Martin	Ire-240
Jacob	Sto-130	Gilbert	Rob-218	Michael	Bur-107
Jacob	Sto-151	Harrison	Cha-216	Mire	Ora-125
Jacob	Sto-151	Henry	Ora-119	N	Glf-163
John	Sto-107	Henry	Bun- 92	Nathan	Fra- 88
John	Sto-152	Henry	Bun- 88	Nicholas	Mec- 41
John	Sto-143	Henry Sen	Ora-171	Orion	Sur-164
John	Sto-130	Hepsebeth	Pas-186	Patience	Bft- 37

Cook,Perry Green	Sam-152	Cooke,John	Dup- 20	Cooper,Joel	Glf-157		
Peter	Sur-178	Thomas	Car-170	John	Ons-107		
Pheby	Ans- 24	William	Brt- 62	John	Glf-182		
Philip	Lnc-328	William	Dup- 20	John	Tyr-212		
Philip	Sto-135	Wm	Grn-136	John	Nsh- 81		
Phillip	Cas- 51	Cooksey,Jessee	Bun- 95	John	Mon- 50		
Richard	Ire-250	Cooley,Edward	Sto-126	John	Nsh- 75		
Richard	Grn-136	G	Bla- 10	John	Ons- 98		
Richard D	Grn-137	John	Fra- 81	John	Cas- 52		
Robert	Sam-155	Cooly,Edward	Fra- 95	John	Dup- 11		
Robt	Mec- 50	Stephen	Fra- 93	John	Hrt-213		
Roland	Grn-125	Stephen	Fra- 80	John Senr	Per-138		
Rolly	Fra- 77	Coombs,John	Way-252	Jonathan	Row- 46		
Shim Senr	Grn-130	Coomer,Berry	Sto-122	Jonathan	Brt- 45		
Shimuel Junr	Fra- 97	Berry	Sto- 93	Jonathan	Cum-247		
Stephen	Mec- 42	John	Sto- 93	Jonathan	Sam-156		
Stephen	Mec- 42	John	Sto-122	Joseph	Mon- 50		
Stephen	Way-243	Coon,Widow	Lnc-328	Joseph	Tyr-213		
Stephen Jr	Way-242	John	Rth- 94	Lorton	Mar- 10		
Tempy	Fra- 96	Coonce,Abraham	Ons-101	Mark	Nsh- 81		
Thomas	Wil-262	Henry	Row- 67	Matthew	Rch-201		
Thomas	Ire-240	Peter	Row- 67	Michael	Roc- 18		
Thomas	Hal-102	Coone,Jacob	Row- 66	Nehemia	Row- 53		
Thomas	Grn-143	Coop,Wm Docktry	Rob-226	Nelly	Bur-114		
Thomas	Sto-156	Coopening,Albert	Bur-113	R	Ash- 8		
Thomas	Way-243	Cooper,A	Mon- 50	Rachel	Sur-188		
Thos	Mec- 50	Adam	Bun- 80	Reuben	Rth- 92		
Thos	Sam-157	Allen	Cas- 51	Robert	Fra- 79		
Thos	Glf-170	Archd Buie	Cum-269	S	Cam-160		
William	Glf-186	Benj	Cur- 90	S	Cam-163		
William	Row- 74	Benjn	Nsh- 75	Saml	Row- 55		
William	Sto-114	Benjn	Dup- 10	Sarah	Pit-235		
William	Sto-156	C	Ora-135	Sollomon	Edg- 42		
William	Sur-185	Cader	Brt- 45	Stephen	Row- 56		
William	Sur-188	Coor	Sam-156	Susana	Rth- 95		
William	Sur-168	David	Row- 73	Thomas	Row- 69		
William H	Sur-177	David	Mar- 4	William	Row- 68		
William	Way-244	Dorcas	Tyr-207	William	Hrt-208		
William	Cas- 51	Edward	Nsh- 76	William	Sur-162		
William	Rth- 93	Elias	Sam-158	William	Rch-199		
William P	Fra- 84	Eliz	Nsh- 82	William	Rth- 92		
William Sr	Row- 74	Fleet	Sam-156	Willie	Fra- 90		
Willm	Fra- 89	George	Rth- 94	Wm	Ora-119		
Wm	Grn-130	George	Joh-287	Wm	Mec- 25		
Wm	Cum-240	George	Nsh- 81	Wm	Pit-241		
Wm	Cha-210	Hardy	Way-251	Wm	Nsh- 80		
Wm	Mon- 24	Henry	Mar- 10	Willouby	Cur- 87		
Wm	Cha-200	Isaac	Mon- 50	Wilson	Cum-265		
Wm	Brt- 44	Isham	Nsh- 83	Coopper,Benjn	Ran-161		
Wm	Mec- 51	J	Glf-172	James	Ran-162		
Wm	Ora-116	Jacob	Mon- 50	Jeremiah	Ran-160		
Cooke,Dempsey	Brt- 62	Jacob	Sam-156	Jeremiah	Ran-163		
Elisha	Brt- 62	James	Sto-125	Sterling	Ran-160		
Ephraim	Rth- 94	James	Mar- 10	Coor,Harphrey	Way-235		
Ephraim	Rth- 94	James	Rth- 94	Hopton	Way-235		
Henry	Dup- 17	Jesse	Mar- 8	Henry	Way-237		
Hugh	Rth- 92	Jles	Hal-100	Jemijah	Sam-161		
Isaac	Bur-115	Joel	Rob-239	Stephen	Way-235		
James	Rth- 92	Joel	Brt- 56	Thomas Sr	Way-234		

Coor,William	Way-234	Coppage,Charles	Fra- 95	Corn,Philip	Row- 87
Coots,Jas	Glf-175	Chas	Ans- 6	Cornealious,John	Sto-130
Cope,Andrew	Row- 70	Jesse	Fra- 98	Cornealous,Jerimah	Sot-128
Isabel	Bur-114	Moses	Ans- 17	Robert	Sto-128
Jacob	Row- 81	William	Prq-215	Cornelison,John	Row- 84
John	Row- 60	Willm	Fra- 86	John	Ran-159
John	Row- 68	Wilmoth	Edg- 65	Cornelius,Benj	Lnc-358
John	Fra- 89	Copper,John	Pas-185	Cornell,James	Row- 60
Philip	Row- 66	Micajah	Pas-185	Cornelus,J	Ash- 3
Rachel	Rob-232	Thos	Pas-185	Corner,Henry	Lnc-355
Samuel	Rch-213	Coppis,Christo	Pas-185	Cornet,Ned	Pas-186
Thomas	Fra- 96	Copsin,John	Ran-162	Cornish,William	Edg- 66
Copeland,David	Gat-113	Copy,C	Glf-173	Cornwall,Benjn	Nor- 63
David	Cha-211	Zebelon	Glf-153	Edward	Sur-190
Dempsey	Nor- 63	Coram,Champ	Roc- 10	Francis	Roc- 30
Elisha	Hrt-217	Eli	Roc- 11	Cornwell,Jesse	Hay-194
Elizabeth	Cha-211	Henry	Cab-136	Corothers,James	Glf-184
Henry	Prq-215	Richard	Roc- 12	Corpage,Isaac	Mon- 38
Holliwill	Hrt-216	William	Roc- 10	Corpening,Jacob	Bur-124
Hugh	Ire-248	Corban,Nancy	Hal-101	Corpensey,Abram	Bur-122
Iry	Nor- 63	Corbet,Elias	Way-234	Corpinging,John	Bur-130
Isaac	Sur-164	James	Brt- 53	Corprew,George	Wsh-225
James	Hrt-215	John	Ons- 98	Jas	Bft- 19
James	Ire-266	Joshua	Way-233	John	Wsh-225
Jas	Rob-234	Josiah	Way-248	Malachi	Wsh-225
Jas	Cho-228	Josiah	Way-254	Mary	Bft- 20
Jesse	Prq-215	Meradith	Rch-208	Samuel	Wsh-226
John	Sur-166	William	Ons-108	Correck,John	Row- 83
John	Nor- 63	Corbett,Jas	Ora-134	Correl,Edward	Ran-160
John	Cha-199	Samuel	Way-248	Jacob	Row- 70
Mark	Cha-210	Corbit,Bryant	Pit-253	Correll,John	Row- 68
Peggey	Ora-128	Dempsey	Pit-253	Corril,Marian	Rth- 93
Reuben	Lnc-336	Hardee	Pit-253	Corsey,John	Rth- 95
Sarah	Lnc-342	John	Pit-253	Corsy,Thos	Glf-170
Sarah	Cho-227	Richard	Rch-208	Cortner,Adam	Lnc-341
Thomas	Mar- 6	Winifred	Edg- 52	David	Lnc-332
Thos	Hrt-206	Corbitt,J	Col- 20	David	Lnc-341
Thos	Cho-227	J	Col- 20	Geo	Glf-177
William	Nor- 63	Lewis	Cas- 51	Jacob	Lnc-341
William	Row- 76	Nicholas	Edg- 52	John	Lnc-332
Coplelen,Kader	Hal-101	Cord,W	Col- 16	Mat	Glf-178
Copelin,Chas Jr	Joh-272	Corder,Archabald	Sur-185	Michl	Lnc-341
Charles Senr	Joh-272	Baley	Sur-178	Thos	Lnc-332
J	Glf-178	Joseph	Sur-162	Thos	Lnc-332
S	Bru-234	Cording,Hosea	Hyd-222	Coruthers,Sam	Ora-130
Copey,N	Glf-172	Jacob	Bft- 19	Coryer,David	Row- 70
Copland,Easter	Gat-110	Joseph	Hyd-212	Coryins,Elizabeth	Cha-201
Henry	Gat-115	William	Hyd-253	Cosan,Benjn	Ran-162
Jacob	Way-244	William	Hyd-223	Cosand,Benjamin	Prq-215
James	Gat-107	Core,Arthur	Cum-265	Gabriel	Prq-215
Cople,Philip	Row- 42	Corey,Joseph	Pas-185	John	Prq-215
Copley,Geo	Ora-118	Martin	Mar-10	Cosby,James	Ora-168
George	Ora-150	Simon	Mar- 6	Tho	Bur-131
Jno	Ora-149	Winefred	Mar- 6	Wm	Grn-119
Jno Jr	Ora-149	Woollard	Mar- 9	Coshatt,John Jr	Cha-205
Tho	Ora-165	Corgan,Patrick	Pas-186	Cosner,Henry	Sto-133
Coplin,Jas	Ans- 27	Cork,Thomas	Roc- 29	Henry	Sto-101
Wm	Mor- 61	Cormack,Wm	Mon- 23	John	Sto-102
Coppage,Chales	Fra-100	Corn,Adam	Bun- 95	John	Sto-102

Cosoon,Kezia	Pas-185	Cotton,Roderick	Edg- 55	Covell,Augustine	Car-185
Cosort,Thomas	Per-136	Rocrick	Cha-202	Lydia	Hyd-233
Cossett,John	Glf-156	Saml	Cho-224	Coventon,John	Rth- 92
Costam,George	Glf-155	Samuel	Edg- 59	Richard	Rth- 94
Costen,Isaac	Gat-106	Seth	Cha-195	William	Rth- 93
Isaac	Dup- 31	Solomon	War-180	Cover,Hezekiah	Lnc-329
James	Dup- 31	Spencer	Edg- 40	Covey,Matthew	Roc- 17
James	Dup- 22	Starky	Fra- 97	Covinington,Wm	Sto-106
James	Gat-106	Whitmil	Hal-101	Covington,Baseley	Rch-209
James	Gat-107	Wm	Cha-191	Benjamin	Rch-197
Jas	Mec- 37	Cottrain,J	Glf-172	Benjamin	Rch-210
Jno	Mec- 24	James	Mar- 8	Benjamin	Rch-208
Costle,Frederick B	Row- 53	John	Mar- 9	Benjamin H	Rch-197
Costner,Peter	Lnc-345	Cottral,Thomas	Cas- 52	James	Rch-213
Coston,Ahab	Ons-108	Cottrell,John	Ire-243	John	Roc- 8
James	Ons- 97	William	Roc- 6	John	Rch-207
John	Ons-104	Couburn,Walter	Mec- 40	Josiah	Rth- 96
Mathew	Ons-108	Couch,Edwd	Ora-142	Mattheq	Rch-208
Robert	Ons-103	Isaac	Ora-151	Samuel	Rch-210
Stephen	Ons-108	J	Ash- 7	Samuel	Rch-201
Stephen Junr	Ons-108	J	Ash- 8	Samuel	Rch-203
Thomas	Ons-108	M	Glf-163	Sarah	Cas- 51
Costrill,William	Edg- 50	S	Ora-157	Sarah	Rch-210
Cotanch,Wills	Mar- 15	Sam	Ora-117	William	Rch-196
Cotaunch,Mchl	Bft- 33	Saml	Glf-164	William	Rch-209
Cotes,Willie	Row- 51	Saml	Ora-151	William	Sto-140
Coth,Edward	Rth- 96	Couland,Jonathan	Brt- 52	Covy,L	Glf-159
Cothen,Wm	Grn-143	Coulston,John	Bft- 36	Cowan,Alexander	Row- 73
Cotner,David	Ora-172	Coulter,Hannah	Rch-206	Benjn	Row- 72
Peter	Ora-133	Jesse	Rch-206	Benjn	Row- 73
R	Ora-172	Martin	Lnc-375	David	Row- 73
Rosa	Ora-133	Phillip	Lnc-375	David	Row- 72
Cotrell,Mark	Grn-119	William	Rch-206	David	Mec- 35
Saml	Grn-135	Coun,Blackburn	Bur-109	Henry	Row- 72
Thomas	Wil-274	Council,David	Hal-100	James	Row- 75
William	Wil-282	Dicy	Edg- 54	James	Lnc-352
Cotten,Temperance	Nor- 63	Eliz	Nsh- 74	Jeney	Row- 74
Cotter,Timothy	Pas-184	Robt	Cha-201	John	Row- 74
Cottingim,Jew Lamar	Bun- 93	Willie	Edg- 53	John	Row- 74
Cottle,Abner	Dup- 30	Councill,Ann	Mar- 16	John	Bla- 4
Jonah	Dup- 31	Councilmen,Mary	Ora-171	John Senr	Row- 72
Josiah	Cha-200	Counsel,Charles	Rob-223	Joseph	Bur-125
Robert	Dup- 32	Charles Senr	Rob-224	Joseph	Row- 74
Thomas	Dup- 32	Isham	Rob-223	Richard	Lnc-366
Cotton,Arthur	Hrt-216	John	Rob-223	Robert	Row- 76
Barnaby	Way-250	Michel	Rob-223	Samuel	Row- 75
Elijah	Way-250	Willis	Rob-223	Sarah	Row- 74
Ephraum	Way-249	Coupee,Francis	Row- 89	Sollomon	Edg- 71
Frederick	Edg- 59	Coupland,John	Ora-170	Stephen	Ire-266
Gabriel	Cha-195	Couple,Peter	Cab-146	Thomas Jr	Row- 74
Henry	Edg- 42	Court,James	Wsh-223	Thomas Senr	Row- 71
Isom	Way-250	Courtney,Jas	Lnc-330	Thomas L	Row- 89
Jesse	Cum-259	John	Row- 74	William (B L)	Row- 74
John	Way-249	John C	Grn-132	William	Ire-250
John	Sam-158	Courtny,J	Ora-157	Wm G S	Row- 72
John	Edg- 47	Cousins,Grief free man of		Cowand,David	Hrt-216
Lewis	Brt- 56	colour	Ran-187	Coward,Benjamin	Rth- 94
Mary	Edg- 60	Coutch,Thos	Ora-142	Benjamin	Rth- 94
Micajah T	Way-177	Coval,Jacob	Rth- 92	Elizabeth	Cha-214

Name	Loc	Name	Loc	Name	Loc	Name	Loc
Coward,James	Rth- 94	Cox,Eli		Ons-104	Cox,Jonathan		Cur- 92
James	Rth- 94	Eli Junr		Ons-101	Joseph		Pit-236
James Sr	Rth- 93	Elijah		Lnc-334	Joseph		Sto-147
Jeremiah	Bur-102	Elisha		Lnc-332	Joseph		Edg- 48
John	Jon-295	Elizth		Hyd-222	Joseph		Sto-110
John	Roc- 26	Ezekiel		Brt- 54	Joseph		Ran-160
Peter	Rth- 95	Ferby		Rob-235	Joseph Jr		Prq-216
Cosdan,John	Ire-262	Fleet		Lnc-366	Joseph Sr		Prq-215
Cowden,James	Bur-110	Geo		Mor- 66	Joshua		Ran-159
Cowel,B	Bru-234	George		Mec- 55	Joshua Jnr		Sto-121
Cowell,Berey	Cur- 91	George		Lnc-366	Joshua Jnr		Sto- 92
Bernard	Edg- 47	George		Brt- 54	Joshua Ser		Sto- 92
Henry	Bft- 19	Gilbert		Rob-235	Joshua Ser		Sto-121
James	Cur- 91	Hannah		Ons-104	Josiah		Way-234
William	Cur- 86	Hardy		Ons- 98	Josiah		Ons- 95
Wm	Bft- 19	Harmon		Rob-233	Kader		Ons- 99
Cowen,E	Glf-153	Harmon		Len-315	Lancaster		Way-242
Elisha	Glf-154	Henry		Mor- 67	Levi		Rob-233
George	Brt- 61	Henry		Glf-152	Lucey		Lnc-366
John	Brt- 60	Hermon		Cha-214	Lucy		Wil-284
Wm	Brt- 53	Holden		Mor- 57	Mariam		Cho-222
Cowey,Charles	Mar- 7	Isaac		Ran-161	Marm		Len-310
Cowin,Adam	Bun- 74	Isaac		Cha-194	Martha		War-177
David	Mec- 28	Isaiah		Sur-174	Mary		Ons-104
Cowper,Caleb	Prq-215	Isham		Rob-235	Mathew		Bur-130
Cox,A	Ash- 7	Isuai		Bur-116	Merril		Mor- 66
Aaron	Pit-238	J		Ash- 7	Micjah		Way-234
Aaron	Wil-278	J		Ash- 3	Mildred		Sto- 94
Aaron	Jon-295	Jacob		Pas-185	Mildred		Sto-123
Abel	Ran-159	Jacob		Ran-161	Moses		Ora-121
Abner	Way-234	Jame		Sto-113	Moses Junr		Jon-294
Abner	Jon-295	James		Row- 85	Moses Senr		Jon-294
Abner	Ran-161	James		Jon-295	Nathaniel		Ran-160
Abraham	Pit-236	James		Sto-113	Odom		Ans- 29
Andrew	Jon-294	James		Sto-154	Peggy		Cho-220
Arey	Cur- 88	James		Len-314	Peregrine		Len-315
Aron	Ons-104	Jas		Rob-235	Pheby		Len-322
Barbara	Bur-116	Jane		Sto-153	Philip		Roc- 12
Benj	Len-314	Jarvas		Cur- 90	Reuben		Wil-278
Benjamin	Pit-236	Jason		Ans- 30	Richard		Hyd-227
Betsy	Cas- 51	Jesse		Rob-233	Richd		Way-233
Boling	Ora-112	Jesse		Row- 57	Risley		Cha-214
Budey	Cur- 92	Jesse		Ans- 31	Robert		Lnc-332
Caleb	Glf-182	Jessey		Cur- 84	Saley		Cur- 90
Caleb	Ran-160	Joel		Nor- 63	Saml		Mec- 54
Caleb	Cur- 90	Jno		Ans- 12	Samuel		Dup- 20
Canaan	Bft- 33	John		Rob-242	Sarah		Hal-102
Charles	Ons-104	John		Ons-104	Sarah		Len-315
Charles	Jon-294	John		Lnc-366	Shadk		Bft- 20
Chas	Ran-161	John		Way-236	Simon		Rob-233
D	Cam-158	John		Ire-262	Simon		Rob-233
Daniel	Pit-251	John		Len-323	Smithon		Way-242
Danl	Bft- 33	John		Cab-146	Solomon		Ran-159
Danl	Ran-162	John		Bft- 30	Stephen Jr		Ran-159
David	Bur-114	John		Bft- 36	Susanna		Way-242
Davise	Cur- 90	John		Brt- 55	Thena		Hal-101
Devenport	Cum-252	John		Cur- 90	Tho		Bft- 30
Edmond	Cha-213	John		Ran-161	Thomas		Mor- 67
Edwd	Cur- 90	John W		Ran-161	Thomas		Wil-284

Name	Ref	Name	Ref	Name	Ref	Name	Ref
Cox,Thomas	Ran-159	Crafford,William	Gat-115	Crandell,Elijah	Car-180		
Thomas	Way-242	Craford,Henry	Gat-116	Carne,Enoch	Tyr-205		
Thomas	Row- 61	Jas	Mec- 39	James	Wil-283		
Thomas Dr	Ran-161	William	Gat-113	John	Wil-283		
Thomas Junr	Row- 61	Craft,Catherine	Jon-295	Thomas	Tyr-205		
Thos	Cur- 90	Charlott	Glf-161	William	Wil-283		
William	Nor- 63	Henry	Mar- 7	Craner,Jos	Glf-182		
William	Ons-102	John	Sur-193	Moses	Glf-187		
William	Ran-160	John	Glf-161	Cranford,Alexr	Ran-162		
William	Way-233	Matthew	Joh-277	John	Mon- 18		
William	Sur-192	Michl	Lnc-337	John	Ran-163		
William	Jon-294	Presly	Sur-168	Ked	Ran-162		
William of B	Ran-162	Presly	Ire-252	Lear	Ran-162		
William Jr	Ran-160	Sally	Joh-290	Leonard	Mon- 18		
William Jnr	Ran-162	Saml	Grn-148	Nathen	Ran-162		
Wm	Len-315	Crafton,Matthew	Pit-237	Saml	Ran-159		
Wm	Mor- 58	Crage,Capt	Mec- 33	Sauney	Ran-163		
Winefred	Way-242	Adam	Rob-226	William	Ran-162		
Zachariah	Cho-203	Eubella	Mec- 30	Crank,James	Cur- 87		
Coxe,David Senr	Bur-115	Henry	Wil-274	Crankfield,Jonathan	Row- 63		
William	Bur-116	Hugh	Wil-285	Crasey,John	Rth- 95		
Coxey,William	Rth- 95	Jas D	Mec- 33	Crathc,Wm	Brt- 59		
Coxk,John	Pas-186	Margaret	Ire-249	Craton,Jacob	Row- 54		
Coyl,John	Bur-119	Moses	Mec- 30	Jas	Cab-137		
Coziah,Lodwick	Sur-190	Roger	Ran-161	Thomas	Wil-278		
William	Sur-191	Sarah	Wil-285	Wm	Cha-204		
Cozle,James	Bun- 82	Cragg,Elisha	Bur-126	Crause,Samuel	Row- 57		
Crab,Benjn	Joh-283	Isachiah	Bur-103	Craven,Danl	Ran-159		
James	Cur- 89	Pleasant	Bur-111	Elizabeth	Ran-162		
Crabb,James	Hal- 99	Rachd	Ora-168	Henry	Ran-161		
Jared	Wil-270	Samuel	Bur-126	Henry Jr	Ran-162		
Ozborn	Ire-255	Theodus	Ons-100	Jacob	Ran-162		
Crabtee,Abraham	Ora-138	W	Bru-236	John	Ran-160		
Andrew	Ora-168	Crago,John	Lnc-342	John Jr	Ran-162		
Benjamin	Wil-272	Craig,Abreham	Ora-143	Joshua	Ran-161		
Eliz	Ora-177	Alex	Ora-114	Joshua	Ran-160		
F	Ora-156	Alexdr	Ora-151	Peter Snr	Ran-162		
Haynes	Ora-130	Archabald	Row- 77	Robert	Ran-160		
James	Ora-165	David	Row- 76	Saml	Ran-160		
James Jr	Ora-168	Isaac	Ora-158	Samuel	Ran-162		
John	Ora-943	James Jr	Ora-151	Sarah	Ran-161		
Richd	Ora-165	Jas J	Ora-122	Sarah of T	Ran-162		
Saml	Ora-168	Jas Sen	Ora-158	Solomon	Ran-162		
Tho	Ora-177	Jno Esq	Ora-117	Thomas	Cha-215		
Wm	Ora-168	Jno Sen	Ora-143	Thomas	Ran-162		
Wm Jr	Ora-168	Mary	Ora-158	Craver,Jacob	Row- 37		
Cracker,William	Joh-282	Sam Jr	Ora-158	Jacob	Row- 83		
Craddock,Thos	Sam-154	Thomas	Orw- 76	Joel	Row- 85		
Cradel,Jas	Hyd-231	Thomas	Bun- 74	John	Row- 50		
Craderick,Joseph	Tyr-211	Wm	Ora-123	Michl	Row- 55		
Cradle,Frances	Hyd-231	Wm	Ora-143	Philip	Row- 48		
Cradlebough,Thos	Row- 47	Cragg,Mary	Hyd-232	Phillip	Row- 38		
Cradock,Joh Sr	Tyr-211	Craiglow,William	Row- 70	William	Row- 83		
Mary	Tyr-212	Crain,Geo	Glf-181	Cravy,Hugh	Cum-260		
Simon	Tyr-212	John	Bun- 92	Crawford,Adam	Roc- 4		
Stephen	Tyr-212	William	Rth- 96	Ann	Cum-239		
Willm	Tyr-211	Craker,L	Bru-234	Archd	Rob-242		
Crafford,John	Bun- 90	Cranay,Andrew	Sto-102	Arthur	Way-249		
Washington	Bun- 90	Cranboc,Elisha	Rob-219	Arthur Sr	Way-249		

Name	Ref	Name	Ref	Name	Ref
Crawford,Charles D	Hyd-234	Creakmon,Tim	Nsh- 83	Cretisfieser,Henry	Row- 56
David	Cab-136	Creamer,Danl	Bft- 28	Crew,Andrew	Nor- 63
David	Ire-237	Jas	Bft- 28	Elisha	Nor- 63
David	Ans- 17	Creas,Phillip	Cab-145	Henry	Nor- 64
Duncan	Rob-243	Creasman,Abraham	Bun- 97	Isaac	Nor- 63
Francis	Rth- 93	Adam	Bun- 83	Jacob	Nor- 63
George	Hay-194	Cowin	Bun- 83	Josiah	Ire-269
Henry	Way-237	Creath,Samuel	War-180	Crews,Ashley	Sto-150
James	Ire-240	Creaton,Wm	Cab-147	Caleb	Grn-143
Jas Sn	Ora-113	Crecy,William	Per-215	David	Sto-132
Jno	Ora-112	Creech,Benj	Len-321	David Ser	Sto-132
John	Rth- 92	Benjn	Dup- 26	David Ser	Sto-101
John	Rth- 93	Cleveland	Cum-241	Gideon Jr	Grn-148
John	Rch-195	Edward	Len-313	Gideon Sr	Grn-148
John	Pit-256	Ezekiel	Len-312	Haridg Junr	Per-136
John	Dup- 10	Ezekiel	Dup- 26	James Ser	Sto-110
John	Ire-237	Jno	Len-322	James Ser	Sto-148
Jos	Cab-136	John	Len-322	Joseph	Sto-133
M	Row- 82	William	Dup- 26	Joseph	Rch-213
Michael	Ans- 31	Creecy,Fredk	Cho-224	Lewis	Grn-148
Michael	Ans- 31	Joseph	Cho-224	Reuben	Sto-111
Neill	Rob-223	Joshua S	Cho-224	Thomas	Sto-134
Peter	Roc- 29	Leml	Cho-224	Thomas Ser	Sto-150
Richd F	Ans- 17	Nathan	Cho-224	Thomas Ser	Sto-112
Robt	Way-233	Thos	Prq-215	William	Sto-148
Sam	Ora-116	Creed,Bartlett	Sur-174	Crezine,Alex	Cab-139
Samuel	Rth- 92	Bennet	Sur-179	Crezine,Alex	Cab-139
Thomas	Way-240	Bennet Ju	Sur-179	Geo	Cab-146
Thomas	Rch-195	Colby	Sur-163	John	Cab-146
Thomas	Ire-255	Colby Ju	Sur-179	John	Cab-146
Thomas	Sur-189	Cornelious	Ons-104	Saml	Cab-146
Thos	Mon- 25	John	Sur-181	Cribb,A	Col- 20
Washington	Rth- 94	Robert	Sur-179	J	Col- 20
Washington	Rth- 95	Creekeman,Forasnan	Cur- 91	L	Col- 20
Washington	Rth- 94	Creekmer,David	Nsh- 86	Shadk	Bla- 12
William	Cum-253	Creekmon,Batchelor	Nsh- 85	T	Col- 21
William	Pit-261	Creekmore,Moses	Cur- 88	Cricher,John	Grn-145
William	Pas-184	Samuel	Cur- 88	Crickmore,Caleb	Hal-101
Crawfort,Archd	Rob-241	Creekner,Robert	Nsh- 85	William	Hal-101
Crawfurd,C D	Bft- 31	Creel,Charles	Len-136	Crider,Barnabas	Row- 90
Crawley,Benjamin	Hal-100	D	Per-141	C	Ash- 8
Bird	Hal-100	Laz	Len-316	C	Ash- 7
David Sr	Hal-101	Nathan	Len-316	Henry	Roc- 14
Green	Hal-100	Rachel	Len-312	Jacob	Row- 69
Thomas	Sur-178	Solomon	Rob-220	Jacob	Bur-126
Crawmer,Gattlich	Sto- 91	Crenshaw,David	Mec- 32	Leonrd	Row- 88
Gottlieb	Sto-120	Henry	Mec- 31	Peter	Row- 89
Crawsett,Wm	Ora-173	Little B	Mec- 49	Philip	Row- 68
Cray,Edward	Bun- 91	Cresain,Levy	Row- 74	Cridle,Daniel	Hyd-231
Hannah	Bun- 81	Cresemore,Henry	Lnc-370	John	Hyd-231
Crayter,John	Cha-197	Henry	Lnc-368	Joseph	Hyd-231
Creach,Ezekiel	Joh-277	Creson,Joshua	Sur-178	William	Hyd-231
Jessey	Joh-280	Cress,Daniel	Row- 89	Crier,Sarah	Nor- 63
Joshua	Joh-280	Crestinbery,Jas	Mec- 48	Criger,Frederick	Sto-127
Joshua Jr	Joh-280	Nicholas	Mec- 48	Crigers,Thomas	Sto-102
Lewis	Joh-280	Crestinberry,Moses	Mec- 48	Crigers,Thomas	Sto-102
Cread,Mary	Cur- 90	Creswell,James	Ire-259	Criles,John	Lnc-355
Sales	Cur- 81	Robert	Ire-256	Crinfield,William	Sur-174
Creaf,Isaac	Row- 60	Sally	Ire-257	Criscow,Geo	Mon-46

Criscow,Jno	Mon- 47	Cronister,Jas	Lnc-363	Crossman,Jonah	Bft- 39		
Wm	Mon- 47	Phillip	Lnc-363	Crosswhite,Henry	Sto-130		
Crise,Jonathan	Cur- 85	Crony,Meriam	Jon-295	Crotsen,David	Row- 78		
Crisel,Jeremiah	Wil-264	Crook,Comfort	Bun- 90	Crotser,Jacob	Row- 86		
Crisman,Geo	Sto-127	Dudley	Sur-162	Crotz,Jacob	Row- 41		
George	Sto- 97	James	Sto-131	Crouch,Jacob	Wil-278		
Crisp,Bray	Bun- 75	James	Sto-138	John	Wil-273		
Charles	Pit-245	Jeremiah	Sto-144	John Junr	Rch-201		
Chisly	Bur-112	John	Rth- 93	John Senr	Rch-201		
Franciss	Mar- 13	Crooks,Andrew	Rth- 95	Samuel	Rch-201		
Isaac	Bun- 73	Jeremiah	Sto-108	Thos	Glf-175		
Jessee	Edg- 53	Croom,Argent	Len-312	Wm	Ora-176		
Joel	Bur-111	Charles	Way-251	Crouchfield,John	Glf-186		
John	Cas- 51	Jesse Sr	Way-251	Crouder,Elizabeth	Per-150		
Micajah	Bur-129	Joshua	Len-317	Crouner,Jacob	Cab-142		
Present	Edg- 53	Major	Len-317	Crous,A	Ash- 14		
Singleton	Pit-245	Major	Way-251	H	Ash- 14		
Spicers	Edg- 53	Mary	Len-311	Crouse,Benj	Lnc-377		
Thomas	Pit-245	Nancy	Way-237	George	Wil-259		
Thomas	Cas- 51	Richd G	Len-316	J	Ash- 14		
William	Edg- 52	Wm	Len-323	John Esq	Lnc-334		
William	Bur-127	Crooms,Abraham	Len-312	Crow,Abraham	Rth- 93		
Criss,Jacob	Cab-141	Crosby,William	Row- 71	Anna	Way-247		
Crisson,Andrew	Bun- 78	Crosemore,John	Bur-110	Francis	Bun- 95		
Crisswell,William	Row- 81	Croser,Rosena	Row- 78	James	Bun- 72		
Cristle,George	Lnc-345	Croset,Jane	Cas- 51	Jessee	Cha-210		
Cristoper, Nancy	Glf-168	Crosewhite,William	Sto- 99	John	Rth- 92		
Criswell,A	Ora-154	Crosine,Eli	Lnc-355	John	Cha-206		
Jno	Ora-123	Cross,Abraham	Lnc-355	John	Bun- 88		
Jno	Ora-122	Abraham	Gat-108	John H	Lnc-336		
Critchfield,John	Sur-178	Asel	Wil-267	Jonathan	Bun- 72		
William	Sur-197	Benj	Ora-162	Levi	Bun- 72		
Crites,Jacob	Lnc-363	Benjn	Gat-115	Reuben	Cha-214		
Peter Jr	Lnc-363	Charles	Sto-149	Richard	Lnc-339		
Peter Senr	Lnc-363	Christena	Row- 86	Robert	Lnc-337		
Crittenden,Henry decd		David	Gat-115	Thomas	Lnc-339		
(col)	Nor- 67	David	Row- 87	Crowal,Jno	Mec- 29		
Crocker,Bailey	Fra- 77	David	Row- 85	Crowder,Abner	Mon- 25		
Benjn	Fra- 94	David	Row- 86	Bartlet	Rth- 95		
Croe,Enoch	Ran-162	Elijah	Bun- 81	Charles G	Sto-146		
James	Ran-162	George	Row- 86	Isaac	Roc- 27		
Joshua	Ran-162	Hanah	Row- 87	J	Mon- 37		
Reuben	Ran-162	Hanah	Row- 86	James	Bun- 90		
Croel,Samuel	Hal-100	Hardy	Gat-115	Jarrett	Rth- 93		
Croft,Nathan	Sto-107	James Sen	Edg- 58	John	Roc- 30		
Nathan	Sto-143	Jas	Bft- 32	John	Mon- 25		
Croll,Widow	Mec- 33	John	Gat-115	Mary	Bun- 93		
Crom,John	Sto-152	John	Bur-131	Neal	Grn-128		
Cromarty,Alex	Bla- 12	John	Gat-107	Peter	Cas- 51		
Jas	Bla- 12	Joseph	Bun- 82	Pleasant	Roc- 30		
P	Bla- 12	Joseph Senr	Bun- 82	Randolph	Nor- 63		
Cromwell,Elisha	Edg- 71	Miles	Hal-100	Robert	Rth- 95		
John	Bun- 86	Parish	Cha-193	William	Nor- 63		
Peggy	Edg- 71	Peter	Row- 86	William	Rth- 93		
Cronan,James	Bun- 85	R. Jessee	Nor- 63	William Jr	Rth- 93		
Cronce,Daniel	Row- 84	Riddick	Gat-116	Wm	Mon- 25		
John	Row- 84	Stephen	Edg- 58	Crowel,Benj	Hal-101		
Croner,Christian	Cab-142	Taylor	Gat-113	Charles	Mec- 46		
Cronister,Daniel	Lnc-363	Crossins,Robert	Bur-119	Edward	Hal-100		

Crowel,George	Mec- 44	Crumpler,Micajah	Sam-163	Culbertson,William	Cas- 51
James	Nsh- 87	Redman	Sam-162	Culbirth,Alexr	Sam-153
Jno	Mec- 30	West	Joh-285	Archd	Sam-153
Jno	Mec- 44	West	Nsh- 90	Cornelia	Sam-153
John	Nsh- 88	West	Nsh- 87	Daniel	Sam-153
Peter	Mec- 30	William	Joh-286	Neil	Sam-157
Peter	Row- 86	Crumplin,Benj	Nsh- 92	Culbreath,John	Cum-266
Samuel	Row- 69	Crumpton,Hezekiah	Wil-275	Lauchlan	Cum-250
Simon	Mec- 46	John	Dup- 18	Neill	Cum-250
Wm	Mec- 44	Crumwell,Andw	Cab-143	Peter	Cum-265
Crowell,Geo	Mon- 43	John	Cab-143	Culbreth,Archd	Rob-228
John	Mon- 44	Crunkelton,Jno	Lnc-358	David	Cum-264
Moses	Mon- 43	Crunkilton,Jno	Lnc-363	Culchalow,James	Hrt-211
Wm	Mon- 44	Cruse,Adam	Cab-145	Culipher,-----	Tyr-209
Crows,Andrew	Sto-131	Andw	Cab-145	Cull,William	Dup- 22
David	Sto-100	Andw	Cab-146	Cullendon,Wm	Mon- 37
John	Sto-100	Benjamin	Per-140	Culler,John	Sto-130
John	Sto-107	Hardy	Per-138	Cullifer,Abraham	Brt- 45
John	Sto-132	Henry	Cab-145	Capt Nathl	Brt- 45
John	Sto-143	Stephen	Per-140	Nathl Jun	Brt- 45
John Jur	Sto-153	Tobias	Cab-145	Nathl Sen	Brt- 45
Crowson,Elisha	Mon- 23	Cruskull,John	Cha-203	Pathenia	Hyd-226
J	Col- 18	Crutchfield,Anderson		Thomas	Brt- 47
James	Rch-208		Cha-199	Thomas	Brt- 49
John	Rch-196	Elizabeth	Cha-208	Cullins,Jacob	Cho-228
R	Col- 18	M	Ora-143	Nathan	Gat-114
William	Rch-211	Milley	Cha-198	Cullum,Jeremiah	Hal-101
Crud,Matthew	Wil-262	Richard	Ons-102	Jesse	Hal-101
Cruise,H	Glf-164	Wm	Ora-114	Matthew	Hal-117
Peter	Row- 67	Thomas	Cha-198	Thomas	Row- 74
Crum,David	Bun- 79	Wm	Cha-213	William	Hal-100
Godfrey	Row- 84	Crutchlon,James	Bur-130	William Senr	Hal-100
John	Brt- 52	Cruteshfuts,Stapleton		Cullumber,Barban	Wil-265
Cruman,J	Glf-178		Cha-203	Cully,Lucretia	Car-181
Crumbey,Archd	Ans- 16	Cruthers,James	Ran-162	Philip	Car-181
Isaac A	Ans- 18	John	Ran-162	Culp,Elizabeth	Cab-146
Crummell,Winifred	Brt- 63	Wm	Bft- 33	Geo	Cab-146
Crumney,Anne	Rth- 92	Cruver,P J	Ora-145	Geo	Cab-145
Crump,Charles	Nor- 63	P · S	Ora-145	Henry	Cab-146
Conrad	Bur-107	Cry,David	Mec- 32	Peter	Cab-146
Henry	Mec- 43	William	Bur-125	Peter	Cab-141
James	Mon- 18	Cuckland,Jesse	Rth- 94	Culpeper,Jno	Ans- 5
James	Nor- 63	Cudd,Jonathan	Rth- 92	Peter	Cur- 91
Jas	Mon- 37	Cuff,John	Gat-107	Culpepper,Alsey	Nsh- 77
John	Cha-210	Mason	Gat-114	Erasmus	Nsh- 77
John	Mon- 20	Smith	Gat-114	John	Nsh- 76
Josiah	Nor- 63	Culberson,Abraham	Bun- 89	M	Cam-163
Mack	Row- 37	Anselm	Hrt-210	Mat	Nsh- 74
Stephen	Mon- 37	Isaac	Wsh-216	N	Cam-164
William	Roc- 22	James	Cha-198	S	Cam-160
Wm	Cha-206	Jno	Mec- 45	Culserhouse,Thos	Grn-125
Crumpler,Asery	Joh-286	Joseph	Bun- 89	Culver,Jane	Ire-262
Ben	Nsh- 87	Josiah	Mor- 59	M	Row- 86
Benjamin	Edg- 64	Saml	Cha-215	Cumbo,R	Bru-226
Blackman	Sam-163	William	Bur-121	Sol	Bru-226
Edmon	Joh-285	Wm	Cha-204	Cumboe,Elijah	Rob-231
Jacob	Sam-161	Culberthson,David	Ans- 8	Gilby	Rob-231
John	Sam-162	Culbertson,Samuel	Row- 82	Jno	Rob-231
Matthew	Sam-161	Hyram	Cas- 51	Cumbor,Wm	Cha-210

Cumbs,Phebe	Nor- 63	Curby,James	Cha-202	Curry,Ezekael	Grn-119		
Cumans,Joshuay	Cur- 91	Wright	Cha-202	Ezekiel	Roc- 6		
Cummings,Alex	Pas-185	Curch,John	Cur- 89	Hugh	Grn-142		
Cummins,Aron	Sam-157	Curd,Benjamin	Cha-204	J	Bru-232		
Asa	Sto- 95	Ezekiel	Sto-152	James	Brt- 65		
Danl	Cha-211	Isaiah	Sto-152	Jas	Bla- 9		
Enoch	Rob-232	Curee,Wilson	Per-150	Jno	Rob-228		
George	Dup- 18	Cureton,Mrs.	Brt- 55	Jno	Rob-224		
Isaac	Row- 67	John	Fra- 98	John	Hal-101		
John	Per-127	Curinton,Wm	Mec- 32	John	Cas- 51		
Jessee	Ire-265	Curl,Elizabeth	Gat-116	John	Wil-263		
Robert	Roc- 17	Geo	Cha-213	Lauchlin	Rob-219		
Sally	Dup- 22	Isham	Nor- 63	Lemuel	Grn-137		
Thomas	Dup- 18	J. John	Cas- 51	Mal	Rob-225		
William	Ire-263	John	Cha-216	Malachi	Brt- 65		
Cummons,E	Glf-176	Nophlet	Nsh- 78	Mary	Rob-221		
Geo	Glf-184	Sophiah	Nsh-643	Randal	Rob-244		
Jos	Glf-186	Willis	Edg- 62	Robert	Lnc-368		
Thos	Glf-186	Wm	Cha-215	Robert	Cab-144		
Thos	Glf-180	Curle,Benja	Len-314	Sarah	Rob-226		
Thos	Glf-176	John	Hrt-212	William	Wil-266		
Cumons,Robt	Glf-176	Curlee,Jno	Ans- 14	Willie	Brt- 65		
Cunigham,John	Cum-235	Obediah	Ans- 21	Cursweel,Ros	Bur-104		
Cuningham,Abraham	Sur-190	Wm	Ans- 14	Curtes,Mary	Ons-107		
Alexr	Per-136	Curles,Thos	Cur- 83	Curtice,James	Bun- 87		
George	Hay-193	Curlet,Robt	Mec- 40	James J	Cas- 51		
George Jur	Hay-193	Curliles,Clark	Mar- 5	John	Bun- 87		
Griffith	Row- 85	Curlin,John	Hal-100	Curtis,Anne	Hal-101		
Humphrey	Hay-194	Thomas	Hal-100	Ben	Bur-120		
Jeremy	Glf-166	Curling,Seth	Fra- 92	Bennett	Mon- 19		
John	Hay-194	Curnutt,Margaret	Wil-267	Caleb	Bur-124		
Nathaniel	Ran-161	Currel,Daniel	Cab-146	D	Ash- 6		
Nathineal	Mec- 49	John	Cab-145	David	Bur-120		
Richd	Sur-168	Currell,William	Wsh-225	Elijah	Ans- 29		
William	Sur-176	Curren,John	Grn-140	Henry	Cas- 51		
William Sr	Sur-187	Wm	Ans- 20	Henry Jr	Cas- 51		
Wm	Row- 59	Current,Hugh	Ire-265	J	Ash- 12		
Cunningham,Benj	Wil-262	John	Ire-265	James	Bur-120		
George	Fra- 88	Currey,James Esqr	Cas- 51	James	Bur-103		
J	Glf-174	Capt James	Cas- 51	Jas	Ans- 27		
James	Lnc-367	Joseph	Cas- 51	John	Ons-107		
Jas	Cho-219	Currie,Archd	Mor- 63	Joshua	Bur-117		
Jas	Mec- 34	Duncan	Mor- 61	Nancy	Ans- 27		
Jesse	War-173	Hugh	Ora-158	Robert	Grn-142		
John	Glf-178	Lochlin	Mor- 60	Sigly	Ons- 98		
John	Wil-263	Lochlin	Mor- 62	T	Ash- 6		
John	Rch-198	Mary	Mor- 63	Curtiss,Patty	Wil-279		
John	Rch-206	Murdoch	Mor- 65	Samuel	Wil-282		
Langston	Wil-283	Curron,Wiley	Grn-132	Curtus,Henry	Mec- 30		
M	Glf-156	Curry,Widow	Mec- 51	Curtz,Jacob	Row- 68		
Mathew	Bun- 74	Allen	Mec- 51	Cuscik,W	Glf-153		
Samuel	Sur-163	Angus	Rch-213	Cushing,T	Cum-239		
Wm	Mec- 33	Angus	Rob-227	Custard,M	Ash- 13		
Cunp,Jonathan	Cur- 84	Angus	Rch-198	Custers,Jas	Mec- 29		
Cuntence,Elisebeth	Cur- 84	Archd	Rob-224	Custis,John	Ran-160		
Cuny,Flora	Ire-238	Charles	Bla- 9	John Jr	Ran-160		
Cupples,A	Mon- 36	Dugald	Rob-227	Lavey	Ran-160		
Cups,Jacob	Mon- 49	Duncan	Rob-227	Moses	Mon- 45		
Jno	Mon- 49	Edward	Rob-227	Richd	Glf-159		

Name	Ref	Name	Ref	Name	Ref
Custis,Saml	Ran-160	Dage,William	Cur- 89	Daman,Thomas	Hay-194
T V	Bft- 36	Willowby	Cur- 91	Damerell,David	Lnc-329
Cutchens,Joshua	Edg- 44	Dagles,Archibald	Grn-127	Dameron,B George	Cas- 53
Thomas	Edg- 63	Dail,John	Prq-216	Batt	Cas- 53
Cutchons,Samuel	Edg- 45	Penelope	Prq-216	Geo	Lnc-368
Cutler,Aaron	Bft- 23	Penlope Jr	Prq-216	Gideon	Hal-102
John	Bft- 23	Daile,Andrew H	Dup- 14	John	Lnc-334
John Jun	Bft- 23	Frederick	Dup- 26	Josseph Jnr	Cas- 52
Moses Jun	Bft- 23	Hardy	Dup- 26	Joseph Sr	Cas- 52
Moses Sen	Bft- 23	Henry	Dup- 26	Samuel	Cas- 52
Robert	Bft- 23	Isaac	Dup- 26	Sarah	Cas- 52
Robert Jun	Bft- 23	John	Dup- 34	Tegnel	Grn-137
Susanh	Bft- 23	John	Dup- 26	Thomas	Lnc-368
Cutrell,Andrew	Hyd-226	Thomas	Dup- 26	Dames,George	Hyd-233
Benjamin	Hyd-226	Dailey,--afcut	Cur- 91	Danal,L P	Cam-159
Binjamin	Hyd-226	Jesse Junr	Pas-187	Danald,Kediah	Bur-104
Charles	Hyd-229	Jesse Senr	Pas-187	Danaldson,William	Edg- 40
David	Hyd-232	Rachel	Cur- 90	Danaly,Robert	Wil-263
Eleazer	Hyd-226	Wm	Hyd-223	Dance,Dred	Nsh- 72
Elizth	Hyd-232	Daily,Abram	Lnc-376	Dancey,David	War-170
Henry	Hyd-226	E Esq	Cam-154	Wm	Row- 40
Jacob	Hyd-226	Daker,Samuel	Ire-240	Dancy,Edward	Wil-267
Jacob	Hyd-226	Dale,Abner	Prq-216	Edwin	Edg- 41
Joseph	Hyd-226	Isaac	Ora-132	Francis	Nor- 65
Joseph	Hyd-226	William	Hal-103	Francis L	Edg- 41
Peter	Hyd-226	Daley,Jno	Len-310	James	Edg- 60
Cutril,John	Bft- 20	Dallas,Petter	Rob-226	William	Edg- 59
Cutter,Moses	Bur-119	Dalrymple,Archd	Mor- 69	Danesy,John	Ran-163
Cutts,Lucretia	Cum-262	James	Mor- 66	Danforth,William	Rth- 96
Sherod	Cum-261	John	Mor- 66	Daniel col	Fra-100
William	Cum-262	Wm	Mor- 66	Alexander	Row- 65
Cuzzens,Richd	Hyd-222	Dalton,Carter	Cas- 53	Anehibel	Cur- 83
Cyrus,Frederick	War-171	Charles	Sto-159	Ann	Bla- 11
James	Roc- 23	David	Rth- 96	Archibald	Hal-102
James Junr	Roc- 34	David Jr	Sto-105	Ard	Bla- 8
		David Jur	Sto-140	Asa	Edg- 49
Dabb,Wm	Ans- 9	David Ser	Sto-109	B	Mon- 43
Dabbs,Jno	Ans- 8	Elijah	Rth- 97	Belcher	Cur- 83
Josiah	Ans- 20	Elizabeth	Rth- 96	Brittain	Hal-102
Nathl	Ans- 6	Isaac	Sto-125	Buckner	Row- 49
Wm	Ans- 6	Isaac	Sto- 96	C	Ora-157
Dabney,Samuel	Cas- 52	Isham	Cas- 52	Chisley	Grn-132
Dade,Elizabeth	Car-169	Jesse	Cas- 52	Chisley Jr	Grn-124
Daffin,Darlin	Dup- 33	John	Roc- 22	Crecy	Len-321
John	Hal-103	John	Bun- 98	Cudbert	Row- 49
Dafford,Wm	Cha-213	John	Cas- 52	Curtis	Way-237
Daffren,Thomas	Lnc-363	John	Rth- 96	David	Way-242
Dage,Denis	Cur- 93	John	Rth- 96	David	Mar- 7
Evin	Cur- 92	Jonathan	Sto- 98	David	Nsh- 79
James	Cur- 93	Jonathan	Sto-128	David	Cur- 80
Joab	Cur- 89	Nicholas	Roc- 23	Dency	Way-250
Job	Cur- 90	Samuel	Roc- 21	Drewry	Hal-103
John	Cur- 92	Thomas	Roc- 24	Drury	Row- 65
John	Cur- 92	Thomas	Rth- 98	E	Bla- 10
Phillip	Cur- 93	Travis	Rth- 97	Edward	Sur-164
Phillup	Cur- 89	William	Rth- 96	Elias	Sam-152
Richerd	Cur- 90	Wm	Mon- 34	Elihu	Cur- 85
Rile	Cur- 91	Daly,Geo	Bur-104	Elisha	Row- 48
Samuel	Cur- 91	Thos	Per-137	Elizabeth	Sto-140

Daniel,Elizabeth	Sto-106	Daniel,Robert	Pit-261	Darden,Abraham	Nor- 64
Ephraim	Edg- 66	Robert	Bun- 73	David	Nor- 64
Ephraim	Way-246	S	Bla- 10	Hariot	Sam-157
Ephriam	Row- 87	Safley	Cur- 83	Jethro	Hrt-212
F	Bla- 10	Sarah	War-180	John Junr	Nor- 64
George	Grn-132	Siam	Row- 48	John Senr	Nor- 64
Hanah	Mar- 5	Simon	Mar- 10	Joseph	Sam-154
Hannah	Pit-233	Spencer	Cur- 80	Luke	Ans- 5
Hyram	Bun- 73	Stark	Grn-119	Lydia	Nor- 64
Isham	Cha-198	Stephen	Sur-193	Mary	Sam-157
Jacob	Way-243	Thomas	Pit-239	Mary A	Dup- 35
Jacob	Sam-151	Thomas	Pit-261	Mill	Per-128
James	Per-128	Thomas Jr	Grn-132	Redick	Nor- 64
James	Cas- 52	Thomas Senr	Grn-132	William	Sam-154
James	Nor- 65	Trury	Edg- 67	Dardon,Elijah	Hrt-214
James	Edg- 67	Wille	Pit-241	Elisha	Hrt-214
James	Len-313	William	Per-137	Henry G	Hrt-213
James	Grn-141	William	Way-237	Pleasant	Hrt-214
Jas	Bla- 10	William	Bun- 82	Dark,Alex	Ora-132
Jas	Bft- 24	William	Mar- 7	Joseph	Mor- 63
Jesse	Cha-191	William	Cur- 80	Joseph	Cha-197
Job	Mon- 22	William Snr	Cur- 83	Saml	Cha-197
Jno	Rob-237	Wm	Mon- 23	Sarah	Mor- 64
Jno	Ora-150	Wm	Grn-124	Susana	Cha-197
Jno S	Mec- 28	Willie	Hal-102	Thos	Cha-204
John	Row- 65	Willis	Hal-102	Darley,Granger	Per-137
John	Per-137	Woodson	Ora-170	John	Per-137
John	Nor- 65	Woodson	Grn-132	Darnal,Mrs.	Mec- 50
John	Bla- 8	Yerby	Ire-264	Joseph	Mec- 30
John	War-173	Zedock	Grn-140	William	Pas-186
John	Bla- 10	Daniels,Clement	Hyd-226	Darnall,Abdel	Wil-267
John Esq	Per-129	Jas	Bft- 34	Anne	Wil-268
Jonathan	Sam-160	John	Bft- 35	Benjamin	Wil-267
Joseph	Grn-134	John	Car-173	John	Wil-268
Joseph Jr	Cur- 85	Manley	Hyd-224	Joshua	Wil-275
Joseph Snr	Cur- 85	Morras	Hyd-228	Thomas	Wil-285
Joshua	Grn-125	Randel	Car-173	William	Wil-275
Josia	Row- 64	• Randle	Hyd-226	Darnel,James	Mon- 31
Josiah Senr	Grn-124	S	Bru-238	John	Ire-252
Lanier	Pit-239	Danil,Chesley	Grn-134	Jordan	Lnc-340
Lemuel	Edg- 49	Rhodia	Nsh- 78	Jos	Lnc-340
Lemuel	Edg- 48	Jeptha	Nsh- 77	Moses	Lnc-340
Leonard	Rth- 96	Danils,Shadrach	Hyd-226	William	Lnc-340
Lewis	Hal-102	Thomas	Hyd-226	Zac	Row- 64
Littleton	Cha-197	Danily,Flora	Rob-229	Darnold,John	War-175
Major	Row- 55	Dank,John	Sto- 98	Joseph	Sto- 97
Martha	Hal-103	Dankin,D	Cam-154	Joseph	Sto-127
Martin	Grn-124	Danley,Jo	Ora-154	Raleigh	Sto-127
Mary	Cur- 83	Nancy	Sur-186	Darr,Henry	Row- 82
Mary	War-177	Danly,John	Mor- 56	Darrach,John	Cum-254
Mathew	Per-150	Dannel,Wm	Ora-127	Malcom	Cum-254
Meriday	Per-137	Dannell,Jas	Glf-184	Darrow,Danl	Cha-213
Molley	Way-246	Will	Dup- 14	Darter,Joal	Mec- 42
Molley	Way-246	Dannelly,James	Ora-159	Obediah	Mec- 42
Nancey	Cur- 83	Danner,Fedk	Bft- 29	Saml	Mec- 42
Nathan	Rob-236	Darbey,James	Cas- 53	Sampson	Mec- 42
Old	Pas-187	Darby,Charles	Rth- 20	Thos	Mec- 42
Owen	Way-237	Daniel	Cas- 52	Dartin,Jas	Mec- 42
Peter	Row- 49	Sarah	Rch-210	Dashiell,Tubman	Tyr-201

-78-

Dasier,P	Bru-228	Davenport,Ephraim	Wsh-222	Davie,Cryderally	Nor- 65
Datty,Wm	Cha-199	George	Lnc-367	Davies,Absolam	Rob-224
Daub,Henry	Sto-130	Hetty	Wsh-221	Frederick	Rob-224
Jacob	Sto-152	Isaac	Wsh-220	James	Sur-180
John	Sto-128	Isaiah	Wsh-220	Jas	Rob-233
Daudy,W	Cam-163	Jacob	Wsh-219	Jno	Rob-227
Dauge,A	Cam-158	James	Wsh-222	Jno	Rob-233
B	Cam-157	John	Lnc-366	Thos Snr	Rob-239
C	Cam-158	Jonas	Bur-116	Daviess,Garrot	Bun- 84
D	Cam-157	Martin	Bur-113	Davinal,John	Ran-164
D	Cam-164	Robert	Bur-113	Davinport,Elias	Joh-280
E	Cam-158	Thos	Bur-115	Davis,Mrs.	Mec- .32
J	Cam-157	William	Row- 76	Aaron	Cab-144
J	Cam-155	William	Wsh-220	Abel	Nsh- 76
J	Cam-154	William	Wsh-218	Abijah	Jon-295
J E	Cam-158	William	Lnc-366	Abner	Cha-193
J Esq	Cam-158	William	Len-316	Abraham	Ans- 12
J Esq	Cam-158	Major William	Wil-276	Abraham	Bun- 81
M	Cam-157	William Junr	Wsh-222	Abram	Pas-187
Samspon	Pas-187	Daverson,James	Ran-163	Absalem	Grn-148
Dauges,M	Cam-163	James Snr	Ran-163	Adam	Sto-112
Daugharty,Amilia	Wil-272	John	Ran-163	Adam	Sto-154
Daugherty,Ann	Sam-151	Joshua	Ran-164	Adam	Ran-163
John	Roc- 29	Silas	Ran-164	Alexander	Lnc-360
John	Cha-191	William Jnr	Ran-163	Amelia	Bun- 90
Saml	Glf-180	William Snr	Ran-163	Anderson	Ora-130
Wm	Glf-180	Davey,Elizebeth	Per-128	Andrew	Ire-248
Daughorn,George	Sam-162	John	Per-150	Andrew	Ire-245
Daughterage,James	Edg- 61	William	Per-128	Andrew Junr	Cab-144
Daughtery,Eliz	Edg- 61	David,Lewis	Sto-139	Andrew Senr	Cab-144
Mary	Edg- 62	Lewis	Sto-104	Andw	Cab-143
Daughtredge,Benj	Nsh- 80	Davidson,Andrew	Mec- 28	Ann	Mar- 12
Daughtrey,Elisha	Nor- 64	Benj	Bun- 98	Anna	Sur-176
Jeremiah	Nor- 64	Caleb	Way-241	Anthony	Car-178
John	Nor- 64	D	Ora-154	Anthony	Car-176
Joseph	Nor- 64	Elender	Edg- 64	Archable	Hyd-229
Mary	Nor- 64	Ephraim	Ire-257	Archbd Esq	Fra- 92
Milly	Nor- 64	G W	Mon- 39	Aron	Ons-102
Sarah	Nor- 64	George	Ire-257	Arth	Pas-186
William	Nor- 65	George L	Ire-239	Arthur	Way-244
Daughtry,Abraham	Sam-159	Green	Mon- 41	Arthur	Nor- 64
Ann	Sam-159	Hugh	Hay-194	Arthur	Nsh- 87
Arthur	Way-233	J	Ash- 6	Arthur	Row- 80
J	Ora-141	Jno	Mec- 24	Arthur	Tyr-212
Dauherty,George	Mec- 32	Jno	Mec- 24	Augustin	Grn-135
Daukens,John	Rch-208	John	Cha-202	Auther	Bft- 34
John	Rch-195	Joseph	Ire-237	B	Bru-234
Samuel	Rch-208	Lucy	Ora-123	Bailey	Pas-187
Samuel	Rch-208	Margaret	Cha-214	Bartlet	Bun- 80
William	Rch-195	Margarett	Mec- 46	Baxter	Bla- 6
Daukins,Jean	Rch-205	Mary	Ire-256	Baxter	Bun- 89
Dauley,William	Cur- 92	Richd	Mon- 41	Benj	Pas-187
Dauterg,Elijah	Brt- 58	Samuel	Bun- 80	Benj	Car-175
Dautry,Jacob	Joh-281	Sarah	Bun- 85	Benj	Hyd-225
Davas,Ichabod	Rob-236	Thomas	Ire-256	Benj Jr	Len-318
Davaul,Saml	Ran-163	William R	Ire-258	Benjn	Prq-216
Davenport,Abm	Lnc-327	Wm Charlotte	Mec- 25	Benjamin	Pit-260
Aron	Wsh-220	Wm Mitchell	Hay-194	Benjamin	Bun- 88
Asa	Wsh-223	Wm S	Mec- 52	Benjamin	Rth- 96

-79-

Davis,Benjamin	Rth- 98	Davis,Elizabeth	Hyd-224	Davis,James		Cas- 52
Benjamin	Hay-194	Elizabeth	War-170	James		Bun- 87
Benjn	Hal-102	Elnathan	Cha-210	James		Hal-103
Benjn	Car-184	Enoch	Hal-103	James		Row- 63
Blake	Hrt-212	Enoch	Glf-155	James		Mor- 54
Buckner	War-169	Enoch	Jon-295	James		Sto-108
Burwell	War-169	Enoch Jnr	Ran-163	James		Sam-159
C	Len-320	Ephraim	Wil-277	James		Grn-134
Calep	Nsh-643	Ephraim	Rth- 96	James		Car-171
Catharine	Lne-320	Ephram	Jon-295	James		Car-175
Caty	Rth- 96	Evan	Row- 56	James		Fra- 85
Charles	Edg- 40	F	Bla- 11	James		Cha-200
Christian	Edg- 50	Fred	Pas-187	James		Len-310
Chs	Per-128	Freeman	Car-175	James		Sto-145
Clem	Bun- 75	G\	Bru-230	James		Sto-133
Clement L	Jon-295	Gabriel	Sur-166	James		Sto-101
Clifford	Car-176	Geo	Cab-144	James		Ora-167
D	Len-320	Geo	Cab-141	James		Sur-168
D ḋ	Bru-234	George	Har-137	James		Nor- 65
Daffun	Ran-163	George	Bun- 88	James		Wsh-225
Daniel	Car-175	George	Pas-187	Jas		Glf-184
Daniel	Mec- 53	Grace	Len-320	Jas		Ora-136
Danise	Prq-216	Hanah	Bla- 11	Jas		Mec- 25
David	Pas-187	Hanah	Bla- 5	Jehu		Pit-240
David	Pas-188	Hardy	Hrt-212	Jesse		Rth- 96
David	Pas-186	Harmon	Bun- 96	Jesse		Rth- 97
David	Cas- 52	Henry	Cas- 52	Jesse		Rth- 97
David	Rth- 96	Henry	Roc- 10	Jesse		Sto-135
David	Dup- 23	Henry	Pit-253	Jesse		Sto-102
David	Gat-110	Henry	Rth- 96	Jesse		Ran-163
David	Sam-153	Henry	Sto-133	Jesse		Hyd-224
David	Sto-125	Henry	Sur-193	Jobe		Ran-163
David	Bun- 81	Henry	Bla- 11	Job		Mon- 37
Davis	Pas-187	Henry	Bla- 8	Joel		Ran-163
Davy	Mec- 53	Henry	Bla- 3	Jno		Ora-144
Davy	Mec- 51	Isaac	Wil-285	Jno		Ora-130
Devotion	Mor- 62	Isaac	Ora-125	Jno		Mec- 39
Dorcas	Pas-187	Isaac	Bun- 85	Jno		Rob-234
Downing	Wsh-226	Isaac	Lnc-331	Jno		Per-128
Dred	Lnc-355	Isaac	Sur-182	John		Pas-186
Drewry	Nsh- 76	Iseral	Mec- 24	John		Bun- 90
Drewry	Nsh- 76	Isham	Sto-148	John		Cas- 52
Duke W Esq	Fra- 88	Isham	Ans- 6	John E C		Pas-187
E	Mon- 34	Isom	Bun- 86	John		Bun- 88
E	Bla- 11	J	Bru-236	John		Bun- 85
Edmd	Pas-186	J	Cam-163	John		Row- 64
Edmond	Pit-260	J	Ora-148	John		Row- 48
Edward	Hal-102	J	Bla- 11	John		Row- 55
Edward	Lnc-339	J	Bla- 11	John		Cab-147
Edward	Row- 77	J	Bla- 10	John		Rth- 96
Edward	Nor- 64	J B	Bru-240	John		Grn-122
Edwd	Bla- 3	J Junr	Bla- 13	John		Gat-111
Eldred	Brt- 59	Jack	Pas-187	John		Bur-119
Elijah	Sur-181	Jackson	Sur-195	John		Bur-110
Elijah	Bun- 82	Jacob	War-175	John		Edg- 49
Elijah	Hay-194	Jacob	Car-185	John		Grn-149
Elisha	Tyr-209	Jacob	Len-318	John		Grn-140
Elisha	Bun- 86	Jacob	Sur-174	John		Grn-136
Elizabeth	Bun- 88	Jacob	Ran-163	John		Ans- 9

Davis,John	Sto-125	Davis,Marry	Sto-128	Davis,Richard		Hyd-224
John	Sur-162	Martha	Hal-103	Richard		Hyd-224
John	Nsh- 76	Mary	Cas- 53	Richard Jr		Hyd-225
John	Lnc-360	Mary	Hal-103	Richd		Ans- 19
John	Bla- 9	Mary	Sto-114	Robert		Cab-148
John	Bla- 6	Mary	Len-317	Robert		Sur-193
John	Bla- 4	Mary	Sto-157	Robert		Hay-194
John	Bun- 81	Mary	Sto- 98	Robt		Way-241
John	Ran-164	Mary	Sur-165	Robt		Mon- 24
John	Ran-163	Mary	Tyr-210	Robt		Cab-144
John	Hyd-234	Mary	Tyr-203	Robt		Mec- 32
John	Hyd-234	Mathew	Ons- 99	Robt		Mor- 62
John	Hyd-224	Mathew	Cha-191	S		Ora-157
John	Hyd-224	Matthew	War-177	Sally		Lnc-355
John	Hyd-224	Matthew	Sur-160	Sampson Senr		Bla- 13
John	Way-237	Matthew Sr	Sur-181	Saml		Pas-187
John B	Jon-295	Maurice	Row- 85	Saml		Row- 47
John Jr	Way-246	Merith	Brt- 58	Saml		Glf-165
John Junr	Nor- 64	Meshack	Bun- 81	Saml		Dup- 19
John Sr	Sur-177	Micajah	Bla- 6	Saml		Hyd-225
John Senr	Nor- 64	Michael	Jon-295	Samuel		Mec- 39
John Senr	Bla- 6	Mildred	Nor- 65	Samuel		Bun- 88
John Sr	Way-243	Miles	Pas-187	Samuel		Bun- 85
Jonathan	Mon- 48	Miles	Mar- 3	Samuel		Dup- 27
Jonathan	Cab-144	Mirick	Row- 40	Samuel		Car-179
Jonathan	Sur-163	Molley	Way-243	Samuel		Car-177
Jonathan	Fra- 94	Molly	Mec- 30	Samuel		Jon-295
Jordan	Car-175	Moses	Gat-108	Samuel		Sur-177
Joseph	Row- 40	Moses	Cab-144	Samuel		Ons-101
Joseph	Sur-165	Nancy	Pas-187	Samuel		Sur-196
Joseph	Glf-189	Nancy	War-178	Samuel		Nor- 64
Joseph Jnr	Ran-164	Nathan	Lnc-341	Sarah		Per-219
Joseph P	Grn-148	Nathan	Edg- 51	Sarah		Row- 63
Joseph Senr	Car-184	Nathaniel	Bun- 85	Sarah		Gat-110
Joseph Snr	Ran-164	Oner	Ran-164	Sarah		Bur-119
Joshua	Pas-187	Patty	Fra- 85	Sena		Ons-104
Joshua	Way-232	Patty	Way-253	Shadrack		Pas-187
Joshua	Wil-265	Penelope	Wsh-219	Sidny		Pas-187
Josiah	Nsh- 87	Penney	Mar- 13	Simon		Pas-187
Josiah	Pit-260	Peter	Mor- 56	Simon		Rth- 97
Josiah	Car-176	Peter	Glf-171	Smith		Wsh-225
Jourdan	Cah-202	Peter	Mon- 40	Solly		Per-128
Lemuel	Nor- 64	Peter R	War-184	Solomon		Row- 47
Leonard	Sto-128	Phillip	Cas- 53	Solomon		Rth- 96
Leonard	Sto- 98	Phillip	Rth- 96	Solomon		Rth- 97
Letty	Roc- 14	Phillip	Rth- 98	Solomon		Bla- 6
Levi	Pas-187	Polly	Pas-187	Solomon		Ire-250
Lewis	Dup- 32	Polly	Pas-186	Staton		Ora-159
Lewis	Nor- 64	Powell	Way-233	Stephen		Mor- 69
Lewis	Pit-260	R	Bru-236	Stephen		Rob-242
Lewis Jnr	Pit-260	Rachel	Len-313	Suger		Mec- 47
Losson	Jon-295	Rachel	Nor- 64	Susanna		Mor- 59
Lowry	Pas-187	Ralph	Mor- 58	Susanna		Lnc-329
M	Bla- 13	Reason	Bun- 75	Syrus		Grn-126
M	Ash- 14	Recia	Bla- 9	T		Cam-165
Mabel	Pas-187	Reubin	Pas-186	T		Glf-176
Major	Cha-192	Rew (Hatter)	Pas-187	Thomas		Wil-279
Major	Cum-253	Rew	Pas-187	Thomas		Pas-187
Marey	Cur- 84	Richard	Tyr-206	Thomas		Pas-187

Davis,Thomas	Hal-103	Davis,Wm		Car-178	Day,Francis	Per-137
Thomas	Rth- 98	Wm		Len-319	Henry	Per-128
Thomas	Dup- 28	Wm (S)	Bla- 7	Henry E	Wsh-227
Thomas	War-181	Wm (B)	Bla- 6	Henry Junr	Per-150
Thomas	War-181	Wm C	Bla- 3	Henry Senr	Per-137
Thomas	Car-175	Willis	Pas-187	James	Sto-111
Thomas	Sur-182	Wilson	Sur-162	James	Sur-166
Thomas H	Sur-181	Windal	Len-317	James	Sto-148
General Thomas	Bla- 12	Winfield	Hyd-224	James	Bur-112
Thomas	Cum-240	Winifred	Bla- 7	Jesse	Per-131
Thomas	Ire-250	Winifred	Bla- 13	Jesse	Sto-147
Thomas	Cum-251	Zach	Len-315	Jessee	Grn-149
Thomas	Way-254	Zachariah	Bur-105	John	Grn-149
Thomas	Hay-194	Davise,John	Cur- 84	John	Bur-112
Thomas	Ran-163	John	Cur- 83	John	Car-173
Thomas Esq	Rth- 20	Neley	Cur- 90	John Junr	Per-137
Thos	Pas-187	Davison,James	Hyd-226	John Senr	Per-137
Thos	Glf-161	Jas	Ora-124	John Senr	Bur-112
Thos	Cab-143	Richard	War-184	Lewis	Lnc-355
Thos	Mon- 24	William H	Rch-197	Mary	Hal-103
Thos	Cha-194	Wm	Bft- 34	Nicholas Jur	Bur-112
Thos	Bla- 13	Daviss,Benjamin	Nor- 65	Nicholas Senr	Bur-112
Thos	Bla- 8	Davy,Edwd	Per-128	Richd	Glf-169
Thos Jn	Sur-160	Gabl son of James	Per-137	Richd	Row- 45
Thos Senr	Cab-144	Gabl Senr	Per-137	Sarah	Nor- 65
Upshear	Lnc-355	Samuel	Per-137	Thomas	Sto-109
Uriah	Ire-250	Daws,Ephraim	Edg- 42	Thomas	Sto-110
Walter	Mec- 33	Dawson,General	Hal-103	Thomas	Wil-282
Waymouth	Pas-186	Daniel	Ran-163	Thomas	Sur-168
Wellington	Car-175	David	Hal-102	Thomas	Sto-150
Will	Pas-188	Ezeciel	Rob-242	Thomas	Sto-151
William	Bun- 88	Hardy	Len-312	Valentine	Row- 85
William	Way-244	Henry	Hal-103	William	Mar- 12
William	Hal-102	Isaac	Mor- 67	William	Car-173
William	Lnc-327	Isaac	Glf-181	William Jr	Sur-166
William	Hal-122	Isaaih	Cha-193	William Sr	Sur-194
William	Rth- 97	James	Wil-285	Wm	Glf-169
William	Bur-113	James	Rch-209	Dayley,Edmund	Car-171
William	Bur-113	Jesse A	Hal-102	Dayton,Wm	Mor- 60
William	Cha-197	John	Len-312	Daze,Darcy	Cur- 88
William	Sto- 96	John	Nor- 64	Enoch	Cur- 86
William	Sto-125	John	Cas- 53	Dea,Daniel	Mec- 41
William	Sur-174	Jonas	Bun- 85	Deadman,Mark	Rth- 97
William	Sur-191	Joseph	Sam-155	Deakins,John	Hrt-215
William	Joh-281	Joshua	Ran-163	Deal,Adam	Pas-186
William	Hay-194	Lenard	Hyd-227	Daniel	Sur-171
William	Hay-194	Mary	Hal-102	Daniel	Pas-187
William	Ran-163	Rebecca	Ora-162	Eli	Edg- 71
William	Hyd-233	Robert	Ons- 99	George	Lnc-377
William	Hyd-224	Thomas	Wil-270	George Jr	Lnc-352
William	Wsh-226	Thomas Jr	Len-312	George Senr	Lnc-352
William D C	Sur-178	Thos Senr	Len-312	Harry	Bur-122
Wm	Row- 47	William	Nor- 64	Jacob	Bur-122
Wm	Bru-228	Wilson	Mor- 65	Jacob	Lnc-352
Wm	Pas-186	Dawthirt,Abraham	Row- 55	Jacob Jr	Lnc-377
Wm	Pit-232	Day,Asael	Bur-112	Jacob Senr	Lnc-377
Wm	Brt- 49	Asel	Bur-126	James	Pas-187
Wm	Bft- 30	Benjamin	Nor- 65	John	Bur-126
Wm	Car-175	David	Hal-103	John	Pas-187

Name	Ref	Name	Ref	Name	Ref
Deal,John	Sto-128	Deatherage,George	Roc- 32	Debrular,M G	Ora-148
John	Lnc-345	John	Sto-122	Debrure,Edward	Jon-295
John	Lnc-377	Lewis	Sto-155	Debutz,G	Cum-237
Joseph	Row- 62	Lewis	Sto-109	Deck,Jacob	Rth- 98
Malachi	Pas-187	Matt	Sto-109	Decker,Christopher	Lnc-352
Tho	Bft- 37	Matthew	Sto-145	George	Lnc-328
William	Lnc-352	Milly	Sto-137	Decks,Leonard	Rth- 97
William	Bur-122	Philip	Sto-137	Dedmon,Edmon	Row- 62
William Jr	Lnc-352	Rachel	Sto-141	James	Row- 64
William Jr	Lnc-352	Solomon	Roc- 24	Thomas	Row- 65
William Senr	Lnc-352	William	Sto-122	William	Row- 62
Deale,Olive	Pit-238	William	Sto- 93	Deek,Adam	Lnc-332
Dean,Anthony	Bun- 97	Deaton,Burrel	Mor- 69	George	Lnc-332
Bartley	Nsh- 89	Burril	Mor- 58	Deekins,John	Cha-191
Betty	Way-251	Clayburn	Cha-207	Deer,B	Glf-174
David	Grn-141	Dison	Mon- 34	C	Glf-175
F	Glf-163	Dison	Mon- 29	Franky	Glf-186
George	Way-251	Eldridge	Bun- 76	James	Sur-180
Henry H	Sur-162	Jackson	Cha-207	John	Lnc-376
James	Cum-260	John	Cha-196	Jonathan	Nsh- 88
James	Roc- 4	Joseph	Mon- 28	Deering,William	Roc- 4
James	Way-244	Levi	Mor- 69	Dees,Jesse	Wil-264
Jeams	Nsh- 86	Matthew	Mor- 69	Levi	Rob-242
Jessee	Grn-141	Nathan	Bun- 76	Marke	Bun- 90
Jethro	Way-232	Thos	Mon- 27	Patsey	Sam-156
John	Cha-204	Thos	Cab-136	Samuel	Rch-203
John	Way-248	Wm	Cha-197	William	Rch-203
John	Way-251	Deaver,Alexander	Dup- 28	Deevine,Maj Edwd	Sam-164
Joshua	Pit-239	Penelope	Edg- 60	Defer,Walter	Lnc-329
Mary	Brt- 59	William	Row- 61	Defrees,D	Ash- 14
Moses	Way-248	Debard,John	Rth- 97	Defreese,George	Rth- 20
Nancy	Hal-102	Debenport,L	Col- 19	Degernite,Daniel	Sur-176
Nancy	Hal-103	Deberry,Allen	Nor- 64	Munford	Ans- 17
Robert	Ran-163	B	Mon- 35	Deggers,Job	Rob-235
Sol	Glf-163	Benjamin	Pit-260	Deggins,William	Pit-255
Tamsey	Ran-163	Benjamin	Nor- 64	Degraffensaidt,Vincent	
Thomas	Len-310	Charlotte	Nor- 64		Roc- 5
William	Len-316	Edmd	Mon- 23	Dehart,Elijah	Ire-247
William E	Len-316	Holland	Nor- 64	Dehority,James	Edg- 44
Deans,D	Glf-184	John	Mon- 23	Deibs,Widow	Lnc-352
Danl	Brt- 57	Iamuel	Pit-263	Deirmon,Henry	Ire-255
James	Hrt-214	Lemuel	Mon- 23	Deits,Jacob	Sto-129
Jas	Glf-180	Matthias	Nor- 64	Jacob	Sto- 98
John	Nsh- 81	Nelly	Nor- 64	Deitz,Frederick	Lnc-377
Penelope	Hrt-213	Sarah	Mon- 23	Jacob	Lnc-377
Saml	Brt- 57	Thomas	Nor- 65	Solomon	Lnc-377
Thos	Hrt-212	Debnam,Charles	Fra- 88	Dejornet,Ford	Row- 64
Dearborn,John	Cur- 82	Deboard,Benjamin	Wil-280	Delamot,Henry	Mon- 21
Dearing,James	Sto-107	Jesse	Wil-283	Delaney,John	Rch-213
James	Sto-142	John	Wil-280	Delany,Turner	Bft- 30
Dearmand,Jas	Mec- 27	Joseph	Wil-272	Delap,Daniel	Row- 48
Dearmond,Allen	Mec- 49	William	Wil-277	Danl	Row- 48
Deas,Daniel	Ans- 15	Debord,George	Bur-113	Henry	Cas- 53
Jas	Ans- 28	Isaac	Ire-255	Hugh	Row- 48
Deason,Abraham	Ans- 7	J	Ash- 11	Delay,Burges	Roc- 18
William	Ans- 11	Jacob	Ire-253	James	Roc- 18
Wm	Ans- 7	James	Bur-113	Deleany,Jno	Mec- 32
Deatherage,Byrd	Roc- 22	Debow,Solomon	Cas- 52	Deleney,Lemuel	Nor- 65
Elizabeth	Roc- 24	Debricks,John	Mar- 4	Delihay,John	Per-137

Name	Ref	Name	Ref	Name	Ref	Name	Ref
Delliard,Theo	Len-315	Denney,Joseph	Roc- 31	Denton,Arthur	Sto-157
Dellinger,Adam	Lnc-338	William	Sur-194	Edward	Hal-102
Barbary	Lnc-377	William	Sur-183	Isaac	Sto-157
George	Lnc-338	Denning,George	Way-248	James	Fra- 81
Henry	Lnc-345	Jonas	Way-248	Jesse	Fra- 80
Henry	Lnc-329	Molley	Way-248	John	Rth- 97
Jacob	Lnc-377	Simon	Cas- 53	John	Rth- 97
Jacob	Lnc-342	William	Way-248	Levy	Edg- 58
John	Lnc-375	Dennis,Anderson	Cha-214	Samuel	Hay-194
John	Lnc-377	Andrew	Mon- 21	Thomas	Rth- 97
John Senr	Lnc-374	Andrew Jr	Mon- 22	Thomas	Rth- 97
Martin	Lnc-376	Edw	Cab-147	Thomas	Hal-102
Michael	Lnc-345	Francis	Car-182	William	Fra- 97
Peter	Lnc-338	James	Car-182	Wm	Cum-235
Phillip	Lnc-344	John	Pit-239	Depreast,William	Rth- 97
William	Lnc-347	Joseph	Bun- 88	Deprust,William	Rth- 96
Dellingham,Arthur	Lnc-339	Mary	Cha-214	Deputy,John	Wil-285
Delmore,Jno	Mec- 43	Nancy	Car-182	Derr,Adam	Lnc-352
Deloach,Britain	Joh-286	Richard	Cha-195	Andrew	Lnc-363
Francis	Nor- 64	Richard	Wil-279	Dervel,Matthew	Lnc-328
Joseph	Joh-277	Ruben	Car-182	Desern,Ephriam	Sur-171
Michael	Nor- 64	William	Ran-163	Deserne,Elijah	Sur-187
Sarah	Nor- 65	William	Glf-181	Deshaser,Hardy	Lnc-363
Thomas	Nor- 64	William Jnr	Ran-163	Detter,Mary(wid)	Lnc-345
William	Nor- 65	Wm	Mon- 33	Deucart,Isaiah	Cab-138
William	Nor- 64	Denny,Geo	Glf-158	Devan,Jeremiah	Brt- 45
Delon,Henry	Pas-186	Geo Jr	Glf-158	Devan,Jeremiah	Brt- 45
Sally	Pas-186	George	Wil-269	Devany,Mrs Alsey	Fra- 78
Sally	Pas-187	Harold	Sur-187	Devaryn,Elijah	Joh-283
Simeon	Pas-186	Henry	Sur-170	Devaugh,Saml	Nsh- 90
Delone,Henry	Hyd-229	Iseriah	Sur-187	Devaughn,John	Nsh- 90
John	Hyd-229	James	Wil-269	Devaul,John	Dup- 34
Delony,Anne	Nor- 65	James	Sur-172	Merian	Ire-261
Edward	Nor- 65	James Jr	Wil-269	Thos	Tyr-207
Delow,Peter	Row- 67	Jas	Lnc-333	Devenport,C	Ora-140
Delpost,Elizebeth	Ans- 28	Jas	Glf-158	Deborah	Tyr-204
Demcy,Patience	Prq-216	Jas Jr	Glf-158	Falket	Tyr-211
Demmery,Shadrach	Nor- 64	John	Wil-269	Fredk	Tyr-211
Wright	Nor- 64	John	Grn-122	J	Tyr-206
Demmit,John	Row- 66	Thos	Glf-161	John	Mar- 14
Dempsey,Edmund	Brt- 47	William	Sur-170	John	Tyr-211
Joshua	Brt- 47	William	Glf-156	John	Rth- 97
Martha	Nor- 64	Wm	Glf-173	John	Rth- 97
Melvin	Hal-103	Denson,Bennett	Fra- 87	Moses	Tyr-211
Demsy,Anne	Hal-103	Bruffet	Row- 58	N	Ora-140
Eliza	Hal-103	John	Nsh- 76	Sarah	Ran-163
James	Hal-103	John E	Fra- 83	William	Pit-262
John	Hal-103	Jordan	Fra- 87	Zail	Tyr-212
Johnson	Hal-103	Massey	Nsh- 76	Dever,John	Bla- 13
Uriah	Hal-103	Shaderek	Ans- 16	Polly	Hay-194
William	Hal-103	Shaderick	Ans- 30	Deveron,Dennis	Brt- 58
Denbey,Elijah	Fra- 87	Willson	Fra- 99	Devers, F Esq	Cam-158
Denby,John	Roc- 14	Dent,James	Fra- 99	Deverson,Amos	Brt- 50
Denham,Susa	Ora-126	John	Fra- 99	George	Brt- 50
Wm	Row- 51	John	Fra- 94	John	Brt- 50
Denmark,John	Dup- 12	John B	Row- 76	Dew,Allen	Hal-102
Denney,Iley	Sur-196	Michael	Fra- 93	James	Fra- 84
James	Sur-194	Thomas H	Row- 76	John	Edg- 66
Jesse	Sur-196	Townsen	Row- 76	John	Hal-102

Dew,L	Bla- 10	Dickerson,Henry	Nsh- 90	Dicks,William	Ran-163
Selah	Edg- 62	Jno	Ora-152	Dicksan,John	Per-129
William	Edg- 67	John	Grn-132	Mary	Per-129
Zachariah	Edg- 68	John	Grn-128	Dickson,Widow	Cab-143
Dewauld,Jacob	Cab-145	Nat	Ora-152	D	Ash- 3
Dewault,Jacob	Cab-142	Ransome	Fra- 90	D	Ash- 4
Michael	Cab-142	Terry	Cas- 52	David	Lnc-339
Dewberry,John	Hal-102	W	Ora-152	Edmond	Per-150
Dewbery,Daniel	Hal-102	Wm	Grn-128	Edward	Cum-264
Deweese,Shadrick	Grn-121	Dickey,Alex	Lnc-330	Hugh	Joh-285
Dewert,Hesekiah	Mec- 51	Anthony	Rth- 98	J	Ash- 8
Marchant	Mec- 51	Anthony Sr	Rth- 98	James	Ora-177
Dewist,Jonathan	Mec- 24	Catharine	Ora-163	James	Lnc-376
Dewitt,William	Roc- 14	David Esq	Rth- 96	James	Cab-143
Dewpree,Jesse	Hal-102	Davis	Ire-260	James M	Cab-144
Dezern,Thos	Ora-150	Elizabeth	Ire-260	Jeremiah	Rch-196
Dial,John	Sto- 98	George	Rth- 96	John	Lnc-339
Peter	Rob-231	Hasten	Ran-163	John	Bur-126
Wm	Ora-156	James	Row- 75	John	Ora-171
Diamond,Jas	Mec- 28	James	Ora-163	John col	Cum-266
Dick (col)	Rch-199	John	Ora-162	John	Sam-157
Dick,Catherine	Mon- 39	John	Row- 73	John Ray	Cum-266
James	Cum-237	John	Glf-161	Joseph	Dup- 12
Jas	Glf-173	Moses	Rth- 96	Joseph	Wil-184
Jno	Ans- 8	R I	Ora-148	M	Ash- 5
John	Lnc-328	Robert	Hay-194	Nat	Ora-171
Jonathan	Ans- 8	Samuel	Cas- 52	Nrm	Ora-177
Manuel	Car-178	W	Glf-155	Robert	Lnc-339
Nathen	Ran-163	William	Row- 75	Robt	Cab-143
Pritchards	Pas-187	William	Row- 75	Saml B	Ans- 28
Sheduck	Rch-191	Wm	Ora-163	Simon	Wil-271
Thos	Glf-179	Zacha	Ora-161	T	Ash- 7
William	Ran-163	Dickings,Thomas	Cha-195	Thomas	Lnc-335
Dicken,Anne	Hal-103	Dickins,Richard	Ire-254	Thomas	Lnc-336
Benjamin	Hal-103	Saml	Hrt-214	William	Per-150
Bennet	Hal-103	William	Hrt-214	Williams	Dup- 7
Jacob	Hal-102	Wm	Grn-141	Wm	Bur-102
James	Hal-102	Dickinson,Benj	Way-246	Die,Martin	Mor- 67
Jesse	Hal-102	Daniel	Way-246	Diffy,Jno	Mon- 33
John	Hal-102	Isaac	Way-246	Diggs,David	Ans- 13
Matthew	Hal-102	Jesse	Way-247	David	Ans- 29
Richard	Hal-103	John	Hrt-208	Dudley	Ans- 29
William	Hal-102	Jonathan	Way-232	Jno	Ans- 32
William	Edg- 57	Jos F	Hrt-209	Jno	Ans- 32
William	Hal-102	Dr. M	Brt- 56	Jno	Ans- 29
Willm Senr	Hal-102	Marshall	Pit-255	Marshal	Ans- 8
Dickens,Gideon	Cha-200	Robt	Mor- 63	Marshall	Ans- 32
Jesse	Per-137	Shadrick	Way-246	Marshall	Ans- 29
Saml	Cab-138	Thomas	Edg- 46	Pleasand	Ans- 27
Dickenson,Daniel	Car-183	Wila	Sur-166	Pleasant\	And- 32
Elizabeth	Car-184	William	Way-244	Sol	Ans- 13
Joel	Bft- 37	Wm	Mor- 63	Wm	Ans- 32
John	Car-184	Withel	Way-232	Wm	Ans- 32
Micajah	Ire-267	Dickison,David	Wil-276	Digner,John	Hyd-220
Dickerson,Arthur	Ans- 16	Isom	Wil-262	Dilback,Jacob	Rth- 96
B	Ora-144	Jeremiah	Mor- 55	Dilda,James	Hal-103
Epapoditus	Grn-128	Dickky,William	Ran-163	Dilday,Joseph	Hrt-215
Garland	Rth- 96	Dicks,Lurenar	Pas-187	Dildy,Arthur	Edg- 52
Griffith	Bun- 96	Peter	Ran-153	Jesse	Pit-260

-85-

Name	Ref	Name	Ref	Name	Ref	Name	Ref
Dildy,Mary	Hal-103	Dinkens,James	Way-241	Dixon,Geo	Cha-207		
Robert	Nor- 64	James	Wil-265	George	Hyd-233		
Dill,Archa	Cas- 52	Jas	Mec- 25	George R	Car-173		
Edward	Car-182	Jesse	Fra-100	Henry	Bft- 32		
John	Car-170	John	Mec- 27	Henry	Nsh- 92		
John	Cas- 52	John	Sur-191	Henry	Ons-102		
Dillahunt,Susanna	Jon-295	John	Glf-174	Henry	Car-180		
Thomas	Jon-295	Joshua	Mec- 28	J	Ora-141		
Dillard,Isaac	Sur-168	Susanna	War-181	Jacob	Per-128		
James	Sto-139	Dinney,John	Sur-169	Jacob	Per-128		
John	Bun- 90	Dinnis,Reuben	Ons-104	James	Row- 64		
John	Sur-170	Thos	Mec- 35	James	Ora-165		
John Junr	Bun- 90	Dirrybusy,John	Bur-114	James	Cha-198		
John Sn	Sur-178	Disen,Basil	Row- 64	James Junr	Car-174		
Thomas	Bun- 90	Disham,James	Ire-250	James Senr	Car-174		
Thomas	Hay-194	Dishaser,Clement	Per-137	Jas	Bft- 32		
Willis	Ora-150	Edmund	Per-137	Jas	Ora-118		
William	Bun- 90	Richd	Per-137	Jesse	Cha-212		
Dillback,John Jr	Rth- 98	Robert	Per-137	Jesse	Cha-212		
John Jr	Rth- 98	Dishman,Kessiah	Wil-265	Jno	Ora-123		
John Sr	Rth- 98	Lewis	Wil-272	Jno	Ora-177		
Mary	Rth- 96	Dishmany,Jephthru	Ire-253	John	Per-137		
Dillen,Mrs.	Lnc-358	Dishon,Augt	Ora-122	John	Sur-191		
John	Tyr-206	G Sen	Ora-132	John	Fra- 84		
Dilliard,Elizabeth	Edg- 60	Jacob	Ora-151	John	Cha-195		
John	Edg- 48	Lewis	Ora-163	John	Glf-154		
Reddock	Pit-248	Luke	Ora-125	John	Sur-182		
William	Nor- 64	Dismaker,George	Cha-192	Jos	Glf-159		
Willis	Ora-117	Wm	Cha-202	Joseph	Car-180		
Dillingham,Absalom	Bun- 94	Dismal,Daniel	Len-319	Nathan	Cha-213		
Hiram	Bun- 94	Jesse	Len-311	Nehemiah	Pit-243		
Dillo,Jacob	Row- 67	John Jr	Len-319	Olive	Edg- 58		
John	Row- 80	John Senr	Len-317	Penelope	Pit-233		
Dillon,Benj	Glf-187	Dismuker,Elisha	Cha-214	Robert	Pit-263		
Jane	Lnc-329	Dison,E	Col- 20	Robert	Pit-243		
John	Roc- 19	J	Col- 20	Robert	Jon-295		
John	Glf-151	J	Col- 20	Robt	Ora-118		
Nathan	Glf-185	Divan,Thomas	Sam-160	Samuel	Row- 73		
Dills,Bartlet	Rth- 20	Divine,Jno	Mec- 30	Sanford	Per-137		
John	Rth- 87	John	Joh-289	Sarah	Edg- 66		
Peter	Rth- 97	Patrick	Mec- 39	Solomon	Cha-195		
Thomas	Rth- 20	Diviney,Jas	Glf-179	Solomon	Car-173		
Dilworth,Benjamin	Roc- 20	S	Glf-179	Stewart	Ora-130		
John	Roc- 32	Dix,James	Cas- 52	Susan	Per-128		
John	Roc- 27	Joshua	Glf-187	Sylvanus	Car-173		
John	Roc- 20	Dixen,John	Sto-136	Tho	Bft- 32		
Nancy	Roc- 32	Dixon,Aaron	Cha-209	Thomas	Edg- 66		
Thomas	Roc- 20	Adam	Ora-174	Thomas	Edg- 43		
Dimit,William	Wil-273	Ann	Car-173	Thos	Cha-195		
Dimmiry,Daniel	Ans- 26	Aron	Ons-102	Uriah	Car-174		
Micajah	Ans- 26	Benjn	Cha-195	Walter	Pit-243		
Dimond,John Jr	Grn-128	Burrel	Ons- 99	William	Glf-160		
John Snr	Grn-128	Clifford	Car-173	William	Sur-190		
Margaret	Roc- 30	Cofield	Edg- 42	William	Edg- 43		
Thos	Grn-128	Elizabeth	Edg- 58	William	Gat-111		
Dinkens,Reuben	Wil-285	Elizabeth	Edg- 57	Wm	Ora-120		
Celia	Sam-152	Ephraim	Bft- 32	Wm	Bft- 31		
Federick	Mec- 25	Fed	Bft- 30	Dixson,Henry	Per-150		
Fedk	Bft- 29	Geo	Bft- 21	Jethro	Nsh- 75		

Dizer,John	Car-184	Dodson,Edward	Ora-112	Dollerhide,Asel	Ran-163
Doak,Hannas	Glf-171	Lewis	Roc- 14	Eliza	Roc- 24
J	Glf-184	Obadiah	Sto-137	James	Per-137
Doake,Elias	Cha-199	Obadiah	Sto-155	Dollison,J	Glf-160
Wm	Glf-153	Obadiah	Sto-112	Dolton,David Ser	Sto-151
Doan,J	Bla- 11	Ralph	Roc- 12	Nathan	Roc- 17
Jesse	Sur-171	Richd	Glf-158	Domingo,Segnor	Mec- 35
John	Cha-212	Stephen	War-180	Dona,Nathen	Ran-163
Dobbins,Alexdr	Row- 72	Thomas	Cab-147	Donald,James	Roc- 29
Hugh	Row- 73	Thos	Lnc-332	William	Roc- 19
Jacob	Sur-173	Washington	Sto- 95	Donaldson,Alex	Row- 71
James	Rth- 97	Washington	Sto-124	Arthur	Cab-136
Jno	Mec- 34	William	War-182	Henry A	Cho-220
John	Ire-266	Dofs,Charles	Sto- 93	Hugh	Bun- 73
Jonathan	Rth- 96	Dogahard,Henry	Lnc-352	John	Row- 71
William	Sur-168	Dogan,Joseph	Ran-164	Joseph	Row- 70
Dobbs,Henry	Mec- 30	Dogget,George	Rth- 20	Spencer	Prq-216
Dobbyns,John	Row- 73	Jeremiah	Hal-102	Donaldson,Andrew	Row- 70
Dobins,John	Sur-172	Richard	Hal-103	William	Ire-253
John	Cas- 52	William	Hal-102	Donathan,Benjamin	Wil-277
Dobson,Drury	Rth- 97	Doggett,Bushrod	Rth- 96	Elizebeth	Sur-178
Easther	Ire-261	Charles	Rth- 20	Jacob	Sur-173
Henry B	Sto-148	William	Rth- 97	Dondy,J	Cam-157
Hezekiah	Dup- 8	Dogl,Adam	Grn-140	Done,Ebenezer	Cha-194
James	Ire-262	Doherty,David	Mec- 52	Ephraim	Cha-195
John	Hay-194	Edmond	Cha-207	Jacob	Cha-204
John	Ire-261	George	Mec- 52	James	Bun- 94
John	Lnc-367	James	Bur-124	Donnako,Mrs. Eve	Per-137
Jos	Bur-103	James	Ora-128	Donnaldson,J	Glf-183
Joseph	Ire-261	Jno	Mec- 47	James	Ire-269
Robert	Rth- 96	John	Rth- 20	John	Ire-269
William	Sto-132	John	Roc- 25	William	Ire-267
William Ser	Sto-149	John C	Lnc-376	Donnason,Jas	Brt- 58
Wm	Glf-172	Patrack	Row- 62	Donnedisee,S Lewis	Hyd-223
Doby,John	Rth- 98	Solomon	Bun- 92	Donnell,Adly	Glf-158
Dockery,Elijah	Bur-131	Dokes,Roddy	Ran-163	Andrew	Glf-154
George	Bur-105	Dolby,Dick	Grn-137	Andy	Glf-159
James	Bun- 73	Jarrett	Nor- 64	D Jr	Glf-175
John	Ora-161	John	Nor- 64	Danl	Glf-175
Thomas	Rch-197	John	Grn-136	Geo	Glf-175
Dockings,Jessee	Ire-266	Knight	Grn-120	John	Glf-173
William	Ire-242	William	Cum-257	John	Glf-154
Dockins,Allen	Row- 58	Doles,Benjamin	Nor- 65	Latham	Glf-158
Doda,Geo	Ans- 26	Fanny	Hal-103	Robt Jr	Glf-175
Dodd,Alsey	Ora-112	Jessee	Nor- 65	Robt Snr	Glf-175
Ben	Cha-199	John	Hal-103	Robt Snr	Glf-161
Bennet	Joh-278	Rebekah	Hal-103	Saml	Glf-156
David	Sam-157	Thomas	Hal-102	Thos	Glf-175
Demsey	Joh-291	William	Nor- 65	William	Glf-153
Geo	Cha-199	Dolison,William	Sto-101	Donoho,Thomas	Cas- 52
Jonathan	Joh-273	Doll (sic)	Pas-186	William	Cas- 52
Mary	Roc- 34	Dollar,Elija	Ora-151	Donon,John	Sam-155
William Snr	Joh-291	James	Ora-150	Donoway,Samuel	Cas- 52
Dodgen,Amos	Bun- 95	Jno	Ora-149	Donsway,Enoch	Cas- 53
William	Bun- 95	John	Sam-158	Doogan,George-free man of
Dodson,Agnes	Sto- 95	Thos	Sam-157	colour	Ran-188
Agness	Sto-124	William	Sam-157	Dookbey,Absalom	Rob-242
Charles	Glf-158	Wm	Ora-146	Doolin,Henry	Cab-145
Daniel	Roc- 14	Dollehite,John	Cum-261	Rice	Cab-143

Name	Loc	Name	Loc	Name	Loc
Dooling,John	Sur-189	Dough,Frederick	Cur- 83	Dowden,John	Edg- 68
William	Sur-161	George	Cur- 83	John	War-176
Dooy,Richd	Row- 59	John	Cur- 84	Jonathan	Edg- 69
Dorcas,Old	Pas-187	Richard	Cur- 83	Mathew	Edg- 65
Dorek,Lewis	Nsh- 76	Samson	Cur- 84	Dowdey,Elias	Cur- 87
Wm	Nsh- 78	Samuel	Cur- 82	John	Cur- 87
Dorington,Patrick	Bur-131	Wm	Cur- 84	Josiah	Cur- 87
Dorlan,Britain	Cha-191	Doughdy,Daniel	Hrt-211	Thos	Cur- 86
Charles	Cab-148	Dougherty,Danl	Cab-139	Thos	Cur- 87
Dorman,Clary	Edg- 41	James	Cab-139	William	Cur- 86
Dormon,Jeraldus	Edg- 63	Doughetry,Jas	Hrt-210	Dowdle,John	Rth- 97
Dorrel,Patrick	Bun- 76	Wm	Hrt-210	Dowdy,Amos	Mor- 58
Dorrill,Fras	Cho-222	Doughie,Edward	Gat-114	Babam	Cha-203
Dorset,Francis	Bur-106	Doughtie,William	Gat-116	Bartley	Cha-204
Dorsett,Nancy	Ora-133	Douglas,Abel	Fra- 78	Daniel	Cur- 83
Dorsey,Damon	Bur-122	Abel	Fra- 91	James	Mor- 58
Jereh	Fra- 93	Angus	Rch-213	James	Mor- 63
Solomon	Fra- 93	Daniel	Rch-203	Joab	Cha-189
Solomon	Fra- 79	Geo	Cab-138	John	Cha-216
Dorson,Joseph	Rth- 98	Jas	Ans- 5	Joseph	Cha-189
Dorth,Young	Ora-151	John	Lnc-331	Thomas Junr	Cha-203
Dortmire,Isaac	Ire-246	John	Cho-223	Thos Jnr	Cur- 87
Dorton,Benj	Mon- 23	John	Fra- 77	Tomas Sr	Cha-189
Clayborn	Cas- 52	Solomon	Ire-256	William	Cha-189
Henry	Rob-236	William	Ire-256	Wm	Cha-215
Doset,Clem	Bur-130	Wm	Ans- 28	Dowe,Jno	Mec- 28
Doss,Charles	Sto-121	Douglass,Adam	Ora-128	Dowel,James	Row- 58
Henry	Roc- 25	Benj	Lnc-355	James	Bla- 9
Matthew	Sto-126	David	Ora-170	Joshua	Wil-269
Matthew	Sto- 97	H	Ora-135	Peter	Wil-262
William	Rth- 97	Jas	Ora-135	Peter	Row- 58
William	Bun- 82	John	Mar- 5	Richard	Wil-262
Zachariah	Sto-114	John	Per-137	Robert	Bla- 9
Zachariah	Sto-155	Leary	Ora-165	Dowell,George	Bur-127
Dossett,Francis	Cha-191	Thomas	Sur-172	James	Bur-127
Henry	Cha-191	William	Roc- 32	James	Ire-254
Hezekiah	Cha-205	Douse,Eliza	Hal-103	Joel	Hrt-214
John	Cha-203	Douthard,Isaac	Sto-108	John	Row- 57
Dossitt,Solomon	Cha-195	Isaac	Sto-143	Walker	Cas- 52
Doster,Wm	Mec- 30	Isaac	Sto-153	William	Ire-254
Dotson,J	Ash- 6	Philip	Sto-144	Dowin,Wm	Mec- 53
Lucy	Grn-141	Douthet,Jacob	Row- 56	Dowland,John	War-175
R	Ash- 12	James	Row- 56	Dowlass,Elisha	Bla- 6
Staphan	Grn-140	John	Row- 57	Down,Howell	Edg- 71
Rev.William	Wil-285	John Sr	Row- 57	Downer,Jno	Ans- 23
William Jr	Wil-285	Joseph	Row- 61	Downes,N	Cam-158
Dotty,Isaac	Lnc-339	William	Row- 56	Shadk	Bft- 28
Doty,Samuel	Ons- 99	Dove,Caleb	Cab-141	Downey,Charles	Row- 71
Doud,Corne	Mor- 69	Simon	Ons-104	D	Bla- 10
Doudey,Caleb	Cur- 84	Dow,F	Col- 17	James	Grn-119
Daniel	Cur- 84	Dowd,James	Mor- 56	James Jr	Grn-119
John	Cur- 85	Jno	Rob-243	James Sr	Grn-119
J	Cam-162	John	Cah-215	John	Grn-132
S	Cam-154	Patrick	Mor- 56	Richard	Wsh-223
Willm	Tyr-209	Richd	Cha-203	Samuel	Cur- 87
Douers,John	Brt- 58	Saml	Cha-193	Sarah	Grn-119
Dough,Beney	Cur- 82	Dowde,Saml	Hyd-221	William	Row- 22
Benj	Cur- 87	Dowden,Anthony	War-167	Yerin	Ire-240
Daniel	Cur- 84	Elizabeth	Edg- 70	Downie,M	Bla- 10

Name	Loc	Name	Loc	Name	Loc	Name	Loc
Downing,George	Edg- 54	Drake,Jordan	Ans- 24	Driver,Charles	Brt- 56		
James	Edg- 54	Martin	Row- 57	Giles	Mec- 52		
John	Hrt-210	Mat	Nsh- 72	James	Fra- 98		
Stevens Esqr	Wsh-224	Richard	Nsh- 87	Thomas	Fra- 81		
Downs,Isaac	Pit-247	Richd	Cha-206	William	Hrt-216		
Leaven	Cas- 53	Silas	Rob-220	Wm	Nsh- 91		
Nehemiah	Pit-245	Trussum	Hal-102	Worren	Nsh- 88		
Saml	Mec- 25	William	Edg- 68	Drizle,John	Brt- 59		
Thos	Mec- 34	Wm	Nsh- 73	Drownburger,Lud	Ora-131		
William	Rth- 98	Wm	Cha-202	Drum,John	Lnc-355		
Downy,Patrick	Lnc-374	Winny	Bun- 72	Peter	Lnc-352		
Samuel	Rth- 97	Drans,Matt	Hrt-209	Phillip	Ire-247		
Dowthert,Thos	Row- 56	Draper,Betsy	Per-129	William	Lnc-355		
Dowty,Elisha	Bft- 32	Chalkly	Prq-216	Drummon,Fanny	Hal-103		
Jas	Bft- 34	Hannah	Cas- 52	Rachel	Hal-103		
John	Bft- 31	Jesse	Prq-216	Thomas	Hal-102		
Lodwk	Bft- 31	Josiah	Ran-163	Drummons,Thomas	Edg- 58		
Peter	Bft- 31	Nathen	Ran-163	Drury,Fanny	Nor- 64		
Teakle	Bft- 31	Presley	Per-128	Jno	Mec- 28		
Tho	Bft- 31	Samuel	Prq-216	Druskell,E	Glf-179		
Dox,William	Cur- 89	Solomon	Per-137	E	Glf-175		
Doxey,James	Cur- 89	Thomas	Nor- 64	Dry,Andw	Cab-141		
John	Cur- 88	Thos	Prq-216	Jacob	Cab-141		
Doxy,John	Joh-282	William	Nor- 64	John	Cab-141		
Sandford	Cur- 90	William	Gat-114	Martin	Cab-141		
Doyal,Daniel	Sur-188	Willis	Wsh-223	Owen	Cab-141		
John	Sur-188	Draughan,George	Cum-259	Peter	Cab-141		
Doyle,David	Rth- 97	James	Edg- 45	Phillip	Cab-141		
James	Rth- 97	Magnus	Bla- 9	Dryman,Henry	Bun- 75		
Dozier,James	Cum-260	Robert	Cum-260	Henry Senr	Bun- 75		
John	Nsh- 76	Thomas	Edg- 44	Ducart,Ezekiel	Glf-158		
Richard	Edg- 58	Wells	Edg- 62	Jos	Glf-160		
Richd	Nsh- 77	William	Edg- 43	Duck,Alexr	Bur-104		
Tho	Nsh- 77	Drauhn,Jacob	Sto-137	John	Bur-104		
Timothy	Lnc-342	John	Glf-178	Tabitha	Joh-278		
Wm	Nsh- 77	Drawhn,Jesse	Glf-187	Wm	Bur-104		
Dozur,Zediah	Prq-216	John	Glf-187	Wm	Bur-105		
Drahorn,Hardy	Sam-155	Drawhorn,Richard	Joh-276	Ducket,Jacob	Bun- 74		
Drake,Benja	Nsh- 77	Drawn,Michl	Row- 47	Richard	Bun- 74		
Caswell	War-169	Drean,Asiniah	Cur- 81	Sarah	Bun- 74		
David	Ora-112	Dresser,Sarah	Pas-187	Duckett,Christopher	Wsh-223		
Deliah	Nsh- 74	Drew,J	Bru-228	Ducksmith,Joseph	Mor- 57		
Drury	Edg- 68	J Sr	Bru-228	Duckworth,Abel	Bun- 72		
Dyer	Nsh- 74	Jno	Ans- 13	George	Mec- 52		
Eli	Mec- 43	Jno Jr	Bru-230	John	Mec- 53		
Ethelbert	Grn-139	John	Brt- 43	Keziah	Bun- 98		
Exum	Nsh- 88	John Jr	Hal-103	Robt	Mec- 52		
Francis	Hal-103	Joshua	Hal-102	Simon	Mec- 52		
Francis	Nsh- 73	Solomon	Hal-102	Thos	Mec- 53		
Francis	Cha-198	Thomas	Hal-102	William	Bun- 72		
Geo	Cha-202	William	Hal-103	Wm	Mec- 52		
Goodson	Fra- 89	Drewry,Eve	Rob-234	Wm	Mec- 52		
Grey	Edg- 70	Henry	Nsh- 76	Dudley,Charles	Sur-175		
Harbet	Mec- 42	James	Hal-102	Chrisr Esqr	Ons-109		
Herbert	Hal-102	Sarah	Rob-234	Cleed Esqr	Ons- 95		
Jesse	Hal-102	Wm	Rob-234	Daniel	Sam-163		
Jno	Rob-220	Driskill,John Jr	Rth- 96	David	Car-184		
John H	Nsh- 79	John Sr	Rth- 96	Elizath	Ons-101		
Jonas	Nsh- 76	Driver,Benj	Nsh- 84	George	Hyd-234		

Name	Ref	Name	Ref	Name	Ref
Dudley,George H	Car-179	Dugless,William	Cas- 52	Dulany,Thomas	Ons-106
James	Cur- 92	Duglis,Eufamy	Cur- 91	Dulen,Daniel	Mec- 45
James	Pit-240	James	Cur- 88	Jno	Mec- 41
Jehu	Car-178	Mary	Cur- 82	Suger	Mec- 40
John	Car-178	Duham,James	War-173	Dulin,David	Row- 82
John	Rch-200	Duke,Andw	Cur- 86	Duly,Martha	Cha-204
Laban	Sam-155	Buckner	Cas- 52	Richd	Per-128
Levy	Sam-156	Burwell Jr	War-168	Dumas,Amos	Rch-199
Malecky	Cur- 92	Burwell Sr	War-168	Benjamin Junr	Rch-199
Needham	Sam-156	Clevas	Grn-127	Benjamin Senr	Rch-199
Rebecca	Ons-102	Dabney	Fra- 91	David	Mon- 26
Richd	Cum-247	Daniel	War-170	David	Rch-199
Robert	Sur-181	Eli	Gat-112	Jemima	Rch-199
Thomas	Ons-105	Eliga Merm	Cur- 84	Jeremiah	Rch-199
William G	Edg- 40	Green	War-172	Moses	Rch-199
Dudly,Abraham	Jon-295	Green B	War-171	Zachariah	Mon- 26
Caleb	Cur- 84	Guilford	War-172	Dun,Mary	Row- 76
Christopher	Jon-295	Jacob	Row- 69	Nathan	Rob-221
Jacob	Jon-295	John	Gat-112	Simon	Lnc-334
John	Jon-295	John	Ora-163	Thomas	Row- 52
L	Bru-236	John	Row- 84	Dunagan,Elijah	Sur-184
Dudney,Jno	Mon- 39	Lewis P	War-177	Jesse	Sur-184
Due,A	Col- 19	Mark	Grn-138	John	Sur-186
Duff,Benjn	Dup- 23	Mary	War-177	Tyre	Sur-179
George	Row- 73	Matthew	War-177	William	Sur-186
John	Bun- 89	O	Glf-183	Dunaho,David	Ire-242
John	Dup- 21	Richard	War-179	Dunaway,Abraham	Per-150
Duffee,Jno	Mec- 45	Richerd	Cur- 90	John	Row- 82
Robt	Mec- 45	Robert	Ora-166	Dunbar,Betty	Bft= 27
Saml	Mec- 45	Taylor	Ora-125	Robt	Bft- 29
Wm	Cha-206	Thomas	Cab-146	Dunbarr,Thos	Tyr-208
Duffie,Jno	Mec- 44	Tyree	Ora-943	Duncan,Absolum	Lnc-358
Duffle,William	Cum-258	William	War-184	Alamander	Sto-140
Duffy,George	Car-177	William P	War-183	Charles	Bur-106
John	Rth-102	Wm	Ora-159	Christian	Roc- 9
Sarah	Hal-103	Wm	Glf-183	Cmore	Ora-136
Dufingham,Archd	Rth- 20	Wm	Glf-183	E	Col- 21
Dugald,Charles	Rob-230	Dukens,Saml	Per-128	Edmund	Cum-264
Dugan,Thomas	Bun- 88	Dukes,Harwood	Nor- 65	George	Dup- 14
William	Bun- 88	John	Cum-265	Henry	Joh-290
Duggan,James	Mar- 12	Jesse	Cum-265	J	Ash- 3
John	Mar- 15	Joseph	Car-182	Jacob	Rob-220
John	Mar- 12	Joshua	Ran-163	Jacob	Dup- 13
Swain	Mar- 11	Priscilla	Hal-103	James	Ire-265
William	Mar- 9	Talitha	Hyd-227	James	War-175
Duggaus,John	Sto-139	Dukkens,Samuel Esq	Per-128	James	Cha-190
John	Sto-105	Duks,Daniel	Gat-107	James	Per-128
William	Sto-104	Dukson,Alexander	Dup- 8	Jane	Ire-251
Duggar,C	Col- 20	Benedict	Dup- 9	Jno	Rob-221
J	Col- 20	James	Dup- 10	John	Cum-248
Dugger,B	Ash- 6	Lewis	Dup- 3	John	Cha-190
D	Ash- 6	Sally	Dup- 7	John Senr	Lnc-363
Duggins,William	Sto-138	William	Dup- 5	M	Col- 21
Duglas,Danl	Rob-219	Dula,Bennet	Wil-275	Mary	Bur-121
Joseph	Mec- 52	John	Wil-282	Micajah	Cha-190
Rachel	Cha-196	Thomas	Wil-279	Nathan	Ire-250
Samuel	Prq-216	William	Wil-276	R	Ora-147
Duglass,Mary	Sur-189	Dulan,Thos	Mec- 45	Sarah	Bur-114
Dugless,T	Ash- 7	Dulany,Daniel M Esq	Ons- 97	Thomas	Car-169

Duncan,Thomas	Sto-104	Dunn,Hezekiah	Ans- 26	Dupoister,Joseph	Ire-267
Thomas	Bun- 86	Isaac	Ans- 17	Duport,William	Bur-119
Thos	Sto-139	James	Dup- 5	Dupree,Cordall	Nor- 65
Duncean,Harison	Grn-141	Jas	Mec- 55	Jacob	Nor- 65
John	Grn-141	John	Sto-101	James Jr	Nor- 65
John	Grn-145	John	Sto-132	James Senr	Nor- 65
Duncum,Willie	War-182	John	Jon-295	Roderick	Way-233
Dunelo,John	Hal-103	John	Mor- 57	Duprey,Benjamin C	Pit-254
Dunford,Philip	Edg- 51	John	Mor- 64	Benjamin Sr	Pit-254
Thomas	Edg- 51	John	Ora-127	Edmond	Pit-253
Dunham,Henry	Rth- 97	Jonas	Edg- 46	Peter	Joh-276
Henry Jr	Rth- 97	L	Col- 20	Robert	Pit-253
Thomas	Rth- 97	Lawrana	Edg- 44	Thomas	Pit-253
William	Rth- 98	Lemon	Edg- 44	Durden,Jacob	Bft- 20
Wm	Cha-202	Mary	Mec- 36	Durdenoe,Cetiah	Way-246
Dunhum,John	Glf-161	Nicholas	Edg- 45	Henry	Way-246
Duning,Samuel	Edg- 44	Numan	Pit-231	Thomas	Way-246
Dunken,E	Col- 20	Phebe	Bun- 86	Dure,Leven	Hrt-216
George	Hal-103	Rachl	Bft- 31	Durgan,Wm	Mon- 41
George	Per-137	Red	Mon- 35	Durgear,Wm	Cha-195
J	Col- 20	Richd	Ans- 26	Durham,Acles	Rth- 97
Wm	Hal-103	Robt	Mec- 54	Archd	Ora-146
Dunkin,Alexander	Ire-256	S	Ora-135	Aron	Ora-121
Charles	Ran-163	Saml	Dup- 6	Charles	Rth- 97
D	Col- 19	Samuel	Mor- 65	Daniel	Per-150
D	Cam-155	Thomas	Ans- 31	Gregory	Cas- 53
J	Cam-154	Thomas	Fra- 80	Hardy	Joh-290
Sally	Pas-186	Thomas	Hal-103	Henry	Cas- 52
W	Cam-154	Thomas	Way-239	Henry	Cas- 52
Z	Cam-153	Thomas Sr	Way-240	Isaac	Ora-113
Dunkins,J	Cam-163	Waller	Len-322	Isaac	Cas- 53
Dunlap,-----	Sto-104	William	Fra- 80	James	Wil-266
Widow	Lnc-342	Wm	Mor- 64	James	Joh-290
Alexander	Ire-243	Wm	Mor- 59	James	Sru-172
Christian	Ora-167	Dunnagan,Ashby	Ora-943	James Jr	Sur-172
David R	Ans- 16	Charles	Ora-164	John	Bur-128
Geo	Ans- 16	Dicey	Ora-165	John	Roc- 17
Jesse	Sto-138	Sarah	Ora-165	John	Per-137
Jas	Mor- 57	Sarah	Ora-943	John	Cas- 53
John	Mor- 66	Wm	Ora-943	Mark	Ora-147
John	Sto-105	Dunnavin,John	Ora-167	Martin	Cas- 53
John	Sto-139	Dunning,Eli	Brt- 54	Mary	Roc- 14
William	Sto-119	Elisha	Pit-260	Matthew	Wil-270
Dunmore,David	Hal-103	James Jr	Glf-170	Mitchell	Bur-127
Dunn,Widow	Mec- 29	John	Bft- 62	Newmon	Cas- 52
Aaron	Ans- 21	Samuel	Row- 81	Redford	Cas- 52
Andrew	Mec- 25	Dunsmore,David	Bun- 85	Richard	Rth- 98
Andrew	Mec- 54	Dunstan,Alcey col	Fra-101	Samuel	War-181
B	Mon- 35	Dunston,Abram	Wsh-218	Thomas	Wil-270
Bartholemew	Mor- 64	Edmund	Brt- 46	W R	Bla- 4
Benj	Way-239	John	Cur- 83	William	Rth- 98
Benjn	Way-234	Dunton,Director	Cur- 86	William	Sto-122
Drury	Ora-167	Francis	Cur- 88	Wm	Ora-126
Edwin	Sto-134	Levin	Cur- 88	Wm	Sto- 93
Edwin	Sto-102	Dunts,James col	Fra-101	Durkins,Wm	Brt- 57
Elizabeth	Len-314	Patty col	Fra-101	Durley,Chas	Ans- 6
Elizabeth	Bun- 74	Dunwiddy,John	Lnc-333	Horatia	Ans- 18
Frances	Bft- 30	Duplis,Hubbard	Glf-160	Durnbush,John	Ire-254
Francis	Wil-274	Dupoister,John	Ire-267	Durnin,N	Ora-140

Name	Ref	Name	Ref	Name	Ref	Name	Ref
Durr,Ormon	Joh-277	Eades,Ezekiel	Row- 83	Earnest,G	Ash- 15		
Durram,Henry	Rth- 98	Eagerton,Charles	Ons-101	Henry	Wil-279		
Durrum,Geo	Bun- 74	Eagle,Elizabeth	Roc- 6	Earnhart,Henry	Row- 86		
Durwell,Philip	Row- 84	Tabitha	Edg- 69	Earp,Abednego	Wil-273		
Durybury,Michael	Bur-122	Eagles,Jo	Bru-226	Josiah	Cas- 53		
William	Bur-122	Eakel,Henry	Row- 56	Earwood,Edmund	Rth- 99		
Duse,Daniel	Joh-183	Henry	Row- 55	John	Rth- 99		
Dutheran,Michael	Bun- 82	Eaker,Christian	Lnc-328	Thos	Lnc-376		
Dutton,Jarrol	Grn-135	Christy	Lnc-328	Will	Lnc-326		
John	Grn-132	Christy	Lnc-327	Easland,Joshua	Cha-192		
Z	Bru-232	Daniel	Lnc-331	Easley,Allen	Hal-104		
Zachariah	Grn-132	Jacob	Lnc-329	D	Mon- 37		
Duty,Jabez	Grn-148	John	Lnc-330	Jno	Mon- 37		
Mathew	Cha-212	John	Lnc-331	Jno	Mec- 36		
William	Cha-212	John P	Lnc-331	Joseph	Sto- 92		
Wm	Cha-212	Michl	Lnc-328	Joseph	Sto-121		
Duval,Archibald	Ire-262	Peter	Lnc-338	William	Sur-160		
Francis	Edg- 40	Peter	Lnc-327	Easom,Gideon	Sam-154		
William	Edg- 42	Eakes,Mary	Roc- 14	Eason,Abner	Edg- 49		
Duvall,F	Col- 17	Eakin,George	Rth- 99	Abner	Brt- 65		
Duvatt,Wm	Glf-175	John	Rth- 98	Edy	Nsh-643		
Dwane,Punsin	Cur- 79	John Jr	Rth- 20	Elizabeth	Gat-112		
Dwiggans,Lyddia	Glf-185	John Sr	Rth- 20	Federick	Gat-109		
Robert	Sto-149	Joseph	Rth- 20	Hardy	Gat-109		
Robert	Sto-110	Samuel	Rth- 20	Isaac	Edg- 40		
Dwiggin,Daniel	Row- 59	Eaks,Widow	Mec- 37	Isaac Jr	Edg- 50		
Dwiggins,John	Row- 61	Zach	Grn-147	J	Cam-160		
Dwryor,T O	Hrt-209	Ealand,David	Glf-186	Jacob	Gat-108		
Dycas,James	Rth- 97	Earhart,Abram	Lnc-376	Jno	Ora-123		
Larkin	Rth- 98	Earl,John	Grn-148	John	Joh-287		
Dycus,William	Rth- 97	Earle,Aspan	Rth- 99	John	Joh-291		
William	Rth- 97	Laurence	Wsh-228	John	Brt- 65		
Dye,Elizabeth	Roc- 32	Peter	Wsh-227	Joseph	Brt- 58		
Dyer,A	Ash- 5	Rebekah	Rth- 99	Joseph Jnr	Brt- 63		
Adry	Lnc-339	Earles,Barnet	Lnc-339	Joshua	Edg- 51		
Caleb	Wil-278	Bennet	Lnc-327	Mary	Pit-233		
Elijah	Wil-276	Joshua	Lnc-327	Mills	Sto-142		
Frederick	Glf-152	Joshua	Lnc-338	Mills	Mar- 12		
John	Rth- 97	Nathan	Rth-100	Nathan	Edg- 51		
John	Lnc-339	Pleasant	Rth-100	Reuben	Mar- 5		
Jonathan	Sur-172	William	Lnc-327	Solomon	Gat-106		
Luke	Glf-154	William	Lnc-339	Zilphey	Gat-108		
Minoah	Wil-284	Earley,William	Hrt-215	East,John	Sur-177		
Samuel	Lnc-339	Wilson	Hrt-211	Thomas	Sto-126		
William	Lnc-339	Earls,Obed	War-178	Thomas	Sto- 97		
Dyke,Jas	Mon- 40	Early,Asa	Brt- 62	Easten,Michal	Row- 79		
Dykes,Isom	Ire-248	Benjamin	Brt- 62	Eastep,Jacob	Row- 59		
Dyson,Barton	Ire-243	Elizabeth	Rth- 99	Thomas	Ire-266		
Isaac	Rch-196	Elizabeth	Rth- 99	Easter,James	Hyd-232		
Joseph	Ire-243	James	Brt- 62	Margryt	Hyd-233		
Polly	Ire-261	Jeremiah	Sur-170	Susanah	Hyd-232		
William	Ire-243	John	Brt- 62	Wm	Bft- 38		
Dyzard,Federick	Mec- 24	John	Rth- 99	Easterling,Wm	Len-318		
		John	Grn-136	Eastis,Bartlett	Cas- 53		
E-esin?,Richard	Cas- 53	Thomas	Rth- 99	Sarah	Cas- 53		
Eackerd,Adam	Lnc-352	Thomas	Rth- 99	Eastwood,Abraham	Hyd-229		
Martin	Lnc-352	Earnest,Andrew	Bur-130	Charles	Grn-138		
Simon	Lnc-352	C	Ash- 3	Isaack	Hyd-229		
Eaden,Samuel	Rth- 99	D	Ash- 3	John	Grn-138		

-92-

Name	Ref	Name	Ref	Name	Ref
Eastwood,Mary	Grn-138	Eborn,Margryt	Hyd-220	Edmond,Wm	Hal-104
Peggy	Bft- 39	Martha	Hyd-225	Edmonds,Elizabeth	Nor- 65
Eatman,Allen	Nsh- 90	William	Hyd-220	Howell	Nor- 65
John	Nsh- 88	Zachary	Hyd-223	James	Hal-102
Noel	Nsh- 90	Ebourn,Moses	Bft- 23	William	Bun- 93
Thomas	Joh-284	Eccherd,Geo	Lnc-374	William	Nor- 65
Eatmon,Irven	Nsh- 86	Eccles,Gilbert	Cum-235	Edmondson,Bryan	Way-241
Joel	Nsh- 87	John	Ora-164	Elisha	Ons- 95
Sarah	Nsh- 86	John	Cum-239	James	Roc- 31
Robert	Nsh- 86	Echols,Wm	Bft- 34	John	Edg- 53
Theophilus	Nsh- 86	Eckleston,Mary	Hrt-210	John	Roc- 31
Eaton,A William	Nor- 66	Ecock,Jno	Mec- 40	John	Way-241
Abraham	Hay-195	Ector,James	Ora-164	Orpha	Edg- 53
Benjamin	Row- 60	Jos	Ora-164	Pollard	Edg- 53
Charles R	Grn-127	Saml	Ora-164	Thomas	Roc- 30
Christopher	Sto-155	Edder,William	Ire-263	William	Roc- 31
Christopher	Sto-113	Edding,Joseph	Cas- 53	Edmonton,Bazel B	Bun- 59
Daniel	Hay-195	Eddins,Abigail	Mon- 29	Robert	Bun- 83
George	Lnc-358	Jno	Ans- 26	Wm	Bun- 89
Isaac	Hay-195	Sterlen	Rth-100	Edmont,John	Ire-239
John	Lnc-360	William	Cas- 53	Samuel	Ire-238
John	Hal-104	Eddleman,David	Lnc-347	Edmonton,John	Bun- 88
John	Grn-128	John	Lnc-366	Edmudson,S	Ora-154
John R	Grn-140	Peter	Lnc-366	Edmunds,Robert	Wil-269
Joshua	Row- 76	Peter	Row- 67	Edmundson,Penney	Way-240
Peter	Row- 59	Philip	Row- 67	Edney,Asa	Bun- 72
Peter	Row- 60	Eddy,Jacob	Cum-266	J	Cam-162
Peter	Sur-175	Edelman,Boston	Ire-250	N	Cam-164
Rebecca	Nor- 66	Edens,Ezekiel	Ons-107	R	Cam-164
Rebekah negr	Hal-104	John	Ons-102	Samuel	Bun- 72
Ro	Ora-110	Robert E	Brt- 43	Edrug,N	Cam-158
Samuel	Hay-195	Sarah	Ons-107	Eds,Isaac	Sto-145
William	Roc- 3	Edes,Isaac	Sto-108	Lindy	Sto-113
William	Hay-195	Edey,--fun	Cur- 91	Lindy	Sto-154
William	War-183	Jemimey	Cur- 86	Robert	Sto-124
Wm A	Hal-104	Edge,Drussilla	Bla- 8	William	Sto-138
Eavans,John	Cha-203	Frank	Pas-188	Edson,Barnabas	Ire-262
Eaveritt,Nathl	Ons-108	Jack	Pas-188	Edward	Ire-261
Eaves,Andrew	Rth- 99	Willis	Nor- 65	Gross	Ire-261
Burrell	Rth- 98	Edgerton,James N	Rth- 99	Joseph	Ire-262
Jonathan	Rth- 99	John	Rth-100	Edward,Eliza	Hal-104
William	Rth- 99	Thomas	Way-254	Ransom	Hal-104
Eavins,Jesse	Rth- 99	William	Rth- 99	Edwards,A	Glf-164
William	Rth-100	William	Way-254	Abel	Glf-156
Eazell,John	Hrt-215	Edgins,John	Lnc-347	Abel	Sto-127
Lewis	Hrt-211	Edgley,Jno Junr	Len-311	Absalom	Glf-164
Eberheart,John L	Sto-146	Ediner,Frederic	Wil-270	Allin	Ora-136
Ebern,Zach	Cho-224	Edings,Thomas	Sto-143	Ambros	Way-236
Ebersole,John	Wil-267	Thomas	Sto-108	Anuel	Glf-181
Ebert,John	Sto-134	Edlemon,Jacob	Sur-190	Arthur	Rth- 99
John G	Row- 57	Edlon,David	Nor- 66	Arthur	Rth- 99
Eblin,Lewis	Row- 52	Edminton,William	Bur-128	Benj	Joh-279
Ebold,J	Mon- 38	Edmiston,George	Bur-126	Benj	Lnc-355
Eborn,Ann	Hyd-220	George	Bur-119	Benjamin	Rob-237
Ann	Hyd-224	Saml	Cab-136	Benjamin	Cum-257
Ann	Hyd-223	Edmond,Benj	Hal-104	Benjamin	Rth- 99
Arkadia	Hyd-223	Charles	Hal-104	Briton Jr	Edg- 69
Henry	Hyd-222	John	Hal-104	Birtton	Bft- 29
Littleton	Hyd-220	Willm	Hal-104	Britton Sr	Edg- 69

Name	Code	Name	Code	Name	Code
Edwards,Bryant	Edg- 69	Edwards,Jas	Glf-162	Edwards,Polly	Nor- 65
Canless	Hay-195	Jas	Rob-231	Polly	Grn-135
Charles	Bla- 6	Jere	Ora-129	R	Ora-139
Charles	Grn-132	Jesse	Rth- 99	R	Ash- 14
Charles	Rth- 99	Jno	Ora-167	Roland	Rob-220
Collin	Wil-275	Jno	Ora-114	Ryal	Bft- 29
D	Ash- 13	Jno	Ans- 21	S	Ash- 13
Daniel	War-170	Joel	Nor- 65	S	Ora-146
Daniel	Fra- 91	John	Lnc-360	Saml	Bft- 29
David	Way-236	John	Bft- 29	Saml	Rob-220
David	Bun- 92	John	Tyr-205	Samson	Way-236
David	Glf-185	John	Sur-194	Samuel	War-180
David Jnr	Bft- 29	John	Bun- 73	Samuel	Row- 61
David Sen	Bft- 29	John	Bun- 77	Sarah	Prq-217
Dempsy	Nor- 65	John	Edg- 66	Sarah	Nor- 65
E	Ash- 14	John	Grn-149	Sarah	Bft- 28
E N	Bft- 37	John Jnr	Ran-164	Selah	Prq-217
Edmond	Bun- 78	John Jr	Nor- 65	Seley	Edg- 50
Edmond	Edg- 68	John Snr	Ran-164	Simeon	Edg- 66
Edward	Sto-126	John Senr	Nor- 65	Solomon	Nsh- 78
Edward	Sto- 97	John Senr	Lnc-358	Stephen	Way-236
Edwin	Nsh- 77	John Senr	Bun- 77	Stokes	Cha-203
Edwin	Nsh- 74	Jonas	Edg- 44	Susannah	Cum-258
Ekels	Bft- 29	Jonathan	Ran-164	Tho	Ora-118
Elias	Rob-220	Jonathan	Ran-164	Thomas	Roc- 24
Elizabeth	Rob-243	Jonathan	Hay-195	Thomas	Joh-281
Elizabeth	Bun- 73	Joseph	Way-239	Thomas	Bun- 94
Ellis	Bun- 82	Joshua	Glf-186	Thomas	Rob-233
Enoch	Rth- 20	Joshua	Cha-207	Thomas	Rth- 20
Etheldred	Edg- 61	Joshua	Cum-248	Thos	Rob-221
Gedion	Sur-181	Josiah	Ons-108	Thos	Glf-181
George	Nsh- 78	Lemmon	Edg- 68	Titus	Fra- 86
Gideon	Fra- 91	Littleton	Grn-127	W	Ash- 14
Henry	Ora-114	M	Ora-156	Walkr	Bft- 29
Hugh	Cha-206	Manl	Bft- 28	William	Bun- 95
Hugh Jr	Cha-216	Martha	Nor- 65	William	Glf-171
Isaac	Bft- 29	Martha	Cha-215	William	Joh-281
Isaac	Mec- 48	Martin	Rth- 20	William	Roc- 30
Isaac	Hal-104	Mat	Lnc-355	William	Nor- 66
Isaac	Nor- 66	Matthew	Nor- 65	William	Nor- 65
Isaac Senr	Nor- 65	Matthew	Dup- 32	William	Pit-243
Isaac	Ran-164	Merit	Ons-102	William	Lnc-366
Isham	Per-137	Micajah	Joh-280	William	Sur-185
Isom	Way-236	Micajah Jr	Joh-280	William	Bun- 77
Israel	Pit-244	Michael	Nor- 65	William	Rth- 99
J	Glf-162	Michael	Nor- 65	Wm	Ora-130
J	Col- 18	Moses	Cum-248	Wm Eno	Ora-118
J	Col- 20	N	Bru-222	Wm	Brt- 60
Jacob	Ran-164	N	Glf-162	Wm	Ans- 19
Jacob	Tyr-205	Nancy	Nor- 65	Wm	Ans- 13
James	Roc- 24	Nathan	Ora-114	Willis	Nor- 65
James	Way-236	Nathan	Edg- 45	Y	Ash- 13
James	Lnc-356	Nathan	Cha-207	Y	Ash- 14
James	Bun- 78	Nathl	Lnc-358	Zedekiah	Fra- 82
James	Grn-132	Nathl	Len-316	Edwell,Dick	Cas- 53
James	Rth- 98	Newman	Dup- 32	Efferet,Martin	Cab-140
James	Cha-207	Patsey	Lnc-342	Martin	Cab-140
James Jr	Nor- 65	Peter	Dup- 32	Effland,John	Ora-159
James Senr	Nor- 65	Philip	Mon- 21	Efflin,Davd	Ora-144

Efland,David	Ora-115	Elison,Thos	Cur- 90	Ellington,Worshum	.Joh-274
Eflin,Jacob	Ora-172	Elkins,Benj Sr	Cha-204	William T	Roc- 6
John	Ora-116	Gabriel	Bun- 77	Wright	Grn-140
Egerton,John J	War-176	James	Bun- 78	Ellinor,Benjamin	Edg- 56
Martha	War-178	Jesse	Bur-115	Etheldred	Edg- 56
Wilmot	War-183	John	Cha-197	Francis	Gat-107
Eggers,C	Ash- 11	John	Bun- 76	James	Edg- 56
D	Ash- 5	Saml	Mor- 57	Elliot,Widow	Row- 87
D	Ash- 6	Saml	Cha-207	Amos	Roc- 11
H	Ash- 9	Saml	Rob-243	Ebenezer	Cha-190
H	Ash- 6	Stephen	Cha-208	Enoch	Mon- 22
J	Ash- 11	Thomas	Bun- 83	James	Mon- 18
L	Ash- 11	Willis	Cha-214	John	Roc- 9
S	Ash- 6	Wm	Cha-214	John	Ire-244
Eggmont,Lott	Cas- 53	Elks,Jacob	Pit-243	Nimrod	Sur-169
Egleton,Margryt	Hyd-223	Samuel	Pit-243	Robt	Ans- 15
Mary	Hyd-225	Samuel Sr	Pit-243	Sally	Pas-188
Noah	Hyd-223	William	Pit-243	Saml	Cha-190
Ehart,Leonard	Bur-120	Ellbeck,Dorothy	Hal-104	Thomas	Pas-188
Eisenhouer,Daniel	Lnc-352	John	Hal-104	Thomas	Pas-188
George	Lnc-352	Montfort	Hal-104	Washington	Sur-167
John Jr	Lnc-352	Ellebey,Thos	Ans- 31	Wm	Ora-161
John Senr	Lnc-352	Elledge,John	Wil-272	Elliott,Abraham	Ran-164
Volumtine	Lnc-352	Joseph	Wil-273	Abram Jr	Prq-217
Ekes,Dudley	Glf-189	Ellen,Loderick F	Nsh- 78	Abram Sr	Prq-216
Eks,Isham	Grn-126	Salley	Nsh- 90	Andrew	Mec- 46
Elame,Robert	Cas- 53	Eller,Conrad	Row- 85	Benja	Prq-216
Elder,James Jnr	Ran-164	Geo	Row- 50	Benjamin	Ran-164
James Snr	Ran-164	H	Ash- 7	Benjn	Cho-220
Jno M	Ans- 4	J	Bru-236	Caleb	Prq-216
John	Ran-164	J	Ash- 10	Charles	Prq-216
John	Ire-264	J	Ash- 8	Dick	Ran-164
Elders,Jeremiah	Lnc-338	James	Bur-105	Elizabeth	Prq-217
John	Lnc-338	John (Staton)	Row- 77	Ephm	Cho-227
Mary	Hay-195	Mary	Bun- 90	Ephraim	Prq-216
Eldredge,M	Ash- 5	P	Ash- 8	Exom	Ora-134
Eldridge,Damnott	Grn-132	Robt	Bft- 23	Foster	Prq-217
Saml	Joh-289	Ellesander,Simeon	Mar- 7	Gabriel	Prq-216
William	Sto- 95	Elleson,Richd	Cum-248	Henry	Prq-216
William	Sto-125	Ellett,Jno	Ans- 14	Hugh	Mec- 55
Eleman,John	Cab-145	Ellickson,William	Grn-132	Hushe	Prq-216
Eley,Barshaba	Nsh- 89	Ellidge,Jacob	Wil-283	Isaac	Prq-216
Josiah	Fra- 88	Elligood,Absm	Bft- 24	Isaac	Ran-164
Messers	Nsh- 89	Ben	Bft- 25	J	Glf-177
Michael	Fra- 89	Franc	Bft- 25	Jacob	Prq-216
Eli,Cate	Bft- 30	Jacob	Bft- 25	Jacob	Ran-164
Samuel	Rch-208	John	Bft- 24	Jacob	Ran-164
Sarah	Cho-223	John	Bft- 25	James	Prq-216
Elice,Judey	Cur- 90	John	Bft- 25	James	Ran-164
Elington,Danl	Cha-199	Rebeca	Bft- 25	Jas F	Lnc-338
Geo	Cha-193	Ellington,Ader	Joh-237	Jeremiah	Ran-164
James	Grn-134	Bevy	Grn-136	Jesse	Bft- 22
John	Grn-134	Daniel	Roc- 12	Jesse	Rth- 99
Jourdin	Grn-134	James	War-173	Jesse of Nn	Prq-216
Eliot,George	Per-128	James	Joh-285	Jesse of P	Prq-216
John	Sam-154	Jesse	Joh-274	Joab	Prq-216
Wm	Mor- 64	John	Roc- 12	Jno	Ora-133
Eliott,Axum	Sur-168	Paschal	Roc- 11	John	Prq-216
Elison,John	Per-137	Waite	Grn-140	John	Fra- 85

Elliott,John	Car-182	Ellis,Delilah	Nor- 66	Ellis,Lewis	Ons-100
Joseph	Ran-164	Delinno	Car-177	Marthey	Cas- 53
Joseph	Ran-164	Dennis	Edg- 50	Mary	Bla- 8
Joseph	Len-311	Dixon	Edg- 65	Mary	Cum-249
Joseph Jr	Prq-216	E Esq	Col- 18	Micael	Grn+139
Joseph Jnr	Ran-164	Eli	Ons-109	Michael	Mar- 9
Joseph Sr	Prq-216	Elias	Nor- 66	Moley	Gat-110
Joshua	Prq-216	Elijah	Ora-127	Monin	Gat-110
Josiah	Prq-216	Elisha	Edg- 50	Nancy	Len-310
Lemuel	Fra- 92	Eliza	Len-313	Patty	Ons-100
M	Glf-159	Elizabeth	Cum-251	Philip	Cum-248
Martin Sr	Rth-100	Ephraim	War-171	Ransom	Row- 55
Mary	Cum-246	Etheldred	Pit-257	Reddick	Nsh- 87
Miles	Cho-230	Etheldred	Sur-173	Richard	War-180
Mordeca	Prq-216	Evan	Bla- 13	Samuel	Bur-126
Moses	Glf-171	Evan	Rob-221	Saul	Ire-269
Myles	Prq-216	Evin	Row- 57	Scipean	Ons-100
Nathen	Ran-164	Francis	Row- 51	Sherrod	Mar-446
Nimrod	Bur-121	Grey	Edg- 41	Stephen	Ora-127
Nixon	Prq-216	Ira	Roc- 14	Stephen	Bla- 8
Peter	Ran-164	Ira	Ora-173	Susanah	Hyd-234
Peter Jun	Bft- 22	Isaac	Row- 59	Thomas	Nor- 65
Peter Sen	Bft- 22	J	Col- 17	Thomas	War-181
Robert	Fra- 85	J	Col- 18	Turner	Ons- 99
Robert	Fra- 99	J	Row- 87	Walter	Hay-195
Robert	Grn-119	J D	Bru-224	William	Ire-266
Robt	Mec- 54	Jacob	Edg- 51	William	Way-244
Saml	Mec- 36	James	Ire-250	William	Edg- 67
Samuel	Rth- 99	James	Row- 61	William	Edg- 49
Samuel	Rth- 99	James	Row- 87	William	Edg- 41
Samuel Jnr	Ran-164	James	Rth-100	William	Rth-100
Sarah	Ran-164	James	War-173	William	Ire-250
Sarah	Nor- 65	James	Cum-245	William	Ire-260
Solomon	Cho-225	Jeph	Ire-241	Wm	Cha-216
Spencer	Glf-171	Jermon	Joh-288	Wm	Cho-230
Theophilus	Prq-217	Jerry	Bur-112	Wm	Bla- 4
Thomas	Bur-107	Jesse	Row- 62	Willie	Row- 55
Thomas	Car-182	Joel	Way-242	Willie	Hal-104
Thos	Mec- 35	Jno	Bla- 2	Willis	Row- 51
Thos	Mec- 53	John	Row- 62	Willis	Wil-269
Townsend	Prq-216	John	Joh-273	Ellison,Charles	Per-128
William	Rth- 99	John	Row- 51	David	Wil-275
Willis Sr	Prq-216	John	Hrt-212	David Esq	Ora-174
Winslow	Prq-216	John	Hyd-227	Hannah	Ran-164
Ellis,A	Ash- 13	John	Ora-127	Hazekiah	Hay-195
Amos	Way-241	John	Pit-258	Hugh	Bun- 92
Anderson	Row- 51	John	Ons-100	James	Wil-281
Ann	Row- 60	John	Row- 87	James	Ora-175
Aprilla	Way-242	John	Gat-110	John	Wil-275
Benjamin	Row- 55	John Senr	War-174	John	Rth- 99
Benjamin	Rth-100	John Snr	Row- 59	John	Rth- 99
Benjn	Car-177	Joseph	Pit-257	John Jr	Rth- 99
Betsey	Nor- 66	Joseph	Bur-113	Lucrea	Bft- 25
Britton	Ons- 99	Joseph	Grn-127	Martha	Ora-175
Charles	Hay-195	Joshua	War-175	Moses	Rth- 99
Christopher	Ire-268	Joshua	Ire-265	S	Ash- 8
Cornelius	Bla- 4	Josiah	War-175	Thomas	Bft- 32
Daniel	Ons-109	Josiah	Gat-110	W	Ash- 15
Dehority	Edg- 65	Laney	Way250	William Jr	Wil-274

Name	Ref	Name	Ref	Name	Ref
Ellison,Wm	Bft- 23	Embertson,George	Row- 74	Ennett,Nathaniel	Ons- 97
Z	Glf-166	Richard	Row- 82	Ennis,James	Edg- 49
Ellisson,Daniel	Wil-284	William	Row- 74	Thomas	Edg- 51
Thomas	Wil-283	Emerson,William	Cha-198	William	Row- 76
William Jr	Wil-283	Emery,Aaron	Pit-262	Enoch,Mary	Cas- 53
Ellmore,John	Cas- 53	Shedrick	Car-173	Ruse	Cas-. 53
Peter	Cas- 53	Emmanuel,Morris	Pas-188	Enochs,Jones	Row- 50
Thomas	Cas- 53	Emmerson,Rewben	Lnc-360	Ensley,Anderson	Hay-195
Ellor,Christain Sr	Row- 79	Wilson	Pas-188	Dinah	Hyd-227
Frederick	Row- 78	Emmery,Stephen	Ran-164	Solomon	Hyd-228
Hormelchar	Row- 78	William	Lnc-346	Eperson,Mary	Brt- 47
Jacob	Row- 80	Zachy	Hyd-225	Epling,Henry	Row- 53
John	Row- 87	Emmins,Isaac	Bur-110	Eply,Daniel	Lnc-346
John	Row- 87	Emond,Thomas	Cas- 53	Jacob	Lnc-347
John	Row- 86	Emory,Lewis	Grn-126	Peter	Lnc-346
John (Mel Son)	Row- 78	Martha	Grn-126	Eppe,Joel	Glf-187
John Senr	Row- 77	Emry,John	Row- 82	Epperson,Mary	Pit-238
Ellot,Charity	Row- 58	Endsby,James	Bur-120	Epps,Edward	Mor- 58
Thomas	Row- 46	Endsley,Alex	Lnc-337	John	Nor- 66
Elmore,Abednego	Wil-277	Andrew	Sto-111	Pleasant	Mon- 18
Artha	Sur-169	Andrew	Sto-147	Richard	Hal-104
Edward	Lnc-341	Archd	Lnc-337	William	Nor- 65
Elizabeth	Wil-276	John	Sto-150	Erdson,Creighton	Edg- 44
Jas	Ora-123	John	Lnc-342	Ernhart,Peter	Cab-143
Jas	Ora-137	John	Sto-110	Ernst,Katherine	Sto-146
Jesse	Per-128	Sarah	Glf-185	Erps,Elijah	Lnc-363
Jno of Peter	Ora-147	England,Mrs.	Cum-238	Phillip	Lnc-363
John J	Ora-137	Daniel	Bur-126	Walter	Lnc-363
John	Way-250	James	Bur-121	Errexon,John	Ons-109
P	Ora-152	Jeribella	Bur-116	Ervin,Edward	Dup- 28
Susanna	War-180	Joseph	Bur-125	Edward	Ons- 99
William	Bun- 93	Joshua	Bur-115	Erwin,Afrolem	Jon-296
William	Cha-210	Thos	Bur-122	Alex Jr	Bur-115
Elms,Henry	Hal-104	William	Cum-238	Alexander Senr	Bur-108
Jesse	Sam-153	William	Bur-119	Arthur	Bur-115
John	Rth- 99	William	Bur-125	Christopher	Ire-261
Elonore,Susanna	Way-247	William Jr	Bur-118	David	Bun- 82
Elrod,A	Ash- 8	Engle,George	Glf-155	David	Ire-238
Adam	Row- 55	John	Lnc-376	Elizabeth	Ire-269
Adam	Row- 55	English,Mrs.	Fra- 90	Elizabeth	Ire-256
Christopher	Row- 56	Andrew	Row- 62	Enoch	Ire-268
Conrod	Bur-112	Henry	Bur-113	Gavin	Rth- 99
Jacob	Row- 55	James	Hyd-230	Geo	Bun- 93
John	Row- 55	James	Rth- 98	George	Ire-248
Peter	Wil-274	Joseph	Car-173	Isaac	Lnc-367
Robert	Sto-112	Leah	Pit-256	James	Bun- 98
Robert	Sto-152	Lovey	Hyd-231	James	Roc- 21
Stephen	Sto-137	Engram,Edw	Len-323	James	Rth-100
Elveson,James	Row- 80	Isaac	Len-314	Jno	Len-320
Elwel,John	Cum-248	James	Len-317	John	Ire-238
Elwell,B	Bla- 13	Enis,Jas	Bur-102	John	Hay-195
Emberson,Ben	Cha-209	Lukeriah	Bur-102	John	Bur-115
Eli	Cha-205	Enloe,Abram	Rth- 99	Joseph	Ire-255
Harry	Mec- 27	Enlows,James	Hyd-223	Margrat	Row- 74
Henry	Mec- 28	Ennes,Raymond	Cum-262	Mary	Ire-249
James	Cha-205	Ennet,Benj	Ons-107	Patrick	Ire-239
Jas	Mec- 36	Joseph	Ons-107	Robt	Glf-172
Jesse	Cha-214	Thomas	Ons-108	Saml	Glf-172
Margaret	Row- 71	Ennett,Joseph R W	Ons-100	Saml	Glf-157

-97-

Name	Ref	Name	Ref	Name	Ref
Erwin,Thomas	Bun- 85	Etheridge,Abel	Cur- 91	Ethridge,Samson	Cur- 84
Thomas	Ire-238	Abel	Cur- 91	Samson	Cur- 84
William	Bun- 93	Abel	Cur- 91	Samuel	Cur- 84
William	Bun- 86	Adam	Cur- 80	Etter,John	Nor- 66
William	Ire-238	Adam	Cur- 85	Ettris,Saml	Lnc-327
William	Ire-239	Asert	Cur- 84	Samuel	Lnc-339
William	Ire-256	Caleb	Cur- 79	Ettriss,Henry	Lnc-327
William Jr	Len-316	D	Cam-157	Eubank,Crusey	Cas- 53
William Senr	Len-316	Daniel	Cur- 86	George	Cas- 53
Wm	Bur-129	David	Cur- 91	Eubanks,Benjamin	Jon-295
Wm W	Bur-102	Demcey	Cur- 91	Daniel	Ons- 98
Esex,free man of colour		Elijah	Wsh-225	Daniel Junr	Ons-103
	Ran-187	F	Cam-166	Edward	Jon-296
Eskridge,Richard	Rth- 99	Holowell	Cur- 90	Elijah	Ons-100
Richd	Cas- 53	J	Cam-157	Elijah	Jon-295
Eslick,Francis	Ons-106	James	Cur- 91	Elisha	Ons-103
Esom,Hardy	Cum-257	James	Pas-188	Ezekiel	Jon-296
Eson,Ezaas	Nsh- 80	James Senr	Cur- 91	George	Ons-103
Wm	Nsh- 81	Jesse	Cur- 91	Isaac	Ons- 98
Espey,Saml	Lnc-336	Josiah	Cur- 91	J	Ora-153
Samuel	Lnc-342	Juley	Cur- 91	John	Ons-103
Essery,James	Bun- 84	Kesiah	Cur- 80	John	Jon-296
Thomas	Bun- 84	Lovey	Cur- 89	Levy	Jon-296
Essex,Jacob	Row- 79	Mallicki	Mar- 13	Lot	Jon-296
Essig,John	Sto-144	Matisky	Cur- 91	Solomy	Ons-103
Esslemen,James	Ire-245	Mathias	Cur- 91	T	Ora-153
Estep,Widow	Row- 66	Nancey	Cur- 91	Thomas	Ons-104
Abraham	Row- 59	Peter	Cur- 91	Thomas	Cha-198
J	Ash- 6	S	Cam-157	Eupanks,J	Glf-178
M	Ash- 6	Sabeney	Cur- 80	Eurl,Blake	Gat-113
Samuel	Row- 65	Samuel	Cur- 92	Charles	Gat-113
Estes,L	Ash- 12	Samuel	Cur- 91	Charny	Gat-114
Leonard	Bur-110	Samuel	Cur- 93	Daniel	Gat-112
Lott	Bur-103	Samuel Junr	Cur- 93	Demsy	Edg- 50
Esther (sic)	Pas-188	Sandland	Cur- 80	Elisha	Gat-112
Esthers,Peter	Lnc-328	Thos	Cur- 89	Elizabeth	Gat-113
Estis,Daniel	Grn-122	Thos	Cur- 91	Elizabeth	Gat-111
Elisa	Ora-112	Tulley	Cur- 91	Jethro	Gat-113
Labon	Bur-128	W	Cam-162	John	Gat-116
Langston	Bur-128	William	Cur- 90	Lepiand	Gat-114
Larkin	Bur-110	William	Cur- 89	Livey	Gat-108
Nathl	Grn-122	William	Cur- 88	Mills	Gat-108
Reuben	Bur-128	William C	Cur- 89	Righ	Gat-112
Sarah	Grn-122	Wm	Brt- 49	Samuel	Gat-114
Thomas	Grn-122	Wm	Cur- 82	Samuel	Gat-112
Wm	Grn-122	Wm	Cur- 85	Sephen	Gat-113
Estoll,William	Rth- 99	Willis	Cur- 88	Stephen	Gat-112
Estrage,Nathan	Ire-250	Willowby	Cur- 91	Whitmill	Gat-113
Estridge,Boroughs	Ora-127	Etherridge,Jona	Bft- 35	Evanes,Peter	Edg- 68
H	Glf-164	Ethrage,Edward	Cum-261	Stephen	Edg- 48
Etcheson,Walter	Row- 61	Emelia	Cum-261	Evans,Widow	Lnc-327
William	Row- 61	Ethridge,George	Per-137	Aaron	Cha-192
Etchison,Edmon	Row- 61	Giles	Cur- 83	Abraham	Nsh-644
Etherage,Caleb	Edg- 57	Henry	Nsh- 74	Absolam	Hrt-206
Mariam	Edg- 41	I	Col- 19	Alexr	Rob-222
Nathan	Edg- 65	Matthew	Nsh- 76	Amos	Way-244
Etheredge,John	Hal-104	Nathan	Cur- 85	Amos	Pit-232
Samuel	Ans- 23	Peter	Nsh- 82	Ann	Cas- 53
Etheridge,Abeah	Cur- 90	Peter	Nsh- 84	Ann	Edg- 49

Name	Loc	Name	Loc	Name	Loc	Name	Loc
Evans,Ann	Nsh- 81	Evans,John		Bru-226	Evans,William		Lnc-339
Anthony	Cha-193	John		Rch-211	William		Bun- 80
Archd Junr	Rob-223	John		Prq-216	William		Cum-261
Archd Senr	Rob-223	John		Edg- 56	Willm		Lnc-327
Azariah	Pas-188	John		Dup- 23	Wm		Brt- 50
B	Ash- 10	John		War-176	Wm		Hrt-206
Bartholm	Pas-188	John		War-174	Wm		Glf-164
Benj	Hrt-206	John		Sam-158	Zach		Cho-230
Benjamin	Pit-236	John		Sto-109	Evanson,E		Col- 18
Benjamin	Prq-217	John		Sto-151	Evenes,Beng K		Cur- 84
Benjamin	Bla- 11	John		Sto-152	Evens,Beng		Cur- 86
Berrel	Hal-104	John		Cum-247	Henery		Cur- 84
Byrd	Nor- 65	John Junr		Car-184	John		Cur- 86
Caleb	Bft- 38	John Senr		Car-184	Samuel		Ran-164
Charles	Rch-198	Joseph		Prq-216	Thos		Cur- 86
Charles	Bun- 80	Joseph		Bun- 94	W		Ash- 5
Charles	Cha-193	Josiah		Hrt-206	William		Ran-164
Charles	War-169	Josiah		Cum-266	Eventon,John A.		Rth- 99
Daniel	Dup- 8	Joshua		Brt- 49	Everage,Duke		Rob-230
Daniel	Joh-284	L		Glf-178	John		Cum-261
Daniel	Row- 54	Leven		War-177	Everatt,Epp		Cas- 53
Danl	Rob-224	Levi		Dup- 22	Samuel		Cas- 53
David	Wil-273	Lewis		Roc- 12	Everedge,Thomas		Joh-276
David	Dup- 22	Loyd		Glf-164	Everet,David		Hal-104
David	Cum-269	Margret		Pit-252	Demsy		Cum-247
David	Cum-266	Mary		Cas- 53	Henry		Cum-248
Dred	Brt- 49	Mary		Cho-228	John		Hal-104
Edon	Hrt-208	Matthew		War-177	Mills		Cum-249
Elexander	Pit-262	Media		Brt- 50	John		Roc- 29
Eli	Row- 57	Michael		Ans- 31	John		Wsh-225
Elijah	Per-137	Mily		Cum-240	John		Way-253
Elijah	Bur-121	Morris		Ans- 31	Joseph		Wsh-225
Elisha	Cas- 53	Nancy		Hal-104	Laurence		Rch-208
Elizabeth	War-171	Nelly		Bun- 90	Mary		Nor- 66
Elizabeth	Dup- 9	Owin		Sto-136	Micaj		Bft- 34
Ellis	Cas- 53	Peter		Wsh-227	Myles		Cho-224
Evan	Pas-188	Pheraby		Way-247	Thos		Ans- 17
Francis	Hrt-208	Philemon		Cum-259	Everhart,Christian		Row- 79
Frances	Hrt-210	Richard		Pit-256	Jacob		Row- 79
George	Dup- 18	Richard		Bun- 75	Peter		Row- 41
George W	Cum-247	Richard		Cha-201	Everidge,William		Joh-277
Henry	Nor- 65	Samuel		Row- 74	Everit,Dr.		Bru-236
Henry	Cas- 74	Samuel		Bun- 89	Saml		Hrt-209
Isaac	Nsh- 81	Samuel		Dup- 20	Everitt,Asia		Wsh-228
Isaac	Bur-107	Sharward		Nsh-643	Epps		Hyd-224
Isom	Way-246	Solomon		Bun- 79	Hardy		Wsh-226
J. Sr	Bru-240	Starkey		Hrt-210	James		Edg- 54
James	Sto-113	Theophilus		Cum-249	James		Mar- 12
James	Sto-153	Tho		Ora-165	Jeresiah		Wsh-226
James	Bun- 78	Thomas		Prq-216	Jeresiah		Wsh-227
James	Roc- 4	Thomas		Dup- 36	Jesse		Wsh-226
Jas Jnr	Cho-230	Thomas		Edg- 49	John		Edg- 69
Jas Snr	Cho-230	Thomas		Len-313	Joseph		Way-235
Jeremiah	Hrt-210	Thomas		Cha-204	Joseph Senr		Wsh-226
Jesse	Glf-161	Thos		Ans- 18	Keton		Edg- 50
Jesse	Per-137	W		Cam-159	Nathaniel		Wsh-226
Joel	Way-246	William		Rch-2111	Silas		Edg- 71
Joel	Hal-104	William		Joh-283	Simon		Mar- 15
Jno	Brt- 50	William		Prq-217	Turner		Mar- 8

-99-

Name	Ref	Name	Ref	Name	Ref
Everitt,William	Mar- 5	Ezzard,Elizabeth	Ran-164	Faircloth,Thomas	Sur-192
William	Mar- 14	Ezzell,Benjn	Sam-162	Fairer,Frederick	Edg- 52
Evernton,Miles	Cur- 87	Frederick	Dup- 24	Fairis,William	Cum-241
Saml	Cur- 87	Hansell	Dup- 16	Fairley,Alexander	Rch-202
Thos	Cur- 87	Kosiah	Dup- 3	Angus	Rch-192
Evers,James Junr	Bla- 4	Priscilla	Hal-104	John	Rch-202
James Senr	Bla- 4	Reuben	Dup- 17	John	Rch-192
Wm	Bla- 4	Sarah	Dup- 17	Peter	Rch-202
Everton,Thomas	Sur-195			Robert	Rob-226
Evins,Alexander	Sur-177	Faber,Reubin	Sto-111	Faison,Elias	Dup- 6
Benjamin	Sto-149	Faddes,John	Ora-110	Elisha	Sam-163
Edwin	Sto-103	Faddis,A	Ora-160	Henry	Sam-152
Henry	Hay-195	Alex	Ora-118	Isom	Dup- 6
Isam	Hay-195	Faddrel,Charles	Sto-145	James Jnr	Sam-152
Isam	Hay-195	Fagan,Easter	Wsh-225	James Senr	Sam-152
Jacob	Hay-195	Levi	Wsh-227	Faithfull,David	Edg- 58
James	Sur-173	Richard	Wsh-225	William	Edg- 59
James Jr	Row- 48	Stephen	Mar- 14	Falconer,Alex Esq	Fra- 77
John	Ons- 96	Thomas	Wsh-224	Bartholomew	War-168
John	Grn-130	William	Wsh-226	Haray	War-172
John	Gat-114	Fagg,Charles	Roc- 5	Hardy	Grn-127
Joseph	Row- 84	Joel	Roc- 5	John	War-174
Lydia	Cur- 89	Samuel	Roc- 5	Robert	War-179
Samuel	Ons- 99	Fagleman,Christr	Cab-141	Falk,George	Sto-143
William	Ons-100	Geo	Cab-141	William	Sto-143
William	Hay-195	Faglen,Philip	Sto-107	William	Sto-152
William	Sur-182	Fagot,Daniel	Cab-141	Falkener,William	War-184
Evis,Isaac R	Dup- 12	Danl	Cab-140	William A K	War-184
Evitt,John Jun	Bft- 32	Geo	Cab-140	Falkner,Hardy	Len-322
John Snr	Bft- 32	Geo	Cab-141	Isaac	Len-323
Lott	Bft- 32	Jacob	Cab-140	James	Len-321
Tho	Bft- 30	Valintine	Cab-140	Jno	Len-312
Wm	Bft- 30	Fail,Dixon	Joh-289	Lewis	Len-321
Evregan,Tom	Pas-188	Ellick	Joh-289	Olive	Lne-320
Ewalt,George	Bur-111	Jonathan	Joh-289	Robt Jr	Way-236
Ewas,George	Bur-111	Mercer	Bun- 85	Robt Sr	Way-236
Ewel,Thomas	Row- 75	Osborn	Joh-290	Rollin	Cum-263
Ewell,Conner	Pit-249	William	Joh-289	Wm	Len-321
James	Pit-260	Fain,David	Bun- 85	Fall,Andrew	Lnc-336
Ewert,Joseph	Mec- 51	Ebenezar	Bun- 85	Ephraim	Bur-102
Joseph	Mec- 51	Joel	War-176	Falls,George	Lnc-338
Ewin,Alexr	Mec- 30	Nancy	War-178	Gilbreath	Lnc-330
Isaac	Rch-206	Tyre	War-181	James	Lnc-332
Martha	Mec- 33	William	War-183	John	Ire-239
Samuel	Rch-206	Fair,Samuel	Ire-247	John	Lnc-330
Ewing,Alexander	Ire-260	Fairchild,Abijah	Wil-274	John Junr	Lnc-338
James	Ire-260	C	Ash- 8	John Senr	Lnc-338
Nathaniel	Ire-260	Faircloth,Arther	Sam-153	Sarah	Lnc-330
Exum,Etheldred	Edg- 57	Caleb	Sam-153	William	Ire-240
F Henry	Nor- 65	Davis	Sam-153	William	Lnc-338
James	Nor- 65	Eliza	Sam-153	Wm	Lnc-330
Priscilla	Edg- 58	Fanny	Cum-246	Famor,William	Dup- 33
Salley	Way-238	Hardy	Sam-153	Fancher,---eleny	Cur- 93
William	Way-236	Isaam	Sam-153	Davies	Cur- 90
William	Edg- 57	J	Cam-157	Faney	Cur- 90
Ezell,Buckner	Ora-113	John	Sam-161	Moses	Cur- 90
George	Grn-122	John Senr	Sam-161	Ryling	Cur- 91
Jas	Ora-113	Smid	Sam-153	Fanin,Zachariah	Cha-196
Taylor Sen	Edg- 46	Solomon	Sam-153	Fann,Eliza	Ora-129

Name	Location	Name	Location	Name	Location
Fann,Mack	Ora-113	Farmer,Joseph	Ans- 32	Farrall,J	Cam-163
Fannan,Lewis	Cha-206	Joseph	Edg- 40	N	Cam-161
Fanney,Anna	Gat-111	Joseph	Ran-164	R	Cam-155
Fanning,Bettee	Lnc-358	Joseph	Brt- 61	Farange,W	Cam-158
John	Wsh-219	Othreel	Grn-129	Farrar,Cathrine	Cha-196
William	Roc- 34	Othreel	Grn-130	Elizabeth	Cha-199
Fansler,Adam	Sto-101	Nathan	Sur-168	John	Lnc-360
Adam	Sto-133	Peter	Glf-155	John,Fauble Creek	Per-138
Far,Robt	Cab-144	Robert	Row- 63	Samuel	Lnc-360
Farbanks,D	Glf-183	Samuel	Edg- 67	William	Lnc-360
D	Glf-159	Samuel	Ire-264	Farraw,Tincher	Ons-105
Farber,Elizth	Brt- 60	Samuel	Rth-101	Farrel,Hutchens	Nsh- 85
Fare,Michael	Sto-110	Solomon	Ran-165	James	Nsh- 85
Michael	Sto-148	Sucky	Joh-281	Farrell,Francis	Cha-202
Farecloth,Thos	Hrt-214	Susanna	Edg- 68	Henry	Way-245
Fareless,Nicholas	Edg- 61	Thomas	Sur-189	Henry	Way-238
Farer,Henry	Cab-141	Thomas	Wil-280	Sarah	Way-252
Fargussan,James	Wil-279	Thomas	Ire-264	William	Way-245
John	Wil-278	William	Brt- 63	Farrer,Abel	Grn-148
John Jr	Wil-278	Zilpha	Edg- 66	William	Joh-281
Joseph	Wil-279	Zilpha	Edg- 67	Farrier,James	Fra- 95
Moses	Wil-279	Farnell,Benj	Ons-103	Farril,Ancel	Nsh- 85
Richard	Wil-281	Benj Jr	Ons- 96	Farrington,Joshua	Roc- 25
Thomas (H C)	Wil-272	Fanny	Ons-103	Farrior,Bryan	Dup- 30
Faringston,Jonathan	Glf-185	Farow,Christopher	Cur- 79	John	Dup- 32
William	Glf-188	Edw	Cur- 79	Farris,Ezekel	Hyd-231
Farington,Wm	Glf-188	Eukiah	Cur- 79	Moses	Bur-117
Faris,Walter	Mec- 28	Hansey	Cur- 81	Wm	Bft- 37
Farlar,John	Bur-121	Jacob	Cur- 81	Wm	Cho-220
Farlass,Charlton	Hrt-210	Farowe,Celab	Cur- 79	Farrish,Thos	Cha-202
Farley,John	Cas- 54	Eliga	Cur- 81	Farrow,Amediah	Roc- 4
Marthey	Cas- 54	Francis	Cur- 81	Benj	Ons-107
S. Daniel	Cas- 54	Isas	Cur- 81	Esther	Per-129
Stephen	Cas- 54	John	Cur- 81	Jeremiah	Hyd-229
Farlow,George	Ran-165	Joseph	Cur- 81	John	Cha-202
Isaac	Ran-165	Lot	Cur- 81	John	Cha-210
Jos	Ora-133	Thos	Cur- 81	Nathineal	Mec- 55
Jos	Ora-144	Farows,Farowe	Cur- 81	Peter	Cha-192
Michael	Ran-165	Farquhar,Wm	Lnc-338	Thos	Cha-208
Nathen	Ran-165	Farr,Widow	Bun- 87	Farson,Harwood	Nor- 67
Uriah	Ran-165	Conrad	Glf-180	Thomas	Nor- 66
Farmer,Absalom	Edg- 66	Henry	Cab-143	Turner	Nor- 66
Aneas	Edg- 66	Jno	Mec- 38	Fartherly,Stephen	Pit-239
Asa	Edg- 66	Lenard	Mor- 56	Farthing,Dudly	Ora-167
Asael	Edg- 65	Richard	Ons-108	Farver,Thos	Ans- 4
Barshaby	Joh-282	Saml	Mec- 51	Faucet,R	Ora-157
Benjamin	Edg- 67	Saml	Cab-143	Faucett,David	Ora-161
Daniel	Per-138	Sarah	Ons-103	E	Ora-160
David	Rth-101	Titus	Ons- 98	G	Ora-155
Dew	Edg- 67	William	Hyd-221	G	Ora-160
Elisabeth	Mon- 30	Farrah,Edward	Cha-215	George	Ora-163
Freddrick	Ran-164	Obediah	Grn-120	Henry	Ora-115
Henry	Sto- 95	Tempy	Grn-121	James	Ora-115
Isaac	Ire-264	Farral,G	Cam-158	James Sen	Ora-116
James	Grn-143	Farrall,D	Cam-159	Jas	Ora-161
Jesse	Ans- 28	G	Cam-152	John	Ora-943
Jessee	Edg- 67	J	Cam-158	M	Ora-155
John	Joh-282	J	Cam-158	Ralph	Ora-125
John	Sur-165	J	Cam-165	Ralph	Ora-126

-101-

Name	Ref	Name	Ref	Name	Ref
Faucett,Ralph	Ora-115	Fees,J	Ash- 13	Fender,Michael	Sur-165
Ralph	Ora-163	J	Ash- 7	N	Ash- 14
Richd	Ora-118	Feete,John	Ran-165	Fenilleson,Anqus	Cum-242
Robt	Ora-118	Fegens,Henry Jr	Rth-100	Fennel,Frederick	Row- 77
William	Ora-163	Feimster,John	Ire-248	Fennell,Anne	Nor- 66
Wm T.	Ora-170	William	Ire-248	J	Ora-141
Tho	Ora-127	Feiser,George Jr	Row- 87	Joham	Nor- 66
Fauguson,Eli	Sto-120	Feke,Wm	Cha-191	John	Row- 67
Fauguzson,John	Sto-109	Felcher,John	Row- 68	John	Nor- 66
Faulcon,Jesse N	Hal-104	Felker,Peter	Lnc-376	M	Cam-157
John	War-174	Fell,Samuel	Car-182	Fenner,Dr.Richd	Fra- 89
John Jr	War-174	Fellow,John	Way-240	Robert	Hal-104
Faulk,E	Col- 18	Robt Jr	Way-248	Fenney,Thos	Mec- 30
J	Col- 18	Robt Jr	Way-241	Jno	Mec- 32
J	Col- 17	William	Way-241	Fenright,G	Bru-224
J	Col- 19	Fellows,John	Sam-154	Fentress,Edward	Ran-165
J	Col- 19	Jonathan	Pit-238	Faroah	Ran-165
J	Col- 18	Susanna	Sam-157	Freddrick	Ran-165
J	Col- 18	Felmet,Davis	Hay-195	Thomas	Ran-165
J	Col- 18	Felps,Ezekel	Row- 80	William	Ran-165
P	Col- 19	Jacob	Joh-296	Fentris,Lott	Pas-189
R	Col- 18	Jane	Row- 53	Ferate,Thomas	Ran-165
S	Col- 18	Koelan	Row- 53	Ferbee,Daniel	Cur- 89
W	Col- 18	Mary	Row- 81	Samuel	Cur- 89
W	Col- 18	Samuel	Row- 88	Thomas	Cur- 89
William	Edg- 63	Seth	Tyr-206	Ferebee,Joseph	Cur- 88
Faulkner,Betsey	Glf-187	William	Cas- 55	P	Cam-161
Fauls,John	Lnc-352	Felton,Ann	Cho-229	Fergerson,Ferremiah	Bun- 79
Faun,Lany	Cha-191	Charles	Gat-107	Fergeson,Matt	Cas- 54
Fauntsly,Robert	Ora-155	Elisha	Hrt-215	Fergins,George	Rth-100
Faure,Francis	Per-129	Elisha	Edg- 51	Fergus,Job	Hay-195
Faust,C	Glf-173	Job	Edg- 50	Ferguson,A	Cum-240
Danl	Glf-180	John	Cho-228	Alexander	Cas- 55
John	Ran-165	John	Way-239	Alexr	Brt- 47
Fausts,Nicholas	Row- 79	Kader	Prq-217	Benj	Len-321
Favel,Javis	Lnc-366	Leah	Cho-229	Daniel	Cum-263
Faw,Isaac	Sto-137	Noah	Gat-108	David	Roc- 4
J	Ash- 8	Richard	Hrt-208	Duncan	Rob-225
Fawn,Mrs. Elizh	Fra- 78	Thos	Prq-217	Henry	Rth-101
Fay,Andrew	Roc- 22	William	Prq-217	James	Ire-240
Fays,John	Ire-256	Felts,Aaron	Wil-264	James	Cum-253
Feagan,Danl	Mor- 56	Aaron Jr	Wil-264	James	Lnc-328
Richd	Mor- 56	Hardy	War-172	James	Lnc-333
Wm	Mor- 56	Henry	War-172	Jas	Lnc-333
Feagen,Peter	Nor- 66	James	Wil-269	Jno	Rob-225
Fearis,Jenny	Mec- 40	Jesse	Wil-267	John	Rch-213
Joseph	Mec- 22	John Esqr	Wil-264	John	Mor- 65
Robt	Mec- 51	Nathaniel	War-178	John	Lnc-330
Featherston,Merryman		Olliver	War-184	John	Rch-193
	Bun- 72	Rowland	War-179	John	Car-185
Richd	Lnc-368	Tillman	War-182	John Jun	Roc- 4
William	Roc- 30	William	War-182	John Sen	Roc- 4
Wm	Lnc-340	William	War-184	Jos	Lnc-330
Fecket,Henry	Ran-165	William	Fra- 98	Mal	Rob-225
Fedrick,J	Mon- 35	William	Way-242	Margaret	Cum-252
John	Per-129	William	Wil-270	Mary	Lnc-333
Lewis	Cas- 54	Fender.A	Ash-146	Moses	Lnc-338
S	Mon- 35	Gabriel	Sur-166	Murdock	Mor- 60
Fees,D	Ash- 13	Henry	Sur-165	Neill	Rob-225

-102-

Ferguson,Phares	Ire-269	Fidler,John	Sto-102	Fife,Samuel	Wil-262		
Robert	Bun- 73	John	Sto-135	Fifer,A	Ora-145		
Sarah	Lnc-333	Peter	Sto-135	Mathias	Row- 85		
Thomas	Fra- 99	Peter	Sto-103	Figg,Joseph	Nor- 66		
William	Roc- 4	Field,Jas	Ans- 23	Willis	Gat-113		
Wm	Mec- 27	Mary	Sto- 95	Figgers,Elizabeth	Hrt-208		
Feribrant,Ann	Cho-223	William	Ran-165	Marthrus	Hrt-211		
Ferington,Solomon	Row- 50	Wm W	Glf-174	Richard	Hrt-211		
Ferlaw,Betsey	Wsh-219	Fielder,Absolom	Row- 59	Fight,Conrad	Row- 79		
James	Wsh-219	Samuel	Roc- 32	Henry	Row- 80		
Mourning	Wsh-217	Fielding,Jacob	Car-175	Fike,John Jr	Cha-206		
William	Wsh-219	Jno	Ans- 29	Tyre	Cha-198		
Ferral,Catharine	Cab-143	Wm	Ans- 29	File,Geo	Cab-146		
Ferrall,T	Cam-158	Fields,Abram	Cha-211	Henry	Cab-141		
Ferrand,William	Jon-296	Adam	Roc- 32	Henry	Cab-145		
William Esqr	Ons-105	Allen	Roc- 33	Jacob	Cab-142		
Ferrel,Harvy	Cas- 55	Ansolm	Roc- 33	John	Cab-140		
William	Cas- 55	Aron	Ons-103	Phillip	Cab-145		
William	Mon- 39	Barbara	Way-250	Filer,Joseph	Sto-144		
Ferrell,Allsey	Fra- 82	Bartholomew	Len-313	Moris	Len-311		
Capt. Cordy	Fra- 80	Bennet	Cha-197	Thomas	Sto-142		
Ephraim	Joh-274	Brice	Ons-103	Filgo,William	Joh-273		
Jacob Jr	Joh-272	Charity	Cha-211	Fillback,George	Rth-100		
Capt. James	Fra- 84	Council	Ons-103	Fillpott,Saml	Bft- 32		
John	Ora-159	David	Cha-190	Filly,Alex.	Bur-119		
Micaja	Row- 53	G	Col- 17	Filps,Thomas	Cas- 54		
Theoderick	Fra- 84	Isaiah	Wil-269	Filups,Garland	Grn-132		
Turner	Fra- 80	J	Col- 17	Fincanin,John	Bur-126		
Ferril,John	Cas- 54	Jacob	Ons-103	Paul	Bur-126		
John	Ire-243	James	Cha-216	Peter	Bur-126		
Ferrill,Isaa	Bur-102	Jeremiah	Ran-165	William	Bur-126		
Veasy	Ora-166	Jeremiah	Cha-214	Fincanna,Isaac	Bur-129		
Ferrington,Floyd	Rth-101	John	Sto-122	Fincannon,John	Bur-131		
John	Cha-216	John	Roc- 33	Fincanon,Isaac	Bur-104		
Saml	Row- 50	John	Glf-167	Finch,Allen	Nsh- 86		
Ferrol,Elisebeth	Mec- 4P	John	Ons- 97	Claborn	Nsh- 85		
Geberal	Mec- 48	L	Col- 18	George	Grn-124		
Ferry,John	Cas- 54	Lamuel	Jon-296	Hambleton	Sur-165		
Ferson,Jno	Mec- 41	Levi	Cha-196	Isham	Mon- 41		
Fesier,Geo	Row- 50	Mills R	Gat-107	Isham	Mon- 39		
Geo	Row- 37	Moses	Ons-103	James	Grn-145		
Fesler,Andrew	Sto-156	Nathan	Jon-296	John	Grn-122		
John	Sto- 97	Nathaniel	Roc- 35	John	Ire-259		
Peter	Sto-156	Peter	Glf-180	John T	Grn-121		
Fesperman,Frederick	Cab-142	Rebecca	Ons-103	John	Sur-195		
Henry	Cab-145	Reuben (Y R)	Wil-275	Mileton	Sur-195		
John	Cab-145	Richard Senr	Cha-203	Richard	Fra- 92		
Festerman,Jno	Mec- 41	Robt	Glf-179	Richardson	Fra- 94		
Fetherby,Benjn	Row- 49	Robt	Row- 59	Fincher,Ben	Mec- 31		
Fetherty,John	Sto-134	Samuel	Ran-165	Ben	Mec- 31		
Fetter,Jacob	Row- 55	Shad	Len-311	Elijah	Mec- 41		
Fetts,Jessee	Nor- 67	William (B E)	Wil-268	Jas	Mec- 31		
Few,Lucrea	Bft- 24	William	Nor- 66	Jas	Mec- 24		
Fewel,Benjamin	Roc- 4	William	Cha-204	Jaushua Snr	Mec- 31		
Fewels,John	Hrt-217	Wm (Y R)	Wil-275	Jno	Mec- 31		
Fhyte,Jacob	Mec- 37	Wm	Glf-172	Jno	Mec- 31		
Jno	Mec- 37	Fife,John	Wil-261	Jno	Mec- 31		
Fidler,George	Sto-152	Lillenezer	Len-215	John	Ran-165		
Godfrey	Sto-136	Sally	Wil-271	Joshua	Mec- 31		

Name	Ref	Name	Ref	Name	Ref
Fincher,Wm	Mec- 41	Fish,William Senr	Lnc-355	Fisher,William Jun	Car-171
Findleson,Daniel	Cum-267	Fishel,Adam	Sto-136	William Senr	Car-183
Findley,Alex	Ora-160	Fishell,Jacob	Sto-104	Wm	Mec- 22
James	Ora-126	Jacob	Sto-137	Fisinger,Peter	Row- 83
Jno	Ora-176	Fisher,Adam	Mec- 41	Fisler,John	Sto-127
John	Glf-156	Benjn	Ran-165	Fismire,Anna	Bur-131
Wm	Ora-116	Benj T	Tyr-213	Fisurs,Adam	Sto-103
Findly,A	Glf-177	Betsy	Pas-189	Fitch,-----	Mec- 22
Charles Senr	Bur-124	Betsy	Car-177	Felix	Bur-115
Geo	Glf-174	Boling	Sto-138	James	Ora-167
Geo	Glf-176	Boling	Sto-104	John	Cas- 54
Mary	Glf-182	Charles	Mec- 42	Tho	Ora-117
T	Glf-175	Conrad	Row- 53	Thos	Ora-167
Findlyson,Malcom	Cum-242	David	Hyd-230	W	Ora-153
Fine,Christen	Ran-165	Elizabeth	Row- 68	William	Cas- 54
Finger,Daniel	Lnc-346	Ezekial	Lnc-358	Fitchet,C	Col- 17
Daniel Senr	Lnc-346	George	Row- 86	Fite,Leonard	Lnc-373
Henry	Lnc-376	George	Lnc-374	Peter	Lnc-367
Henry	Lnc-326	George	Lnc-377	Fitsgerald,Benj	Ire-243
Jacob	Lnc-376	George	Sto-135	David	Ire-243
John	Lnc-376	George	Len-318	Henry	Ire-243
Peter	Lnc-346	George	Sto-103	John	Ire-243
Fink,Geo	Cab-141	George Jr	Row- 78	William	Ire-242
Finley,Charles	Mec- 30	Gorge	Cur- 88	Fitts,Henry	War-172
Jas	Lnc-334	Geo	Cab-145	Fitzgerald,James	Sur-170
Jenny	Mec- 30	Henry	Glf-158	John	Rth-100
Jno	Mec- 33	Henry	Cab-145	Peter	Sur-175
John	Wil-257	Hezekiah	Prg-217	William	Ire-238
Robert	Lnc-336	Jacob	Row- 82	Fitzpatrick,Hugh	Sto-101
Robert	Rth-100	Jacob	Mec- 42	Hugh	Sto-133
W	Ash- 7	John	Row- 82	Mary	Row- 89
Finly,Charles	Bur-124	John	Lnc-358	FitzRandoph,Benj	Bla- 3
Wm	Mec- 30	John	Lnc-358	Fiveash,Fedrick	Joh-284
Finna,Mary	Hrt-211	John	Sam-153	Jno	Rob-222
Finney,Joseph Jn	Sur-167	John	Cha-198	Jno	Rob-233
Finnie,Robert	Nor- 66	John	Row- 68	N	Cam-160
Finnin,John	Ora-161	John	Rth-101	Fizer,Joseph	Sto-131
Finny,Alexr	Mec- 42	John	Row- 53	Peter	Sto-100
Drewry	Hal-104	John	Cur- 86	Peter	Sto-131
James	Hal-105	Joseph	Lnc-374	Flack,Andrew	Rth-101
Joseph	Sur-160	Joseph	Lnc-377	Andy	Glf-175
Robert	Wil-263	Joshua	Ran-164	Elijah	Glf-189
Fipps,George	Bur-127	Halowell	Cur- 86	George	Rth-101
John	Row- 39	Harmon	Row- 68	Jas	Glf-175
Fires,Wm	Hal-104	Lewis	Cab-141	Michael	Ire-248
Firr,Joseph	Bur-113	Littleton	Mon- 44	Flake,Emanuel	Pit-249
Fiscus,Adam	Sto-130	Maxsy	Cur- 86	Jordon	Ans- 32
Adam	Sto- 99	Molestin	Glf-183	Mansell	Pit-254
Adam	Sto-127	Nancy	Wil-283	Flanagin,James	Pit-259
Frederic	Sto-128	Peter	Rth-101	John	Pit-259
Frederick	Sto-127	Polly	Mec- 42	Thomas	Pit-259
Fisens,Frederick	Sto- 98	Richard	Lnc-358	Flanekin,Charles	Mec- 24
Fish,Berry	Sto-124	Stephen	Lnc-358	David	Mec- 49
Isaac	Lnc-355	Thomas	Cas- 54	Jno	Mec- 49
Jasper	Bur-104	Thomas Senr	Lnc-377	Wm	Mec- 23
John	Len-316	Thos	Sam-153	Planican,Tulley	Cur- 91
Salathial	Lnc-355	Thos Junr	Sam-157	Flanigan,Phillip	Lnc-346
Tho	Len-323	William	Lnc-358	Flanikin,Adlia	Mec- 35
William	Lnc-355	William	Cur- 86	Isaac	Mec- 49

Name	Loc	Name	Loc	Name	Loc	Name	Loc
Flanikin,Wm	Mec- 50	Fletcher,Mrs.	Bru-234	Flood,Phil		Bft- 32
Flannagan,John	Dup- 34	Aaron	Pas-188	Willie		Hal-104
Will	Dup- 33	Edward	Grn-122	Flora,Winifred		Edg- 65
Flannekin,Saml	Mec- 49	Enoch	Wil-282	Florey,Will		Cur-90
Flatcher,Jeremiah	Cas- 54	Exum	Edg- 55	Floryd,J		Mon- 38
Flaw,David	Mec- 44	Frederic	Pas-188	Flourance,Obid		Cas- 54
Thos	Mec- 44	J	Ash- 8	William		Cas- 54
Flecher,Lewis	Grn-136	James	Sur-193	Flours,Ben		Nsh- 86
Major	Grn-124	James	Wil-258	Benj		Nsh- 90
Thomas	Sto-139	James	Ire-253	Edward		Nsh- 86
Fleece,Jesse	Hrt-213	James	Bur-106	Michael		Nsh- 86
John	Hrt-212	Jesse	Prq-217	Flow,Jas		Mec- 23
Fleeming,Jas	Bla- 13	John	Bun- 89	Flowers,Asher		Way-235
Fleetwood,Ashley	Brt- 47	John Esq	Wil-266	Burwell		Way-250
Edmund	Brt- 47	Mary	Pas-189	G		Col- 18
Hatten	Brt- 44	Mary	Ire-255	George		Ire-250
Henry	Prq-217	Ralph	Way-238	Green		Cha-215
John	Hrt-209	Reuben	Bun- 94	Hardy		Edg- 44
Wm	Brt- 43	Reuben	Ire-253	Henry		Way-247
Flemin,George	Pit-231	T	Ash- 13	Hugh		Rob-220
Fleming,Abram	Bur-122	Thomas	Sur-187	J		Bru-236
Allen	Sam-160	Thomas	Hal-104	Jacob		Sam-154
Arch	Lnc-363	Thomas Esq	Wil-277	Jacob		Joh-291
Archd	Lnc-358	William	Bun- 82	Jacob		Cha-193
Benjamin	Pit-254	William	Bun- 88	Jesse		Way-234
Catey	Cab-147	William	Row- 56	Jno		Ans- 28
Charles	Edg- 69	William	Sur-185	John		Roc- 29
Charles	War-169	William	Row- 74	John		Way-234
Daniel	Hay-195	William	Grn-136	John		Ire-250
David	Pit-254	William	Sto-139	John		Cur- 79
George	War-171	William	Fra- 78	Josiah		Wsh-227
J	Glf-184	Fleth,D	Cam-158	Kitey		Cur- 81
John	Lnc-363	Flewellen,Demsy	Hal-104	Muphrey		Way-250
John	Pit-253	Richard	Hal-104	Nathan		Cha-210
John	Pit-254	Flim,J	Bru-236	Ransom		Nor- 66
Milly	Grn-139	Flimmon,John	Cha-195	Saml		Way-234
Mitchel	Cab-138	Flin,Ebenr	Cab-138	Simon		Rob-221
Peter	War-178	Jesse	Rth-100	Thomas		Joh-288
Rob	Bur-130	John	Glf-187	Thomas		Nsh- 87
Thomas	War-181	John	Rth-100	Thos		Ans- 27
William	Sur-162	Flinchum,John	Sto-106	U		Col- 18
William	Edg- 65	John	Sto-141	W		Col- 18
William	War-182	Robert	Sto- 94	Will		Dup- 14
Wm	Cab-138	Thomas	Sto-141	William		Way-234
Flemings,John	Edg- 67	Thomas	Sto-106	Floyd,A		Col- 21
Flemming,Alexr	Sam-159	Flinn,Benj	Hyd-224	B		Col- 21
John	Ire-256	D	Col- 21	Caleb		Sto-153
John	Sam-159	Enoch	Hyd-224	George		Grn-127
Saml	Row- 39	Joseph	Mec- 40	Halsey		Prq-217
Saml	Row- 56	Wm	Mec- 24	Henry		Sto-155
Samuel	Ire-239	Flint,Thomas	Ora-138	Henry		Sto-113
Flemmon,Allison	Row- 71	Flinthem,John	Ora-165	Hickman		Grn-129
George	Rth-101	Flipper,Lewis	Roc- 28	Jno		Mon- 28
John	Rth-101	Flipps,Joseph	Cas- 54	John		Brt- 62
Flemons,David	Sur-176	Floid,Randolph	Brt- 55	M		Col- 20
Jesse	Sur-171	Floman,John	Pit-247	Nancy		Bft- 27
Job	Sur-192	Flood,Benjn	Hal-104	Peirce		Bur-118
John	Sur-188	Jesse	Hal-104	Penuel		Nsh- 75
Fletcher,Mrs.	Cum-240	John	Pit-236	S		Ash- 15

Floyd,Tho	Bft- 20	Fokle,Christian	Sto-131	Forbes,D	Cam-159
Viney	Bft- 27	Samuel	Sto-155	D	Cam-163
W	Col- 18	Foleston,Benoni	Bun- 76	D	Cam-160
Wm	Cho-226	Folesum,Benj	Way-242	F	Cam-160
Wm	Grn-127	Foley,Catey	Cas- 54	Henery	Cur- 85
Wm Sr	Grn-145	Folger,Lathan	Sto-134	J	Cam-154
Floyed,Francis	Row- 86	Lathron	Sto-102	J	Cam-157
Fredk	Fra- 89	Reubin	Sto-147	J	Cam-157
Griffin	Mar- 6	Folick,John	Row- 72	J	Cam-157
Margret	Dup- 12	Folk,Adam Jnr	Sto- 97	J	Cam-160
Thomas	Fra- 88	John	Sto- 97	Janach	Cur- 85
Flud,Enoch	Nsh- 88	S	Bru-230	L	Cam-155
Enoch Sr	Nsh- 88	William	Sto-107	M	Cam-154
Fluellen,Archey	Joh-275	Folke,Adam	Sto- 96	M	Cam-157
Sarah	Joh-275	Mary	Brt- 58	M Jnr	Cam-160
Flury,Henry	Cho-220	Folkner,Elizebeth	Ans- 10	P	Cam-160
Fly,Enoch	Nor- 66	Jno	Ans- 31	Quincy	Cur- 88
Enos	Nor- 66	John	Fra- 79	Robert	Pit-255
John	Nor- 66	Mos	Ora-136	S	Cam-154
Mary	Nor- 66	Folks,Benjm	Brt- 46	S	Cam-154
Peggy	Nor- 66	Wm	Mon- 44	S	Cam-156
Flyn,Thomas	Sto- 91	Folley,Allen	Roc- 27	S	Cam-155
Flynchum,Jacob	Sto-123	Elkanah	Bun- 76	William	Pit-242
Robert	Sto-122	Follin,Jacob	Gat-111	Forbors,E	Cam-163
William	Sto-123	Folsom,George	Cum-263	Forbus,A	Glf-153
William	Sto- 94	Israel	Cum-260	Auther	Edg- 50
Flynn,Francis	Sur-181	Stephen	Edg- 49	David	Rth-101
James	Sur-176	Thomas	Joh-290	Eli	Glf-155
John	Sur-171	William	Dup- 11	George	Glf-173
Leonard	Sur-177	William	Cum-256	Jearbny	Glf-153
Mary	Sur-189	Winder	Edg- 70	Jesse	Glf-154
Thomas	Sto-120	Folson,D	Bru-228	John	Edg- 50
William	Sur-186	Folts,Jacob	Sto-131	Forchand,J	Cam-155
Flynt,Perry	Sto-125	Foman,John	Sur-183	Ford,Absalem	Grn-142
Perry	Sto- 96	Fonderen,John	Rth-101	Absalom	Grn-138
Roderic	Sto-140	Fonds,Daniel	Ans- 7	Archa	Sur-191
Rocerick	Sto-105	Fonvielle,Brice	Ons- 98	Auston	Lnc-330
Thomas	Sto-125	Fonville,David	Jon-296	Dan	Mon- 46
Thomas	Sto- 96	Fred	Ora-124	Ezekiel	Cum-251
William	Sto-119	Hatcher	Ora-119	Fred	Lnc-332
William	Sto-129	Jeremiah	Jon-296	George	Roc- 13
Foard,Rebecah	Cas- 54	Foort,Charlotte	Nor- 67	George	Mec- 30
Fodrel,John	Sto-124	Elias	Nor- 67	J	Ash- 3
Fodrey,Willm	Car-183	Fooshee,Joseph Hill	Cha-215	John	Lnc-329
Fodry,Thos	Hyd-231	Foot,George	Roc- 16	John	Lnc-335
Fogg,Joseph	War-174	William	Sur-178	John	Cab-147
Fogleman,David	Ora-120	Foote,Henry	War-172	Jos	Cho-230
David	Glf-177	Footman,Dempsey	Cho-228	Lamuel	Roc- 13
H	Ora-172	Foraman,John	Row- 65	Larkin	Cas- 55
Hen	Ora-131	Forbas,A	Glf-171	Leay	Cas- 55
James	Ora-121	Hap	Glf-151	Lemuel	Roc- 15
Jno	Ora-131	Hugh	Mec- 32	Mathew F	Grn-133
John	Ora-172	Forbes,A	Cam-157	Mumrod	Cas- 54
Peter	Ora-131	Arthur	Pit-263	Nathan	Lnc-329
Peter Jr	Ora-131	B	Cam-154	Richard	Ire-250
Fogles,Philip	Sot-142	Benjamin	Pit-260	Richd	Mon- 46
Foin,John	Row- 42	Benjamin	Pit-257	Richd	Mon- 46
Peter	Row- 80	C	Cam-154	Simon	Cas- 55
Peter	Row- 42	Caleb	Cur- 84	Suckey	Row- 88

-106-

Name	Ref	Name	Ref	Name	Ref
Ford,Teddy	Lnc-332	Forkner,Joseph	Sur-181	Fort,Turner	Ans- 12
Thos	Lnc-332	Lewis	Sur-185	Wilie	Way-246
William	Lnc-366	Martin	Sur-176	Forte,W	Cam-156
Wm	Cho-230	Pleasant	Sur-160	Forten,Jesse	Mar- 13
Wm	Mon- 33	Susanna	Sur-161	Fortescue,Luke	Hyd-221
Wm	Row- 40	Thomas	Sur-161	Moses	Hyd-233
Woodly	Lnc-332	Forksey,Elliott	Cho-227	Richard	Hyd-232
Fordham,Benj Jr	Jon-296	J	Cam-156	Thos	Hyd-233
Benjamin Senr	Jon-296	J Esq	Cam-159	William	Hyd-221
John	Jon-296	N	Cam-157	Zachariah	Hyd-233
William	Jon-296	W	Cam-154	Fortesque,Simon	Bft- 35
Fore,Francis	Roc- 2	Forkum,Peter	Sto-153	Wm	Bft- 19
Nancy	Joh-290	Forkur,Thomas	Row- 63	Fortey,Lavis	Cab-145
Forehand,D	Cam-164	Formal,V	Ora-152	Fortias,Wm	Glf-155
David	Edg- 69	Forman,James	Bur-131	Fortin,John	Rth-100
David	Edg- 65	Forney,----l M.	Lnc-371	Pleasant	Rth-101
James	Len-320	Abram	Lnc-358	Richard	Rth-100
Jesse	Dup- 15	Peter	Lnc-366	William	Rth-101
Lewis	Way-233	Forquher,William	Per-138	William	Rth-100
Sarah	Pas-189	Forquhr,John	Per-129	William	Rth-100
Thos	Cho-229	Wm	Per-219	Fortinberry,William	Rth-101
James	Ora-120	Forrans,Thos K	Sam-164	Fortinbury,James	Rth-100
Foreman,Alexander	Car-170	Forrest,Eliza	Mon- 44	John	Rth-100
Amas	Bft- 19	George	Way-240	Fortner,Aaron	Wil-285
Benjamin	Hyd-233	Isaiah	Ora-167	Dread	Wil-278
Benjn	Hal-104	John	Mon- 44	Plood	Wil-285
Cornelius	Edg- 56	John	Roc- 10	Ford	Bur-126
Harmon	Hyd-221	Nathan	Mon- 44	J	Ash- 8
James	Car-184	Thomas	Cas- 44	Levi	Wil-275
Jeremiah	Edg- 57	Forrester,Benj	Lnc-358	Micajah	Wil-278
John	Pit-254	John	Wil-277	Seegar	Wil-285
Joshua	Hyd-222	John Jr	Wil-280	Solomon	Wil-285
Noah	Hyd-222	Shad	Ora-115	Thomas	Ire-247
Penelope	Pit-254	Thomas	Bur-105	Thomas	Ire-247
Prudence	Pit-253	Forshee,William	Cha-211	Fortunberry,Jacob	Bun- 84
Russel	Car-184	Porster,John	Glf-185	Fortune,Jessee	Ire-247
Uriah	Hyd-233	Forsyth,Benjamin	Sto-157	Laurence	Wsh-219
Foreshee,Gabriel	Cha-202	Benjn	Sto-116	Richard	Bur-110
Foreston,Nathl	Cha-203	Hugh	Mec- 23	Foscue,Frederic	Jon-296
Forgason,Anthony	Hrt-212	Jno	Mec- 45	Lewis	Jon-296
Murdock	Mor- 65	John	Ire-243	Richard	Jon-296
Robert	Cab-146	Wm	Ora-164	Simon Junr	Jon-296
Wm	Cab-147	Forsythe,Bernard	Ora-117	Simon Senr	Jon-296
Forgerson,Alexr	Glf-169	John	Ora-117	Foshee,Elijah	Cha-198
George	Ran-164	Robert	Lnd-333	Elijah Sen	Cha-16
John	Ran-164	William	Grn-136	Joseph	Cha-209
William	Ons-105	Wm	Ora-142	Joseph	Cha-191
Forgoon,Alexr	Cab-143	Port,Elias Senr	Hal-104	Foskue,William	Ons-100
Forgoson,Wm	Cab-146	Elizabeth	Edg- 56	Fosler,William Sr	Bun- 94
Forguson,Micajah	Wil-274	Elizabeth	Edg- 41	Foss,John	Wil-272
Robert	Sur-188	French	Cha-194	Fosset,Sam	Ora-151
Forgussan,John	Wil-284	George	Edg- 41	Fossett,James	Hal-104
Thomas (Y R)	Wil-283	John Junr	Bla- 9	James	Hal-105
Forister,Hezekiah	Sur-181	John Senr	Bla- 8	John	Ora-170
James	Sur-178	Lewis	Edg- 47	John	Hal-104
William	Sur-177	Nancy	Way-246	Nancy	Hal-104
Forkner,Isaac	Sur-161	Ricks	Hal-104	Richd	Ora-143
James	Sur-174	Sherwood	Rob-234	Will	Ora-170
John	Sur-181	Thomas	Rob-234	Fossit,Robt	Row- 41

Foster,Andrew	Roc- 15	Foster,Samuel	Row- 74	Fowler,J	Col- 21		
Anthony	Sur-171	Samuel	Rth-100	James	Per-138		
Anthony	Wil-280	Sucky	Pas-188	John	Per-129		
Asel	Rth-101	T	Glf-177	John	Grn-143		
Christopher	Fra- 79	Thomas	Bun- 89	John	Grn-129		
Colby	Cas- 54	Thomas	Wil-280	John	Grn-127		
Daniel	Fra- 85	Thomas	Cas- 54	Joshua	Fra- 87		
Daniel	Roc- 26	Thomas	Edg- 72	M	Ora-147		
Daniel	Rth-101	Thomas Jr	Wil-283	Pleasant	War-184		
David Jr	Row- 72	Thomas Senr	Bun- 96	Richd	Per-129		
David Senr	Row- 72	William	Row- 84	Robt	Mec- 42		
Edison	Wil2-85	William	Glf-186	Saml	Sto-148		
Edmund	Rth-101	William	Bun- 89	Saml	Grn-149		
Edmund	Rth-101	Wm	Ora-123	Samuel	Sto-111		
Edmund	Rth-101	Fouch,Elijah	Rth-101	T	Col- 19		
Francis Jr	Prq-217	Jonathan	Rth-101	Thomas	War-181		
Francis Sr	Prq-217	William	Rth-101	W	Col- 20		
Geo	Ora-162	William	Rth-101	William	Prq-217		
George	Bur-106	Fouch,Elijah	Rth-101	Fox,Abram	Bur-121		
George Jr	Wil-276	Jonathan	Rth-101	Allen	Bur-108		
Hasens	Rth-101	William	Rth-101	Barney	Cha-205		
Henry	Mec- 23	William	Rth-101	Benjamin	Nor- 67		
Henry	Lnc-376	Foumson,Wm	Bft- 37	David	Ran-165		
Henry	Mec- 45	Fountain,Fanny	Ons-104	David	Cha-197		
Henry P	War-172	Franky	Pas-189	Elijah	Bur-104		
Isaiah	Ons-104	Henry	Dup- 34	Francis	Wil-283		
J	Glf-158	James	Edg- 55	George	Pas-189		
James	Pas-189	James	Sto-149	George	Ran-164		
James	Glf-189	James	Sto-111	Hugh	Ire-264		
James	Cas- 54	Jane	Sto-111	Hugh	Bur-106		
Jno	Mec- 24	Joab	Dup- 34	Isham	Fra- 83		
Joel	Sto-151	John	Dup- 34	Jacob	Cha-212		
Joel	Sto-109	Nathan	Dup- 35	Jacob	Cha-197		
Joel	Gat-106	Saml	Glf-168	Jacob	Cha-212		
John	Wil-264	William	Edg- 55	James	Bur-108		
John	Wsh-222	Fourel,Elisebeth	Mec- 40	James	Bur-105		
John	Pas-188	Jno	Mec- 41	James	Bun- 73		
John	Glf-176	Foust,Andrew	Ran-165	Jane	Per-217		
John Esq	Fra- 89	Danl	Ora-172	Jno	Mec- 39		
John	Row- 64	Geo	Ora-170	John	Bur-108		
John B	Prq-217	Jacob	Ran-165	John	Bur-121		
John Jr	Wil-277	Mary	Ora-172	John	Cha-197		
John T	Fra- 79	Philip	Ran-165	John	Row- 61		
Joseph	Row- 72	Fousts,Peter	Row- 80	John Jr	Cha-208		
Joshua	Wsh-227	Fouts,David	Lnc-339	Joseph	Pas-189		
Joshua Sr	Prq-217	J	Ash- 7	Larkin	Bur-126		
Lettis	Cas- 54	J	Ash- 15	Leonard	Ran-165		
Lewis	Ons-104	L	Ash- 8	Michael	Ran-165		
Lewis	Cas- 54	Foutz,John	Row- 80	Moses	Bur-106		
Lott	Ons-100	Fowler,A	Col- 20	Nicholas	Cha-205		
Nancy	Cas- 55	Abram	Rth-100	Prissillah	Ran-165		
Richard Jr	Row- 75	Arthur	Per-129	Rebecah	Ran-165		
Richd	Row- 72	Daniel	Per-219	Robt	Nor- 66		
Robert	Row- 84	David	Mon- 25	Robert	Bun- 74		
Robert	Wil-283	Eliza	Sam-153	Samuel	Sto- 91		
Robert	Row- 72	Francis	Roc- 4	Samuel	Sto-109		
Robert	Cas- 55	Gabrael	Grn-141	Samuel	Sto-120		
Robert Senr	Row- 65	Gabriel	Per-129	Sark	Fra- 93		
S	Glf-185	J	Col- 21	Stephen	Mec- 39		

Fox,Thomas	Ran-165	Frank,Peter	Row- 83	Frazer,George Jnr	Ran-165
Thomas	Cum-258	Franklin,Mrs.	Mec- 50	Isaac	Glf-157
Thomas Jr	Wil-279	Archibald	Hal-104	J	Glf-176
Foxhall,Robert	Edg- 59	Bernard	Sur-175	J	Glf-170
William	Edg- 58	Chesterfield	Per-138	James	Glf-168
Foxwell,Edward	Cas- 55	Edward	Dup- 17	James	Glf-157
Poy,Enoch	Jon-296	Henry	Rth-100	Jas Sen	Glf-158
James	Ons-107	James	Sto-130	John	Ons-101
John	Lnc-340	James	Sto-127	John	Sto-133
Lewis	Jon-296	Jason	Gat-110	John	Glf-168
Foye,Frederick Esq	Ons-100	Jesse	Sur-160	Jonathan	Ran-165
Foyle,James Sr	Ons- 95	John	Sur-180	Joshua	Rth-100
Jesse	Ons-100	John	Bur-111	Lowel	Sto-133
Frack,William	Row- 81	John	Bur-127	Lowel	Sto-101
Frady,Charles	Sru-190	John E	Sto- 99	M	Glf-183
Ephraim	Sur-190	John E	Sto-127	Robert	Sto-147
Henry	Sur-190	John E	Sto-130	Robert	Sto-110
John	Sur-190	John Senr	Bur-111	Solomon	Ran-165
Fraisor,Barnet	Grn-142	Jonathan	Bur-111	Stephen	Sto-149
Howell	Grn-143	Lewis	Rth-100	Stephen K	Sto-111
John	Grn-143	Little B	Wil-258	Thomas	Ran-165
Ransom	Grn-139	Malechi	Sto- 98	Thomas Jnr	Ran-165
Ransom	Grn-145	Maleki	Sto-127	Wateman	Way-235
Shade	Grn-145	Meshach	Sur-189	William	Mor- 66
Wm	Grn-143	Moses	Bur-111	Frazier,Alexander	Nsh- 84
Wm (On)	Grn-123	Noah	Nor- 66	Alexander	Car-180
Fraless,Wm	Hrt-210	Saml	Bur-130	Charles	Sur-194
Fraley,George	Row- 77	Sarah	Pas-189	James	Ons- 97
George	Row- 78	Shad	Sur-162	Jane	Row- 42
John	Row- 80	Thomas	Rth-100	John	Car-183
John	Row- 86	Walter	Sur-180	Sally	Sur-196
Praly,Henry	Row- 50	William	Joh-275	William	Ons-106
Jacob	Row- 50	Franks,Rebeca	Bft- 19	William	Sur-194
Frame,John	Brt- 56	Richard	Bun- 93	Frazor,Widow	Mec- 47
Frames,Anthony	Cur- 92	Wm	Cha-202	Isaac	Mec- 54
France,Sarah	Roc- 35	Frankum,James	Bur-129	Jas	Mec- 39
William	Wil-281	Wm	Bur-129	Frazure,James	Bun- 97
Frances,Burrel	Hal-105	Fraser,H	Mon- 28	Frear,H	Glf-173
C	Ash- 8	Isreael	Cab-138	Frears,James	Grn-129
Francis,Bartlett	Sto-121	James	Dup- 31	Freaze,John	Row- 39
Daniel	Rth-101	John	Mon- 23	Frederick,Felix	Dup- 3
David	Rth-101	John	Cab-136	James	Sam-162
Fred	Brt- 51	Simon	Mon- 29	Peter	Sam-162
Frederick	Sto-155	Wm	Cab-139	William Sr	Dup- 8
Frederick	Sto-113	Frasher,Angus	Hal-104	Fredericke,Sarey	Cur- 83
John	Sto- 93	George	Ire-253	Fredericks,William	Dup- 4
John	Ire-262	James	Ire-259	Freeland,Alexander	Ire-260
John	Sto-156	James	Ire-240	Andrew	Ire-260
John	Sto-121	Prashure,James	Jon-296	Chas	Ora-143
Micajah	Sto-121	John	Jon-296	James	Ora-177
Micajah	Sto- 91	Frasier,John Esqr	Wsh-224	James	Ire-260
Micajah	Sto- 93	Frasor,James	Hrt-206	James Jr	Ora-124
Micajah	Sto-119	Frasure,Alexander	Rch-205	Jno	Ora-151
Thomas	Ire-263	James	Wil-269	Jno	Ora-117
William	Nsh- 89	Frazel,Samuel	Ons-100	Jos	Ora-137
Franciss,Thos	Tyr-202	Frazer,Aaron	Sto-134	Samuel	Ire-260
Frank (sic)	Pas-189	Abel	Glf-170	Tho	Ora-124
Edward	Jon-296	Benjn	Ran-165	Thomas	Ire-260
John	Row- 70	George Snr	Ran-165	Walter	Ire-260

Freeland,William	Ire-260	Freeman,Joshua	Sto-156	Frew,David	Pas-189
Freeling,Henry	Row- 65	Josiah	Edg- 47	Isaac	Pas-189
Freeman,Widow	Mec- 46	Larry	Sam-164	Friadle,H	Ora-121
Aaron	Bun- 75	Lend	Row- 52	Friar,W	Glf-177
Aaron Junr	Bun- 75	Malone	Rth-100	Frick,Henry	Sur-172
Abraham Senr	Bla- 6	Martha	Brt- 61	Jacob	Row- 78
Abraham Junr	Bla- 6	Mary	Brt- 52	Mathias	Row- 78
Allen	Rth-100	Mary	Brt- 49	Frickey,John	Cab-138
Allen	Rth-100	Mat	Nsh- 75	Friday,Andrew	Lnc-332
Allen	Mec- 44	Michael	Bur-126	Jonas	Lnc-344
Arch	Pas-189	Moses	Bun- 92	Martin	Lnc-344
Benjamin	Rob-243	Nathan	Sto-154	Friddle,J	Ora-121
Benjamin	Rth-100	Olive	Grn-136	John	Row- 85
Benjamin Jnr	Rob-243	Peter	Rth-101	Friel,Henry	Ora-150
Charles	Brt- 51	Poley	Gat-112	Wm	Ora-150
Cleben	Mec- 45	R	Mon- 43	Friend,Joseph	Wil-268
D Jr	Ora-134	Reuben	Mor- 59	Frieze,Henry	Row- 70
Daniel	Joh-282	Reubeon	Mec- 36	Jacob	Row- 73
David	Sur-187	Robert	Sur-175	Jacob	Row- 71
David	Mec- 44	Robert	Fra- 97	Peter	Row- 70
Davy	Joh-282	Robert	War-179	Samuel	Row- 70
Deen	Ora-134	Robertson	Rth-100	Frilas,Jesse	Glf-157
Dugger	Rth-100	Salley	Gat-108	Frink,S	Bru-226
Edmond	Grn-136	Saml	Ora-176	W	Col- 19
Elizth	Ons-103	Saml	Bft- 28	Frinks,A	Col- 19
Elizabeth	Sur-170	Saml	Bla- 6	T	Col- 19
Elizh	Bru-228	Samuel	Wsh-220	Frisby,Wm	Cho-224
Evin	Grn-136	Sarah	Len-322	Fritz,Geo	Row- 41
Fatherman	Rth-100	Sarah	Ora-123	Henry	Lnc-337
Francis	Way-234	Thomas	Gat-107	John	Row- 41
George	Gat-106	Thomas	Grn-126	Frizby,Abraham	Bun- 96
George	Cha-207	Thomas	Bun- 75	Josiah	Bun- 84
Gideon	Grn-136	Timothy	Gat-108	Samuel	Bun- 83
Jacob	Rob-243	Tyre	Sur-170	Frizzell,Patcey	Mar- 13
James	Fra- 92	William	Edg- 59	Frizzle,John	Bur-129
James	Sto-153	William	Way-234	John	Pit-238
James	Brt- 51	William	Rth-100	Jonathan	Pit-239
James	Sto-113	William	Fra- 94	Frocler,Geo	Ora-120
James Esqr	Wsh-220	William	Bur-126	Frohock,John	Ire-256
Jas	Mec- 37	Wm	Ora-145	Alexr	Row- 37
Jas	Mon- 40	Wm	Mor- 59	Frolinger,Henry	Ora-120
Jesse	Bun- 75	Wm	Brt- 52	John	Ora-120
Jesse	Hrt-209	Wm Junr	Fra- 94	Frombarger,Caty	Lnc-331
Jno	Len-322	Freemon,Abner	Sur-163	John	Lnc-331
Jno	Ora-134	Freer,Robert	Hal-104	John	Lnc-331
Jno	Ans- 22	Freesland,Fredk	Cab-143	Frons,John	Bft- 37
Jno	Rob-243	Freeze	Row- 69	Frosman,Esther	Jon-296
John	Edg- 63	Freezon,Thos	Sam-153	Frost,Barbary	Jon-296
John	Bla- 6	Freman,Anderson	Grn-143	Ezekiel	Sto-116
John	Bun- 76	Eds	Cur- 87	Ezekiel	Sto-156
John	Bun- 76	Elisebeth	Cur- 84	Hopkins	Roc- 21
John	Ons-103	French,Jeremiah	Cas- 54	James	Lnc-337
John	Brt- 52	William Esq	Ons- 95	James P	Cha-210
John	Rth-101	Freshwartes,James	Ons-106	James Snr	Joh-290
John	Mon- 40	Thomas	Ons-106	John	Row- 61
John	Mon- 23	Freshwater,Jem	Pas-189	Jonas	Roc- 21
John	Cur- 87	John A	Pas-188	Penelope	Car-179
Joseph	Gat-107	Sarah	Ora-130	Robert	Lnc-337
Joshua	Bun- 75	Thadds	Pas-188	Robert Junr	Lnc-340

-110-

Name	Ref	Name	Ref	Name	Ref
Fruar,Elizabeth	Nor- 66	Fulford,Benjn	Car-177	Fuller,Ezekiel	Fra- 91
Richard	Nor- 66	Clifford	Car-176	F	Glf-177
Frur,Thomas	Nor- 66	James	Car-177	Gideon	Sto-126
Fry,Amos	Ran-164	Joseph	Car-177	Isaac	Per-138
Bethsheba	Mor- 57	Josiah	Cur- 90	Isaih	Per-138
Briant	Row- 42	Samuel	Car-172	James	Cas- '54
Elizabeth	Sto- 96	Sarah	Car-178	John	Fra- 91
Elizabeth	Sto-125	Stephen Senr	Car-177	John	Grn-122
George	Mor- 58	Uriah	Car-177	Jonathan	Grn-127
George	Row- 54	Fulghum,Anthony	Way-248	Jones	Fra- 93
George	Rth-101	Benj	Way-247	Joseph	Grn-122
George Jr	Row- 53	Jacob	Way-243	Levy	Cas- 54
George Junr	Lnc-348	Jesse	Way-234	Mary	Nor- 66
George Senr	Lnc-348	John	Way-243	Mary	Car-171
Henry	Row- 81	Joseph	Way-248	Moses	Cas- 54
Henry Jr	Row- 81	Matthew	Way-243	Moses	Per-138
Jacob	Lnc-348	Winefred	Way-247	Phillip	Rth-101
James	Row- 81	Fulgum,John	Hal-104	Samuel	Glf-185
James	Mor- 57	Pulk,Adam	Sto-126	Solomon	Car-185
James	Mon- 45	Adam Jun	Sto-127	William	Fra- 78
John	Sto- 93	Andrew	Sur-173	William	Cas- 54
John	Lnc-346	Andrew	Sto-127	William	Hal-105
John	Sto-122	Jacob	Sur-187	Wm	Grn-127
John	Sto-125	John	Sur-187	Wm	Grn-130
John	Sto- 96	John	Sto-126	Wilson	Car-185
John Jr	Lnc-374	Joseph	Sto-127	Fullerton,Andw	Bft- 19
Joseph	Mor- 58	Leonard	Sto-127	Pullington,James	Cas- 54
Michael	Sto-132	Peter	Sto-130	Pullinton,John	Cho-228
Michael	Sto-101	William	Row- 86	Fulmore,Andrew	Rob-238
Nathan	Row- 81	Fulks,Charles	Lnc-342	Pulp,George	Sto-148
Nathan	Mor- 58	Fullar,Henry	Cas- 54	Michael	Sto-148
Nicholas	Lnc-374	William	Per-138	Peter	Sto-137
Peter	Lnc-374	Fullard,Crafford	Len-312	Peter	Sto-147
Phillip	Lnc-378	Fullbright,Widow	Lnc-352	Peter	Sto-103
Phillip	Lnc-348	Andrew	Lnc-352	Peter	Sto-111
Thomas	Mor- 56	Jacob	Lnc-355	Peter Snr	Sto-149
Thos Jun	Mor- 56	Jacob	Lnc-352	Solomon	Sto-147
Valentine	Sto-150	Jacob	Lnc-352	Fulsher,Reuben	Jon-296
Valingtine	Sto-109	John	Lnc-355	Fulshire,Jesse	Car-176
Vincent	Row- 41	John	Lnc-352	Levy	Car-179
Wm	Mon- 45	William	Lnc-352	Reuben Senr	Jon-296
Fryer,A	Col- 20	Fuller,Widow	Mec- 50	Thomas	Car-179
George	Rth-100	Archibald	Ran-165	Fulton,Alexander	Glf-174
Jessee	Edg- 47	Aron	Per-138	D	Ora-155
Jonathan	Sam-163	Alexander	Ire-264	Francis	Sto-142
Mary	Edg- 47	Beliher	Car-171	Francis	Sto-106
Willis	Brt- 60	Benjn	Ran-164	Geo	Glf-174
Fuell,James	Roc- 6	Betton	War-168	Jessee	Ora-170
Fuget,Susanna	Wil-260	Brittin	Ran-165	John	Row- 89
Fugler,Michael	Mar- 6	Crafford	Grn-122	Robert	Sto-140
Fulbright,John	Hay-195	Daniel	Grn-122	Robert	Sto-105
Martin	Hay-195	David	Grn-130	S	Glf-174
William	Hay-195	David	Hyd-228	S Jr	Glf-174
Fulcher,Joseph	Cur- 81	David Jr	Grn-122	Saml	Ora-155
Fulder,Samuel	Cas- 54	Demsey	Grn-122	Thos	Ora-155
Fulerton,Tho	Bur-130	Derling D	Ran-165	Fults,Jacob	Sto-153
Fulford,Abihail	Car-177	Ejah	Grn-122	John	Sto-142
Absalom	Car-177	Elizabeth	Ran-165	John	Sto-107
Benjamin	Hyd-228	Ezekiel	Fra- 87	Peter	Sto-104

Fults,Peter	Sto-136	G., Widow	Lnc-327	Gaither,Edward	Ire-268
Fultz,Frederick	Row- 53	G----,John Junr	Jon-297	Edward B	Ire-243
Fulwider,Ellina	Row- 66	G----,Jessy	Jon-297	Jerimiah	Ire-266
Fulwood,William	Bun- 87	Gabby,Jonathan	Hay-195	John	Ire-268
Funderburg,Francis	Cab-141	Gabor,James	Cab-138	John	Ire-268
Funkhowser,Henry	Bun- 84	Gabriel,Abram	Lnc-358	Lebetous	Ire-243
Fur,John	Row- 69	Emanuel	Car-184	Reasin	Ire-242
Henry	Cab-142	James	Car-184	Zacharia	Ire-267
Paul	Cab-141	Zilphia	Car-184	Galaher,Alex	Ora-175
Furbush,Adam	Pas-189	Gadberry,Green	Row- 51	James	Ire-258
Peter	Pas-189	James	Row- 47	Galaspie,Bothie C	Jon-297
Thomas	Pas-188	Nat	Row- 51	Duncan	Cum-237
Furer,Jno	Mon- 49	Gadd,James	Rth-103	Galaway,Ann	Edg- 49
Furgason,Daniel	Nsh- 88	Joseph	Mon- 31	C	Bru-230
Wm	Row- 43	Joseph	Rch-199	N	Bru-228
Furgerson,Alexr	Bun- 93	William	Rch-200	Galbrath,J	Glf-178
Furgeson,Hugh	Row- 76	William	Bun- 80	J	Glf-172
Furgison,John	Row- 58	Gadden,Ephram	Joh-283	J Snr	Glf-172
Furr,Charles	Mor- 66	Gaddis,Alsey	Rth-103	Jas	Glf-166
Jacob	Mor- 62	Ansel	Ran-166	John	Glf-155
Lenard	Mor- 62	Jas	Mec- 32	Galbreath,Thos	Glf-156
Furrington,Abraham	Row- 43	Jesse	Ran-166	Walter	Ora-123
Furster,Charles	Cur- 81	John	Bun- 87	Galconer,Thos	Grn-120
Fusel,John	Grn-134	John	Ran-166	Gale,John	Cum-247
Fussel,Aaron	War-167	Gaddy,Frederick	Ans- 13	Gales,Sam	Mon- 33
Fussell,Benjn	Dup- 23	Jas	Ans- 10	Galespie,John	Mor- 57
Eliza	Dup- 21	Jeremiah	Ans- 30	Gallaspey,Wilson	Bun- 90
Harrison	War-172	Thos	Ans- 12	Gallaspy,John	Bun- 96
Fusset,John	Ons-104	Thos	Ans- 18	Silas	Bun- 92
Futeral,Moore	Ons-104	Wm	Ans- 13	Gallaugher,Wm	Per-219
Futerel,Laurence	Sam-161	Gadger,Banjamin	Bun- 87	Gallaway,J	Col- 18
Futreel,James	Way-252	Gadis,Archabald	Row- 87	Mary	Bft- 29
Futrel,Needham	Joh-280	Gady,James	Cum-267	Thomas	Cha-203
S	Col- 18	James Junr	Cum-267	Gallehee,Hugh	Ire-250
Futrell,Benjamin	Mar- 12	John	Cum-267	Matthew	Ire-239
David	Nor- 66	Thomas	Cum-245	Gallemore,Abel	Ran-166
Dempsey	Nor- 66	Gaemil,Joshuay	Cur- 83	Elisha	Sur-187
Dempsey Jr	Nor- 66	Gaffin,John	Hal-105	John	Ran-167
Elizabeth	Nor- 66	William	Hal-105	William	Sur-188
Elliott	Nor- 66	Gage,Jacob	Rth-103	Gallen,Edward	Ran-166
Enos	Nor- 66	James	Grn-136	Gallent,Daniel	Mec- 25
Ephraim	Nor- 66	Wm	Grn-136	Gallet,Matthew	Cho-223
John	Nor- 66	Gaham,Robert	Ora-165	Galleway,Moses	Bur-109
John Jr	Nor- 66	Gail,William	Hal-105	Gallian,Samuel	Sur-162
John Senr	Nor- 66	Gailord,Stephen	Cur- 85	Young	Sur-163
Martha	Nor- 66	Gainer,Arthur	Mar- 6	Gallimore,John	Row- 70
Milly	Nor- 66	Elisha	Roc- 26	Gallion,Tho	Bur-104
Nathan	Nor- 66	Joseph	Pit-239	Thomas	Bur-125
Noah	Nor- 66	Martha	Hal-106	Gallison,Richard	Rth-102
Penelope	Nor- 66	Shubel	Ran-166	Galloop,Esekiah	Cur- 83
Sampson	Nor- 66	Gaines,Johnson	Roc- 25	Hughes	Cur- 83
Sarah Jr	Nor- 66	Susanah	Bft- 26	Johnghs	Cur- 87
Sarah Senr	Nor- 66	Thomas	Sto-121	Peter	Cur- 82
Sherrard	Nor- 66	Gains,James	Mor- 62	Willis	Cur- 83
Thomas	Nor- 66	Joseph	Per-138	Gallop,A	Cam-159
Willie	Nor- 66	Thomas	Per-138	A	Cam-165
Futril,M	Ora-147	Thomas	Roc- 9	A	Cam-154
Pyfe,John	Cho-220	Gaither,Basil	Ire-268	Anthony	Ons-107
		Burgess	Ire-267	C	Cam-165

Gallop,E	Cam-156	Gann,Saml Senr	Roc- 23	Gardner,Letty	Bft- 38
J	Cam-157	Ganner,A	Glf-174	Lewis	Dup- 35
J	Cam-160	Gannon,Al	Glf-154	Luke	Mar- 13
J	Cam-162	B	Glf-154	Martin	Edg- 43
J Jnr	Cam-154	Perry	Glf-154	Martin	Edg- 44
M	Cam-159	Gans--,Wm Sr	Bru-224	Mary	Pit-249
Galloway,Mrs.	Bru-234	Gant,Charles	Fra- 86	Nancy	Car-183
Charles	Row- 61	Henry	Glf-174	Paul	Glf-171
Edward	Pit-251	Henry	Lnc-355	Rustin	Sto-112
Henry	Tyr-202	J	Glf-178	S	Glf-164
Hosea	Pit-234	J	Ora-139	Samuel	Sur-187
Jno	Mec- 48	James	Ora-137	Saml	Mar- 10
John	Ire-260	Jeremiah	Fra- 98	Sarah	Mar- 10
Robert	Roc- 34	John	Lnc-351	Solomon	Glf-188
Thomas	Ire-243	John	Ora-137	Sylvinas	Glf-188
William	Bun- 97	Sarah	Ora-137	Thadias	Glf-187
Gally,William	Ire-253	Wm	Ora-118	Thomas	War-181
Galord,Aaron	Cur- 80	Zach	Ora-124	Thomas	Mar-445
Gambel,John	Glf-152	Gantly,Mary	Ora-161	Thomas	Bun- 78
Gambell,James	Glf-153	Ganus,W	Col- 21	William	Edg- 43
Jesse	Wil-255	Gappius,S	Ora-160	William	Car-183
John	Wil-266	Will	Ora-171	William	Car-182
John Jr	Wil-259	Gardan,John	Wil-258	William	Sto-110
William	Glf-153	John W	Wil-257	Wm	Glf-186
William	Wil-259	Nancy	Wil-258	Wm	Sto-149
Gambil,John	Cas- 55	Gardener,Jas	Cab-136	Willis	Way-252
Gambill,J	Ash- 4	Josiah	Hal-105	Zachariah	Pit-236
M	Ash- 7	Lias	Rch-208	Gardnur,Jno	Mec- 48
W	Ash- 7	Wm	Brt- 67	Wm	Mec- 47
Gamble,John	Lnc-330	Wm	Brt- 65	Gare,Michael	Wil-273
Gambling,J	Cam-164	Gardneir,Brazilla	Mec- 28	Garganus,Henry	Ons-102
L	Cam-165	Gardner,Cela	Brt- 54	Reuben	Pit-261
P	Cam-165	Demsey	Edg- 69	Robert	Pit-261
Gambrol,James	Prq-218	Edward	Pit-236	Garish,James	Car-171
Games,William Jnr	Cas- 55	Edward	Pit-251	Saml	Bur-117
William Senr	Cas- 55	Edward	Pit-250	Garison,Garret	Bur-105
Gamewell,C	Cam-159	Elia	Bla- 11	Henry	Bur-105
John	Mon- 24	Elizabeth	Pit-250	Garland,Daniel	Bun- 76
Gammon,James	Hal-106	Everett	Brt- 63	Jonathan	Hal-105
Jesse	Hal-105	Francis Junr	Car-183	Joseph	Cas- 56
Patsy	Hal-105	Francis Senr	Car-183	Josiah	Cha-202
Polly	Pas-190	George	Nsh- 75	Garling,Jacob	Lnc-351
Gammy,John	Lnc-333	Hardy	Mar- 10	Garlington,J	Cam-163
Gan--,John	Sto-138	Henry	Cho-220	Garman,Charles	Wil-283
Gancy,S	Bru-226	Hez	Glf-169	Garmen,Michael	Cab-147
Gandy,Amos	Nsh-643	Isaac	Bft- 19	Gammon,William	Pit-262
Edward	Nsh-644	Isaac	Mar- 8	Garmon,Geo	Cab-147
Ganer,Wm	Nsh- 77	Isaac	Glf-171	Isaac	Bun- 74
Ganey,Abram	Sam-160	James	Glf-187	John	Cab-147
Bartholemew	Sam-160	James	Mar- 6	Garner,Aaron B	Lnc-446
Elias	Sam-160	Jemimah	Cur- 86	Benjamin	Row- 61
J	Bru-240	Jesse	Pit-250	Bradley	Mor- 65
Jacob	Sam-160	Jessee	Edg- 69	Burgis	Row- 60
John	Joh-290	John	Bun- 78	David	Row- 82
S	Bru-240	John	Edg- 44	David	Row- 69
Wm	Sam-160	Jonathan	Edg- 69	David	Bur-114
Wm	Mon- 25	Jonathan	Glf-170	Elisha	Joh-283
Gann,John	Roc- 23	Jose	Way-237	Eve	Sur-191
Samuel	Bun- 95	Lazarus	Edg- 46	Fereby	Mor- 61

Name	Loc	Name	Loc	Name	Loc
Garner,Gutridge	Bur-114	Garrawood,James	Row- 84	Garrot,John	Bun- 81
Henry	Row- 83	Garrell,Hovey	Cur- 85	Lewis	Sur-185
Henry	Sur-191	Thomas	Sto-135	Welcom	Sur-179
Jacob	Row- 42	Garrep,Joshua	Way-254	William	Bun- 88
Jacob	Lnc-344	Garret,Pugh	Pit-250	William	Ons-101
Jacob	Sur-191	William	War-183	Garroth,Jessey	Grn-129
James	Ran-167	Garrett,Betsey	Wsh-226	Garrott,E	Cam-161
Jane	Row- 82	Bradley	Wsh-225	Henry	Ora-172
Jeremiah	Lnc-360	Cable	Glf-163	Henry Sen	Ora-172
Jno	Mor- 59	Carter	Ora-166	J	Glf-177
John	Sur-191	Caysoan	Edg- 54	J	Cam-154
John	Cas- 56	Enoch	Bft- 23	J	Cam-159
John	Lnc-360	Eveard	Hrt-206	James	Ora-151
John	Cum-266	Green	War-171	Jess	Cur- 90
John	Nor- 67	James	Edg- 47	Levren	Prq-217
John	Row- 83	Jemia	Tyr-207	Nancy	Car-182
John	Row- 42	Jesse	Brt- 62	S	Cam-155
John	Row- 69	Jno	Ora-159	S	Cam-160
John	Row- 69	John	Wsh-225	Stephen	Grn-122
John	Row- 60	Joseph	Gat-114	Tyra	Ora-164
John	Ran-167	Joseph	Wsh-225	W	Cam-155
John Jnr	Ran-167	Mrs. Mary	Brt- 51	Garrowood,Wm	Row- 62
Josiah	Cum-266	Mary	Cho-230	Garton,Elizabeth	Ire-269
Lucy	Len-314	Peggy	Edg- 64	James	Ire-269
Mathias	Row- 68	Rebeca	Bft- 31	Garvin,R	Bla- 4
Moses	Joh-284	Samuel	Cas- 56	Garvis,Austin	Cur- 87
Nathan	Ans- 13	Thos	Tyr-203	John	Cur- 87
Needham	Dup- 15	William	Wsh-224	Samuel	Cur- 87
Peter	Mor- 60	Garrick,Mary	Cum-246	Thos Senr	Cur- 87
Philip	Row- 82	Garris,-----	Cur- 86	Garvy,Thomas	Dup- 30
Randolph (col)	Nor- 67	George	Nor- 67	Garvys,A Jr	Glf-177
Reubin	Sto-147	Henry	Nor- 67	Gary,Abijah	Ons-109
Robert	Row- 86	James	Nor- 67	Gilbert	Bft- 39
Robt	Row- 39	Joseph	Nor- 67	Henry	Nor- 67
Saml	Cha-193	Lovet	Cur- 93	John	Hal-105
Samuel	Nor- 67	Lucy	Nor- 67	Wm	Hal-105
Silene	Sto-147	Solomon	Cur- 93	Gash,Ann	Bun- 94
Simeon	Dup- 16	Garrison,Absalom	Bun- 83	John	Bun- 94
Stephen	Cum-263	Edmon	Row- 47	Martin	Bun- 83
Thomas	Rth-103	Garret	Rth-103	Gask,John	Nor- 67
Thos	Lnc-330	Geo	Ora-124	Gaskey,John	Row- 88
Valentine	Grn-126	Geo Sr	Ora-120	Gaskill,Abraham	Car-174
Wilie	Dup- 26	Jacob	Ora-124	Addam	Hyd-228
William	Nor- 67	James	Row- 47	Anson	Car-172
William	Lnc- 360	Jas	Mec- 48	Jacob	Hyd-229
William	Sur-188	John	Lnc-341	Jacob	Hyd-229
William	Rth-103	John	Cab-146	James	Car-172
Wm	Cha-193	William	Bun- 94	John	Car-172
Garns,Daniel	Hrt-212	Garriss,Alin	Len-319	Joseph	Car-172
Dol	Hrt-212	Thomas	Way-250	Joseph Junr	Car-174
Gidden	Hrt-216	William	Dup- 25	Robert	Car-172
Garood,Burket	Cur- 82	Garron,Andrew	Bun- 98	Thomas	Car-172
Garott,Betsey	Cur- 91	Daniel	Bun- 80	William Junr	Car-174
Catey	Cur- 88	John	Bun- 79	William Senr	Car-174
Edwd	Cur- 91	Joseph	Bun- 80	Gaskin,James	Hal-105
Thos	Cur- 90	Garrot,Dan	Mon- 28	Gaskins,Absalom	Car-182
Garrason,Nancy	Dup- 33	Henry	Roc- 33	Caswell	Car-171
Thomas	Dup- 8	Humphrey	Mon- 31	David	Brt- 49
Garrawood,Jacob	Row- 84	John	Ons-106	George	Brt- 44

-114-

Name	Ref	Name	Ref	Name	Ref	Name	Ref
Gaskins,Jacob	Car-172	Gattis,Alex	Ora-160	Gaylard,Jer	Bft- 19		
John	Brt- 44	James	Ora-142	Lucretia	Hyd-223		
John	Lnc-327	Jas	Ora-156	Neone	Hyd-223		
John Jnr	Car-172	Jno	Ora-156	Neome	Hyd-220		
John Snr	Car-172	Jno	Ora-142	Rebeckah	Hyd-224		
Joseph	Car-173	Samuel	Rth-102	Zachariah	Hyd-223		
Nathl	Lnc-327	Tho	Ora-170	Gaylor,George	Dup- 14		
Nosh	Car-173	Thos	Ora-156	Gays,James	Fra- 96		
Sarah	Cho-220	Gatton,Benjamin	Row- 64	Geans,Francis	Cur- 90		
Thos	Brt- 49	Jeremiah	Ire-268	Gears,James	Row- 64		
Thos	Pas-189	Joseph	Ire-243	Gee,Charles	Hal-105		
William	Pas-190	Gatts,John	Nor- 67	Drury	Nor- 67		
William	Car-173	Gatwood,Dudley	Cas- 55	James Ecor (col)	Nor- 67		
Gasper,Conrad	Row- 39	Gaulteny,Daniel	Lnc-376	Mary	Cum-269		
Henry	Row- 39	Nathan	Lnc-376	Nevill	Hal-105		
Gasperson,John	Bun- 81	Gaultney,William	Ire-250	Geer,David	Rth-102		
Gassom,George	Rth-102	Gaultny,John	Ire-251	John N	Wil-278		
Gastin,Tom	Ons-105	Nathan	Ire-251	Geering,Jabesh	Roc- 29		
Gaston,Authur	Bft- 37	Gause,B	Bru-226	Gelden,Charles	Cur- 90		
Gately,Elisabeth	Rch-201	Eleanor	Bru-222	Genett,William	Way-239		
Isaac	Rch-201	J	Bru-226	Wm	Cur- 81		
Isaac	Rch-201	John J	Bru-226	Gennett,Betsey	Way-239		
Thomas	Rch-201	N. Jr	Bru-230	Joseph	Way-239		
Gates,Fred	Ora-165	N. Senr	Bru-226	Gentle,Samuel	Row- 60		
George	Roc- 5	P	Bru-232	Thos	Row- 58		
Joseph	Wil-262	S	Bru-226	Gentry,Abednego	Sur-170		
Marian	Cum-268	Wm Jr	Bru-226	Allen	Sur-194		
Peter	Rth-102	Gavin,Anne	Sam-152	Allen	Wil-268		
Philip	Roc- 7	Edward C	Sam-152	Jonathan	Wil-268		
Richd	Per-129	Gay,Bailey	Fra- 94	Joseph	Sur-163		
Samuel	Edg- 53	Benjamin	Pit-259	Joseph W	Roc- 33		
William	Lnc-348	Charles	Hrt-212	Matthew	Wil-268		
Gatewood,Griffin	Ans- 30	Demsey	Edg- 52	Nicholas	Wil-259		
Robt	Ans- 17	Elias	Nor- 67	Meshack	Sur-165		
Thomas	Cas- 55	Elijah	Cum-264	Reuben	Sur-195		
Gather,Burrel	Row- 65	Henry	Nor- 67	Richard	Sur-194		
Elizabeth	Row- 64	J	Col- 21	Shelton	Sur-163		
Nicholas	Row- 66	James	Ire-242	Watson	Roc- 22		
John	Row- 63	James	Hrt-214	William	Sur-169		
Johnsey	Row- 64	John	Edg- 61	Geoch,Jesse	Mec- 26		
Walter	Row- 66	John	Ire-242	George,Altin	Cha-215		
Gatlen,John	Len-317	Jonathan	Nor- 67	Brice	Jon-297		
Gatlin,Franky	Dup- 25	Jonathan	Ran-166	D	Ora-141		
Garner	Ran-166	Jonathan	Ran-166	Daniel	Jon-297		
J----	Hrt-214	Kinchen	Edg- 43	David	Roc- 28		
James Snr	Ran-167	Lucy	Edg- 52	David	Jon-296		
Jardon	Hrt-212	Martha	Fra- 89	David	Joh-289		
Jesse	Ran-166	Osborn	Fra- 94	David	Len-320		
Jethro	Hrt-212	Richard	Edg- 49	Emsley	Cha-191		
Lewis	Hrt-207	Richard	Edg- 48	Henry	Bla- 6		
Patrick	Hrt-209	Robert	Row- 89	Isaac	Sto-125		
Gatling,Edward	Edg- 46	Sherwood	Edg- 48	Isaac	Sto-106		
James	Gat-115	Solomon	Nor- 67	Isaac	Sto-141		
John	Gat-116	Thomas	Nor- 67	James	Sto-154		
John	Gat-116	Thomas	Fra- 81	John	Edg- 56		
Miles	Gat-115	Thomas Junr	Fra- 96	Michael	Edg- 57		
William	Gat-112	William	Edg- 49	Ned	Pas-190		
William	Edg- 46	Gaylard,Elme	Hyd-232	Old	Pas-190		
Gator,Samuel	Edg- 54	Hona	Bft- 21	Presley	Cha-216		

-115-

George,Reubin		Sto-155	Gibbs,Benj		Len-316	Gibson,David	Lnc-332
T		Glf-179	Benj		Hyd-231	David	Lnc-332
Thomas		Rch-201	Benj		Hyd-229	David	Lnc-328
Willm Blunt Q		Pas-189	Benj		Hyd-227	Edward	Bur-111
Wm		Mec- 53	Benjamin		Hyd-228	Elizabeth	Sto- 93
Wm		Cha-203	Brinson		Hyd-227	Elizabeth	Roc- 34
Gerald,Alexander		Roc- 10	Cason		Hyd-228	Elizabeth	Sto-122
Lewis		Roc- 10	Cason Junr		Hyd-229	Ezekiel	Sto-120
Mary		Roc- 11	Charles		Dup- 12	Francis	Row- 71
William		Roc- 11	Cornelius		Bur-131	George	Row- 71
Gerding,Geo G		Lnc-376	Daniel		Hyd-230	Gilbert	Rch-208
Geren,A		Glf-151	Delitha		Hyd-228	Guin	Cas- 56
Gerison,Jno		Mec- 47	Elizabeth		Hyd-227	Henry	Tyr-206
Gerkin,Fedk		Bft- 24	Elizabeth		Hyd-227	Hugh	Lnc-334
Hannah		Wsh-221	Gilead		Hyd-229	Jennings	Ora-116
Nelly		Bft- 22	Henry		Bft- 35	Jno	Ora-113
German,Widow		Fra- 96	Henry		Hyd-229	John	Glf-182
Emory		Cum-253	Henry		Hyd-226	Joel	Wil-260
John		Lnc-346	Hugh		Bur-121	John	Ran-166
Wm		Ans- 6	Ivia		Hyd-227	John	Rch-195
Gerrard,Geo		Bft- 30	James		Rth-103	John	Mec- 53
Gerred,Mrs		Mec- 28	James		Rth-103	John	Lnc-346
Gerrell,J		Cam-154	Jane		Hyd-228	John	Glf-173
S		Cam-163	Jesse		Hyd-228	John Jnr	Ran-166
Geruson,Arthur		Mec- 48	John		Cha-07	Joseph	Bur-106
Geseften,Joseph M		Bur-116	John		Fra- 79	Joseph	Row- 71
Gessage,William		Cas- 55	John		Cha-205	Luke	Rch-194
Gessett,Lea		Cas- 56	John		Ire-255	Moses	Glf-173
Getchrist,Archd		Rob-218	John Jr		Dup- 13	Nancy	Rch-195
Geter,Robert		Grn-123	Joseph		Hyd-228	Nathan	Rch-194
Gethen,Jas		Ans- 20	Joseph		Hyd-227	Nathaniel	Rch-195
Geurin,Isaac		Roc- 19	Nancy		Rth-103	Nathen	Bur-130
Nathan		Roc- 19	Raybon		Fra- 79	Nelson	Rch-195
Gewen,Asa		Ans- 15	Rebecca		Dup- 13	Nelson Junr	Rch-194
Asa		Ans- 15	Reuben		Hyd-227	Nelson Senr	Rch-194
Jeremiah		Ans- 15	Robert		Hyd-227	Obadiah	Sto-126
Gewin,Jno		Ans- 26	Saml		Hyd-230	Pleasant	Roc- 25
Thos		Ans- 30	Samuel		Hyd-227	Rhody	Cas- 55
Gheen,Elizabeth		Row- 76	Thomas		Hyd-227	Robert	Rch-202
James		Row- 76	Thos		Ans- 33	Stephen	Bur-108
Thomas		Row- 76	Uriah		Hyd-227	Thomas	Edg- 56
Gholson,Mrs Fanny		Fra- 90	Washington		Hyd-228	Thomas Snr	Ran-166
Gibb,James		Bur-125	Watson		Hyd-228	Thos	Cum-239
Willis		Mec- 39	Whitley		Mar- 8	Thos	Lnc-331
Gibbins,John		Sto-143	Wiasington		Hyd-226	William	Ire-260
John		Sto-107	William		Hyd-226	William	Rch-194
Gibble,Frederick		Car-184	William		Cha-196	William	Row- 71
Gibbon,Jno		Mec- 31	William		Lnc-355	William	Sto- 96
Patty		Row- 84	William		Bur-121	William	Bur-111
Stephen		Dup- 19	Willm		Bru-230	William	Lnc-328
Gibbons,Catharine		Ons-107	Gible,Dedrick		Car-169	William Junr	Ons-103
George		Ons- 95	Gibney,Jno		Mec- 36	William Jnr	Sto-125
John		Cho-224	Nicholas		Mec- 35	William Senr	Ons-103
John		Mec- 29	Gibson,A		Glf-173	William Sen	Sto-125
Gibbs,Abia		Hyd-227	Archa		Ons-104	Wm	Ora-123
Alie		Bft- 39	Armon		Bur-130	Giddens,Elizth	Ons-102
Ambrose		Hyd-228	Champ		Roc- 25	Isaac	Way-238
Anson		Hyd-227	Charles		Way-251	Giddins,Basil	Ire-243
Bartee		Hyd-231	Daniel		Ons-103	Basil	Ire-243

Giddins,Thomas	Ire-243	Gilburt,Aaron	Glf-168	Gillaspie,D	Glf-151
Gideon,Eliza	Bur-128	James	Hal-105	D 2n	Glf-153
Moses	Bft- 30	Gilchey,Frederick	Row- 84	Jas	Mec- 52
Gideons,Edward	Wil-279	Gilchrist,Angus	Rch-191	Jas	Glf-172
James	Wil-279	Flora	Rob-225	Jno	Mec- 52
Gifferd,John	Way-245	Gilbert	Rob-224	Jno	Mec- 52
Giffers,Rubin	Ora-161	J	Glf-174	P	Glf-172
Gifford,Jonathan	Ran-166	Jno	Rob-227	Gilleland,Jacob	Bur-120
Levi	Ora-133	R	Glf-174	John	Roc- 2
Giger,Adam	Sto- 98	S	Glf-184	Joseph	Cha-197
Adam	Sto-129	Wm	Rob-225	Robert	Roc- 2
Adam Jnr	Sto- 99	Gilder,Daniel	Cab-142	Gillem,Wm	Cab-147
Jacob	Sto-131	Gilbert	Bun- 77	Gillemun,Willm	Cab-142
John	Sto-129	Giles,Amy	Jon-297	Gillespie,David	Bur-116
Gilaspey,Elijah	Sur-177	Anthony	Row- 64	Isaac	Row- 72
Gilbert,Widow	Lnc-344	Crispin	Bur-122	John	Bur-116
Abraham	Sam-159	Crispen D	Bur-110	Joseph	Dup- 7
Alexanderick	Rth-102	Eliz	Tyr-211	Richd	Row- 72
Asa	Edg- 63	Franklin	Ons- 99	Robert	Row- 73
B	Cam-159	John	Jon-297	Thomas	Row- 73
Edward M	Jon-297	John	Row- 89	Thomas	Row- 73
Elvy	Rob-218	John Senr	Bun- 94	Willison	Hay-195
Francis	Mar- 12	William	Ran-166	Gilley,C	Ash- 12
Gideon	Wil-284	Gilespie,David	Bla- 11	Charles	Bun- 75
J	Cam-153	Gilford,Jacob	Cur- 91	Gilliam,Burwell	Ora-126
J	Cam-154	Gilisan,Perimah	Sto-132	Burwell	Ora-125
J	Mon- 35	Robert B	Sto-151	Harbert	Grn-130
James	Cum-258	Gilky,Robert	Rth-102	Henry	Prq-217
James	Bur-128	Gill,Allen	Ire-261	Howell	Ans- 20
James	Cha-202	David	Ire-250	Jno	Ora-112
Jeremiah	Wil-284	Edward	Brt- 47	John	Wil-262
Jessey	Jon-297	Mrs.Elizah	Fra- 88	John	Ran-166
Joel	Glf-168	James	Hal-105	JOrdan	Nor- 67
Jno	Mon- 46	James	Ora-130	Nancy	Nor- 68
John	Cha-215	John	Grn-126	Sesley	Grn-134
John	Bru-230	Joseph	Grn-122	William	Wil-261
John	Pas-190	Micajah	Cum-248	Wm	Grn-134
John	Sam-152	Richard	Grn-130	Gilliams,Epaphaditus	
John Senr	Jon-297	Robert	Fra- 94		Hay-195
John Senr	Sam-152	Robt	Per-129	Gillihan,Mary	Row- 73
Joseph	Jon-297	Susanah	Ire-261	Gilliken,Alice	Car-178
Joshuah	Cha-207	Thomas	Brt- 66	Betsy	Car-183
Josiah	Pas-190	Thos	Ora-134	Enoch	Car-178
Josiah	Glf-168	Willm A	Fra- 90	Francois	Car-178
Michael	Bur-128	William T	Edg- 65	George Junr	Car-178
Phebie	Bru230	Wm	Brt- 43	George Senr	Car-177
Robert	Jon-296	Wm	Grn-141	James	Car-177
Sabra	Cha-204	Gillam,Drury	Row- 83	Jesse	Car-177
Spencer	Rob-242	Drury	Fra- 86	Thomas	Car-178
T	Bru-236	Ephraim	Fra- 97	Uriah	Car-178
Thos	Glf-168	Marcus	Fra- 97	William	Car-177
W	Cam-154	Mason	Cha-196	Gilliland,Aron	Mec- 47
William	Jon-297	Moses	Brt- 67	James	Lnc-355
William	Rob-218	Nancy	Fra- 96	Jno	Mec- 51
William	Prq-217	William	Fra- 87	Robert	Bur-120
Wilson	Cha-204	Wm	Cha-213	Thomas	Lnc-358
Gilbreath,Thomas	Rth-103	Gillasby,William	Cas- 55	William	Lnc-355
Gilbreth,Angus	Rob-232	Gillaspie,Alexr	Mec- 24	Gillis,Alexr	Cum-242
Gilbs,R	Bru-236	Charles	Mec- 32	Angus	Rob-231

Name	Ref	Name	Ref	Name	Ref
Gillis,Angus	Mon- 28	Giner,John	Joh-283	Glasgo,Samuel	Ran-166
Archd	Mor- 60	Gingles,Jas	Lnc-335	Glasgow,Richard	Grn-127
Archibald	Rch-213	Jno	Mec- 46	Sally	Pas-189
Dan	Mon- 28	Saml	Lnp-330	Glass,Danl	Cha-202
Daniel	Rch-205	Ginkins,Sanford	Cha-206	Henry	Bur-120
Danl	Mor- 68	Ginn,Mace	Way-237	Joab	Cha-207
Danl	Mor- 64	Ginnans,Charles	Wil-264	John	Cha-203
John	Rch-205	Thomas	Wil-264	John	Bur-117
John	Cum-242	Ginning,E	Ash- 8	Johnson	Cha-207
John	Mon- 28	Gipson,Bert	Cur- 85	Josiah	Cha-199
John P C	Cum-251	Gideon	Cur- 86	Josiah	Cha-190
Malcom	Rch-192	Jacob	Cur- 86	Margarett	Mec- 33
Malcom	Cum-269	John	Mor- 64	Phillip	Wil-266
Malcom	Mon- 28	Moses	Mon- 34	Robt	Mec- 38
Norman	Rob-232	Peter	Cur- 86	P	Glf-177
Norman	Rob-232	Thos	Cur- 86	Stephen	Ora-159
Roderick	Cum-255	Thos	Cur- 85	Thos	Mon- 38
Suine	Cum-250	Wm	Mon- 34	Glaze,Polley	Cas- 55
Gillison,Ann	Row- 43	Girken,Benj	Bft- 22	Glazebrook,John	Bur-107
Gillispie,Alexr	Cas- 56	Rchd	Bft- 22	Glazebrooks,James	Sur-194
James	Cas- 56	Gisin,Henry	Car-180	Glazner,Abraham	Bun- 97
Gillmore,Wm Senr	Hal-105	Githen,Jno	Ans- 29	Geo	Bun- 97
Gillem,Conrod	Row- 89	Philip	Ans- 7	Giles	Bun- 85
Gillon,Wm Ham	Cas- 56	Gittel,Seth	Jon-296	Jonas	Bun- 97
Gillum,E	Ora-140	Thomas	Jon-297	Gleeson,Matt	Bft- 37
E	Ora-140	Given,Elias	War-170	Glemp,George	Grn-126
Edmond	Ora-162	George	Lnc-363	Glen,Charles	Per-129
Harris	Bur-118	Saml	Mec- 32	David	Lnc-332
Magnyard	Bur-118	Givens,Cotsen	Ran-166	George	Per-129
W	Ora-140	Robert	Lnc-332	Jeremiah	Sur-181
William	Hal-105	Thos	Lnc-342	John	Lnc-332
Wyat	Hal-105	William	Bur-118	Robert	Lnc-332
Gillvin,Mason	Lnc-327	William Sr	Bur-118	Sampson	Per-138
Gilman,Harbert	Joh-286	Wm	Lnc-333	Thomas	Sur-181
Gilmen,John	Dup- 20	Gladden,Jerremiah	Bun- 80	Thompson	Sur-170
Gilmore,Charles	Hal-105	John	Bun- 80	Wm	Per-138
Delilah	Cha-214	Moses	Lnc-338	Glenn,Abraham	Roc- 23
Hugh	Cur-240	William	Bun- 80	Daniel	Roc- 34
Jacob	Dup- 15	Gladen,George	Ons-167	David	Ora-142
Jno	Mec- 23	Joseph	Lnc-338	James	Fra- 83
John	Glf-154	Saml	Lnc-338	James	Roc- 22
Josiah	Cab-136	Thompson	Lnc-338	James Esqr	Ons-105
Nat	Cab-136	Gladis,Wm	Hal-105	Jere	Ora-127
Polly	Mor- 63	Gladson,Ana	Glf-171	Jno	Ora-149
Robt	Glf-179	Burges	Pit-242	John	Lnc-327
Stephen Junr	Cum-246	D	Glf-173	John	Sto- 96
Thomas Esq	Cum-245	Dempsey	Pit-242	John	Sto-136
Wm	Cha-206	L	Glf-161	John	Grn-112
Wm	Mec- 36	Glancey,Archibald	Car-177	Nancy	Roc- 24
Gilpin,Benjamin	Sur-189	Glandon,Josiah	Sur-181	Robt	Ora-116
Gilreath,Alexr	Wil-262	Glascock,Elizabeth	War-170	Thomas	Ons-105
George	Wil-264	George	Mor- 55	Thompson	Bla- 5
Henry	Wil-262	James	Row- 64	Tyree	Ora-166
Jerimiah	Wil-264	John M	Bun- 73	Wm	Ora-167
Joanna	Wil-264	Martram	Row- 46	Glidewell,M	Ash- 12
William	Wil-273	Patsy	Mor- 56	Gliffeth,James	Jon-297
William Jr	Wil-264	Peter	Row- 63	Glissen,Sarah	Mar- 5
Gilston,D	Ora-155	Scarlat	Row- 62	Glisson,Bryan	Dup- 25
Gimmings,John	Cas- 56	Glasgo,Caleb	Cur- 91	Celey	Mar- 4

-118-

Glisson,Daniel	Dup- 25	Godfrey,W	Cam-154	Goin,Fanny	Per 138
James	Mar- 15	Goding,Ezekiel	Tyr-212	William	Glf-185
John	Dup- 25	Godley,Chas	Bft- 28	Goines,John	Cas- 55
Lewis	Dup- 25	Joseph	Bft- 28	Going,Allin	Per-129
William	Dup- 13	Mary	Bft- 20	Anthony	Sur-152
Glossin,David	Cha-206	Tho	Bft- 26	Benjamin	Sur-185
Glosson,Joseph	Cha-211	Godphrey,Sarah	Pas-189	Burges	Ran-166
Saml	Cha-211	Godsey,John	Roc- 5	Burtin	Ran-166
Gloster,Thomas B	War-182	Thomas Junr	Roc- 5	Edmond	Per-129
Glover,Christian	Row- 77	Thomas Sen	Roc- 5	Edward	Grn-143
Daniel	Gra-140	William	Roc- 7	Elsabeth	Ran-166
Darnold	Hal-170	Godward,Ellender	Mar- 15	Etherige	Per-151
Jones	Nor- 68	Fredrick	Mar- 16	Frederick	Roc- 21
Mary	Hal-105	George	Mar- 9	Jessee	Roc- 24
Ransom	Grn-140	Godwin,A	Bru-228	John	Cas- 55
Sarah	Elg- 64	Allen	Cum-261	Joseph	Sur-179
Sarah	Nor- 68	Barnaba	Hrt-210	Joseph Sr	Sur-179
Thomas	Cum-245	D	Col- 18	Nathan	Sur-179
Wm	Cab-139	E	Col- 18	William	Sur-186
Glovier,John	Nsh- 83	Elleck	Joh-284	Zepheniah	Roc- 35
Goare,J	Col- 19	George	Hrt-216	Goings,Thomas	Hal-305
J	Col- 19	Henry	Sam-156	Goins,Jno	Rob-232
Gobble,Frederick	Row- 81	Henry	Cha-194	Jno Jnr	Rob-232
Jacob	Row- 81	J	Col- 20	Jno Snr	Rob-239
John	Row- 81	J	Col- 20	Thomas	Roc- 8
John Sr	Row- 81	J	Col- 18	Wm	Rob-232
Gobel,Cornelius	Lnc-351	J	Col- 19	Zeph	Roc- 26
John	Lnc-352	Jacob	Sam-161	Golaher,Benj	Bur-115
Gober,Molley	Grn-124	James	Hrt-215	Gold,Daniel	Rth-102
Goble,Cable	Ire-246	John	Sam-156	Goldby,William	Bur-112
Corbin	Ire-264	Jonathan	Sam-155	Golden,Jackey	Sto- 96
Godcus,William	Cas- 55	Nathen	Ran-166	Jacob	Ons-100
Godden,Aaron	Joh-289	R	Col- 20	Thomas	Sur-162
James	Joh-274	S	Col- 18	Wm	Sur-160
Marget	Jon-297	Selby	Tyr-206	Goldman,Jacob	Lnc-329
Nancy	Joh-282	Will	Sam-155	John	Bun- 75
William	Joh-274	Goelet,John	Wsh-224	Goldsberry,Ignatius	
Goddin,Mason	Sam-155	Goff,Eliza	Dup- 21		Fra- 97
Solomon	Sam-155	Ellison	Mon- 32	Goldsmith,Saml	Cum-241
Godett,Abram	Ans- 12	Henry	Pit-256	Goldson,Sarah	Cha-214
Godfree,William	Cum-238	James	Sur-190	Golff,Josiah	Cur- 90
Godfrey,David	Prq-217	James	Glf-182	Gollihorn,Asa	Mon- 21
E	Cam-157	John	Pit-262	Gollomon,Judiath	Hrt-211
Francis	Prq-217	Rachael	Brt- 57	Golson,James	Nsh- 86
J	Cam-156	Saml	Glf-159	Jonas	Nsh- 90
J	Cam-156	Saml	Glf-182	Goltony,John	Rth-104
J	Cam-159	Saml	Dup- 25	Gomillion,Abraham	Joh-298
J	Cam-159	Starling	Mon- 33	Gones,David	Cur- 89
James	Mar- 16	William	Roc- 5	Gooch,Amas	Grn-138
James	Sur-195	William	Pit-257	Daniel	Grn-141
John	Bur-106	Goforth,Ezekiel	Bur-118	Dafiel	Grn-138
Joseph	Prq-218	George	Lnc-338	Francis	Cas- 56
L	Cam-153	Presley	Rth-102	John	Per-129
S	Cam-157	Preston	Lnc-338	John	Cas- 56
S	Cam-163	Thomas	Wil-277	John	Crn-138
Thos	Prq-218	Wm	Mec- 49	John	Hay-195
Thos	Ans- 7	Goganus,Robert	Pit-242	Nathanl	Cas- 56
Tully	Prq-218	Gogin,Fanny	Ora-172	Pomfret	Grn-138
W	Cam-164	Goin,Arkless	Eun- 80	Rowland	Grn-141

-119-

Name	Loc	Name	Loc	Name	Loc
Gooch,Sally	Grn-138	Goodman,W	Bru-232	Gorden,Jacky	Sto-125
Thomas	Grn-136	William	Gat-116	James	Glf-167
Will Junr	Cas- 56	William	Gat-107	James	Per-129
William-Sr	Cas- 55	William	Sto-107	James	Row- 79
Wm	Grn-138	William	Sto-142	James	Bla- 6
Wm	Grn-135	Wm	Row- 42	John	Sto-121
Good,Edward	Bur-121	Winefred	Len-319	John	Sto- 97
George	Sto-140	Goodner,E	Glf-161	John	Glf-187
James	Hal-105	Goodnight,Michael	Cab-143	Jonathan	Mec- 24
Piget	Cur- 90	Michael	Cab-139	Jonathan	Mec- 30
Sollo	Bur-102	Goodrich,Henry	Ora-166	Joseph	Row- 79
Thomas	Rth-103	Goodrum,John	Ire-240	Josua	Rth-104
Goodbread,Joseph	Bur-118	Goodson,James	Nor- 67	Luke	Cur- 87
Joseph	Rth-101	Joel	Lnc-363	Mary	Rth-103
Mary	Rth-102	John	Lnc-376	Nathaniel	Prq-217
Phillip	Rth-102	Manden	Nor- 67	Randall	War-179
Goode,Abram	Rth-104	Mat	Lnc-357	Richd	Glf-169
Edward	Rth-104	Sarah	Bur-118	Saml	Mec- 30
Hailey	Ora-120	Goodsum,Thos	Grn-138	Samuel	Rth-104
Henry	Sto-140	Goodwin,Alsy	Cha-193	Wm	Row- 57
John	Rth-102	Caleb	Prq-217	Gordin,William	Per-151
Joseph	Rth-102	Demsy	Cha-193	Gordon,Alexander	Cas- 56
Richard	Rth-104	Edum	Cho-228	Bowen	Car-169
Goodesin,Oliver	Car-174	Epepharm	Hay-195	Chapman	Wil-262
Reesy	Car-174	George	Hal-105	Charles	Glf-165
Gooding,Fras	Len-323	Gideon	Cha-197	Charles	Row- 58
James	Len-314	James	Cha-194	Christian	Ire-251
Jno	Len-319	Jas	Cho-229	David S	Cum-246
Mary	Jon-297	Jas	Cho-228	George	Ire-250
Goodloe,Henry	Fra- 93	Jno	Cho-230	George	Ire-244
Mrs. Nancy	Fra- 89	Job	Prq-217	George	Hrt-209
Goodlow,David	Grn-122	John	Prq-217	James	Bft- 27
Henry	Ora-115	John Jr	Prq-218	Jas	Glf-170
Goodman,Ambros	Cha-213	Jonathan	Car-169	Jas	Lnc-330
Christopher	Row- 78	Lemuel	Grn-141	Jas	Ans- 17
Cypuan	Tyr-211	Louis	Wil-258	Jas	Ans- 26
D	Col- 21	Richard	Prq-217	Jesse	Fra- 87
David	Brt- 43	Robinson	Lnc-358	John	Rth-103
E	Col- 20	Thos	Cho-228	John	Rch-195
Geo	Cab-145	Wiley	Ans- 20	Jonathan	Glf-167
Geo Senr	Cab-145	William	Prq-217	Mary	Rch-194
Henry	Gat-115	William	Cha-201	Mary	Cho-222
Henry	Row- 84	Wm	Cha-193	Samuel	Sur-186
Isaac	Lne-319	Wm	Cha-213	Sarah	Wil-262
J	Ash- 15	Wm	Cha-201	Thomas	Sur-161
J	Col- 19	Gooff,John	Pit-255	Mrs. Willa	Fra- 87
Jacob	Joh-288	Gordan,Abrm	Pas-190	William	Ire-260
James	Len-319	Arthur	Pas-189	William	Sur-179
John	Fra-140	Betsy	Pas-189	William	Cas- 55
John	Row- 77	James	Hal-106	Gordy,Jacob	Ons-106
John	Ran-166	John	Pas-189	Lizannah	Ons-106
John	Row- 73	Lydia	Pas-190	Moses	Row- 45
Michael	Cab-148	Thomas	Pas-190	Nelly	Row- 45
Michael	Cab-142	Willm	Bft- 27	Gore,Geo	Cha-202
Nancy	Len-318	Gorden,Archibald	Grn-133	Isaac	Dup- 6
Seth D	Pas-190	Benjamin	Gat-107	J	Col- 20
Solomon K	Ran-166	Branch	Glf-160	John Jr	Dup- 6
Thos	Cab-145	C	Glf-160	John Sr	Dup- 6
Tobias	Cab-139	Frankey	Cur- 93	Lewis	Dup- 4

-120-

Name	Ref	Name	Ref	Name	Ref
Gore,Will	Dup- 6	Gowin,Benjamin	Rth-103	Graham,Danl	Mor- 60
Gorgess,Job	Sur-191	James	Rth-104	Danl	Rob-230
Gorham,Hez	Cho-220	James	Rth-103	Dugald	Rob-219
Sarah	Pit-235	William	Rth-104	Dugald	Rob-229
Thomas	Pit-239	Goyne,Edward	Mor- 64	Dugald	Rch-205
William	Pit-263	Henry	Mor- 64	Duncan	Rob-223
Goring,Isam	Ora-156	Levi	Mor- 64	Duncan	Rch-213
Gorman,Rosey	Roc- 19	Wm	Mor- 64	Elexr	Cum-243
Gornto,David Esqr	Ons- 97	Grace (sic)	Pas-190	Elizabeth	Lnc-327
John	Ons- 97	Abel	Sur-175	Ezekiel	Rth-103
Gorrell,David	Glf-156	Mary	Len-323	Forcus	Row- 69
Ralph	Glf-156	Matthew	Way-241	Geo	Mor- 63
Robt	Glf-167	Thomas	Car-173	George	Lnc-373
Wm	Glf-174	Wm	Row- 52	Gen. George	Mec- 36
Gosage (sic)	Cab-139	Wm	Car-172	George	Rch-202
Gosden,Peter	Cur- 85	Gracy,Robert	Ire-243	J	Col- 19
Goslin,William	Sto-153	Graddy,Alex Jr	Dup- 27	J	Col- 20
Goss,Danl	Row- 87	Alexander Sr	Dup- 27	James	Row- 74
David	Row- 83	Durham	Way-235	James	Row- 73
David	Row- 87	Frederick	Dup- 25	James	Row- 74
Ephriam	Row- 87	Fredrick Sr	Dup- 27	James	Row- 72
Frederick	Row- 87	Henry Jr	Dup- 27	James	Row- 75
George	Row- 87	Henry Sr	Dup- 27	James	Rch-205
Jacob	Row- 85	James	Sup- 27	James	Rch-212
John	Row- 85	Jno	Len-319	James	Lnc-373
Joseph	Row- 87	Thomas	Dup- 25	Jno	Rob-227
Lenord	Row- 87	Timothy	Dup- 28	John	Ire-250
Michal	Row- 85	Wm	Len-319	John	Row- 75
Thos	Grn-138	Gradiless,John	Bft- 20	John	Mor- 65
Wm	Grn-141	Gradman,William	Gat-115	John	Row- 39
Gosset,Abm	Bur-130	Grady,Jno	Ans- 16	John	Rth-104
Elijah	Ran-166	Reuben	Roc- 6	John	Lnc-338
John	Ran-166	Reuben Jun	Roc- 10	John	Ran-166
William	Ran-166	William Senr	Roc- 30	John	Rch-204
Gossett,Thomas	Cas- 56	Gragg,James	Bur-107	John	Rch-212
Thomas	Glf-157	W	Ash- 12	John	Rch-196
Gossom,Joseph	Rth-103	Will	Bur-128	John	Cum-247
Goswick,George	Fra- 87	William	Bur-128	John Esq	Rch-202
John	Fra- 88	Gragston,Wm	Ora-147	John Esq	Rch-204
Joseph Junr	Fra- 87	Graham,Alexander	Rch-205	Jonathan	Ire-266
Gote,William	Per-138	Alexr	Cum-243	Joseph	Row- 71
Gott,Richd	Ora-130	Alex	Rob-219	Margaret	Mor- 64
Gouch,Mary	Bun- 83	Alexr	Rob-226	Mary	Ora-171
Gouge,John	Bur-114	Annanias	Rch-204	Moses	Row- 72
Gouger,Henry	Wil-278	Archd	Cum-243	Neill	Mor- 65
Gough,Francis	Bun- 86	Archd	Lnc-338	Neill	Rch-205
Robin	Pas-190	Archd	Cum-269	Nelly	Hrt-209
Gould,Daniel	Ans- 19	Archd Maj	Cum-244	Peter	Rch-203
Goulding,George	Car-176	Archibald	Rch-213	Richard	Mec- 53
John	Car-176	Archibald	Rch-191	Richard	Sto-131
Thomas	Car-174	Bedford	Cas- 55	Richard	Ire-242
Gouls,Cresey	Rob-221	Benj	Mor- 60	Richd	Row- 74
Goun,John	Cha-202	Burl	Rch-204	Robert	Cum-247
Gourly,Hugh	Bun- 91	Chanchy	Hrt-209	Robt	Mec- 41
John	Glf-188	Chauncy	Len-317	Sally	Nor- 68
Gowan,William	Ro2- 73	Daniel	Cum-270	Sarah	Cum-269
Gower,William	Joh-274	Daniel	Cum-268	Thomas	Lnc-338
Zachariah	Joh-274	Daniel	Cum-244	Thos	Mor- 55
Gowin,Alexander	Rth-103	Daniel Jnr	Cum-244	Walter	Cum-248

Graham,William	Rch-203	Grantham,James	Way-240	Gray,A Jr			Glf-173
William	Ire-242	Joel	Way-240	A Snr			Glf-173
William	Rth-104	John	Prq-218	Anne			Wil-284
William	Rth-103	Joseph	Rob-238	Alexander			Per-138
Wm	Mec- 52	Joshua	Rob-239	Alexr			Ran-166
Zach	Mor- 60	Joshua	Rob-239	Andw			Ora-162
Grain,Daniel	Hal-106	Molley	Way-240	Betsey			Wsh-224
Grames,Conrad	Row- 51	Moses	Ran-166	Beverlay			Cab-147
Granberry,James	Nor- 67	Needham	Way-239	C			Cam-157
Langley	Brt- 56	Rachel	Bun- 75	David			Ans- 23
Lucy	Nor- 67	Sion	Way-240	David			Rth-102
Granbery,Mary	Cho-220	Solomon	Way-239	David			Ire-240
Thos	Prq-217	Thomas	Way-240	Dingly E			Jon-297
Grandy,A	Cam-163	Uriah	Rob-240	Elizebeth			Ans- 20
D	Cam-154	William	Bun- 75	Ephraim			Bur-121
F	Cam-160	Granthan,James	Hrt-213	Ferneler			Jon-296
J	Cam-155	Granthon,Jardon	Hrt-212	George			Wil-273
J	Cam-153	Grau,Henry	Sur-190	Gilbert			Ran-166
M Esq	Cam-154	John	Sur-190	Henry			Per-129
S	Cam-160	Peter	Sur-190	Henry			Wsh-224
Granes,John	Cur- 88	William	Sur-190	Hugh			Ire-240
Grange,J	Bru-232	Graves,Arouch (ST)	Cas- 55	Hugh			Ire-240
J	Bla- 11	Azariah (col)	Cas- 56	I			Cam-156
Granger,G	Cam-162	Azariah Jr	Cas- 55	J			Cam-163
John	War-175	B	Bru-232	J			Glf-162
Grans,Nancy	Per-129	B Snr	Bru-236	James			Gat-112
Granstham (sic)	Nsh- 90	Barzillia Sr	Cas- 56	James			Cab-147
Grant,Absalom	Nor- 67	Benjn	Ran-166	James			Rth-104
Andrew	Rth-102	Boston	Ora-171	James			Wil-273
Charity	Way-250	David	Grn-120	James			Cur- 82
Bazel	Ons-103	Elijah J B	Cas- 55	James			Cab-136
D	Len-314	George	Ran-166	James	(K C)		Wil-274
Edward	Ons-101	George	Row- 66	James Jr			Wil-271
Elisha	Nor- 67	Hardy	Rob-221	Jas			Glf-163
J	Glf-184	J	Ora-131	Jas			Glf-165
J	Bru-234	J	Ora-132	Jas			Glf-168
James	Nor- 67	Jacob	Cas-. 55	Jas			Glf-173
James	Cas- 56	James	Sur-173	Jean			Ran-166
John	Wil-269	James	Cas- 55	Jesse			Glf-161
John	Ons-108	John	Cas- 55	Jno			Mec- 25
John	Ons-106	John	Sur-174	Jno			Ans- 20
John	Rch-193	John	Ran-166	John			Cur- 81
John	Cas- 55	John	Cha-209	John			Len-313
Joshua	Roc- 14	John	Grn-124	John			Len-316
Mary	Nor- 67	Nathl	Grn-120	John			Sur-194
Micajah	Way-250	Peter	Sur-187	John			Hal-105
Polly	Nor- 67	Ralph	Grn-120	John			Wsh-224
Richard	Nor- 67	Richd	Ans- 6	John			Bun- 97
Stephen	Way-250	Samuel Snr	Ran-166	John Senr			Len-316
Stephen	Ons-103	Samuel Jnr	Ran-166	Joseph			Pas-189
Susanna	Rth-103	Solomon	Cas- 55	Joseph			Pas-189
Thomas	Rth-103	Thomas	Sur-187	Joseph			Cur- 87
Thomas	Way-250	Thomas	Cas- 55	Joseph			Cur- 82
Thomas	Per-129	Thos	Ora-144	Joseph			Pit-235
Tolo E	Ons- 95	William	Rth-102	Joseph			Len-318
William	Nor- 68	William	Ran-167	Joseph			Rth-104
Grantham,David	Sam-160	William	Cas- 75	L			Cam-155
Edward	Rob-240	Wm	Grn-120	Lodwick			Len-316
Jacob	Way-240	Wm	Grn-124	Mary			Hal-105

Gray,Molly	Pas-190	Grean,Boen	Cur- 84	Creen,J		?sn- 2?
Nancey	Cur- 86	James	Cur- 84	J		Asn 2
Nathan	Ons-101	James	Cur- 84	J		Ash- 9
Nelson	Mec- 47	William	Cur- 87	J		Ash- 9
Ransom	Mec- 48	Greanway,Sarah	Grn-119	J		Col- 19
Reuben	Ons-105	Greaves,Elizabeth	Cur- 94	Jacob		Ans-'24
Richard	Cur- 82	J	Cam-157	James		Hrt-206
Robert	Cur- 82	Jobe	Cur- 84	James		Rth-103
Robin	Pas-190	Green (sic)	Mon- 51	James		Bur-114
Sampson	Mec- 46	A	Mon- 42	James		Jon-297
Samuel	Rth-102	A	Col- 20	Jas		Ans- 4
Samuel	Ran-166	Aaron	Gat-105	Jeremiah		Roc- 3
Samuel	Wil-271	Abner	Ora-167	Jeremiah		Poc- 31
Samuel	Bun- 74	Abraham	Gat-106	Jessey		Joh-287
Shered	Mec- 24	Abraham	Joh-277	Jessey Jr		Joh-287
Stephen	Ora-943	Allan	War-167	Joel		Mon- 29
Susanah	Cas- 56	Allen	Ire-260	Jno		Mon- 31
T	Glf-173	Allen	Hal-105	John		Glf-159
Tho	Jen-322	Amos	Rth-103	John		Grn-126
Thomas	Ire-240	Archibald	Car-180	John		Rth-102
Thomas C	Lan-316	Arthur	Hal-105	John		War-176
Thornton	Pas-189	Asey	Grn-126	John		Bur-113
Thornton	Pas-189	B	Ash- 6	John		Bur-117
Thos	Cur- 81	Benjn	Hal-105	John		Grn-136
Thos	Cur- 87	Berry	Grn-124	John		Edg- 61
William	Glf-167	Bethe	Bur-117	John		Ons-105
William	Bun- 83	Bryan	Joh-287	John		Cum-202
William	Row- 82	C	Col- 20	John		Ire-266
William	Cur- 82	Conrad	Sto-103	John		Nsh- 76
William	Cum-249	Conrad	Sto-137	John		Bur-131
William	Wil-264	D	Col- 17	John		Glf-157
William	Sur-195	D	Mor.- 43	John C		War-174
William b	Sur-179	Daniel	Grn-126	Jonathan		Jon-297
William Lee	Brt- 43	David	Mon- 20	Jos		Glf-164
Wm	Len-316	David	Hyd-231	Joseph		Rth-102
Wm	Mec- 47	David Sr	Hyd-231	Joseph		Hrt-207
Wm	Mec- 45	Demsey	Joh-287	Joseph (sergt)		War-174
Wm	Cur- 85	Edward	Cum-263	Joseph T		War-175
Wm	Cur- 82	Edwd	Cho-223	Leonard		Ans- 24
Willis	Mor- 64	Elijah	Bur-118	Lewis		Fra- 83
Graybill,H	Ash- 13	Elijah	Grn-137	Littleberry		Hal-105
H	Ash- 7	Elijah	Grn-139	Lizia		Rob-243
P	Ash- 13	Enoch	Edg- 46	Luis		Ran-166
P	Ash- 7	Gedian	Mon- 49	Luke		Gat-106
Grayham,Elizabeth	Hal-106	George	Rth-104	Major		Per-138
George	Cas- 55	George	Nsh- 90	Marshal		Ran-166
John	Cas- 55	George	Hal-105	Martin		Mon- 28
Micajah	Cas- 55	H	Bru-232	Mary		Hal-105
Richard	Sto-100	Hardy	Ans- 24	Mary		Wil-282
Richd	Cas- 55	Henry	Rth-103	Mary Anne		Hal-105
Grayson,Benjamin	Rth-102	Henry	Rth-100	Meshack		Pth-103
Isaac	Rth-102	Henry	Rth-104	Moses		Mec- 36
John	Wil-281	Isaac	Gat-116	Obediah		Fra- 84
Joseph	Rth-102	Isaac	Ire-265	Patty		Cna-200
William	Wil-281	Isaac	Hrt-215	Philip		Sto-103
William	Rth-102	Isaac	Rth-104	Philip		Sto-107
William	Rth-102	J	Ash- 6	Philip		Sto-143
Greaer,John	Ons-108	J	Ash- 6	Philip Sen		Sto-137
Zadock	Ons-102	J	Ash- 11	Polly		Jon-297

Green,R	Mon- 42	Greene,Samuel	Dup- 19	Gregory,Mitchel	Cur- 89
R	Ash- 6	Timothy	Dup- 19	Peter	Cur- 89
Rachal	Hrt-211	Greenlee,Ephraim	Bur-131	Richard	Cur- 89
Richard	Bur-105	James	Byn- 77	Thos	Cur- 84
Richard	Wil-279	Saml	Bur-104	Gregory (sic)	Mon- 51
Richard	Sur-195	William	Bur-116	A	Cam-160
Richard Jr	Bur-106	Greens,Jacob	Mon- 49	Abram	Per-138
Richd	Mon- 32	Greenstreet,Eliz	Wil-271	Absalem	Rth-102
Richd Sr	Mon- 32	Jesse	Wil-271	C	Mon- 42
Ro	Ora-129	Greenwood,Abner	Sur-173	C	Mon- 42
Robt	Mon- 30	James	Sur-166	C	Cam-159
Robt	Ans- 25	John	Sto- 95	Charles	Ons- 97
Robt	Cha-199	John	Sto-124	D	Cam-159
Robt	Mec- 37	Robert	Sto- 95	David	Pas-190
Robt	Row- 50	Robert	Sto-124	E	Cam-155
Robt	Way-252	Thomas	Sur-174	Eda	Bun- 90
S	Col- 16	William	Sto- 95	Elizabeth	Bun- 90
Samuel	Gat-105	William	Sto-124	G	Mon- 42
Samuel	Gat-109	Greer,Alexr	Mec- 25	Hardy	Ons- 97
Selah	Edg- 47	Annanias	Roc- 30	Hardy	Nor- 67
Shadrach	Bur-113	D	Bru-238	Hosea	Lnc-334
Shadrach Jr	Bur-113	David	Bun- 78	J	Cam-153
Simon	Fra- 83	Francis	Bun- 87	J	Cam-161
Sion	Joh-287	Freeman	Roc- 30	J	Cam-154
Solomon	War-180	George B	Bun- 72	Jacob	Rth-102
Thomas	War-181	Isaac	Mec- 35	James	Bun- 83
Thomas	Bur-106	J	Ash- 11	James	Joh-273
Thomas	Wil-263	Jacob	Ora-116	James	Ire-262
Thomas	Hal-105	Jas	Mec- 26	James	Ire-262
Thos	Bur-117	Jas	Mec- 41	James	Brt- 48
Thos	Glf-155	Jas Jnr	Mec- 28	Jason Esqr	Ons- 97
Turner	Nor- 79	John	Row- 45	John	Brt- 46
Ursula	Row- 75	Luke	Roc- 30	John	Rth-102
W	Mon- 42	Mary	Bun- 90	John	Prq-218
Welthey	Joh-287	Nathen	Mec- 27	John	Bun- 80
William	Bur-118	Robert	Sto-125	Joseph	Wil-261
William	Sto-145	S	Ash- 11	L	Cam-157
William	Grn-137	Samuel	Cas- 56	L	Cam-152
William	Way-250	Thomas	Roc- 30	L	Cam-159
William	Hay-195	Thos Jnr	Mec- 26	Lott	Sam-152
William Junr	Fra- 83	Thos Esq	Mec- 25	Lucy	Dup- 4
Willm	Bft- 19	W	Ash- 5	Luke	Cur- 84
Willm Esq	Fra- 88	Greeson,J	Glf-177	M	Cam-155
Wm	Cab-139	Gregg,Banester	Rth-103	M	Cam-154
Wm	Cha-200	Frederick	Rth-102	Margaret	Ons-104
Wm	Mon- 32	Jesse	Rth-102	Mary	Edg- 41
Wm	Mon- 30	John	Bur-128	Mary	Gat-105
Wm	Mon- 28	William	Sto-157	Mary	Joh-273
Wm	Grn-139	Greggs,Eliza	Hal-105	Mary	Cho-227
Wm H	Brt- 53	Gregorey,Caleb	Cur- 89	Mathew	Rob-218
Wilson	Hal-105	Frankey	Cur- 89	Mercam	Cur- 89
Zachariah	Ire-260	Gideen	Cur- 89	N	Cam-157
Zacheus	Car-180	Gracey	Cur- 86	N	Cam-159
Greenaway,John	Rth-103	James	Cur- 90	Phoeby	Sur-184
Greene,George	Pit-263	John	Cur- 89	R	Cam-161
John	Bun- 86	John	Cur- 89	Richd	Cha-210
Joseph	Dup- 6	Leml	Cur- 86	Richd	Row- 55
Richd	Mon- 50	Leml	Cur- 89	Robert	Bun- 90
S	Dup- 19	Matthew	Cur- 86	S	Cam-158

-124-

Name	Loc	Name	Loc	Name	Loc	Name	Loc
Gregory,S	Cam-156	Griffen,Simon	Mar- 5	Griffin,Jetty	Edg- 44
Saml	Cho-224	William	Pas-189	Jno	Ans- 8
Saml	Cam-158	Zachariah	Edg- 47	Jno B	Cho-230
T	Cam-153	Griffeth,Edward	Ire-250	John	Rth-102
Thomas	Ire-265	J	Ash- 7	John	Edg- 45
Thos	Sam-154	John	Ire-255	John	Hay-195
Uz	Joh-274	S	Ash- 8	John	Mar-446
W	Cam-155	S	Ash- 8	John	Cum-260
W	Cam-152	Saml	Len-310	John	Mor- 67
W	Cam-154	W	Ash- 8	John	Cur- 86
William	Ons- 98	Griffey,Isaac	Ora-171	John	Way-243
Willm	Pas-190	Griffin,Abraham	Ans- 21	John M	Grn-139
Wm	Cha-207	Alexander	Mar- 15	Joseph	Bur-104
Wm	Lnc-334	Alexander	Cas- 56	Joseph	Edg- 61
Gregson,Amos	Row- 87	Amos	Ans- 8	Joseph	Roc- 27
Greives,Hannah	Ons-107	Amos	Roc- 6	Joseph	Prq-217
John	Ons-107	Mrs. Ann	Brt- 49	Joseph	Nor- 67
Gresham,Elizabeth	Cha-208	Ann	Roc- 6	Joshua	Mar- 9
John	Bun- 72	Ann	Cas- 56	Josiah	Prq-217
Gressitt,J	Col- 19	Archd	Nsh- 77	Josiah	Pit-241
Grey,Benjamin	Edg- 44	Arthur	Nor- 67	Lawrence	Mor- 67
Charles	Edg- 61	Benjamin	Jon-297	Lewis	Edg- 46
James	Edg- 47	Benjamin	Nor- 67	Lewis	Cha-193
Jessee	Edg- 43	Berrell	Gat-115	Lot	Sur-176
Nancy	Nor- 67	Caleb	Way-249	Luis	Ran-166
S	Ora-152	Charles	Sto-105	M	Cam-156
Gribble,Jas	Mec- 34	Charles	Sto-139	Martin	Mar- 10
Thos	Mec- 41	Clayban	Hal-105	Mary	Mar- 13
Thos	Bur-118	David	Wsh-223	Mary	Nsh- 77
Thos	Mec- 29	David	Ans- 15	Mat	Per-129
Grice,Alexr	Sam-157	David	Len-314	Matthew	Mar- 12
Charles	Pas-190	Dempsey	Nor- 67	Med	Pas-190
Jacob	Joh-283	Dency	Way-241	Michajah	Mar- 12
James	Lnc-363	Edward	Bun- 92	Millicent	Prq-218
James	Sam-153	Elias Jr	Prq-217	Nathan	Prq-217
Reuben	Lnc-363	Elias Sr	Prq-217	Nathaniel	Prq-218
Robert	Sam-153	Elizabeth	Roc- 9	Patty	Pas-190
Sally	Pas-189	Elizabeth	Prq-218	Pearce	Nsh- 73
Stephen	Joh-284	Enoch	Ans- 21	Pearty	Edg- 47
William	Cum-266	Ezekel	Row- 63	Priscilla	Prq-217
Grider,Cornelius	Lnc-351	Fredk	Ans- 21	Reuben	Mar- 6
Cunrad	Lnc-352	Geo	Ans- 21	Robert	Nor- 67
Frederick	Lnc-352	George	Glf-154	Robt	Way-243
Jacob	Cas- 56	George	Sto-153	Sadoc	Row- 75
John	Lnc-352	George	Sto-154	Sam J C	Pas-190
Valent	Bur-104	George	Sto-112	Saml	Cha-207
Gridley,John	Bur-124	Hardy	Way-250	Sarah	Nor- 67
Grieg,William	Sto-154	Henry	Edg- 43	Scothey	Roc- 18
Grieson,D	Ora-131	Isaac	Bur-129	Seth	Nor- 67
Grieves,Jeremiah	Pas-189	Isaac	Pas-189	Sion	Fra- 94
John	Pas-190	Isabel	Nor- 67	Sion	Fra- 86
Olly	Pas-189	J	Col- 17	Solomon	Ans- 19
Rhoda	Pas-190	J	Cam-156	Tho	Ora-113
Griffa,Thomas	Wil-266	J	Glf-172	Thomas	Nsh- 78
Griffen,Asa	Mar- 6	Jacob	Nsh- 73	Thomas	Pit-239
George	Edg- 41	James	Prq-217	Thomas	Pas-190
Henry	Mar- 10	Jas	Ans- 15	Thos	Ans- 9
John	Mar- 7	Jesse	Prq-218	Thos	Glf-159
Joseph	Bur-122	Jessee	Nsh- 72	William	Edg- 46

Griffin,William	Row- 60	Grimes,Lewilling	Mar- 14	Grist,Wm	Bft- 38
Wm	Ora-120	Luben	Brt- 43	Griste,William	Row- 82
Wm	Prq-217	Luke	Ora-160	Grisum,Richard	Grn-129
Yance	Mor- 67	Maxamilian	Wsh-227	Grizzard,Hulon	Nor- 67
Yoklet	Row- 56	Michael	Cum-253	Jesse	Pit-259
Zadock	Roc- 26	Moses	Bla- 6	Grizzle,John	Rth-102
Griffis,Wm	Mor- 67	Nancy	Row- 59	Grogan,Bartho	Roc- 25
Griffith,Mrs.	Cum-236	Patrick	Ire-260	Bartlet	Roc- 25
Aron	Mec- 35	Peter	Row- 41	Daniel	Roc- 24
Benjamin	Sur-181	Sampson	Dup- 16	Elijah	Roc- 9
Chisholm	Bun- 79	Samuel	Row- 89	Francis	Roc- 25
D	Ash- 5	Thomas	Dup- 11	Henry Jun	Roc- 9
David	Mec- 37	Thomas	Mar- 14	Henry Sen	Roc- 9
Edward	Sur-162	Thomas	Cum-239	John	Roc- 25
Evan	Len-317	Thomas	Bla- 6	Richard	Roc- 24
H	Ash- 3	William	Dup- 24	Samuel	Roc- 9
J	Ora-160	William	Edg- 53	Samuel	Roc- 35
John	Bun- 76	William	Joh-282	Thomas	Roc- 9
Jonathan	Mec- 24	William	Sur-196	Thomas	Roc- 25
Josa	Len-217	Wm	Cho-222	William	Roc- 11
JOseph	Rth-103	Wm	Glf-177	William	Roc- 9
Mason	Cha-203	Wm	Ora-113	Grogen,Thomas	Rth-103
Reuben	Hal-105	Willie	Edg- 67	Grogery,Hosey	Gat-109
Richard	Mec- 42	Grimmer,Drury	Pit-247	Groles,William	Sto- 98
Thomas	Rth-103	Jacob	Pit-247	Groom,Lott	Len-319
Thomas	Rth-103	Mary	Hal-106	Zachariah	Cas- 55
W	Ora-160	Mildred	Hal-106	Grooms,Amelia	Bun- 93
William	Sto-153	Robert	Hal-105	Grose,B	Ash- 13
William	Cha-203	Grimsby,Thomas	Wil-259	Christy	Lnc-346
William	Lnc-373	Grimsley,Ervin	Rob-237	Henry	Lnc-346
Grifin,Joseph	Mor- 67	George	Rob-236	Gross,Adam	Lnc-374
Wm	Grn-124	James	Dup- 15	Christian	Lnc-329
Grifith,Charles	Mec- 42	Lewis	Rob-236	D	Glf-159
Griges,Gorge	Cur- 92	Wm	Rob-236	Daniel	Lnc-329
John	Cur- 92	Grinaway,Will	Bur-112	Henry	Lnc-329
Grigg,Burrell	Rth-104	Grindstaff,Isaac	Bur-114	Henry	Lnc-374
Griggory,George	Per-129	Grindstead,Lydia	Hal-105	Henry Jr	Lnc-374
Griggs,Henry	Bun- 91	Grinsted,James	Per-134	James	Cum-237
Jno	Ans- 27	Grisam,Barnabas	Ire-261	John	Lnc-374
Thomas	Grn-126	Elizebeth	Ans- 22	John	Bur-105
Grigory,Charls	Per-138	David	Ans- 17	Thomas	Hay-195
Grigs,William	Sto-113	George	Ora-149	Grou,Jacob	Sur-194
Grim,T	Ora-148	Robert	Ora-149	Mazy	Sur-189
Grimes,Adam	Row- 48	Grison,John	Cha-202	Grouse,Simon	Sur-170
Allen	Jon-296	Grissel,Arthur	Nsh- 86	Grove,Simon	Sur-168
Ann	Pit-235	Bannister	Joh-283	William B	Cum-240
Christen	Row- 41	Grissett,G	Col- 20	Groves,Widow	Lnc-331
Cutliff	Row- 42	G	Col- 20	Abraham	Ire-240
Eliza	Ora-169	Pricad	Bru-224	George	Rth-104
Geo	Bft- 36	Wm J	Bru-222	Joseph	Dup- 17
Geo	Row- 41	Grissom,Ben	Lnc-330	Sampson	Bla- 6
J	Ash- 7	Stephen	Mon- 22	Thos	Lnc-334
James	Dup- 15	Thomas	Jon-296	Grub,George	Row- 83
James	Brt- 54	Grissum,Benj	Grn-148	Grubb,C	Ash- 7
James Senr	Brt- 64	John	Grn-127	Conrad	Row- 79
John	Ora-113	Mary	Grn-148	John	Row- 79
John	Dup- 8	Grist,Fedk	Bft- 28	Grubs,William	Sto-128
John	Edg- 53	John	Bft- 29	Grumwood,John	Bun- 94
Joseph	Dup- 11	Ready	Bft- 28	Grune,Eliza	Dup- 21

-126-

Name	Location	Name	Location	Name	Location	Name	Location
Grune,John	Dup- 21	Gullett,Isaac	Glf-156	Gupton,John	Fra- 98		
Grunler,James	Bru-122	Jesse Sr	Wil-281	Robert	Fra- 86		
Grunt,Adam	Lnc-352	John	Glf-157	Mrs. Sarah	Fra- 88		
Gryst,Theophilus	Nsh- 87	Gulley,John	Joh-283	Stephen Junr	Fra- 86		
Gualtney,Henry	Pit-234	Robert	Joh-281	Stephen Senr	Fra- 87		
John	Pit-234	Robert Sr	Joh-287	William	Fra- 86		
William	Pit-234	Gullich,John	Lnc-336	Gurganes,Mary	Hyd-225		
Gualtny,Robert	Ire-263	John Jun	Lnc-336	Gurganess,Milly	Hyd-223		
Guarant,Thomas P	Roc- 12	Gullick,Jonathan	Lnc-330	Sarah	Hyd-223		
Guarland,Elizabeth	Way-237	Gulloway,Agness	Mec- 48	Gurganus,Aron	Hyd-225		
Isaac	Way-237	Daniel	Mec- 48	Eliza	Bft- 21		
Gudger,James	Bun- 84	Jas	Mec- 48	Hona	Bft- 23		
William	Bun- 94	Gully,Jesse	Dup- 13	Jesse	Ons+1		
Guen,A	Bla- 12	John	Dup- 13	Jesse Junr	Ons-108		
Guess,Moses	Ora-158	William	Dup- 14	Joel	Ons-108		
Wm	Ora-150	Gum,John	Cur- 92	John	Bft- 21		
Guest,Joseph	Cum-246	Robin	Sam-159	John	Ons-108		
Neill	Cum-245	Gummers,P Junr	Ora-145	Natl	Bft- 21		
Gueyn,James	Wil-261	Gump,William	Bun- 90	Nicodeomus	Ons-102		
Gueyse,Richard A	Wil-258	Gums,Abraham	Nor- 67	Zachariah	Ons-102		
Guffer,James	Mon- 23	Humphrey	Nor- 67	Gurley,Aaron	Way-233		
Guffin,Timothy	Ran-167	Nathan	Nor- 67	Arthur	Way-234		
Gufford,Stephen	Dup- 25	Gun,James	Rob-226	Charles	Joh-280		
Guffy,James	Rth-102	Jno	Rob-218	Frederick	Way-244		
John	Rth-102	Gunad,Nancy	Jon-297	Henry	Bun- 73		
Thomas	Rth-102	Gunn,Alexander	Ire-247	Isam	Hay-195		
William	Rth-101	Danl	Cha-214	James	Mon- 47		
Gugott,James	Bft- 38	Griffin	Cas- 55	Jonathan	Joh-279		
Guifford,Stephen	Row- 47	James	Cas- 55	Lewis	Way-249		
Guilford,Joseph	Bft- 29	Jas	Ora-145	Morris	Joh-279		
Guin,Farlow O	Rob-231	John	Grn-143	Patience	Joh-281		
J	Ora-148	Samuel	Nor- 68	Peterson	Hrt-210		
James	Edg- 51	Thomas	Cas- 55	William	Hal-106		
Jno	Per-129	Gunston,James	Sur-167	Willis	Ans- 8		
Simeon	Glf-151	Gunter,Abner	Cha-200	Wm	Ans- 25		
Thornton P	Sto-109	Abner	Edg- 58	Wm	Ans- 25		
Guinn,Edward	Ons-102	Archibald	Hal-105	Wm	Ans- 21		
Hardy	Ans- 11	Ben	Cha-211	Gurry,William	Rth-103		
Jno	Ans- 27	Clary	Cha-193	Gurthridge,West	Hal-105		
Polly	Ire-265	David	Bun- 81	Gurwash,Mrs.	Bru-234		
Thomas	Roc- 14	Elisabeth	Mor- 67	Gustell,J Snr	Glf-173		
Thos	Ora-150	Isaac	Cha-211	Guthrey,Archibald	Car-169		
Thornton	Sto-145	John	Cha-195	Benjn	Car-181		
William L	Rth-103	John	Row- 46	Charles	Car-185		
Guins,John	Cas- 55	John	Mor- 58	Charles Senr	Car-179		
Guion,Thomas	Edg- 41	Judith	Hal-105	Elijah	Car-179		
Guither,John	Wsh-228	Malcom	Mor- 68	Frederick	Car-171		
Guiton,J	Col- 19	Mary	Jon-296	John	Car-170		
Guiwn,Saml	Bur-104	Richd	Cha-215	Levy	Car-179		
Gulbreath,Barbra	Cum-266	Thos	Cha-211	Samuel Senr	Car-179		
Gullage,Joel	Ans- 10	William	Hay-195	Stephen	Car-179		
Wm	Ans- 27	Willis	Cha-211	Stephen	Car-176		
Wm	Ans- 13	Willis	Cha-210	William	Car-179		
Gullery,James	Rth-104	Wm Junr	Hay-195	Zebedee	Car-179		
Gullet,George	Row- 58	Gupton,Cooper	Fra- 86	Guthrie,Beverley	Cha-202		
George	Row- 84	David	Fra- 86	Boyd	Hay-195		
William	Row- 58	Isaac	Fra- 86	Claban	Cha-202		
Gullett,Daniel	Wil-277	James	Fra- 85	J W	Bft- 24		
Ezekiel	Glf-156	Jesse	Fra- 86	Samuel	Car-184		

-127-

Name	Ref	Name	Ref	Name	Ref
Guthrie,Wm	Cha-202	Gypson,Wm	Mon- 28	Hadley,Jacob	Cha-203
Wm	Bft- 37	Gyton,James	Cum-251	Jeremh	Cha-199
Guthrin,Garret	Per-129			Jeremiah	Cha-214
Gurthry,Wm	Bla- 13	H----,Adam	Stp-128	Jeremiah	Cha-213
Guthridge,Joseph	Nsh- 75	Habbard,Solomon	Glf-157	Jno	Ora-129
Guttell,Joshua	Glf-180	Hachet,Thomas	Jon-298	John	Cha-195
Guttery,Francis	Bun- 89	Hack,William	Cum-237	John	Cha-209
John	Bun- 94	Hackel,Thomas	Cum-241	Joseph Jr	Cha-204
Guttin,Patrick	Hrt-210	Hacket,Anne	Rth-106	Joseph Sr	Cha-204
Guttrey,Carter	Lnc-358	Thomas	Glf-155	Joshua	Cha-204
Nelson	Lnc-363	William	Ran-168	Joshua	Ran-168
Thos	Lnc-363	Hackett,James	Glf-155	Joshua	Cha-215
Guy,Alexander	Ire-256	James	Wil-258	Simon	Cha-203
Benjamin	Ire-246	Oliver	Glf-155	Simon	Sur-168
Brian	Cum-268	Oliver	Glf-173	Thomas	Sur-174
Enoch	Ire-250	Wm	Glf-155	Thos	Cha-194
Henry	Joh-282	Hackins,Austin	Bur-103	William	Rch-198
James	Cum-268	Hackney,Charles	Cha-216	Wm	Row- 39
James	Ire-247	Danl	Cha-204	Wm	Cha-194
James	Ire-248	Jinnings	Nsh- 75	Hadlin,Nathan	Bun- 96
Jesse	Dup- 3	John	Cha-199	Hadly,Elisha	Bur-105
John	Ire-248	John	Cha-211	John	Ora-166
Joseph	Ire-260	John Jr	Cha-216	John	Cum-240
Leml	Dup- 4	Joseph	Cha-198	Hadnot,Libues	Ons- 97
Mary	Pas-190	Joseph Jr	Cha-214	Stephen	Car-179
Samuel	Ire-256	Lott	Cha-202	Whitehurst	Ons-101
Thomas	Cum-245	Robt	Cha-207	William G	Ons- 95
Vines	Ora-115	Wm	Cha-214	Hadocks,William	Row- 63
William	Ire-256	Wm Jr	Cha-205	Hafer,Lewis	Lnc-344
William	Joh-282	Hacles,Robert	Rob-218	Hafford,James	Pit-257
William Jr	Dup- 4	Hadain,David	Bun- 97	Hafman,Peter Jr	Glf-180
William Snr	Dup- 4	Hadan,Joseph	Row- 87	Hagan,Penney	Mar- 9
Guyer,Jo	Glf-163	Hadder,Nehemiah	Rch-204	Hagans,Jesse	Edg- 45
Guynn,Iverson	Cas- 56	Haddick,Drury	Bla- 9	Priscilla	Edg- 66
Sarah	Rth-103	Henry	Bla- 9	Hagar (sic)	Pas-191
Guyre,Aron	Prq-217	Haddock,Andrew	Cas- 57	Harden,Mary	Mec- 55
Jesse	Prq-217	Charles	Pit-231	Hagee,David	Row- 53
Nathan	Prq-217	Charles	Pit-260	Jacob	Row- 53
William	Prq-217	David	Cas- 57	James	Per-139
Guyther,John	Mar- 8	Henry	Sur-183	Lazarus	Row- 53
Guyton,John	Bla- 6	John	Pit-261	Hagen,Peter	Bft- 33
Wm	Bla- 5	John	Pit-237	Hagens,John	Ran-168
Gwaltney,John	Pit-249	Nancy	Cum-266	Joseph Snr	Ran-168
Robert	Pit-249	Richard	Cas- 57	Hager,Christy	Lnc-360
William	Pit-248	Shadrack	Edg- 52	Fred	Lnc-331
William	Pit-249	William	Pit-236	George	Lnc-360
Gwil,Philip	Bun- 95	Haden,Mrs.	Bru-236	John	Lnc-360
Gwin,John	Hrt-211	Billy D	Row- 62	Jonathan	Lnc-360
Johnson	Sur-179	George	Ire-245	Joseph	Lnc-360
William Jr	Bur-120	James	Cas- 58	Robert	Lnc-360
Gwinn,Saml	Pas-190	Jesse	Row- 52	Simeon	Lnc-360
Gwynn,Daniel	Cas- 56	Joseph	Rth-107	William	Lnc-360
Nathaniel	Bur-121	Robert	Row- 77	Wm	Lnc-332
Philip	Bur-126	Hadeson,Archd	Ran-167	Hagerman,J	Ash- 6
Gy,Theophilus	Cum-265	Hadgan,Henry	Glf-157	J	Ash- 6
Gyman,Isaiah	Sto- 97	Hadgen,Isaiah	Glf-157	Hagerty,Patrick	Gat-109
Isaiah	Sto-127	Jas	Glf-157	Hagey,Conrad	Glf-156
Thomas	Sto-127	Hadin,Dr.Anthony	Wil-265	Henry	Row- 41
Gypson,Moses	Mon- 28	Hadley,George	Ran-167	Haggard,James	Brt- 61

-128-

Name	Ref	Name	Ref	Name	Ref
Haggard,Jesse	Brt- 61	Haines,William	Edg- 62	Hale,Edward	Way-232
John	Brt- 61	Hainline,Jacob	Row- 83	Elizth	Brt- 61
Haggathy,John	Brt- 50	John	Row- 84	Enoch	Bla- 8
Haggeson,Cotencey	Ran-168	Nathan	Row- 83	Joshua	Brt- 60
Henry	Ran-168	Hains,Abraham	Sur-195	N	Bla- 8
Richard	Ran-168	David	Sur-160	Palser	Lnc-354
Hagie,George	Row- 79	Eaton	Hal-107	Stephen	Bun- 92
George Jr	Row- 79	George	Row- 55	Zachariah	War-184
John	Row- 79	Herbert	Sur-165	Hales,Chapman	Joh-285
Valentine	Row- 52	Isaac	Glf-163	Henry	Joh-286
Hagins,Christph	Bft- 30	Jacob	Lnc-333	Haley,Charles	Roc- 14
Darby	Bft- 30	John	Row- 56	Isam	Rch-208
Holland	Bun- 78	Jonathan	Sur-174	Jacob Sr	Grn-137
I b	Bft- 28	Joseph	Sur-184	John	Rch-210
John	Bun- 78	Joshua	Glf-163	Jonathan	Rch-208
William	Bun- 78	Lucy	Hal-106	Silas	Rch-211
Haglar,Jno	Ans- 21	Martin	Row- 56	Thomas	Ora-167
Philip	Ans- 24	Nathan	Sur-186	William	Row- 53
Haglen,Jno	Mec- 28	Philip	Row- 55	Halford,Lucy	Rth-108
Hagler,J	Mon- 42	Philip Jr	Row- 54	Haliburton,Thos	EsqPer-139
J	Mon- 42	Simeon	Sur-184	Haliday,Robert	Cum-237
John	Wil-276	Thomas	Sur-195	Hall,A	Bru-238
William	Wil-285	William	Sur-196	Abram	Dup- 30
Hagles,John	Cab-141	Hainy,Jesse	Hal-107	Amey	Wil-264
Hagood,B	Mon- 36	Hair,David	Ire-242	Andw	Glf-169
B	Mon- 36	Joseph	Ire-242	Ann	Jon-298
J-..	Mon- 36	John	Grn-136	Armajah	Sam-151
Jesse	Mon- 36	Nicholas	Lnc-329	B	Glf-176
John	Mon- 27	Rebaca	Mec- 38	Barnabas	Sam-153
P	Mon- 36	Thomas	Ire-241	Benj	Ons-106
T	Mon- 36	Wm	Ans- 19	Benjamin	Hyd-229
Hague,John	Lnc-376	Wilson	Ans- 23	Bn	Bru-222
Marth	Row- 75	Hairston,Peter	Sto-116	Caleb	Way-244
Hail,Andrew	Hal-106	Peter	Sto-157	Catherine	Row- 78
Benjn	Hal-107	Haithcock,James	Cha-202	Charles Senr	Sam-159
James	Hal-107	Jeffrey	Hal-107	Charles Senr	Sam-153
James	Cum-253	Reuben	Hal-107	David	Sam-163
Jesse	Hal-107	Hal,Burton	Per-130	David	Sto-104
John	Hal-106	Halbert,Daniel	Sto- 96	David	Sto-138
Jonathan	Cum-265	Joel	Sto-105	Davidson	Ire-261
Joseph	Fra- 80	Joel	Sto-140	Demcy	Gat-113
Mary	Edg- 47	John	Rth-106	Edward	Prq-219
Richard	Hal-107	John	Sto- 95	Edward	Edg- 41
William	Hal-107	Halbrook,William	Sto- 96	Edwd	Bft- 37
Haile,Joseph	Len-312	Halcay,Mary	Cur- 89	Everard	Bft- 29
Hailey,Ansel	Mon- 31	Halcock,Jesse	Mec- 32	Ezekiel	Cum-260
David	Cas- 57	Halcom,Larany	Sur-165	F	Mon- 20
Elizabeth	Nor- 69	Philip	Bun- 89	Forney	Dup- 26
Holliday	Nor- 68	Halcomb,George	Sur-176	George	Hay-196
Jno	Ans- 32	James	Sur-173	George	Wil-270
Haily,William	Cas- 58	John	Sur-168	George W	Ons-101
Hain,Howell	Grn-149	Larance	Sur-165	George	Ire-241
Hainer,William	Lnc-351	Leroy	Sur-169	Harison	Sur-187
Haines,Francis	Rob-236	Phillip	Sur-165	Henry	Ora-149
James	Lnc-358	Shadrach	Sur-170	Henry	Ora-150
John	Glf-167	Thomas	Sur-169	Henry	Ora-149
Joseph	Row- 84	Haldor,John	Sto-151	Hugh	Ire-261
Laurence	Rob-236	Hale,Allan	Bla- 8	Isaac	Row- 75
William	Roc- 8	E	Bla- 8	Isaac	Dup- 18

-129-

Hall,Isaac	Ora-164	Hall,Lewis	Dup- 32	Hall,W	Cam-159		
Isaac	Wil-270	Lewis	Sam-153	W	Ora-140		
Isham	Wil-263	Lewis	Sur-182	W Junr	Bru-238		
J	Ora-140	M	Ash- 4	W Snr	Bru-238		
J	Glf-176	Marium	Way-253	W G	Glf-165		
J	Ash- 6	Mary	Hrt-216	William	Dup-'33		
J	Ash- 8	Mary	Roc- 31	William	Row- 75		
Jadoth	Cas- 57	Morgan	Cab-139	William	Sto-101		
James	Roc- 21	Morris	Cum-249	William	Bun- 91		
James	Roc- 3	Moses	Rth-106	William	Hyd-228		
James	Dup- 31	Nancy	Cur- 85	William	Ire-242		
James	Dup- 32	Nathan	Sam-153	William	Ora-161		
James	Bun- 91	Nathan	Bla- 13	William	Hal-107		
James	Hyd-226	Philip	Sto- 92	William	Sto-133		
James	Ran-168	Philip	Sto-121	William Jnr	Ran-169		
James	Ire-261	Philip	Per-139	William Jnr	Ran-169		
James	Rch-213	Pleasant	Hal-107	William Snr	Ran-169		
James H	Ire-265	Pleasant	Cas- 57	Willm	Fra- 80		
James Junr	Sam-153	Philladelphia	Ons-106	Willm Senr	Sam-159		
James Sen	Ire-261	Polly	Ons-106	Wm	Row- 38		
Jas	Sam-153	R	Ash- 7	Wm	Mec- 49		
Jas	Mec- 45	R	Ash- 4	Wm	Nsh- 72		
Jesse	Bur-125	Rachel	Prq-219	Wm	Cho-227		
Jesse	Wil-276	Raford	Bla- 8	Wm	Mon- 20		
Jo	Row- 39	Randal	Sto-121	Halley,Sherwood	Cha-213		
Joel	Grn-122	Randal	Sto- 93	Halling,Magness	Sto-146		
Joel	Sam-153	Richard	Fra- 78	Hallmon,Anthony	Lnc-346		
Joel	Nor- 69	Richard	Rth-105	Henry	Lnc-348		
Jno	Ora-174	Robert	Cas- 57	Jacob	Lnc-346		
Jno	Ans- 31	Robert	Wil-270	Halloway,David	Grn-136		
John	Glf-171	Robert Jr	Wil-260	David	Pit-253		
John	Row- 75	Robt	Ora-122	George	Bur-128		
John	Glf-161	Robt	Ora-174	William	Row- 86		
John Esq	War-176	Saml	Cha-196	Hallsy,Denney	Cur- 91		
John	Glf-166	Saml	Bru-230	Halowel,William	Cur- 87		
John	Bur-125	Samuel	Row- 74	Halse,D	Cam-159		
John	Ire-241	Samuel	Roc- 31	Halsey,Elizabeth	Prq-219		
John	Nor- 68	Samuel	Ran-168	Henry	Cho-231		
John	Ora-136	Samuel	Ons-106	Mala	Cho-230		
John	Ora-163	Samuel	Bun- 83	Halsoe,John	Dup- 34		
John	Cur- 85	Samuel	Ire-261	Halstead,Andrew	Pas-191		
John	Fra- 80	Sarah	Bur-122	Benjn	Pas-191		
John	Mon- 20	Sarah	Cas- 57	Jessey	Cur- 91		
John	Ire-261	Sarah	Mec- 34	John	Pas-191		
John	Rch-199	Shadrach	Ons-108	Halsted,Joshuay	Cur- 91		
John	Sur-176	Simon	Car-173	Marey	Cur- 91		
John H	Edg- 41	Solomon	Row- 74	Milberey	Cur- 90		
John Junr	Sam-154	T	Ash- 7	Haltom (sic)	Mon- 51		
John Junr	Sam-153	Tho	Ora-177	Elijah	Mon- 19		
John P	Sur-186	Thomas	Jon-298	Joseph	Mon- 33		
Johnston	Ons-103	Thomas	Edg- 49	Ham,Berryman	Grn-129		
Joseph	Jon-298	Thomas	Rth-105	Elisha	Fra- 85		
Joseph	Mon- 20	Thomas	Ran-167	Hezekiah	Glf-187		
Joshua	Bur-127	Thomas	Wil-282	Jesse	Cha-184		
Josiah	Sam-153	Thomas	Hal-107	Joel	Mon- 37		
Laury	Bla- 8	Thomas	Sur-182	John	Ire-242		
Lazarus	Bla- 8	Thomas	Ire-249	Phillip	Glf-164		
Leml	Pas-191	Thos	Ora-135	Reuben	Fra- 86		
Levy W	Cur- 87	Thos	Bla- 11	Solomon	Fra- 86		

Ham,Willm	Fra- 86	Hamilton,Reuben	Lnc-355	Hammond,John	Ons-100
Haman,Elizebeth	Cur- 90	Robert	Car-174	John	Ran-169
Hamblet,Francis	Per-151	Robert	Rth-106	Mary	Roc- 22
James	Per-151	Robert	Buń- 98	Matthias	Ire-244
Hambleton,James	Wsh-226	Sanders	Car-179	Peter	Ons- 96
Jessee	Nsh- 92	Sarah	Rth-104	Sucky	Ons-100
Lazarus	Wsh-226	Srah	War-181	Hammonds,Benjamin	Wil-266
Thomas	Nsh- 84	Sarah	War-181	Eliz	Nsh- 83
Hamblett,Peter	Mon- 38	Stephen	Mon- 21	James	Ire-254
Richard	Cas- 57	T	Glf-175	Jessee	Nsh- 84
Robert	Cas- 57	T	Glf-174	Jno	Mec- 27
Thos	Cas- 58	Thomas	Hyd-229	Willey	Roc- 25
William	Cas- 58	Wat	Mon- 19	Wm	Nsh- 84
Hamblin,Magness	Sto-104	William	Bun- 87	Hammons,Burwell	Edg- 56
William	Sur-171	William	Rth-106	Charles	Fra-100
Hambrick,David	Rth-108	Hamlet,Anne	Hal-106	E	Cum-238
Elijah	Rth-108	Byrd	Roc- 28	Elijah	Edg- 58
George	Rth-109	Byrd	Roc- 26	Elisha	Rch-210
Henry	Rth-108	Elisabeth	Rch-200	James	Edg- 58
Henry	Sur-166	Henry	Rch-200	Isham	Fra- 96
Isaac	Rth-108	James	Cha-197	J	Cum-237
James	Rth-108	Re	Ora-156	Capt.James	Fra- 99
Jeremiah	Rth-108	Hamlett,R	Ora-146	Jeremiah	Row- 80
John	Rth-108	Wm Jr	Cha-198	Jesse	Fra- 96
Nathan	Rth-108	Hamlin,Eleakim	Bun- 85	Jno	Rob-220
Reuben	Rth-108	Joseph	Per-148	Jno Sr (col)	Rob-241
Rice	Rth-108	Magness	Sto-139	John	Bun- 78
Samuel	Rth-108	Richd	Per-139	Milly	Cum-251
Hamby,Samuel	Wil-283	Uam	Per-139	Oliff	Edg- 57
Hamel,Nancy	Hal-108	Wood J	Hal-107	P	Col- 17
Nelson	Hal-105	Hamm,Benjn	Way-237	Shadrach	Edg- 58
Hamilton,Alexr	Lnc-367	Ezekiel	Way-251	Willas	Rob-220
Andrew	Rth-107	Henry	Way-236	Willis	Edg- 58
Archd	Lnc-355	Jacob	Sto-147	Hamms,Abm	Ran-168
Barnaby	Way-243	Mary	Sto-111	Hamock,John	Ran-167
Claudias	Way-253	Mary	Sto-149	Hamon,Ambrose	Sur-183
Eliz	Len-316	Mordiac	Sto-148	Rachael	Sur-184
Elizabeth	Bun- 88	Richd	Way-236	Hamons,Elijah (col)	Rob-241
Gatsey	Len-323	Spyers	Way-249	Henry (col)	Rob-241
Geo	Glf-175	Stephen	Way-236	James	Sur-186
Gustavus	Roc- 4	Wrest	Way-236	Jno (col)	Rob-241
Horatio	Sto-103	Zach	Way-236	Joseph	Sur-163
Horatio	Sto-136	Hammack,Robert	Sur-160	Samuel (col)	Rob-241
Hugh	Bun- 93	Wm	Cha-191	William	Sur-179
J	Ora-152	Hammens,William	Ire-245	Hamphill,Hue	Per-130
Jacob	Row- 84	Hammer,John	Ran-167	Hampton,David	Row- 39
James	Car-174	John	Row- 65	David	Ire-261
James	Grn-135	Hammilton,John	Roc- 13	Edward	Cha-201
Jesse	Rth-106	William	Roc- 13	Ephraim	Row- 39
John	Cab-138	Hammon,Gec	Ans- 25	Ezekiel	Bun- 77
John	Pas-191	Jno	Ans- 25	Geo	Mec- 28
John	Way-233	Jourdon	Cha-201	Henry	Sur-170
John	Lnc-373	Lewis	Hal-108	Jacob	Wil-280
Joseph	Rth-104	Wm	Ans- 5	James	Sto-125
Martha	Len-316	Hammond,Barte	Bft- 19	Jeremiah	Wil-280
Noble	Rth-105	Edward	Ons- 95	Joel	Lnc-376
Patrick	Grn-138	Edwd	Ora-175	John	Rth-108
Peggy	Way-249	Eliz	Ons- 96	John	Row- 53
Preson	Hyd-229	Jno	Mec- 24	Jonathan	Rth-104

-131-

Hampton,Livingston	Wil-280	Hanes,John	Rth-105	Hanrahan,Michl	Bft- 36
Micajah	Bun- 96	Saml	Cha-209	Walter	Bft- 36
Noah	Rth-104	Haney,Francis	Rth-105	Hansel,James	Lnc-376
Obedia	Row- 39	Hezekiah	Ans- 9	William	Lnc-366
Robt	Row- 39	John	Rth-107	Hansell,Squire	Mec- 44
Stephen	Sur-179	Lewis	Edg- 64	Hansen,Joseph	Sto- 98
Thomas	Wil-280	Reuben	Bur-120	Hansill,William	Mar- 14
Turner	Wil-276	Robert	Rth-108	Hansly,Evin	Ons-107
Welcome W	Wil-277	Shadrach	Bur-127	John	Ons-107
William	Row- 89	William	Rth-106	John Junr	Ons-107
William	Lnc-376	William S	Roc- 6	Hanson,Bartlett	Bur-103
Wm	Row- 67	Hank,D	Ash- 7	Hantsucker,George	Mor- 55
Wm Sr	Row- 67	D	Ash- 10	Hany,Henry	Ons-107
Hamrick,George	Wil-268	G	Ash- 10	Hezekiah	Ons-109
John	Wil-285	Hankins,Eliz	Cho-220	Hape,Mrs.	Bru-234
Hamton,Thomas	Sur-165	Lewis	Ire-262	Hapron,William	Per-130
Hanan,Giden	Cur- 90	Hanks,Fanny	Grn-140	Harald,Jesse	Rob-230
Hanby,Gabriel	Sur-172	James	Wil-259	Harben,Allen	Row- 61
Reuben	Wil-281	John	Lnc-367	Harbert,Allen	Rch-202
Hancel,Joseph	Rch-208	John	Ora-175	Charles	Cur- 88
Hanchey,D	Col- 19	Richd	Lnc-367	Charles	Rch-202
Hancock,Benj	Cha-201	Thos	Lnc-327	John	Rch-200
Gaberal	Ons-102	Willm	Fra- 87	John	Hal-107
James	Jon-298	Willm	Fra- 87	John	Hal-107
John	Mon- 20	Hanky,John	Sto-131	W	Ash- 7
Lewis	Cha-197	Hanley,Fanny	Wil-279	Harbesop,William	Lnc-351
Sam	Mon- 22	Henry	Wil-280	Harbin,Hansin	Ire-246
Saml	Ora-111	John Jr	Wil-276	Resin	Ire-246
Thos	Ans- 31	John Senr	Wil-276	Wates	Row- 62
Thos	Ans- 30	Simpson	Wil-277	William	Ire-265
William	Ons- 97	William	Wil-277	Harbison,William	Bur-108
Zebedee	Ons-106	William Jr	Wil-277	Wm	Mec- 45
Hand,Aaron	Lnc-336	Hanly,Benjamin	Ire-246	Harbourd,Priscilla	Jon-298
Christopher	Roc- 34	Henry	Ire-246	Hardaster,Elisha	Ran-169
Isaiah	Tyr-209	Hann,N	Ora-138	Hardcastle,Eliz	Rob-233
William	Roc- 5	Hanna,James	Sur-160	James	Joh-274
Handcock,Calvin	Car-177	Hannah,Alexander	Hay-196	Shadrack	Joh-274
Caswell	Car-177	Samuel	Ire-258	Hardee,Abraham	Pit-262
Cromwell	Car-176	Thos	Lnc-373	Abraham	Pit-233
Harman	Pit-236	William	Ran-168	Alfred	Pit-233
James	Pit-236	William Jnr	Ran-169	Elizabeth	Pit-262
James	Pit-236	Hanner,James	Glf-171	John	Pit-255
John	Car-183	James	Row- 64	John	Pit-251
Joseph	Car-178	James	Nsh- 88	John	Hal-106
Josiah	Len-323	Jesse	Glf-154	Thomas	Pit-236
Margeret	Car-176	Jo	Glf-176	William	Hal-107
Handkins,Denny	Bru-230	John	Glf-161	William	Pit-262
Handley,Isaac	Way-251	Joseph	Glf-154	Harden,Abel	Rth-109
James	Way-249	R	Glf-177	Benjamin	Row- 64
John	Ora-130	Robert	Row- 64	Benjamin	Rth-109
Handly,I	Col- 19	Robert	Glf-173	David	Lnc-341
Hanes,Abraham	Sam-151	Hanners,Hannah	Way-246	David	Rth-109
Armistead	Cha-214	Hannon,Edwin	Rth-107	Edmund	Rth-107
Daniel	Rth-105	Nancy	Hal-106	Edmund	Rth-109
Ely	Rth-104	Thomas	Mor- 63	Elijah	Lnc-338
Harbert	Cha-202	Thomas	Mor- 56	Frederick	Rob-237
Herbert	Cha-210	William	Rth-106	Gabrl	Mor- 62
Herbert	Cha-213	William	Rth-107	Hardy	Rth-109
Jesse	Rth-106	Hannor, R	Ash- 4	Henry	Cas- 58

-132-

Name	Ref	Name	Ref	Name	Ref	Name	Ref
Harden,Isaac	Hal-107	Hardison,Eliza	Bft- 26	Hare,John		Gat-112
James	Mor- 62	Ezekiel Esqr	Wsh-227	John		Sam-162
Jas	Lnc-341	Frederic	Wsh-225	John Jun		Mor- 56
John	Lnc-338	Harman	Edg- 69	Jonathan		Cum-247
Mark	Ran-167	James	Mar- 10	Joseph		Gat-110
Mark	Roc- 6	Jesse	Ons-107	Martin		Sam-162
Mark	Rth-109	Jesse Junr	Ons-108	Moses		Hrt-216
Nichs	Ora-125	John	Mar- 10	Rachel		Wsh-228
Patsey	Rth-109	John	Mar- 10	Thos Ed		Brt- 51
Peter	Roc- 31	Joshua	Mar- 16	Harelson,Anderson		Roc- 15
Peter	Hal-108	Lemuel	Ons- 99	Harget,Nancy		Jon-298
Robert	Rth-109	Luke	Mar- 8	Hargett,Casper		Mec- 43
Robt	Mor- 62	Nancy	Wsh-227	Henry		Mec- 43
Sarah	Ora-121	Samuel	Wsh-227	Jas		Mec- 30
Solomon	Rob-239	William	Dup- 26	Henry		Mec- 43
Steward	Glf-154	Hardister,Samuel	Lnc-351	Jno		Mec- 43
Thomas	Rth-105	Samuel	Ran-168	Joseph		Mec- 44
William	Ire-255	Hardiway,Joseph	Edg- 47	Seany		Mec- 44
Young	Rth-109	Hardwick,John	Roc- 4	Wm		Mec- 43
Hardens,Benjn	Sam-156	Hardy,Andrew	Edg- 64	Hargis,Abrham		Per-148
Sion	Sam-156	Benjn	Brt- 43	Dennis		Per-139
Harder,Jos	Ora-119	Carter	War-169	Jane		Per-139
Hardesill,John	Rth-106	Charles	Brt- 48	Joseph		Per-130
Hardeson,Joseph	Hyd-222	David	Hal-107	Nathan		Per-139
Hardesty,Benjn	Car-183	Henry	Sur-189	Shadrack		Per-139
Burton	Car-183	Isaac	Len-310	Tho		Ora-175
Hardey,Edwd	Cur- 86	Jesse	Dup- 27	Tho L S		Ora-110
Hardgrove,Aron	Sam-154	John	Sto- 95	Thomas		Per-139
Arther	Sam-157	John	Len-313	William		Per-151
Hardin,Ben	Lnc-327	John	Sto-123	Hargrams,Chairity		Edg- 44
Benj	Bft- 28	John	Ed- 71	Hargrave,Saml		Glf-166
Benjamin	Row- 62	John	Way-232	Hargron,Israel		Grn-140
Elisha	Bur-116	Joseph	Len-317	Hargrove,Augustus		Fra- 94
H	Ash- 8	Martha	Brt- 47	B		Col- 17
Isa	Bft- 28	Michael	Edg- 72	Emanuel		Nor- 69
John	Glf-154	Miles Esqr	Wsh-222	Gillam		Cha-203
John	Bur-107	Nancy	Mar- 16	Jesse		Row- 88
John	Bur-118	Nancy	Len-314	Lemuel		Nor- 68
Jonathan	Rth-109	Robert	Edg- 71	M		Glf-162
Joseph	Rth-109	Hardison,Joshua	Mar- 16	Hargroves,John		Dup- 9
Lavina	Bft- 28	Hardy,Robert	Edg- 41	William		Cas- 58
Moses	Bur-109	Tempy	War-181	Wm		Grn-140
Peggy	Wil-280	Thomas	War-181	Haris,Aaron		Ire-265
Stephen	Bur-116	William J	Brt- 47	Elisha		Cha-197
Thomas Jnr	Brt- 47	Wm	Len-317	Halsey		Cho-230
Thomas Senr	Brt- 47	Wm	Len-322	John		Cur- 90
William	Bur-117	Hare,Aaron	Cum-249	John		Cha-209
Hardin,F Ransford	Nor- 68	Aaron	Hrt-209	Harison,Aliz		Cur- 84
John	Nor- 69	Briant	Hrt-214	Gideon		Hal-106
Presley	Nor- 68	Daniel	Cum-267	Henry		Glf-182
Renney	Sur-175	Easter	Gat-109	James		Grn-134
Sterling	Grn-129	Hasey	Gat-115	Jno C		Mec- 33
William	Nor- 68	Isaac	Sam-162	John		Cho-227
Hardison,Asa	Wsh-227	Jesse	Cum-265	Jonathan		Gat-105
Benjamin	Mar- 7	Joel	Sam-161	Joseph		Sur-175
Charles	Ons-108	Jno P	Hrt-216	Robert		Grn-127
Cullen	Mar- 10	Jno Sen	Mor- 56	William		Row- 77
David	Mar- 9	John	Gat-108	Winefred		Hal-106
Edward	Mar- 10	John	Cum-264	Harke,Jno		Mec- 40

Harker,Anson	Car-179	Harner,Joshua	Sto-126	Harrald,Wilson	Ons- 99
Belcher	Car-179	Harney,Jarvis	Cur- 87	Harralson,H	Per-139
Clarisa	Car-177	Harp,Isaah	Joh-288	Harramond,William	BWsh-225
James	Car-179	John	Sur-195	Harrard,E	Cam-161
Zachariah	Car-179	Joseph	Nsh- 92	Harrel,Aaron	Gat-114
Harkey,David	Cab-140	Kessiah	Wil-265	Aaron	Gat-113
Henry	Cab-146	William	Ire-269	Abner	Gat-107
Jacob	Cab-141	William	Joh-287	Abraham	Gat-107
Martin	Ire-238	Harp,Williamson	Joh-288	Charles	Gat-106
Harkfield,Jacob	Fra- 82	Harper,Ambrose	Hal-108	David	Cho-230
Harkin,John	Bun- 85	David	Row- 39	Elisah	Gat-116
Harkins,Thoney	Bun- 88	David	Row- 81	Elisha	Gat-113
Harkman,Geo	Cab-139	Edmd	Ora-112	Elisha	Rob-235
Harkness,Mrs.	Mec- 26	Edward	Cha-206	Elizabeth	Gha-200
Harky,Jno	Mec- 40	Eliphlite	Sto-153	Jesse	Rob-235
Harlad,David	Hal-107	Elizabeth	Cha-194	Jesse	Gat-114
Harley,James	Sam-159	Francis	Hyd-228	Noah	Gat-108
Joel	Mon- 21	G	Col- 19	Peter	Gat-116
Harlin,David	Row- 45	Higdon	War-172	Reuben	Gat-114
Joshua	Wil-261	James	Fra- 98	Robert	Gat-113
Harlow,Joseph	Hal-106	James	Rth-105	Samuel	Gat-106
Mary	Hal-107	Jesse Jr	Len-320	Thomas	Gat-107
Obed	Ora-176	Jesse Senr	Len-320	Thomas	Gat-115
Harly,Hugh	Glf-168	John	Joh-289	William	Gat-114
John	Glf-168	John	Ran-167	Harrell,Abraham	Gat-109
Harman,Hezekiah	Cha-206	John	Cha-210	Amos	Brt- 50
Joseph	Cha-206	John	Row- 38	Arthur	Brt- 54
M	Glf-173	John	Hal-106	Asa	Gat-112
Harmer,Hoddy	Glf-154	Joseph	War-173	Benjamin Junr	Mar- 11
Harmon,A	Ash- 6	Josiah	Bur-130	Benjamin Senr	Mar- 11
Abraham	Hrt-208	Judathen	Ran-167	Cason	Ans- 30
Amos	Wil-277	Lot	Bun- 80	Charity	Prq-219
B John	Nor- 68	Martha	Roc- 27	Christopher	Brt- 55
C	Ash- 9	Mary	Wil-267	Christr	Edg- 70
Danl	Row- 52	Rachael	Roc- 16	Daniel	Sam-154
Demsey	Ran-168	Reubin	Edg- 59	Eli	Hrt-216
E	Glf-177	Saml	Row- 40	Elijah	Hrt-211
George	Lnc-348	Saml	Row- 38	Elisabeth	Mar- 5
Geo	Cha-215	Samuel	War-180	Eliza	Dup- 6
James	Way-233	Samuel	War-180	Elizabeth	Rth-105
John	Wil-277	Samuel Jr	Row- 81	Ezekiel	Mar- 5
Jonathan	Brt- 63	Sarah	Len-320	Francis	Joh-289
Joseph	Rth-105	Stephen	Hal-107	Francis	Rth-108
Joshua	Brt- 65	Vicy	Hal-107	Gabriel	Brt- 58
M	Ash- 6	Vincent	Hal-108	Geo D	Brt- 55
Michael	Lnc-348	W	Col- 20	George	Brt- 54
Nicholas	Brt- 63	W	Col- 18	Gilbert	Rth-106
Peter	Lnc-348	William	Sto-140	Henry	Joh-290
Philip	Row- 52	William	Cha-215	Hodges	Brt- 54
Rebeckah	Cha-211	William	Sto-106	Isaac	Brt- 51
Valentine	Row- 50	William	Sto-153	Isaac	Brt- 51
William	Lnc-348	Wm	Len-320	Jacob	Mar- 11
William Jr	Lnc-348	Wm B	Nsh- 80	James	Brt- 55
Harn,Sion	Cum-265	Zephiniah	Sto-153	James	Mar- 11
Harna,Sylva	Pas-191	Harpis,Wm	Cur- 83	James	Dup- 20
Harnchy,Martin	Dup- 20	Harrald,Benjn	Cha-200	James	Brt- 51
Harned,Joshua	Sto- 96	Britton	Ons-109	James Senr	Brt- 55
Harnell,Isham	Wil-266	David	Pas-191	Jerh	Brt- 55
Harner,John	Row- 74	Stephen	Ons-102	Jesse	Hrt-211

Harrell,Jno	Ans- 18	Harris,B	Glf-181	Harris,Henry		Pit-234
Jno	Ans- 6	B	Bru-224	Henry		Pit-253
Jno R	Ans- 7	Barnill	Sur-185	Henry		Mec- 42
John	Brt- 50	Bazeal	Sur-175	Henry		Fra- 90
John	Len-323	Ben	Cha-207	Henry		War-172
John	Rth-108	Benjn	Ans- 26	Herbert		Fra- 85
John	Rth-106	Benj Sen	Cha-215	Hiram		Lnc-336
John	Pit-253	Benjamin	Grn-133	Howel		Mon- 30
John	Mar- 7	Bennet	Ire-254	Howel		War-172
Jos	Brt- 51	Bennet	War-169	Howell		Roc- 32
Joseph Jr	Prq-218	Brantly	Mon- 19	Hugh		Bur-124
Josiah	Brt- 58	Bridget	Cum-261	Hugh		Mec- 28
Josiah	Brt- 51	Brittain	Fra- 94	Hutson		Rch-201
Kadar	Dup- 20	Burwell	War-168	Irey		Grn-135
Levi	Mar- 11	Cason	Hyd-231	Isaac		Rth-106
Lewis	Mar- 5	Charles	Roc- 33	Isaac		Pas-190
Luvy	Joh-289	Charles	Cab-137	Isham		War-173
Mills	Ans- 7	Charles	Grn-145	Isham Senr		War-173
Moring	Way-242	Charles	Grn-133	Isham		Grn-134
Moses	Mar- 4	Claiborn	Mon- 21	Isham	(Entered)	Grn-134
Parker	Mar- 15	D	Glf-167	Jacob		Sur-174
Powell	Brt- 54	Daniel	Fra- 80	Jacob		War-173
Richard	Rth-105	Daniel	Car-180	Jacob		Pit-233
Samuel	Edg- 51	Daniel	War-169	James		Pas-190
Silas	Prq-219	Daniel	Rth-109	James		Fra- 98
Silas Sr	Prq-219	David	Grn-133	James		Mon- 31
Solomon	Rth-104	David	Gat-109	James		Fra- 96
Starky S	Hrt-208	Dread	Cha-199	James		Mon- 20
Streel	Rth-106	Capt E	Ora-135	James		Glf-161
Thomas	Prq-219	E	Ash- 11	James		Row- 75
Thomas	Mar- 4	Ed D	Cab-145	James		Roc- 25
Thos	Brt- 54	Edmund	War-171	James		Roc- 12
William	Joh-289	Edward	Hyd-230	James		Ora-164
William	Brt- 55	Elender	Roc- 26	James		Grn-145
William	Mar- 15	Elijah	Grn-149	James		War-175
Wm	Bft- 36	Elijah	Sur-175	James		Rth-106
Zachariah	Ans- 18	Elijah	Grn-122	Jas		Bft- 21
Harrelson,Thomas	Cas- 58	Elizabeth	Hyd-223	Jas		Glf-158
Harril,Matthew	Mon- 24	Elsey	Pit-235	Jas		Cab-137
William	Cas- 57	Epheram	Cur- 91	Jas		Mec- 51
Harrill,Lemuel	Nor- 68	Ephraim col	Fra-101	Janey		Hyd-231
Harrilson,Forbus	Cas- 57	Etheldred	Mon- 20	Jessee		Bun- 76
Jere	Cas- 58	Fieldman	Ora-124	Jessey		Grn-123
Harrington,Mrs.	Cum-240	Firy	Grn-149	Jesse		Hyd-232
Isaac	Cha-209	Frederick	War-171	Jesse		Row- 41
Jacob	Ons-105	Geo	Row- 37	Jessey	(mover)	Grn-123
S	Cam-158	Geo	Cab-137	Joel		Mon- 29
Harris (sic)	Mon- 51	George Jr	Grn-148	Joel		War-173
A	Bru-232	George Senr	Car-184	Joel		Glf-185
Abner	Ire-247	George W	Grn-145	Jno		Mon- 29
Aggustin	Grn-127	Gibson	Hyd-222	Jno		Mec- 24
Allen	Mon- 20	Gibson	Sur-186	John		Bur-128
Alsey	Fra- 95	Gideon	Grn-148	John		Bun- 91
Amy	Pit-234	Gilliam	Mec- 42	John		Pas-190
Andrew	Cha-201	Green	Mon- 20	John		Nor- 68
Ann	Pit-234	Hamlin	Nor- 68	John		Ran-167
Arthur	Mon- 30	Hardy	Grn-134	John		Hyd-226
Arthur	Mon- 20	Harwell	Nsh- 78	John		Mec- 27
Asa	Pit-237	Henry	Nor- 68	John		Cha-197

Harris,John	Mar- 12	Harris,Paten	Bun- 78	Harris,Thomas	Pit-232
John	Bla- 9	Precilla	Grn-139	Thomas	Grn-137
John	Bft- 21	Pricila	Grn-123	Thomas	Bur-127
John	Rch-197	R	Ora-139	Thomas	Car-185
John	Roc- 33	Randle	Mon- 19	Thomas	Car-169
John	Row- 74	Ransom	Grn-148	Thos	Mon- 22
John	Row- 58	Rich	Bru-228	Thos	Grn-148
John	Bur-131	Richard	Grn-130	Thos S	Cab-144
John	Bun- 74	Richard	Pit-249	Thompson	Roc- 13
John	Bur-116	Richard	Pit-253	Timothy	Pit-258
John	Grn-133	Richard	Ire-266	Turner	Mon- 19
John B	Roc- 12	Richard	Pas-190	Tyre	Cum-258
John E	War-176	Robert	Per-130	W	Ash- 7
John Glen	Bun- 84	Robert	Sur-174	West	Mon- 20
John Jun	Per-130	Robert H	Grn-137	Wiley	Ran-169
John Junr	Roc- 27	Robt	Ora-128	William	Nor- 68
John Senr	Roc- 26	Robt	Row- 57	William	Pit-233
John Sen	Pas-190	Robt	Cab-143	William	Pit-258
John Senr	Per-130	Robt	Mon- 22	William	Gat-105
John (moved)	Grn-123	Roling	Grn-134	William	Roc- 27
Jonathan	Hyd-226	Rowland	Mon- 44	William	Roc- 12
Jonathan	Mec- 23	S	Bru-224	William	Rth-106
Jonathan	Rch-210	Saim	Grn-130	William	Rth-107
Joseph	Hyd-231	Salley	Bft- 31	William Jr	Nor- 69
Joseph	Pit-238	Saml	Grn-136	Willm	Cho-220
Joseph	Roc- 12	Saml	Glf-159	Wm	Mon- 21
Joshua	Mon- 30	Saml	Row- 58	Wm	Mon- 30
Joshua	Row- 59	Saml	Mec- 52	Wm	Grn-129
Josiah	Hyd-231	Samuel	Mec- 23	Wm	Grn-122
Josiah	Pas-190	Sarah	Hyd-226	Wm	Cab-144
Josiah	Car-183	Sarah	Roc- 33	Wm	Cab-137
Kizze	War-177	Sarah	Bur-128	Wm	Mon- 44
Lard H	Mec- 23	Selah	Nor- 69	Wm	Ora-149
Leonard	War-177	Sherwood	Grn-136	Williamson	Row- 79
Leven	Roc- 26	Sherwood	Grn-123	Willis	Grn-134
Lewis	Bur-128	Sherwood	Cum-246	Wooten	Rth-104
Littleton	Mon- 20	Silas	Mon- 30	Harrison,A	Cam-152
Lucy	Roc- 16	Silas	Sur-180	Andrew Jr	Cas- 57
Major	Pit-233	Silvenis	Pit-233	Andrew Senr	Cas- 57
Major	Pit-240	Simon	Car-183	Aron	Wsh-222
Mary	Ire-248	Solomon	Hyd-227	Benjn	Nor- 69
Mary	Roc- 32	Solomon	Mec- 44	Benjamin	Jon-298
Mary	Mon- 44	Soveron	Pit-233	Benjamin	Wsh-226
Mary	Mec- 46	Spears	Grn-144	C	Col- 17
Mary	Ora-169	Starling Esq	Ora-128	C	Cam-156
Matthew	Roc- 6	Stephen	Hyd-227	Charles	Cas- 57
Micajah	Grn-129	Sterling	Grn-133	Charles	Nor- 68
Mildred	Nor- 68	Sterling	Rth-106	D	Cam-165
Milly	Sto- 93	Stokely	Car-184	Danl	Len-315
Mitchell	Per-130	Susanna	Mor- 63	Densey	Nsh- 86
Moses	Pit-233	T	Ora-139	Elijah	Wsh-225
Moses	Pit-258	Tarlton	Rth-108	Elizabeth	Jon-298
Moses	Nsh- 77	Taylor	Mon- 27	Elizabeth	Wsh-226
Nancy	Pas-190	Theophilus	Gat-108	G	Cam-156
Nathan	Nor- 69	Thomas	Sur-194	George	Grn-145
Nathan col	Fra-101	Thomas	Pas-190	Hasmon	Wsh-227
Nathan	Mon- 29	Thomas	Ire-240	Hedley	Cas- 58
Oliphis	Cab-138	Thomas	Hyd-226	Henry	Nsh- 76
P	Bru-234	Thomas	Wil-284	Issabel	Ora-112

-136-

Name	Ref	Name	Ref	Name	Ref
Harrison,J	Cam-159	Harrison,Zachariah	Roc- 15	Harrold,John Jr	Wil-270
J Esq	Cam-159	Harriss,Alice	Hal-107	Richard	Sto-112
J	Cam-156	Amos	Brt- 45	Richard	Sto-150
James	Jon-297	Amos	Dup- 33	Richard Jnr	Sto-147
James	Cas- 58	Ary	Hal-108	Stephin	Cho-229
James	Sur-172	Benjn	Hal-107	Harroway,John	Cas- 57
James	Mar- 11	Benjn	Hal-107	Harruch,J	Col- 21
James	Hrt-211	Carter	Hal-107	Harry,Widow	Lnc-328
James	Bur-131	Charles	Hal-107	Jacob	Sto-134
James	War-174	Claybourn	Sto-130	Harsell,Anderson	Ora-163
Jeremiah	Ire-251	Elisha	Brt- 62	Harshaw,Ann	Bur-111
Jerremiah	Bun- 84	Eliza	Hal-107	Harstings,H C C	Ora-136
Jesse	Bft- 30	Elizabeth	Edg- 53	Harsy,Charles W	Gat-108
Jesse	Hal-107	Elizth	Tyr-210	Hart,A	Glf-178
Jessee	Roc- 20	George	Edg- 70	Barnae	Hal-106
Jethro	Nsh- 89	Hamilton	Hal-108	Benjamin	Edg- 41
John	Cas- 57	Hellery	Bru-228	Betty	Hal-108
John	Nsh- 76	Henry	Cha-216	Cath	Ora-127
John	Roc- 20	Isaac	Bur-108	Charny	Hrt-210
John	Prq-219	James	Hal-106	Christian	Sto-129
John Jr	Nor- 69	James	Hal-106	Creusey	Wil-266
John Senr	Nor- 69	John	Cha-196	David	Wil-267
Joseph	Pas-191	John	Edg- 54	E	Ash- 15
Joseph	Ire-251	John	Cha-215	Elizabeth	Cas- 57
Joseph	Bun- 75	John	Brt- 46	Etheldred	Nor- 68
Joseph	Hrt-213	Joseph	Tyr-210	H	Glf-178
Joseph	Jon-298	Mark	Hal-107	Henry	Hrt-214
King	Mar- 11	Mary	Edg- 57	Henry	Sto-122
Levy	Jon-298	Michael	War-177	Henry	Sto- 93
Lucy	Len-322	Milley	Sto-122	Henry Junr	Nor- 69
Mary	Row- 74	Newet	War-178	Henry Senr	Nor- 68
Matthew	Wil-276	Newsom	War-178	J	Ash- 4
Nathaniel	Nor- 69	Oren	Hal-106	J of Step	Ora-153
Nathaniel	Bun- 81	Phill	War-179	James	Cha-197
Nathaniel	War-178	Priscilla	Hal-107	James	Ire-261
P	Cam-163	Ransom	War-179	James	Ora-163
Prudy	Jon-298	Robert	Dup- 30	James	Ora-115
R	Cam-159	Robert	War-179	James	Grn-120
Reubin	Brt- 54	Ruthen	Hal-108	Jas	Lnc-335
Richard	Edg- 59	Samuel P	Mar- 12	John	Nor- 68
Robert	Prq-219	Thomas	Edg- 53	John	Cha-197
Robt	Mec- 45	Thomas	Edg- 41	John	Cha-207
Rosamond	Ons-104	Timothy	Edg- 69	John	Hrt-209
Saml	Mec- 34	Warren	Hal-123	John	Sto- 93
Samuel	Row- 80	West	Cha-191	John	Grn-124
Samuel	Rth-106	William	Edg- 71	John Jnr	Sto-122
Simmons	Jon-298	William	Gat-113	John Ser	Sto-122
Stephen	Jon-298	William	War-183	John Senr	Nor- 68
Susanna	Jon-298	Wm	Hal-108	Joseph	Grn-124
Thomas	Cas- 57	Yerba	War-184	Joseph	Cha-198
W	Cam-156	Harrisson,Joseph	Wsh-226	Morgan	Ora-116
William	Cas- 57	Lois	Wsh-224	Moses	Ans- 13
William	Sur-170	Lovick	Wsh-224	Nancy	Grn-133
William	Roc- 15	Harrod,Elijah	Sto-101	P	Ash- 5
William	Jon-298	T	Bru-224	P	Ash- 10
Willm	Fra- 92	Harrold,Elijah	Sto-133	Pleasant	Grn-124
Wm	Nsh- 87	Hugh	Bur-114	Rachel	Sur-185
Wm Esq	Fra- 93	John	Sto-148	Richard S	Edg- 59
Wm Senr	Roc- 20	John	Wil-270	Robert	Ons- 98

Name	Loc	Name	Loc	Name	Loc
Hart,Samuel	Way-253	Hartness,James	Ire-254	Harvey,Wm	Car-172
Spencer	Edg- 48	Harton,Burwell	War-169	Wm	Bft- 24
Succy	Ora-161	Gideon	War-171	Harvil,Holly	Rth-107
Thomas	Grn-120	William	Rth-106	Harvill,David	Sur-169
Thos	Cha-214	Hartsawy,John	Row- 73	James	Sur-170
Thos	Ora-147	Hartsell,Geo	Cab-140	Moses	Sur-167
W	Ash- 10	Geo	Cab-141	Squire	Sur-167
Warren	Nor- 69	Hartsfield,Ahym	Len-322	William	Sur-169
Warren Junr	Nor- 68	Ben	Len-311	Harvy,George	Ire-265
Harte,Jacob	Bur-129	Jno	Len-311	James	Ons-103
Harten,Jacob	Sto-113	Saml	Len-311	John	Pit-258
Hartgrove,Ben	Mec- 54	Shad	Len-322	Sarah	Ons-103
Howel	Sto- 96	Hartsley,Jno	Mon- 47	Thomas	Sur-166
Howel	Sto-125	Hartsoah,Paul	Lnc-326	Thomas	Ons- 97
James	Sto-109	Hartson,Isaac	Cha-201	William	Pit-258
James	Sto-151	Jno	Cha-211	Harwel,Samuel	Ire-258
James	Sto-157	Hartt,Widow	Mec- 51	Harwell,D	Bru-232
James Jnr	Sto-126	Andrew	Mec- 24	Francis	Lnc-357
M	Ora-155	Jas Esq	Mec- 26	Fredk	Lnc-357
Suckey	Sto- 96	Matthew	Mec- 24	Gardner	Lnc-357
Sucky	Sto-125	Hartwick,Anthony	Mec- 40	Harbert	Lnc-357
Susannah	Sto-109	Jno	Mec- 40	Jeremiah	Ire-257
Susannah	Sto-151	Koonron	Mec- 40	John	War-174
Thompson	Mec- 54	Hartzog,D	Ash- 11	John	Ire-257
William	Sto-125	G	Ash- 9	Marcus	Hal-108
Hartin,Hardy	Ans- 14	Harvard,Britan	Cha-193	Nancy	Ire-258
Hartis,Henry	Mec- 41	Harvel,James H of M	Cum-260	Nathaniel	Ire-257
Lewis	Mec- 22	Mason	Joh-277	Rawly	Lnc-368
Hartley,Benjamin	Row- 81	Mellury	Cum-263	Rebekah	Hal-108
Burrel	Sam-159	Rheuben	Nsh- 77	Robert	Hal-106
James	Sam-152	Thos	Mor- 69	Samuel Senr	Lnc-357
Labon	Row- 81	Harvell,Moss	Joh-277	Thomas	Lnc-357
R	Ash- 8	Harvey,A E	Bft- 23	Willm	Hal-108
Thomas	Row- 80	Bosha	Roc- 24	Harwood,Absolom	Mon- 49
Hartly,George	Bur-107	David	Hyd-221	Henry	Row- 80
Hannah	Bur-120	David	Ora-167	Howel	Mon- 49
James	Bur-122	David	Ora-163	John	Row- 66
John	Bun- 74	Ezekiel	Sto-139	Lewis	Row- 80
Labon	Row- 40	Henry	Bft- 20	Malichi	Mon- 49
William	Bur-112	Isaac	Glf-152	Philip	Row- 65
Hartline,G	Row- 39	J	Glf-160	William	Row- 81
Hartman,Geo	Cab-142	James	Cur- 89	Hascott,Mat	Bft- 32
George	Sto-102	Jeremiah	Nsh- 90	Hase,Reuben Sr	Way-254
George	Sto-135	Jesse	Ran-167	Samuel	Row- 62
George	Row- 54	John	Bft- 20	Zach	Way-250
George	Row- 69	John	Row- 73	Hasel,Joab	Cum-240
Harmon	Sto-126	John	Ran-167	Hasell,Isaac	Mar- 6
Henry	Row- 55	John	Hal-108	John	Cur- 87
Jacob	Row- 53	John B	Lnc-344	William H	Mar- 11
Jacob	Row- 85	Jon	Ora-124	Haselston,WM	Ran-168
John	Row- 86	Joseph	Mar- 4	Hash,J	Ash- 7
John	Row- 77	Michael	Ran-167	W	Ash- 9
John	Row- 77	Michael	Ran-169	Haskens,Sylvenus	Ons- 97
John	Sto-135	Nathan	Ora-128	Hasket,Abraham	Ran-169
John	Sto-103	R	Bla- 12	Anthony	Prq-218
John Senr	Sto-135	Richard	Hyd-225	Henry	Prq-218
Michl	Row- 68	Thomas	Len-321	Jesse	Car-183
Peter	Row- 55	William	Glf-157	Jesse	Prq-218
Hartmus,Peter	Cho-325	William	Car-184	Jesse	Ran-168

Hasket,John	Prq-218	Hastings,J	Cam-158	Hathcock,Peter	Cas- 58
John	Ran-168	Jos Sen	Ora-136	Rachel	Hal-108
John Sr	Prq-218	Joshua	Way-233	Stephen	Cha-201
Joseph	Prq-218	Hasty,Elijah	Rch-197	Surry	Hal-107
Joseph	Ran-169	John	Rch-198	Tarlton	Cha-201
Joseph Jnr	Ran-168	Joseph	Way-241	Wm	Hal-108
Joseph Jr	Prq-218	Matthew	Rch-197	Hathhorn,Jno	Rob-220
Joshua	Prq-218	Mima	Way-241	Nathaniel	Rob-242
Josiah	Prq-218	Peeples	Ans- 8	Hathorn,J	Ans- 9
Malem	Ran-168	Stephen	Ans- 14	John	Mon- 22
Rebecah	Ran-168	Williby	Nor- 68	Joseph	Mon- 32
Sampson	Pas-191	Haswell,Thomas	Fra- 95	Thomas	Mon- 32
Silas	Prq-218	Hatch,Alex	Ora-113	Hatinger,Jacob	Row- 77
Thomas	Car-184	Anthony Junr	Jon-297	Hatley,Abner	Cha-214
Thomas	Prq-218	Anthony Senr	Jon-297	Joab	Cha-201
William	Prq-219	Asey	Jon-297	Josiah	Sur-169
William Jr	Prq-218	Durant	Jon-297	Mark	Cha-194
Haskett,Oliver	Glf-156	Edmond Junr	Jon-297	Sherwood	Cha-194
Haskey,Wm	Grn-122	Edmond Senr	Jon-297	Sherwood	Cha-208
Haskins,Benj	Ons- 97	Haskil	Jon-297	Wm	Cha-202
James	Grn-136	Henry	Len-317	Wm	Cha-194
John	Grn-136	Joseph	Jon-297	Hatly,Stardy	Mon- 49
Purnel	Ons- 87	Thos	Ora-122	Uriah	Cha-214
William Junr	Ons- 97	Hatchel,Bartlett	Per-130	Wm	Mon- 49
William Senr	Ons-103	Hatcher,John	Mon- 19	Hatmaker,M	Ora-145
Hasky,Isaac	Grn-123	Peggy	Bun- 90	Hatoway,Shadrach	Pit-253
Thomas	Grn-122	William	Cas- 57	William	Pit-253
Haslen,Stephen	Ran-169	Wm	Ans- 22	Hatrick,Robert	Glf-172
Hasley,Joseph	Sto-112	Hatchet,W	Ora-140	Hatsan,Daniel	Rch-210
Hasling,Stephen	Ran-168	W Jr	Ora-140	David	Bur-130
Hass,David	Lnc-336	Hatchsell,David	Ons-105	Hatsell,Armsted	Car-180
Mary	Lnc-336	Richard	Ons- 98	Henrietta	Car-179
Hassel,Enoch	Tyr-206	Hately,H	Ash- 6	William	Car-180
Fanny	Wsh-222	M	Ash- 6	Hatten,Robert	Pit-234
Isaac	Tyr-206	Hater,Angus Ray	Cum-269	William Dowdy	Cha-203
James	Tyr-204	Hatfield,Elizabeth	Wsh-228	Hattin,Frances	Edg- 53
John	Tyr-206	George	Hay-196	Taylor	Cur- 79
Joseph	Tyr-203	John	Prq-219	Hatton,Charles	Ire-264
Joseph Sen	Tyr-206	John	Tyr-213	David	Pit-233
Solomon Junr	Tyr-206	John	Tyr-213	John	Ire-264
Hassell,James	Tyr-212	Nancy	Prq-219	Hatwood,Tho Jr	Ora-113
Jesse	Cho-224	Salley	Hrt-209	Haudkins,Ts	Bru-228
Joshua	Tyr-213	William	Prq-218	Haughton,Chas	Cho-224
Joshua	Mar- 14	Hathaway,Burten	Tyr-205	Edwd	Cho-227
Joshua	Wsh-224	Edmund	Cum-246	Henry	Cho-220
Levi	Wsh-217	Jas	Cho-220	Jas	Cho-228
Myles	Cho-224	Woolsey	Tyr-205	John	Cho-224
Sarah	Wsh-228	J	Cam-162	Jona Jun	Cho-224
Solomon Sr	Tyr-213	Hathcock,Aron	Nor- 69	Jona Sen	Cho-224
Hasser,Joab	Ran-169	Bartlet	Nor- 68	Lamuel	Prq-219
Haste,Saml	Brt- 50	Curtis	Hal-108	Richard	Prq-219
Hasten,Jos R	Grn-132	D	Ora-156	Richd	Cho-222
Joshua	Ran-167	Dempsy	Mor- 67	Thomas B	Wsh-223
Hastey,George	Rch-207	Henry	Hal-108	Haukins,Saml	Bru-240
Hasting,Henry	Ora-943	Jacob	Ora-125	Wm	Bru-240
Jas	Ora-170	John	Hal-108	Hauks,James	Bun- 74
Hastings,C	Cam-158	John	Ora-164	Haun,Christian	Lnc-374
D	Cam-155	John	Cha-215	David	Lnc-374
Henry	Ora-151	M	Ora-156	Jacob	Lnc-374

-139-

Name	Ref	Name	Ref	Name	Ref	Name	Ref
Haun, Peter	Lnc-374	Hawkins, David	Lnc-329	Hawley, Mrs. E	Cum-234		
Haunchy, Will	Dup- 23	Edward	Rth-106	Jacob	Grn-137		
Hause, E	Bru-222	Elizabeth	Jon-298	Nathan	Grn-147		
Hauser, Abraham	Sto-103	Ezeriah	Ons- 97	William	Nor- 68		
Abraham	Sto-137	Grimes	Rth-106	Hawn, Frederick	Lnc-348		
Benjn	Sto-129	Harberd	Rth-105	Haws, George	Lnc-348		
Benjamin	Sto- 98	Henry	Hal-106	Henry	Hal-106		
Christian	Sto- 99	Henry	Hal-106	Henry	Lnc-348		
Christian	Sto-130	Isaac	Bur-124	John	Hal-106		
Daniel	Sto-107	Isham	Hal-106	Simon	Lnc-348		
Daniel	Sto-142	James	Wil-267	Susannah	Ons-107		
Geo P	Sto-128	James	Bun- 75	Hay, Charles	Sam-158		
George	Sto-145	Jesse	Edg- 52	David	Cum-240		
George	Sto-109	Jessy	Jon-298	Frederick	Glf-162		
Henry (cons)	Sto-128	Jno	Mec- 34	George	Rth-105		
Henry (sad)	Sto-128	John	Ons-106	John	Jon-298		
Henry	Sto- 98	John (S F)	Wil-280	Mary	Jon-298		
John	Sto-152	John	Row- 83	Thomas	Jon-298		
Johṇ	Sto-103	John	Wil-272	Hayes, Mrs.	Mec- 36		
John	Sto-135	John D Esq	Fra- 83	Arthur	Fra- 91		
Joseph	Sto-128	John H	War-174	Arthur	Roc- 5		
Joseph	Sto-152	Joseph	War-173	Charles	Fra- 91		
Laurance	Sto-107	Joseph	Ons- 99	Charles	Mec- 45		
Laurance	Sto-142	Joseph	Rth-108	Elizabeth	Roc- 16		
Martin	Sto-129	Joseph Junr	Hal-108	Hugh	War-172		
Martin	Sto- 98	Joseph Senr	Hal-108	Jno	Mec- 25		
Michael	Sto-128	Joshua	Wil-284	John Senr	Fra- 88		
Michael	Sto-114	Josua	Rth-107	Joseph	Mec- 51		
Peter	Sto-145	Littleton	Jon-298	Reuben	Mec- 33		
Peter	Sto-109	Major	Bft- 24	Ruth	Brt- 56		
Hausphus, Robert	Rth-105	Major Jr	Bft- 19	Saml	Brt- 56		
Hauthen, Jas N	Mec- 24	Mary	Bft- 22	Sarah	Mec- 33		
Hauzer, Jacob	Row- 57	Micajah T	War-178	Sarah	Brt- 57		
Havard, George	Cur- 86	Michael	Rth-106	Streetor	Hrt-210		
Havener, Jacob	Lnc-336	Nanny	Hal-108	Willie	Nor- 68		
Martin	Lnc-330	Phill (col)	War-178	Willis	Joh-275		
Nichl	Lnc-337	Phill (Majr)	War-178	Wm	Mec- 49		
Nicholas	Lnc-330	Phillemon	War-179	Hayle, Ezekiel	Lnc-340		
Haver, Casper	Sto-142	Phillip	Grn-134	Hayles, Saml	Bla- 8		
Geo	Row- 42	Ready	Bft- 39	Haynds, Hugh	Ire-256		
Havins, Eliz	Ons-102	Robert	Sur-175	Haynes, Bat	Mec- 36		
Henery	Cur- 89	Saml	Lnc-329	Christn	Row- 49		
Havor, J	Cam-163	Saml	Bur-124	Eaton	Mor- 68		
Hawkings, Elzy	Edg- 54	Saml	Bft- 25	Joseph	Mec- 36		
Hawkens, James	Cur- 91	Samuel	Hal-108	Robert	Lnc-363		
Hawkings, Ephraim	Per-129	Sarah	Wsh-228	William	Hay-196		
Wm	Per-130	Solomon	Hal-108	William	Roc- 12		
Hawkins, Ann	Jon-298	Terhanan	Bur-124	Hayns, William G	Sto-151		
Asher	Ons-106	Urial	Ons-104	Hays, Mrs.	Fra- 97		
Ben	Bft- 22	Whitehurst	Ons-101	Absalom	Nor- 69		
Benj	Len-314	William	Jon-298	Ayne	Wil-281		
Benjn	Dup- 34	William	Wil-263	Bazill	Cha-211		
Benj Esq	Fra- 91	Wm	Mec- 35	Benjamin	Gat-114		
Benjamin	Bun- 93	Wm	Mec- 34	C	Bru-236		
Benjamin	War-168	Wm	Grn-134	David	Bur-111		
Benjamin	Sto-124	Hawks, Benjamin	War-169	Edmond	Ran-167		
Benjn	Sto- 95	Jeremiah	War-175	Edward	Hay-196		
Benjn	Hal-108	John	War-174	Elisha	Gat-106		
Burrel	Lnc-329	Hawley, Dicey	Joh-283	Greenbury	Ire-268		

-140-

Hays,Hance	Gat-109	Hazard,John	War-175	Heath,John	Way-241	
Hartwell	Wil-265	Lewis	War-177	John Jr	Glf-167	
Henry	Grn-142	Lot	Grn-138	Martin	Sto-138	
Ja	Bru-222	Thos	Mec- 34	Martin	Sto-104	
Jacob Jr	Bru-228	Haze,W	Col- 21	Moses	Mec- 32	
James	Cha-189	Hazelip,John	Mar- 9	Saml	Glf-158	
James	Bur-128	Hazleman,Henry	Bur-131	Saml	Sto-139	
James	Per-139	Hazlet,John	Lnc-340	Samuel	Sto-104	
James	Glf-181	Hazlewood,Anne	War-167	Samuel	Grn-127	
James	Wil-267	David	War-169	Samuel B	Jon-297	
Jerda	Cum-263	Warrick	War-183	T	Glf-179	
Jessey	Grn-129	Hazlip,Abner	Mar- 15	Thomas	Sto-141	
Jno	Bru-222	Heacock,Charles	Roc- 27	Thomas	Sto-106	
John	Cha-204	John	Roc- 26	Thos	Cur- 86	
John	Bur-128	Sarah	Roc- 26	William	Sto-138	
John	Bur-126	Head,George	Sur-182	William	Sto-104	
John	Bur-124	Jno	Ans- 27	Heathcock,John	War-174	
John	Grn-145	Jno	Rob-233	John Sr	War-174	
John	Lnc-330	John	Sur-182	Thomas	Rch-204	
John	Bun- 87	William	Sur-188	Heathe,Alexander	Dup- 8	
John	Cas- 58	Headen,Thos	Lnc-355	John	Dup- 10	
John	Gat-107	Headley,James	Cab-146	Levi	Dup- 18	
Joseph	Row- 69	Stephen	Cab-146	Thomas	Dup- 9	
Josiah	Grn-127	Headpeath,Abhm	Nsh- 74	William	Dup- 9	
Matthew	Lnc-342	Headson,Aaron	Cha-199	Heatherly,Geo	Bun- 95	
Nelly	Bur-127	Joab	Cam-155	John	Bun- 95	
Peece	Ran-167	Heady,Daniel	Car-176	Heathman,Ezekiah	Row- 76	
Peyton	Grn-141	John	Ons-105	Heavens,Jonathan	Hyd-233	
Reuben	Wil-272	Richard	Grn-144	Heavill,W	Cam-158	
Richd	Ora-115	Heagpeth,Solomon	Grn-147	Hebert,Mary	Cum-239	
Robert	Bun- 73	Heane,Howell	Pit-247	Heckstall,John	Brt- 45	
Saml	Grn-145	Mary	Pit-247	Hedding,Andrew	Cha-197	
Saml	Grn-129	Heard,Stansel	Edg- 53	Phebe	Cha-212	
Simson	Grn-146	Hearn,Joseph	Joh-288	Hederick,Francis	Row- 87	
Solomon	Ire-267	William	Ran-169	Francis	Row- 82	
Stephen	Cha-212	Hearne,Edmund	Rth-106	Hedgeman,Lewis	Dup- 10	
Thomas	Bur-128	G	Mon- 43	Hedgepeth,Abraham	Hrt-214	
William	Gat-116	Mary	Pit-248	Avis	Bun- 87	
William	War-183	Heart,Mickal	Bur-130	Noah	Way-233	
William	Row- 69	Hearthaway,John	Pit-247	William	Hrt-213	
William	Bur-126	Heartsfeild,R	Bru-236	Williby	Nor- 68	
William	Bun- 85	Heasley,Danl	Row- 41	Hedgman,Henry	Edg- 42	
Wm	Ora-171	Heath,Amasiah	Glf-166	Hedgpeth,John	Edg- 67	
Haysley,Joseph	Sto-150	Baxter	Sto-138	Hedick,Jonas	Lnc-344	
Haystin,Lidia	Mar- 15	Baxter	Sto-104	Hedlow,Andrew Jr	Rth-105	
Hayth,Jacob	Glf-158	Curhbert	Glf-166	Hedpeath,Holiday	Nsh- 77	
Wm	Glf-159	Enos	Glf-166	Hedrick,Adam	Row- 41	
Hayward,Saml	Row- 44	Ezekiel	Glf-166	Adam Jr	Row- 85	
Haywood,Henry	Edg- 41	Henry	Glf-182	Geo	Row- 81	
James	Way-249	Henry	Len-320	Jacob	Row- 85	
Josiah	Mor- 67	James	Joh-284	John	Lnc-351	
Wm	Fra- 79	John	Ire-267	Philip	Row- 85	
Hayworth,Eli	Glf-169	John	Bun- 86	Hedricks,Saml	Cho-225	
Geo	Glf-170	John	Sto-141	Heelsepeck,Jacob	Sto-129	
H	Glf-169	John	Sto-139	Heeth,J	Glf-174	
Jeremia	Row- 44	John	Sto-138	J	Glf-174	
Michl	Row- 45	John	Sto-106	W	Cam-163	
Richd	Glf-170	John	Jon-298	Hefley,John	Hay-195	
Hazard,George	Ons-107	John	Glf-167	Mary	Hay-196	

-141-

Name	Ref	Name	Ref	Name	Ref
Heflin, Charles	Grn-130	Hemphill, David	Per-130	Henderson, John	Glf-169
Joab	Rth-107	J	Glf-179	John	Cha-192
John	Pth-107	J	Glf-172	Joseph	Rth-105
Wm	Grn-122	J Jr	Glf-172	Josiah	Ons- 97
Hafner, Daniel	Bun- 98	James	Bur-119	Lawson	Lnc-336
Elizabeth	Bun- 97	S	Glf-179	Leonard	Grn-140
Frederick	Bun- 84	S	Glf-172	Lewis	Cha-208
Geo	Bun- 85	Thomas	Bur-110	Logan	Lnc-373
Jacob	Lnc-351	Henbey, Elizebeth	Ans- 10	Mary	Cum-238
John Jr	Lnc-351	Henby, Elisha	Prq-218	Mary	Hyd-228
John Senr	Lnc-351	John	Prq-218	Matthew	Mec- 52
Michael	Lnc-351	Joseph	Ans- 16	Milly	Bur-111
Phillip	Lnc-351	Joseph	Ans- 16	Moses	Rth-108
Samuel	Bun- 86	Nathan	Prq-218	Nancy	Dup- 14
Hegden, Lenord	Row- 72	Sylvanus	Prq-218	Nanney	Gat-109
Heggie, John	Grn-124	Thos	Prq-218	Neal	Bft- 25
Heinze, Christian	Sto-146	Henchee, Thos	Cha-212	Plea	Ora-130
Heist, John	Ora-150	Hencock, Stephen	Dup- 35	Rem	Mec- 39
Heither, William	Roc- 15	William	Roc- 28	Richard	Roc- 17
Helderman, Gullet	Lnc-376	Hendocock, Numial	Hrt-212	Richard	Mec- 54
Jacob	Lnc-363	Thos	Hrt-213	Richard Junr	Roc- 19
Nicholas	Lnc-363	Henderick, Augustus	Ans- 26	Saml	Cas- 58
Helford, M	Cam-162	Henderin, Anderson	Pow- 84	Saml Jr	Cas- 57
Heliphar, Henry	Row- 66	Henderix, Abraham	Row- 61	Samuel	Ire-253
Hellebrand, Conrad	Lnc-326	William	Row- 62	Samuel	Ire-253
Conrad.	Lnc-337	Henderson, Abner	Cha-205	Sarah	Car-174
Henry	Lnc-334	Alexander	Row- 63	Stephen	Ons- 97
Hellen, Brian	Car-171	Alexander	Ons-101	Thomas	Ons- 99
Helley, Wm C	Ora-156	Alexr	Mec- 53	Thomas	Roc- 5
Hellin, William	Ons- 97	Andrew	Mec- 47	Thomas Esqr	Ons-100
Hellon, George	Row- 65	Archd	Row- 89	Doct Thos	Mec- 28
Helm, Michael	Wil-262	Archd	Rob-219	William	Cas- 57
Helmes, Jacob	Lnc-329	Arnold	Rth-107	William	Ons-100
John	Lnc-328	Benjamin	Rth-105	William	Lnc-360
Helmon, Caleb	Glf-181	Charles	Ons- 95	William	Ire-251
Helms, ---ebb	Mec- 22	Daniel	Rch-192	William	Rth-106
Abraham	Mec- 42	Daniel	Rch-206	William	Rth-105
Burrel	Mec- 43	Dunc	Bla- 7	William	Rth-105
DAvid	Mec- 43	Ezekiel	Ons- 98	William	Rth-107
George	Mec- 42	Gabriel	Rth-107	William	Dup- 35
Isaac	Mec- 43	Isaac	Mec- 35	Willm	Glf-168
Jacob	Mec- 43	Isaac	Rth-105	Wm	Mec- 53
Jacob	Lnc-327	Isaac	Cha-191	Hendley, John	Sto-111
Jno	Mec- 43	Jacob	Cas- 57	John	Sto-146
Jno	Mec- 43	James	Cha-214	John	Sto-143
Joal	Mec- 43	James	Bun- 88	William	Row- 63
Tilghman	Mec- 43	James	Wil-269	Hendour, Josiah	Bla- 12
Wm	Mec- 43	James	Glf-168	Hendrakes, Samuel	Ran-167
Wm	Mec- 42	Jas	Mec- 38	Hendraks, Samuel	Ran-167
Helmstetter, Peter	Row- 80	Jno	Mec- 22	Tobias	Ran-168
Helmstitler, Peter	Row- 85	Jno	Ora-142	William	Ran-167
Helsepech, Jacob	Sto- 38	Jno	Ora-117	Hendrick, Ezekiel	Sur-193
Heltebran, Conrad	Bur-105	Jno	Ora-156	Isaac	Nsh- 84
Helton, Mrs.	Fra- 99	Jno	Mec- 55	Jas S	Ans- 17
J	Ora-131	Jno	Rob-228	Oxney	Nsh- 82
Robt	Ire-251	Jno	Mec- 54	Stephen	War-180
Wintrop	Hal-106	John	Cha-210	Hendricks, Amey	Ora-149
Hemp, Joseph	Cha-195	John	Cha-210	Frederick	Row- 61
Hemphill, Andrew	Bur-119	John	Roc- 19	Nicholas	Sto-148

-142-

Name	Ref	Name	Ref	Name	Ref
Hendricks,£... ...n	Row- 83	Hennings,Adam	Sto- 98	Hensley,Thomas	Cas- 58
Hendrik,Iriqmis	Nsh- 84	Henrahan,Walter	Pit-232	Wm	Cha-195
Hendrix,Abranam Jr	Row- 62	Henry,Fanny	Non- 46	Hensly,Benj	Bun- 79
Benjamin	Wil-280	Geo	Cha-198	Berrey	Bun- 79
Daniel	Row- 66	Harmon	Roc- 13	Harry	Bun- 78
Darby Esqr	Wil-282	Isaac	Lnc-367	Henry	Bun- 79
David	Row- 62	Isaac M	Ire-238	James	Bun- 79
Dorcas	Prq-219	Isam	Rch-206	John	Bun- 78
H	Glf-157	James	Lnc-330	Washington	Bun- 78
Henry	Row- 63	James	Brt- 49	Henson,Archibald	Bun- 92
Hester	Cha-204	James	Rth-105	Toseph	Ran-168
Isaac	Ire-267	James	Rth-106	Hensy,Richard	Roc- 7
Isaac	Brt- 65	Jas	Mec- 46	Henton,John	Mon- 45
Isaac	Row- 65	Joel	Ran-168	Herben,John	Roc- 32
James	Row- 65	John	Lnc-373	Herbin,Stephen	Glf-169
James	Glf-157	John	Hyd-227	William	Roc- 32
James	Rth-106	John	Lnc-333	Herbst,John H	Sto-146
Job	Prq-218	John	Lnc-334	Jonas	Sto-146
John	Ire-269	John	Dup- 6	Herden,Zick	Mec- 30
John	Row- 65	John	Hay-196	Herder,Niccolas	Per-148
Jonathan	Bur-107	Joseph Junr	Bun- 94	Herdlow,Michl Jr	Rth-105
Joshua	Row- 61	Joseph Snr	Bun- 89	Herdon,Abner	Cha-214
Levi	Prq-218	Malcolm	Hay-196	Herell,David	Glf-174
Micajah	Wil-282	Malcomb	Bun- 84	Stephen	Glf-174
Nicholas	Sto-111	Martha	Brt- 49	Herine,Nehemiah	Mon- 50
Seth	Prq-218	Philip	Ans- 18	Herington,Moring	Hyd-222
Solomon	Prq-218	Rebecca	Len-310	Herman,Andrew	Lnc-338
William	Bur-131	Reuben	Sto-138	David	Lnc-338
Hendrixon,John	Bur-120	Robert	Brt- 49	Jacob	Lnc-338
Hendrixson,Josiah	Bur-176	Robert	Hyd-227	Henry	Lnc-338
Hendsley,Jas	Cho-226	Robt	Row- 71	Peter	Lnc-338
William	Ire-251	Posanna	Lnc-333	Richard	Lnc-338
Henegin,Dennis	Mec- 30	Samuel	Ire-255	Hermon,Merryman	Cha-209
Henery,Mrs.	Cum-238	Sarah	Hal-107	Tacehosiah	Cha-193
James	Cur- 90	Stephen	Ans- 11	William	Prq-219
Henley,Elias	Ran-168	Stephen	Roc- 12	Hern,E	Ora-157
Gabrel	Ran-168	William	Bun- 89	Eben	Mon- 20
J-	Mon- 35	William	Ire-255	Hefler	Cha-194
Jesse	Ran-169	Wm	Bru-226	J	Ora-157
John Snr	Ran-167	Wm	Ans- 20	James	Edg- 65
Joseph	Ran-167	Wm	Mec- 47	Jesse	Mon- 18
Marey	Cur- 91	Hensell,E	Glf-176	Joshua	Lnc-363
Stephen	Ran-169	Henshaw,Benjn	Ran-167	Ley	Mon- 18
Wm	Hal-106	Banj	Sto-134	Michael	Edg- 41
Henly,B	Mon- 39	Jesse	Ran-168	Nehimiah	Mon- 39
Christopher	Ire-247	John	Sto-148	S	Ora-157
Edmd	Mon- 29	Seth	Ran-168	Sally	Mon- 49
Eladian	Mon- 49	Thomas	Ran-168	Selby	Mon- 21
Henry	Ire-247	Thomas	Ran-167	Thos	Mon- 20
Henry	Grn-122	William	Ran-167	Thos	Ora-150
James	Mon- 25	Hensiham,Walter	Pit-255	Wm	Mon- 20
Jas Dunbar	Per-139	Hensley,Colberd	Bun- 81	Benj	Ora-170
John	Grn-122	David	Roc- 21	D	Ora-153
John	Pas-191	Enoch	Roc- 21	Edmond	Cas- 57
Jonathan	Ire-266	James	Bun- 77	El	Ora-157
Stephen	Ire-247	John Jnr	Ran-167	G	Ora-153
Wm	Ora-169	Lewis	Bun- 86	John	Cha-211
Hennegan,Widow	Mec- 31	Michl	Row- 51	John	Lnc-362
Hennigin,Saml	Mec- 29	Michl	Ora-127	John	Ire-264

Hern,Lewis	Ora-116	Herring,Stephen	Sam-152	Hester,Ann	Fra- 92	
Pompt	Ora-131	Stephen	Len-316	Benj	Grn-148	
Red	Ora-157	Stephen B	Sam-151	Benj	Grn-148	
Herne,Thos	Bla- 13	W	Cam-165	Charles	Grn-149	
Herod,Mary	Sam-156	Whitfield	Dup- 26	Drury	Grn-124	
Heron,Betsey	Nor- 68	William	Len-312	Elizabeth	Grn-126	
Herrald,R	Glf-183	William H	Dup- 28	Frances	Grn-145	
Reuben	Glf-165	Herrington,Chrles	Hyd-222	Francis	Grn-124	
Herrantine,Jas	Sam-153	Henry	Pit-235	Garland	Grn-145	
Herren,Berry	Hay-196	Hosea	Hyd-222	Graves	Grn-120	
Fielding	Sur-163	James	Bla- 5	James	Fra- 92	
Francis	Sur-179	Jamima	Pit-233	James	Grn-124	
John	Joh-280	Jas	Bft- 30	John	Bla- 6	
Matchet	Joh-280	Joab	Pit-238	John	Sto-146	
Wm	Rob-240	M '	Cam-153	John	Sto-110	
Herricks,Efthea	Cho-223	Paul	Pit-239	John	Sto-111	
Herrill,John	Bur-115	Simon	Pit-235	John	Rth-107	
Herriman,Archd	Mon- 40	Thos	Cam-157	John	Rth-107	
Herrin,Christopher	Sur-175	Herrintine,Stephen	Sam-156	John	Grn-125	
George	Sur-174	Herrintone,Jas	Sam-163	John	Grn-122	
Moses	Lnc-327	Herris,Jno	Ora-149	Joseph (B O)	Bla- 6	
Stephen	Rch-203	Herritage,Wm	Cas- 58	Joseph Junr	Bla- 6	
William	Bur-112	Herrod,Jesse	Sto-156	Joseph Senr	Bla- 6	
William Senr	Bur-112	Herron,Mrs.	Mec- 27	Michael	Rth-108	
Herring,Alexd	Dup- 5	David	Roc- 26	Robert	Grn-124	
Anne	Sam-152	Isaac	Mec- 25	Robert	Sto-149	
Asia	Len-315	Jarn	Roc- 28	Robt	Cha-206	
Benj	Way-249	Richard	Bur-112	Thos	Grn-120	
Benj	Dup- 25	Herson,Allen	Mec- 37	Thos Junr	Bla- 6	
Benjn Jr	Dup- 14	Hertel,Fred Wm	Sto-136	Thos Senr	Bla- 6	
Daniel	Dup- 26	Hervey,George	Pas-191	Wm	Grn-120	
Elisha	Dup- 5	Gideon	Hal-106	Wm	Bla- 6	
Eliz	Len-316	James	Cur- 89	Wm	Grn-141	
Enoch	Sam-164	Ocney	Hal-106	Wm Jr	Grn-147	
Fredk	Sam-154	Paton	Hal-106	Zac Sr	Grn-135	
Gabrel	Sam-164	Robert	Hal-106	Zachariah	Grn-141	
George	Way-252	Thomas	Hal-106	Hesters,Jno	Rob-218	
Graddy	Way-250	Thos	Cur- 89	Wm	Rob-220	
Henry	Nor- 68	William	Hal-106	Hethcock,Benj	Mon- 38	
Henry	Way-251	Wm M	Pas-191	D	Mon- 38	
Ichabod	Way-250	Wm Senr	Hal-106	Demsy	Mon- 49	
Jacob	Way-249	Hervy,Levina	Prq-219	James	Mon- 38	
James	Way-240	Stephen	Hal-106	Hethpath,E	Cum-237	
Joel	Sam-160	Hesler,John (B L)	Sto-147	Hewell,Jacob	Hyd-234	
Joel	Way-247	Robert	Per-151	Hewet,John	Ons-102	
John	Dup- 28	William	Per-151	Josephus	Nor- 68	
John	Len-318	Heslip,Andrew	Rth-106	Josiah	Nor- 68	
Joseph	Way-238	Andrew	Rth-106	Nancy	Ons-105	
Joshua	Sam-162	John	Rth-106	Rigdon	Ons-105	
Joshua	Sam-152	Hess,Daniel	Cab-142	Hewett,A	Cam-161	
Lewis	Dup- 27	Daniel	Row- 70	Hewey,Rebekah	Rth-107	
Major	Rth-107	Henry	Row- 68	Hewie,S B	Cum-239	
Molley	Way-253	John	Row- 78	Hewit,D	Bru-232	
Nathan	Sam-162	Hessey,H	Ora-152	D Junr	Bru-238	
Nathl	Len-316	Hessler,Barbary	Row- 80	D Snr	Bru-238	
Simon	Way-238	Christopher	Row- 80	E	Bru-238	
Simon	Len-312	Henry	Row- 80	J	Bru-232	
Stephen	Dup- 26	Salome	Sto-146	J	Bru-238	
Stephen	Sam-164	Hester,Abram	Rth-107	John	Bun- 73	

Hewit,F	Bru-238	Hickman,Jos	Sur-175	Hicks,Thomas		Rth-105
P Snr	Bru-238	Penelope	Cum-245	Thomas		Cha-199
R	Bru-238	Saml L	Bru-222	Thos		Grn-143
R	Bru-238	Stephen	Cum-245	Thos		Sam-152
Rigden	Jon-297	W	Bru-226	William		Cas- 57
W	Bru-238	William	Cum-245	William		Nor- 69
Hewitt,D	Bru-226	Wm B	Glf-157	William		Rth-104
E	Bru-240	Wyatt	Ora-174	William		Fra- 81
Ezekl	Bru-240	Escom	Sur-180	William		Ran-168
J	Bru-240	Hickmon,Joseph Jn	Sur-191	William		Ire-261
Jo	Bru-240	S	Col- 19	Wm		Mon- 33
P Jr	Bru-230	Thomas	Sur-180	Wm		Cho-230
S	Bru-240	Wm	Sur-161	Wm		Grn-146
Silas	Bru-222	Hickmore,Wm	Grn-146	Zachariah		Edg- 68
Thos	Bru-228	Hicks,Abner	Grn-148	Hicky,Sarah		Hay-196
Wm	Bru-226	Absalem	Grn-147	Hide,Benjamin		Rth-107
Hews,Dellilah	Dup- 12	Andrew	Rth-107	Benjamin		Hay-195
Jessee	Bun- 78	Asa -	Fra- 80	Jno		Ora-158
John Senr	Bun- 76	Benjamin	Rth-105	John		Hay-195
Robert	Bun- 80	Berry	Mon- 30	Hider,Benjamin		Rth-104
William	Dup- 12	Daniel	Cas- 57	Benjamin Jr		Rth-104
William	Bun- 75	Daniel	Sam-152	Hiett,Asa		Ans- 25
Heyley,Leond	Lnc-335	Daniel	Cas- 57	Higden,Eliz		Row- 72
Hiatt,Benjamin	Glf-180	Davis	Ran-167	Walter		Row- 75
Christopher	Glf-180	Elias	Nor- 68	Higdon,Charles		Cha-201
E	Glf-184	Elizabeth	Sto-110	Danl		Cha-205
Enos Jr	Glf-167	Elizabeth	Sto-150	Jane		Bur-125
Evans	Glf-167	George	Rch-197	John		Bur-103
Francis	Cur- 92	Harris	Grn-147	John		Cha-205
Geo	Glf-163	Howel	Mor- 61	John		Bur-104
Isaac	Glf-167	Jacob	Grn-137	Leo		Bur-104
Isham	Glf-182	James	Edg- 70	Phillip		Cha-205
J	Glf-183	James	Bur-117	Thomas		Bun- 96
Joel	Glf-187	James	Way-251	Higgans,Elizabeth		Wil-268
John	Gat-115	James	Wil-272	John		Wil-261
Joseph	Sur-176	James	Lnc-362	Mary		Wil-271
Linnsey	Tyr-212	James	Sur-166	Higgins,Ananias		Bun- 77
T	Glf-184	James	Rch-198	John		Bun- 88
William	Glf-182	Jasper	Grn-143	Michael		Car-182
William	Sto-133	Jesse	Cha-214	Miles		Bur-117
Hibbart,John	Hay-195	John	Nor- 69	Higgs,Jacob		Hal-107
Hibbits,Robert	Ire-255	John	War-176	Jonathan		Ons-109
Hibbs,Jonathan	Car-182	John	Grn-127	Kenelim		Grn-146
Hichcock,Thomas	Sto-134	John	Bun- 73	Reubin		Brt- 58
William	Sto-134	Jonathan	Bun- 87	Samuel		Hal-107
Hickcock,B	Glf-168	Jonathan Snr	Bun- 87	Authern		Grn-146
John	Glf-168	Joshua	Mon- 33	Theophilus		Brt- 55
Jos	Glf-167	Josiah	Fra- 97	Wm		Brt- 54
Joshua	Glf-167	Luke	Cas- 57	High,E		Col- 17
Wm	Glf-167	Matt	Ora-114	Gardiner		Ans- 22
Wm Jr	Glf-167	Micajah	Ora-128	J		Col- 18
Hickerson,David	Wil-280	Miles	Fra- 93	Jno		Ans- 17
David Jr	Wil-280	Rebeka	Cha-198	Julius		Bla- 6
John	Wil-262	Robert	Mon- 33	L		Col- 16
Thos	Prq-218	Samuel	Sur-170	Robert		Fra- 95
Hickman,Edwin	Sto-113	Stephen	Joh-286	Highfeth,Arthur		Rob-236
Edwin	Sto-154	Susanna	Way-252	Highfield,H		Glf-160
J	Glf-179	Thomas	Bun- 95	Highmiller,Coonrod		Ire-247
Jas	Glf-157	Thomas	Nor- 68	Highsmith,Jacob		Pit-255

-145-

Highsmith,John	Pit-255	Hill,David		Car-174	Hill,John		Sto-122
Mosses	Pit-255	Durham		Fra- 83	John		Brt- 44
William	Dup- 19	Dutton		Roc- 9	John		Roc- 9
Hight,Alsey	Nsh- 90	E		Col- 19	John		Ire-261
Hannah	Fra- 96	Eli		Ora-165	John		Sur-189
Herbert	Fra- 88	Eli		Car-183	John		Rch-208
Johnathan	Grn-127	Elizabeth		Gat-111	John		Cha-204
Nathl	Fra- 91	Ephraim		Rth-107	John		Cha-199
Mrs. Polly	Fra- 89	Felix K		Sam-164	John H		Car-180
Polly	Fra- 91	Geo		Bft- 30	John Junr		Car-174
Reed	Bur-128	George		Row- 54	Johnson		Hrt-215
Samuel	Fra- 97	George W		Hrt-215	Jordan Esq		Fra- 83
Hightower,Allin	Cas- 58	Gracey		Cur- 89	Joseph		Row- 62
Charsial	Cas- 58	Green		Sto-125	Joshua		Bft- 30
Daniel	Cas- 57	Green		Sam-160	Lazus		Dft- 28
Epephrodiuts	Bun- 98	Green		Rth-106	Leonard		Sur-189
Epphr	Cas- 57	Green Esq		Fra- 89	Luke		Cur- 92
Francis	Cas- 58	Henry		Nor- 69	M		Col- 19
John	Cas- 58	Henry		Bur-127	Marget		Jon-298
Richard	Cas- 57	Henry		Cha-216	Mrs. Martha		Fra- 79
Robt	Cas- 57	Herman		Nor- 69	Martin		Mon- 25
Thomas	Cas- 57	Herman		Bft- 28	Matthew		Sto- 94
Higs,Barnet	Grn-149	Hinchen		Fra- 98	Matthew		Sto-122
Johanthan	Grn-127	Hosbert		Hal-108	Merilla		Sur-163
Leonard	Grn-127	Isaac		Car-180	Michl		Bft- 29
Nathan	Nsh- 77	Isaac		Sur-187	Miles		Gat-105
Higson,John	Bft- 36	J		Ash- 14	Mills		Cho-230
Hiland,Henry	Bur-115	J		Col- 20	Moses		Rob-239
Hilbern,F	Bru-234	James		Ons-101	N		Ora-140
Hilburn,H	Col- 18	James		Wil-274	Nancy		Ora-165
Vayllen	Rob-219	James		Rth-106	Nathl		Ora-167
Hildrith,David	Ans- 26	James		Cur- 88	Noah		Rob-240
Hilegh,Henry	Row- 68	James		Lnc-336	Peoples		Edg- 62
John	Row- 68	James		Row- 53	Peter		Car-174
Michl	Row- 67	James		Mor- 56	Peyton		Edg- 64
Hileman,John	Row- 73	James		Hrt-215	Polly		Car-180
Hill,Aaron	Ran-168	James		Ire-247	Priscilla		Rth-107
Aaron	Ran-169	James		Ire-161	Mrs. Rebecca		Fra- 95
Abraham	Row- 69	Jas		Rob-240	Reuben		Rth-104
Abraham	Ire-248	Jas		Lnc-340	Richard		Len-314
Alce	Gat-111	Jas J Esq		Fra- 87	Richard		Roc- 13
Amos	Mor- 62	Jeane		Dup- 7	Richard		Fra- 94
Aron	Ran-169	Jeremiah		Lnc-363	Richard		Sur-175
Asa	Wsh-221	Jesse		Rth-108	Richard Sr		Sur-187
Asa	Rth-106	Jesse		Cur- 92	Richland		Fra- 98
Asa	Rth-107	Jesse		Sur-187	Ritchman		Mec- 41
Bartlett	Sur-173	Jno		Mec- 46	Robert		Rth-106
Benj	Hrt-215	Jno		Mec- 53	Robert		Sto-129
Benjamin	Sur-183	Jno Junr		Per-130	Robert		Fra- 79
Benjn	Joh-286	Jno Senr		Per-130	Robert		Sto-126
Bennet	Sam-159	Joel		Cab-144	Robert		Sto- 96
Buckner	Car-180	John		Ran-168	Robert C		Fra- 82
Caleb	Sto-125	John		Rth-107	Rubin		Row- 69
Caleb	Sto- 96	John		Bur-122	S		Col- 18
Charles	Rth-107	John		Gat-114	S		Col- 18
Charles	Rth-107	John		Edg- 61	Samuel		Ran-169
Clem	Gat-111	John		Car-176	Samuel		Car-177
David	Ire-248	John		Car-180	Samuel		Sto-112
David	Ire-262	John		Cur- 92	Samuel		Roc- 26

Name	Loc	Name	Loc	Name	Loc
Hill,Sarah	Row- 54	Hilliard,James	Hal-108	Hines,Benjn	Hal-106
Sarah	Hrt-214	James	Nsh- 74	Bryant	Nsh- 77
Sealy	Tyr-208	John	Nsh- 75	Daniel	Dup- 10
Seth	Row- 69	John	Nor- 68	Daniel	Len-318
Simon	Mar- 3	John	Rch-196	Federick	Row- 47
Sion	Sam-160	Priscilla	Edg- 56	Felix	Sam-157
Slaughter	Rob-239	Robt C	Nsh- 76	Frederick	Row- 55
Stephen	Ire-248	Silas	Mor- 63	Fredk	Dup- 27
Sterling	Fra- 38	Thomas	War-181	George	Ire-264
Susanna	Way-241	Willm	Fra- 87	Hartwell	Nsh- 79
Swenfold	Bur-114	Hilling,Ann	Pit-234	Hartwell	Nsh- 78
Sydney	Car-175	Hillitsan,Conrod	Bur-104	Jacob W	Row- 40
Thomas	Rob-239	Hillman,Jacob	Cab-145	Joel	Len-318
Thomas	Hal-107	Jesse	Hal-108	John	Mar-446
Thomas	Ran-167	Hillomon,John	Hrt-216	John	Mar- 14
Thomas	Dup- 7	Hills,Eben	Bft- 29	John	Sur-164
Thomas	Wil-268	Hillsman,James	Fra- 97	John	Way-238
Thomas	Fra- 79	Mrs. Martha	Fra- 84	John	Way-239
Thomas	Lnc-360	Hillyard,Benj	Grn-144	July	Sto-143
Thomas	Wsh-217	Hilman,Joshua	Roc- 18	Lewis	Nsh- 78
Thomas	Sur-181	Hilmon,E	Glf-183	Little B	Nsh- 78
Thomas	Sur-193	Hilton,Berck	Bur-130	Micajah	Edg- 47
Thos	Ans- 13	Eliphus	Bur-130	Needham	Dup- 6
Thos	Cha-215	Freman	Ire-253	Patsey	Len-310
W	Ash- 5	Hernan	Bur-131	Peter	Edg- 50
Webb	Way-253	James	Row- 45	Peter	Way-242
Whitmill	Gat-108	James	Row- 44	Richard	Edg- 68
Whittmill	Rob-240	Jerri	Bur-130	Rosanna	Edg- 69
William	Ran-168	Jesse	Bur-130	Sharewood	Pit-237
William	Dup- 5	Joseph	Row- 56	Stephen	Way-238
William	Rth-106	Peter	Bur-130	William	Ire-264
William	Bur-114	Robert	Rth-105	William	Mar- 14
William	Cur- 83	Sterling	Cha-216	Williams	Edg- 68
William	Car-180	Thomas	Sur-177	Willis	Dup- 24
William	Jon-298	Thos	Row- 57	Willis	Way-241
William	Fra- 80	Hilyard,Ezekiel	Cha-205	Hineson,Joseph	Ons- 98
William	Row- 54	Hincanin,William	Bur-125	Hinkle,Widow	Lnc-366
William	Row- 60	Hinchan,Benjn	Cha-195	Anthony	Row- 50
William	Mar- 8	Hinchemen,Leonard	Cab-141	Anthony	Lnc-374
William	Sur-179	Hinchen,Absolam	Cha-212	Benjn	Row- 58
William	Sur-175	Hinchey,David	Ora-151	Gasper	Row- 49
William Esqr	Ons- 98	John	Rch-200	Hannah	Lnc-366
William W	Edg- 66	Levi	Ora-151	Jacob	Lnc-366
Wm	Rob-240	M	Ora-152	Jacob Jr	Lnc-366
Wm	Car-180	Mikel	Ora-151	John	Lnc-376
Wm	Row- 38	Hinchy,Ezekiel	Ora-151	Joseph	Row- 58
Wm	Cha-199	Hanah	Cha-212	William	Lnc-360
Wilsy	Bft- 28	Hindman,Jacob	Cab-143	Hinnant,James	Joh-283
Winney	War-184	Hindmon,William	Bur-173	John	Joh-287
Hillard,Jacob	Bur-104	Hindon,Wm	Bla- 4	Jonathan	Joh-283
Wm	Cum-240	Hinds,Joseph	Wil-259	Josiah	Joh-284
Hillburn,Henry Sr	Bla- 6	Nancy	Bur-129	Mary	Joh-283
Woodward	Bla- 4	Samuel	Wil-259	William	Joh-283
Hillem,John	Sto-134	Hindsley,John	Brt- 44	William Jr	Joh-282
Hillen,James	Cum-259	Hine,John	Sto-144	Hinnon,Charles	Cha-204
William	Cum-260	Hinemon,Robert	Sur-195	Hins,Bolen	Cha-193
Hillhouse,Jas	Lnc-340	Hines,Alexander	Sur-168	Hinshaw,Jacob	Sur-166
Hilliard,Epps	Ora-126	Allen	Nsh- 77	Jesse	Cha-194
Isaac	Hal-107		Fra- 88	Jonathan	Sur-165

Name	Ref	Name	Ref	Name	Ref	Name	Ref
Hinshaw,Joseph	Sur-177	Hinton,John	Cas- 57	Hix,West	Jon-298		
Thomas	Cas- 58	John	Gat-110	William	War-183		
Thomas	Sur-170	John	Joh-274	Hixon,Willoby	Hyd-229		
Thomas	Sur-168	Jos B	Bft- 37	Hize,John	Cab-148		
William	Sur-192	Joseph	Joh-274	Hoagland,Tunis	Hay-196		
Hinshke,John F	Sto-146	Lewis	Cha-193	Hoard,Wiley	Mar- 8		
Hinsley,Benj	Cha-211	Malacy	Joh-287	Hobay,E	Glf-159		
Benjamon	Bur-107	Mary	Gat-111	Hobb,John	Sam-159		
John	Cas- 57	Noah	Gat-111	William	Bur-112		
Mackfield	Cas- 57	Noah	Brt- 63	Hobbert,Joseph	Cum-249		
Hinsly,Amos	Bur-117	Reuben	Edg- 45	Hobbs,Abigal	Hyd-223		
Ben	Bur-117	Reubin	Gat-110	Amos	Gat-107		
Hinson,Aaron	Cha-207	Sally	Bft- 27	Berneby	Ran-167		
Aron	Len-311	William	Cas- 57	Charlot	Hrt-210		
Bartlet	Ans- 30	William	Brt- 63	Charlton	Brt- 52		
Bartlet Sr	Bur-103	William	Gat-107	David	Gat-108		
Benjn	Ans- 12	William	Joh-286	Edmon	Gat-108		
Benjn	Ans- 32	William	Joh-288	Edward	Ons-107		
Chas	Ans- 24	William S	Pas-190	Elisha Jnr	Ran-169		
Chas	Ans- 30	Wm	Hal-108	Elisha Snr	Ran-169		
Daniel	Hay-196	Willis	Joh-288	George	Sam-156		
David	Hay-195	Hiott,Elizabeth	Nor- 68	Hardy	Bla- 4		
Edward H	Ans- 23	Hipkenstall,Wm	Hal-108	Hetty	Ora-177		
Elijah	Mon- 38	Hipp,Andrew	Mec- 55	Isaac	Gat-105		
F	Mon- 38	David	Mec- 54	Isaac	Cas- 57		
Francis	Ans- 19	Jacob	Mec- 54	J	Col- 17		
Geo	Mon- 38	Jno Snr	Mec- 54	James	Ire-256		
Hearty	Len-311	Volentine	Mec- 55	Jemima	Ons-108		
J	Mon- 39	Hipps,George	Bur-122	Jesse	Gat-107		
James	Ire-241	Jacob	Bur-122	Jessy	Ire-259		
Jesse	Rob-237	John	Bun- 75	Jno	Ans- 32		
Jesse	Len-311	Hipworth,Jno	Mec- 37	Jno	Ora-145		
Jno	Ans- 28	Hire,Leonard	Sto-143	John	Ora-170		
Jno	Ans- 29	Hisa,Andrew	Bur-112	Joseph	Bla- 12		
Jno	Mon- 38	Hise,Daniel	Bur-115	Letia	Way-245		
John	Len-316	George	Bur-111	Lewis	Sam-151		
Jos	Len-313	Jacob Jr	Bur-115	Lydia	Way-245		
Josua	Rob-236	Lee	Bur-130	Michael	Sam-152		
Martha	Cha-209	Hislett,David	Cha-194	Miles	Cho-227		
Mary	Cha-209	Hislop,James	Ran-167	Moses	Cho-227		
Merril	Mon- 46	Hislor,Michl	Row- 86	Reddick	Ire-259		
Nathan	Ans- 8	Hitchcock,Asell	Row- 48	Samuel	Brt- 62		
Obediah	Ans- 6	Eliza	Row- 47	Samuel	Gat-108		
Pamela	Ons-105	Thomas	Sto-101	Sarah	Hrt-208		
Phillip	Rth-105	Hiter,John	Cur- 83	Sarah	Hrt-211		
Ruth	Cha-209	Hix,A	Col- 19	Simon	Ons-107		
S	Mon- 39	Alexander	Jon-298	Simon Junr	Sam-159		
Sampson	Ans- 25	Chas	Ans- 18	Simon Senr	Sam-159		
Sarah	Rth-104	Daniel	Per-130	Thomas	Gat-107		
Wm	Ans- 29	Eliza	Row- 51	Thos	Cho-227		
Hinton,Old	Grn-126	Henry	Ire-265	William	Ire-256		
Christopher	Cas- 58	Jesse	Bur-119	William	Ran-168		
David	Bun- 77	Jno	Ans- 16	William Senr	Sam-152		
Eliza	Brt- 50	John	Rth-107	William Senr	Sam-162		
Fedrick	Gat-107	John	Sur-189	Wm	Cho-228		
George	Joh-288	Joshua	Mon- 28	Wm	Ora-114		
Hardy	Joh-274	Lewis	Row- 61	Wylie	Mec- 53		
Hardy	Joh-288	Robert	War-179	Hobby,Reuben	Joh-276		
Jno	Mon- 41	S	Ash- 12	Sary	Joh-290		

-148-

Hobby,William	Joh-282	Hodges,Elizabeth	Pit-248	Hogan,Mary		Hal-107
Hobgood,Elizah	Hal-108	George	Pit-235	Thos		Ora-156
Mikajah	Hal-106	Henry	Prq-218	Thos Jr		Ora-151
Hobly,Alexr	Cha-202	Isaiah	Bft- 33	William		Ran-167
Hobs,Daniel	Glf-182	James	Sur-160	Zac		Mon- 30
Hobson,David	Sur-182	James	Bft- 26	Hogen,Marthew		Cah-214
David Sr	Sur-174	Jas	Bft- 20	Hogg,James		Ora-130
Nathan	Sur-188	Jesse	Brt- 57	John		Ran-168
Silas	Sur-192	Jno	Mec- 34	Sarey		Nsh- 88
William	Sur-181	John	Brt- 57	Thomas		Cum-267
Hoby,William	Rob-218	Joseph	Sur-163	Hoggans,James		Lnc-334
Hockada,Warwick	Hal-107	Joseph	Bla- 5	Hoggard,Winefred		Brt- 62
Hockady,James	Grn-122	Joseph	Prq-219	Wm		Brt- 66
Wm	Grn-122	Josiah	Hyd-230	Hoggatt,Hezekiah		Glf-172
Hockeday,Saml	Mec- 28	Lanier	Pit-240	Jas		Glf-172
Hockton,Abner	Sam-164	Mitchum	Hal-107	Joseph		Glf-168
Hocut,Benj	Hrt-210	Oration	Pit-253	N		Glf-168
William	Joh-286	Philemon	Cum-246	W		Glf-183
William B	Joh-285	Portlock Jnr	Pit-253	Hogges,Anthny		Edg- 60
Hodam,George J	Dup- 14	Portlock Sr	Pit-253	James		Edg- 54
Hodg,David	Cas- 47	Richd	Bft- 26	Sarah		Edg- 60
Isaac	Cas- 57	Richd Just	Bft- 26	Hogghead,David		Ire-240
Hodge,Alexr	Mec- 34	Seth	Pit-240	Hoggs,Rebekah		Rth-105
D	Glf-183	Tho	Bft- 22	Saml		Grn-148
Francis	Roc- 30	Thomas Jr	Nor- 69	Hoggshead,Robert		Ire-244
Geo	Glf-160	Thomas Senr	Nor- 68	Hogshead,Samuel		Bun- 97
George	Bur-129	Thos	Len-312	Walter		Bun- 85
George	Row- 77	Welcom	Sur-163	Hogsten,Archebald		Ire-251
Icabad	Mon- 25	William	Sur-163	Hogwood,Howel		War-173
Isaac	Glf-160	William	Hal-107	John		War-173
James	Cum-260	Willie	Pit-260	Lucy		War-177
James	Roc- 31	Hodgeson,Joseph	Dup- 18	Runyon		Ora-122
Jas	Mec- 34	Hodgeston,John	Bft- 34	William		War-184
Jesse	Cum-268	Hodson,Jas	Glf-184	Hoileman,Geo		Bur-130
John	Row- 78	Jesse	Glf-170	Hoine,Tho		Ora-128
John	Row- 78	Jonathan	Glf-160	Hoke,Fredk		Lnc-344
John	Bur-118	Robt	Glf-169	Henry		Lnc-326
John	Bur-129	Thos	Glf-169	Hokett,Richard		Edg- 49
John	Wil-282	William	Glf-172	Holbert,Daniel		Sto-125
John	Pit-262	William	Glf-160	John		Sto-125
Philip	Ora-125	Hoel,Elias	Bft- 36	Holbrook,Ezekiel		Sto-148
Robert	Bur-118	Hoelet,Jesse	Brt- 54	Hargiss		Wil-259
S	Glf-183	Hoff,Thomas	Wsh-226	James		Sto-101
Sam	Ora-130	Zilpha	Wsh-226	James		Sto-132
Samuel	Cas- 57	Hoffler,Francis	Gat-109	James Jnr		Sto-132
Susan	Bur-119	James	Gat-107	John		Sto-111
T	Glf-183	John	Gat-108	John		Sto-148
T	Ash- 12	Thomas	Gat-108	Jere		Wil-259
W	Ash- 6	Hofner,John	Row- 77	Joseph		Sto-148
William	Bur-118	Hog,Nanny	Hal-108	Joseph		Sto-110
Wm	Bla- 6	Pinkney	Row- 83	Larkin		Sur-180
Hodgen,Jo	Glf-176	Robert	Hal-107	Randolph		Wil-260
Hodges,Bartholomew	Sur-162	Hogan,Dan	Ora-156	Robert		Sur-170
Ben	Bft- 26	Danl	Ora-142	William		Wil-259
Benjamin	Dup- 5	Isaiah	Mon- 29	William		Sto-125
Dilinea	Wil-276	J	Glf-176	William Jr		Wil-264
Drury	Bft- 26	James	Edg- 63	Holcom,George		Sur-172
Edmon	Sur-162	John	Roc- 7	Holcomb,Branch		Sur-192
Edy	Bft- 33	John	Lnc-376	George		Cas- 58

Holcomb,John	Bun- 92	Holdness,Sarah	Cas- 57	Holland,Richard	Bun- 77
John Senr	Bun- 92	Holdriten,William	Bur-125	Richard	Nsh- 80
Lewis	Sur-195	Holdsclaw,Henry	Bur-106	Richard	Mor- 69
Mary	Bun- 92	James	Lnc-357	Sarah	Bft- 26
Holdbrook,Vetch	Cab-139	Joseph	Bur-106	Stephen	Glf-182
Holden,B	Bru-226	Holdway,Henry	Wil-267	Thomas	Sto-143
Federick	Mec- 42	John	Wil-260	Thos	Sam-162
Isaac	Ora-117	Holebough,Susana	Row- 78	William	Rth-109
James	Bru-240	Holehouser,Andrew	Row- 66	Hollandsworth,Eliz	Cum-248
Jas	Mec- 32	Holehower,Winnie	Ire-239	John	Cum-249
Job	Bru-238	Holeman,Absolum	Wil-280	Samuel	Cum-248
John	Ora-116	David	Ire-243	Stephen	Cum-266
John	Sto-103	J	Glf-179	Hollaway,John	Cha-193
John	Jon-297	Jacob	Cab-143	John	Wil-259
Mathew	Cha-190	Jacob	Row- 63	Holleman,Samuel	Hrt-211
Saml	Mec- 42	James	Row- 62	Hollemon,Josiah	Hrt-215
Samuel	War-181	Richd	Ora-162	Holler,Christian	Row- 71
Tho	Ora-128	Thomas	Wil-283	Henry	Lnc-351
Wm	Bru-226	William	Wil-277	Jacob	Lnc-346
Holder,Aron	Brt- 65	William	Row- 63	John	Lnc-351
Charles	Sto- 97	Holesay,Richd	Grn-132	John	Lnc-351
Charles	Sto-127	Holeway,Abner	Ire-269	Moses	Pit-242
Davis	Sur-162	Holfsclaw,J	Ash- 12	Zachr	Lnc-346
Dempsey	Wil-280	J	Ash- 12	Hollerday,Jonathan	Mar- 7
E	Glf-159	Holifield,Voll	Sur-170	Thomas	Mar- 5
Elisha	Brt- 65	Voll Jn	Sur-171	Hollewell,John	Mar- 12
Ezekiel	Brt- 65	Holinsworth,Mary	Way-248	Miles	Mar-445
Frederick	Sto-151	Hollack,Mary	Roc- 28	Holley,Absolem	Ans- 14
George	Sam-157	Holladay,John	Brt- 46	Edward	Ans- 21
George V	Sam-161	John	Roc- 2	James	Sam-160
H	Ora-157	Thos	Cha-195	James	Way-234
Henry	Sto-152	Hollaman,Mark	Sto-151	John	Sam-160
Henry	Sto-131	Holland,Anthony	Bur-116	Josiah	Brt- 49
Henry Jnr	Sto-137	Arnold	Ire-262	Moore	Brt- 52
John	Sto-137	Basil	Ire-265	William	Sam-162
Jonathan	Joh-286	Betsey	Wsh-224	Winefred	Way-245
Joseph	Ran-167	Chas	Bft- 27	Holliday,Reuben	Pit-262
Joseph	Sto-129	Daniel	Sam-161	Wm	Ora-128
Joseph	Sto-131	Elisha	Way-244	Robt	Ora-128
Joseph	Sto- 99	Enos	Way-244	Saml	Cha-192
Josiah	Joh-285	Exum	Edg- 50	Hollidy,Joshua	Ran-168
Margrett	Sto-153	Henry	Edg- 68	Robert	Ran-169
Penney	Joh-286	Henry	Edg- 41	Hollimon,Federick	Joh-286
Presly	Sur-164	Isaac	Lnc-331	Fedrch Jr	Joh-286
Solomon	Hay-196	James	Edg- 51	Jesse	Joh-285
Spencer	Sur-164	James	Edg- 69	Tobias	Joh-286
Thomas	Brt- 65	James	Dup- 29	William	Joh-285
William	Sur-187	John	Sto-146	Hollingsworth,Amos	Bun- 95
William	Way-247	John	Sur-179	Enoch	Hay-196
Hoderfield,Ava	Bur-115	John	Ran-167	Henry	Sam-157
Daniel	Wil-284	John	Bft- 38	Henry Senr	Sam-152
Danl	Bur-115	John	Hay-196	Jacob	Bun- 95
Isaac	Rth-105	Julias	Lnc-329	James	Sam-157
Jacob	Rth-107	Marcus	Rth-105	Thos	Sam-152
William	Rth-105	Matthew	Way-235	William	Glf-160
William	Rth-105	Matthew	Lnc-331	William	Dup- 35
Holdhouser,Andr	Row- 39	Oliver	Lnc-331	Willm	Sam-157
M	Row- 39	Peggy	Edg- 62	Zebulon	Sam-152
Holdman,Chrls	Per-130	Phil	Bft- 27	Hollinsworth,J	Ash- 12

Hollinsworth,J	Ash- 12	Holly,Henry	Hal-107	Holt,Ephram	Sto-102
Joseph	Sto-123	Jesse	Sam-162	Ephraim	Sto-135
V	Ash- 12	Jesse	Hal-106	Etheldred	Joh-280
W	Ash- 12	John	Brt- 64	Fetherston	Sto- 94
Hollis,Edward	Wsh-226	Jonathan	Sam-155	Francis	Sto-122
Jesse	Cas- 57	Leonard	Lnc-374	Francis	Ora-159
Holliwell,Stephen	Way-234	Osburn	Sam-155	Francis	Sur-179
Hollman,Henry	Lnc-335	Reddick	Sam-156	Geo	Ora-117
Hollock,William	Roc- 27	Sherod	Sam-156	Harvey	Hal-108
Holloman,Exum	Cha-193	Holmes,Archd	Cum-264	Henry	Ora-171
Jedediah	Edg- 42	Archd	Pas-191	Hez	Ora-171
Nathan	Brt- 62	Benjn	Joh-286	Isaac	Roc- 23
Hollomon,Aaron	Hrt-213	Frederick	Way-240	Isaac Esq	Ora-118
Ann	Hrt-213	Gabriel	Sam-163	Israel	Ora-119
Briant	Hrt-215	George	Dup- 8	James	Ora-119
Cornelus	Hrt-215	Hardy	Way-240	Jean	Ora-171
D Thomas	Nor- 68	Hardy	Sam-156	Jno Jun	Ora-118
Exum	Nor- 68	James	Cum-268	Jno Sen	Ora-171
George	Hrt-215	James	Sam-163	John	Joh-277
Howell	Hrt-212	James	Ora-172	John	Sur-184
Isom	Edg- 45	Jeremiah	Cum-256	John	Row- 60
Josiah	Mor- 56	Jno	Ora-119	John	Nor- 69
Wright	Hrt-215	John	Way-240	John	Wil-280
Holloway,D	Glf-159	Joseph	Bru-240	Joseph	Hal-107
J	Ash- 15	Mary	Bla- 11	Maj J	Ora-171
James	Per-139	Mary	Sam-157	Michael	Ora-171
John	Prq-218	Owen	Sam-163	N Senr	Ora-144
John	Prq-219	Sam	Ora-159	Nathan	Sur-172
Jos Esq	Per-139	Wm	Cho-224	Peter	Bur-111
Obid	Cas- 58	Holms,G	Col- 17	Ryon	Bru-236
Reuben	Rth-107	James	Ire-265	S	Cam-159
Robert	Per-139	Rubin	Row- 37	Saml	Joh-288
Samuel	Nor- 68	Thomas	Row- 89	Samuel	Nor- 69
T	Ora-138	Holomon,ChristopherWay-247		Capt W	Ora-171
Hollowel,Absalom	Pas-190	Ezekiel	Way-247	Wiat	Bun- 83
Jno Jnr	Cho-227	Jeremiah	Way-247	William	Ons-107
Mary	Pas-191	Thomas	Way-240	William	Ora-120
Miriam	Pas-191	Holoway,Brim	Ora-150	William	Joh-290
Samuel	Pas-191	Holowell,Edwin	Way-244	Wm of Ncls	Ora-121
Hollowell,Benj	Hyd-223	Holpher,Jacob	Row- 66	Holteman,Crun	Cab-142
Dicey	Brt- 57	Holsclaw,William	Bur-113	Holton,Widow	Bun- 97
Dinson	Hyd-223	Holsen,Nicholas	Sto-138	Abell	Bla- 5
Exum	Way-249	Holsenbask,Abram	Cas- 57	David	Cab-146
Henry	Prq-218	Holshouser,Jacob	Row- 67	Eph	Bft- 33
Ira	Hyd-230	Mary	Row- 68	Isaac	Glf-170
James	Prq-219	Michl	Row- 68	James	Cum-266
John	Cho-228	Holson,Bask John	Per-147	Jean	Cum-266
Joseph	Way-244	Holsower,Henry	Row- 77	Jesse	Glf-170
Luke	Cho-227	Holsted,Jolif	Cur- 89	Nathl	Glf-170
Rachel	Prq-219	L	Glf-171	William	Cum-266
Reddick	Prq-219	Holston,Averytt	Joh-278	William	Cum-248
Silas	Way-243	Holt,Ambrose	Wil-274	Homer,N	Cam-158
Thomas	Way-237	Anne	Roc- 23	Robt	Ora-149
Thomas	Joh-279	Barnett	Hay-196	Homes,Esther	Bft- 28
William	Prq-219	Benjamin	Wil-273	Gerthan	Bft- 36
William	Way-237	Burwell	Nor- 68	Jezekiah	Grn-132
Wm	Brt- 57	Danl	Ora-144	J	Bru-240
Zadock	Hyd-223	David Esq	Cum-258	Jas	Ans- 10
Hollowl,Moses	Cho-228	Eliz	Ons-103	Richard	Grn-132

Homes,Richard	Grn-149	Hooker,Hardy	Ans- 32	Hoover,Henry	Lnc-363
William	Way-240	Jacob	Ran-169	Jacob	Ire-238
Homesley,Ben	Lnc-331	John	Tyr-204	John	Cab-142
Stephen	Lnc-331	Stephen	Pas-191	Philip	Row- 54
Honbarrier,Daniel	Row- 68	William	Dup- 16	Solomon	Lnc-326
Henry	Row- 67	William	Sto-112	Hope,Abner	Cab-136
John	Row- 68	William	Sto-155	Benj	Grn-137
Honey,Charity	Nsh- 74	Wm	Tyr-205	Catey	Cab-137
Robt	Ans- 15	Hooks,Benjamin	Mec- 43	Henry	Lnc-330
Honeycut,Britain	Joh-275	David	Dup- 6	Has	Cab-138
Drury	Joh-276	Drusilla	Way-243	Samuel	Rth-105
John	Sam-161	E	Col- 18	Thos	Mec- 48
Nancy	Joh-276	Eliza	Grn-122	Hopgood,Ezekiah	Grn-141
Rowel	Ire-258	Ephraim	Way-243	Fowler	Grn-138
Siddy	Joh-276	G	Col- 20	John	Grn-141
William	Joh-275	Jacob	Mec- 23	Thos	Grn-141
Honeycutt,Ambrose	Mon- 49	Jno	Mec- 44	Hopis,Adam	Lnc-376
Eli	Mon- 48	John	Way-252	Hopkins,Alexander	Bur-119
Elisha	Mon- 49	R	Col- 17	Alexander	Wsh-223
James	Sam-161	Robert	Way-245	Alsey	Nsh- 91
John	Sam-157	Robt	Way-253	Ann	Grn-144
Moses	Bun- 77	Susan	Dup- 6	Arnold	Pit-245
W	Mon- 38	Washington	Way-249	Betsey	Mon- 18
Willm Senr	Sam-161	Whitmill	Mec- 45	Charles	Grn-143
Wm	Sam-157	William Jr	Way-253	Charles	Ran-169
Hood,A	Cam-158	William Sr	Way-252	Crafford	Nsh- 91
Bole R	Way-239	Hooper,Widow	Lnc-344	Daniel	Edg- 71
Britton	Way-250	Abraham	Bun- 77	Frederick	Edg- 60
Bryan	Joh-274	Abraham	Wil-265	George	Hyd-229
Charles	Joh-288	Absolam	Hay-195	George	Grn-144
Edward	Way-247	Benjamin	Cas- 57	Hampton	Mon- 19
Jesse	Cas- 57	Biddy	Wil-271	Hezekiah	Hal-106
Jerry	Mec- 41	C	Bru-230	Jesse	Bur-131
Jno	Mec- 40	Charles	Ire-255	John	Sur-183
John	Roc- 21	D	Bru-230	John	Lnc-360
John	Bur-130	Ezekel	Cur- 81	John	Brt- 53
John	Glf-181	Hannah	Bun- 97	John	Bft- 39
John	Hay-196	James	Ire-248	John	Mon- 44
Nathaniel	Joh-279	James	Bun- 86	John	Grn-138
Reubeon	Mec- 41	James	Rth-104	John	Grn-137
Richard	Wil-274	John	Ire-249	Jonathan	Roc- 19
Solomon	Ire-247	John	Hay-196	Joseph	Nsh- 83
Thomas	Len-312	Noul	Cur- 81	Joseph	Brt- 47
Thomas	Per-139	Susanah	Cas- 57	Joseph	Sto-153
Turnus	Mec- 39	Woodley	Cas- 57	Joseph	Wsh-228
William	Joh-278	Zachariah	Cas- 72	Joshua	Glf-181
William	Len-311	Hoopper,Elijah	Sto-152	Josiah	Brt- 46
Hoodenpile,Philip	Bun- 94	Hoose,David	Ons-103	Lewis	Sto-108
Hoods,Robt	Mec- 40	Hooser,John	Sur-188	Lewis	Sto-144
Robt	Mec- 22	Hooten,Charles	Hyd-221	Philip	Tyr-213
Hoof,John	Fra-100	Joseph	Hyd-221	Richd	Mon- 18
Hook,Charles	Dup- 5	Salley	Bft- 33	Robert	Hyd-227
John	Cab-142	William	Hyd-222	Sally	Rth-107
Mathias	Cab-142	Hoots,Anthony	Sur-191	Thomas	Tyr-206
Michael	Hay-196	Daniel	Sur-191	Thomas	Roc- 19
Hooker,David	Sto-145	Henry	Sur-191	Thos Jr	Tyr-209
Eli	Ran-168	John	Wil-263	William	Cha-195
Eliza	Tyr-210	Hoover,Adam	Sur-182	William	Edg- 71
Francis	Pas-191	Daniel	Lnc-362	Wm	Ora-118

Hopkins, Wm	Hyd-231	Horn, Joel	Sam-153	Horny, Phillip Jr	Glf-167
Willie	Fra- 99	John	Edg- 64	Horrilson, Abner	Per-130
Hopper, Anne	Wil-271	John	Sur-184	Horse, Widow	Lnc-340
Charles	Bur-116	Joseph Sr	Ora-142	Anthony	Lnc-336
Darby Jun	Roc- 9	Joshua Jr	Ora-142	Christian	Lnc-334
Darby Sen	Roc- 9	Josiah	Edg- 60	Jacob	Lnc-339
Jasper	Bur-116	Laurence	Rch-195	John	Lnc-338
Jeremiah	Roc- 9	Lee	Nsh- 86	Peter	Bur-106
John	Roc- 10	Lurana	Edg-284	Horseford, John	Roc- 16
Joseph Jun	Roc- 9	Mary	Row- 60	Richard	Roc- 16
Joseph Sen	Roc- 9	Meshack	Way-245	Horten, Eldridge	Cas- 58
Joshua Sen	Roc- 9	Michael	Cum-264	Elisha	Mar- 9
Thomas	Roc- 9	Michael	Ans- 9	Jacob	Sto-154
Zechariah	Bur-116	Nicholas	Sur-177	James	Mar-446
Hoppers, John	Sur-195	Peter	Roc- 14	James	Cas- 58
Hoppus, D	Ash- 14	Pheraby	Way-245	John	Cas- 58
Hopson, Charles	Cha-212	Nathaniel	Rob-240	Zachariah	Cas- 58
E	Ora-141	Silas	Joh-284	Horton, Anthony	Rth-107
George	Cha-194	Stephen	Mon- 22	Benjn	Cha-192
Henry	Way-250	Sukey	Gat-110	Geo	Bun- 82
Henry Jr	Rth-105	Thomas	Ons- 98	George	Cas- 57
Isaac	Cha-212	Thomas	Nsh- 89	Howel	Rth-105
J	Ora-133	Thomas	Nsh- 89	James	Ora-164
John	Cha-08	William	Edg- 55	James	Nor- 68
Joseph	Cha-210	William	Nor- 68	Jesse	Cha-191
Joshua	Cha-205	William Senr	Ora-169	John	Car-176
Stephen	Cha-212	Wm	Ora-142	John	Cas- 57
William	Ora-166	Wm	Nsh- 89	John (H)	Cas- 57
Wm	Cah-194	Wm	Nsh- 89	Joshua	Wil-269
Y	Ora-141	Hornady, Chris	Ora-133	Julius	Hal-106
Hopston, Ginny	Jon-298	J	Ora-133	Lewis	Cha-193
William	Jon-297	Hornbuck, James	Cas- 58	Mary	Hrt-213
Horah, Hugh	Row- 89	Hornbuckle, Eliz	Cas- 72	N	Ash- 3
Horbacker, Christian	Cab-140	Horne, Abel	Ora-123	Willeford	Hrt-211
Hordry, Wens	Glf-180	Archd	Ora-117	William	Cha-199
Horn, Absalom	Edg- 60	Elisha	Hal-106	William	Rth-106
Amos	Edg- 69	Mrs. Sally	Fra-100	William Sr	Cha-203
Ann	Edg- 61	Turner	Brt- 54	Wm	Ora-164
Bythal	Edg- 55	Wm	Ora-152	Wm	Ora-111
Charity	Nor- 68	Wm Junr	Ora-126	Willis	Per-148
Elijah	Edg- 61	Horner, Geo	Ora-128	Zepheniah	Bun- 78
Edward	Edg- 62	George	Ora-163	Hosea, Hugh	Prq-218
Elias	Mon- 47	James	Ora-164	James	Nor- 68
Elijah	Edg- 60	John	Ora-151	Sally	Pas-191
Elizabeth	Way-245	Tho Jun	Ora-174	Thos	Prq-218
Elizabeth	Row- 80	Hornerdy, Lewis	Ora-132	Hosey, Thomas	Joh-286
Henry	Edg- 66	Sol	Ora-132	Hoskins, A	Glf-183
Henry	Ons- 95	Hornesley, Joseph	Lnc-337	Baker	Prq-219
Henry	Nsh- 86	Horney, --ittes	Cur- 87	Bartten	Tyr-203
Isaac	Nsh- 89	Jeffery	Row- 46	Chas	Tyr-202
J	Ora-148	Jessey	Glf-169	E	Glf-183
Jacob	Edg- 67	John	Glf-165	Edmd	Cho-220
Jacob	Nsh- 77	M	Glf-167	Eli	Glf-172
James Jr	Ora-142	Horniblow, Eliz	Cho-220	Hanner	Glf-182
James Junr	Nor- 68	Horniday, Simon	Ora-119	James	Tyr-206
James Senr	Nor- 68	Horning, Betsy	Pas-191	Jno	Cho-230
Jesse	Sur-176	Horns, Abisha (Negro)		John	Glf-182
Jesse	Ora-142		Edg- 62	John	Glf-171
Joel	Joh-284	Horny, Phillip	Glf-170	Moses	Glf-172

-153-

Name	Ref	Name	Ref	Name	Ref
Hoskins,Richd	Cho-226	Houston,Archibald	Cab-138	Howard,Elijah Senr	Brt- 63
Wm	Cho-226	David	Ire-257	Elisha	Hrt-214
Hosong,John	Bur-115	David	Mec- 29	Eliz	Ons-106
Hossee,Clem	Ora-159	Elenor	Cab-139	Elizabeth	Sur-164
Nathl	Ora-129	George	Med- 39	Elizabeth	Hyd-220
Hossom,Coonrod	Rth-107	Henry	Mec- 39	Francis	Cas- 57
Hottsdaw,Sussey	Rob-234	James	Ire-257	Geo	Bun- 94
Hough,Jas	Ans- 5	James	Row- 73	Geo	Row- 44
Moody	Ans- 6	Jas	Mec- 29	George	Wil-275
Wm	Ans- 12	Jno	Mec- 29	Graves	Cas- 58
Houk,Fredk	Bur-130	John	Mec- 34	Grenbury	Ire-268
Geo	Bur-129	John	Jon-298	Hardy	Edg- 63
Jacob	Row- 48	John	Cab-138	Henry	Cum-262
John	Row- 48	Joseph	Ire-244	Henry	Row- 57
Houpt,Catharine	Ire-261	Mary	Mec- 29	Henry	Ons-106
Jacob	Ire-261	Nancy	Cab-138	Henry	Cas- 57
John	Ire-261	Placebo	Ire-267	Hyrum	Mon- 28
House,Dudley	War-170	Samuel	Ire-245	I H	Bft- 37
Dudley Jr	War-170	Samuel	Ire-245	J	Cam-159
Elias	Cab-140	Thos	Mec- 39	James	Edg- 63
Elisha	Sam-159	William	Ire-246	James	Row- 81
George	Sam-159	Wm	Mec- 40	James	Rch-197
Green (moved)	Grn-123	Wm	Cab-139	James	Cum-265
Israel	Edg- 56	Houze,Green	Fra- 83	James	Len-319
Isham	War-174	James	Fra- 94	James	Hyd-223
James	Brt- 56	Mrs. Martha	Fra- 83	Jas	Mec- 30
John	Cab-140	William	Fra- 83	Jesse	Sur-171
John	Sam-150	Hovater,Jacob	Ire-265	Jessee	Edg- 62
John	Pit-254	Hover,Henry	Mec- 54	Jo	Lnc-374
John Junr	Sam-160	Jacob	Row- 54	John	Grn-133
Peter	Ora-150	Andrew	Lnc-373	John	Row- 57
Simon	Len-321	Hovery,Seth	Hyd-222	John	Row- 47
Thomas	Pit-245	Hovis,Frederick	Lnc-329	John	Ora-158
W	Ora-141	George	Lnc-340	John	Len-319
William	Pit-245	John	Lnc-376	John	Len-315
Housen,David	Ora-167	How,R Esq	Bru-232	John	Row- 82
Houser,Henry	Lnc-329	Howard,Alexn	Ans- 13	John	Wil-272
Jacob	Lnc-335	Allen	Lnc-362	John	Car-172
John	Lnc-338	Allen	Grn-141	John Jr	Row- 82
John	Lnc-338	Ann	Car-172	John Jr	Wil-272
Peter	Lnc-335	Arthur	Jon-298	Jonathan	Bur-104
Housten,Edward	Dup- 29	Bally	Bft- 38	Joseph	Bur-125
Eliza	Dup- 29	Barnet	Grn-141	Joseph	Ons- 99
Elizabeth	Dup- 29	Barnet	Len-315	Joshua	Wil-282
George E	Dup- 10	Benjn	Sam-161	Josia	Row- 44
Henry	Dup- 30	Benjamin	Row- 82	Josiah	Jon-298
James	Dup- 29	Benjamin	Brt- 63	Leven	Row- 63
Jno	Mec- 29	Benjamin	Ons- 97	Littleton	Cum-257
Saml	Mec- 48	Benjamin	Wil-276	Luke	Hrt-214
Samuel	Dup- 29	Benjamin Jr	Wil-275	Mathew	Row- 78
Stephen	Dup- 29	Brodie	Grn-141	Micaja	Row- 44
Thos	Mec- 38	Charles	Sur-164	Mincon B	Sam-162
Will H	Dup- 30	Christian	Row- 57	Mordacai	Lnc-362
William	Row- 82	Christopher	Wil-272	Modecai	Lnc-357
William A	Dup- 29	Clabon	Sur-176	Phillip	Sur-183
Wm	Mec- 38	Durkas	Cha-199	Phillup	Wil-262
Wm	Mec- 29	Edmon	Row- 66	Polley	Nsh- 90
Wm	Mec- 29	Edmond	Jon-297	Richard	Lnc-363
Houston,Andw	Cab-138	Elijah Jnr	Brt- 63	Saml	Len-320

-154-

Howard,Samuel	Lnc-363	Howell,Eppy	Bur-126	Howland,Christopher	Car-175
Simon	Car-171	Exum	Nor- 68	William	Car-175
Stephen	Hrt-213	Fanny	Nor- 69	Zepheniah	Car-175
Stephen	Edg- 50	Henry	Way-249	Howlet,John	Per-151
Test---	Ons-101	Henry	Way-252	Obediah	Roc- 28
Thomas	Hyd-231	Henry	Way-251	Howlett,A	Glf-160
Thos S	Ora-147	Holliday	Nor- 69	Harmon	Glf-181
William	Sur-189	Jacinth	Way-254	Howlin,Anala	Bft- 21
William	Cum-265	James	Way-252	Howling,John	Bft- 31
William	Row- 57	James	Bur-115	Redk	Bft- 32
William	Lnc-363	James	Mar-446	Howse,Lawrence	Ons- 98
William	Row- 63	John	Way-237	Howser,John	Row- 86
Wm	Mec- 30	John	Edg- 53	Howson,John	Hal-108
Wm	Mon- 28	John	Rth-109	Howze,Isaac	Fra- 96
Wm	Ans- 30	John	Way-233	Isaac Junr	Fra- 96
Wm	Row- 58	John	Hay-196	Hoy,Charles	Nsh- 86
Wm Jnr	Car-172	John	Glf-187	Hoyle,Adam	Lnc-373
Wm Senr	Car-172	John	Way-253	and Esq	Lnc-336
Williby	Edg- 64	John	Way-251	David	Rth-108
Willis	Edg- 63	John	Mon- 44	Henry	Rth-108
Wilson	Edg- 54	John Junr	Nor- 69	Jacob	Lnc-335
Howcott,Nathl	Cho-226	John Senr	Nor- 69	Jacob	Lnc-329
Howe,Mrs.	Brt- 49	Jordan	Way-232	John	Lnc-332
Author	Cho-223	Joshua	Rth-109	John	Rth-108
Howel,Bartin	Cum-264	Jourdan	Mon- 40	John Jr	Rth-108
David	Joh-281	Lewis	Way-252	Martin	Rth-108
David	Sur-189	Mary	Roc- 18	Peter	Lnc-342
Edmund	Wsh-219	Mills	Way-253	Hoyles,John	Bla- 8
Eli	Cab-147	Mills	Way-233	Huabbard,Gade	Rob-219
Henry	Mon- 47	Paul	Bur-111	Hubbard,Benjamin	Wil-273
James	Sur-174	Ralph	Way-233	Betsey	Cas- 57
Joseph	Cab-148	S	Cam-160	E	Ash- 13
Joseph	Cab-147	Samuel	Bur-127	Frumory	Cas- 57
Joseph	Row- 59	Stephen	Way-233	Henry	Joh-277
Marmaduke	Rob-242	Thomas	Rth-109	Isaac	Hal-108
Mills	Cum-268	Thos	Mon- 44	Isham	Wil-273
Osborn	Joh-281	Thos	Grn-143	James	Joh-277
Ralph	Rob-242	Whittock	Mar- 5	Jere	Ora-171
Rebeca	Grn-143	William	Edg- 54	Jo	Ora-160
Robert	Sur-184	William	Way-237	John	Glf-164
Robt	Cha-212	Woodard	Way-252	John	Cas- 57
Shadrick	Rob-242	Woodward	Way-232	Joseph	Per-139
Thos	Cha-211	Wright	Way-237	Nathaniel	Wil-273
Wm	Cab-147	Howerton,Ezekiel	Edg- 57	R	Ash- 13
Zachariah	Hal-107	T	Glf-160	Ralph	Cas- 57
Howell,Amy	Edg- 45	Thomas	Edg- 57	Solomon	Car-184
Ann	Edg- 40	Howet,Ben	Pas-191	W	Ash- 7
Archelus	Way-251	Howett,Ann	Tyr-213	William	Cas- 57
Arthur	Way-242	William	Tyr-213	Woodson	Per-139
Arthur	Way-249	Howie,George	Mec- 24	Hubbel,Hillard	Wil-257
Arthur	Way-236	Jas S	Mec- 30	Hubbert,Burges	Ans- 8
Benjn	Cas- 57	Robt	Mec- 24	Jno	Ans- 20
Benjn	Way-235	Saml	Mec- 38	Wm	Ans- 8
Burwell	Way-252	Samuel	Cum-267	Huber,Danl	Lnc-326
Caleb	Way-235	Wm	Mec- 39	Thos	Lnc-326
Dancel	Way-251	Wm	Mec- 30	Huchins,David	Sto-123
Daniel	Fra- 80	Wm	Mec- 24	John A	Grn-140
Eli	Edg- 63	Howington,John	War-176	Huchison,Joshua	Grn-145
Elizebeth	Ans- 28	Riley	Roc- 17	Huckaba,Bartlett	Mon- 45

-155-

Huckaba,Thos	Mon- 45	Hudson,Thomas	Row- 65	Huffman,Martin	Lnc-348
Thos	Mon- 45	Thomas	Row- 72	Martin	Lnc-374
Wm	Mon- 45	Thomas	Hal-108	Mary	Ons-104
Huckabey,John	Fra- 90	Uriah	Prq-219	Michl	Row- 78
Huckaby,John	Rth-104	Wilie	Ire-241	Philip	Sto-135
Huckeby,Benj	Mor- 57	William	Row- 59	Philip	Sto-102
Joshua	Bun- 96	William J	Ire-242	Huffner,Martin	Row- 67
Huckins,John	Sto-122	Hudsperth,Carter	Sur-169	Hufham,John	Dup- 21
Huddleston,Jonathan	Glf-167	David	Sur-178	Hufhines,Danl	Ora-145
Huddlestone,Chas	Rth-104	Giles	Sur-177	Jacb	Ora-145
David	Rth-105	Morgan	Sur-177	John	Sur-189
David	Rth-104	Hudspeth,George	Su-r170	P	Ora-145
John	Rth-105	Hue,George	Bur-108	Hufman,Benj	Grn-126
Hudgins,Abner	Dup- 10	Jacob	Bur-108	Dan	Ora-137
Harison	Sto-100	Huel,Allen	Pit-249	Jacob	Lnc-351
Humphrie	Gat-113	James	Pit-254	Jacob	Grn-126
J	Ora-141	Solomon	Pit-254	Jacob Senr	Lnc-351
Jno	Ora-150	Huey,Peter	Cab-144	Michael	Lnc-351
John P	Gat-113	Hugg,Betsy	Car-175	Hufmire,Clec	Pas-191
Joseph	Gat-107	Daniel	Sur-176	Hufstotler,George	Lnc-332
Moses	Ora-150	Israel	Sur-167	Henry	Lnc-329
Right	Rth-107	J	Ash- 12	Henry	Lnc-332
Samuel	Sto-100	Jacob	Row- 40	Jacob	Lnc-331
Thomas	Per-130	Jesse	Sur-167	John	Lnc-332
Thos	Ora-150	John	Sur-168	John	Lnc-332
Hudler,King	Len-310	John	Sto-134	Mich	Lnc-332
Hudleston,Dnl	Mec- 28	Jonathan	Sur-167	John	Lnc-327
Robt	Mec- 28	Joshua	Sur-169	Huges,M	Col- 19
Jessey	Grn-139	Philip	Bun- 85	Huggins,Alexander	Ire-261
Hudleston,John	Grn-123	Reuben	Fra- 88	Cooper	Ons- 97
Hudley,Elizabeth	Per-130	Richard	Car-175	Easther	Dup- 9
Hudnal,John	Cas- 58	Thomas	Way-248	Edward	Bun- 98
Hudnell,Cullen	Bft- 33	William	Sur-192	Elizabeth	Jon-297
Whitce	Bft- 33	Huffhine,Daniel	Sto-152	Ja	Ora-153
Wm	Bft- 33	Jacob	Sto-152	Jacob	Ons- 97
Hudson,Abel	Roc- 13	Huffhines,Jacob	Ora-120	Jacob	Jon-297
Abiah	Row- 64	Hufhum,Ann	Bla- 11	Jacob	Ora-127
Alexr	Lnc-374	Huffman,Adam	Row- 77	James	Jon-297
Charnol	Cha-201	Anthony	Row- 54	James	Lnc-328
Danl Jr	Lnc-374	Chrisn	Ons-104	John	Lnc-331
Edward	Hal-108	Christor	Lnc-351	John	Rth-104
J	Bru-224	Daniel	Row- 51	John	Ire-241
James	Row- 74	David	Row- 38	Luke	Dup- 11
Jeremiah	Ire-251	David	Row- 50	Luke	Ons- 96
Jeremiah	Cas- 57	David	Row- 54	Luke Junr	Ons-103
Joel	Roc- 18	Geo	Glf-177	Penny	Jon-297
Joel Senr	Roc- 18	George	Lnc-348	Robert	Lnc-331
John	Fra- 94	George	Sto-144	Robert	Ire-240
John	Lnc-374	George	Sto-108	Sarah	Lnc-328
John	Cas- 58	Henry	Sto-108	William	Dup- 26
Jonathan	Lnc-363	Henry	Sto-144	Hugh,J	Ash- 15
Joseph	Mec- 55	Henry	Lnc-348	Hughbanks,Mary	Mar- 15
Mary	War-178	J	Ora-140	Hughes,Chas	Ora-111
Richd	Row- 56	Jacob	Row- 53	E	Cam-163
Robert	Roc- 12	Jacob	Ons-104	Elizabeth	Row- 89
Robert	Roc- 14	John	Lnc-329	James	Cas- 57
Rodey	Sam-160	Joseph	Lnc-348	John	Roc- 8
Starlin	Sur-162	Lewis	Sto-108	John	Sur-163
T	Bru-224	Lewis	Sto-144	John	Row- 82

Hughes,John	Cas- 57	Hulin,William	Row- 76	Humphries,Thomas	Pas-191
John	Ora-125	Hull,Benjamin	Lnc-333	Thomas	Roc- 31
Joseph	Bur-107	John	Cha-212	William	Bur-111
Judith	Row- 84	John	Glf-185	Humphry,Jas	Rob-235
Sarah	Cas- 58	Joseph	Rch-209	Jno	Rob-235
Thomas	Row- 66	Samuel	Sto-155	Lucia	Rob-235
Wiley	Cas- 57	Saml	Lnc-331	Thomas	Sto-151
William	Roc- 8	Hulm,Hamlin	Hal-106	Wm	Rob-235
Hughey,Andrew	Row- 75	Hulme,Jesse	Wil-272	Hundle,William	Gat-109
Isaac	Row- 71	Joseph	Wil-277	Hundley,Humphy	Bft- 38
Henry S	Row- 73	Moses	Wil-277	James Sr	Way-237
James	Bun- 88	Majr William	Wil-275	John	Sto-108
James	Ire-241	Humble,David	Mon- 33	John	Sto-157
Joseph	Bun- 93	Mary	Mon- 32	Hunings,Thos	Tyr-203
Hughs,Alexander	Ire-240	Humbles,John	Hyd-222	Hunley,Abner	Bun- 80
Allen	Brt- 44	Humpher,John	Row- 62	Hunnings,Edward	Tyr-209
Annaretta	Brt- 52	Humphes,James	Rth-106	Patsey	Tyr-209
Benjn	Way-233	Humphlet,A----	Ons- 96	Hunnycut,Hardy	Hay-195
Christopher	Ire-241	Humphres,David	Rth-108	Hunnycutt,Henry	Mec- 29
Cornelius	Brt- 50	John	Rth-108	Huns,James	Way-240
D Joseph	Per-130	Samuel	Rth-108	Hunsucker,George	Bur-114
Edith	Way-236	William	Rth-108	John	Bur-114
Eliz	Brt- 53	Humphress,Peggy	Bft- 27	Hunt,A	Mon- 37
Evan	Cha-204	Humphrey,Asa	Ons-104	Abel	Row- 51
Francis	Mec- 35	David	Ora-162	Abner	Glf-164
George	Hay-195	Francis	Ons-104	Abraham	Row- 40
Henry	Brt- 53	Henry	Glf-171	Abraham	Rth-104
Hillery	Brt- 51	Jacob	Ons-104	Ale-	Glf-163
Isaac	Wil-276	John	Wil-275	Alexr	Mor- 67
J	Ora-139	John (L F)	Wil-283	Allen	Glf-164
J Snr	Ora-139	John	Ons-109	Anderson	Sur-162
James	Ire-240	Joseph	Ons-104	Archd	Cha-200
James	Hay-195	Lewis	Ons-104	Arthur	Bun- 87
John	Cha-214	Lott	Ons-105	Benjn	Fra- 90
John	Hay-195	Owen	Wil-275	Berrymon	Cas- 58
Joseph	Hay-196	Penelope	Ons-107	Charles	Roc- 32
Josiah	Brt- 53	Polly	Wil-279	Charles	Row- 87
Lydia	Lnc-335	Thos	Cas- 57	Daniel	Row- 59
Margaret	Rch-191	Whitehead	Ons- 99	David	Row- 40
Mary	Brt- 46	William	Row- 83	David	Nsh- 88
Ralph	Bun- 74	Willm	Cas- 57	David	Sur-185
Saml	Ora-137	Humphreys,Collins	Cas- 57	Drew	Hrt-211
Samuel	Hay-196	Elisha	Prq-218	Edward	Grn-124
Stephen	Brt- 52	Ezekiel	Edg- 54	Eleazer	Glf-165
Sterling	Per-130	H	Glf-152	Eleazor	Glf-182
Whitmell	Brt- 49	Hal	Per-130	Elija	Row- 40
William	Per-129	Hal	Per-130	Enoch	Row- 87
Wm	Cha-204	Owen Jr	Wil-276	Grissom	Mor- 67
Hughlet,John	Cas- 57	Humphries,A	Cam-163	Henry	Fra- 99
Hughster,George	Cas- 57	D	Cam-157	Henry	Ora-118
Hugrey,Henry	Row- 74	David	Bur-118	Henry	Lnc-360
Huie,James	Row- 89	Hansel	Ora-162	Isaiah	Glf-162
Huit,Henry	Pas-191	Isaiah	Sur-190	Isum	Cur- 85
Lewis	Lnc-346	J	Cam-163	Jacob	Glf-186
Hulgin,Robert	Roc- 21	J	Cam-155	James	Lnc-337
Stephen	Roc- 21	James	Bur-111	James	Glf-161
Hulin,Arthur	Row- 82	John	Cas- 57	James	Grn-127
John	Row- 76	Jonathan	Pas-191	James	Nsh- 75
William	Row- 82	M	Ash- 8	Jas	Rob-221

Name	Ref	Name	Ref	Name	Ref
Hunt,Jesse	Fra- 94	Hunter,Jacob	War-174	Huntsucker,Wm	Mor- 59
Jesse	Glf-162	Jacob	Fra- 94	Huraby,Richd Esq	Cum-254
John	Grn-145	James	Roc- 21	Hural,Rachal	Gat-111
John	Cab-138	James	Rth-108	Hurdle,Abram	Prq-219
John	Ora-116	James	Rch-209	Cader	Cho-228
John	Nor- 68	James	Glf-155	Hardy	Ora-120
John Jr	Grn-144	James	Hal-108	Harmon	Cho-228
Johnathan	Grn-132	Jas	Mec- 47	Harmon Snr	Cho-229
Jonathan	Bun- 77	Jno	Mec- 48	Henry	Cho-228
Joseph	Row- 45	Joab	Dup- 34	James	Ora-124
Mary	Grn-127	John	Fra- 80	Jos	Cho-230
Mrs. Mary	Fra- 95	John	Sto- 98	Joseph	Gat-110
Mary	Glf-185	John	Brt- 52	Moses	Prq-219
Mat	Nsh- 72	John	Row- 66	Reuben	Cho-229
Nathaniel	Row- 45	John	Dup- 10	Hure,Leonard	Sto-107
Nathl	Grn-124	John	Rth-106	Hurley,Absolum	Wil-285
Oliver	Row- 51	John	Sto-128	Amos	Cha-193
Onesoforus	Ons-108	John	Bun- 82	Clement	Wil-285
Patience	Nor- 69	John B	Mar-445	Daniel	Mon- 22
Rhodia	Nsh-643	Joseph	Mec- 39	Darkis	Joh-289
Sarah	Grn-144	Josiah	Lnc-333	Edward	Mon- 22
Semie	Cur- 85	L Charles	Cas- 57	Elijah	Cha-214
T Snr	Glf-184	Lewis	Rth-109	Francis	Wil-266
Thos	Ora-146	Libius	Car-179	James	Mon- 22
W	Glf-162	Margeret	Mec- 39	James	Rch-198
William	Rth-108	Margerett	Mec- 48	John	Wil-284
William	Rth-107	Mary	Mec- 36	John	Cha-191
William K	Rth-108	Micheal	Mec- 28	Joshua	Mon- 22
William Jr	Glf-162	Nancy	Ora-121	Josiah	Cha-211
Wm	Grn-140	Nathan	Bun- 90	Larkin Jr	Wil-285
Wm	Glf-182	Peter	Rth-106	Moses	Rch-198
Z	Glf-164	Prisiller	Nsh- 77	Rachel	Wil-285
Zebelin	Row- 45	Rachel	Roc- 32	Stephen	Mon- 22
Hunter,Abner	Bur-124	Richard	Lnc-357	William	Wil-284
Absalem	Grn-136	Robert	Roc- 23	Wm	Mon- 22
Andrew	Bur-124	Robert	Bun- 80	Hurndon,E	Ora-141
Andrew	Ora-114	Rosey	Row- 66	Hurry,Sterling	Ora-161
Aron	Ora-158	Saml	Glf-160	Hurst,Hardy	Mar- 9
Benjn	Sto-128	Thos	Mec- 39	James	Mar- 15
Cader	Brt- 51	Timothy	Brt- 51	John	Way-241
Cloe	Gat-106	Valitine	Row- 65	Wm	Len-318
Cordal	Nsh- 77	William	Gat- 31	Hurste,Andrew	Dup- 10
David	Mar-445	William	Sto- 98	Will B	Dup- 6
Drewry	Nsh- 77	William	Rth-107	Hurt,Jesse	Mon- 29
Edw	Dup- 34	William	Dup- 33	Joel	Sur-177
Edward	Gat-105	William	Dup- 35	John	Sur-193
Elizabeth	Cha-209	William	Sto-128	Robert	Sur-172
Elizabeth	Sto- 99	William	Bun- 89	William	Sur-172
Elizabeth	Joh-290	William B	Mar-446	Zacheus	Per-139
Elizabeth	Sto-130	Huntington,Roswell	Ora-115	Zachius	Per-130
Ephraim	Ans- 30	Huntley,Elijah	Ans- 18	Hurte,James	Wil-263
George	Roc- 25	Robt	Ans- 10	Hurton,Edwd	Lnc-329
Henry	Mec- 48	Stephen	Ans- 11	Husay,S	Glf-165
Henry	Mec- 23	Huntsacer,Davolt	Lnc-351	Thos	Glf-165
Hogan	Dup- 7	John	Lnc-351	Husband,William	Rch-195
Humphry	Lnc-373	William	Lnc-351	Huse,Archd	Mor- 61
Isaac	Gat-105	Huntsinger,H	Ash- 6	Benjamin	Rth-108
Isaac	Gat-106	J	Ash- 10	John	Bur-130
Isaac	War-174	Huntsucker,Geo	Mor- 64	Phillip	Rth-108

-158-

Huse,William	Rth-108	Hutchins,John	Nor- 68	Hux,Benjamin	Hal-108
Wm	Mor- 68	John Jr	Sur-171	Nathan	Hal-107
Young	Rth-108	John Sr	Sur-191	Hyat,Shadrack	Bun- 93
Husey,John	Cab-146	Jonathan	Sur-175	Hyatt,Edward	Hay-196
Hushett,Nathaniel	Cha-210	Josiah	Sur-172	Elijah	Hay-196
Husk,Jo	Ora-157	Nathaniel	Cur- 89	Hezekiah	Bur-124
John	Cum-241	Nicholas	Sur-175	John	Row- 49
Huske,Allen	Ora-111	Partrick	Sur-171	Meshack	Bun- 88
Huskers,Nancey Y	Cur- 89	Peter	Cur- 89	Shadrick	Hay-196
Huskins,Robert	Lnc-376	Richard	Cur- 89	Simon	Bur-121
Robert	Lnc-366	Robert	Sto-140	Hyde,Harry	Ons-101
Husky,Wm	Grn-149	Samuel	Sto-131	James	Row- 73
Huson,Benj Lee	Brt-209	Sarey	Cur- 89	John	Row- 73
Thomas	Lnc-336	Sarey	Cur- 89	Luther	Ons-101
Hussey,John E	Dup- 31	Strangmon	Sur-172	Susanna	Ans- 16
Joseph	Row- 55	Thomas	Sur-176	William	Bur-125
Judeah	Ran-168	William	Hrt-214	Hyer,Isaac	Row- 54
Miles	Cum-241	William	Sur-176	Hyman,Hugh	Mar- 3
Thomas	Hyd-234	William	Sur-172	Joel	Brt- 46
William	Ran-167	Hutchison,-----	Mec- 25	John	Edg- 45
Husstoller,Henry	Lnc-337	J	Ora-160	Lamiel	Mar- 7
Hussy,John	Cum-269	Jesse	Row- 61	Lewis	Mar- 12
Hust,George	Bun- 94	R	Ora-160	Olive	Mar- 3
Penelope	Cho-220	Hutson,Abel	Hyd-230	Thomas	Mar- 3
Sarah	Per-139	Aquale	Hyd-230	Thomas	Mar- 10
Huston,DAvid	Lnc-336	Archable	Hyd-232	Thomas	Mar- 10
Thos	Mec- 28	Crusey	Cas- 57	William	Mar- 3
Zadok	Ora-124	Elijah	Hyd-230	William Jr	Edg- 53
Husy,Samuel	Cab-146	Elijah	Hyd-230	William Sr	Edg- 53
Hutchens,James	Ora-128	Elizabeth	Hyd-230	Hynsley,Robt	Cha-198
Walice	Cur- 89	J	Glf-178	Hypock,Polly	Jon-298
Hutcherson,Asariah	Sto-123	James	Cab-144	William	Jon-298
Hezekiah	Ans- 33	James	Hyd-233	Hyson,John	Jon-298
Jas	Ans- 33	Jesse	Mar- 11	Hyter,Asa	Pas-191
Jno K	Ans- 33	Joakim	Ans- 21	John	Pas-191
John	Roc- 10	John	Len-321	Tom	Pas-191
Philip	Ans- 33	Jos	Cho-228	Hwet,A	Cam-163
Richard	Sto-123	Joseph	Mec- 49		
Richard	Sto- 94	Joseph	Ran-167	Iams,Thomas	Row- 45
William	Sto-123	Jos	Cho-230	Iceler,Barbara	Rth-109
Wm	Sto- 94	Moses	Hyd-231	Icenhower,Martin	Bur-105
Wm	Glf-158	Richard	Mec- 54	Ichabud (sic)	Pas-193
Hutcheson,Widow	Mec- 35	Saml	Cab-139	Ictum,Benedict	Lnc-360
David	Mec- 36	Seth	Cab-144	Iddings,James	Glf-167
Jas	Mec- 35	Tabitha	Cha-205	Jonathan	Glf-161
Jno	Mec- 35	Thomas	Rth-105	Jos	Glf-169
Hutchings,Eliz	Len-321	Uriah	Cho-231	Mack	Glf-169
John	Sto-147	William	Bur-131	Wm	Glf-168
Simon	Len-321	William	Hyd-230	Idle,Barnet	Row- 48
Hutchingson,Peter	Grn-133	Wm	Ans- 12	Nathan	Row- 48
Hutchins,Benjamin	Sur-175	Hutt,Charles	Cha-205	Idlet,Evan	Pas-193
James	Sur-176	Hutton,Mary	Ire-242	John	Pas-193
Fedric	Sto- 94	Sarah	Brt- 59	Idol,Michael	Sto-137
Frederick	Sto-123	Wm	Cab-137	Idolett,Shadrach	Glf-185
George	Sto-105	Huver,Andrew	Ran-168	Idor,Geo	Glf-167
Harison	Sto-131	David	Ran-168	Ijams,Beal	Row- 64
John	Sto-110	Jacob	Ran-168	Brice	Row- 62
John	Sto- 94	John	Ran-168	Vachell	Row- 62
John	Bft- 27	Jones	Ran-168	Iles,Charles	Hal-109

Iles,John	Hal-109	Ingram,Thomas	Nor- 70	Irwin,Peggy	Mec- 49
Nich	Lnc-342	Thomas	Bun- 74	Robt	Mec- 26
Rodom	Hal-109	Vaichel	Cas- 58	Robt	Mec- 41
Susanna	Hal-110	Walter	Roq- 14	Saml	Mec- 53
Imler,John	Row- 43	William	Joh-281	Saml	Mec- 41
Mary	Row- 43	William	Nor- 70	Thos	Mec- 41
Ing,Christopher	Edg- 56	William	Bur-114	William	Mec- 48
Jacob	Edg- 55	William	Hay-196	Wm	Mec- 48
Inge,Richard	Grn-140	William Jnr	Ran-169	Wm	Mec- 26
Ingle,Jacob	Lnc-344	William Snr	Ran-169	Wm	Mec- 40
M	Ora-145	Wm P	Ans- 20	Isaacks,D	Ash- 12
Martin	Lnc-370	Ingrum,Edwin	Rch-199	E	Ash- 12
Michael	Lnc-344	Jesse	Rch-199	Elisha	Sur-180
Ingler,David	Row- 84	Wiley	Rch-199	R	Ash- 6
Ingold,J	Glf-177	Inloe,Anthony	Bun- 83	Isaacs,Jacob	Ire-245
Jacob	Glf-155	Inman,Amos	Bun- 91	Isan,John	Hay-196
P	Glf-177	Fanny	Bun- 80	Isbel,Peter	Hal-109
Peter	Ora-131	Henry	Bur-121	Isbell,John	Row- 59
Wm	Glf-177	Jeremiah	Nor- 70	Littleton	Sur-183
Ingram,Abner	Sam-160	Josiah	Rob-235	Richard	Sur-176
Abraham	Cum-267	Inmond,J	Col- 19	Temple	Sot-121
Alexr	Cum-248	Inscors,Reuben	Grn-146	Temple	Sto- 93
Archd	Cas- 58	Insley,Davd	Row- 47	Thomas Esqr	Wil-283
Beezely	Cum-259	Irby,Charles	Lnc-331	Isehoos,Michael	Cab-139
Benjn	Ans- 9	John	Grn-120	Isehower,Nics	Cab-139
Benjn	Fra- 95	John	Lnc-331	Peter	Cab-145
Charles	Cum-259	Peter	Grn-120	Iseler,Adam	Rth-109
Clement	Ran-171	William	Hal-109	Isely,B	Glf-178
D	Ash- 6	Wm	Grn-120	Christian	Glf-180
Elisha	Cas- 58	Wm	Mon- 38	Isler,John Junr	Jon-298
George	Mon- 45	Iredell,Hannah	Cho-220	John Senr	Jon-299
Goldman	Hay-196	Ireland,Abednigo	Glf-181	William	Jon-299
Ingram	Joh-290	Daniel Junr	Car-173	Williams	Jon-299
Isham	Ans- 16	Daniel Senr	Car-173	Isley,Boston	Ora-125
J	Cum-239	Meriah	Cur- 92	J Jr	Ora-132
James	Nor- 70	Sarah	Hrt-210	John	Ora-171
James	Cas- 58	William	Ora-162	Malh	Ora-144
Jeremiah	Ans- 26	Ireon,Fredrick	Roc- 33	Isons,Harman	Hay-196
John	Cas- 58	Sarah	Roc- 33	Israel,Eliza	Bft- 38
John	Ans- 20	Iresin,William	Ire-247	Johnston	Bun- 89
John	Sam-160	Irvin,George	Row- 74	Mary	Bun- 94
John	Cum-238	Henry	Row- 73	Michael	Bun- 82
John Esq	Sam-163	John A	Edg- 42	Michael Senr	Bun- 82
Joseph	Joh-281	Joseph	Row- 73	Solomon	Bun- 82
Joseph	Ans- 12	Lindsey	Cab-138	Isreal,John	Rob-220
Joseph	Ans- 17	Samuel	Nor- 69	Lemuel	Rob-220
Larken	Ans- 19	Samuel	Cab-144	Sarah	Rob-241
Leml	Ans- 26	Thomas	Wil-266	Ivay,Thos	Rob-235
Matthew	Mon- 26	Thos	Cab-138	Ivens,David	Nsh- 75
Merit	Fra- 81	William (B S)	Row- 73	Iver,Duncan	Mor- 68
Moody	Ans- 9	William	Row- 73	Iverns,James	Row- 47
Nancy	Cum-249	Irvine,Abram	Rth-111	Ivery,T	Glf-160
Needham	Joh-281	James	Rth-111	Ives,Hardy	Jon-298
Patsey	Nor- 70	Irving,John	Grn-143	Jesse	Glf-154
Polly	Nor- 70	Irwin,Alexr	Mec- 40	Job	Len-314
Robert	Bun- 87	James	Ire-261	Sarah	Jon-298
S	Cum-241	Jas	Mec- 41	Thos	Cur- 87
Saml	Sam-160	Jenny	Mec- 50	Thos	Glf-188
Stephen	Cas- 58	Michael	Ire-267	Timmy	Cur- 87

-160-

Ivester,George	Rth-109	Jackson,Andrew	Ran-170	Jackson,J		Ash- 12
Ivey,B	Bru-224	Arthur	Pas-192	J		Ash- 6
Charles	Rob-218	Bailey	Pas-192	Jacob		Glf-167
David Jr	Joh-276	Bailey Esq	Pas-192	Jacob		Ora-177
Edey	Rob-218	Bartholomew	Cas- 58	Jacob		Len-314
Edward	Fra- 80	Benjamin	Pas-192	Jacob		Ran-170
Elizabeth	Rob-219	Benjamin	Wil-269	James		Glf-170
Hartwell	Joh-277	Boysten	Glf-167	James		Pas-193
Isham	Rob-233	Carter	Glf-167	James	J	Ora-177
Isham	Rob-233	Christian	Mor- 63	James		Ora-128
James	Joh-277	Colbey	Hay-196	James		Sto-124
James Snr	Joh-277	Colby	Ora-159	James		Mon- 26
Jessey (col)	Rob-241	Craft	Glf-169	James		Roc- 26
Jno	Ora-146	Daniel	Cas- 58	James		Mor- 64
John	Way-249	Daniel	Wil-277	James		Sur-171
Joshua	Rob-237	Daniel	Nor- 69	James		Cho-230
Josiah	Rob-238	David	Fra- 84	James		Ran-170
Lewis	Rob-235	David	Prq-219	James		Ran-170
Lidia	Bru-226	David	Rth-111	Jas		Sam-155
Lovet	Joh-276	Edward	Bur-119	Jas		Glf-157
Mary	Rob-238	Edward	Hal-108	Jas		Ora-177
Mirick	Joh-276	Edwd	Bft- 26	Jas Sen		Ora-177
Paton	Joh-277	Edwin	Sam-156	Jane		Cas- 58
Prissilla	Rob-235	Eleanor	Len-314	Jehu		Sur-185
Reaves	Joh-277	Elias	Rth-110	Jesse		Ans- 14
Robt	Len-315	Eliza	Row- 40	Jesse		Len-314
S	Bru-222	Ely	Rth-110	Jesse		Cum-247
Silas	Rob-233	Ephraim	Bun- 72	Jessee		Edg- 66
Thomas	Rob-219	Ezekael	Grn-141	Jim		Ora-151
William	Joh-273	Francis	Roc- 11	Jno		Ans- 18
Ivins,Edward	Row- 58	Francis	Car-171	Jno		Ora-129
Ivy,Eliz	Bla- 12	Franky	Sto-139	Joel		Edg- 61
J	Col- 16	Frederick	Edg- 58	John Esq		Sam-162
Robert	Hal-109	Gabriel	Rth-111	John		Sam-155
Ruffin	Wil-269	Gabriel	Bur-127	John		Rth-111
Turner	Bla- 3	George	Roc- 23	John		Rth-110
Zoe	Bft- 34	George	Mor- 56	John		Roc- 33
Izell,Jaylon	Edg- 47	George	Car-171	John		Glf-157
Izzard,Federick	Mec- 29	Gillace	Sam-159	John		Prq-219
		H	Ora-177	John		Pit-239
J----,Ezekiel	Rth-110	Habran	Sam-151	John		Roc- 25
J----,Jacob	Jon-299	Henry	Mon- 33	John		Fra- 89
J----,----am	Jon-299	Henry	Lnc-334	John		Len-314
Jack (Negro)	Way-239	Henry	Sto-164	John		Sur-193
Lockwood	Pas-192	Henry	Sto-138	John		Cha-215
Jacks,Jane	Sur-193	Henry	Mon- 33	John		Ran-170
Job	Sur-165	Hezekia	Pas-193	John		Cum-249
Richard N	Sur-169	Isaac	Ans- 6	Jonathan		Grn-142
Richard Sr	Sur-172	Isaac	Glf-170	Jonah		Sam-155
Solomon	Sur-168	Isaac	Fra- 87	Joseph		Rth-110
Jackson,Abia	Pas-192	Isaac	Ora-165	Joseph		Prq-219
Abner	Wsh-227	Isaac	Ora-117	Joseph		Pit-239
Allen	Mon- 24	Isaac	Bft- 22	Joseph		Mor- 63
Alsey	Fra- 88	Isaac	Edg- 61	Joseph		Mor- 58
Alsey	Fra- 85	Isaac	Ran-169	Joseph		Sur-185
Amer	Sto-113	Isaac Sen	Ora-176	Joseph Jr		Pit-239
Ames	Sto-153	Isham	Len-317	Josiah		Fra- 88
Amos	Bur-119	J	Ora-154	Juthas		Rob-222
Andrew	Mor- 68	J	Col- 20	Leml		Pas-193

-161-

Jackson,Lemuel	Pas-192	Jackson,Thos Jnr	Ran-169	James,Mrs.		Bru-234
Leonard	Roc- 32	Walter	Len-321	Abner		Ora-132
Lewis	Rth-111	Warren	Sam-162	Abram		Dup- 16
Lewis	Pas-192	William	Prq-219	Allen		Brt- 48
Lewis	Joh-289	William	Pas-193	Andrew		Brt- 57
Lowe	Fra- 88	William	Pas-192	Aul		Cur- 90
M	Glf-174	William	Pas-192	Bartlett		Mon- 33
Malach	Pas-193	William	Fra- 82	Benjn		Row- 60
Malachi	Pas-192	William	Sur-176	Benjn		Hal-109
Malachi	Pas-192	William	Edg- 61	Benj Junr		Hal-109
Mararet	Rth-109	William	Wil-269	Benjn Senr		Hal-109
Margrett	Mar- 5	William	Nor- 69	Betsy		Cho-223
Martha	Wil-269	Willm	Sam-156	Bridges		Rth- 91
Mary	Prq-219	Willm Junr	Fra- 89	Carson		Sto-151
Mary	Cas- 58	Willm Senr	Fra- 89	Daniel		Dup- 17
Mary	Pas-193	Wm	Row- 40	Daniel		Dup- 14
Mary	Cum-248	Wm	Ora-177	Daniel		Pit-241
Michael	Ran-170	Wm	Mor- 68	Darcas		Cho-223
Middleton	Sam-156	Wm	Mor- 58	Edward		Bun- 79
Miles	Pas-193	Wm	Grn-138	Edwards		Bur-104
Mordecai	Pas-192	Wm	Ora-160	Elias		Dup- 23
Mordecai	Pas-193	Wm	Ora-159	Elisha		Hal-109
Mourning	Wah-228	Wm	Ora-118	Eliza		Dup- 21
Nathan	Sam-160	Wm	Cho-230	Frederick		Brt- 48
Nathan	Sam-155	Wm	Nsh- 72	Geo		Mon- 33
Nathen	Ran-170	Wm Jr	Ora-164	George		Row- 61
Needham	Cum-266	Zach	Pas-193	Hardy		Hal-110
Obed	Sam-159	Jackston,Stephen	Ran-170	Henry		Ans- 25
Orren	Fra- 96	Jacobes,David	Cur- 92	Holland		Pit-239
Penny	Pas-192	Jacobs,Abraham	Row- 89	Hosey		Ans- 21
Randal	Mor- 68	Benjamon	Per-139	James		Row- 60
Rew	Pas-193	Caleb	Per-139	Jessee		Ora-152
Richd	Sam-156	Christian	Row- 37	John		Dup- 17
Robert	Cas- 58	E	Bru-236	John		Sto-129
Robert	Edg- 61	Elizabeth	Rob-231	John		Row- 46
Sabara	Pas-193	George	Per-130	John		Pit-261
Sally	Pas-192	J Junr	Bru-234	John		Pit-239
Saml	Mon- 44	J Snr	Bru-234	John		Pit-235
Saml	Grn-138	Jacob	Nor- 69	John		Brt- 48
Sarah	Prq-220	Jessy	Per-139	John		Sto-104
Sarah	Cha-194	Jno	Per-130	John		Sto-104
Sarah	Cha-200	Kindal	Row- 78	John		Sto-156
Seth	Sam-155	Lewis	Row- 76	John		Ons-107
Seth	Pas-193	Richard	Per-130	John		Rch-204
Shadrach	Pit-239	S	Bru-234	John		Hyd-223
Solomon	Rth-110	Shad	Bla- 9	Jonathan		Brt- 48
Wolomon	Rth-110	Susannah	Nor- 69	Jonathan		Wsh-227
Stephen	Ans- 18	William	Nor- 69	Joshua		Pit-240
Susannah	Car-171	William	Ire-261	Judith		Roc- 18
Tandy	Rth-111	Wm	Ora-162	Kesiah		Bft- 19
Thomas	Pas-192	Zachariah	Ire-261	Leml		Pas-192
Thomas	Roc- 26	Jacocks,Jannett	Brt- 47	Levina		Pas-193
Thomas	Roc- 24	Jonathan	Brt- 45	Martin		Rch-212
Thomas	Car-171	Jaolett,Benj	Glf-180	Mary		Dup- 7
Thomas	Tyr-201	O	Glf-180	Mary		Joh-276
Thomas	Rch-198	Jaottell,Jos	Glf-176	Matthew		Rth-110
Thomas	Ran-170	Jagart,Jas Esq	Mec- 36	Nancy		Roc- 23
Thomas	Hyd-224	Jalock,William	Cas- 58	Nancy		Bft- 26
Thos	Rob-234	James (sic)	Bla- 8	Nancy		Edg- 60

-162-

Name	Code	Name	Code	Name	Code	Name	Code
James,Nic	Row- 55	Jarman,Robert	Ons-105	Jasper,Richd	Bft- 34		
Nic Sr	Row- 55	Susannah	Ons- 99	Sedan	Hyd-232		
Nilanor	Dup- 36	William Senr	Jon-299	William	Car-171		
Philip	Rch-196	Jarnigan,Miles H	Hrt-215	Jassler,Abner	Cha-200		
Polly	Pas-192	Mills	Hrt-215	Jastion,Jno	Rob-234		
Priscilla	Nor- 70	Seth	Hrt-211	Jay,Bennet	Hay-196		
Reubin	Brt- 48	Jarrald,Ishom	Ons-102	David	Bun- 89		
Robert	Pit-241	Jarrel,Sarah	Hal-110	James Junr	Per-139		
S	Ash- 14	Jarrell,David	Dup- 36	James Senr	Per-139		
Samuel	Row- 59	John	Joh-283	John	Per-139		
Solomon	Pas-192	William	Roc- 10	Joseph	Rth-110		
Thomas	Pit-235	Jarret,Widow	Lnc-326	William	Per-139		
Thomas	Bur-111	Daniel	Bun- 88	Jayroe,G	Col- 20		
Thomas	Lnc-362	Enoch	Cum-268	Jeal,Jesse	Glf-185		
Thomas	Sam-158	John	Ran-170	Jeames,John	Sto- 98		
Thomas	Nor- 70	John	Row- 85	William	Sto- 98		
William	Dup- 19	Margrat	Row- 88	Jean,Martha	Sto-100		
William	Sto-129	Mary	Row- 85	Martha	Sto-132		
William	Pit-241	Moses	Bun- 88	Nathan	Fra- 93		
William	Lnc-351	Saml	Lnc-326	Wiley	Sto-100		
William	Lnc-376	Wiley	Row- 85	Wiley	Sto-131		
William	Cum-266	Jarrett,Daniel	Bun- 94	William	Sto-100		
William	Hay-196	John	Bun- 96	William	Sto-132		
Wm	Ans- 24	Killiam	Bur-125	Wm	Ora-112		
Wm	Mon- 33	Jarrison,Jesse	Row- 43	Jeans,William	Hrt-216		
Jameson,Alexander	Bur-124	Jarrold,Elijah	Wil-280	Jearnegan,James	Dup- 15		
Jas	Cab-138	Jarrot,Isaac	Ons-108	Jesse	Dup- 25		
John	Row- 70	John	Cum-238	Zelpha	Dup- 24		
Saml	Cab-138	Jarvis,Bennet	Sur-167	Jeffers,Samuel	Rth-109		
Samuel	Bur-121	Daniel	Sur-175	Jefferson,Daniel	Sur-166		
Jamison,Geo	Ora-119	David	Hyd-231	Henry	Cha-198		
James	Row- 71	Foster	Hyd-231	Major	Pit-259		
John	Ora-160	Foster	Hyd-231	Obedh	Bft- 24		
Mary	Mec- 54	Jabez	Bun- 93	Richd	Cha-207		
William	Row- 71	James	Wil-270	Thomas	Nor- 69		
Jane (sic)	Pas-192	James	Row- 55	Jeffery,William	Sur-177		
Phillip	Glf-185	James	Sto-135	Jeffres,James	War-175		
Smyth	Glf-186	Jas	Sur-163	R	Ora-138		
Janes,James	Rth-109	Jesse	Bur-103	Jeffreys,Fanny	Cas- 58		
John	Rth-109	Jonathan	Hyd-231	John	Cas- 58		
John	Rth-111	Joseph	Hyd-228	Joshua	Cas- 58		
Lydia	Len-315	Levy	Sur-170	L	Ora-135		
Thomas	Rth-109	Lydia	Bft- 33	Mrs. Mary	Fra- 93		
Thomas	Rth-111	Patience	Ire-255	Osbn Senr	Per-139		
William	Rth-110	R	Cam-152	Simon	Fra- 92		
Janner,Thos	Mec- 30	S	Cam-163	Simon G	Fra- 93		
Jardon,William	Hrt-216	S	Cam-158	Thomas	Per-130		
Jarman,Ann	Ons-102	Samuel	Hyd-227	Jeffries,Anson	Nor- 69		
Ben	Ons-105	Semian	Ons-107	Middy	Nor- 70		
Berry	Ons- 98	Stephen	Sur-172	Simon	Nor- 69		
Emanuel	Jon-299	Thos	Cur- 87	Tho	Ora-126		
Hardy	Jon-299	William	Sur-180	William	Per-139		
Henry	Tyr-208	William	Row- 61	Evan	Ora-136		
Jno	Ans- 12	William	Cur- 87	Jeffryes,Thomas	Cas- 59		
John	Jon-299	Zachy	Hyd-231	Jefries,Brock	Grn-131		
John	Ons-104	Zadoc	Row- 55	Green	Grn-131		
Josiah	Tyr-202	Jasher,David	Cha-197	Wm Senr	Grn-131		
Penelope	Ons-105	Jasper,John B	Hyd-233	Jeghour,John	Row- 77		
Rachel	Jon-299	Jonathan	Hyd-232	Jelk,Robert	Hal-109		

-163-

Name	Location	Name	Location	Name	Location
Jelks,Jarrell	Joh-287	Jenkins,Willie	Fra- 78	Jernegan,Winefred	Way-253
Jemison,Arthur	Mec- 37	Wm	Lnc-331	Jernigan,E	Col- 18
Robt	Mec- 25	Winborn	Brt- 54	Godwin	Brt- 61
Jempston,James	Pas-192	Winborne	Nor- 69	Lewis	Brt- 61
Richard	Pas-192	Winifred	Hal-108	Phebe	Brt- 57
Jeneret,J	Col- 19	Jennett,Isaac	Wsh-223	Saml	Brt- 63
Jenings,Eliza	Bur-111	Jesse	Bla- 3	Wm	Brt- 61
Jenkens,Demsey	Edg- 44	John	Hyd-228	Jervis,James	Sto-102
Jenkins,Abner	Rch-197	Nathan	Hyd-228	James	Ire-253
Abraham	Brt- 55	Robert	Hyd-228	Jesher,Darkes	Cur- 92
Ben	Lnc-331	Robert Jr	Hyd-228	Jesop,Thos	Prq-219
Benja	Nor- 69	Solomon	Hyd-228	Jessop,C	Ora-134
Benjamin	Rob-2-5	Jennings,Abigail	Pas-192	Caleb	Glf-183
Cannon	Hal-110	Betsy	Pas-192	Caleb	Sur-185
Charles	Ans- 16	Daniel	Cas- 58	Eli	Sur-185
Charles	Pit-239	David	Pas-192	Elijah	Sur-185
Edward	Rob-235	Demsey	Pas-192	Jacob	Sur-177
Elisha	Ran-170	Ebenezar	Pas-193	Joseph	Glf-187
Green	Fra- 85	Ebenezar	Pas-193	Joseph	Sto-154
Henry	Pit-245	Elisha Jun	Pas-193	Joseph	Sto-113
Henry	Grn-140	Elisha Sen	Pas-192	L	Glf-162
Ja--	Lnc-340	James	Pas-191	T	Glf-169
James col	Fra-101	James	Pas-192	Thos	Glf-163
Jas	Ans- 23	Jervis	Pas-192	Timothy	Sto-154
Jenky	Lnc-342	Jno	Ans- 13	William	Glf-171
Jesse	Hal-109	John	Pas-192	William	Sto-113
John	War-174	John	Pas-192	William	Sto-154
John	Lnc-340	John Jun	Pas-191	William	Sto-153
John	Lnc-340	John Sen	Pas-191	Jessup,Abraham	Cum-247
John	Edg- 65	Leml	Pas-191	Geo	Bft- 37
John	Nor- 70	Leml	Pas-191	Jester,Ebenezr	Hyd-232
John Jnr	Ran-170	Levi	Pas-192	Jacob	Sur-172
Jos	Lnc-340	Lyddia	Pas-191	Maskel	Glf-168
Louis	Rob-235	Lydia	Pas-192	N	Glf-164
Miland	Edg- 46	Thomas	Pas-193	Jestin,Jarrison	Grn-137
Nancy	War-178	William	Pas-191	Jesture,James	Bun- 93
Noah	Edg- 68	William	Roc- 23	Jeter,Edmont	Ire-261
Osburn	Edg- 50	Willm	Pas-192	Jethro,Thomas	Wsh-221
Patty	Ran-170	Jennitt,Hezekiah	Edg- 69	Jetton,ASoph	Mec- 24
Pherlbe	Edg- 69	Jent,Rebaca	Mec- 43	Lewis	Mec- 53
Reuben	Lnc-340	Jerald,Garland	Roc- 10	Jewel,Absolom	Ire-244
Reubin	Nor- 70	Jermwild,A	Col- 18	Jewell,Stephen	Hyd-228
Rigdon	Brt- 58	Jerden,John	Sto-149	Stephen	Bur-117
Robert	Pit-245	Jernegan,A	Col- 18	Thomas	Ons- 97
Robert	Grn-140	Asa	Way-235	Jherd,Phillip	Lnc-346
Saml	Brt- 54	Barnaby	Way-233	Jhert,Elizabeth	Lnc-347
Saml	Lnc-333	Benjn	Way-238	George	Lnc-347
Saml	Lnc-330	David	Way-235	Lawrance	Lnc-347
Samuel	Lnc-328	Elizabeth	Way-250	Jiggets,John	Hrt-212
Thomas	Grn-137	Etheldred	Way-233	Jiggetts,Edward	Hrt-211
Thomas	Edg- 72	George	Way-233	Jiles,Jeremiah	Tyr-205
Thomas	Nor- 70	Kedar	Way-240	Jeremiah	Rth-109
Thomas	Ran-170	Lewis	Way-234	Medow	Bun- 94
Thomas Jr	Grn-137	Mills	Way-235	William	Bun- 86
Wat	Grn-140	Page	Way-239	Jimison,John	Ora-169
Wiatt	Lnc-341	Phebe	Way-233	Jims,Edmund	Wil-278
William	Glf-156	Richd	Way-233	Jines,Thomas	Wil-260
William	Fra- 84	W	Col- 18	Jinings,John	Sur-173
William	Hay-196	W	Col- 18	Jink,Peter	Row- 48

Jinkins,Alkanon	Sur-195	Jobe,Thomas	Row- 57	Johnson,David	Edg- 44		
Aron	Row- 73	Jobling,William	Cas- 58	David	Joh-277		
Charles	Hrt-209	Jock,B R	Bru-230	David	Hyd-223		
Clay	Hrt-217	Joe (sic)	Pas-193	Dempsey	Sur-188		
D	Glf-179	Joe,Major	Pas-192	Dempsey	Nor- 69		
Daniel	Mar- 8	John of colour	Mar- 3	Drury	Joh-275		
David	Ons-104	E	Ora-153	Dudley	Hal-109		
Edward	Row- 54	Lackey	Edg- 71	Duncan	Rob-228		
Francis	Sur-174	Johns,Zachariah	Rth-109	E	Glf-179		
George	Brt- 63	Johnson,----tel	Cur- 93	Edward	Prq-220		
Henry	Hrt-207	A	Ash- 8	Elias	Rch-213		
Henry	Glf-157	Abel	Joh-278	Elias Senr	Nor- 69		
Hugh	Lnc-366	Abram	Mar- 8	Elijah Jr	Len-323		
Irwin	Hrt-215	Absolam	Rob-237	Elijah Senr	Len-316		
James	Brt- 63	Absolam	Per-139	Elisha	Ans- 11		
James	Mar- 15	Ackrel	Hal-108	Elisha	Edg- 69		
James	Ons-108	Alexr	Rob-231	Eliza	Row- 56		
Jas	Hrt-208	Alexr	Rob-227	Esther	Edg- 52		
John	Brt- 62	Alexr	Rob-225	Ezl	Len-323		
John	Ons-107	Allen	Joh-277	Fanny	Sur-184		
John	Ora-152	Ambrose	Wil-262	Fereby	Joh-273		
John	Grn-149	Amos	Joh-274	George	Roc- 16		
John	Hrt-213	Amos	Edg- 69	George	Row- 79		
John	Grn-130	Amy	Sur-182	George	Wil-263		
Joseph	Sur-169	Anderson	Grn-130	George Jr	Wil-263		
Lewis	Ons-107	Andrew	Nsh- 91	George W	Wil-262		
Lewis	Row- 63	Andrew	Wil-268	Gideon	Roc- 5		
Lodwick	Brt- 63	Andy	Glf-180	H	Ahs- 14		
Mansfield	Grn-130	Angus	Rob-232	Hardwick	Wil-270		
Mary	Hrt-208	Ann	Pit-256	Hardy	Grn-142		
Moses	Lnc-366	Anthony	Nor- 70	Henry	Joh-276		
Polly	Grn-131	Archa	Sur-171	Henry	Joh-275		
Ternyon	Cur- 90	Archer	Grn-144	Isaac	Mon- 24		
Thomas	Grn-123	Archer Jr	Grn-144	Isaac	Joh-275		
Thos	Hrt-207	Archibald	Rch-206	Isaiah	Len-323		
Tom	Ora-157	Arthur B	Joh-285	Isaiah	Len-322		
William	Bun- 80	Ashly	Sur-170	J	Ash- 3		
William	Wil-271	Ashly	Sur-196	J O	Ash- 3		
Wm	Ora-150	Azeal	Tyr-206	Jacob	Edg- 48		
Wm	Grn-123	Baraby	Nor- 70	Jacob	Sur-170		
Winbern	Gat-112	Barsha	Gat-112	Jacob	Joh-275		
Winburn	Ans- 24	Benjamin	Edg- 48	James	War-174		
Zachariah	Hrt-207	Benjamin	Sur-166	James	Row- 56		
Jinks,Burrl	Cha-191	Benjn	Row- 58	James	Glf-167		
John	Row- 61	Benjn	Sur-166	James	Pit-253		
Matthew	Cum-258	Benjamin (Clay Bank)		James	Car-171		
William	Bur-115		Wil-266	James	Bur-114		
Jinnings,Anthony	Sur-180	Benjamin Jr	Sur-169	James	Bur-105		
John	Wil-260	Benjamin (R R)	Wil-259	James	Edg- 48		
Luke	Wil-260	Boston	Nor- 69	James	Grn-141		
William	Wil-260	Cador	Sur-167	James	Joh-275		
Jissup,Isaac	Bla- 9	Caleb	Glf-165	James	Wil-263		
James	Bla- 9	Charles	Nor- 70	James	Wil-266		
Saml	Bla- 9	Chas	Sur-169	James	Glf-180		
Jnocon,Johnathan	Grn-129	Chs E	Cho-230	James	Ran-171		
Joalett,D	Glf-159	Cullen	Joh-276	James C	Quar	Pas-193	
Joans,Charles	Ran-169	Danl	Len-322	James R		War-175	
Thomas	Ran-170	Darden	Nor- 69	Jas		Ans- 27	
Job,T	Glf-177	David	Bur-105	Jas		Ans- 23	

Name	Ref	Name	Ref	Name	Ref
Johnson,Jane	Hal-110	Johnson,Mary	War-177	Johnson,Solomon	Bla- 4
Jeremiah	Hyd-224	Matthew	Sto-127	Solomon	Rch-200
Jeoffery	Wil-263	Matthew	Sur-182	Solomon	Joh-286
Jesse	Glf-162	Matthew	Nsh- 91	Solomon	Joh-285
Jesse	Wil-262	Matthew	Nor- 70	Starling	Joh-276
Jessee	Nor- 69	McAllister	Roc- 16	Stephen	Grn-131
Jessee	Edg- 44	Michael	Cha-195	Stephen	Cha-215
Joab	Cha-203	Michael	Cha-203	Stephen	Nsh- 91
Joel	Roc- 30	Milly	Joh-273	Sterling	Hal-109
Joel	Mar- 8	Moses	Wil-271	Strangmon	Sur-167
Jno	Rob-244	N	Glf-169	Sugan	Fra- 79
John	Grn-133	Nathan	Edg- 67	Susanna	Hal-109
John	Row- 56	Nathaniel	Row- 69	Talton	Glf-169
John	Prq-219	Needham	Mon- 25	Tralton	Grn-129
John	Roc- 14	Neill	Rch-193	Thomas	Grn-129
John	Fra- 97	Noel	Grn-134	Thomas	Sto-121
John	Grn-140	Noel	Grn-148	Thomas	Sto-119
John	Grn-138	Obed	Joh-291	Thomas	Roc- 15
John	Cha-203	Obedience	Nor- 70	Thomas	Edg- 53
John	Sur-166	Oliver	Nor- 70	Thomas	Sto-144
John	Sur-181	Parananas	Grn-129	Thomas	Sur-174
John	Tyr-203	Patience	Grn-146	Thomas	Ed- 67
John	Joh-277	Peter	Rch-204	Thomas	Wil-260
John	Wil-259	Peter	Rob-226	Thos	Glf-180
John	Nor- 70	Philip	Joh-276	Thos	Glf-171
John H	Gat-113	Phillip	Cha-208	Thos	Mon- 23
John R Esqr	Wil-281	Phillip	Grn-144	Trisey	Nsh- 87
Jonah	Hal-109	Polly	Joh-276	Turner	Grn-129
Jonathan	Grn-146	Rachel	Wil-263	W E Estate of	War-176
Jonathan	Sur-196	Randol	Hal-109	Walter	Roc- 26
Jonathan	Joh-275	Randolph	Rth-111	Warren	Joh-285
Joseph	Sur-167	Randolph	Edg- 69	William	Sto-134
Joseph	Cha-216	Rebecca	Joh-275	William	Pit-259
Joseph	Nor- 69	Redden	Joh-287	William	Pit-253
Joseph	Hal-109	Reuben	Roc- 7	William	Sto-102
Joshua	Glf-168	Richard	Joh-273	William	Fra- 91
Joshua	Glf-162	Richard Jr	Nor- 70	William	Edg- 52
Joshua	Fra- 90	Richard Senr	Nor- 70	William	Edg- 48
Joshua	Mar- 8	Richard W	Edg- 68	William	Sur-167
Joshua	Mar- 13	Richd	Ans- 7	William	Sur-173
Joshua	Joh-277	Richd	Row- 57	William	Sur-171
Josiah	Nsh- 74	Richd	Cha-211	William	Sur-184
Judy	Row- 65	Robert Jr	Nor- 69	William	Rch-204
Juidken	Car-169	Robert R	War-179	William	Rch-213
Kemp	War-177	Robert Senr	Nor- 70	William	Joh-289
Lenard	Edg- 66	Robt	Cha-213	William (H C)	Wil-272
Leonard	Cha-195	Sally	War-180	William (R R)	Wil-259
Lewis	Wil-270	Saml	Bft- 39	William R	War-183
Lewis Senr	Wil-281	Saml	Bur-118	William Esqr	Wil-277
Louis	Rob-236	Saml	Grn-144	Wm	Ans- 28
Lucy	Joh-277	Saml	Joh-278	Wm	Row- 56
Lucy	Nor- 69	Saml	Rob-236	Wm D C	Sur-175
MDuke	War-177	Saml Snr	Bur-118	Wm	Hal-109
Manchester	Row- 69	Samuel Esq	Wil-259	Wm Jr	Grn-146
Maridith	Ans- 10	Samuel H	Sur-189	Wm Sr	Grn-146
Mark	Joh-290	Samuel Jr	Wil-263	Willie	Joh-275
Martha	Pit-256	Sarah	Bur-112	Willis	Hal-108
Martha	Nor- 70	Sarah	Hal-109	Zacaria	Row- 81
Mary	Roc- 16	Sile	Joh-272	Johnston,Mrs.	Cum-234

Johnston,Adam	Ire-244	Johnston,Hardy	Cum-259	Johnston,John		Lnc-351
Alex H	Brt- 60	Haskiah	Ons-104	John		Ire-253
Alexr	Cum-262	Henry	Brt- 56	John		Ire-265
Allen	Bun- 84	Henry	Rth-109	John		Cum-264
Andrew	Ire-253	Henry	Cha-197	John		Ran-170
Andrew	Mec- 53	Henry	Ons- 98	John		Way-235
Angus	Cum-243	Henry	Ran-170	John		Per-134
Ann	Brt- 46	Hiram	Ran-169	John		Cum-262
Ann	Ons-105	Hugh	Cum-241	John		Cum-255
Ann	Brt- 67	Isaac	Cas- 58	John		Mar- 7
Asa	Ire-261	Isaac	Cha-207	John		Lnc-346
Ashley	Ire-268	J	Bru-240	John D		Ire-243
Aurthur	Mor- 63	Jack	Bun- 73	John Junr		Ons- 98
B	Ora-138	James	Cas- 58	John Senr		Ons-109
Baker	Ire-268	James	Bun- 96	John	(wag)	Cas- 58
Barbary	Joh-299	James	Ora-137	Jonas		Ons-102
Barnabas	Cum-256	James	Sam-158	Jonathan		Brt- 64
Barnabas	Cum-257	James	Dup- 12	Joseby		Sam-158
Benj	Ons-100	James	Lnc-360	Joseph		Lnc-329
Benjamin	Rth-110	James	Ire-265	Joseph		Dup- 22
Benjamin	Ire-267	James	Way-249	Joseph		Mor- 57
Benjamin	Ire-265	James	Glf-188	Joseph		Cum-257
Benjamin	Ire-265	James	Cum-254	Joseph		Ran-170
Benjamin	Ire-243	James	Bun- 73	Joshua		Lnc-360
Benjamin	Cum-262	James	Brt- 67	Joshua		Cha-210
Benjamin Senr	Per-139	James C	Mar- 8	Kader		Cum-261
Benjn	Per-134	James Junr	Bun- 95	L		Ora-148
Benjn	Ran-170	Jas	Mor- 61	Lanslet		Cas- 59
Benjn	Dup- 6	Jas	Bft- 25	Lazarus		Way-247
Catharine	Cum-256	Jas	Ora-113	Levi		Cha-198
Charles	Ran-170	Jarvis	Ire-265	Levy		Brt- 46
Darcy	Way-240	Jason	Rth-111	Lewis		Sam-151
Daniel	Cum-244	Jeremiah	Brt- 47	Lewis		Lnc-357
Daniel	Rth-111	Jesse	Rth-109	Littleton		Brt- 65
Danl	Ora-120	Jesse	Cha-212	Lochlin		Mor- 61
David	Mec- 38	Jessee	Ire-269	Malcom		Cum-255
David	Lnc-339	Joab	Rth-110	Mark		Sam-153
David	Rth-111	Joel	Rth-109	Mason		Ons-107
Dora	Cha-212	Joel	Bla- 11	Miah		Ire-246
Duncan	Cum-243	Jno	Bur-107	Michael		Mor- 63
Ecol	Per-130	Jno	Ora-113	Michael		Sam-153
Edward	Cha-213	Jno Esq	Mec- 39	Moses		Ran-170
Eli	Cha-196	John	Cas- 58	Nancy Rachal		Mec- 54
Elijah	Hay-196	John	Cas- 58	Nathan		Sam-158
Elisabeth	Per-139	John	Cas- 58	Nathaniel		Bun- 97
Feby	Cas- 59	John	Bun- 93	Patrick		Mec- 53
Ford	Lnc-334	John	Cab-144	Phil		Mor- 68
Ford	Lnc-333	John	Row- 64	Philip		Bur-126
Francis	Ire-251	John	Sam-158	Phillip		Rth-109
Frederick	Rth-111	John	Rth-109	Pleasant		Cas- 59
G C	Ora-156	John	Dup- 15	Randle		Cum-244
G St	Ora-156	John	Dup- 11	Rebecca		Brt- 59
Geo	Ora-170	John	Row- 37	Reuben		Bun- 98
George	Lnc-336	John	Sam-153	Richard		Cum-260
Greenbury	Ire-243	John	Cha-207	Richard		Cas- 58
H	Col- 18	John	Cha-200	Richd		Bla- 11
Hannah	Cas- 58	John	Bla- 7	Richd		Lnc-374
Hannah	Jon-299	John	Cum-243	Robert		Lnc-339
Harbert	Cum-256	John	Cum-243	Robert		Row- 74

Johnston,Robert	Row- 60	Johnston,Wm	Mec- 53	Jolly,James	Rth-111
Robert	Dup- 11	Wm	Per-134	James	Pit-257
Robert	Lnc-360	Wm Esq	Bla- 10	Jesse	Hyd-232
Robert	Ire-244	Wm W	Brt- 56	John	Bft- 26
Robert	Ran-170	Willis	Bun- 75	Jonan	Bft- 26
Robt	Mec- 53	Johnstone,Andrew	Lnc-373	Joseph	Pit-241
Robt	Bla- 4	John	Lnc-362	Kenneday	Pit-261
Robinson	Lnc-374	John	Mor- 63	Martha	Pit-245
Rosanah	Ran-170	Lewis	Mor- 58	Sarah	Hal-110
Ruben	Dup- 13	Robt	Lnc-373	William	Ire-264
Rufus	Mec- 45	Robt Senr	Lnc-373	William	Rth-111
Sally	Mor- 65	William	Lnc-362	Jonagan,Britton	Ans- 23
Saml	Mec- 38	Johson,Richard	Pit-252	David	Ans- 23
Saml	Mec- 53	Johston,M	Mon- 37	Samuel	Ans- 23
Samuel	Cas- 59	Joiner,A	Col- 18	Wm	Ans- 7
Samuel	Row- 74	Aaron	Pit-259	Jonakin,George	Nor- 70
Samuel	Rth-111	Abraham	Pit-256	Jacob	Fra- 91
Sill	Cum-262	Abraham	Pit-257	Jonas,Bassel	Jon-299
Simon	Cum-263	Amos	Pit-260	Nathan	Jon-299
Simon	Way-249	Ben	Sam-160	Jone (sic)	Pas-192
Solomon	Sam-158	Blount	Hal-109	Jones,Mrs.	Cum-235
Taply	Cum-257	Darcas	Pit-238	Mrs.	Cum-241
Theodrick	Cas- 59	Drury	Edg- 52	Mrs.	Brt- 62
Theophilus	Bun- 74	Eli	Hal-110	---elaus	Cur- 92
Thomas	Cas- 58	Elisha	Edg- 55	A	Cum-235
Thomas	Dup- 32	Elizabeth	Edg- 63	A B	Bru-238
Thomas	Ire-251	Francis	Way-240	Aaron	Grn-137
Thomas	Ran-170	James	Pit-259	Aaron	Ran-170
Thomas	Wsh-223	James	Pit-260	Abigail	Car-177
Thos	Cab-139	Joel	Way-240	Abraham	Hyd-229
Thos	Brt- 45	Joel	Hal-109	Abraham	Hrt-215
Thos	Dup- 8	John	Hal-109	Abraham	Hrt-212
Turner	Cha-196	John	Pit-260	Allen	Fra- 93
Vincent	Cum-265	Joseph	Ire-267	Allen	Edg- 53
Will	Dup- 11	Joseph	Rth-110	Allen	Rth-110
William	Brt- 45	Joshua	Sur-171	Allen	Pit-263
William	Lnc-338	Moses	Fra- 97	Allen	Cha-212
William	Row- 74	Robert	Hal-109	Allen	Jon-299
William	Sam-158	Samuel	Rth-110	Allen	Hal-109
William	Rth-111	Selah	Sam-160	Allen	Hal-109
William	Rth-109	Susannah	Cho-222	Alsey	Fra- 88
William	Rth-110	Turner	Hal-109	Alsey	Fra- 83
William	Rth-110	Willis	Sam-156	Alsy	Cha-190
William	Dup- 13	Joinner,Nelson	Hrt-211	Ambrose	Hyd-228
William	Way-249	Jokeley,Wm	Ora-127	Ambrose	Wil-283
William	Ran-170	Jolley,Fredrick	Mar- 16	Ambrose	Car-176
William	Ran-170	Jesse	Mar- 12	Ambrose	Len-318
William	Way-240	Jesse Senr	Mar- 13	Ambrose	Per-130
William	Cum-262	John	Ora-114	America	Grn-137
William	Cum-259	Noah	Mar- 14	Amos	Fra- 79
William	Mar- 8	Peter	Mar- 9	Amos	Ran-170
William Senr	Brt- 65	Jolly,Allen	Ire-255	Amos Esqr	Ons- 95
Wm	Bru-228	Ann	Pit-239	Andrew	Nor- 69
Wm	Mec- 38	Charles	Ire-255	Ann	Nsh- 78
Wm	Mec- 38	Charles	Ire-250	Anne	Rth-111
Wm	Mec- 22	Elizabeth	Pit-261	Aquilla	Ora-123
Wm	Ora-128	Henry	Pit-243	Aquilla	Ora-112
Wm	Mor- 63	Isom	Pit-262	Arial	Jon-299
Wm	Mec- 54	James	Cum-246	Arter	Cur- 90

-168-

Name	Ref	Name	Ref	Name	Ref	Name	Ref
Jones,Arthur	Dup- 14	Jones,Daniel		Grn-144	Jones,Furnifold		Len-323
Arthur	Way-236	Daniel		Sur-186	Gabrael		Grn-133
Atlas	Mor- 69	David		Rth-111	Gabriel		Wil-277
Augustin	Dup- 23	David		Dup- 25	George		Roc- 14
B	Cam-159	David		Gat-114	George		Lnc-355
Bain	Cur- 85	David		Cur- 92	George		Cum-267
Bartie	Jon-299	David		Mor- 62	George		Wil-264
Bath	Pas-192	David		Mor- 62	George W		Wsh-222
Benj	Hrt-214	David		Mor- 61	George W Senr		Wsh-227
Benj	Cha-202	David		Fra- 84	James		Ora-112
Benjamin	Sto-133	David		Edg- 48	James		Bla- 4
Benjamin	Rth-111	David		Ran-170	James		Lcn-355
Benjamin	Sto-108	David		Hyd-228	James		Edg- 71
Benjamin (L F)	Wil-280	David		Cum-257	James		Edg- 56
Benjamin	Bun- 91	David		Mar- 13	James		Row- 76
Benjamin	Sto-101	Dempsy		Ons- 99	James		Row- 80
Benjamin	Fra- 83	Demsey		Gat-106	James		Row- 80
Benjamin Esqr	Wil-263	Diana		Grn-138	James		Ire-256
Benjamin Jr	Wil-263	Drury		Row- 61	James		Hal-109
Benjn	Row- 48	E		Cum-241	James		Hal-109
Benjn	Sam-155	E		Cum-240	James		Nor- 70
Benjn	Sto-143	Easter		Gat-109	James		Way-235
Benjn	Hal-109	Eathon		Hyd-228	James		Way-244
Benlon	Cho-230	Ebed		Bun- 96	James		Per-134
Berry	Rth-110	Ebenezer		Row- 59	James C		Fra- 95
Betsy	Pas-192	Edmd		Cha-205	James Esqr		Wsh-223
Bilson	Edg- 47	Edmd		Cho-227	James T		Pas-193
Biram	Hay-196	Edmd		Nsh- 74	Jas		Cho-226
Brantty	Cha-197	Edmond		Hal-109	Jas		Ans- 9
Briant	Cas- 58	Edmond		Grn-137	Jas		Mec- 30
Brice	Mon- 29	Edmund		Rth-110	Jas		Bla- 8
Briton	Pit-241	Edmund Colo		Wil-276	Jane		Row- 43
Briton	Pit-233	Edward J		War-171	Jane		Nor- 69
Britton	Edg- 58	Edwd		Cha-192	Jarvis M		Ons- 98
Bruington	Grn-138	Elias		Bun- 74	Jeremiah		Roc- 31
C	Col- 18	Elijah		Fra- 78	*Jesse		Dup- 8
Carter	Nor- 70	Elijah		Jon-299	Jesse		Pit-242
Carteret	Ons- 98	Elis		Cur- 79	Jesse		Bft- 30
Cathr	Dup- 24	Elisha		Dup- 14	Jesse		Sur-183
Capt Catlett	Wil-277	Elisha		Lnc-332	Jesse		Rch-200
Charity	Row- 56	Eliza		Row- 63	Jesse		Way-236
Charity	Way-236	Elizabeth		Ire-250	Jesse F		Mar- 4
Charles	Sam-160	Elizabeth		Ran-169	Jesse Senr		Bla- 4
Charles	Rth-111	Emanuel		Grn-123	Jessee		Nor- 70
Charles	Nsh- 90	Epps		War-170	Joal		Mec- 51
Charles	Lnc-355	Erasmus		Wil-273	Joel		Brt- 54
Chas	Mon- 44	Evin		Cur- 92	Jno		Ans- 22
Chas	Ora-113	Evin		Sur-185	Jno		Ans- 4
Christeen	Ire-239	Ezekiel		Roc- 16	Jno		Ans- 4
Churchill	Per-134	Ezekiel		Jon-299	Jno		Mec- 30
Clayton	Cas- 58	Febey		Jon-299	John		War-175
Clem	Bft- 20	Federick		Gat-105	John		Rth-111
Corban	Tyr-208	Francis		War-171	John		Rth-110
Cullen	Cho-230	Francis		Grn-136	John		Rth-110
Cutler	Fra- 84	Francis		Cha-198	John		Grn-124
D	Cam-163	Francis		Cho-222	John		Rth-110
D	Cam-161	Frederick		Rob-238	John		Sto-137
Daniel	Ans- 23	Frederick Jr		Len-318	John		Prq-219
Daniel	Rth-110	Fredk		Len-318	John		Cas- 59
					*Jesse		Len-318

Name	Loc	Name	Loc	Name	Loc	Name	Loc
Jones,John	Pit-261	Jones,Joseph (L R)	Wil-278	Jones,Moses			Grn-126
John	Pit-260	Joseph	Cho-230	Moses			Cas- 59
John	Bun- 95	Joshua	Bun- 94	N			Col- 19
John	Pas-193	Joshua	Roc- 34	Nancy			Cas- 58
John	Brt- 55	Joshua	Prq-219	Nancy			Grn-123
John	Bft- 30	Joshua	Row- 61	Nancy			Ora-131
John	Hrt-207	Joshua	Fra- 88	Nathan			Bla- 8
John	Roc- 30	Joshua	Wsh-222	Nathan			Rch-201
John	Roc- 11	Joshua P	Fra- 99	Nathan			Way-237
John	Car-171	Josiah	Bla- 9	Nathanl			Cas- 58
John	Fra- 98	Josiah	Prq-219	Nathaniel			Gat-106
John	Grn-136	Josiah Jr	Prq-220	Nathaniel			Joh-274
John	Sto-157	Juval	Glf-168	Nelly			Bft- 27
John	Ons-101	Kilby	Jon-299	Nelly			Row- 64
John	Sur-196	Kilby	Ons-104	Newman			Roc- 11
John	Bla- 4	Kilby	Ons-106	Oakley			Roc- 15
John	Nsh- 79	L	Cam-153	Patiance			Mec- 30
John	Bft- 20	Latucy	War-177	Peggy			Fra- 95
John	Rch-203	Leonard	Fra- 90	Phillip			Hrt-213
John	Joh-282	Levy	Sur-179	Polly			Cum-236
John	Hal-109	Levy	Bla- 4	Prissillah			Ran-169
John	Glf-186	Levy Jnr	Bla- 8	Rachel			Sam-152
John	Nor- 69	Leweling	Grn-127	Ralph			Grn-139
John	Way-236	Lewis	Len-321	Ralph			Grn-137
John	Way-243	Lewis	Rth-110	Reading			Len-320
John	Mar- 8	Lewis	Cha-212	Rebecca			Car-184
John	Mar- 9	Lewis	Nor- 70	Rebeckah			Hyd-?24
John	Bun- 74	Lewis	Gat-110	Redding			Ons-105
John	Bun- 73	Lewis Esq	Cum-267	Reddon			Sam-155
John J	Nor- 70	Lewis Jr	Dup- 15	Reuben			Grn-133
John Jr	Dup- 15	Lewis Sr	Dup- 15	Reuben			Cas- 58
John Jnr	Ran-169	Lewis Sen	Ora-112	Rhoda			Fra- 91
John Jnr	Pit-258	Littleberry	Rth-111	Richard			Cas- 58
John M	Sam-162	Loduc	Pas-193	Richard			Row- 64
John M Esqr	Wil-278	Lucy	Per-130	Richard			Fra- 87
John Sr	Dup- 15	Lucy	Hal-110	Richard			Ons-105
John Sr	Prq-219	Luis	Ran-170	Richard			Cum-236
John Senr	Rch-204	Luis	Ran-169	Richard			Mar- 5
John Snr	Pit-258	Luraney	Roc- 30	Richard			Hal-110
John Snr	Ran-169	M	Cam-161	Richard			Ran-170
John W	Glf-184	M	Ora-147	Richard			Len-323
Jon Sen	Ora-113	Malecky	Cur- 92	Richd			Cha-190
Jonas	Jon-299	Marshal	Mor- 62	Richd			Ora-116
Jonathan	Dup- 15	Mary	Dup- 27	Richd Esq			Cha-202
Jonathan	Ran-170	Mary	Ons-106	Richd Senr			Len-323
Jones	Grn-128	Mary	Len-319	Ridley			Hal-109
Jones	Sam-154	Mary	Cur- 82	Robert			Rth-111
Jordan	Bun- 76	Mary	Hyd-228	Robert			Rth-111
Joseph	Row- 45	Matthew	Joh-275	Robert			Grn-127
Joseph	Row- 48	Matthew	Cum-263	Robert			Row- 60
Joseph	Prq-219	Micajah	Glf-187	Robert			Bur-110
Joseph	Row- 46	Michael	Dup- 30	Robert			Fra- 95
Joseph	Cas- 59	Miles	Pas-193	Robert			Row- 84
Joseph	Gat-111	Morras	Hyd-222	Robert			Hal-110
Joseph	Hrt-212	Morris	Hyd-223	Robert			Bun- 73
Joseph	Bur-113	Morton	Wil-277	Robert (Cooper)			Per-139
Joseph	Nsh- 91	Moses	Ora-128	Robert H			War-184
Joseph	Bft- 24	Moses	Bla- 4	Robert Senr			War-179
Joseph	Wil-268	Moses	Hay-196	Robert Senr			Grn-127

Jones,Robt	Way-250	Jones,Thomas	Roc- 28	Jones,William Junr	Nor- 70
Robt	Per-134	Thomas	Row- 80	William of Cole	Prq-220
Roland	Row- 58	Thomas	Cum-268	William Senr	Nor- 70
Roxey	Cur- 92	Thomas	Hal-109	William Senr	Roc- 29
S	Cam-157	Thomas	Hal-109	Willm	Fra- 98
S	Col- 20	Thomas	Ran-170	Wm	Grn-134
S	Ash- 13	Thomas	Ran-170	Wm	Brt- 45
Salley	Hrt-216	Thomas	Bun- 73	Wm (Long)	Len-323
Sally	Ons-103	Thomas (B M)	Wil-274	Wm	Mon- 45
Samson	Way-245	Thomas (L R)	Wil-285	Wm	Mor- 61
Saml	Dup- 16	Thos	Ans- 28	Wm	Bur-104
Saml	Pas-193	Thos	Len-318	Wm	Len-320
Saml	Per-130	Thos	Mec- 52	Wm	Bla- 4
Samuel	Row- 38	Thos	Cho-226	Wm	Nsh- 92
Samuel	Cur- 87	Timothy	Tyr-202	Wm (Short)	Len-321
Samuel	Sto-147	Tobias	Way-243	Wm Jnr	Cho-226
Samuel	Sur-179	Travis	Glf-188	Wm Senr	Cho-226
Samuel	Ran-169	Vilet	Nsh- 73	Wm Snr	Grn-126
Samuel	Bun- 83	Vinkler Jr	Grn-134	Willie	Nor- 70
Sanisford	Rth-111	W	Bru-234	Willie	Fra- 89
Sarah	Hyd-220	W	Cam-163	Willis	Way-236
Sarah	Ora-124	W	Cam-161	Willis	Bur-116
Sarah	Rth-110	W	Cam-157	Willis	Hal-109
Sarah	Tyr-201	Wallace	Rth-111	Willis	Hal-109
Seth	Sur-189	Walter	Bft- 30	Wilson	Per-130
Shade	Jon-299	Wilaby	Pit-259	Jonikin,Lewis	Joh-288
Shaderick	Mor- 62	Wiley	Cas- 58	Jonson,Joshuay	Cur- 87
Shadr	Dup- 16	Wiley	Gat-107	Jonston,Easter	Gat-110
Shadrach	Cum-259	Wiley	Wil-271	Noble	Row- 48
Silas	Rch-205	Wiley	Per-139	Jordan,Abm	Cho-226
Silas	Glf-188	Wilie	Pit-257	Arthur	Nor- 70
Simon H	Gat-108	Wilie	Pit-260	Batte	Nor- 70
Smith	Pas-193	Wilie	Way-232	Benjamin	War-168
Smith	Row- 59	Willey	Grn-138	Caleb	Cho-229
Solomon	Rth-110	William	Rth-110	Cambun	Fra- 87
Solomon	Dup- 16	William	Prq-219	Charles	Way-237
Solomon	Sur-190	William	Cas- 58	Charles	Brt- 55
Solomon	Mar- 10	William	Cas- 58	Chs	Cho-230
Standiford	Rth-111	William	Pit-258	Chs	Ora-154
Stephen	Bun- 88	William	Pit-233	Clark	Cho-227
Stephen	Per-130	William	Bur-125	Dempsey	Cho-230
Stephen	Per-134	William	Cur- 91	Dillon	Cum-241
Stephen	Dup- 16	William	Roc- 29	Dinah	Hyd-221
Sterling	Rth-110	William	Roc- 11	Dixon	Joh-286
Sugar	Cha-198	William	Car-171	Dorcas	Hyd-221
Susana	Len-319	William	Fra- 94	Edmond	Hal-109
Mrs. Susanah	Fra- 93	William	Fra- 81	Edmond	Fra- 84
Susanna	War-180	William	Jon-299	Emelius	Sam-154
Sylvester	Ora-113	William	Joh-288	Enos	Ora-175
T	Glf-177	William	Joh-281	Evans	Fra- 99
Tamsey	Bft- 39	William	Joh-277	Frederick	Way-237
Tho	Ora-114	William	Joh-272	George Jr	Nor- 70
Thomas	Dup- 16	William	Edg- 58	George Senr	Nor- 70
Thomas	War-182	William	Wil-272	George W	Hyd-232
Thomas	Gat-113	William	Way-236	Hana	Cho-230
Thomas	Sto-133	William	Mar- 6	Hezekiah	Nor- 70
Thomas	Wil-274	William Esq	Hrt-213	Ichabud	Prq-220
Thomas	Bun- 89	William Esqr	Ons- 98	Jacob	Cho-228
Thomas	Brt- 56	William G F	Roc- 30	Jacob	Cho-230

Jordan,James	Brt- 58	Jordon,Jon	Ora-124	Joyner,Andrew	Mar- 8
James	Wsh-226	Joseph	Bun- 85	Ann	Nsh- 82
Jas	Bla- 10	Susanah	Bun- 85	Benj	Mar- 3
John	Hyd-230	Jorey,Elkin	Mor- 65	Bennet	Nsh- 80
John	Hyd-225	Joseph,Solomon M	Car-173	Burrel	Nsh- 80
John	Cho-228	Josey,Frederick	Row- 68	Curtis	Nsh-644
John	Bla- 10	John	Row- 67	David	Sur-182
Jos	Cho-228	Stephen	Nor- 69	Drewry	Nsh-643
Jos	Cho-226	William	Nor- 69	Giles	Nor- 70
Joseph	Prq-219	Wm	Row- 39	Giles	Sur-189
Joseph Jnr	Brt- 46	Willis	Nor- 69	Hardy	Nsh- 79
Joseph Senr	Brt- 46	Jourdan,Cornelius	Edg- 67	Henry	Nsh- 80
Jude	Rob-219	Edy	Edg- 67	Jessee	Nsh- 80
Martha	War-177	Francis	Mon- 32	Jonathan	Sur-178
Mrs. Mary	Brt- 47	Grey	Edg- 60	Jordan	Nsh- 87
Matthew	Len-315	Henry	Edg- 67	Lewis	Nor- 69
Matthew	Len-313	Jno	Mon- 28	Lewis	Nsh- 79
Matthew	Prq-219	Jno	Mon- 32	Matthew	Nsh- 80
Meady	Cha-214	Joshua	Edg- 66	Mills	Sur-178
Morning	Cho-228	Randolph	Edg- 43	Nathan	Nsh- 81
Nathan	Cho-229	Thos	Mon- 28	Nathan	Nsh- 81
Richard	Hyd-234	Thos	Mon- 32	Thomas	Nor- 70
Richard	Pas-192	Jourden,J	Mon- 43	Whitney	Mar- 16
Richard	Pit-253	J	Mon- 43	Wm	Nsh- 80
Robert H	Roc- 25	Margret	Ran-170	Willis	Sur-176
Robert	Roc- 25	Wm	Mec- 32	Jucy,Henchen	Ran-169
Rothias	Hyd-221	Jourdin,Thomas	Grn-134	Judah (sic)	Bft- 38
Samuel	Roc- 27	Jovanso,John	Ons-105	Judd,John	Wil-261
Seth	Fra- 92	Jowers,Geo	Ans- 26	Nathaniel	Wil-267
Thomas	Hyd-234	Geo	Ans- 4	Nathaniel Jr	Wil-260
Thomas	Nor- 70	Joseph	Ans- 23	William	Wil-261
Thomas	Cum-248	Joyce,Alexander	Roc- 34	Jude,John	Sur-180
Thomas	Ora-161	Alexr	Sto- 94	Judge,James	Hal-109
Thomas	Pas-192	Alexr	Sto-123	James	Dup- 30
Thomas	Pit-241	Ambrose	Roc- 23	John	Hal-109
Thomas N Creek	Pas-192	Andrew	Roc- 24	Judkins,C	Glf-162
Uriah	Nor- 70	Elisha	Roc- 33	Edmd	Bft- 37
Valentine	Pit-241	George	Roc- 23	Gray	Bft- 37
William	Hyd-234	Isaac	Sto-153	Joel	Glf-162
William	Sam-158	Isaac	Sto-113	John	Nor- 69
Wm	Nsh- 85	James	Roc- 24	Nathaniel	Hal-109
Wm	Cho-226	John	Roc- 25	Rebekah	Hal-109
Wm	Cho-230	John Coon	Roc- 23	Thomas	War-181
Wm	Ora-117	John P	Roc- 23	Juett,Thomas	Cas- 59
Willie	Nor- 70	Martha	Roc- 20	Jukes,John	Gat-110
Winefred	Way-237	Martin	Mar- 12	Julen,Bohan	Ran-170
Woodford	Roc- 24	Pleasant	Roc- 23	Isaac	Ran-170
Zacheriah	Rob-229	Robert	Roc- 33	Tobias	Ran-170
Jorden,Hannah	Cur- 87	Samuel	Roc- 23	Julin,George	Rth-110
Jonathan	Ora-163	Thomas	Sto-123	Jesse	Ran-169
Jonathan	Hrt-215	Thomas S of C	Roc- 24	Julius,Samuel	Rth-109
Jordin,Jacob	Gat-109	Thomas S of E	Roc- 22	Jump,John	Len-318
John	Gat-108	Thomas Senr	Roc- 22	Junima,John	Dup- 28
Joseph	Gat-109	Thos	Sto- 94	Jurdan,Jerimiah	Gat-108
William	Gat-109	William	Sto- 94	Jurden,Butten	Ran-170
Jordon,Adam	Bur-120	William	Sto-122	Charles	Sto-129
Geo	Ans- 9	William	Roc- 24	George	Sto-108
Jas	Ans- 22	Joyner,Abraham	Nor- 70	George	Sto-144
John	Bun- 77	Amos	Nsh- 80	James	Ran-169

Jurden,John	Sto-109	Keahey,Samuel	Rch-205	Keeland,J		Ora-154
Jury,W E	Bru-234	Sarah	Rch-205	W Jr		Ora-153
Juschore,Wm	Ora-161	Keahy,James	Rch-205	Keele,Jacob		Brt- 50
Justice,Allen	Cha-208	Keair,Mary	Bft- 32	Keeling,Carlton		Wil-257
Amos	Bun- 72	Milley	Bft- 32	Thomas		Wil-257
Comfort	Ons-108	Keais,Amey	Bft- 31	Keemore,James		Nor- 70
Elijah	Ons-108	Clary	Bft- 31	Keen,Anna		Roc- 32
Ephraim	Bun- 81	Keal,John	Pit-262	George		Joh-278
Francis	Ons-108	Keale,Samuel	Pit-262	Isaac		Joh-284
Isaac	Bur-131	Simon	Pit-256	James		Brt- 54
James	Bun- 72	Kean,Leonard	Sto- 97	John		Cas- 59
James	Rth-111	Solomon	Hrt-215	John		Cum-259
Jarrad	Rth-110	Kearney,James	War-173	Lamuel		Gat-113
John	Bur-131	Sarah	War-180	leonard		Sto-127
John Junr	Bun- 72	William K	War-183	Sasser		Joh-284
John Senr	Bun- 72	Kearns,Joseph	Ran-171	William		Sam-155
Joseph	Bun- 80	Kears,Henry	Bft- 37	Keenan,Isaac		Ran-171
Peter	Lnc-351	Salley H	Bft- 37	Silas		Ran-171
Stephen	Cha-205	Silva	Bft- 37	Keener,Adam		Lnc-370
Thomas	Bun- 72	Keath,J	Bru-234	Jacob		Lnc-370
William	Bun- 72	William	Row- 53	John		Lnc-370
William	Lnc-346	Wm	Bru-228	John Jr		Lnc-370
William	Bun- 72	Keating,Robert	Cho-220	Michael		Lnc-370
Justin,Benjn	Ran-170	Keaton,Alexander	Dup- 27	Keep,James		Nor- 70
Henry	Ran-170	Benja	Pas-194	Keepler,David		Lnc-370
Henry	Bur-129	Betsy	Pas-194	Keetan,Clifton		Wil-273
Thomas	Bur-105	Deba	Pas-194	John		Wil-264
Justiss,Benjn	Hal-110	Isaac	Pas-194	John Jr		Wil-262
John	Hal-109	Joel	Ire-253	Lucy		Wil-265
Joseph C	Hal-110	John	Pas-194	Peter		Wil-262
Robert	Hal-108	Joseph	Prq-220	William		Wil-262
Wm	Hal-109	Joseph Jun	Pas-193	Keeter,Henry		Rth-112
Juvell,James	Bur-120	Julius	Ire-254	James		Rth-112
		Julius	Ire-254	Jesse		Hal-110
Kack,H	Ora-131	Miles	Ire-253	John		Rth-112
Kahoon,Benjamin	Jon-300	S	Cam-159	Josua		Rth-112
Kale,Elisha	Lnc-355	Silas	Pas-194	Lemuel		Brt- 47
Robert	Hrt-210	William	Pas-194	Keeth,Elizabeth		Nsh- 80
Kalvel,Edmon	Row- 47	William	Pas-194	Keetor,N		Bru-230
Kanady,Aaron	Sur-180	William	Ire-254	Keever,Thos		Lnc-376
John	Glf-185	Yerb	Ire-255	Keileigh,Sam		Cab-136
John	Glf-158	Keator,J	Cam-165	Wm		Cab-137
Keziah	Sur-180	L	Cam-165	Keilly,George		Cas- 59
Nathan	Glf-185	Keblet,Jacob	Lnc-355	Keisiter,Paul		Lnc-344
Samuel	Sur-180	Kee,Achilles	Sur-187	Keisler,Jacob		Row- 72
Kap,Lucy	Sto-154	Henry	Edg- 63	John		Row- 72
Karr,John	Bur-126	John	Mor- 60	John		Cab-139
Kasey,James	Rob- 22	Jonathan	Jon-299	Keit,Martha		Edg- 72
Kations,Joseph	Cha-203	Joseph	Jon-299	Keith,Gabriel		Bun- 93
Katon,Nellie	Ire-269	Rice	Sur-184	George		Grn-126
Kay,James	Grn-137	Sarah	Mor- 60	Hugh		Mor- 60
John	Nor- 70	William	Sur-187	Sion		Ans- 32
Kaylor,George	Lnc-347	Keeber,Wm	Brt- 43	Keithly,Jonathan		Dup- 25.
Keach,Jasper	Hyd-222	Keel,Hardy	Bft- 32	Kelan,John		Row- 84
John	Hyd-222	Howell	Car-185	Keland,W Sen		Ora-153
Stephen	Hyd-222	Isaac	Mar- 10	Kelgaw,James		Row- 82
Keachey,John	Rch-195	Minchey	Hrt-211	Kell,Rebecca		Ora-164
Keacht,John H	Mar- 11	Keeland,Elizabeth	Mor- 62	Thomas		Sur-195
Keagle,Jno	Mec- 46	F	Ora-153	Wm		Ora-174

Kellam,Henry	Glf-185	Kelly,Edward	Roc- 16	Kellyham,Cornelius	Bla- 12
John P	Glf-166	Edward	Hal-110	Kelman,Henry Sen	Roc- 10
Saml	Glf-158	Eliza	Hal-110	Kemer,William	Hal-110
Shed	Glf-158	Enoch S	Lnc-357	Kemmery,Frederick	Rth-112
Kellar,Christian	Bur-131	Henry	Rth-112	Kemp,A	Cam-161
Jacob	Bur-108	Henry	Cha-194	Barnett	Cas- 59
Jacob	Bur-119	Hugh	Mor- 68	Benjamin	Sur-191
John	Bur-118	Hugh	Cum-243	D W	Bla- 13
Joshua	Glf-181	Hugh	Cum-269	Green	War-171
Leonard	Bur-107	J	Bla- 11	James	Cur- 88
Martin	Bur-126	James	Rth-113	John	Row- 83
Michael	Bur-122	James	Bft- 39	Mary	Bla- 13
Keller,John	Lnc-351	James	Mon- 25	Squire	Ire-254
Michael	Lnc-351	James	Mor- 63	Wm	Bla- 13
Robt	Row- 44	James	Cas- 59	Kempe,Christy	Lnc-327
Rosanna	Sur-164	James	Rch-200	Kenady,Agnus	Rch-210
Kellet,Alexr	Sam-163	James	Sto-140	J	Cam-156
Kelley,A	Cam-161	Jas	Mor- 61	W	Cam-160
Charles	Mar- 14	Jas	Rob-230	Kenan,Danl L	Dup- 6
Garrett	Sto-141	Jas	Bla- 7	Martin	Bun- 82
J Esq	Cam-154	Jas Junr	Bla- 7	Sarah	Dup- 6
James	Sto-106	John	Roc- 31	Thomas	Dup- 6
Jno	Ora-128	John	Mor- 63	Kencey,Danl	Sam-163
John Jr	Joh-272	John	Mor- 68	Kendal,Benjn	Row- 44
John Jr	Joh-272	John	Row- 86	Kendall,James	Mon- 41
Joseph	Edg- 72	John	Bla- 7	James	Wil-275
Joshua	Bun- 86	John	Rch-213	Jas	Mon- 37
Labin	Bft- 22	John	Bun- 87	R	Mon- 37
M	Cam-161	John	Sur-178	Wm	Mon- 37
Mat	Cam-158	John	Rth-112	Kendel,Benj	Mon- 40
Met	Bft- 29	Joseph	Mor- 67	John	Mon- 39
Patrik	Sto-141	Joseph	Mor- 68	Saml	Mon- 44
Polley	Bft- 21	Joseph	Cha-201	Wm	Mon- 44
Sabry	Joh-274	Margaret	Hal-110	Kendle,Nancy	Pas-194
Sally	Joh-274	Mary	Mor- 68	Kendrick,Thos	Lnc-336
William	Cas- 59	Mathew	Rob-230	Kendrix,William	Lnc-367
Kellis,Louis	Rch-200	Matthew	Bla- 7	Kendy,David	Mec- 54
Kellom,Noa	Row- 43	Patrick	Sto-106	Kenedy,Gilbreath	Lnc-330
Thomas	Ora-162	Patrick	Rob-228	Henry	Len-321
Kellon,Abraham	Row- 66	Patrick	Bla- 13	Isaac	Bur-120
James	Row- 53	Peter	Mor- 63	James	Per-130
Kellor,John	Row- 65	Peter	Sur-164	Jas	Mec- 35
Kellry,David	Gat-107	Reuben	Cha-202	Jas	Mec- 51
Kells,Tho	Ora-124	Sally	Brt- 60	Jesse	Len-311
Kellum,David	Roc- 24	Thomas	Sur-185	Jno	Mec- 34
Edmond	Jon-300	Thomas	Bun- 87	Jno	Len-311
Elijah	Jon-300	W D	Bla- 7	John	Lnc-333
John	Roc- 24	William	Rch-211	John Senr	Mar- 12
Spencer	Roc- 24	William	Rch-212	Joshua	Len-311
William	Roc- 24	William	Rch-199	Lemuel	Mar- 12
Kelly,And	Bla- 7	William	Bun- 86	Mary	Len-314
Angus Esq	Cum-256	William	Rth-112	Ruth	Mar- 6
Barbee	Cha-193	William	Sam-154	William	Cum-255
Curtis	Bft- 22	Wm	Mor- 67	Wm	Mec- 45
Danl	Mor- 61	Wm	Hal-110	Keniday,Robert	Grn-133
Danl	Mor- 65	Wm	Cho-230	Wm	Grn-123
Danl	Rob-232	Wm	Bla- 11	Kennada,James	Brt- 59
Duncan	Mor- 68	Wm	Cha-197	Patrick	Sam-159
Edmond	Mor- 68	Wm C	Mor- 68	Kennaday,Rev. Andrew	
					Wil-261

Name	Loc	Name	Loc	Name	Loc
Kennaday,Martin	Wil-268	Kerby,Samuel	Sto-144	Kerr,Wm	Mec- 54
Nancy	Rth-112	Wiley	Cha-190	Wm	Mec- 25
William (B C)	Wil-267	William	Sur-173	Wm	Mec- 37
Kennady,James	Row- 45	William --ke	Sur-193	Kerrell,Phillip	Row- 70
John	Row- 44	Kerethers,James	Row- 82	Kerriker,Henry	Row- 70
John	Row- 45	Kerfuse,Caleb	Row- 39	Kerringer,George	Mor- 62
John	Cum-237	Kerk,George	Per-140	Kerrn,Conrad	Row- 82
Sherwood	Row- 45	Kerklin,Sarah	Roc- 3	Kerrse,Alexander	Sur-188
William	Row- 45	Kerley,Samuel	Sto-108	Kersey,David	Cas- 59
Kenneday,David	Pit-250	Samuel Jnr	Sto-108	Drury	Sur-179
John	Pit-239	Kerlock,Mellisan	Lnc-355	James	Cas- 59
Kennedy,Alexr	Mor- 65	Kermichal,Archd	Ora-125	John	Cas- 59
Archibald	Dup- 7	Kern,Daniel	Row- 85	John	Car-173
Celia	Cho-222	Philip	Row- 85	John Jr	Cas- 59
Daniel	Cum-255	Richard	Row- 85	Richard	Car-172
Daniel	Dup- 31	Kernega,Abraham	Jon-300	Samuel	Cas- 59
Daniel Senr	Cum-255	Kerner,Joseph	Sto-137	Thomas	Car-172
David	Mor- 58	Joseph	Sto-103	William	War-182
David	Dup- 5	Kerney,Catharine	Fra- 85	Kerson,Jno	Mec- 47
Edward	Mor- 59	John	Sto-128	Kersy,A	Glf-170
George	Mor- 59	Kernoy,Christian	Row- 84	B	Glf-170
James	Dup- 30	Geo	Row- 42	Jesse	Glf-169
Jas	Bft- 19	John	Row- 42	Wm	Glf-169
John	Mor- 61	Philip	Row- 42	Kesishke,Frederick	Sto-114
John	Cum-255	Kerns,Alexr	Mec- 33	Kesler,Christian	Row- 79
John	Bft- 27	Daniel	Mec- 32	John	Row- 77
John	Dup- 30	John	Row- 40	Kessey,Amos	Glf-167
Joseph	Dup- 31	Wm	Mec- 46	Kessler,J	Ash- 13
Rebecca	Wsh-224	Kernuss,Noah	Row- 77	J	Ash- 8
Robt	Mor- 57	William	Row- 77	Kester,Paul	Bun- 76
Thomas	Dup- 32	Kerny,David	Ire-266	William	Sto-101
Will	Bft- 37	Kerr,Abraham	Row- 50	William	Bun- 98
Wm Plantation	Bft- 35	Absolem	Sur-182	William	Sto-133
Kenney,Crawford	Fra- 99	Alexander	Sur-182	Ketcham,David	Ons-105
Thomas	Rch-207	Bazillia	Cas- 59	Jonathan Esqr	Ons-105
Kennick,David	Row- 59	Elener	Ire-241	Ketchey,John	Row- 78
John	Row- 60	Elizabeth	Ire-263	Ketchy,John	Row- 68
Kennisec,John	Bur-104	Hugh	Rth-113	Keter,James	Hal-110
Kenny,Christian	Row- 84	Hugh	Mec- 46	L	Bru-234
John	Row- 58	James	Row- 39	Mary	Hal-110
Kenrick,Geo	Row- 58	James	Ire-257	Nancy	Rth-112
Kent,Burrel	Nsh- 86	Jas	Mec- 29	Uriah	Hal-110
James	Row- 80	John	Cas- 59	Ketner,Francis	Sto-100
Nelson	Nsh- 86	Jno	Mec- 47	Frederick	Sto-103
Richard	Ire-268	Joseph	Mec- 54	Matthew	Sto-103
Wilie	Nsh- 86	Matthews	Sur-182	Kettle,Joel	Glf-180
William	Mar- 3	Moses	Mec- 34	Kever,Henry	Mec- 36
Kenyan,Sally	Lnc-340	Peter	Row- 78	Jno	Rob-239
Keply,Henry	Row- 87	Richard	Mec- 47	Kew,James	Ire-238
Ker,David	Mec- 23	Robt	Mec- 46	Kewell,John	Bft- 35
Faith	Edg- 55	Saml	Mec- 46	Key,Criswell	Roc- 29
Richard	Mec- 22	Saml	Mec- 47	Garland	Roc- 26
Kerby,Isaac	Cha-199	Saml	Mec- 34	George	Nor- 70
James Jun	Cha-190	William	Rth-113	John	Roc- 27
Jesse	Sur-184	William	Ire-239	Samuel	Hal-110
Jesse	Sto-144	William	Ire-239	Thomas	Roc- 29
John	Sur-177	William	Glf-155	Vinson	Mon- 29
Peter	Sur-193	Wm	Mec- 46	Keykendall,Abraham	Bun- 98
Phillip	Sur-180	Wm	Mec- 44	Jacob	Bun- 95

Name	Ref	Name	Ref	Name	Ref
Keykendall,James	Bun- 94	Killion,Daniel	Bun- 93	Kimbell,Seegan	War-180
Peter	Bun- 84	Daniel	Ire-245	Nathl	Fra- 78
Simon	Bun- 95	David	Lnc-351	William	War-183
Keys,James H	War-176	David	Lnc-370	Willie	War-182
John	Sur-177	Henry	Lnc-345	Kimble,Charles	Sto-127
John	Mor- 55	Jacob	Lnc-370	Harris	Row- 77
Joseph	Sur-173	Jacob	Lnc-362	Jacob	Row- 83
William Junr	Nor- 70	Jacob	Lnc-370	Kimbol,George	Roc- 9
William Senr	Nor- 70	John	Lnc-351	Kimborough,Jas	Ans- 8
Kibbell,Walter	Fra- 91	John	Lnc-347	Kimbro,Andrew	Cas- 59
Kichen,Joseph	Rob-220	Mathias	Lnc-362	Aron	Row- 45
Kid,Benjamin	Sur-181	William	Ora-167	E	Ora-155
John	Ire-257	Killo,Isaac	Roc- 28	George	Sur-183
Kidd,Moses	Cha-204	Killow,Josify	Roc- 32	Moses	Row- 43
William	Ora-167	Killpatrick,Robt	Cab-143	Ormon	Sur-183
Kidwell,Elijah	Rth-112	Killup,William	Gat-108	Solomon	Sto-141
Elijah	Rth-112	Killy,J	Cum-241	Thomas	Row- 45
Kie,Robt	Bla- 11	James C	Cum-239	Kimbrough,Betsey	Cas- 59
Kieoller,Henry	Lnc-326	John	Cum-241	F	Ora-145
Kiesler,John	Row- 73	Mary	Cum-238	Goldman Esq	Wil-263
Kiestler,George	Lnc-326	Kilman,Aaron	Roc- 12	Jno	Ans- 20
Jacob	Lnc-326	Henry Jun	Roc- 10	John	Cas- 59
Jacob	Lnc-326	James	Roc- 11	Nancy	Roc- 21
Kiff,James	Mar- 14	Kilparick,James	Rth-112	Nathl	Ans- 18
Kiger,Jacob	Sto-129	Kilpatrick,Andrew	Bun- 96	Wm	Cas- 59
Kight,David	Pit-236	Andrew	Ire-259	Kimbull,Pleasant	Grn-132
Henry	Pit-251	Fras	Len-321	Kime,David	Ran-171
John	Pit-250	Hugh	Rth-113	Kimmer,Henry	Mon- 38
Samuel	Pit-251	Isler	Len-322	Kimmons,Thomas	Rth-113
Samuel Jr	Pit-251	J D	Row- 75	Kimmy,Mason	Ons-102
Stephen	Pit-251	James	Bun- 84	Kimzey,Agness	Bun- 88
Kilbourn,E	Ash- 6	James	Rth-112	Benj	Bun- 91
Kilby,Abraham Esq	Wil-267	James	Rth-112	William	Bun- 88
Henry	Wil-260	Joseph	Bun- 97	Kinamon,John	Grn-149
Humphrey	Wil-266	Joshua	Ire-263	Kincade,Andrew	Row- 75
James	Wil-267	Robert	Row- 73	Archd	Bur-130
Reuben	Wil-266	William	Rth-112	Archd	Row- 75
William	Wil-260	William	Row- 72	James	Bur-130
William Jr	Wil-285	Wm W	Bun- 73	James	Row- 82
Kilibrew,Rabeckah	Edg- 51	Kilyier,Jacob	Grn-143	James Sr	Row- 75
Kililes,Robt	Cha-208	Jacob	Grn-138	John	Row- 76
Robt Jr	Cha-208	Kimbal,George Junr	Roc- 34	Joseph	Row- 64
Killams,Thos	Ans- 21	Jessee	Roc- 34	Kincaid,David	Lnc-360
Killebrew,Hinchy	Jon-300	John	Hal-110	James Senr	Bun- 72
William	Jon-300	Kimball,A	Mon- 43	John	Lnc-360
Killet,John	Way-248	Abington	Grn-148	John	Bur-127
Killian,Adam	Hay-196	Buck	Mon- 43	Robert	Bur-115
Daniel	Sto-103	Drury	Grn-148	William	Bur-127
Daniel	Sto-136	Drury	Lnc-365	Kincanon,Andrew	Sur-174
Michael	Sto-136	John	Bun- 95	Kincey,Christopher	Jon-299
Killingsworth,Freeman		John	Bun- 95	John	Jon-299
	Joh-287	Joseph	Bun- 95	Joseph Junr	Jon-300
Henry	Rch-209	Sion	Fra- 84	Joseph Senr	Jon-299
John	Joh-280	Wm	Mon- 43	Lewis	Jon-299
Joseph	Jon-300	Kimball,Benjamen	War-169	Kinchen,Ben	Cha-194
Shadk	Bft- 26	Edmund	War-170	Ben	Cha-211
Wm	Hal-110	James	War-172	Leonard	Nor- 70
Killion,Andrew	Lnc-351	Joseph	War-173	Kindal,Elisha	Ans- 12
Barbary	Lnc-347	Leonard	War-177	Jno	Ans- 16

-176-

Kindal,Wm	Mor- 59	King,Daniel	Rth-113	King,John		Sam-159
Kindell,John	Wil-282	Darcas	Len-311	John		Sto-120
William	Wil-274	David	War-170	John		Bur-126
Kinder,Adam	Lnc-376	David	Mar- 4	John		Roc- 4
Conrad	Lnc-376	David	Dup- 29	John		Hal-110
Henry	Lnc-357	David	War-170	John		Sto- 91
Jacob	Row- 88	Drury	Rth-112	John		Ons-104
Jacob	Inc-365	E	Ash- 3	John		Ora-120
John	Sto-136	Edward	Hal-110	John		Ons-101
John	Lnc-336	Edwin	Nor- 79	John B		Grn-138
Peter	Lnc-336	Elenor	Ora-131	John H		Brt- 56
Kindle,Geo	Mon- 39	Elihu A	Ire-248	John Junr		Sam-154
John	Ran-171	Elijah	Roc- 14	John Junr		Roc- 25
Thomas	Ran-171	Eliphlet	Pit-234	Johnson		Sto-151
Kindred,Saml	Ans- 12	Eliza	Ora-164	Johnson		Sto-109
Kindrick,Saml	Cas- 59	Elizebeth	Ans- 26	Johnston		Bur-105
Thomas	Cas- 59	Ephaim	Hrt-212	Jonathan		Rth-112
Kineday,John	Way-242	Ephraim,	Ons-100	Jonathan		War-176
King,Mrs.	Cum-237	George	Jon-299	Jonathan		Bun- 82
A	Ora-156	George	Rth-112	Joseph		Bun- 82
A	Col- 18	George	Hal-110	Joseph		Wsh-228
Abner	Rth-113	Gorge	Grn-129	Joseph		Lnc-355
Abraham	Pit-253	Hallod	Hal-110	Julias		Mec- 31
Absalem	Rth-112	Hekerson	Ans- 21	Julin		Nsh- 78
Alexander	Ire-263	Henry	Ora-124	Levy		Roc- 17
Alexander	Sto-155	Henry	Cum-268	M		Bru-236
Alexr	Sto-114	Henry	Nor- 70	Mary		Hal-110
Allen	War-167	Henry	Ora-134	Mary		Ons-108
Allen	Way-245	Henry	Roc- 17	Micajah		Ons-102
Ambrose	Roc- 25	Henry	Roc- 29	Micajah		Sto-119
Andrew	Ire-248	Henry	Brt- 64	Michael		Wsh-223
Andw	Ora-142	Henry	Ora-163	Michael Junr		Sam-154
Anne	Hal-111	Hezekiah	Ans- 26	Michael Senr		Sam-154
Anthony	War-168	Hiram	Hal-110	N		Ora-156
Anthony	Hal-110	J	Ora-156	Nathan		Cum-246
Ard	Bla- 11	James	Ire-248	Nathan		Roc- 32
Armor Jr	Ora-163	James	Lnc-362	Nathan		Ons-101
Armor Sr	Ora-163	James	Sto-140	Nathaniel		Sur-185
Armoser	Ora-124	James	Edg- 50	Nathl		Ora-142
Arthur	Hal-110	James	Rth-113	Nathl		Ora-170
B	Glf-179	James	Wil-279	Nehemiah		Roc- 4
Baxter	Ora-142	James	Ons-102	Nehemiah		Roc- 18
Baxter	Ora-156	James	Ons-100	Norman		Cho-230
Benajah	Ons-108	James	Per-131	Parnal		Gat-114
Benjamin	Bun- 89	James	Ora-164	Peter		Ran-171
Benjamin	War-169	Jas	Ans- 26	Polly		Sur-192
Bennett	Mec- 32	Jeremiah	Sur-187	Priscilla		Rth-112
Boling	Ran-171	Jesse	Row- 62	R		Ash- 7
Briton	Pit-258	Jessee	Ire-264	R		Ora-154
C	Glf-186	Joel Esq	Fra- 83	Rachel		Hal-111
Cader	Brt- 59	Jno	Len-322	Rachel		Ire-261
Celia	Len-315	Jno	Mec- 24	Richard		Ons-102
Charles	Ora-131	Jno	Ans- 28	Richard H		Ire-263
Charles	Dup- 12	Jno	Ans- 30	Rigdon		Ons-105
Charles	Sam-163	John	Lnc-362	Robert		Mar- 7
Charles	War-169	John	Ran-171	Robert		Cas- 59
Charles	Hal-110	John	Nor- 71	Robt		Mor- 54
Charles Jnr	Brt- 64	John	Fra- 77	Robt		Mon- 29
Charles Senr	Brt- 64	John	Grn-132	S		Bla- 10

King,Sam	Ora-124	King,Wm	Hal-110	Kirby,Salley	Nsh- 74	
Sampson	War-181	Wm	Glf-174	Thomas	Hal-110	
Saml	Ora-163	Wm	Ora-122	Thomas	Joh-284	
Samuel	Hal-110	Wm	Ora-124	Wiley	Cha-199	
Samuel	Hal-110	Winifred	Hal-110	Will	Sam-163	
Samuel	Ire-263	Wood	War-184	William	Cha-199	
Samuel	Ire-239	Zachariah	Roc- 24	William	Prq-219	
Samuel Junr	Bun- 98	Kinghton,Betsey	Cas- 59	Kirckman,Levin	Glf-181	
Samuel Snr	Bun- 89	Kiniday,John	Grn-139	Kirk (sic)	Mon- 51	
Sarah	Ora-120	Kinlaugh,Wm	Rob-243	Danl	Mon- 43	
Sarah	Ora-164	Kinlaw,Benjamin	Rob-243	Elisha	Ora-147	
Simon	Gat-108	Robert	Rob-243	Geo Jr	Cha-205	
Solomon	Bla- 6	Kinley,John	Cur- 87	Isaac	Ora-126	
Stephen	Ons-101	Joshua	Cab-138	Isaac	Cas- 59	
Stephen	Sam-156	Kinn,Christian	Ran-171	James	Ora-172	
Tabby	Dup- 25	David	Ran-171	James	Mon- 24	
Tho	Ora-114	Kinnaday,William	Wil-268	Jno	Mec- 39	
Thomas	Bur-107	Kinnaman,John	Sto-134	Jno	Mec- 38	
Thomas	Jon-300	Walter	Sto-134	Jno L	Ora-143	
Thomas	Bur-111	Kinnebrew,James	Cas- 59	John	Roc- 3	
Thomas	Dup- 12	Kinnega,Isaac	Jon-300	John Esq	Mon- 45	
Thomas	Roc- 17	Kinneman,John	Sto-137	Joseph	Cha-204	
Thomas	Pit-253	Samuel	Sto-137	Parham	Mon- 43	
Thomas	Ire-239	Kinnery,William	Rth-112	Parkarch	Ora-147	
Thomas D	Sam-160	Kinney,Thomas	Wsh-227	Sarah	Ora-114	
Thomas Junr	Ons-102	Kinniman,Thomas	Sto-102	Wm	Ora-137	
Thomas Senr	Roc- 20	Thomas	Sto-134	Kirkdall (sic)	Mon- 51	
Thomas Senr	Ons- 98	Kinninson,James	War-173	Kirkham,Peter	Brt- 48	
Thos	Bur-103	Kinnion,Anthy	Bft- 29	Kirkland,James	Nor- 71	
Wiatt	Roc- 12	Kinnon,Joel	Cas- 59	Jesse	Rth-112	
Wilie	Way-244	William	Cas- 59	Jo	Ora-160	
William	Ire-264	Kinnup,John	Row- 67	Joseph Jr	Ora-151	
William	Lnc-362	Kinsauls,Bethia	Pit-240	Joseph	Ora-151	
William	Nor- 71	Francis	Pit-241	Nathan	Rth-112	
William	Pas-194	Henry	Pit-261	Wm	Ora-143	
William	Gat-105	John	Pit-239	Wm	Ora-160	
William	Bur-122	Racheil	Pit-241	Kirkman,D	Glf-173	
William	Sur-190	Kinsbrach,Jno Esq	Mec- 25	E	Glf-161	
William	Sto-119	Kinsday,John	Grn-137	Geo	Glf-165	
William	Roc- 11	Kinsey,Henery	Cur- 81	George	Glf-161	
William	Roc- 22	John	Dup- 8	J	Glf-182	
William	Roc- 20	Mary	Cur- 81	Jos	Glf-165	
William	Row- 60	Thomas	Hay-196	Levin	Glf-183	
William	Pit-253	Kinsland,Rebecca	Hay-196	Thomas	Ran-171	
William	Cas- 59	Kinsworthy,Joshua	Hay-196	Kirkpatrick,Eliz	Cum-248	
William	Bun- 82	Kinyon,Benja	Prq-220	H	Glf-166	
William	Bun- 81	Jos	Cho-226	Hugh	Mec- 24	
William	Sto- 91	Levi	Prq-220	Jas	Mec- 50	
William	Ons-102	Kipp,A	Cam-158	Sam	Ora-112	
William C	Edg- 57	Kipps,Seth	Hyd-222	Thos	Mec- 50	
William Jur	Sto-120	Kirbey,Gideon	Cha-196	Thos	Mec- 51	
William Junr	Jon-299	Wm	Ans- 18	Valentine	Cab-143	
William Junr	Sam-154	Kirby,Daniel	Bur-122	Kirksey,Elijah	Ire-241	
William Rumplus	Sam-154	Eliza	Bur-122	Kirly,Jesse	Sto-108	
William Senr	Jon-299	James	Bur-131	Kirnega,Robert	Jon-300	
William Senr	Sam-154	James	Joh-284	Kirty,Samuel Jnr	Sto-253	
Wm	Hal-110	James	Cha-199	Kirven,Whitmil	Cum-259	
Wm	Ora-163	John	Bur-112	Kiser,John	Sto-156	
Wm	Brt- 59	Josiah	Bur-117	John	Sto-116	

Kiser,John Jnr	Sto-116	Kline,Peter	Sto-129	Knolley,Jacob	Edg- 61	
Manas	Sto-156	Kluge,John P	Sto-154	Knotgrass,J	Ora-168	
Philip	Sto-114	Knapper,Hugh	Wil-276	Knott,-----	Glf-186	
Philip	Sto-155	Kneland,Jesse	Wsh-225	Bartlet	Grn-120	
Kisler,John	Sto-156	Kng,John	Way-243	Ephraim	Wil-270	
Kisney,Saml M	Bur-113	Knight,A	Glf-160	James	Grn-142	
Kitchen,David	Bun- 85	A	Glf-163	James	Glf-186	
Easter	Cas- 59	Abel	Glf-164	James Jr	Glf-186	
Elizabeth	Edg- 63	Abel	Glf-185	Jethan	Glf-186	
Elizabeth	Mor- 65	Abner	Hal-110	John	Per-132	
Jesse	Fra- 93	Arthur	Edg- 71	John	Brt- 43	
Kintchen	Mor- 65	Charles	Edg- 63	Nathan	Glf-186	
Lovitt	Edg- 46	Charles W	Edg- 47	Nathl	Brt- 60	
Oren	Edg- 60	D	Glf-162	William	Sto-110	
Kitchens,Ephraim	Bun- 97	Elias	Glf-164	William	Sto-111	
Kitchesides,Polly	Lnc-327	Evans	Cas- 59	William	Sto-150	
Kite,H	Cam-160	Garrett	Edg- 49	Knotts,Absolem	Ans- 23	
J	Cam-164	H	Glf-184	Knowle,Jas	Bla- 3	
Nancy	Pas-194	Henry	Glf-186	Knowles,David	Lnc-336	
W	Cam-164	Henry	Cum-253	James	Dup- 21	
Z	Cam-159	Isaac	Cas- 59	John E	Dup- 21	
Z	Cam-156	James	Wil-273	William	Dup- 19	
Kiteral,John	Pit-239	James	Edg- 57	Knowls,Abner	Prq-220	
Kith,Jon	Ans- 30	Jessee	Edg- 70	Elizabeth	Prq-220	
Kitian,John	Sur-182	John	Roc- 15	Knows,Liddy	Bft- 27	
Kitle,Wm	Grn-131	John	Glf-164	Rhoda	Bft- 26	
Kitner,Francis Sr	Sto-131	John	Mor- 67	Knox,Mrs.	Mec- 27	
Frederic	Sto-136	John	Hal-124	Alderson	Pit-256	
George	Row- 69	John	Edg- 62	Alexander	Pit-257	
Henry	Sto-152	John	Grn-131	Allison	Mec- 53	
Henry	Sto-131	John Senr	Hal-110	Allison	Jon-300	
Matthew	Sto-136	Johnathan (dead)	Grn-131	Andrew	Ire-255	
Peter	Row- 68	Jonathan	Grn-138	Adnrew	Pas-193	
Kitrell,Isaac	Grn-129	Jonathan	Glf-164	Benjamin	Ire-255	
Isham	Grn-128	Joseph	Cas- 59	David	Mec- 28	
John	Grn-146	Judith	Grn-149	George	Pit-255	
Johnathan	Grn-129	Moses	Rch-208	Harry	Pas-193	
Ruth	Grn-128	Peter	Edg- 63	Hugh	Pas-193	
Saml	Grn-128	Robert	Roc- 7	James	Brt- 55	
Wm	Grn-129	Saml	Lnc-334	Jas	Mec- 26	
Kittle,Cade	Grn-132	Sampson	Roc- 7	Jno	Mec- 28	
Kittrel,Elizabeth	Gat-115	Stephen	Hal-110	Joseph	Ans- 9	
Joshua	Fra- 91	Thomas	Roc- 17	Milly	Edg- 72	
Kittrell,Belson	Brt- 67	Thomas	Wil-278	Noah	Bft- 28	
Bryant	Ora-117	Thomas	Rch-203	Robert	Lnc-357	
George	Gat-112	Thos	Glf-159	Saml	Ans- 28	
Standley	Brt- 58	Thos	Glf-164	Samuel	Mec- 26	
William	Gat-107	Walker	Fdg- 54	William	Pit-261	
Willm	Fra- 91	William	Cum-253	William	Pit-254	
Kivet,Barberna	Ran-171	William	Roc- 3	William	Ire-258	
Jacob	Ran-171	William	Cum-253	Koen,Daniel	Pas-193	
John	Ran-171	William	Bun- 84	John	Pas-193	
John	Ran-171	Willis	Edg- 71	Kook,Nicholas	Rth-112	
Peter Jnr	Ran-171	Zachariah	Roc- 18	Koonce,Benjamin	Jon-300	
Peter Senr	Ran-171	Knighton,John	Bun- 74	Edward	Jon-300	
Kizer,David	Cab-147	Knights,Thomas	Pas-194	Elijah	Jon-300	
Frederick	Cab-147	Knites,Cader	Jon-299	Emanuel	Jon-300	
Geo Junr	Cab-147	Joseph	Jon-299	Frederic	Jon-300	
Geo Senr	Cab-147	Knoling,Milly	Mon- 38	George	Jon-300	

-179-

Name	Ref	Name	Ref	Name	Ref	Name	Ref
Koonce,Jacob	Jon-300	Kuykendall,Peter	Bun- 72	Lacy,John	Roc- 2
John	Jon-299	Kyle,Charles	Bun- 87	Mary	Prq-220
Penice	Jon-300	Hamilton	Bun- 87	Pheby	Rth-116
Richard	Jon-299	Richard	Bun- 83	William	Prq-220
Richard	Jon-300	Robert	Bun- 98	Lad,Thomas	Per-134
Tobiah	Jon-300	Thomas	Bun- 98	Ladd,Diner	Glf-165
William	Jon-300	Thomas	Bun- 87	Jessey	Grn-126
Zenos	Jon-300	Kyser,Adam	Lnc-337	Jno	Mec- 37
Koons,G	Ash- 7	Adam	Lnc-332	Joseph	Roc- 3
G	Ash- 10	Christy	Lnc-327	Mary	Sto-125
William	Lnc-351	Christy	Lnc-328	Mary	Sto- 96
Koontz,John	Row- 79	Henry	Lnc-328	Moses	Roc- 3
Michl	Row- 79	John	Lnc-338	William	Rch-198
Kornegay,Abram	Dup- 14	John	Lnc-328	Wm	Mec- 36
Basil	Dup- 14	Joseph	Lnc-328	Laden,Betsy	Pas-195
Daniel	Way-250	Joseph	Lnc-328	Ladyman,Leven	Roc- 28
David	Sam-157	Joseph	Lnc-328	Laferight,J	Glf-176
David	Dup- 25	Lawrence	Lnc-328	Laffoon,Dennis	Sur-163
George F	Dup- 25	Ruth	Lnc-332	James	Sur-163
George Sr	Dup- 14			Laftly,David	Mon- 44
Isaac	Dup- 25	L----;Thomas	Cas- 60	David	Mon- 45
Jacob	Way-248	Laboyteaux,William	Pas-194	Laggin,Joseph	Wil-277
John	Dup- 14	Lacenbury,Henry	Ire-243	Laghinaur,George	Sto-102
Joseph	Dup- 3	Joshua	Ire-243	Laghinnour,Jacob	Sto-136
Martin	Dup- 7	Robert	Ire-243	Laginaur,Jacob	Sto-103
Mary	Dup- 14	Robert	Ire-243	Lagle,John	Row- 64
Morning	Way-248	Laceter,Frankey	Rch-209	Lahern,Hugh	Bur-124
Will	Dup- 25	Lacewell,William	Rth-114	Mary	Bur-124
Will Sr	Dup- 25	Lacey,Eliza	Ora-125	Laiders,Abram	Grn-137
Korney,Jacob	Dur-109	Hannah	Per-221	Laiding,John	Glf-182
Korth,Thomas	Ran-171	John	Row- 54	Lain,Benjamin	Cas- 61
Kramsh,Samuel G	Sto-146	Robt	Ora-125	Cady	Prq-221
Krauth,Charles J	War-184	Lack,Benjamin	Bla- 9	Caleb	Prq-220
Kraws,John	Sto-112	John	Grn-139	Charles	Bun- 98
Kresort,William	Row- 77	Lackey,Alex	Ora-160	Ezekiel	Prq-221
Kriger,Adam Jnr	Sto-130	John	Bur-121	Jacob	Prq-221
Anna Mary	Sto-146	Joseph	Edg- 60	Jemima	Prq-220
George	Sto-130	Thomas	Brt- 52	John	Prq-221
George	Sto- 99	Solomon	Bur-120	John	Glf-159
Henry	Sto- 99	William W	Ire-246	John Jr	Prq-220
Henry	Sto-130	Lackky,Alexander	Ran-171	Joseph	Hal-111
Jacob	Sto- 98	Lacklear,Wm	Rob-220	Joseph Jr	Prq-220
Krite,George	Row- 77	Lacklock,Wm	Ora-137	Joseph Sr	Prq-220
Krizer,An. Marg	Sto-111	Lacky,Alexander	Ire-252	Mary	Prq-221
Krows,Andrew	Sto-134	Amos	Ire-252	Rachel	Prq-220
Kruser,Conrad	Sto-146	George	Ire-253	Randel	Bur-126
Kudge,Mary	Hal-111	George	Ire-251	Reuben	Prq-220
Kulbreath,Edward	Rth-112	James	Ire-251	Rhoda	Prq-221
Kulp,Adam	Row- 77	John M	Ire-251	Ruth	Prq-221
Kumes,July	Sto-107	Thomas	Ire-251	Sarah	Prq-221
Kuntra,Theophilus	Gat-106	William	Ire-251	Sitterson	Prq-221
Kurbow,John	Wil-279	William	Ire-252	Laine,Daniel	Row- 66
Kurley,John	Wil-275	William	Ire-246	James	Ons- 99
Joseph	Wil-275	Lacock,Thomas	Ora-137	Sally	Ons-108
Larkin	Wil-275	Lacy,Adam	Hyd-232	William	Ons-107
Larkin Jr	Wil-275	Batte C	Roc- 33	Lair,Peter	Lnc-347
Samuel	Wil-279	Benj	Ons-106	Lake,Daniel	Bun- 84
William	Wil-275	Griffith	Ans- 9	Lemuel	Joh-275
Kuykendall,Abraham	Bun- 72	Jesse	Ans- 8	Lakey,Anna	Sur-192

Lakey,Francis	Sur-177	Lamb,Lott Snr	Glf-179	Lampley,Joseph	Rch-207
James	Mor- 59	M	Col- 18	Lancaster,Aaron	Way-237
James	Sur-182	Manna	Cha-212	Hart	Mor- 68
John	Bun- 87	Martha	Rob-233	James	Edg- 62
Manor	Bun- 87	Miriam	Prq-220	John	War-173
Susanna	Sur-191	Nancy	Rob-233	John	War-173
Lalistadt,Jane	Bla- 10	Nathan	Ran-172	Jonathan	Way-240
Lam,James	Row- 70	Odun	Rch-201	Laurence	War-177
Lamair,Ozburn	Ran-173	Penuel	Rob-231	Levi	Nor- 71
Laman,Neill	Mor- 68	Restore	Prq-220	Levie	Way-238
Lamar,Hosea	Dup- 34	Reuben	Ran-172	Robert	Edg- 42
Jacob	Dup- 34	Richard	Ran-172	Willis	War-182
James	Dup- 36	Richard	Rob-242	Willm	Fra- 89
Thomas	Dup- 23	Robert	Glf-156	Lance,Bostian	Row- 67
Lamash,Wm (col)	Rob-240	Saml	Glf-158	Jacob	Cab-146
Lamb,A	Cam-160	Saml	Glf-169	John	Bun- 91
Abraham	Rob-240	Silas	Way-232	John Junr	Bun- 91
Abraham Jr	Way-245	Thomas	Way-245	Peter	Bun- 91
Abraham Sr	Way-245	Thomas	Ran-172	Valentine	Bun- 91
Albert	Ran-172	W	Cam-158	Lancer,Sampson	Roc- 17
Ann	Ran-172	William	Rch-201	Land,Charles	Edg- 43
Armejah	Prq-220	William	Prq-220	Isaac	Hay-197
Arthur	Rob-238	Lamberson,Daniel	Nor- 71	James	Wil-278
Arthur	Rob-234	James Junr	Nor- 71	James	Hay-197
Barnabas	Rob-236	James Senr	Nor- 71	Jeremiah	Cur- 88
Benjn	Ran-172	John	Nor- 71	Jeremiah	Hay-197
Betty	Nor- 71	Kent	Col- 17	Jonathan	Wil-284
Campble	Rob-238	Lambert,Ezekiel	Roc- 30	Lemuel	Hal-111
Cornelius	Ran-172	John	Row- 41	Littleberry	Edg- 42
David	Way-245	John	Ran-173	Mary	Dup- 35
Doratha	Prq-220	John	Joh-275	Nancy	Wil-284
Eliza	Ora-152	Joseph	Roc- 21	Reuben	Glf-165
G	Cam-158	Lavy	Rth-115	Landberry,Jacob	Cum-252
Gabrael	Ran-172	Mary	War-178	Landcaster,John	Ons-104
Gabriel	Ran-172	Moses	Row- 41	Landen,Enos	Bun- 98
Henry	Ran-172	Nuy	Mor- 67	Landerlin,M	Cam-152
Henry	Sur-187	Richardson	Cha-210	Landers,Barny	Bun- 80
Henry Sr	Sur-187	Saml	Row- 41	Larkin	Cas- 60
Hulda	Ran-173	Saml	Row- 41	Elisha	Edg- 55
Isaac	Way-245	Sarah	Roc- 31	James	Ons-109
Isaac	Ran-172	William	Glf-158	Littleton	Bft- 34
Isaac	Glf-187	Lamberth,John	Cha-197	Landinham,Z	Glf-181
Isaac	Rob-235	Thos	Cha-191	Landish,David	Grn-142
J Esq	Cam-154	Lambertson,J	Col- 21	George	Grn-142
Jacob	Way-232	Lambeth,B	Col- 19	John	Grn-140
Jacob	Prq-220	R	Col- 19	John	Grn-142
James	Row- 69	Lamkin,Leanna	War-177	John Sr	Grn-142
Jesse	Ora-128	Lewis A B	Nsh- 87	Landley,Saml	Cha-194
Jesse	Ora-119	Mathias	War-178	Landmon,Jno	Ans- 29
Joab	Ran-172	Samuel	Nsh- 89	Landon,James	Sto-126
John	Cur- 89	Lammon,Alex	Bla- 14	James	Sto- 97
John	Prq-220	D	Bla- 10	William	Sto-126
Jonathan	Way-245	Daniel	Rch-206	William	Sto- 97
Jonathan	Rob-231	Mal	Rob-226	Landreath,Martha	Glf-156
Joseph	Mor- 56	Wm	Hal-111	Simon	Glf-156
Joseph	Ran-172	Lamon,Keneth	Rch-213	Landreth,Thomas	Rch-191
Joshua	Way-232	Lampkin,Peter	Glf-159	Landridth,John	Glf-154
Josiah	Ran-172	Lampla,Wm	Grn-137	Landrum,Abner	Mor- 68
L	Cam-162	Lampley,Benjamin	Rch-207	Benj	Mor- 63

Name	Loc	Name	Loc	Name	Loc
Lane,Abraham	Cha-193	Lanear,John	Dup- 34	Langston,Simson	Way-251
Allen	Glf-171	Stephen	Dup- 35	Timothy	Gat-113
Benj	Cho-228	Lanery,Salley	Gat-109	Uriah	Way-251
Bryan	Way-241	Lang,James	Pit-260	Uriah	Gat-112
Cardy	Edg- 59	John	Pit-260	William	Hrt-214
Cullen	Way-241	Langdale,Sarah	Brt- 46	Willis	Nor- 71
David	Brt- 51	Langford,Delilah	Lnc-330	Langwell,Thomas	Roc- 17
David	Sur-176	Eli	Bun- 95	Lanier,Adams	Mar- 15
Gisbon	Roc- 6	Elias	Nor- 71	Benjn	Ans- 17
Hiram	Row- 46	Elisha	Fra- 90	Benjn	Sam-158
Isaac	Ran-172	George	Bur-124	Benjn	Fra- 85
Jack	Pas-194	Gorge	War-171	Elisabeth	Mar- 9
James	Brt- 51	Joab	War-176	Fanny	Bft- 20
James	Wil-285	John	War-174	Isaac	Ans- 7
Jesse	Glf-170	Rollay	War-179	James	Mar- 15
Jno	Ran-172	Langhhorn,William	Cha-203	Joab	Bft- 26
Jno	Mec- 53	Langle,Lam	Cur- 84	Jno	Ans- 24
John	Jon-300	Langley,Demsey	Nsh- 87	John	Row- 61
John	Edg- 64	Francis	Joh-283	Robert	Pit-241
John	Wil-267	Geo Jun	Bft- 36	Robert	Grn-126
John	Wil-271	Hezekiah	Edg- 51	Sally	Mon- 41
John	Ran-172	Isaac	Joh-283	Sarah	Mar- 7
John	Ran-172	Isaiah	Edg- 50	Starling	Mec- 54
John	Way-241	Jacob	Way-233	Thomas Esq	Fra- 89
John	Roc- 4	James	Joh-283	William	Mar- 10
John	Row- 62	James	Joh-283	Willm	Bft- 39
Jonathan	Glf-171	Jas W	Cho-225	Wm	Grn-134
Joseph	Way-246	Jesse	Row- 81	Wm	Row- 39
Joseph	Ran-172	John	Edg- 52	Lanjans,Thomas	Sto-131
Joseph	Rch-211	John	Ons-100	Thomas	Sto-100
Leml	Pas-195	John	Cas- 61	Lank,Mary	Gat-111
Lemuel	Nor- 71	John	Nsh- 81	Thomas	Gat-110
Leven	Jon-300	Jonathan	Cha-210	Lankaster,Hartwell	Edg- 43
Lucy	Way-237	Joseph	Cas- 61	Lankford,Anthony	Rth-114
M	Bru-240	M	Ash- 3	John	Rth-114
Mary	Nor- 71	Martha	Edg- 56	Robert	Rth-114
Nancy	Way-241	Mary	Nsh- 90	Thomas	Sto-122
Ransom	Nor- 71	Miles	Way-232	Thomas	Sto- 93
Reuben	Glf-182	Nat	Bft- 23	West	Sto-122
Richd	Glf-152	Oswell	Way-243	West	Sto- 93
Saml	Cho-229	Sephn Jun	Bft- 23	William	Sto-106
Samson	Way-252	Shadrack	Edg- 51	William	Sto-141
Susana	Glf-168	Stephen	Bft- 23	Zach	Mor- 60
Talor	Sur-193	Thomas	Wsh-219	Lanmetz,Jacob	Sto-103
Tamar	Pas-194	Wm	Nsh- 80	Lanning,John	Bun- 91
Tidings	Ran-172	Langlie,Ann	Pit-241	Lannon,Enos	Row- 40
William	Row- 62	Langly,Allen	Ran-172	Lansdale,Benjamin	Bla- 5
William	Way-238	James	Pit-241	B C	Cum-237
William	Row- 86	Wm	Ran-172	Lansdown,Mary	Wil-285
William	Sur-182	Langmead,Charles	Prq-220	Nathl	Bur-127
William	Jon-301	Langsdon,John	Cum-237	Reuben	Wil-285
Wm	Cho-220	Langston,Dorothy	Len-314	Lansing,Elizabeth	Mec- 35
Wm	Glf-157	Isaac	Hrt-214	Jacob	Mec- 35
Lanear,Aaron	Dup- 36	Jesse	Len-315	Lanston,John	Cho-226
Benjn	Dup- 33	Jesse	Way-248	Lanter,Evan	Ran-171
Isom	Dup- 34	Levie	Way-253	Lantern,Charity	Hal-112
James	Dup- 34	Mace	Way-251	James	Hal-111
Jesse	Dup- 34	Needham	Way-251	Lantinaw,Jacob H	Sto-146
Jesse Sr	Dup- 35	Simeon	Len-315	Lappins,Edward	Roc- 27

Name	Ref	Name	Ref	Name	Ref
Larance,Samuel	Sur-161	Lasseter,John	Rch-207	Latham,John	Row- 66
Larcy,Jos	Bft- 33	Thomas	Mar- 6	Noah	Bft- 26
Lard,David	Hay-197	Lassiter,Aaron	Gat-111	Phin	Bft- 23
William	Bun- 98	Allen	Cho-224	Tho	Bft- 26
Largate,Jacob	Glf-170	Amos	Gat-111	William	Ran-171
Largcaut,James	Rth-113	Amos	Gat-111	Lathem,Anthony	Ran-173
Largen,Elijah	Bur-102	Aron	Nor- 71	Cornelius	Ran-173
Largin,James	Bur-130	Blake	Gat-109	Enoch	Ran-173
Larimore,James	Sto-105	Cloe	Gat-111	James	Mor- 59
James	Sto-139	Deliley	Gat-111	James	Ran-173
Thomas	Sto-138	Elias	Nor- 71	James	Ran-173
Thomas	Sto-104	Elijah	Joh-276	James	Ran-173
Larin,Jarrus	Cas- 61	Enoch	Nor- 71	John	Ran-173
Larkin,Thomas	Roc- 20	Enos	Nor- 71	Lathmore,Jas	Cho-222
Larkins,Aaron	Bla- 11	Everett	Nor- 71	Lathrom,Saml	Mec- 33
Benj	Bla- 11	Ezekiel	Gat-112	Lathry,Anne	Wil-267
George	Bla- 11	Federick	Gat-113	Latimore,John	Rth-114
James	Bla- 11	Green	Nor- 71	John	Rth-114
Moses	Bla- 11	Henry	Nor- 71	John	Rth-114
Larky,James	Ire-264	Henry	Gat-108	Latin,Joshua	Rth-114
Larrance,C	Glf-160	James	Gat-108	Marigan	Rob-234
Elisha	Hrt-210	James	Gat-111	Latta,J	Ora-138
J	Glf-160	James Junr	Nor- 71	J Junr	Ora-144
Lartz,A	Glf-184	James Senr	Nor- 71	James	Ora-160
Lary,Henry	Sto-151	John	Nor- 71	James Jr	Ora-149
Lasater,James	Cha-206	John	Gat-107	Jas (of Tho)	Ora-117
Laseter,Isaac	Ans- 10	Jonathan	Gat-107	Jas	Mec- 46
Joseph	Rch-211	Joseph	Nor- 71	Jno	Ora-164
Mary	Rch-211	Josiah	Gat-111	Jno of Thos	Ora-164
Micajah	Rch-208	Judith	Nor- 71	Jno of J	Ora-177
Lash,Abraham	Sto- 98	Mary	Nor- 71	Jno Sen	Ora-118
Abraham	Sto-128	Matthew	Nor- 71	John	Ora-117
Christian	Sto- 98	Micajah	Ran-171	John Esq	Ora-116
Christian	Sto-114	Moses	Gat-106	Jos	Ora-176
Christian	Sto-128	Nancy	Gat-111	Tho	Ora-117
George	Sur-183	Rachel	Gat-111	Wm	Ans- 28
George Ju	Sur-189	Reuben	Cho-227	Lattimore,George	Lnc-367
Harmon	Sur-189	Robert	Sam-160	Lattis,Wylie	Rth-113
Jacob	Sto-128	Robert	Gat-108	Lauchanour,G P	Lnc-351
Nathaniel	Sto-108	Sanders	Nor- 71	Lauchon,Joel	Mor- 56
Nathaniel	Sto-144	Seth	Gat-112	Laughinghouse,Andw	Bft- 28
Lashley,Benjamin	Nor- 72	Silas	Nor- 71	Edward	Pit-263
Bernard	Ora-121	Stephen	Len-313	J	Cam-161
Elizabeth	Nor- 72	Will	Ran-171	Jno	Pit-263
Thomas Jr	Ora-165	Winney	Gat-111	Tho	Bft- 28
Thos	Glf-155	Wm	Brt- 51	Laughlin,William	Roc- 7
Wm	Ora-163	Lasslie,Jas	Ora-128	Laughter,James	Bun- 72
Lashmet,Elias	Sto-103	Lasster,Hardy	Cha-211	John	Bun- 72
Lashmit,Elisas	Sto-135	Laster,Jacob	Mor- 65	John	War-175
Lasiter,John	Brt- 51	Laston,Jno	Mec- 24	Samuel	Bun- 72
Wm	Grn-133	Latham,Alexr	Bft- 26	William	War-183
Wm	Cha-215	Botheas	Bft- 26	Laughton,Wm	Brt- 44
Lasley,Daniel	Rch-196	Chs	Bft- 27	Launcis,Jacob	Sto-136
Laslie,Robert	Pit-255	Cornelius	Ran-171	Launies,Henry	Sto-119
Laspier,B	Bru-236	James	Bft- 23	John	Sto-119
Lassater,Jotham	Cum-262	Jas	Bft- 20	Laurance,G	Ash- 11
Lassel,Ben	Pas-194	Jas	Bft- 26	Jessee	Nsh- 74
Lasseter,Hardy	Cum-261	Jesse	Hyd-220	Robert	Hrt-208
Jesse	Rch-207	John	Bft- 21	Thomas	Nsh-.72

Laurance,Wm	Nsh- 74	Lawrance,Micheal	Mec- 55	Lawson,Joshua	Sto-123	
Laurenc,Charity	Pit-257	Lawrence,Abigail	Car-178	Moses	Sto-123	
Laurence,Abram	Grn-126	Abner	Brt- 47	Moses	Sto- 94	
David	Edg- 64	Adam	Ine-267	Patsey	Cas- 60	
Elisha	Nor- 71	Crecy	Brt- 50	Sherrod	Sto-155	
Eliz	Ons-103	David	Brt- 47	Sherwood	Sto-112	
George	Edg- 72	David	Bun- 85	Thomas	Sto-121	
Henry	Grn-126	David	Car-178	Thomas	Ire-241	
James	Edg- 70	Edward	Ran-173	Thomas	Bun- 78	
Jas	Ora-133	Frederick	Brt- 45	Thomas	Sto- 93	
John	Nor- 71	Jeremiah	Brt- 47	Thomas	Sto- 92	
John	Edg- 69	Jessy	Ran-173	Thomas	Sur-181	
John	Edg- 72	Jno	Ans- 10	Thos	Car-183	
John Jr	Edg- 72	John	Car-178	William	Roc- 16	
Joshua	Edg- 59	Jonathan	Ran-173	Lax,William	Ran-171	
Leml	Nor- 71	Jos	Brt- 49	Laxton,Jane	Bun- 73	
Lemuel	Edg- 70	Nancy	Brt- 47	Levi	Wil-273	
Mary	Nor- 71	Nancy	Ran-173	Lay,Bird	Cas- 60	
Peter P	Cho-220	Needham	Ran-173	Burwell	Roc- 13	
Pheba	Hal-111	Peter	Ran-173	David	Cas- 61	
Ricks	Nor- 71	Reuben Jnr	Brt- 45	Eliz	Cho-222	
Riddick	Edg- 71	Reuben Sen	Brt- 45	J	Bru-224	
Silas	Edg- 72	Watson	Car-178	J	Col- 16	
Sollomon	Edg- 72	William	Bur-131	J	Col- 19	
Sollomon	Edg- 70	Wm	Brt- 60	Jno	Mec- 31	
Wm	Grn-126	Wm	Ran-173	Patsey	Cas- 61	
Wm T	Grn-123	Wm	Brt- 45	Reuben	Bur-106	
Willis	Edg- 72	Lawrey,Henry Junr	Nor- 78	Theophilus	Roc- 22	
Laurens,Henry	Wil-262	Lawrie,George	Row- 56	William	Ire-247	
John	Wil-263	Laws,E	Ora-135	Laycock,Thomas	Ora-166	
Thomas	Wil-263	Elizabeth	Ora-151	W	Ora-152	
Laury,Joseph	Rth-115	Geo Jr	Ora-164	Laydur,Elizabeth	Prq-220	
Lavant,Isaac	Lnc-351	James(son of David)		William	Prq-220	
Lavendor,Wm L	Bft- 36		Wil-283	Laymore,J	Cam-156	
Lavills,T	Cam-155	Jane	Ora-174	J	Cam-156	
Law,Andrew	Glf-154	Jno	Rob-239	S	Cam-156	
Robert	Sto-123	L	Ora-135	Laythem,A	Ash- 12	
Robt	Glf-173	Moses	Ons-101	Layton,Hillery	Sam-155	
Doctr Wm	Brt- 48	Shadrach Jr	Wil-285	James	Cum-259	
Lawder,John	Glf-169	W	Ora-139	John	Sam-156	
Lawhon,John	Way-249	Lawson,---rose	Sto-121	Saml	Glf-180	
Lawhorn,Pheraby	Way-240	Agnes	Ire-251	William	Sam-155	
William	Way-249	Burrell	Sto-112	Lazenbury,Joshua	Ire-241	
Lawing,Andrew	Mec- 24	Burrill	Sto-155	Lea,A	Ora-153	
Lawler,Ann	Mor- 58	Christopher	Dup- 30	Abner	Per-131	
Eli	Cha-205	David	Sto-121	Archibald	Per-140	
John	Cha-207	David	Sto- 92	Barnet	Per-140	
John	Cha-197	David	Cas- 60	Benjamin	Per-131	
Lawless,Benjamin	Rth-116	Elisha	Sto- 93	Benjamin	Cas- 60	
Presly	Sur-170	Elisha	Sto-122	Carter Esq	Per-140	
Lawly,Joseph	Ran-172	Francis	Per-140	Catharine	Cas- 60	
Lawman,Lewis	Bur-104	Francis	Per-131	Gabriel B	Cas- 60	
Lawrance,Abram	Lnc-350	J	Ora-148	Gabriel Sr	Cas- 60	
Alexander	Lnc-351	Jas	Ora-171	George col	Per-131	
Daniel	Lnc-350	John	Sto-123	James	Per-131	
Isaac	Lnc-354	John	Sto- 94	James	Cas- 60	
Isaac	Lnc-351	John	Per-131	James	Cas- 60	
Jacob	Lnc-353	Jonas	Sto-122	James	Cas- 61	
Jo	Lnc-350	Jonas	Sto- 93	Jeremiah	Cas- 60	

Name	Ref	Name	Ref	Name	Ref
Lea,Jesse	Per-131	Leary,Job	Len-320	Ledbetter,Wm Jr	Cha-208
Jessey	Rob-218	John	Cho-227	Ledenham,Eben	Glf-157
John (C B)	Cas- 60	John	Brt- 52	Thos	Glf-157
John Junr	Per-140	John Esqr	Wsh-224	Ledford,Edwd	Bur-117
John	Per-131	Joshua	Wsh-224	Elias	Bur-120
John little	Per-131	Miles	Wsh-220	Frederick	Rth-116
Mrs. Nancy	Per-131	Prudence	Wsh-224	Frederick	Bun- 73
Reuben	Per-131	Salathel	Hyd-231	George	Bun- 87
Richerd	Per-131	Sarah	Cho-224	James	Bur-120
Thomas	Cas- 60	Thos	Brt- 49	John	Sto-142
Vincent	Per-140	William	Brt- 52	John	Sto-107
William	Cas- 60	Leaser,Daniel	Row- 71	John	Bun-. 73
Leach,Clary	Ran-172	John Sr	Row- 71	La----	Sto-103
Danl	Rob-222	Martin	Row- 71	Lewis	Rth-115
Dugald	Mor- 65	Leash,James	Sur-182	Mary	Row- 42
Dugald	Rob-231	Leatch,M	Mec- 22	Moses	Ran-173
Duncan	Cum-244	Leath,Arthur	Per-140	Obediah	Bun- 84
Jean	Ran-172	Coleman	Cas- 61	Peter	Bur-120
Jno	Rob-219	Joel	Cas- 60	Sarah	Bur-117
John	Ran-173	Saml	Bft- 34	Squire	Sto-136
John	Joh-275	Susanah	Hyd-232	Thomas	Rth-116
John Senr	Rch-192	Leatherman,Chn	Row- 53	William	Bur-120
Levi	Ran-172	Danl	Row- 52	William	Lnc-338
Malcolm	Mor-.66	Isaac	Row- 53	William	Lnc-333
Neill	Cum-244	John	Bun- 77	Lednum,John	Brt- 43
Richard	Row- 88	John Junr	Bun- 77	Ledwell,Wm	Ran-173
Richd	Row- 39	Nicholas	Bun- 77	Lee,Doct	Bft- 22
William	Sur-176	Leathers,Fielding	Ora-149	Ahimiah	Cur- 90
Wm	Ran-172	J	Ora-138	Anna	Dup- 19
Zadock	Row- 64	Jas	Ora-135	Anna	Dup- 21
Leachfield,Francis	Cur- 92	John	Cum-245	Arnus	Cur- 90
Jacob	Cur- 86	Moses	Ora-164	Aron	Sam-160
William	Cur- 92	Peter	Row- 81	Ball	Edg- 49
Leachman,Thomas	Cas- 61	Travers	Roc- 31	Benj	Hrt-216
Leadbetter,Alesy	Cha-210	Wm	Ora-149	Benj	Hrt-216
Matthew	Hay-196	Leatherwood,Edwd	Bur-116	Genl Benjamin	Rob-237
Leagle,Adam	Lnc-337	John	Hay-196	Betsey	Cur- 91
George	Lnc-335	Samuel	Hay-197	Blanch	Bft- 22
League,Wm	Glf-168	Leavey,Alexr	Cum-236	Budget	Sam-159
Leak,Caty	Rth-116	Leazen,Jacob	Row- 70	Charles	Joh-288
Isaac	Pas-195	Ledberry,John	Mon- 24	Charles	Joh-287
Joel Jun	Pas-195	Ledbetter,Coleman	Ora-130	Crucy	Rth-116
Joel Sen	Pas-195	David	Nor- 72	Curtis	Sam-160
Leake,Walter	Rch-206	E	Glf-164	Daniel	Cur- 90
William P	Rch-195	E Jr	Glf-185	David	Hrt-210
Leanderman,Henry	Wil-263	G	Mon- 40	David Snr	Joh-290
Leonard	Wil-263	Henry	Mon- 43	Deruy	Cur- 90
Leany,Jno	Mec- 29	Isaac	Rth-114	Durham	Jon-300
Jno	Mec- 24	Joel	Mon- 39	Edward	Edg- 71
Leapar,John	Cas- 60	John	Rth-114	Edward	Joh-289
John	Cas- 60	John	Cha-194	Edward	Bur-128
Leary,C	Len-320	Johnston	Rth-114	Edward	Joh-287
Chas	Cho-224	Layburn	Rth-115	Elijah	Bun- 83
Enoch	Wsh-224	Richard	Rth-113	Elisha	Bun- 96
Ephraim	Hyd-234	Richard	Rth-114	Eliza	Bft- 32
Ezekiel	Wsh-223	Roland	Ans- 27	Ephraim	Sam-159
Frederic	Wsh-223	Thomas	Bun- 89	Fred	Glf-180
Jesse	Wsh-222	Walton	Rth-114	Geo	Mon- 45
Job	Cho-230	Wm	Cha-199	Henry	Brt- 56

Name	Ref	Name	Ref	Name	Ref
Lee,Henry	Row- 61	Lee,Richd	Ans- 5	Legate,Erick	Rob-236
Henry	Rth-115	Robt	Cab-147	Jereh	Bft- 26
Henry	Edg- 47	Robt	Ans- 18	Legates,Danl	Bft- 25
Henry	Edg- 52	S	Ora-157	Leger,Samuel	Cas- 60
Hezekiah	Roc- 6	Saml	Cha-212	Legett,Alexander	Brt- 46
Hillery	Row- 59	Samuel	Way-250	Ester	Mec- 42
Hopkin	Cum-260	Samuel	Joh-289	Jas	Mec- 42
Isaac	Glf-185	Samuel	Rch-212	John	Brt- 46
Isaac	Rob-235	Saphn	Rob-238	Jonathan R	Brt- 66
Isaac	Gat-113	Stephen	Joh-289	Mrs. Lear	Brt- 46
Isaac	Sam-151	Stephen	Gat-114	Nazary	Brt- 60
J	Ora-140	Stephen	Jon-300	Robt	Mec- 42
J	Ora-141	Thomas	Row- 51	Capt Wm	Mec- 42
Jacob	Rob-235	Thomas	Jon-300	Legget,John	Cum-247
James	Joh-289	Thos & Deruy	Cur- 90	Leggett,Daniel	Wsh-233
James	Nsh- 85	also see Lee,Deruy		Luke	Wsh-225
James	Edg- 70	Thos	Cur- 91	Leggitt,Benjamin	Mar- 7
James	Cab-147	Vichl	Bft- 19	David	Mar- 11
James Jr	Lnc-357	W	Bru-236	Josiah	Mar- 5
James Senr	Lnc-357	Westbrook	Sam-160	Noah	Edg- 53
James Snr	Joh-289	William	Joh-289	Titus	Mar- 14
Jas	Bft- 27	William	Gat-115	Legrand,H	Mon- 36
Jas	Ans- 22	William	Sto-154	J	Mon- 36
Jerry	Joh-289	William	Rth-114	Jno	Mon- 41
Jesse	Sam-160	William Senr	Sam-162	William	Rch-199
Jesse Jnr	Rob-233	Wm	Mon- 38	Legraves,Daniel	Mon- 26
Jessey Snr	Rob-238	Wm	Bft- 22	Lehn,John	Bru-228
Joel	Joh-290	Wm	Hal-111	Leigh,Benjn	Prq-220
Jno	Ans- 12	Wm	Cab-147	Jessee	Edg- 72
Jno	Ans- 22	Wm Junr	Sam-159	John	Dup- 19
Jno B	Ora-117	Willis	Joh-289	John	Ora-142
John	Ran-173	Willowby	Roc- 29	Richard	Prq-220
John	Joh-289	Zachariah	Joh-276	Stephen	Edg- 72
John	Mar- 3	Zachariah	Rth-116	Thos	Tyr-203
John	Hal-111	Leeberry,Moses	Mec- 54	Leighton,James	Brt- 49
John	Hal-111	Leebeugue,Lewis	Row- 60	Lemay,John	Grn-136
John	Rth-116	Leecraft,Susannah	Car-170	Lewis	Grn-131
John	Jon-300	Leek,Henry	Nor- 71	Lewis	Grn-148
John	Edg- 44	Josiah	Nor- 71	Richard	Grn-148
John	Bur-116	Leep,William	Cur- 86	Lembough,Henry	Bur-126
Jonathan	Jon-300	Leeper,Eliz	Lnc-367	Lemet,Jacob	Cho-223
Joseph	Rob-236	James	Hay-196	Leming,Abram	Lnc-370
Joseph	Sto-139	Matthew	Lnc-367	Lemly,Widow	Row- 87
Joseph	Rth-115	Leese,Mary	Mec- 49	Lemmican,Jno	Mec- 25
Joseph	Edg- 43	William	Ire-259	Lemmon,Mrs.	Cum-240
Joseph	Cha-192	Wm	Mec- 51	Alexander	Roc- 8
Joshua	Glf-174	Leetan,Jesse	Mon- 25	David	Roc- 7
Kedar	Sam-162	Leetch,Jas	Mec- 27	David	Roc- 20
Lemuel	Joh-276	Lefferly,Cane	Ora-140	George	Roc- 20
Letishe	Cur- 90	Leffers,Samuel	Car-169	James	Roc- 8
Linton	Cur- 90	Lefler,Thos	Cab-140	James	Roc- 20
Linton Sen	Cur- 90	Lefner,J	Mon- 42	John	Roc- 7
Lunday	Sam-159	Leftwitch,Robert	Roc- 9	Joseph	Roc- 19
Mary	Cha-189	Legat,David	Pit-234	Moses	Ire-266
Nathan	Row- 59	John	Pit-240	Samuel	Roc- 8
Owen	Rth-116	Martin	Pit-261	Talitha	Roc- 9
Peter	Sam-160	Martin	Pit-261	Thomas	Roc- 19
Peter	Sam-152	Sarah	Pit-234	William	Roc- 19
Rachel	Ans- 17	Legate,Elisha	Bft- 26	Lemmonds,Robt	Mec- 25

Name	Ref	Name	Ref	Name	Ref
Lemmonds,Wm	Mec- 29	Leonard,Philip	Lnc-326	Lewing,William	Rth-116
Lemmons,Caty	Mon- 28	Philip Jr	Row- 79	Lewis,Aaron	Bla- 7
David	Rth-116	Phillip	Row- 41	Aby	Lnc-336
Jacob	Ora-110	Thos	Glf-170	Allen	Pit-253
Jno	Mec- 44	Thos Esq	Bru-222	Amos	Edg- 71
John	Mon- 28	Val	Row- 40	Ann	Car-176
Mars	Mec- 44	Vallentine Jr	Row- 79	Archibald	Car-179
Neil	Mon- 28	Vann	Fra- 86	Asa	Rth-116
Robert	Rth-114	Willm	Fra- 85	Bartholomew	Edg- 57
Lemon,Elizabeth	War-170	Leopard,Christian	Row- 86	Ben	Bft- 32
Joseph	Grn-129	Lepard,Henry	Row- 68	Benjamin	Nor- 71
Samuel	Lnc-330	Lepherd,John	Ire-255	Benjamin	Wil-265
Lenard,Jacob	Row- 52	William	Ire-259	Benjamin	Bun- 72
Jacob	Ran-173	Lepperd,Frederick	Cab-145	Benjn	Hal-111
Lenchicom,Thos	Glf-157	Peter	Cab-145	Berry	Roc- 12
Lenhart,Lawrence	Lnc-328	Leroy,Lewis	Bft- 36	Bryant	Nsh- 84
Lennard,John	Sto- 91	Lerry,Aron	Mec- 48	Charles	Rth-115
Lennon,D	Col- 20	Lesley,E	Cam-157	Charrity	Hrt-211
George	Bla- 7	Leslie,Daniel	Cum-246	Chloe	Hal-111
M	Col- 20	Duncan	Cum-250	Cornelius	Edg- 71
Lennox,John	Roc- 31	James	Ire-256	Crowel	Hal-111
Lenoir,Buckner	Cum-257	John	Cum-243	Cullen	Hal-111
Thomas	Hay-197	Malcom	Cum-250	Daniel	Hyd-230
Genl William	Wil-276	William	Ire-239	Daniel	Ire-243
William B	Wil-276	Lessley,George	Lnc-333	David	Hal-111
Lenords,Robert	Row- 71	Lester,Banester	Ons-109	David	Gat-114
Lenosey,Eleanor	Lnc-335	H D	Ora-148	David Jr	Rth-115
Lenter,Stephen	Lnc-340	Jacky	Pas-194	David Sr	Rth-115
Lenton,Isaac	Tyr-205	Jacob	Pas-194	Derrum	Bla- 6
John	Dup- 16	Jeremiah	Pit-239	Edmond	Grn-126
Lents,Davoll	Row- 81	John	Brt- 45	Edward	Roc- 11
Peter	Row- 68	Moses	Edg- 52	Edward	Roc- 13
Lentz,John	Row- 86	Lethco,Joseph	Row- 52	Edward	Cas- 60
Lenvill,Aaron	Sto-110	Letherman,Jonas	Row- 53	Edward	Grn-124
William	Sto-110	Lethworth,Fredk	Pit-251	Egbert	Hal-111
Leonard,Chas	Row- 66	Letts,Jacob	Lnc-347	Elephis	Edg- 45
Dicy	Bru-228	Leuviner,Isaac	Rch-213	Elizabeth	Wil-265
E	Bru-240	William	Rch-213	Elvy	Hal-111
Eliza	Row- 66	Levans,Andrew	Cha-200	Exper	Way-238
Fredk	Fra- 85	Polly	Cha-200	Exum	Edg- 57
G	Bru-238	LeVicoat,Lark	Row- 52	F	Gat-116
H	Bru-240	Levins,Richd	Cha-215	Gielding	Ora-149
J W	Bru-228	Levister,David	Grn-131	Fielding	Ora-170
Jacob	Row- 41	John	Grn-131	Fielding	Cas- 60
Jacob	Row- 41	Lewallen,Jonathan	Ran-172	Francis	Grn-124
James	Glf-168	Shadrick	Ran-172	Francis	Mec- 35
James	Pas-194	Thomas	Ran-171	G	Ash- 7
James	Glf-189	Lewark,John	Car-173	G	Ash- 8
James Jr	Glf-189	Lewarke,John	Cur- 87	George	Nsh- 82
Jas	Glf-183	Lewdwick,Henry	Cab-145	George	Lnc-329
John	Sto-120	Nics	Cab-145	George	Wil-260
John	Glf-189	Lewellen,Lyson	Nor- 72	George	Lnc-341
John Junr	Fra- 86	Thos	Roc- 23	George Jr	Wil-278
John Senr	Fra- 85	Thos Senr	Roc- 23	Green	Edg- 57
Jos	Glf-157	Lewellin,J	Ora-148	H	Col- 17
Jos	Glf-161	Lewelling,Sarah	Edg- 65	Harbert	Cha-206
Joseph	Row- 44	Lewin,James	Rth-114	Hayes	Roc- 30
Michal Jr	Row- 79	Lewing,David	Lnc-359	Henry	Mec- 35
Michl	Row- 79	William	Rth-115	Henry	Ora-149

-187-

Name	Code	Name	Code	Name	Code
Lewis,Henry	Ora-159	Lewis,Lewis	Hal-111	Lewis,Washington	Sto-157
Henry	Cab-140	Luke	Hrt-208	Watson	Hrt-208
Henry	Nsh- 86	Lutin	Gat-116	William	Bun- 90
Henry	Cha-212	Lutin	Gat-113	William	Wil-265
Henry G	Bun- 72	Major	Nsh- 90	William	Cas- 60
Hezekiah	Wsh-221	Martha	Mec- 30	William	Hal-111
Howell	Grn-120	Mary	Sur-180	William	Car-175
Hyram	Cas- 61	Mary	Grn-148	Wm	Mor- 56
J	Ash- 7	Michael	Lnc-351	Wm	Grn-140
J	Ash- 13	Mills	Gat-113	Wm	Bft- 31
Jacob	Rob-237	Mordecai	Bur-112	Wm	Bft- 33
Jacob	Ire-245	Morgan	Hal-111	Wm	Ora-149
Jacob	Cab-142	Moses	Bal- 13	Wm	Hal-111
Jacob	Lnc-351	Nancy	Roc- 21	Wm	Cha-210
James	Wil-284	Nathaniel	Wil-265	Williamson	Mec- 35
James	Nor- 71	Nathl	Grn-133	Willis	Pit-244
James	Hal-111	Nicholson	Way-252	Willis	Grn-120
James	Ran-172	Nics	Cab-140	Winiford	Pit-249
James	Joh-291	Peter	Row- 39	Worner	Sur-185
James	Grn-140	R	Bal- 11	Lewiston,James	Grn-123
James	Edg- 50	Richard	Wil-282	John	Bun- 91
James	Bur-112	Richard	Rth-113	Lewman,Aaron	Ire-265
James	Car-179	Richd	Row- 48	Lewter,Sarah	Nor- 72
James Jnr	Grn-140	Richd	Cum-251	Libass,David	Roc- 33
Jas	Ora-145	Robert	Bun- 72	Libby,Mrs.	Cum-239
Jas	Bft- 28	Robert	Lnc-376	Libertine,Daniel	Sur-175
Jane	Dup- 8	Robert	Nsh- 90	Lichfield,John	Bft- 38
Jennit	Ora-149	Robt	Ran-172	Licht,Chas	Cab-140
Jesse	Wsh-220	Robt	Bla- 6	Lide,Henry	Ans- 7
Jessee	Bun- 79	Robt	Bla- 7	Lides,Jacob	Bur-125
Jessee	Edg- 69	S	Ora-162	Ligett,James	Brt- 46
Joel	Mor- 61	Sally	Mor- 69	Lighteker,Conrad	Cab-141
Jno	Rob-237	Saly	Mor- 62	Lightfoot,Bartholomew	
John	Bft- 32	Samuel	Ran-171		Cha-211
John	Hrt-207	Samuel	Row- 76	Taply	Glf-167
John	Mor- 64	Sarah	Roc- 34	William	Nor- 71
John	Ran-172	Sarah	Wsh-221	Like,Christian	Lnc-362
John	Ran-171	Sarah	Roc- 30	Jacob	Lnc-357
John	Nsh- 90	Sherrod	Nsh- 90	Joseph	Lnc-362
John	Nsh- 82	Simion	Lnc-374	Lile,Wm	Bru-230
John	Gat-113	Simn	Bru-228	Liles,B Junr	Bru-236
John	Lnc-331	Sina	Brt- 63	David	Ans- 30
John	Cha-210	Surles	Cha-195	Edward	Hrt-209
John	Rth-114	Theo	Roc- 34	Eli	Ans- 12
John	Car-175	Thomas	Ire-248	Elijah	Ans- 23
John	Car-175	Thomas	Car-175	Jackson	Fra- 99
John M	Ran-172	Thomas	Car-176	Jas	Ans- 30
Jonas	Edg- 71	Thomas Senr	Car-179	Jno	Ans- 7
Jos	Bft- 31	Thos	Mec- 29	Jonas	Rth-114
Joseph	Grn-133	Thos	Ans- 22	Joseph	Ans- 23
Joseph Esqr	Wsh-221	Thos B	Grn-148	Stepn	Bru-226
Josiah	Bla- 7	Tobiah	Hal-111	Thos	Cho-227
Josiah	Nsh- 83	Ullen	Way-236	Lillanine,Elijah	Edg- 70
Judith	Wsh-226	Urban	Way-236	Lillard,Joshua	Roc- 10
Kedar	Way-236	Uriah	Hyd-230	Morgan	Roc- 10
L	Cam-152	Uriah	Car-175	Moses	Roc- 10
Laben	Way-234	W	Ora-137	Lilley,Daniel	Mar-13
Lazarus	Hal-111	W	Col- 17	David	Mar- 9
Levi	Pit-262	Warner	Hal-111	Elizabeth	Gat-110

-188-

Lilley,Henry	Gat-105	Lindsay,William	Nor- 71	Link,Philip	Row- 79
Jas	Rob-240	Wm	Glf-166	Linke,John	Lnc-354
Jos	Bft- 21	Lindsey,Atha	Ora-116	Linker,Henry	Cab-142
Josiah	Mar- 10	Caleb	Ora-127	Linkley,John	Cha-203
Kedar	Mar- 5	Caleb	War-169	Linley,Aaron	Cha-194
Lilly,Amsd	Mon- 41	David	Cur- 86	Abraham	Cha-216
Cady	Prq-221	Edward	Hal-111	David	Cha-204
Edwd	Mon- 24	Eli	Ora-114	James	Cha-204
Elijah H	Mon- 41	James	Cur- 87	Jonathan	Cha-199
Elizabeth	Mon- 24	James	Ora-127	Joshua	Cha-195
John	Mon- 24	James	Rth-116	Thos	Cha-213
John Sr	Mon- 40	Jno	Ora-127	Thos	Cha-199
Mills	Prq-220	John	Row- 49	Thos Sr	Cha-204
Nat	Mon- 24	John	Roc- 8	Linn,Allen	Bur-104
Nathan	Prq-220	Jonathan	Cur- 86	Henry	Lnc-339
Reuben	Prq-221	Joshua	Roc- 8	John	Lnc-339
Thomas	Sto-105	Josiah	Hal-111	Linnings,James	Cha-205
Thomas	Sto-139	Noah	Ans- 23	Linnins,Thos	Cha-201
Lily,J	Mon- 42	Robt	Ora-125	Linsey,Anderson	Sur-195
Limbough,Peter	Bur-130	Lindsy,Robert	Fra- 99	John	Cha-208
Limeberry,James	Cha-209	Lineback,Benjn	Sto-130	Labon	Sur-166
Limebury,Francis	Ran-172	Christian	Sto-137	Rsd Collen	Rob-225
George	Ran-172	John	Sto-146	Tibby	Grn-149
Jacob	Ran-172	John	Sto-107	Walter	Bun- 98
Samuel	Ran-172	John	Sto-114	Lint,Isaac	Ora-116
Samuel	Ran-172	John	Sto-114	Lintecum,Daniel	Sto-148
Lin,Nancy	Lnc-327	Joseph	Sto-134	Linthicum,Richd	Glf-157
Lincer,Henry	Cab-141	Joseph	Sto-128	Linton,Burge	Bft- 34
Linch,Edmond	Ora-151	Joseph	Sto-102	Danl	Bft- 35
Elabeth	Ora-148	Peter	Sto-129	J	Cam-157
Elizebeth	Ans- 17	Linebarger,Fredk	Lnc-373	J	Cam-158
Good	Ora-157	John	Lnc-327	Lemuel	Pas-194
James	Bun- 77	Lewis	Lnc-340	Lemuel	Brt- 57
James	Bun- 76	Lineberrier,Peter	Row- 85	Luke Jun	Bft- 34
John	Car-184	Lineberry,Jno	Ora-133	Luke Sen	Bft- 34
John	Lnc-376	John	Lnc-373	Malica	Bft- 34
John	Row- 73	John	Lnc-357	Saml	Bft- 34
Olive	Edg- 57	John Jr	Lnc-362	Lints,Benjamin	Row- 77
Oren	Edg- 57	John Senr	Lnc-362	Jacob	Row- 77
William	Hal-111	Michael	Lnc-357	Michal	Row- 77
Lincher,Henry	Cab-141	Linegar,Isaac	Rch-204	Linty,Devoll	Row- 67
Lind,J	Ora-131	Lingafelt,John	Lnc-327	Lintz,Devol	Row- 67
Linden,Abram	Cas- 60	Linger,Wm	Row- 53	Peter	Row- 67
John	Cas- 60	Linget,Adam	Bur-111	Linvell,Aaron	Sto-147
Mary	Roc- 7	Lingle,Anthony	Row- 39	Barbary	Sto-132
Linder,John Junr	Roc- 21	Casper	Row- 68	David Jnr	Sto-147
John Senr	Roc- 21	Francis	Row- 67	Moses	Sur-186
Jonathan	Ora-128	Francis	Cab-145	Robert	Sto-134
Joshua	Cha-212	Paul	Cab-145	Wm	Sto-150
Owen	Ora-117	Lingo,Jno	Ora-149	Linvill,Brace	Sur-186
Thos of Jos	Ora-145	Joseph	Ora-166	John	Sur-187
Wm	Cah-199	Lingwith,Dederniah	Car-176	S	Ash- 6
Lindly,Saml	Cha-213	Link,Frederick	Bur-115	Linzey,Jacob	Bun- 87
Lindsay,Isaac	Rch-197	Jacob	Lnc-376	Nathan	Nsh- 81
James	Nor- 71	John	Row- 79	Salley	Nsh- 82
Josiah	Nor- 72	John	Per-131	Wm	Nsh- 82
Nancy	Glf-167	Katy	Lnc-376	Lion,Nathl	Row- 62
Robt	Glf-181	Nancy	Row- 76	Lions,Elijah	Gat-110
Samuel	Glf-173	Philip	Row- 75	Lipe,Geo	Cab-140

Lipe,Godfred	Cab-140	Little,J	Bru-222	Litton,Joseph	Bur-106
John	Cab-140	Jacob	Ans- 12	Michael	Bur-130
Leonard	Mon- 49	Jacob	Ans- 13	Thomas	Bur-105
Lipman,Phillup	Cur- 90	Jacob	Lnc-350	Lively,Lucy	Rth-114
Lippe,C	Mon- 42	James	Pit-241	Livengood,Christian	Row- 41
Lips,Jacob	Wil-280	Jessee	Edg- 70	Christian Sr	Row- 41
John	Wil-280	Jno	Rob-222	Hartman	Row- 84
Lipscomb,Archd	Per-140	Capt Jno	Rob-224	Hartman	Row- 80
Pheby	Cas- 60	John	Edg- 64	Jno	Row- 50
Thos	Per-131	John	Ire-264	Michl	Row- 41
Wm	Per-134	John	Cho-221	Robias	Row- 50
Lipsey,Isaac	Ons- 87	John	Rth-115	Liveratt,Thomas	Rth-113
James	Jon-301	John	Roc- 27	Liverett,Robert	Rth-113
Rasco	Jon-301	John	Ora-123	Liverman,Dempsey	Tyr-201
Sarah	Jon-300	John	Mec- 23	James	Tyr-207
Liscom,Wilson	Hal-112	John	Pit-246	John Jr	Tyr-202
Liscomb,John	Bft- 19	John	Row- 66	John Senr	Tyr-201
Wm	Brt- 45	Jonah	Bft- 26	Joseph	Tyr-207
Liscus,Adam	Sto- 97	Lewis	Lnc-350	Livermon,Asa	Hrt-211
Lisenbey,Jno	Ans- 27	Margaret	Row- 60	Asa	Hrt-212
Vinney	Asn- 27	Mary	Hrt-213	Edoment	Hrt-211
Lisk,Benj Stitt	Mon- 24	Michael	Ans- 33	Haney	Tyr-207
Martin	Sto-144	N	Col- 21	Jestice	Tyr-208
Timothy	Bur-108	Nahum	Pit-253	S	Tyr-207
Wm	Ans- 22	Nancy	Roc- 27	Thos	Tyr-207
Lister,Israel	Pas-195	Noah	Edg- 71	Wm	Tyr-202
Jesse	Sur-164	Peter Junr	Lnc-350	Livingston,Mrs.	Cum-236
John	Row- 70	Peter Senr	Lnc-350	Duncan	Rch-202
Minny	Pas-195	Pleasant	Ans- 13	Duncan	Rch-205
Nathan	Glf-151	Reading	Pit-247	Duncan	Rch-211
Liteker,Jacob	Cab-141	Robert	Nor- 71	John	Wil-273
Litle,Jno	Ans- 13	Robert	Rob-233	John O	Wil-284
Litt,John	Mor- 63	Stephen	Pit-240	Peter	Rob-227
Litten,Elijah	Lnc-354	T	Bru-224	Sol	Glf-182
Fanny	Lnc-354	Thomas	War-181	Lloyd,D	Glf-184
Isaac	Lnc-354	Thomas	Roc- 19	David	Bla- 9
James	Lnc-354	Thos	Glf-162	David	Glf-186
Wesley	Lnc-354	William	Pit-235	Edward	Glf-181
Litteral,Eliz	Roc- 32	William	Pit-241	L	Ora-136
James	Cas- 60	William P	War-182	Mary	Ora-146
Jerins	Cas- 61	Wm	Ans- 28	S	Ora-135
Little,Alexr	Rob-233	Littlejohn,Eliz	Rth-116	Thomas	Sto-137
Archd	Rob-222	Ephraim	Rth-116	Lloyed,Steward	Jon-300
Archd	Cha-211	Ephraim	Rth-115	Loath,Archd	Cho-223
Archd Senr	Rob-224	Joseph	Grn-146	Lochlin,James	Ran-173
Asa	Edg- 64	Thomas	Rth-115	John	Ran-173
Catharine	Ran-173	Thos B	Grn-144	Lochinour,Geo	Sto-135
Crandal	Pit-241	Wm Sen	Cho-220	Lock,Alexander	Ire-259
David	Roc- 27	Littleton,Benj	Ons- 96	D	Bla- 11
Dempsey	Pit-246	Huton	Ons-109	Eliza	Grn-147
Duncan	Rob-219	Rheuben	Jon-301	Ezekiah	Grn-146
Duncan	Rob-223	Samuel	Ons- 96	George	Ire-267
Edmond	Pit-247	Solomon	Ons-102	Francis	Ire-266
Etheldred	Pit-257	Thomas	Ons-100	Isaac	Rob-237
Exum	Edg- 70	Thomas	Ons- 97	James	Ire-265
George	Lnc-357	Thos	Mon- 44	James	Hal-111
Grey	Edg- 71	William W	Ons- 96	James	Bur-103
Isaac	War-176	Zach	Ons- 96	Jessey	Grn-128
J	Col- 20	Litton,A	Cam-153	Jonathan	Grn-126

Lock,Susana	Hal-111	Locus,Elic	Nsh- 89	Loller,Wilie	Rth-114	
Thomas	Hal-111	Henry	Nsh- 88	Lomar,Moses	Roc- 17	
Lockalear,Saml	Hal-111	John	Nsh- 88	Lomax,Abel	Glf-186	
Lockamy,Aron	Sam-155	Kinchen	Nsh- 89	Robert	Glf-186	
Ely	Sam-155	Stepen	Nsh- 88	Robt	Glf-182	
Ely	Sam-162	Lodge,Lewis	Edg- 48	Lon,William	Hrt-214	
Hugh Senr	Sam-156	Robert	Edg- 47	London (sic)	Pas-194	
Jacob	Sam-162	Lodwick,P	Glf-178	Amos	Sur-170	
Jacob	Sam-155	Loe,Burrel	Rob-237	Henry	Rth-114	
Jas	Sam-153	Danl	Rob-238	Isaiah	Mon- 34	
Joseph	Sam-155	John	Rob-220	John	Wil-269	
Moses	Sam-162	Joshua	Wil-278	Livingston	Rth-114	
Moses Senr	Sam-162	Samuel	Bun- 75	Swepstone	Rth-116	
Odom	Sam-155	Willis	Rob-237	William	Ire-263	
William	Sam-156	Loflin,Joseph	Hay-197	Long,Mrs.	Bru-234	
Locke,Alexander	Row- 82	Loften,Eldridge	Lnc-354	Adam	Ora-120	
Elizabeth	Row- 68	James	Lnc-357	Adam	Ans- 24	
Francis	Row- 87	L	Glf-178	Alexand	Ire-267	
James	Row- 69	Loftin,Jeremiah	Len-315	Alexander	Row- 86	
James	Row- 72	Jno	Len-323	Ann	Ora-144	
John	Grn-145	Joel	Len-316	Anthony	Lnc-359	
John	Row- 69	Joseph	Len-315	B	Ash- 15	
Mathew	Row- 82	Jsa	Len-317	Barney	Row- 49	
Richard	Row- 68	Leond	Len-314	Benjamin	Wsh-225	
Robert	Row- 68	Lewis	Jon-300	Benjamin	Rch-208	
Lockelaur,Robert	Hal-111	Needham	Len-317	Benjamin	Wsh-219	
Lockenhour,John	Row- 48	Shadrach	Len-319	Conrad	Ora-138	
Lockhart,Adam	Ans- 14	William	Len-317	D	Cam-157	
Andrew	Bun- 72	Lofton,James	Ran-173	Delilah	Wsh-219	
James	Ora-112	John	Ran-173	Edward	Edg- 41	
Jas	Ans- 14	Robt	Ran- 73	Elza	Hal-111	
John	Nor- 72	T	Glf-176	Felix	Row- 49	
John	Bun- 72	Logan,Andrew	Rth-113	Frederick	Nor- 71	
Saml	Grn-138	Drury	Rth-115	Frederick	Sur-165	
Sarah	Ora-112	Drury	Rth-115	Frederick Sr	Sur-165	
William	Sur-185	Drury	Rth-113	G	Col- 20	
Wm	Glf-174	Francis	Rth-113	Geo	Cab-148	
Lockheart,Carry	Joh-273	Francis	Rth-115	George	Row- 49	
Elam	Joh-273	Hugh	Sur-188	George	Row- 79	
Hannr	Joh-273	James	Sur-183	George	Sur-165	
Osborn	Joh-274	James	Rth-115	George	Joh-278	
Polly	Joh-273	James	Rth-113	George	Sur-195	
Thomas	Joh-273	John	Ire-241	Gloud	Rth-115	
Locklear,Charly	Rob-221	John	Sur-177	Henry	Sto-107	
Gade	Rob-232	John	Rth-115	Henry	Sur-165	
Hugh	Rob-231	John	Bur-120	Henry	Mec- 45	
Joseph	Rob-230	John	Rth-115	Henry	Lnc-328	
Levi	Rob-231	John	Rth-113	Henry	Sto-143	
Matt B	Rob-232	Larkin	Rth-115	Henry	Rth-114	
Rhody	Rob-219	Mary	Sur-188	Henry W	Hrt-206	
Robert	Rob-230	Mary	Rth-115	Israel	Sto-148	
Samuel	Rob-231	Moses	Rth-113	J	Ash- 15	
Sarah	Rob-232	Loghinour,Geo Jnr	Sto-137	J	Bla- 11	
Wm	Rob-232	Loid,Henry	Pit-241	J	Col- 19	
Locklier,John	Rch-192	Loid	Per-140	Jacob	Ora-124	
Lockman,David	Lnc-362	Lokery,Thomas	Ire-266	Jacob	Row- 79	
Isaac	Lnc-362	Loller,Archibald	Rth-113	Jacob	Mec- 45	
Moses	Sam-161	Isaac	Rth-114	Jacob	Rob-234	
Locus,Charles	Nsh- 88	Thomas	Rth-114	Jacob	Sto-142	

Name	Ref	Name	Ref	Name	Ref
Long,James	Per-140	Long,William	Wsh-222	Louis,Jas	Rob-236
James	Joh-277	William	Prq-220	John (P R)	Wil-278
James	Wsh-220	William	Cas- 61	John (son of David)	
James	Hal-111	William	Rth-115		Wil-280
James	Cab-147	William R	Edg- 53	John (miller)	Wil-282
Jasper	Ora-124	Wm	Mon- 48	Joseph	Wil-277
Jesse D	Gat-111	Wm	Per-135	Joseph Jr	Wil-282
John	Cab-142	Zilpha	Wsh-222	Martin	Rob-233
John	Row- 49	Longard,Curtis	Roc- 27	Shadrach	Wil-273
John	Ran-172	Longbottom,Joseph	Wil-272	Welcome W	Wil-283
John	Per-140	Longest,Joshua	Car-185	William	Wil-275
John	Sur-165	Longmin,Wm	Grn-144	Wm	Rob-237
John	Cas- 61	Wm Jr	Grn-144	Lourance,Andrew	Row- 73
John	Rch-209	Longmire,John	Bun- 96	John	Row- 72
John	Rch-210	Longon,James	Fra- 83	Love,Alexander	Nor- 72
John	Wsh-220	Lonsford,Payton	Ans- 20	Angus	Rob-224
John	Lnc-334	Lontey,George	Lnc-337	Christopher	Ire-248
John	Lnc-335	Jacob	Lnc-337	Danl	Mor- 61
John	Lnc-342	Saml	Lnc-337	David	Sur-185
John	Rth-115	Loofman,Arna	Glf-188	David	Mec- 55
John	Rth-114	Loomiss,Nathl Esq	Ons- 97	Duncan	Mor- 57
John	Rth-113	Looper,Biggy	Rob-238	Elizabeth	Nor- 71
John	Edg- 46	Sarah	Ire-251	George	Lnc-342
John	Bur-121	William	Ire-254	George B	Sto- 94
Joice	Nor- 71	Loops,James	Edg- 61	George B	Sto-123
Jonathan	Lnc-357	Zachariah	Edg- 46	James	Sto-110
Joseph	Mar- 5	Loorey,Eve	Row- 81	James	Cab-147
Josiah	Lnc-339	Lootey,Jacob	Cab-145	James	Sto-149
Josiah	Edg- 41	Lop,Jacob	Row- 40	John	Ran-172
Leml	Hal-111	Peter	Row- 41	John	Nor- 71
Leonard	Lnc-357	Lopach,Christopher	Sto-143	John	Bun- 72
M	Col- 20	Lorance,Daniel	Row- 70	John	Len-323
Mary	Hal-111	Joshua	Row- 72	John	Bun- 75
Mary	Ire-239	William	Lnc-328	John C	Sto-149
Mary Senr	Hal-111	Loray,-----	Mec- 25	John C	Sto-110
Nathan	Bft- 29	Lord,E	Bru-236	Jonah	Cab-148
Nicholas	Fra- 85	J	Bru-228	Jonathan	Sur-185
Prettyman	Lnc-362	Jacob	Glf-155	Michael J	Sam-152
R	Bru-224	Joseph	Wil-277	N	Col- 20
Rachael	Lnc-362	William	Cum-264	N	Cum-241
Rebukah	Ans- 26	Lordon,Nimshar	Roc- 14	Peggy	Wil-268
Reuben	Prq-220	Loretey,Andrew	Lnc-332	Robert	Hay-197
Reuben	Lnc-334	Lorngston,Betholemy	Joh-288	Samuel	Ire-259
Reuben Senr	Per-140	Isaac	Joh-289	Samuel	Rth-116
Reubin	Sto-148	Joseph	Joh-289	Samuel	Bur-112
Rhuben Junr	Per-140	Lorton,John	Hal-111	Thomas	Ora-167
Richard	Nor- 71	Mary	Hal-111	Thomas	Hay-197
Richd	Lnc-341	Losson,Abraham	Rob-235	Thomas	Sur-185
Robert	Cas- 60	Losswoser,Adam	Row- 88	Thos	Mec- 46
Rubin	Ans- 20	Lotharp,Francis	Joh-290	William	Row- 83
Samuel	Lnc-362	Lott,free man of colour		William	Ora-167
Sarah	Prq-220		Ran-187	William	Rch-207
Sarah	Nor- 72	Louder,Samuel	Wil-264	William	Sur-185
Silas	Wsh-222	Loudermilk,Henry	Bur-106	William	Lnc-342
Silas	Nor- 72	John	Ran-172	William	Rth-116
Simeon	Prq-220	Loughenhour,Jacob	Row- 49	William Jn	Sur-185
Thomas	Wsh-224	Louis,Benjamin	Rob-234	Lovecey,John	Lnc-373
Thomas	Lnc-357	David	Wil-277	Lovecy,Shade	Lnc-372
Thos	Prq-220	James	Wil-280	Loveingood,Samuel	Hay-197

Name	Ref	Name	Ref	Name	Ref	Name	Ref
Lovel,C	Bru-232	Low,Nathan	Ran-172	Loy,Henry	Ora-159		
Elizebeth	Mec- 49	Nathan	Ran-172	Jacob	Ora-119		
Lovelace,Archibald	Wil-272	Orph	Pas-194	Jno Senr	Ora-145		
Cassy	Ire-267	Thomas	Pas-194	Martin	Ora-118		
Erasmus	Ire-268	Thomas	Ran-172	Robt	Cha-213		
Isaac	Row- 81	William	Pas-194	Loyd,David	Grn-123		
Pryor	Cas- 61	Lowder,Caleb	Ran-173	Edward	Ans- 31		
Rhoda	Cas- 60	Thos	Mon- 39	Edward	Grn-124		
Sally	Ire-266	W	Mon- 42	Ezekiel	Ons-108		
Saml	Ora-162	Lowdermilk,Jacob	Ire-264	F	Cam-160		
Thomas	Ire-243	Lowe,D	Glf-177	Henry	Hyd-224		
Lovelass,Elias	Roc- 16	D Jr	Glf-177	Henry	Ora-116		
Samuel	Roc- 16	Daniel	Ans- 32	Isaac	Grn-123		
Young	Roc- 16	Daniel	Roc- 28	Isaac	Grn-149		
Lovell,Abner	Roc- 18	David	Roc- 30	J	Glf-158		
William	Sto-154	Eve	Row- 44	John	Roc- 7		
Loven,William	Way-244	Green	Lnc-362	John	Row- 81		
Loverel,William	Ire-266	James	Row- 37	John	Ons-100		
Lovet,Barney	Joh-284	James	Roc- 5	Johnson (moved)	Grn-123		
Benjamin	Rob-233	Jesse	Lnc-376	Joseph	Edg- 47		
Charles	Cur- 92	John	Roc- 30	Martha	Ora-131		
John	Ons-107	Kittey	Roc- 5	Nicholas	Edg- 63		
John	Car-183	L	Glf-177	Stephen	Sur-182		
Patrick	Gat-110	Thomas	Roc- 5	Thomas	Roc- 5		
Lovett,Aaron	Glf-158	Thomas	Ran-171	Thomas	Ora-130		
Jos	Glf-171	Thomas	Hal-111	Valentine(moved)	Grn-123		
Moses	Glf-171	Thomas Jr	Lnc-362	Wels	Grn-138		
Lovick,Wm	Len-317	Thomas Senr	Lnc-362	Wm	Grn-129		
Loviet,Moses	Rob-221	Thomas Senr	Hal-111	Wm	Grn-134		
Richard	Rob-222	Thos	Ans- 31	Zedock	Grn-120		
Wm	Rob-222	Wm	Hal-111	Loyed,David	Hrt-210		
Lovill,Edward	Sur-177	Lower,W	Ash- 3	Loysel,Peter	Bft- 36		
James	Sur-174	Lowerance,Abraham	Ire-259	Luallen,Jesse	Ans- 15		
Lovin,Laeresa	Bun- 91	Lowery,J Snr	Glf-184	Lucabell,John	Row- 81		
Loving,Bryant	Rch-194	W	Glf-177	Lucas,Charles	Bla- 9		
John	Bur-110	Lowes,Jas	Rob-236	Elias	Sam-153		
Reddick	Rch-195	Lowie,John	Ire-245	George	Bla- 11		
William	Bur-128	Lowman,----	Bur-105	Henry	Bla- 3		
Lovins,Hugh	Ora-149	A Jr	Glf-178	Hugh	Mec- 53		
Hugh	Ora-149	J	Glf-175	Isham	Len-311		
James	Bur-125	Lowndes,John	Bft- 33	Jas	Glf-175		
Lovist,Annes	Rob-220	Lowrance,Alexdr	Row- 72	Jas	Mec- 53		
Lovit,Ethrelbred	Nsh- 89	Lowrey,Thos	Lnc-327	Jesse	Hyd-228		
J	Col- 20	Lowrie,James	Bun- 74	John	Ran-171		
Lovitt,Henry	Len-216	Saml Esq	Mec- 55	William	Rth-113		
Herod	Len-311	Lowry,Alex	Bur-116	William	Rth-116		
Moses	Len-311	Benjn	Pas-194	William	Glf-175		
Lovlass,James	Sur-197	Celia	Rob-219	Wm	Mon- 33		
Lovsit,Coleson	Rob-240	Eli	Ans- 11	Luceferr,Elish	Ire-248		
Henry	Rob-237	Elizebeth	Ans- 11	Lucelby,David	Row- 82		
Low,Aaron	Pas-194	John	Pas-194	Luck,Edmund	Ran-172		
Barnet	Pas-194	John	Glf-187	James	Per-220		
David	Ora-159	John	Sto-149	Lucket,Samuel	Rth-116		
Ezekel	Ire-251	Joseph	Pas-194	Luckey,Richard	Row- 74		
James	Pas-195	Noah	Pas-194	Robert	Row- 74		
James	Ran-172	Thomas	Rob-220	Samuel	Row- 74		
Jesse	Way-243	Thomas	Hal-111	Lucky,George	Ire-267		
Mads	Ora-137	Thomas	Pas-194	Hugh	Lnc-359		
Nancy	Ire-254	Loy,George	Ora-145	William	Row- 74		

Name	Ref	Name	Ref	Name	Ref
Lucous,Richd	Tyr-210	Lurenar (sic)	Pas-194	Lyles,David	Rth-116
Lucus,Daniel	Way-245	Lurey,W	Cam-165	David	Rth-115
John Sr	Way-254	Lurrey,E	Cam-155	Drury	Joh-286
Joseph	Way-245	J	Cam-155	Exum	Nor- 71
Mary	Cha-210	Lurry,N	Cam-156	J	Ash- 7
Ludkins,Chas	Ans- 30	Lusk,Hugh	Lnc-347	James	Rth-115
Ludwick,Daniel	Sto-127	Joseph	Hay-197	Jessee	Nor- 71
Jacob	Sto-149	Saml	Row- 43	John	Rth-116
William	Sto-149	Samuel	Bun- 94	Larkin	Rth-116
Ludwig,Jacob	Sto-110	William	Bun- 94	Mary	Nor- 71
Luere,J	Mon- 37	Luske,William	Bun- 81	Thomas	Rth-115
Lufcy,Jno	Ans- 12	Lusly,Nathan	Rth-116	Lyn,Isral	Row- 39
Lumbeth,Counsel	Row- 42	Luster,John	Mar- 5	Lynch,Anny	Lnc-376
Lumley,Thos	Lnc-332	Luten,H R	Hrt-210	Arthur	Joh-281
Lumly,William	Lnc-373	John	Mar- 13	Claxton	Rth-113
Lumpkin,Anthony	Grn-125	Luter,Giles	Nor- 71	Cornelius	Joh-290
Anthony	Grn-120	Jonathan	Nor- 71	Demsey	Joh-288
Edmund	Grn-120	Mary	Nor- 71	Elias	Rth-113
Joseph	Grn-120	Thomas	Nor- 71	Elijah	Bun- 72
Richard	Glf-160	Lutes,Adam	Lnc-327	Elijah	Roc- 8
Wm	Grn-133	Daniel	Lnc-327	Henry	Mar- 5
Lumsden,John	Cum-240	Luthaland,Roderick	Rob-229	Hugh	Roc- 19
Lumurd,J	Glf-175	Luther,Christian	Ran-173	James	Roc- 10
Lund,James	Ora-131	David	Cab-142	Jesse	Glf-178
Lundin,Mrs. S	Cum-235	George	Ran-187	Jno	Ora-176
Lundy,Elijah	Ire-269	Godfrey	Ran-171	Jno	Ora-119
Ezekiel	Sto-153	Hardy	Cha-200	John	Mar- 5
Saml	Cum-240	Henry	Cha-200	John	Sur-188
Thomas	Ire-267	Jacob	Ran-171	John	Ora-165
Lunee,L	Ash- 12	Jonathan	Ran-171	John	Ora-166
Lunett,John	Sto-146	Michael	Ran-172	John	Ora-166
Lunmons,John	Bur-121	Peter	Mon- 33	John	Ora-160
Lunsford,Abraham	Bur-107	Saml	Cab-142	Moses	Ora-128
Daniel	Rth-115	Lutin,King	Cho-227	Polly	Hal-111
Eaton	Fra- 98	Luton,Enoch	Cur- 86	Robert	Roc- 19
Eli	Ire-254	Fanny	Cho-223	Saxton	Rth-113
Elijah	Wil-272	Fredk	Cho-224	Susanah	Mar- 4
Elisha	Wil-272	Henry	Ans- 17	William	Joh-273
Ezekiel	Wil-267	Hervey	Pas-194	Lyndon,Josiah	Ran-187
Jacob	Wil-266	Miriam	Pas-194	Lyne,Henry	Grn-134
Jesse	Bur-126	Lutz,Charity	Lnc-370	Lynn,Alexr	Roc- 16
Jesse	Per-140	George	Lnc-370	John	Roc- 15
Jesse	Per-131	Henry	Lnc-370	John	Row- 67
John	Bur-126	John	Bur-130	Lyns,James	Grn-140
Jonathan	Wil-270	Luveling,John	Edg- 54	Lyon,Clement	Grn-126
Joseph	Per-140	Lyday,Abraham	Bun- 84	Edmond	Cas- 60
Michael	Ire-253	Andrew	Bun- 84	Jacob	Wil-259
Nimrod	Bur-131	Jacob	Bun- 72	James	Wil-264
Samuel	Per-140	John	Bun- 98	James	Sto- 92
William	Wil-265	William	Bun- 84	James Jnr	Sto-121
William	Fra- 98	Lyeres,John	Row- 87	James Jnr	Sto- 93
William	Bur-107	Lyerley,Peter	Row- 67	James Snr	Sto-121
Lupton,Allen	Car-174	Lyerly,Henry	Row- 78	John	Grn-126
Elizabeth	Car-174	Jacob	Row- 82	John	Wil-271
John	Car-174	Lyle,C	Mon- 42	John	Roc- 17
Jonah	Car-173	Thomas	Grn-123	Leonard	Bur-129
Silas	Car-174	Z	Mon- 42	Richard	Per-140
Luras,Henry	Hyd-220	Lyles,Balton	Rth-115	Robt	Bla- 7
Samuel W	Hyd-224	Bird	Rth-116	Temsey	Cas- 72

Name	Ref	Name	Ref	Name	Ref
Lyon,Thomas	Edg- 57	Mackey,William	Wsh-224	Madison,Peyton	Grn-143
William	Wil-259	Mackins,A	Mon- 43	Madith,Jas	Glf-165
William	Cas- 60	Mackling,Matthew	Sto-133	Madkin,John	Cas- 62
William	Sur-161	Maclamore,Joel H	Hal-113	Madkins,Richard	Pas-195
William V	Wil-259	MacLean,Mrs.	Cum-236	Madrey,Richard	War-179
Wm	Len-322	Maclemore,John	Rch-200	Madrin,Effia	Pas-195
Zachariah	Grn-126	Maclen,Benjamin	War-169	John	Pas-197
Lyons,Robert	Sur-182	John	War-175	Joseph	Pas-195
William	Sur-191	Macman,David	Ire-268	Lydia	Pas-195
Lype,Jacob	Row- 69	Macom,Patsey	Nsh- 91	Richd	Pas-195
Jonas	Mon- 50	Macomb,Matth	Hal-113	Thomas	Pas-195
Lyrely,C	Mon- 42	Macon,George W	War-171	Madry,Elizabeth	Nor- 73
Lyster,Robert	Row- 65	Gideon	Ran-175	John	Nor- 72
Lytaker,Jacob	Row- 68	Gideon	War-171	John	Hal-113
Lytle,James esqr	Lnc-360	Mary H	War-177	John	Prq-221
John	Lnc-359	Nathaniel	War-178	Mary	Nor- 72
John	Lnc-360	Nathl	Fra- 85	Peter	Nor- 72
Robt	Bla- 14	Wm	Mon- 28	William	Nor- 72
Saley (wid)	Lnc-359	MacQuean,Neill	Cum-270	William Jr	Nor- 72
William	Lnc-362	MacRae,Daniel Senr	Cum-270	Mage,Stithe	Rth-123
Lyttle,George	Bur-110	F	Cum-235	Magee,Elias	Bur-122
Millington	Bur-125	Macy,David	Glf-183	James	Jon-301
Thos	Bur-119	E	Glf-161	William	Hal-113
		George	Glf-187	Magett,Nicholas	Nor- 72
M----,Hardy	Jon-301	H	Glf-183	William	Nor- 72
M--hant,---lly	Tyr-209	H	Glf-159	Maggee,Henry	Glf-185
Maberry,John	Lnc-365	John	Glf-169	Maggett,John	Hrt-214
Randolph	Ire-251	Laban	Glf-161	William	Hrt-214
Mabery,Luke	Row- 78	Mathew	Row- 53	Maggle,William	Glf-181
Philips	Roc- 11	Nathl	Glf-161	Magilbery,Mary	Mor- 68
Randolph	Cha-202	O	Glf-156	Magilbry,Angus	Mor- 64
Sol	Mon- 41	Paul	Glf-180	Maglaulin,Robt	Row- 72
Wilkinson	Edg- 63	Paul	Glf-161	Maglilin,James	Row- 70
Mabin,D	Glf-171	Reuben	Sur-195	Magness,Benjamin	Rth-120
Mabley,Levane	Row- 58	Reubin	Sto-147	Benjamin	Rth-123
Mabry,Charles	War-169	Robt	Glf-161	Jacob	Rth-118
Deth	War-169	Stephen	Sto-150	Wm	Lnc-341
Green	Nor- 73	Thad	Glf-159	Mahaffey,William	Hay-197
Matthew	War-177	Thadias	Glf-188	Mahan,Began	Mec- 49
Reps	War-179	Thos	Glf-183	James	Cas- 62
Maca,John	Car-170	Zach	Glf-162	James	Row- 69
Macarn,Abraham	Row- 83	Madcaf,Elizabeth	Ire-254	John	Row- 70
Michl	Row- 83	Madd,Jonathan	Row- 63	Mahathew,James	Ire-254
MaCasland,Matthew	Lnc-345	Madden,And	Ora-154	Mahew,John	Ire-268
William	Lnc-345	Andw	Ora-127	Mahon,Henry	Cas- 62
Macay,Elizabeth	Row- 86	Ar	Ora-154	Sarah	Cas- 62
Mace,Francis	Car-183	George	Ora-155	Maiden,John	Ire-269
Sarah	Car-183	Jno	Ora-127	Richard	Ire-269
Maceal,Jno Jr	Ora-142	S	Ora-154	Maies,William	Ire-241
Macharney,James	Cur- 87	William	Row- 64	William	Ire-256
Macints,Jacob	Sto-106	Maddin,Mary	Rth-119	Maile,-----	Sto-94
Mack,Gravnor	Glf-157	Maddux,Benjn	Pas-195	John	Sto- 94
James	Roc- 12	Jesse	Pas-195	John	Sto-123
Mackey,David	Roc- 19	Made,Nancy	Rth-121	Lloyd	Sto-124
John	Sur-168	Maden,Thomas	Edg- 53	Lloyd	Sto- 95
Joseph	Pas-196	Maderas,William	Bur-110	Philip	Sto-155
Mary	Roc- 30	Maderis,David	Roc- 4	Philip	Sto-112
Samuel	Bur-121	John	Glf-181	Reuben	Sto-123
Tho	Pas-196	Mades,Mary	Jon-301	Robert	Sto-124

-195-

Maile,Robert	Sto- 95	Mallposs,John	Dup- 28	Mangrum,James	Hal-113
Robert Jnr	Sto-155	Malom,Thomas	Cas- 72	John	Grn-123
Main,James	Per-151	Malone,Charles	Nor- 72	Josiah	Grn-138
John	Cum-254	Daniel	Per-145	M	Glf-158
John	Bla- 5	Daniel	Cas- 62	Pleasant	Grn-138
Mainemar,John	Lnc-335	Daniel	Roc- 14	Saml	Grn-123
Mainer,Aron	Edg- 55	John	Per-141	William	Grn-123
Jethrow	Edg- 56	L	Ora-153	Wm Jr	Grn-139
Roady	Edg- 56	Lewis	Cas- 62	Wm Sr	Grn-139
Wills	Edg- 55	Mildred	Nor- 73	Wingfield(moved)	Grn-123
Zachariah	Edg- 55	Nancy	Roc- 16	Mangum,Arthur	Ora-128
Mainor,Charity	Dup- 30	Nathl	Cas- 61	Blasam	Nor- 73
John	Dup- 15	Stephen	Cas- 62	Joseph	War-175
John	Sam-157	William	Rth-117	Wm	Ora-117
John	Way-233	Wm	Ora-153	Wm P	Ora-150
Josiah	Sam-160	Malory,Charles	Grn-144	Manica,Joseph	Sto-120
Josiah Senr	Sam-161	Wm	Grn-144	Manin,Elijah	Pit-238
Penelope	Dup- 24	Malsbey,Mrs.	Cum-240	Sarah	Pit-238
William	Dup- 27	Man,Ader	Cur- 85	Maning,Calib.	Cru- 89
Mainord,George	Joh-274	Betsy	Pas-195	Charles	Hal-112
Maira,Arthur	Hyd-232	Jane	Per-141	Eliza	Hal-116
Mairs,Nancy	Cha-215	John	Grn-128	John	Edg- 57
Major,John	Cha-199	Leonard	Car-183	John	Pit-245
Wm	Cha-215	Peter	Grn-123	John	Pit-254
Majors,John	Bur-128	William	Way-197	Judith	Edg- 72
Makessinson,Eufaney	Cur- 91	Manalin,Samuel	Prq-221	Nancy	Hal-113
Makinhamer,Abm	Cab-140	Mancel,W	Col- 19	Reuben	Pit-245
Geo	Cab-140	Mancell,Robert	Sto- 98	Reuben	Pit-245
Jacob	Cab-140	Mancil,E	Col- 21	Richard	Pit-245
Makit,Benjamin	Jon-301	Manders,Burgess	Nor- 73	Sarah	Hal-112
Malaby,Elizabeth	Joh-288	Mandevill,Y	Cam-161	Thomas	Edg- 56
Malcan,Joseph	Sto- 98	Mandley,Furneford	Way-248	Manis,David	Bur-112
Malcom,Joseph	Sto-128	Manduell,Elizabeth	Hyd-223	Mankin,John	Cur- 89
Malett,Mrs.	Cum-237	Elizth	Hyd-223	Mankins,Stephen	Sur-196
Joseph	Ora-158	John	Hyd-223	William	Ora-162
Maley,Hugh	Row- 85	Lydia	Hyd-223	Manley,Bazel	Cha-203
Malford,W B	Bla- 13	Maner,Hector	Mor- 63	Joshua	Roc- 12
Malicar,Richd	Cas- 62	Maners,Abednego	Mor- 59	Maning	Hrt-209
Mall,Uriah	Hrt-208	Ambrose	Mor- 58	Margett	Hrt-209
Mallard,Danl Senr	Jon-302	Ambrose	Mor- 64	Moses	Hrt-209
James	Dup- 36	Danl	Mor- 64	Manlove,John	Glf-162
James	Jon-302	Danl	Mor- 64	Jonathan	Row- 46
John Jr	Dup- 20	Daniel	Mor- 60	Will	Glf-157
John Junr	Jon-302	Elizabeth	Mor- 59	Wm	Row- 47
John Senr	Jon-302	James	Mor- 57	Manly,Benjn	Nor- 73
John Sr	Dup- 20	James	Mor- 62	Hardy	Hal-113
Joseph	Dup- 9	James	Mor- 56	James	Row- 52
Lawson	Jon-302	Meshat	Mor- 59	Mary	Hrt-213
Samuel	Rch-199	Wm	Mor- 60	Moses	Hal-113
Mallet,Peter	Row- 66	Wm	Mor- 57	William	Hal-114
Mallison,Ann	Hyd-221	Maney,Samuel	Wil-268	Mann,Arnold	Cum-253
Christopher	Hyd-223	Manford,Catey	Cur- 93	Claborn	Nsh- 87
George	Ire-262	Mangrove,Henry	Hal-113	Charles	Nor- 72
John	Hyd-220	Mangrum,Benj (moved)		Christian	Tyr-205
William	Hyd-223		Grn-123	Daniel	Nsh- 88
Winnifred	Hyd-234	Gray	Grn-139	Henry	Mon- 50
Mallord,William	Dup- 10	James	Grn-123	Isam	Cha-194
Mallory,Thomas	Cas- 63	James	Grn-139	James	Per-141
Wm	Hal-112	James	Ire-253	James	Cum-253

Mann,John	Cho-221	Manuel,Shada	Sam-161	Marks,Wm	Cha-214
John	Nor- 73	Troy	Sam-156	Markum,John	Sto-139
John	Bur-119	William	Sto-105	John	Sto-104
John	Nor- 72	Wm	Sto-139	Markus,Jane	Cha-208
Jonathan	Cum-252	Manuell,Hugh	Roc- 23	Wm	Cha-207
Malachi	Mon- 50	Maples,James	Mor- 55	Marley,Alexander	Ran-174
Nathan	Ora-163	Mard	Lnc-354	John	Ran-174
Rachel	Cas- 61	Wm	Ran-174	Benjn	Cha-194
Rolin	Cha-208	Marbery,Jacob	Mon- 45	Bowling	Edg- 55
Saml	Mon- 50	John	Mon- 45	Jas	Sam-150
Solomon	Tyr-205	Tabitha	Mon- 45	John	Wil-285
Theoderick	Nor- 72	Marbra,Benjamin	Bun- 95	Marlin,David	Row- 82
Thomas	Cho-223	Marbuck,Paul Ser	Sto-149	Elija	Row- 82
Thomas	Per-141	Marces,John	Edg- 45	James	Row- 82
William	Nor- 72	March,George	Row- 84	John	Row- 82
Wm	Cha-208	Jacob	Row- 84	John Jr	Cas- 75
Mannen,Eliz	Bft- 38	John Sr	Row- 83	Joseph	Row- 82
Manning,Abiah	Nsh- 82	Marchant,Elesebeth	Mec- 49	Joseph	Row- 76
Alexander	Nsh- 82	Marcim,Mary	Cas- 62	Marlow,Elijah	Ire-252
Benj	Nsh- 83	R	Ora-157	Elijah	Ire-268
Chas	Cho-222	T	Ora-157	James	Ire-251
Dursiller	Nsh- 82	Marcum,Thos	Ora-159	Jno	Mec- 43
Edwd	Brt- 43	William	Bur-110	John	Ire-252
Eli	Mar- 14	Mardree,Elizabeth	Brt- 48	Mark	Ire-252
Isom	Mar- 8	Joseph	Brt- 43	Mark	Ire-253
James	Nsh- 75	Michl	Brt- 44	Martha	Bun- 86
James	Mar- 10	Mare,William	Hyd-227	Mary	Wil-265
Jos	Cho-221	Maremoon,Elizabeth	Nor- 73	Miles	Ire-251
Joseph	Hyd-224	Margeret,Didah	Car-176	N	Col- 19
Mathias	Nsh- 81	John	Car-176	Nathan	Edg- 68
Merrit	Dup- 35	Marine,John	Rch-203	Smallwood	War-180
Milley	Nsh- 78	Mariner,Abitha	Tyr-210	Thomas	Rth-122
Preggin	Nsh- 81	Abitha Jr	Tyr-210	Thomas	Ire-268
Reuben	Mar- 15	John	Tyr-210	Marly,Catherine	Ran-173
Tucker	Nsh- 83	Peter	Tyr-210	Marman,Benjamin	Ran-174
William	Mar- 7	Maris,John	Ora-129	Marmey,Christian	Lnc-327
William	Mar- 8	S	Glf-162	George	Lnc-334
Wm	Cho-221	William	Edg- 65	George	Lnc-327
Manor,Henry	Ons-100	William	Jon-301	Jacob	Lnc-340
Jesse	Sam-160	Mark,James G	Mon- 21	Jacob	Lnc-327
John	Cum-265	Markel,Peter	Cho-222	John	Lnc-327
Lurany	Ons-101	Markham,Anthony	Pas-196	Marmon,Thomas	Ire-269
Willis	Mon- 50	Clarky	Pas-195	Marner,Poley	Gat-109
Manring,Andrew	Sto-153	Nancy	Pas-195	Maron,Nat	Mon- 34
Mansard,John Bap	Pas-197	Robt	Pas-197	Marple,George	Cas-295
Mansell,Robert	Sto-128	Thomas	Pas-196	Marr,Jereithan	Roc- 27
Mansfield,Lucy	Cas- 62	Thomas	Pas-196	John	Roc- 11
Thomas	Sto-123	Markin,John	Sto-145	Sarah	Roc- 27
Thomas	Sto- 95	Markit,Frederic	Jon-301	Marriner,Dempsey	Wsh-224
Manship,Charles	Glf-157	Joseph	Jon-301	John	Wsh-222
E	Glf-172	Markland,Nathanl	Sto-108	John	Lnc-336
N	Glf-173	Nathaniel	Sto-135	Peter	Wsh-220
Manuel,Gilson	Roc- 23	Nathaniel	Sto-102	Marrs,Nimrod	Mec- 29
Jesse	Sam-162	Robert	Sto-136	Marry,Presley	Sto- 96
Jesse	Cum-236	Marklin,John	Row- 55	Marsbune,Matthew	Dup- 36
Jesse	Cum-251	Marks,James	Cha-201	Marsh,Charles	Cha-209
John	Sam-163	John	Cha-211	Charles	Cha-215
John	Sto-139	John	Cha-215	Clabon	Sur-170
Nichs	Sam-163	Thomas	Edg- 57	Daniel	Sur-178

Name	Ref	Name	Ref	Name	Ref
Marsh,Danl	Bft- 36	Marshall,Wm	Ans-16	Martin,Edwd	Per-131
David W	Edg- 41	Wm	Grn-140	Eliza	Row- 65
James Junr	Cum-251	Wm Sen	Ora-134	Elizabeth	Ire-251
James Senr	Cum-250	Willson M	Per-151	Elijah	Bft- 21
John	Bft- 36	Marshborne,Willm Jr	Nor- 72	Enoch	Roc- 18
John	Cum-250	Marshburne,Jethro	Dup- 34	Etheldred	Nor- 72
John	Cha-215	Marshell,Joseph Esq	Ons- 99	Etheldred Jr	Nor- 72
John	Sur-174	Purnel	Ons- 97	Geo	Sto-126
Mary	Sur-164	Marsingail,M	Col- 17	Geo	Mon- 18
Miner	Sur-164	Marston,Rev Thomas	Wil-270	Geo	Cha-209
Samuel	Sur-168	Thomas Jr	Wil-261	George	Sto- 97
Solomon	Ans- 19	Martain,Mrs.	Mec- 33	George	Ire-259
Thomas	Sur-164	Abraham	Mec- 47	George	Row- 70
William	Sur-164	Coleman	Mec- 41	George	Roc- 23
Wm	Cha-193	Elisha	Hrt-215	George	Sur-176
Marshal,Benjamin	Sto-110	Epheram	Mec- 22	George	Lnc-372
Charles	Hal-112	Gabril	Hrt-216	Henry	Rth-122
F	Ora-145	Jno	Mec- 42	Henry	Wil-261
George	Bun- 72	John	Mec- 46	Henry	Ora-167
Humphrey	Row- 90	John	Cum-241	Henry	Bla- 14
Isaac	Ire-250	Peggy	Mec- 47	Henry	Roc- 30
Jacb	Ora-145	Richard	Hrt-215	Hosea	Hyd-220
James	Hal-112	Robt	Mec- 47	Hugh	Sto-155
Jas	Mec- 36	Sally	Mec- 33	Hugh	Sto-112
Jesse	Mec- 37	Thos	Mec- 54	Isaac	Wil-261
John	Rth-122	Wm	Mec- 52	Isaac	Glf-165
Martin	Sto-100	Marterage,A	Hrt-209	Isaac	Bur-131
Robert	Hal-113	Martial,Ichobad	Lnc-354	Isabella	Roc- 21
Sackby	Cas- 62	Martin,Widow	Lnc-367	Israel	Nor- 72
Samuel	Ran-173	Abraham	Sto- 95	Jacob	Rth-121
Thomas	Sto-131	Abraham	Roc- 24	James	Gat-111
William	Sur-173	Abraham Ser	Sto-124	James	War-173
Wm	Ora-145	Absalom	Car-180	James	Bur-108
Marshall,Aaron	Sur-174	Alex	Mor- 64	James	Sto-145
Ben	Cha-209	Alexander	Roc- 5	James	Per-131
Benjamin	Sto-148	Alexander	Bun- 88	James	Per-151
Charles	War-169	Alexander	Rch-199	Capt James	Wil-264
Chas	Lnc-335	Alexr	Cum-242	James	Sto- 95
David	War-170	Ally	Bla- 10	James	Cas- 61
Dixon	War-170	Ambrose	Wil-261	James	Lnc-370
Eleazor	War-170	Andrew	Roc- 26	James	Hal-113
Eliza	Hal-113	Asa	Bur-109	James (B M)	Wil-262
John	Ons- 97	Bailey	Roc- 26	James	Roc- 21
Henry	Ans- 16	Barrot L	Sur-176	James	Roc- 28
Jas	Ans- 14	Benj	Hyd-225	James	Cab-139
John	Gat-109	Benjn	Joh-275	James	Lnc-336
John	Ora-171	Benjamin	Wil-264	James	Sto-124
John Jr	Ora-166	Benjamin	Pit-236	James	Glf-167
Jonathan	Ons-102	Benjamin H	Roc- 6	Jas	Ans- 31
Martin	Sto-132	Benjamin H	Sur-169	Jesse	Gat-111
Mary	Car-184	Burrel	Sur-171	Jesse	Rth-123
Matthew	War-177	Burwell	Way-254	Jesse	Way-247
Matthew	Sto-132	Caleb	Ora-126	Jesse	Bur-131
Nancy	War-178	Cordy	Cha-200	Jno H	Ans- 18
Richard	Sto-149	Daniel	Rch-194	John	Bur-104
Ruth	Sur-192	David	Sto-149	John	Bur-104
Stephen	War-180	David	Roc- 18	John	Sto-155
Thomas	Sto-100	David	Sto-110	John	Rth-120
William R	War-182	Edmond	Mar- 14	John	Ora-129

Martin,John	Pas-195	Martin,Richard	Rth-118	Mary,Auston	Joh-275	
John	Way-241	Richard	Roc- 24	John	Cha-196	
John	Rch-192	Richard	Cab-139	Maryhue,Mary	Jon-301	
John	Lnc-359	Richd	Cas- 62	Masey,Martin	Bun- 78	
John Majr	Wil-263	Robert	Sur-188	Mash,Derias	Ran-175	
John	Brt- 62	Robert	Cas- 62	Elizebeth	Ans- 19	
John	Sur-168	Robert	Bun- 88	Jno	Ans- 13	
John	Sur-184	Robert	Lnc-336	Simeon	Ans- 15	
John	Sur-195	Robert Esqr	Wil-268	Thos	Ans- 15	
John	Bla- 7	Robert Jun	Roc- 5	Mashal,John	Cha-212	
John	Cas- 61	Robert Sen	Roc- 5	Mashborn,David	Bur-117	
John	Ire-267	Rothean	Hyd-234	David	Bur-118	
John	Hal-113	Saml	Cha-205	Drury	Bur-117	
John	Roc- 21	Saml	Sto- 94	Edward	Cha-194	
John	Roc- 23	Saml	Bur-140	Elijah	Bur-117	
John	Roc- 27	Samuel	Ran-175	Elisha	Bur-124	
John	Mor- 56	Samuel	Lnc-362	Mary	Bur-124	
John	Sto-126	Samuel	Lnc-367	Matthew	Bur-117	
John	Sto-127	Samuel	Sur-182	Wm	Bur-117	
John	Sto- 97	Samuel	Sto-123	Mashborne,Benj	Ons-104	
John	Sto-114	Sarah	Rth-121	Daniel	Ons-108	
John	Row- 63	Sarah	Bla- 14	Henry	Ons- 99	
John	Row- 65	Sarah	Mar- 6	Polly	Ons-105	
John Jr	Nor- 72	Thomas	Rth-123	Thomas	Ons-102	
John Jr	Wil-261	Thomas	Nor- 72	William Senr	Nor- 72	
John Sr	Sur-192	Thomas	Wil-261	Mashburn,Daniel	Jon-302	
John Senr	Wil-269	Thomas	Roc- 22	James	Mor- 59	
John Senr	Nor- 72	Thomas	Bur-127	James Junr	Jon-302	
Johnson	Joh-274	Thomas	Sto-126	James Senr	Jon-301	
Jopah	Cha-209	Thomas	Sto- 97	John	Mor- 62	
Joseph	Way-243	Tincanin	Bur-107	Samuel	Mor- 61	
Kinchen	Ans- 12	Vallentine	Roc- 29	Thos	Mor- 65	
Leonard	Roc- 13	Walter	Roc- 17	Masin,Na	Ora-157	
Leonard	Roc- 15	William	Sto-128	Masingale,Daniel	Ans- 28	
Lewis	Ran-173	William	Sto-135	Masingill,George	Joh-277	
Lidda	Sur-181	William	Len-315	Henry	Joh-276	
Margart	Rch-197	William	Way-241	Mask,Dudley	Rch-200	
Martin	Rth-119	William	Wil-273	John	Rch-200	
Martin	Rob-234	William	Cas- 62	John	Mon- 31	
Martin	Mor- 63	William	Ire-267	John D	Rch-200	
Martin Jnr	Rob-225	William	Mar- 6	Pleasant	Rch-200	
Mary	Sam-156	William	Roc- 27	Saml	Ans- 22	
Michael Junr	Roc- 29	William	Roc- 29	Silas	Ans- 22	
Michael Senr	Roc- 30	William	Bur-131	Mason,Abner	Nsh- 76	
Milly	Roc- 23	William	Sto- 98	Abraham	Row- 49	
Molly	Roc- 24	William	Sto-102	Affa	Tyr-205	
Moses	Bft- 21	Willm	Bft- 21	Alexr	Ora-170	
Murdoch	Mor- 65	Wm	Cha-212	Anna	Ons-108	
Nancy	Ire-255	Wm	Grn-140	Benj	Hyd-231	
Nancy	Roc- 27	Wm	Rob-225	Benja	Nsh- 75	
Neill	Rch-192	Wm	Mor- 54	Benjamin	Cum-256	
R	Bru-228	Wm	Lnc-341	Benjn	Hal-112	
Obediah	Sur-176	Wm Jr	Bft- 21	Daniel	Hal-112	
P	Cum-238	Willis	Way-247	David	Car-175	
Peter	Edg- 47	Zacheus	Nor- 72	David	Cas- 61	
Philip	Bur-105	Zadock	Wil-279	Edward	Hyd-232	
Polly	Rth-120	Martindale,Saml	Mor- 56	Foster	Nsh- 75	
Rebecka	Cha-207	Stephen	Dup- 29	Foster	Cum-245	
Rebekah	Roc- 18	Marting,Marey	Cur- 92	Fred	Hyd-232	

Mason,H	Ora-148	Massengale,Walker	Nsh- 73	Masters,Nicholas	Sur-183	
Henry	Cha-204	Worren	Nsh- 73	Thomas	Bun- 97	
Henry	Hal-113	Massengel,M	Ash- 14	William	Sur-167	
James	Grn-131	Massengell,D	Ash- 13	Mastin,John	Sto-135	
James	Hyd-229	J	Ash- 14	John	Sto-103	
James	Ire-262	Masser,John	Joh-275	Mathias	Sto-102	
James	Cur- 80	Surget	Lnc-374	Matthias	Sto-134	
James	Bft- 33	Massey,Ab	Ora-157	Mataw,John R	Row- 54	
James J	Hal-112	Abel	Fra- 82	Matchet,Will	Dup- 18	
Jas	Ora-134	Aben	Ire-245	Matherly,Joseph	Wil-281	
Jas	Hyd-231	Adkins	Tyr-211	Matheson,Malcolm	Mor- 64	
Jno	Per-131	Asa	Fra- 82	Norman	Mor- 64	
John	Car-174	Avery	Bun- 80	Neill	Mor- 64	
John	Hyd-225	Benjamin	Lnc-354	Mathew,Danl	Rob-227	
John	Hyd-231	Berekias	Fra- 81	Isham	Rob-240	
John	Ons-108	Drury	Lnc-334	Mathews,Anabella	Rob-224	
John	Cum-246	Drury	Lnc-340	Anderson	Gat-114	
Joshua	Car-174	Henry	Mec- 32	Andrew	Bun- 83	
K	Cam-161	Hezekiah	Lnc-331	Aron	Mec- 34	
K	Cam-161	Lowell	Cas- 62	Christian	Mor- 66	
Little Berry	Roc- 12	Isaac	Glf-158	Clement W	Gat-115	
Littleberry	Nor- 72	Isham	Fra- 82	Cornelius moved	Grn-123	
Lydia	Hal-113	James	Cha-198	Edward	Cha-197	
Mark	Rch-200	Joab	Bun- 80	Hugh	Rob-227	
Marmiduke	Nsh- 77	John	Hay-197	Isaac	Sam-158	
Martha	Hal-113	John	Cas- 62	James	Sam-158	
Michael	Bur-124	John	Joh-280	James	Mor- 66	
Miles	Brt- 43	John	Lnc-331	Jeremiah	Edg- 69	
Nancy	Ora-151	John	Row- 57	Jno Junr	Rob-224	
Nancy	Bft- 33	Jordan	Cas- 62	Jno Senr	Rob-224	
Patrick	Per-131	Mark	Lnc-340	John	Gat-114	
Peter	Bun- 88	Nathan	Roc- 17	John	Cum-241	
Philip	Ora-118	Ralf	Joh-281	John	Bun- 94	
R	Ora-133	Richard	Fra- 81	John	Row- 72	
Reuben	Row- 50	Russell	Cha-210	Joseph	Mon- 40	
Robert	Ora-172	Sampson	Fra- 81	Lodowick	Gat-114	
Robert	Ire-261	Simeon	Fra- 82	Malcolm	Rob-227	
Salley	Nsh- 76	Thomas	Roc- 18	Matt	Gat-114	
Sarah	Hyd-229	William	Nor- 73	Neill	Rob-223	
Sarah	Bur-128	Willm	Fra- 95	Tandy	Sto- 96	
Thomas	Cha-194	Massick,Randsome	Rth-117	Thomas	Row- 72	
Thomas	Per-131	Massiner,Ben	Bft- 39	Thomas	Edg- 65	
Thomas	Per-141	Massingal,Joseph	Hal-112	Thos	Sam-159	
Thomas	Hyd-227	Massy,Azol	Ons- 97	William	Gat-115	
Thomas	Hyd-232	Drury	Cum-262	William	Sto-145	
Thomas	Lnc-357	Edward	Ons-100	Willy	Cha-197	
Thomas	Cum-246	Gui	Ire-268	Mathewes,Ezekiel	Cas- 61	
Thos	Hyd-231	John	Ire-253	Mathewis,Charles	Cas- 62	
Uriah	Car-174	Rebecca	Ons-105	Patsey	Cas- 61	
Wiley	Cas- 61	Stephen	Cum-265	Mathewson,Alexr	Rob-226	
William	Wsh-220	William	Cas- 62	Daniel	Bun- 93	
Wm	Nsh- 75	Master,John	Lnc-365	Mathias,John	Gat-110	
Mass,James	Way-248	Michael	Lnc-365	Thos	Cho-226	
Massee,Abner	Ora-150	Masters,Aron	Bur-114	William	Gat-108	
Massenburg,Nancy	Fra- 96	Geo	Cab-139	Mathis,John	Roc- 29	
Massengale,Henry	Nor- 72	Henry	Bur-114	Lazarus	Joh-274	
Heza	Nsh- 72	John	Bun- 97	Solomon	Roc- 17	
James	Nsh- 73	John	Cab-147	Thomas	Roc- 17	
Reddick	Nsh- 73	Joseph	Hyd-229	Thomas Senr	Roc- 18	

Name	Ref	Name	Ref	Name	Ref	Name	Ref
Mathis,William	Roc- 17	Matthews,Saml	Mec- 34	Maxfield,James	Ora-117		
Mathison,Thomas	Bur-129	Saml	Lnc-335	Maxley,Nathaniel	Roc- 33		
Matier,James	Roc- 29	Samuel	Lnc-342	Samuel	Roc- 33		
Matin,William	Glf-152	Silas	Pit-245	Maxwel,Daniel	Cum-268		
Matiseck,Thompson	Cas- 62	Simon	Cum-262	David	Row- 64		
Matlock,John	Roc- 26	Stephen Esq	Wil-267	Maxwell,Andrew	Bun- 72		
Sarah	Cha-211	Tandy	Sto-125	Ben	Mec- 53		
Wm	Cha-211	Thomas	Ran-174	C	Ash- 12		
Mattcaw,Andrew	Sur-183	Wiley	Ran-175	George	Mec- 22		
Matthews,Aaron	Sur-188	William	Rch-196	Hugh	Dup- 9		
Amos	Cum-262	William	Wil-268	James	Fra- 77		
Ansel	Wil-271	William	Hal-112	James	Roc- 20		
Benjn	Fra- 96	William	Pit-233	James	Dup- 7		
Berry	Sur-189	Wm	Glf-154	Jas	Mec- 22		
D	Glf-155	Wm	Mec- 25	John	Dup- 30		
David	Rth-121	Wm	Ran-174	John	Cum-268		
David	Cum-257	Matthewson,Alex	Ire-247	John	Dup- 21		
Etheldred	Gat-112	Charles	Ire-262	Joseph	Mec- 51		
Ford	Rch-196	Donnald	Ire-264	Robt	Mec- 41		
Gideon	Hal-112	Francis	Ire-264	Samuel	Roc- 17		
Guilford	Hal-112	Gillum	Ire-254	T	Ash- 6		
Hardy	Cum-258	John	Ire-264	Thomas	Row- 64		
Henry	Rch-196	Nathan	Edg- 40	Thos	Sam-162		
Henry	Pit-245	Matthias,Elisha	Gat-107	W	Ash- 14		
Hezekiah	Sur-176	Matthis,Arthur	Dup- 17	Wm	Mec- 41		
Hopkins	War-172	Enouch	Mar- 13	Wm	Mec- 41		
Isham	Hal-112	Ezekiel	Dup- 17	May,Benjamin	Pit-259		
Jacob	Cum-263	Herring	Dup- 28	Benjamin	Pit-244		
Jacob	Cum-263	Jacob	Dup- 17	Benjn	Fra-100		
James	Dup- 28	Jacob	Dup- 18	Benjn	Ans- 9		
James	Sur-176	John	Dup- 16	D Senior	Ora-132		
James	Sur-167	John	Dup- 21	Daniel	Ans- 30		
James	Lnc-335	John	Lnc-350	Danl	Ora-120		
Jas	Mec- 49	Luke	Mar- 15	Enoch	War-171		
Jason	Hal-112	Sarah	Dup- 12	Frederick	Sur-196		
Jno	Mec- 43	William	Mar- 15	Fredrick	Pit-246		
Joel	Bur-117	Mattock,Benj	Cas- 62	Frederick	Pit-246		
John	Rth-122	Nicholas	Cas- 62	Gardner	Pit-238		
John	Rch-196	Mattocks,Edward	Rth-118	H	Glf-178		
John	Nsh-644	John	Ons-103	J	Ash- 5		
Jordon	Rch-196	Talton	Cha-191	J	Glf-178		
Joseph	Pit-253	Mattucks,George	Wil-259	Jacob	Pit-246		
Joseph	Mec- 34	Maudlin,Benj	Per-221	James	Pit-246		
Kesiah	Ora-163	George	Wil-266	James	Pit-259		
Mary	Nsh- 80	Jesse	Wil-269	James	Bun- 88		
Mary	Hal-114	John	Per-221	Jeptha	Pit-246		
Moses	Hal-113	John	Wil-269	Jeremiah	Pit-246		
Mussenane	Ire-259	Joseph	Per-221	Jno	Ans- 4		
Needham	Cum-252	Mark	Ran-187	Jno	Ans- 12		
Neily	Fra-100	Sarah	Way-252	Jno	Ans- 25		
Olive	Rch-196	Mauk,Henry	Sur-189	John	Pit-249		
Reuben	Sur-182	Peter	Sur-184	John	Roc- 7		
Richard	Hal-112	Maulbay,Peter	Wil-274	John	Cha-198		
Richison	Rch-196	Maulby,William	Wil-284	John	Row- 86		
Riddick	Gat-112	Maulpus,H	Bru-230	Joseph	Cha-205		
Robert	Ire-241	Maumore,Mary	Sur-197	Nathan	Pit-256		
Robt	Mec- 47	Mauney,Jacob Sen	Lnc-332	Pleasant	Ans- 10		
Robt	Mec- 54	Michl	Lnc-328	Reuben	Mon- 25		
Saml	Pas-196	Peter	Lnc-328	S	Ora-139		

-201-

Name	Ref	Name	Ref	Name	Ref
May,Shade	Pit-246	Mayoes,Edward	Way-244	McAnnally,Charles	Sto-151
Southerland	Ora-167	Mays,James	Bft- 33	Elizabeth	Sto-142
Sterling	Pit-244	Jesse	Sur-163	Elizabeth	Sto-107
Thomas	Fra- 99	Jona	Bft- 30	McAns,Hezekiah	Roc- 25
Tobias	Ora-120	Leml	Cur- 84	McAnulty,Joseph	Cab-148
Vinson	Cha-198	Roland	Bft- 33	McArthur,Mrs.	Cum-239
W	Ash- 8	William	Rch-191	Alexr	Cum-266
Willie	Fra- 98	Mayson,William	Ire-243	Alexr	Rob-228
Woodson	Row- 39	Maze,David	Wil-271	Catharine	Rob-231
Mayberry,Abel	Wil-266	Levy	Row- 76	Colen	Rch-213
Frederic	Wil-261	Mazer,Henry	Sto-144	Daniel	Cum-254
James	Wil-270	Mazingo,Edwd	Len-313	Daniel M	Cum-269
Thomas	Lnc-376	Pearce	Len-313	James	Mor- 59
William	Bun- 82	Wm	Len-313	John	Cum-245
Maye,Joseph	Pit-256	Mazy,Stephen	Cha-201	Marthew	Mon- 21
Susannah	Pit-260	Mc---ten,Thomas	Bur-124	Mary	Rch-206
Mayer,Widow	Cab-140	McAdam,Hugh	Ora-114	Mary	Rob-229
Mayes,Aaron	Cha-204	James	Pas-195	Neill	Rob-231
Benjamin	Ire-242	James	Ora-115	Peter	Rob-230
Elijah	Mec- 30	McAdams,George	Ons- 98	Peter	Rob-229
Harman	Mon- 48	John	Bur-131	Peter Junr	Cum-250
James	Ire-242	Tinnen	Ora-123	Peter Senr	Cum-250
John B	Ire-242	McAden,James	Cas- 61	McArty,Alexr	Bla- 4
Robert	Ire-242	Jinnett	Cas- 62	Neill	Bla- 5
William	Lnc-357	John	Cas- 62	McAtte,Zacaria	Row- 51
Mayfield,Benjn	Fra- 82	McAdow,D	Glf-173	McAuley,Dan	Mon- 31
Edmund	War-171	Margarett	Glf-155	Jno	Mon- 31
Jacob	Wil-278	Wm	Glf-156	Malcom	Rch-213
John	War-175	McAfee,John	Bur-119	Murdock	Mor- 59
John	Grn-131	Robert	Rth-119	Murdock	Mor- 59
John	Grn-131	Samuel	Rth-122	Murdock	Mor- 55
Mary	War-178	McAffee,Jas	Lnc-327	McAusland,Mrs.	Cum-239
Nathaniel	Rth-121	McAhay,James	Roc- 18	McAuslin,John	Ran-175
Samuel	Rth-121	McAlester,Daniel	Rch-210	Wm	Ran-175
Stephen	Bur-107	McAlister,Alexr	Cum-260	McBain,Wm	Per-131
Stephen	Rth-122	Alexr	Cum-263	McBane,Catharine	Ora-163
Thomas	War-181	Alexr Senr	Cum-267	Wm	Cah-198
Voluntine	Grn-131	Archibald	Rch-203	Wm B	Ora-115
William	Rth-122	Charles	Cum-265	McBaritt,Joseph	Mec- 22
Mayhew,Aaron	Lnc-357	John	Rch-191	McBee,Vardy	Lnc-344
Maynard,Sally	Wil-271	Neill	Cum-260	McBeth,Walter	Mor- 54
Maynas,Jno	Ans- 10	McAllister,Bk	Bru-228	McBrayer,David	Rth-117
Peter	Ans- 9	H	Bru-228	William	Rth-117
Richard	Ans- 20	Isabella	Cum-267	McBrian,Isaiah	Glf-180
Richd	Ans- 9	Leven	Roc- 26	McBrid,J	Ash- 14
Mayne,Charles	Wil-285	Malcom	Dup- 19	McBride,Alexr	Rob-232
Henry	Wil-285	McAlpan,Angus	Cum-265	Andrew	Mec- 28
Mayo,David	Edg- 72	Daniel	Cum-251	Angus	Rob-225
Drury	Edg- 71	Malcom	Cum-265	Daniel	Sur-167
Henry	War-172	McAlpen,Danl	Rob-228	Duncna	Rob-225
John W	Edg- 54	Mal	Rob-225	J	Glf-161
John	Car-172	Neill	Rob-243	J	Cam-162
Jolly	Pit-262	Neill	Rob-226	J	Cam-162
Joseph	Edg- 40	Robert	Rob-243	James	Glf-153
Levi	Edg- 52	McAlroy,James	Roc- 7	James	Wil-265
Micajah	Edg- 53	William	Roc- 20	Jno	Rob-231
Nathan Jr	Edg- 54	McAnes,James	Roc- 25	John	Sur-191
Nathan Sen	Edg- 54	William	Roc- 25	John	Rob-225
Peter	Pit-261	McAnnally,Charles	Sto-109	Melcom	Cab-143

-202-

Name	Ref	Name	Ref	Name	Ref
McBride,Niell	Ans- 27	McCallister,Jas	Lnc-327	McCarver,David	Lnc-372
Peter	Bla- 8	McCallum,Angus	Rob-229	David	Lnc-372
Robt	Mec- 29	Angus	Rob-229	James	Lnc-33
Samuel	Sur-107	Angus	Rob-232	John	Lnc-327
Sarah	Wil-265	Archd	Rob-221	McCashill,Alexr	Mor- 69
Wakeman	Sur-183	Barnabas	Ran-173	McCaskell,Alex	Mon- 28
William	Ire-256	Danl	Rob-222	Dan	Mon- 28
William	Sur-194	Duncan	Mor- 61	Finly	Mon- 28
William	Wil-265	G	Mon- 34	John	Mon- 28
McBroom,Andrew	Ora-127	J	Mon- 34	John	Mon- 28
Jane	Row- 73	James	Ran-173	McCaskey,Edward	Mar- 12
John	Row- 73	Jno	Rob-232	Eli	Mar-446
McBryde,Archd	Mor- 54	John	Ran-173	McCaskill,Angus	Rch-198
Archibald	Rch-197	Jonathan	Ran-173	Jno	Mor- 62
Duncan	Rch-203	McCally,Roderick	Mec- 40	John	Mon- 30
Henry	Mor- 62	McCalop,Daniel	Sam-163	Keneth	Mor- 64
James	Mor- 62	McCalvie,Wm	Mec- 35	Kenneth	Rch-198
McCabb,Jas	Cab-138	McCaly,James	Row- 73	McCaskle,Daniel	Ire-244
John	Cab-138	McCamie,Jas	Ora-119	McCaugnahay,James	Row- 72
McCabe,Amos	Hay-197	McCamish,John	Hay-198	McCaul,Alexander	Lnc-359
Grace	Bft- 31	McCan,James	Bur-129	Archd	Lnc-372
John	Bft- 19	James	Glf-156	James	Lnc-372
Samuel	Hay-198	McCanamon,Richard	Bur-121	John	Lnc-372
Zachariah	Hay-197	Young	Bur-121	Robert	Lnc-372
McCadams,Isaac	Ora-121	McCanly,DAvid	Ire-252	McCauley,A	Ora-154
McCaddams,C	Ora-160	McCann,Hugh	Dup- 22	Adw	Ora-170
Hugh	Ora-163	John	Wil-259	Andw	Ora-143
Wm	Ora-160	John	Dup- 22	Bill	Ora-170
McCagg,J	Glf-176	Nathl	Dup- 22	Jas	Ora-115
McCahran,Hacter	Cab-143	Polly	Bun- 85	Jno Jr	Ora-143
McCain,Alexr	Cas- 62	William	Dup- 20	Jno	Ora-122
Andrew	Mec- 33	McCardey,John	Cab-148	Jno Jr	Ora-142
Andrew	Mec- 33	McCarkle,Thos	Mec- 53	Math Jr	Ora-151
H	Glf-182	McCarmage,Duncan	Rob-221	Mathew	Ora-142
Hugh	Mec- 33	Gilbert	Rob-221	Robt	Ora-122
Hugh Jnr	Mec- 33	Jno Jnr	Rob-221	Tho	Ora-115
Hugh Snr	Mec- 33	Jno Snr	Rob-221	Wm	Ora-117
Jno	Mec- 33	John	Rob-221	McCaulley,A	Mon- 35
John	Cas- 62	McCarn,Archibald	Rch-202	D	Mon- 35
Joseph	Mec- 33	Hugh	Rch-191	F	Mon- 36
Joseph	Roc- 31	John	Rch-191	McCauly,Chty	Ora-156
Michael	Ora-151	Neill	Rch-191	Daniel	Mec- 52
Wm	Mec- 33	McCarquedale,Danl	Sam-155	McCausley,Mathew	Ora-131
McCaless,J	Ora-169	McCarrol,George	Roc- 21	McCawley,Jas	Glf-183
McCall,D	Cum-238	McCarron,James	Cab-148	McCay,Anglis	Row- 74
Dugald	Cum-255	Robert	Cab-148	Jas	Mec- 25
Hugh	Ire-256	Thomas	Cab-149	John	Mec- 31
Hugh	Mec- 40	McCarson,David	Bun- 95	John	Row- 72
James	Bun- 97	David Senr	Bun- 95	Thos	Mec- 54
Jas	Mec- 41	James	Bun- 72	Wm	Mec- 30
John	Bur-126	McCarter,Aaron	Sto-154	McCharty,Jno	Mec- 23
Matthew	Mec- 40	Aaron	Sto-113	McCindley,John	Cab-144
Robert	Bun- 98	E	Cam-154	McClain,Allen	Mec- 49
Rote	Bur-129	McCarty,Cornelius	Lnc-338	Charles	Rth-121
Samuel	Bur-111	Jacob	Lnc-331	Ephraim	Bun- 88
Samuel	Bun- 85	Jacob	Lnc-338	George	Roc- 30
Wm	Mec- 40	James	Bun- 93	George	Mec- 48
McCallam,James	Roc- 7	John	Bun- 96	James	Glf-155
McCalliam,Jno	Rob-229	McCarver,Alex	Lnc-333	John	Ire-251

Name	Ref	Name	Ref	Name	Ref
McClain,John	Pas-197	McClintock,J	Glf-161	McColl,Dugald	Cum-269
Jos	Glf-171	John	Glf-177	Dugald P C	Cum-244
Joseph	Roc- 30	Robt	Glf-158	Duncan	Rch-203
Joseph	Ire-250	Saml	Glf-180	Duncan	Rch-203
Michael	Glf-155	Wm	Glf-174	Duncan	Bla- 12
Moses	Glf-156	McCliston,Jane	Rth-121	Duncan	Rch-198
Nancy	Roc- 30	McCloed,John	Sam-155	Duncan	Rch-212
R	Glf-153	Neil	Sam-155	Duncan	Rch-192
T	Glf-173	McClore,Richard	Rth-120	Duncan Esq	Rch-198
William	Glf-154	McClose,Arthur	Rth-118	Gilbert	Cum-267
McClalen,Isaac	Cab-143	John	Rth-118	Hugh	Rch-198
McClam,B	Col- 19	McCloskey,Hugh	Cab-139	Hugh	Rch-198
McClamarach,Geo	Row- 64	McCloud,Daniel	Mec- 41	Hugh	Rch-197
McClane,Daniel	Row- 71	Hector	Ire-270	John	Rch-192
John	Row- 71	John	Ire-260	John	Rch-193
John	Rth-123	John	Wil-279	John	Cum-268
McClarney,Henry	Cas- 61	Reubin	Hyd-230	Nellie	Rch-199
McClarty,Barbara	Mec- 45	McClowrath,Robert	Bur-125	Sol	Rob-219
McClatchy,Hambelton	Ire-249	McCluneth,Jacob	Bur-131	McCollar,Duncan	Bla- 9
McClatthey,John	Bun- 93	McClure,Alexander	Hay-197	McCollins,Caud	Rth-120
McClay,Henry	Lnc-374	Alexr	Mec- 35	McCollister,Ezekl	Roc- 21
McClean,Daniel	Ire-244	Andrew	Hay-198	McCollum,Alex	Bla- 13
John	Ire-245	Andrew Jnr	Hay-198	Caty	Sur-191
McCleary,Andrew	Mec- 25	David	Mec- 35	Daniel	Mec- 41
Ann	Mec- 28	David	Grn-147	Duncan	Cum-244
Jas	Mec- 27	James	Ora-125	Duncan	Rch-193
Robt	Wsh-217	Jas	Mec- 28	Duncan	Cha-205
Wm Charlotte	Mec- 25	Jas	Mec- 35	Edwd	Mon- 27
McCleay,Micheal	Mec- 55	Jas	Lnc-336	James	Ire-249
McClees,John	Tyr-203	Jno	Mec- 54	Henry	Ora-111
Jos	Tyr-203	Jno	Mec- 35	Macom	Mon- 27
McClehatton,Polly	Glf-174	John	Hay-197	Macom Jr	Mon- 27
McClelan,Charles	Cab-139	John	Lnc-333	Malcom	Mec- 30
John	Cab-144	John	Mec- 35	Matthew	Mec- 40
Joseph	Cab-149	Mary	Ora-125	Matthew	Mec- 40
Wm	Cab-144	Matthew	Mec- 47	Neill	Bla- 13
McCleland,M	Mon- 35	Thomas	Hay-198	P	Bla- 8
McClellan,George	Brt- 49	Thos	Mec- 47	McColman,Malcom	Cum-268
McClelland,John	Ire-265	William	Hay-198	McColough,Hugh	Bft- 37
McClelland,John	Ire-265	William	Lnc-333	McComb,Jas	Mec- 46
John	Ire-259	Wm	Grn-135	John	Lnc-365
John	Ire-264	McClurg,John	Hay-197	McCombs,Major	Rth-117
John	Ire-266	McCluskey,Edwd	Ora-147	Martin	Rth-119
John	Ire-248	Wm	Ora-152	Robt	Mec- 40
Joseph	Ire-264	Ed	Ora-132	Capt Saml	Mec- 36
William	Ire-259	Ed	Ora-155	Wm	Mec- 38
Wm Ross	Ire-248	McCoalsky,A	Col- 20	McCommon,Joseph	Mec- 31
Margaret	Mec- 50	McCobins,Nancy	Cas- 61	Wm	Mec- 32
McClendon,Alex	Mon- 30	McCochren,Ard	Bla- 7	McCone,Mary	Pit-240
Dan	Mon- 30	McCockburn,John	Cum-241	McConn,Keziah	Car-171
Keneth	Mon- 30	McCoclin,David	Pas-195	McConnel,Alexr	Ire-262
McClennahan,Ruben	Ire-255	McColin,David	Pas-184	James	Ire-268
McClennehan,Alexr	Ire-238	McColl,Alexander	Rch-198	John	Ire-266
McClenney,Polley	Bft- 39	Angus	Cum-250	John	Ire-262
McClennon,Mary	Prq-221	Ard	Bla- 12	Walter	Ire-166
McCleod,Daniel	Ire-244	Daniel	Rch-212	William	Ire-266
Robert	Ire-244	Daniel	Cum-264	William	Hay-198
William	Ire-245	Daniel	Rch-203	William	Ire-265
McCleoud,J	Mon- 34	Dolly	Rch-212	McConnell,Benjamin	Ire-258

-204-

Name	Location	Name	Location	Name	Location
McConnell,Jane	Ire-256	McCrackan,Robert	Ran-175	McCreary,Joseph	Bur-111
Thomas	Ire-256	Sam	Ora-170	McCree,Thomas	Row- 71
McCoquedale,Hugh	Sam-155	Sam	Ora-121	McCremmon,Daniel	Mor- 65
McCord,Widow	Mec- 54	Saml	Bur-108	Malcolm	Mor- 54
Hannah	Mec- 54	Thos	Ora-121	Norman	Mor- 54
Jno	Mec- 54	McCrackin,Ab	Ora-165	McCrery,David	Ire-257
Capt John	Wil-257	Ab	Ora-124	James	Ire-266
Susan	Ora-169	Alex	Ora-161	Moses	Hay-198
Thos	Mec- 31	George	Hay-197	Samuel	Ire-258
William	Cas- 62	Jane	Glf-189	McCrimmin,Angus	Cum-244
Wm	Mec- 55	Joe	Ora-161	Daniel	Cum-251
McCorkadal,Daniel	Cum-266	John	Hay-197	John	Cum-243
McCorkle,Alexander	Lnc-357	Joseph	Hay-198	Roderick	Cum-244
Alexdr	Row- 72	Quilla	Hay-198	McCroky,Hugh	Mec- 32
Elizabeth	Lnc-357	Robt	Ora-161	McCrory,David	Ora-122
James	Ire-266	Step	Ora-161	Hugh	Mec- 25
Jas	Mec- 24	Tho	Ora-118	Hugh	Mec- 33
Jas	Mec- 31	McCraney,Danl	Rob-243	J Senr	Ora-160
Jas	Lnc-333	Mal	Rob-228	John	Ora-116
Jno	Mec- 31	McCranie,Archd	Cum-263	Wm	Mec- 33
Joal	Mec- 53	Hugh	Cum-254	McCrossky,Francis	Mec- 25
Joel	Row- 72	John	Cum-242	McCrray,Jno	Row- 40
Matthew	Lnc-357	John	Cum-269	Wm	Row- 40
Matthew	Mec- 31	Murdoch	Cum-263	Wilson	Row- 40
McCormac,Daniel	Rth-118	Murdoch	Cum-253	McCrum,Mrs Rachel	Mec- 25
John	Cum-246	Murdoch	Cum-242	McCrummon,Roderick	Rch-213
McCormack,Jas	Mec- 32	Neill	Cum-242	McCuag,Alexr	Cum-269
Wm	Mec- 35	Neill	Cum-252	McCubbin,Sophia	Roc- 13
McCormaig,Angus	Rch-194	McCrarey,Malcom	Bun- 77	William	Roc- 13
Daniel	Rch-212	McCrary,Boyd	Bun- 79	McCuiston,Eliz	Glf-181
Duncan	Rch-192	Elijah	Bun- 79	Robt	Glf-181
John	Rch-192	Hugh	Bun- 99	Thos	Glf-181
McCorman,Robert	Lnc-342	Hugh	Row- 40	Wlater	Glf-158
McCoy,James	Ire-250	Joel	Bun- 79	McCulleans,Brain	Cum-265
Joseph	Prq-215	John	Ora-151	McCullen,Asher	Way-250
Joshua	Prq-215	Margaret	Bun- 91	Benjn	Sam-156
Maben	Prq-221	Roderick	Rob-223	John	Sam-156
Rachel	Len-314	Tho	Bur-130	John Junr	Sam-156
Samuel	Ire-251	William	Bun- 99	McCuller,R	Ora-153
Thomas	Row- 89	McCraven,Duncan	Ire-266	Z	Ora-154
Willis	Prq-221	McCraw,Benjamin	Sur-163	McCullers,John	Joh-275
Wm	Brt- 67	Byard	Rth-117	McCulley,Robt	Ora-121
McCoye,A	Cam-164	Francis	Sur-179	McCulloch,Andrew	Ora-163
F	Cam-154	George	Sur-161	Andw	Ora-117
F	Cam-165	Jacob	Sur-161	Benjn	Hal-113
J	Cam-158	James	Sur-160	Charles	Row- 85
J	Cam-165	Samuel	Sur-160	Elijah	Mec- 34
M	Cam-158	Samuel	Rth-117	George	Row- 86
R	Cam-165	William	Sur-161	Isaac	Mec- 49
S	Cam-164	McCray,James	Ora-163	James	Ora-175
T	Cam-161	Jas	Ora-121	James	Row- 82
W	Cam-164	John	Tyr-210	Jas	Mec- 50
W	Cam-165	Sarah	Ora-163	Jno	Mec- 49
W	Cam-162	McCrayer,Andrew	Bun- 95	Jno	Mec- 31
Z	Cam-155	David	Bun- 82	John	Ire-240
McCracin,Margret	Cas- 62	James	Bun- 88	Robert	Lnc-331
McCrackan,Elizth	Mec- 54	John	Bun- 88	Samuel	Row- 82
James	Row- 76	Samuel	Bun- 80	Thos	Glf-157
John	Bur-108	Samuel Snr	Bun- 88	Wm	Ora-173

McCullock,George	Ora-165	McDaniel,John	Ran-174	McDonald,Archd	Cum--50
John	Ora-165	John	Ran-173	Archd	Rob-219
Jos Jr	Ora-165	John Junr	Jon-301	Ard	Bla- 4
Jos Sr	Ora-165	Jonathan	Mop- 45	Cathrine	Mor- 66
Robt	Ora-137	Malcom	Bla- 4	Caty	Mor- 69
McCulloh,James	Lnc-331	Mary	Ons-107	Daniel	Cum-265
John	Ire-248	Matthias	Roc- 11	Daniel	Cum-269
Linzey	Lnc-354	Miles	Ran-173	Daniel	Rch-208
Margaret	Ire-249	Milly	Sur-181	Daniel	Cum-254
McCulpan,Duncan	Ire-245	Nace	Row- 66	Daniel	Cum-257
McCulpen,Michael	Ire-244	Neill	Cum-266	Daniel	Cum-250
McCunn,Daniel	Cum-245	Patrick	Hal-102	Daniel	Cha-213
McCurday,Alexander	Ire-250	Pattson	Bft- 37	Daniel	Rch-198
James	Ire-252	Peter	Nor- 72	Daniel	Rch-200
Samuel	Cab-147	Reuben	Sur-169	Daniel	Rch-192
McCurdey,Archibald	Cab-144	Risden Senr	Jon-301	Daniel	Mor- 60
McCurdy,Archabald	Cab-148	Risden	Jon-301	Daniel	Mor- 64
William	Ire-254	Risden Junr	Jon-301	Daniel	Mor- 55
Will	Dup- 5	Theoderick	Roc- 23	Daniel	Mor- 56
McCurry,Jacob	Rth-121	William	Jon-301	Danl	Mor- 60
John	Rth-122	William	Bur-111	Danl	Mor- 60
Micajah	Rth-121	William	Cas- 62	Danl	Mor- 61
T	Glf-178	McDannal,David	Mec- 36	Danl	Mor- 65
Wm	Ran-173	McDannald,William	Wil-273	Danl	Rob-227
McDade,Benjamin	Ran-175	McDannel,Eli	Ora-119	Danl	Rob-228
E	Ora-144	Eli Jun	Ora-120	Danl	Mor- 55
James	Ran-174	Eliz	Ora-129	Donald	Bla- 5
James	Ran-175	Jas	Ora-119	Donald	Mor- 64
Jno	Ora-126	Jno	Ora-114	Duncan	Cho-221
Plie	Row- 71	Melch	Ora-113	Eli	Rch-200
Willis	Edg- 60	Wm	Ora-114	Flora	Bla- 5
McDaniel,Abraham	Ran-175	McDannold,Wm Jr	Wil-261	Hugh	Cum-269
Allen	Row- 66	McDanold,Benjn	Cha-203	Hugh	Rch-212
Amos	Ran-174	Reubin	Rth-119	Hugh	Cum-242
Amos	Ran-174	T	Mon- 35	Hugh	Rch-194
Angus	Cum-242	McDaris,Mary	Glf-186	Hugh	Mor- 60
Ard Junr	Bla- 4	McDavy,Andrew	Bur-109	Hugh	Mor- 63
Bartley	Nor- 72	McDearmid,Angus	Cum-256	J	Cam-164
Charles	Hal-114	McDermad,Jno	Rob-228	Jacob	Cha-192
Chs	Row- 57	McDermid,Angus	Rob-231	James	Rch-193
Daniel	Ons- 98	Farquha	Rob-222	James	Rch-200
Daniel	Way-250	Mary	Rch-191	James	Cha-197
Daniel	Wil-271	McDermor,Seth	Glf-163	James	Cha-205
David	Bur-110	McDill,Samuel	Glf-157	James	Mor- 65
Durenza	Roc- 12	Mcdivit,Mary	Ire-241	James	Wsh-221
Elisha	Nor- 72	McDonald,Mrs.	Cum-240	Jno	Cha-213
Frederick	Nor- 72	Alexander	Rch-206	Jno	Rob-224
Geo	Tyr-207	Alexr	Cum-238	Jno	Mor- 64
Henry	Sur-196	Alexr	Cum-241	Jno	Rob-229
Ira	Ran-174	Alexr	Mor- 60	John	Cum-246
Isaac	Ran-174	Alexr	Mor- 63	John	Cum-265
J	Bru-236	Alline	Mon- 30	John	Pas-195
James	Sur-187	Angus	Cum-269	John	Cum-269
James	Row- 84	Angus	Cum-254	John	Cum-252
James Junr	Jon-302	Angus	Rch-192	John	Rch-195
James Senr	Jon-301	Angus	Mor- 61	John	Rch-197
John	Ire-263	Angus	Mor- 61	John	Mor- 60
John	Sur-170	Angus	Mor- 65	John	Mor- 64
John	Jon-301	Angus	Mor- 64	John	Rob-227

Name	Ref	Name	Ref	Name	Ref
McDonald,John	Mor- 57	McDuffee,Archd	Cum-244	McEachern,Mal	Rob-231
John	Cum-243	Archd	Cum-246	Margaret	Rob-229
John Senr	Cum-244	D	Mon- 27	Neill	Rob-223
John Senr	Cum-252	Dan	Mon- 28	Patrick	Rob-224
M	Cum-238	Dugald	Rch-191	Nancy	Rch-205
Macolm	Sam-155	Elisabeth	Rch-191	McElmerray,Saml	Bun- 88
Malcolm	Mor- 57	George	Cum-269	McElmery,William	Rth-117
Margaret	Rch-197	John	Rch-206	McElroy,Adam	Mor.- 23
Mary	Ire-245	John	Cum-251	Henry	Mon- 23
Mary	Cha-205	John	Rch-193	J	Ash- 9
Mary	Mon- 24	John	Mor- 63	McElvoy,John	Bun- 78
Merthur	Cha-211	Malcom	Cum-269	McElwrath,Christian	Bur-129
Neill	Cum-251	Mary	Cum-246	McEnnsice,William	Rth-122
Neill	Mor- 64	Neil	Mon-27	McEntire,Aaron	Rth-117
Neill	Mor- 61	Neill	Rob-228	Archibald	Rth-117
Peter	Cha-205	McDuffie,Daniel	Mor- 66	Bird	Rth-120
Roderick	Rch-212	Danl	Rob-235	James	Bur-102
Sterling	Rch-199	Duncan	Cum-242	James	Rth-117
McDonel,James	Bun- 83	Duncan	Mor- 68	Jno	Mec- 25
McDonnal,Widow	Mec- 41	Jennet	Rob-228	Jonah	Rth-117
McDonnald,Alexand	Ire-264	John	Mor- 59	William	Rth-117
McDonold,James	Rth-117	Neill	Mor- 68	McEwen,William	Ire-239
John	Rth-123	McDugal,Archd	Mor- 54	McEwin,Daniel Esq	Wil-274
John	Rth-121	McDugald,Alexr	Cum-252	Duncan	Rob-232
Joseph	Rth-119	Alexr	Rob-244	James	Wil-278
Joseph	Rth-118	Allen	Cum-252	John	Bla- 12
McDougal,Thomas	Ire-239	Angus	Cum-253	M Junr	Bla- 12
McDough,Duncan	Rch-191	Ann	Bla- 12	M Senr	Bla- 12
McDowel,Mrs.	Mec- 37	Archd	Rob-226	Saml	Mec- 28
Charles	Bur-103	Archd	Cum-252	Will	Bla- 12
George	Mec- 39	Daniel Tay	Cum-252	McFadian,Archd	Cum-268
Hugh	Mec- 37	Daniel	Mor- 66	McFadrin,Neill	Mor- 66
James	Wsh-223	Daniel M	Cum-253	McFail,A	Cum-240
Jno	Mec- 25	Danl	Mor- 65	Abraham	Sam-155
Michael	Wil-257	David B	Cum-252	Malcom	Cum-253
William	Rch-212	Duncan	Mor- 62	McFall,John	Bur-131
Wm	Bun- 93	Hugh	Cum-253	P	Cum-238
McDowell,Alexr	Bla- 3	Hugh	Bla- 12	McFalls,Delilah	Bur-117
Catharine	Brt- 67	Hugh	Cum-243	Durham	Bur-116
David	Hay-197	Jno	Mor- 65	McFarland,Alexr	Rch-205
Delilah	Nor- 72	John	Cum-245	Archd	Cum-244
Eliager	Hay-197	John	Cum-252	Daniel	Rch-193
Fredrick	Mar- 13	John	Mor- 62	David	Hay-198
John	Hay-198	Malcom	Cum-246	Dugald	Rch-193
John	Bur-104	Mary	Cum-253	Dugald	Rch-198
John	Hay-198	Mary	Rob-244	Dugald	Mor- 55
John	Edg- 58	Mary B	Cum-253	Duncan	Rch-193
Mary	Hay-198	Ranald	Rob-220	Henry	Grn-137
Nancy	Hay=198	Saml	Rob-228	Jacob	Mec- 37
Stephen	Brt- 51	McEachearn,Daniel	Cum-255	Jacob	Hay-197
William	Rth-118	McEachen,Archd	Rob-224	James	Ire-244
William	Hay-198	McEachern,Danl	Rob-238	James	Hay-197
William	Hay-198	Duncan	Rob-229	James	Rch-191
McDuel,Thomas	Pit-240	Flora	Rob-226	James	Grn-137
Thomas	Pit-232	Hector	Rob-223	James	Rth-120
McDuffee,A	Mon- 36	Jno	Rob-230	Jesse	Hay-198
Angus	Cum-244	Jno	Rob-225	John	Ora-166
Angus	Rch-213	Mal	Rob-229	John	Rch-214
Angus	Mon- 27	Mal	Rob-238	John	Rch-205

McFarland,John	Hay-197	McGee,Robt	Sam-151	McGlochon,Elisha	Hrt-215	
John	Rch-193	Tabley	Ora-169	McGloshon,George	Hrt-215	
John	Hay-197	Thomas	Lnc-365	James	Hrt-215	
John	Rth-123	Thomas	Dup- 7	Luke	Hrt-212	
L	Ora-146	Will	Dup- 9	McGlunnegal,James	Ire-268	
Malcolm	Mor- 57	William	Cum-247	McGogan,Archd	Ans- 28	
Parland	Mor- 61	William	Ire-257	McGomery,J	Bru-230	
Patrick	Rth-123	Wm	Ran-173	McGomry,James	Lnc-333	
Reuben	Hay-198	McGeehe,Thomas	Per-131	Joseph	Lnc-330	
Walter	Hrt-211	Wm	Per-131	McGoogan,John	Rch-212	
William	Hay-198	McGehe,John A	Sur-170	McGound,Job	Tyr-207	
William	Rth-119	Joseph	Per-151	McGowan,Robt	Sam-151	
McFarlane,Baker	Hrt-213	McGehee,Banks	Grn-131	McGowdy,James	Glf-181	
McFarlin,Thomas	Cas- 62	Benj	Grn-131	McGowen,Fredk	Bla- 7	
McFarling,Lyria	Glf-187	Cavils	Grn-132	James	Dup- 7	
McFatridge,D	Glf-169	Craford	Grn-131	John	Dup- 9	
Saml	Glf-170	John Esq	Per-141	Mary	Dup- 7	
McFAtter,Archd	Bla- 5	Josiah	Grn-131	William	Dup- 9	
D	Bla- 10	Josiah	Grn-123	McGowns,Jas	Hyd-231	
Daniel	Bla- 5	Lewis	Grn-139	John	Hyd-229	
Stevin	Bla- 12	Mich	Grn-137	Joseph	Hyd-231	
McFerson,Archd	Ans- 28	Nathan	Grn-131	Martha	Hyd-231	
Lewis	Len-314	Shem	Grn-131	Nancy	Pit-234	
Jno	Ans- 7	Thomas	Grn-123	Wm	Hyd-231	
Joseph	Len-314	McGilberry,Daniel	Rch-192	McGrady,Isaiah	Wil-260	
McFurson,William	Sam-163	McGill,Allen	Rch-193	Jacob Esqr	Wil-268	
McGachey,Peter	Rob-223	Angus	Rch-193	McGrauy,Wm	Cab-146	
McGaha,Abbey	Mec- 34	Archd	Rob-231	McGraw,Enoch	Cab-147	
Alexr	Mec- 52	Archibald	Rch-193	James	Cab-146	
McGahan,Alexdr	Row- 74	Dan	Mon- 30	John	Cab-147	
McGahee,J	Ora-154	Daniel	Rch-192	John	Cab-146	
McGahey,Jeremiah	Rth-121	Danl	Rob-225	Nics	Cab-147	
John	Sur-160	Hector	Mon- 30	McGregan,Daniel	Cum-267	
John	Rth-119	John	Cum-260	McGregar,Archd	Cum-255	
John	Rth-119	Neill	Rob-231	McGregor,Anthony	Ans- 27	
Mima	Rth-122	William	Wil-277	Chloe	Hal-112	
Mima	Rth-122	McGimsey,T	Ash- 9	Duncan	Cum-251	
Thomas	Rth-123	McGin,Thos	Mec- 54	McGregory,Jno	Ora-172	
William	Rth-118	McGinis,John	Bur-111	McGrew,John	Bun- 94	
McGallard,John	Bur-129	McGinn,Thos Jno	Mec- 55	William	Bun- 94	
McGans,Jno	Cho-230	McGinness,Jas	Lnc-365	McGrigor,Hector	Mor- 68	
McGeachy,Alexr	Rob-223	McGinnis,Widow	Lnc-338	William	Nor- 73	
McGebony,D	Glf-180	Charles	Cab-143	Wm	Nsh- 75	
McGee,Andrew	Glf-158	Jas Jr	Lnc-365	McGrimes,John	Cab-143	
Archibald	Rch-204	Joseph	Mec- 25	McGrunta,John	Bur-124	
Duncan	Cum-253	Rebecca	Sto-150	McGuffey,Edmond	Bun- 95	
Blueford	Wil-275	Rebecka	Sto-110	McGugan,Archd	Cum-269	
Catharine	Lnc-365	McGinty,Hanah	Mec- 38	Hugh	Rob-223	
David	Wil-275	McGirt,Archd	Rob-230	Jno	Rob-228	
Drury	Sur-174	Jno	Rob-229	Mal	Rob-223	
Harmon	Sto-110	McGislen,Thos Jr	Bur-120	McGuier,Wm	Row- 40	
Harmon	Sto-148	McGlammery,George	Rth-119	McGuire,Alexander	Rth-121	
Hartwell	Sto-149	McGlandin,Martha	Cho-221	Andrew	Ire-242	
James	Wil-273	McGlanhon,Jerry	Brt- 44	David	Row- 65	
John	Ire-265	Wm	Brt- 43	Eliza	Row- 40	
John	Ire-251	McGlasson,John	Bur-119	Geo	Bun- 97	
Micajah	Cha-197	McGlaulin,Samuel	Row- 72	Henry	Row- 40	
Patrick S	Bur-117	McGlemery,Edward	Sur-188	James	Row- 65	
Ralph	Wil-284	John	Sur-189	James G	Ire-242	

Name	Ref	Name	Ref	Name	Ref	Name	Ref
McGuire,John	Sur-170	McIntire,John	Ire-245	McIver,Nancy	Mor- 65
Patrick	Ire-243	John	Cum-240	Sarah	Cha-207
Philip	Cho-231	Mary	Cum-237	McIves,Alexr	Cha-191
Richard	Ire-242	McIntosh,Aleck	Mor- 67	McKalb,Jas	Rob-226
Thomas	Rth-118	Alexr	Cum-251	McKalep,Hugh	Sto-101
McGuirt,Isom	Mec- 45	Alexr	Mor- 64	Hugh	Sto-132
McGullen,Thomas	Jon-302	Alexr	Mor- 63	John	Sto-132
McGumery,J	Glf-172	Alexr	Mor- 66	John	Sto-137
McHairy,James	Glf-165	Angus	Rch-196	McKalip,Elizabeth	Sto-112
McHaley,Wm	Row- 41	August	Ire-245	McKallum,David	Roc- 5
McHan,Matthew	Rth-118	Catharine	Ire-245	McKamons,Isaac	Sur-177
McHargue,Alexander	Ire-262	Daniel	Rch-196	McKaney,James	Sur-186
James	Ire-262	Daniel	Rch-209	James Sr	Sur-185
James	Ire-262	Daniel	Ire-245	Jesse	Sur-177
James	Ire-255	Danl	Mor- 68	McKany,Mattw	Sur-174
John	Ire-252	Duncan	Mor- 62	McKarran,Ard	Bla- 10
McHedie,Ausbun	Mec- 39	John	Ire-245	McKaskell,John	Rch-209
McHenry,Archibald	Hay-198	John	Cum-268	McKaskil,Keneth	Mor- 65
Henry	Row- 74	John	Cha-203	McKaskill,Daniel	Rch-212
Jesse	Mon- 40	John	Mor- 64	John	Rch-192
Mchevin,Jno	Mec- 40	Keneth	Mor- 68	McKaskle,George	Ire-245
Mchinney,Samuel	Bun- 77	Margaret	Ire-245	William	Ire-260
McHoiney,W	Cam-157	Murdoch	Mor- 64	McKay,Adam	Rob-222
McIlwinnen,Fanny	Sam-150	Murdock	Mor- 64	Alexander	Ire-245
McInis,Angus	Rch-205	Neill	Mor- 69	Alexander	Ire-245
Archibald	Rch-202	Peter	Mor- 68	Alexander	Rch-205
Daniel Esq	Rch-196	McIntyre,Andw	Cha-203	Alexr Esq	Cum-246
Duncan	Mor- 57	Archd	Cum-267	Alexr	Rob-222
Finlak	Rch-202	Daniel	Cum-268	Alexr	Rob-226
Hugh	Rch-202	Daniel B	Cum-269	Angus	Ire-270
James	Rch-202	Dugald	Cum-267	Ann	Cum-246
John	Rch-205	Duncan	Cum-269	Archd	Rob-232
John	Rch-209	Duncan	Rch-202	Archibald	Rch-194
John	Rch-207	Elizabeth	Cum-269	Archibald	Rch-193
Murdoch	Rch-205	Hugh	Cum-267	Ard	Bla- 3
Murdock	Rch-198	John	Cum-250	August	Ire-245
Neill	Rch-209	Malcom	Cum-267	D (J F)	Bla- 8
McInish,Miles	Cha-213	Nicholas	Cum-268	Daniel	Ire-245
McInnis,Daniel	Cum-270	McInvail,Turner	Fra- 98	Daniel	Ire-245
Daniel	Cum-244	McIver,Mrs.	Cum-238	Daniel	Rch-206
Duncan	Cum-254	A	Bla- 13	Daniel	Rch-203
Jno	Rob-232	Alexr	Mor- 62	Daniel	Ire-239
Jno	Rob-219	Alexr	Mor- 69	Danl	Bla- 9
John	Cum-256	Angus	Mor- 68	Donold	Ans- 27
Mal	Rob-219	Cathrine	Cha-207	Duncan	Rch-202
Murdock	Rob-219	Cathrine	Mor- 65	Duncan	Rch-194
Roderick	Rch-196	Daniel	Mor- 66	Duncan	Ans- 27
McInnish,Donald	Cum-238	Danl	Mor- 57	Edward	Cum-254
McInnon,Jno	Rob-222	Danl	Mor- 68	Elizabeth	Rob-222
McInny,Murdock	Cha-193	Duncan	Mor- 68	George	Cum-250
McIntagert,Danl	Rob-227	Duncan	Mor- 66	Gilbert	Mor- 64
Gilbert	Rob-227	Duncan	Mor- 61	Gilbert	Rob-227
McIntire,Mrs.	Mec- 47	Evander	Cum-238	Hugh	Rch-191
Alexr	Cum-237	John	Rch-192	Hugh	Rob-226
Andrew	Dup- 7	John	Cha-207	J	Col- 17
Alexander	Hay-198	John	Cha-207	James	Mon- 27
James	Cum-239	John little	Cha-204	Jane	Ans- 28
Jas	Mec- 22	John	Mor- 57	Jl (F)	Bla- 10
Jerem	Roc- 32	John	Mor- 68	Jno	Mon- 27

Name	Location	Name	Location	Name	Location	Name	Location
McKay,Jno	Rob-227	McKeethuns,John	Mor- 63	McKibben,Jno	Mec- 30		
John	Ire-244	McKeever,T	Glf-172	McKibbon,Arthur	Mec- 29		
John	Ire-264	Mckefre,James	Bun- 84	Margaret	Mec- 30		
John	Ire-264	McKelep,Elizabeth	Sto-150	McKie,Chas	Bla- 8		
John	Rob-219	McKellar,Archd B	Cum-250	McKieb,Betsey	Wsh- 22		
John Junr	Cum-246	Archd Senr	Cum-250	McKimmey,Aaron J	Car-181		
John Senr	Cum-246	Archibald	Rch-195	Aaron Senr	Car-181		
Malcom	Cum-269	Daniel	Rch-195	Isaac	Car-181		
Margaret	Cum-244	Dugald	Rob-221	McKimmy,Jas	Tyr-203		
Murdock	Cum-269	Duncan	Cum-268	Jos	Tyr-204		
Nancy	Rch-191	Jno	Rob-221	Wm	Tyr-204		
Neil	Ire-245	John	Cum-268	McKindley,Charles	Cab-148		
Neil	Ire-239	John	Cum-255	David	Cab-149		
Neil	Ire-239	Peter	Cum-254	David	Cab-139		
Neill Esq	Cum-253	Peter Esq	Cum-268	Rebeccah	Cab-144		
Robert	Ire-245	McKemmy,J	Glf-179	McKinley,Wm	Mec- 54		
Thomas	Ire-241	McKennan,Hugh	Sam-155	McKinly,Robt	Mec- 54		
William	Ire-245	John	Sam-155	McKinney,Burnes	Rth-120		
William	Ire-239	Murdoch	Sam-162	Daniel	Rth-120		
McKean,John	Glf-157	McKennel,Danl	Mor- 62	Ellender	Wil-277		
McKeay,Wm	Cab-129	McKenney,John	Roc- 8	George	Rth-119		
McKee,Abraham	Cab-139	McKennon,Alexr	Rch-201	Henry	Rth-119		
Alexander	Ire-247	Alexr	Mor- 59	Peter	Cas- 62		
David	Bla- 3	Daniel	Rch-205	William	Cas- 62		
Isaac	Lnc-332	Jno	Mor- 61	William	Rth-122		
Jesse	Cas- 62	John	Mor- 64	William	Bun- 96		
James	Ire-246	John	Mor- 59	McKinnis,Thos	Lnc-338		
James	Lnc-367	Lauchlan	Rch-205	McKinnon,Alexr	Cum-269		
James	Bur-120	Neill	Rch-206	Alexr	Cum-243		
James	Hay-197	Norman	Mor- 59	Charles	Mor- 61		
Jas	Mec- 27	Phillip	Cha-194	Christian	Rch-196		
Jas	Rob-219	Randel	Rch-212	Daniel	Rch-203		
Capt Jno	Mec- 33	McKenny,Howel	Cum-257	Duncan	Cum-250		
John	Ire-245	John Capt	Cum-256	Hector	Cum-244		
Morrison	Mec- 34	Sarah	Cum-252	Hector	Rch-194		
Rankin L	Ora-117	McKensey,Jno	Rob-224	John	Cum-244		
Robert	Cas- 62	McKenzie,Alexr	Cum-252	Keneth	Rob-223		
S P	Bla- 2	Daniel	Cum-270	Lauchlan	Rch-196		
Samuel	Lnc-367	Daniel	Cum-252	Peter	Rch-203		
Theo	Row- 38	Duncan	Cum-243	Roderick	Rob-227		
William	Ire-260	Hugh	Cum-252	McKinny,Charity	Glf-172		
William	Sur-168	James	Ire-241	Charles	Bur-107		
Wm	Mec- 27	John	Mor- 63	Courtney	Nsh- 85		
Wm	Ora-174	John	Rch-198	Eliza	Ons-103		
Wm	Bla- 7	Keneth	Rch-211	George	Glf-185		
Wm Junr	Ora-168	Kenneth	Rch-197	John	Bur-109		
Winslow	Mec- 46	McKeowen,Nancy	Rth-117	John	Bur-114		
McKeeb,James	Tyr-206	McKerall,Wm	Ora-168	John	Bun- 95		
McKeel,Ann	Bft- 25	Mckern,Luke	Bun- 87	John	Jon-302		
Benjamin	Edg- 51	McKerrs,James	Ire-247	Thos	Bur-113		
Carney	Bft- 23	McKethen,Archd	Cum-246	William	Bur-113		
Ed	Bft- 24	John	Cum-267	Willson	Bur-113		
John	Bft- 23	John	Cum-245	Mckins,John	Hyd-225		
Mary	Bft- 38	Neill	Cum-244	Nimrod	Hyd-233		
Merkh	Bft- 25	McKetheons,Dugald	Mor- 55	McKinsey,Donald	Cum-237		
Milly	Edg- 51	Mckey,Joel	Bun- 84	John	Cum-238		
Olive	Bft- 30	John	Bun- 84	Keneth	Bur-110		
Wm	Bft- 24	Robert	Hyd-230	McKinsie,Alexander	Ire-245		
McKeethin,A	Bru-222	Wm	Bft- 33	John	Sam-151		

Name	Ref	Name	Ref	Name	Ref
McKinsie,Rhodeham	Roc- 15	McLain,Thomas	Lnc-367	McLean,Daniel	Cum-243
McKinzey,Duncan	Ans- 29	McLairty,James	Cab-148	Daniel	Rch-196
McKinzie,Alexander	Wil-257	McLam,Joel	Sam-160	Daniel	Rch-211
Andrew	Ire-259	Robt	Sam-160	Daniel	Cum-253
Angus	Ire-260	Spivey	Sam-159	Danl	Rob-232
G	Bru-232	McLaMoore,Jno	Bur-124	Danl	Rob-242
Gilbert	Cum-250	McLanamore,John	Bur-121	Danl	Rob-229
J B	Bru-236	McLane,Hugh	Cab-137	Danl	Rob-229
Jenny	Mor- 64	John	Bun- 72	Dugald	Cum-252
Katharine	Cum-251	McLannan,Neil	Ans- 18	Duncan	Mor- 62
Kines	Ire-264	McLaran,John	Cum-239	Duncan	Mor- 61
William	Mar- 8	McLaren,Neil	Ans- 28	Duncan	Cum-254
Wm	Mec- 23	McLarren,Jno	Ans- 31	Duncan	Mor- 60
McKinzy,Keneth	Mon- 27	McLartey,Archd	Cab-147	Duncan Maj	Cum-253
Wm	Glf-188	McLauchlan,Isabella	Cum-244	Effy	Mor- 60
McKisack,Jonathan	Per-145	John	Cum-243	Eliz	Lnc-320
Robt	Per-145	John	Rch-194	Hector	Rob-229
Wilson Senr	Per-145	Neill	Cum-269	Hector	Mor- 64
McKissick,Daniel	Bun- 94	McLauchlin,Alen	Rob-222	Hector	Rob-227
James	Ire-256	Archd	Rob-224	Hector	Rob-225
John	Bun- 94	Archibald	Rch-191	Hugh	Rch-211
McKithen,D	Col- 19	Collin	Rob-230	Hugh	Cum-237
M	Bru-240	Danl	Rob-218	Hugh	Cum-254
McKnight,George	Sto-103	Dugald	Mor- 58	Hugh	Rch-253
Goerge	Sto-135	Dugald	Rob-226	Hugh H	Cum-252
Hugh	Ire-241	Duncan	Rob-226	James Tay	Cum-254
Hugh	Row- 71	Isabella	Rch-191	Jno	Rob-224
James	Ire-241	Jno	Rob-230	Jno	Rob-229
James	Ire-241	Jno	Rob-232	Jno	Rob-229
Jas	Mec- 25	Nincolas	Rob-218	Jno	Rob-228
John	Glf-159	Robert	Rob-224	Jno	Rob-229
John	Row- 71	Robt	Mor- 54	Jno	Rob-242
Robt	Mec- 36	McLaurin,Angus	Rch-193	John	Cum-255
Robt	Mec- 37	Daniel	Rch-203	John	Rch-204
Roger	Row- 55	Daniel	Rch-204	John	Rch-205
Thos	Mec- 46	Daniel	Rch-191	John	Cum-243
William	Ire-259	Duncan Senr	Rch-202	John	Rch-198
William	Sto-151	Duncan Maj	Rch-202	John	Rch-191
William	Sto-144	Duncan Pond	Rch-202	John	Rch-197
Wm	Row- 71	Hugh	Rch-193	John	Rch-211
Wm	Glf-158	Hugh	Rhc-193	John	Ire-244
Wm	Glf-184	John	Rch-212	John	Rch-213
McKoy,Farquhard C	Cum-268	Laurin	Rch-205	John Esq	Cum-263
Hugh	Ire-246	McLaurtey,Alexr	Cab-147	Lauchlan	Cum-253
Major John	Bla- 13	McLawrin,L	Cum-237	Lauchlen	Rob-229
McKraghan,Hugh	Row- 44	McLay,Jno	Mec- 22	Lauchlin	Rob-229
McKraney,Keneth	Rch-192	McLean,Alexr	Cum-252	Lauchlin	Cum-250
McKrimmon,Danl	Rob-228	Alexr	Mor- 66	Malcom	Cum-254
McKuller,Dunc	Bla- 7	Allen	Cum-237	Mary	Rob-232
McKume,Barnaby Jr	Way-249	Allen B S	Cum-246	Nancy	Rob-229
Barnaby Jr	Way-247	Allin	Mor- 69	Neill	Rob-229
John	Way-235	Angus	Rch-192	Neill	Rob-222
Michael	Way-239	Ann	Cum-252	Neill	Mor- 61
Richd Jr	Way-251	Archd	Rob-229	Neill	Mor- 66
Richd Sr	Way-235	Archd	Mor- 54	Neill B	Cum-253
Robt	Way-239	Archd	Rob-222	Neill F	Cum-252
Salley	Way-239	Archd B	Cum-252	Neill Mill	Cum-253
William	Way-236	Archd Senr	Cum-252	Peter	Bla- 8
McKuthrow,A J	Bla- 10	Daniel	Cum-255	Rory	Cum-253

McLean,Sarah	Mor- 66	McLeod,John	Mor- 60	McMahan,Andw	Cab-145		
Wm	Lnc-336	John	Mor- 66	Archibald	Bun- 76		
McLear,Archd	Rob-219	John	Cum-263	Bernard	Row- 62		
John	Per-143	John	Sam-155	Eli	Bun- 78		
Jon	Per-151	John Esq	Rch-196	Eliza	Ora-168		
Sarah	Per-131	John Junr	Cum-261	Geo	Row- 62		
McLelan,A	Bru-226	John Senr	Rch-196	James	Row- 61		
McLellan,Daniel	Cum-259	Mal	Rob-244	James	Bun- 76		
Malcom	Cum-267	Malcom	Bla- 12	James	Cab-145		
Mary	Bla- 5	Malcom	Cum-263	Mary	Row- 62		
Mary	Bla- 3	Margaret	Cum-263	Morgan	Row- 61		
McLemore,Abram	Fra- 89	Margaret	Cum-263	Samuel	Row- 62		
Atkins	War-167	Mary	Mor- 60	Stephen	Bun- 79		
Charles	Sam-162	Murdoch	Rch-191	Mcmahon,Barbara	Bft- 19		
Charles	Sam-156	Murdoch	Rch-192	Sarah	Bft- 20		
Drury	Bla- 8	Murdoch B D	Cum-244	Tho	Bft- 24		
E	Bla- 8	Murdoch Senr	Cum-244	McMain,M	Ora-153		
Nathl	Fra- 96	Nancy	Mor- 64	McManiss,Laurance	Cha-198		
Wm	Bla- 8	Neill	Mor- 56	Nathan	Cha-198		
Young	Fra- 83	Neill	Mor- 57	McManus,Aaron	Cha-204		
McLendal,Jesse	Ans- 6	Neill	Mor- 59	McMarth,Wm	Cha-215		
Joel	Ans- 10	Neill	Mor- 61	McMaster,Margt	Bla- 12		
Mary	Ans- 6	Norman	Rch-213	Wm	Bla- 6		
McLendon,Dennis	Rch-199	Norman	Cum-242	McMasters,Andrew	Ran-173		
Edwd	Mon- 23	Norman	Mor- 64	Daniel	Ran-173		
James	Rch-202	Norman	Cum-262	Lewis	Ran-173		
James	Sam-154	Norman	Mon- 27	Jonath	Cha-204		
Samuel	Rch-199	Norman	Rob-229	Saml	Ran-174		
Wm	Mon- 23	Norman	Ans- 7	Simeon	Ran-173		
McLennan,William	Cum-239	Norman	Ans- 31	William	Cha-204		
McLennon,Allen	Mor- 58	Norman	Mon- 30	McMath,James	Cha-211		
John	Rch-207	Norman Snr	Mon- 27	Wm	Cha-213		
John	Mor- 59	Roderick	Rch-208	McMickal,Archibald	Glf-159		
McLoad,Hugh	Mon- 29	Roderick	Cum-254	Thos	Glf-159		
John	Mon- 27	Roderick	Ans- 7	McMilan,Duncan	Rob-227		
McLeod,Alexander	Rch-207	William	Rch-191	McMill,Stelair	Sur-197		
Alexander	Rch-209	William	Cum-255	McMillan,Mrs	Cum-241		
Alexander	Rch-196	McLeoud,J Jnr	Mon- 36	Alexander	Rch-203		
Alexr	Mor- 62	McLeran,Duncan	Cum-241	Alexander	Rch-193		
Alexr	Mor- 57	McLerran,Archd	Cum-265	Angus	Bla- 4		
Alexr	Mor- 59	Daniel	Cum-267	Archd	Rob-243		
Angus	Rch-213	Duncan	Cum-267	Archd	Rob-226		
Angus	Rch-209	McLerren,John	Cum-266	Ard	Bla- 4		
Angus	Rob-224	John	Cum-264	Danl	Rob-223		
Archebald	Rch-206	Neill	Cum-266	Danl	Rob-224		
Archibald	Rch-192	McLester,Danl	Mon- 50	Danl	Rob-227		
Catharine	Rch-213	Jas Esq	Mon- 39	Danl	Rob-225		
Christin	Cum-244	Jno	Ans- 31	Dugald	Bla- 13		
Daniel	Cum-255	McLilly,Anne	Hal-113	Dugald	Rob-225		
Danl	Mor- 60	McLinnen,John	Rch-213	Dugald	Rob-226		
Danl	Mor- 61	Mcllain,Jno	Mec- 23	Duncan	Bla- 4		
Duncan	Rch-195	McLoad,Donald	Cum-238	Duncan	Rob-225		
J	Bla- 10	Norman	Cum-239	Duncan	Rob-228		
James	Rch-193	McLod,Murdock	Mon- 25	Duncan	Rob-225		
Jno	Mec- 24	McLooms,Gabriel	Ran-174	Duncan Senr	Rob-225		
Jno	Mor- 69	McLsie,Hugh	Ire-268	Edward	Rch-203		
John	Cum-242	McLuen,Solomon	Ons- 97	Effie	Rch-199		
John	Cum-243	McLur,Jno	Per-141	Effy	Bla- 9		
John	Rch-195	McMackins,M	Mon- 42	Flora	Rob-228		

-212-

McMillan,Gilbert	Rob-233	McMillion,Joseph	Hay-198	McNaught,Barbra	Cum-270
Gilbert	Rch-202	Polly	Hay-198	McNeal,Benjamin	Wil-281
Hector	Rch-203	Samuel	Hay-197	James	Wil-266
Hector	Rob-226	McMin,Elihu	Glf-171	John	Per-141
Iven	Bla- 10	Samuel	Lnc-362	Joseph	Wil-281
J	Ash- 7	McMining,A	Ora-153	Pryor	Per-141
James	Ire-244	McMiniway,Alexr	Cas- 62	William	Wil-277
Jas	Rob-243	McMinn,Elizabeth	Bun- 95	McNealey,John (Tad)	Row- 73
Jno	Rob-229	McMooring,Will	Pit-240	McNealy,Archad	Row- 72
Jno	Rob-221	McMullen,Mrs	Cum-238	Isaac	Row- 68
Jno	Rob-231	McMullin,James	Cas- 62	James	Row- 72
Jno	Rob-222	John	Cas- 62	John	Row- 72
Jno	Rob-226	Nathan	Fra- 80	Saml	Row- 72
Jno	Rob-226	Ran	Ora-162	Thomas	Rch-206
John (M)	Bla- 2	Robert	Edg- 63	McNear,Duncan	Cum-248
John	Cum-237	McMullins,James	Rth-118	Hugh	Bla- 12
John (S R)	Bla- 9	Micajah	Fra- 87	McNell,Duncan	Cum-237
John	Rch-213	McMunroe,Peter	Cum-270	Wm L	Cum-237
Mal	Rob-219	McMurray,John	Glf-173	McNeeley,Adam	Per-141
Mal	Rob-226	McMurry,Eliza	Glf-178	James	Roc- 28
Malcom	Bla- 4	James	Per-151	McNeely,Adam	Ire-257
Malcom	Rch-197	Jno	Per-141	Andrew	Mec- 36
Malcom	Rch-193	Jno	Mec- 45	Jno	Mec- 30
Mary	Rob-222	Robt	Cab-144	John	Rth-119
Nancy	Mon- 29	Samuel	Per-151	John	Ire-241
Neil	Bla- 5	William	Glf-159	John	Ire-258
Neill	Bla- 13	McNab,Sally	Grn-139	Roderick	Mor- 60
Peter	Rch-193	McNabb,Ard	Bla- 12	Samuel	Ire-241
Robert Senr	Bla- 9	Jas	Rob-234	Samuel	Bur-126
Thomas	Cum-250	Jno	Rob-234	McNees,John	Len-312
Wm	Rob-223	McNair,Alexander	Rch-212	McNeial,Hoze	Cas- 62
Wm	Bla- 11	Daniel	Rch-203	McNeill,Agnes	Cum-246
McMille,Dougle	Sur-172	Daniel	Rch-193	Agnes	Cha-214
Martha	Sur-173	Donald	Mor- 63	Alexr	Rob-228
McMillen,Alexr	Mor- 68	Duncan	Rob-225	Alexr	Rob-226
Angus	Mor- 58	Edward	Rob-222	Angus Esq	Rch-202
Arch	Mor- 65	Edward	Rch-203	Ann	Cum-267
Arch	Mor- 55	Edward	Rch-191	Archd	Cum-261
Archd	Mor- 60	Edward	Edg- 62	Archd	Cum-250
Archd	Mor- 58	Enoch	Lnc-333	Archd	Cum-252
Catharine	Cum-265	Gilbert	Rch-203	Archd	Rob-244
Daniel	Cum-243	James	Lnc-333	Archd	Mor- 62
Daniel	Cum-244	Jennette	Rch-203	Archibald	Rch-211
Daniel	Cum-265	Jno	Rob-222	Daniel	Cum-261
Daniel	Cum-244	Jno	Rob-222	Daniel	Cum-250
Danl	Mor- 57	Jno	Rob-242	Daniel	Cum-242
Dugald	Cum-264	John	Rch-205	Daniel	Rch-194
Edward	Cum-266	John	Rch-192	Daniel Jr	Cum-251
Eli	Hal-113	John Esq	Rch-192	Danl	Mor- 62
James	Cum-268	Malcom	Rch-193	Danl	Rob-234
John	Cum-267	Nathl	Rch-205	Danl	Rob-227
John Esq	Cum-251	Neill	Rch-193	Danl	Rob-235
Malcolm	Mor- 56	Neill Esq	Rch-212	Duncan	Rob-226
Murdock	Cha-201	Ricd Matw	Roc-218	Duncan	Mor- 57
Neill	Mor- 54	Roderick	Rob-218	Geo	Ora-111
Neill	Cum-243	McNatt,Eliza	Ora-164	Hector	Cum-264
McMillian,Jno	Rob-227	Fred	Ora-164	Hector	Cum-250
McMillion,Amon	Ans- 14	Joshua	Ora-164	Hector	Cum-245
Jas	Ans- 14	McNaught,Alexr	Cum-270	Hector	Mor- 60

-213-

Name	Ref	Name	Ref	Name	Ref
McNeill,Hector	Mor- 54	McOrosy,Nancy	Rob-226	McPherson,W	Cam-158
Hector	Rob-227	McOrvey,Edward	Rob-230	William	Rch-192
Hector Junr	Cum-255	Jno	Rob-230	McQuage,Mal	Rob-233
Hector S	Cum-255	McPerson,Abigail	Cha-107	McQuean,Daniel	Cum-260
Hector Senr	Cum-255	John	Cha-203	Daniel	Cum-250
Henry	Cum-253	McPeters,Charles	Row- 69	John	Cum-260
James	Mor- 62	David	Hay-198	John	Rch-192
James	Cum-267	Jonathan	Hay-198	Malcom	Cum-259
Jas Esq	Rob-244	McPhail,Dougle	Sam-151	Murdoch	Rch-205
Jean	Cum-251	Dugald	Cum-267	Norman	Cum-259
Jno	Cum-251	Duncan	Sam-152	Roderick	Rch-192
Jno	Mor- 61	Jno	Rob-223	McQueen,Alexr	Cum-267
Jno	Mor- 69	John	Cum-267	Angus	Mor- 62
Jno	Rob-228	McPhater,Archd	Rob-224	Angus	Mor- 58
Jno	Rob-218	Jno	Rob-225	Angus	Rob-228
Jno Jnr	Rob-226	McPhaul,Danl	Rob-223	Danl	Mor- 64
Jno Senr	Rob-226	James	Cum-268	Elisha	Sam-155
John	Mor- 61	Mary	Rob-244	Hugh	Sam-155
John	Cum-255	McPhaull,Jno	Rob-244	James	Rob-219
John	Bla- 9	McPhautin,Danl	Rob-237	John	Mor- 66
John	Rch-193	McPherson,Alexr	Cum-251	Murdoch	Mor- 61
John R	Cum-245	Archd	Mor- 68	Murdock	Cha-214
John Scotch	Cum-253	B	Cam-162	Peter	Mor- 65
Joseph	Cum-252	Colin	Cum-250	McQuerry,John	Wil-261
Lauchlan	Rch-202	D	Cam-162	McQuesten,Joseph	Mec- 29
Malcom	Cum-255	Daniel	Pas-197	McQuilken,Neill	Rob-244
Malcom	Mor- 63	Danl	Cha-212	McQuire,Jas	Mec- 31
Malcom	Rob-231	Danl	Rob-225	McQurry,William	Wil-267
Malcom	Rob-230	Duncan	Mor- 68	McRackan,James	Cum-240
Mary	Cum-250	E Jun	Ora-129	James	Cum-238
Neill	Cum-244	Enoch	Cha-213	McRackin,Wm	Ran-175
Neill	Rch-196	Enoch	Ora-128	McRae,Alex	Mon- 26
Neill	Rob-226	Grice	Cum-250	Alexander	Rch-198
Neill	Rob-226	J	Cam-165	Alexander	Rch-198
Neill	Rob-219	J	Cam-165	Alexander	Rch-201
Capt Neill	Cum-251	J	Cam-164	Alexander	Rch-191
Neill Esq	Cum-255	James	Hrt-216	Alexn	Ans- 23
Neill Ferry	Cum-253	Jas	Ora-129	Alexn	Ans- 20
Neill Junr	Cum-252	Jno	Mor- 63	Alexn	Ans- 21
Neill Senr	Cum-252	John	Ire-259	Alexr	Ans- 20
Prior	Per-151	John	Bla- 13	Alexr	Ans- 30
Sarah	Cum-243	John	Cha-212	Alexr	Ans- 28
Tabitha	Mor- 63	John	Rch-194	Anguish	Ans- 30
Wm	Rob-221	John B	Cum-250	Anguish	Ans- 28
Wm	Rob-227	John R	Cum-250	Chrisr	Ans- 29
McNely,Robert	Ire-257	Joseph	Hal-121	Christopher	Ans- 30
McNider,James	Prq-222	Joseph	Sto-102	Christopher Jr	Rch-206
John	Prq-221	Joseph	Sto-134	Christopher Sr	Rch-198
Thos	Prq-221	Manan	Rob-228	Collin	Mon- 26
McNiel,G	Ash- 5	Matthew	Ire-258	Colin	Cum-250
McNielle,Henry	Per-131	Nancy	Pas-197	Dan & Dan	Mon- 26
McNight,Hugh	Mor- 56	Neill	Rch-213	Dan	Mon- 26
McNinch,Archd	Cum-247	Noah	Pas-197	Daniel	Ans- 28
McNorton,C	Bla- 7	O	Cam-162	Daniel	Ans- 27
J	Bla- 12	Othniel	Cha-213	Daniel	Cum-268
Neill	Bla- 3	Peter	Pas-197	Donold	Ans- 4
Neill	Bla- 6	Robert	Ire-258	Duncan	Ans- 28
Sarah	Bun- 91	S	Cam-162	Duncan	Ans- 28
McNulty,Wm	Cab-148	T	Cam-165	Duncan	Rch-198

Name	Ref	Name	Ref	Name	Ref
McRae,F	Mon- 36	McWarter,Aron	Mec- 32	Mears,Joel	Bun- 93
Farquhard	Ans- 30	Jno	Mec- 31	Jona	Bla- 4
Farquhard	Ans- 28	Moses	Mec- 30	Naomi	Bla- 4
Farquhard	Ans- 23	McWhorter,Saml	Lnc-342	Philip	Sto-138
Gilbert	Cum-269	McWilliams,Clement	Hal-114	Meas,Matthias	Hay-198
James	Rch-198	George	Edg- 40	Measells,Mark	Dup- 35
Jno	Ans- 28	John	Bft- 37	Meason,Mrs	Mec- 28
Jno	Ans- 28	John	Hyd-224	Henry	Mec- 36
Jno	Ans- 28	Peter	Hyd-224	Jas	Mec- 26
John	Rch-201	McWorter,Fanny	Mec- 30	Meatherly,Levi	Bun- 76
John Brick	Cum-250	Jas	Mec- 35	William	Bun- 77
John Senr	Cum-250	Meacham,Celia	Nor- 73	Mebane,David	Ora-123
Mal	Rob-229	Henry	Nor- 73	Jas Esq	Ora-147
Malcom	Rch-205	James	Rch-201	M	Ora-152
Malcom	Cum-254	John	Rch-201	Robt	Ora-147
Murdoch B S	Cum-244	Rank	Mec- 25	Wm	Ora-134
Norman	Rch-191	William	Rch-201	Mechum,Jacob	Hal-114
Peter	Rch-192	Meachum,Jesse	Cha-198	Mary	Hal-114
Philip	Ans- 30	Meador,Jas	Ans- 11	Paul	Hal-114
Philip	Cum-255	Jason	Ans- 8	Meck,Francis	Rob-242
Roderick	Cum-250	Jason	Ans- 12	Meclanins,James	Cur- 90
Sarah	Rch-198	Jno	Ans- 15	Mecoy,Cornelous	Cur- 86
McRainey,James	Ran-173	Jobe	Ans- 11	Medders,Benjamin	Jon-301
McRath,Nellie	Rch-200	Levi	Ans- 27	Jeremiah	Jon-301
McRea,Duncan	Cum-237	Lewis	Ans- 7	John	Jon-301
Jno	Rob-219	Moridca	Ans- 6	Millington	Jon-301
McReady,Wm	Lnc-333	Meadows,Abram	Grn-139	Thomas Junr	Jon-301
McRee,James	Ire-257	Daniel	Ire-252	Thomas Senr	Jon-301
William	Ire-258	E	Bru-222	Tobe	Jon-301
McReece,J	Glf-172	Elias	Car-181	Zadoc	Jon-301
McRorie,William	War-184	Isaac	Car-181	Meddlin,Bryan	Dup- 28
McShehigh,John	Prq-221	Isham	War-176	Meddows,Daniel	Per-131
McSperrian,Jas	Mec- 34	James	Grn-139	Nathaniel	Rch-209
McSwain,Alexr	Rob-223	Jessy	Grn-139	Medearis,Abrham	Per-131
Angus	Cum-268	John	Grn-139	Medford,Daniel	Mar- 3
C	Mon- 38	Mikael	Grn-139	Jeptha	Mon- 33
Danl	Rob-222	Randol	Wil-283	Jonah	Hay-197
Geo	Mon- 38	Riley	Grn-139	Medfort,Henry	Mar- 5
Jno	Rob-224	William	Dup- 23	James	Mar- 5
Jno	Ans- 26	Wm	Grn-138	Medillor,John	Glf-186
John	Wil-277	Meaghers,Martin B	Pas-195	Judioth	Glf-186
Mal	Rob-223	Meagitt,N	Cam-158	Medley,Bryan	Way-246
Malm	Rob-222	Meagles,Jasper	Len-312	John	Mon- 48
Roderick	Rob-226	Meakens,Daniel	Cur- 83	John	Hal-113
McSwane,Benjamin	Rth-117	Jeremiah	Cur- 82	Rubin	Ans- 16
McSwein,Angus	Rch-209	John	Cur- 90	Smith	Ans- 17
Angus	Rch-195	Marget	Cur- 82	Medlin,Bradley	Fra- 98
Daniel	Rch-194	Mealer,James	War-173	Eleanor	Len-316
Finlak Junr	Rch-194	Peter	Cab-138	John	Mor- 56
Finlak Senr	Rch-194	Means,Alexander	Ire-259	Matthew	Fra- 92
McSwine,William	Rth-117	Benjamin	Ran-175	Nicholas	Len-313
McTae,Edwd	Row- 51	James	Cab-139	Shadrack	Fra- 82
McVa,Hamilton	Ran-175	Jno	Mec- 25	William	Fra- 81
McVay,John	Per-141	John	Cab-139	Medlock,Charles	Bur-114
McVeely,Henry	Mec- 34	Robert Senr	Roc- 24	Henry	Bur-114
McVery,Danl	Ora-134	Wm	Glf-173	Sarah	Bur-113
McVey,Daniel	Bun- 93	Wm	Cab-139	Medyett,Elisha	Cur- 82
McVicar,Jno	Rob-218	Wm	Mec- 33	Meeds,Benjamin	Pas-195
Wm	Rob-228	Mears,Joab	Bla- 4	John	Pas-195

Name	Loc	Name	Loc	Name	Loc
Meedy, Wm	Cha-194	Meloy, Wm Ap	Mec- 30	Melvin, Tho	Ora-159
Meek, Adam	Mec- 48	Melord, Stephen	Bur-107	Memory, George	Bla- 3
Robt	Mec- 23	Melson, Charles	Nsh- 78	Men, Thos Meirs	Cur- 87
Meekins,----	Tyr-212	Edmond	Ons-106	Mendenhall, Benjamin	Ran-174
Isaac	Tyr-207	Jos	Cur- 84	Daniel	Glf-166
Joseph	Tyr-201	Polly	Tyr-209	Elisha	Ran-175
Thomas	Tyr-206	Rebecca	Cho-222	Enos	Glf-167
Meeks, Benjamin	Edg- 44	Sally	Tyr-209	Isaac	Ran-173
Britton	Ans- 18	Taylor	Car-181	Isaac	Glf-169
Caleb	Pit-243	Melton, Anderson	Sur-172	Isaiah	Glf-167
Henry	Pit-245	Ansel	Mor- 56	James	Glf-159
J	Col- 20	Benjamin	Rth-123	Jas	Glf-162
John	Ons-102	Boling	Fra- 96	Jas	Glf-168
Joshua	Pit-244	Boling	Fra- 97	John	Glf-169
Little Berry	Ans- 26	Cornelius	Rth-119	Jonas	Glf-168
Mereman	Edg- 53	Daniel	Rth-123	Jonathan	Sto-150
Reddan	Bla- 12	Daniel	Rth-123	Judidth	Glf-166
Reuben	Ons-102	David	Nsh- 80	Mos	Glf-168
S	Col- 18	Edward	Ons-101	Moses	Glf-187
Megginson, John	Mon- 25	Isham	Sur-182	Moses	Glf-168
Sam	Mon- 24	Isham	Ans- 11	N	Glf-166
Thos	Mon- 24	Jemimah	Edg- 62	Nathl	Lnc-334
Meggs, Jno	Ans- 19	Jesse	Ans- 11	Richd 2nd	Glf-168
Meglawhorn, Adam	Pit-238	Jesse	Ons- 96	Robt	Lnc-334
Arthur	Pit-238	Jesse	Sto-101	Seth	Glf-168
George	Pit-260	Jesse	Rth-123	Stephen	Rch-212
Jeremiah	Pit-238	Jesse	Rth-123	Mendingall, Jesse	Bur-119
Unity	Pit-238	John	Nsh-644	Mendinghall, Jos	Sto-111
Megrery, D	Ora-139	John	Grn-135	Joseph	Sto-146
Megs, Dolley	Cur- 90	John	Rth-120	Menedy, Thos	Mec- 25
Megwart, John	Bun- 94	John	Rth-118	Meng, William	Cum-238
Mehaffa, Thomas Jr	Sur-196	John	Rth-117	Menin, Henry	Dup- 6
Thomas Sr	Sur-196	Jonathan	Ons- 99	Menis, Frederick	Row- 68
Mehaffey, James	Wil-272	Joseph	Ons-107	Menster, John	Row- 71
Mehaffy, Joseph	Lnc-347	Joshua	Rth-123	Menyon, John	Ire-241
Mehala, Garrot	Sur-168	Josiah	Nsh- 84	Menzies, John	Roc- 8
Mehona, Jesse	Hal-112	Mathew	Ora-133	Mequagar, Duncan	Ans- 30
Mehorney, Phillip	Cur- 91	Naomi	Cha-200	Meradeth, Sanders	Rch-199
Meizle, John Jnr	Brt- 65	Plury	Nor- 73	Merady, Alexander	Dup- 33
John Senr	Brt- 53	Reubin	Rth-119	Mercer, C Junr	Cam-157
Jos	Brt- 53	Reuben	Rth-123	C Snr	Cam-155
Meizles, James	Brt- 60	Reubin	Rth-123	J	Cam-159
Mekins, James	Hyd-233	Richard	Ons-106	Jacob	Edg- 52
Meland, John	Cha-197	Robert	Fra- 82	Jeremiah	Cur- 88
Melay, Appleton	Lnc-327	Robert	Fra- 95	Jeremiah Jr	Cur- 88
Melcher, John	Cab-140	Robert	Rth-122	John	Dup- 30
Melholland, John	Ire-241	Ruth	Ons-102	L	Cam-163
Melicar, E	Glf-170	Silas	Rth-119	Linsey	Cur- 87
Melkear, Barrus	Cur- 91	Samuel	Ons-106	Mason	Cur- 93
Mellis, Elizabeth	Car-181	William	Rth-120	R	Cam-159
Mellon, Edwd	Lnc-335	Melven, Comfort	Ons-107	T	Cam-159
John	Cup- 21	Melvin, Danl	Bla- 10	T Esq	Cam-154
Jonn	Lnc-335	George	Bla- 8	W	Cam-155
Meloan, Joseph	Cha-196	George	Bla- 7	William	Edg- 44
William	Cha-196	Henerey	Cur- 84	Merchent, Gidun	Cur- 90
Melone, Brindes	Per-151	James	Ora-125	Marey	Cur- 92
Mark	Per-151	John	Ora-125	Merchison, Mrs	Cum-238
Melony, Wm	Len-318	John	Bla- 8	Alexr	Cum-238
Meloy, Wm	Mec- 30	John Jnr	Bla- 8	John	Cum-239

Mercilliot,Jacob	Roc- 31	Merril,Andw	Row- 52	Messick,Leonard		Sur-169
Peter	Roc- 31	Moses	Lnc-354	Richard		Sur-157
Mereday,Jas	Bft- 32	Merrill,Amos	Row- 52	Wm		Bft- 34
Mereddy,James	Bla- 13	Arthur	Car-184	Messner,M		Glf-161
Meredith,Elisha	Sto-134	Benjn	Row- 80	Messor,A		Col- 20
James	Sto-110	Jonathan	Row- 52	Metcalf,Danzee		Rth-118
James	Sto-149	Lytle	Ran-174	Warner		Rth-118
John	Sto-134	Merriman,Bryan	Mon- 43	William		Rth-119
John	Joh-274	Malcom	Mon- 43	Methias,Simon		Cur- 89
W H	Bla- 13	Mark	Wil-278	Metzler,John		Row- 52
Meret,Benjamin	Pit-255	Merrit,Absalom	Sam-158	Mewbern,Sarah		Cho-224
Joseph	Ora-171	Benj	Mon- 24	Wm		Cho-230
Wilie	Ora-171	Burwell	Sam-158	Mewburn,Wilson		Cho-224
Mergall,Paul	Ora-151	Charlote	Dup- 23	Mews,Wm		Ora-137
Mergan,S	Ora-156	Daniel	Dup- 16	Mewshace,Wm		Cha-200
S	Ora-156	David	Sam-157	Mggee,Becham		Glf-188
Mergon,Martin	Ire-254	Fred W	Sam-158	Miager,Ambrose		War-168
Reuben	Ire-269	Gabrjel	Sam-158	Mials,Elizabeth		Edg- 56
Merideth,Jno	Cho-231	Green	Grn-129	Ezekiel		Ran-174
Meridith,Elisha	Sto-102	Jacob	Sam-158	Mical,John		Rth-121
Merion,Bartholomew	Sur-171	James	Jon-302	Mice,Benjamin		Row- 53
Daniel	Sur-173	James	Mon- 23	Micer,Jacob		Row- 66
Meriott,Lovet	Hal-114	John	Mon- 23	Michael,Benjn		Hal-112
Nancy	Hal-114	Joseph	Ora-152	Jerry		Row- 81
Richard	Hal-112	Levy	Sam-158	Samuel		Row- 81
Shadrach	Hal-112	Michael	Sam-158	Thomas		Rth-122
Thomas	Hal-112	Michl	Dup- 7	Michaels,Peter		Lnc-328
Thos	Hal-113	Nancy	Dup- 5	Thomas		Sur-182
William Senr	Hal-113	Patrick	Dup- 7	Michal,Frederick		Row- 87
Wm Junr	Hal-113	Sam	Sam-158	Jacob		Row- 54
Merit,Hezekiah	Jon-301	Merritt,Benjn	Fra- 92	John		Row- 41
Meritt,Jessee	Tyr-209	Daniel	Cas- 62	Peter		Row- 41
Meroney,Wm	Cha-214	James	Fra- 91	Wm		Row- 54
Merony,Henry	Gat-108	John	Fra- 92	Micham,Geo		Cha-213
Meroon,Jacob	Rth-117	Patsy	Ora-165	Micheau,J		Cam-154
Merrel,Abner	Row- 38	Solomon	Cas- 62	Michel,Cady		Rth-123
Azariah	Row- 87	Wilie	Ora-150	David		Wil-257
Benjamin	Bun- 80	Wilie	Ora-142	Jno Alexr		Tyr-209
Danl	Ran-175	Wm	Cah-191	John Jun		Cha-201
John	Cur- 84	Merry,W	Cam-162	John Jr		Row- 85
John	Cur- 84	Meshaw,Joel	Bla- 12	Ransom		Cha-190
John	Bun- 91	Sion	Bla- 12	Richard		Gat-110
Rebekkah	Mon- 49	Messer,Burwell	Ans- 17	Wm		Row- 53
Merrell,Jacob	Bun- 79	Coleman	Rob-241	Michenor,Thos		Bur-127
John	Bun- 84	Horis	Dup- 14	Michle,Nichl		Row- 40
William	Bun- 84	Jacob	Rob-220	Mickel,Nazreth		Rob-238
Merres,Alexander	Ran-174	Jeremiah	Ans- 20	Reuben		Cha-194
Merress,Peggy	Rth-122	Jno	Rob-242	William		Ire-264
Merret,William	Sam-152	Joshua	Rob-220	Mickle,Jerry		Bur-124
Merrett,Joel	Sto-151	Joshua	Dup- 29	Mickum,John		Sto-148
Joel	Sto-109	Maradeth	Rob-220	Micky,Julianna		Sto-131
John	Sto-156	Noah	Rob-220	Julianna		Sto-100
John Jnr	Sto-156	Noah	Jon-302	Lewis		Sto-131
John Jnr	Sto-114	Richard	Rob-242	Lewis		Sto-100
Thomas	Sto-157	William	Joh-276	Mictery,Joseph		Ran-175
William	Sto-156	William	Joh-282	Midcalf,Absalom		Bun- 86
Wm H	Ora-117	William Junr	Jon-301	James		Bun- 93
Merrick,John	Pas-195	William Senr	Jon-301	James Senr		Bun- 93
Merridy,James	Row- 45	Messick,George	Sur-196	Joseph		Bun- 92

Name	Ref	Name	Ref	Name	Ref
Middleton,David	Dup- 8	Mikel,H	Ash- 7	Miller,Adam	Row- 76
Isaac	Dup- 8	Milam,Adam	Wil-280	Alexander C	War-184
James	Wil-259	John	War-176	Andrew	Mec- 22
John	Rch-211	William	Wil-280	Andrew	Rth-118
Robert	Dup- 8	Milar,James	Sto-138	Andrew	Lnc-354
Thomas	Hay-197	Milborn,Arnold	Brt- 58	Andw	Cur- 88
Wm	Cho-224	Mrs. S	Brt- 48	Barbary	Row- 78
Midget,Joseph	Car-185	Milborne,Saml	Row- 46	Benjn	Brt- 44
Sally	Joh-273	Milbourn,John	Edg- 69	Betsey	Wil-281
Midgett,Banister	Hyd-229	Miler,Ezekiel	Sto-141	C	Ash- 10
Christ	Hyd-231	Miles,Aaron	Ran-174	C	Ash- 10
John	Tyr-209	Abner	Hal-112	Caleb	Cur- 88
Levi	Hyd-231	Benjn	Hal-112	Christian	Sur-166
Mary	Hyd-231	Drury	Ran-173	Chritian	Row- 67
Moriss	Tyr-208	Isaac	Bun- 75	D	Ash- 3
Robert	Hyd-229	Isham	Rth-122	D	Ash-10
Sparrow	Hyd-230	Jacob & Moth	Cas- 61	Daniel	Sur-169
Willm	Tyr-209	James	Cas- 62	Danl	Row- 78
Miell,Jacob	Bur-104	James	Cas- 61	David	Mec- 45
Peter	Bur-104	Jas	Ora-144	David	Bun- 82
Miers,Christian	Row- 79	John	Cas- 61	David	Row- 85
Danl	Row- 42	Jonathan	Cha-199	David	Lnc-335
David	Row- 42	Tho	Bft- 30	Mrs E	Cum-237
David	Row- 80	Thomas	Hal-112	Elisha	Brt- 51
Geo	Row- 42	Thomas	Pas-197	Enoch	Cur- 81
Geo	Row- 42	William	Nor- 73	Ephraim	Brt- 45
Geo	Row- 43	Milesady,John	Glf-180	Federick	Row- 39
Geo	Row- 42	Milhollan,James	Ire-241	Fergus	Ire-266
Henry	Row- 80	Milican,J	Col- 20	Francis	Cab-139
Jacob	Row- 42	S	Col- 20	Frederic	Wil-281
Jacob	Row- 42	Miligan,James	Rth-119	Frederick	Sto-112
Jacob	Row- 43	Thomas	Rth-118	Frederick	Sto-152
Jacob	Row- 41	Miliken,Jas	Ora-113	Frederick (son)	Sto-153
Jacob	Row- 79	Ro Sen	Ora-113	Frederick	Row- 83
John	Cho-224	Millakin,Hardy	Hal-113	Frederick Jnr	Sto-154
John	Row- 42	Millar,Charles	Sto-138	Frederick Ser	Sto-154
John	Row- 81	Henry	Roc- 10	Fredk	Bla- 4
John	Row- 84	James	Roc- 19	G	Ash- 8
Marmeduke	Ans- 13	John	Roc- 10	Geo	Cab-140
Marmeduke	Ans- 10	John	Roc- 33	Geo	Cab-145
Peter	Row- 42	Martin	Roc- 11	George	Row- 67
Peter	Row- 42	Thomas	Roc- 19	George	Bur-105
Philip	Row- 42	William	Roc- 19	George	Dup- 29
Thomas	Cho-224	Millard,Bethany	Sam-152	George	Row- 83
Thos	Ans- 4	Jacob	Dup- 13	George	Row- 89
Miezle,Aaron	Brt- 53	Jesse	Dup- 12	Godfrey	Sto- 98
Cader	Brt- 52	John	Sam-160	Godfrey	Sto-129
Hannah	Brt- 51	Stephen	Dup- 11	H	Ash- 3
Hezekiah	Brt- 52	Mille,William	Sur-177	Haman	Ran-174
Isaac	Brt- 44	Millen,Stephen	Sur-187	Haman	Ran-174
Jerry	Brt- 44	Millender,James	Wil-281	Harmon	Sto- 99
Josiah	Brt- 67	Samuel	Wil-281	Harmon	Sto-130
Thomas	Brt- 53	W B	Bru-228	Henry	Wil-266
Thomas	Brt- 53	William	Wil-278	Henry	Lnc-350
Timothy	Brt- 44	Milles,William	Cas- 63	Henry	Ire-246
William	Brt- 44	Miller,Widow	Lnc-331	Henry (L F)	Wil-277
Mige,Fred	Ora-167	Abigail	Mon- 21	Henry	Bur-104
Mihane,Micajah	Sto-144	Abraham	Mec- 38	Henry	Row- 67
Mikel,D	Ash- 4	Abraham	Row- 85	Henry	Cab-146

-218-

Miller,Isaac		Gat-113	Miller,Joshua		Jon-301	Miller,Wm	Ran-174
Isaac		Cur- 86	Lewis		Brt- 52	Wm	Len-310
J		Ash- 13	Malachi		Brt- 45	Wm	Mec- 39
J		Cam-161	Martin		Jon-302	Millers,Mrs	Mec- 26
J		Ash- 7	Mary		Per-221	Milles,William	Ons-106
J		Ash- 9	Mary		Rth-119	Milleton,J	Ora-156
J		Ash- 9	Mary		Row- 87	Millican,A	Bru-222
J		Ash- 9	Mary		Row- 81	B	Bru-224
Jacob		Sto-112	Mary		Edg- 72	Benjamin	Ran-175
Jacob		Bur-125	Mary		Ire-251	H	Bru-222
Jacob		Sur-166	Matthew		Mec- 41	J	Bru-224
Jacob		Ran-174	Michl		Row- 55	S	Bru-222
Jacob		Cab-140	Michl		Ran-174	Milligan,Alexr	Ire-247
Jacob		Sto-134	Nathl		Cho-225	David	Hay-197
Jacob		Sto-152	Nathl		Brt- 43	Fergus	Ire-248
Jacob	(H)	Sto-153	Nicholas		Lnc-370	Fergus	Ire-247
Jacob	(Gen)	Sto-152	Nicholas		Row- 41	Gilbert	Lnc-347
Jacob		Bun- 81	Peter		Mon- 40	James	Ire-246
Jacob		Row- 85	Peter		Row- 57	Milliken,Samuel	Ran-175
Jacob		Row- 78	Philip		Row- 67	Millikin,John	Nor- 73
James		Sto- 96	Philip		Sot-152	Ro Jnr	Ora-112
James		Cab-147	Phillip		Lnc-374	Samuel	Ran-175
James		Sto-150	Phillip		Len-311	Sterling	Nor- 73
James		Jon-302	Prisiller		Cur- 81	Millins,William	Bur-113
James		Sto-155	Rachel		Jon-302	Millis,Edw	Glf-156
James	Genl	Rth-118	Reuben		Brt- 43	James	Glf-179
James		Ora-177	Reubin		Gat-109	Nicholas	Glf-156
James		Ran-174	Richard		Ire-266	Thos	Glf-179
Jas		Mec- 38	Richard		Wsh-226	Milloby,Marvel	Rth-121
Jane		Ora-175	Richd		Ran-174	Millon,John	Lnc-335
Jesse		Wil-278	Robert		Rth-123	Mills,Ambrose	Rth-119
John		Sur-168	Robert		Dup- 7	Amos	Glf-165
John		Cho-223	Robert		Gat-109	Andrew	Ans- 27
John		Sto- 98	Robt J		Bur-112	Benjn	Bru-222
John		Row- 67	Saml		Lnc-329	Benona	Glf-164
John		Row- 67	Saml		Row- 73	Charles	Ire-239
John		Row- 59	Samuel		Row- 82	Charles	Ire-239
John		Per-221	Samuel Sr		Row- 72	Claban	Hal-112
John		Row- 55	Samith		Cho-226	Daniel	Ons-104
John		Row- 39	Sarah		Hay-198	Edward	Ire-257
John		Sto-128	Sarah		Brt- 52	Eliza	Dup- 31
John		Sto-153	Smith		Lnc-357	Ezekiel	Ran-175
John		Bun- 81	Solomon		Cur- 92	Fedk	Bft- 29
John		Bun- 83	Solomon		Row- 78	Frederick	Pit-237
John		Row- 77	Susanna		Row- 54	Frederick	Pit-237
John		Dup- 7	Susanna		Rth-118	George	Ons-105
John		Bur-115	Thaney		Cur- 80	Henry	Glf-174
John		Ran-175	Thos		Cur- 88	Henry	Roc- 28
John		Row- 83	Tobiah		Row- 77	Henry	Glf-167
John		Ire-238	Tobiah		Row- 63	Henry	Pit-236
John		Ire-246	Valintine		Row- 53	Henry	Pit-234
John		Lnc-347	William		Row- 69	Henry	Pit-242
John		Brt- 60	William		Row- 70	Henry	Pit-251
John Senr		Bun- 81	William		Row- 72	J	Col- 20
Jonathan		Brt- 52	William		Per-221	J	Col- 20
Jonathan		Sto-152	William	(W C)	Wil-273	J	Glf-178
Joseph		Sto-126	William		War-183	James	Mon- 26
Joseph		Sto-153	William		Gat-108	Jas	Glf-155
Joseph		Wil-277	William Jr		Wil-274	Jane	Bru-222

Mills, Jane	Edg- 52	Mimiler, William	Rth-123	Minter, John	Cha-189
Jeremiah	Glf-152	Mimms, John	Cas- 61	Joseph	Cha-192
Jesse	Rth-121	Joseph	Cha-195	Minton, Benjn	Brt- 54
John	Hal-112	Mary	Cas- 61	Cader	Brt- 62
John	War-174	Needham	Cha-195	James	Wil-282
John Esq	Rth-120	Yong	Cha-200	Jesse	Wil-283
John Jr	Rth-121	Mims, D	Col- 20	John	Wil-281
John Senr	Row- 61	Davin	Cha-204	John	Nsh- 78
Jonathan	Glf-165	J	Col- 20	John	Nsh- 75
Jonathan	Row- 83	Mary	Rch-208	Meredith	Wil-283
Jos	Glf-163	Wm	Cha-205	Sarah	Brt- 54
Joseph	Pit-251	Minatilor, Richd	Glf-159	Sarah	Brt- 55
Joshua	Ons- 99	Mince, William	Rth-122	Willis	Brt- 54
Kinchey	Mon- 25	Minehew, Bryan	Dup- 14	Mints, Henry	Bru-226
Lewis	Ons-108	Bond	Gat-106	J	Bru-230
Lewis	Ons-104	Miner, Enfancy	Cur- 89	J	Bru-224
M	Glf-176	Miney, Ducy	Per-131	T	Bru-230
Mary	Ans- 24	John	Per-131	Mirack, Francis	Mor- 56
Maryan	Jon-302	Thomas	Per-131	Mires, David	Mec- 43
Naman	Edg- 65	Ming, Frans	Cho-228	Jacob	Sto-135
Nancy	Roc- 17	James	Cho-225	Mirony, Wm	Bla- 3
Nasby	Pit-242	Jos	Ora-125	Mise, David	Rch-206
Samuel	Pit-243	Jos	Ora-128	Miseinhamer, Jacob	Cab-141
Sarah	Roc- 15	Mingels, Cunrod	Lnc-350	Jacob	Cab-142
Sarah	Pit-251	Henry	Lnc-350	Jacob	Cab-141
Stephen	Ons- 99	Mary	Lnc-347	John	Cab-141
Stephen	Dup- 19	Minges, George	Hay-197	John	Cab-142
Tarner	Cum-268	Jacob	Hay-197	John	Cab-141
Thomas	Pit-251	Mingleburgh, Jo	Row- 89	John	Cab-141
Waitman	Roc- 7	Mingo, free man of colour		John	Cab-145
William	Pit-258		Ran-187	Labian	Cab-147
William	Bun- 72	Mingo (free Negro)	Len-318	Peter	Cab-141
William	Pit-237	Mingy, Dudly	Grn-136	Misinhamer, Jacob	Cab-140
William	Wil-279	Mining, Frederic C	Sto-146	Misner, Jonn	Mon- 49
William Junr	Ons-101	Lewis	Sto-145	Misschen, Charles	Rth-121
William Senr	Ons- 99	Minkler, Conrad	Bur-103	Missemore, Francis	Ire-245
Wm Esq	Bru-222	Minn, Wmson	Grn-147	Missens, Nickles	Hrt-212
Willis	War-183	Minnes, Jno	Ora-122	Misser, Redd	Bru-228
Milly (sic)	Pas-195	Minnis, Jas	Ora-114	Mitchal, David	Mec- 51
Milner, Benjamin	Per-151	John	Ora-116	Wm W	Mec- 50
Mrs Jacobina	Fra- 83	Jno	Ora-134	Mitcham, Elizabeth	Glf-160
James	Per-151	Wm	Ora-153	Mary	Roc- 7
James	Per-143	Minnish, James	Sur-169	Mitchel, A	Ahs- 14
Milrama, Joseph	Sur-189	Thomas	Sur-168	Benj	Grn-144
Milsaps, Joseph	Ran-175	Minor, John	Grn-144	Benjn	Grn-124
Joseph	Ire-251	John Jr	Grn-145	Charles	Per-141
Joseph	Ire-251	Randal	Grn-144	David	Cab-142
Thomas	Ire-254	Samuel	Ire-241	Drury	Wil-267
William	Ire-252	Mins, David	Per-221	Eby	Mec- 39
Milson, Robert	Wil-285	Minsey, Jacob	Ans- 13	Elijah	Grn-135
Milsted, William	Sur-174	Minshaw, Bryan	Way-234	Gideon	Grn-137
Milton, James	Bun- 74	Jesse	Way-242	Hannah	Mec- 38
Jesse	Sto-132	Nathan	Way-234	Henry	Nsh- 74
John	Mon- 24	Patsey	War-178	Henry	Rth-122
Joseph	Mon- 24	James	Way-242	Howel	Cha-191
Mills	Hrt-216	John	Way-242	I	Ash- 13
Polley	Cas- 62	Minster, Frederick	Cab-147	Jacob	Lnc-347
Robert	Mon- 45	Michal	Cab-142	James	Rth-117
Stephen	Grn-133	Minter, Abner	Cha-210	James	Pas-195

-220-

Name	Loc	Name	Loc	Name	Loc	Name	Loc
Mitchel,James	Ire-251	Mitchell,Hardy	Cum-236	Mitchl,J	Cam-156		
Jas	Mec- 36	Henry col	Fra-101	Mitchum,Henry	Ans- 6		
Jesse	Cho-230	Isaac	Bft- 25	Mittere,James	Gat-111		
Joel	Hal-113	Isham	Roc- 18	Mittz,Fredk	Len-317		
Jno	Mec- 37	Isham	Ans- 7	Mixner,William	Cur- 89		
Jno Jr	Cho-231	J	Glf-164	Mixom,Jermh	Cho-224		
John	Rth-121	Jacob	Ans- 13	Mixon,Elijah	Bft- 19		
John	Cho-230	Jacob	Edg- 41	Geo	Bft- 19		
John	Cas- 62	James	Mar- 8	Jas	Bft- 34		
John	Cab-142	James	Brt- 65	Lucrea	Bft- 19		
John	Cha-202	James	Nor- 73	Mary	Bft- 19		
John	Grn-137	James Jnr	Brt- 63	Michl	Bft- 34		
John	Pas-197	Jesse	Glf-188	Zed	Bft- 34		
Jonathan	Wil-267	Jno	Ora-122	Mize,Fred	Ora-149		
Joseph	Rth-118	John	Glf-187	Jeremiah	Roc- 11		
Joshua (J L)	Wil-278	John	Cas- 62	John	Wil-264		
Joshua Jr	Wil-273	John	Sto-112	Randol	Row- 55		
Joshua Senr	Wil-274	John	Hrt-212	Wm	Ora-126		
Joyey	Hal-114	John	Sto-145	Mizell,Charles	Mar- 6		
Mary	Wil-265	John	Fra- 83	Chloe	Mar- 13		
Mathias	Cab-143	John	Bur-117	Dianah	Mar- 11		
Michael	Grn-129	John	Way-249	Durant	Mar- 7		
Misniah	Grn-136	John	Brt- 61	Edward	Mar- 13		
Moses	Ire-254	Jonas	Brt- 61	Hardy	Mar- 10		
Nancy	Mec- 38	Joseph	Ons- 96	Luke	Mar- 9		
Patsey	Rth-121	Mary	Way-251	Mark	Mar- 9		
Pleasant	Grn-137	Mrs Mourning	Fra- 87	Mourning	Mar- 11		
R	Ash- 13	N	Ora-155	William	Mar- 6		
Rachel	Pas-197	Nancy	Roc- 18	Mobley,Allin	Sam-152		
Robert	Ora-163	Nicolas	Ons-103	Ben	Fra-100		
Robert	Cum-237	Penry	Ora-122	James	Cha-214		
Sally	Ire-268	Peter	War-184	John	Mar- 14		
Thomas	Pit-241	Polly col	Fra-101	Mary	Dup- 36		
Thomas	Wil-273	Prissy col	Fra-100	Terril	Sam-155		
Thomas	Grn-134	Rachael	Brt- 53	Wallace	Sam-156		
Tom	Pas-197	Reuben	Way-253	Wiley	Sam-157		
Wheler	Wil-276	Robert	Lnc-350	William	Roc- 10		
William	Ire-251	S	Cam-156	William	Mar- 9		
William	Ire-254	Saml	Glf-182	Mobly,Fredrick	Pit-241		
William Jr	Wil-285	Saml	Brt- 64	Mock,Jacob	Row- 50		
Wm	Grn-124	Samuel H	Ons- 97	Jacob	Row- 47		
Zack	Grn-132	Segar	Hrt-215	Michal	Row- 70		
Mitchell,Abby col	Fra-100	Shad	Ora-123	Peter	Ire-246		
Adam	Glf-152	Stephen	Edg- 67	Philip	Row- 46		
Cader	Brt- 66	Thomas	Edg- 54	Philip	Row- 46		
Cealy	Grn-124	Thos	Cur- 89	Stephen	Tyr-207		
Charles	Cas- 61	Thos	Brt- 66	Thos	Cab-139		
Daniel	Ons-105	William	Ons- 95	Mocy,Robert	Nsh- 89		
David	Cas- 62	William	Roc- 24	Mode,Jacob D	Cho-221		
Dred	Dup- 5	William	Pit-249	Modgling,Henry	Cha-203		
Elizabeth	Nor- 73	Wiliam	Per-151	Modlen,Joseph	Ran-187		
Esther col	Fra-100	William	Way-253	Modlin,Charles	Mar- 14		
F	Cam-154	William Senr	Wil-276	Dempsey	Brt- 61		
Geo	Ora-117	Wm	Grn-129	William	Sur-194		
Geo	Ora-158	Wm	Brt- 63	Mody,Philip	Nsh- 76		
George	Ons-102	Zadock	Brt- 63	Moffet,John	Ran-173		
George	Way-242	Mitchem,Nathl	Lnc-328	Moffit,Aaron	Ran-174		
George W	Ons- 97	Mitchen,Quaintain	Cha-215	Adam	Ran-174		
H	Cam-155	Mitchener,Saml	Joh-282	Charles	Ran-175		

Name	Loc	Name	Loc	Name	Loc
Moffit, Charles	Ran-175	Monroe, Alexr	Rob-244	Moody, Isaac	Rth-117
David	Rth-119	Angus	Rob-230	Isaac	Hay-197
David	Ran-175	John	Row- 50	Jesse	Bur-105
Hugh	Ran-175	Mal	Rob-223	John	Fra- 89
Mary	Ran-175	Peter	Rob-229	John	Sur-173
Robert	Ran-175	Montague, Henry	Rth-119	John	Lnc-365
Saml	Ran-174	Latinue	Grn-120	John	Hay-197
Moffitt, John	Bur-119	Young	Grn-144	John	Ire-269
Mofit, Robert	Row- 43	Monteith, Alexr	Mec- 51	John	Roc- 21
Mohaughn, Jesse	Cha-201	Natl	Cab-137	Joseph Senr	Bun- 94
Mohorn, Ed	Cha-201	Samuel	Bur-129	Mary	Bur-122
Rebekah	Hal-113	Wm	Mec- 46	Micajah	Bur-108
Mohun, Jesse	Brt- 43	Montfot, Ann	Ons- 97	Moses	Bun- 94
Joel	Brt- 47	Edward	Ons- 96	Nancy	Ire-269
Moirisson, John	Ire-244	Martha	Hal-113	Rebecca	Nor- 73
Moiser, Adam	Cha-208	Sally	Hal-113	Reuben	Hay-197
Moldin, Thomas	Rth-117	William	Ons- 96	Surrill	Nor- 72
Moll, Barbara	Bur-126	Wm A	Hal-112	Thomas	War-181
Molleston, John	Ons-103	Montgomery, Alexr	Cas- 63	Thomas	Cum-237
Old Molley	Bft- 38	David	Bur-112	Thomas	Ire-269
Mollison, Ebenezer	Car-180	Hugh	Ora-167	Thos	Glf-160
Molloy, Duncan	Rob-223	James Sr	Cas- 62	William	Dup- 28
Jno	Rob-225	Jas	Mec- 40	William	Nor- 73
Jno	Rob-224	Jas	Mec- 45	William	Cum-248
Molone, Thos	Hrt-214	Jno	Mec- 48	Wm	Ran-174
Moloy, Charles	Cum-244	Jno	Mec- 23	Mooer, William	Bun- 89
Duncan	Cum-266	Jno	Mec- 25	Mool, Abram	Lnc-374
Molsby, James	Bla- 5	Jo	Cas- 63	Daniel	Lnc-374
Thos	Bla- 9	John	Bun- 97	Henry	Lnc-374
Molton, Abraham	Cum-247	John	Wil-285	John	Lnc-374
Wm	Ans- 19	John	Row- 46	John Jr	Lnc-374
Moly, John	Lnc-332	John	Hay-197	John Senr	Lnc-373
Momfred, Bryan	Jon-302	John	Cha-189	Peter	Lnc-374
Edward	Jon-301	John	Bur-111	Moon, Andrew	Bur-131
Monday, Christopher	Wil-270	John	Ire-263	Jacob	Cha-195
Elisha	Ran-173	Mary	Hrt-213	James	Cha-195
Hal	Per-131	Michael	Cas- 61	James Senr	Sam-154
Robert	Edg- 49	Robert	Cum-246	John	Brt- 59
William	Ire-264	Robt	Mec- 46	John	Cha-212
Monden, Jesse	Glf-167	Robt	Mec- 44	Lawrence	Ran-174
Peter	Edg- 48	Robt	Mec- 40	Leo	Cha-209
Mondine, James	Jon-302	Robt	Glf-169	Richd	Glf-182
Money, Isaac	Sur-183	Saml	Mec- 49	Simon	Cha-209
J	Col- 18	William	War-182	Simon	Glf-182
J	Col- 21	William	Bun- 97	Thomas	Cha-212
Jacob	Sur-194	Wm	Glf-169	Wm	Ran-174
James	Sur-166	Wm	Glf-175	Wm	Cha-209
Jesse	Glf-164	Wm	Ora-142	Mooneham, David	Edg- 43
John	Sur-178	Montieth, Widow	Mec- 53	Mooney, Adam	Rth-120
Morgan	Sur-169	Montigue, C	Cam-160	Barbary	Bla- 3
Wm	Sur-166	Moode, Nancy	Rth-122	Christer	Rth-123
Mongomery, J	Glf-173	Moody, Benj	Cha-207	Dafiel	Rth-119
Hugh	Ora-169	Benjamin	Wil-272	David	Rth-118
Monk, Daniel	Sam-152	Benjn	Hal-113	David	Rth-123
Daniel	Cum-250	David	Joh-274	Jacob	Rth-119
Jacob	Dup- 23	David	Joh-279	James	Rth-122
James	Mor- 58	E	Ash- 12	M	Col- 20
Thomas	Mar- 7	Epps Esq	Fra- 93	Peter	Rth-118
Monnan, Sarah	Bft- 27	George	Bur-104	W	Col- 19

-222-

Name	Code	Name	Code	Name	Code	Name	Code
Mooney,William	Roc- 28	Moore,Audlin		Row- 78	Moore,Frederic		Lnc-370
William	Wil-274	Azariah		Len-321	Gedeon		Mor- 59
Mooningham,Shadrach	Sur-172	Azh		Ora-127	George		Ora-166
Moor,Widow	Bun- 86	Barnet		Roc- 33	George		Edg- 45
Aaron	Sto-114	Ben		Bur-116	George		Rob-218
Abraham	Bun- 86	Benjamin		Edg- 51	George		Hal-112
Barbara	Bun- 86	Benjamin		Cum-260	George		Mor- 58
David	Sto- 93	Benjamin		Roc- 26	George		Row- 62
David	Mec- 45	Benjamin		Pit-262	George Esq		Rth-122
Edward	Bun- 76	Benjamin		Pit-235	George L		Grn-137
Elizabeth	Mar- 4	Briton		Cas- 62	Gideon		Hyd-227
Isaac	Bun- 97	Bryan		Len-315	Giles		Bft- 33
James	Mar- 6	Burwell		Fra- 98	Goodrich		Ire-261
James	Mar- 7	Callum		Fra- 98	Hardy		Cum-260
James	Mar- 6	Cam		Glf-165	Henry		Rch-199
Jesse	Mar- 7	Cason		Pit-262	Henry		Roc- 19
John	Mar- 14	Cason		Pit-233	Henry		Pit-235
John	Bun- 98	Catharine		Ans- 27	Henry		Pit-243
John	Per-221	Charles		Wsh-226	Henry		Hyd-222
Morriss	Mar- 7	Charles		Ire-262	Higdon		War-172
Moses	Mar- 8	Charles		Rob-218	Isaac		Roc- 18
Nathaniel	Mar- 6	Charles		Roc- 20	Isaac		Brt- 49
Rustun	Sto- 94	Charles		Roc- 25	J		Bru-224
Samuel	Mar- 9	Charles		Mec- 37	Jacob		Pit-259
Thomas	Bun- 75	Charles		Prq-221	Jacob		Pit-242
Thomas Sr	Cha-216	Charles		Glf-165	James		Ora-162
William	Bun- 79	Clary		Ora-147	James		Ora-165
William	Bun- 77	Cornelius		Prq-221	James		Sur-170
William	Sto-155	Cornelius		Nor- 72	James		Bla- 3
William Junr	Bun- 75	Cullen		Len-322	James		Ire-244
Moore,----	Ora-171	Dan		Mec- 54	James		Bur-121
-----	Sto- 93	Daniel		Sur-195	James		Ans- 7
Mrs	Mec- 28	Danl		Bur-128	James		Sto-142
A	Ora-154	David		Mec- 29	James		Sto-156
Aaron	Sto-155	David		Sto-121	James		Len-315
Aaron	Cum-259	Dempsy		Pit-240	James		Rth-120
Aaron	Hrt-214	Edmond		Pit-262	James		Hal-113
Abel	Pit-239	Edmond		Pit-235	James		Roc- 20
Abel Senr	Cum-259	Edward		Sur-162	James		Pit-262
Abraham	Pit-258	Edward		War-170	James		Sto-107
Abraham	Cha-215	Edward		Pit-235	James		Hrt-215
Adam	Bur-130	Edward		Mor- 66	James Esq		Hrt-206
Alexander	Lnc-365	Eleazr		Bft- 22	James G		Cha-192
Alexander	Bur-106	Eli		Row- 48	James Sen		Ora-171
Alexr	Cum-269	Eli		Pit-259	Jas		Bft- 22
Alexr	Sto-155	Elijah		War-171	Jas		Sam-162
Alexr	Cha-210	Elijah		Edg- 45	Jas.		Mec- 43
Alexr	Sto-114	Elijah		Ons- 95	Jas.		Hrt-210
Alfred	Bru-226	Elijah		Bur-128	Jas		Mec- 39
Allen	Pit-240	Elisha		Pit-255	Jas Esq		Ora-118
Allen	Hrt-207	Elizabeth		Nor- 72	Jas Jr		Sam-157
Alped	Lnc-340	Elizabeth		Prq-221	Jane		Hyd-222
Amos	Edg- 59	Enoch		Edg- 59	Jeremiah		Brt- 53
Andrew	Mec- 48	Evitchell		War-170	Jesse		Sto- 94
Ann	Mon- 32	Ezekiel		Rth-120	Jesse		Hal-113
Anny	Lnc-358	Fainsess K		Hyd-232	Jesse		Bur-128
Arthur	Bla- 3	Fannon		Mor- 62	Jesse ·		Sto-122
Arthur	Lnc-350	Francis		Rth-117	Jesse		Glf-163
Ashly	Pit-232	Fred		Bur-130	Jesse Senr		Bur-128

-223-

Moore,Jessee	Nor- 72	Moore,Lewis	Sam-163	Moore,Sally	Brt- 65		
Joel	Bft- 32	Lucy	Bft- 30	Saml	Len-320		
Joel	Sur-178	M Esqr	Bru-238	Saml	Bft- 32		
Jno	Ora-157	Major	Grp-149	Samuel	Edg- 43		
John	Rth-122	Margarett	Mec- 47	Samuel	Rth-119		
John	Sur-187	Margt	Bft- 30	Samuel	Cas- 61		
John	Grn-123	Mark	Rth-121	Samuel	Roc- 28		
John	Nor- 72	Mark	Mon- 23	Samuel	Prq-221		
John	Hyd-222	Mary	Ora-120	Sarah	Mon- 26		
John	Len-315	Mary	Ire-249	Sarah	Rth-122		
John	Grn-139	Mary	Car-179	Sarah	Nor- 73		
John	Rth-119	Mary	Rob-218	Seth	Cha-200		
John	Rth-118	Mary	Rob-233	Sol	Ora-114		
John	Hal-113	Mary	Hal-113	Spencer	Pit-235		
John	Cum-260	Mary	Row- 62	Susan	Bft- 30		
John	Lnc-370	Mathias	Pit-240	Susanna	Pit-234		
John	Lnc-372	Matthew	Cum-260	Theophilus	Edg- 42		
John	Roc- 19	Maurice	Bla- 3	Tho	Len-322		
John	Roc- 21	Micajah	Mec- 35	Tho	Ora-120		
John	Roc- 25	Milly	Pit-240	Thomas	Cum-239		
John	Mor- 58	Moab	Pit-237	Thomas	Ire-262		
John	Pit-241	Molley	Bft- 30	Thomas	Ire-262		
John	Pit-243	Morris	Hrt-206	Thomas	War-181		
John	Pit-239	Moses	Ans- 8	Thomas	Edg- 52		
John	Len-323	Moses	Pit-261	Thomas	Sto-142		
John	Bft- 31	Moses	Brt- 56	Thomas	Roc- 12		
John	Hrt-207	Moses	Lnc-340	Thomas	Roc- 20		
John	Glf-166	Nancy	Bur-110	Thomas	Bun- 95		
John	Glf-159	Nathan	Prq-221	Thomas	Sto-107		
John C	Cum-261	Nathaniel	Way-245	Thomas	Mon- 32		
John R	Nor- 73	Needham	Cum-260	Thomas	Hyd-222		
John Jr	Rth-117	Capt O	Ora-171	Thos	Mon- 24		
John Sr	Rth-117	Partins	Per-141	Thos	Prq-222		
John Sr	Rth-122	Patsay	Hrt-213	Thos	Glf-169		
John Sr	Rth-120	Patty	Dup- 6	Thos	Per-141		
Jonathan	Rth-117	Penny	Brt- 48	Thos C	Glf-165		
Jones	Grn-137	Phillip	Rth-119	Thos Jr	Cha-193		
Jordan	Cum-260	Presly	Cha-201	Titus	Brt- 66		
Jordan Senr	Cum-260	R	Mon- 37	Toney	Bft- 31		
Jorden	Rob-242	Rachel	Rth-122	Vol	Mon- 22		
Jos	Brt- 60	Rachel	Rth-121	Walker	Len-323		
Joseph	Rth-123	Reading	Pit-261	William	Sur-179		
Joseph	Ora-171	Reading	Pit-235	William	Ons-102		
Joseph	Rch-197	Reuben	Hal-112	William	Per-141		
Joseph	Rob-236	Reuben	Roc- 27	William	Ire-262		
Joseph	Row- 75	Reuben	Sto-123	William	Sto- 95		
Joseph	Row- 75	Richard	Rth-121	William	Len-315		
Joseph	Prq-221	Richard	Pit-240	William	Rth-120		
Capt Joseph	Sam-162	Richd	Len-311	William	Cas- 61		
Joshua	Ire-262	Ro	Ora-113	William	Pit-257		
Joshua	Prq-221	Robert	Ran-174	William	Pit-260		
Josiah	Prq-221	Robert	Per-141	William	Lnc-336		
Kenneday	Pit-241	Robert	War-179	William	Sto-123		
Kiddy	Brt- 54	Robert	War-180	William	Row- 62		
Lambt S	Per-141	Robt	Mor- 62	William	Lnc-333		
Lamuel	Pit-259	Rodham	Sur-161	William Doctr	Row- 89		
Lawrence	Ans- 4	Mrs S	Brt- 47	William E	Nor- 72		
Lemuel	Rth-120	Salley	Bft- 33	William Esq	Hrt-206		
Leuticca	Sto-158	Sally	Ire-261	William Esq	Fra- 77		

Moore,Wm		Ora-112	More,James		Hay-198	Morgan,Enoch	Glf-181
Wm		Ans- 25	James		Per-131	Enoch	Cab-144
Wm		Rob-222	James		Per-127	Ezekiel	Ran-175
Wm		Rob-233	John		Ire-260	Ezekiel	Ran-173
Wm		Rob-234	John		Ire-244	Fredk	Sam-156
Wm		Rob-223	John D		Per-151	H	Glf-174
Wm		Mec- 52	Lewis		Per-131	Hardy	Mon- 21
Wm		Mon- 21	Marget		Jon-301	Hardy	Hrt-209
Wm		Mec- 34	Pegey		Cur- 93	Henry	Cum-262
Wm		Bft- 32	Philips		Per-131	Henry	Brt- 45
Wm		Glf-166	Capt Robert		Per-151	Hugh	Prq-222
Wm	(little)	Bft- 30	Simmeon		Jon-302	Isaac	Pas-195
Willis		Cum-259	Tarlton		Per-131	Isaac	Bur-110
Willoby		Bft- 31	William		Brt- 66	Isham	Len-314
Woody		Pit-259	Wm		Nsh- 86	J	Row- 87
Zachariah		Sto-142	Wm Plath		Per-131	J	Glf-175
Moorehead,James		Rch-199	Morefeal,W		Ash- 12	J	Cam-157
Mooreman,Archibald		Rch-206	Morefield,Mary		Sur-178	J	Mon- 35
Benjamin		Rch-207	Morehead,Ann		Cas- 62	James	Sur-170
Benjn		Ans- 29	John		Roc- 12	James	Row- 65
Jennette		Rch-207	Moreland,Betsey		Lnc-327	James	Row- 87
Mary		Rch-211	James		Sur-190	James	Edg- 58
Susanah		Rch-207	John		Bun- 75	James	Row- 77
Tarlton		Rch-207	Joseph		Sur-183	James	Rth-120
Wm		Ans- 29	Lewis		Ora-164	James	Mor- 69
Moorhead,James		Rth-120	William		Sur-184	James	Hrt-212
Mooring,Christian		Nor- 72	William		Lnc-354	James	Cab-148
John		Cha-211	Moreman,Gabl		Row- 62	James Sr	Sur-188
John		Edg- 53	Morey,James		Lnc-376	Jane	Edg- 41
John		Pit-249	Jeremiah		War-176	Jesse	Ran-175
Thomas		Way-241	John		War-176	Jesse	Len-314
William		Pit-234	Morfit,George		Row- 87	Jesse	Joh-276
Moorman,Rachel		Wil-265	Jacob		Ran-174	Joel	Nor- 72
Moors,Sarah		Cas- 62	Lewis		Row- 87	Jno	Ora-146
Mooten,David		Rch-200	Morgain,James		Gat-110	John	Rth-121
James		Rch-199	Joseph		Gat-112	John	Sur-190
Mophett,James		Cha-196	Morgan,A		Cam-157	John	Nor- 73
Mophis,John		Cha-211	Abraham		Gat-116	John	Edg- 65
Moran,Henry		Hal-112	Amos		Cum-257	John	Cum-262
Martha		Hal-113	Aron		Dup- 7	John	Rth-118
Morass,John		Hal-114	Austin		Roc- 12	John	Hrt-210
Mordah,James		Ire-259	Becky		Jon-302	John	Brt- 49
James		Ire-259	Ben		Pas-196	John	Glf-157
Jane		Ire-259	Ben		Pas-197	Jonah	Hal-113
John		Ire-259	Benjamin		Sto-139	Jonathan	Mon- 47
Joseph		Ire-255	Benjamin		Sto-145	Jordan W	Hrt-206
Robert		Ire-246	Benjamin		Sto-104	Joseph	Mor- 69
William		Ire-255	Betsy		Pas-195	Joseph	Mon- 21
Mordecai,Jacob		War-184	Cador		Pas-195	Joshua	Wil-284
Mordicai,Isaac		Nsh- 73	Charity		Gat-110	Josiah	Fra- 99
More,Abraham		Per-131	Charles		Pas-196	Josiah	Fra- 92
Adam		Ire-256	Charles		Mon- 21	M	Cam-157
Andrew		Ire-244	Claudeus		Pas-195	Mark	Mon- 47
Charles R		Jon-301	Daniel		Wil-258	Mary	Pas-197
Grizay		Per-131	Daniel		Cas- 63	Mary	Car-171
Isaac		Pas-197	David		Ran-175	Matth	Hal-113
Isaac		Pas-196	Dennis		Edg- 71	Matthew	Cum-262
J		Ash- 7	Edward		Sam-156	Milly	Nor- 72
James		Ire-241	Elija		Row- 82	Nathan	Row- 66

Name	Ref	Name	Ref	Name	Ref
Morgan,Nathan	Row- 78	Moris,John	Mor- 61	Morris,George	Hay-198
Nathan	Row- 82	John	Glf-164	George	Rth-118
Nathan	Mor- 69	Rachel	Cur- 86	George	Pas-196
Patience col	Fra-101	Morisey,Willm Esq	Sam-159	Halen	Rth-122
Patsey	Cas- 61	Morison,Widow	Mec- 29	Hanah	Hyd-232
Perments	Rth-120	Alexr	Mor- 56	Henry	Nor- 73
Peter	Edg- 71	Archd	Rob-228	Henry	Grn-144
Pheribee	Cha-205	Danl	Rob-228	Henry	Grn-146
Polly	Mor- 59	Heriman	Sur-167	Henry	Rth-120
Prudence	Nor- 73	James	Sur-167	Henry	Mor- 61
Reuben	Dup- 19	Jas	Mec- 23	Hugh	Ora-149
Reuben	Ire-267	Jno	Rob-228	Isaac	Ran-174
Richard	Rch-200	Jno	Rob-232	Isaac	Row- 80
Robert	Row- 68	Jno	Mec- 23	Isaac	Row- 42
Robert	Hay-197	Jno	Mec- 38	J	Ora-153
Robt	Pas-197	John	Rth-117	J	Ash- 9
Rudd	Bun- 83	Malcolm	Mor- 61	J	Mon- 37
Sally	Mon- 31	Margrat	Row- 74	Jacob	Pas-197
Sarah	Cho-221	Maurice	Mor- 58	Jacob	Mor- 61
Seth	Pas-196	Nathaniel	Sur-194	James(son Chrst)	Pas-197
Seth	Gat-114	Norman	Mor- 60	James	Dup- 24
Sol	Ora-146	Norman	Rob-231	James	Rth-119
Stephen	Bun- 84	Robt	Mec- 38	Jas	Mec- 41
Thomas	Ora-138	Thos	Mec- 38	Jehosapl	Pas-197
Thomas	Wil-281	Moriss,Asa	Ons- 99	Jeremiah	Way-242
Thos	Glf-164	Mork,Strawhorn	Mar- 16	Jessee	Nsh- 73
W	Ora-138	Morley,Henry	Wil-278	Job	Pas-197
W	Bru-240	Sibbella	Bla- 3	Jno	Mec- 38
Wil	Mon- 35	Morman,Frederic	Mon- 47	John	Ora-160
William	Nor- 73	Morn,Hardy	Rob-239	John	Pas-196
William	Edg- 58	John	Row- 42	John	Pas-197
William	Cas- 61	Mornal,Robt	Per-131	John	Ran-173
William	Hay-197	Morning,Bennet	Row- 47	John	Jon-301
William	Rch-200	Moromey,Marthey	Gat-109	John	Way-245
William	Joh-277	Morphis,John	Cha-206	John	Bur-117
William	Bun- 97	Morris,Aaron	Pas-197	John	Hal-113
William Jr	Cas- 61	Aaron Jun	Pas-197	John	Hay-197
Wm	Rob-234	Alsey	Nsh- 74	John Jr	Nor- 72
Wm	Ans- 11	Aron	Row- 45	John Sr	Grn-144
Wm P	Hrt-209	Arthur	Pas-196	John Senr	Nor- 72
Willis	Hal-112	Benjn	Pas-196	Jonathan	Tyr-207
Willis	Roc- 12	Benjamin	Ran-173	Josa	Pas-196
Willis	Hrt-211	Celiah	Way-243	Joseph	Pas-197
Zacha	Mon- 21	Charles	Dup- 10	Joseph	Ran-175
Morgen,Caty	Ire-254	Chrissy	Pas-197	Joseph	Row- 45
Morgin,Allin	Per-131	Christo	Pas-196	Joshua(son Nath)	Pas-196
Fieldes	Cur- 81	Demsey	Prq-221	Joshua(ox merd)	Pas-196
John	Nsh- 92	Densey	Nsh- 73	Lennard	Per-131
John Jr	Nsh- 86	Edmund	Rth-121	Lorance	Sur-172
Joseph	Cur- 81	Edward	War-170	Lurenar	Pas-197
Wm	Nsh- 92	Eli	Pas-197	Major	Mec- 32
Morgon,John	Ire-251	Elias	Mon- 22	Mark	Pas-196
Morice,Mary	Mor- 68	Elijah Esq	Rch-206	Mary	Ran-174
Peter	Mor- 66	Elizabeth	Mec- 41	Mary	War-177
Stephen	Mor- 66	Emanuel	Pas-196	Matthew	Cum-254
Moridy,David	Glf-165	Fedrick	Mor- 61	Micajah	Rth-118
Morine,Archibald	Car-181	Fr	Ora-136	Morda Jun	Pas-196
John	Car-181	G	Cam-159	Mordeca Sen	Pas-196
William	Car-181	George	Rth-119	Nancy	Cab-144

Morris,Nathan	Pas-197	Morrison,John	Rch-192	Morriss,Silvia	Ons-102
Nathan	Pas-196	John	Rch-196	Thomas	Ons-106
Nathan	Pas-195	John	Rch-212	Thomas	Edg- 66
Nathl	Fra- 94	John	Cum-267	Thomas	Cas- 62
Philemon	Mec- 41	John	Ire-247	William	Edg- 66
Presley	Sot-126	John	Rch-201	William	Bun- 90
Pritchard	Pas-197	John	Cum-255	Wm	Glf-168
R	Mon- 37	John	Cab-143	Wm	Brt- 62
Reuben	Ran-175	John Senr	Rch-193	Willoby	Hal-113
Richard	Nor- 72	Keneth	Rch-213	Zadock	Brt- 52
Richd	Ora-114	Malcom	Rch-193	Morrisson,Alexr	Lnc-331
Seaton	Mec- 32	Mark	Glf-168	Andrew	Ire-259
Shadrak	Sto-142	Murdoch	Rch-213	George	Ire-256
Shadrach	Sto-107	Norman	Cum-255	George	Ire-259
Solomon	Hay-197	Norman	Rch-192	Henry	Ire-246
Solomon	Mec- 32	Norman	Rch-196	James	Ire-244
Stephen	Grn-144	Norman	Rch-196	James	Ire-259
Tery	Grn-139	Norman	Rch-212	James	Ire-245
Tho	Pas-196	Robt	Cab-143	John	Ire-259
Tho	Bft- 30	Roderick Senr	Cum-253	Thomas	Ire-259
Thomas	Ran-174	Rory	Cum-245	Morrow,Alexander	Ran-174
Thomas	Jon-301	Saml	Cab-143	Allin	Row- 74
Thomas	Rth-119	Shaw	Rch-192	Arthur	Roc- 6
Thos	Grn-138	Thomas	Ire-247	Daniel	Grn-120
Thos	Mon- 28	William	Rch-192	David	Bun- 80
Tony	Pas-197	William	Rch-196	David	Mec- 50
Will(Ivy Thicket)	Pas-195	William	Ire-248	David	Mec- 23
William	Rth-121	William	Ire-248	George	Row- 77
William	Hyd-224	William	Ire-247	George	Mec- 52
William	Bur-117	William	Ire-264	J of Jas	Ora-160
William	Ans- 20	William	Lnc-335	J of Walton	Ora-160
William	Jon-301	Wm	Cab-143	James	Rth-123
William	Hrt-208	Wm	Ora-129	James	Bun- 87
Wm	Ora-163	Morriss,Aquila	Hal-112	James	Ora-114
Wm	Nsh- 92	Archl	Brt- 44	James	Hay-198
Wm	Ora-122	Dunstan	Hal-112	James	Row- 74
Wm	Grn-144	Elijah	Brt- 52	James Jr	Rth-118
Wm	Rob-239	Emanuel	Ons- 98	James Junr	Hay-198
Wm	Mec- 41	Facthy	Hal-113	Jno Jnr	Ora-122
Wm	Bft- 30	George	Hal-112	Jno W	Mec- 52
Morrisett,C	Cam-157	George Junr	Hal-112	John	Ora-170
Peter	Cam-160	Henry	Hal-112	John	Row- 64
W	Cam-157	Hillery	Hrt-213	John	Bun- 74
Morrison,Abner	Lnc-331	Isham	Hal-112	Martha	Mec- 52
Alexr	Cum-254	J H	Bla- 8	Patrick	Rth-120
Andrew	Ire-247	James	Hal-113	Robert	Bun- 83
Andrew	Row- 74	James	Hal-114	Robt	Ora-115
Andrew S	Rth-122	James C	Hal-113	Thos	Lnc-341
Carson R	Cab-144	John	Ons-103	William	Bur-109
Daniel	Lnc-372	John	Edg- 66	Wm	Per-131
Duncan	Rch-191	John	Hrt-216	Wm B C	Ora-134
Francis	Ire-268	Joseph	Brt- 52	Morse,Abigail	Car-169
Hugh	Ire-248	Joseph	Hal-112	Arter	Cur- 92
Hugh	Cum-244	Matthew	Brt- 52	Blandina	Car-178
James	Rth-121	Mosses	Brt- 62	Cranes	Cur- 90
James	Cab-143	Nancy	Cas- 62	Daniel	Car-178
James	Cab-144	Philip Junr	Hal-112	Danl	Bla- 11
Jas	Mec- 49	Philip Senr	Hal-113	Francis	Ons- 99
John	Cum-242	Rhoda	Brt- 62	George	Car-170

Morse,Helesy	Cur- 89	Mosely,Albert	Ran-174	Moss,Wm	Mon- 44		
Isaac	Ons-106	Benjamin	Cum-246	Mosse,Hezekiah	Cha-202		
Jacob	Car-178	Cuthbert	Nor- 73	Mosses,William	Ire-262		
James	Car-178	Lydia	Nor- 73	Most,A	Ash- 7		
John	Ons-106	Martha	War-178	J	Ash- 6		
John	Car-169	Matthew	Len-317	J	Ash- 12		
John	Cur- 92	Zeph	Ire-251	Mosteller,David	Lnc-344		
John Junr	Ons-105	Moser,Francis	Lnc-350	George	Lnc-374		
Jos	Lnc-336	Henry	Lnc-350	John	Lnc-344		
Joseph	Ons-106	Henry	Sto-130	Jonas Jr	Lnc-344		
Joshua	Car-178	Henry	Sto- 99	Michael	Lnc-328		
Josiah	Car-178	Henry	Sto-108	Peter	Lnc-344		
Peter	Cur- 90	Jacob	Lnc-350	Peter	Lnc-344		
Theodore	Car-178	Michael	Lnc-350	Motley,Tabitha	Hal-114		
William	Ons-106	Peter	Sto-130	Thomas	Hal-113		
Willowby	Cur- 92	Peter	Sto- 99	Thos	Mon- 49		
Zack	Cur- 89	Peter Jur	Sto-130	Wm	Mon- 47		
Mortimore,D	Glf-159	Moses (sic)	Pas-196	Motsinger,Alex	Row- 48		
Robt	Glf-160	Moses,free man of colour		Danl	Row- 50		
Morton,Alex	Mon- 23		Ran-187	J	Ash- 10		
Anderson	Cas- 62	Moses & Simon & C	Mec- 22	Jacob	Row- 46		
Ann	Car-177	Moses,Widow	Cab-141	Moughon,John	Nor- 73		
Asa	Ons- 98	David	Lnc-339	Peyton	Nor- 72		
Benj Junr	Ons- 97	Fred	Ora-172	Moulder,Christiana	Ire-267		
Benj Senr	Ons- 97	Henry	Lnc-350	Susanah	Ire-267		
Ezekiel	Mon- 49	James	Bur-125	Mount,Harris	Roc- 19		
Ge	Mon- 27	Jno	Ora-172	John	Roc- 19		
George	Per-141	John	Lnc-350	John Junr	Roc- 20		
Jacob	Ora-124	Molly (Old)	Fra- 84	Matthias	Roc- 19		
Jas	Mon- 40	Saml	Bur-104	William	Roc- 19		
John	Ons- 97	William	Fra- 84	Mounticue;Nancy	Pas-196		
John	Ire-239	Mosley,David	Edg- 65	Pernal	Pas-196		
John	Cha-211	Henry	Sur-164	Will	Pas-196		
John T	Car-183	Fortine	Sur-172	Mounts,Jacob	Sto-141		
Josiah	Cas- 61	West	Sur-164	Michael	Sto-141		
Mary	Cas- 61	Moss,Anthony	Ire-238	Mourey,John	Row- 79		
Meshack	Cas- 61	Arslie	Mec- 53	Mourning,Jane	Brt- 57		
Micajah	Ons- 98	David	War-170	Mouser,John	Lnc-347		
Olliver	Mar- 8	Gideon S	War-171	Mower,Jacob	Row- 67		
Patrick	Sur-184	Henry	Sto-135	William Jr	Bur-117		
Peggy	Mon- 25	Howell	Grn-135	Mowerie,Peter	Row- 67		
Peter	Ora-124	Howell	Grn-140	Mowery,Frederick	Row- 67		
Peyton	Cas- 61	Howell	Hay-198	John	Row- 67		
Richard	Ons- 98	James	Rch-211	Mowrie,Henry	Row- 68		
Richard Junr	Ons- 97	John	Ran-175	Mowring,Andrew	Sto-113		
Robert	Bun- 74	John	Cha-191	Mowry,Jacob	Sto-140		
Rosanna	Car-183	Milly	Wsh-225	Moxley,D	Ash- 14		
Step	Cas- 62	Patsy	Mon- 44	Henry	Hal-113		
Stephen	Mon- 32	Polly H	War-178	Thomas	Roc- 4		
William	Sur-171	Reuben	Grn-135	W	Ash- 14		
William	Cas- 61	Richard	Hal-112	Moye,George	Pit-235		
Wm	Mon- 31	Richardson	Prq-221	Gideon	Pit-262		
Mosby,William	Sur-189	Robt	Mon- 44	Joel	Pit-260		
Moseley,Jonathan	Sam-163	Saml	Grn-135	John	Pit-232		
Mary	Pas-197	Samuel	Sur-195	Mary	Pit-252		
Miriam	Pas-196	Stith	Row- 42	Robert	Nsh- 88		
Tally	Len-322	Thomas	Sur-196	Sarah	Pit-256		
William	Roc- 13	Turner	Grn-135	William	Pit-263		
Wm	Len-322	William	Hyd-230	William	Pit-256		

Name	Ref	Name	Ref	Name	Ref
Moyers,Frederick	Lnc-362	Mullins,Thomas Sr	Roc- 16	Munroe,Duncan	Mor- 65
Geo	Cab-140	William	Rth-122	John Senr	Cum-270
John	Lnc-362	Mullis,George	Ire-267	John Esq	Cum-268
John	Cab-140	Stephen	Sur-169	Malcom	Cum-242
Mozingo,Winnefred	Len-316	Muls,Matthew	Bla- 7	Malcom	Mor- 58
Muckleroy,Jas	Mec- 32	Mulver,Jno	Mec- 50	Malcolm	Mon- 31
Wm	Bft- 28	Mulwer,Jas	Mec- 34	Malcolm	Mon- 30
Wm	Mec- 32	Wm	Mec- 35	Neill Esq	Cum-268
Mudey,Barbra	Cha-205	Mumford,Mrs	Cum-238	Neill M C	Cum-269
Riley	Cha-205	George	Row- 66	Neill Junr	Cum-268
Mudlin,Thomas	Way-252	Jahue	Ons-105	Peter	Cum-243
Muimey,Sarey	Cur- 86	Robeson Junr	Cum-237	Robert	Rch-197
Mulder,Kader	Hal-112	Robeson Senr	Cum-237	Muns,Jacob	Cho-230
Thos	Cur- 90	William	Edg- 68	Joseph	Prq-221
Mulford,Sarah	Bla- 4	William	Pit-251	Thos	Cho-230
Mulhollan,Hugh	Ora-121	Munce,Mathew Junr	Bla- 5	Wm Jnr	Cho-230
Hugh Sr	Ora-159	Mund,Alexander	Dup- 26	Wm Sen	Cho-230
Mulhollon,John	War-175	Munday,Jere	Lnc-362	Munson,Wm	Mec- 49
Mulkey,J	Ash- 4	Munden,Charles	Pas-196	Munsy,Eli	Row- 50
Mull,Benedick	Row- 67	Elisha	Prq-221	Muntce,M	Bla- 14
John	Row- 77	Levi Jr	Prq-221	Murchison,Alexr	Mor- 64
Thomas	Row- 88	Levi Sr	Prq-221	Christian	Mor- 64
Tobias	Row- 88	Nathan	Prq-221	Dan	Mon- 28
Mullace,Jas	Ans- 24	Nathaniel	Prq-221	Danl	Mor- 68
Jno	Ans- 14	Simon	Pas-196	Danl	Mor- 64
Mary	Ans- 24	Thomas	Way-247	Duncan	Mor- 55
Sol	Ans- 14	Willm	Pas-196	Duncan	Mor- 63
Mullakin,Lewis	Row- 55	Munds,William	Dup- 26	Jno	Cha-196
Mullen,Charles	Ran-174	Munfield,J	Glf-174	Keneth	Cha-196
Clem	Mec- 46	Munford,Lydia	Ans- 18	Keneth	Mor- 64
Jacob	Ran-175	Munger,James	Nor- 73	Wm	Mor- 58
Jno	Mec- 51	Jessee	Nor- 73	Wm	Mor- 62
John	Pas-146	John	Nor- 72	Murden,Frances	Fra- 79
Joseph	Pas-197	Wilson	Nor- 73	J	Cam-158
Levi	Prq-221	Mungo,Joseph	Fra- 78	John	Nor- 72
Wm	Ran-175	Spell	Fra- 78	Robt	Pas-197
Zadock	Prq-221	Mungomery,Wm	Ora-169	Sylvas	Pas-197
Mullenex,Green	Ran-174	Munkers,James	Sur-162	Murdock,And	Ora-123
Mullens,Daniel	Rth-120	Eliza	Sur-163	Eliza	Ora-174
Mathias	Rth-120	Munly,Elisha	Row- 52	James	Ora-175
Nicholas	Rth-120	Munn,Alexr	Cum-255	Ro	Ora-128
Valentine	Rth-121	Daniel	Bla- 4	Tho	Ora-120
Mullin,Bettee	Lnc-372	Danil	Mon- 27	Wm	Ora-175
Greenberry	Brt- 59	Duncan	Mon- 27	Murdaugh,John	Brt- 57
Thos	Cha-207	James Jr	Mon- 27	Lemuel	Brt- 56
Wm	Len-318	Jas	Mon- 27	John	Hay-198
Mullins,Abner	Bun- 96	Jno	Mon- 27	Mure,Joseph M	Hal-112
Ahab	Bun- 96	John	Cum-269	Murfree,Drury	Fra- 86
Charles	Rth-118	Nedum	Rch-212	Wm H	Hrt-209
J	Ash- 11	Neill	Cum-266	Murfrey,Malacha	Joh-287
Jno	Per-131	Wm	Per-141	Murkison,Alex	Mon- 28
John	Bur-115	Munnerlin,Joseph	Rch-197	Alexr	Cum-256
John Ch	Bur-115	Munroe,Alexr	Cum-244	John	Cum-256
Kinchen	Fra- 85	Archd	Mor- 63	Kenneth	Cum-269
Nathan	Row- 40	Ard	Bla- 4	Murphay,William	Roc- 11
Oren	Fra- 82	Dan	Mon- 30	Murphey,A D	Ora-145
Richard	Rth-123	Daniel	Rch-193	Alex (H C)	Cas- 61
S	Ash- 11	Daniel	Rch-196	Alexander	Cas- 61
Thomas Junr	Roc- 16	Dugald	Mor- 58	Alexander	Cas- 62

Murphey,Ann	Cas- 62	Murphy,Murdock	Rch-203	Murril,D		Cum-239
Archibald	Wil-278	Nickos Junr	Fra- 82	Geo		Row- 49
Casly	Bft- 30	Nickos Senr	Fra- 88	Robert		Lnc-362
Daniel	Dup- 22	Neill	Rob-230	Murrill,Ann		Nor- 72
Daniel	Ans- 13	Neill	Bla- 4	John		Nor- 72
Daniel	Ans- 30	Niell Esq	Rob-222	Mary		Nor- 72
Elizabeth	Wil-276	Parker	Fra- 85	Winborne		Nor- 72
Isaac	Ans- 32	Patsey	Sur-189	Murrow,Jno		Per-141
Isaac	Ans- 27	Robert	Cum-237	Murry,Ann		Row- 65
James	Roc- 16	Sion	Fra- 85	Barnes		Cha-194
James	Rth-118	Thomas	Sur-196	Charles		Cas- 62
James	Roc- 26	Thomas	Cum-267	Isan		Cha-190
James	Wil-282	Thomas	Jon-301	James		Cas- 62
James	Cas- 62	Thomas Junr	Cum-267	James		Fra- 90
John	Cas- 62	William	Cum-259	Jas		Mec- 37
John	Roc- 13	Wm	Bur-104	Jas		Ora-137
John	Glf-161	Wm	Grn-140	John		Nsh- 85
Jonathan	Glf-172	Murr,Easter	Row- 89	John		Cas- 62
Joséph	Roc- 17	Murrah,Peggy	War-179	John		Ora-121
Joseph	Cas- 61	Murray,Also	Ora-124	John		Row- 83
Joseph	Sur-183	Arthur	Dup- 33	John Jr		Grn-137
Matt	Cas- 61	Asa	Dup- 18	Milly		Ora-172
Miles	Roc- 17	Bethuel	Wsh-223	Nicholas		Row- 75
Moses	Lnc-337	Daniel	Dup- 20	Phillip		Fra- 97
Rachael	Ans- 27	Elijah	Ran-174	Robt	F	Ora-136
Samuel	Ire-245	James	Ons- 99	Sally		Ora-137
Silas	Wil-282	James	Bun- 82	Samuel		Hay-198
Timothy	Dup- 24	James	Dup- 37	Wm		Nsh- 92
Uriah	Wil-279	James	Cab-143	Willis		Nsh- 89
William	Pas-197	James	Bun- 95	Muse,Daniel		Mor- 58
Wm S	Pit-231	Jas	Ora-172	James		Mor- 61
Murphy,Archd	Rob-228	Joel	Glf-159	Jason		Mor- 61
Archd	Cas- 61	John	Bun- 82	Jesse		Mor- 57
Christian	Rob-230	John	Bun- 91	Joshua		Hyd-225
Danl	Row- 43	John C	Roc- 19	Thomas		Mor- 55
David	Sto-138	Jonathan	Roc- 27	Thos		Mor- 69
Edward	Hrt-209	Margret	Ora-163	Will T		Pas-197
Effie	Cum-269	Martha	Car-169	Wm T		Cho-225
Eliza	Dup- 24	Nathl D	Roc- 17	Muselwhite,Leonard		
Gorge	War-171	Nelanor	Dup- 20			Ans- 21
Hugh	Bla- 12	Richd	Ora-121	Musgrave,Abby		Way-234
Isaac	Glf-179	Robert	Len-319	Abraham		Way-242
J	Ans- 11	Robert	Bun- 95	Agga		Way-239
James	Rch-207	Samuel	Bun- 91	Andrew		Way-242
James	Cum-266	Samuel	Bun- 91	James Jr		Way-234
James	Fra- 95	Wm	Ora-163	James Sr		Way-234
James	Rth-120	Murrel,L	Bru-230	John		Way-233
Jas	Bur-104	M	Bur-232	Joshua		Way-239
Jesse	Cum-259	Murrell,Henry	Ons- 98	Moses		Way-239
John	Rob-234	John	Ons-100	Richd		Way-234
John G	Grn-130	William	Ons-101	Robt		Way-239
John	Cum-269	Murrelt,L	Bru-232	Musgrove,J		Bru-240
John S	Cum-264	Murrey,Jabus	Rth-120	Music,Austen		Rth-120
Joseph	Sur-183	Jessee	Cha-216	Jonathan		Rth-118
L	Cam-162	Mathew	Ons-109	Louellen		Rth-121
Luke	Car-175	Sarah	Hyd-230	Musick,David		Sto-138
Martin	Ora-169	Thomas	Grn-128	David		Sto-104
Miles	Ran-173	Walter	Ora-147	John Jnr		Cur- 86
Murdock	Rob-228	William	Hyd-230	John Snr		Cur- 86

Name	Ref	Name	Ref	Name	Ref
Muson,William	Ora-121	Nailer,John	Row- 61	Nash,T	Cam-165
Musshont,Joshua	Ons- 97	Nailing,Nelson	Grn-131	William	Ans- 24
Musslewhite,Jonah	Rob-242	Naill,James	Bur-104	Wm	Ans- 25
Leonard	Rob-242	Nailor,Joshua	Ran-176	Nasworthy,Osborn	Pit-246
Milbey	Rob-241	Joshua	Ran-175	Natall,John	Grn-131
Nathan	Rob-241	Nathan	Sam-154	Nathum,Edith	Wil-279
Thos	Rob-242	Nall,Ann	Mon- 21	Nations,Christr	Sto-129
Thos	Rob-242	Henry	Row- 64	Christopher	Sto- 98
Mustepha (sic)	Pas-196	John	Cha-202	Naylor,Hezekiah	Mon- 20
Mustian,Jesse	War-175	Nathan	Cha-202	Jos	Mon- 22
Rea	War-179	Nicolas	Mor- 56	Sam	Mon- 19
Mustion,Moorning	Ans- 17	Thos	Cha-196	Nea---,John	Bft- 30
Mustipner,Mary	Cho-222	William Snr	Sto-147	Neagle,Jno	Lnc-367
Muyr,William	Nor- 73	Nance,D	Col- 18	Loyd	Ire-264
Muzell,Henry	Edg- 45	David	Roc- 35	Neal,Aaron	Car-181
Muzzall,William	Cas- 62	E	Col- 18	Amos	Hyd-230
Myars,Miles	Way-238	Federick	Grn-123	Brooks	War-169
Mydett,Banister	Cur- 82	Frederick	Roc- 31	Cudbeth	War-169
Betsey	Cur- 82	Hudson	Ran-176	Edward	War-171
Doritey	Cur- 82	John	Grn-126	Elizabeth	War-171
Jacob	Cur- 82	John	Wil-265	Henry	Ora-165
Morrey	Cur- 81	John	Glf-188	J	Bru-238
Wolomon	Cur- 81	John	Cas- 63	John	War-174
Wm	Cur- 81	Joseph	Bla- 6	John	Hyd-228
Mydgett,John	Tyr-205	Mary	Roc- 35	Lucy	Hyd-229
Lewis	Tyr-205	Peter	Sur-173	Milly	Row- 42
Samuel	Tyr-204	Thomas	Ran-176	Moses	Fra- 92
Samuel Sen	Tyr-205	W	Col- 17	Reuben	Grn-135
Myers,David	Bun- 89	Wiett	Ans- 22	Richard	War-179
Elias	Lnc-370	William	Roc- 28	Thomas	Roc- 2
John	Row- 79	William	Wil-265	William	Hyd-229
Peter	Sur-175	Nanny,Abner	Rth-123	William	Hyd-229
Peter	Row- 86	Polly	Rth-124	William	Sto-105
Saml	Brt- 62	Robert	Row- 64	William Sen	Roc- 4
Thomas	Bun- 95	Nantz,Clem	Lnc-359	Wm	Mon- 38
Wm	Brt- 61	Eliz	Lnc-359	Willis	Hyd-230
Myes,John	Ire-254	Frank	Lnc-359	Neale,H	Bru-226
Myhand,Silus	Sam-156	Richard	Lnc-359	John	Dup- 10
Myrack,Moses	Cha-198	Napier,Robert	Roc- 5	S	Bru-226
Myres,Coty	Sur-191	Naridike,Aden	Sto-150	Nealy,E	Col- 18
George	Hay-198	Naridikie,Aden	Sto-112	Nearn,Jesse	Bft- 38
James	Sur-196	Narnold,Ceziah	Gat-110	Nease,F	Ora-132
Joseph	Sur-196	Naron,Equilla	Joh-285	Geo	Ora-132
Myrick,Charles	War-169	John	Nsh- 87	J	Ora-132
Edmond	Hal-112	Thomas	Nsh- 87	Neaze,Marn	Ora-144
James	War-174	Wm	Nsh- 87	Neblock,George	Row- 75
Jesse	Cha-210	Narsworthy,John	Nor- 73	Ned Negro	Way-239
Mary	Cha-198	Nathan	Nor- 73	Nedd col	Rch-211
Matthew	War-178	Saml	Joh-287	Needham,Franky	Ran-176
Moses	War-177	Nash,Caleb	Cho-226	Isaac	Ran-175
Susanna	War-180	Fred	Ora-112	John	Ran-176
Tapley	Cha-196	Griffith	Ans- 17	John	Ran-176
		J	Cam-158	John	Ran-176
Nail,George	Lnc-373	J	Cam-160	Susannah	Ran-176
Jno	Ora-133	Jonathan	Ans- 8	T	Cam-156
Nelly	Ora-150	Joseph	Ans- 25	Thomas	Ran-176
Philip	Row- 66	Michael	Ans- 15	William	Ran-176
Wm	Bur-104	Peggy	Cas- 63	Wm	Mor- 59
Nailer,Batson	Row- 61	S	Cam-158	Neel,Adam	Lnc-334

Name	Loc	Name	Loc	Name	Loc	Name	Loc
Neel,Alex	Lnc-341	Nelson,Elijah	Sto-124	Nelson,William	Cas- 63		
E	Ora-148	Elsy	Pit-242	William Snr	Sto-122		
Hannah	Rth-124	Garret	Bft- 29	William Snr	Sto- 94		
James	Rth-124	Giles	Pit-231	William Senr	Bun- 81		
Jas	Lnc-334	Hezekiah	Nor- 73	Wm	Glf-178		
Jesse	Mec- 23	Hugh	Wil-282	Wm Junr	Bun- 81		
Jno	Mec- 54	Isaac	Sto-120	Nelums,David	Per-141		
Jno	Mec- 47	Isaac	Sto- 92	Nelvin,Hosa	Hrt-213		
John	Lnc-334	James	Lnc-332	Neovell,Samuel	Rth-124		
John	Rth-124	James	Sto-105	Nerny,Nickles	Hrt-208		
John D	Rth-124	James	Car-174	Nerrel,Mrs	Cum-235		
Joseph Esq	Lnc-330	James	Sto-155	Nerris,Thomas	Gat-109		
Paton	Rth-124	James	Nor- 73	Neryton,Hardy	Ons- 97		
Saml	Mec- 26	James	Ran-175	Nesbet,William	Lnc-350		
Thomas	Rth-124	James	Cas- 63	Nesbit,John	Ire-260		
William	Roc- 33	Jas	Ora-120	John Sen	Ire-260		
William	Rth-124	Jas	Glf-181	Nesbitt,Thos	Bur-119		
Neelhall,Daniell	Mec- 44	Jesse	Cha-209	Nesfield,Miss	Cum-239		
Neels,Philip	Roc- 16	Jesse	Rch-195	Nester,Abraham	Mec- 33		
Neely,Mrs	Mec- 26	Jesse	Glf-185	Netherby,Mary	Bur-112		
Henry	Mec- 48	Joel	Sto-122	Nethercut,Loftin	Dup- 30		
Hugh	Hay-198	John	Sto-155	Will	Dup- 33		
Hugh	Mec- 23	John	Sto-140	Netherly,Sam	Bur-112		
Jno	Mec- 48	John	Pit-263	William	Bur-112		
John	Cab-148	John	Nor- 73	Netson,P	Ora-157		
Moses	Mec- 26	John	Glf-188	Nettle,Allen	Edg- 68		
Samuel	Mec- 26	John	Hay-199	John	Edg- 68		
Sarah	Bur-128	John Snr	Sto-122	Nettles,Solomon	Hay-199		
Thomas	Cab-148	John Snr	Sto- 94	Nettleton,O	Bru-230		
Thos	Mec- 26	Joseph	Car-174	Nevans,Robert	Row- 75		
Negus,William	Way-250	Joshua	Ire-241	Nevell,Wiley	Cha-209		
Neighdiver,Geo	Bun- 74	Joshua	Sto-123	Neven,William	Cum-253		
Neil,Andrew	Ire-240	Kathe	Bft- 28	Nevil,John	Grn-123		
Geo C	Bun- 85	Malinda	Row- 66	Nevill,Benjn Jr	Hal-114		
George	Sto-124	Martha	Bft- 29	Benjn Senr	Hal-114		
Gilbreth	Ire-239	Martin	Pit-242	Edmond	Hal-114		
Mary	Sto-124	Mary	Car-172	Goodman	Hal-114		
Robert	Sto-140	Moses	Row- 64	Hardy	Hal-114		
William	Sto-140	Moses	Row- 83	Jesse	Hal-114		
William	Lnc-354	Naboth	Pit-242	Jesse Junr	Hal-114		
William	Ire-257	P	Bru-234	John	Hal-114		
Neill,J	Glf-178	Polly	Sur-186	Sol	Ora-127		
Threshley	Cha-198	Sam	Ora-122	Thomas Senr	Hal-114		
William	Cha-216	Samuel	Ran-176	William	Hal-113		
Neilson,J	Ora-155	Sarah	Jon-302	Neville,G	Ora-143		
Neily,A	Bla- 12	Sarah	Pit-242	Jesse	Ora-144		
Nekins,Jonathan	Dup- 28	Shadrach	Nor- 73	S	Ora-144		
Nelms,Chloe	Hal-114	Susanah	Sto-104	New,John	Dup- 10		
Elias	Fra- 96	Susanah	Sto-138	John	Sto-100		
Jonah	Hal-114	Tapley	Sto-123	John	Sto-131		
Presley	Ans- 31	Thomas	Rch-195	Joseph	Bla- 8		
Nelson,--muel	Ran-176	Thomas	Ire-241	Wm	Sam-160		
Abraham Jr	Nor- 73	William	Row- 64	Newbern,Lydia	Len-312		
Abraham Senr	Nor- 73	William	Sto-122	Nichs	Cho-226		
Abraham	Ire-241	William	Sto-104	Newberry,Benjamin	Cum-249		
Christ	Hyd-231	William	Car-174	Isaac	Cum-247		
David	Hay-199	William	Sto-138	Isaac	Cum-249		
David	Car-174	William	Nor- 73	James	Rch-211		
Ebenezer	Row- 64	William	Ran-176	Jesse	Rch-210		

Name	Loc	Name	Loc	Name	Loc
Newberry,Jesse	Cum-247	Newel,Wm	Cab-148	Newson,Harison	Row- 83
John	Wsh-221	Newell,Adam	Way-235	Henry	Nor- 73
John	Bla- 14	Anne	Roc- 13	James	Nor- 73
Jonathan	Rch-210	Edward	War-170	James M	Edg- 70
Jonathan Senr	Rch-199	John	Way-233	Joab	Way-243
Joseph	Rob-220	Landon	Roc- 13	Joel	Hrt-216
Stevens	Wsh-221	Nancy	Way-250	Joel	Nor- 73
William	Rch-210	Newhall,Ebenezer	Ons- 96	Joel	Way-232
Newbery,Mary	Rob-234	Newill,John	Roc- 13	Joel Sr	Way-243
Newbold,Elijah	Ons-105	Newison,Ethelred (col)		John	Hrt-211
Sally	Ons-103		Rob-241	Joseph	Way-245
Samuel	Prq-222	Newkirk,Henry	Dup- 31	Lampson	Edg- 56
Thomas	Ons-105	Newland,Benjamin	Bur-107	Laurance	Hrt-208
Newborn,Eliza	Brt- 49	Jacob	Cha-199	Laurence	Edg- 70
Thomas	Brt- 67	Joshua	Cha-207	Moses	Nor- 73
Newbourn,George	Edg- 52	Newley,John	Ora-168	Nathaniel	Nor- 73
Newbowls,Saml	Pas-198	Wilka	Cho-230	Semore	Nor- 73
Newby,Exum	Prq-222	Newlin,James	Ora-128	Thomas	Edg- 48
Exum Jr	Prq-222	James	Ran-176	William	Row- 83
Francis	Prq-222	John	Ora-128	Willis	Way-246
Francis Jr	Prq-222	Nathl	Ora-128	Newson,William	Way-243
Frederick	Ran-175	Thomas	Ran-176	William	Way-243
Gabriel	Ran-176	Newman,Avery	War-167	Newsum,Gillum	Glf-185
Gabriel	Prq-222	Avery	War-167	Newton,Abram	Dup- 23
Gideon	Ran-176	Charles	Sto-141	Benjamin	Rth-124
James	Glf-168	Daniel	War-170	Daniel	Ons- 97
Jesse	Prq-222	David	Hrt-210	Easter	Gat-110
Jesse	Way-246	James	Sto-106	Ebenezer	Rth-124
John	Pas-198	James	Sto-141	Ebenezer	Rth-124
Joseph of F	Prq-222	Jason	Rth-124	Ebenezer	Rth-124
Joseph of J	Prq-222	Jesse	Sto-106	Elinor	Dup- 3
Joseph Sr	Prq-222	Jno	Len-322	Eliza	Dup- 5
Joshua	Ran-176	John	Sam-161	Enoch	Dup- 17
Kezia	Pas-198	John	Sto-106	Garnett	Per-141
L	Cum-240	John	Sto-124	Geo	Bun- 88
Mark	Prq-222	John	Sto-141	Elizebeth	Ans- 25
Mary	Prq-222	John	Sto- 95	H	Ora-169
Mary Jr	Prq-222	John	Glf-183	James	Dup- 21
Max	Pas-198	John	Glf-176	Jesse	Dup- 8
Nathan	Prq-222	Jos	Glf-169	Jessee	Hyd-230
Rachel	Prq-222	Joseph	Sto-141	John	Pit-252
Sally	Pas-198	Joseph	Sto-141	Mary	Ora-169
Saml	Ran-176	Joseph	Sto-106	Mary	Dup- 4
Saml	Ran-176	Suzanah	Bun- 90	Melona	Mor- 64
Thomas	Ran-175	Will	Sam-163	Robert	Rth-123
William	Prq-222	William	Rth-124	Robt	Ora-169
William	Ran-175	Willm	Bft- 38	Sterling	Hyd-230
Newcom,Julius	Rth-124	Wm	Ora-112	William	Rth-124
W	Ora-155	Newsom,Amos	Nor- 73	Wm	Ans- 19
Jacob	Glf-152	Benjamin	Nor- 73	Wm	Grn-140
Newel,David	War-169	Charles	Hrt-216	Wm	Ans- 26
David	Cab-144	Daniel	Brt- 59	Younger	Rch-193
Francis	Cab-148	David	Way-243	Niccols,Write	Per-141
J	Bru-230	David	Hrt-215	Nicholas,Edmond	Nor- 73
John	War-173	David Jr	Way-243	Francis	Ire-260
Johnston	Cab-148	Devenport	Row- 83	James	Ire-267
Peter	Mec- 42	Ephraim	Way-246	James	Bur-118
T	Bru-236	Ephraim	Edg- 67	John	Nor- 73
William	War-183	Gillum	Hal-114	John	Ire-243

-233-

Nicholas,John	Ire-242	Nichols,Thos	Mon- 33	Nicolas,Resdon	Rch-207
Joseph	Mec- 55	Tom	Pas-198	Nicoll,Andrew	Bun- 95
Mary	Ora-169	Whitley	Pit-258	Nicols,James	Car-169
Nott	Hrt-206	William	Pit-257	Nicolson,Alexr	Rch-194
William	Wil-263	Willm	Sam-155	Daniel	Mor- 66
Nichold,Julius	Rth-124	Willm	Pas-198	Daniel	Mor- 65
Nicholds,A	Col- 18	Wm	Cho- 22	Daniel	Rch-206
C	Col- 17	Willis Jr	Per-132	Duncan	Mor- 66
E	Col- 18	Willis Senr	Per-132	John	Mor- 66
Jacob	Wil-274	Willoughby	Ran-175	John	Rch-195
John	Wil-273	Wright	Per-132	John	Bla- 2
John Jr	Wil-281	Wright	Hrt-208	Mal	Rob-228
Natt	Hrt-213	Nicholson,A	Ora-131	Malcom	Rch-206
William Senr	Wil-276	Alex	Mon- 30	Mary	Rch-213
Nicholdson,Abel	Wil-265	Archd	Cum-238	Matthew	Per-222
John	Sto-111	Atkin	Fra- 84	Peter	Rch-206
John	Glf-181	Charles	Mar- 8	Peter	Mor- 68
Joshua	Sto-146	Charity	Hal-114	Niel,Honore	Cho-221
Samuel	Wil-269	Gassaway	Row- 87	James	Brt- 48
Nicholes,Allin	Cas- 63	Gilford	Nsh- 77	Nifong,Adam	Row- 48
Fielder	Cas- 63	Gorge	War-172	Night,Benjamon	Sto-105
Nicholls,Benajah	Brt- 45	James	Fra- 92	Demcey	Gat-111
George	Wsh-227	James	Ora-121	Rachal	Gat-111
Jehu	Brt- 43	John	Mar- 6	William	Row- 64
Nichollson,John	Bun- 85	John	Hal-114	Nileigh,Margaret	Bun- 91
Nichols,Amos	Ora-174	Jos	Cur- 88	Nines,John	Mar- 5
Arther	Ans- 27	Josiah	Cur- 88	Ninon,John	Glf-168
Arthur	Ans- 8	Lazarus	Ire-253	Nippen,Solomon	Grn-122
Benj	Nsh- 90	Leml	Cur- 89	Nipper,Jams	Cas- 63
Benjamin	Sur-178	Mary	Nsh- 75	William	Cas- 64
David	Nsh- 87	Nathan	Prq-222	Nirney,John	Gat-106
E	Col- 18	Nathl	Fra- 83	Nisbet,Ross	Ire-239
Griffin	Hal-114	Penelope	Edg- 58	Nisen,Christian	Sto-137
H	Pas-198	Samuel	Ran-175	Nisler,David	Cab-142
Isaac	Ans- 13	Thomas	Hal-114	John	Cab-142
Jacob	Ire-267	Thomas	Hal-114	Nics	Cab-142
James	Nsh- 90	Urban	War-182	Nivan,Danl	Cha-200
James	Ran-176	Zachariah	Ran-175	Nives,W	Ash- 15
Jane	Ora-177	Nickall,Alexander	Roc- 28	Nix,John	Rth-123
Jeremiah	Pas-198	John	Roc- 28	William	Rth-123
Jeremiah	Nsh- 87	William	Roc- 21	Nixon,-----	Per-222
Jerry	Pas-198	Nickalls,Jeremiah	Roc- 21	Abigale	Glf-169
Jerusha	Pas-198	Nickerson,Sarah	Cho-223	Anna	Pas-198
Jessee	Nsh- 87	Nickins,Betsy	Pas-198	Barnaby	Get-105
Jno	Ora-177	Edward	Hrt-211	Daniel	Ons-107
John	Mon- 33	Willis	Hrt-216	Francis	Prq-222
John	Nor- 73	Nickleson,Lewis	Grn-140	George N	Prq-222
Laurance	Nsh- 90	Nickless,Joseph	Rth-124	Isaac	Pas-198
Leml	Pas-198	Nickolds,Isaac	Glf-166	Jacob	Sur-170
Martha	Hal-114	Nickols,Biddy	Roc- 13	James	Lnc-359
Mary	War-177	J	Ash- 15	Jno	Cho-229
Mary	Mon- 33	William	Roc- 13	John	Cho-224
Mary	Pit-240	William	Roc- 15	Leach	Pas-198
Micaja	Per-132	Nicks,Edward	Hay-199	Phineas	Prq-222
Rose	Pas-198	Geo	Glf-165	Reubin	Gat-125
Stephen	Pas-198	George Jr	Glf-159	Robert	Lnc-359
Stephen	Nsh- 77	Q	Glf-175	Robt	Cho-230
Thomas	Row- 78	William	Rth-124	Ruth	Gat-108
Thos	Pas-198	Nickson,Phenehas	Ran-176	Samuel	Prq-222

Nixon,Sarah	Lnc-359	Nolen,Daniel	Lnc-367	Norman,Patty	Dup- 10
Thos	Ans- 16	Noles,William	Bun- 91	Ro	Ora-129
William	Lnc-359	Nolliby,Bareby	Nsh-644	Robert	Roc- 8
Zachariah Jr	Prq-222	Nolly,Needham	Sam-163	Sarah	Wsh-218
Zachariah Sr	Prq-222	Nolue,Daniel	Cum-245	Thomas	Wil-274
Noals,Edward	Roc- 16	Nonnon,Benj	Cas- 63	Thomas	Sur-189
Noble,Ann	Pit-231	Nooles,William	Roc- 31	Thomas Esar	Wsh-220
Benjamin	Pit-238	Nooncaster,Betty	Row- 79	Wm	Sur-162
Colmon	Sur-196	Noossman,Paul	Cab-145	Wm	Ora-129
George W Esqr	Ons-107	Norcum,Edmd	Cho-225	Normant,William	Rob-218
John	Pit-231	Fredk	Cho-225	Normon,George	Grn-120
John	Ora-170	John	Cho-225	Isbell	Sur-192
John	Ora-154	Norden,John	Cum-262	John	Glf-171
Joshua	Pit-254	Malehijah	Cum-262	Matthew	Sur-180
Martain	Rob-237	Robert	Cum-262	Thomas Sr	Grn-148
Sally	Pit-254	Thomas	Cum-262	William	Sur-191
Samuel	Ons- 99	Nored,Alice	Car-176	Norrel,Henry	Rth-124
Shadrach	Pit-262	Tabitha	Car-179	Norrell,Sarah	Rth-124
Simon	Pit-255	Norfleats,Isaac	Mar- 7	Norris,G	Ash- 8
William	Rth-124	Norfleet,Abm	Cho-227	Isom	Dup- 22
Wm	Mon- 44	Elisha	Cho-221	J	Ahs- 8
Nobles,Ariel	Bft- 36	Isaac	Edg- 47	James	Joh-290
Catharine	Lne-320	James	Cho-221	James	Cum-260
Geo	Len-320	John	Brt- 56	James	Hyd-226
H	Col- 17	Kinchen	Gat-109	Jno	Mec- 25
Isaac	Bft- 29	Marmaduke	Nor- 73	John	Lnc-371
Isaac Jun	Bft- 29	Marmaduke	Hal-114	John	Cum-260
J	Col- 19	Mrs Mary	Brt- 56	John	Pit-257
Jerimah	Jon-302	Mary G	Brt- 56	John	Fra- 80
Jesse	Bft- 29	Thomas	Brt- 56	Joseph	Fra- 81
John	Bft- 29	Norflett,Nathl	Per-141	Joseph	Cum-260
Phelpena	Len-319	Norington,Nelly	Mor- 67	Mary	Dup- 22
Polly	Len-320	Noriss,Jessie	Tyr-208	Mary	Len-316
Rachel	Len-316	Norkite,Nicholas	Ans- 25	Mathew	Car-184
Richd	Len-319	Norman,Abner	Bft- 32	Matthew	Joh-276
Susana	Len-316	Anna	Sur-180	Miriam	Pas-198
Tennison	Jon-302	C	Glf-176	Reuben	Dup- 22
William	Len-316	C Jr	Glf-176	Robert	Cum-260
Noblet,John	Bur-118	Charles	Wsh-221	Robert	Edg- 45
Joseph	Bur-117	Elizabeth	Roc- 35	Sinson	Hyd-226
Noblett,John	Ora-129	Frank	Ora-134	William	Roc- 30
Noblette,Robt	Cha-195	George	Rth-124	Zachariah	Car-180
Nockwork,Brittain	Cha-200	Hannah	Wsh-219	Norriss,Henry	Edg- 72
Noe,James	Car-171	Henry	Tyr-212	North,Daniel	Sur-174
Leticia	Car-171	Isaac Jr	Wil-269	John	Sur-176
Peter	Ora-159	Isaac Senr	Wil-271	Thomas	Cas- 63
Peter	Car-171	Isaiah	Wsh-219	Northam,George	Rch-212
Saml	Ora-113	James	Wsh-221	Northcutt,Anthony	Hrt-215
Nolan,James Jr	Row- 64	James	Wil-269	John	Hrt-216
Noland,E	Glf-172	Joanna	Wsh-219	Northerd,Edmund	Bur-113
Henry	Wil-273	Job	Glf-161	Solomon	Bur-112
James	Row- 64	John	Wsh-218	Northington,Jesse	Cum-253
Jno	Mec- 34	John	Wil-269	Jesse Junr	Cum-252
Patiance	Mec- 34	John	Lnc-333	Northon,John	Hyd-227
Peter	Wil-273	John	Roc- 17	Norton,David	Bun- 92
Phillip	Sur-171	Lucy	Roc- 24	George	Ons-107
Pierce	Wil-278	Martha	Wsh-221	Isom	Rch-204
Stephen	Row- 62	Milly	Wsh-226	James	Rch-204
William	Wil-273	Nehemiah	Wsh-222	Martin	Rch-203

-235-

Name	Ref	Name	Ref	Name	Ref
Norton,Nicholas	Sur-172	Nox,George	Row- 73	Oakes,John	Sto-142
Richd	Ran-176	James	Row- 72	Oakley,Francis	Hay-199
Willie	Hal-114	John	Row- 73	Jesse	Per-132
Norval,Aneas	Edg- 68	Noxon,Martha	Cho-221	John	Grn-142
Hardy	Edg- 50	Noyes,W	Col- 19	P	Cam-159
James	Edg- 69	Noys,Mrs	Bru-226	Richard	Roc- 25
Theophilus	Edg- 51	Nuckols,Solomon	War-180	Stephen	Grn-142
Norwill,Benj	Hrt-213	Nucom,William	Sur-196	Thomas	Cas- 64
Winneford	Hrt-213	Nucomb,Mary	Roc- 4	Thos	Grn-142
Norwood,Aron	Ire-241	Thomas	Sto-158	Walter	Per-142
Benj	Grn-140	Nucome,Julius	Rth-123	Williamson	Roc- 25
Burwell	Nor- 74	Nuley,Granett	Cas- 63	Wm Sr	Grn-142
Geo	Cha-197	Null,Adam	Bur-108	Oakly,James	Grn-139
Henry	Cha-209	George	Lnc-354	Oaks,Elliott	Glf-182
John	Fra- 81	Jacob	Sto-100	James	Bur-120
John	Cha-206	Jacob	Sto-132	Lemuel	Glf-183
John	Ire-258	James	Cha-215	Thomas	Row- 39
Joseph	Nor- 73	John	Lnc-350	William	Hay-199
Jourdin	Grn-140	John	Sto-143	Oasty,Stephn	Bft- 27
Laban	Nor- 74	John	Sto-145	Oates,Jethro	Sam-151
Moses	Nor- 74	Presly	Cha-194	John	Sam-154
Nathaniel	Nor- 73	Robert	Ora-164	Stephen	Sam-154
Samuel	Nor- 74	Nullman,John	Cab-140	Oats,Jethro	Way-248
Tabitha	Nor- 74	Num,A	Glf-173	Jno	Mor- 69
Thos	Mon- 26	Geo	Glf-173	John	Lnc-341
William	Nor- 74	Geo Snr	Glf-173	Michael	Mec- 42
William	Cha-216	J	Glf-173	William Senr	Lnc-341
Wm	Ora-171	Numan,Benjamin	Lnc-351	Wm	Lnc-334
Wm	Grn-136	Joel	Per-141	Wm Junr	Lnc-341
Wm	Grn-143	John	Pit-232	Oatsville,Charles	Cha-19
Norwoods,John	Grn-143	Nun,Cotton	Per-132	Obeths,John	Row- 55
Norsworth,Barsheba	War-169	Nunam,Edward	Roc- 26	OBrian,Ephm	Ora-129
Norworth,James	Gat-107	John	Roc- 20	Joseph	Per-132
Thomas	Gat-107	Nunely,Alexr	Cum-248	Obriant,John	Grn-148
Nothen,Arther	Cur- 90	Nunery,Amos	Cum-265	Patrick	Grn-139
Denny	Cur- 90	Henry	Cum-265	OBryan,Elizabeth	Edg- 41
Jas	Cur- 90	William	Cum-265	Ephraim	Ora&120
Patrick	Cur- 90	Nunley,P	Mon- 43	Laury	Edg- 41
Phillip	Cur- 90	Nunn,Elisa	Ora-116	William	Per-142
Nothern,George	Row- 83	Fras	Len-319	Obryant,Desails	Grn-142
J	Ash- 8	Joshua	Len-315	John	Rch-197
John	Wil-262	Malcom	Cum-254	Laurance	Rch-194
Samuel	Row- 86	Stephen	Len-318	Robert	Grn-142
Notsen,Eliza	Row- 65	William	Len-314	Tillotson	Rch-198
Nott,John	Hrt-209	Nunnaly,Levy	Bur-126	Ochiltree,Elizabeth	
Nowel,James	Joh-287	Nunns,William	Sto-144		Cum-270
Joel	Row- 65	William	Sto-108	Odam,Angey	Nor- 74
Matthew	Roc- 32	Nuton,John	Per-141	Darling	Mec- 42
Nowell,Dismay	Hrt-210	W	Col- 17	Geo	Lcn-350
Ephraim	Cas- 63	Nutt,David Sen	Ora-134	Isham	Nor- 74
Isom	Edg- 71			Josiah Jr	Nor- 74
John	Hrt-210	Oak,John	Lnc-330	Josiah Senr	Nor- 74
Lemuel	Mar- 11	Thos	Lnc-330	Mills	Nor- 74
Nowey,J Jr	Ora-132	Oakeley,McFarland	Per-142	Moses Jr	Nor- 74
Jno Sen	Ora-132	Moses	Per-132	Moses Junr	Nor- 74
Nowland,David	Rth-124	Thos	Per-132	Moses Senr	Nor- 74
David	Rth-124	Wat	Per-132	Noah	Nor- 74
James	Rth-124	Wat Senr	Per-132	William	Nor- 74
Nox,Benjn	Row- 72	Wm	Per-132	William	Lnc-350

Name	Ref	Name	Ref	Name	Ref
Odam,Winborne	Nor- 74	Ogelsby,Thomas	Car-182	Oliver,Stephen	Per-152
ODanal,J	Cam-166	Oggley,William	Row- 54	Stephen	Joh-279
ODaniel,Bartel	Bur-110	OGilby,Ann	Cas- 64	Tam	Lnc-350
John of H	Ora-147	Ogle,John	Bun- 94	Thomas	Sur-184
John Sen	Ora-158	Ogleby,Asea	Bur-103	William	Car-170
Sar	Ora-132	Richard	Per-132	William	Roc- 11
ODannel,Henry	Ora-129	Richd	Per-142	Willis	Mor- 67
Saml	Ora-114	Oglesby,Bethel	Cum-247	Willia	Mor- 67
ODannell,Alexr	Dup- 25	Micajah	Sur-161	Winifred	Joh-282
Owen	Dup- 30	Ware	Sur-163	Olliver,Elijah	Sur-183
Odell,Benj	Bun- 85	William	Sur-185	Everett	Nor- 74
Elizabeth	Bun- 97	Oglethorpe,Sarah	Bur-116	James Jr	Nor- 74
Henry	Roc- 8	OHarrow,Andw	Cab-144	James Senr	Nor- 74
Isaac	Glf-159	Okelly,James	Cha-213	John	Nor- 74
James	Row- 48	Okerman,Barberry	Sto-154	Joseph	Nor- 74
James	Bun- 85	Okey,Nancy	Sto-107	Mallica	Ons-107
Jeremiah	Roc- 9	V	Glf-153	Thomas	War-181
Jessee	Roc- 25	Old Luck (sic)	Pas-206	William	Sto-127
John	Row- 48	Old,H Esq	Cam-154	Olphin,James	Nor- 74
John	Glf-167	H Esq	Cam-154	OMalley,M	Cho-221
Lewis	Roc- 8	Oldfield,Richard	Jon-302	Oman,Dennis	Ons-100
Lewis Junr	Roc- 34	Vicey	Jon-302	Jesse	Ons-100
Nathaniel	Roc- 8	Oldham,John	Cha-211	John	Ons-102
Uriah	Roc- 8	Richd	Cha-213	Philip	Ons-100
William	Roc- 8	William	Cha-199	Omerry,Charles	Grn-126
Oden,Chas	Bft- 21	Olendorf,Henry	Row- 89	Chassity	Bft- 35
Holland	Bft- 21	Oliphant,Joseph	Ire-260	Jacob	Bft- 25
Richd	Bft- 21	Josiah	Bla- 7	Omery,Jessey	Grn-127
Robert	Hyd-220	Thomas	Sur-186	Richard	Grn-126
Wm	Bft- 20	Wm	Glf-159	Omit,Amos	Jon-302
Odham,Jeremiah	Fra- 80	Olivant,Joseph	Per-142	Enoch	Jon-302
Odiam,Thos	Cha-192	Oliver,Abijah	Bur-130	James	Jon-302
Odin,Thomas	Bft- 20	Abraham	Roc- 7	Susanna	Jon-302
Odineal,John	Roc- 6	Alexander	Wsh-210	Omitt,Daniel	Ons-105
Odinn,Thomas	Cha-196	Alexander	Rch-208	Oneal,Abner	Car-172
Odle,Benjamin	Hay-199	Andrew	Mec- 33	Anny	Joh-285
Isaac	Ran-176	Andrew	Wsh-229	Bateman	Car-172
Odom,Benjn	Gat-116	Asey	Joh-279	Benjn	Joh-286
Demsey	Edg- 55	Benjamin	Bun- 97	Bridgers	Joh-285
Eldred	Brt- 62	Daniel	Car-185	C	Bla- 10
Jacob	Hrt-215	Demsey	Joh-274	Christ	Hyd-229
Jacob	Nsh- 79	Geo	Lnc-372	Christopher	Hyd-229
Jacob	Sam-159	Henry	Joh-283	Christopher	Cur- 82
John	Edg- 56	Isaac	Roc- 5	Christopher	Lnc-341
John	Gat-116	James	Roc- 6	Christopher	Car-172
Jonah	Hal-114	James	Jon-302	Elizabeth	Car-171
Richard	Edg- 56	Jno	Rob-231	Federick	Joh-286
Odum,Jacob	Sam-162	John	Lnc-365	Fieldes	Cur- 82
OFarrell,Barny	Ora-110	John	Grn-124	Frans	Car-171
Ogbourn,John	Rch-209	John	Rth-125	Frans Snr	Car-172
William	Rch-208	John	Jon-302	Hugh	Row- 66
Ogdon,Benj	Mon- 23	John Elias	Roc- 12	Isom	Joh-285
Ogeley,William	Row- 54	John R	Jon-302	James	Joh-285
Ogelsbey,Abner	Car-183	Joseph	Wsh-228	James	Row- 64
Benjn	Car-181	Martha	Roc- 7	John	Hyd-229
Ogelsby,Absalom	Car-182	Needham	Joh-280	John	Cur- 82
John	Car-182	Peter	Roc- 2	John	Lnc-342
Levy	Car-182	Richd	Mor- 61	Jos	Cur- 79
Rebecca	Car-182	Sarah	Dup- 13	Joseph	Cur- 82

Name	Ref	Name	Ref	Name	Ref	Name	Ref
Oneal,Lodowick	Joh-285	Orr,Jas	Mec- 40	Ottam,Jorge	Gat-106		
M	Bla- 10	Jas	Mec- 38	Otten,Josiah	Mec- 36		
Nathan	Cur- 82	Jas	Mec- 23	Ottery,Archd	Sam-162		
Nathan	Cur- 87	Jno	Mec- 40	Sterling	Sam-162		
Patrick	Joh-285	Jno H	Mec- 22	Ottry,Alexr	Sam-156		
Richard	Car-171	John	Bun- 98	Oules,Edwd	Cur- 92		
Ryas	Joh-286	John	Lnc-329	Ousling,David	Cha-198		
Saml	Joh-285	Jonathan	Mec- 22	Outland,Cornelius	Way-244		
Saml	Joh-285	Nathan	Mec- 39	Eleaus	Cur- 81		
Samuel	Cur- 88	Nathan	Mec- 47	Exum	Way-244		
Thomas	Joh-286	Nathen	Mec- 39	Exum	Nor- 74		
Thophilus	Joh-285	Robert	Bun- 84	Jeremiah	Nor- 74		
Warren	Joh-285	William	Bun- 84	John	Nor- 74		
William	Joh-285	Wm	Bft- 36	Jonathan	Way-237		
Willm	Car-171	Orrel,Danl	Row- 57	Josiah	Nor- 74		
Wm	Nsh- 74	Edger	Row- 57	Luke	Way-237		
Oneale,Henery	Cur- 81	James	Row- 57	Robert	Nor- 74		
Oneil,Emond	Edg- 59	Jha	Bft- 30	Thomas	Nor- 74		
Isom	Edg- 59	Wm	Bft- 30	Thomas	Way-237		
Lazarus	Edg- 58	Orrell,James	Ons-102	William	Nor- 74		
Patrick	Bur-104	Orren,John	Roc- 7	Outlaw,Aaron	Brt- 50		
Oneils,Elisha	Edg- 59	Orten,James	Row- 75	David	Brt- 55		
ONiel,Benjn	Ans- 25	Orton,James	Ire-247	David	Gat-109		
Kindred	Ans- 22	Jesse	Wil-265	Edward	Brt- 66		
Right	Ans- 22	Thomas	Bun- 94	Edward C	Brt- 52		
Wm	Ans- 22	Orum,Thomas	Jon-302	George Esq	Brt- 66		
Onley,Edwin	Gat-105	Orval,Lemonteban	Grn-149	George Jnr	Brt- 67		
Only,Mrs	Fra- 87	Ory,Nathan	Sto-142	J	Bru-224		
Levi	Glf-172	ORyan,Peter	Sam-150	Jacob	Brt- 51		
Zadock	Prq-222	Osbern,George	Ora-145	James	Brt- 52		
OQuinn,Alexr	Cum-267	J	Ora-177	James	Gat-108		
Orain,John	Mar- 3	Jas	Ora-145	John	Brt- 52		
Thomas	Mar- 4	Osborn,Adlai	Ire-241	Joshua	Brt- 52		
William	Mar- 4	Christopher	Cab-147	Lewis	Gat-116		
Orand,Wm	Cha-210	Christopher	Mon- 47	Mary	Brt- 53		
Orbison,Nancy	Ire-240	E	Ash- 12	Rachal	Gat-111		
Orbon,Fulkerd	Lnc-368	Ephraim	Ire-241	Ralph	Brt- 61		
Ordy,Henry	Mon- 39	Geo	Bun- 98	Ralph	Brt- 53		
Ore,John	Roc- 2	John	Pit-246	William	Hrt-215		
William	Roc- 22	R	Ash- 12	Outtan,Edwd	Dup- 27		
Orick,Samuel	Ire-264	Osborne,John	Row- 46	James	Dup- 27		
ORilly,Benjamin	Bun- 98	John	Bun- 73	Outterbridge,Burr	Mar- 16		
Jno	Ora-136	Newman	Bun- 73	Mrs Polly	Fra- 88		
Orman,Michael	Ran-187	Stephen	Row- 46	Stephen Esq	Fra- 77		
Ormond,Aron	Mec- 45	Osborun,Wm	Bft- 22	Outton,Alexander	Dup- 27		
Betey	Mec- 31	Osburn,Alexr	Mec- 30	Benjn	Dup- 14		
Jas	Mec- 31	Alexr	Mec- 31	Jesse	Dup- 15		
Jas	Mec- 31	Jonathan	Hay-199	John	Dup- 27		
Jno	Mec- 31	Osly,Conrad	Mon- 49	Overby,Joab	Roc- 21		
Mary	Bft- 19	Osmond,Ben	Lnc-333	Lewis	Per-133		
Robt	Mec- 29	Ostun,Robert	Bun- 76	Smith	Roc- 28		
Sebenah	Mec- 35	Solomon	Bun- 98	Sterling	Roc- 15		
Wm	Bft- 19	Thomas	Dup- 35	Overcast,Daniel	Row- 67		
Orr,David	Mec- 44	Oten,Mary Ann	Bun- 91	Geo	Cab-139		
David	Mec- 44	Meshack	Bun- 96	Henry	Cab-139		
Franklin	Mec- 39	Otis,Nathl	Bft- 28	Jacob	Row- 70		
Isaac	Mec- 40	Otrey,Cornelius	Cum-265	John	Cab-139		
James	Cas- 64	Theophilus	Cum-265	Lenord	Row- 70		
James Jr	Cas- 64	Otridge,Nancy	Way-247	Michl	Row- 71		

Overcast,Peter	Cab-142	Overton,J		Cam-165	Owen,Medford	Mor- 60
Overley,David	Joh-280	J		Cam-164	Owens	Hay-199
Overman,Aaron	Way-242	J		Cam-164	Richd	Ora-111
Ben S	Pas-198	J		Cam-164	Tignal	Cha-199
Chalkley	Way-242	J		Cam-164	William	Cas- 64
Charles	Ran-176	J		Cam-164	William	Rth-125
Charles	Prq-222	J		Cam-164	Wm	Cha-206
Henry	Prq-222	J		Cam-162	Wm	Tyr-204
Henry	Pas-198	Jacob		Hrt-216	Owens,A	Glf-187
Isaac	Pas-199	Jesse		Pas-199	A	Ash- 11
James	Pas-199	John		Jon-302	Abel	Bun- 83
James	Ora-134	Jona		Cho-223	Abraham	Tyr-204
James	Pas-198	K		Cam-164	Amron	Tyr-204
Jesse	Way-238	L		Cam-164	B	Ash- 10
Jesse	Prq-222	L		Cam-164	Basil	Bft- 27
John	Ran-176	L		Cam-164	Bathsheba	Ire-268
John	Ran-176	Lamuel		Per-222	Benj	Ons-106
John	Way-244	Leml		Pas-199	Charles H	Bur-122
John	Prq-222	Lovey		Pas-198	Demsy	Edg- 51
John	Way-238	M		Cam-161	Elijah	Edg- 50
John	Pas-198	Matthias		Hrt-216	Elisha	Edg- 51
Joshua	Pas-199	Moses		Fra- 98	Elizabeth	Tyr-205
Mordeca	Pas-198	Osborn		Fra- 91	Elizabeth	Rth-125
Nathan	Pas-199	P		Cam-164	Ezekiel	Sam-153
Nathan	Pas-198	Polly		Pas-199	Frederick	Tyr-204
Phebe	Pas-198	R		Cam-165	George	Wil-267
Reuben	Prq-222	R		Cam-164	George	Hay-199
Rew	Pas-199	R		Cam-164	Isaac	Tyr-204
Robt	Pas-199	R		Cam-164	Jacob	Rth-125
Thomas	Way-246	R		Cam-162	James	Bun- 85
Thomas	Pas-198	Rachel		Pas-198	James	Bur-127
Thos	Prq-222	Richard		Roc- 8	Jas	Tyr-204
Thos	Pas-198	Samuel		Prq-222	Jehu	Tyr-204
Wm	Pas-198	Susa		Pas-198	Jesse	Hay-199
Overstreet,Elias	Rch-209	Thomas		Roc- 2	John	Tyr-205
James	Hal-114	Thure		Pas-198	John	Rth-125
Jno	Rob-222	Titus		Cum-264	John Jr	Rth-125
McGelbery	Rob-230	William		Roc- 7	Johnson	Wil-267
Rebecca	Rch-191	Winneford		Hrt-206	Lott	Edg- 50
Overton,Aaron	Fra- 91	Overturn,S		Bru-234	Lovey	Cur- 83
Anne B	Roc- 5	Oweins,Uriar		Hyd-227	Mary	Nsh- 85
Asa	Hrt-213	Owen,Bazil		Row- 66	Mosly	Bun- 91
B	Cam-158	Benjamin		Row- 86	Owen	Tyr-204
Benjn	Prq-222	Edward		Roc- 18	Owen	Sam-163
Betsy	Cho-223	Elias		Edg- 50	Patience	Brt- 57
Chery	Cum-265	Henry		Row- 66	Pleasant	Ire-268
Christopher	Brt- 50	J		Ora-157	Rachel	Wil-284
D	Cam-164	James		Bla- 3	Raleigh	Rth-125
Dyer	Cum-249	Jno		Per-133	Richard Esq	Wil-274
E	Cam-164	John		War-175	Sally	Ire-267
E	Cam-164	John		Mor- 56	Thomas	Hay-199
Elec	Pas-199	John		Joh-277	Thomas	Ons-100
Elisha	Hrt-216	John		Row- 66	Thomas	Rth-125
Francis	Prq-222	John		War-176	Thos	Tyr-204
G	Cam-164	John		Grn-121	Thos	Sam-153
George	Roc- 2	John Junr		Roc- 20	William	Car-185
Goshen	Pas-199	John Junr		Grn-133	William	Bun- 80
H	Cam-165	John Senr		Grn-133	William	Lnc-354
H	Cam-165	John Senr		Roc- 20	William	Edg- 52

Owens,William	Sam-153	Ozburn,Jno	Mec- 31	Padrick,John	Cur- 87
Wm	Tyr-204	Jno	Mec- 24	Pafford,Thomas	Sto-109
Wilson	Bun- 83	Capt Jno	Mec- 24	Page,Benjn	Ran-177
Zacheriah	Cur- 84	John	Joh-275	Benjamin	Ran-176
Owensby,Tom	Lnc-365	Nathan	Mar- 14	Catherine	Brt- 57
Owin,Alexr	Mec- 37	Wm	Mec- 31	Ephraim	Sam-150
Efford	Row- 40	Wm Snr	Mec- 31	Jacob	Mon- 21
Evan	Sto-155	Ozier,Jacob	Mon- 32	James	Pit-259
Harmon	Row- 85	Jeremiah	Ran-176	James	Cas- 65
Hezekia	Row- 40	John	Mon- 28	James	Per-132
Margrett	Sto-153	Wm	Mon- 31	John	Edg- 50
Nancy	Row- 86	Ozment,D	Glf-183	John	Mar- 14
Peter Jr	Row- 85	Howard	Glf-166	John	Cas- 65
Peter Sr	Row- 85	J	Glf-183	John	Joh-275
Ralph	Row- 85	James	Glf-171	Joseph	Rob-240
Richd	Row- 40	Richd	Glf-158	Joseph	Pit-236
Robert	Row- 85	Samuel	Glf-171	Laurence	Edg- 65
William	Row- 86	Ozmint,C	Glf-164	Mary	Brt- 57
Owing,Joseph	Row- 76	Jonathan	Glf-157	Meltisha	Pit-259
Norman	Row- 62			Nathan	Brt- 57
Owins,John	Bur-131	P----,-----	Sto- 91	Samuel	Roc- 33
John	Sto-136	P--ttard,Samuel	Cas- 65	Silas M	Roc- 24
Samuel	Bur-112	Pace,Burrell	Rth-127	Sion	Sam-155
William	Cur- 87	Cornelius	Rth-127	Thomas	Cas- 65
Owles,David	Cur- 86	Jerremiah	Bun- 82	Thomas	Edg- 65
Ownby,Arthur	Rth-125	John	Sur-181	Tobias	Joh-274
James	Rth-125	Jonathan	Rth-127	Uriah	Mon- 48
John	Rth-125	Jos B	Ora-164	Whitehead	Cas- 65
John	Rth-125	Richard	Bun- 81	William	Pit-259
Ownsby,James	Rth-125	Pack,Azarea	Row- 84	William	Pit-236
Owry,Geo	Mon- 47	Joseph	Row- 84	William	Brt- 55
Oxendine,Charles	Rob-232	Mary	Row- 84	William	Cas- 65
David	Rob-230	Reason	Row- 84	Wm	Cha-216
Jesse	Rob-232	William	Row- 84	Pagett,Benjamin	Bur-120
John	Cum-237	Packer,Clenny	Jon-303	John	Sur170
Moses	Rob-232	H	Glf-179	Thomas	Sto-102
Oxford,Able	Bun- 93	John	Rth-127	Paggett,Thomas	Sto-135
Jacob	Bun- 78	John B	Way-236	William	Sto-119
James	Bur-108	Joseph	Ire-267	Paid,Andrew	Per-132
Jonathan	Bun- 88	Lewis	Sam-159	George	Per-132
Samuel	Lnc-350	Will	Glf-158	Richard	Per-132
Oxley,Eliza	Brt- 44	Packston,Elisebeth	Mec- 29	Pain,Edward	Tyr-204
Hardy	Brt- 53	Pacshall,John Jr	Roc- 28	Horden	Per-132
John	Brt- 44	John Senr	Roc- 28	Igerfy	Mor- 63
Jonas	Len-314	Padget,Benjamin	Dup- 33	Isaac	Row- 44
Oxly,Amy	Len-314	Ephraim	Rth-126	James	Bun- 81
John	Jon-302	Jacob	Rth-126	John	Tyr-205
Ozbon,Richard	Sur-196	Joab	Dup- 34	John	Sur-171
William N	Sur-195	John	Rth-126	John	Sur-180
William Sr	Sur-196	John	Dup- 32	John	Bun- 90
Ozborn,Andrew	Sto-127	Nehemiah	Rth-126	John	Per-142
D	Glf-165	William	Dup- 36	Mary	Row- 44
Jas	Glf-157	William	Rth-126	Moses	Sur-180
John	Glf-160	Padgett,Edmund	Rth-126	Nelly	Row- 44
Peter	Glf-156	Ephraim	Sur-195	Stephen	Sur-179
W	Glf-158	John	Tyr-210	Thomas	Tyr-205
William Jr	Glf-185	Padrick,Benjamin	Ons-106	Thomas	Bun- 81
Wm Snr	Glf-184	Jesse	Cur- 87	Paine,Esther	War-171
Ozburn,Edwin	Mec- 53	John	Ons-107	Isaac	Rth-127

Name	Ref	Name	Ref	Name	Ref
Paine,James	War-176	Palmer,Will	Pas-199	Parish,David	Cab-137
James	Per-142	Wm	Ora-116	David	Glf-158
John	Cur- 82	Palnick,Spencer K	Rch-210	Dempsey	Cho-231
Joseph	Cur- 82	Pamalle,Jane	Hyd-233	Humphry	Rth-126
Robert	Per-142	Timothy	Hyd-233	Jesse	Lnc-357
Solomon	Per-142	Pane,Barnabas	Row- 45	Jesse	Ora-127
Thomas	Ran-176	Benjn	Row- 47	John	Grn-146
Thos	Cur- 82	David	Hyd-229	John	War-176
Wm	Per-142	Isaac	Pas-200	John	Joh-274
Pains,John	Row- 65	Isaah	Row- 49	Johnston	Cha-215
Painter,George	Rth-125	John	Row- 46	Johnston	Lnc-362
Henry	Bur-130	John	Row- 45	Jos	Chos-231
Jacob	Lnc-334	Mary	Row- 44	Lankford	Grn-129
Jacob	Rth-125	Prudence	Per-132	Leon	Grn-137
Leonard	Rth-127	Ruth	Row- 46	Leroy	Mor- 61
Saml	Bur-130	Stephen	Row- 47	Mary	Cha-195
West	Per-142	Tarisen	Row- 47	Mary	Cas- 65
Pair,Bathsa	Pas-200	Thompson	Row- 46	Nelson H	Mor- 60
Richerd	Cur- 91	Wm	Row- 49	Noel	Glf-159
William	Cur- 91	Pankay,Edward	Sto-148	Obed	Ire-264
Pairam,Mathew	Rob-223	Pankey,Stephen	Rch-210	Patsey	War-170
Pairtree,Easter	Hyd-222	Panther,Nathiel	Per-142	Peggy	Lnc-362
James	Hyd-222	Pao,Christen	Row- 55	Pleasant	Grn-148
Noah	Hyd-222	Paquinett,Eliz	Car-170	Presley	Grn-128
Sabra	Hyd-222	John	Car-184	R	Glf-159
Paisley,James	Glf-156	Par,M	Col- 19	Ransom	Grn-137
John	Glf-173	Paradise,William	Ons-100	Ransom	Grn-142
Samuel	Glf-173	Paramore,Joseph	Wsh-221	Shaderack	Grn-129
William	Glf-156	Pardue,Arkins	War-167	Smith	Nor- 74
Wm	Glf-174	Patram	War-179	Stephen	Len-315
Paisly,John	Glf-156	William	War-182	Susan	Dup- 7
Palin,Sarah	Pas-200	William	War-183	Thomas	Per-142
Tho	Pas-200	Pare,Joseph	Prq-223	Toply	Cab-137
Paling,Pernace	Cur- 88	Parham,Cannon	Grn-146	Valentine	Mec- 36
Palmer (sic)	Mon- 51	Edward	Grn-144	Wm	Ora-126
Amasa	War-168	Federick	Grn-146	Parisher,Camel	Car-183
Betsy	Pas-200	George	Grn-146	Samuel	Car-183
Betsy	Pas-200	John	Cha-213	Park,Ebenezer	Row- 77
Demarius	Mon- 49	Kipy	Grn-130	Jesse	Row- 78
Edward	War-171	Lewis	Grn-146	Joseph	Prq-223
Edward	Bun- 90	Parham	Grn-139	Noah	Row- 78
Henry	Pas-200	Saml	Grn-146	Robert	War-180
James	Brt- 48	Thornton	Grn-129	Uriah	Row- 60
James	Cum-268	Thos	Grn-146	Parke,David	Ora-118
James	Ora-115	Thos W	Grn-146	Wm	Ora-177
Jerry	Pas-199	Wiley	Grn-146	Parker,A	Col- 17
Jessee	Bun- 82	Williamson	Grn-146	A	Ora-146
John	Bur-110	Paridge,John	Cur- 83	Abby	Dup- 22
John	Bun- 82	Parie,Malcolm	Mor- 56	Abner	Per-132
John	Wil-264	Paris,Henry	Ora-115	Abner	Per-132
John	Pas-199	Robert	Cur- 83	Abraham	Len-315
John	Mon- 50	Thos	Cur- 83	Abraham	Hrt-212
Luke	Cas- 64	Parish,Abel	Per-142	Abraham	Gat-107
Martin	Ora-115	Augn	Grn-148	Abraham	Gat-113
Robert	Mon- 18	Averylla	Joh-276	Alen	Cha-215
Samuel	Hyd-234	B	Glf-159	Alexander	Dup- 22
Tho	Ora-163	Bettee	Lnc-362	Alexander	Pit-237
Thomas	Wsh-228	Calm	Ora-143	Alexander	Nor- 74
Thomas	Pas-200	Charles	Joh-273	Amelia	Brt- 64

Parker,Amos	Gat-110	Parker,Isaac		Gat-114	Parker,John Senr	Ons-100
Ann	Edg- 63	Isaac		Mec- 47	Jona	Cho-227
Ann	Sam-158	Isaac		Way-246	Jonathan	Gat-114
Archa	Ons-109	J		Bru-226	Jonathan	Glf-184
Aron	Nor- 74	J		Cam-157	Jonathan	Joh-289
Arthur	Way-248	J Senr		Bla- 11	Joseph	Hrt-207
Asa	Lnc-332	Jacob		Dup- 20	Joseph	Cur- 91
Benj	Cur- 86	Jail		Prq-223	Joseph	Gat-107
Benj	Hrt-207	James		Pit-263	Joseph	Sam-160
Benjamin	Cum-244	James		Wil-281	Joseph	Hal-116
Brady	Gat-113	James		Gat-107	Joseph	Pas-201
Briton	Nor- 74	James		Gat-108	Josiah	Nor- 75
Buckner	Ire-267	James		Mar- 9	Josiah	Gat-111
Celia	Nor- 75	James		Cum-266	Kader	Gat-110
Charles	Cab-147	James		Hal-115	Kader	Cum-260
Christy	Lnc-337	James		Edg- 63	Kader	Per-132
Cullin	Hrt-211	James		Ons-100	Kader	Nor- 75
Damaris	Per-142	James		Way-249	Kedar	Mar- 9
Daniel	Sam-162	James		Ran-177	King	Hrt-210
Daniel	Gat-107	James		Nor- 74	Lamuel	Hrt-211
Daniel	Brt- 66	Jas		Ans- 10	Lancaster	Edg- 66
Darius	Nor- 75	Jas		Hrt-207	Laz	Hrt-211
David	Row- 65	Jas		Mon- 43	Lemuel	Nor- 74
David	Ora-151	Jeremiah		Nor- 74	Levi	Lnc-335
David	Wil-267	Jesse		Way-245	Lewis	Nor- 75
David	Grn-139	Jessee		Cur- 87	Lucy	Grn-123
David	Nor- 75	Jessee		Edg- 65	Lucy	Nor- 74
Drury	Mon- 43	Jethro		Gal-115	Luke	Brt- 55
E	Col- 17	Job		Cho-229	Luke	Gat-114
Edward	Row- 65	Job		Nor- 74	Luke	Sam-153
Edward	Gat-107	Jno		Ans- 17	Mary	Lnc-335
Elijah	Hrt-207	Jno		Ans- 29	Mary	Cha-200
Elisha	Gat-116	Jno		Per-142	Matthew	Joh-283
Elisha	Hrt-207	Jno		Ans- 9	Micajah	Rth-127
Elisha	Brt- 54	John		Hrt-210	Mikajah	Hal-115
Elisha	Cho-223	John		Prq-223	Miles	Row- 65
Elisha	Cho-231	John		Roc- 14	Miles	Gat-112
Eliz	Cho-228	John		Roc- 15	Moses	Rch-193
Elizabeth	Prq-223	John		Hrt-208	Moses	Rob-236
Elizabeth	Mon- 43	John		Lnc-337	Nathan	Cur- 87
Enoch	Lnc-337	John		Brt- 55	Nicholas	Sam-153
Enoch	Dup- 34	John		Len-316	P S	Row- 39
Faithy	Hal-114	John		Cha-203	Peter	Cur- 87
Francis	Nor- 74	John		Gat-106	Peter	Gat-108
Francis	Hal-116	John		Gat-107	Peter	Dup- 16
Francis	Hal-116	John		Fra- 87	Peter	Ans- 9
Francis	Rob-243	John		Lnc-362	Reuben	Gat-113
G	Mon- 37	John		Nsh- 88	Reubin	Brt- 64
G	Col- 17	John		Cum-250	Richard	Sam-158
Gabriel	Len-316	John		Hal-116	Richard	Wil-265
George	Sur-186	John		Ora-169	Richd	Row- 78
Hardy	Dup- 34	John		Sur-173	Robert	Prq-223
Hardy	Dup- 18	John		Hal-115	Robert	Gat-112
Hardy	Edg- 63	John		Ire-238	Robert	Gat-114
Henry	Lnc-335	John		Ons-109	Robt	Cha-199
Henry	Wil-264	John		Wil-271	Rubin	Row- 63
Humphrey	Gat-107	John		Ran-177	S	Cam-157
Humphrey	Lnc-341	John Moor		Bun- 92	S	Col- 17
Isaac	Brt- 55	John Junr		Ons-100	Saml	Hrt-216

Parker,Saml	Cho-229	Parkes,William	Cas- 65	Parks,Thomas	Nor- 75
Samuel	Cum-261	Parks,Abigal	Prq-223	Thos	Mec- 38
Samuel	Sur-181	Alford	Cas- 65	Thos	Cha-191
Samuel	Nor- 75	Ambrose Esqr	Wil-274	William	Bur-108
Sarah	Brt- 59	Amos	Row- 78	William	Bur-110
Sarey	Cur- 84	Bedy	Hal-114	Wm	Nsh- 92
Seth	Prq-223	Benjamin	Hay-199	Wm	Mec- 39
Seth Jnr	Cho-226	Benjamin	Wil-264	Wm Sr	Nsh- 92
Seth Snr	Cho-226	Casiah	Nor- 75	Parmelle,William	Hyd-234
Silas	Hrt-212	Cela	Brt- 50	Parmer,James	Row- 50
Solomon	Nsh- 89	David	Mec- 49	John B	Row- 58
Squire	Sur-195	David	Mec- 38	Parnal,Acy	Joh-281
Stephen	Per-132	Elisha	Nor- 75	Benjn	Joh-281
Stephen	Ons-100	Elizabeth	Wil-272	Jeremiah	Joh-283
Stephen	Ire-239	Elizabeth	Nor- 75	Parnel,John	Joh-281
Ted	Cum-253	George	Bur-109	Parnell,Edward	Row- 50
Theophilus	Edg- 41	Giles	Nor- 75	Parr,David	Cur- 89
Thindred	Gat-113	Hal	Way-237	Isah	Cur- 88
Tho	Sam-153	Hugh	Mec- 25	Jesse	Cur- 89
Tho	Bur-130	Hugh	Row- 70	Jesse	Cur- 88
Thomas	Per-133	Humphrey	Nor- 75	Jos	Cur- 89
Thomas	Rth-126	Hyram	Cas- 64	Parram,William	Rth-127
Thomas	Gat-110	Jacob	Row- 82	William	Rth-126
Thomas	Rth-127	James	Bur-108	Parrik,Bazzle	Rth-126
Thomas	Cum-266	James	Sur-168	James	Rth-126
Thomas	Rch-204	Jas	Mec- 38	Parrimoore,Amos	Ans- 12
Thomas	Nor- 75	Jas Snr	Mec- 39	Parris,Robt	Cha-197
Thomas B	Hal-115	Jess	Cas- 64	Parrish,Allen	Ora-117
Thos	Ans- 29	Jethroe	Nor- 75	Gillam	Cha-196
Weeks	Edg- 44	Jno	Mec- 38	James	Cho-231
Wilie	Cum-252	Jno	Mec- 39	Joel	Ora-147
Wilkey	Prq-223	Jo	Row- 40	John	Roc- 9
William	Pit-248	John	Hay-199	Jonas	Roc- 9
William	Wil-274	John	Rth-126	Luke	Way-254
William	Dup- 19	John	Grn-131	Mourning	Nsh- 88
William	Lnc-362	John (L E)	Wil-262	R	Bla- 11
William	Cum-256	John (H C)	Wil-269	Sarah	Cho-230
William	Cum-266	John (W O C)	Wil-268	Sherwood	Cha-204
William	Hal-117	John	Row- 40	Johs	Cha-204
William	Hal-117	Joseph	Mec- 38	Parrot,Benj	Len-317
William	Edg- 62	Joseph	Nor- 74	Hannah	Len-321
William	Per-142	Joseph	Way-237	Jacob	Len-321
William	Ire-241	Larkin	Bur-107	Joseph	Len-316
William	Ons-100	Major	Way-237	Lewis	Per-132
William	Bun- 97	Moses	Mec- 34	Lucy	Per-132
William H	Gat-114	Nathan	Prq -223	Reuben	Per-142
Willm	Sam-153	Reuben Esqr	Wil-264	Simon	Len-321
Wm	Mon- 43	Robert Colo	Cas- 65	Wm	Nsh- 84
Wm	Cur- 84	Robt	Mec- 25	Wm	Grn-141
Wm Junr	Hal-115	Robt	Mec- 29	Parrum,Michl	Row- 49
Wm Jr	Mon- 24	Robt	Mec- 38	Parsley,John	Glf-155
Wm Sr	Mon- 23	Ruben Jr	Wil-263	Parsnul,James	Mon- 33
Williamson	Rth-126	Saml	Bur-104	Parson,John	Grn-128
Willis	Gat-115	Saml	Mec- 39	John	Cha-196
Willis	Cho-231	Samuel	Wil-266	Sarah	Row- 72
Zachariah	Nor- 75	Sarah	Prq-223	Parsons,Asa	Prq-223
Zilpha	Edg- 62	Solomon	Cas- 65	Geo	Glf-176
Zorey	Cur- 84	Thomas	Bur-108	Geo Jr	Glf-176
Parkes,Isaac	Bur-130	Thomas	Wil-261	George	Wil-275

Parsons,J	Ash- 11	Paschall,Thomas	War-181	Paterson John	Mor- 60
James	Glf-172	Thomas Sr	War-181	John Sr	Sur-165
Jno	Ans- 28	Ward	War-182	Joseph	Grn-148
John	Wil-282	William	War-183	Kennedy	Row- 52
Johnson	Mar- 8	Paschell,C	Glf-177	Mary	Mor- 60
Joseph	Mon- 32	Pasely,John	Wil-282	Mary	Ran-177
Joseph	Sto-150	Paskall,John	Grn-123	Rebeca	Sur-165
M	Ash- 7	Paskell,John Senr	Roc- 29	Rebecca	Dup- 6
Richard	Sur-166	Paskill,John	Roc- 27	Sarah	Mor- 64
S	Ash- 4	Pasmoore,Jno	Ans- 5	Turner	Cas- 65
Samuel	Mon- 27	Pasmore,A	Ash- 14	William	Sur-167
Tabitha	Mor- 58	Pass,Holloway	Cas- 65	William	Cas- 65
Thos	Mon- 29	Nathan	Cas- 65	William	Sur-173
Vincent	Ans- 28	Passinger,Thos	Cab-138	Wm	Mor- 57
William	Sur-193	Passmore,John	Nsh- 74	Pateshaull,Benjn	Cha-208
Part,Step	Ora-110	Passons,Jeremiah	Jon-303	Patillo,Priscilla	War-179
Partee,Charles	Grn-139	Patch,John	Cas- 65	William	War-183
Lockhart	Grn-139	Pate,Anthony	Len-323	Patishall,Wm	Cha-215
Noah	Row- 70	Asa	Ans- 19	Wm Jr	Cha-215
Parten,Benjn	Ran-177	Bryan	War-251	Patram,Peter	Ora-120
Bettee	Lnc-356	Catherin	Row- 50	Patrick,Ann	Bft- 28
Henry	Cum-263	Charles	Rob-241	Ebenezer	Roc- 20
James	Lnc-357	David	Way-252	Hugh	Roc- 19
Jinny	Lnc-357	Elias	Rch-204	Isaac	Wsh-223
William	Hal-116	Elias	Way-251	James	Roc- 19
Partin,Benjn	Hal-117	Isom	Way-251	Jemima	Rch-204
C	Ora-157	James Jr	Way-252	Joel	Pit-231
Chas	Ora-142	Jno	Rob-241	John	Hal-114
Henry	Glf-167	John	Way-252	John	Wsh-223
James	Hal-117	Joseph	Way-251	Joseph	Wsh-221
Jean	Ora-131	Lewis	Way-252	Joshua	Pit-255
John	Mon- 19	Nancy	Joh-275	Selby	Tyr-209
Lenn	Ora-131	Nathan	Dup- 5	Thomas	Rth-128
Lucy	Nor- 75	Saml	Bft- 34	Uriah	Tyr-209
Nancy	Hal-117	Samuel	Rch-204	William	War-183
Nathl	Mon- 19	Shadrick	Way-252	Wm	Cha-200
Randle	Mon- 18	Stephen	Rch-212	Patridge,Jesse	Cur- 87
Robert	Hal-116	Thomas	Way-251	Sarah	Cha-200
W	Ora-160	Thorogood	Rch-196	Patterson,A	Bla- 3
Wealthy	Hal-117	Travis	Joh-275	Alex	Lnc-340
Partree,Coleman	Hyd-222	Wilaby	Way-252	Alexander	Rch-191
Partridge,John	Cha-195	William	Jon-303	Alexr	Cab-139
John	Hal-116	Wm	Bft- 22	Alexr	Rob-226
Parum,Lewis	Mor- 67	Zach	Len-320	Angus	Rob-223
Pary,John	Nsh- 85	Zachariah	Rob-241	Archd	Cum-244
Pasamore,Ezekiel	Pit-243	Paterick,John A	Tyr-207	Archibald	Rch-202
Joel	Pit-251	Paterson,Charles	Ran-177	Arthur	Lnc-341
Pascall,Willm	Fra- 79	Charles	Ran-177	C P	Ora-118
Paschal,Alexr	Cas- 65	Daniel	Mor- 60	Charles	Ran-187
Elish	Cas- 64	Duncan	Mor- 60	D	Ora-146
Isaah	Cas- 64	Duncan	Mor- 57	Daniel	Cum-243
Jesse	Cas- 64	Duncan	Mor- 56	Daniel	Bla- 4
William	Cas- 64	Geo	Cha-193	Daniel	Cum-254
Paschall,Dennis	War-170	Gilbert	Sur-165	Daniel	Rch-191
Elisha	War-170	Jacob	Cur- 85	Daniel B S	Cum-244
James	War-173	James	Row- 73	Danl	Rob-244
John	War-175	Jesse	Sur-170	David	Rth-126
Mrs Nancy	Fra- 99	Joel	Sur-169	David	Wil-262
Samuel	War-180	John	Sur-173	David	Nor- 76

Patterson,Duncan	Cum-254	Patton,Abigail	Bun- 98	Payne,John Jr	Bur-106
Greenberry	Glf-187	Alex	Ora-113	Jonas	Wil-282
Henry	Ire-250	Andrew	Ora-170	Joseph	Roc- 8
Hugh	Cab-138	Charles	Mec- 46	Robert	Bur-106
Isaac	Ora-131	Elijah	Bur-124	Robert	Cas- 64
James	Rth-127	Elijah	Rth-125	Thomas	Cas- 64
James	War-175	Geo	Bun- 83	William	Bur-127
James	Rth-127	Heuston	Bun- 99	William	Roc- 29
James	Ire-252	James	Bun- 89	Paynes,Thos	Cur- 85
James	Rch-193	Col John	Bun- 88	Payson,J	Bur-230
James	Bun- 75	John	Ora-130	Payton,Thomas	Cum-245
James	Ire-255	John	Ora-137	Pea,Lidia	Mec- 50
James	Ora-119	Joseph	Bun- 98	Peaby,James	Bur-130
James	Row- 51	Joseph	Bur-109	Peace,John	Bun- 98
Jas	Lnc-341	Joseph	Cab-139	John Senr	Grn-129
Jarratt	Nor- 76	Mary	Bun- 99	Jos	Ora-159
Jarrott	Roc- 33	Mathew	Bun- 99	Joseph	Grn-129
Joab	Bun- 92	Mathew	Ora-130	Saml	Grn-129
Jno	Rob-223	Robert	Bur-129	Wm	Glf-165
Jno	Rob-222	Robert	Bun- 83	Peacock,Abm	Ran-177
Jno	Mec- 25	Sam	Ora-134	Abram	Rth-125
John	Sto-134	Zachariah	Bur-124	Daniel	Way-254
John	Rth-128	Pattrick,Purnal	Ans- 28	David	Joh-289
John	Cum-254	Pau,Edmon	Sur-164	George	Wsh-226
John	Ire-262	Hardy	Cha-212	Isaac	Bft- 38
John	Ire-246	Reubin	Sur-164	Jacob	Joh-286
John	Bun- 75	Richard	Cha-200	Jesse	Way-253
John D	Wsh-227	Paul,Abraham	Rob-232	John	Lnc-371
Jordan	Ire-268	Ezeochael	Ans- 32	John	Way-244
Joseph	Bun- 75	Ezra	Bft- 19	John	Way-242
Joseph	Bur-119	Hona	Bft- 20	John Jr	Way-252
Joseph	Ire-268	Jacob	Ans- 7	John Sr	Way-252
Jourdin	Grn-128	Jacob	Ans- 32	Luke	Ora-172
Mann	Ora-126	Jacob	Hyd-224	Needham	Way-252
Mathew	Bun- 85	James	Cas- 64	Noah	Way-244
Michael	Glf-154	John	Ora-161	Peter	Way-246
Mordeca	Sto-132	Redmon	Hyd-233	Raeford	Way-244
Mordica	Sto-100	Sarah	Ans- 29	Richd	Wsh-224
Piety	Bun- 74	Stephen	Rob-232	Saml	Grn-125
Robert	Lnc-330	Thomas	Sur-164	Seth	Way-245
Robert	Lnc-341	Wm	Rob-232	Simon	Way-244
Robert	Rth-128	Paull,Edward	Wsh-227	Stephen	Way-244
Robert	Bun- 75	Paulson,Joseph	Glf-187	Theophilus	Bla- 7
Robert	Bun- 76	Paumer,Thos	Cur- 89	Uriah	Way-243
Robert Sr	Rth-128	Paxton,Johnson	Pit-242	Wm	Mon- 36
Robt	Cab-139	Richd	Cho-224	Wm	Ran-177
Samuel	Bun- 98	William	Bun- 98	Pead,James	Prq-223
Simmons	Sto-112	Payn,Daniel	Cas- 65	Patience	Prq-223
Simmons	Sto-147	Jesse	Cas- 65	Peagram,D	Glf-186
Susanna	Edg- 40	Payne,Abner	Bur-131	John	Glf-186
Kent	Joh-291	Barny	Bur-107	Peake,William	Bun- 81
Thomas	Grn-127	Catharine	Bur-131	Peaks,Rachal	Row- 55
Thos	Cha-208	Charles	Cas- 75	Peal,Abram	Mar- 7
Wm	Ora-119	Daniel	Bur-131	Amos	Mar- 9
Wm	Row- 51	Ebenezer	Cho-221	Andrew	Mar- 11
Wm	Mec- 36	George	Wil-281	James	Mar- 13
Wm	Mec- 37	John	Bur-131	Jesse	Sto-131
Wilson	Glf-160	John (T)	Cas- 64	John	Mar- 9
Patton,Aaron	Bun- 83	John Esq	Cas- 64	Kitey	Cur- 81

Peal,Moses	Mar- 11	Pearce,Lazarus	Len-318	Pearson,Jesse A	Row- 84
Reuben	Mar- 14	Levi	Ans- 20	Job	Way-242
Riddick	Gat-110	Lovet	Joh-284	John	Roc- 27
Sary	Gat-111	Mary	Mon- 27	John	Rth-125
Stephen	Mar- 9	Mary	Ans- 22	John	War-173
Tabitha	Rch-204	Mary	Joh-284	John	Row- 88
Thomas	Mar- 11	Moses	Ans- 17	Joseph	Glf-182
William	Hyd-224	Moses	Ans- 21	Joseph	Row- 90
Peale,Hillary	Pit-257	Nathan	Fra- 81	Lewis	Rth-128
John	Pit-261	Nathan	Cum-236	Nathanl	Row- 87
John	Dup- 15	O	Cum-241	Richmond	Row- 66
Pealer,Anthony	Row- 66	Obadh	Per-132	Richmond Sr	Row- 87
Christian	Row- 77	Orion	Mec- 34	Saml	Row- 44
Lewis	Row- 67	Philip	Joh-279	Stephen	Bur-108
Michl	Row- 67	Phillip	Fra- 80	Thos	Cha-199
Pear,Allen	Mec- 32	Rachal	Gat-109	William	Bur-115
Ann	Mec- 43	Rhody	Mon- 38	Wm	Row- 44
Cleben	Mec- 32	Saml	Cum-237	Peasour,George	Lnc-341
Eli	Hal-116	Sarah	Wsh-223	Peaterson,James	Cas- 64
Jno	Mec- 32	Simon	Joh-283	Joseph Jnr	Cas- 64
Jones	Hal-116	Simon Jr	Joh-280	Joseph Snr	Cas- 64
Miol	Mec- 27	Slade	Bft- 37	Mary	Cas- 64
Pearc,Daniel	Gat-105	Snowden	Dup- 35	Thos	Cas- 64
Pearce,Abner	Bft- 28	Stephen	Fra- 81	Peavy,C	Bru-236
Abner	Gat-106	Stevens	Wsh-222	J	Bru-234
Abram	Prq-223	Thomas	Gat-105	N	Bru-236
Alexr	Sam-158	Thos	Prq-223	T	Bru-234
Ansel	Ran-177	William	Gat-105	Peavy,Ambrous	Roc- 10
Asey	Joh-279	William	Gat-105	George	Roc- 33
Bettee	Lnc-365	William	Ran-176	James	Roc- 32
Cader	Joh-280	Wm	Ans- 23	John	Roc- 33
David	Prq-223	Wm	Ans- 22	Rebourn,Tho	Bft- 37
Elijah	Sto-154	Wm	Mor- 61	Pecas,Peter	Bft- 39
Elijah	Ans- 22	Winsor	Ran-176	Peck,Adam	Row- 51
Elisha	Nor- 75	Zebiah	Prq-223	Devall	Row- 51
Elizabeth	Sur-182	Pearcy,Cader	Brt- 51	Geo	Row- 51
Elizabeth	Way-234	Peare,William	Gat-115	Geo	Row- 52
Elizebeth	Ans- 31	Peariman,Isaac	Roc- 17	Henry	Row- 80
Ephram	Joh-284	Pearker,Holms	Car-181	Henry	Row- 51
Everit	Fra- 80	Pearles,Joseph	Bft- 30	Jacob	Row- 84
Federick	Gat-106	Pearly,Charles	Lnc-361	Jacob	Row- 80
George	Sto-116	Pearsall,Edwd Jr	Dup- 10	Jacob	Row- 52
George	Sto-156	James Jr	Dup- 11	John	Cab-146
Hambelton	Ran-177	James Sr	Dup- 11	John	Row- 57
Hardy	Ans- 13	Pearse,Aaron	Gat-115	John	Car-169
Isaac	Gat-109	Isaraeil	Hyd-224	Nancy	Grn-147
Isom	Mec- 36	Pearson,Barnaby	Way-244	Philip	Row- 51
J	Cam-162	Bartley	Nor- 75	William	Bun- 84
Jacob	Nor- 75	Benjamin	War-169	Peckler,Joseph	Row- 65
James	Glf-186	Benjamin	Row- 89	Pedler,John	Row- 67
Jas	Bft- 34	Charles	Bur-103	Peebles,Benjamin	Pit-246
Jesey	Joh-279	Elizabeth	Prq-223	George	Hal-116
John	Prq-223	Francis	Rth-128	Henry	Nor- 75
John	Joh-283	George	Sto-102	Henry Senr	Nor- 75
John	Roc- 34	Ichabod	Way-244	Howell	Nor- 75
John	Fra- 86	Isaac	Ora-114	Jesse	Hal-115
John	Ran-177	Isaac	Ran-177	John	Nor- 75
Jona	Bft- 34	Jacob	Roc- 31	John	Hal-116
Joshua	Joh-280	James	Wil-275	Seth	Nor- 76

Name	Ref	Name	Ref	Name	Ref
Peebles,Sterling	Nor- 75	Peggs,Elizabeth	Roc- 26	Pendleton,Abigail	Pas-199
Turner	Nor- 75	Pegram,George	War-172	Dina	Pas-200
William	Pit-244	George Sr	War-172	George	Pas-200
Peed,Gaing	Bft- 32	Gideon	War-172	Henry	Pas-201
Geo	Cho-221	Henry	War-172	Hiram	Lnc-365
John	Bft- 31	William	War-184	John	Pas-199
Laml	Bft- 32	William	Cum-258	Nehem	Pas-199
Peede,Cyrus	Lnc-354	Pell,Jonas	Hrt-209	Peggy	Pas-200
Peeden,Amus	Joh-279	Jonathan	Sur-164	Saml	Pas-199
James	Joh-280	William	Rth-128	Samuel	Pas-201
Nuet	Joh-281	William Jr	Rth-125	Timothy	Pas-200
Patrick	Pit-252	Wm	Cho-221	Pendry,John	Sur-167
William	Joh-279	Pelly,Alphred	Cha-197	Penian,Benjamin	Wil-283
Peek,Frederick	Cab-141	James	Row- 58	Penick,Henry	Lnc-337
Peel,Catherine	Edg- 49	James Junr	Row- 58	Phebe	Lnc-328
Danl	Bft- 31	Pelt,James	Brt- 52	Penigar,Mathias	Sto-151
Demsy	Edg- 46	Jno V	Mec- 35	Penington,A	Ash- 8
Elisha	Edg- 68	Pelts,Wm O & Simon	Mec- 35	David	Mon- 44
James	Edg- 46	Pemberton,James	Bla- 13	E	Ash- 7
John	Edg- 46	John	Rch-199	E	Ash- 6
John	Edg- 48	Rich	Mon- 29	E	Ash- 15
John	Cum-241	Pence,Catharine	Cab-144	Edwd	Mon- 44
John Jr	Edg- 46	Palestine	Cab-146	Kinchen	Mon- 44
Willis	Edg- 43	Pender,David	Edg- 62	L	Ash- 8
Willis	Fra- 97	Drury	Edg- 62	M	Ash- 8
Willis	Way-237	Edmund C	Way-235	W	Ash- 13
Peele,Axum	Brt- 54	Edwin	Edg- 64	W	Ash- 4
Edmond	Nor- 74	Elisha	Brt- 59	William	Hay-199
Jethro	Nor- 74	Jethro	Hrt-210	Penion,John	Bur-124
Joel	Nor- 74	John	Edg- 47	Stokes	Ans- 24
John	Nor- 75	John C	Way-235	Penix,John	Cas- 65
Mark	Wil-269	John C Jr	Way-249	Overton	Sur-178
Reuben	Wil-269	Joseph	Edg- 65	William	Cas- 65
Thomas	Nor- 74	Josiah	Edg- 41	Penland,Alexander	Bur-109
Peeler,Anne	Rth-126	Paul	Way-254	Elizabeth	Bun- 88
Chrissy	Ora-150	Reddick B	Hal-114	Geo	Bun- 96
Jacob	Row- 85	Right	Edg- 55	Geo Senr	Bun- 93
Peter	Rth-126	Sollomon	Edg- 41	George	Bur-109
Sam	Ora-160	Stephen	Brt- 46	James	Bur-108
Peell,Mills	Bft- 25	Thomas	Way-243	John	Bun- 74
Peelle,Dempsey	Brt- 56	Thomas	Joh-286	Peter	Bun- 97
Josiah	Brt- 56	Wm	Brt- 46	Robert	Hay-199
Lawrence	Brt- 54	Pendergast,Ed	Ora-129	Robert	Bur-107
Mary	Brt- 49	Jno	Ora-130	William	Bur-109
Wm	Brt- 58	Jno	Ora-130	Penley,Benjamin	Wil-275
Peelor,Saml	Ora-118	Mary	Ora-130	Jonathan	Wil-276
Peeples,Abner	Joh-290	Wm	Ora-129	William	Wil-279
Abraham	Glf-182	Wm	Ora-170	Penly,John	Bur-116
D	Glf-166	Pendergras,Nimrod	Ire-246	Joshua	Bur-116
Hastead	Glf-186	Pendergrass,Charcull		William	Bur-115
John	Glf-186		Bur-117	Penner,Winney	Lnc-341
Lewis	Roc- 18	Isaac	War-174	Pennery,James	Row- 76
Nathanl	Row- 86	Jas	Per-132	Penney,Jessey	Joh-273
Thomas	War-182	Jesse	War-174	Pennigar,Peter	Sto-151
William	Row- 88	John	Bun- 98	Penninger,Geo	Row- 68
Wyatt	Glf-186	Jon	Ora-136	Jno	Mec- 31
Peerman,Whitmil	Fra- 94	Jos	Per-132	Pennington,Jacob	Sur-187
Peerson,Joseph	Ran-177	Joseph	Bur-117	Jordan	Dup- 5
Peg,John	Row- 48	Luke	Ora-154	L	Ora-159

Name	Loc	Name	Loc	Name	Loc
Pennington,Noel	Sam-155	Perkens,Elisabeth	Rch-211	Permenter,Saml	Ans- 32
Robt	Cha-194	Wm Senr	Hal-115	Pernell,Jno	Rob-242
Pennion,Elias	Bur-106	Perkins,Abram	Ora-165	John	Hal-117
Penny,Alexdr	Row- 71	Alexander	Bur-109	Margaret	Rob-234
Edward	Cum-263	Allen	Way-244	Wm	Hal-116
James	Brt- 60	Barney	Row- 49	Peron,Anda	Ran-177
Pennwill	Joh-276	Benjamin	Lnc-362	Perrel,Johb	Row- 53
William	Joh-278	Bigin	Lnc-357	Perrey,Demsey	Joh-287
Pennywill,John	Ons-104	Bigin Jr	Lnc-356	Reuben	Joh-287
Penrice,Clerky	Prq-223	C Esq	Cam-154	Perriman,John	Row- 50
Penright,Jesse	Sur-167	Charles	Sto-126	Perrin,Nathaniel	Hay-199
Jonathan	Sur-192	Charles	Sto-109	Perrisher,Joshua	Pas-200
Penry,James	Row- 64	David	Lnc-354	Perritt,Demsey	Ans- 30
Samuel	Row- 64	Dempse	Lnc-354	Jacob	Cha-213
Thomas	Row- 64	E	Cam-153	Perry,A	Bru-236
Pentergast,George	Cas- 65	Eli	Lnc-350	Aaron	Glf-156
Thomas	Cas- 65	Elijah	Bur-104	Abner	Ora-130
Penturf,Hannah	Lnc-375	Ephraim	Lnc-350	Adonijah	Jon-303
Peoler,Benj	Ora-150	Fanny	Cho-225	Benja	Prq-223
Jacob	Ora-142	George	Rch-207	Benjn	Brt- 50
Richard	Ora-149	Henry	Cas- 64	Benjn	Fra- 94
Saml	Ora-150	Henry	Hal-115	Betty	Pas-200
Thos	Ora-150	Henry Snr	Cas- 64	Brittain	Nsh- 85
Peoples,Drury	Row- 80	Israel	Bur-102	Burrel Senr	Fra- 80
Henry	Pit-257	J	Cam-154	Cader	Pas-200
Jno	Mec- 47	Jacob	Rch-207	Celia	Mon- 50
John	Cha-215	Jacob	Cur- 89	Daniel	Prq-223
Joseph	Cum-262	James	Cas- 64	Daniel	Hay-199
Pepinger,Abraham	Row- 86	Jas	Glf-163	Drewly	Rob-237
Pepkin,Solomon	Rob-240	Jemimah	Cur- 89	Ebenezer	Glf-188
Pepper,John	Hal-115	Jeremiah	Way-244	Edwd	Cha-199
Stephen	Hal-116	Jesse Jnr	Cas- 64	Eldridge	Brt- 52
Stephen Junr	Hal-116	Jesse Sr	Cas- 64	Eli	Glf-171
Peram,J	Glf-174	John	Cas- 64	Elijah	Mon- 50
Peran,John	Glf-184	Jos	Bur-102	Elijah	Ora-163
Peras,Alexr	Ran-177	Joseph Snr	Glf-185	Eliz	Cho-229
Saml	Ran-177	Lamuel	Pit-262	Enos	Fra- 96
Perce,Benjamin	Hal-114	Mary	Bft- 39	Francis	Mec- 55
Percell,Thomas	Cas- 65	Moses	Row- 49	Hardy	Jon-303
Percival,R	Ash- 3	Richard	Cas- 64	Hardy	Bun- 75
Percy,Mary	Bur-115	Richd	Lnc-354	Hardy	Pas-200
Perdu,George	Grn-135	Thomas	Sur-161	Hemerick	Brt- 44
Perdue,Benj	Glf-154	W T	Cam-152	Henry	War-172
Bevel	Wil-269	William	Lnc-341	Isaac	Edg- 40
Dennis	Len-313	William	Hal-117	Isaac	Prq-223
Francis	Fra- 90	Wm Jun	Bft- 24	Isaac	Fra- 83
James	Glf-181	Wm Sen	Bft- 21	Israel	Pas-200
Joel	Wil-269	Perkinson,Eli	War-171	J	Ash- 9
John	Sur-195	Levi	War-177	Jacob	Mar- 10
Thomas	Sur-196	William	Roc- 7	Jacob	Rob-237
Perey,Demsey	Cur- 87	Perlear,Isaac	Wil-264	Jacob	Fra- 97
John	Cur- 87	John	Wil-283	Jacob	Pas-200
Joseph	Cur- 87	Permair,John	Rch-201	Jacob	Hrt-209
Josiah	Cur- 83	Permairs,Wm	Mon- 31	James	Edg- 44
Thos	Cur- 83	Permenter,Jas	Ans- 31	James	Fra-100
Perisher,Bosot	Tyr-206	Jas	Ans- 31	James	Ora-169
Perisho,John	Prq-223	Jno	Ans- 23	James	Hal-115
Perkens,Benjn	Hal-115	Nathaniel	Edg- 44	James	Mon- 21
Charles	Hal-115	Nathaniel	Edg- 45	Jeptha	Fra- 82

Name	Ref	Name	Ref	Name	Ref
Perry,Jerie	Cha-190	Perry,W	Ash- 15	Peters,Sarah	Pit-251
Jereh Esq	Fra- 80	William	Mar- 6	Peterson,Archd	Sam-156
Jereh	Fra- 83	William	Cum-260	Bartholomew	Hal-116
Jeremh (ridge)	Fra- 81	William	Per-223	Benjamin	Nor- 75
Jeremiah (R H)	Fra- 84	Willm	Pas-200	Chas	Cho-223
John	Brt- 44	Willm Senr	Fra- 84	Elisha	Sam-157
John	Jon-303	Wm	Mor- 59	Henry	Brt- 64
John	Cha-198	Wm	Nsh- 85	Humphry	Grn-135
John	Cha-199	Wm	Brt- 50	Jno	Rob-226
John	Fra- 98	Wm	Cha-213	John	Sam-156
John (fflt)	Fra- 80	Wm Sr	Cha-194	Joseph	Sam-157
Capt John	Fra- 83	Winefred	Edg- 41	Mabel	Sam-156
John	Bla- 12	Person,Amey	War-167	Nakcin	Cum-243
John	Way-249	Benjamin	Nor- 75	Matthias	Lnc-347
John	Mon- 50	Bob	Grn-138	Moses	Sam-164
John	Sto-134	Charles	Hal-116	Nicolas Snr	Car-170
John	Sto-102	Francis	Fra- 79	Robt	Brt- 60
John of Miles	Prq-222	George	Sto-134	Simon Peter	Rch-199
John Jr	Prq-223	Hubbert	Ans- 31	Thos	Sam-158
John Sr	Prq-223	Jackson	Mec- 35	William	Sam-156
Joseph	Hal-116	Jesse	Fra- 87	Peterwood,John	Grn-121
Joseph	Hrt-209	John	Fra- 85	Pethone,Jno	Rob-223
Joshua	Fra- 96	John	Ons- 98	Peticord,Greenbury	
Joshua (f)	Fra- 80	John Junr	Ons- 97		Sto-135
Joshua Esq	Fra- 88	Lidia	Wil-281	William	Sto-102
Josiah	Prq-223	Mason	Sur-192	William	Sto-135
Josiah	Brt- 51	Peterson	War-178	Petiford,Archd	Sto-147
Laurance	Prq-222	Presley	Fra- 79	Archelaus	Sto-111
Lewelly	Wsh-226	Thomas	Grn-131	Drury	Sto-147
Lige	Jon-303	William	War-184	T	Cum-238
Mary	Edg- 41	William	Way-252	Thomas	Sto-146
Mrs Mary	Fra- 98	Willm	Fra- 93	Thomas	Sto-110
Mary	Hal-117	Zachariah	Grn-133	Thomas	Sto-149
Mary	Hal-114	Persons,Thomas	Way-238	Petifrew,E farm	Tyr-212
Mary	Prq-223	Perune,Blackman	Glf-180	James	Grn-137
Milhunt	Prq-222	Pervey,Wm	Rob-221	William	Grn-137
Nathan	Prq-223	Perviance,David	Cab-147	Wm Senr	Grn-127
Nathl	Fra- 96	John	Cab-139	Petillo,James	Lnc-354
Noah	Mar- 12	Simson	Cab-139	Ton	Lnc-354
Nodelay	Gat-108	Perviane,Robt	Cab-146	Petoway,John	Ons-101
Peter	Cum-239	Pervis,Henry	Rob-238	Maberry Esqr	Ons- 99
Peter	Cha-210	Pesser,Zach	Ran-177	Peyton	Ons-100
Prisse	Gat-110	Peter,free man of colour		Robert	Ons-100
R	Ash- 9		Ran-187	Petre,John	Cab-141
Reubin	Prq-223	Peter,free man of colour		Petree,Jacob	Sto- 96
Robert	Prq-223		Ran-187	Petrie,Daniel	Sto-132
S	Ash- 9	Peter,free man of colour		Henry	Sto-116
Salley	Hrt-213		Ran-187	Henry	Sto-157
Saml	Cho-229	Peter,Cullen	Hal-115	Jacob	Sto-125
Samuel	Mor- 62	Hervey	Pas-200	Solomon	Sto-126
Silas	Jon-303	Jacob	Cab-148	Solomon	Sto-157
Solo	Cho-229	Jo	Ora-157	Petry,John	Lnc-375
Solomon	Grn-126	Simon	Sto-154	Pettet,Gedeon	Ons- 98
Solomon	Fra- 89	Peters,---- Sands	Pas-200	Samuel	Bur-125
Solomon	Fra- 82	George	Sam-162	Petteway,Micajah	Edg- 64
Tamor	Fra- 96	Gilliam	Nor- 75	Petteyford,Wm	Ora-149
Tilmon	Cha-211	Henry	Nor- 75	Pettifoot,CollinsGrn=121	
Turner	Cha-199	John	Nor- 75	Pettigrew,W	Ora-148
W	Ash- 13	Reading	Pit-251	Ebenezer	Wsh-216

Name	Ref	Name	Ref	Name	Ref
Pettijohn,Abram	Cho-222	Phelps,Charles	Wsh-224	Philips,David	Edg- 50
Abraham	Cho-225	Charles	Tyr-212	Elias	Bun- 73
Job	Cho-225	Cuthbert	Wsh-225	Elizabeth	Roc- 29
John	Cho-225	Devias	Tyr-212	Enoch	Row- 78
Pettillo,John T	Grn-121	Edward	Wsh-219	Ezekel	Row- 56
Pettis,David	Way-242	Enoch	Wsh-219	Ezekiah	Mon- 39
Horatio	Grn-124	Evan	Wsh-216	Ferebe	Len-315
Pettit,Benjamin	Sur-181	Frederic	Wsh-220	Joster	Sto-129
Pettits,Mills	Bur-119	George	Wsh-220	Frederick M	Edg- 55
Pettitt,Benjamin	Sur-193	Hannah	Tyr-212	Gemma	Roc- 27
George	Sur-173	Henry	Wsh-219	Geo	Ans- 6
Mark	Rch-194	Henry	Brt- 48	Henry	Way-248
Thomas	Sur-173	Isaac	Wsh-216	Irby	Ora-111
Thomas	Sur-183	James	Wsh-220	Isaac	Bur-115
Pettitts,John	Bur-119	James	Brt- 48	Jacob	Bun- 86
Petty,Abraham	Cha-210	James	Gat-110	Jacob	Ans- 13
Abram	Cha-211	Jeremiah	Tyr-210	James	Ans- 23
Ambrose	Cha-191	Jessee	Tyr-212	James	Edg- 55
Eli	Wil-274	John	Wsh-223	James	Ora-115
Isaa	Cha-191	John	Wsh-225	James	Roc- 23
James	Cha-211	John	Tyr-210	Jas	Ran-177
James	Rth-127	John	Mar- 7	Jobe	Ans- 31
James	Rth-125	John	Ire-255	Jno	Mec- 32
Jesse	Cha-216	John Junr	Wsh-217	Jno	Ans- 29
John	Sto-140	Joseph	Wsh-221	John	Row- 84
John	Cha-210	Joseph	Tyr-211	John	Joh-280
John	Cha-216	Joseph Esqr	Wsh-219	John	Sto-140
Joseph	Rth-126	Joseph Jr	Tyr-212	John	Sto-143
Lewis	Cha-211	Joshua	Tyr-211	John	Sto-143
Polly	Rth-127	Lizza	Wsh-219	John	Hay-199
Reuben	Cha-206	Luben	Brt- 61	John	Row- 69
Stephen	Cha-193	Micajah	Brt- 43	John	Sto-105
Thomas	Cha-205	Nancy	Wsh-219	John	Sto-107
William	Rth-126	Noah	Wsh-219	John	Sto-108
William Esqr	Wil-274	Robt	Brt- 43	John	Sto-152
William Jr	Cha-210	Uriah	Wsh-218	Klochlin	Sam-162
Wm Jr	Cha-205	Wm	Brt- 45	Lazarus	Bun- 76
Zachariah	Sur-166	Pheobus,J	Bla- 11	Lazrus	Bun- 77
Zachariah	Ans- 11	Phifer,Bradley	Hay-199	Lazarus Senr	Bun- 77
PettyJohn,John	Sur-169	Caleb	Cab-138	M	Mon- 38
Pew,Damason	Hyd-229	David	Mec- 24	Margaret	Cum-267
Francis	Hal-116	Geo	Cab-139	Mathew	Edg- 56
Little John	Hyd-229	Godfree	Mec- 41	Mordecai	Sto-128
Nancy	Cum-238	Henry	Mec- 40	Nancy	Edg- 46
Thomas	Cha-203	Jno	Mec- 46	Robert	Hay-199
Pewe,Jean	Ran-177	John	Cab-146	Robert	Roc- 23
Thomas	Ran-177	Nicholas	Mec- 40	Ruben	Ans- 6
Peyton,Nancy	Edg- 62	Peter	Mec- 41	Saml	Ran-177
Pfohl,Thomas	Sto-158	Philhour,Nicholas	Row- 71	Samuel	Sto-143
Phabon,Elijah	Rth-127	Philip,Foster	Sto- 99	Susannah	Cum-259
Phares,Isaac	Cum-265	Mary	Row- 60	Thomas	Ire-244
Lucretia	Cum-264	Philips,Abraham	Roc- 19	Thrower	Bun- 77
Samuel	Cum-265	Adam	Bun- 73	William	Ons-106
Pharris,Saml	Cab-143	Angus	Cum-245	William	Bun- 73
Phaul,Danl	Rob-229	Beddo	Row- 65	William	Ons-100
Phebe (sic)	Cho-223	Benj	Ora-138	William	Joh-280
Phelps,Asa	Tyr-210	Benjn	Hal-116	William	Bur-115
Benjamin	Wsh-219	Daniel	Sam-155	Wm	Mec- 54
Benjamin	Wsh-220	David	Sam-158	Wm	Mec- 45

Philips,Wm	Mec- 33	Phillips,Phebee	Cha-198	Phobus,J Senr	Bla- 13
Wm	Row- 57	Philemon	Glf-161	Pickard,Alex	Ora-147
Wm Senr	Bun- 73	Phillip	Ire-243	Isaac	Ora-165
Phillip,David	Glf-153	Phillip	Sur-193	Isaac Senr	Ora-165
Phillipps,John	Glf-156	R	Ora-139	James	Ora-129
Phillips,Abner	Sur-193	Reading	Len-314	Jno S	Ora-147
Abraham	Sur-171	Reuben	Wil-285	Michael	Ora-121
Ann	Hyd-224	Reuben	Len-322	Rd	Ora-147
Ann	Ora-146	Robt	Cha-198	Pickel,Henry	Ora-168
B	Ora-139	Robert	Wil-268	Pickelsimer,Henry	Bun- 88
B	Glf-184	Richard	Sur-181	Henry Jun	Bun- 88
Benjn	Sam-151	Samuel	Dup- 12	Pickens,Alexr	Cab-144
C	Cam-158	Sibil	Mor- 66	Andrew	Bun- 74
D	Cam-158	Sion	Cha-198	Hugh	Cab-144
David	Lnc-365	Solomon	Lnc-347	Saml	Mec- 44
Dennis	Cha-207	Solomon	Sur-173	Pickern,Naman	Jon-302
Drury	Nor- 75	Stephen	Rth-126	Picket,Abraham	Row- 83
Duncan	Cum-267	Stephen	Rth-125	Charles	Row- 49
E	Ash- 11	Steven	Wil-268	Dawson	Dup- 34
Edmon	Sur-182	T	Ora-140	Edwd	Ora-170
Eli	Mor- 58	T	Ora-140	James	Dup- 31
Elizabeth	Cha-204	Thomas	Sur-192	James	Dup- 18
Ephraim	Sur-163	Thomas	Cas- 65	John	Ran-177
Exum	Nsh- 79	Thomas	Grn-139	John	Dup- 18
Fanny	Len-313	Thomas	Wil-284	Mary	Row- 49
Fred	Pas-200	Thomas	Len-315	Micajah	Rth-127
Hezekiah	Mor- 65	Thomas	Dup- 9	Wm	Row- 49
Isaac	Mar- 12	Thos	Len-315	Wm	Ora-170
Isaac	Bur-109	Thos	Cha-207	Pickett,Benjn	Ran-177
J	Ash- 11	Thos	Ora-121	Carter	Ire-259
James	Rth-126	Weller	Ran-177	Charity	Glf-166
James	Cha-207	William	Sur-171	Elijah	Ire-259
Jas	Glf-167	William	Wil-285	Jacob	Ora-173
Jery	Mor- 63	William	Len-315	Jasper	Cur- 86
Jesse	Mor- 63	William	Cha-204	Jas	Ora-150
Jessee	Nor- 75	William W	Wil-284	Jesse	Ora-130
Joel	Glf-170	Wm	Mor- 69	John	Ran-177
Joel	Mor- 66	Phillipy,Luke	Glf-180	John	Ora-127
John	Per-142	Phillops,B	Bru-234	Jos	Glf-166
John	Mor- 66	Phillpott,James	Grn-142	Joseph	Ans- 5
John	Wil-273	John	Grn-142	Judy	Ora-149
John	Cab-147	Thos	Grn-142	Mark	Ora-150
John	Cha-204	Wm	Grn-142	Martin	Ans- 4
John	Cup- 8	Phillups,Samuel	Cur- 87	Nicholas	Sto-129
Lazarus	Cha-196	Philpot,John	Mar- 8	Thos	Ora-150
Lewis	Cha-207	Philps,Abraham	Gat-110	Wm R	Ans- 6
Lewis	Mor- 66	Philyaw,James	Ons- 99	Pickette,James	Rch-210
Mark	Mor- 56	James Junr	Ons- 99	Pickhard,Henry	Ora-158
Mark	Bla- 3	Martin	Jon-302	Pickhart,Henry	Cha-213
Mark	Len-314	Phipes,Jas	Glf-154	Wm	Cha-213
Mathew	Mor- 63	Phips,Aaron	Glf-155	Pickins,Elisebeth	Mec- 49
Meredith	Cha-196	George	Sur-166	Jerrard	Glf-186
Mordecai	Sto- 98	J	Ash- 5	John	Glf-186
Nathan	Cab-143	J	Ash- 5	Wm	Mec- 45
Nathaniel	Wil-285	Joseph	Glf-154	Pickle,Anthony	Row- 53
Nice	Len-313	Joseph	Glf-155	Elijah	Roc- 20
P	Ash- 11	S	Ash- 5	Jacob	Roc- 19
Patrick	Cha-205	Wm	Glf-160	Jacob	Len-319
Peter	Len-314	Phisarius,John	Cha-214	Jessee	Roc- 20

-251-

Name	Ref	Name	Ref	Name	Ref
Pickle,Mary	Ora-174	Pigott,John	Car-177	Piner,Thomas	Car-178
Michl	Len-319	Levi	Car-177	Pinhorton,Robert	Bun- 87
Valentine	Row- 54	Levi	Car-177	Pinion,William	Sur-187
Valentine	Row- 84	Wm	Char-209	Pinkert,Thomas	Sur-188
William	Roc- 21	Zechonias	Car-170	Pinkerton,David	Bun- 80
Picott,Julian	Mar- 6	Pigram,Patsey	Glf-181	Jas	Row- 40
Pidgeon,Charles	Row- 44	Pigue,John Sen	Ora-133	Pinket,John	Pit-240
Pierce,Charrity	Hrt-211	Wm	Ora-133	Zachariah	Pit-234
Daniel	Brt- 45	Pike,David	Way-253	Pinkham,Jane	Car-176
E	Ora-146	Ephraim	Hrt-207	Nathaniel	Car-177
Elijah	Ora-146	George	Nor- 75	Pinkleton,Wm	Row- 80
Elza	Hal-116	J Jr	Ora-133	Pinkley,Michl	Bur-129
Isom	Hrt-211	Jesse	Pas-201	Pinkston (sic)	Mec- 47
Jehu	Mar- 8	John Jun	Pas-200	Aron	Row- 77
Job	Hrt-208	John Sen	Pas-200	Edward	Row- 75
Joel	Nor- 75	Jonathan	Way-253	Meshack	Row- 77
John	Hal-116	Joseph	Sur-185	Micaja	Row- 76
John	Ire-266	Maky	Cha-200	Richard	Row- 76
Jonachan	Ire-251	Nath	Pas-200	Thomas	Row- 77
Joseph	Hal-115	Nathan	Way-253	William Sr	Row- 77
Kinchen	Glf-188	Richardson	Nor- 75	Wm	Row- 37
Lemuel	Joh-284	Sam	Ora-132	Pinnegar,John	Sto-141
Matthew	Brt- 45	William	Sto-101	William	Sto-141
Phillip	Cas- 65	William	War-182	William	Sto-106
Richard	Hrt-211	William	Hal-116	William Jur	Sto-141
Walter	Hal-115	William	Sto-132	Pinnell,Royal	Fra- 79
William	Mar- 7	Piland,Edward	Gat-112	Washington	Fra- 79
Wm	Brt- 47	James	Gat-107	Pinner,Arthur	Hrt-215
Zadock	Hrt-210	Robt	Cha-214	John	Nor- 74
Piercy,James	Wsh-226	Wm	Cha-216	Joseph	Nor- 74
Piere,Joseph J	Hal-115	Pile (sic)	Cum-237	Natt	Hrt-215
Pierse,J	Col- 20	Piles,Caleb	Ora-125	Thos	Hrt-215
Piersey,Blake	Bun- 76	Jeremiah	Ire-261	W	Bru-224
Pierson,Christopher	Bur-122	Pilgrim,Isaac	Bft- 38	Pinron,Joel	Bur-110
Hannah	Bur-122	John	Lnc-339	Thomas	Bur-110
Isaac	Bur-103	Michael	Bun- 73	Pinson,Aaron	Hay-199
John	Cas- 64	Prisilla	Pit-261	Abijah	Sur-186
Michael	Bur-122	Pilkenton,N	Glf-160	Richard	Sur-173
Susannah	Bur-122	Wm	Glf-160	Piper,Jno	Ora-135
Thomas	Bur-122	Pilkington,James	Bun- 87	Mary	Pas-200
Piget,Wm	Row- 46	William	Wil-266	Peter McArthur	Cum-269
Pigg,Clabon	Sur-164	Pilkinton,John	Rth-127	Sam	Ora-158
Jas	Glf-163	John	Joh-281	Sol	Ora-138
Martin	Glf-164	Richard	Joh-280	W	Ora-157
Nathan	Sur-164	Samuel	Cha-196	Wm	Ora-142
Paul	Sur-177	Wm	Cha-210	Pipins,Nelson	Ire-251
R	Glf-162	Pilley,Eliza	Bft- 23	Pipkin,Arthur	Way-247
V	Glf-164	Hillery	Bft- 21	Asher	Way-247
William	Sur-164	John	Bft- 23	Charles	Way-240
William	Wil-271	Tho	Bft- 20	Elisha	Way-240
Wm	Glf-163	Pillgreen,James	Pit-241	Elisha	Way-235
Piggit,John	Cha-204	Pilmon,D	Glf-162	Isaac	Gat-116
Piggott,Jeremiah	Cha-194	Pinchback,Wm	Cas- 65	Isaac	Len-318
Wm	Cha-212	Pincum,Jesse	Bft- 25	Jesse	Dup- 15
Piggter,J	Col- 16	Sarah	Bft- 25	Jesse	Len-318
Pigott,Abraham	Car-171	Pinegar,Mathias	Sto-109	John	Way-248
Cevil	Car-177	Piner,Nancy	Car-185	John	Nor- 74
Culpeper	Car-177	Joel	Hyd-231	Joseph	Way-248
Elijah	Car-177	Joseph	Car-176	Joseph	Way-247

-252-

Pipkin,Lovard	Way-240	Pitman,Matthew	Dup- 35	Pitts,Henry	Hal-117
Matthew	Way-248	Matthew	Mec- 40	Isaac	Sto-111
Needham	Way-240	Matthew	Mec- 35	Isaac	Sto-146
Peggy	Way-240	Micaja	Row- 77	James	Lnc-357
Philip	Way-247	Michael	Mec- 31	Jesse	Sto-101
Tabitha	Nor- 75	Randolph	Edg- 67	Jesse	Sto-132
Willis	Way-240	Sally	Edg- 62	John	Hal-116
Pippen,Banister	Fra- 95	Samuel	Edg- 42	Mark	Nsh- 74
Isaac	Fra- 80	Samuel	Hal-115	Martha	Nsh- 79
John	Edg- 64	Samuel	Rch-212	Philip	Bur-126
Loftis	Fra- 81	Sarah	Mec- 50	Rigdon	Ons- 97
Pippenger,Cornelius	Bun- 84	Selah	Hal-116	Samuel	Sto-147
Pippers,Joshua	Car-180	Thomas	Rob-240	Samuel	Sto-112
Pippin,Arthur	Sur-175	Thomas	Hal-115	Walter	Nsh- 76
Elijah	Edg- 71	Thomas	Edg- 64	Piver,Daniel	Car-171
Joseph	Edg- 70	Thomas	Row- 77	George	Car-171
Noah	Edg- 71	Thomas	Bun- 97	James	Car-171
William	Edg- 63	Pitmon,Sampson	Ans- 20	Johannas	Car-171
Pirchet,James	Ran-177	Pitsford,Drury	Sto-110	Peter	Car-182
Pirkins,Martin	Cas- 65	Pitt,Ann	Edg- 56	Zachariah	Car-182
Pistol,Robinson	Ans- 21	Archibald	Edg- 47	Plammons,K	Cum-236
Pit,Thomas	Ons-109	David	Edg- 44	Plares,Tho	Bur-130
Pitcher,Daniel	Sur-176	James	Edg- 44	Plaster,Charlotte	Mec- 25
James	Sur-183	Jesse	Mon- 26	John	Bur-115
John	Roc- 34	Joseph	Edg- 47	John	Row- 70
Pitchford,Daniel	War-170	Mary	Edg- 44	Plat,Adam	Dup- 22
Elijah	War-171	Richard	Edg- 56	Platt,Joshua	Dup- 22
Ezekiah	War-170	Thomas	Edg- 45	Pleas, J J	Cam-164
Sterling	War-180	Pittard,Elijah	Fra- 83	Pleasnt,Blewford	Cas- 65
Thomas	War-182	John	Per-142	Micajah	Cas- 64
Zachariah	War-184	Samuel	Per-142	Stephen	Per-142
Pitman,Amos	Dup- 33	Pittman,Absolam	Rob-240	Tho	Ora-118
Arthur	Hal-115	Britan	Rob-239	Wm	Cas- 65
Blake	Hal-115	Elias	Rob-237	Pleasants,Robert	Fra- 83
David	Edg- 63	Hardy	Rob-239	Pledger,John	Nor- 75
Demsey	Hal-115	Isham	Rob-240	John	Tyr-203
Demsey	Rch-197	Isham	Rob-237	Joseph	Tyr-203
Demsey Senr	Rch-207	Jacob	Rob-222	Robt	Tyr-204
Edward	Edg- 65	Jas	Rob-221	Pleming,John	Bun- 75
Felix	Edg- 67	Jessee	Rob-239	John	Bun- 75
Francis B H	Ons-100	Jessee	Rob-221	John	Bun- 96
George	Row- 77	Jethro	Joh-282	Pless,Henry	Cab-146
Grisham C	Edg- 58	Joel	Rob-240	Henry	Cab-145
Harrison	Edg- 58	John	Bur-120	Peter	Mon- 48
James	Hal-115	Joseph	Bur-114	Pliler,Henry	Cab-141
Jeremiah	Ons- 99	Mallekiah	Rob-240	Jacob	Mec- 44
Jesse	Rch-210	Mary	Rob-240	Plimer,David	Sur-164
Jessee	Edg- 67	Moses	Rob-229	Pliming,John	Bun- 87
John	Jon-303	Nathan	Rob-221	Peter	Bun- 84
John	Edg- 61	Nevile	Rob-234	Thomas	Bun- 84
John R	Hal-116	Noah	Rob-218	Pliss,John	Bur-109
John Senr	Hal-116	Noah	Rob-236	Ploi,John	Row- 55
John Senr	Hal-115	Josiah	Rob-237	Plot,Elias	Lnc-371
Jordan	Ons-101	Robert	Rob-221	George	Lnc-371
Joseph	Edg- 58	Sampson	Rob-221	Isaac	Cab-147
Joseph	Edg- 45	Pitts,Anne	Hal-117	Jesse	Cab-147
Levina	Way-241	Cadwalter	Sto-112	Plott,Henry	Hay-199
M	Bru-234	Cadwalter	Sto-147	Ploughaman,John	Row- 79
Matth	Hal-115	Cunrad	Lnc-347	Plowman,Jacob	Bun- 80

Plowmon,Mary	Sur-190	Poff,Peter	Sto-130	Pollock,Lewis	Ons- 97
Plumbly,Abraham	Bur-121	Peter	Sto- 99	Polson,John	Gat-110
Plumer,Ezekiah	Grn-146	Saml	Sto-130	Jos	Glf-164
John	Row- 42	Samuel	Sto- 99	William	Gat-109
Plumly,Josiah	Nor- 74	Pofford,Thomas	Sto-150	Polston,Daniel	Ora-163
Obediah	Nor- 74	Thomas	Sto-151	J	Ora-154
Plummer,Aaron	Bla- 7	William	Sto-123	Pond,Griffin	Wil-280
Abednego	Row- 44	Pogue,Joseph	Wil-280	Josiah K	Ans- 22
Abiezer	Roc- 3	Joshua	Cas- 65	Ponder,Daniel	Bun- 87
Alexr	Cum-248	Poindexter,Arcabald	Sur-182	Hezekiah	Rth-127
Baruch	Roc- 3	David	Sur-175	Ponds,Morning	Edg- 46
Charles	Roc- 18	David	Sto-140	Pone,D	Bru-238
Elias	Bla- 6	David	Sto-106	Ponns,Jno	Ora-124
Hemp Neg	Hal-117	Elizabeth	Sur-177	Ponns,Jno	Ora-124
J	Ash- 6	Jane	Sur-184	Ponsciton,John	Rth-127
Jeremiah	Bla- 7	John	Sur-182	Pool,Alexander	Rth-127
John	Grn-146	John G	Sur-175	Arter	Hay-199
John Senr	Bla- 7	John Stray	Sur-188	Betsy	Pas-199
Joseph	Rth-128	Richard	Brt- 47	Burges	Grn-133
Kimp	War-184	Robert	Sur-188	Collin	Mon- 27
Moses	Bla- 6	Samuel	Pas-199	George	Rth-126
Richd	Cum-266	Thomas W	Sur-177	Harry	Joh-278
Samuel	Bla- 3	William	Sur-188	Henry	Mon- 27
Thomas	Roc- 3	Poiner,David	Cas- 65	Isham	Mon- 24
William	Row- 76	David Snr	Cas- 65	Jacob Sr	Row- 78
Wm	Bla- 7	Joel	Bft- 34	James	Ran-177
Wm	Bla- 6	Pointerent,P	Col- 19	James Jun	Pas-199
Plumor,Mashaih	Ran-177	Poland,Henry	Nsh- 82	Jas	Per-132
Plunk,Jacob	Lnc-350	John	Nsh- 81	Jas Sen	Pas-199
Jacob	Lnc-332	John	Nsh- 80	Jesse	Bur-131
John	Lnc-350	Polisfield,J	Ora-154	John	Row- 78
Peter	Lnc-330	Polk,Catharine	Row- 86	John	Pas-199
Plunket,Houston	Cab-139	Charles	Mec- 46	John	Ran-177
James	Cab-139	Charles	Mec- 44	John Snr	Joh-291
James	Cab-144	James	Glf-156	Logustin P	Grn-133
Pluson,Starling	Ora-131	Jno	Ans- 31	Matthew	Car-182
Pluto,Wm	Bft- 24	Mickal	Mec- 30	Peggy	Pas-200
Podau,Jacob	Cab-146	Nancy	Mec- 25	Phillip P	Grn-133
Poe,Ben	Cha-201	Shelvy	Ans- 14	Reuben	Cha-216
David	Cha-207	Thos	Ans- 4	Richd Jun	Pas-200
Hatings	Cha-202	Wm	Mec- 46	Richd Sen	Pas-200
J	Ash- 7	Pollard,Benjamin	Pit-249	Robt	Pas-199
Jacob F	Cha-194	Elizabeth	Pit-248	Samuel	Mon- 33
Jesse	Cha-189	George	Mar- 6	Seth P	Grn-133
James	Glf-165	J	Mon- 37	Simon	Ran-177
John	Wil-268	James	Pit-248	Theophilus	Joh-273
Joseph	Cha-215	James	Pit-249	Tho Sen	Pas-200
M	Ash- 7	John	Lnc-365	Thoms Jun	Pas-200
Raleigh	Sur-178	John	Pit-249	William	Bur-105
Randolph	Cha-201	Jordan	Pit-249	Wm	Ran-177
Robt	Cha-196	Thos	Mon- 40	Poole,Danl	Len-315
Robt Jr	Cha-208	Zachariah	Sto- 94	David	Row- 67
Robt Sr	Cha-208	Zachariah	Sto-123	Elis	Cur- 86
Stephen	Cah-199	Pollock, Mrs.	Brt- 58	Fras	Len-313
W	Ash- 7	B	Ons- 98	Jacob	Row- 67
William	Glf-163	H	Glf-171	John	Row- 67
William	Wil-268	James	Jon-302	Josiah	Len-312
Poff,Isaac	Sto-130	John	Jon-303	Saml	Len-322
Isaac	Sto- 99	John Esqr	Ons- 99	Wm	Len-311

-254-

Name	Ref	Name	Ref	Name	Ref
Poor,Aaron	Mon- 27	Pope,William	Per-142	Porter,Mary	Hal-115
Caleb	Bur-122	Winkfield	Way-252	Matthew	Sam-161
George	Sto-119	Popeland,James	Ora-119	Moody	Edg- 58
James	Mon- 27	Popelston,Jno	Cho-221	Nathan	Joh-277
Sol	Mon- 27	Poplin,Geo	Mon- 41	Penelope	Roc- 8
Poore,Edward	Glf-171	H	Mon- 38	Robert	Rth-126
Jeremiah	Gul-168	J Jr	Mon- 38	Robert	Edg- 63
Robert	Sur-181	Jos	Mon- 39	Samuel	Rth-128
Pope,Alexr	Sto-150	Mary	Cha-189	Samuel	Edg- 63
Amey	Nor- 75	R	Mon- 38	Spencer	Rob-224
Archibald	Edg- 56	Wm	Mon- 38	Thomas	Rth-126
Barnaby	Nor- 75	Popplin,Jno	Mon- 39	Thomas	Rth-127
Benjn	Hal-115	Porch,Eaton	Joh-291	Thos	Ran-177
Blackman	Sam-158	Fedrick	Grn-121	William	Lnc-357
Charles	Row- 45	Henry	Fra- 97	William	Rth-126
David	Way-254	Independent	War-174	William	Rth-126
Davolt	Lnc-350	James	Mon- 22	William	Bur-118
E	Ash- 13	Sarah	Edg- 69	William Col	Rth-125
Elijah	Hal-116	Port,John	Bla- 10	William	Rth-127
Elijah	Nor- 75	Porten,Jas	Glf-152	William	Rth-127
Elizabeth	Sto-133	Porter,Alexr	Bur-118	William	Hyd-226
Frederick	Rob-238	Alexr	Mec- 25	William	Hay-199
Geo W	Row- 44	Alexr	Mec- 36	Wm	Lnc-338
George	Row- 45	Archabald	Mec- 37	Wm	Mec- 33
Hardy	Roc-233	Barnabas	Ans- 16	Capt Wm B	Mec- 26
Hardy	Edg- 56	Chrsitopher	Bun- 79	Wm Jnr	Mec- 27
Harris	Bla- 11	Christopher Sr	Bun- 79	Wm Snr	Mec- 28
Harwood	Fra- 94	David	Rth-128	Porthune,Murdock	Mor- 57
Henry	Lnc-370	David	Bur-117	Portin,Benjamin	Hay-199
J	Ash- 13	Drury	Ans- 10	Portis,Jas	Glf-169
Jacob	Hal-114	Dudley	Roc- 2	Jeremiah	Fra- 96
Jacob	Ans- 16	Eli	Edg- 40	John	Fra- 96
Jacob Big	Sam-158	Elizabeth	Edg- 64	Wm	Glf-170
James	Row- 43	Etheldred	Rob-223	Portlock,James	Pas-200
Jaremiah	Ans- 17	Francis	Wil-258	W	Cam-163
Jesse	Way-245	Henry	Bur-118	Portress,Jre	Nsh- 77
Jessey	Joh-288	Henry	Dup- 18	Sarah	Hal-117
John	Nsh- 79	Henry	Sam-162	Posay,C	Cam-160
John	Edg- 55	Hugh	Mec- 37	Posey,Benjamin	Bun- 88
John	Way-254	Hugh	Mec- 36	Francis	Bun- 82
John	Way-252	J	Glf-172	Humphrey	Bun- 99
Jonathan	Sam-153	J Esq	Col- 16	James	Bur-127
Joseph	Edg- 63	James	Mec- 46	Posponer,Berey	Cur- 87
Joseph	Nsh- 78	James	Mec- 25	Posten,John J	Row- 72
Mary	Len-316	James	Ire-243	Postill,Francis	Bun- 87
Micajah	Ans- 12	James	Rth-127	Postin,Charles	Row- 60
Nathanel	Row- 48	Jas	Mec- 31	Postion,Jno	Ans- 23
Osborn	Grn-123	Jas B	Mec- 32	Poston,John	Bun- 88
Pool	Cum-259	Jno Snr	Mec- 36	Sarah	Ire-256
Reddin	Dup- 16	John	Rth-128	Posttton,Mrs	Mec- 28
Richd	Cha-212	John	Car-182	David	Mec- 28
Solomon	Way-238	John	Ons-106	Poteate,Miles	Cas- 64
Stephen	Cum-257	John	Mec- 26	Poteet,Col James	Bun- 78
Thos	Sam-159	John	Mor- 66	James Senr	Bun- 78
Unch	Mor- 63	John Junr	Sam-161	John	Bun- 78
West Junr	Sam-163	Joseph	Wil-258	Poter,Benj	Hrt-211
William	Hal-116	Joseph Jr	Wil-271	Thos	Hrt-214
William	Edg- 55	Joshua	Roc- 30	Pots,George	Row- 84
William	Edg- 67	Martin	Edg- 63	Peter	Row- 84

Name	Ref	Name	Ref	Name	Ref
Pots,William	Row- 84	Powe,Simon	Ans- 14	Powel,Wm	Nsh- 77
Pott,Wm	Mec- 24	Thos	Ans- 14	Wm	Ans- 27
Potte,Capt Jas	Mec- 25	Powel,Aden	Joh-282	Wm Senr	Hal-117
Potter,Abram	Rth-127	Allison	Nsh- 75	Willis	Hal-117
Ann	Ons-105	Barnabas	Rob-239	Zilphey	Gat-110
Danl	Len-311	Daniel	Hal-116	Powell (col)	Col- 21
David	Mec- 29	Daniel Senr	Hal-116	A	Col- 17
Elias	Roc- 10	Danl	Rob-239	A Esq	Col- 19
Gorden	Mec- 34	David	Gat-111	Ann	Col- 20
J Junr	Bru-236	Demsey	Rob-221	Benjamin	Edg- 70
J Snr	Bru-236	Duglas	Rob-239	Benjamin	Nor- 74
James	Bru-236	Elijah	Cha-201	Benjamin	Bur-126
Jas	Mec- 33	Elijh	Ran-177	Bodey	Sam-161
Joseph	Roc- 30	George	Hal-116	Brittain	Dup- 23
Littleton	Bft- 34	Hampton	Hal-116	Cader	Brt- 54
M	Glf-183	Henry	Cha-196	Cader	Hrt-207
M	Bru-238	Honrias	War-172	Cela	Brt- 55
Moses	Roc- 16	Isaac	Joh-282	Charles	Cha-210
Natl	Bft- 34	Jacob	Gat-109	Charles	Hrt-217
R	Ash- 12	Jacob	Ran-177	Cotten	Mar- 3
R	Bru-238	James	War-173	Daniel	Edg- 45
R Esqr	Bru-234	Jesse	Hal-116	Danl	Len-314
Richard	Prq-223	Jno	Rob-223	David	Hay-199
Robert	Grn-142	Jno	Rob-218	E	Ash- 12
S	Bru-234	Jno	Rob-235	Edward	Grn-129
Stephen	Sur-162	John	Rch-201	Eldred	Brt- 46
Thomas	Grn-144	John	Sam-151	Eli	Ran-176
Wm	Len-311	John	Gat-109	Elias	Nor- 75
Wm	Lnc-334	John	Hal-115	Elijah	Dup- 17
Potts,Agness	Mec- 29	John B	War-175	Elijah	Dup- 19
Fras	Len-317	Kezany	Hal-116	Ellus	Bur- 127
Henry	Ire-249	Mark	Sam-158	Enos	Way-253
J	Cum-235	Mary	Hal-116	George	Bur-112
J	Bru-236	Mary	Hal-116	George	Dup- 20
James	Ire-260	Mary	War-177	Henry	Brt- 63
James	Len-321	N	Ora-140	Hezekiah	Prq-223
Jas	Mec- 25	Nathan	Nsh- 76	J	Col- 19
Jonathan	Mec- 52	Nathan	Mon- 31	J	Col- 20
Margaret	Ire-249	Nathaniel	Rob-239	J	Cam-163
Mary	Len-314	Niclas	Rob-238	Jacob	Edg- 64
Peter	Ire-264	Orren	Hal-115	James	Cas- 65
Ralph	Bft- 36	Ptollemy	Hal-117	James	Cha-208
Robert	Ire-249	Richard	Rob-236	James	Nor- 76
Robt	Mec- 51	Robert	Rch-200	James	Cas- 65
Stringer	Len-314	Ruth	Joh-290	Jesse of Halifax	
Susanna	Len-314	Ruth	War-179		Brt- 56
William	Ire-248	S	Ora-155	John	Cas- 65
Pound,Jno	Ans- 12	Salley	Gat-109	John	Bla- 11
Saml	Ans- 18	Solomon	Hal-116	John	Len-321
Thomas	Roc- 10	Sophia	Cha-197	John	Cas- 65
William	Cha-196	Steven	Joh-278	John	Pit-248
Pounds,J Junr	Bru-236	Thomas	War-181	John	Roc- 20
John Sr	Bru-226	Thos	Mon- 30	Lamuel	Prq-223
Wm	Bru-226	Thos	Cha-196	Lewis	Sam-158
Povoh,Benj	Ons-106	William	Wil-272	Lewis	Hrt-208
Mark	Ons-106	William	Joh-290	Lewis	Bur-109
Powals,Maryan	Cas- 65	William	Prq-222	Lewis Jr	Bur-115
Powe,Jas	Ans- 14	William	Lnc-341	Luke	Sam-159
Jas	Ans-14	William Junr	Hal-117	M	Col- 17

Name	Loc	Name	Loc	Name	Loc
Powell,Mary	Brt- 51	Powers,Samuel	Cur- 91	Preslar,Daniel	Ans- 9
Matthew	Nor- 74	Sarah D	Rch-209	Jno	Ans- 10
Miles	Nor- 74	Susanna	Brt- 59	Jno	Ans- 24
Ransom	Rth-125	W	Cam-155	Joshua	Ans- 9
Ransom	Row- 61	William	Hal-115	Salathial	Ans- 9
Ransom	Nor- 75	William	Roc- 2	Stephen	Ans- 9
Reubin	Edg- 57	William	Cur- 91	Wm	Ans- 9
Robert	Gat-108	Powles,Adam	Row- 67	Presley,Jesse	Rob-233
Robert	Grn-129	Powsis,David	War-170	Preslor,Elias	Ans- 9
Rodk	Bft- 26	Poyner,Adam	Cur- 88	Presnal,Stephen	Ran-176
Salley	Gat-112	Even	Cur- 88	Presnall,Danl	Ran-176
Sally	Nor- 75	Gorge	Cur- 88	Elijah	Ran-177
Saml	Brt- 46	Isah	Cur- 88	Esau	Ran-176
Silas	Bft- 22	James	Cur- 88	James	Ran-176
Silas Jr	Nor- 74	Joel	Cur- 88	John	Ran-176
Silus Senr	Nor- 75	Lovey	Cur- 88	Stephen	Ran-176
Stapleton	Pit-262	Lydia	Cur- 86	Wm	Ran-177
T	Col- 17	Mary	Cur- 86	Presnell,Absalom	Bur-126
Thos	Ora-144	Polley	Cur- 91	Pressa,Robt	Ans- 21
William	Way-234	Powers	Cur- 88	Presscoat,Benj	Ons-102
William	Brt- 64	Robert	Cur- 88	Pressley,Anthony	Bun- 94
William	Pit-234	Thomas	Cas- 75	Jno	Mec- 43
Wm	Grn-129	Tina	Cur- 90	Levi	Mec- 43
Wm	Brt- 57	Poytress,Celia	Nor- 75	Peter	Bun- 94
Wm	Ans- 11	Odam	Nor- 76	Richard	Mec- 43
Wm	Ans- 25	Prack,J	Ora-140	Voluntine	Mec- 43
Wiley	Cha-216	Practer,Thos	Ire-265	Pressly,David	Bun- 80
Willis	Edg- 58	Praither,Thomas	Ire-266	Presson,Saml	Ans- 21
Powels,Richard	Gat-109	Prance,Joseph	Cum-264	Stephen	Rth-128
Power,John	War-176	Polly	Cum-241	Preston,WinnefredSur-197	
Thomas	War-181	Prather,Leo	Ora-122	Prevatt,Peter	Rob-221
Powers,Absalom	Hal-115	Prator,Amos	Rth-125	Prevett,Antho	Cho-231
Barnabas	Rch-208	William	Sto-120	Irven	Ire-250
Benj	Pas-199	Pratt,Elizabeth	Roc- 33	Wm	Cho-231
C	Col- 17	George	Ora-143	Previtt,Cader	Ire-254
C	Cam-162	James	Ora-168	Nancy	Ire-253
Clarey	Cur- 91	James Jr	Ora-943	Willis	Ire-252
Elizabeth	Sto-139	John	Wsh-222	Prewitt,Anne	Rth-126
Ephrim	Tyr-207	John	Roc- 33	Benjamin	Bun- 91
Henry	Cha-213	Lott	Wsh-221	James	Bun- 91
Henry	Hal-115	Nehemiah	Roc- 22	Joel	Wil-271
J	Col- 17	Richard	Ire-263	John	Rth-127
J	Col- 17	Robert	Sto-131	John	Rth-128
James	Cur- 91	Robert	Sto-100	John	Wil-259
Jas	Mec- 52	Saml	Ans- 7	Joseph.	Wil-271
Jesse	Joh-272	William	Pit-255	Spencer	Rth-127
Jesse	Pit-252	William H L	Roc- 17	Prewitt,HambletonCas- 65	
John	Tyr-208	William	Roc- 33	William	Cas- 65
John	Sto-139	Wm	Ans- 7	Price,Aaron	Pas-200
John	Cur- 91	Zebulon	Cho-225	Abra	Bft- 19
Joshua	Tyr-210	Predie,George	Grn-131	Abram	Cas- 65
Josiah	Tyr-211	Robert	Grn-131	Asa	Mar- 7
Kezia	Wsh-218	Thomas	Grn-131	Benjn	Ans- 26
Moses	Hal-115	Thomas	Grn-132	Benjamin	Row- 64
Nancey	Cur- 91	Wm	Grn-131	Betsy	Pas-199
Nancy	Rob-243	Pregan,J	Bru-230	David	Bur-106
Polly	Tyr-210	Prescot,Jesse	Car-180	Doctrin	Cho-227
Priscilla	Wsh-219	Willoughby	Car-180	Drury	Roc- 34
R	Col- 17	Preslar,Amos	Ans- 9	Gideon	Cha-199

Price,Gillam	Rth-127	Price,Thomas	Mar- 8	Prim,Jno	Mec- 51	
Hardy	Edg- 55	Thos	Ans- 13	Thos	Mec- 47	
Henery	Cur- 82	Thos	Dup- 16	Primrose,Thos	Grn-139	
Henry	Mec- 40	Thos W	Ora-173	Prince,Hamilton	Cum-253	
Irvin	Joh-286	W	Ash- 12	Isem	Cum-257	
Isaac	Roc- 10	Walter	Bur-107	Mary	Nor- 76	
Isaac	Mec- 25	Will	Dup- 24	Nathan	Cum-258	
Isaac	Mec- 47	William	Cas- 65	Nicholas	Cha-202	
Isabella	Lnc-331	William	Rth-125	Oliver	Cha-202	
J	Col- 17	William	War-183	Richd	Ans- 27	
James	Ire-259	William	Edg- 56	Richd	Ans- 15	
James	Joh-286	William	Way-248	William	Rth-125	
Jas	Mec- 26	William	Mar- 8	Priner,Thomas	Roc- 34	
Jessee	Edg- 56	William D	Rth-128	Pringle,Charles	Car-183	
Joel	Edg- 55	Willm	Bft- 19	Prior,Pleasant	Mon- 40	
Jno	Mec- 35	Wm	Ora-143	Samuel	Row- 82	
Jno Junr	Ora-143	Wm	Hal-115	Prisly,James	Bur-105	
John	Cas- 65	Wm	Lnc-333	John	Bur-105	
John	Prq-223	Willis	Edg- 55	Jonathan	Bur-105	
John	Rth-126	Zachariah	Joh-280	Nathan	Bur-107	
John	Rth-127	Prices,Moses	Edg- 60	Pritchard,A	Cam-165	
John	Bun- 75	Prichard,Abso	Cho-227	Ann	Brt- 58	
John	Sur-195	E	Ora-140	Benj	Pas-200	
John J	Cas- 65	Prickett,Jeremiah	Glf-174	Benj	Pas-200	
Jonathan	Edg- 55	JOsiah	Bla- 7	Christopher	Brt- 63	
Jonathan	Mec- 26	Pridden,John	Nor- 75	D	Cam-162	
Joseph	Edg- 61	Priddie,John	Grn-149	David	Pas-201	
Josiah	Mec- 47	Priddle,John	Mor- 58	Edward	Cha-214	
Lemuel	Roc- 18	Priddy,John	Grn-130	Elijah	Ora-114	
Lewis	Mor- 61	Pride,Frederick J	Hal-116	Elisha	Pas-199	
Lucy	Joh-285	Hock J	Hal-109	Enoch	Pas-199	
Major	Cas- 64	John	Bun- 74	H	Cam-162	
Margt	Bft- 27	Oliver	Bun- 91	Hardy	Nor- 75	
Mark	Joh-285	Pridgeon,Lanson	Bla- 11	Hugh	Pas-199	
Marthy	Mar- 5	M	Bla- 13	James	Bur-126	
Mary	Wil-265	Matthew	Bla- 12	Jesse	Sur-163	
Matt	Bft- 36	Wm	Bla- 11	Jesse	Fra- 87	
Meridith	Cas- 64	Pridit,Wm	Grn-146	John	Pas-200	
Nancey	Cur- 81	Pridy,George	Sto-124	Jonathan	Brt- 63	
Nathl	Dup- 15	George	Sto- 95	Jos	Pas-200	
Peter	Way-236	James	Sto-124	Joseph	Pas-199	
Philip	Bun- 96	James	Sto- 95	Joseph	Sur-192	
Philip Senr	Bun- 96	John	Sto-145	Joshua	Nor- 75	
Pinewill	Jon-303	Lewis	Sto- 95	Leml	Pas-199	
Race	Roc- 34	Lewis	Sto-124	Lidey	Mon- 50	
Rachel	Cho-223	Priest,Angus	Rch-193	Moses	Pas-200	
Rederick	Ans- 9	D	Bla- 10	Peggy	Nor- 75	
Reese	Lnc-333	David	Len-312	Pelig	Pas-199	
Reese	Mec- 51	John	Len-312	Phillip	Sur-179	
Richard	Hal-115	John	Cum-243	Presley	Nor- 76	
Richard	Joh-285	Thomas	Roc- 33	Richd	Pas-199	
Richard	War-179	Priggen,Bajah	Nsh- 82	Ruth	Pas-199	
Richd	Cum-247	David	Nsh- 80	Saml	Pas-199	
Ruth	Pas-200	Jessee Sr	Nsh- 89	Thaddeus	Pas-199	
Ryas	Joh-285	Peter	Nsh- 89	Thos	Mon- 29	
Samuel	Pas-199	Priggin,Hardy	Nsh- 92	Wm	Ora-143	
Soln	Bru-228	Hardy	Nsh- 85	Zacka	Sur-163	
Thomas	Joh-273	Jessee Jr	Nsh- 89	Pritchet,Isaac	Roc- 30	
Thomas	Edg- 58	Prim,James	Sur-182	James	Cum-260	

Name	Loc	Name	Loc	Name	Loc
Pritchet,Jeremiah	Roc- 30	Propes,Henry	Cab-142	Pugh,Eaton	Mar- 15
Jno	Ora-152	Michael	Cab-142	Eaton	Nor- 76
Joseph	Roc- 30	Propet,Michl	Lnc-326	Eaton	War-171
Margaret	Roc- 31	Prophet,James	Bun- 79	Eaton Negroe	Hal-116
Nathaniel	Jon-303	Propst,Jacob	Lnc-345	Eliza Jun	Brt- 43
Stephen	Ora-151	Jacob	Lnc-370	Eliza Senr	Brt- 59
Thomas	Roc- 30	John	Lnc-347	Francis	War-171
Pritchett,Abish	Bft- 19	Prosser,James	Mon- 19	Majr Francis	Fra- 78
Asa	Tyr-204	Prout,Joshua	Ans- 17	G	Cam-165
Jeptha	Hal-115	Pruatt,Thomas	Grn-123	Henry	Gat-112
John	Fra- 87	Pruden,David	Brt- 66	J	Cam-157
Peter	Bft- 33	Jacob	Brt- 66	Jacob	Cha-204
Priscilla	Hal-115	Lodwick	Brt- 66	James	Cur- 83
Margaret	Hal-116	Nathenial	Gat-107	James	Sam-152
Sterling	Hal-115	Pruit,Harrod B	Row- 65	Jeremiah	Nsh- 91
William	Hal-115	Pleasent	Row- 56	John	Ora-130
Wm	Hal-114	William	Rth-128	John	Car-177
Wm	Bft- 33	Pruitt,Burrel	Sur-190	John	Hal-117
Z	Glf-175	John	Grn-123	Joseph	Brt- 59
Prithee,Noah	Way-254	Nancy	Sur-189	P	Cam-156
Privet,John	Prq-223	William	Sur-189	Paul Sparrow	Cur- 82
Privett,Harris	Ire-254	Willis	Sto-105	Rachal	Edg- 47
Jacob	Ire-253	Willis	Sto-139	Reuben	Lnc-376
John	Ire-253	Prust,Dempsey	Roc- 22	Sampson	Ora-122
John	Ire-253	Pryor,David	Row- 85	Stephen	Pit-237
Nancy	Ire-255	Ezra	Hal-115	W	Cam-155
Richard	Ire-255	John	War-176	Whitmell H	Brt- 58
Privit,Williford	Wil-270	John H	Sto-126	William	Pit-231
Privitt,Manarias	Ire-248	John H	Sto- 96	William	Brt- 64
Pro,Chs	Row- 56	Joseph	Hal-114	Puit,Frances	Bur-128
Probitt,Lewis	Bur-127	Peter	Hal-114	Joseph	Bur-128
Proby,Paul	Pas-200	Thomas	Row- 85	William	Bur-128
Wm	Pas-200	Pslamon,Vincent	Way-240	Puitt,Mary	Bur-126
Prock,Sarah	Bur-112	Psalter,Ananias	Car-175	Puket,Priscilla	Dup- 36
William	Bur-112	Christopher	Car-175	Pullam,John	Fra- 96
Procker,Joseph	Grn-121	James	Car-174	Kinchen	Glf-155
Procter,Joseph	Ora-137	Rebecca	Car-175	Nelson	Fra- 84
Proctor,Aaron	Edg- 61	Richard	Car-175	Pullem,Elibth	Per-132
Amey	Ans- 25	William	Car-174	James	Per-132
Ann	Edg- 45	Pucket,Chatham	Lnc-341	Pulley,Lida	Mar- 15
Benj	Lnc-359	Joel	Roc- 22	Pulliam,Barnet	Grn-139
Giles	Roc- 11	John	Cas- 72	Elizabeth	Grn-148
Hardy	Edg- 45	Parham	Dup- 18	Pulliem,John	Sto-105
Jesse	Edg- 44	William Sr	Dup- 35	Pullom,John	Bur-125
John	Rth-126	Puckett,Isham	Sur-177	Margit	Rth-127
Jonathan	Edg- 46	James	Ire-257	Pullum,Bird	Per-132
Mary	Edg- 44	Joseph	Sur-186	Curren	Mon- 31
Mary	Edg- 43	Richard	Sur-176	Joseph	Cas- 65
Reuben	Prq-223	Thomas	Sur-186	Pully,Charity	Hal-115
Reubin Jr	Rth-126	Zachariah	Sur-185	David Junr	Hal-116
Reubin Sr	Rth-126	Pue,Arnal	Joh-286	David Senr	Hal-116
Richd	Ora-149	Benjamin	Bur-129	Frederick	Hal-116
Solomon	Cha-199	Simeon	Joh-286	James	Fra- 93
Thomas	Sto-152	Puff,Andrew	Rob-223	Jesse col	Fra-100
Profit,Larkin	Mon- 23	Pugh,Amos	Lnc-375	John	Joh-287
Profitt,John	Wil-271	Austin	Brt- 58	Joseph	Hal-116
Samuel	Wil-258	Curnelous	Cur- 82	Mary	Nor- 75
Thomas	Wil-283	E	Cam-159	Robert	Rch-206
William	Wil-283	Easter	Brt- 66	Robert Jr	Nor- 75

-259-

Name	Location
Pully,Robert Sr	Nor- 75
Spittle	Cha-200
William	Hal-115
Pulmer,Henry	Cum-234
Pultom,Zechariah	Bur-129
Pumphrey,Henry	Wil-260
John	Wil-266
Larkin	Wil-261
Pricilla	Pit-233
Reading	Pit-233
Punch,Matthew	Ire-249
Puntch,James	Lnc-370
Thomas	Lnc-347
Purcell,William	Roc- 18
Purdam,Benjamin	Row- 56
Purdie,J S	Bla- 10
Purdom,Elisha	Sur-183
Henry	Sto-144
Mary	Sur-183
Thomas	Sto-152
Purdy,Mary	Cho-221
Purgear,Daniel	Grn-125
John	Grn-125
Purkins,Allen	Way-245
J	Ash- 11
James	Pit-262
James	Nsh- 87
James	Nsh- 91
L	Ash- 11
Saml	Ans- 15
T	Ash- 13
W	Ash- 8
Purlee,Benjamin	Per-134
Purrington,John H	Hal-116
Pursel,Jno	Rob-224
Neill Junr	Cum-264
Pursell,George	Roc- 18
Purser,David	Bft- 33
Jerry	Mec- 46
Jno	Mec- 46
Marian	Cum-265
Mary	Bft- 33
Neill Senr	Cum-264
Robt	Mec- 46
Robt	Bft- 33
Zedh	Bft- 33
Purvines,David	Mec- 23
Joseph	Mec- 23
Purvis,Gabrial	Edg- 54
Moes	Brt- 55
William	Brt- 66
Purviss,Rodrick	Mar- 8
Puryear,Barnes	Grn-133
Robert	Grn-133
Sarah	Sto-137
William	Grn-133
Wm Senr	Grn-133
Pustle,Henry	Ire-255
Putman,Benjamin	Rth-127
Putman,Elias	Rth-128
George	Rth-128
John	Rth-128
William	Rth-128
Wilson	Rth-128
Putnal,Joshua	Pit-252
Putney,Anthony W	Nor- 75
Richard	Nor- 76
Pyant,Thos	Mec- 44
Pybern,Christopher	Bun- 74
Pyburn,Sarah	Hay-199
Pyett,Joseph	Bur-121
Pyland,Martha	Nor- 75
Richard	Nor- 74
Pyle,James Junr	Ora-125
James Sen	Ora-125
John	Ora-125
John	Ora-120
Wm	Ora-125
Pyram,Charles	Sur-189
Pyrant,Wm	Mon- 50
Wm	Mec- 46
Quait,Robert	Glf-172
Quakingbush,Peter	Cha-211
Qualls,C	Ora-132
Sam	Ora-122
Sarah	Grn-123
Wm	Grn-123
Quarter,Baker	Hrt-213
John Odem	Hrt-213
Quartimus,Eliz	Pit-234
Quary,Mrs	Mec- 47
Mes	Mec- 41
Mrs	Mec- 40
Jonathan	Mec- 46
Robt	Mec- 38
Robt	Mec- 44
Wm	Mec- 44
Wm	Mec- 46
Quaslv (sic)	Pas-201
Quean,John	Row- 66
Queen,David	Ire-252
Hugh	Rth-128
Hugh Sr	Rth-128
Joseph	Ire-252
Moses	Bur-131
R	Mon- 36
Richard	Rth-128
Richard	Bur-131
S	Mon- 36
Samuel	Bun- 96
William Junr	Rth-128
William Sr	Rth-128
Query,James	Cab-137
Quey,Philimon	Cha-209
Quicley,Elizabeth	Cur- 82
Jacob	Cur- 81
John	Cur- 81
Quicley,Joseph	Cur- 81
Wm	Cur- 82
Quiggle,Michael	Lnc-345
Quillham,Mary	Cab-137
Quilling,John	Sto-110
Quilman,Geo	Cab-140
Quimby,Jonas	Way-237
Quin,Abner Junr	Car-183
Abner Senr	Car-183
Edward	Bft- 36
Quinby,John	Glf-160
Quinerly,Edward	Pit-250
Patrick	Pit-250
Quinn,Caleb	Dup- 30
David	Dup- 10
John	Mar- 8
Loftin	Dup- 32
Thomas	Dup- 32
Quinton,Samuel	Bun- 73
Quiry,John	Bur-125
Quisby,Peter	Bun- 73
Quitt,William	Ire-252
Qullen,John	Sto-147
Thomas	Sto-150
Qury,Dolphine	Cum-235
R----,Jeremiah	Jon-303
R----,Saml	Ran-178
Rabey,Addom	Gat-114
Rabon,D	Bru-236
Rabone,Hodge	Bur-117
Raby,Blake	Brt- 56
Elisha	Hrt-207
Luke	Brt- 56
Peter	Bur-130
Race,Jessie	Grn-131
John	Grn-131
Rachel,Free	Ons-106
Sterling	Rch-204
William	Rch-213
Rackly,Jno Sr	Mon- 26
Racow,Dorcas	Hyd-226
Rader,Adam	Lnc-370
William	Lnc-370
Radford,Eli	Fra- 88
Jesse	Sto-124
John	Bun- 76
John	Bun- 87
Joseph	Bun- 76
Polley	Way-238
Robt	Way-239
William	Sto- 95
Wm	Sto-124
Radgon,Hugh	Mec- 23
Rae,Angus	Rob-231
Archd	Rob-218
Eliza	Rob-225
Flora	Rob-225
Lauchlin	Rob-231

-260-

Raeford,James	Mon- 25	Rains,Wm	Ran-179	Ramsey,Wm	Bla- 12
John	Way-233	Rainwater,William	Sur-163	Wm	Cum-240
Matthew	Mon- 25	Rainwatter,John	Rch-206	Ramsom,John	Lnc-337
Philip	Way-233	Raison,Elizabeth	Roc- 31	Ramsour,David	Lnc-326
Raford,Robert	Joh-280	Raker,Frederick	Row- 49	David	Lnc-345
Ragan,Jesse	Per-133	Rakestraw,John S	Pit-252	Henry	Lnc-345
Ragen,David	Ora-173	Nancy	Roc- 7	Henry	Lnc-371
Raggsdail,Richard	Rth-130	Rakley,Elijah	Cum-259	John	Lnc-345
Ragister,Henry	Per-143	Ralagh,Michael	Sto-153	Ramsower,Henry	Ran-178
Ragland,Evin	Grn-142	Ralay,Michael	Sto-112	Mchl	Ran-178
Robt	Cha-215	Ralesback,Jacob	Row- 49	Ramsy,Benj	Ons-104
Theoderick	Cha-192	Henry	Row- 59	Isaac	Ons-101
Thos	Cha-194	Raley,Abner	Roc- 15	Wm	Per-133
Wm	Cha-197	Raling,Gorge	Cur- 89	Ranalds,A	Col- 20
Ragsdale,DAvid	Grn-135	Rall,Rachel	Wsh-219	D	Col- 17
Edward	Grn-133	Rallings,James	Cha-200	Rand,Abraham	Sto-132
Edwin	Rch-201	Rallins,Joseph	Tyr-205	Abraham	Sto-100
Jones	Grn-134	Ralls,David	Way-233	William	Sto-100
Thomas	Rch-202	Ralph,J	Cam-159	William	Sto-132
William	Rch-200	Joseph	Cur- 89	Randal,Richd	Ans- 16
William	Glf-186	Rolin	Glf-185	Randall,John	Rth-129
Raiford,Jno	Ans- 16	Tapley	Glf-185	John	Wil-282
Philip	Cum-239	Thomas	Gat-110	Peter	War-178
Robert	Cum-239	Ralston,Samuel	Pit-242	Robert	Rth-130
Raily,Andrew	Lnc-365	Ram,Amos	Jon-303	Randel,Johnston	Ran-179
John	Lnc-365	William	Jon-303	Ransom	Ran-178
Rainer,Henry	Lnc-328	Rama,Joseph	Sur-162	Randle,Benager	Mon- 32
Seaton	Cum-266	Rambau,Gorge	Cur- 92	Douglas	Mon- 41
Rainey,Ben	Ora-128	Ramey,Randol	Grn-147	Elijah	Jon-303
Cath	Bft- 39	Ramsam,Phillip	Rth-131	Fred	Mon- 39
David	Ora-115	Ramsay,Henry	Hrt-213	J	Mon- 39
Hall	Nor- 76	Samuel	Bur-110	Jabel	Mon- 32
Isaac	Cas- 67	William	Bun- 92	Jas	Mon- 39
James	Ora-128	Ramsey,Andrew	Ire-239	John	Ire-248
James	Cas- 66	Ann	Cha-214	John	Lnc-342
John	Cas- 67	David	Ire-259	John	Mon- 39
Sarah	Ans- 19	David	Jon-303	Jonas	Mon- 39
Thomas	Nor- 76	George	Rth-129	Letty	Mon- 44
William	Cas- 66	J	Bru-224	Nehemiah	Jon-303
William	Lnc-342	James	Bun- 93	Noah	Mon- 32
Wm	Ora-128	James	Bur-129	Peter	Mon- 39
Rainor,Daniel	Dup- 33	James	Lnc-339	Silas	Rth-131
David	Sam-160	Joel	Bun- 76	Smith	Rth-130
John	Dup- 34	John	Nor- 76	Thos	Mon- 39
Richard	Sam-160	John	Bun- 93	Wiat	Mon- 41
Stephen	Dup- 36	John	Lnc-336	William	Rth-130
Rains,Ambros	Cha-207	John	Cum-237	Randleman,John	Sto- 96
Anthony	Ran-179	Lewis	Per-133	John	Sto-126
Henry	Bun- 84	Mial	Cha-202	Randles,James	Ire-255
Henry	Joh-279	Neill	Rob-229	John	Ire-256
James	Ran-179	Richd	Bur-130	William	Ire-256
Jno	Ans- 12	Robert	Lnc-336	Randly,Hugh	Ire-264
John	Cas- 67	Robert	Ire-239	Randolph,David	Edg- 40
John	Ran-179	Saml	Lnc-330	James	Cas- 66
John	Ran-179	Simon 2	Bun- 77	James	Pit-263
Luellen	Ran-179	Stark	Ans- 25	Jesse	Pit-263
Robt	Ran-178	Thomas	Lnc-345	Lary	Cas- 67
Robt	Ran-179	William	Car-160	Malachi	Nor- 76
Saml	Ran-179	Wm	Lnc-336	Paul	Edg- 40

Name	Ref	Name	Ref	Name	Ref
Randolph,Robert	Cas- 66	Ranyolds,Sally	Mor- 63	Ratliff,Abraham	Wil-279
Samuel	Bun- 90	Rape,Henry	Mec- 44	Aron	Len-320
Samuel	Bun- 76	John	Mec- 31	Benjamin	Bun- 83
William	Cas- 66	Peter	Mep- 31	Elam	Len-317
Willis	Pit-246	Peter	Mec- 44	Jesse	Ans- 23
Randrick,Widow	Lnc-338	Samuel	Mec- 44	Job	Sur-178
Randsom,Richard	Cas- 66	Raper,Benj	Pas-201	Joseph	Sur-167
Ranes,John	Joh-284	Caleb	Pas-201	Joshua	Wil-261
Raney,David	Per-133	Cornels	Pas-201	Moses	Len-320
Edmon	Row- 65	David	Pas-201	Richard	Sur-168
Jane	Sur-190	Henry	Pas-201	Thomas	Sur-168
Thomas	Per-133	Henry M	Prq-224	Thos	Ans- 17
William	Row- 75	John	Pas-201	Thos	Ans- 29
Rangold,John	Cha-207	Joseph	Prq-223	Thos	Ans- 28
Ranier,Robt	Mec- 30	Robt	Way-246	Thos	Cha-207
Ranises,William	Bur-127	William	Glf-167	Wm	Ans- 29
Rank,Elizabeth	Sto-154	Raphel,James	Dup- 8	Wm	Ans- 18
Gottlieb	Sto- 99	Rapier,Henry	Prq-224	Ratliffe,Rachel	Rob-238
Gottlieb	Sto-129	Rarey,George	Row- 75	Rats,Godfrey	Row- 40
John	Sto-130	Rasberry,Jno	Ans- 20	Godfrey	Row- 38
Rankhorn,Amos	Prq-224	Josiah	Hrt-215	Henry	Row- 38
James	Pas-201	Richard	Hrt-210	Raupaw,David	Wil-272
John	Pas-201	William	Hrt-211	Hillair	Wil-258
Joseph	Ans- 24	Rascoe,Danl	Brt- 46	Hiram colo	Wil-264
Sarah	Prq-224	Eliz	Brt- 46	Raven,Abram	Bft- 39
Willm	Pas-201	John	Brt- 46	Ravens,John	Per-143
Rankin,Alexr	Lnc-372	Peter	Brt- 66	Raw,William	Joh-284
Denny	Ire-259	Rasedon,John	Ran-179	Rawley,James	Roc- 13
Geo	Glf-161	Rasener,Elias	Lnc-345	Rawlins,Richd	Brt- 52
J	Glf-174	Rasens,M	Ash- 13	Sarah	Dup- 21
J	Glf-184	Rash,Asa	Wil-270	Rawls,Charity	Brt- 55
James	Ire-259	Daniel	Wil-272	Daniel	Mar-446
James	Glf-156	James	Ire-253	David	Mar- 12
Jas	Glf-180	John	Sur-177	David	Hrt-213
Robert	Ire-257	Joseph	Wil-284	Drucilla	Brt- 62
Robt	Glf-161	Levi	Wil-269	Frury	Hrt-213
Robt Jr	Glf-184	Luke	Wil-270	James	Mar-446
Saml	Glf-171	Perry	Wil-283	John S	Hrt-208
Samuel	Lnc-372	Thomas	Ire-253	Jonas	Brt- 62
William	Lnc-354	Rason,John	Lnc-331	Moriah	Brt- 50
William	Lnc-372	Rasor,Josiah	Brt- 67	Randol	Hal-117
Rankings,John	Sto-152	Ratchford,Moses	Lnc-330	Thomas	Edg- 51
Rankins,Duncan	Rch-197	Ratcliffe,William	Roc- 19	William	Mar- 11
Saml	Mec- 46	Rathbone,Penal	Bun- 79	William	Hrt-208
Rann,Mikajah	Hal-117	Rathobone,Andrew	Bun- 79	Williams Junr	Mar- 14
Ransan,Thomas	Sto- 99	Rathrock,Frederick	Sto-136	Rawson,John	Ran-178
Ransom,John	Sur-196	Philip	Sto-135	Joseph	Ran-178
Joseph	Sto-129	Philip	Sto-135	Ray, A B	Ora-147
Martin	Rob-222	Philip	Sto-103	Archd	Mor- 61
Richard	War-179	Ratley,Fed	Mon- 24	Archd	Mor- 65
Seymoure	War-180	Fed Snr	Mon- 25	Archd	Cum-264
Simon	Rob-222	Francis	Nsh-644	Archd Senr	Cum-269
William	Roc- 35	Fredk	Sam-164	Ard	Bla- 13
Willis	Rob-222	Jas	Sam-163	Christen	Cum-269
Ransome,William	Fra- 93	Matthew	Nsh- 84	D	Bla- 12
Ranson,Benjn	Sto-128	Parson	Nsh- 81	Daniel	Cum-270
Thomas	Sto-131	Passons	Nsh- 83	Daniel Capt	Cum-264
Ranssan,Capt Wm	Wil-263	Shade	Mon- 25	Danl	Cum-240
Rany,Thomas	Per-143	Ratlif,Cors	Ran-177	Darling	Mar- 4

Ray,David	Ora-122	Ray,Samuel	Mar- 4	Read,Anne	Hal-118	
David H F	Ora-112	Stephen	Ora-943	Arther	Ran-179	
Duncan	Cum-255	Stephen	Ora-117	Asa	Hal-118	
Duncan	Cum-243	Tho	Ora-118	Benjamin	Gat-111	
Duncan	Mor- 57	Thomas	Ora-169	Bird	Cas- 66	
Duncan Esq	Cum-269	Thomas	Bun- 78	Blewford	Cas- 66	
Francis	Cas- 66	Thomas Senr	Bun- 79	Clement	Hal-117	
Geo	Ora-177	Thos	Ran-178	Ezekil	Hyd-229	
George	Sto-131	W	Ora-155	George	Cas- 66	
George	Sto-100	W	Ash- 3	James	Cas- 66	
Henry	Ora-113	William	Ora-161	James	Gat-108	
Henry	Brt- 49	William	Brt- 44	James	Car-180	
Hiram	Bun- 76	Wm	Ora-173	Jesse	Hal-117	
Hugh	Cum-254	Wm	Cab-139	John	Cur- 86	
Hutson	Ran-178	Wm Sen	Ora-114	John	Pit-255	
Isaac	Ora-113	Wilson	Bun- 73	John	Cas- 67	
J	Ash- 6	Wilson	Mor- 62	John	Cas- 67	
J	Col- 17	Rayfield,Lovet	Bla- 5	John	Hal-117	
J	Col- 17	Rayl,Geo	Glf-166	John	Rth-130	
James	Ora-123	Geo Jr	Glf-166	John	Rth-130	
Capt James	Ora-174	Matthew	Glf-185	Joseph	Bun- 85	
James of Jno	Ora-177	N	Glf-206	Lewis	Row- 47	
James	Bun- 92	Wm	Glf-166	Lucy	Cum-239	
James	Cas- 67	Rayley,Benj	Hrt-216	Micajah	Gat-116	
James	Mar- 7	Etheldred	Hrt-206	Rhesa	Hal-117	
James	Bun- 83	Raymer,George	Row- 70	Robert	Prq-224	
James	Wil-280	Jacob	Row- 82	Sally	Rth-130	
James	Ran-178	Raynalds,W	Bru-222	Sarey	Cur- 92	
Col'd John	Ora-171	Rayner,Amos	Brt- 47	Thomas	Pit-256	
Jno	Ora-128	Elijah	Brt- 44	Thomas	Cas- 66	
Jno Jun	Ora-112	Enoch	Brt- 43	Thomas	Cas- 67	
John	Ran-178	Joshua	Brt- 52	Thos	Hal-117	
John	Ran-178	Miles	Brt- 49	William	Hal-117	
John	Mor- 61	Samuel	Edg- 72	William	Jon-303	
John	Mor- 61	Samuel	Brt- 52	Willis	War-182	
John Hatter	Ora-161	William	Edg- 52	Winifred	Hal-118	
John	Ora-161	William	Brt- 51	Reader,Rober	Rth-129	
John	Cum-269	Raynes,John	Pas-202	Thomas	Rth-130	
John	Cum-264	Raynold,Georg	Rth-130	Reading,John	Wil-271	
John	Cum-260	Raynor,James	Sam-155	William	Wil-268	
John	Cum-243	Judeath	Hrt-208	William Jr	Wil-268	
John	Cum-242	Zadock	Hrt-209	Reagan,John	Roc- 5	
John	Bun- 76	Rea,Andrew	Mec- 30	Reak,Martin	Grn-125	
John	Lnc-337	David	Mec- 34	Real,William	Bur-109	
John	Ran-178	Enoch	Row- 47	Reamer,Jacob	Cab-145	
John C	Cum-242	James	Cho-225	Reams,Caleb	Nor- 76	
Joseph	Bun- 76	James	Hrt-215	Elijah	Nor- 76	
Joseph	Ora-161	Jno	Rob-242	John	Nor- 76	
Joseph	Ran-178	Jno	Mec- 24	Peter	Nor- 76	
Lonard	Sur-180	Jno	Mec- 34	William	Nor- 76	
M	Ora-139	John	Mec- 29	Reap,Henry	Bur-109	
Malcom	Cum-251	John	Mec- 30	Susannah	Bur-112	
Margaret	Cum-243	Joseph	Mec- 34	Rease,Roger	Nsh- 80	
Neill	Cum-268	Neal	Mec- 33	Thomas	Bun- 80	
Payton	Glf-160	Robert	Prq-224	Reaser,John	Row- 71	
R	Ora-153	Sally	Nor- 76	Reason,Rauley	Edg- 50	
Robert	Bun- 99	Saml	Cho-225	Reaons,James	Way-234	
Robt	Ora-117	Thomas	Cho-223	Reath,John	Grn-135	
Robt Jun	Ora-175	Reace,Nany	Grn-132	Reaves,Benj	Mon- 20	

-263-

Name	Ref	Name	Ref	Name	Ref
Reaves,David	Row- 63	Reddick,Mourning	Bun- 87	Redmon,Harmon	Sto-105
Edward	Bla- 9	Noah	Mar- 9	Harmon	Sto-140
G	Col- 18	Obadiah	Prq-224	Jacob	Sto-142
Isaac	Wil-272	Robert	Prq-224	Redmond,Daniel	Edg- 41
J	Bru-222	Rue	Edg- 48	Jams	Bft- 38
James	Bun- 82	Seth	Prq-224	Redmond,Jno	Ora-149
James	Row- 75	Sollomon	Prq-224	Redwell,Robert	War-180
Jesse	Mon- 18	Thomas	Mar- 9	Thomas	War-181
John	Cha-197	William	Prq-224	Redwine,Mich Jr	Mon- 22
Josiah	Mon- 18	William	Wsh-226	Michael	Mon- 22
Lewis	Grn-135	William	Mar- 11	Redyard,Josiah	Cha-207
Mary	Row- 63	Willis	Prq-224	Ree,Jack	Hrt-209
Robert	Bla- 9	Willis	Mar- 11	Reece,Abraham	Sur-165
S	Col- 19	Reddicks,John	Bur-120	Abraham Ju	Sur-177
Saml	Grn-135	Reddin,Johnson	Joh-282	Caleb	Glf-166
Samuel	Mon- 18	Levi	Mor- 61	Daniel	Sur-174
Samuel	Ire-252	Robert	Cum-258	Jarret	Cum-245
Tho	Ora-128	William	Cum-258	Jesse	Sur-166
Thomas	Cha-203	Redding,John Jr	Wil-261	Joel	Sur-168
William	Bla- 9	Richard R	Nsh- 80	John	Ons-102
William	War-182	Saml	Pas-202	Josiah	Ans- 25
Reavis,David Jr	Rth-130	Tho	Ora-168	Levy	Sur-171
Davis	Rth-129	Thos	Ora-153	Peter	Lnc-345
Edward	Rth-130	William	Mar- 14	Thos	Glf-168
John	Rth-130	Redditt,Alex	Bft- 31	Wm	Ran-177
Joseph	Rth-130	Aquilla	Brt- 44	Reed,Mrs	Brt- 49
Martha	Rth-130	Josiah Jun	Brt- 44	Abram	Bur-119
Sarah	Rth-130	Josiah Sen	Brt- 44	Allen	Mec- 25
Reavs,David Sr	Rth-128	Lewis	Bft- 31	Archibald	Bun- 82
Reberson,Jeremiah	Grn-128	Redfarne,Isaac	Ran-179	Betsy	Pas-202
Rebeson,Edward	Cum-252	Saml	Ran-179	Charles	Sto-102
Record,David	Cha-190	Redford,James	Glf-169	Coonrod	Cab-148
Rector,Benjamin	Ire-245	Jno	Mec- 29	David	Row- 78
John	Ire-267	Wm	Mec- 29	David	Mec- 25
Lewis	Bun- 81	Redforn,Nimrod	Ans- 27	Eldad	Bun- 79
Red,Lewis	Hal-117	Redicks,Cornelius	Bur-119	George	Row- 81
Redd,Kincy	Ons-100	Reding,John	Ora-170	George	Bur-109
Sigby	Ons-107	Stephen	Ora-138	George	Bur-116
Whittiker	Ons-107	Tho	Ora-126	George	Car-182
William	Ons-100	Thos	Ran-178	Hannah	Bun- 91
Reddack,John	Ran-179	Wm	Ran-178	Henry	Cab-148
Teby	Ran-179	Redinhour,Adam	Sto-144	Henry	Bur-105
Redden,Jno	Mec- 31	Henry	Cab-140	Hugh	Mec- 24
Reddett,Peter	Bft- 21	Jacob	Cab-140	J	Ash- 12
Reddick,Henry	Cho-231	Nics	Cab-140	J	Ash- 12
Henry	Prq-224	Redland,Thomas	Bla- 5	Jacob	Sto-103
James	Hrt-208	Redman,Francis	Ire-254	Jacob Jur	Sto-137
Job	Prq-224	Hosea	Ire-254	James	Hay-200
Jno	Cho-231	Joel	Ire-253	James	Edg- 58
John	Mar- 9	John	Ora-159	James	Bur-106
John	Mar- 12	John	Ire-253	James	Bur-119
John	Sto-133	Stephen	Bun- 92	Jas	Mec- 34
John Junr	Mar- 9	Thomas	Ire-254	Jas Snr	Mec- 34
Kenneth	Mar- 15	William	Rth-129	Jeremiah	Cha-200
Martin	Mar-445	William Jr	Rth-129	Jesse	Bur-108
Mills	Mar- 9	Redmane,J	Ora-140	Jno	Mec- 25
Mills	Mar- 12	Redmon,Abraham	Sto-151	Jno	Mec- 34
Morning	Sto-142	Abraham	Sto-109	Jno	Mec- 36
Morning	Sto-107	Benjamin	Sto-140	John	Sur-187

Reed,John	Wil-269	Reeves,Jas	Ora-136	Relfe,Anne	Pas-201	
John	Row- 72	John	Way-239	Joseph	Pas-201	
John	Row- 77	John D	Sur-187	Josiah	Pas-201	
John	Cab-147	Lovard	Way-238	Thos	Pas-201	
John	Cab-136	Michael	Ora-151	Thomas	Pas-201	
John D	Brt- 46	Morgan	Row- 74	Will T	Pas-201	
Joseph	Mec- 50	Reuben	Cha-215	Relliam,John	Grn-135	
Joseph	Mec- 34	Richard	Fra- 98	Relps,Isaac	Glf-163	
Joseph	Cab-137	William	Fra-100	Relton,Botton	Rth-130	
Loall	Bur-109	Willis	Ora-132	Rembling,Barny	Row- 54	
Miles	Edg- 51	Regan,Charles	Lnc-361	Remer,Michael	Cab-140	
Noah	Row- 78	Jno Jnr	Rob-241	Remmington,James	Ire-248	
Peter	Bun- 91	Jno Snr	Rob-243	Ren,James	Per-143	
Robert	Hay-200	Josep	Rob-241	John	Ran-178	
S	Ash- 12	Morgan	Lnc-335	Joseph	Bun- 80	
S	Ash- 12	Regens,P	Ash- 14	William	Per-152	
Saml	Mec- 50	Reggin,Charles	War-169	Renalds,Jones	Sur-168	
Saml	Mec- 53	Fanny	War-171	William	Sur-185	
Samuel	Bur-122	Francis	War-171	William Ju	Sur-185	
Shaderick	Hrt-212	Francis Snr	War-171	Renard,James	Sur-167	
Tho	Pas-201	Samuel	War-181	Rench,John	Cum-267	
Thomas	Bun- 84	Reggo,N	Cam-161	Rencher,Elijah	Row- 62	
Thos	Hrt-213	Register,Benj	Bla- 6	Samuel	Row- 75	
William	Hrt-209	Burwel	Sam-158	Thomas	Row- 74	
William	Ons-107	John	Sam-158	William	Row- 74	
William	Bur-126	Joseph	Sam-158	Renches,J N	Ora-141	
William	Bur-108	S	Bru-226	Rendleman,Jacob	Row- 66	
Wm	Mec- 51	Thos	Sam-157	John	Row- 69	
Reede,DAniel	Roc- 25	Reickel,George G	Sto-145	Renegor,George	Sur-190	
Daniel	Roc- 23	Reid,Alexander	Lnc-359	Henry	Sur-190	
Elisha	Roc- 26	Archd	Mor- 55	Joseph	Sur-190	
Hugh	Roc- 26	Belany	Ire-268	Joseph Ju	Sur-190	
John	Roc- 25	Burrell col	Fra-100	Renfrew,James	Cum-263	
John	Roc- 26	David	Mor- 66	Renfro,Joel	Joh-283	
Thomas	Roc- 4	George	Ire-266	Stephen	Joh-284	
William	Roc- 25	James	Lnc-356	William	Joh-284	
Reedling,Barbara	Bur-112	John	Lnc-361	Renfrow,John	Bun- 74	
Reeks,Zilphey	Gat-110	Robert	Lnc-365	Renhardt,Joseph	Lnc-335	
Reel,George	Lnc-375	William	Lnc-353	Renn,Henry	Edg- 70	
Reep,Adam	Lnc-329	Reider,Conrod	Bur-113	Renny,Elisebeth	Cur- 86	
Adolph	Lnc-328	Reiley,Edwards	Cho-221	Renoir,Thomas	Cum-258	
Mich	Lnc-332	Reiner,Nicholas	Cum-257	Renshaw,Abraham	Bur-126	
Rees,A	Ash- 9	Reinhardt,Ch	Lnc-345	Charles	Grn-125	
J	Ash- 6	Ch	Lnc-345	Rentfrow,Jacob	Way-245	
John	Ran-177	Cunrod	Lnc-373	Jacob Jr	Way-245	
N	Ash- 6	David	Lnc-345	James	Way-245	
Reese,James	Car-178	George	Lnc-371	Reonato,Samuel	Bun- 94	
Richard	Nor- 76	Jacob	Lnc-328	Rep,David	Cab-138	
Mrs Suhia	Fra- 93	John	Lnc-374	Rerves,Joseph	Row- 73	
Thomas	Car-178	Jos	Lnc-339	Respess,Lang	Bft- 21	
Reeves,A	Ora-156	Reinhart,Christr	Cab-140	Richd	Bft- 21	
Edward	Cha-216	Reins,Ambrus	Joh-279	Tho	Bft- 21	
F	Ora-136	John	Joh-279	Ressaberry,Daniel	Hay-200	
George Sen	Ora-116	Oliver	Joh-279	Reveal,Matthew	Hrt-211	
Hardy	Way-238	Oliver Jr	Joh-280	Revel,Burl	Rob-220	
J	Ora-155	Reise,Jessee	Ire-254	M	Cum-239	
J B F	Ora-136	Rejester,J	Col- 19	Sarey	Cum-246	
J P	Bla- 13	Reley,Dorrel	Row- 60	Revell,Anne	Nor- 76	
James	Bla- 12	Relfe,Ann	Pas-202	Betty	Way-245	

-265-

Revell,Hardy	Way-232	Reynolds,Perl	Lnc-333	Rhodes,Reddick	Sam-161
Mary	Way-238	Richard	Jon-303	Reuben	Ora-168
Micajah	Way-232	Robert	Row- 64	Robert	Brt- 55
Michael	Way-245	Robt	Sam-161	Sandford	Roc- 34
Solomon	Way-238	Solomas	Sto-111	Sarah	Lnc-340
Revels,Elisha col	Rob-241	Solomon	Sto-149	Taylor	Dup- 13
Micajah	Sam-161	Thomas	War-184	Thomas	Brt- 56
Nathaniel	Rob-240	Wm	Glf-161	Thomas	Bun- 82
Revely,Stephen	Grn-132	Reynols,John	Ran-178	Thomas Junr	Bun- 95
Reves,J	Ash- 7	Reysell,Hannah	Hyd-234	Thos	Glf-160
Jno	Ora-144	Rhea,Andrew	Ora-130	Thos	Ora-152
Thomas	Ora-155	J	Ora-148	W	Ora-148
W	Ash- 7	Jas	Mec- 34	Will	Dup- 21
Revil,Barney	Nsh- 78	Thos	Mec- 34	William	Dup- 13
Mat	Nsh- 78	Rhew,John	Ora-165	William	Roc- 18
Revill,Hezekiah	Ora-165	Rhoad,Jacob	Hrt-208	William	Sam-154
Ky	Ora-165	Rhoades,Abraham	Edg- 48	William	Jon-303
Geo	Bun- 83	Arthur	Wsh-223	Woodhouse	Ons- 98
Revis,Jesse	Sur-197	John	Wil-264	Rhodesouth,Geo	Row- 39
John	Bun- 95	John	Edg- 54	Rhoeds,Salley S S G	
Mary	Sur-168	Joseph	Edg- 54		Hal-118
Whitfield	Grn-135	Rhoads,John	Tyr-212	Rhuark,M	Bru-234
Revus,James	Way-250	Simeon	Tyr-212	Rhym,David	Lnc-341
Rew,Beville	Hyd-232	Rhodes,Aaron	Ora-150	Rhyme,Michl	Lnc-341
Fred	Hyd-233	Abraham	Hay-200	Rhymer,Jesse	Hal-117
Fred Jnr	Hyd-233	Allen	Cha-198	Rhyne,Adam	Lnc-340
Lovey	Hyd-233	Andrew	Bun- 80	Jacob	Lnc-340
Reubin	Hyd-233	Anna	Way-235	Jacob	Lnc-340
Sothey	Hyd-233	Aquilla	Ora-142	John	Lnc-340
Solomon	Hyd-232	Benj	Ora-150	John	Lnc-372
Rewes,Zachariah	Cum-249	Christy	Lnc-365	Martin	Lnc-340
Rex,Edmond	Pit-248	Cornl	Pas-201	Philip	Lnc-340
George	Row- 76	Eliz	Brt- 60	Thomas	Lnc-372
Reyenalds,C	Bru-224	Fredk	Lnc-365	Rhyns,Michael	Lnc-340
Reynels,Abner	Ran-179	Henry	Brt- 55	Rhyser,Michl	Lnc-329
David	Ran-179	Henry	Lnc-326	Peter	Lnc-329
Francis	Ran-179	Henry	Ora-149	Rials,Hardy	Cum-261
Jeremh	Ran-179	Hesekiah	Ora-150	Martha	Cum-261
Jerh	Ran-179	Jacob	Brt- 60	Richd	Cum-262
Jesse	Ran-179	Jacob	Rob-219	Richeson	Cum-261
John	Ran-179	James	Jon-303	Wm	Ora-142
Luis	Ran-179	James	Dup- 3	Rible,Jacob	Row- 38
Wm	Ran-179	James	Roc- 26	Riblin,Peter	Row- 67
Reynier,Geo	Cab-142	John	Brt- 46	Ricacs,James	Bun- 79
Reynodls,Abraham	Bun- 74	John	Ran-178	Ricard,Jesse	Glf-159
Ann	Bun- 82	John	Bun- 79	Michal	Row- 70
Anne	Wil-258	John	Ora-150	Riccard,John	Row- 83
Archablad	Sto-128	Maj Jno	Ora-118	John Sr	Row- 83
Benjamin	Edg- 47	John F	Dup- 29	Rice,Abigal	Cas- 67
Charles	Cum-124	John Jnr	Brt- 53	Archibald	Cas- 67
Coleman	Jon-303	Joseph	Sam-163	Arthur	Mon- 41
David	Glf-187	Joseph T	Dup- 31	Arthur	Mon- 41
Edward	Roc- 4	Joshua	Bun- 90	Benj	Nsh- 85
Elisha	Wil-267	Leven	Tyr-205	Ciziah	Gat-111
J	Glf-183	Martha	Brt- 56	David	Rob-236
J Jr	Glf-183	Mary	Brt- 55	Edmond	Cas- 67
James	Jon-303	N	Ora-148	Frances	Cas- 67
John	Wil-258	P	Glf-160	Francis	Row- 75
Patience	Edg- 44	Peter	Bun- 84	H William	Cas- 66

Name	Code	Name	Code	Name	Code
Rice,Harnes	Grn-141	Richards,Durrit	Cas- 66	Richardson,J	Cam-162
Holeman	Row- 61	Evans	Nor- 76	J	Ash- 4
Hopkins	Nsh- 85	George	Fra- 90	Jacob	Pas-201
Ibzan	Cas- 66	Isaac	Ran-178	James	Hal-117
J	Bla- 11	J H	Bla- 8	James	Cas- 66
James	Brt- 66	James	Lnc-337	James	Bla- 7
James	Bun- 74	James	Grn-129	James	Cas- 66
Jas	Mon- 41	James	Hyd-232	Jas	Mec- 27
Jeptha	Roc- 16	Jas	Lnc-335	Jesse	Rth-129
Jessee	Bun- 93	Jas	Bru-222	Jesse	Hal-117
Jno Sen	Ora-143	Jesse	Fra- 81	Jno	Cho-222
John	Nsh- 84	John	Fra- 85	John	Cha-194
John	Pit-251	John	Dup- 7	John	Rth-130
John	Grn-148	John	Hay-199	John	Mor- 66
John	Cas- 66	John Junr	Jon-303	John	Mor- 59
John	Cas- 66	John Junr	Nor- 77	John	Roc- 20
John	Joh-290	John Senr	Jon-303	John	Tyr-203
Joseph	Bun- 97	John Senr	Nor- 77	John	Nsh- 72
Joseph	Per-143	Major	Fra- 83	John	Joh-285
Leweling	Grn-147	Morris	Sur-176	John	Hal-117
Mary	Row- 80	Nancy	Fra- 96	John	Hal-118
Nathan	Roc- 31	Nancy	Bft- 28	Jonathan	Joh-285
Philip	Row- 82	Mrs Nanny	Fra- 95	Joseph	Wil-262
Price	Joh-285	Pricelle	Hyd-232	Joseph	Roc- 22
Sarah	Cas- 66	Reuben	Rth-129	Joseph	Ire-268
Stephen	Ire-244	Richd	Hyd-232	Joseph	Joh-285
Thomas	Mon- 45	Sarah	Hyd-234	Josiah	Pas-201
Thomas	Gat-115	Sarah	Hyd-225	Josiah	Cha-214
Tignal	Joh-283	Shadrach	Hyd-232	Levi	Pas-202
William	Bun- 93	Stephen	Fra- 90	M	Col- 18
William	Cas- 67	Thomas	Hyd-232	M	Pas-201
William	Grn-279	Waller	Row- 50	Martha	Per-143
William Jun	Lnc-331	Wherry	Pit-261	Mary	Mor- 59
William Sen	Lnc-331	William	Nor- 76	Mary	Pas-201
Williamson	Cas- 67	Willm	Fra- 85	Mary	Roc- 21
Wm	Mon- 41	Willm	Fra- 84	Mary	Hal-117
Wm	Mec- 40	Willis	Fra- 85	Mary	Row- 81
Zebia	Cas- 67	Richardson,Absalom	Hal-117	May	Cha-216
Rich,Mrs	Cum-241	Allen	Joh-285	Meason	Mec- 42
Christian	Sto-135	Alsey	Nsh- 72	Miles	Pas-201
David	Ans- 5	Amos	Bla- 3	Millington	Fra- 87
John	Row- 61	Benjn	Hal-117	Moses	Hal-117
John	Glf-163	Binklely	Mec- 42	Pheriba	Pas-202
John	Ran-179	C	Ash- 7	Robt	Ora-163
John	Sam-158	Cata	Mec- 42	S	Cam-165
John	Sto-131	Charles	Rth-130	Saml	Glf-185
John	Nor- 76	Charles	Row- 81	Saml N	Bla- 7
Lewis	Sto-136	Charles Jr	Rth-129	Samuel	Roc- 24
Moses	Ran-180	D	Cam-162	Sarah	Roc- 22
Peter	Ran-178	Danl	Pas-202	Solomon	Hal-118
Peter	Ran-179	David	Mor- 69	Stephen	Mor- 57
Peter	Ran-178	Drewry	Mor- 61	Stephen	Row- 81
Robert	Rth-130	Edmond	Mec- 42	Stephen	Pas-202
S	Col- 19	Edward	Mor- 58	Thomas	Joh-283
S	Cum-241	Elisha	Wil-259	Thomas	Wil-260
Saml	Glf-163	Ellis	Wil-270	William	Rth-129
Richard,Silas	Car-184	George	Mec- 42	William	Joh-287
Richards,Charles	Grn-129	H	Ash- 6	William	Cas- 67
Charles	Row- 50	Hardy	Hal-117	Wm	Nsh- 74

Name	Location	Name	Location	Name	Location
Richardson,Wm Snr	Joh-285	Ricks,Henry		Edg- 62	Riddle,William	Roc- 25
Wm	Hal-118	Irven		Nsh- 88	William Jr	Cha-203
Wm	Bla- 2	Isaac		Nor- 76	Wm Sr	Cha-206
Wm S	Cha-216	Isaac		Hal-117	Ridenour,Jacob	Way-235
Richarson,Bryan	Joh-285	Isaac		Edg- 62	Rider,Adam	Row- 87
Hardy	Joh-284	J		Glf-176	Jacob	Sto- 97
John	Row- 88	Jacob		Nsh- 80	Jacob	Sto-126
Riche,Warren	Sur-182	Joel		Nsh- 79	Wm	Ran-178
Richer,Michl	Row- 67	John		Hal-117	Wm	Ora-110
Richerds,Dianer	Cur- 86	John		Grn-146	Rides,Fred	Bur-102
Richerson,Arther	Ran-178	John		Grn-148	Ridge,Caleb	Ran-177
Chen	Ran-177	Josiah		Nsh- 80	Jas	Ran-179
Drury	Ran-177	Lary		Grn-147	Peter	Ora-132
Lewis	Grn-130	Mary		Nor- 76	Riding,John	Ran-178
Lucey	Ran-178	Miqajah		Nsh- 80	Joseph	Ran-178
Richd	Ran-178	Morning		Nsh- 88	Joseph	Ran-178
Wm	Ran-179	Mourning		Nsh- 88	Ridings,David	Sur-188
Richeson,Hardy	Rch-202	Phebe		Edg- 62	Jesse	Sur-176
Thomas	Cum-249	Sary		Nsh- 80	John	Sur-188
Richey,Daniel	Cab-140	Wilie		Nsh-643	Ridle,Stephen	Sto-107
Geo	Cab-145	William		Sur-182	Ridley,Howell S	Grn-142
Henry	Cab-140	Wm		Nsh- 79	James	Grn-133
Henry	Cab-145	Rictor,Ephraim		Cur-126	Ridlin,John	Row- 69
Joseph	Bur-117	Riddick,David		Gat-115	Ried,Alexander	Ire-244
Michael	Cab-146	Henary		Gat-112	Brice	Ire-244
Richmond,Ann	Cas- 67	Isaac		Gat-105	James	Ire-244
Daniel	Cas- 66	Isaiah		Gat-105	John	Ire-266
James	Cas- 67	Jethro		Gat-112	Rigby,Jonathan	Ons-108
Jessee	Bun- 91	Jo		Gat-105	Owen	Ons- 98
John	Cas- 67	Job		Gat-106	Rigdon,Benjn	Car-183
John	Cas- 67	John		Gat-108	Rigg,John	Sto-141
John	Cas- 67	John		Sto-101	John	Sto-106
Joseph	Cas- 67	Lassiter		Gat-106	Samuel	Sto-139
William	Cas- 67	Macajah		Cat-113	Samuel	Sto-104
Wm	Cas- 67	Nathan		Gat-105	Riggains,Ruth	Ora-150
Rick,Jeremiah	Cha-200	Reubin		Gat-105	Riggan,Charles	Cha-201
Rickets,Elisabeth	Rch-212	Robert		Gat-110	Joel	Wil-283
Ricketts,Anthony	Mon- 21	Robert		Gat-109	Peter	Wil-282
Benj	Mon- 34	Thomas		Gat-112	William	Wil-282
Jno	Ans- 10	William W		Gat-108	Riggen,Daniel	War-170
John	Bur-120	Riddle,Benjamin		Row- 62	Daniel	War-170
Moses	Sto-127	Brittan		Cha-211	Gillum	Row- 43
Moses	Sto- 97	Cato		Cha-189	Jacob	War-176
Reason	Mon- 22	James		Row- 65	John	War-175
Reason	Ans- 6	James		Sur-170	Wm	War-182
Richd	Ora-113	John		Bun- 78	William	War-184
Saml	Ora-114	John		Cha-211	William P	War-183
Wm	Ans- 17	John		Mor- 68	William W	War-183
Wm	Ora-114	John		Row- 44	Wm	Cha-212
Wm	Ora-115	John		Row- 60	Riggens,C	Ash- 12
Rickles,Benjamin	Rth-129	John		Roc- 25	Ephraim	Cha-208
Jesse	Mon- 44	Overton		Sto-138	Isham	Row- 44
Ricks,Abraham	Nsh-643	Richd		Cha-194	J	Ahs- 13
David	Nsh- 80	Samuel		Row- 65	James	Row- 43
Dempsey	Nor- 76	Stephen		Sto-143	Rigging,Darby	Pit-263
E	Glf-169	Tabitha		Cha-211	Riggins,Jas	Ora-122
Edwin	Nor- 76	Tere		Sto-113	Riggs,David	Ons- 99
Eli	Edg- 61	Tere		Sto-154	David	Sur-181
Elia	Nsh-644	Thos		Cha-198	G	Cam-156

Riggs,Hugh	Ora-174	Riley,James		Cum-237	Ripper,Sallathol	Rob-239
Isaac Junr	Car-183	James		Row- 83	Rippey,John	Ora-165
Isaac Senr	Car-184	James		Ora-167	Jos	Ora-124
J	Cam-157	Jas		Ora-155	Ripple,Henry	Sto-144
James	Ora-125	Jane		Per-133	Henry	Sto-107
John	Ons-101	Jane		Per-133	John	Sto-136
John	Ora-174	Jno		Ora-176	Martin	Row- 84
Lot	Sur-173	Jno		Mec- 22	Rippy,Ed	Ora-165
M	Cam-163	Jno		Mec- 22	Edward	Rth-131
N	Cam-163	Jno		Mec- 38	J	Ora-163
Saml	Ora-115	John		Ora-151	John	Rth-131
Samuel	Ora-169	John		Cum-265	Mat	Ora-165
Sarah	Ora-169	Michael		Sto-107	Thos	Ora-163
Silas	Sur-181	Peter		Ora-126	Risdesell,Phillip	Lnc-345
T	Cam-156	W		Ora-138	Risen,James	Bla- 6
T	Cam-166	Will		Ora-171	Risley,Timothy	Hrt-214
Thomas	Cas- 67	William		Per-133	Rissato,David	Bur-103
William	Ons-103	William		Ora-943	Ristan,Bazel	Wil-273
Zadock	Sur-177	Willm		Fra- 80	Ritch,Daniel	Mec- 43
Righ,Jacob	Row- 48	Wm		Mec- 22	Daniel	Mec- 43
Righly,Michal	Sto-142	Rilke,Allison W		Cab-142	Demey	Mec- 43
Right,Benjamin	Sto-140	Rily,James		Ire-269	Edmond	Mec- 30
John	Row- 40	Wm		Per-133	Jno	Mec- 30
John	Sto-139	Rimmer,John		Per-143	Ritchardson,D	Ash- 15
John	Sto-105	Phebe		Per-152	J	Ash- 5
M	Ash- 10	Thomas		Per-152	Ritcheson,Rich	Ora-119
Sarah	Cas- 66	Rimor,Nicholas		Row- 68	Ritchey,Abrm	Cab-140
Whitely	Sto-101	Rina,Christopher		Roc- 32	John	Cab-140
Whitely	Sto-133	Rinat,Thomas Jr		Sur-184	Ritchmond,Charles	Mec- 49
William	Sto-133	Rine,Eales		Lnc-350	Rite,Jonathan	Cur- 90
William	Sto-101	Rinehart,Andrew		Row- 69	Ritenhouser,J	Mon- 42
William Jur	Sto-133	Charles		Row- 70	Ritt,James	Ons-104
Wm	Grn-139	Jacob		Row- 68	Rittenhouse,Nicholas	
Wm	Cho-229	Rineheart,Daniel		Rth-130		Sto- 94
Wm	Cho-225	Rineir,Jno		Mec- 33	Nicholas	Sto-123
Rights,John	Sto-146	Ring,Elisha		Pit-243	Ritter,James	Sur-185
Rightsman,Chrr	Ran-178	Francis		Lnc-370	Jesse	Mor- 56
Davd	Ran-178	John		Sto- 91	Jno	Len-313
Jacob	Ora-134	John		Lnc-369	John	Mor- 59
Rigs,George	Lnc-329	John Jur		Sto-132	M	Ash- 13
Saml	Pas-201	John Ser		Sto-100	Moses	Mor- 60
Rigsbey,D	Ash- 14	John Ser		Sto-132	Thos	Mor- 69
John	Cah-210	Martin		Sur-187	William	Edg- 50
Josiah	Brt- 46	Richard		Sto-132	Rivels,Nathaniel	Sam-156
Rigsby,Josiah	Ora-150	Thomas Jur		Sto-132	Stephen	Sam-156
Lewis	Cha-205	Thomas Jur		Sto-100	Rivenbark,Eliza	Dup- 5
Luke	Cha-104	Thomas Ser		Sto-100	Fredk	Dup- 6
Oldham	Cha-194	Thomas Ser		Sto-132	W M W	Dup- 19
Russel	Cha-199	William		Sto-148	Rivens,Alexr	Rob-244
T	Ash- 14	Ringgold,James		Pit-238	Rivers,Joel	Fra- 93
William	Sur-191	John		Pit-238	Richard	Joh-276
Riker,George	Mec- 23	Ringstaff,Adam		Mor- 57	Richd	Fra- 93
Riland,Benoni	Pit-257	Conrod		Ora-177	William	Joh-278
Riley,Absalom	Cum-265	Peggy		Ora-177	Zachariah	War-184
Charles	Sto-150	Ripley,Sarey		Cur- 92	Rix,Jonas	Glf-169
Charles	Sto-110	Wm		Car-184	Thos	Glf-170
Daniel	Wil-263	Riply,Anne		Pas-201	Rilegrove,H	Glf-178
J	Ora-152	Sally		Pas-201	Roach,Gideon	Roc- 5
Jacob	Ora-126	Rippee,J		Ash- 8	James	Roc- 11

Name	Ref	Name	Ref	Name	Ref
Roach,Jno	Ans- 7	Robason,Mat	Bft- 24	Roberson,Henry	Row- 78
Jno	Ora-112	Noah	Mar- 9	Higson	Grn-129
Jno	Ora-112	Simon	Bft- 26	J	Bru-238
John	Rth-129	Simon	Mar- 16	James	Grn-140
Joseph	Rth-130	Tho	Bft- 22	James	Pit-234
Joseph	Rth-129	William	Mar- 9	John	Len-312
M	Cum-239	Willis	Mar- 23	John	Pit-246
Rabin	Ora-142	Robb,Wm	Mec- 23	John	Way-253
Thos	Ran-178	Robberds,Richard	Jon-303	Joseph	Hrt-208
Wm	Ora-112	Robbins,A Junr	Bru-222	L	Bru-234
Wm	Bft- 33	A Senr	Bru-222	Lasey	Pit-258
Roads,George	Lnc-340	Absolem	Bru-222	Leond	Grn-140
Jacob	Lnc-340	Elijah	Edg- 43	Lewis	Len-312
John	Joh-290	Elisha	Edg- 43	Moses	Pit-246
K	Cam-164	Elizabeth	Edg- 67	Nathl	Grn-144
Sally	Nor- 76	F	Bru-222	Nathl	Grn-140
Samuel	Sto-131	Frederick	Edg- 66	P W	Bru-232
Thomas	Nor- 76	J	Bru-222	Priscilla	Bun- 98
W	Cam-163	Jacob	Edg- 43	Robert	Grn-128
Wizeman	Bur-104	Joel	Bru-222	Robert	Pit-246
Roan,Benjamin	Hal-118	John	Edg- 43	Sarah	Bun- 77
Clem	Mec- 27	John	Brt- 64	Thomas	Row- 75
Francis	Bla- 5	John	Prq-224	Valentine	Bun- 91
Henry	Mec- 42	Joseph	Prq-224	William	Bun- 92
James	Per-143	Kenchin	Edg- 43	William	Bun- 74
Jas	Mec- 42	Sarah	Bru-222	William	Row- 78
Jno	Mec- 42	Stephen	Edg- 64	Robert,Benj	Hrt-209
John	Cas- 66	Thomas	Edg- 67	William	Bur-107
Lewis	Hal-118	William	Edg- 64	Roberts,Abel	Cur- 88
Raford	Bla- 5	William	Way-235	Ann	Cho-221
Saml	Mec- 27	William	War-183	Arthur	Per-143
Thomas	Cas- 67	William	Edg- 42	Asa	Prq-223
William	Hal-117	Robbs,Angel	Ora-124	Benj	Glf-167
Wm	Mec- 27	Roberds,Chas	Ora-149	Benjamin	Ire-264
Roane,Thomas	Roc- 15	James	Bun- 81	Benjn	Bru-230
Roark,C	Ash- 12	John	Bun- 96	Britain	Joh-282
Judith	Sto-119	John	Bun- 90	C	Ora-141
Judith	Sto- 91	John Senr	Bun- 90	Charles	Car-181
T	Ash- 12	Joshua	Bun- 90	Charles	Car-174
Timothy	Sto-113	Robert	Bru-236	Chars	Pas-201
Robards,Mary	Grn-145	Samuel	Bun- 81	Chas	Bft- 29
Wm	Grn-141	W	Bru-232	Christr	Cho-227
Robason,Amos	Mar- 9	William	Bun- 96	Claxton	Nor- 76
Benjamin	Mar- 12	Roberson,Benj	Len-312	Cyrus L	Roc- 8
David	Mar- 10	C	Bru-238	Daniel	Row- 46
David	Mar- 12	Charles	Bun- 76	Daniel	Row- 47
David	Mar- 6	Clabourn	Grn-131	David	Ire-264
Dorcas	Mar- 5	Debey	Gat-108	Duke	Per-133
Henry	Mar- 13	Edward	Bun- 76	Edward	Wil-276
Henry	Mar- 5	Elijah	Jon-303	Elender	Prq-224
Henry	Mar- 7	Elijah	Grn-128	Elias	Nor- 76
Jasper	Bft- 26	Eliphas	Bun- 92	Elisha	Ons- 97
Jesse	Mar- 9	Enoch	Pit-246	Ellis	Roc- 8
Jesse	Bft- 33	Geo	Bun- 77	Eph	Ora-167
John	Mar- 9	George	Grn-144	Esther	Nor- 76
Joshua	Mar- 5	George	Row- 76	Ethelred col	Rob-241
Luke	Bft- 33	George	Grn-120	George	Prq-224
Lurane	Bft- 38	George Jr	Grn-144	George	Roc- 15
Mark	Mar- 5	Henry	Row- 75	George	Ire-264

Roberts,Henry	Way-249	Roberts,Mary col	Rob-241	Robertson,Isaac	Hay-200
Houston	Ons- 97	Mary A G	Roc- 8	Isaac	Rth-129
Hugh	Prq-224	Matthew	Ire-254	Isaac Jnr	Hay-200
Humphrey	Cas- 75	Morris	Rth-131	Isham	War-174
Isaac	Prq-224	Pascil	Cas- 66	Israel	Rth-129
Isaac	Way-249	Peter	Cur- 88	James	War-173
Ishmael	Cha-195	Phil	Ora-164	Jane	Brt- 57
J	Cam-155	Plasant	Ora-161	Joab	Per-143
J	Ora-148	James	Ora-164	John	Roc- 31
Jacob	Wil-281	Pleasant	Sur-171	John	Row- 47
James	Nor- 76	Polly	Wil-281	John	Hay-200
James	Roc- 34	Richard	Nor- 76	John	Roc- 6
James	Hay-200	Richard	Ons- 99	John	Sur-184
James	Hay-200	Robert	Row- 65	John	Row- 80
James	Sur-160	Rylen	Ran-178	John	Brt- 50
Jemima	Car-182	S	Ora-139	John	War-176
Jesse	Ora-163	S	Ash- 11	Jonathan	Rth-130
Jno	Per-143	S	Ora-146	Jos	Per-133
John	Car-181	Sally	Sur-19?	Luke	Rth-129
John	Car-174	Sarah	Car-174	Lydia	Cur- 89
John	Dup- 15	Sarah	Per-224	Margart	Pas-201
John	Lnc-328	Step	Rth-131	Mark	Roc- 21
John	Dup- 27	Thomas	Lnc-341	Martha	Rth-129
John	Fra- 95	Thomas	Roc- 34	Mary	Hay-200
John	Gat-110	Thomas	Cas- 66	Mary	Hal-118
John	Pas-201	Thomas	Wil-257	Mary	Edg- 52
John	Prq-224	Thomas	Cas- 67	Nathan	Cur- 88
John	Wil-276	Warrin	Row- 38	Nathan	Cha-210
John	Cur- 89	William	Rth-131	Peter	War-178
John	Row- 75	William	Dup- 27	Peter	Edg- 55
John	Cha-214	William	Nor- 76	Rebekah	Roc- 35
John	Cas- 67	William	Roc- 34	Sarey	Cur- 81
John	Sur-173	William	Prq-223	Southern	Pit-248
John	Sur-160	William	Joh-275	Susanna	Pas-201
John flat foot	Bun- 90	William	Cur- 88	Thos	Ora-147
John Sr	Prq-224	William	Cas- 66	Tulley	Cur- 88
John Senr	Lnc-328	William	Wil-264	V	Ora-156
John col	Rth-131	Wm	Row- 43	William	Hay-200
Johnathan	Row- 43	Willis	Nor- 76	William	Ire-253
Jonathan	Nor- 76	Willis	Per-143	William	Cas- 67
Jonathan col	Rob-241	Willis	Per-133	William	Car-174
Jonathan	Sur-179	Willis	Ora-164	William	Car-174
Joseph	Rth-131	Robertson,Andrew	Ora-165	William	Rth-129
Joseph	Wil-266	Betsey	Cas- 67	William	War-183
Joshua	Lnc-335	Burwell	War-169	William	War-182
Joshua	Pas-201	Clark	War-169	William H	Ire-269
Joshua	Sur-161	Charles	Rob-241	Wm	Row- 46
Josiah	Roc- 7	Christopher	Cur- 81	Roberttson,George	Bur-115
Kinchen	Nor- 76	Christopher	Cur- 81	Robeson,Doctr	Cum-239
Knchen	Cha-195	Crisortion	Cur- 81	Mrs	Mec- 25
Laurance	Row- 66	David	Ons-106	Aron	Mec- 28
Leaoin	Cas- 66	Davd	Row- 46	B	Bla- 10
Lucy	Pas-202	Edward	Roc- 34	Catherine	Bla- 12
Ludwick G	Car-178	Elijah	Edg- 51	Charles	Bla- 12
M	Ash- 13	George	Rth-129	Daniel	Mec- 41
Martin	Rth-131	Gid	Per-133	David	Mec- 35
Martin	Roc- 2	Giles	Ons-107	Downs	Mec- 34
Mary	Per-133	Holeway	Cur- 89	Fanny	Cum-260
Mary	Cho-227	Hugh	Row- 46	Henry	Mec- 51

Robeson,James		Bla- 6	Robins,Reuben	Sur-186	Robinson,Lewis		Cum-257
Jas		Mec- 54	Richard	Sur-186	N	H K	Ora-172
Jas		Mec- 34	S	Col- 21	Orpha		Prq-224
Jas		Mec- 29	Salley	Gat-111	Peggy		Cas- 67
Jno		Mec- 27	Thomas	Wil-282	Penty		Mon- 25
Jno		Mec- 25	Thomas Jr	Wil-276	Peter		Mon- 29
Jno M		Mec- 38	William	Rth-130	Randle		Cum-252
Joel		Cum-258	Wm	Ran-179	Richard		Sur-163
Jona		Bla- 5	Robinson,-----	Sto-115	Salley		Lnc-373
Jonathan		Wsh-220	Alex	Lnc-334	Sally		Sto-113
Malcom		Cum-265	Amos	Lnc-336	Sally		Sto-155
Matthew		Mec- 35	Andrew	Sto-125	Saml		Lnc-336
Ozburn		Mec- 33	Archibald	Car-182	Squires		Rch-200
Peter		Cum-236	Arthur	Rch-200	Susa		Ora-171
Rachel		Mec- 51	Charles	Sto-101	Teringem		Car-169
Richard		Mec- 28	Charles	Sto-132	Thomas		Nor- 76
Robert Esq		Mec- 38	Daniel	Rch-206	Thomas		Car-173
Robt		Mec- 35	Daniel	Cas- 67	Thos		Prq-224
S		Bru-240	Elijah	Lnc-353	Upshire		Mon- 32
Saml		Mec- 34	Ezekiel	Lnc-334	Wallace		Car-174
Sarah		Mec- 35	George	Ire-251	William		Lnc-331
Starkey		Cum-257	George	Ire-260	William		Wil-283
Thos		Mec- 34	Henry	Mon- 32	William		Sur-186
Thos J		Cum-240	Henry	Cas- 67	William		Lnc-359
William		Cum-260	Isaac	Lnc-354	William		Rch-203
Wm		Mec- 37	Israel	Sto-132	William		Sur-173
Wm		Mec- 48	Jacob	Sto-101	Wm		Bft- 36
Wm		Bla- 13	Jacob	Sto-132	Zach		Lnc-334
Wm		Ora-127	James	Lnc-334	Zachariah		Ans- 32
Wm		Mec- 24	James	Lnc-329	Zod		Ans- 20
Zekiel		Mec- 38	James	Roc- 14	Robison,Alexander		Bur-124
Robinett,Allen		Wil-257	James	Lnc-354	Daniel		Mor- 68
Isaac H		Wil-257	James	Lnc-371	G Andrew		Hay-199
James		Wil-275	James	Cas- 67	Jeremiah		Cum-257
Jesse Esq		Wil-257	James	Ora-162	John		Bur-120
Jesse Jr		Wil-257	James	Ora-119	John		Bur-116
Robins,Danl		Ran-178	James	Car-174	John		Cab-137
Danl		Ran-179	Jas	Lnc-334	Mark		Bur-120
Darcas		Gat-111	Jas	Lnc-334	Thos		Sam-158
Enoch		Hyd-223	Jas	Ora-122	William		Bur-120
Esther		Cur- 86	Jas	Lnc-336	Wm Senr		Ora-162
Ezl		Ran-179	Jesse	Lnc-329	Robley,John		Row- 76
G		Col- 21	Jesse	Lnc-373	Lewis		Row- 51
Isaac		Ran-179	Jesse	Cas- 66	Robruck,Jo		Row- 47
Jacob		Gat-111	Job	Lnc-334	Robson,Edw		Ora-130
James		Gat-111	Job Sen	Lnc-336	M		Ora-156
James		Hyd-224	Jno	Mon- 31	Solomon		Pit-258
James Senr		Ran-180	John	Lnc-336	Wm		Ora-136
Jas		Ran-180	John	Wil-282	Roby,George		Lnc-361
John		Ran-179	John	Sur-191	John B		Ire-241
John		Ran-179	John	Lnc-359	Henry		Ire-260
Jonathan		Ran-180	John	Sur-163	Truman		Sur-191
Joseph		Ran-179	John	Sur-162	Rochel,Kinchen		Hrt-207
Joseph		Ran-179	John	Sur-182	Rochet,John		Lnc-373
Lewis		Gat-111	John Sen	Ora-128	Rock,John		Ire-247
Mills		Fra- 98	Joseph	Car-173	John Butler Jr		Cum-247
Moses		Ran-180	Joseph	Car-171	Rockett,Richd		Lnc-365
Nancy		Gat-111	Joshua	Lnc-354	Rodelander,Maryan		Ans- 10
Phillip		Rth-130	Katy	Lnc-354	Peter		Ans- 10

Name	Loc	Name	Loc	Name	Loc
Roderick,Raleigh	Mar- 15	Roebuch,George	Mar-445	Rogers,Lott	Mor- 63
Rodes,J	Col- 19	Rof,Henry	Sto-130	Mark	Dup- 13
J	Col- 19	Rogan,Thomas	Ora-169	Martha	Roc- 23
M	Col- 19	Rogers,Absalum	Cha-213	Martha	Bun- 83
Nathaniel	Sur-188	Absolam	Pit-246	Matthew	Hay-199
P	Glf-178	Allen	Rth-129	Nancy	Dup- 23
Randolph	Cha-214	Ananias	Car-185	Nicholas	Dup- 9
Thomas	Mor- 63	Asa	Dup- 14	Peleg	Dup- 9
Rodger,David	Hrt-211	B	Bru-224	Polly	Sto-157
Rodgers,Mrs	Mec- 24	Bartlet	Bun- 77	R	Ash- 14
Widow	Mec- 55	Benjamin	Nor- 76	Randle	Ran-179
Carson	Cab-139	Daniel	Joh-274	Robert	Row- 58
Edmond	Mec- 46	David	Rth-130	Robert	Bun- 74
Etheldred	Edg- 57	David	Rth-129	Robert Snr	Bun- 89
Geo	Cab-139	David Jr	Rth-131	Sally	Per-143
Hannah	Mec- 45	Drewry	Pit-256	Samuel	Bun- 86
Henry	Cha-199	Drury	Pit-259	Sarah	Way-233
Hugh	Mec- 32	E	Col- 18	Sarah	Rch-209
James	Edg- 48	Elizabeth	Hal-118	Shadr	Mor- 63
James	Hrt-213	Ellenor	Ora-120	Shadrach	Hal-117
Jas	Mec- 44	Everitt	Mar- 15	Simon	Mar- 13
Jas	Mec- 32	Ezekiel	Wsh-225	Sion	Cha-203
Jno	Mec- 44	Fredk	Brt- 46	Stephen	Cur- 83
Jno	Mec- 32	Frederick	Brt- 47	Stephen	Mar- 10
Jno	Ora-132	George	Bun- 93	Sterling	Mar-445
John	Cab-139	George	Fra- 93	Susan	Dup- 25
John	Hrt-208	Hannah	Bur-114	Thomas	Fra- 81
Joseph	Ire-259	Hannah	Bun- 87	Thomas	Bun- 75
Joseph	Cab-139	Henry	Mar-445	Tobias	Cha-214
Josiah	Cha-204	Hugh	Hay-200	W	Mon- 42
Josiah	Edg- 48	Hugh	Bun- 87	Whitehead S	Cur- 83
Letisha	Tyr-211	Isaac	Bun- 72	William	Car-185
Levy	Edg- 49	Isaiah	Dup- 15	William	Cur- 92
Moses	Cab-139	J	Mon- 43	William	Pit-259
Needham	Ire-257	Jacob	Pit-259	William	Hal-117
Robt	Mec- 24	Jacob	Glf-171	William	Mar- 4
Seth	Cab-139	Jacob	Nsh- 74	William	Mar- 15
Stephen	Edg- 49	Jacob	Cha-216	William	Bun- 77
Thos	Cab-142	James	Dup- 20	William Senr	Mar- 13
Thos	Mec- 55	Jerremiah	Bun- 87	Wm	Cur- 83
Turner	Hrt-211	Jesse	Mor- 56	Z	Mon- 43
Wm	Mec- 32	John	Dup- 32	Rogerson,Asa	Prq-224
Wm Jr	Ora-132	John	Grn-131	Daniel	Prq-224
Wm Sen	Ora-132	John	Dup- 13	Daniel	Mar- 5
Willis	Edg- 48	John	Pit-259	David	Mar- 6
Roditt,Jno	Cho-231	John	Pit-259	Hezekiah	Prq-224
Rodman,Francis	Ire-240	John	Per-143	Jeremiah	Prq-224
Rodney,Isaac	Brt- 37	John	Mor- 63	Jesse	Prq-224
Rodwell,James	War-176	John	Cur- 83	Job	Mar- 11
John	War-176	John	Cas- 66	John	Prq-224
Rody,J	Col- 19	John	Mar-445	Jonathan	Gat-113
Roe,Elizebeth	Ans- 20	John	Wsh-220	Josiah	Mar- 6
Jacob	Nsh- 89	John	Joh-274	Simon	Mar- 11
Jane	Nsh- 90	Jonas	Rth-129	Solomon	Prq-224
John	Bft- 32	Jonathan	Wil-263	William	Mar- 5
Joseph	Cas- 66	Jos	Cho-231	William	Mar- 10
Matthew	Fra- 92	Joseph	Grn-128	Roggers,Benjn	Ans- 26
Robert	Nor- 76	Joseph	Grn-146	Daniel	Ons-105
Robt	Bft- 32	Joseph	Cat-139	Elijah	Ons-102

-273-

Name	Ref	Name	Ref	Name	Ref
Rogers,Elizabeth	Ans- 24	Ronsley,John	Cha-199	Rose,Mathew	Edg- 55
Henry	Ans- 15	Ronsone,Jos	Bft- 36	McKill	Hyd-230
Humphery	Ans- 26	Rook,Benjamin	Nor- 76	Molly	Sto-145
Jesse	Ans- 13	Daniel	Nor- 77	Molly	Sto-109
Jno	Ans- 25	James	Hrt-210	Ola	Pas-202
Jobe	Ans- 21	James	Nor- 76	Philip	Roc-' 8
Lamir	Ans- 26	Loven	Row- 46	Reddick	Nsh- 77
Mark	Ans- 21	Martin	Nor- 76	Robert	Edg- 56
Richard	Ons- 97	S	Glf-170	Saml	Glf-188
Robbert	Ans- 9	Rooke,Jacob	Sur-184	Samuel	Hay-200
Sampson	Ans- 27	Rooker,William	Rth-130	Sarah	War-180
Thos	Ans- 21	Rooks,Jethro	Hrt-216	Stephen	Nor- 76
Zach	Ons-100	Michael	Mec- 43	Sterling	Wil-261
Roglin,Wm	Grn-148	Nancy	Way-253	Theophilus	Way-245
Rolan,Findle	Cas- 66	Roose,Daniel	Row- 67	Timothy	Ran-178
Roland,Charles	Bun- 77	Roper,Anne	Nor- 76	Warners	Pas-201
Geo	Bun- 77	Charles	Nor- 76	William	Row- 69
Henry	Bun- 78	Cyrus	Hal-117	William	Way-233
Willie	Fra- 98	David	Bur-127	William	Hyd-230
Roler,E	Mon- 42	Fredrik	Hyd-227	William	Pas-201
Rolernd,A	Mon- 35	Henry	Cas- 66	William	Edg- 55
Rolimon,Teddy	Mon- 31	James	Bur-104	Wm	Nsh- 75
Rolland,John	Cha-195	James	Rch-202	Roseamon,Georgw	Row- 68
Young	Cha-191	John	Cha-213	Roseberry,William	Roc- 27
Rollet,Ezekel	Row- 44	John	Cas- 66	Rosel,William	Sto-157
Rollin,Charles	Pit-261	John	Mec- 31	Rosemerry,Joseph	Car-174
John	Pit-262	Joshua	Cha-196	Roshers,Ruben	Rob-242
Reuben	Pit-262	Thomas	Rch-213	Ross,Widow	Mec- 55
Robert	Hay-200	Thomas	Rch-211	A	Cam-156
Rollings,Jesse	Cah-195	Wm	Rob-224	A	Glf-177
Rollins,Aggatha	Ran-178	Rora,Jas	Ans- 11	Alexander	Mec- 25
Betsey	Cur- 87	Rosamon,George	Row- 70	Ann	Edg- 62
David	Ran-179	Peter	Row- 82	Benj	Glf-154
David	Ran-177	Rosan,John	Bun- 74	Benj	Bft- 31
George	Ran-179	Rosborough,John	Row- 75	Benjamin	Bur-122
George	Rth-130	Rosbrough,Saml	Row- 75	Benjamin	Bun- 89
Isham	Mon- 48	Rose (sic)	Pas-202	C	Mon- 30
Jas	Ran-178	Aaron	Edg- 55	Charles	Sur-181
John	Ran-179	Abner	Sur-178	D	Col- 20
Mary	Hyd-224	Amos	Nsh- 84	Daniel	Ans- 21
Wm	Ran-179	Anderson	Per-143	David	Mec- 47
Rolls,William	Hal-117	Benjamin	Bur-108	David	Ans- 13
Rom,Widow	Lnc-338	Benjn	Joh-289	Donold	Ans- 5
Isaac	Lnc-342	Burwell	Edg- 55	Ebenezer	Ans- 8
Rome,Jos	Len-323	Christian	Edg- 56	Edward	Hyd-222
Rominger,Cornelius	Row- 53	Duncan	Per-143	Elias	Grn-132
Jacob Jur	Sto-137	Mrs Eunice	Per-143	Elijah	Hyd-221
Jacob Jr	Sto-102	Francis	Hay-199	Francis	Bft- 34
Martin	Sto-134	Francis	Sur-177	Francis	Cab-139
Michael Jur	Sto-134	Isaiah	Bur-114	George	Rth-129
Michael Sr	Sto-143	J	Ash- 9	George	Rth-129
Philip	Sto-136	Jacob	Bur-114	George	Mec- 38
Romungers,Michael	Sto-108	James	Nor- 76	Griffin	Ans- 15
Rone,Jane	Cas- 67	James	Joh-288	J	Ora-140
M	Ora-146	John	Bur-114	James	Rth-131
Roney,Anne	Ora-124	John	Sur-194	James	Car-170
Ben	Ora-123	John Jr	Way-233	James Sr	Rth-131
Ben Sen	Ora-123	Jonathan	Bur-115	James Senr	Fra- 80
Ronsley,James	Cha-203	Littlebury	Row- 66	James Jr	Rth-131

-274-

Name	Ref	Name	Ref	Name	Ref
Ross,Jas	Ans- 10	Roughten,J	Ans- 8	Rowark,Timothy	Sto-154
Jas	Glf-155	Roulhac,William	Mar- 7	Rowe,Chrisn	Ons-103
Jas	Cab-136	Roundtree,Eliz	Way-247	Gaius	Ons- 98
Jas	Cab-138	Francis	Way-247	James	Ons- 99
Jas	Mec- 52	Hannah	Len-313	John	Pas-202
Jno	Mec- 49	Joseph	Ora-162	John	Row- 78
John	Fra- 95	Kedar	Way-247	Nancy	Pit-258
John	Grn-129	Moses	Bft- 33	Rowel,B	Bru-232
John	Bft- 31	Thomas	Ora-162	Bn Jr	Bru-222
John	Cab-138	Rounsoford,David	Ire-247	Rowell,Jacob	Way-238
John	Bur-104	John	Ire-247	W	Bru-232
John	Bft- 25	Rountree,Abner	Gat-112	Rowland,A	Ash- 13
John	Ire-244	Charles	Gat-107	Alfred	Rob-218
John Senr	Row- 67	Charles	Ora-162	David	Mon- 50
Joseph	Cab-139	Chas	Ora-169	Henry	Grn-135
Josiah	Bft- 32	Elizabeth	Per-224	J	Ash- 13
Kinchen	Ans- 15	Jesse	Pit-239	Jesse	Bft- 22
Levin	Glf-159	John	Per-143	Jessee	Edg- 63
Levin	Glf-180	John	Gat-114	Joel	Mon- 49
Luke	Mar-446	Miles	Gat-109	Martha	Rob-238
Martin	Ans- 19	Moab	Pit-257	Mary	Mon- 49
Martin	Prq-224	Selia	Gat-108	Pleasant	Grn-147
Moses	Rth-131	Willie	Edg- 67	Saml	Rob-238
Q	Glf-176	Rourke,Wm	Bru-222	Sherwood	Mon- 49
R	Ash- 14	Rouse,Burwell	Way-236	Thomas	Grn-135
Samuel	Cab-138	D	Mor- 69	Thomas	Rth-130
Samuel	Rth-131	George	Dup- 20	Wm	Mon- 49
Silvy	Ans- 20	Henry	Way-248	Rowly,Elias	Glf-187
Solomon	Rth-129	Jno	Len-312	Roxberry,John	Ora-171
T	Glf-174	Jno	Len-311	Royal,Joseph	Sur-181
Thomas	Cha-194	John	Len-321	Willm	Sam-161
Thomas	Mar- 14	John	Way-238	Royall,Joseph	Grn-138
W	Mon- 40	Jonathan	Len-316	Royals,Laban	Sam-161
Wm	Ans- 13	Joshua	Len-312	William	Sam-155
Wm	Bft- 36	Michael	Roc- 32	Royer,Saml	Ran-178
Wm	Nsh- 88	Rebecca	Len-312	Royster,Francis	Grn-125
Zachariah	Bun- 89	Richd	Len-310	John	Grn-125
Rossamon,Eliz	Lnc-350	Samuel	Roc- 32	Joseph	Per-133
Henry	Lnc-350	Simon Jr	Len-311	Wm Jr	Grn-133
Laveney	Lnc-350	Simon Senr	Len-322	Wm Senr	Grn-125
Rossell,Isham	Cha-200	Solomon	Dup- 13	Rozel,John	Roc- 20
Rosser,Benonius	Cha-215	William	Dup- 9	Rratliff,Henry	Hyd-224
Horris	Ans- 8	Routen,Agnes	Tyr-209	Rubly,J	Glf-173
Joshua	Ans- 8	John	Tyr-209	Rudd,Eliza	Hal-118
Wm	Cha-216	Richd	Tyr-209	John	Hal-118
Rossmasan,Coonrod	Rth-130	Routledge,Thos	Dup- 8	Nancy	Cas- 67
Rotan,James	Row- 82	Routon,Ann	Tyr-203	Wm	Hal-117
Rothrock,George	Sto-144	Rover,J	Col- 21	Ruddock,Jane	Glf-167
Philip	Sto-136	Row,James	Bur-131	Rude,Charles	Sto-135
Rothrok,Patrick	Cha-196	John	Per-133	John	Sto- 96
Roton,James	Sur-196	John	Cha-216	John	Sto-126
Josiah	Sur-167	Nicholas	Bur-131	John	Sto-138
Thos	Cur- 86	Solomon	Cha-192	Rudisale,Jacob	Bur-129
Wm	Cur- 86	Rowan,John	War-175	Rudisell,Henry Jr	Lnc-375
Rottenberry,Wm B	War-184	Thomas	Cum-249	Henry Senr	Lnc-375
Rouch,Peter	Lnc-350	Rowark,Edward	Cas- 67	John	Lnc-337
Rough,Daniel	Row- 85	Elisha	Cas- 67	Michl	Lnc-337
Roughten,D	Ans- 13	Ezekiel	Cas- 67	Phillip	Lnc-371
J	Ans- 13	John	Cas- 67	Phillip Jr	Lnc-371

-275-

Name	Ref	Name	Ref	Name	Ref
Rudisell,Phillip Jr	Lnc-371	Runnels,Jacob	Mon- 32	Rushing,Robt	Ans- 11
Rudser,Jacob	Sto-137	James	Mon- 32	Sol	Ans- 11
Rue,Ruben	Car-180	James Snr	Mon- 32	Stephen	Ans- 7
Southy	Car-180	Jno	Mon- 32	Wm	Ans- 8
Thomas	Car-180	John	Rth-129	Russ,David	Bla- 3
Ruff,Danl	Bft- 31	Nicholas	Bun- 86	David Junr	Bla- 5
John	Edg- 48	Thomas	Rth-131	E	Bla- 8
Wm	Bft- 24	William	Hrt-210	Hugh	Bla- 6
Ruffe,Charles	Wil-274	Wm	Mon- 32		Bru-238
Ruffen,Doctr Wm H	Brt- 48	Willis	Sam-152	J	Bla- 11
Ruffin,Etheldred	Edg- 62	Runnian,Abraham	Bun- 92	J	Bla- 10
Henry	Brt- 57	John	Bun- 88	J Sr	Bru-240
James	Brt- 57	Joseph	Bun- 92	James	Lnc-365
Guy	Edg- 61	Thomas	Bun- 92	Jas Esqr	Bru-222
Jessee	Edg- 69	Runnolds,Hanner	Hrt-209	John	Bru-222
John	Edg- 46	Jas	Hrt-209	John	Bla- 11
John	Brt- 57	Jesse	Hrt-209	John M	Bla- 5
John Jr	Edg- 45	Payshan	Hrt-209	Joseph	Bla- 5
Joseph	Edg- 46	Runnols,David	Hrt-216	Joseph	Bla- 11
Lemon	Edg- 46	Runsfell,Henry	Lnc-332	M	Bla- 10
Robert	Edg- 46	Runyall,Mary	Nor- 65	M	Bru-228
Robert	Roc- 15	Runyalls,Jeffery	Mor- 65	R	Bru-240
Samuel	Edg- 50	Runyan,Jeremiah	Rth-131	S	Bru-222
Sarah	Edg- 62	Will	Lnc-342	Sympo	Bru-226
Sterling	Roc- 16	Rupard,John	Row- 58	T	Bru-240
Tho	Ora-160	Peter	Row- 57	William	Tyr-208
Thomas	Brt- 57	Ruretthers,John	Row- 73	Wk	Bla- 5
William	War-184	Rusell,China	Way-240	Russel,Archd	Mon- 22
Rufrey,James	Roc- 20	Richd	Ans- 17	Aron	Mon- 25
Rufty,George	Row- 89	Rush,Asel	Ran-178	B	Cam-158
Rulis,J	Mon- 36	Ben	Mon- 29	Cele	Cab-144
Rumage,Geo	Mon- 41	Benjn	Ran-178	Charles	Roc- 14
Geo Jr	Mon- 41	Benjn	Ran-178	David Junr	Car-181
Nathan	Mon- 41	David	Bur-129	David Senr	Car-181
Rumbly,Aron	Ora-125	George	Lnc-345	Gabl	Ran-179
Edw	Ora-125	Joseph	Bur-129	Gabl	Ran-179
Henry	Ora-125	Lemuel	Grn-149	George	Rth-129
J	Glf-173	Michael	Ran-178	Habakuh	Car-181
John	Ora-125	N	Ora-137	Hamilton	Cab-148
Nathan	Ora-125	Noah	Ran-178	Henry	Row- 61
Rumbold,Fredreck	Ire-249	Peter	Bur-121	James	Cab-143
Rumfelt,John	Lnc-372	Saml	Grn-129	James	Mon- 20
Rumley,Clement	Car-171	Wm	Mon- 31	John	Mor- 56
Gilbert	Car-170	Rusher,Jacob	Row- 79	John	Pas-202
Jacob	Car-170	Rushing,Abraham	Ans- 11	John	Wil-275
John	Car-170	Archd	Ans- 9	John	Mon- 21
Marian	Glf-172	Brina	Ans- 11	John Snr	Mon- 20
Rachel	Car-178	David	Ans- 11	John Snr	Mon- 21
Rumph,Mr	Mon- 24	Hardy	Ans- 11	Joseph	Cab-137
Rumple,Daniel	Row- 72	Jason	Ans- 11	Leonard	Mon- 20
Philip	Row- 71	Jno	Ans- 7	Lot	Car-184
Runals,Archilus	Bun- 93	Jno	Ans- 7	M	Ash- 11
Runnells,John	Lnc-338	Jno	Ans- 6	Major	Rob-218
Lewis	Sam-161	Joseph	Ans- 12	Mark	Rob-224
Runnels,A	Mon- 31	Matthew	Ans- 11	Mary	Rth-130
Elijah	Rth-129	Paul	Ans- 7	Micajah	Ons- 98
Hamilton	Rth-129	Philip	Ans- 11	Moses	Mon- 21
Henry	Mon- 31	Philip	Ans- 11	Thomas	Car-176
Hugh M	Rth-130	Richd	Ans- 11	Thos	Mor- 56

Name	Ref	Name	Ref	Name	Ref
Russel,Thos	Mon- 20	Ruth,John	Row- 63	Ryde,Wolsan	Mon- 43
Timothy	Grn-139	Ruth	Bun- 92	Rye,J	Bru-238
Wm	Mon- 20	Rutherford,Widow	Lnc-329	Rygan,Charles	Cha-199
Russell,A	Glf-162	David	Bur-109	Rymer,David	Bun- 91
Alexander	Roc- 2	David	Row- 75	Henry	Row- 69
Alexr	Glf-154	James	Bun- 75	Ryndles,Wm	Lnc-336
Alexr	Ora-121	James	Rth-131	Ryon,John	Sur-163
Benj	Hyd-233	John	Bur-125	William	Hyd-224
Benj Snr	Hyd-233	Rutland,Abednego	Hal-117		
Charles	Sur-176	David	Nor- 76	S-----,John	Jon-304
David	Cab-146	J	Bru-230	S---t-,John	Row- 71
David	Hay-200	James	Nor- 76	S-ygen,William	Hal-118
Eliz	Hyd-233	James	Brt- 56	Sabiston,David Sr	Car-171
J	Glf-162	Mashcik	Nor- 76	Robert	Car-182
J	Glf-183	Narsworthy	Nor- 76	Sabo,Catoe	Way-238
J	Ora-160	Orren	Nor- 76	Sach,Joseph	Sto-143
James	Hay-200	R	Bru-228	Sackey,James	Lnc-335
James	Roc- 6	Watson	Nor- 76	Saddler,Philip	Mec- 36
James	Bun- 79	Whitmell	Brt- 54	Sadler,Anderson	Lnc-365
James	Nor- 76	Rutledge,Abel	Row- 74	Henry	Lnc-359
John	Car-184	Elijah	Sto-156	Henry	Lnc-372
John	Joh-288	Elijah	Sto-114	James	Lnc-365
John C	Fra- 87	George	Lnc-365	Jere	Lnc-359
John Senr	Grn-142	James	Row- 63	John	Hyd-231
Joseph	Ans- 19	James	Lnc-365	Nathl	Lnc-365
Matthew	Bun- 74	James	Sur-196	Richard	Hyd-229
Richard	War-180	Joel	Sur-169	Saml Junr	Hyd-229
Salley	Hrt-212	Isaac	Sur-167	Samuel	Hyd-227
T	Glf-183	John	Sur-192	Sarah	Hyd-231
Talbot	Sur-171	John	Lnc-333	Shadrach	Hyd-230
William	Cum-235	Sarah	Lnc-365	Will R	Lnc-365
William	Cas- 67	William	Sur-196	Cap William	Rth-133
William	Sur-183	Rvers,Joshua Jr	War-176	Cap William	Rth-131
William Junr	Cum-235	Joshua Sr	War-176	William Esq	Rth-132
Wm	Glf-181	Ryal,Ede	Car-171	Zachariah	Lnc-359
Wm	Glf-184	James	Bla- 12	Saffield,Lindy	Ire-269
Russil,Ann	Ons-106	Lewis	Sam-158	Safford,Thomas	Cas- 69
Thomas Esqr	Ons- 99	Marmaduke	Car-179	Sage,Sarah	Ons-108
William	Ons-106	Noah	Sam-161	Sailot,Henry	Sto-130
Russle,James	Cab-147	Owen	Sam-159	Peter	Lnc-361
James	Jon-303	Stephen	Bla- 8	Sails,Cornelius	Bun- 97
Jaa	Mec- 44	Ryals,Britain	Joh-277	Saine,Frederick	Row- 64
Jean	Cab-147	Hardy	Sam-160	Gasper	Row- 64
Jerry	Mec- 33	Isam	Sam-163	George	Row- 64
Jesse	Cha-195	Marmaduke	Sam-158	Jacob Junr	Lnc-328
John	Cab-147	Owen	Sam-162	Joseph	Row- 66
Mary	Cab-147	William	Joh-275	Saint,Benjn	Ans- 8
Thos	Mec- 49	Young	Sam-163	Isham	Ans- 9
Wm	Mec- 32	Ryan,Mrs Eliz	Brt- 46	William	Prq-225
Russon,Wilson	Row- 59	Joel	Glf-166	St.Clair,Archd	Rch-191
Russum,Vinum	Glf-154	John	Gat-115	C Thomas	Hay-200
Rust,Jeremiah	Grn-131	John	Glf-157	John	Wil-257
Saml	Grn-123	Michael	Wil-261	St.Goin,Richd	Per-144
Rustin,George	Ran-179	Patrick	Dup- 13	St.John,Abram	Cas- 70
Henry	Ran-179	R	Glf-176	Edmondson	Fra- 79
Jas	Ran-179	Will	Glf-151	Willm	Fra- 86
John	Ran-179	Ryassan,Stephen	Sto-145	St.Lawrence,Eliz	Cha-193
Wm	Ran-179	Ryche,Ben	Ora-119	Henry	Nor- 77
Ruth,Jacob	Ran-178	F	Ora-177	Sale,Anne	Wil-268

Sale,Cornelius	Wil-261	Samuel,George	Cas- 69	Sanders,Jesse	Gat-116
James	Wil-261	Henry	Sto-125	Jesse	Bur-120
John	Wil-272	James	Cas- 69	Joel	Glf-188
John Jr	Wil-264	Jeremiah	Cas- 69	Jno	Rob-239
Leonard	Wil-261	John	Sto-131	Jno	Ans- 17
Robert	Wil-261	Josiah	Cas- 69	John	Way-242
Salemon,Jacob	Sto-124	Lewis	Wil-261	John	Ran-181
Sales,Anthony	War-167	Micajah	Stu-167	John	Hrt-215
Armstead	Cur- 88	Mordecai	Wil-261	John	Nsh- 82
Polly	War-178	Reubin	Sto- 96	John	Nsh- 86
Wm	Cab-147	Reubin	Sto-126	John	Ons- 98
Sallenger,John	Mar- 15	Sarah	Cas- 69	John	Sur-179
Sallinger,Stephen	Mar- 7	Samy,George	Row- 87	John	Glf-187
Salmon,David D	Cum-241	Sandaford,Noah	Rch-206	John	Gat-111
Jacob	Sto- 95	Sandars,Jacob	Nsh- 90	John	Car-180
James	Sur-170	Thomas	Nsh- 89	John	Joh-290
Jonathan	War-176	Sanderlin,A	Cam-159	John	Tyr-206
Joseph	Sur-196	C	Cam-153	John	Cha-215
Richard	Sam-152	Chs	Cho-226	John Jr	Prq-225
William	Dup- 25	F	Cam-157	John Sr	Prq-225
William	War-184	J	Cam-154	Joseph	Way-254
Salmons,Willoughby	Car-181	J	Cam-156	Joseph	Grn-126
Salter,Ann	Bla- 13	J	Cam-157	Joshua	Prq-225
James	Bla- 14	L	Cam-155	Luke	Mon- 22
John	Pit-237	T	Cam-161	Lyon	Nsh- 87
Margaret	Pit-240	W	Cam-163	Marey	Cur- 87
Mary	Wsh-228	Sanderling,B	Cam-159	Martha	Glf-167
Sarah	Prq-226	Sanders,Abednego	Wil-269	Mary	Wil-285
Wm	Bla- 13	Abraham	Pit-259	Mary	Prq-225
Saltonstall,G T	Cum-236	Abram	Prq-225	Mary	Nsh- 90
Salusbury,John	Wsh-227	Alexr	Dup- 12	Mason	Cas- 69
Salvy,Edwd	Row- 59	Ann	Prq-224	Mills	Bur-120
Salyer,Samuel	Cur- 87	Aron	Cas- 69	Nancy	Cha-207
Old Sam (sic)	Pas-206	Benjn	Ran-182	Nathan	Prq-226
Sam,Betty	Bft- 30	Berry	Sto-125	Nimrod	Mon- 22
Sammon,Agnus	Bla- 13	Betty	Way-254	Patsey	Cas- 69
Sammons,Robert	Hyd-232	Byrant	Gat-115	Phillip	Cha-194
Sarah	Row- 71	Charles	Pas-203	R	Ora-146
William	Ons-107	David	Wil-285	Reuben	Joh-274
Sample,Jas	Mec- 46	Elizabeth	Hrt-210	Rhoda	Pas-204
Joseph	Mec- 25	Ellick	Joh-281	Richard	Ons-109
Wm	Mec- 35	Geo	Glf-165	Richard	Edg- 48
Sampler,James	Bur-112	George	Grn-127	Richd	Way-254
Samples,William	Bur-128	H	Glf-165	Richd	Cas- 69
William Jr	Bur-128	Josea	Pas-204	Robert	Pit-257
Sampson,Michl Esq	Sam-150	Isaac	Ons-103	Robert	War-179
Polly	Car-182	Jacob	Mon- 22	Robert	Gat-115
Sidny	Pas-203	James	Bun- 93	Robert	Cas- 69
Thomas	Cum-241	James	Row- 76	Samuel	Car-180
Sams,Berdit	Bun- 88	James	Nsh- 90	Sarah	Prq-224
Edmond	Bun- 87	James	Ons-108	Sarah	Prq-226
Hackly	Bun- 87	James	Cas- 69	Shadr	Bur-104
John	Bun- 76	James	Gat-116	Stephen	Mon- 22
Reuben	Bur-131	James	Fra- 82	Stephen	Roc- 4
Sams,Rice	Roc- 13	James Jr	Cas- 69	Susanah	Sto-125
Samuel,Anderson	Grn-141	Jesse	Mon- 22	Susannah	Sto- 96
Archd	Cas- 69	Jesse	Mor- 55	Susannah	Car-183
Edmend	Sto-109	Jesse	Glf-168	Sythe	Cas- 69
Edmund	Sto-151	Jesse	Ons-106	T	Col- 19

Name	Loc		Name	Loc		Name	Loc
Sanders,Taylor	Cas- 69		Sanford,Willis	Nor- 78		Satterswaite,Tho	Bft- 31
Thomas	Fra- 79		Sankston,Jno	Ora-159		Satterthwaithe,Abram	Hyd-225
Thos	Prq-225		Sanlin,Lewis	Bun- 75		Abrm	Hyd-225
Thos	Sam-153		Santee,John Junr	Bla- 3		John	Hyd-224
Thos	Cha-215		John Senr	Bla- 3		Mary	Hyd-224
Vincent	Fra-100		Sap,Benjn	Ran-181		Saml	Hyd-225
William	Roc- 16		Jesse	Ran-181		William	Hyd-224
William	Prq-226		Sapenfield,John	Row- 79		William	Hyd-225
William	Ons-108		Sapingfield,Geo	Lnc-373		Wm	Hyd-225
William	Fra- 79		Sapp,Elizabeth	Sto-150		Zach	Hyd-225
Wm	Ans- 8		Newel	Row- 48		Satterthwatie,Jeremiah	
Wm	Nsh- 90		Sarah	Glf-162			Hyd-221
Wright	Way-242		Sarcy,Sulley	Cur- 90		Satterthwite,Abrm	Hyd-225
Zepheniah	Roc- 15		Sargent,Daniel	Per-144		Satterwhite,Howell	Grn-147
Sanderson,Benj	Cur- 86		James	Rth-114		James	Grn-147
Benjamin	Hyd-228		Thomas	Bur-111		James Jr	Grn-143
Caleb	Cur- 86		Sarnett,Anaretta	Edg- 47		Mitchel	Grn-133
Celia	Rob-243		John	Edg- 47		Rethen	Grn-133
Charles	Glf-161		Joshua	Edg- 47		Smith	Grn-133
Daniel	Cur- 86		Zachariah	Edg- 47		Wm	Grn-132
Henery	Cur- 87		Sarrock,Dempsey	Hal-120		Sauceman,Daniel	Cab-148
Jessey	Cur- 85		Sartain,James	Wil-260		Jacob	Cab-148
John	Cur- 86		Sarte,Tobias	Glf-156		Sauls,Benj	Way-241
Jonathan	Rob-243		Saser,Mary	Ans- 20		Benj	Way-251
Leml	Cur- 86		Jno	Ans- 18		David	Joh-272
Nancey	Cur- 86		Sasser,Abel	Joh-284		Green	Nor- 77
Richerd	Cur- 87		Arthur	Joh-283		Henry	Nor- 77
Samuel	Hyd-228		Edward	Way-235		Henry Jr	Way-241
Sanders	Hyd-228		Henry	Way-250		Henry Sr	Way-241
Thomas	Ons-101		Henry	Joh-283		John	Bur-121
Thos	Cur- 86		John	Way-253		Pereby	Joh-272
Thos	Cur- 87		John Jr	Way-253		Rayman	Way-237
Thos	Cur- 85		Joseph	Way-239		Redden	Joh-273
Sandford,Robt Jr	Grn-133		Lewis	Joh-290		Warren	Nor- 77
Stephen	Grn-133		Ruth	Way-235		Saunders,Anne	Rth-135
Wm	Fra- 79		Stephen	Way-233		Benjamin	Nor- 78
Sandifer,Elemeleck	Nor- 78		William	Way-233		Benjn	Cah-213
John	Nor- 77		William	Joh-282		Benjn	Ran-180
Joseph	Sam-160		Satchwell,James	Hyd-225		Edward	Lnc-375
Sandiford,Saml	Fra- 82		John Jur	Hyd-223		Francis	Ran-180
Sandlin,Ezekiel	Bun- 75		John Sr	Hyd-223		Francis	Nor- 77
James	Hay-201		Sater,Henry	Sur-183		George	Ran-180
John	Hay-201		John	Sur-183		Jacob	Jon-304
John	Fra-100		Joseph	Sur-174		James	Cha-210
John	Tyr-205		Saterfd,Betsy	Per-133		James	Roc- 5
Nicholas	Dup- 32		Betsy Jr	Per-133		James	Cho-225
Samuel	Dup- 32		Saterfield,Amos	Cas- 69		James Senr	Roc- 20
Will	Dup- 33		Isaac	Per-144		John	Roc- 15
William	Hay-201		Saterwhite,Horace	BRow- 89		John	Rth-133
Sandling,Jesse	Ons-105		Satter,Ann	Bft- 28		John	Rth-131
Lewis	Ons-101		Henry	Hyd-228		John	Bft- 20
Sandmon,John	Dup- 24		Wiley	Glf-175		Joseph	Cha-210
Sandorson,Thomas	Hyd-227		Satterfiel,John	Per-133		Josh	Ran-180
Sandreth,S	Ash- 5		Satterfield,James	Per-144		Josh	Ran-180
W	Ash- 5		Jas	Cho-226		Josh	Ran-180
Sandrews,Sarah	Hal-119		Kinchen	Glf-188		Katy	Lnc-349
Sands,J	Ash- 6		Thos	Cho-231		Mark	Wsh-227
Samuel W	Hal-118		Wm	Cho-221		Moses	Jon-303
Saner,Peter	Row- 55		Wm	Per-144		Polly	Wsh-221

Saunders,Reuben	Mar- 10	Sawyer,C	Cam-153	Sawyers,Jos	Try-207
Richard	Ran-180	C	Cam-155	Joseph	Hyd-230
Robert	Hal-118	Caleb	Pas-206	Joseph	Hyd-231
Saml	Lnc-334	Calep	Try-208	Leven	Tyr-204
Saml	Lnc-334	Con	Cam-160	Lewis	Bun- 82
Sarah	Jon-304	Chris	Tyr-208	Lewis	Bun- 82
Thomas	Lnc-346	D	Cam-161	M	Cam-158
Wm	Cho-225	D	Cam-163	M	Cam-152
Wm	Roc- 19	D	Cam-157	M	Cam-157
Wm	Ran-180	D W	Cam-158	M Esq	Cam-152
Saunderson,Benj	Jon-304	Daniel	Tyr-202	Malac	Pas-206
Elijah	Jon-304	David	Pas-202	Mashal	Cur- 83
Ephr	Len-318	David	Pas-205	Matt E	Cho-221
William	Len-318	Dem Esq	Cam-152	Miles	Tyr-208
Saundrews,Matthew	Hal-119	Densi	Tyr-207	N	Cam-164
Saur,Yalton	Way-244	E	Cam-158	Nancy	Pas-205
Saurey,Jas	Hrt-211	E	Cam-158	Nathan	Jon-304
Sauser,B	Col- 17	E	Cam-157	Noah	Pas-204
F	Col- 17	E	Cam-163	Noah	Pas-205
J	Col- 17	E	Cam-156	Owen	Wsh-222
Richd	Ans- 18	Elijah	Hyd-226	P	Cam-158
Savage,Abraham	Edg- 59	Elisha	Hyd-226	P	Cam-161
Allen	Edg- 54	Elisha	Hyd-230	Patsy	Pas-205
Charles	Edg- 64	Enoch	Pas-205	Peter	Hyd-226
Charles	Dup- 23	Enoch Esq	Cam-159	Polly	Tyr-208
Drewry	Nsh- 84	F Snr	Cam-158	R	Cam-158
Jacob	Dup- 22	F	Cam-162	R	Cam-161
James	Edg- 58	Fred	Pas-202	Randell	Hyd-226
Jesse	Gat-115	Fred B	Pas-205	Richerd	Cur- 90
Joel	Way-238	Gr:.ffith	Pas-202	Robin	Tyr-207
John	Bla- 4	H	Cam-158	Robin Sr	Tyr-208
John	Ran-180	H	Cam-160	S	Cam-160
John	Ran-181	Halowell	Cur- 86	S	Cam-152
John	Ran-181	Isaac	Hyd-226	S J	Cam-160
Love	Dup- 9	Isaac	Pas-204	Saml	Ran-181
Mary	Ran-180	Isaac	Tyr-207	Saml	Pas-204
Pryer	Gat-113	J	Cam-158	Samuel	Ran-182
Randal	Nsh- 84	J	Cam-160	Steph	Tyr-207
Samuel S	Row- 89	J	Cam-160	Sungon	Cur- 83
Warren	Edg- 63	J	Cam-160	Susan	Pas-204
Wm	Bft- 38	J	Cam-162	T	Cam-158
Savill,M	Cam-165	J	Cam-161	T	Cam-158
Robt	Mec- 28	J	Cam-161	T	Cam-160
Savits,Catherine	Row- 68	J	Cam-155	T	Cam-161
Sawel,J	Mon- 36	J	Cam-154	Thomas	Pas-204
Sawers,John	Row- 55	Jacob	Cur- 86	Thomas	Hyd-226
Sawrey,Henry Senr	Nor- 77	Jacob	Tyr-203	Thos	Cam-158
Sawyer,A	Cam-161	James	Cur- 86	Vina	Pas-205
A	Cam-161	James	Cas- 70	W	Cam-160
A	Cam-161	Janach	Cur- 85	W	Cam-161
A	Cam-154	Jenny	Hyd-226	William	Bun- 86
Abel	Pas-204	Jessey	Cur- 86	William	Cas- 70
Abel	Tyr-202	Jessey	Cur- 85	William Sr	Cas- 69
Abner	Tyr-207	Joel	Pas-205	Willie	Hyd-226
Absolam	Cas- 70	John	Pas-202	Willm	Tyr-208
Baley	Sur-190	John	Hyd-226	Z	Cam-158
Betsy	Pas-203	John	Hyd-226	Zabeniah	Cur- 85
C	Cam-158	John	Cha-201	Zephalia	Hyd-226
C	Cam-160	John	Cas- 70	Sawyers,Mary	Wil-276

Name	Ref	Name	Ref	Name	Ref
Sawyers,Joseph	Row- 69	Scarlet,To	Ora-157	Scott,David	Nor- 78
William Jr	Cas- 69	Scarlett,James	Ora-168	Elender	Ons- 96
Sayer,Jacob	Cas- 75	Scarlot,J	Ora-138	Eliza	Pas-205
Saymour,Robert	Per-133	Mary	Ora-138	Elizabeth	Rth-135
Saxton,E	Cam-161	Stephen	Ora-138	Elly	Nor- 78
Samuel	Hal-119	Scarlott,Steph	Ora-149	Emanuel	Cum-263
Thos	Ran-181	Thos	Ora-142	Exum	Nor- 77
Scabold,Henry	Lnc-349	Scath,James	Hyd-225	Francis	Hrt-212
Scadlack,James	Cur- 92	Schaw,Dan	Bla- 10	Geo	Bun- 74
Scaff,David	Pas-204	John	Bla- 12	Hannah	Edg- 55
Joseph	Hal-118	John	Bla- 7	Harrey	Grn-121
S	Cam-164	Schohan,Malcom	Bla- 12	Heliry	Rth-133
W	Bru-236	Scismore,Jesse	Bur-114	Henry	Bft- 36
Scaglor,Angelico	Ans- 10	Scissor,Betty	Mor- 62	Henry	Prq-226
Scales,Absalom	Roc- 25	Scoffield,J	Glf-176	Isaac	Hal-120
Augustus	Cur- 83	Scofield,Jesse	Pit-250	Isham	Hal-119
Cynthia	Roc- 23	Scoggin,Burges	Rth-134	Isom	Edg- 54
Daniel	Roc- 23	Ezekiel	Rth-134	Israel	Edg- 72
Henry	Roc- 8	Ezekiel	Rth-134	James	Cha-198
James	Roc- 21	Jemima	Rth-133	James	Rth-132
Joseph H	Roc- 22	Jno	Ora-149	James	Bun- 79
Nathaniel	Roc- 31	John	Per-144	James	Nor- 77
Nathaniel	Roc- 33	Scoggins,Charles	Rth-133	James	Ire-252
Thomas	Roc- 22	R	Ora-140	Jas	Cab-142
Scalf,Benjamin	Ire-267	Samuel	Rth-133	Jas	Cur- 90
David	Ire-267	Scogin,Aaron	Per-144	Jemima	Rch-203
Scalfs,Lewis	Wil-258	Joseph	Per-144	Jesse	Hal-119
William	Wil-271	Scold,Samuel	Bur-119	Jno	Ora-145
Scals,John	Sur-188	Scolds,Joseph	Bur-118	John	Cab-136
Scamore,John	Per-133	Scoles,William	Hal-120	John	Row- 48
Scarbaus,Abselam	Cur- 79	Scott,Hector	Hyd-225	John	Nor- 78
Aney	Cur- 82	Isaac	Cha-210	John	Rth-133
Chaney	Cur- 81	John	Hal-119	John	Bur-103
Eufan	Cur- 82	M	Ora-137	John	Ons- 96
Jacob	Cur- 81	Mitchel	Cur- 90	John	Cur- 80
Joshuay	Cur- 82	Richard	Hal-119	John	Cas- 69
Nancey	Cur- 82	Wm	Cur- 83	John	Nor- 77
Patey	Cur- 79	Scot,Ann	Mor- 64	John	Hal-120
Scarber,Gideon	Cur- 79	Hardy	Hal-119	John	Ire-241
Scarboro,Benjn	Dup- 33	John	Bun- 94	John	Ire-247
Nathan	Dup- 35	W	Ora-140	John	Ire-249
Scarborough,Daniel	Roc- 27	Scott & Jos Tally	Mec- 34	Joseph	Prq-225
Edward	Lnc-361	Scott,Ab	Pas-203	Joseph	Bun- 78
Elizabeth	Car-172	Abm	Pas-202	Joseph	Cas- 69
Isaac	Edg- 51	Abram	Lnc-368	Joseph Sqnr	Bun- 79
James	Edg- 51	Adam	Glf-174	Leonard	Sto- 98
James	Roc- 27	Alexander	Nor- 78	Leonard	Sto-129
James	Wil-284	Alexander	Ire-248	Lott	Sam-162
Kincheon	Sam-164	Alexr	Cab-144	Malai	Pas-206
Wm	Car-172	Andrew	Way-254	Marina Esq	Pas-204
Scarbrough,Ben	Mon- 23	Aron	Cab-142	Mary	Pas-205
J	Cam-156	Britain	Joh-280	Mary	Bur-102
John	Mon- 23	Charles	Way-251	Mary	Ora-123
Saml	Mon- 23	Charles	Ons- 96	Micaja	Row- 60
Thrift	Ora-124	Daniel	Sto-120	Miles	Ora-126
Wm	Mon- 25	Daniel	Sto- 91	Obediah	Ons-101
Wm	Mon- 23	Daniel	Sur-183	Polly	Pas-204
Scarlet,John	Ran-180	Danl	Ran-180	Polly	Lnc-368
Stephen	Ran-182	David	Roc- 29	Priscilla	Hal-119

Scott,R	Ora-155	Scrmes,Franky	Dup- 14	Sears,John Sen	Grn-147	
Rhoda	Hal-120	Scrugs,Brett	Sto-155	Joseph	Grn-147	
Robert	Bun- 98	Scruter,Jno	Ans- 32	Rosa	Ora-146	
Robert	Bun- 78	Scudders,Moses	Sur-181	William	Gat-112	
Robt	Glf-171	Scull,Alexr	Cum-266	William	Hyd-233	
Robin	Pas-205	J G	Bru-226	Wm	Mor- 63	
S	Ash- 14	Scurlock,Joseph	Cha-215	Wm	Grn-146	
S	Ash- 10	Mary	Hal-119	Seat,John	Cha-197	
Saml	Ora-163	Wm	Grn-141	Seaton,Juda	Pas-204	
Saml	Mec- 53	Scurr,Betsey	Cur- 88	Ransom	War-179	
Samuel	Bun- 85	Sea,Elizabeth	Hrt-213	Seatton,W Junr	Bla- 10	
Sarah	Rch-204	Seabolt,John Senr	Lnc-370	Seawal,Gedeon	Mor- 58	
Stephen	Sto-127	Seaborn,Frederick	Cum-257	James	Mor- 54	
Stephen	Sto- 97	Seabrooks,Daniel	Hyd-228	Joseph	Mor- 67	
Stephen	Pas-206	Thomas	Hyd-233	Seay,Eliz	Brt- 55	
S̶t̶e̶p̶h̶e̶n̶	Pas-206	Seabury,Raleigh	Dup- 16	S̶e̶a̶y̶b̶r̶o̶u̶g̶h̶,̶W̶m̶	Mon- 35	
Stephen Jun	Pas-205	Secrease,Christian	Row- 84	Sebastan,Benjamin	Wil-272	
Stephen Sen	Pas-205	Thomas	Row- 84	Elisha	Wil-262	
Susan	Mon- 21	Seachrist,George	Row- 79	William	Wil-262	
Thomas	Bur-109	Seaglar,Geo	Ans- 22	Sebaugh,Margaret	Lnc-326	
Thos	Pas-205	Seagle,John	Lnc-327	Sebern,Jesse	Cur- 87	
Thos	Ora-145	Seagraves,Wm	Ans- 22	Sebine,Mary	Wil-268	
Vela	Hal-119	Wm	Ans- 8	Seborn,Joseph	Hyd-225	
Will	Pas-205	Seagrove,Phobe	War-178	Sechoan,Isaac	Rob-242	
William	Sto-136	Seal,Joshua	Ans- 18	Seckler,Frederick	Row- 70	
William	Sto-103	Seals,John	Wsh-227	Rudolf	Row- 69	
William	Roc- 11	Seales,Joseph	Sto-119	Secler,Daniel	Row- 53	
William	Bur-109	Sion	Cab-147	Secreets,Andrew	Mec- 43	
William	Bur-118	Sythea	Sto-139	Francis	Mec- 30	
William	Edg- 71	Thos	Brt- 46	Jacob	Mec- 42	
William	Ons- 96	Seany,Archablad	Mec- 22	Jacob	Mec- 29	
William	Sur-183	David	Mec- 43	Jno	Mec- 30	
William	Ora-162	George	Mec- 44	Wm	Mec- 30	
William	Lnc-368	Titus	Mec- 44	Sedberry,G	Mon- 36	
William	Ire-248	Searcey,Wm H	Grn-145	J	Mon- 36	
Wm	Ran-180	Searcy,David	Rth-134	W	Mon- 36	
Wm	Mec- 24	John	Rth-131	Sedon,Antealy	Row- 84	
Wm	Mec- 46	Lemuel	Joh-276	George	Row- 84	
Scotten,James	Ran-181	Reuben	Rth-134	Seduce,Edward	Car-173	
John	Ran-180	Richard	Rth-132	Seemore,Thomas	Way-238	
Soctts,George	Row- 54	Thomas	Roc- 5	Seey,Benjn	Cha-215	
Screws,Benjamin	Ons-100	William	Ran-182	Seferate,Geo	Cab-145	
David	Dup- 34	William	Rth-132	Michael	Cab-145	
James	Dup- 35	Searle,Stephen H	Ran-181	Sefferate,Wm	Cab-145	
Jesse	Dup- 34	Searles,Edward	Len-311	Sefferth,Barn	Cab-140	
John	Dup- 24	Jonathan	Cur- 92	Sefford,John	Lnc-361	
Joseph	Dup- 35	Major	Dup- 15	Leonard	Lnc-361	
Robert	Dup- 35	Robert	Len-311	Sefort,Geo	Cab-143	
Scriggs,Richard	Rth-132	Robt	Len-317	Segars,John	Mor- 65	
Robert	Rth-132	Searls,Coolr	Bft- 30	Josiah	Mor- 67	
Scriven,Jane	Bla- 7	Edwd	Bft- 30	Martin	Mor- 65	
Scrivner,Benjamin	Row- 86	Wm	Bft- 30	Southard	Cum-255	
Scroggs,David	Hay-201	Sears,Abner	War-167	Seipper,James	Cum-263	
James	Ire-247	Anderson	Grn-146	Seitz,Abram	Lnc-373	
James	Ire-245	Barbee	Cha-200	George	Lnc-373	
Jeremiah	Ire-247	David	Mor- 63	George Senr	Lnc-373	
John	Ire-347	George	Hrt-215	Thomas	Lnc-373	
William	Bun- 95	H	Ora-146	Selah, Philip	Pas-204	
Scrom,Jno	Ans- 29	John Jr	Grn-147	Selby,Ann	Hyd-228	

Name	Ref	Name	Ref	Name	Ref
Selby,Henry	Bft- 37	Selos,Elisha	Cha-198	Sessoms,Robert	Edg- 59
John	Hyd-228	Selph,Wm B	Ora-143	Saml	Brt- 50
John	Hyd-229	Selters,James	Bru-228	Solomon	Sam-153
Mary Ann	Hyd-223	Semon,John	Lnc-369	Thomas	Cum-264
Saml	Hyd-229	John Jr	Lnc-369	William	Hrt-215
William	Hyd-229	Semore,David	Cur- 82	Setliff,John	Sur-165
Self,Aaron	Rth-134	Sen,James A L	Brt- 59	Sally	Sur-188
Abram	Per-133	Senate,Claban	Wsh-226	Setonthorn,Wm	Bft- 24
B	Ora-139	Isham	Wsh-225	Setser,Adam Jr	Bur-122
Elisha	Bur-106	Seniard,James	Bun- 85	Adam	Bur-122
Ewell	Glf-185	Senseng,William	War-183	Jacob	Bur-122
Francis	Bun- 96	Senter,Fereby	Cum-246	John	Bur-122
Francis	Cha-197	Joel	Lnc-341	Lawrence	Bur-122
John	Cum-237	John	Sur-163	Setterson,Charles	Prq-226
Parish	Bur-106	Mary	Cum-258	James	Prq-225
Walter	Fra- 95	Mary	Cum-258	Settlemere,David	Lnc-369
William	Rth-135	Moses	Row- 37	Martin	Lnc-369
Wm	Cha-193	Stephen	Cum-257	Settles,Mace	Cas- 70
Sell,Enis	Ran-181	Zacha	Sur-163	Matthew	Hal-119
John	Sto-133	Sentill,Guilford	Bun- 84	Setzer,Easter	Lnc-370
Jonathan	Sto-133	William	Bun- 84	Jacob	Lnc-370
Jonathan	Sto-101	Sep Negro	Way-238	Jacob Senr	Lnc-370
P	Mon- 42	Serews,James	Nsh- 74	John	Lnc-349
Sellars,Cuzzy	Joh-282	John	Nsh- 76	John Senr	Lnc-370
Elijah	Dup- 14	Serey,Aaron	Cum-261	Mathias	Lnc-369
George	Lnc-328	George	Cum-261	William	Lnc-349
Jacob	Dup- 21	John	Cum-261	Sevan,John D	Row- 75
James	Joh-287	Lemuel	Cum-263	Sevenson,Levi	Dup- 24
John	Dup- 16	Segant,James	Cas- 70	Sever,F	Ash- 8
Joseph	Bur-125	Sergent,Henry	Per-144	Severn,John Snr	Car-170
Sampson	Mon- 30	Sermon,Jethro	Pit-237	Sevitz,George	Row- 70
W	Bru-224	John	Pit-256	Sexton,Amos	Pas-204
Yong	Cha-207	Samuel	Lnc-334	Asa	Pas-202
Seller,Cunrad	Lnc-349	Sernous,Anthony	Cur- 88	Frederick	Bur-125
Sellers,A	Bru-226	Serraker,Jacob	Row- 50	Happy	Wsh-225
Cathrine	Bla- 9	Serrat,Allen	Lnc-356	J	Cam-163
E	Bru-240	John	Lnc-371	Jeremiah	Pas-202
Elijah	Rth-134	Robert	Rth-133	Jerry	Pas-205
George	Cum-259	Robert	Rth-133	John	Pas-205
Gilbert	Rob-244	Serreleson,Richd	Cas- 70	M	Mon- 36
James	Bur-110	Service,Thos	Lnc-333	Mark	Pas-205
John	Bla- 9	Sesar On Radics Land		Mark	Nor- 78
John	Mor- 57		Pas-204	Montillian	Cum-256
Joseph	Nsh- 90	Sessions,I	Col- 20	Peggy	Nor- 78
L	Bru-240	Reuben	Cho-227	Peter	Cha-195
M	Bru-222	Ricd	Cab-146	Robt	Pas-204
Mary	Bru-226	Richard	Sam-164	Samuel	Tyr-203
N	Bru-240	Sessom,Henry	Cum-264	Samuel	Cum-250
Nancy	Bur-131	Sessoms,Alexander	Edg- 60	Tamar	Pas-202
Robert	Bur-122	David	Edg- 59	Thomas	Nor- 78
T	Bru-222	Elisha	Hrt-211	Will	Bft- 24
W	Bru-240	Elmore	Hal-119	Seymore,Jno	Len-311
William	Bur-122	Ge W	Hrt-209	Jno	Len-313
Sellivan,Comfort	Len-314	Isaac	Sam-153	M	Cam-165
Sellors,A	Col- 20	James	Hrt-209	Robt	Per-144
J	Col- 18	John	Hrt-209	Shaber,Gottlieb	Sto-115
Sells,Faithy	Hal-119	Josiah	Edg- 60	Shackelford,Jacky	Ons-101
G	Ash- 11	Nancy	Edg- 60	John	Ons-103
John	Hal-119	Nathan	Edg- 68	Maryann	Ons-104

Shackel,Charles	Roc- 27	Sharp,Christ	Ora-120	Shaw,Alexander	Rch-191
Shackleford,Thos	Roc- 5	Danl Jr	Row- 81	Alexander	Rch-201
Shadden,Henry	Way-236	Isaac	Ora-120	Angus	Mor- 58
Shaddy,Jacob	Ora-172	Isham	Roc- 22	Angus	Bla- 7
Jacob	Ora-144	Jacob	Hrt-208	Angus	Cum-262
Jno	Ora-144	James	Nsh- 79	Angus	Rob-228
Shade,David	Mon- 45	James Sen	Roc- 22	Archd	Rob-237
Horner	Way-246	Jas	Mec- 34	Archd	Cum-244
Shadman,Nathan	Cha-201	Jno	Mec- 34	Archd	Cum-262
Shadrich,Henry	Cha-191	John	Ora-121	Benj	Glf-185
Shadwick,Hardy	Roc- 28	Joseph	Bft- 30	Charles	Cum-243
John	Roc- 28	Joshua	Edg- 72	Charles	Ora-131
Martin	Roc- 28	Ned	Mec- 35	Christian	Ans- 33
Mary	Grn-123	Peter	Ora-143	Christopher	Ans- 26
Saml	Grn-123	Richard	Mec- 49	Colin	Cum-241
Shafer,John	Lnc-327	Samuel	Sto-119	Dan	Mon- 30
Shaffer,Andrew	Glf-155	Starky	Hrt-206	Daniel	Rch-192
John	Sto-139	Thomas	Edg- 65	Daniel	Cum-256
Shafner,Richard	Glf-177	William	Roc- 23	Daniel Junr	Cum-261
Shagfulth,Charles	Hrt-208	Sharpe,Adam	Roc- 5	Daniel Senr	Cum-263
Shakespear,Martha	Pas-203	Adlai	Ire-252	Danl	Lnc-368
Shakleford,James	Car-179	Amos	Ire-262	Danl	Rob-228
Stephen	Car-176	Azel	Ire-254	Danl	Rob-227
Shallington,Wm H	Joh-286	Black	Ire-263	Duncan	Cum-253
Shally,Mary	Lnc-361	David	Ire-263	Dushee	Cum-262
Shalor,James	Hyd-221	Henry	Roc- 7	E	Ora-156
Shamel,John	Sto- 99	James	Ire-263	Ellet	Hal-120
Shamill,John	Sto-131	James M	Ire-263	Gardner	Ran-180
Shandley,Stephen	Sam-152	John	Ire-263	George	Row- 45
Shandry,John	Cab-140	Joseph	Ire-254	Gilbert	Cum-268
Shank,Monas	Cab-142	Levi	Ire-254	H	Glf-177
Shankle,Beverly	Mon- 41	Silas	Ire-263	Haley	Ran-182
Eli	Mon- 41	Thomas	Bur-107	Henry	Hal-119
Geo	Mon- 41	Thomas	Ire-252	Hugh	Glf-177
Mary	Mon- 40	William	Ire-263	J	Col- 18
Val	Mon- 41	Sharrock,Bashaba	Brt- 56	James	Sur-166
Shanks,C	Ora-140	David	Brt- 57	James	Glf-154
Chas	Ora-117	Saml	Brt- 53	James	Hal-120
John	Grn-139	Stephen	Hal-119	Jas	Glf-185
Robert	Grn-121	Shatchy,Andrew	Wil-266	Jesse	Ran-180
Thomas	Cas- 70	Shause,Frederick	Sto- 99	Jno	Ans- 7
Shanning,Lovey	Cur- 82	Shavener,John	Hyd-223	Jno	Rob-228
Shannon,J	Cam-155	Shaver,C	Glf-173	Jno	Rob-225
Jane	Mec- 32	Christian	Sto-129	Jno	Rob-224
John	Pas-203	Federick	Mec- 40	Jno Junr	Rob-228
Shannonhouse,Jas L	Pas-204	John	Row- 77	Jo	Ora-154
Thos	Pas-204	Joseph	Ire-262	Jo Jrn	Ora-176
Shanwell,Elisha	Rth-133	Joseph	Ire-261	John	Rch-203
Sharborough,Miles	Cha-216	Pegga	Hrt-208	John	Cum-237
Shardel,John	Cab-143	Reuben	Mec- 41	John	Glf-185
Sharebut,Benjamin	Bun- 95	Shavers,Benjamin	Bla- 5	John	Brt- 47
Shareman,Benj	Ora-162	Erasmus	Bla- 5	John	Pas-203
Shark,Daniel	Row- 80	Joel	Row- 78	John C C	Cum-244
Sharke,J	Ash- 7	Morris	Bla- 5	Jonas	Hrt-208
Sharman,James	Lnc-332	Shadek	Bla- 5	Joseph	Ora-115
Sharmer,Peter	Sur-191	Shaves,James	Grn-123	Joseph	Cha-200
Sharp,Abraham	Edg- 65	Shaw,Mrs	Cum-241	Joseph B	Ora-123
Benjamin	Edg- 46	Adam	Pas-204	Levi	Ora-130
Bosten	Ora-171	Adamson	Ire-268	Mahorn L	Cum-253

-284-

Shaw,Malcom	Cum-261	Sheaser,Fed	Ora-131	Shelton,Willis	Hal-118
Malcom	Rch-201	Sheats,David	Row- 58	Sheltor,Nelson	Lnc-359
Malcom	Rch-205	Sheck,Adam	Row- 40	Shelvey,Jonathan	Ans- 14
Malcom C	Cum-254	Sheets,A	Ash- 8	Reece	Ans- 24
Mary	Cum-244	Andrew	Sur-173	Shelvy,Even	Mec- 46
Matthew	Glf-186	Frederick	Sur-187	Moses	Mec- 53
Michl	Row- 59	J	Ash- 14	Shemborough,Peter	Mor- 65
Murdock	Rob-242	Reuben	Mor- 58	Shenburger,John	Mor- 59
Neill	Rob-227	Shehorn,Widow	Mec- 43	Peter	Mor- 59
Neill	Rob-227	Morris	Mec- 43	Shenck,Henry	Lnc-345
Noble	Glf-188	Peggy	Mec- 43	Shenk,Betty	Edg- 41
Norman	Cum-250	Wm	Mec- 43	Shepard,Elijah	Roc-220
Norman	Cum-244	Wm	Mec- 41	Elizabeth	Car-182
Norman	Cum-262	Sheitos,Able	Sto-108	George Esqr	Ons-107
Ralph	Sur-168	Sheley,John	Pas-203	Henry	Len-319
Robt	Glf-156	Shelhorn,Jacob	Row- 55	Jamima	Ans- 15
Sheon	Mor- 65	Shell,Benj	Lnc-373	Jamima	Ans- 15
Stephen	Ons-101	Charles	Lnc-369	Marian	Car-170
Stephen	Mec- 34	Henry	Lnc-370	Wm	Ans- 13
Thos	Ans- 27	Saml	Lnc-373	Sheperd,Cypheus	Cur- 89
Wiley	Ora-126	Stephen	War-180	Shephard,John	Cum-256
William	Roc- 16	Shelly,Benjn	Ire-262	Shepherd,Ann	Pit-255
William	Ire-268	Jas	Glf-168	Bird	Rch-209
William	Sur-167	Jesse	Glf-170	Geo	Cab-146
William	Ons-107	John	Ire-254	James	Mar- 6
William	Glf-186	John	Glf-188	James	Sur-187
Wm	Glf-176	M	Glf-170	John	Mor- 67
Wm	Pas-203	Nancy	Hal-120	John	Gat-109
Wm	Mec- 29	Richard	Ire-261	John	Bun- 79
Wm	Mor- 66	Shelpher,John Jr	Jon-303	Jordan	Pit-256
Wm	Ora-117	John Senr	Jon-205	Laney	Jon-303
Shawn,Neill H	Cum-263	Jessey	Jon-205	Lewis	Glf-180
Sheaks,Jacob	Row- 58	Luke	Jon-304	Nancy	Bft- 38
Sheappard,Lewis	Cas- 69	Shelton,Armstreet	Bun- 81	R	Col- 18
Shearen,Joseph	Glf-186	Bennett	Mon- 22	Robert	Hal-118
Sheares,Elijah	Mon- 33	David	Bun- 81	Solomon	Hrt-213
Shearin,Daniel	War-170	Edmond	Per-144	Starlin	Ire-257
Frederick	War-171	Edward	Sto-140	Thomas	Rch-210
Gardner	War-171	Edward	Sto- 96	Thomas	Grn-125
Isham	War-176	Elijah	Roc- 7	Thomas	Bun- 76
James	War-175	George	Cas- 70	Thos	Cab-136
John	War-174	George	Bun- 72	Will B	Pas-203
Joseph	War-175	Isaac	Bun- 72	William	Ire-257
Lewis	War-177	John	Roc- 7	William	Sur-187
Lucy	War-177	Martin	Sto-145	William	Bun- 90
Moses	War-178	Martin	Bun- 81	Z	Glf-160
Sterling	War-180	Roderick	Bun- 81	Sheppard,Andrew	Wil-257
Thomas	War-181	Spencer	Sto- 95	Austin	Wil-262
William	War-183	Spencer	Roc- 7	Elijah	Ons- 98
Wm	Grn-137	Spencer	Sto-124	George Junr	Ons- 99
Zachariah	War-184	Stephen	Bun- 72	Hardy	Ons-102
Shearing,Aaron	Grn-126	Temple	Lnc-361	Hosa	Ons-102
Jessee	Grn-126	William	Row- 71	James	Wil-262
John	Grn-126	William	Edg- 70	John	Wil-260
Joseph	Grn-126	William	Sto- 95	John	Roc- 5
Shearley,William	Hal-124	William	Sto-123	John	Ons- 99
Shears,John	Mor- 67	William	Bur-120	John	Mon- 29
Shearwood,Benjn	Row- 81	Wm Jur	Sto- 75	Lucrecy	On2-104
Thos	Cur- 80	Wm Jur	Sto-124	Robert	Wil-261

Name	Ref	Name	Ref	Name	Ref	Name	Ref
Sheppard,S	Ash- 6	Sherril,Joseph	Lnc-354	Shields,Wm	Mec- 48
Sarah	Wil-261	Joshua	Lnc-356	Shiff,David	Roc- 13
Selah	Ons-109	Joshua Junr	Lnc-356	Shifler,Christian	Bur-108
Stephen	Wil-266	Joshua Senr	Lnc-356	Shiford,Christian	Rob-234
William	Roc- 5	Levi	Lnc-356	Shilcutt,E	Glf-158
William	Bur-131	Michael	Lnc-356	Shill,John	Bur-103
Shepperd,Chs	Ran-181	Moses	Lnc-356	Shin,Catharine	Cab-142
David	Cum-239	Moses Junr	Lnc-353	Jean	Cab-147
J	Ora-141	Moses Senr	Lnc-354	Joseph	Cab-147
James	Row- 78	Nicholas	Lnc-356	Levy	Sur-196
James	Pit-232	Sherrill,Isaac	Bur-111	Saml	Cab-142
James	Ora-163	Ulbe	Bur-122	Shine,Francis	Sam-163
Jno	Ora-128	William	Bur-107	James	Jon-305
John	Row- 70	Sherrin,Aaron	Ire-251	James	Hal-119
Volumtine	Way-239	Sherrod,Benjn	Fra- 89	Willis	Hal-118
W	Ora-141	Benjn	Way-238	Shines,Francis	Jon-304
Wm col	Ora-126	James	Fra- 94	John	Jon-304
Wm	Ran-181	James	Way-238	Shingleton,Baths	Bft- 25
Wm	Ran-181	John	Way-246	Jason	Ons- 99
Sheppord,Thomas	Dup- 9	Salathiel	Mar- 8	Polly	Dup- 12
Sheraden,Geo	Ora-134	Col. Thomas	Fra- 83	Williby	Edg- 51
Sherel,Nathaniel	Cur- 84	William	Way-238	Wm	Bft- 25
Sherell,George	Hay-201	Wilson	Mar- 14	Wm	Mor- 69
Samuel	Hay-201	Sherrow,Andrew	Rth-135	Shinn,Isaac	Cab-147
Sheren,C	Glf-166	James	Rth-133	Benj	Cab-147
Jos	Glf-166	John	Rth-135	John	Sur-166
Sheridan,Louis	Bla- 3	Richard	Rth-135	John	Lnc-354
Sherley,Benj	Len-313	William	Rth-135	Silas	Cab-147
Richard	Edg- 68	William	Rth-132	Shinoll,Benjamin	Sur-185
Sherlin,Isom	Mec- 24	Sherward,Jordan	Nsh-644	Richard	Sur-185
Wm	Mec- 32	Wm	Ora-115	William	Sur-185
Sherling,Jno	Mec- 32	Sherwood,D	Glf-161	Ship,Ann	Sam-150
Sherlock,George	Fra- 91	Daniel	Glf-157	Peter	Hal-118
Mary	Pas-203	H	Glf-161	Thomas	Sto-113
Sherly,Moses	Len-312	John	Edg- 47	Shipman,Danl	Bla- 12
Sherman,Squire	Grn-139	Noah	Car-182	Edward	Bun- 94
Sherrard,Arthur	Nor- 77	Sheshire,Burch	Row- 57	Hezekiah	Bun- 84
James	Nor- 77	Shetly,Andrew	Lnc-364	Jas	Bla- 12
John	Nor- 77	John	Lnc-364	John	Bun- 94
Sherrel,Eli	Lnc-356	Peter	Lnc-365	Shipp,Bartlett	Sto-126
Sherren,Abner	Hal-119	Shettle,Anthony	Lnc-328	Reading	Pit-251
Sherrer,A	Ash- 3	Shetwell,E	Glf-175	Robert	Sur-162
C	Ash- 8	Elkins	Glf-176	Thomas	Sto-155
R	Ash- 8	Geo	Glf-174	William	Pit-250
Sherril,Aaron	Lnc-356	J	Glf-174	Shire,Christian	Row- 42
Alexander	Lnc-356	Shever,Jacob	Mec- 40	Shireman,Michael	Lnc-326
Aquilla	Lnc-354	Shew,Henry	Cab-140	Shires,Jacob	Wil-266
Benjamin	Lnc-349	John	Cab-141	Phillip	Wil-266
Calbert	Lnc-349	Susanah	Cab-140	Shirley,Henry	Edg- 41
David	Lnc-349	Shicer,John	Mor- 56	James	Edg- 41
David	Lnc-354	Shield,James	Cha-205	Shirly,Daniel	Pas-203
Eli	Lnc-349	Shields,Abel	Sto-143	Kelly	Sto-138
Elisha	Lnc-356	Archd	Mor- 54	Shirr,Moses	Mor- 57
Eliz	Lnc-349	Betsy	Mec- 39	Shive,Martin	Cab-139
Enos	Lnc-349	David	Mec- 23	Phillip	Cab-142
Evan	Lnc-356	Enos	Bun- 78	Shiver,William	Ons- 96
Jacob	Lnc-370	Patrick	Mor- 66	Shivers,Brinson	Dup- 33
Jeptha	Lnc-356	Neill	Mor- 62	Shoaf,Christian	Row- 41
Jessey	Lnc-356	Thomas	Hal-119	Geo	Row- 41

Shoaf,Jacob	Row- 41	Shores,Henry	Sto-136	Shufford,Jacob Sr	Lnc-373
Jacob Senr	Row- 41	Jacob	Sur-190	Shuford,Daniel	Lnc-329
Shoafe,Geo	Row- 41	John	Sur-172	David	Lnc-329
Shoalers,Levi	Dup- 35	Livy	Sur-167	Geo	Bun- 84
Solomon	Dup- 35	Simeon	Wil-263	Jacob	Lnc-329
Thomas	Dup- 35	Shorry,Fasly	Bur-115	John	Lnc-329
Shoat,Edward	Bur-109	Short,A	Glf-160	P----	Lnc-326
Shoeck,Abraham	Ire-244	Daniel	Ans- 28	Shugars,Hannah	Ora-128
Shoemake,Sally	Mec- 43	Eliza	Bur-114	Isaac	Ora-129
Shoemaker,Joel	Ire-255	James	Hal-120	Shugart,George	Sur-174
John	Ire-255	Joab	Roc- 17	Shuler,Abraham	Row- 43
John	Ire-253	John	War-173	Adam	Row- 43
Reanold	Ire-253	John	War-174	Adam	Row- 87
Sharah	Ans- 15	John	Wsh-228	Daniel	Row- 43
Tarlton	Ire-255	Jonathan	Glf-171	George	Hay-200
Thomas	Ire-263	Lewis	Nor- 77	George	Hay-200
William	Ire-254	M	Glf-179	Georger	Row- 87
Shoeman,John	Row- 40	Milly	Nor- 78	John	Hay-200
John	Row- 66	Rebecca	Nor- 78	Michl	Row- 43
Shoemate,Elizabeth	Wil-267	Richd	Bft- 26	Peter	Row- 43
Shoeping,Jacob	Row- 70	Robt	Cha-214	Shull,Chas	Lnc-327
Michl	Row- 67	Rollen	Hal-120	F	Ash- 12
Nicholas	Row- 70	William	Lnc-369	S	Ash- 12
Shoepink,Andw	Cab-139	William O	Roc- 17	Shults,Casper	Sto- 99
Shoffner,Jno	Mon- 47	Wm	Ans- 28	Christian	Row- 87
Shofner,Fed	Ora-131	Wm	Ans- 28	George	Row- 87
Jno	Ora-139	Willis	Hal-118	Godfrey	Sto-146
Jno	Ora-145	Shoup,Christopher	Sto-129	Henr	Sto- 99
Shole,Edward	Bur-116	Jacob	Sto-142	John	Sto- 99
Sholur,Gottlieb	Sto-146	Peter	Bur-105	Samuel	Sto-146
Shomaker,E	Glf-173	Shoupe,Jery	Bur-116	Shumaker,Harman	Bun- 80
Shook,Abraham	Hay-200	Shouse,Elizabeth	Sto-107	Shuman,George	Row- 85
Andrew	Lnc-349	Elizabeth	Sto-143	Shunklin,Jas	Ora-161
Fredk	Lnc-349	John	Sto-107	Shurk,Mary	Bun- 98
George	Hay-200	Shrantz,John	Lnc-371	Shurman,Robert	Bur-121
George	Lnc-326	Shreve,John	Roc- 6	Shuston,Sophia	Cab-142
George	Lnc-350	Shrines,Daniel	War-170	Shutt,George	Sto-103
Polly	Hay-201	Shroat,Christian	Row- 88	George	Sto-136
Shooleberrier,Casehart		Shrom,Henry	Lnc-340	Henry	Ora-110
	Row- 69	Shropshire,St.John	Roc- 34	Jacob	Sto-103
Fred	Row- 69	Shrote,Adam	Row- 76	Jacob	Sto-135
Shoolenberrier,David		Shrott,Andrew	Mec- 29	Shy,Ely	Cas- 70
	Row- 69	Shrye,James	Cur- 87	Sibbet,W	Col-18
Shooler,Abraham	Row- 79	Shucaff,James	Hrt-213	Sibley,Widow	Mec- 43
Adam	Row- 79	Wm	Hrt-213	Elijah	Mec- 42
Daniel	Row- 79	Shurfell,Evan	Ans- 13	Jno	Mec- 43
Michl	Row- 80	Shuffield,Amos	Dup- 17	Jno	Mec- 43
Shoolts,Mark	Row- 82	Ephraim	Nor- 77	Robt	Mec- 42
Shope,John	Bun- 83	John	Dup- 24	Siddal,Ira	Cas- 69
Shore,Henry	Sto- 99	Joseph	Nor- 77	Siddle,Jobe	Cas- 69
Henry	Sto-129	Lincoln	Dup- 32	Sides,Andrew	Lnc-369
Jacob	Sto- 99	Mary	Nor- 77	Chas	Ans- 22
Jacob	Sto-129	Shuffill,Wm	Ans- 20	Christopher	Mon- 49
John	Sto-130	Shuffle,Everet	Mor- 60	Daniel	Row- 77
John	Sto- 99	Isaac	Mor- 60	Eve	Lnc-359
Peter	Sto-143	Isham	Mor- 57	George	Sto-137
Peter Ser	Sto-129	Isham	Mor- 60	George	Sto-104
Shores,Abyram	Sur-184	John	Mor- 60	Henry	Lnc-375
Henry	Sur-169	John	Mor- 55	Jacob	Lnc-365

Sides,Jacob	Lnc-329	Sillivan,Turner	Wil-262	Simmons,J		Bru-224
Jacob	Bur-125	William	Wil-285	J		Col- 1o
John	Sto-102	Sills,Thomas	Hal-124	J		Col- 19
John	Sto-135	Silor,James	Cha-203	J		Col- 20
John	Lnc-359	John	Cha-202	J		Col- 20
Leonard	Cab-140	Josiah	Cha-208	James		Hal-119
Michael	Cab-146	Phillip	Cha-203	James		Jon-205
Nics	Cab-140	Richard	Cha-195	James		Mon- 33
Peter Jr	Lnc-365	Silver,Geo Junr	Bun- 76	James		Ire-264
Peter Senr	Lnc-365	George	Bun- 76	James		Rth-132
Philip	Sto-144	John	Bun- 76	Jas		Mec- 48
Siford,Abraham	Row- 67	Silverthorn,John	Hyd-231	Jesse		Sto- 94
George	Row- 68	John S	Hyd-232	Jesse		Edg- 65
Peter	Row- 67	Robert	Hyd-232	Jesse		Hal-118
Sigman,Barnet	Lnc-349	Joshua	Hyd-233	Jesse		Mon- 33
Barnet	Lnc-349	Silas	Bft- 32	Jesse		Sto-122
Christor	Lnc-349	William	Pit-243	Joel		Hrt-209
Daniel	Lnc-349	Silverton,Miriam	Prq-226	Jno		Mec- 49
George	Lnc-349	Silvey,Edward	Sto-153	John		Sto- 93
George	Lnc-349	Thomas	Sto-123	John		Row- 83
George Junr	Lnc-349	Thos	Sto- 95	John		Nsh- 90
John	Lnc-349	Sim---,Pheby	Rth-134	John		Ran-182
Polser	Lnc-349	Simeon,John	Ire-269	John		Sto-121
William	Lnc-349	Simins,Geo	Glf-180	John		Brt- 48
Sigmon,George	Lnc-370	Simmerman,Danl	Row- 50	John		Tyr-208
John	Lnc-345	Simmonds,J	Bru-222	John		Sam-153
John Jr	Lnc-369	L	Col- 19	Jos		Ora-113
John Senr	Lnc-369	T	Col- 19	Joseph		Cur- 87
Martin	Lnc-370	Simmons,A	Col- 19	Lavendor		Jon-303
Stophel	Lnc-374	Abram	Cas- 70	Lydia		Mar- 7
Sikes,A	Cam-159	Adam	Mon- 33	Malachi		Fra- 84
Aaron	Cha-210	Asea	Hyd-224	Nancy		Ons-103
Abraham	Car-181	Averitt	Ons- 95	Nathan		Mar- 12
Allen	Ora-122	B	Bru-224	Needham		Jon-305
Henry	Cum-259	Bell	Sto-121	Paul		Bla- 9
Henry	Ons-107	Benj	Mon- 28	Philip		Hal-120
Joab	Fra- 97	Benj Sr	Bru-224	Richard		Rth-132
Jno	Ans- 16	Benjamin	Jon-303	Richard		Rth-132
John	Sam-163	Benjamin	Hay-201	Samuel		Hal-119
Joshua	Pas-205	Bill	Sto- 93	Samuel		Hal-118
Joshua	Ans- 21	Catharine	Bur-122	Sanders		Cum-264
Matthew	Nsh- 83	Charles	Sur-181	Sherod		Sam-152
P	Cam-160	Charles	Rth-132	T		Col- 20
Sherwood	Ans- 22	D	Col- 20	T		Mon- 35
W	Ash- 3	Daniel Senr	Jon-304	Thomas		Jon-303
W	Cam-158	Danniel Junr	Jon-305	Thos		Cha-206
William	Cum-261	Deborah	Prq-226	Thos		Cur- 87
Silance,William	Ons-107	Elijah	Ons- 96	Waitstill		Jon-304
Silby,Jeremiah	Hyd-229	Elijah	Jon-304	William		Bru-224
Silcock,Amos	Roc- 14	Elizabeth	Jon-304	Willm		Tyr-208
Richard	Roc- 13	Ephraim	Sto- 93	Wm		Cab-137
William	Wil-265	Ephraim	Sto-121	Zadock		Ans- 17
Silechar,John	Row- 37	G	Mon- 37	Simms,Benj		Bla- 4
Siles,M	Col- 18	George	Cas- 70	Benj		Way-246
Sill,James	Mon- 18	Graves	Row- 69	Benjamin		Edg- 49
Sillery,William	Rth-134	Hillery	Jon-304	Britton		Way-246
Silliman,Saml	Row- 73	Israel	Bur-124	Edmund		Way-235
Sillivan,John	Wil-262	Israel	Bur-125	John		Cho-222
Samuel	Wil-273	J	Mon- 37	John		Way-241

Simms,Martha	Edg- 67	Simpson,Isaac	Ons- 95	Sims,Brigs	Grn-130	
Martha	Way-232	Isaac	Hyd-224	Briton	Wil-275	
Sarah	Bla- 5	J	Bla- 11	Buckner	Ire-267	
Shadrack	Way-245	Jacob	Car-178	Charles	Grn-133	
Williams	Edg- 66	James	Mar- 7	Chesley	War-169	
Simmsial,Samuel	Rth-134	James	Car-176	Dial	Wil-279	
Simon & Moses & C	Mec- 22	James	Cas- 70	Elijah	Cas- 70	
Simon & Wm O Pelts	Mec- 35	Jas	Mec- 45	Elisha	War-170	
Simons,Widow	Mec- 49	Joab	Pas-206	Isaac	Cum-248	
Anthony	Cur- 92	Jno	Mec- 41	J	Col- 18	
Benjamin	Sur-186	Jno	Mec- 46	James	Cum-248	
Denis	Cur- 93	John	Roc- 28	John	Roc- 20	
George	Brt- 48	John	Pas-205	John	Joh-277	
Isaac	Prq-226	John	Bla- 8	John	War-174	
James	Lnc-375	John	Car-178	John	War-173	
Jas	Mec- 49	John	Car-180	John Jun	Roc- 4	
Jos Jnr	Brt- 59	John	Row- 81	John Sen	Roc- 4	
Joseph Senior	Brt- 48	John	Ons-103	Littleton	Rth-133	
Marey	Cur- 91	John	Ora-127	M	Col- 19	
Mattw	Ran-182	John	Cas- 69	M	Col- 20	
Mitchel	Cur- 86	Joshua	Cas- 70	Mary	Sur-164	
Mitchel	Cur- 93	Joshua	Car-175	Sarah	War-180	
Robert	Cur- 91	Luke	Ora-125	Thomas	War-181	
Robert	Cur- 93	Mary	Mar- 16	W	Col- 19	
Sally	Nor- 77	Milley	Mar- 16	William	Wil-274	
Samuel	Cur- 91	Moses	Cas- 70	William	Joh-276	
William	Car-181	Moses	Cas- 70	William	Sur-187	
Willis	Cur- 91	N	Mon- 41	William	War-182	
Simonton,Gilbreth	Ire-239	Nathaniel	Roc- 17	William	Row- 86	
James	Ire-260	Nathl	Glf-158	Simsal,Francis R	Mec- 27	
John	Ire-260	Nathl Jr	Glf-182	Simson,Basil	Row- 87	
Robert	Ire-258	Oliver	Cas- 70	Benjamin	Row- 81	
Smith	Ire-258	Polly	Pas-205	Benjamin	Row- 87	
Thomas	Ire-255	Richard	Ons-108	Benjn	Row- 87	
William	Ire-260	Richd	Glf-182	Francis	Cur- 92	
William Sen	Ire-260	Robin	Pas-205	John	Row- 87	
Simpkins,Abel	Bur-115	Robt	Cho-231	Joshuay	Cur- 84	
Jas	Sam-160	Robt	Pas-204	Nancey	Cur- 86	
Susan	Bur-126	Roger	Car-178	Teague	Row- 52	
William	Joh-272	Roger	Ora-163	Wm	Cur- 84	
Simpson,A	Col- 20	Rossetta Junr	Car-178	Zack	Cur- 93	
A J	Bru-222	Rossetta Senr	Car-178	Simsons,Simeon	Cho-225	
Abraham	Car-178	Sam	Ora-124	Wm	Cho-225	
Absalom	Car-178	Saml	Pas-203	Sinclair,Alfred	Ans- 6	
Alexander	Jon-304	Sarah	Cho-231	Andrew	Rob-223	
Ann	Bla- 12	Solomon	Ons-103	Daniel	Cum-251	
Asariah	Car-169	Thomas	Dup- 13	Duncan	Mor- 65	
Bazil	Row- 81	Thomas	Jon-304	Duncan	Rob-243	
Ben	Ora-124	Thos	Glf-182	Eliz	Cho-222	
Charon	Wsh-222	Thos	Mec- 45	Jas	Ans- 20	
Chs	Cho-226	Will	Pas-203	John	Mor- 64	
E	Col- 17	William	Roc- 17	John	Ans- 4	
Edward	Joh-278	Willm	Pas-203	John	Cum-250	
Elisandney	Cur- 86	Wm	Mec- 45	Lot	Cha-211	
Eliza	Pas-206	Willis	Pas-205	Mary	Rob-228	
Exum	Cho-231	Zibed	Car-185	Peter	Mor- 68	
George	Mec- 53	Sims,Ambrose	Cum-259	Peter	Cha-196	
Hezekia	Pas-205	Anderson	Cab-136	Peter	Ans- 5	
Hugh	Bla- 8	Benjamin	War-168	Sing,Stephen	Mor- 62	

Sing,Wm	Ora-133	Sism,David		Rth-135	Skipper,Henry		Way-250
Singletary,B	Bru-240	Sissel,George		Ran-187	Isaac		Bru-230
B J	Bla- 10	Julia		Row- 43	J Snr		Bru-236
Benj Junr	Bla- 6	Thos		Row- 45	Jas		Bru-222
David	Bla- 13	Sitaker,John		Row- 70	John		Way-250
J	Bru-240	Sitts,Zebulon		Cha-196	John		Ons-104
J	Bla- 11	Sitz,David		Nsh- 72	John Jr		Bru-228
J	Bla- 10	Sitz,Wm		Grn-136	Joseph		Ons-104
James (L)	Bla- 5	Sizemore,David		Bun- 76	M		Bru-224
James (Short)	Bla- 7	E		Ash- 7	Nathan		Ons-104
Johnson	Bla- 7	G		Ash- 4	Simon		Len-321
Jona Junr	Bla- 7	Geo		Bun- 76	Thomas		Rch-209
Joseph	Bla- 6	John		Sto-126	Skittletharpe,Arthur		
Joseph B	Bla- 11	John		Sto- 97			Wsh-224
Joseph (Long)	Bla- 5	John		Sto-156	Betsey		Wsh-222
Josiah	Bla- 6	Sally		Rth-133	Charles Junr		Wsh-222
Mary	Bla- 6	William		Sur-184	Charles Senr		Wsh-221
R	Bla- 10	William		Sto-156	Edmd		Wsh-221
S--ondon	Bla- 6	William		Sto-116	Isaac		Wsh-222
Sarah	Bla- 13	Sizer,Jabez		Car-170	Jno		Wsh-222
Thomas	Bla- 7	Skeen,A		Glf-179	Slack,John		Ran-180
Wm C	Bla- 13	J		Glf-179	Nicholous		Cur- 90
Singleton,Christr	Mon- 23	Jesse		Len-312	David Lott		Hyd-233
Edmd	Mon- 27	Sketoe,John		Way-244	Ebenezer		Mar- 7
Hansel	Sam-158	Skidmore,Abraham		Sur-178	Slade,Ebenezer		War-171
Martha	Ora-165	Thos		Lnc-372	Eden		Car-180
Nathen	Mec- 55	Skiles,John		Brt- 59	Ezekiel		Cas- 69
Phillip	Per-144	John		Row- 76	Hannah		Cas- 69
W	Bru-232	Wm		Brt- 58	Henry		Mar- 10
William	Cas- 75	Skiliton,John		Cab-137	Henry		Hyd-234
Wm	Mec- 55	Skilliton,Jas		Cab-137	Henry		Bft- 34
Sink,Cristean	Row- 85	Skinner,Mrs Anna		Fra-100	Jeremiah		Mar- 10
Geo	Row- 43	Benjn		Prq-225	John		Hyd-234
Jacob	Row- 43	Charles W		Prq-226	Lear		Hyd-233
Jacob	Row- 85	Demsey Jr		Edg- 52	Mary		Hyd-233
Michal	Row- 85	Demsey Sr		Edg- 52	Nathan		Cas- 70
Michl	Row- 43	Dolly		Cho-221	Reasen		Bft- 34
Michl	Row- 43	Elizabeth		Nor- 77	Saml		Bft- 34
Sinkler,Hezekiah	Cha-202	Evan		Wsh-223	Thomas		Cas- 70
Sinnas,Jacob	Way-240	Henry		Edg- 52	Thomas Jr		Cas- 75
Sinter,John	Ran-181	James		Hrt-214	Turner		Hyd-233
Sipe,Abram	Lnc-350	James		Prq-225	William		Cas- 69
Daniel	Lnc-349	Jas		Cho-231	William		Mar- 6
Henry	Lnc-349	John		Cho-225	Wm		Cho-221
Jacob	Lnc-349	John		Edg- 67	Sladel,Mary		Hyd-225
John	Lnc-349	John		Prq-226	Slagle,John		Row- 81
Paul	Lnc-350	Jos		Cho-221	Slarter,Mrs		Brt- 49
Sipple,James	Roc- 10	Jos B		Cho-221	Slate,John		Hay-200
Sired,Richard	Mec- 42	Joshua Jr		Prq-225	Slater,David		War-184
Sisclave,Philip	Row- 49	Joshua Sr		Prq-226	Elisha		Sto-136
Siscliff,Arehart	Row- 48	Martha		Nor- 77	John		Sto-135
Sisk,Allen	Sur-194	Nathan		Prq-226	Slatey,Christian		Cha-194
Elijah	Sur-194	Nathl		Len-312	Slaton,William		Hal-119
Isaac	Sur-167	Rachel		Prq-225	Slatonstat,William		Cur- 89
James	Sur-194	Stephen		Prq-226	Slatter,Lewis		Hal-118
Jeremiah	Sto-124	Thomas		Row- 61	Solomon		Hal-119
Jesse	Sur-167	Wm J		Cho-231	Slaughter,Abram		Grn-142
Robert	Rth-135	Skiper,Josiah		Rch-211	Isaac		Grn-142
Thomas	Sur-194	Skipper,A		Bru-236	Jacob		Grn-142

Name	Ref	Name	Ref	Name	Ref
Slaughter, John	Joh-283	Slocumb, Stephen	Sam-164	Smelley, Ezekel	Nsh- 90
Matthew	Pit-237	Slone, Jas	Mec- 48	Smelly, Evret	Nsh- 90
Owen Senr	Rch-197	Sloop, Conrad	Row- 69	Smelty, Moses	Nsh- 86
Owin Senr	Rch-201	John	Row- 69	Smiley, Andrew G	Grn-131
Peter	Joh-282	Peter	Row- 69	Smilie, James	Cum-242
Tebetha	Rch-210	Slough, Daneil	Cab-140	Smith, A	Ash- 13
William	Rch-210	Jacob	Bur-111	A	Ash- 3
Wm	Brt- 47	Slown, William	Cur- 92	A	Mon- 42
Wm	Brt- 47	Sluder, Isaac	Bun- 97	Aaron	Joh-275
Zebelen	Rch-210	Slughten, Richard	Hyd-222	Abm	Ran-181
Zebelen	Rch-210	Slughter, Henry	Row- 89	Abm	Pas-202
Slaving, William	Ire-244	Sluntsford, Arey	Rch-209	Abm	Pas-205
Slawter, J	Col- 19	Sluther, Henry	Bun- 75	Abner	Joh-274
Lewcy	Sto-141	Slyers, Samuel	Sto-136	Abner	Pit-262
William	Sto-141	Slyth, Jonathan	Sto-135	Abraham	Bla- 11
Slaytor, Henry	Sto-144	Richard	Sto-135	Abraham	Lnc-340
Sleage, James	War-173	Small, Abm	Ran-180	Abraham	Sto-141
Sherrod	War-180	Benjn	Car-183	Abraham	Pit-261
Sleagle, Charles	Lnc-340	Benj Jnr	Cho-226	Abram	Bur-104
Fed	Lnc-333	Benj Snr	Cho-227	Abram	Lnc-340
Sled, William	Rch-198	Benjamin	Jon-305	Absalom	Cha-215
Sleddin, Wm	Cha-209	David	Gat-108	Adam	Bur-105
Sledge, Joel	Fra- 90	Eliz	Cho-221	Adam	Ran-180
John	Cab-139	Jonas	Car-184	Adam	Sto-110
Mary	Hal-120	John	Cum-255	Adam	Bur-125
Person	Fra- 99	John	Gat-109	Adam	Cha-209
Willis	Hal-118	Joseph Jnr	Cho-227	Adam	Sto-149
Sleep, Sarah	Cho-222	Joseph Snr	Cho-227	Alex	Lnc-333
Sleight, John Esqr	Wsh-221	Joshua	Gat-108	Alex	Mon- 26
Sline, Patrick	Glf-186	Joshua	Pas-203	Alexandrew	Hrt-209
Slinkerd, Henry	Lnc-375	Matthew	Way-253	Alexr	Grn-121
Sloan, Mrs	Mec- 37	Moses H	Gat-107	Alexr	Rob-226
David	Ora-111	Nathan	Bur-103	Allen	Rch-210
Jas	Mec- 47	Reuben	Cho-227	Allen	Way-249
Jas	Mec- 23	Thos	Cho-226	Alln	Ran-181
Jeremiah G	Ire-252	William	Roc- 21	Ambrose	Cho-227
Jno	Mec- 52	William	Ran-182	Ambrose	Cha-198
John	Mor- 65	Wm	Rob-240	Amos	Brt- 44
John	Row- 85	Wm	Ran-181	Anderson	Grn-128
M	Ora-135	Smallwood, Chas	Bft- 20	Andrew	Row- 80
Mary	Ire-241	Elijah	Sur-181	Ann	Edg- 56
Robt	Mec- 51	Elijah Sr	Sur-175	Anne	Wil-267
Robt	Mec- 36	Jonathan	Sur-164	Anthony	Bur-126
Samuel	Ire-264	Wm	Sur-162	Archd	Cum-245
Sarah	Mec- 51	Smally, Abner	Bur-126	Archd	Rob-231
Thomas	Ire-254	Smart, Leroy	Row- 65	Archd	Rob-230
William	Wil-272	Lucy	Cho-223	Archd	Mor- 67
Sloane, David	Dup- 8	Stephen	Mon- 21	Asa	Mon- 50
David	Dup- 37	William	Rth-134	Asy	Joh-288
Edward	Dup- 23	Smartt, Mrs	Mec- 25	Austin	Sto-131
Gibson	Dup- 16	Francis B	Mec- 23	B	Ash- 13
John	Dup- 18	Mrs. Geo	Mec- 27	B	Glf-178
John	Dup- 18	L B	Mec- 50	B	Cam-154
Robert	Dup- 7	Smaw, Henry	Bft- 24	Genl B	Bru-222
William	Dup- 20	Henry	Bft- 31	Barbara	Rob-228
William	Dup- 22	Tho	Bft- 24	Barbara	Lnc-329
Slocum, Tho	Bft- 24	Wm	Bft- 31	Barton	Rth-133
Slocumb, Ezekiel	Way-237	Smayers, John	Lnc-371	Barton	Cha-208
Jesse	Way-235	Smelledge, John	Ons- 95	Bassel	Jon-304

-291-

Name	Loc	Name	Loc	Name	Loc	Name	Loc
Smith,Batson	Nsh-644	Smith,D	Cam-162	Smith,Edward	Rch-204		
Benj	Way-249	D	Bru-228	Edwd free man of colour			
Benj	Hyd-233	Daniel	Cum-255				Ran-187
Benj	Bla- 12	Daniel	Cum-242	Edwd	Lnc-341		
Benjamin	Cum-243	Daniel	Rch-210	Edwin	Joh-290		
Benjamin	Edg- 53	Daniel	Rth-134	Edwin	Sto- 92		
Benjamin	Row- 81	Daniel	Rth-132	Edwin	Mec- 36		
Benjamin	Hal-118	Daniel	Cas- 69	Edwin	Sto-121		
Benjamin	Rob-241	Daniel	Sur-179	Eleazer	Row- 47		
Benjamin	Pit-258	Daniel	Wil-268	Elexander	Bun- 82		
Benjamin	Roc- 25	Daniel	Mec- 25	Elie	Way-234		
Benjn	Joh-273	Daniel	Bun- 89	Elih	Tyr-208		
Benjn	Ran-181	Daniel	Roc- 25	Elijah	Bur-116		
Benjn	Prq-225	Danl	Mor- 68	Elijah	Bur-108		
Benjn	Row- 51	Danl	Cha-212	Elijah	Dup- 29		
Benjn	Row- 50	Danl	Bur-129	Elisha B	Hal-118		
Benjn	Tyr-210	Danniel	Jon-304	Elisha B	Ans- 18		
Benjn	Ans- 21	Danniel Junr	Jon-303	Eliza	Bur-118		
Bennet	Nsh- 85	Davd	Ran-181	Eliza	Dup- 17		
Bennet	Grn-141	David	Cum-243	Eliza	Bft- 38		
Bennit	Sur-174	David	Cum-241	Elizabeth	War-170		
Bookajah	Way-249	David	Ire-263	Elizabeth	Pit-252		
Britain	Joh-274	David	Lnc-365	Elizabeth	Nor- 78		
Britton	Way-242	David	Bur-115	Ellender	Roc- 3		
Bryan	Joh-291	David	Mec- 51	Ellick	Joh-275		
Burn	Rch-204	David	Row- 84	Enoch	Lnc-341		
Caleb	Ons-103	David	Ran-182	Enoch	Lnc-338		
Caleb	Row- 78	David	Mec- 34	Esther	Edg- 52		
Capt Caleb	Wil-260	David	Lnc-340	Etheldred	Nor- 78		
Caleb Junr	Ons-103	David	Mon- 41	Everit	Mor- 69		
Cannon	Bft- 29	David	Cha-207	F	Glf-175		
Cannon	Grn-146	David	Len-318	Fanny	Mon- 41		
Cannon	Pit-235	David	Sto-143	Fleet	War-171		
Catharine	Cum-254	David	Pit-251	Francis	Cas- 70		
Catharine	Bur-105	David	Pit-231	Francis	Cur- 83		
Catlett	Sur-163	David	Cum-257	Francis	Sto-125		
Caty	Pit-250	David	Cum-251	Francis	Jon-304		
Charity	Cum-259	David Junr	Cum-251	Francis	Roc- 25		
Charles	Bla- 8	Davis	Pas-205	Francis Jr	Cas- 69		
Charles	Gat-109	Drew	Dup- 29	Frederick Jr	Dup- 29		
Charles	Grn-133	Drew	Hal-119	Frederick Sr	Dup- 29		
Charles	War-169	Drury	Way-250	G W	Hrt-206		
Charles	Sur-179	Drury	Way-247	Gasper	Row- 86		
Charles	Ire-239	Drury	Sto-105	Gasper	Row- 39		
Charles	Pit-242	Drury	Sto-139	Geo	Cab-140		
Charles	Pit-231	Drury	Ans- 20	Geo	Cab-147		
Charles	Pit-234	Drury	Roc- 25	Geo	Mon- 45		
Charles	Mor- 63	Drury	Nor- 78	Geo	Row- 60		
Christena	Bur-129	Duncan	Rob-232	Geo	Ans- 25		
Christian	Sto-108	Duncan	Rob-222	Geo	Row- 39		
Christian	Sto-144	Duncan	Cab-144	Georg	Cas- 70		
Coonrod	Cha-212	Duncan	Cum-243	George	Bur-106		
Cornelias	Row- 52	E	Bru-228	George	War-172		
Courtney	Nor- 78	E	Ora-131	George	Row- 86		
Cullen	Way-252	Ebenezer	Brt- 57	George	Row- 84		
Cullen	Hyd-224	Echred	Mon- 47	George	Ran-181		
D	Ash- 14	Ed	Mec- 27	George	Jon-305		
D	Ora-154	Edward	Hal-118	George	Pit-251		
D	Cam-164	Edward	Sur-170	Goodman	Fra- 88		

Name	Location	Name	Location	Name	Location	Name	Location
Smith,Gordon	Roc- 26	Smith,Jabez			Tyr-207	Smith,Jas	Rob-228
H	Ash- 6	Jack		Mec- 27		Jas	Cab-136
H	Ora-133	Jacob		Sur-187		Jas P	Cab-137
H	Ora-131	Jacob		Rth-132		Jane	Bla- 8
H	Mon- 42	Jacob		Car-175		Jarret	Bur-119
H	Mon- 42	Jacob		Sur-173		Jerch	Tyr-207
H	Bru-234	Jacob		Row- 84		Jeremiah	Rth-132
Hannah	Hal-119	Jacob		Cab-148		Jerimiah	Ans- 22
Hardy	Pit-231	Jacob		Jon-304		Jerry	Lnc-342
Harris	Bft- 37	Jacob		Sto-141		Jery	Bur-120
Hartwell	Hal-118	Jacob		Hay-200		Jesse	Sur-164
Haster	Mor- 63	Jacob		Mor- 59		Jesse	Cha-196
Henry	Ire-245	Jacob		Row- 70		Jesse	Ans- 23
Henry	Bur-119	James	(C P)	Bla- 11		Jesse	Pit-238
Henry	Bur-104	James	(E C)	Bla- 7		Jesse	Row- 47
Henry	Brt- 57	James	(D C)	Sur-191		Jessee Jr	Nor- 78
Henry	Way-239	James		Rch-204		Jessee Senr	Nor- 77
Henry	Pas-204	James		Joh-289		Jno	Rob-222
Henry	Sto-108	James		Ire-269		Jno	Mec- 34
Henry	Brt- 44	James		Ire-252		Jno (B C)	Ora-127
Henry	Cha-197	James		Ire-249		Jno	Mon- 37
Henry	Sto-144	James		Lnc-368		Jno	Len-313
Henry	Bur-111	James		Bur-105		Jno	Ans- 24
Henry	Pit-252	James		Fra- 95		Jno	Ans- 24
Henry	Pit-240	James		Rth-134		Jno	Ans- 19
Henry	Nor- 77	James		Rth-135		Jno	Ans- 18
Henry	Pit-258	James		Dup- 25		Jno (S C)	Ora-127
Henry	Hay-200	James		Grn-133		Jo	Ora-176
Henry	Hay-200	James		War-176		Job	Cum-262
Henry Junr	Lnc-345	James		Sur-162		Joel	Grn-141
Henry Jr	Way-237	James		Bun- 72		Joel	Hal-118
Henry Ser	Sto-144	James		Wil-266		Joel Esq	Rth-131
Hezekiah	Sur-163	James		Ran-182		John	Cum-259
Hugh	Cab-144	James		Ran-182		John	Cum-238
Hugh	Cum-260	James		Hyd-233		John	Cha-212
Irby	Grn-133	James		Hyd-224		John (C S)	Bla- 8
Isaac	Joh-285	James		Hal-119		John	Grn-123
Isaac	Ire-250	James		Hal-120		John	Gat-115
Isaac	Way-233	James		Rob-241		John	War-176
Isaac	Rob-241	James		Ora-127		John	Ora-119
Isaac	Bft- 36	James		Mon- 24		John	Sur-162
Isaac	Mon- 40	James		Cha-209		John	Ons-106
Isaac	Cha-198	James		Ans- 33		John	Row- 87
Isaac	Mor- 66	James		Pit-252		John	Row- 89
Isaac	Jon-305	James		Hrt-213		John	Row- 88
Isaiah	Dup- 30	James		Prq-226		John	Bun- 79
Israel	Prq-225	James		Hay-200		John	Ran-182
Dr J	Bla- 13	James		Roc- 30		John	Ran-180
J	Col- 20	James		Roc- 28		John	Ran-181
J	Col- 17	James		Mor- 62		John	Ire-244
J	Bla- 8	James		Mor- 56		John	Hyd-224
J	Ash- 14	James		Row- 39		John	Way-241
J	Glf-178	James		Cur- 92		John	Way-247
J	Glf-176	James		Row- 74		John	Hal-119
J	Ora-141	James Junr		Hal-124		John	Hal-119
J	Cam-162	James W		Grn-121		John	Bun- 93
J Esqr	Bru-232	Jas		Cho-228		John	Bun- 89
J Senr	Ora-160	Jas (C S)		Bla- 8		John	Bur-130
J G Esq	Col- 19	Jas		Bft- 20		John	Lnc-341

Smith,John	Len-323	Smith,Jos	Bur-105	Smith,Mary		Len-310
John	Mon- 44	Joseph	Lnc-361	Mary		Jon-304
John	Mon- 24	Joseph	Fra- 91	Mary		Ans- 31
John	Jon-304	Joseph	Rth-134	Mary		Ans- 23
John (T)	Bla- 8	Joseph	Car-174	Mary		Pit-250
John Short	Joh-291	Joseph	Gat-116	Mary		Hay-201
John	Joh-289	Joseph	Mec- 41	Mary		Mor- 58
John	Joh-275	Joseph	Wil-259	Mary		Row- 46
John	Rch-194	Joseph	Way-250	Mary		Row- 47
John	Rch-194	Joseph	Hyd-223	Matthew		Mec- 30
John	Ire-252	Joseph	Way-233	Michael		Sto-141
John	Ire-252	Joseph	Way-238	Michael		Sto-106
John	Ire-252	Joseph	Ora-132	Michl		Row- 78
John	Cum-266	Joseph	Sto-113	Mildred		Nor- 78
John	Lnc-349	Joseph	Sto-155	Miles		Hal-119
John	Lnc-368	Joseph	Ans- 19	Molly		Sto-141
John	Bur-105	Joseph	Pit-250	Mordeca Jun		Pas-202
John	Bur-105	Joseph	Nor- 78	Mordeca Jun		Pas-205
John	Dup- 30	Joshua	Roc- 22	Morris		Cum-259
John	Rth-135	Joshua	Fra- 92	Moses		Edg- 59
John	Rth-135	Joshua	Wil-266	Moses		Cha-207
John	Cum-243	Josiah	Prq-225	Moses Jur		Sto-142
John	Rth-131	Josiah	Jon-304	Moses Jur		Sto-107
John	Rth-133	L	Ash- 12	Moses Ser		Sto-143
John	Rth-133	Landen	Hal-118	Moses Ser		Sto-107
John	Glf-154	Laurence	Fra- 89	Nancy		Pas-203
John	Grn-136	Laurence	Nor- 77	Nancy		Pit-256
John	Grn-129	Lazarus	Way-247	Nancy		Roc- 30
John	Pit-250	Lazerus	Pit-258	Nancy		Roc- 23
John	Glf-158	Lenard	Mor- 54	Nancy		Mor- 67
John	Roc- 22	Lenord	Row- 84	Nathan		Bur-108
John	Roc- 16	Lenord	Row- 84	Nathan		Nsh- 89
John	Roc- 9	Leonard	Ora-133	Nathan		Mon- 26
John	Mor- 69	Levi	Row- 58	Nathan		Cha-207
John	Mor- 60	Levy	Cho-225	Nathan		Cha-205
John	Row- 51	Lewis	Dup- 19	Nathan		Hay-201
John	Row- 70	Lewis	Pit-251	Nathan		Mor- 69
John Shff	Row- 66	Lewis	Joh-289	Nathaniel		Nor- 77
John-A	Mon- 41	Lewis	Hay-200	Nathl		Glf-182
John A	Joh-291	Lewis	Cum-249	Nedom		Sur-197
John B	Cab-139	Lilly	Pas-203	Needham		Joh-289
John F	Mon- 39	Littleton	Ran-182	Needham		Cha-208
John M R	Rth-135	Lucretia	Bft- 19	Neill		Rob-232
John P	Grn-133	Luke	Ans- 31	Neill		Rob-228
John P	Ora-121	Malcom	Cum-246	Neill		Rch-202
John Jr	Prq-225	Mallechi	Mar- 15	Nicholson		Way-237
John Sr	Prq-226	Margaret	Wil-257	Nimrod		Cha-196
John Senr	Bun- 93	Marian	Cum-255	Noah		Pit-256
John W K	Joh-278	Mark	Cha-196	Noble		Bla- 14
John Snr	Joh-275	Marmaduke	Gat-107	Obedia		Row- 52
Jona	Bla- 3	Martha	Lnc-340	P		Cam-163
Jonathan	Cum-259	Martha	Roc- 16	Patsey		Sur-189
Jonathan	Joh-276	Martin	Cha-191	Patsey		Cha-205
Jonathan	Gat-113	Martin	Row- 40	Peggy		Cas- 70
Jonathan	Brt- 43	Mary	Car-175	Penelope		Wsh-227
Jonathan	Cha-207	Mary	Dup- 11	Peter		Bla- 8
Jonathan	Prq-225	Mary	Mec- 53	Peter		Lnc-364
Jonathan	Mor- 69	Mary	Edg- 72	Peter		Cas- 69
Jones	Dup- 29	Mary	Wsh-226	Peter		Row- 87

Smith,Peter	Row- 84	Smith,Saml R		Ora-112	Smith,Tamar		Pas-205
Peter	Rob-230	Saml		Brt- 58	Tarlton		Rth-135
Peter	Sto-107	Saml		Mec- 25	Telmelak		Hal-118
Peter	Cha-203	Saml		Pas-202	Temperance		Nsh- 90
Peter	Sto-152	Saml of J		Ora-134	Tho		Bft- 31
Peter	Sto-142	Saml		Bur-130	Thomas		Sur-186
Peter	Pit-243	Saml		Mon- 45	Thomas		Ire-253
Peter P	Cha-216	Saml		Row- 60	Thomas		Gat-106
Philip	Mon- 50	Saml		Grn-141	Thomas		Car-176
Philip	Row- 87	Saml		Pas-205	Thomas		Cas- 69
Philip	Row- 80	Saml		Roc- 14	Thomas		Cas- 69
Preter	Jon-304	Saml		Row- 56	Thomas		Cas- 70
Prudence	Mec- 50	Saml G		Joh-282	Thomas		Sur-181
R	Bla- 8	Saml Jr		Joh-282	Thomas		Way-237
R	Bru-234	Sampson		Mor- 65	Thomas		Bun- 97
R Senr	Ora-147	Sampson		Mor- 64	Thomas		Sto- 77
Ralph	Sto-150	Samuel		Rob-231	Thomas		Sto-126
Rebekah	Hal-118	Samuel		Dup- 25	Thomas		Sto-134
Reuben	Car-179	Samuel		Cum-253	Thomas		Hyd-233
Reuben S	Ora-126	Samuel		Cha-216	Thomas		Roc- 15
Reuben	Mon- 34	Samuel		Ire-252	Thomas Jr		Rth-131
Reubin	Grn-140	Samuel		War-180	Thomas Sr		Rth-131
Richard	Nsh- 85	Samuel		Cas- 70	Thos		Ans- 7
Richard	Hal-118	Samuel		Cas- 70	Thos		Mec- 25
Richard	Hal-119	Samuel		Nsh- 78	Thos		Hrt-207
Richard	Gat-114	Samuel		Row- 61	Thos		Cas- 70
Richard	Wsh-220	Samuel		Bun- 75	Thos		Bla- 13
Richard	Sto-141	Samuel		Pit-242	Thos (S R)		Bla- 8
Richd	Cas- 69	Samuel		Pit-233	Thos Jr		Cas- 70
Richd	Cas- 70	Samuel Junr		Car-175	Thos Jr		Cho-228
Richd	Cas- 70	Samuel Senr		Car-175	Thos R		Mec- 25
Richd	Cas- 70	Sandy		Cas- 69	Thos Sen		Bla- 8
Richd	Cha-208	Sarah		Grn-121	Thompson		Sto-102
Richd	Cha-210	Sarah		Cas- 69	Tobias		Ora-132
Richd	Glf-158	Sarah S C		Ora-126	Tryon		Bla- 12
Richd	Len-311	Sarah		Ora-121	Tully		Pas-202
Richd Sen	Ora-118	Sarah		Ans- 32	Turner		Joh-275
Ridden	Dup- 29	Sarah		Ans- 28	Turner		Brt- 57
Ridley	Way-252	Sarah		Pit-250	Uriah		Hal-119
Robert	Gat-114	Sarah		Mor- 69	Uriah		Mon- 48
Robert	Rth-133	Sephy		Hrt-213	Vachel		Rth-135
Robert	Cum-243	Sherwood		Grn-133	W		Col- 19
Robert	Rth-134	Sherwood		Mon- 50	W S		Ora-155
Robert	Cas- 69	Silas		Hrt-210	W L		Hrt-209
Robert	Sto- 93	Silas		Pit-239	Whitfield		Cum-259
Robert	Ire-238	Silus		Brt- 57	Wiley		Cha-196
Robert	Sto-125	Simpson		Glf-155	Will		Pas-203
Robert	Lnc-331	Solomon		Car-175	Will		Dup- 23
Robert	Sto-121	Solomon		Nor- 77	Will Short		Ora-136
Robert R	Hal-119	Sparkman		Pit-257	William		Joh-274
Robt	Ora-173	Step		Ora-174	William		Cum-259
Robt	Mon- 45	Stephen		Cho-231	William		Cum-243
Robt T	Pas-205	Stephen		Row- 85	William		Tyr-201
Robt W	Cab-137	Stephen		Hyd-224	William		Joh-275
Rosanna	Lnc-367	Stephen		Roc- 8	William		Rch-194
S	Cam-156	Stephen		Dup- 27	William		Ire-264
S Esq	Col- 20	T		Bru-240	William		Ire-264
Saley	Way-237	T A		Bru-226	William		Bur-118
Salley	Way-239	Tabitha		Way-249	William		Rth-134

Name		Ref	Name	Ref	Name	Ref
Smith,William		Rth-133	Smith,Wm	Mon- 38	Smotherman,Jesse	Ran-182
William		Rth-133	Willis	Cha-199	Wm	Ran-183
William		War-182	Winifred	Hal-119	Wm	Ran-182
William		War-182	Wyatt	Grn-123	Smothers,Elizabeth	Roc- 4
William		Cas- 69	Y V R	Pas-193	Jacob	Row- 89
William		Cas- 70	Zach	Ora-118	Smoyer,John Senr	Lnc-370
William		Sur-162	Zach	Rth-131	Smyth,John	Sam-164
William		Ons-106	Zachariah	Mor- 57	Wm	Sam-159
William		Ons- 99	Zachariah	Hal-118	Snall,Hugh	Mec- 34
William		Row- 78	Zebn	Tyr-207	Snead,Charles	Ons- 99
William		Way-249	Smitheal,John	Row- 82	Jane	Per-133
William		Hal-118	Smither,Gabriel	Wil-271	Lemuel	Per-133
William		Bun- 75	Samuel	Roc- 16	Sneaden,William	Ons-107
William		Hal-119	William	Wil-271	Sneador,Thos	Cur- 88
William		Bun- 98	Smitherman,John	Ran-180	Sneed,Alexander	Roc- 34
William		Sto-106	Saml	Ran-180	Benjamin	Sur-176
William		Cab-141	Thos	Ran-181	Henly	Rch-204
William		Sto-141	Smithers,John	Row- 77	John	Rch-212
William		Wil-278	William	Row- 77	Samuel	Rch-197
William		Pit-258	Smithey,John	Cas- 70	Solomon	Rch-212
William		Roc- 29	Reubin	Cas- 70	Solomon	Rch-204
William		Roc- 27	Smithson,Aaron	Pas-204	Stothen	Grn-136
William		Roc- 26	Adam	Pas-203	Thomas	Per-144
William		Roc- 25	E	Cam-158	William	Rch-212
William		Roc- 16	John	Pas-204	Wm M	Grn-144
William		Cur- 92	Malac	Pas-204	Zadock	Nsh- 78
William		Cur- 89	Matthias	Pas-202	Sneede,Ann	Jon-304
William		Row- 75	Miles	Pas-204	Sneling,Hugh	Grn-131
William Junr		Rch-196	Sally	Pas-205	Snell,Abijah	Wsh-222
William Jr		Prq-229	Thomas	Pas-204	Ann	Wsh-222
William Jr		Prq-226	Smithwick,Davd	Bft- 32	Asael	Wsh-222
William Senr		Cum-250	Ebenezer	Mar- 5	Elisebeth	Mec- 45
William Sr		Prq -225	Edmond	Mar- 5	Henry	Wsh-228
Willie		Mon- 24	Edmond	Brt- 64	Hiram	Wsh-227
Willie		War-182	Edmond Senr	Mar- 6	Isham	Wsh-222
Wm		Mor- 69	Edward	Mar- 15	James	Wsh-222
Wm		Mor- 69	Edwin	Mar- 10	James	Cur- 83
Wm		Mor- 67	Henry	Mar- 13	Jas	Mec- 38
Wm		Mor- 60	Humphrey	Prq -224	Jeremiah	Wsh-227
Wm		Glf-169	Joel	Mar- 6	John	Wsh-220
Wm		Hrt-213	John	Mar- 16	Kezia	Wsh-224
Wm		Ans- 22	John Senr	Mar-445	Polly	Wsh-222
Wm		Cha-201	Lenard	Brt- 46	W	Bru-236
Wm		Cha-202	Mark	Bft- 32	Snelling,Barnet	Grn-149
Wm		Mon- 21	Rebecca	Mar- 6	Leml	Grn-123
Wm		Mon- 45	Simon	Mar- 6	Snelson,Marshal	Bun- 83
Wm		Mon- 47	Swain	Mar- 10	Thomas	Bun- 87
Wm		Bur-130	Washington	Mar- 13	Snider,Adam	Row- 39
Wm		Mec- 28	William	Mar- 15	Barnet	Lnc-354
Wm		Mec- 33	Smittick,James	Hal-120	David	Sto-136
Wm		Ran-181	Smmers,Alexander	Pit-262	David	Sto-103
Wm	L	Ora-113	Smoot,Alexander	Row- 64	Geo	Row- 38
Wm		Ora-116	Caleb	Row- 79	George	Lnc-354
Wm		Glf-182	James	Wil-264	Henry	Row- 57
Wm		Ora-149	Jenifer	Row- 62	Jacob	Row- 80
Wm		Grn-121	John	Row- 64	John	Lnc-354
Wm		Grn-128	Thomas	Row- 64	John	Sto-144
Wm		Cha-193	William Jr	Row- 64	John	Row- 58
Wm		Cha-214	Smother,Henry	Lnc-370	Lewis	Row- 82

Snider,Martin	Sto-134	Soals,B	Col- 20	Sothern,John	Sto-140
Mary	Sto-143	J	Col- 20	Jsohua	Sto-140
Philip	Sto-137	J	Col- 17	Lord	Sto-104
Philip	Sto-144	J	Col- 19	Reubin	Sto-105
Philip	Row- 57	N	Col- 21	Stephen	Sto-140
Snipe,Elisha	Hrt-216	T	Col- 20	William	Sto-123
Thomas	Per-144	Soary,Andrew	Edg- 42	South,William	Brt- 46
Sniper,Wm	Cha-196	Mikajah	Hal-118	Southall,Daniel	Gat-115
Snipes,Billison	Dup- 26	Robert	Edg- 60	Faney	Nsh- 76
James	Grn-144	Sollomon	Edg- 44	Henry	War-172
Jesse	Joh-282	Willoby	Hal-119	Southard,Henry	Sur-193
Jessee	Grn-147	Socard,Henry	Rth-132	Isaac	Sur-193
John	Cha-209	Sockwell,J	Glf-178	J	Ora-140
John	Nor- 78	John	Glf-180	Martin	Sur-178
Matthew	Glf-186	Solars,Saybert	Bun- 81	Micajah	Lnc-349
Nancy	Joh-276	Solice,James	Way-234	Souther,Henry	Wil-264
Nathanl	Cas- 70	Sollts,Benjamin	Roc- 27	Capt Joshua	Wil-264
Needham	Joh-288	Solomon,Bennet	Mon- 45	Michael	Rth-131
Robert	Nor- 77	Goodwin	Mon- 45	Southerland,Alexr	Rch-191
Thomas	Cha-201	Leveter J	Sur-191	Ann	Cum-237
Thomas Jr	Cha-208	Lucy	Mec- 48	Daniel	Dup- 31
Thos Jr	Cha-208	Luke	Grn-128	George	Dup- 5
William	Nor- 78	Willm	Fra- 87	James	Edg- 42
Snodon,Francis	Cur- 89	Wm	Mon- 40	Jenry	Dup- 7
Snody,Thomas	Ire-246	Somerhill,Wm	Grn-146	Lucy	Roc- 6
Snotherly,Jacob	Ora-159	Somerill,Benjamin	Edg- 69	Mordecai	Ora-149
Snotterly,H	Ora-132	Henry	Edg- 68	Phillip	Dup- 9
H	Ora-121	Somerlin,Edward	Edg- 66	Robert	Dup- 32
Snow,Ann	Cas- 70	James	Edg- 68	Will	Dup- 33
Benjamin	Sto-141	Somers,Fary	Cas- 69	Southern,Reubin	Sto-140
Benjamin	Sto-111	James	Cas- 69	William	Sto- 94
Benjn	Sto-149	Somerville,Mary	Grn-141	Sowel,Asou	Mor- 56
Fielding	Sur-162	Somirs,John	Cas- 69	Charles	Mor- 62
Frost	Sur-160	Sommerlin,Barnes	Edg- 45	Jesse	Mor- 54
Frost L	Sur-163	Jacob	Edg- 64	John	Mor- 57
Henry	Row- 57	James	Edg- 68	William	Cum-265
Ice	Sur-163	Sonaino,Peter	Wsh-227	Sowell,Mrs	Brt- 52
John	Sto-151	Sooner,Alsey	Jon-304	Charles	Brt- 44
John	Sto-109	Sorells,Wm	Bur-104	Clery	Hrt-211
Larkin	Sur-180	Sorrel,John	Cum-245	Daniel	Ons-108
N	Cum-238	Sorrell,Ann	Brt- 50	Ezekiel	Brt- 53
Obed	Sur-180	Priscilla	Edg- 48	Fredk	Sam-154
Sarah	Cum-249	Rhoda	Brt- 50	George	Hrt-207
Thomas	Sur-162	Thos	Hrt-209	James	Hrt-209
W	Ash- 9	Sorrells,John Sr	Rth-134	John	Brt- 46
William	Sur-162	John	Rth-131	Lewis	Brt- 50
Xanthus	War-184	Sorrels,Charles	Rth-135	Moses	Mar- 10
Snowden,E	Cam-163	Edward	Sur-197	Obed	Hrt-211
Henry	Pas-203	Joseph	Hay-200	Shadrach	Ons-108
Leml	Pas-203	Sarah	Hay-201	William	Brt- 54
N Esq	Cam-152	Wally	Rth-132	Sowerby,Sally	Nor- 77
S	Cam-160	Walter	Bur-104	Sowers,Geo	Row- 41
Thad	Pas-203	Washington	Hay-200	Jacob	Row- 41
W	Cam-157	William	Hay-200	John	Row- 79
Wm	Pas-203	Sorsby,Alexander	Nsh- 79	Michal	Row- 79
Snowe,Isaac	Cur- 87	Benja	Nsh- 76	Philip	Row- 79
Snugg,John	Mon- 39	Soster,R W (Charlotte)		Valentine	Row- 79
Snuggs,Richd	Ans- 27		Mec- 25	Spach,Gottlieb	Sto-137
Snyder,John	Cab-146	Sothern,Ford	Sto-138	Gottlieb	Sto-103

Spach,John	Sto-137	Sparks,Jery	Bur-115	Speer,Aaron	Sur-172
John	Sto-103	John	Roc- 18	Drury	Sur-189
Joseph	Sto-108	John Esq	Wil-258	George	Sur-182
Spadia,Peter	Hyd-225	John Jr	Wil-259	Jacob	Sur-167
Spaight,Christian	Lnc-337	Levi	Wil-273	John	Sur-171
Spain,Berry	Sur-188	Matthew	Sur-167	Leven	Sur-182
Thomas	Cum-257	Matthew	Sur-177	Rachel	Sur-188
Fred	Hyd-231	Reuben	Wil-266	Shadrach	Sur-189
Hezekiah	Edg- 41	Richard	Rth-133	Speight,William	Brt- 49
John	Pit-248	Richard	Ire-252	Speirs,Joseph E	Cab-143
Joshua	Pit-244	Samuel	Edg- 56	Spell,Deliah	Nsh- 92
Patience	Nor- 77	Samuel	Sur-161	John Jr	Edg- 68
Thomas	Pit-246	Solomon	Wil-261	John Sr	Edg- 70
William	Pit-248	Solomon Jr	Wil-268	Lewis	Sam-156
Spainhour,Henry	Sto-130	Thomas	Sur-167	Selah	Edg- 48
Henry	Sto- 97	W	Ash- 7	Spellar,Thomas	Mar- 7
Henry	Sto-126	Sparrow,Abram	Lnc-375	Speller,Henry	Brt- 46
Henry	Sto- 99	Benj	Hyd-230	Thomas	Brt- 59
Jacob	Sto-126	John	Ora-116	Spellings,Britton	Edg- 71
Jacob	Sto- 97	Thomas	Rth-133	Spelman,Ailsy	Pas-205
Jacob	Sto- 96	Wm	Ora-146	Courtny	Pas-204
Jacob Jur	Sto-127	Spaugh,Adam	Row- 54	Janey	Cur- 80
John	Sto-130	John	Row- 54	Nancy	Pas-204
John	Sto-127	Spaush,Jacob	Row- 54	Rachel	Pas-204
Joseph	Sto- 97	Speagle,Danl	Lnc-326	Sarah	Pas-203
Joseph	Sto-127	Debault	Lnc-326	Spence,A	Cam-164
Michael	Sto-129	John	Lnc-326	Aaron	Glf-180
Michaiel	Sto- 99	Martin	Lnc-339	Abigal	Cur- 91
Spalter,Lemuel	Car-172	Michl	Lnc-329	Anne	Nor- 77
Span,Anne	Hal-120	Philip	Lnc-339	Artis	Cur- 89
James	Cur- 90	Samuel	Lnc-329	D	Cam-158
Richard	Hal-119	Speaks,Lucky	Ire-254	D	Cam-161
Spangler,Jacob	Lnc-327	Martin	Row- 74	Danl	Pas-204
Peter	Bur-131	Spear,Benton	Rob-238	David	Row- 59
Peter	Lnc-327	Byrd	Ans- 10	David	Pas-205
Peter	Lnc-328	Elisha	Cab-143	Henery	Cur- 90
Spann,John M	Roc- 20	James	Pit-240	Isaac	Dup- 13
William	Bun- 73	Jno	Ans- 18	J	Cam-161
Spargar,John W	Sur-177	John	Bur-102	J	Cam-162
Sparger,Phillip	Sur-179	John	Pit-240	J	Cam-164
Sparkes,A	Hal-120	John	Pit-233	James	Pas-205
Sparkman,Ann	Edg- 49	John	Pit-233	James	Glf-182
Charny	Ons- 99	Peggy	Pit-233	James	Sam-154
James	Way-244	Solomon	Cab-144	James Jun	Pas-204
James	Brt- 53	William	Sto-113	John	Jon-303
Jas	Brt- 49	Wm	Ans- 17	Joseph	Pas-204
Lewis	Gat-108	Speares,Phillip	Rob-237	Kessiah	Wil-268
Reddick	Edg- 68	Spearman,Sarah	Jon-304	L	Cam-162
Reuben	Edg- 51	Spears,Isaiah	Cab-143	Malicky	Cur- 90
Wm	Brt- 44	J	Cam-158	Mark	Pas-202
Wm Sen	Brt- 43	Joseph	Hal-119	N	Cam-164
Sparks,Benjamin	Sur-194	John	Pit-256	N	Glf-159
David	Row- 38	John	Grm-128	Newton	Pas-205
Edmond	Cas- 70	Richard	Mec- 31	Peggy	Pas-205
Eliza	Bur-122	William	Sto-154	Robt	Pas-205
George	Wil-269	Wm W	Cab-143	Rodey	Sam-158
George	Sur-168	Willis	Nsh- 77	Thornton	Pas-205
Hampton	Row- 38	Speck,David	Cab-145	Timothy	Dup- 16
James	Wil-271	Speed,Elizabeth	Rch-208	Will	Pas-203

-298-

Spencer,Absolum	Lnc-369	Spice,John	Sto-130	Spoon,C	Glf-169
Benj	Hyd-227	Spicer col	Fra-101	Chen	Ran-180
Benj	Hyd-227	Spicer,Ester	Ons-108	Davd	Ran-180
Benj	Hyd-230	James	Edg- 45	John	Ora-131
Benjamin	Lnc-370	John E	Ons-107	John	Ran-180
Benjamin	Hyd-227	Joseph	Wil-259	John	Glf-170
Benjamin	Tyr-202	Moses	Edg- 60	Peter	Glf-168
Caleb	Tyr-203	Samuel	Wil-270	Spooner,John	Cho-221
Christ Sr	Hyd-227	Sarah	Edg- 61	Reuben	Ons-106
Christopher	Hyd-227	William	Edg- 60	Spoonhower,Peter	Bur-108
Daniel	Cas- 70	William	Wil-259	Spradling,John	Wil-273
Edward	Hyd-227	Spicey,Dickson	Joh-283	John Jr	Wil-285
Frisbey	Hyd-227	Spier,Mary	Bft- 28	Spraker,George	Row- 79
Hannah	Mon- 33	Spiers,Parthena	Pas-202	Sprall,Hugh	Lnc-333
Isaac	Ran-181	Robt	Ans- 8	Spranhower,Peter	Bur-115
James	Grn-144	Spight,Pleasent	Gat-112	Sprat,Solo	Cur- 92
John	Sto-139	Spights,Sharp	Jon-305	Spratt,James	Ora-116
John	Sto-105	Simon	Jon-305	Samuel	Rth-132
John	Sur-174	Thomas	Jon-305	Sprawls,Elijah	Rch-201
Jones	Hyd-230	Spikes,Jeremiah	Prq-225	Perry	Rch-197
Joseph	Tyr-207	Spillings,Wm	Bft- 36	Solomon	Rch-206
Mahala	Hyd-227	Spilmon,John	Sur-171	Solomon	Rch-201
Mary	Hyd-228	William	Sur-171	Spreberry,Archd	Mec- 32
Mary	Mec- 46	Spinks,Enoch	Ran-182	Ben	Mec- 32
Nathan	Hyd-227	Lewis	Ran-182	Jack	Mec- 32
Nathan	Sto-131	Luis	Ran-180	Jas	Mec- 32
Nathan	Sto-100	Spinner,Wm	Brt- 59	Sprewel,John	Rth-133
Nathan	Tyr-203	Spires,Elisha	Hrt-214	Sprewell,Ann	Edg- 70
Rebeckah	Hyd-227	Mary	Len-315	Isaac	Bft- 20
Robert	Tyr-203	Mary	Hrt-209	John	Tyr-211
Saml	Ans- 31	Thomas	Hrt-212	Nathn	Tyr-210
Samuel	Hyd-228	Spivey,David	Brt- 61	Rebeca	Bft- 38
Sarah	Bur-103	James	Fra- 94	Samuel	Mar- 11
Selby	Hyd-227	Jonathan	Brt- 53	Sprewill,Benjn	Tyr-211
Symore	Mon- 32	Matthew	Nor- 77	Charles	Tyr-211
Thomas	Hyd-227	Rachal	Gat-109	Fredk	Tyr-211
Thomas	Hyd-229	Richard	Fra-100	Hezh of Simn	Tyr-211
Thos	Grn-144	Sary	Gat-11	Hosanah	Tyr-210
William	Hyd-227	Seth	Gat-110	Martha	Tyr-210
William	Hyd-229	William	Nor- 77	Obediah	Tyr-212
William	Bur-126	William	Gat-108	Stephen	Tyr-211
William	Sur-183	Wm	Sam-158	William	Tyr-210
Willm	Lnc-332	Wm	Bur-105	Spright,Fullington	Gat-113
Wm	Bur-129	Wm	Cha-205	Jerimiah	Gat-115
Wm	Ans- 4	Wm	Brt- 61	Thomas	Gat-114
Zach	Lnc-340	Wm B	Brt- 57	William	Gat-112
Spendlove,Jannet	Bla- 12	Spivy,Aaron	Brt- 66	Spring,Aaron	Bft- 34
Rober	Bla- 12	John	Mor- 59	Benjaman	Cur-/82
Sperberry,Wm	Mec- 32	Jonas	Bun- 84	Springer,Adam	Ora-133
Sperlen,Isaac	Rch-210	Moses	Brt- 66	Stephen	Glf-187
Sperlock,Wm	Grn-143	William	Bun- 84	Springfield,Moses	Per-144
Sperry,Jos	Cho-229	Wm	Mon- 24	Thos	Cha-199
Sperue,John	Cum-258	Splawn,James	Rth-134	Springle,Ichabud	Bft- 34
Spewell,Samuel Jr	Tyr-210	James	Rth-134	Nancy	Bft- 35
Spewill,Hezekiah	Tyr-211	Moses	Rth-133	Springs,Adam	Mec- 35
Joseph	Tyr-211	Riggy	Rth-133	Andrew	Mec- 28
Thos H	Tyr-210	Spoolman,Ephriam	Row- 44	Capt Jno	Mec- 35
Lois	Tyr-210	Federick	Row- 44	S	Bru-236
Spice,John	Sto- 99	Spoon,Adam	Ora-121	Sprinkle,George	Sto-128

Name	Ref	Name	Ref	Name	Ref
Sprinkle,George	Sto- 98	Spvie,Aaron	Ans- 15	Stafford,Samuel	Way-240
John	Sto-128	Squire,Rogers	Nor- 78	Samuel	Sto-113
John	Sto- 98	Squires,Appleton	Bft- 21	Samuel	Sto-153
Peter	Sur-166	D	Cam-156	Step	Pas-202
Petee	Sur-190	Elizabeth	Car-176	Thomas	Ran-182
Moses	Sur-177	J	Cam-155	Thos	Ran-181
Samuel	Sur-190	Robt	Mec- 40	William	Prq-225
William	Bun- 92	Squrs,Thos	Ora-136	William	Glf-161
Sprott,Jas	Mec- 25	Srum,John	Lnc-341	Wm	Cab-144
Jas Snr	Mec- 37	Peter	Lnc-346	Staggs,William	Ora-162
John	Pas-205	Stacey,Aaron	Lnc-356	Stagner,Benj	Mon- 25
Thos	Mec- 50	Benjamin	Lnc-356	Gob	Mon- 47
Capt Thos	Mec- 36	Mack	Lnc-356	Henry	Bun- 91
Sprouse,Jessee	Bun- 79	Malon	Cas- 69	Stainback,John	Nor- 78
Sprout,James	Roc- 28	Wm	Cho-231	Stainton,John	Bla- 6
Spruberry,Jno	Mec- 24	Stack,David	Glf-158	Stalcup,Eliza	Ora-162
Sprue,Sarah	Glf-156	Thos	Glf-161	Jno	Ora-123
Spruel,Jesse	Tyr-205	Stackbarger,John	Sto-129	Staley,Adam	Wil-271
Richard	Tyr-203	Joseph	Sto-129	Eve	Wil-271
Samuel	Tyr-204	Stacker,John	Ran-181	Martin	Ora-131
Uri	Tyr-204	Thos	Ran-181	Stallians,James	Edg- 56
Spruill,Aaron	Wsh-216	Stackhouse,Thos	War-183	James	Edg- 50
Andrew	Wsh-222	Stacks,Abraham	Pit-236	John	Edg- 52
Dempsey	Wsh-219	Sarah	Pit-260	Josiah	Edg- 45
Ebenezer	Wsh-220	Stacy,Bruckner	Mon- 23	Lott	Edg- 55
Evan	Wsh-220	Robert	Prq-225	Philip	Edg- 44
Henry	Wsh-218	Samuel	Prq-225	Simcan	Edg- 56
Hugh	Wsh-218	Stadler,Mary	Cas- 70	Stalling,Seth	Gat-108
James	Wsh-218	Stafford,A	Glf-174	Shadrick	Gat-108
John	Wsh-210	Adam	Cas- 69	Simon	Gat-108
Joseph	Wsh-221	Benjamin	Bur-122	Z	Joh-272
Lemuel	Wsh-218	Betty	Way-239	Stallings,Elias	Cho-227
Miles	Wsh-217	Dolly	Pas-205	Elijah	Fra- 88
Susanna	Wsh-218	Elis	Cas- 69	Elisha	Fra- 88
Sylvanus	Wsh-216	Elisha	Jon-304	Hardy	Fra- 77
Uriah	Wsh-227	Geo	Ora-133	Henry	Prq-224
William	Wsh-221	Geo	Ora-129	Jesse	Prq-224
Zebedee	Wsh-218	George	Mec- 38	Jesse	Mar- 6
Zebulon	Tyr-212	Gray	Hal-120	John	Dup- 24
Spry,Enoc	Row- 58	Henry	Cas- 70	John	Prq-226
Francis	Row- 58	James	Per-144	John	Fra- 90
John	Row- 58	James	Cab-144	Joseph	Prq-224
John	Row- 58	James	Glf-151	Kenneth	Mar-446
Spurgen,Eli	Row- 44	John	Pas-202	Mary	Edg- 72
Jo	Row- 43	John	Sto-102	Meshick	Dup- 22
John	Row- 83	John	-226	Miles	Cho-229
Joseph	Row- 43	John	Sto-135	Millicent	Prq-224
Josia	Row- 43	John	Bur-106	Mrs Polly	Fra- 84
Saml	Row- 44	John	Bur-122	Rachel	Cho-229
Squire	Row- 43	John Sr	Prq-225	Reubin	Fra- 98
Spurgin,Isaah	Row- 43	Joseph	Cas- 70	Reubin Junr	Fra- 97
Spurlin,Elijah	Lnc-341	Labon	Cas- 70	Reuben	Prq-224
John	Lnc-338	Labon Jr	Cas- 69	Shade	Dup- 17
Spurling,Hugh	Lnc-341	Malachi	Pas-202	Shadrach Jr	Dup- 22
J	Ash- 14	Mariam	Prq-226	Stallins,Jesse	Brt- 53
J	Ash- 14	Moses	Cab-143	Josiah	Brt- 55
Z	Ash- 14	Nathan	Bun- 93	Stallion,Abraham	Bur-127
Z	Ash- 14	Revel	Ran-182	Stallions, Hardy	Mar- 5
Spurlock,Wm	Cha-193	Robt	Glf-167	Matthew	Ans- 31

Stallions,Reuben	Bur-109	Standley,Jacob	Sam-152	Stanly,Isaac	Glf-185
Thos	Row- 56	John	Cas- 69	Isaiah	Glf-164
Stallons,Joel	Roc- 31	John	Sto-127	J	Glf-164
Wm	Cab-141	John	Sto-134	James	Jon-305
Stallsworth,Saml	Ora-118	John	Sto-114	Jas	Glf-162
Stally,C	Glf-177	John	Sto- 98	Jesse	Len-317
C	Glf-177	John	Brt- 60	Jesse	Glf-163
Geo	Glf-181	L	Cam-160	Jesse	Glf-162
Stam,George	Grn-137	P	Cam-161	Jesse	Glf-161
Stamey,Daniel	Lnc-373	Thomas	Sto-110	John	Jon-305
Henry	Lnc-373	William	Sam-155	John	Pas-205
John	Lnc-373	William	Brt- 63	Joseph	Glf-167
Peter	Lnc-332	Standly,Daniel	Ons-101	Joseph	Row- 62
Stamley,Wm	Ora-150	Garrett	Sto-156	M	Glf-162
Stamper,J	Ash- 10	Jesse	Sto-116	Major	Way-249
J	Ash- 10	Jesse	Sto-155	Malor	Glf-188
J	Ash- 4	John	Sto-156	Michael	Glf-164
Jesse	Wil-267	Thomas	Sto-149	Moses	Dup- 16
Joel	Wil-260	Stanfield,Hal	Per-153	Moses	Way-249
Joel	Wil-270	John	Per-133	Nathaniel	Jon-304
John	Hal-119	John	Glf-162	Robert	Jon-305
Jonathan	Wil-272	Luret	Per-133	Shadrach	Wil-265
Nathaniel	Wil-264	Mason	Sur-163	Thomas	Ire-252
Richard	Wil-260	Robt	Per-133	William	Jon-305
Robert	Hal-119	Stanford,J	Glf-177	Wm	Glf-159
S	Ash- 10	Jas	Ora-173	Stansberry,David	Wil-283
W	Ash- 10	Jonathan	Mec- 52	Nathan	Wil-274
Wm	Grn-138	* Linas	Lnc-375	Stansbury,Aaron	Wil-278
Stamps,John	Cas- 70	Richd	Ora-115	Luke	Bur-129
Stanall,J H	Glf-160	Robt	Ora-170	Moses	Wil-284
Stancil,Noble	Pit-261	Saml	Mec- 52	Stansel,Nathan	Edg- 70
Peter	Rch-195	Saml	Dup- 9	Stansell,John	Joh-285
Stancill,Charlotte	Nor- 78	Stange,Abraham A	Wil-279	Stanshin,John M	Grn-128
Everett	Nor- 77	Stanley,Christopher	Sto- 94	Stansil,Godfrey	Pit-244
Samuel	Nor- 78	Elijah	Edg- 46	Peter	Cum-260
Standard,Henry	Cas- 70	Elizabeth	Wil-265	William	Cum-260
Standback,David	Rch-200	Freeman	Hyd-232	William	Pit-244
Forester	Cas- 70	James	Sur-176	Stansill,Godfrey	Joh-286
George	Rch-200	James	Joh-277	John	Joh-286
Thomas	Rch-199	Joel	Wil-273	Nathan	Joh-286
Standen,Jesse	Prq-225	John	Grn-125	Stansul,John	Bun- 73
William	Prq-225	John	Sur-184	Stansypher,John H	Wil-277
Standfield,Abram	Cas- 69	John	Wil-264	Stanton,Benjn	Ran-181
John	Cas- 69	John Jr	Wil-266	David	Ran-181
Standford,E	Ash- 8	Jona	Bla- 3	Frederick	Nor- 78
Joseph	Ora-149	Mary	Joh-277	Green	Fra- 92
Standin,Hendn	Cho-221	Nathan	Wil-271	James	Car-170
Standland,D	Bru- 37	Richard	Glf-164	James	Wil-275
H	Bru- 37	Richd	Ora-125	James	Edg- 48
J	Bru- 37	Richd	Ora-124	John	Ran-181
J	Bru- 37	Samuel	Glf-165	John	Bun- 81
L	Bru-222	Will	Dup- 24	L	Glf-183
P	Bru-240	Willm	Pas-204	Owen Junr	Car-184
S	Bru-226	Stanlon,Jas	Cab-138	Owen Senr	Car-184
T	Bru-226	Stanly,Charles	Bur-117	Saml	Ran-181
Standley,Barnabas	Sam-152	Edwd	Glf-186	Thos	Prq-225
Christopher	Sto-123	Hannah	Jon-304	Willis	Edg- 48
E	Cam-158	Henry	Jon-305	Stapelton,Thos	Glf-159
Elisha	Cas- 69	*Stanford,Moses	Mec- 40	Staples,John	Bur-112

-301-

Staples,R	Cam-155	Staton,Thomas	Mar- 15	Steel,Patience	Cha-201
T	Cam-159	Thomas	Mar- 7	Phillip	Rth-134
Star,Adam	Row- 56	William	Edg- 53	Robert	Hal-119
Casper	Row- 60	Windfield D	Edg- 52	Robert J	Rch-199
Christopher	Ire-242	Staway,Phillip	Lnc-349	Robt	Mec- 51
Jasper	Row- 56	Stawler,Lucy	Sto-106	Saml	Cum-238
Joseph	Dup- 28	Stawls,Bond	Mar- 15	T	Ora-141
Starak,John	Lnc-368	James	Mar- 14	Thomas	Sto- 97
Starbuck,E	Glf-165	Miles	Mar- 14	Thomas	Sto-127
Gayer	Glf-188	Mills	Mar- 15	Thos	Ora-172
Hezekiah	Glf-188	Stead,James	Wil-282	Thos	Cha-210
Matthew	Glf-166	Thomas	Wil-282	William	Sto- 91
Paul	Sto-110	Steadman,E	Cum-239	William	Row- 76
Steward	Glf-187	Winship	Cha-203	William	Sto-155
Thos	Glf-188	Steagall,Absolem	Ans- 10	William	Sto-120
Wm	Glf-163	Geo	Ans- 21	Wm	Ora-121
Wm Jr	Glf-163	Jas	Ans- 22	Steele,Henry	Ora-120
Stark,Elisha	Ans- 15	Jno	Ans- 14	Henry	Ire-241
John	Grn-135	Moses	Ans- 25	James	Bur-106
Starke,Ruth	Ora-120	Sol	Ans- 8	John	Bun- 73
Starkey,Abram	Cas- 70	Thos	Ans- 21	John	Ire-239
Jonathan	Cas- 69	Steal,Sarah	Jon-304	John	Bur-124
Joseph	Hay-201	Stealey,Peter	Ran-182	Joseph	Ire-246
Starkweather,Nancy	Bft- 38	Stealy,Abm	Ran-181	Joseph	Ora-112
Starling,Celiah	Way-253	Abm	Ran+181	Ninian	Ire-244
J	Col- 18	Danl	Ran-180	Ninian	Ire-243
J	Col- 18	John	Ran-181	Ninian	Ire-242
Nazareth	Way-236	Josh	Ran-180	Ninian	Ire-241
Robt	Way-253	Leo	Ran-181	Samuel	Bur-106
T	Col- 17	Martin	Rn-181	Thos	Mon- 21
William	Joh-285	Steaphens,Anthony	Cas- 69	William	Ire-241
William	Way-239	George	Cas- 69	Wm	Brt- 49
Starns,Federick	Mec- 42	Samuel	Cas- 69	Steelman,William	Row- 63
Jno	Mec- 29	Thomas	Cas- 69	Steelmon,Betsey	Sur-192
Joseph	Cab-141	Stedham,D	Ash- 7	Charles	Sur-168
Starr,Adam	Ora-118	J	Ash- 4	Charles Sr	Sur-192
D	Glf-177	S	Ash- 4	George	Sur-192
Henry	Sto-143	S	Ash- 4	Jeremiah	Tyr-212
Henry	Sto-142	Steed,Benjn	Ran-180	Steely,Edmund	Wsh-223
Henry	Tyr-210	Callton	Ran-180	Frederic	Wsh-224
Henry Ser	Sto-143	Charles	Ran-182	Jeremiah	Wsh-227
Jacob	Lnc-370	Clatin	Ran-180	Michl	Bft- 22
Philip	Lnc-370	Helkiah	Mon- 22	Lovick	Lnc-359
Starratt,J	Glf-175	Jedethan	War-186	Steener,Abraham	Sto-145
Wm	Glf-175	John	Ran-180	Steers,Daniel	Roc- 10
Starret,John	Lnc-326	Moses	Mon- 22	Steerwalt,Tobiah	Cab-145
Starrot,Alexander	Bun- 75	Sam	Mon- 22	Steerwault,Tobias	Cab-143
Starterick,Seth	Sto-148	Steel,Abram	Rth-133	Stegall,Jeremiah	Roc- 3
Stasny,Danl	Bur-104	Edwards	Sto- 97	John	Roc- 3
Staten,Griffin	Rob-239	Francis	Sto-155	Stegnar,John	Roc- 6
Statin,Benjamin	Rth-132	Francis	Sto-112	Steller,Peter	Row- 68
Elisha	Sto-103	James	Car-180	Step,Betsy	Per-133
Staton,Arthur	Edg- 52	Jas	Mec- 51	James	Nor- 78
Bythal	Edg- 53	Jas	Mec- 48	Joshua	Nor- 78
Ezekiel	Edg- 54	Jas	Mec- 33	Joshua	Per-133
Fredk	Ans- 8	John	Row- 88	Stephen,Elizabeth	War-170
James	Edg- 53	John	Ran-181	Mary	Rob-243
Jessee	Edg- 54	John	Rth-134	Robert	Hrt-214
Nehemiah	Edg- 52	Martin	Mec- 51	Stephens,Abraham	Nor- 77

Stephens,Alexander	Row- 83	Stephenson,Hardee	Pit-249	Stevens,David		Joh-274
Arthur	Nor- 77	James	Jon-305	E		Col- 18
Asa	Ons-105	James	Hay-200	Edward		Joh-288
B	Ora-147	James	Ire-260	Ferebe		Len-321
Barnabis	Mor- 66	James	Ire-250	Hardy		Mon- 26
Barnabas	Sam-154	James	Ire-252	Henry		Joh-288
Benj	Cas- 70	James	Ire-252	Henry		Joh-274
Benjamin	Cum-244	Jno	Mec- 34	J		Cam-157
Berry	Cur- 91	John	Hay-200	J		Col- 20
E Jr	Glf-162	John	Ire-260	J		Col- 19
Edward	Cum-264	John	Ire-260	Jacob		Joh-282
Edwin	Cum-241	John Sen	Ire-260	James		Mor- 58
Eliz	Nsh- 82	Mosses	Ire-260	Jno		Mon- 31
Etheldred	Way-234	Thomas	Mar- 13	Jno		Len-311
Geo	Glf-162	William	Nor- 77	John		Joh-288
George	Edg- 44	William	Hay-201	John		Len-318
Henry	Ora-122	William	Ire-252	John Jr		Joh-282
J	Glf-162	William	Ire-260	M		Col- 20
James	Cum-257	William	Ire-260	M		Col- 17
James	Cum-263	Stephins,Jenkins	Nor- 77	Mildred		Sam-163
James C	Nor- 77	John	Cur- 88	P		Bru-224
Jesse	Mec- 29	Urias	Glf-164	Rebeca		Mon- 32
John	Pit-243	Stepney,Major	Prq-225	Richd		Mor- 67
John	Wil-283	Samuel	Prq-225	Roderick		Cum-257
Joshua	Grn-137	William	Prq-225	Samson		Row- 62
Leachman	Roc- 13	Stepp,James Junr	Bun- 73	Thos		Ora-147
Loveck	Rch-206	James Junr	Bun- 73	W		Bru-224
Nelly	Jon-304	John	Bur-110	William		Joh-288
R	Mon- 35	Joseph	Bun- 73	William		Joh-275
Richard	Ons-104	Phebe	Bun- 95	Stevenson,James		Row- 71
Richard	Ons- 98	Thomas	Wil-279	John		Row- 61
Richard	Row- 83	William	Bun- 73	John		Row- 62
Robert	Bur-131	Sterdevant,Jno	Ans- 4	John		Joh-276
Sarah	Way-232	Stergeon,Jno	Mec- 49	Jonathan		Cum-257
Sarah	Mec- 29	Stergison,Wm	Cab-143	Joseph		Rth-135
Sherrod	Bur-114	Sterling,Jas	Mec- 35	Solomon		Joh-275
Silas	Cha-214	Robt	Mor- 65	Stevins,H		Bla- 13
Silas	Cha-214	Wm	Mor- 65	S		Col- 19
Squire	Mec- 29	Wm	Rob-236	Steward,Bitha		Hrt-208
Mrs Sucky	Fra- 88	Sternes,John	Bur-108	Jacob		Bun- 87
T	Glf-161	Sterns,David	Mec- 42	Joshua		Bun- 86
Theo	Sam-159	Federick	Mec- 42	Nathaniel		Bun- 82
Tho	Ora-118	Jacob	Mec- 41	Nathaniel Junr		Bun- 82
Thomas	Bun- 87	Jno	Mec- 22	Ralph		Ire-249
Welcom	Bun- 76	Jno	Mec- 41	Sampson		Glf-153
William	Cas- 70	Nicholas	Mec- 50	Stephen		Row- 44
William	Ons-100	Stetman,Samuel	Edg- 41	Stewart at Stewart's Mills		
William	Nor- 77	Stevele,Fred	Bur-103			Wsh-225
William	Pit-233	Stevens (sic)	Bru-224	Stewart,Alex		Ora-177
William	Hay-200	A	Bru-224	Alexr		Mec- 40
William	Roc- 13	A	Col- 19	Alexr	Bigger	Mec- 31
William	Roc- 4	Absalom	Len-316	Allen		Rch-202
William	Sam-154	Archd	Mor- 67	Archd		Rob-223
William Jun	Roc- 14	B	Col- 20	Barnabas		Cha-200
Wm	Grn-141	Benja	Len-310	Bartlet		War-169
Willoby	Ons- 98	Benjn	Joh-281	Capt Benjn		Fra- 86
Stephenson,Anne	Wil-283	Calloway	Mor- 65	Cathrine		Mor- 69
Elam	Ire-251	Charles	Sam-163	Charles		War-169
Esther	Jon-304	Charles	Joh-282	Charles		Mor- 55

Stewart,Chas	Sur-163	Stewart,Moses free man		Stinchecomb,John	Row- 84
Christian	Rob-225	of colour	Ran-187	Stine,Elias	Lnc-349
D	Bru-232	Nelly	War-178	Henry	Lnc-349
Daniel	Sam-155	Norman	Rob-229	Jacob	Bur-105
DAnl	Rob-227	P	Cum-241	John	Lnc-349
Dunkin	Ire-238	Peter	Nor- 78	John Junr	Lnc-349
Edward	Mor- 54	R	Glf-153	Stinnet,Dabner	Rth-132
Edwd free man of colour		Reubeon	Mec- 40	Stinsen,Joshua	Row- 61
	Ran-187	Robert	Edg- 40	Stinson,Aaron	Sur-184
Elijah	Bft- 21	Robt	Ora-126	Alexr	Mec- 47
Everet	Hal-102	Robt	Glf-167	David	Mec- 38
George	Mor- 60	Saml	Glf-181	Hugh	Mec- 47
Gitbe	Mor- 58	Saml L R	Ora-117	Jno	Mec- 37
Isaiah	Sur-171	Saml	Cha-203	John	Cha-193
James	Dup- 28	Thomas	Ire-252	John	Cha-196
James	Cas- 69	William	Glf-178	Michael	Mec- 47
James	Bun- 86	William	Cas- 69	Moses	Sur-178
James	Wil-275	William	Edg- 56	Robt	Cha-195
James	Row- 68	William	Nor- 78	Willm	Glf-161
James	Rch-202	William	Rth-134	Wm	Glf-169
James	Ire-255	William	Ire-255	Stipe,Henry	Sto-152
Jas	Ans- 14	William	Mar- 6	Stirewalt,Adam	Row- 69
Jas	Mec- 33	Wm	Mec- 52	Frederick	Row- 69
Jas	Rob-224	Wm	Mec- 35	John	Row- 69
Jas	Mec- 32	Wm	Mec- 35	Michl	Row- 70
Jno	Mec- 41	Wm	Ans- 14	Stiring,Elisha	Tyr-206
Jno	Rob-223	Zach	Hay-200	Stirl---k,Paul	Sto-114
Jno	Rob-229	Stewentor,Fredk	Lnc-373	Stison,Littlejohn	Car-172
Jno	Rob-229	Stewert,Wm	Ans- 15	Stites,Brittain	Dup- 36
Jno	Rob-225	Stice,Chares	Rth-134	Stith,Jesse	Sto-142
Jno	Mec- 38	Charles	Rth-134	Jesse	Sto-107
Jno	Mec- 33	Phillip	Rth-134	Stitt,Jene	Mec- 29
John	Cha-191	Stigall,Jesse	War-176	Jno	Mec- 34
John	Dup- 27	Raban	Hal-118	Wm	Mec- 25
John	Sam-155	Stighler,Geo	Cab-145	Stiverson,James	Prq-226
John	Glf-187	Stiles,Benjamin	Lnc-356	John	Prq-225
John	Sur-182	Geo	Mon- 44	Stoakes,Andrew	Dup- 10
John	Mon- 21	James	Hay-200	Will Sr	Dup- 9
John	Cha-203	John	Ons- 98	Stoball,John Jr	Grn-125
John	Glf-167	John	Hay-200	John Senr	Grn-125
John	Row- 49	John	Lnc-356	Stockard,Jonathan	Glf-162
John	Row- 70	Thomas	Hay-201	Stockbarger,John	Sto- 99
John	Glf-154	William	Hay-200	Stocks,Hilory	Pit-251
John	Ire-267	William	Hay-200	Isaac	Pit-252
John	Rch-198	Still,Boaz	Bun- 72	Levi	Pit-260
John	Ire-249	John	Cab-142	Margaret	Pit-260
John Jr	Glf-164	John	Jon-303	Sarah	Pit-260
Johnthn	Row- 49	Stiller,Henry	Row- 68	Stockton,David	Rth-133
Jos	Lnc-341	Stillwell,Elijah	Mec- 29	Douty	Sto-101
Joseph	Hal-120	Elisha	Mec- 29	Joseph	Sur-195
Joseph	Mec- 32	Jeremiah	Hay-201	Mary	Sto-133
Josiah	Ans- 25	Jesse	Mec- 29	Thomas	Rth-133
Jourdan	Cha-193	Jno	Mec- 40	Stoddard,Agness	Sur-186
Lincoln	Mec- 31	Shadrach	Bur-121	Stodle,John H	Bur-102
Mal	Rob-225	Stilly,Levi	Bft- 31	Stoghdel,William	Hay-201
Margaret	Rch-198	Sarah	Jon-305	Stokely,Lyddia	Pas-202
Mary	Hal-120	Stilsebough,Danl	Lnc-371	Stoker,Matthew	Rth-132
Moses free man of colour		Stilwell,Jery	Bur-131	Stokes,Allen	Mon- 50
	Ran-187	Thomas	Joh-280	Alpheus	Pit-246

Stokes,Ambrose	Mon- 50	Stone,John	Sto-120	Story,Robert	Bun- 82
Anne	Nor- 78	John	Fra- 92	Robert	Wil-278
D	Glf-174	John	Rth-131	Wm	Mec- 29
Dempsey	Nor- 78	John	Rth-132	Wm	Cur- 82
Demsy	Edg- 50	John	Glf-155	Stotesbury,John P	Hyd-224
E	Glf-175	John	Cum-263	Stots,Jacob	Sur-163
Edmund	Prq-225	Joseph	Sur-187	Peter	Sur-180
Elizabeth	Pit-255	Jonathan	Fra- 91	Samuel	Sto-145
Frederick	Prq-225	Jonathan	Prq-226	Stott,Jehue	Jon-304
Herbert	Nor- 78	Mary	Cas- 69	John	Nsh- 87
Hugh	Prq-225	Merrit	Fra- 96	Thomas	Pas-203
Isaac	Pit-256	Randal	Ans- 12	Willm	Pas-203
James	Pit-236	Richd	Mon- 40	Stough,Geo	Cab-142
Joel	Pit-246	Seml	Pas-203	Martin	Cab-142
John	Pit-251	Serenius	Cha-202	Michael	Cab-142
John Sen	Pit-237	Solathiel	Row- 44	Samuel	Cur- 82
Montford	Row- 89	Solomon	Wil-264	Stout,Aaron	Cha-209
Genl Munfort	Wil-282	Solomon	Brt- 53	Chs Jr	Ora-133
Nathan	Pas-204	Sparkman	Brt- 50	Chs Sen	Ora-133
Richd	Mon- 50	Thos	Pas-203	Francis	Cha-209
Robt	Mon- 50	Thos	Cha-209	Jacob	Ran-180
Sally	Nor- 78	Uriah	L 341	Jacob	Ran-180
Silvanus	Cas- 69	William	Mon- 45	Jas Jr	Ora-134
Thomas	Fra- 98	William	Cum-263	John	Ran-180
Thos	Cha-193	William	Sur-196	John	Ran-181
Thos	Glf-175	William	Sur-187	Jonathan	Wil-272
Willm	Fra- 98	William	Sur-186	Jonathan	Ran-180
Wm	Mon- 43	Willm N	Fra- 91	Joseph Sen	Ora-133
Wm B	Cha-192	Wm	Cab-148	Josh	Ran-180
Stokton,Douty	Sto-132	Zedekaih	Brt- 67	Nelly	Row- 44
Stoll,William E	Rth-131	Stoner,John A	Row- 79	Peter Jr	Ora-133
Stone,Alexr	Cha-198	Michl	Row- 78	Peter Sen	Ora-133
Anderson	Per-144	Peter	Row- 78	Saml	Ran-180
Asey	Cha-213	Peter	Ora-133	Sol	Ora-133
Benjamin	Cum-262	Stonesipher,E	Ash- 6	Wm	Cha-209
Benjn	Brt- 52	S	Ash- 6	Zac	Row- 44
Burges	Roc- 3	Stonestreet,Margat	Row- 60	Stover,Francis	Sto-130
Cornelus	Prq-226	Stonstreet,Butler	Ire-247	Francis	Sto- 99
Cutberth	Wil-259	Elisha	Row- 60	Stow,Abraham	Sur-173
Daniel State	Cur- 81	Stores,R	Cam-162	Abraham	Sto-128
David	Rob-224	Stork,Charles	Row- 70	Andrew	Mon- 48
Edward	Brt- 49	Storm,Jno	Rob-219	Andrew	Mon- 48
Enoch	Sur-174	Samuel	Rob-219	John	Sur-189
Epp	Cas- 69	Stornsill,Jesse	Mec- 29	Stowe,Abram	Lnc-329
Francis	Cha-208	Story,A	Mon- 36	Dinyl	Cur- 79
Henry	Bur-130	Andrew	Bun- 82	Jacob	Lnc-329
Isaac	Prq-226	Ben	Mec- 29	Jeremiah	Cur- 81
James	Sur-163	Clary	Wil-284	Wm	Cur- 82
James	Ons-108	Daniel	Ans- 15	Stowed,William	Rth-135
James	Sur-186	Geo	Bun- 82	Stowers,John	Cas- 75
Jas	Rob-242	J	Mon- 34	Stowvall,Fedrick	Cas- 70
Jas	Rob-223	James	Mon- 31	J	Ora-148
Jesse	Cha-210	James	Cha-198	Strader,A	Glf-178
Jno P	Ans- 16	Jas	Mec- 29	H	Glf-178
John	Cha-190	Jesse	Wil-274	Strain,Alex	Ora-125
John	Sur-180	Jessee	Nor- 77	Dav	Ora-122
John	Sto- 91	John	Cha-198	David	Ora-156
John	Per-144	Mary	Bft- 38	David	Ora-142
John	Pas-203	Rachel	Cum-251	John	Ora-142

Name	Ref	Name	Ref	Name	Ref
Strainge,Owin	Row- 87	Strickland,Elias	Rob-232	Strider,Jacob	Ran-181
Straly,Gottlieb	Sto-154	J----	Way-241	Strinfield,Joseph	Dup- 21
Strange,Charrity	Ons-105	Jacob	Rob-232	Stringer,Geo	Mon- 47
James	Roc- 4	John	Way-240	J	Ash- 5
John	Ons- 98	Joseph	Way-240	John	Rch-197
Julius	Row- 87	Josiah	Rth-135	Stringfellow,Enoch	Rch-202
William	Roc- 21	Kinsman	Fra- 81	William	Rch-202
Wm	Row- 39	Lewis	Rob-229	Strong,James	Roc- 12
Strater,John G	Sto-146	Nathan	Nor- 77	John	Roc- 33
Strather,Peter	Cas- 70	Obediah	Fra- 81	John Sen	Roc- 88
Stratton,Benjamin	Roc- 12	Sampson	Fra- 82	Nathan K	Cho-222
John	Roc- 9	Stricklen,Lott	Ans- 29	Sneed	Roc- 7
William	Roc- 28	Strickler,Alexander	Bur-126	Zachariah	Roc- 8
Straughan,Alix	Bla- 12	Wm	Ans- 23	Stroop,Adam	Sto-130
Straughn,Fielding	Cha-213	Stricklin,Absalom	Cum-245	Saml	Sto-130
Isaiah	Cha-202	Archebald	Rch-207	Samuel	Sto- 99
John	Cha-194	Benjamin	Joh-281	Strother,Alex	Lnc-340
Reuben	Cha-191	Elisabeth	Rch-211	Catp James	Fra- 85
Richd	Cha-191	Harman	Sam-161	Stroud,Christr	Ire-244
Steven	Cha-206	Harman	Jon-304	David	Bur-117
Tapley	Cha-210	Holley	Sam-162	George	Grn-129
Strawbridge,Wm	Mar- 15	Isaac	Sam-155	Hannah	Dup- 28
Strawn,Crispin	Cha-202	John	Sam-160	John	Ora-165
Larkin	Sur-162	John	Hal-120	Lewis	Len-319
Strawther,Jno	Ans- 31	John	Jon-304	Peter	Bur-117
Strayhon,Gilbert	Ora-143	John	Rch-209	Peter Jr	Bur-117
Wm	Ora-143	John Senr	Sam-162	Richard	Ire-269
Strayhorn,C	Ora-148	Joseph	Joh-288	Thomas	Ire-244
David	Ora-168	Lazarus	Hal-119	Stroup,Adam	Lnc-375
G	Ora-144	Marmaduke	Hal-119	Daniel	Lnc-375
James	Ora-168	Marmaduke	Jon-304	David	Lnc-375
Jno	Ora-144	Mary	Hal-120	Jacob	Lnc-341
W Junr	Ora-144	Matthew	Dup- 8	John	Lnc-375
Wm	Ora-128	Matthew	Sam-151	Joseph	Bun- 83
Strayhorne,Jas	Ora-158	Richd	Dup- 8	Michael	Lnc-375
Street,Anthony	Rth-134	Robt	Sam-156	Phillip	Lnc-375
Edwd	Dup- 22	Saml	Sam-160	Strowd,Anderson	Ora-125
John Esq	Ora-111	Saml	Joh-282	John	Ora-115
Moses	Per-144	Thomas	Hal-120	William	Sur-195
Nimrod	Rth-132	Thos	Sam-160	Strown,Ailsey	Cur- 82
Peter	Lnc-371	Uriah	Joh-281	Strube,John	Cab-138
R	Ora-139	Strickling,Arnal	Nsh- 85	Struckler,Taylor	Edg- 59
Richd	Mor- 54	Ausborn	Nsh- 84	Strudwick,Martha	Ora-126
Simon	Rth-134	Burrel	Nsh- 91	Strukten,Abraham	Ans- 26
Will	Dup- 23	D	Col- 18	Strum,Bartholw	Grn-141
William	Per-144	Elie	Nsh- 86	Christian	Grn-121
Streeter,Edward	Ans- 6	Giddion	Nsh- 85	Ezekiah	Grn-121
Wm	Ans- 29	Hardy	Nsh- 88	Strunk,D	Ash- 13
Streety,Wm	Bla- 3	Ishamel	Nsh- 85	Struther,Christian	Cas- 69
Stricker,Daniel	Cab-139	J	Col- 18	David	Cas- 69
Stricklan,Jesse	Cum-267	Joseph	Nsh- 79	Struttan,Hezekiah	Wil-276
Nathan	Joh-290	Lazrus	Nsh- 91	Joel	Wil-275
Thos	Mec- 48	Lazrus	Nsh- 91	Reuben	Wil-279
Strickland,Aaron	Way-248	Lazrus	Nsh- 91	Strutton,Absalom	Bur-125
Alsy	Nor- 77	Mark	Nsh- 85	Stuard,James	Grn-129
Aron	Rob-232	Noer	Nsh- 89	John	Grn-129
Brazilla	Fra- 81	Osborn	Nsh- 86	William	Cur- 89
Brinkley	Fra- 81	P	Col- 18	Stuart,Alexr	Cum-255
Britton	Way-248	Simson	Nsh- 85	Alexr	Cum-267

Name	Code	Name	Code	Name	Code
Stuart,Charles	Car-177	Stults,Adam	Sto-100	Suddith,William	Bur-107
Daniel	Mor- 64	Adam	Sto-131	Sugars,Jasper	Cho-222
Daniel	Cum-252	Casper	Sto-100	Sugart,John	Sur-177
Daniel	Cum-244	Casper	Sto-129	Zachariah	Sur-192
David	Row- 68	Casper	Sto-131	Sugers,Leonard	Sur-191
David	Cum-256	Daniel	Sto-153	Sugg,Harbert	Mon- 33
Dugard	Cha-191	Henry	Sto-151	Isaac	Mon- 33
Duncan	Cum-253	Henry	Sto-129	Jno	Mon- 33
Ephraim	Roc- 30	John	Sto-100	John	Mon- 21
Francis	Car-182	John	Sto-131	Peter	Pit-254
George	Roc- 11	John	Sto-129	Thos	Mon- 33
George	Cum-257	John	Sto-129	Wm	Mon- 33
Hector	Cum-266	Katharine	Sto-152	Suggs,A	Bru-222
James	Per-153	Philip	Sto-107	Alagood	Bla- 8
John	Hay-201	Philip	Sto-142	Curtis	Rob-236
John	Hay-201	Stunfield,Saml	Glf-168	George A	Edg- 69
John	Roc- 25	Sturdevant,Edward	Pit-238	J	Col- 19
John	Mon- 20	Sturdivant,Anderson	Hal-118	Jas	Rob-236
John	Cum-256	Benjamin	War-169	John	Bla- 12
John	Cum-253	Edmond	Hal-119	Josh	Len-321
Joseph	Cum-261	Lucy	Hal-118	Reading	Edg- 41
Joseph	Mon- 19	Sturgell,F	Ash- 12	Sarah	Rob-243
Norman	Cum-243	J	Ash- 9	Wm	Bla- 11
Peyton	Row- 89	J	Ash- 7	Sugs,A	Col- 19
Rachel	Car-177	J	Ash- 4	Leban	Lnc-336
Ranald	Cum-255	R	Ash- 4	Solomon	Mor- 67
Reuben	Cum-256	W	Ash- 9	Uriah	Dup- 19
Robert	Row- 68	Sturgeon,Henry	Mec- 35	Suit,John	Grn-126
Robert	Roc- 6	Jno	Mec- 49	Polly	War-178
S	Cum-237	Sturtz,Nicholas	Bur-114	Rebekah	Hal-119
Samuel	Sto-152	Stuther,William	Bun- 91	Suite,William	Cas- 69
Silas	Mon- 20	Stutt,T	Bru-236	Suits,C	Glf-179
Thomas	Per-133	Stuttle,Anthony	Lnc-333	Christian	Wil-266
Thomas	Sto-152	Benjamin	Rth-133	Jacob	Glf-175
Wm	Mon- 19	Stutts,Christopher	Mor- 59	Sulevant,John	Row- 85
Stubbins,Jo	Ora-116	Henry	Mor- 59	Sulgrove,James	Glf-167
Stubblefield,Carter	Roc- 16	Jacob	Mor- 59	Sulifin,Alexr	Mec- 46
Hugh	Roc- 15	Lenard	Mor- 58	Wm	Mec- 47
Richard	Roc- 15	Styron,Amasa	Car-173	Wm	Mec- 49
Wyett	Cas- 70	Christopher	Car-172	Sulivan,James	Lnc-334
Stubbs,Archibald	Wsh-216	Frnas	Car-175	Joseph	Mor- 67
G	Col- 17	George	Car-173	Saml	Lnc-334
George	Wsh-225	James	Car-174	Sulleighead,S	Ora-154
J	Col- 20	John	Car-174	Sullen,John	Glf-167
J	Col- 17	John Junr	Car-174	Sullers,Willis	Ora-121
James	Wsh-223	John Senr	Car-174	Sullins,Zachariah	Rth-134
Levi	Bft- 22	Lasan	Bft- 35	Sullivan,Mrs	Cum-239
Micajah	Wsh-223	Lemuel	Car-173	Azel	Glf-156
Richd	Bla- 9	Lemuel	Car-179	C	Glf-172
William	Hyd-223	Sabra	Car-173	D	Glf-172
William	Wsh-222	Simon	Car-174	Daniel	Lnc-371
Wm	Bft- 23	Styers,Samuel	Sto-103	Daniel	Bur-121
Studdard,B	Glf-179	Styles,Zaccheus	Fra- 99	Danl	Bru-238
William	Sto-102	Styner,Jacob	War-184	Dukson	Dup- 24
William	Sto-134	Stype,Henry	Sto-144	E	Bru-232
Studdevent,Randel	Ran-180	Styres,Samuel	Sto-137	F	Bru-228
Studivent,Thos	Cha-205	Samuel	Sto-103	G B	Bru-230
Studman,John	Rth-132	Suddith,Alex	Bur-130	George	Sto-147
Joseph	Rth-135	Tho	Bur-130	Hampton Jr	Dup- 26

Name	Loc	Name	Loc	Name	Loc
Sullivan,Jas	Glf-158	Summerset,J	Col- 21	Sutherland,T	Ash- 9
John	Lnc-335	Selah	Ons-108	Sutliff,Jo	Row- 50
M	Bru-222	Summerville,John	Nor- 78	Suton,King	Cho-221
Maee	Bft- 25	Samuel	Nor- 77	Sutten,Groge	Nsh- 83
Martha	Bru-222	Summit,Christian	Lnc-353	Sutter,John	Row- 80
Milly	Dup- 15	Francis	Lnc-353	Lott	Row- 80
R	Bru-232	Francis	Lnc-349	Sutterweigh,Chas	Cha-216
Saml Jr	Glf-158	Jacob	Lnc-361	Suttin,Campbell	Sto-134
Samuel	Glf-156	Summy,Christopher	Bun- 73	Suttle,Bushrod	Rth-133
Smith	Glf-157	Frederick	Lnc-371	Henry	Rth-132
Sol	Glf-158	Jacob	Row- 79	Isaac	Rth-132
Stephen	Glf-171	Sumner,Charlotte	Nor- 77	Joseph	Rth-132
Thomas	Sto-109	Edwin	Nor- 77	Joseph	Rth-132
Thomas	Sto-151	James	Nor- 77	Reuben	Wil-268
Thos	Ora-167	James	Prq-226	Suttlemire,Jacob	Bur-129
Wm	Glf-156	James B	Gat-107	Suttles,George	Rth-132
Wm	Row- 43	Jethro	Gat-110	Robert	Rth-132
Zachariah	Hal-118	Jethro	Gat-116	Thomas	Bur-113
Sullivant,Drury	Fra- 83	Lucy	Nor- 77	Sutton,---eby	Rth-133
Isaac	Ans- 12	Luke	Hrt-214	Anthony	Ons- 98
Owen	Nsh- 87	Lurany	Ons-101	Beman	Bla- 13
Sulliven,Martin	Brt- 59	Mary	Cho-227	Benja	Len-311
Sullivent,Whitney	Ran-180	Matthew	Dup- 32	Benjamin	Pit-255
Sumerill,Faithy	Edg- 70	Moses	Hrt-215	Catharine	Nsh- 84
Sumerlin,James	Len-320	Richard	Bun- 80	Christopher	Bla- 5
Tho	Len-323	Susanna	Gat-108	David	Pit-255
Sumers,Maning	Sur-172	William	Hrt-215	Dumpsey	Grn-139
Waitmon	Sur-173	Sumpter,Henry	Bur-112	E	Bru-234
William	Sur-170	Thos	Mec- 55	Elias	Sam-163
Sumey,Michl	Row- 42	Sumro,Daniel	Lnc-371	F	Ora-139
Peter	Row- 42	Henry	Lnc-371	George	Prq-225
Summerhill,Eliz	Rth-135	Henry	Lnc-371	James	Sam-158
John	Rth-135	Michl	Lnc-345	James	Way-250
Summerlin,Allen	Dup- 26	Suquire,John	Rth-116	James	Cas- 70
Dennis	Dup- 26	Surat,Mary	Mon- 19	James	Cas- 70
Frederick	Dup- 26	Surgeoner,James	Rch-198	James	Cho-225
James	Dup- 26	John	Rch-212	Jas	Lnc-329
James Jr	Edg- 68	William	Rch-194	Jeremiah	Prq-225
Michl	Dup- 12	Surman,Isaac	Hyd-231	Jno	Len-311
Patsey	Pit-244	Joseph	Hyd-231	John	Rth-133
Susan	Brt- 67	Joseph Sr	Hyd-231	John	Len-316
Winburn	Wil-282	Peter	Hyd-230	John Junr	Bla- 5
Summers,Basil	Ire-242	Surrat,E----	Per-153	John Sr	Prq-224
Basil	Ire-265	Jenny	Wil-279	Joseph	Sam-154
Benjamin	Ire-244	Surratt,Abel	Row- 83	Joseph E	Prq-224
Charles	Ire-258	Absolam	Row- 83	Lemuel	Wsh-228
F	Glf-178	Jonathan	Row- 83	P	Ora-139
Jacob	Ora-132	Thomas	Row- 83	Peggy	Bft- 31
Jno	Ora-120	Suter,John	Roc- 19	Philip	Bun- 96
M	Ora-145	John	Nor- 77	Philip Junr	Bun- 96
Nancy	Ire-265	Lucy	Nor- 78	Richard	War-179
Paul	Wil-280	Mildred	Nor- 77	Samuel	Prq-225
Peter	Glf-178	William E	Roc- 29	Simeon	Dup- 26
Rachel	Ire-244	Sutes,Abereham	Cur- 85	Susana	Len-313
Sally	Ire-266	Elisebeth	Cur- 85	Susanna	Row- 88
Thomas	Sur-164	Sutherland,J	Ash- 7	Tho	Ora-165
William	Sto-154	James	Hal-120	Tho	Bft- 29
William J	Ire-266	John	Way-234	Thomas	Brt- 45
Zachariah	Ire-244	John	Grn-123	Thos	Prq-225

-308-

Sutton,Thos Junr	Sam-154	Swan,James	Row- 71	Swett,George	Sur-183
Thos Senr	Sam-154	Jesse	Row- 63	J	Bru-238
Vinson	Nsh- 82	John	Cas- 69	William Jr	Sur-178
William	Rth-132	Mathew	Row- 71	William Sr	Sur-183
William	Rth-132	Moses	Mec- 26	Swift,A George	Cas- 70
William	Brt- 66	Moses	Lnc-342	Anthony	Cas- 69
William	Len-321	R	Glf-161	E	Ash- 6
William R	Prq-225	Rolin	Row- 59	Flower	Ran-180
Wm	Mon- 19	Samuel	Rth-134	Francis	Cas- 70
Wm Senr	Bla- 13	Sarah	Ire-244	John	Cas- 70
Swafford,Jas	Ran-181	Thomas	Cas- 69	Joshua	Wsh-221
Swaim,Jesse	Sto-143	Thomas	Ire-244	Major	Bru-234
Jonathan	Sto-136	Thomas	Row- 72	S	Ash- 6
Michael	Wil-282	W	Cam-165	Sarah	Cas- 70
Moses	Sto-143	William	Cas- 69	Swain	Wsh-221
William	Sto-136	William S	Row- 75	Thomas	Cas- 70
Swain,Abraham	Tyr-206	Zephaniah	Ire-244	Thos	Ran-180
Andrew	Bur-117	Swaner,Henry	Mar- 13	Swift's M Soldiers	Bru-234
Anneretta	Brt- 58	Joel	Cha-211	Swilly,Zenos	Jon-305
Benjn	Tyr-212	William Senr	Mar- 12	Swilson,Palmore	Ran-181
C	Bru-238	Swaney,Jas	Ran-181	Swim,Al	Glf-156
Eleakim	Tyr-213	John	Bun- 98	Ashley	Ran-181
Eleazer	Wsh-220	Lida	Ran-181	Cher	Ran-181
Elias	Tyr-203	Thos	Ran-181	Enoch	Bun- 87
Geo	Glf-152	Swann,Benj	Cas- 69	Jas	Ran-181
George	Bun- 94	Dorcas	Mec- 51	John	Ran-181
J	Glf-183	Edward	Cas- 69	John	Ran-181
J	Glf-183	Jno	Mec- 50	Levi	Bun- 87
J	Bru-228	John	Cas- 69	M	Glf-154
J	Bru-238	Joseph	Mec- 49	M	Glf-157
J	Bru-228	Joseph	Mec- 27	M D	Ran-181
James	Tyr-204	Joseph	Cas- 70	Marmaduke	Glf-156
James	Mar- 11	Wm	Mec- 49	Michael	Sur-166
James	Mar- 9	Swanner,Jesse	Bft- 25	Moses	Sur-166
Jessee	Tyr-212	Jesse Jun	Bft- 26	Silas	Row- 80
John	Tyr-203	John	Bft- 27	Wm	Glf-154
John	Mar- 10	William	Mar- 14	Wm	Glf-161
John	Wsh-222	Swanson,Elijah	Fra- 85	Wm	Glf-161
Joseph Jr	Tyr-212	John	Wil-281	Swindal,J	Col- 17
Joseph Sr	Tyr-212	William	Wil-281	M	Col- 20
Joshua	Tyr-210	Swarengen,George	Ran-180	A Esq	Col- 20
Kussy	Bur-119	Swaringam,Eliza	Mon- 40	Swindell,Benj	Hyd-225
Lemuel	Wsh-221	Swath,John	Cur- 86	Benjamin	Hyd-226
Lydia	Wsh-222	Swatheander,Philip	Row- 61	Christiana	Hyd-229
Paul	Ire-253	Sweany,Barnabaa	Bla- 4	Foster	Hyd-226
Peter S	Wsh-221	Mial	Joh-278	Fredrick	Hyd-226
Richd	Brt- 58	Searingam,Elijah	Mon- 40	Hardy	Hyd-229
S	Glf-183	Swearingham,Van	Lnc-333	Jacob	Hyd-225
Simon	Wsh-222	Swearingin,Samuel	Hay-201	Joel	Hyd-229
Stevens Junr	Wsh-221	Sweat,Abraham	Hal-120	John	Hyd-230
Stevens Senr	Wsh-221	Delilah	Hal-120	Jonathan	Hyd-228
T	Wsh-220	Virtue	Row- 63	Joseph	Hyd-226
Thomas	Wsh-220	William	Nor- 78	Margryt	Hyd-229
Whitmell	Brt- 53	Sweatman,Will	Dup- 23	Robert	Hyd-227
Swaine,James	Cho-221	Sweeten,Charles	Wil-284	Silas	Hyd-227
Swainey,Daniel	Hay-200	Sweney,Darbey Esq	Rch-211	Vallentine	Hyd-230
Swan,Asa	Ire-244	Swenney,Bryant	Row- 80	Volentine	Hyd-226
Charles	Row- 76	Swett,Edward	Sur-178	Wade	Hyd-226
James	Bun- 74	Edward Sr	Sur-184	William	Hyd-229

Name	Loc	Name	Loc	Name	Loc
Swindell,William Jr	Hyd-228	Sykes,Joseph Senr	Bla- 13	Tage,Moses	Row- 46
Willis	Hyd-230	Kinchen	Nor- 77	Taggert,Thos	Bur-121
Willis	Bla- 9	Mary	Bla- 13	Tague,Emma	Ire-264
Swindle,C	Ora-146	Samuel	Prq-225	Francis	Ire-264
Chris	Ora-118	Thomas	Nor- 77	Michael	Sur-186
John	Roc- 32	Thos	Bla- 13	Tailor,Andrew	Rth-136
Swing,Conrad	Glf-155	William Jr	Nor- 77	Taite,Caswell	Cas- 72
J	Glf-177	William Senr	Nor- 78	Sarah	Cas- 72
Swink,Christian	Row- 76	Syler,Benj	Mor- 56	William	Cas- 72
Daniel	Row- 78	Wymer	Bun- 74	Zepheniah	Cas- 72
George	Row- 76	Symon,Peter	Cab-145	Talbert,Pheby	Nsh- 76
George	Row- 76	Symond,Henry	Cab-143	Thomas	Per-144
Henry	Row- 77	Symons,Abm	Pas-203	Talbot,Jesse	Ran-182
John	Bur-105	Ben	Pas-206	Joshua	Sur-169
Peter	Row- 37	Isaac	Pas-204	Josiah	Ran-183
Swinney,Daniel	Row- 60	Jehosaphae	Pas-203	Talbott,John	Glf-168
Isaiah	Edg- 59	Jacob	Pas-203	Talent,Aaron	Lnc-339
Swinnry,Austin	Dup- 14	Jesse	Pas-203	Taliaferro,Chas	Sur-160
Swinny,Edmon	Sur-189	Penny	Pas-203	Talkum,Joseph	Row- 64
Jno	Per-133	Tony	Pas-203	Tall,J	Ash- 4
Levi	Per-133	Willm	Pas-204	Tallant,Richd	Ans- 31
Robt	Per-133			Taller,Benjamin	Nor- 78
Swinson,Eben	Dup- 8	Tabb,James	Row- 75	Eli	Nor- 78
Jesse	Dup- 15	Thos	Row- 40	James	Nor- 78
John	Bla- 12	Vincent	Row- 65	Priscilla	Nor- 78
John	Dup- 9	Taber,Elijah	Rth-136	Talley,Reuben	Grn-146
John A	Dup- 26	Elisha	Rth-137	Sterlg	Ora-112
Richard	Wsh-222	Elizabeth	Rth-136	William	Wil-270
Richd	Dup- 29	Elizabeth	Rth-137	Talleys,Andrew	Wil-260
Theophilus	Dup- 8	Jonathan	Rth-137	Tally,Fedk	Cha-202
Swisegood,Adam	Row- 81	Mary	Rth-136	Frederick	War-171
Andrew	Row- 81	Robert	Rth-136	Geo	Mon- 45
Philip	Row- 81	Thomas	Rth-136	Henry	War-172
Swisher,G	Glf-178	Taborn,Burrel	Nsh- 92	Joel	War-175
J	Glf-178	Burton	Grn-145	Jos	Mec- 34
Jacob	Row- 76	Sollomon	Nsh- 92	Jos & Scott	Mec- 34
Swisler,Robert	Bur-110	Tabourn,Wm	Grn-140	Rachell	War-179
Syales,H	Mon- 42	Wm Jr	Grn-140	Thomas	War-181
Syhorn,David	Car-176	Taburn,Henry col	Fra-101	Talor,Arabold	Sur-186
Sykes,Anne	Nor- 77	Tacker,Jacob	Row- 45	Henry	Per-153
Briton	Nor- 77	John	Row- 45	Luke	Sur-188
Crecia	Hal-118	S	Glf-166	Matthew	Sur-182
Fanny	Hal-119	Tacket,William	Row- 87	Talton,Cullen	Joh-284
Harbert	Len-315	Tackett,Wm	Ora-124	Hardy	Joh-284
Isaiah	Bla- 10	Tader,Wm	Hrt-209	Nancy	Joh-291
Israel	Bla- 7	Tadlock,Absalom	Brt- 67	Needham	Joh-284
J	Bla- 13	Absalum	Prq-226	Sally	Joh-291
J	Bla- 12	Demcy	Prq-226	William	Joh-284
Jacob	Hal-120	James	Pas-207	Taltoul,Jonathan	Rth-137
James	Bla- 13	James	Prq-226	Tamar (sic)	Pas-206
James	Hal-120	Jesse	Prq-227	Tamplin,E	Cam-155
Jas	Ora-159	Joseph	Ran-182	Taner,John Jr	Sur-181
Jethroe	Nor- 77	Joshua	Prq-227	Taney,Aaron	Wil-275
Jno	Ora-122	Miles	Prq-226	Taneys,William	Hay-201
John	Prq-225	Tabitha	Way-239	Tanglessan,John	Sto-150
John Jr	Tyr-208	Taff,Elias	Pit-233	Tangulsan,Eli	Sto- 91
John Senr	Tyr-208	Taford,Samuel	Cum-253	Tanhesly,Charles	Bun- 73
John Senr	Bla- 13	Taft,Meritt	Tyr-203	Tankard,Geo	Bft- 22
Joseph	Nor- 77	Tagart,John	Cab-139	Tanner,Daniel	Rth-136

Tanner,Dorcas	War-170	Tarr,Christian	Row- 89	Tatom,Jesse	Bla- 10
Frederick	Sur-191	Melcher	Row- 42	Labin	Sam-164
Frederick J	Sur-190	Tarry,James	Cha-203	Nathaniel	Bun- 78
Howell	Nor- 78	Saml	Cha-193	R	Col- 18
Jacob	Sto-126	Tart,Eneas	Edg- 65	William	Car-174
John	Sur-181	James	Brt- 61	William	Sto-100
John	Cab-138	John	Joh-289	William	Sam-152
Josep	Car-175	N L Est of	Edg- 65	Tatum,Berry	Cur- 88
Joseph	Bur-118	Nathan	Brt- 61	Caleb	Cur- 88
Joseph	Nor- 79	Nathan	Edg- 42	Daniel	Cur- 88
Margaret	Cab-138	Thomas	Sam-161	Ed	Glf-166
Michael	Rth-136	Thomas Junr	Sam-161	Ed Jr	Glf-166
Peter	Sur-191	Tarter,John	Bur-130	Halowell	Cur- 91
Samuel	Nor- 78	John	Bur-130	Harteack	Glf-188
Susannah	Nor- 78	Tarver,Billingsley	Ans- 32	Henry	Hal-121
Tail	Sot- 97	Micajah	Ans- 30	Henry	Glf-186
Tansel,Edward	Fra- 83	Michael	Asn- 32	John	Sto-100
Tansey,William	Sur-185	Samuel	Nor- 79	John	Cur- 88
Tansil,John	Fra- 83	Tash,Adam	Row- 48	Jonathan	Glf-160
Tap,George	Per-144	Goerge	Row- 49	Nathan	Cur- 87
Lewis	Per-144	John	Row- 50	Sihor	Glf-185
Vincent	Per-144	Taskonton,Zebulon	Tyr-205	William	Cur- 91
William	Per-144	Tate,A	Glf-179	Taunt,Abram	Lnc-348
Tapley,Mason	Ora-119	David	Bur-102	Andrew	Lnc-348
William	Cas- 72	Francis	Hal-120	George	Lnc-348
Taply,Henry	Ran-182	Geo	Ora-136	Mary	Bft- 27
James	Ran-182	George	Roc- 18	Sion	Fra-100
Tapp,Abner	Ora-113	Hugh	Bur-104	Taunton,John	Glf-162
Taprest,William	Cas- 72	J J C	Ora-154	Taurus,Lodwick	Grn-126
Tapscott,Educy	Cas- 72	James	Ora-121	Taw,Joseph	Per-226
Henry Jr	Cas- 72	James Jnr	Ora-163	Tax,Saml	Sto-151
Henry Sr	Cas- 72	James Sr	Ora-163	Tayborne,Allen	Nor- 79
Tar,Agnis	Ora-170	Jos of Wm	Ora-173	Nathan	Nor- 79
Henry	Row- 85	Joseph	Bur-114	Wyatt	Nor- 79
Tarber,Samuel	Joh-272	Owen	Sur-182	Tayler,Samuel	Sto-152
Tarbutton,Joseph	Mon- 31	Randall	Rth-137	Tayloe,Ann	Brt- 52
Joseph	Rch-198	Robert	Ora-167	Richard	Mar- 8
Taretels,C	Glf-165	Robert	Sto-150	Taylor,A	Col- 17
Tarkenton,Benj	Wsh-218	Robert	Sto-156	Abel	Cas- 72
Isaac	Tyr-213	Samuel	Sur-181	Abm	Lnc-335
Joseph	Per-227	Samuel	Rth-137	Abraham	Mec- 27
William	Wsh-217	Thos	Ora-118	Abraham	Edg- 43
William	Wsh-220	W	Ora-140	Abs	Lnc-334
Zebedee	Wsh-218	Wm	Bur-103	Aily	Dup- 24
Tarkinton,Easter	Tyr-213	Wm	Glf-178	Alexander	Cas- 72
Enoch	Wsh-219	Tatem,Betsy	Pas-206	Allen	Edg- 44
John	Tyr-210	Tates,Caleb	Cur- 87	Amos	Rob-221
Joseph	Tyr-206	Jaocb	Cab-148	Ann	Ons-106
Susanna	Wsh-221	James	Cur- 84	Ann	Pit-263
Tarlington,Israel	Sam-150	John	Cab-143	Ann	Hrt-215
Sarah	Brt- 65	Methias	Cur- 84	Arthur	Mon- 48
Tarlon,Thos	Ans- 6	Peter	Cab-148	Arthur	Nsh- 88
Abner	Ans- 12	Samuel	Pit-263	Benj	Cur- 86
Britton	Ans- 27	Sarey	Cur- 84	Benjamin	Nor- 78
D	Ora-157	Tatham,Thomas	Hay-201	Benjamin	Lnc-353
James	Ire-264	Tatom,Dickson	Sam-164	Berry	Mon- 39
Jno	Ans- 12	Edward	Sto-100	Betsey	Cur- 79
Wm	Ans- 11	G	Ora-157	Blake	Rob-220
Tarr,Ben	Nsh- 92	Haley	Row- 39	Boyakin	Fra- 99

-311-

Taylor,Bytha	Edg- 53	Taylor,J		Cam-165	Taylor,John		Mar- 12
Charles	Grn-145	J		Cam-159	John		Mar- 4
Chas	Ans- 9	J		Ash- 13	John		Rch-202
Chr	Len-315	J		Ash- 13	John		Rch-194
Cornelius	Nsh- 83	J		Col- 17	John		Nsh- 90
D	Bla- 10	Jacob		Lnc-353	John		Lnc-368
Daniel	Nsh- 83	Jacob		Cum-237	John		Lnc-349
Daniel McLeon	Cum-244	James		War-175	John		Bla- 10
Danl	Bla- 7	James		Roc- 16	John		Cho-225
David	Hal-120	James		Roc- 32	John		Nsh- 84
Davis	Cab-144	James		Pit-262	John	Eno	Ora-117
Dempsey	Dup- 25	James		Len-318	John Harper		Roc- 26
Dempsey	Roc- 3	James		Rth-136	John McRae		Cum-269
Dempsey	Nor- 78	James		Brt- 66	John Jnr		Grn-141
Demsey	Nsh- 75	James		Nor- 78	John Junr		Bun- 77
Demsey	Nsh- 91	James		Hyd-228	John Shaw		Cum-259
Demsey	Nsh- 86	James		Cas- 72	John Sr		Way-236
Dormon	Cas- 72	James		Cas- 72	John Snr		Grn-141
Edmond	Grn-136	James		Mar- 12	Jonathan		Ans- 15
Edmond	Ire-258	James		Ire-256	Jonathan Jr		Way-241
Edney	Cur- 86	James		Cha-215	Jonathan Sr		Way-242
Edward	Nsh- 80	James D		Roc- 31	Joseph		Gat-110
Edwd	Mon- 20	Jas		Bft- 28	Joseph		Roc- 32
Eleanor	Len-314	Jas		Cho-225	Joseph		Len-316
Elijah	Ons- 99	Jas		Bft- 32	Joseph		Dup- 29
Elisha	Pit-244	Jas		Rob-237	Joseph		Car-185
Elizabeth	Jon-305	Jeremiah		Pit-245	Joseph		Per-153
Elizabeth	Glf-188	Jesse		Bur-112	Joseph		Edg- 69
Elza	Edg- 43	Jesse		Gat-109	Joseph Jr		Grn-133
Ezecial	Rob-240	Jesse		Ons-105	Joseph S		Cab-149
Fort	Nsh- 89	Jesse		Len-320	Joseph Sr		Way-236
Capt Francis	Fra- 87	Jesse		Rth-136	Joseph Sr		Grn-145
Franskey	Cur- 88	Jessee		Edg- 55	Joshua		Car-180
Fred	Ora-116	Jno		Mec- 25	Joshua		Lne-313
Frederick	Ans- 22	Jno miller		Ora-143	Joshua		Edg- 43
Fredk	Lnc-348	Jno Sen		Ora-130	Joshua		Edg- 43
G	Cam-159	John		Bur-105	Joshua		Mar- 3
Gemima	Lnc-316	John		Cur- 92	Josiah		Cur- 88
George	Sam-157	John		Row- 63	Josiah		Pas-206
George	Hrt-215	John		Roc- 16	Josiah		Sto-119
George	Ora-143	John		Glf-159	Josiah		Jon-305
George	Ora-112	John		Pas-207	Josiah		Rob-242
George	Sto-139	John		Pit-244	Josua		Rth-136
George	Cas- 72	John		Pit-244	Keziah		Hal-120
George (Gs R)	Wil-266	John		Ora-112	Keziah		Hal-121
George Senr	Wil-279	John		Len-318	Kinchen		Hrt-207
Gilbert	Rob-232	John		Rth-136	Kinchen		Mar- 5
Harras	Rob-237	John		Rth-137	Kinchen		Nsh- 75
Henry	Nor- 79	John		Edg- 53	Kit		Nsh-644
Henry	Rob-243	John		Edg- 43	Lemuel		Rob-237
Hillery	Cho-228	John		Dup- 29	Lewis		Rth-137
Hudson	Mon- 39	John		Bun- 77	Lewis Jr		Grn-131
Hudson	Hal-121	John		Nor- 78	Lewis Senr		Grn-131
Isaac	Hrt-210	John		Ran-183	M		Cam-165
Isaac	Sto-123	John		Cas- 72	M		Ash- 15
Isaac	Len-318	John		Hal-120	Malachi		Hal-121
Isaac	Sto- 94	John		Glf-185	Malicka		Hrt-207
Isaac	Ire-242	John		Cum-267	Manl		Bft- 28
Isaac Jr	Len-313						

Taylor,Margaret	Hal-121	Taylor,Tho	Ora-130	Taytom,John	Sto-131
Mary	Bft- 28	Tho	Ora-116	Thomas	Sto-131
Maxey	Cur- 86	Thomas	Edg- 53	Tatum,Edward	Sto-131
Merrill	Edg- 44	Thomas	Brt- 67	William	Sto-131
Micajah	Ans- 22	Thomas	Joh-284	Teabo,A	Bru-230
Micajah	Ans- 9	Thos	Cur- 88	Teachey,Timothy	Dup- 37
Miles	Pas-206	Thos	Grn-145	Timothy	Dup- 23
Mills	Grn-147	Thos	Bla- 3	Timothy Jr	Dup- 22
Mills	Rob-243	Thos	Cho-225	Teag,Abraham	Row- 50
Molly	Gat-110	Volentine	Lnc-369	Aron	Row- 48
Moses	Ons-105	W	Cam-165	Isaac	Row- 48
Moses	Len-319	W	Cam-164	Jacob	Row- 47
Nancey	Cur- 87	Warner	Grn-129	James	Row- 47
Nancy	Rth-137	Wilbey	Rob-237	Joab	Row- 50
Nathaniel	Gat-107	Wiley	Nsh- 85	John	Row- 48
Nathl	Grn-132	Will	Pas-206	John	Row- 44
Nehemiah	Pit-244	William	Gat-108	Moses	Row- 47
Nemiah	Ons-100	William	Car-181	Ruth	Row- 47
P	Mon- 42	William	Dup- 12	Teage,Ezekel	Row- 48
Patty	Nsh- 86	William	Cur- 86	Teague,David	Cha-195
Paul	Edg- 54	William	Row- 62	Edward	Bur-109
Penelope	Hrt-211	William	Roc- 31	Elisha	Bur-106
Polly	Cur- 86	William	Pit-261	George	Sto-127
Rachl	Bft- 39	William	Sto-104	Isaac	Mor- 62
Raney	Bft- 28	William	Sto-138	Isaac Esqr	Wil-275
Reubin	Edg- 55	William	Edg- 47	Isaac Sr	Cha-204
Reubin Sr	Cas- 72	William	Bun- 88	Jacob	Chs-203
Rheuben	Cur- 88	William	Cas- 72	James	Wa-195
Rhuben	Cur- 86	William	Cas- 72	John	Lns-264
Rhubin	Nsh- 79	William	Way-242	John	Sto-134
Richard	Grn-145	William	Way-237	John	Cha-203
Richard	Sto-138	William	Glf-188	John	Sto-102
Richard Jr	Edg- 53	William	Edg- 64	Joseph	Wil-278
Richard Sen	Edg- 53	William	Mar- 14	Magnue	Wil-278
Robbin	Cho-229	William	Ons- 97	Mary	Cha-204
Robert	Grn-131	William B	War-183	Moses	Mor- 66
Robert	Sto-145	William Senr	Cum-267	Moses	Bur-108
Robert	Rth-136	Willm (S)	Fra- 92	Nimrod	Lnc-351
Robert A	Fra- 87	Wm	Mon- 20	Solo. on	Ire-264
Robt	Ora-117	Wm	Mec- 27	Van	Lnc-350
Robt	Ora-176	Wm	Cab-144	William	Rch-209
S	Bru-238	Wm	Ora-161	William	Wil-278
S	Bru-234	Wm	Len-320	William	Sto-102
Mrs S	Cum-234	Wm	Ans- 14	William	Sto-134
Saml	Bur-104	Wm	Rob-240	Willis	Cha-194
Saml	Bft- 28	Wm	Nsh- 90	Teal,Jacob	Row- 70
Samuel	Fra- 95	Wm	Cho-225	Peter	Row- 70
Sanders	Ans- 21	Wm	Nsh- 92	Thomas	Cha-189
Sarah	Pas-207	Wm P	Grn-142	William	Joh-279
Sarah	Cha-192	Wm Snr	Mon- 20	Teale,Catherine	Pit-249
Sarah	Hal-121	Willis	Rob-240	Jacob	Pit-248
Sarey	Cur- 88	Wiloubey	Cur- 88	James	Pit-248
Shadrach	Len-316	Wilson	Hal-102	John	Pit-248
Simion	Nor- 79	Wilson	Nsh- 88	Joseph	Pit-248
Steph	Ora-176	Wilson Jr	Nsh- 87	Moses	Pit-249
Stephen	Edg- 64	Windal	Len-318	William	Pit-248
Stephen	Joh-284	Young	Ire-257	Teals,Alexr	Edg- 56
Teagle	Edg- 42	Zacheriah	Cur- 86	Teasley,Absam	Ora-164
Temple	Ire-257	Taytom,J	Ash- 11	Danl	Ora-174

-313-

Teasley,John	Ora-164	Templeton,John	Ire-261	Tetterton,Matthew	Wat-251
Teaster,Robert	Ire-244	John	Ire-261	William	Wsh-226
Samuel	Sur-165	John	Bur-118	Wm	Bft- 20
Tecaters,James	Cur- 91	Joseph	Ire-257	Teversan,Thomas	Cas- 72
Tedder,Benjamin	Rch-199	Robert	Ire-262	Tew,Joseph	Mec- 48
Dolly	Edg- 41	Robert	Ire-256	Thacker,Charles	Roc- 27
Elijah	Cum-257	Robert	Ire-246	Charles	Roc- 29
John	Cum-261	Robert	Ire-241	Thagget,George	Cum-247
Saml	Bla- 12	Thos	Lnc-331	Thally,Andrew	Dup- 20
Sion	Cum-261	Tenbough,Aaron	Grn-136	John Sr	Dup- 22
Wm	Bla- 12	Tendil,Joshua	Sam-155	Thames,Cornelius	Cum-247
Wm	Rob-227	Tennesson,Abraham	Bun- 93	David	Cum-248
Winny	Cum-261	Tennison,Benjamin	Row- 78	John	Cum-248
Teder,M	Col- 16	John	Cas- 72	John Junr	Cum-248
M	Col- 16	Lusy	Cas- 72	Joseph	Cum-247
Teel,Benjn	Ans- 30	Thomas	Edg- 48	William	Cum-247
Emanuel	Ans- 7	Tenpeny,Daniel	Row- 88	Thark,Aaron	Glf-182
Lod	Ans- 4	Richard	Row- 87	Tharp,C	Bru-224
Lewis	Ans- 10	Terock,Henry	Wsh-227	F	Bru-224
Richd	Ans- 10	Terpin,Thomas	Rth-136	Jas	Glf-181
Wm	Ans- 18	Terrance,Alexr	Cum-238	Jas	Glf-159
Wm	Ans- 23	Terrel,James	Cum-266	John	Bru-230
Wm	Ans- 29	Terrell,James L	Rth-136	John	Roc- 28
Wm	Ans- 32	Joel	Rth-136	John	Grn-142
Teem,Peter	Cab-141	Joel	War-184	Laban	Glf-159
Teet,Simon	Ans- 23	John	Grn-124	Polly	Sto-145
Teffreace,James	Row- 60	Terrentine,Saml	Ora-164	Polly	Joh-276
Tegars,Joshua	Cha-191	Terril,John	Cas- 72	Sary	Hyd-232
Telfair,David	Edg- 40	John	Grn-126	Thos	Glf-182
Hugh	Edg- 40	Jonathan	Cas- 72	Usly	Glf-183
Hugh	Pit-232	Terry,Benjamin	War-169	Wm Sr	Bru-230
Paulina	Edg- 46	Champnus	Rch-195	Tharpe,William	Ire-268
Temberlin,Edmund	Rth-136	David	War-170	Zadock	Ire-267
Lewis	Rth-135	Eli	Rch-210	Zais	Ire-268
Morris	Rth-135	James	Rch-198	Thatch,Judah	Prq-226
Temple,Allen	Cha-190	James	Rob-236	Rosanna	Prq ·226
Angilica	Pas-207	James	Grn-142	Spencer	Prq-226
Brittain	Pas-207	Jenny	War-174	Thatcherson,Amos	Glf-181
George	Ire-258	John	Hrt-215	Thermon,Milly	War-177
Harmon	Hrt-209	Joseph	Per-134	Therowgood,Paul	Tyr-203
J	Cam-165	Joseph	Sur-191	Therrel,Gable	Bur-130
James Jun	Pas-207	Mathew	Cas- 72	Therwendon,G	Ora-141
James Sen	Pas-207	Matthew	Rch-194	Thigpen,Dennis	Edg- 72
John	Cha-191	Nancey	Cas- 72	Etheldred	Edg- 72
Miriam	Pas-207	Peter	Roc- 7	Gilliad	Edg- 49
Robt	Pas-207	Roland	Grn-136	Isaiah	Edg- 50
Sam	Mon- 38	William	Rch-200	James	Cum-267
Saml	Cha-191	William	Rch-195	James	Edg- 70
Saml	Cha-201	William	Bun- 89	Joab	Dup- 35
Thomas	Pas-207	Zeb	Bft- 31	John	Cum-267
William	Car-182	Tervill,Eddy	Bur-125	John	Dup- 31
Woodall	Cha-200	Tessenden,Benj	Wsh-227	Joshua	Ons-101
Temples,Luke	Mor- 68	Tessler,J	Ash- 5	Samuel	Edg- 71
Robt	Brt- 47	Tester,Stephen	Cum-268	Wilie	Dup- 33
Templeton,David	Ire-245	Teter,Geo	Mon- 47	Thigpin,Ephrum	Nsh- 88
David	Bur-118	Tetman,John	Lnc-332	Thomaker,J	Glf-175
James	Ire-241	Tetterton,Jesse	Bft- 24	Thomans,James	Cur- 84
James	Bun- 78	Jos	Bft- 25	Labin	Cur- 84
John	Ire-258	Keziah	Bft- 35	Labin	Cur- 84

Thomas,A	Ora-144	Thomas,Henry	Cas- 72	Thomas,Joseph	Joh-281
Aaron	Bun- 76	Isaac	Rch-204	Josiah	Cas- 72
Adam	Roc- 33	Isaac J	Cab-136	Josiah	Fra- 86
Alex	Bft- 24	J	Col- 19	Josiah	Bft- 62
Alexdr	Row- 46	J	Col- 18	Josiah Jnr	Brt- 58
Allen	Cha-195	J	Col- 16	Josiah Senr	Brt- 58
Amos	Brt- 62	Jacob	Ans- 14	Lettice col	Fra-101
Anne	Rth-136	Jacob	Row- 79	Lewis	Rob-233
Arch	Dup- 30	Jacob	Edg- 62	Lewis	Sam-156
Arthur	Pit-244	Jacob	Joh-281	Lewis A	Dup- 30
Asa	Ans- 32	Jacob	Per-134	Louis	Rch-203
Asa	Cas- 72	Jacob	Ora-137	Luke	Glf-170
Athanatius	Fra- 95	James	Ora-117	M	Glf-178
Aunanias	Ans- 14	James	Ran-183	M	Ora-135
Bailam	Ans- 24	James	Cab-139	Macaijah	Mor- 57
Barnabee	Cha-192	Jas	Brt- 61	Martin	Cha-191
Barnet	Cha-191	Jas	Ora-137	Mary	Ora-170
Basdil col	Fra-100	Jane	Bla- 8	Mary	Edg- 46
Benj	Mor- 67	Jesse	Ora-159	Micaj	Ora-119
Benj E	Cum-235	Jesse	Cum-239	Midajah	Edg- 49
Benjamin	Edg- 49	Jesse	Mon- 30	Michael	Roc- 33
Benjamin	Glf-185	Jessee	Roc- 33	Minsey	Bun- 81
Benjn	Ans- 14	Jezabud	Edg- 49	Molley	Way-234
Benjn	Ans- 14	Jno	Ans- 24	Morning	Edg- 45
Catherine	Ora-136	Jno W	Ans- 24	Nancey	Cas- 72
Christopher	Cas- 75	John	Cum-235	Nanny	Ora-170
Coteney	Brt- 65	John	Bla- 12	Nathan	Mor- 54
D	Bla- 10	John	Edg- 49	Notty	Bur-105
Daniel	Rch-209	John	Rth-137	Organ	Fra- 90
Daniel	Cas- 72	John	Sto-145	Philip	Cum-258
Danl	Ora-144	John	Len-314	Mrs Phillis	Fra- 83
David	Cas- 72	John	Sto-155	Rebecca	Len-314
David	War-170	John	Joh-285	Richard	Edg- 68
Dempsey	Roc- 29	John	Rch-204	Richard	Roc- 13
Dora	Mer- 62	John	Ire-245	Robt	Ans- 32
E	Ora-147	John	Row- 79	Robt	Ans- 29
Edmond	Ans- 9	John	Row- 87	S	Col- 19
Edw	Ora-125	John	Cas- 72	Samuel	Per-134
Edy	Mon- 31	John	Cas- 72	Samuel	Car-171
Elias	Rob-238	John	Bun- 72	Sarah	Cho-222
Elijah	Roc- 19	John	Fra- 83	Shaderick	Hrt-211
Elijah	Rch-196	John	Grn-121	Simon	Rch-207
Elijah Esq	Rch-207	John	Pit-246	Stephen	Rch-203
Elijah	Rch-204	John	Roc- 31	Thomas	Ora-170
Elisha	Brt- 47	John	Mor- 67	Thomas	Roc- 13
Eliza col	Fra-101	John	Roc- 13	Walker	Roc- 20
Elizabeth	Rob-243	John	Sto-109	William	Dup- 33
Mrs Elizah	Fra- 86	John L	Fra- 95	William	Rch-207
Evan	Row- 65	John R	Len-314	William	Rch-197
Ezeckael	Ans- 21	Johnson	Nor- 79	William	Car-170
Fedr	Cha-200	Jona	Bla- 8	William Junr	Sam-154
Francis	Way-243	Jonathan	Nsh- 78	William Senr	Sam-157
G	Ora-144	Jonathan	Dup- 11	Willm D	Fra- 77
Geo	Ora-164	Jordan	Brt- 58	Willm (F S)	Fra- 96
George	Bla- 11	Jordan	Fra- 80	Willm Senr	Fra- 78
Gregory	Dup- 31	Jos	Glf-162	Wm	Row- 43
H	Ora-144	Joseph	Mor- 68	Wm	Ora-129
Hany	Rch-207	Joseph	Hay-201	Wilson	Edg- 61
Hannah	Ora-123	Joseph	Cha-200	Thomason,Arnold	Rch-199

Thomason,David	Sur-171	Thompson,Elijah	Joh-281	Thompson,John		Ora-158
David	Cha-207	Elijah	Brt- 58	John		Sur-180
Fleming	Sto-148	Elijah	Mon- 31	John		Cum-237
Geo	Row- 40	Elisha	Mon- 23	John		Bla- 11
George	Sto-110	Elizabeth	Edg- 40	John		Ire-248
Jesse	Row- 88	Elizabeth	Nor- 79	John		Rth-136
John	Sto-111	Elizabeth	War-171	John		Rth-137
John Snr	Sto-111	Enoch	Ora-943	John		Sto-135
Pleasant	Sto-111	Enoch Esqr	Ons-100	John		Sto-151
Thomas Snr	Sto-147	Etheldred	Nor- 78	John		Rob-221
Wm	Cha-205	Everett	Way-251	John	(L)	Way-251
Thomasson,Benj	Grn-130	Francis	Way-249	John		Way-234
E	Grn-128	Frederick	Row- 89	John		Ran-183
Fleming	Grn-129	Geo	Cha-202	John		Mon- 40
George	Grn-144	George	Ire-265	John		Cur- 86
George	Sto-147	George	Rob-221	John		Nor- 79
John	Grn-145	Gideon	Rth-136	John		Cha-203
John Jur	Sto-148	H Esq	Ora-111	John Jr		Way-251
Nathl	Grn-128	H Sen	Ora-111	John Sr		Way-251
Nelson	Grn-144	Hanah	Cha-209	Jon		Ora-116
Richard P	Grn-128	Harrod	War-172	Jos		Ora-115
Thos	Grn-128	Henry	Mec- 41	Joseph		Ora-158
Thos Sr	Grn-144	Henry	Ran-183	Joseph		Sur-180
Wm	Grn-128	Henry	Nor- 79	Joseph		Mec- 31
Thomison,James	Cha-196	Henry	Pas-206	Joseph		Row- 73
Richd	Cha-196	Henry	Roc- 28	Joseph A		Ora-129
Thoml,James	Glf-182	Hester	Ons-102	Joseph		Mec- 24
Thompson,-----	Rth-136	Hezekiah	Brt- 63	Joseph Sr		Sur-175
Widow	Mec- 55	Hugh	Rch-203	Joshua		Ora-943
Mrs	Cum-239	I W	Bft- 38	Josiah		Ora-121
Mrs	Mec- 36	Isaac	Bur-104	K		Cum-236
Mrs	Ora-143	Isoom	Lnc-361	Lewis		Joh-281
A	Ora-131	J E	Ora-152	Lewis		Brt- 63
A	Ora-152	J	Ash- 13	Lewis		Ons-104
Abel	Ora-943	J	Glf-179	Margaret		Ire-265
Alexr	Rob-222	James	Ora-943	Margaret		Rob-243
Alexr	Mon- 41	James	Ire-264	Marey		Cur- 88
Andrew	Ran-182	James	Rth-137	Mary		Bun- 83
Aron	Mec- 30	James	Way-249	Mary		Rch-202
Balaam	Cha-197	James	Brt- 63	Mary		Bur-120
Ben	Mec- 31	James	Glf-172	Mary		Pas-207
Benj	Len-317	James	Glf-168	Mary		Cha-191
Benjamin	Rob-241	James	Brt- 50	Money		Cur- 89
Benjamin	Mec- 27	James Esqr	Ons- 99	Moses		Wil-279
Charles	Rob-218	Jas	Mec- 44	Nancey		Cas- 72
Charles	Rob-238	Jas	Mec- 48	Nancy		Way-251
Charles	Nor- 79	Jas M C	Ora-145	Nathan		Hay-201
Charles	Lnc-342	Jas Qu	Ora-145	Neill		Rob-223
Daniel	Roc- 9	Jas Jun	Ora-113	Nicholas		Cas- 72
Danl	Mor- 68	Jas Senr	Ora-145	Peter		Way-251
Danl	Mor- 68	Jethro	Way-251	Peter		Bur-111
David	Way-249	Jno	Rob-221	Phillip		Rth-136
David	Bur-126	Jno	Mec- 31	Polly		Lnc-361
David Jr	Bur-126	Jno	Ora-133	R		Glf-174
Davis	Cur- 89	Jno	Mec- 24	Rachel		Rob-240
Drury	War-169	Jno	Mec- 40	Richd		Ora-111
E	Ora-152	Jno Esq	Ora-129	Richd		Ora-115
Elijah	Sur-180	Jno B C	Ora-147	Richd		Ora-144
Elijah	Rth-137	John	Ora-944	Robert		Bun- 91

-316-

Name	Loc	Name	Loc	Name	Loc
Thompson,Robt	Ora-134	Thomson,Jas	Sam-157	Thornton,Samuel	War-181
Robt	Ora-115	John	Cum-246	Theophilus	Ire-258
S T	Ora-153	John B	Cas- 72	Thos Senr	Sam-160
S of B	Ora-135	Laurence	Dup- 32	William	Sur-176
Sam	Ora-177	Malcom	Cum-245	Wm	Grn-132
Sam	Ora-134	Martha	Hal-121	Thoroton,Sally	Per-144
Saml	Cha-207	Neill	Cum-246	Thorp,Benj P	Grn-133
Saml	Cha-213	Neill	Cum-253	Sally	Per-134
Saml	Ora-114	Rachal	Row- 75	Timothy	Fra- 95
Samuel	Cur- 89	S M	Ora-157	Thorton,James	Sur-176
Samuel	Rob-221	Susanna	Hal-121	Thraneburgh,David	Wil-263
Samuel	Cha-208	William	Sam-164	Jacob	Wil-263
Sarah	Len-320	William	Row- 74	Lewis	Wil-271
Sarah	Ora-137	Wm	Brt- 58	Thrash,Valentine	Bun- 74
Shone	Mon- 23	Thonbury,David	Lnc-349	Threadgill,Geo	Ans- 6
Stephen	Way-254	Thore,Henry	Sto-103	Jas	Ans- 19
Stephen	Rob-234	Thorington,David	Way-248	Jno	Ans- 17
Stephen	Ora-134	Thorn,Aquilla	Row- 77	Jno	Ans- 12
Susannah	Per-144	D	Glf-153	John	Ans- 19
T Ens	Ora-152	Edy	Edg- 66	Randal	Ans- 19
Tho	Ora-116	John	Glf-172	Thos	Ans- 6
Tho	Ora-943	Martin Jr	Edg- 65	Thos	Ans- 16
Thomas	Way-251	Martin Sr	Edg- 65	Wm	Ans- 16
Thomas	Mor- 68	Pegga	Hrt-214	Wm	Ans- 16
Thomas	Roc- 29	Thomas	Edg- 65	Threadkill,Jesse	Cah-200
Thos	Mec- 54	Wm	Glf-154	Thrift,Isham	Ora-116
Thos Senr	Ora-145	Thornborough,Benj	Glf-188	Nathaniel	Nor- 79
Tobias	Sur-189	Henry	Glf-187	Throckmorton,J	Mon- 37
Trinegar	Rob-220	James	Glf-187	Nancy	Mon- 38
Will	Ora-158	Thos	Glf-187	R	Mon- 37
William	Ire-252	Thornburg,Mary	Ran-182	Robt	Mon- 47
William	Joh-282	Thornburgh,Edwd	Ran-182	Thos	Mon- 37
William	Nor- 79	Mattw	Ran-183	Throgmorton,Gabrial	Ans- 22
William	Bur-124	Wm	Ran-182	Robt	Mon- 40
William	Rth-135	Wm	Ran-182	Wm	Mon- 40
William	Sur-178	Thornbury,Thomas	Ran-182	Throgood,John	Hyd-222
William	Lnc-359	Wm	Ran-182	Thronibeyer,Jno	Lnc-329
William	Brt- 67	Thorne,Samuel	Hal-121	Throughgood,Demsey	Mar- 7
William	Car-170	Thornel,Constant	Edg- 43	Throw,Jesse	Cha-200
Willm (place)	Car-178	Thornhill,Joseph	Bun- 98	Thrower,Sarah	Hal-120
Wm	Bla- 3	Thorns,John	Ire-267	Thurmond,Mirideth	Wil-263
Wm	Rob-221	Thornton,Widow	Cho-228	Tial,James	Mar- 9
Wm	Cho-226	Ben	Sam-160	Tiby,Wm	Mon- 40
Wm	Mec- 41	Benjamin	Roc- 25	Tice,Abram	Mar- 16
Wm	Rob-234	Ellinor	Hyd-227	Henry	Row- 50
Wm	Ran-183	F	War-180	Jacob	Row- 50
Wm	Mon- 40	Felix	Sam-160	John	Mar- 12
Wm	Mon- 43	Harrod	Joh-289	Peter	Row- 48
Wm	Mon- 23	Herod	Sam-160	Ticer,Henry	Mec- 24
Wm	Mon- 46	Jacob	Bru-226	Tickle,William	Roc- 15
Wm	Mon- 48	John	Rch-205	Tidder,James	Cha-191
Wm	Cha-209	John	Row- 58	Tier,Ludsick	Ora-123
Willis	Sam-152	John Junr	Sam-160	Ties,Luke	Ora-112
Zadock	Way-236	Mary	Sam-161	Tigast,John	Bur-105
Zecknes	Mec- 31	Moses	Bun- 87	Tigner,Curtis	Sto-149
Thomson,Chas	Brt- 58	Nat Senr	Sam-160	Jonathan	Sto-147
. Duncan	Cum-245	Needham	Sam-160	Tila,John	Cha-193
Elisha	Row- 83	Owen	Sam-161	Tiler,Joseph	Sto-108
James	Row- 66	Richard	Roc- 13	Joseph	Sto-152

Tilghman,Jno	Len-311	Tilsmon,Elijah	Cha-199	Tison,Noah	Pit-242
John	Len-318	Tilton,James H	Gat-113	Saml	Ans- 17
Richd	Len-318	Timberlake,Ephy	Fra- 85	Sharewood	Pit-257
Joseph	Len-318	Francis	Fra- 93	Stephen	Pit-259
Tillery,Ann	Ran-183	James	Fra- 97	Thomas	Pit-263
Isaac	Bun- 81	Timmons,Elisha	Hyd-227	William	Pit-257
John	Nor- 78	Fisher	Bft- 27	Wm	Ans- 16
Prismus	Hal-115	Jeremiah	Sam-156	Tistaman,J	Ash- 13
Tillet,J	Cam-155	John	Mar- 10	T	Ash- 13
R	Cam-156	Thomas	Jon-305	Titterton,Chas Y	Bft- 31
Tillett,Avery	Cur- 82	Tindal,Jas M	Ans- 29	Wm	Bft- 28
Easter	Cur- 82	Nehemiah	Ans- 29	Titus,Reuben	Hal-120
Samuel	Cur- 82	Robert	Roc- 28	Toasley,George	Ora-150
Sarey	Cur- 83	Tindall,James	Dup- 28	Toby,James	Car-179
Thos	Cur- 82	John	Dup- 28	Nancy	Car-179
Tilley,Daniel	Sto-141	Tindel,J	Cam-158	Tod,George	Joh-285
E	Ash- 4	Jeremiah	Sam-155	Todd,Adam	Mec- 55
Edmund	Sto- 92	Tinen,Robert	Ora-152	George	Mec- 55
Henry	Sto- 95	Tinnen,Carns	Ora-137	Gorge	War-171
Joel Jnr	Sto-141	Ezekiel	Glf-168	Hardy	Tyr-211
John	Sto-141	Robert	Ora-116	Hardy	Brt- 44
John	Sto-121	Tinnin,Davd	Ora-134	James	Brt- 53
Lazarus	Ora-167	Tiner,John	Joh-281	Jas	Mec- 54
Lazarus	Hay-201	Willis	Joh-281	Jas	Mec- 54
Stephen	Ora-167	Tinsley,Sarah	Wil-267	Jean	Ire-266
Tillinghast,P J Jr	Cum-239	Thomas	Wil-267	Jno	Mec- 55
P J Senr	Cum-239	Tinsly,Sarah	Jon-305	John	Wsh-221
Tillington,Richd	Cha-209	Tipet,John	Grn-137	John	Roc- 22
Tillman,Ann	Mon- 23	Tippet,Benj	Ons-101	Joseph	Mec- 54
Jarrot	Cha-191	Cenia	Jon-305	Lewis	Edg- 65
John	Cha-202	Samuel	Jon-305	Samuel	Ire-266
Joshua	Cha-190	William	Jon-305	Thomas	Row- 89
Tillor,D D	Glf-184	Tipps,John	Bur-130	W	Bru-236
Tillory,David	Hal-120	Tips,Cunrad	Lnc-369	William	Brt- 53
John	Hal-121	Jacob	Bur-111	William	Roc- 33
Tillston,Joseph	Cha-199	Tipton,Edward	Hal-121	Wm	Row- 49
Tilly,David	Sto-154	Jonathan	Bun- 77	Wm	Mec- 55
David	Sto-113	Jonathan Junr	Bun- 77	Tofebrigt,Phillip	Lnc-345
Edmund	Wil-257	Wylie	Bun- 77	Tolar,Jesse	Way-235
Edmund	Sto-121	Tire,Lewis	Row- 42	Myar	Way-234
Edmund	Bur-112	Tisdal,Edward	Edg- 43	Thomas Sr	Way-235
Edmund Jur	Sto-155	Tisdale,Robt	Mon- 19	Tolbert,John	Mon- 20
Edmund Jur	Sto-112	Tisdel,Joel	Nsh- 91	Kiah	Mon- 21
Henry	Sto-124	Pillander	Nsh- 77	Samuel	Mon- 18
Joel	Sto-154	Randison	Edg- 42	Sarah	Mon- 20
Joel	Sto-113	Tisdell,Elisha	Nsh- 91	Thos	Mon- 19
Joel Jur	Sto-106	Ran	Joh-287	Toler,Jesse	Hay-201
John	Sto-112	William	Nsh- 80	John	Cas- 72
John	Sto-106	Tisner,Frederick	Row- 87	John	Cum-265
John	Sto-155	Tison,Allen	Pit-262	Tolison,Isaac	Per-227
John	Sto- 92	Benjamin	Pit-257	Toliver,C	Per-227
John Jur	Sto-145	Benjamin Jnr	Pit-259	J	Ash- 13
John Snr	Sto-145	Elisha	Ans- 10	J	Ash- 4
John Snr	Sto-155	George	Pit-257	J	Ash- 15
Lewis	Wil-273	Ichabod	Pit-259	J	Ash- 14
Stephen	Wil-273	Jacob	Pit-257	J	Ash- 15
W	Bru-226	Joab	Pit-257	W	Ash- 14
Tilman,John	Mon- 21	Milley	Ans- 16	Tollen,Joseph	Cas- 72
Tilmon,Roger	Per-144	Moses	Pit-259	Toller,Wm	Bla- 7

Name	Ref	Name	Ref	Name	Ref
Tolsom,Benjn	Per-133	Toms,William	Rth-135	Townsend,Dan	Mon- 24
Mary	Per-133	Zachariah	Prq-226	J	Col- 20
Wm	Per-133	Tomson,D	Col- 17	John	Bur-110
Tolson,Asa	Car-173	John	Row- 64	Josiah	Prq-227
Benj	Car-173	Mary	Row- 86	Thos	Rob-240
Gedeon	Car-173	Patcey	Row- 76	William	Hrt-211
George	Car-182	Thomas	Gat-105	Wm	Cab-147
Jesse	Car-173	Tomy,Elizabeth	Cum-266	Townsley,J	Ora-138
Rebecah	Ans- 29	Toney,free man of colour		Oliver	Sur-183
Thomas	Car-172		Ran-187	Towry,Adam	Rth-136
Thomas Senr	Car-173	Toney,free man of colour		Edmund	Rth-136
Wm	Car-173		Ran-187	Trabuthan,Mrs S	Cum-238
Zachariah	Car-173	Toney,Martha	Hal-120	Trace,John	Row- 66
Tom (cook)	Bft- 38	Tony,John	Hal-120	Trader,Suky	Mor- 62
Tom & wife (col)	Mec- 47	Malachi	Cum-249	Trafton,G	Cam-162
Tomas,George	Rob-224	Tooks,J	Col- 19	Trammel,Isaac	Bun- 85
Tomason,Tho	Bft- 32	Tool,Federick	Joh-289	Robert	Roc- 8
Tomberlen,DAvid	Ans- 21	Geraldus	Sam-159	William	Bun- 85
Tomberlin,John	Way-247	Henry	Edg- 72	William	Roc- 12
Thomas	Way-246	Jeraldus	Edg- 64	Trammil,John	Roc- 9
William	Way-247	Tooley,Anthony	Hyd-233	Transue,Abraham	Sto-129
Tomberlinson,StephnWay-246		Tootle,Eden	Wsh-228	Abraham	Sto- 99
Stephen	Way-246	Top,George	War-171	Abraham	Sto- 99
Tomblin,Hugh	Ire-255	Rebeca	Per-134	John	Sto-129
Tomlin,Alexander	Sur-180	Toppin,Thomas	Hyd-223	Peter	Sto-135
Tomlinson,Archd	Wil-257	Topping,Saml	Cho-231	Philip	Sto-130
Edmon	Joh-291	Wm	Cho-231	Tranum,William	Roc- 13
Harris	Joh-278	Torrance,Albert	Tow- 89	Trap,Martin	Bur-130
Humphrey B	Ire-261	George	Mec- 24	Trapnal,William	Cum-259
Jas	Glf-158	Hugh	Mec- 24	Travillian,Joel	Rth-137
John	Ire-265	Robert	Row- 89	Travis,Caleb	Cur- 93
John	Glf-158	Torrans,Elias	Sam-157	Jacob	Row- 86
John	Row- 61	Torrence,Adam	Ire-258	Joseph	Row- 86
Josia	Row- 45	Alexander	Ire-257	Trawick,Henry	Rob-222
Josiah	Row- 45	Hugh	Lnc-334	Patty	Rob-229
Moses	Row- 44	John	Lnc-334	Trayest,Margarett	Cha-193
Perry	Ire-265	Matt B	Lnc-334	Traylor,John	Grn-147
Thos	Row- 45	Sarah	Ire-257	Sarah	Bun- 93
Thos Jr	Mon- 39	Torrentnce,Robert	Ire-255	Trayweek,Berimon	Ans- 25
Wm	Mon- 39	Torry,James	Cum-268	Treace,Henry	Row- 77
Zadock	Glf-181	Touchton,Jonas	Glf-160	Peter	Row- 77
Tomman,Macy	Row- 85	Tough,Mary	Row- 80	William	Row- 79
Tommas,John	Row- 60	Tow,Christopher	Bun- 90	Treadaway,Daniel	Ans- 21
Tommason,Henry	Bft- 31	Ezekiel	Bun- 91	Treas,Daniel	Cab-145
John	Bft- 31	James	Bun- 98	Trease,Peter	Cab-146
Wm	Bft- 31	Reubin	Bun- 80	Treat,Benjamin	Roc- 12
Tommeson,George	Row- 76	Towel,Danl	Ora-129	Treble,Rev William	Wil-281
Richard	Row- 76	Towell,Jesse	Ora-145	Trebothan,Matw	Nsh- 78
William	Row- 76	Jno	Ora-145	Tredaway,R	Ash- 4
William	Row- 76	Towers,Mathew	Rob-242	Tredway,William	Bun- 93
Tommy,Jacob	Lnc-346	Towmy,D	Glf-168	Tredwell,Amos	Mon- 43
Tompkins,James	Wil-262	Town,Joice	War-175	John	Sam-164
Thos	Mon- 41	Townsand,Lewis	Bun- 79	John Senr	Sam-164
Tompson,John	Ire-257	Townsel,William	Rob-218	Obediah	Row- 45
Toms,Anderson	Prq-226	Townsen,John	Mon- 26	Saml	Cho-221
Francis	Prq-227	T	Mon- 35	Samuel	Mar- 8
John	Prq-227	Townsend,Aaron	Cab-148	Stephen	Mon- 43
Joshua	Prq-226	Aaron	Cab-148	Wm	Row- 45
Mary	Prq-226	Alexr	Rob-241	Treece,Michael	Sur-184

Name	Ref	Name	Ref	Name	Ref
Trees,George	Sur-184	Trott,Adam	Ons-103	Trueblood,Jonathan	Pas-207
Trevathan,Henry	Edg- 55	Adam	Ons-103	Joseph	Pas-207
Robert	Edg- 56	Benjamin	Row- 76	Joshua	Pas-206
Sion	Edg- 57	Frizby	Row- 76	Mary	Pas-206
Trevit,John	Row- 62	Hannah	Ons-108	Nathan	Pas-206
Trewil,Sreve	Rth-137	James	Ons- 96	Saml	Pas-206
Trexler,Adam	Row- 67	James	Row- 76	Stephen	Pas-206
Jacob	Row- 79	John	Row- 76	Thomas	Pas-207
John	Row- 89	John	Ons-103	Will	Pas-206
Peter	Row- 77	Murfrey	Ons-103	Trueit,Michl	Lnc-326
Peter	Row- 40	Samuel	Row- 82	Truelove,James	Rth-136
Tribbit,Richard	Row- 63	Thomas	Row- 76	Thomas	Fra- 85
Trice,Ezekiel	Ora-170	Wm C	Glf-180	Timothy	Cum-256
Henry	Ora-136	Winniford	Ons-101	Willm	Fra- 85
Trickey,Wm	Per-144	Trotter,Benjamin	Row- 83	Truhitt,Bright	Len-320
Trifflestead,Peter	Lnc-349	E	Glf-176	Truit,Amey	Roc- 31
Trigleth,Wm	Nsh- 81	E	Glf-172	Trull,Sarah	Ans- 24
Trigstern,Shadrach	Joh-290	Geo	Glf-161	Sol	Ans- 15
Trim,Charles	Per-144	James	Per-144	Stephen	Ans- 25
Robert	Per-133	Joseph	Row- 83	Wm	Ans- 21
Trimble,John	Ora-168	Oldom	Row- 83	Trulove,Aven	Sur-188
Trip,Godfrey	Cur- 83	Richard	Row- 82	Landon	Sur-182
John	Cha-199	Tho	Bft- 27	Michl	Cho-225
Jonathan	Cha-199	Thos	Per-133	Truman,B	Bru-234
Mary	Cha-196	Wm	Per-133	Charles	Cha-203
Tripes,John	Grn-129	Troublood,J	Glf-183	Henry	Cha-193
Triplet,Wm	Cha-207	Troutman,Adam	Row- 67	J	Bru-236
Triplett,Elijah	Wil-274	Adam Sr	Row- 67	J	Bru-234
Ellender	Wil-282	Andrew	Row- 73	John	Cha-194
Jesse	Wil-276	Catharine	Cab-146	King	Rch-211
Jesse (Elk)	Wil-282	Eve	Lnc-346	Richd	Cha-197
Thomas	Wil-282	Jacob	Ire-239	Trumbret,Ruby	Hrt-216
Thos	Bur-116	Joshua	Row- 69	Trummell,Hardy	Brt- 51
William	Sur-166	Martin	Row- 83	Truss,Samuel	Pit-252
Tripp,Caleb	Pit-258	Michl	Row- 68	Warren	Pit-252
Charles	Pit-258	Peter	Cab-140	Truster,William	Wil-264
Jos	Bft- 31	Troutt,John	Wil-267	Trusty,A	Mon- 35
Trisdale,James	Grn-121	Trowton,Catron	Nor- 78	John	Row- 82
John	Grn-121	Troy,Alexn	Ans- 13	William	Sur-182
Tritt,Henry	Lnc-349	John	Ran-182	Truves,John	Cab-138
Jacob	Lnc-349	Mathew	Row- 89	Tuber,John	Bun- 72
Troarbaugh,Jacob	Lnc-329	Rosanah	Rch-209	Tucker,A	Glf-172
Trogdon,John	Ran-182	True,Chs	Ora-157	Amos	Ran-182
Samuel	Ran-182	Ellen	Or--176	Amos	Dup- 16
Solomon	Ran-182	Ha	Ora-157	Andrew	Row- 58
Wm	Ran-182	Harrison	Ora-166	Anthony	Nor- 79
Trogler,Jacob	Ora-120	Jno	Per-133	Aracher	Sur-162
Trolinger,Hi	Ora-124	Tab	Ora-157	Aron	Row- 57
Trollinger,Adam	Roc- 7	Trueblood,Abel	Pas-207	Benjamin	Ran-183
Samuel	Roc- 7	Amos	Pas-207	Benjamin	War-168
Thomas	Roc- 6	Ann	Pas-207	Benjamin	Sur-195
Tropper,Peter	Bun- 83	Asa	Pas-206	Benton	Edg- 59
Trotman,Hezekiah	Gat-106	Ben	Pas-207	Branch	Sur-162
Joseph	Gat-105	Caleb	Pas-207	Brney	Nsh- 81
Noah	Gat-105	Caleb	Pas-206	Corborn	Nsh- 82
Reddick	Gat-108	Caleb	Pas-206	Daniel	Grn-137
Ruth	Gat-109	Eliz	Pas-206	Daniel	Roc- 12
Salley	Gat-108	James	Pas-207	Daniel	Dup- 18
Thomas	Gat-106	John	Pas-207	Daniel	War-170

Tucker,David	Ire-242	Tucker,Valentine	Ire-252	Tunnel,William	Hal-120
David	Ire-242	William	Ran-182	Tunnell,Patsey	Nor- 79
David	Sur-194	William	Cha-196	Wm	Bft- 35
Delilah	Lnc-328	William	Joh-288	Tunstall,Geo Esq	Fra- 89
Eliner	Sto-149	Wm	Sur-160	Paton R	Hal-120
Elijah	Dup- 24	Wood	Ans- 8	Richard	War-179
Elizabeth	War-171	Wright	Pit-242	Turke,John	Bun- 79
Enus	Nsh- 92	Tuggel,Mary	Pit-252	Turley,Gracy	Joh-290
Francis	Sto-149	Tuggle,Frankey	Cas- 72	Turleyfill,John	Lnc-356
Francis	Sto-111	Tugh,Jeremiah	Sam-156	John	Lnc-356
Frederick	Hal-120	Jeremiah Sr	Sam-162	Littleberry	Lnc-356
Garner	Sur-162	John	Sam-162	Lodowick	Lnc-356
Geo	Mon- 48	John Esq	Sam-155	Turlington,Kader	Cum-261
Geo D	Bur-110	Lewis	Sam-156	Suky	Cum-261
George	Lnc-371	Marmaduke	Sam-162	Willis	Cum-262
Gray	War-172	Philip	Sam-155	Turnage,Emenuel	Pit-263
Henry	Row- 84	Willm	Sam-161	Kadar	Dup- 25
Hezekiah	Cas- 72	Tugman,James	Wil-273	Luke	Rch-203
Jacob	Cab-141	Tuke,John	Nor- 79	Jesse	Dup- 25
James	Row- 84	Littleton	Nor- 79	Zachariah	Dup- 24
James	Hal-120	Thomas	Nor- 79	Turnbull,John	Wil-263
James	Row- 57	Tuley,Abel S	Hyd-231	Turner,Aaron	Jon-305
James	Sur-160	Brian	Hyd-232	Aaron	Rch-212
Jesse	Mor- 59	Clinton	Hyd-231	George	Lnc-369
Joab	Nsh- 83	Delilah	Hyd-232	Abraham	Pit-237
John	Ire-242	Dinah	Hyd-232	Ann	Brt- 68
John	Cha-202	Elisha	Hyd-232	Ann	Cas- 72
John	Cab-148	Henry	Hyd-234	Armstead	Juc-353
John	Pit-235	Jacob	Hyd-232	Ben	Ora-132
John	Pit-235	Job	Hyd-231	Benjn	Sam-157
John	Bur-104	John	Hyd-232	Caleb	Pas-206
John	War-173	Jones	Hyd-232	Charity	Brt- 59
John	Lnc-335	Laban	Hyd-233	Charles	Pas-206
John E	War-175	Major	Hyd-231	Charlotte	Nor- 79
John W	War-176	Ormond	Hyd-232	Cherry	Nsh-644
Joseph	Cab-141	Solomon	Hyd-232	Creasa	Ans- 16
Joshua	Pit-237	Susanah	Hyd-233	Dempsey Jr	Nor- 79
Joshua	Pit-234	Thomas	Hyd-231	Demsy	Pas-206
Keley	Pit-238	Tulford,Stephen Jr	Car-169	Dickinson	Way-254
Levi	Glf-171	William	Sur-189	Edward	Nor- 79
Lewis	Way-246	Tull,Abraham	Sto-152	Edward	Wil-262
Lewis	Cab-141	Charles	Len-321	Elias	Sur-174
Luke	Dup- 16	Grorr	Sto-152	Eliz	Nsh- 76
Mary	Bur-112	Isaac	Len-317	Elizabeth	Brt- 67
Nancy	Bur-112	John Senr	Len-317	Elizth	Bla- 9
Nathan	Prq-226	Wm	Len-311	Elsbery	Prq-226
Nathaniel	Mor- 59	Tulloch,James	Cas- 72	Etheldred	Nor- 79
Paschal	Joh-288	Tully,Peter	Hal-120	Ezekiel	Hyd-229
Polley	Rth-136	Sever W	Cho-222	Fanny	Len-317
Reddick	Pit-242	Tuman,David	Ons- 96	George	Prq-226
Robert	Roc- 14	Tumberton,Freeman	Bur-110	Hawkins	Prq-227
Robert	Nsh- 84	Tumbleston,Joseph	Ran-182	Henley	War-172
Robert	Lnc-359	Wm	Ran-183	Henry	Edg- 62
Roby	Ire-244	Tumblin,Freeman	Bur-124	Isaac	Pit-237
Shadrach	Roc- 11	John	Hal-121	Isrial	Ora-150
Thomas	Ran-182	Tumlinson,David	Bun- 75	for self & J	Mon- 35
Thos	Len-312	Tuning,James	Glf-152	Jacob	Edg- 61
Tobias	Row- 61	Tunmire,Peter	Bur-108	James	Hal-121
Tom	Lnc-346	Samuel	Bur-107	James	Cas- 72

-321-

Name	Ref	Name	Ref	Name	Ref	Name	Ref
Turner,James	Fra- 92	Turner,Sarah	Bun- 78	Twiford,William	Cur- 87		
James	Sam-161	Sarrah	Cum-259	Twig,Nancy	Cum-241		
James	War-173	Sary	Joh-272	Twigg,Joshua	Cas- 72		
James	War-174	Silas	Len-320	William	Cas- 72		
James	War-176	Simon	Brt- 48	Twiggs,Timothy	Rth-136		
James	War-176	Simon	Nor- 79	Twindell,Jesse	Hyd-228		
James K	Hal-120	Sledge	War-181	Joshua	Hyd-227		
Jas	Ans- 20	Stephen	War-180	Twine,Elisha	Prq-227		
Jas	Ans- 16	Sugars	Nor- 79	Jesse	Prq-227		
Jas Jun	Ora-113	Teratta	War-181	John	Cho-229		
Jas Sen	Ora-113	Thomas	Hal-120	Thos	Prq-227		
Jesse	Ans- 16	Thomas	Cas- 72	Will	Pas-206		
Jno	Ans- 7	Thomas	Wil-270	Twitington,Thomas	Nsh-643		
John	Row- 83	Vines	Fra- 91	Twitty,Allen	Rth-136		
John	Hal-121	Will	Pas-206	Russel	Rth-137		
John	Rth-137	William	Prq-226	William	War-182		
John	Rth-137	William	Jon-305	William Sr	Rth-136		
John	Jon-305	William	Pit-237	Twity,Daniel Sr	Dup- 22		
John	Nor- 79	William	Hrt-211	Tyer,James	Pit-259		
John	Sam-157	William	Cas- 72	Tyerrell,Wm	Glf-157		
John	Sur-174	William	War-183	Tygart,Andrew	Row- 64		
John	Lnc-353	Wm	Sam-164	Jesse	Row- 45		
John	Row- 76	Wm	Nsh- 75	Richard	Row- 64		
John W	Sam-157	Turney,Gilbert	Sur-162	Tyler,Adam	Cha-197		
John Jr	Joh-272	Turnire,David	Mec- 47	Bartlet	War-169		
John Snr	Joh-272	Turrance,Barnabas	Mec- 52	Charles	Ran-182		
Joseph	Ans- 22	Turrentine,Danl	Ora-115	David	Roc- 15		
Joseph	Pas-207	Danl	Ora-164	Edwd D	Mon- 33		
Joseph	Hay-201	John	Ora-164	Jas	Sam-162		
Joshua	Pas-207	Samuel	Ora-112	John	Brt- 54		
Kezia	Wsh-224	Tutherow,John	Lnc-340	John	Car-176		
Lazarus	Nsh- 76	John	Lnc-340	Owen	Sam-163		
Lovey	Pas-207	Tutle,Abs	Bft- 32	Reuben	Roc- 15		
Mary	Pas-206	Amos	Bft- 32	Richd	Brt- 54		
Mary	Pas-207	John	Sto-106	Thomas	Sto-152		
Mary	Bla- 11	Richard	Rch-191	Tylor,Aaron	Cum-252		
Matt	Bur-130	S-rah	Bft- 32	Jacob	Cum-252		
Matthew	Way-246	Tutor,Etheldred	Rob-232	Tynar,Benjamin	Rob-218		
Matthews	Rth-135	Morris	Rob-232	Tyner,Curtis	Sto-110		
Mial	Ons-108	Owen	Cum-258	Etheldred	Way-234		
Miles	Prq-226	Tutt,Benjamin	Bun- 74	Jacob	Way-233		
Nancy	Dup- 33	Tuttero,David	Row- 66	Jessey	Joh-281		
Nathan	War-178	Joe	Row- 66	John	Nor- 78		
Nathl	Ans- 25	Tuttle,A	Cam-158	John	Sto-150		
Parson	Cum-238	John	Sto- 96	Nicholas	Nor- 78		
Patsy	Pas-206	Thomas	Sto-126	Tynes,West	Brt- 56		
Person	Rth-136	Tuzzall,Moses	Ora-164	Tyrie,G	Ash- 12		
Person	Rth-136	Twaddle,Margt	Bla- 14	T	Ash- 7		
Phereby	Hal-120	Tweed,James	Bun- 88	W	Ash- 14		
Powel	Row- 40	Tweedy,Jonathan	Pas-207	Tyron,Cornelius	Cha-196		
Rebecca	Prq-227	Twiddy,Devotion	Tyr-203	Tyrrell,Jo	Ora-110		
Richard	Prq-226	James	Prq-226	Joel	Fra- 77		
Robert	Hay-201	Jessy	Jon-305	Tyson,Aaron	Hyd-234		
Robt	Mon- 40	Samuel	Tyr-205	Ann	Pit-255		
Robt	Hay-201	William	Prq-227	John	Cha-213		
Robert	Wil-259	Twidy,Benjn	Tyr-210	John	Hyd-234		
Sally	Joh-274	David	Tyr-209	Josiah	Mor- 65		
Samson	Wsh-223	Twiford,Betey	Tyr-205	Lewis	Cha-213		
Sarah	Wil-271	Elizabeth	Tyr-205	Lydia	Mor- 64		

Name	Ref	Name	Ref	Name	Ref
Tyson,M	Bla- 12	Underwood,William	Wil-264	Ussery,Blackwell	Mon- 25
Mary	Hyd-234	William	Nor- 79	David	Mon- 26
Richard	Hyd-224	William	Bun- 97	Elijah	Mon- 25
Sarah	Hyd-225	Wm	Rob-240	Patsy	Mon- 31
Thomas	Mor- 66	Underwoods,Lewis	Mec- 31	Wm	Mon- 25
Tysotus,Sollomon	Edg- 41	Unity,Brittain	Hay-201	Wm	Ans- 13
		Unthank,Allen	Glf-163	Ussory,J	Mon- 36
Ubanks,William	Ire-261	Jas	Glf-164	R	Mon- 37
Ufford,John	Hyd-232	John	Glf-163	Utinoon,Sarah	Bur-121
Ulis,Adam	Ora-172	Jonathan	Sur-161	Utley,Elizabeth	Rob-221
John	Ora-172	Josiah	Glf-165	Utly,Allen	Cum-258
Ullen,Laboon	Cum-264	Upchurch,Allen	Mon- 39	Darcus	Cum-258
Umphleet,James	Way-254	B	Mon- 39	William	Cum-257
Umphret,Sarah	Nor- 79	Benjn	Fra- 81	Utzman,Lewis	Row- 89
Umphrey,John	Way-238	Buckner	Fra- 95	Mary	Row- 86
Umphreys,Joh	Hyd-229	Charles	Fra- 82	Uzzell,James	Len-311
Umphry,Benjamin	Rob-230	George	Ire-253	James	Way-249
Umphsted,William	Gat-113	Gillom	Cha-204	Major	Way-249
Umstead,Danl	Ora-159	Harmon	Mon- 41	Thomas	Len-317
J	Ora-132	James	Fra- 80		
Umsted,J	Ora-146	John	Fra- 93	Vail,Magy	Cho-225
Underhill,William	Dup- 13	John	Cha-200	Thomas	Cho-225
Underwood,Abraham	Roc- 15	Jubel	Fra- 82	Valentine,David	Hrt-210
Bishop	Edg- 55	Moses	Ire-253	David	Wil-283
C	Glf-178	Richard	Fra- 82	David	Cum-262
Danl	Cha-201	Ruffin	Cha-190	Elijah	Grn-130
Danl	Ran-182	Shadrich	Ire-253	Sam	Hrt-210
David	Ora-119	Sherwood	Rth-138	Valiant,Ancel	Glf-152
Elisa	Ora-131	Sion	Fra- 97	Valintine,A	Hrt-209
George	Mor- 67	Stephen	Cha-201	Paul	Hrt-216
Henry	Mon- 49	Upoton,H	Cam-164	Vallentine,Jno	Ans- 20
Henry	Lnc-364	Upp,Jacob	Sto-114	Vals,John	Sto-146
Howell	Fra- 90	Jacob	Sto-156	Valuery,John	Tyr-201
James	Cha-204	Upright,Samuel	Row- 68	Van,Elisha	Edg- 60
Jessee	Nor- 79	Uptegrove,Jesse	Rth-138	John Jr	Dup- 24
Jo	Mon- 46	Upthegrove,Isaac	Sur-178	Vancannon,Jacob	Ran-186
Joel	Sur-160	William	Sur-177	John	Ran-186
Jno	Ora-136	Upton,Delilah	Cha-213	Peter	Ran-186
John	Mor- 67	G	Cam-159	Vance,Ann	Edg- 58
John	Mor- 57	Jesse	Cum-247	David	Mec- 47
John	Nsh- 78	John	Cha-195	Col David	Bun- 93
Jonathan	Nor- 79	John	Glf-169	John	Bur-113
Joseph	Bun- 84	John	Rth-138	John	Sto-149
Josiah	Sam-161	M	Cam-160	John	Sto-111
Levey	Nsh- 78	Mary	Car-171	Samuel	Lnc-369
Lewis	Wil-262	Richard	Mor- 59	Wm	Mec- 26
Lucy	Hal-121	Robert	Rob-234	Vancell,Jacob	Row- 69
Malias	Nsh- 74	W	Cam-154	Vandeford,Jas	Ans- 25
Manuel	Nsh- 76	Urey,Geo	Cab-145	John	Cha-197
Mary	Hal-121	Geo	Cab-140	Wm	Ans- 25
Mary	Rch-206	Urquhard,Allen	Cum-262	Vanderdown,Stephen	Bur-112
R	Glf-179	John	Cum-258	Vanderkool,A	Ash- 12
Reuben	Lnc-364	Norman	Cum-262	Vanderpool,Elijah	Bur-113
Robt	Glf-160	Uryll,Willis	Glf-172	Isaac	Wil-282
Saml	Ran-183	Usher,James	Rch-203	Josiah	Sur-175
Sarah	Sam-162	Samuel	Rch-200	W	Ash- 6
Solomon	Cha-212	Thomas	Rch-198	Vandiforth,Mintey	Cha-204
Thomas	Roc- 11	Usry,Thomas	Rch-197	Vandike,John	Grn-143
Thomas	Ran-183	Welcom	Rch-197	Vandiver,John	Ire-258

Name	Ref	Name	Ref	Name	Ref
Vandiver,Matthew	Ire-242	Vanpelt,Harmon	Hrt-211	Vaughan,James Jr	Nor- 79
Vanduser,Thos	Cur- 89	Job	Edg- 42	James Jr	Cas- 73
Vandyke,John	Lnc-340	John	Pit-251	James Senr	Nor- 79
Vanetter,John	Sur-172	Luke	Hrt-210	Jeremiah	War-173
Vanhook,Aron	Per-133	Simeon	Edg- 69	Jessee	Nor- 79
Jacob	Per-153	Vanstory,John	Glf-176	John	Nor- 79
John	Per-145	Vanzant,Barna	Sur-193	John	Ora-943
Kindal	Per-145	Garrot	Sur-176	John	Roc- 24
Loyd	Per-145	Isaac	Rth-137	John	Rth-137
Robt Esq	Per-153	James	Rth-137	Lewis	Cas- 73
Sarah	Per-133	Vaper,James	Nor- 79	Lystia	Roc- 22
Vanhoose,John	Rth-137	Stiles	Nor- 79	Nichol	Cas- 73
Vanhorn,Abraham	Tyr-204	Willis	Nor- 79	Osbourn	Hal-121
Isaac	Bur-104	Varden,Barnet	Pas-207	Peyton	War-179
John	Bur-104	Charity	Pas-207	Richd	Cas- 73
Vanhoy,Abraham	Sto-147	David	Edg- 64	Sherwood	Lnc-369
Claton	Sur-194	Elizabeth	Edg- 62	Simeon	Roc- 34
Thomas	Sur-195	Hollal	Pas-207	Thomas	Nor- 79
William	Sur-195	James	Pas-207	Thomas	Hal-121
Vankay,Abraham	Sto-111	Jerusa	Pas-208	Thos	Lnc-364
James	Sto-149	John	Pas-207	Thos Jr	Cas- 73
Vanlandingham,Peter	Edg- 43	Lovey	Pas-207	Thos Sr	Cas- 73
Richd	Roc- 9	Thos	Pas-207	Vincent	War-182
Richd	War-179	Tully	Pas-207	William	Nor- 79
Vann,Mrs	Cum-236	Varm,William	Hrt-211	William	Nor- 79
Charles	Gat-115	Varment,Mary	Rth-137	Wm	Ans- 20
Charles	Gat-115	Varnal,Benjamin	Edg- 51	Zebulon	Sto-113
Edward	Gat-115	Varnan,James	Sto-138	Zebulon	Sto-153
Edwd	Sam-154	Johathan	Sto- 95	Vaughn,Caswell	Per-145
Ezekiel	Cum-264	Richard	Sto-138	Granvil	Per-145
James	Nor- 79	Varner,Andrew	Sto-129	Hillery	Hrt-213
James	Sam-154	Andrew	Sto- 99	James	Grn-135
Jessee	Nor- 79	Henry	Row- 86	James	Bur-118
Jesse	Hrt-212	Jacob	Ran-186	John	Hrt-214
John	Gat-115	Jacob	Ran-186	John	Hrt-211
John	Hrt-212	Jacob	Ran-186	John	Per-145
John	Sam-158	John	Ran-186	K	Glf-166
Kedar	Sam-154	Joseph	Ran-186	Saml	Per-133
Leonard	Sam-157	Varnis,Jacob	Row- 54	Samuel	Lnc-358
Thos	Sam-157	Varnum,Isaac	Sto-124	Vaughter,Beverly	Sto-122
Thos	Ans- 8	Vaser,George	Ire-258	Beverly	Sto- 94
William	Sam-158	John	Ire-258	Elizabeth	Sto-105
William	Cum-264	Reuben	Grn-121	John	Sto-104
William Senr	Sam-154	John	Grn-121	John	Sto-138
Willm	Sam-158	Thomas	Grn-121	Russell	Sto-138
Wm	Ans- 8	Thomas	Grn-125	Russell	Sto-104
Vanne,John	Sam-157	Vincent	Roc- 32	Vauld,Mashborn	Bur-117
Vannoy,Andrew	Wil-277	Vassar,Dawson	Edg- 66	Vaun,Ephm	Len-322
Elijah	Wil-281	Martha	Edg- 66	James	Len-322
Francis Esqr	Wil-267	Vaughan,Charlotte	Nor- 79	Lazeras	Ans- 21
Jesse	Wil-280	Cornelius	Roc- 22	Stephen	Dup- 16
John	Wil-281	David	Nor- 79	Wm Jr	Len-322
Sarah	Wil-273	Elisha	Hrt-211	Wm Senr	Len-321
Susanna	Wil-260	Elizabeth	Sto-140	Vause,Nancy	Len-314
Vanorton,Hadrianus	Pit-242	Henry	Roc- 4	Benjn	Row- 84
Vanover,C	Ash- 15	Isaac	Rch-195	Elija	Row- 39
C	Ash- 14	Ishmael	Ora-127	James	Row- 45
S	Ash- 15	J	Ora-139	John	Row- 45
Vanpelt,Danl	Brt- 50	James	Cas- 73	John	Row- 45

-324-

Name	Ref	Name	Ref	Name	Ref
Veail,Mary	Bft- 35	Vest,Obediah	Sto-151	Vickers,Riley	Ora-166
Veal,George	Hyd-228	Samuel	Sto-112	William	Lnc-332
Veale,Eliz	Brt- 58	Samuel Ser	Sto-151	Vickery,Charles	Bun- 81
Wm	Brt- 58	William	Sto- 97	Luke	Bun- 81
Vears,John	Brt- 57	William	Sto-126	Sampson	Bun- 73
John	Wil-266	Vestal,Ben	Cha-212	Victor	Glf-167
William	Wil-266	Danl	Lnc-340	Vickey,Heam	Ran-186
Veasey,Mark	Grn-126	John	Lnc-341	Sampson	Ran-186
Veers,William	Sur-181	Nathan	Cha-212	Vickry,Abm	Ran-186
Veich,Moses	Mec- 33	Sarah	Cha-212	Abm	Ran-186
Velsh,Rayley	Cab-147	Thos	Cha-212	Chrisn	Ran-186
Venable,Daniel	Sur-181	Wm	Cha-212	John	Ran-186
John	Lnc-333	Vestall,Silas	Cha-204	M D	Ran-186
Thomas	Sur-164	Vestell,David	Cha-210	Vicks,John	Edg- 64
William	Sur-164	David	Cha-204	Josiah	Nsh- 78
Vennables,John	Sto- 97	Vester,Benj	Nsh- 84	Victory,Benjn	Cho-223
John	Sto-127	Michael	Nsh- 83	Viddle,Vaun	Rob-219
Venters,Eliz	Ons-100	Wislie	Nsh- 84	Vier,Adam	Row- 46
Mallica	Ons- 99	Vestil,John	Ran-186	Vince,Mrs Cata	Mec- 40
Nancy	Ons-101	Vestill,Isaac	Sur-169	Colintine	Mec- 40
Verble,Daniel	Row- 86	James	Sur-165	Vincent,A	Ora-154
Henry	Row- 88	Jesse	Sur-192	Alex	Ora-154
John	Row- 86	Joseph	Cha-203	Allen	Cha-194
Verhine,Averhart	Ans- 16	Thomas F C	Sur-178	Benjn	Lnc-339
Verling,Samuel B	Sto-145	Thomas	Sur-166	Burket	Hal-121
Verloines,Abram	Cas- 73	Veztur,Eliz	Nsh- 82	Calaster	Hal-121
Thomas	Cas- 73	Vicars,Stephen	Wil-260	Dier	Mec- 42
Vermillion,Samuel	Rth-137	Viccory,Jehu	Row- 45	Drury	Mec- 42
Vermillon,Guy	Roc- 20	Vick,Anne	Hal-121	Hartgrove	Mec- 43
Vernam,Francis	Rob-236	Benjamin	Hal-121	Jacob	Grn-131
Reddan	Rob-236	Benjamin	Hal-121	Jarrett	Hal-121
Vernetson,Leven	Wsh-226	Celia	Row- 49	Letticia	Hal-121
Vernon,Isaac	Roc- 23	Edmond	Ans- 16	Mary	Hal-121
Isaac Senr	Roc- 24	Eli	Nsh- 79	Robert	Hal-121
J	Bru-226	Elijah	Nsh- 79	Rubin	Ans- 24
James	Sto-104	Isaac	Nsh- 81	T	Ora-155
James	Roc- 8	Jacob	Nsh- 85	Thomas	Cha-201
John	Roc- 24	Jesse	Way-242	Thos	Mec- 42
Jonathan	Sto-124	John	Nsh- 79	Vines,Charles	Pit-252
Molly	Roc- 23	John	Hal-121	E	Bru-234
Nehemiah	Roc- 24	John	Nsh- 81	J Snr	Bru-234
Obediah	Roc- 24	Jonah	Hal-121	Saml	Bft- 23
Richard	Roc- 22	Kinchen	Nsh- 85	Samuel	Pit-252
Richard	Roc- 32	Lewis	Nsh-644	Tho	Bft- 23
Tinsley	Roc- 7	Mary	Nsh- 79	Thos	Bru-230
Verrell,Doctr Wm	Fra- 82	Nathan	Mor- 62	Wm	Bft- 20
Verser,William Sr	War-182	Nathan	Nsh- 80	Vinsent,William	Roc- 32
Versor,William	War-182	Providence	Edg- 51	Vinson,Archey	Joh-291
Vertel,Jesse	Ran-186	Robert	Nsh- 85	Benj Jr	Way-249
Vesey,Ezekiel	Grn-127	Robert	Nsh- 92	Benj Sr	Way-251
Frankie	Grn-127	Soseph	Nsh- 79	Daniel	Nor- 79
Wm	Grn-127	Vickas,Elijah	Wil-258	David	Nor- 79
Vest,Absolum	Ire-252	Vickers,--ander	Lnc-371	Drury Snr	Joh-290
Charles	Sto-129	David	Ora-124	Elizabeth	Nor- 79
Charles	Sto-151	J	Glf-178	James	Joh-278
Charles	Sto- 99	James	Rth-137	John	Joh-291
Isham	Sto-130	John	Rth-137	Joshua	Nor- 79
Isham	Sto- 99	R	Ora-139	Paton	Joh-291
John	Sto-131	R	Ora-154	Pleasent	Hrt-211

Vinson,Mrs Sally	Fra- 86	Wade,Allen	Per-134	Wadkins,Lyddall	Rth-140
Saml	Ran-186	Andrew	Mon- 38	Smith	Cha-192
Shadrach	Nor- 79	Caleb	Car-175	Thomas	Row- 60
Susannah	Nor- 79	David	Car-175	Thomas	Row- 60
Tabitha	Pit-238	Downy	Per-146	William	Rth-144
Thomas Jr	Way-251	Edward	Mor- 65	William	Ran-184
William	Nor- 79	Elisha	Roc- 7	William	Rch-208
Vinters,Benjamin	Pit-251	Elizabeth	Car-175	Williams	Rch-207
Virgin,James	Mar-446	Henry F	Ran-183	Wadley,James	Cha-199
Virret,James	Nsh- 87	Horatio H	Rch-210	Wadsworth,Archd	Mor- 57
Vivion,Chas	Ans- 29	Howell	Nor- 80	Egnatious	Mor- 58
Vogler,Christian	Sto-146	Isaiah	Ran-185	Jno	Mor- 65
Voials,Rachel	Cab-147	James	Car-175	John	Mor- 56
Voight,John	Gat-107	James	Dup- 11	Thomas	Mor- 63
Voils,David	Cab-147	Jedidas	Car-175	Wafer,Abner	Lnc-327
Thos	Cab-147	Jno	Len-310	Waff,Geo	Cho-221
Voleny,Nathl	Tyr-207	John Junr	Nor- 80	Sarah	Cho-221
Voliver,Charles	Hyd-226	John Senr	Nor- 80	Wagener,Wm	Cab-140
Vollovey,Elisha	Tyr-206	Lyddia	Ans- 19	Wagg,J	Ash- 13
Volluntine,J	Bru-232	Mark	Mor- 69	Waggerly,John	Bur-109
Voss,Greenberry	Cas- 73	Martha	Nor- 80	Waggoner,A	Ash- 13
Philip	Sto-134	Meeks	Grn-141	Andrew	Lnc-361
Thomas	Sto-101	Moses	Roc- 13	Ben	Bft- 29
Thomas	Sto-133	Rachel Junr	Car-176	Cath	Ora-174
Vowell,Wm	Glf-155	Rachel Senr	Car-176	Caty	Lnc-369
Vuncten,Saml	Row- 66	Richard	Nor- 80	Danl	Row- 37
Vyland,James	Cha-214	Robert	Per-134	Edmond	Lnc-361
		Robert	Per-154	G	Glf-178
Waberton,John	Nsh- 75	Robt	Ran-184	Gabriel	Sto-124
Wacaser,George	Ran-184	Sally	Ons-105	Geo	Bun- 90
Henry	Ran-185	Seth	Ran-184	George	Row- 77
Jacob	Ran-184	Thomas	Per-134	H	Ash- 14
John	Ran-183	Tinslow	Mor- 58	H	Ash- 13
Wadard,Joel	Joh-283	William	Rth-138	Henry	Ora-174
Waddel,William	Joh-283	William	Nor- 80	Isaac	Rth-140
Waddell,Charles	Wil-259	Wm	Ans- 31	Jacob	Bun- 89
Hugh	Bru-228	Wilson	Car-172	Jacob	Row- 41
Hugh	Bla- 7	Windsor	Car-179	Jacob	Row- 72
John	Cha-201	Wadington,Saml	Cab-148	Jno	Ora-174
John	Bru-228	Wm	Cab-147	John	Rth-141
Richd	Way-242	Wm	Cab-148	Mary	Lnc-369
Thos	Cha-189	Wadkins,Ambrose	Rth-140	Peter	Glf-180
Waddenton,John	Cab-139	David	Row- 60	Peter	Glf-180
Waddill,Wm	Mor- 58	David	Wil-268	Thos	Mec- 52
Waddle,Betsey	Cum-258	David	Rch-207	Waggonner,Adam	Sto-152
Edmund	Ran-183	Elizabeth	Bun- 96	Gabriel	Sto- 95
Edmund	Ran-183	Evan	Rth-140	Joseph	Sto-100
George	Mec- 24	Isaac	Cas- 74	Joseph	Sto-132
Henry	Sur-178	Isarael	Rch-207	Lewis	Sto-110
Jacob	Fra- 77	James	Rch-211	Lewis	Sto-147
Jas	Mec- 54	Joel	Rth-140	Wagister,D	Mon- 46
John	Row- 82	John	Row- 63	Wagner,Danl	Row- 40
Luke	Cum-258	John	Row- 81	Wagoner,Adam	Bun- 90
Matthew	Ran-183	John	Rch-211	John	Sur-194
Richard	Sur-178	John	Rch-211	Philip	Cab-140
Wm	Mec- 37	John	Rch-195	Willm	Cab-140
Waddy,Benjn	Fra- 89	John	Rch-208	Wagster (sic)	Mon- 51
James	War-174	Kenchen	Ran-185	Wagster,Jno	Mon- 47
Spence	Fra- 89	Kinchen	Ran-184	Wah,Samuel	Ire-258

-326-

Wahab,Iseral	Mec- 33	Walker,Aaron	Glf-160	Walker,Henry		Hal-123	
Robt	Mec- 32	Abner	Cas- 74	Hugh		Cas- 74	
Wahob,Mary	Car-172	Abner	Roc- 22	Hugh		Mec- 25	
Wainright,James	Pit-256	Abraham	Roc- 31	J		Glf-172	
Richd	Bft- 39	Abraham	Ire-238	J		Mon- 43	
Daniel	Pit-257	Alexander	Cas- 74	J		Glf-174	
Wair,Martha	Brt- 67	Allen	Roc- 20	J Jr		Glf-175	
Waisner,Andrew	Row- 53	Allen	Roc- 5	Jacob		Rth-139	
Jacob	Row- 54	An	Ora-152	Jacob		Glf-159	
John	Row- 67	Andrew	Mec- 24	James		Rth-143	
Waistcoat,Geo	Bft- 39	Andrew	Mec- 25	James		War-173	
J----	Bru-228	Andrew	Ora-127	James		Roc- 26	
John	Bru-228	Andrew	Nor- 81	James		Cab-148	
Waite,Susanna	Wil-271	Any	Cur- 87	James		Cas- 74	
Wakefield,Chas Jr	Bur-127	Archabald	Mec- 22	James		Ire-252	
Chas Senr	Bur-127	Archibald	Cab-148	James		Ire-269	
John	Bur-116	Aron	Wsh-222	James		Bur-112	
Thomas	Bur-109	Aron	Ora-127	James Senr		Grn-127	
Thomas	Bur-116	Arthur	Ire-256	Jas		Mec- 35	
William	Sto-124	Benjn	Row- 59	Jeremiah		Ora-162	
Waker,David	Way-234	Betsey	Cur- 88	Jobe		Rth-141	
Walakens,Wm	Cur- 81	Betsey	Cur- 86	Jobe		Cas- 74	
Walden,Drew	Hal-122	Buck	Ora-127	Jno		Mec- 32	
Drury	Nor- 81	Buckley Junr	Per-146	Jno		Mec- 35	
Eaton free man of		Buckley Senr	Per-146	Jno		Mec- 36	
colour	Ran-187	C	Ora-154	Jno		Ora-129	
Harwood	Nor- 80	Caleb	Cur- 88	Jno		Rob-231	
James	Cha-195	Charles	Rob-229	John		Rth-141	
Jno	Ans- 14	Chay	Ora-143	John		Rth-141	
John	War-173	D	Mon- 43	John		Rth-138	
John	Cha-196	Daniel	Cur- 84	John		Pit-246	
Jonathan	Cha-205	Daniel	Nsh- 77	John	(H C)	Wil-284	
Matthew	Nor- 81	David	Sto-101	John		Wsh-227	
Richd	Ans- 13	David	Sur-196	John		Row- 58	
Stephen	Nor- 81	David	Sur-164	John		Cur- 87	
Stephen	Nor- 81	David	Sto-133	John		Cur- 90	
Thomas	Pas-209	Dianna	Roc- 9	John		Roc- 10	
William	Nor- 80	Dorset	Pit-246	John		Sto-133	
Willis free man of		Edward	Cur- 86	John		Wil-270	
colour	Ran-187	Elizabeth	Roc- 32	John		Bft- 22	
Waldon,Ann	Cha-209	Elizabeth	Cur- 84	John		Car-169	
Waldrap,Daniel	Rth-142	Elizabeth	Sur-164	John		Grn-139	
Ezekiel	Rth-141	Ellis	Grn-139	John Jr		Lnc-359	
Jeconias	Rth-142	Ezekiah	Cur- 88	Joseph		Bun- 86	
Joseph	Rth-142	Fanly	Per-134	Joseph		Cas- 74	
Luke	Rth-141	Felix	Hay-201	Joshua		Ora-123	
Robert	Rth-141	Francis Jr	Cum-256	Josiah		Wil-259	
Waldron,John	Ons-105	Francis Senr	Cum-254	Julius		Grn-128	
Mary	Ons-105	Frederick	Cab-145	Lee		Row- 88	
Wales,George	Ire-268	Geo	Mor- 65	Lem		Nsh- 74	
Henry	Sto- 99	George	Cas- 74	Martha		Wsh-222	
Isaac	Ire-268	George	Wil-284	Martha		Hrt-214	
Samuel	Ire-269	George	Grn-127	Mary		Roc- 29	
Walk,Jonathan	Row- 52	George	Rth-141	Mary		Roc- 30	
Joseph	Row- 54	Green	Fra- 99	Mary		Cum-238	
Martin	Row- 50	Hampton	Cho-225	Maxey		Cur- 88	
Saml	Row- 52	Hardridge	War-172	Micajah		War-177	
Walker,Mrs	Cum-240	Henry	Mec- 35	Micajh		Nsh- 73	
A	Ora-154	Henry	Cab-146	Micajah		Tyr-207	

Walker,Michael	Cab-140	Walker,William	Sto-119	Wall,Michael	Sur-184
Michael	Cab-141	William	Cur- 88	Peter	Roc- 10
Mildred	Roc- 6	William	Sto-133	R	Col- 18
Mysendine	Ire-238	William	Cas- 74	Randle	Mon- 23
Nathan	Cur- 87	William	Cas- 75	Richard	Roc- 21
Odley	Cur- 87	William	Cas- 74	Robert	Rth-142
P	Ora-154	William	Ire-239	Robert	Roc- 22
P	Cum-240	William	Ran-184	Sterling	Row- 86
Patsey	War-178	William	Sto- 91	Thomas	Rth-141
Peter	Ora-152	William	Row- 84	William	Nor- 81
Peter	War-179	William	Lnc-364	William	Glf-186
Phillis	Lnc-353	William	Joh-287	William	Sur-184
Philp	Ora-134	William	War-184	William	Ran-185
Pleasant	War-179	William L	Cum-246	Wm	Mon- 41
Ransom	War-180	William S	Roc- 72	Wm	Ora-112
Rebecca	Nor- 80	William E	Roc- 31	Zachariah	Roc- 22
Richard	Grn-127	Wm	Grn-130	Wallace,Aaron	Cab-148
Richard	Sur-169	Wm	Ora-143	Affeah	Pit-252
Robert	Roc- 19	Wm	Glf-160	Alexr	Mec- 39
Robert	Sto-133	Wm	Ora-129	Alexr	Mec- 50
Robert	Ire-267	Wm	Row- 58	Andrew	Dup- 30
Robert	Ire-268	Wm	Bft- 31	Andrew	Mec- 49
Robert	War-179	Wm	Mec- 49	Bea Z	Bft- 37
Robert Sr	Sur-175	Wm	Nsh- 78	Benjamin	Ons-109
Robt	Mec- 37	Wm	Tyr-206	Daniel	Row- 68
Robt	Ora-123	Wm Senr	Grn-127	David	Car-172
Robt	Ran-184	Walkup,S	Cam-155	David	Ans- 15
Robt	Ran-184	Wall,Abraham	Nor- 80	Edward	Wil-269
Rubin	Bur-104	Anne	Rth-139	Everet	Mor- 59
Sam	Ran-184	Bird T	War-168	George	Pit-262
Saml	Cur- 88	Burress	Grn-126	Hannah	Car-172
Saml	Ran-183	Danl	Mon- 40	James	Rth-141
Saml	Ran-185	David	Roc- 6	James	Dup- 31
Saml	Ran-185	David	Nsh- 84	James	Bun- 83
Samuel	Sur-164	Elizabeth	Nor- 81	Jas	Mec- 48
Samuel	War-181	Henry	Edg- 58	Revd Jas	Mec- 25
Sarah	Bun- 74	Henry	Roc- 13	Jediah	Cab-136
Senr	Lnc-359	Jas	Ans- 31	Jerry	Dup- 31
Solomon	Cum-256	Jessey Jr	Joh-286	Jno	Mec- 48
Susanna	Edg- 46	Jessey Sr	Joh-286	John	Bun- 98
Tandy	Cha-198	Jno	Ans- 31	John	Pit-252
Thadeus	Rth-143	John	Rth-141	John	Lnc-330
Tho	Bft- 31	John	Fra- 93	John	Wil-265
Tho	Bft- 25	John	Glf-171	John	Sur-179
Thos	Cur- 88	John	Roc- 26	John C	Car-172
Thos	Bur-104	John	Hrt-212	Mary Junr	Car-173
Thomas	Wsh-224	John	Roc- 9	Mary Senr	Car-172
Thos	Cur- 92	John	Mon- 40	Matthew	Mec- 39
Thos	Mec- 32	John	Rch-211	Matthew	Mec- 39
Thos Sr	Mec- 52	John	Sur-186	Matthew	Mec- 49
W	Mon- 43	John	Joh-287	Moses	Mec- 35
Wiler	Rth-142	John Jun	Roc- 11	Nathan	Row- 63
William	Rth-141	John Sen	Roc- 11	Nicholas	Mor- 56
William	Rth-139	John Sr	Mon- 40	R	Ash- 5
William	Pit-240	Join	Roc- 26	Rebecca	Car-173
William	Roc- 31	Joseph	Wil-262	Richd	Ans- 13
William	Roc- 32	Joseph	Bft- 28	Richel	Ire-241
William	Sto-101	Joshua	Grn-134	Robert	Dup- 19
William	Sto-101	Mark	Nsh- 83	Robert	Ons- 99

Wallace,Robert	Car-172	Wallis,Nancy	Hal-123	Walton,John	Grn-138
Robin	Car-174	Nathl	Grn-137	John B	Gat-107
Robt	Mec- 39	Richard	Ire-265	Loftin	Per-146
Stephen	Jon-306	Robert	War-180	Margaret	Row- 82
Tho	Bft- 22	Ruth	Rth-143	Phillip	Cas- 73
Thomas	Pit-256	Ruth	Rth-138	Rhuben	Per-146
Thomas	Sur-193	Thomas	Rth-138	Richd	Row- 87
William	Lnc-335	Thomas	Roc- 21	Thomas	Gat-107
William	Ire-241	William	Gat-116	Tilman	Bur-125
William	Ons-102	Zepheniah	Grn-137	Timothy	Gat-109
William	Mar- 14	Wallises (col)	Rch-210	Timothy	Gat-109
Wm	Car-172	Wallton,John	Dup- 21	Timothy	Brt- 50
Wm	Mec- 39	Walls,Edward	Lnc-334	Wm	Cho-231
Wm	Mec- 39	Jacob	Mon- 47	Wm	Hrt-208
Wm	Cab-136	James	Sto- 93	Waltrap,Nancy	Nor- 81
Wm	Mec- 48	James	Sto-121	Waltrop,Edward	Bur-109
Wm	Ora-163	Walraven,Alexr	Sto-154	William	Bur-109
Zekiel	Mec- 39	Walser,Frederick	Row- 80	Wamack,Richd	Row- 40
Walldrap,Edmond	Rth-139	Jacob	Row- 80	Wamble,Amos	Pit-248
Waller,Carhurt	Row- 51	John	Row- 80	Egbert	Pit-248
George	Row- 86	Philip	Row- 81	Henry	Pit-248
Henry	Edg- 46	Walsh,Andrew	Wil-282	John	Cha-198
Henry	Sto-130	John	Wil-262	William	Pit-248
James	Dup- 31	Thomas	Wil-259	Wammack,Jonah	Rth-138
John	Dup- 31	Walston,Ambers	Cur- 89	Wamoc,Archbd	Row- 52
John	Row- 78	Barbary	Edg- 52	Wamock,Archd	Lnc-359
John	Edg- 57	Charity	Edg- 49	John	Cha-191
Lucrecia	Hal-123	George	Pit-259	Richard	Row- 85
Nathan	Dup- 11	Henry	Edg- 48	Rods	Cha-191
Nathan	Dup- 32	Jonas	Edg- 69	Warbin,James	Ire-246
Nathl	Grn-139	Littleberry	Edg- 51	William	Ire-245
Peter	Row- 86	Silas	Edg- 51	Warborton,John	Brt- 46
Rebecca	Edg- 48	T	Cam-159	Ward,Mrs	Bru-234
Rebekah	Roc- 5	Turner	Brt- 59	A	Col- 19
Sterling	Edg- 47	Walten,Thos	Bur-102	Aaron	Brt- 50
William	Rth-138	Walter,Daniel	Per-146	Allen	Nor- 80
Willis	Hal-123	Nicolas	Cab-142	Anthony	Ora-118
Wallice,Penninah	Prq-229	Paul	Cab-142	Antoney	Tyr-209
Wallington,Edward	Cas- 73	W	Ash- 7	Aron	Cho-228
Wallis,Abner	Per-146	Walters,Abraham	Per-146	B	Ash- 5
Adam	Rth-142	Labon	Roc- 12	B	Ash- 12
Charity	Rch-204	Lewis	Hrt-210	Barbary	Brt- 60
Elizz	Mon- 18	Mary	Cha-211	Benj	Ons- 98
Elisha	Rch-204	Needham	Dup- 13	Benjamin	War-169
Hannah	Hal-124	Reason	Roc- 16	Benjamin	Hal-124
Hugh	Rth-143	Waltom,Amos	Ons-108	Benjamin	Hal-122
Hugh	Rth-138	James	Ons-108	Betty	Prq-229
James	Rth-141	Walton,Ed	Ora-117	Campbel	Roc- 14
Jeremiah	Hal-121	Ed	Ora-158	Catharine	Ons- 98
John	Grn-137	Francis	Sto-113	Champion	Brt- 50
John	Rch-213	Francis	Sto-155	Charles	Dup- 10
John	Hal-123	Geo	Cho-228	Charles	Lnc-369
John	Roc- 21	George	Rth-138	Charrity	Ons-101
M	Ora-146	Henry	Rth-140	Cunrod	Lnc-369
Major	Cas- 74	Henry	Gat-106	D	Ash- 7
Marey	Cur- 91	Holady	Gat-105	D	Ash- 6
Martha	Hal-121	Jno	Cho-229	D	Ora-153
Matthew	Ire-265	John	Ons-100	Daniel	Joh-283
Matthew	Ire-265	John	Row- 82	Danl	Row- 39

Ward, David	Car-182	Ward, John		Ons-108	Ward, Stephen		Cha-212
David	Ons- 98	John		Bla- 3	Stephen		Bla- 3
David	Mar- 13	John		Tyr-203	Susy		Ora-133
David	Ire-254	John B		Ire-242	T		Col- 18
Delilah	Sam-157	John		Ran-185	Tamer		Mar- 15
Edward	Ons-106	John P		War-174	Thomas		Mar- 5
Edward Jr Esqr	Ons- 99	Jonathan		Mar- 11	Thomas		Cha-194
Elizabeth	Sto-142	Joseph		Grn-126	Thos		Prq -228
Enoch	Ons- 95	Joseph		Hyd-226	Thos		Ans- 13
Frederick	Lnc-353	Joseph		Hal-123	Thos		Brt- 50
George	Brt- 44	Joshua		Brt- 61	Thos		Mon- 33
George	Mec- 43	Josiah		Ons- 99	William		Sam-158
George	Lnc-348	Josiah		Prq-228	William		Row- 60
Gilbert	Hal-122	Josiah		Wsh-227	William		Sto-107
Hennery	Jon-305	Kesiah		Tyr-208	William		Sto-142
Henry	Cha-193	Labun		Rth-144	William		Bur-131
Henry	Wsh-228	Laven		Row- 59	William		Lnc-353
Henry	Mar- 9	Lemuel		Nor- 81	William		Ire-268
Humphrey	Cho-228	Lewis		Bun- 80	Williams		Row- 85
Isaac	Row- 63	Luke		Pit-261	Wm		Mec- 24
Isaac	Cho-228	Lydia		Row- 63	Wm		Wsh-223
J	Ora-155	Lydia		Cho-229	Wm		Brt- 52
J	Ora-156	Capt M		Hrt-210	Wm		Brt- 60
J	Ora-153	M		Col- 21	Wm Esq		Rob-233
J	Col- 19	Marthy		Mar- 4	Wm		Cur- 81
J	Col- 20	Mary		Cum-251	Wm		Cho-227
J Jr	Bru-222	Matthew		Pit-262	Wm Jnr		Cho-229
J Senr	Bru-224	Matthew		Len-318	Warden, Jade		Bur-114
Jacob	Sto-140	Milcher		Lnc-353	Josiah		Ora-149
James	Dup- 3	Mile		Hrt-210	Mary		Cum-238
James	Pit-262	Morris		Jon-306	Richerd		Cur- 90
James	Bru-224	Moses		Brt- 50	Wm		Cha-192
James	Pas-209	Nancy		Pit-255	Wardlow, James		Roc- 20
James	Brt- 51	Nancy		Ons- 99	John		Roc- 19
James	Hrt-210	Nancy		Cho-222	William		Roc- 27
James	Ran-184	Oleph		Cum-264	Wardon, John		Way-238
James	Mar- 10	Palser		Lnc-353	Wards, E		Bru-222
James T	Cho-221	Patrick		Car-171	Francis Negro		Hal-123
Jas	Brt- 60	Phillip		Bla- 3	Ware, John		Cas- 73
Jas	Ora-118	R		Ora-153	Samuel		Ora-167
Jeremh	Cho-228	Randal		Sto-142	Thomas		Grn-125
Jesse	Car-179	Richard		War-179	Thomas		Cas- 73
Jesse	Sam-154	Richard Esqr		Ons-109	Thos		Mon- 24
Jesse	Ons- 95	Robt		Cha-199	William Jr		Cas- 73
Jno	Cho-228	Ru		Ora-153	William Sr		Cas- 73
Joab	Cha-205	S		Ora-153	Wm		Ans- 6
John	Dup- 3	S		Col- 20	Warf, Patsy		Ire-253
John	Dup- 28	Salley		Mar- 6	Warlick, Danl		Lnc-236
John	Pit-261	Saml		Bft- 23	Danl		Lnc-335
John	Wsh-226	Samuel		Row- 60	David		Lnc-342
John	Ora-126	Seth		War-180	Lewis		Lnc-326
John	Mor- 67	Seth		Ons- 98	Warlock, Absolum		Lnc-371
John	Mor- 57	Shadk		Cho-228	Jno		Lnc-371
John	Sto-106	Silas		Sto-108	Warmott, Thomas		Grn-131
John	Sto-141	Sollomon		Edg- 45	Warmouth, John		Fra- 95
John	Sto-155	Solomon		Car-171	Warner, Abigail		Cho-222
John	Mon- 33	Spellar		Mar- 13	Daniel		Row- 81
John	Row- 83	Spyers		Way-238	Drucilla		Row- 74
John	Edg- 62	Stephen		Ora-133	Harden		Mor- 61

Ward,John	Row- 54	Warren,William	Per-146	Wason,Henry		Bun- 75
John	Bft- 34	William	Ire-246	Wasson,J		Ash- 3
Joseph	Bft- 33	William	Ora-943	William		Ire-259
Saml	Pas-209	Wm	Bft- 32	William		Ire-263
William	Row- 53	Warrick,-----	Sam-151	Waterfield,Aberaham	Cur- 92
Warnick,L	Ora-140	Elijah	Sam-156	Berey		Cur- 92
Warnier,Deborah	Pas-208	Faithy	Rob-243	Berry		Cur- 92
Warnock,Jacob	Cum-257	Herod	Sam-159	Betsey		Cur- 92
William	Cum-257	James	Sam-156	Betsey		Cur- 92
Waroford,Samuel	Row- 79	John	Sam-159	James		Cur- 92
Warpole,Rebecca	Nor- 81	Moses	Sam-155	Jethry		Cur- 92
Warpul,James	Mon- 47	Sarah	Sam-157	John		Cur- 92
Warran,Allen	Hrt-210	Sherod	Sam-159	John		Cas- 74
Joshua	Ire-246	William	Wil-270	Mikel		Cur- 92
May	Ire-246	Warrin,Benjamin	Cas- 74	Mikel		Cur- 92
Robert	Ire-247	Bozwell	Cas- 74	Rheubin		Cur- 92
Warrell,B	Col- 20	G John	Cas- 74	Samuel		Cur- 92
James	Hrt-214	James	Cas- 74	Sarey		Cur- 92
Mary	Hrt-208	Larkin	Cas- 74	William		Cur- 92
William	War-184	Samuel	Cas- 74	William		Cur- 92
Warren,David	Ora-149	Samuel	Cas- 74	Watermon,William	Dup- 11
Edward	Jon-306	Starling	Cas- 74	Waters,Amos		Bft- 21
Edward	Gat-114	Thomas	Cas- 74	Benjn		Sam-152
Edward	Cha-205	William	Cas- 74	Catharine		Cho-223
Edward	Hal-123	William	Cas- 74	Danl		Len-311
Elijah	Joh-281	William	Cas- 74	Deep		Wil-279
Elijah	Sam-152	Warring,Ann	Cho-222	Fedk		Bft- 23
Goolow	Per-134	Warrington,Thomas	Pas-209	Henry		Sam-155
Henry	Ran-184	Warritt,Isom	Hrt-209	Isaac		Wil-280
Henry	Bft- 29	E	Col- 17	Isaac		Bft- 22
Hugh	Lnc-348	Warsham,Daniel	Row- 80	J		Col- 18
James	Wil-261	Heny	Row- 83	Jacob		Grn-149
James	Bun- 73	Warson,Robert	Row- 74	Jer		Bft- 23
James	Ran-183	Warters,Absolem	Rth-142	Jerh		Bft- 25
James	Ora-149	Moses	Rth-142	Jesse		Way-247
Jno	Ora-149	Wartes,Hardy	Ons- 97	Jno		Len-311
Jno	Ora-177	Micajah	Ons- 97	Jno Senr		Len-311
John	Bur-105	Selah	Ons-103	Jo		Bru-230
John	Rth-144	Southy	Ons- 96	John		Edg- 70
John	Gat-115	Wartman,William	Sto-110	John		Bft- 22
John	Pit-246	Warwick,Anne	Nor- 81	John P		Wil-260
John	Hyd-233	Dewey	Way-250	Jonah		Bft- 22
Joshua	Edg- 55	Jacob	Way-236	Joseph		Len-311
Josiah	Sam-155	Sally	Nor- 81	Joseph H		Cha-214
Mary	Nsh- 83	Thomas	Way-248	Joshua		Ans- 15
Michael	Nor- 81	West	Way-235	Micheal		Mec- 44
Needham	Joh-281	Wylie	Mec- 32	Moses Esqr		Wil-280
Robert	NOr- 81	Wasdon,David	Way-236	Needham		Way-248
Robert	Mar- 11	Washam,Widow	Mec- 52	Polley		Bft- 22
Sam	Ora-171	Miles	Mec- 52	Tho		Bft- 22
Sam	Ora-121	Nancy	Bun- 74	Tresyla		Bft- 22
Samuel	Nor- 81	Thos	Mec- 52	Wm		Bft- 21
Samuel	Per-134	Washburn,John	Rth-142	Winfield		Bft- 23
Samuel	Wil-261	Moses	Bur-116	Winfid		Bft- 23
Sarah	Mon- 25	Robert	Rth-143	Watezel,Henry		Bun- 86
Solomon	Sto-132	Washington,John	Grn-142	Jacob		Bun- 86
Thomas	Hal-123	John	Len-323	Watford,Jonas		Len-311
Thomas Senr	Hal-122	Nicholson	Way-253	Wm Jnr		Brt- 61
Vincent	Cas- 73	Wm	Grn-142	Wm Senr		Brt- 61

Wathan,Elisha	Gat-111	Watson,Happy	Sto-158	Watson,R L	Bla- 4
Wathen,James	Gat-111	Hugh	Rth-142	Robert	Bur-116
Watken,Isaac	Sam-150	Hugh	Rth-143	Robt	Cha-203
Watkins,Abijah	Edg- 62	Hugh	Rth-141	Robt B	Brt- 61
Alexr	Sam-163	Isaiah	Ans- 15	Samuel	Way-245
Allen	Joh-284	Israel	Hyd-228	Sarah	Ora-164
Amos	Joh-284	Jacob	Ans- 20	Sherrod	Mar-446
Arthur	Way-243	Jacob	Row- 83	Solomon	Rob-239
Chrisr	Ans- 28	James	Bun- 94	Stott	Nor- 80
David	Sam-163	James	Ora-126	Thomas	Edg- 47
Gillam	Fra- 86	James	Row- 59	Thomas	Hal-123
Isaac	Nsh- 78	James	Roc- 12	W	Bru-236
James	Dup- 12	James	Roc- 12	W	Ora-160
James	Sur-174	James	Roc- 13	W	Bla- 11
Jas	Ans- 14	James	Ora-117	Walter	Mor- 65
Jno	Mon- 37	James	Rch-195	Wentworth	Row- 75
John	Cas- 73	James	Cum-245	Will	Dup- 17
John	Dup- 13	James	Hyd-230	William	Hyd-228
John	Roc- 33	James	Ora-163	William	Rth-138
John	Fra- 92	James	Bla- 11	William	Rth-138
John	War-175	James Sen	Roc- 14	William	War-184
Leven	Dup- 13	Jas	Mec- 29	William	Roc- 22
Lydia	Way-243	Jas	Glf-169	William	Nor- 80
M	Col- 18	Jas	Mon- 40	William	Jon-306
Mitchell	Edg- 67	Jas	Rob-240	William	Sto-148
Nancy	Roc- 25	Jas Snr	Rob-232	William	Glf-179
Richard	War-180	Jas W	Bft- 34	William	Joh-272
Stephen	Rth-140	Jeremiah	Car-180	William	Ons-106
Thomas	Pit-237	Jesse Senr	Per-146	Wm	Rob-222
William	Sam-153	Jno	Mon- 41	Wm	Row- 59
Watkns,Moses	War-178	Jno	Rob-233	Wm	Mor- 67
Watson,A	Ora-146	Jno	Ans- 24	Wm	Cab-148
Adam	Hay-201	John	Glf-154	Wm	Ora-130
Alexander	Rth-138	John	Rth-138	Wm	Mec- 38
Alexander	Rch-202	John	Mor- 55	Wm	Bur-130
Alexander	Rch-195	John	Hay-201	Willie Jr	Hal-122
Alexr	Ans- 33	John	Brt- 53	Willie Sen	Hal-122
Alexr	Cum-261	John	Bur-130	Willis	Joh-282
Anne	Rth-138	John	Roc- 4	Watt,B	Col- 18
Archibald	Rch-194	John	Rob-230	Daniel	Grn-121
Arthur	Mar-446	John	Rch-194	James	Roc- 14
Asa	Ons-108	John	Joh-288	John	Ire-248
Barb	Ora-115	John	Bft- 34	John Senr	Roc- 31
Barbatha	Hrt-211	Jonathan	Rob-239	Robert	Lnc-330
Benjamin	Hyd-229	Joseph	Dup- 16	Sarah	Bru-228
Bennet	Ora-143	Joseph	Bur-109	William	Ire-241
Charles	Per-146	Joshua	Roc- 13	Watterer,Joel	Len-312
Clabon	Glf-188	Laven	Ans- 12	Rhegemshirk	Len-313
David	Bft- 34	Mark	Ora-166	Watters,Ezekiel	Cas- 74
David	Wil-277	Mrs Martha	Brt- 53	Jas	Rob-236
David	Way-246	Mary	Ans- 27	Jno	Len-313
David	Mor- 67	Mathew	Mor- 68	John	Rch-212
David	Hay-201	Mathew	Rob-242	Thos	Rob-236
Edmund	Mfc- 46	Mike	Joh-284	William	Rob-236
Elijah	Per-146	Moses	Car-181	Wm	Rob-233
Elijah	Cum-257	N	Bru-236	Watterson,Eliz	Lnc-342
Elizabeth	Wsh-226	Noah	Ire-247	George	Lnc-342
Fed	Bft- 34	Peter	Bur-130	John	Lnc-342
George Esq	Rth-138	R	Ora-152	Watts,Andrew	Ire-258

Watts,Benjamin	Wil-277	Weatherly,W	Glf-175	Weaver,John	Nsh- 89
Elizabeth	Roc- 34	Wm Jr	Glf-176	Laurance	Nsh- 89
Elizabeth	Ire-258	Z	Glf-160	Lewis	Hrt-214
James	Ire-258	Weatherouth,Aywall	Row- 86	M	Ahs- 12
James	Bur-106	Weathers,Allen	Lnc-340	Mary	Grn-135
John	Ire-258	Edward	Grn-124	Pegga	Hrt-209
John	Mar- 10	Elijah	Cas- 74	Peter	Bun- 85
John Junr	Mar-446	Elisha	Lnc-340	Robert	Grn-135
R	Col- 18	Elisha	Lnc-340	Samuel	Nsh- 89
Rachell	Mar- 4	George	Lnc-341	Sarah	Nor- 81
Thomas	Ire-265	James	Grn-124	Stephen	Sur-188
Thomas	Ire-258	Jno	Mec- 50	Stephen	Row- 47
Thos	Ans- 11	John	Lnc-340	Susinah	Hrt-209
William	Mar-445	John	Lnc-340	Thomas	Sur-173
William	Wil-278	Thos	Lnc-341	Thomas	Ora-131
William	Ire-258	Wm	Grn-124	Tim	Ora-128
Waugh,James	Wil-257	Weathersbee,Bartholomew		Valentine	Bur-111
John	Ire-239		Mar- 10	W	Ash- 4
William	Ire-258	John	Mar- 4	W	Ash- 12
Way,Abel	Cha-212	Shadk	Bla- 8	William	Sur-170
Amos	Cha-212	Thomas	Mar- 3	Wm	Row- 56
Anthony	Cha-196	Weatherspoon,George	Mec- 39	Wm	Grn-135
Benjamin	Ran-184	Thomas	Lnc-353	Willis	Hrt-212
John	Cha-212	Wm	Mec- 50	Weavle,George	Row- 79
Joseph	Cha-194	Weaver,Abraham	Grn-139	Jacob	Row- 47
Sollomon	Cha-196	Adam	Bur-129	John	Row- 47
T	Glf-183	Arthur	Ora-129	Webb,Aron	Ora-129
Wayman,John	Row- 46	Benjamin	Rth-144	B	Ash- 6
Waymire,David	Rn-184	Cannon	Rch-209	Benjamin	Bun- 77
Randolph	Ran-184	Celia	Hrt-209	Caleb	Row- 74
Waymouth,Robt	Pas-208	Charles	Hrt-216	Charity	Wil-276
Thomas	Pas-208	Charles	Row- 53	Clara	Cho-223
Weaden,Nathan	Hal-122	Conrad	Lnc-335	Daniel	Rth-140
Weaks,Benjn	Car-180	Conrad Junr	Lnc-329	Danl	Bru-230
Weant,John	Row- 38	Demsey	Hrt-212	David	Row- 82
Wear,David	Row- 49	Dudley	Grn-135	David	Rth-140
John	Row- 49	Edward	Hrt-208	David	Rth-140
Wm	Row- 48	Frederick	Rch-209	Demcy	Prq-229
Wearon,John	Ora-127	George	Row- 54	Demsey	Edg- 52
Wease,Adam	Bun- 98	Henry	Nor- 80	Demsy	Edg- 51
John	Bun- 98	Henry	Bur-111	Dred	Roc- 28
Weast,Abm	Bur-130	Hugh	Bun- 73	Elias	Rth-141
Weatherby,Aaron	Rth-144	Isaac	Grn-139	George	Hal-122
Levy	Roc- 30	J	Ash- 7	Giles	Mar- 11
Weatherford,Thos	Cas- 73	J	Ash- 12	Gill	Roc- 30
William	Cas- 73	J	Ash- 12	Henry	Rch-200
Weatherington,Abram	Mar- 6	J	Ash- 12	Henry	Lnc-353
Joseph	Mar- 6	J	Ash- 12	Hill	Nor- 80
Weatherly,A	Glf-174	Jacob	Lnc-369	J	Ash- 6
Andy	Glf-175	Jacob	Row- 88	J Junr	Bla- 10
E	Glf-174	Jacob	Row- 55	J Senr	Bla- 10
E Snr	Glf-176	Jacob	Bun- 88	James	Ora-110
Isaac	Hrt-213	James	Hal-122	James	Wil-260
Isaiah	Glf-156	James	Hrt-216	James	Bur-128
Isaiah	Glf-171	Jarrat	Hal-123	James	Per-146
J	Glf-179	Jesse	Hrt-214	James	Ora-123
Jesse	Glf-171	John	Hrt-212	James	Rth-143
Job	Glf-171	John	Bun- 89	Jas	Ora-132
M	Glf-184	John	Nor- 80	Jeremiah	Rth-139

Webb,Jesse	Ran-183	Webster,Chas	Ora-159	Welch,Isaac	Sto-133
Jesse	Ons-102	Henretta	Roc- 30	Isom	Ire-268
Jesse	Fra- 92	James	Ran-185	Jacob	Sur-183
Jno	Ans- 7	James	Roc- 26	James	Ire-261
John	Rch-208	John	Roc- 22	James	Ire-241
John	Rch-197	John	Hyd-223	Jno	Ans- 19
John	Sto- 94	Loyd	Cha-216	Jno	Ans- 8
John	Ons-100	Lucy	Bft- 38	John	Sur-170
John	Bun- 74	Martin	Roc- 20	John	Ire-262
John	Sto-123	Nancy	Roc- 30	John	Hay-201
John	Brt- 47	Nancy	Sto-152	John	Row- 65
John	Bur-128	Nelly	Tyr-212	John	Grn-131
John	Row- 75	Richd	Cha-191	John	Bur-119
John	Bun- 84	Tamsey	Roc- 28	John	Rth-138
John	Bun- 92	W	Cam-157	John	Rth-138
John	Grn-142	William	Ire-265	Joseph	Sto-124
John	Edg- 52	William	Roc- 19	Joseph Cap	Rth-139
John	Fra- 97	Weeden,Jno	Ora-154	Josha	Ora-168
John Jr	Edg- 65	Weedins,J	Bru-238	Mathias	Ran-184
John Jr	Grn-133	Weeks,Archibald	Rth-138	Miles	Cho-229
Johnston	Ora-123	Benjamin	Rth-141	Richard	Rch-208
Jonathan	Rth-139	Charlotte	Edg- 64	Robert	Grn-131
Jonathan	Bun- 93	Elisha	Rth-139	Saml	Cho-229
Laurence	Bft- 26	Jabez	Car-180	Samuel	Sto-141
Lennon	Rch-207	Jacob	Sto-152	Samuel	Sto-106
Mary	Ire-242	James	Edg- 64	Samuel	Prq-229
Moses	Cho-225	James	Edg- 63	Samuel	Ire-269
Nancy	Rth-142	James Sr	Edg- 63	Sarah	Cho-231
Reuben	Bur-128	Jno	Mec- 50	Theodosha	Sto-141
Richard	Edg- 64	John	Ran-185	Theodosia	Sto-106
Richard	Fra- 86	John	Edg- 58	Thomas	Hay-201
Robert	Rth-138	John	Car-181	Thomas	Bur-119
Robert Junr	Rch-207	Sally	Pas-208	William	Hay-201
Robert Senr	Rch-207	Seth	Ons-105	William	Glf-167
S	Bla- 10	Weer,John	Lnc-342	Wm	Bft- 20
S William	Cas- 74	John Junr	Lnc-342	Zachariah	Ans- 12
Samuel	Rch-212	John Senr	Lnc-342	Welcome,Mason	Cho-223
Samuel	Bla- 6	Joseph	Lnc-342	Welden,John	Prq-229
Samuel	Dup- 18	Robert	Lnc-342	Mary	Hal-124
Sarah	War-180	Weever,A	Glf-165	Welding,Joel	Ons-101
Stephen	Bur-116	Asale	Way-254	Weldon,Thomas	Hal-123
Thomas	Per-146	Benjamin	Edg- 43	William Jr	War-184
Thomas	Grn-137	John	Edg- 44	William Sr	War-183
Turner	Rch-207	John	Way-244	Welker,A	Ash- 13
W	Bla- 10	Jonathan	Edg- 65	Welkings,David	Dup- 31
Watson	Rch-201	Jonan	Bft- 39	Well,Geo	Mon- 25
William	Ons- 99	Weir,Jas	Cab-138	Wellaford,Micajah	Sam-155
William	Hal-124	Welb,Zacha	Cho-221	Wellborn,Genl Jas	Wil-273
William	Hal-121	Welbon,Thomas	Roc- 13	John	Wil-269
William	Row- 57	Welbourne,John	Ran-184	Wellbrooks,John	Lnc-348
William	Nor- 80	Welch,Andrew	Hay-201	Wellhelm,Lewis	Row- 69
William	Edg- 50	David	Hrt-206	Wellin,John	Pit-250
William Junr	Ons-100	David Sr	Sur-192	Thomas	Pit-250
Wm	Ans- 7	Demsay	Hrt-211	Wellington,Armsted	Cas- 73
Webber,Casper	Rth-144	Edwd	Cho-229	Wellman,John	Row- 61
Casper	Rth-142	Eli	Cho-228	Wells,----k	Lnc-371
Casper	Rth-143	Elizebeth	Ans- 10	Alexander	Dup- 24
David	Cas- 73	Ephraim	Sur-192	Ann	Edg- 50
Webla,Thos	Glf-182	George	Rth-139	Anne	Nor- 81

-334-

Wells,Benj	Hrt-211	Wels,Stephen	Per-146	West,John	Hal-123		
Benj	Nsh- 86	Welsh,Eliz	Ons-108	John	Bun- 97		
Burwell	Lnc-367	Isaack	Cha-209	John	Nor- 80		
Diannah	Ons-101	James	Car-183	Johnathan	Row- 63		
Eliz	Ons-105	John	Ons-103	Joshuay	Cur- 92		
Featherston	Lnc-367	Joseph	Cab-144	Leonard	Bun- 80		
Frederick	Roc- 10	Lydia	Bft- 22	Levi	Lnc-336		
Frederick	Dup- 24	Michael	Cha-207	Lydia	Nsh- 76		
Humphery	Rth-143	Robert	Car-184	Martin	Mec- 27		
Isaac	Lnc-342	Walter	Cha-196	Mary	Row- 52		
Isaac	Ora-132	Welton,J	Ora-139	Michl	Lnc-353		
J	Ora-153	Thos	Hrt-209	Nathan	Row- 63		
J	Col- 17	Wescott,James	Hyd-233	Noel	Joh-276		
J	Col- 20	Wescout,Miley	Tyr-209	Peggy	Wil-282		
J Jr	Ora-132	Wesley,William	Hrt-216	Penelope	Brt- 48		
Jacob (H)	Dup- 18	Wesner,John	Sur-168	Peter	Grn-134		
James	Lnc-330	Wesson,James	Rth-144	Peter	Bur-104		
James	Jon-306	William	Rth-144	Randol	Hal-122		
Jas Junr	Lnc-331	West,Widow	Bun- 97	Rebecca	Rob-220		
Jeremiah	Nsh- 81	Aaron	Wil-267	Reuben	Lnc-375		
Jeremiah	Rth-143	Alexander Jr	Bur-106	Richard	Cha-213		
Jesse	Ons-106	Alfred	Row- 52	Robert	Lnc-348		
Jno	Ora-133	Barnaby	Nor- 80	Robert	Lnc-353		
John	Nsh- 87	Barny	Lnc-368	Robert	Cur- 84		
John	Bft- 22	Barny Senr	Lnc-368	Robert	Cas- 74		
John	Cas- 73	Ben	Mec- 47	Robert	Brt- 45		
John	Bun- 74	Betsey	Cur- 91	Saml	Dup- 19		
Jonathan	Nsh- 86	C Benj	Cas- 74	Sampson	Fra- 99		
Jos	Ora-134	Cara	Ons-103	Sampson	Fra-100		
Joseph	Prq-228	Charles	Lnc-368	Susaney	Cur- 91		
Josiah	Ons-101	Charles	Ans- 30	Tart	Cum-238		
Martin	Sto-132	Charles	Pas-208	Thomas	Row- 59		
Martin	Dup- 23	Daniel	Wil-265	Vickory	Wil-266		
Mathew	Edg- 49	Daniel	Dup- 7	Vincent	Cum-253		
Michael	Edg- 41	Danl	Row- 41	William	Lnc-368		
Miles	Cas- 74	Delilah	Dup- 21	William	Row- 77		
Miles Jr	Cas- 74	Eastern	Mon- 28	William	Sur-166		
Na	Ora-153	Ephraim	Lnc-353	William	Hal-121		
Nathl	Ora-132	Gabriel	Tyr-206	William	Bun- 74		
Newman	Rth-142	Henry	Mec- 42	William	War-182		
Norman	Rth-143	Henry	Bun- 97	Wm	Bla- 8		
Samuel	Hrt-208	Hezekiah	Hay-201	Wm	Grn-135		
Samuel	Wil-276	Ignatius	Cha-208	Wm Senr	Tyr-206		
Starling	Joh-277	Isaac	Lnc-368	Wm Junr	Tyr-206		
Stephen	Nsh- 81	Isaac	Row- 63	Willis Junr	Sam-161		
Thomas	Cas- 74	Isaac Jr	Lnc-368	Willis Senr	Sam-161		
Thomas	Bun- 74	J	Col- 19	Wilowby	Cur- 90		
Thomas	Hal-123	Jacob	Ire-268	Westall,Thomas	Bun- 93		
Thomas	Dup- 18	James	Bla- 8	Westbroks,Fanney	Cas- 74		
Thomas	Edg- 45	James	Row- 52	Westbrook,Caty	Roc- 22		
W	Ora-153	James	Dup- 7	Charles	Len-317		
W	Ora-133	Jas	Bla- 9	Forney	Sam-161		
William	Ons-106	Jas	Rob-219	Fortney	Sam-152		
Williby	Edg- 63	Jas	Mec- 33	Gray	Len-319		
Willis	Edg- 55	Jerrimiah	Bun- 97	James	Nor- 81		
Wyatt	Fra- 85	Jesse	Cha-209	James	Jon-306		
Zachanah	Ran-184	Jno	Rob-223	James	Len-312		
Wels,Hardy	Sur-195	Jno	Ans- 18	Jas	Bla- 10		
Overton	Grn-121	John	Tyr-206	Jas	Sam-161		

Name	Loc	Name	Loc	Name	Loc
Westbrook,Jessey	Jon-306	Whaley,Samuel	Dup- 33	Wheeler,Richd	Glf-157
John	Bla-'11	Stephen	Dup- 33	Sarah	Roc- 28
John	Jon-306	William	Dup- 33	Stephen	Cho-222
Joseph	Sam-161	Whaly,John C	Ons-103	Wm	Rob-238
Mary	Sam-161	Rigdon	Ons-101	Wheeter,Darden	Nor- 80
Moses	Len-317	Wharry,George	Rth-139	Hezekiah	Nor- 80
Moses	Sam-161	Thomas	Rth-139	James	Nor- 80
Samuel	Jon-305	Wharton,Edmond	Jon-306	Wheler,Benjamin	Per-146
Thomas	Ons-103	Isaac	Jon-306	Eliz	Ora-132
Thomas	Roc- 22	Sarah	Jon-306	Whetsell,Wm	Ora-121
William	Sam-161	Whatwold,Elisha	Nsh- 91	Whicker,Caleb	Glf-164
Wester,John	Sam-157	Whealer,Benjn	Grn-127	John	Glf-188
Western,Amos	Edg- 64	Martin	Grn-137	Thomas	Sto-150
Westmoreland,----	Sto- 96	Nancy	Grn-127	Whickersham,John	Glf-162
Jackson	Mec- 37	Vincent	Roc- 12	Whidbee,Ann	Prq-229
Peterson	Ire-257	Whealus,Henry	Hal-122	Elizabeth	Prq-229
Robert	Ire-259	James	Hal-122	Elizabeth	Prq-229
Robert	Rth-142	Joiner	Hal-123	James	Prq-229
Taylor	Sto-125	Kinchen	Hal-122	John	Prq-229
William	Sto-125	Lemuel	Hal-123	Joshua	Prq-229
William	Bun- 72	Wheatley,Elexander	Mar- 14	Lamuel	Prq-229
Weston,Bently	Dup- 28	Elisabeth	Mar- 13	Robert	Prq-229
Eliza	Dup- 12	George Esqr	Wil-270	Whidbey,John	Cur- 81
Ephraim	Brt- 48	George Jr	Wil-262	Moger	Cur- 81
Jas	Hrt-213	Henry	Mar- 13	Betsey	Wsh-225
John	Bft- 30	John	Wil-270	Whight,John	Ran-185
John	Brt- 48	John	Cur- 90	Thomas	Ran-185
Malachi	Brt- 59	John	Mar-445	Whik,James	Lnc-359
Reuben	Dup- 11	Mary	Wil-270	Joshua	Lnc-369
Reuben	Dup- 28	Simon	Mar- 12	William	Lnc-359
Saml	Hyd-230	Thomas	Mar- 11	Whiles,Tho	Bft- 26
Solomon	Brt- 60	William	Cur- 90	Whiless,Milbry	Nsh- 77
Wiley	Lnc-356	William	Mar-446	Wm Jr	Nsh- 74
Westray,Daniel	Fra- 97	Whedbee,Benjn	Cho-223	Wm Snr	Nsh- 74
Hutson	Fra- 97	Eliz	Cho-222	Whinnery,A	Ora-132
James	Fra- 79	Richd	Cho-225	Whinney,Mary	Cha-195
Samuel	Nor- 81	Thos	Cho-225	Whirlly,Aby	Rth-141
Samuel	Nsh- 80	Thos	Cho-221	Whisenhunt,Geo	Lnc-369
Wm	Nsh- 79	Wheeler,A	Bla- 12	George	Lnc-335
Wetherington,Ambrose		Bud	Lnc-334	George	Ran-184
	Pit-238	Celia	Nor- 80	Henry	Ran-185
Wethermon,Christian	Sur-165	Etheldred	Ire-252	John	Lnc-369
Curtis	Sur-186	Ezekiel	Roc- 28	Nich	Lnc-334
Samuel	Sur-165	H	Glf-178	Whisker,Thos	Glf-163
Wethernton,James	Ons-106	Henry	Glf-167	Whisnant,Adam	Lnc-331
Wetherspoon,Tam	Lnc-348	Henry	Nor- 81	Whitacar,Isaac	Sur-172
Wettz,Eliza	Dup- 12	Henry	Edg- 51	Jonathan	Sur-177
Wever,Abraham	Sur-188	Hulda	Pas-208	William	Sur-177
Whailey,J	Cam-160	James	Hay-201	Whitaker,Abraham	Hal-122
Whaler,Mary	Ons-107	James	Glf-168	Abram	Bft- 26
Whaley,Arch	Dup- 30	Jobe	Hrt-206	Abram	Rth-140
C	Cam-164	John	Cha-190	Cary	Hal-122
Eby	Hal-122	John	Glf-184	Dudley	Hal-123
Ezekiel	Len-313	John	Glf-188	Eli	Hal-122
Isaac	Dup- 31	John	Ons-102	Edward	Hal-123
John	Cum-266	John	Hrt-208	Isom	Mar- 13
Joseph	Ire-244	John Senr	Nor- 81	J	Ahs- 10
Joseph	Ire-245	Manlove	Glf-167	James	Hal-122
S	Cam-165	Manlove Jr	Glf-167	James	Row- 62

Whitaker,James	Bun- 97	White,David	Ora-160	White,James		War-176	
Jno	Ans- 25	David	Mar- 6	James		Grn-128	
John	Hal-123	David	Ire-249	Jas		Rob-230	
John	Bun- 80	David	Cab-143	Jas		Ans- 4	
John	Rth-142	David	Prq-227	Jas		Bla- 7	
John	Bun- 97	Demcy	Prq-227	Jas		Bla- 12	
Joshua	Bun- 91	Dempsey	Brt- 44	Jane		Mec- 44	
Joshua	Hal-123	E	Cam-161	Jeremiah		Rth-143	
Lontsford	Hal-122	Edward	Ons-104	Jeremiah		Gat-109	
Manson	Mar- 12	Edward	Pas-209	Jesse		Wil-267	
Matt C	Hal-122	Edward G	Ire-259	Jesse		Brt- 60	
Peter	Row- 38	Elizabeth	Wil-266	Jesse		Mar- 9	
Peter	Bun- 88	Enous	Ans- 15	Jesse		Lnc-342	
Polley	Bft- 25	Ephraim	Brt- 60	Jesse		Pas-209	
Polley	Bft- 38	Ezekiel	Brt- 59	Jesse Jr		Prq-227	
Richard	Nor- 81	F	Bru-226	Jesse Junr		Prq-227	
Richd	Row- 58	Fedrick	Cur- 88	Jessey		Grn-124	
Robert	Hal-123	Francis	Prq-228	Jessey	(col)	Rob-241	
Robert L	Fra- 83	Frans	Bft- 26	Jo		Ora-157	
Whitmill	Hal-123	Fred	Brt- 60	Joel		Ans- 9	
Thomas	Row- 63	Frederick	Row- 55	Jno		Ora-122	
William	Bun- 80	G	Bru-232	John		Glf-175	
Wm	Bft- 37	G J	Bla- 2	John		Wil-263	
Wm	Bft- 26	Gabriel	Prq-228	John		Brt- 61	
Wm	Ora-117	Ganer	Bla- 5	John		Cur- 92	
Wm	Bun- 79	Geo	Brt- 60	John		Cab-148	
Whitby,Benj	Ora-119	Geo	Cho-231	John		Cha-215	
White,-----	Cur- 86	Geo	Glf-156	John		Bla- 4	
Mrs	Fra- 99	George	Ons- 99	John		Ire-246	
Aaron	Glf-156	George	Pas-209	John		Ire-246	
Adam	Mor- 55	George	Pas-209	John		Ran-183	
Agnes	War-167	George	Ire-258	John		Cab-148	
Agustin	Rth-142	Hannah	Nor- 80	John		Bur-131	
Amos	Brt- 50	Henry	Ans- 8	John		Bur-127	
Andrew	Ire-248	Henry	Prq-228	John		Hay-201	
Andrew	Mor- 58	Henry	Hyd-230	John		Lnc-331	
Ann	Cho-221	Henry	Rth-142	John		Row- 54	
Ann	Pas-208	Henry	Edg- 45	John		Roc- 31	
Archibald	Cab-148	Isaac	Prq-228	John		Row- 42	
Archibald	Cab-148	Isaac	Jon-306	John		Mor- 58	
Archibald	Cab-148	Isaac	Rth-139	John		Pas-209	
Arnold	Prq-228	Isiah	Ans- 6	John		Pas-209	
B	Ora-140	J	Cam-156	John	of John	Prq-227	
Ben	Pas-208	J B Esq	Col- 21	John	of Ben	Prq-227	
Ben	Pas-208	Jacob	Prq-227	John		Glf-165	
Benjamin	Bur-115	Jacob	Brt- 61	John		Pit-242	
Benjamin	Roc- 19	James	Mec- 53	John		Rth-143	
Benjn	Pas-208	James	Brt- 60	John		Edg- 41	
Betsey	Rth-143	James	Cur- 92	John Sr		Prq-227	
Betsheba	Car-178	James	Ire-244	John Sr		Prq-229	
Burges	Sto-123	James	Ire-248	John Junr		Lnc-341	
C	Cam-160	James	Ran-183	John Junr		Cab-148	
Cader	Brt- 44	James	Cur- 87	Jonas		Bur-131	
Catherine	Bla- 3	James	Lnc-328	Jonathan		Ran-184	
Charles	Cha-196	James	Lnc-332	Jonathan		Sto- 94	
Charles	War-169	James	Prq-228	Jonathan		Sto-123	
Cilas	Cho-231	James	Ora-130	Jonathan		Prq-229	
Coley	Grn-131	James	Bun- 92	Jonathan		Tyr-207	
Daniel	Ans- 10	James	Pit-238	Jordan		Prq-228	

White,Jos		Glf-168	White,Rigdon		Len-318	White,Thos	Mec- 30
Jos		Glf-152	Robert		Wil-263	Thos of Josiah	Prq-227
Joseph		Cab-146	Robert		Cur- 86	Thos	Sam-151
Joseph		Pas-209	Robert		Lnc-328	Thos W	Prq-229
Joseph		Tyr-202	Robert		Pas-209	Thos Senr	Cur- 87
Joseph		Hyd-229	Robert		Bur-110	Timothy	Cha-212
Joseph		Ora-130	Robert		Rth-142	Toms	Pas-208
Joseph		Grn-132	Robert		Rth-139	Vine	Cur- 92
Joseph Jr		Ora-142	Robt		Glf-180	W	Ora-157
Joseph Sen		Ora-142	Robt		Ans- 8	W	Bru-240
Joshua		Prq-227	Rubin		Ans- 12	Wallis	Cur- 87
Joshua		Grn-132	S		Col- 18	William	Roc- 13
Joshua	of Geo	Prq-229	Sam		Ora-122	William	Sto-143
Joshua	of B	Prq-229	Samuel		Ire-247	William	Ire-257
Joshua	of Wm	Prq-228	Samuel		Cab-148	William	Edg- 66
Josiah		Bla- 13	Samuel		Prq-229	William	Bur-128
Josiah		Mor- 58	Samuel		Prq-227	William	Sto-108
Josiah	of B	Prq-227	Sarah		Ans- 15	William	Cur- 87
Josiah	of Jacob	Prq-227	Sarah		Prq-227	William	War-183
Josiah Jun		Pas-208	Sarah	of Luke	Prq-229	William	Sur-191
Josiah Sen		Pas-208	Sarah		Pit-252	William	Prq-227
L		Ash- 10	Sarah		Car-169	William	Wsh-226
L		Bru-232	Sary		Nsh- 79	William	War-183
Lettice		Lnc-328	Seth		Prq-227	William	Nor- 80
Littleberry		Nsh- 83	Silas		Ons- 98	William	Bur-115
Ludan		Ora-120	Simeon		Cha-206	William	Rth-144
Magga		Pas-209	Solo		Brt- 53	William	Rth-143
Mariam		Prq-229	Solomon		Hrt-210	William	Edg- 43
Martin		Brt- 60	Solomon		Jon-305	Wm	Brt- 44
Mary		Mon- 27	Stanton		Glf-158	Wm	Bla- 5
Mary		Cha-206	Starling		Glf-181	Wm	Mor- 69
Mary		Ire-256	Stephen		Cha-209	Wm	Ora-142
Mary		Brt- 50	Stephen		Edg- 60	Wm	Grn-139
Mary		Pas-208	Stephen		Pas-209	Wm Senr	Brt- 54
Mary		Prq-228	Stephen		Pas-209	Wm S	Cab-148
Media		Hrt-210	Stephen		Ora-177	Willis	Roc- 4
Molly		Pas-209	Stephen		Rth-141	Willowby	Cur- 88
Nancey		Cur- 92	T---t		Tyr-207	Windsr	Bft- 31
Nathan		Pas-209	T B		Col- 19	Zachariah	Ans- 12
Nathan		Prq-228	Telis		Grn-131	Zachariah	Ans- 15
Nathan Jun		Pas-209	Theophilus Jr		Prq-228	Zedekiah	Ans- 20
Noah		Brt- 60	Theophilus Sr		Prq-228	Whitecar,Jonathan	Sur-187
Noah		Brt- 49	Thomas		Cab-146	Riley	Sur-195
Noah		Brt- 50	Thomas		Cab-147	William	Sur-187
Peggy		Prq-229	Thomas		Bur-128	Whitehall,--sus	Cur- 85
Penninah		Prq-229	Thomas		Cab-148	Elish	Cur- 85
Peter		Brt- 25	Thomas		Wsh-225	Whitehart,Willis	Ora-153
Philip		Row- 54	Thomas		Nor- 81	Whitehead,Allen	Hal-124
Polly		Pas-208	Thomas		Grn-146	Arthur	Cha-203
Polly		Pas-209	Thomas		Rth-139	Arthur	Nsh- 75
Rachel		Rth-142	Thomas		Gat-107	Augustine	Edg- 45
Rebecka		Pas-208	Thomas		War-181	Benj	Hal-123
Rebeca		Pas-209	Thomas		Cha-214	Ebenr	Per-146
Reuben		Prq-229	Thos		Bla- 3	Eliz	Ons-100
Reubin		Brt- 60	Thos		Cur- 86	Henry	Nsh- 75
Reubin		Brt- 60	Thos		Cur- 86	Jacob	Hal-123
Reubin Senr		Brt- 61	Thos	of Wm	Prq-227	Jacob	Cha-208
Richard		Sur-186	Thos	of Ben	Prq-227	James	Pit-250
Richardson		Ire-262	Thos		Prq-227	James	Nsh- 75

Whitehead,James	Edg- 66	Whitemer,Geo	Lnc-369	Whitley,Cager	Mon- 48		
John	Hal-124	John	Lnc-369	David	Hrt-214		
John	Pit-240	Philip	Lnc-329	Elijah	Hrt-207		
John	Pit-258	Whitemore,James	Grn-125	Elijah	Sam-150		
Jon	Nsh- 75	Whites,Jesse Musac Jr		Elisha	Hrt-214		
Joseph	Prq-228		Rob-227	Eliza	Bft- 21		
Joseph	Hal-123	Jesse Musac Senr	Rob-227	Elizabeth	Lnc-328		
Katharine	Hal-123	Whiteside,Mrs	Mec- 27	Enoch	Joh-287		
Lazarus	Cum-246	Jas	Mec- 26	Exodus	Mon- 47		
Lazarus	Nor- 81	Moses	Bun- 83	Filus	Mon- 47		
Lazy	Nsh- 76	Saml	Mec- 26	Geo	Mon- 48		
Mathew	Edg- 43	Whitesides,Adam	Rth-141	George	Edg- 47		
Matthew	Cum-259	John	Rth-139	George	Hrt-214		
Milley	Cur- 90	John	Lnc-330	Hardy	Nsh- 79		
Nathan	Nsh- 74	Thomas	Rth-142	Hardy	Edg- 50		
Robert	Cum-260	William	Rth-144	James	Hrt-212		
Sarah	Hal-123	William F	Rth-141	Job	Mon- 46		
Sarah	Edg- 66	Whitesill,Sam	Ora-171	John	Joh-281		
Silas	Cha-211	Whiteus,Jesse	Cab-144	John	Bft- 21		
Thos	Cha-208	Whitfield,Abraham	Nsh-643	John	Pit-254		
Will	Pit-241	Ann	Nsh- 78	Jonathan	Mon- 48		
William	Sur-192	Benjamin	Edg- 53	Jesse	Cum-265		
William	Cum-246	Bryan Jr	Len-317	Jesse	Bft- 21		
William	Pit-258	Bryan Senr	Len-131	Jesse	Way-233		
Wm	Hal-123	Conste	Len-323	Jesse	Edg- 45		
Whitehous,James	Cur- 88	Deliah	Nsh- 79	Josiah	Nsh-644		
Samuel	Cur- 89	Georg	Per-146	Kager	Mon- 46		
Whitehouse,Anthony	Pas-209	Hardy	Nsh- 77	Mary	Nsh- 89		
Fred	Pas-209	Jacob	Nsh- 78	Micajah	Nsh- 86		
John	Cha-203	James	Per-154	Mills	Nsh- 76		
John	Nsh-643	John	Hal-123	Needham	Mon- 47		
Whitehurst,Arthur	Pit-244	John	Len-318	Needham	Mon- 47		
Bat	Bft- 32	John	Per-146	Patcy	Mon- 47		
Batson	Pit-244	John	Grn-124	Selah	Sam-163		
Batson	Pit-244	Joseph	Dup- 15	Samuel	Pit-254		
Charles	Pit-244	Lewis	Len-316	Simeon	Edg- 48		
H	Cam-163	M	Brt- 48	Sion	Nsh- 78		
Hillery	Bft- 33	Needham	Way-235	Solomon	Nsh- 76		
J	Cam-165	Rhuben	Nsh-644	Stephen	Ans- 26		
J	Cam-165	Rubin	Hrt-212	William	Joh-279		
J	Cam-161	W	Ora-154	Zillah	Way-245		
J	Cam-153	Wiley	Nsh- 77	Whitlock,John	Sto-123		
Joshua	Pit-244	William	Hal-123	John	Sto- 95		
Lydia	Bft- 33	William	Way-235	William	Sur-178		
Richard	Ons-109	Wm	Cas- 74	Whitlow,Henry	Row- 70		
Richard	Car-177	Wm	Ora-125	Jesse	Cas- 74		
Robert	Car-177	Wm Sr	Nsh- 84	John	Cas- 74		
S	Cam-154	Whithed,Wm Sen	Ora-165	Jordan	Cas- 74		
Samuel	Car-172	Whithers,Richard	Pit-243	Joseph	Pas-209		
Thomas	Ons-108	Whiticer,John	Rth-143	Matthew	Mec- 52		
W	Cam-165	Whiting,Saml	Pas-208	Wm	Cas- 74		
William	Pit-244	Whitledge,Ambers	Jon-306	Whitlowe,John	Row- 75		
Williby	Edg- 53	Whitley,Arthur	Mar- 7	Whitman,Henry	Len-311		
Zach	Bft- 33	Auther Jr	Bft- 21	Jacob	Cur- 80		
Whiteman,Fredk	Cho-225	Auther Sen	Bft- 21	John Jr	Dup- 20		
Mattheq	Cho-225	Benj	Nsh- 91	John Sr	Dup- 18		
Whitemer,Stephen	Pas-208	Benjamin	Mar- 15	Whitmill,Thomas	Hal-123		
Ben	Lnc-337	Benjamin	Mar- 15	Whitmore,Charles	Ora-126		
Daniel	Lnc-369	Cader	Joh-279	Howell	Cas- 73		

-339-

Name	Ref	Name	Ref	Name	Ref
Whitmore, Lucy	Cas- 74	Whorton, Dianna	Pas-209	Wiggans, Joshua	Hrt-207
Richd	Cas- 73	E	Glf-176	Katharine	Hal-123
Abm	Pas-208	E	Glf-175	Sarah	Hrt-216
John	Pas-209	Gideon	Glf-154	Thos	Hrt-207
Ransom	Sur-189	J	Glf-172	Willie	Hrt-206
Whitsel, Saml Jr	Ora-137	Saml	Pas-208	Wm	Hrt-207
Whitsell, A Sen	Ora-132	Sarah	Ons-104	Wiggin, E	Bla- 12
Adam	Ora-120	Selah	Edg- 46	Joseph	Bla- 13
C	Ora-177	Watson	Glf-175	Thomas	Gat-113
Henry	Ora-159	William	Pas-208	Wiggins, Archbd	Fra- 98
Ja Sr	Ora-177	Whuley,, B	Ora-153	Arthur	Brt- 55
Jacob	Ora-120	Jno	Ora-153	Arthur	Hal-122
Jacob Jr	Ora-177	Shyght, William	Ran-185	David	Bur-126
James	Roc- 17	Shysenhunt, Adam	Ran-184	Edward	Nor- 80
John	Ora-160	Wian, Peter	Lnc-328	Elias	Fra-100
N	Ora-177	Wiatt, Abraham	Lnc-341	Elihu	Sam-163
S Sen	Ora-155	Demsey	Nsh- 91	Elijah	Sam-163
Whitset, Samuel	Roc- 6	Sarah	Hal-123	Ezekiel	Bur-121
Whitside, Jno	Mec- 27	William	Row- 66	Geo	Len-313
Whitsill, A	Ora-145	Wice, John	Row- 78	Geo	Len-313
Whitson, Joseph	Bun- 89	Michal	Row- 79	Gersham	Len-312
Thomas	Bur-124	Wichard, John	Pit-235	Hardy	Bur-108
Whitston, John	Lnc-337	Wickasen, Jacob	Ran-184	Henry	Edg- 57
Whittaker, Israel	Bur-120	Wicker, Benjamin	Sto-150	Isaac	Bla- 13
Jacob	Ora-168	David	Cha-195	James	Len-313
Patsy	Ora-168	David	Mor- 68	James	Edg- 69
Wm	Ora-168	James	Sto-101	James	Mar- 3
Whittamore, Abraham	Roc- 14	James	Sto-133	Jesse	Gat-110
Clem	Roc- 26	Jesse	Mor- 68	Jesse O	Hal-124
Clement	Roc- 10	Jonathan	Mor- 68	John	Len-312
Lewis W	Roc- 15	Johnson	Mor- 68	John	Len-313
Whitted, Jno	Ora-113	Mathew	Cha-195	John	Edg- 57
Jos	Ora-147	Mathew	Mor- 68	John Sr	Edg- 56
Levi	Ora-126	Milly	Mor- 68	Lewis	Sam-151
Thos Jun	Ora-158	Robt	Cha-195	Mary	Bla- 12
Thos Senr	Ora-147	Tally	Sto-147	Philip	Wsh-227
Wm	Ora-110	Thomas	Sto-150	Sampson	Fra- 96
Whittenton, Leonard	Wil-260	Thos	Cha-195	Samson	Nsh- 73
Whittet, James	Ran-185	William	Sto-133	Samuel	Wsh-223
Whittington, C	Ash- 5	Wickerson, Caleb	Ran-185	Samuel	Nor- 80
Richd	Joh-275	Wickes, Jane	Cur- 92	Sarah	Len-313
Richd Snr	Joh-275	William	Cur- 92	Stephen	Cum-248
Robt	Joh-291	Wicks, H	Mon- 43	Thomas	Edg- 58
Whittock, James	Sur-168	Joseph W	Prq-229	Wm	Hal-122
Thomas	Sur-167	Mathias	Prq-229	Willis	Bur-121
Whitton, Priscilla	Wsh-223	Samuel Jr	Prq-228	Willis	Nsh- 85
Thomas	Wil-285	Samuel Sr	Prq-229	Willis	Sam-151
Whitty, Charles	Jon-306	Shadrick	Prq-228	Wiggons, Eli	Bur-104
Joseph	Jon-306	William Sr	Prq-229	Wiggs, Abner	Len-316
Lewis	Jon-306	Widdop, Wm	Glf-163	Amos	Way-240
Whitworth, A	Glf-184	Widdows, Isaac	Glf-170	Arthur	Way-234
Elizabeth	Roc- 22	Wm	Glf-170	Danl	Sam-159
Jacob	Roc- 4	Wier, Thos	Mec- 38	Henry	Way-250
John	Roc- 32	Thos	Mec- 48	Henry	Way-248
Mary	Roc- 34	Wiggains, Caroline	Hrt-212	Henry Sr	Way-234
Tabitha	Roc- 34	Henry	Hrt-214	Jesse	Way-250
Thomas	Roc- 6	Wiggan, Willis	Hal-123	John	Way-237
William	Lnc-337	Wiggans, Edward	Hal-122	John	Way-233
Whooten, Charles	Pas-208	Henry	Hrt-214	John	Way-234

Wiggs,John Sr	Way-253	Wildere,Nathaniel	Car-180	Wilkerson,Charles	Ran-185	
Jordan	Way-234	Wildin,Hosa	Ons-101	David Jr	Grn-133	
Lewis	Way-252	Wilds,Humphrey	Bur-118	David Sr	Grn-134	
Thomas	Way-233	Wiles,Jacob	Bun- 94	Francis	Pit-244	
William	Way-253	James	Sur-167	Francis	Grn-134	
Wigins,Federick	Grn-135	John	Sur-192	J	Bru-230	
Joseph	Grn-127	Lewis	Sur-166	J	Ora-161	
Rachel	Rob-235	Luke	Sur-191	James	Grn-134	
Thomas	Grn-135	Luke Sr	Sur-190	James Jr	Nor- 81	
Wigs,Obediah	Joh-286	Pinson	Sur-166	James Sr	Nor- 80	
Wike,Jacob	Lnc-348	Stephen	Sur-192	Jas	Ora-161	
Wikle,Michael	Hay-201	Thomas	Sur-192	John	Per-146	
Wil---ing,Ephraim	Sto-104	Thomas Sr	Sur-192	John	Grn-134	
Wilaby,John	Pit-244	Wiley,Alexander	Cas- 73	John	Nor- 81	
Wilber,John	Pas-209	Alexr	Glf-155	John	Row- 42	
Temperance	Grn-137	Cleophas	Wsh-221	John Jr	Grn-135	
Wilborn,Jean	Ran-185	David	Glf-155	Lewis	Per-146	
John	Ran-185	Evan S	Cab-144	Patience	Pit-240	
William	Ran-185	Hardy	Ons-104	Polly	Row- 89	
Wilborne,John	Row- 47	Harvey	Wsh-220	Randol	Grn-135	
Moses	Row- 47	Hugh	Glf-156	Samuel	Row- 89	
Moses	Row- 48	Jas	Glf-153	William	Ran-185	
Wm	Row- 48	Leah	Wsh-224	Wm	Ora-161	
Wilbourn,Jesse	Ran-183	James	Wsh-221	Wm	Grn-134	
John	Ran-183	Moses	Cab-143	Wilkeson,Danl	Rob-222	
Milly	Sur-193	Oliver	Cab-144	Moses	Bur-125	
Wilburn,Lewis	Joh-272	Oliver Junr	Cab-144	Wm	Bla- 7	
Wilcock,Steph	Tyr-204	Robt	Glf-154	Wilkey,Cathrine	Cha-212	
Wilcockson,Daniel	Wil-261	Thomas	Cas- 74	Israel	Cha-210	
Wilcox,Dana	Rob-233	Thos	Glf-152	V	Ora-161	
Lida	Rob-233	Thos	Glf-161	Vinct	Ora-147	
Jerry	Pas-209	Thos	Glf-153	Wilkie,Jo	Ora-119	
Martha	Rob-233	W	Glf-154	Wilkin,J	Cam-163	
S	Ash- 8	William	Glf-156	Jona	Ora-172	
S	Ash- 8	Wilfong,Elisa	Ora-111	Wilkingson,T	Bru-236	
Wilder,Adkin	Brt- 62	Wilford,Arch	Brt- 53	Wilkins,Ann	Sam-151	
Ann	Brt- 61	James	Brt- 54	Charles Jr	Rth-144	
Caty	Joh-287	Wilhelm,Ceo	Cab-141	Charles Snr	Rth-144	
Cullen	Joh-288	Wilhite,Young	Grn-138	David	Wil-264	
Fras	Cho-225	Wiliams,Cary	Per-146	David	Hal-124	
Irwin	Joh-278	Wiliamson,Francis	Cur- 90	Elijah	Ans- 10	
James	Cas- 74	James	Per-146	Elisha	Cum-247	
James	Joh-287	Wilie,Ruannah	Ire-242	Elizth	Hyd-222	
Jesse	Ons-105	Wilken,Geo	Glf-171	Geo	Cha-212	
Jonathan	Ons-104	Wilkens,Alexr	Cha-190	George	Sur-174	
Joseph	Joh-287	Benjn	Way-238	Isaac	Hay-201	
Mary	Joh-274	George	Sto-124	J	Cam-159	
Michl	Cho-227	Jacob	Gat-110	Jacob	Hyd-222	
Moses	Nsh- 83	Jesse	Rob-241	James	Rth-141	
Nathl	Cho-227	John	Sto-124	James	Edg- 68	
Saml	Joh-278	John	Ons-107	John	Hay-201	
Sampson	Cho-225	Patsy	Cur- 91	John	Sto- 95	
Samuel	Ons-105	Samuel	Cur- 83	Jonas	Rob-234	
Stephen	Cum-262	Wm	Ora-130	Lewis	Hal-123	
Till Snr	Joh-287	Zilla	Ons-107	Margryt	Hyd-223	
William	Joh-287	Wilkenson,Jno W	Ora-171	Mildred	Hal-124	
William	Joh-287	Wilkerson,Ann	Pit-233	Nancy	Nor- 80	
Willis	Cho-225	Benjamin	Pit-244	Priscilla	Hal-124	
Wildere,Abraham	Car-181	Caleb	Ran-184	Richard	Rth-144	

Wilkins,Richd	Ora-120	Wilkison,Lemuel	Bur-108	Willhite,Mrs Rachel	Fra- 79
Rothias	Hyd-222	Mathew	Rob-241	Willholm,Henry	Cab-141
S	Cam-161	Neill	Cum-264	William,Catharine	Hrt-211
Samuel	Way-252	Ozburn	Mec- 44	Daniel	Hrt-214
Sophia	Hal-124	Peter	Rch-191	Elisha	Hrt-212
Terrell	Rth-138	Philip	Cum-251	Josiah	Hrt-208
U Nicey	Sam-152	Sally	Rob-230	Wood Senr	Sam-161
West	Hal-122	Thomas	Per-146	Williames,Betsey	Cur- 89
Whitmell	Brt- 64	Wilks,Elijah	Rob-219	John	Cur- 93
William	Edg- 68	Elisha	Rob-219	Stuard	Cur- 93
William	Cas- 74	James	Brt- 56	Williams,-----	Ran-183
William	Hyd-221	John	Jon-306	Williams (sic)	Mon- 51
William	Bur-111	John	Brt- 67	A	Ash- 5
William	Sto-124	John	Rob-224	A	Glf-183
William	Edg- 45	Micajah	Brt- 56	Abigail	Car-171
William	Nor- 80	Solomon	Rob-224	Abner	Per-146
Wm	Grn-126	Stephen	Pit-252	Abner	Nor- 81
Wilkinson,Abram	Hyd-225	Will,Old	Bft- 30	Absolam	Rob-236
Benjn	Car-180	Willard,Augustine	Sur-183	Alair	Per-134
Brian	Hyd-225	Daniel	Prq-228	Alex	Mon- 27
C	Col- 17	George	Sto-101	Alexr	Cum-259
Coleman	Hyd-233	George	Sto-133	Alexr	Row- 54
Edward	Rch-191	John	Sto-137	Alfen	Grn-135
Eliz	Ons-106	John	Sto-104	Allen	Cha-191
Elizabeth	Hyd-224	Jonathan	Sur-189	Allen	Brt- 64
Isaac	Hyd-224	Joseph	Prq-228	Allison	War-167
Isaac	Hyd-224	Martin	Prq-228	Amos	Mon- 24
Isriel	Hyd-225	Willas,George	Rob-220	Amos	Bur-130
James	Lnc-356	James	Rob-220	And	Ora-137
James	Hyd-225	Saml	Rob-220	Ann	Cas- 74
John	Dup- 7	Willborn,Samuel	Wil-264	Anne	War-167
John	Edg- 44	Willcox,Benjamin	Jon-306	Aquilla	Ire-252
John	Lnc-361	John	Jon-306	Arney	War-167
Joshua	Edg- 54	William	Jon-306	Arthur	Fra- 81
Lewis	Rth-140	Willebey,Edward	Ans- 19	Arthur	Prq-229
Marvil	Hyd-225	Willefred,J	Col- 17	Austin	Row- 50
Oden	Hyd-224	Willemson,Henry	Way-243	B	Bru-234
Reuben	Joh-282	Willens,Charles	Joh-279	Bench	Per-134
Richard	Hyd-224	Lucretia	Joh-278	Benet	Per-146
Robert	Hyd-225	Willesom,Joseph	Nsh- 87	Benj	Mon- 24
Thomas	Rth-144	Willet,Demsey	Mon- 26	Benj	Car-171
William	Rth-143	James	Cha-198	Benj	Mor- 54
William	Lnc-356	John	Cha-197	Benj	Ons-108
Zachariah	Hyd-225	Willetts,Gabriel	Sto-146	Benjamin	Ran-184
Wilkinton,Robt	Cha-196	Gabriel	Sto-111	Benjamin	Nsh- 84
Wilkison,Angus	Cum-269	Henry	Sto-111	Benjamin	Brt- 48
Archd	Rob-225	Henry	Sto-146	Benjamin	Rth-138
Christian	Rob-225	Willey,Francis	Ons- 98	Benjamin	Ran-183
Danl	Rob-225	Hillary	Gat-109	Benjamin	Edg- 42
Danl	Ora-127	John	Ons- 96	Benjn	Hal-123
David	Per-134	Thomas	Hal-122	Benjn	Hal-121
Edward	Rob-229	William	Hal-122	Benjn	Row- 60
Edward	Rob-225	Willeybey,Joseph	Ans- 19	Benjn	Sam-151
Jas	Mec- 48	Willfong,Geo Jr	Lnc-369	Benjn	Grn-123
Jno	Ora-122	John	Lnc-369	Benjn	Ans- 30
Jno	Rob-224	Martin	Lnc-369	Benjn	Ans- 9
Jno	Rob-224	Peter	Lnc-369	Betsey	Cur- 88
John	Per-146	Willhite,Ambrose	Fra- 91	Betsey	Cur- 88
Lemuel	Bur-126	Lewis	Fra- 79	Bilgrm	Nsh- 90

Williams,Bingiss	Bur-109	Williams,Edward	Bur-107	Williams,George	Gat-113	
Brice	Ons-104	Edward	Rch-208	George	Rth-142	
Bridges	Grn-124	Edward	Glf-167	George	Rth-140	
Buckner	Nor- 81	Edward Esq	Ons- 96	George	Rth-143	
Burgess	Bur-115	Edwards	Pit-252	George	Rth-144	
Burrell	Cha-200	Edwd	Dup- 28	George	Rth-144	
Burrell	Cha-193	Elias	Fra- 81	George	Dup- 10	
Burwell	Edg- 43	Elijah	Hrt-207	George	Fra- 84	
Burwell	Dup- 28	Elijah	Ans- 8	George	Row- 60	
Byrd	Cup- 23	Elijah	Bur-126	George	Ire-265	
C	Cam-157	Elijah	Bun- 96	George	Cur- 79	
C	Ash- 4	Elijah	Edg- 44	George	Hyd-226	
C	Cum-240	Elijah L	Rth-141	George III	Pit-234	
Catherine	Sam-162	Elirn	Sam-154	George Buch	Pit-234	
Charity	Pit-255	Elis	Nsh- 84	George H	Pit-248	
Charity	Mar- 5	Elisha	Gat-113	George Sorrel	Pit-234	
Charity	Nsh- 86	Elisha	Fra- 82	Gideon	Rth-139	
Charles	Sto-139	Elisha	Hrt-207	Giles	Rob-236	
Charles	Cur- 93	Elisha	Ons-101	Godfy	Bft- 27	
Charles	Cur- 91	Elisha	Brt- 58	H	Cum-238	
Charles	Grn-147	Eliz	Ons- 98	H	Ash- 13	
Charles	Dup- 14	Eliz	Ons-109	Hampton H	Edg- 53	
Charles	Fra- 81	Eliz	Ons-104	Harris	Fra- 88	
Charles	Sto-105	Eliza	Bft- 27	Harry H	Cum-246	
Charles	Lnc-359	Eliza	Bur-122	Hawkins	Sur-187	
Charles	Lnc-339	Eliza B	Cho-222	Helen	Gat-114	
Chloe	Mar- 7	Elizabeth	Pit-248	Henry	Ans- 14	
Cobb	Rth-139	Elizabeth	Mor- 56	Henry	Cha-210	
Cole Joseph	Sur-184	Elizabeth	Edg- 42	Henry	Ans- 30	
Cooper	Nsh- 73	Elizabeth	Cas- 74	Henry	Grn-145	
Craftin	Cas- 73	Elizabeth of Jno	Cas- 74	Henry	Grn-130	
Daniel	Cha-193	Elizabeth	Row- 89	Henry	Fra- 80	
Daniel (Bo Nasty)	Sam-154	Elizabeth	Hal-121	Henry	Nsh- 86	
Daniel	Cur- 82	Ellender	Roc- 6	Henry	Cas- 74	
Daniel	Ons-101	Enoch	Bun- 95	Henry	Bft- 27	
Danil	Mon- 26	Ephraim	Mon- 23	Henry G	War-172	
Danl	Lnc-375	Ephriam	Sur-171	Herod	Edg- 44	
Danl	Ran-183	Eprain	Sto-138	Hezekiah	Nor- 80	
David	Per-146	Evan	Len-316	Hezekiah	Mec- 43	
David	Sto-139	Ezekiel	Cha-212	Hezekiah Esqr	Ons-101	
David	Ans- 30	Ezekiel	Ons-102	Hiram	Rth-144	
David	Dup- 17	F--	Mon- 35	Halowell	Cur- 90	
David	Sam-154	Fed	Lnc-359	Hopkins	Dup- 9	
David	Sto-104	Fereby	Cum-246	Hosa	Ons-102	
David	Hrt-212	Fountain	Jon-305	Howell	Grn-121	
David	Lnc-359	Francis	Mon- 25	Hubbert	Rch-201	
David	Ire-252	Francis	Brt- 50	Humphrey	Bun- 83	
David	Ora-127	Francis	Dup- 10	Isaac	Prq-228	
Demcy	Gat-115	Francis	Roc- 33	Isaac	Ans- 23	
Denney	Bft- 27	Francis	Row- 54	Isaac	Joh-290	
Dennis	Len-317	Frank	Ire-254	Isaac	Lnc-353	
Dred	Brt- 50	Freder	Dup- 17	Isaac	Pas-208	
Drewry	Nsh- 87	Frederick	Lnc-339	Isaac	Pas-209	
Drewry Jr	Nsh- 87	Geo	Ans- 14	Isaac Sr	Prq-228	
Drury	Edg- 42	Geo	Cha-209	Isaac Senr	Cum-259	
Duke	Cas- 73	George	Pit-248	Isae	Cur- 93	
E	Cam-157	George	Pit-247	Isham	Cha-200	
E	Cam-159	George	Bun- 96	Isheamail	Mec- 42	
E	Ora-143	George	Gat-113	J	Cam-162	

Williams,J		Cam-162	Williams,Jno	Ans- 26	Williams,John B		Cho-221
J		Mon- 34	Jno	Ans- 30	John	(C house)	Per-146
J		Cam-154	Jno	Ora-122	John	D	Mar- 5
J		Cam-154	Jobe	Ans- 14	John	Esq	Fra- 81
J		Cam-158	Joel	Sam-161	John	Esq	Sur-173
J		Ash- 5	Joel	Edg- 44	John	Junr	Fra- 81
J		Ash- 4	Joel	Cum-259	John	Jr	Sur-171
J		Col- 19	Joel	Nsh- 88	John	Jr	Row- 78
J		Col- 19	Joel	Lnc-328	John	Senr	Per-134
J		Glf-183	Joel S	Cum-245	Jonas		Glf-168
J		Ash- 14	John	Way-238	Jonathan		Mec- 36
J		Bru-236	John	Cha-206	Jonathan		Gat-115
J B		Mon- 34	John	Cha-196	Jonathan		Gat-114
Jacob		Len-312	John	Cha-199	Jonathan		Gat-114
Jacob		Dup- 29	John	Len-317	Jonathan		Rth-140
Jacob		Dup- 11	John	Roc- 7	Jonathan		Rth-143
Jacob		Cur- 79	John	Roc- 9	Joseph		Cha-199
Jacob		Ran-183	John	Cur- 91	Joseph		Ans- 22
James		Sto-133	John	Brt- 49	Joseph		Len-313
James		Hrt-210	John	Brt- 54	Joseph		Ora-172
James		Pit-252	John	Pit-259	Joseph		Dup- 31
James		Gat-114	John	Pit-261	Joseph		Rth-139
James		Gat-113	John	Pit-244	Joseph		Car-172
James		Dup- 33	John	Grn-126	Joseph		Row- 65
James		Dup- 30	John	Hal-122	Joseph		Cur- 79
James		Nor- 81	John	Row- 51	Joseph		Hal-122
James		Nor- 81	John	Roc- 22	Joseph		Hyd-226
James		Bur-110	John	Glf-157	Joseph	Jr	Dup- 19
James		Rth-139	John	Rth-140	Joseph	Jr	Sur-174
James		Fra- 82	John	Rth-140	Joseph	Sr	Dup- 19
James		Sur-190	John	Rth-140	Joshua		Edg- 44
James		Nsh- 79	John	Rth-144	Joshua		Cha-209
James		Cas- 73	John	Rth-138	Joshua	Jun	Roc- 5
James		Sur-162	John	Grn-149	Joshua	Junr	Roc- 18
James		Ran-183	John	Nor- 81	Joshua	Senr	Roc- 18
James		Ran-183	John	Edg- 43	Joshua	Sen	Roc- 5
James		Ran-184	John	Bur-104	Judd		Pas-209
James		Ire-254	John	Rth-139	Jude		Lnc-375
James		Ire-253	John	Len-323	Kelsey		Edg- 62
James		Hal-122	John	Joh-282	Laurence		Row- 65
James		Roc- 29	John	Joh-274	Leml		Ans- 22
James		Row- 56	John	Nsh- 86	Lemuel		Pit-252
James		Bru-226	John	Sur-172	Leonard		Grn-147
Jane		Edg- 62	John	Ons-107	Levin		Glf-168
Jane		Bru-226	John	Ons-101	Lewis		Mar- 4
Jas		Ans- 26	John	Edg- 64	Lewis		Brt- 66
Jas		Ora-176	John	Edg- 56	Lidda		Sur-196
Jas		Cur- 82	John	Row- 78	Luke		Rth-139
Jas		Bft- 27	John	Row- 78	Lurenar		Pas-209
Jason		Gat-115	John	Ran-183	M		Ora-141
Jerey		Mor- 62	John	Lnc-353	M		Cam-163
Jesse		Hrt-210	John	Bun- 80	M		Mon- 34
Jesse		Dup- 29	John	Brt- 66	M		Ash- 9
Jesse		Sto-154	John	Hal-121	M		Col- 19
Jesse		Rch-211	John	Gat-114	Margaret		Cha-199
Jesse		Ons-101	John	War-173	Mark		Cha-194
Jesse		Sur-172	John	Sam-161	Mary		Pit-234
Jethro		Hrt-211	John	Dup- 21	Mary		Dup- 19
Jethro		Nor- 80	John	Dup- 35	Mary		Bur-122

Williams,Mary	Rch-206	Williams,Robert	Pit-254	Williams,Theo		Sam-159
Mary	Ons-108	Robert	Rth-140	Theophilus		Dup- 27
Mary	Hal-123	Robert	Dup- 11	Tho		Tyr-212
Mary	Pas-208	Robert	Glf-187	Tho		Bft- 26
Mary	Prq-229	Robert	Sto-100	Tho		Ora-175
McCajah	Mec- 31	Robert	Cur- 87	Thomas		Wsh-224
Menase	Sam-154	Robert	Hay-201	Thomas		Edg- 43
Mildred	Dup- 28	Robert	Nsh- 89	Thomas		Dup- 32
Mills	Gat-114	Robert	Per-228	Thomas		Rth-144
Miriam	Pas-209	Robert Jr	Dup- 11	Thomas		Rth-143
Moses	Brt- 49	Robt Junr	Sam-162	Thomas		Nor- 81
Moses	Lnc-358	Robt Junr	Sam-161	Thomas		Fra- 82
Moses	Sur-180	Robt Senr	Sam-162	Thomas		Cum-268
Moses	Ora-114	Rolan	Nsh- 87	Thomas		Cum-262
Mourning	Dup- 30	Roland	Ans- 10	Thomas		Sur-172
Nancey	Cur- 89	Roland	Roc- 18	Thomas	C	Sur-173
Nancy	Mar- 6	Rowland	Rch-199	Thomas		Rcc- 6
Nancy	Lnc-327	Rubin	Ans- 23	Thomas		Len-313
Nathan	Cha-196	S	Mon- 34	Thomas		Bur- 93
Nathan	Nor- 80	S	Cam-154	Thomas		Bun- 92
Nathan	Mec- 29	S	Col- 17	Thomas		Grn-121
Nathan	Hrt-212	S	Ora-146	Thos		Prq-228
Nathan	Nsh- 88	S	Bru-232	Thos		Cha-215
Nathan	Cas- 74	Saml	Ans- 26	Thos		Cur- 86
Nathan	Mec- 48	Saml	Cam-158	Timothy		Ans- 8
Nathaniel	Mor- 65	Saml	Brt- 66	Tully		Prq-229
Nathl	Ans- 21	Saml	Nsh- 85	Uriah		Prq-228
Nathl	Grn-147	Samuel	Per-146	V		Ash- 14
Nathl	Roc- 27	Samuel	Bun- 93	W		Cam-161
Nathl Jr	Grn-135	Samuel	Nor- 80	Warren		Hrt-214
Nehemia	Row- 60	Samuel	War-180	Wesley		Row- 60
Nelly	Mor- 63	Samuel	Mar-446	Wiatt		War-182
Nimrod	Cha-202	Samuel	Nsh- 87	Wiley		Grn-147
Noah	Edg- 43	Samuel	Ire-253	Wiley		Nsh- 89
Obediah	Ran-184	Sarah	Sto-101	William		Wsh-221
Orren	Nor- 81	Sarah	Pas-208	William		Way-239
Owen	Pas-208	Sarah	Sto-133	William		Cha-203
Owin	Sto-133	Semion	Ons- 97	William		Len-316
Owin	Sto-101	Serena	Ons-105	William		Roc- 6
Parrit	Ans- 21	Seth	Pas-209	William		Pit-252
Peter	Joh-288	Sherrard	Nsh- 81	William		Bun- 94
Peter	Ora-113	Silvia	Hal-122	William		Gat-114
Plummer	Rch-209	Simon	War-180	William		Rth-142
Polly	Brt- 65	Stephen	Ans- 10	William		Rth-142
President (col)	Rob-241	Stephen	Len-316	William		Dup- 11
R	Cam-159	Stephen	Dup- 19	William		Edg- 48
R	Glf-184	Stephen	Dup- 8	William		War-183
R	Ash- 14	Stephen	Hay-201	William		Sam-154
Randal	Ans- 26	Stephen	Rch-205	William		Lnc-341
Rebecca	Len-322	Stephen	Ons- 95	William		Hay-201
Reubeon	Mec- 37	Stephen	Ora-167	William		Lnc-364
Rich	Glf-183	Stephen	Ons-104	William		Mar- 14
Richard	Mar- 13	Stephen	Row- 56	William		Mar- 11
Richard	Row- 64	Stephen Esqr	Ons-102	William		Mar- 5
Richard	Pit-263	Stevens	Wsh-224	William		Ons- 98
Richard	Cha-190	T	Cam-157	William		Cas- 74
Richd	Ans- 32	T	Cam-160	William		Sur-179
Robert	Grn-145	Temperance	Dup- 11	William		Cas- 73
Robert	Sto-132	Thedorek	Cha-216	William		Cur- 79

-345-

Name	Ref	Name	Ref	Name	Ref
Williams,William	Sur-161	Williams,James	Dup- 9	Willis,Andrew	Car-176
William	Row- 85	James	Cur- 88	Anne	Hal-122
William	Wil-266	James	Jon-306	Benjamin	Rth-139
William	Hal-121	Jas	Mec- 52	Benjn	Car-182
William	Prq-228	Jas	Mec- 41	Briton	Car-175
William (Gen)	War-183	Jeremiah	Roc- 31	Caleb	Car-176
William (Maj)	War-183	Jeremiah	Jon-306	Daniel Junr	Car-176
William Junr	Roc- 29	Jno	Cho-231	Elijah	Cha-201
William Jnr	Roc- 7	Jno	Mec- 40	Ezekiah	Car-175
William Senr	Roc- 29	Jno	Mec- 36	Daniel Senr	Car-175
Willm	Fra- 96	John	Rch-204	Geo	Row- 52
Willm Esq	Fra- 94	Josiah	Sam-158	Geo Junr	Row- 52
Willm	Fra- 85	Kinchen	War-177	George	Rob-241
Wm	Glf-168	L	Col- 18	George	Car-179
Wm	Cha-200	Lewis	Lnc-367	George	Car-173
Wm	Ans- 19	Lewis	Mor- 59	H	Bru-232
Wm	Ans- 21	M	Col- 19	Henry	Cas- 75
Wm	Ans- 32	M	Col- 19	Icabod	Nor- 80
Wm	Bft- 30	M	Col- 20	J	Cam-158
Wm	Mon- 23	Mark	Hal-124	Jacob	Row- 51
Wm	Ora-134	Matthew	Nor- 81	James	Rth-140
Wm	Grn-130	N	Cum-237	James	Car-176
Wm	Ora-137	Nathan	Cas- 73	James	Row- 52
Wm	Grn-147	Peter L	Hyd-227	Jas	Bft- 27
Wm	Car-172	R	Col- 18	Jeremiah	Cum-247
Wm	Cur- 81	Richard	Nor- 81	Joab	Rth-140
Wm	Ora-113	Richard	Bun- 86	John	Rob-242
Wm	Row- 37	Robt	Cha-205	John	Lnc-342
Wm	Mor- 62	Roland	Ans- 25	Jonathan	Dup- 21
Wm	Per-134	Saml	Hyd-226	Joseph	Pit-239
Wm Esq	Fra- 99	Saml	Hyd-226	Joseph	Rth-139
Wm H	Bft- 39	Solomon	Car-180	Joseph	Car-179
Wm Jr	Mon- 34	Thomas	Nsh- 87	Josiah	Car-176
Wm Sr	Mon- 34	Thomas	Row- 76	Lewis	Hal-121
Willis	Nsh- 82	Upton	Mec- 37	Littleton	Car-175
Wilson	Nsh- 84	Urbane	Jon-306	Marget	Rth-140
Zachariah Jr	Cha-201	W	Col- 19	N	Ora-139
Williamson,--ert	Lnc-371	Will	Sam-163	Nicholas	Cas- 74
Ann	Nsh- 87	William	Cas- 74	Peter	Rth-144
Ann	Cas- 74	William	Cur- 88	Reubin Junr	Car-175
Avery	Hyd-230	William	War-183	Reuben Senr	Car-175
Benj	Cas- 73	William	Row- 75	Richd	Cum-248
Benjamin	Nor- 81	Wm	Mor- 62	Robert	Pit-255
Benjamin	Sur-197	Zackh	Sam-162	Russel	Car-175
Charles	Bun- 86	Williford,Abner	Brt- 62	Samuel	Car-176
Demsey	Hyd-226	Benjamin	Edg- 61	Sarah	Car-176
Dorothy	Hal-122	Benjamin	Edg- 42	Seth	Car-175
Elijah	Bun- 91	Harmon	Edg- 42	Simon	Rob-241
Eliz	Ons-107	John	Edg- 43	Step	Ora-120
Frances	Hrt-213	John	Brt- 62	Thomas	Car-182
George	Hal-122	John	Edg- 65	Thos	Row- 52
George	Cha-198	Meedy	Edg- 44	Wm	Cha-196
Godfree	Mec- 36	Willms,Askenoss	Cha-193	Wm	Cha-216
Hawley	Roc- 31	Willins,John	Hal-122	Wm	Hal-122
Henry	Pit-252	Nathan	Nsh- 89	Wm	Row- 52
Isaac	Rch-204	Willis,Abner	Car-176	Wm	Row- 39
J	Col- 19	Aganes	Car-179	Wilson	Cha-202
J	Col- 18	Ahab	Rob-220	Zachariah	Car-179
James	Mor- 59	Alpheus	Car-176	Williston,Elijah	Car-174

Name	Ref	Name	Ref	Name	Ref
Williston,James	Car-174	Wilson,Alexander	Ire-242	Wilson,Isaac Jr	Prq-228
Willitt,Russel	Cha-209	Alexr	Ran-185	Isaac Sr	Prq-228
Willkins,John	Hal-122	Alfred	Rob-238	Isabella	Len-316
Willoby,Mary	Brt- 62	Amos	Ons-101	Ishmel	Row- 62
Willoughbee,Saml	Hrt-205	Andrew	Ons-105	J	Mon- 35
Wm	Hrt-216	Andrew	Lnc-369	J	Cam-153
Willoughby,Sol	Joh-274	Andrew	Bun- 83	J	Col- 19
Willroy,A	Cam-162	Andw	Ora-118	J	Glf-177
Wills,---es	Way-245	Angeliso	Rth-143	J	Ash- 11
Abraham	Wil-264	Anna	Ora-167	J S	Bla- 11
Cunrad	Lnc-364	Archa	Ons-100	Jacob Jr	Prq-228
Daniel	Lnc-359	B	Glf-183	Jacob Sr	Prq-228
Elisa	Ora-133	Capt B	Mec- 52	James	Way-233
Haborn	Grn-134	Benj	Glf-157	James	Bun- 99
Henry	Cho-222	Benjamin	Rth-142	James	Rth-139
Humphrey	Rth-138	Benjamin	Row- 64	James	Rth-138
Isaac	Lnc-364	Bloomer	Cha-201	James	Cum-250
Jacob	Dup- 21	Boyd	Row- 40	James	Ran-185
James	Cho-222	Caleb	Cur- 91	James	Cum-240
John	Lnc-335	Caleb	Ora-167	James	Ons- 97
John	Lnc-364	Call	Glf-157	James	Ire-242
Robert	Per-134	Charles	Cum-270	James	Ire-252
Will	Dup- 23	Christopher	Prq-228	James	Way-248
Willsocks,Samuel	Bun- 78	Clement	Len-317	James	Lnc-330
Willson,Abner	Cas- 74	D	Glf-158	James	Ora-120
Eliza	Ora-168	Daniel	Rth-142	James Junr	Lnc-353
James	Bur-129	David	Rth-139	James Jr	Brt- 52
James	Bur-117	David	Mec- 52	James Senr	Lnc-353
James	Cas- 74	E	Col- 20	James Senr	Brt- 51
James	Cas- 73	E	Col- 18	Jas	Ans- 23
James W	Edg- 47	Ed	Ora-132	Jas	Glf-161
Jas	Mec- 50	Ed Sen	Ora-134	Jas	Ans- 32
Jas Junr	Ora-168	Edward	Cha-214	Jas	Mec- 39
Jas Senr	Ora-168	Edward	Bun- 79	Jas	Mec- 27
Jesse	Bur-113	Edward Jnr	Bft- 65	Jas	Ora-145
Jesse	Bur-112	Edward Senr	Brt- 65	Jas	Mec- 46
John	Bft- 30	Elijah	War-170	Capt Jas Esq	Mec- 39
John	Ire-112	Elisha M	Sam-154	Jane	Glf-154
Johnston	Cas- 74	Elizabeth	Cum-248	Jery	Mor- 56
Joseph	Bur-117	F	Glf-159	Jesse	Ran-185
Mary	Bur-117	Francis	Pas-209	Jesse	Glf-157
Randel	Bur-127	G	Col- 19	Jessee	Roc- 15
Robert	Bur-125	General	Bur-106	Jno	Ans- 32
Robert	Cas- 73	Geo Junr	Bun- 76	Jno	Mec- 35
Stagy	Bur-117	Geo Junr	Bun- 79	Jno	Mec- 38
Thomas	Ora-168	Geo Senr	Bun- 79	Jno	Ora-143
William	Bur-115	George	Mec- 23	Jno	Lnc-353
William	Cas- 73	George	Bla- 13	Jno	Ora-120
William	Cas- 74	George	Ran-185	Rev Jno M	Mec- 45
Wilmoth,Ezekiel	Sur-162	George	Hrt-210	John	Glf-171
Jabriel	Rth-143	Hartwell	Rth-143	John	Bur-129
William	Rth-143	Hartwill	Rth-142	John	Sto-139
Wilmouth,Nathan	Cas- 75	Henry	War-172	John	Grn-136
Wm	Cas- 75	Hester	Cha-198	John	Mec- 26
Wilscey,J	Cam-155	Hester	Glf-157	John	Bun- 89
Wilson,Mrs	Mec- 37	Humphry	Cha-202	John	Sam-155
Mrs	Mec- 54	Isaac	Gat-113	John	Dup- 15
A	Glf-175	Isaac	Ran-185	John	Dup- 21
A	Glf-179	Isaac	Brt- 60	John	Rth-144

Wilson,John	Sto-105	Wilson,Peggy	Row- 85	Wilson,Solo		Ora-134
John	Lnc-341	Pheraby	Way-250	Stephen		Cha-215
John	Row- 63	Pleasant	War-179	T		Cam-157
John	Ire-239	Plum	Mec- 53	T		Glf-173
John	Mar- 16	R	Cam-157	Theo		Len-312
John	Rch-200	R	Ora-137	Tho		Ora-127
John	Mon- 20	R	Ora-144	Tho		Len-318
John	Cha-214	R	Col- 20	Tho		Ora-127
John	Ora-160	R	Ora-157	Thomas		Grn-121
John	Ons-106	Randall	Rth-139	Thomas		Rth-141
John	Ran-183	Richard	Bun- 96	Thomas		War-181
John	Lnc-353	Richard	War-179	Thomas		Lnc-326
John	Bun- 76	Richard	Bun- 76	Thomas		Sto-143
John	Bun- 82	Ripley	Hal-121	Thomas		Ran-184
John	Wil-272	Robert	Sto-109	Thomas		Bun- 79
John	Hal-122	Robert	Bun- 98	Thos		Sam-162
John	Lnc-337	Robert	Rth-140	Thos		Ran-185
John	Lnc-333	Robert	Sto-145	Thos		Ran-185
John	Lnc-330	Robert	Grn-147	Thos		Glf-183
John	Row- 41	Robert	Rch-211	Thos		Mec- 45
John	Roc- 27	Robert	Ora-167	Thos		Mec- 41
John	Roc- 29	Robert	Row- 81	Thos		Lnc-337
John	Pas-208	Robert	Ire-258	Thos		Lnc-332
John	Hyd-225	Robert	Bun- 82	Thos		Lnc-333
John	Mor- 67	Robert	Lnc-337	Thos		Glf-157
John	Hyd-226	Robert K	Rth-143	W		Glf-177
John Sr	Grn-135	Robert K	Rth-141	Will		Cur- 90
Jonathan	Rth-142	Robert M	Lnc-336	Will		Pas-208
Joseph	Mon- 35	Robert W	Ire-247	William		Way-235
Joseph	Len-312	Robt	Mor- 62	William		Way-239
Joseph	Mec- 36	Robt	Mec- 52	William		Sto-140
Joseph	Bun- 96	Robt	Ans- 29	William (L F)		Wil-281
Joshua	Row- 83	Robt	Way-235	William		Pit-236
Joshua	Lnc-346	Robt	Way-233	William		Nor- 80
Joshua	Bun- 76	Robt	Glf-159	William		Rth-139
Joshua	Hal-121	S	Col- 17	William		Row- 76
Joshua	Way-248	Salley	Nsh- 82	William		Bun- 78
Josiah	Brt- 65	Salley	Way-248	William		Bun- 86
Josiah	Ons-106	Sally	Ons- 99	William		Bun- 76
Lamb	Cur- 90	Sam	Ora-162	William		Wil-265
Lewis	Rob-238	Saml	Cha-199	William		Lnc-327
Lewis	Grn-147	Saml	Mec- 35	William		Glf-179
Littleberry	Hal-123	Saml	Cha-193	William Senr		Bun- 98
Lydia	Prq-227	Saml	Ran-185	Wm		Bur-105
M	Mon- 35	Saml	Mec- 52	Wm		Glf-181
M	Col- 19	Saml	Lnc-334	Wm		Ora-147
M	Col- 21	Samuel	Lnc-342	Wm		Mor- 62
Margaret	Ire-258	Samuel	Mec- 24	Wm B		Row- 62
Mary	Wil-281	Samuel	Bun- 89	Wm G		Ans- 18
Mary	Edg- 46	Samuel	Ran-183	Wm I		Mec- 24
Mary	Ire-256	Samuel	Ire-251	Wm J		Lnc-330
Math	Ora-122	Samuel	Bun- 78	Willis		Pit-236
Mathew	Grn-131	Sanford	Hal-121	Zeblon		Ons-103
Mathew	Sam-156	Sarah	Mec- 33	Wilton,Daniel		Jon-305
Matthew Senr	Lnc-353	Sarah	Row- 41	Susanna		Jon-306
Moses	Lnc-342	Seth	Bft- 26	Wily,John		Glf-154
Nancy	Rth-144	Sherod	War-180	Robt		Glf-152
Nancy	Nsh- 76	Silvenus	Glf-169	Wimberley,Benjn		Brt- 57
Noah	Sam-151	Simgon	Cur- 90	David		Cha-191

Name	Ref	Name	Ref	Name	Ref
Wimberley,George	Joh-287	Windly,Isaac	Bft- 19	Winkler,Joseph	Bur-129
James	Ans- 7	Windorn,Isom	Edg- 43	Matthias	Bur-106
John	Brt- 62	Windos,Eppenitus	Row- 87	Peter	Row- 51
Levy Jnr	Brt- 54	Winds,Elizabeth	Mec- 38	Thomas	Bur-106
Levy Senr	Brt- 54	Windslow,Jesse	Cho-229	Winley,Elizabeth	Hyd-220
Malacha	Joh-288	Job	Cho-229	James	Hyd-223
Wimbly,M	Mon- 37	Pleas	Cho-228	John	Hyd-223
Wimbrough,Michael	Hal-123	Windsor,John	Roc- 31	Levy	Hyd-220
Wimbury,Danl	Pas-208	John	Cas- 74	Thomas	Hyd-221
Enoch	Pas-209	Thomas	Cas- 73	Winn,Andrew	Cur- 82
Wims,James	Cas- 73	Wine,Claret	Len-311	Archelus	Roc- 17
Winagam,Sharp	Per-134	Winebarger,Cunrad	Lnc-348	Tho	Bft- ·26
Winan,Elizabeth	Hrt-209	Winedoff,Daniel	Cab-139	William	Cum-239
Winants,Mrs	Brt- 45	David	Cab-139	Wm	Cha-202
Winben,James	Hrt-216	John	Cab-140	Winne,Ann Jun	Tyr-205
John Senr	Hrt-216	Mathias	Cab-139	Joseph	Tyr-206
Winborn,Abraham	Nsh- 91	Michael	Cab-142	Winningham,Adam	Ran-183
Benjn	Brt- 45	Winet,Norman	Ire-265	Richd	Ran-183
David	Hal-123	Winey,Josiah	Sam-157	Thos	Cha-208
David	Nsh- 85	Winfield,Avis	Hyd-234	Winsette,Joseph	Jon-305
Eliz	Nsh- 91	Brian	Hyd-225	Winslow,Benja	Prq-227
John	Nsh- 91	Charlet	Ans- 16	Caleb	Prq-227
Winborne,Dempsey	Nor- 80	Edward	Ans- 16	Elhazer	Ran-185
James Senr	Nor- 80	Penelope	Hyd-225	Esther	Prq-227
John	Nor- 80	Rhoda	Hyd-225	Henry	Ran-183
Stephen	Nor- 80	Richard	Hyd-232	James	Ran-183
William	Nor- 80	Valentine	Hyd-232	John	Pas-209
Winbourn,David	Ran-184	Winford,Alexr	Row- 57	John	Ran-183
Winburn,Eli	Rch-208	John	Row- 59	John	Cum-241
Henry	Mar- 15	Winfray,John	Mar- 15	John Jr	Prq-228
Wince,Jno	Mec- 40	Winfree,David	Grn-134	John Sr	Prq-227
Winchaster,Thos	Mec- 31	James	Grn-134	Jordan	Prq-227
Winchester,Coleman	Roc- 18	Winfrey,Caleb	Sur-172	Joseph	Ran-183
Daniel	Mec- 31	Isaac	Sur-180	Mary	Glf-186
David	Roc- 18	Job	Sur-180	Millicent	Prq-227
David	Bur-124	Obadiah	Sto-126	Jesse	Prq-227
David	Bur-117	Obediah	Sto- 97	Nathan	Ran-184
Douglas	Bur-121	Wingate,Demcy	Prq-228	Peter	Prq-229
Francis	Bur-117	Henry	Len-317	Samuel	Prq-227
John	Roc- 17	J	Lnc-364	Thomas	Ran-184
Thos	Mec- 41	J	Col- 19	Winsor,Danl	Sur-168
Wm	Mec- 43	Joel	Pit-238	Isaac	Sur-184
Winders,Edwd	Dup- 14	John	Pit-250	Winstead,Charles	Per-146
James	Dup- 3	Joseph	Prq-228	David	Nsh- 88
Windham,Greene	Pit-246	Peggy	Lnc-364	Jeremiah	Edg- 43
Isaah	Pit-244	Wm	Bru-222	Jeremiah	Edg- 42
John	Pit-244	Wm	Ans- 9	John	Per-146
Micajah	Edg- 64	Wingler,Leonard	Wil-266	Peter	Nsh- 82
Peter	Cum-263	Winick,D	Glf-171	Samuel	Nsh- 88
Willie	Joh-274	Winingham,James	Ran-185	Thomas	Nsh- 89
Winding,Elisebeth	Mec- 39	Winker,Jonah	Bft- 28	Winsted,Joseph	Edg- 43
Windley,Henry	Bft- 21	Winkfield,Thomas	Ire-258	Mathew	Edg- 65
Isl Jun	Bft- 20	Winkler,Abm	Bur-130	Samuel	Per-146
John	Bft- 21	Christian	Sto-146	Stanly	Per-146
Moses	Bft- 20	Conrod	Bur-126	William	Per-134
Reed	Bft- 20	Conrod	Bur-104	Winston,Anthony	Fra- 94
Shadrach	Hyd-223	Ephraim	Bur-106	Benjn	Fra- 99
Tho	Bft- 19	Francis	Row- 81	Mrs Edy	Fra- 99
Wm	Bft- 19	Francis	Row- 52	George	Fra- 99

Name	Loc	Name	Loc	Name	Loc
Winston,Isaac	Fra- 99	Wiser,Joel	Cur- 92	Wolf,Ann	Ora-146
Jesse	Fra- 84	Wishong,Conrad	Sur-191	Betsy	Mec- 41
John	Fra- 99	Leonard	Sur-175	Caleb	Bun- 91
Joseph	Sto-109	Leonard Jr	Sur-178	Charles	Way-247
Joseph	Sto-151	Phillip	Sur-190	Charles Jr	Way-247
Mrs Mary	Fra- 99	Wisner,David	Hay-201	Daniel	Sur-180
Moses	Grn-124	Jesse	Sto-134	Frederick	Way-247
Moses	Fra- 99	John	Sto-135	Frederick	Sto- 91
Robert	Sto-125	Michael	Sto-134	George	Mec- 31
Robert	Sto- 96	Wisong,John	Sur-195	Henry	Mec- 31
Silvanus(moved)	Grn-124	Wiswot,Chares	Cur- 82	Jacob	Mec- 32
Thomas	Grn-124	Witcher,Ephriam	Sur-161	Philip	Mec- 31
Willie	Fra- 99	Witherington,Benj	Len-315	Stephen	Way-247
Willm	Fra- 99	Danl	Len-313	Wolfendun,John	Bft- 39
Winter,Mitchm	Lnc-327	Eliz	Len-322	Wolfington,Abram	Glf-170
Robt	Lnc-330	Fredk	Len-321	D	Glf-169
Winters,Ambrose	Hal-121	George	Hrt-210	James	Roc- 21
Jemima	Wsh-227	Jno	Len-315	James	Glf-170
John	Fra- 98	Micajah	Len-315	John	Glf-170
Mary	Hal-124	Miles	Hrt-210	Woliver,Jacob	Cab-141
Mary	Hal-124	Rachel	Hrt-210	Wollace,Jesse	Ans- 6
Ritter	Hal-122	Reuben	Len-315	Wollard,Abs	Bft- 25
Savina	Hal-124	Robert	Len-313	Abs	Bft- 24
Watson	Cas- 73	Wm	Len-316	Alligd	Bft- 23
William	Bur-121	Willis	Len-315	Benjamin	Edg- 50
Wm	Hal-122	Witherow,James	Rth-143	Colem	Bft- 22
Wirley,Richd	Mon- 38	John	Rth-142	Coutn	Bft- 22
Wisanon,L	Glf-178	Sidney	Rth-143	Danl	Bft- 23
Wisdom,Abner	Cas- 74	Withers,Abram	Bft- 19	Danl	Bft- 39
John	Cas- 74	Isam	Rth-144	David	Bft- 25
Wise,Aron	Rob-239	Nathaniel	Rth-144	Elijah	Edg- 69
Benjamin	Bur-121	Willis	Rth-143	Eliza	Bft- 23
Edith	Way-249	Willis	Rth-144	Enoch	Edg- 50
Elisha	Way-236	Witherspoon,David Esqr		Howe	Bft- 24
Geo	Bun- 85		Wil-262	Jaspr	Bft- 22
Henry	Lnc-327	Harison	Bur-130	Jeremih	Bft- 25
Jacob	Lnc-335	Jas	Lnc-336	John	Bft- 24
Jacob	Row- 86	John	Wil-276	Kelite	Bft- 22
John	Lnc-326	William	Ire-239	Kromn	Bft- 25
John	Lnc-337	Withrow,James	Bun- 72	Martin	Bft- 25
Mary	Ons-106	John	Bun- 91	Michl	Bft- 24
Thomas	Ons-106	Witsman,Conrod	Ora-128	Nancy	Pit-233
William	Joh-278	Witsordhouse,Martin	Cab-141	Noah	Bft- 24
Wiseman,Ann	Bur-113	Witt,Edmund	Sto-156	Osbourn	Bft- 22
Isaac	Row- 52	Edmund	Sto-114	Richd	Bft- 25
Timothy	Row- 81	J	Glf-178	Richd	Bft- 24
William Jr	Bur-114	Joshua	Bun- 75	Riley	Bft- 24
Wm	Row- 40	William	Sto-156	Saml	Bft- 25
Wm	Bur-130	Wittenberg,Widow	Lnc-348	Saml Sen	Bft- 25
Wilson	Row- 85	John	Lnc-348	Wiley	Bft- 24
Wisemen,Isaac	Row- 37	Wittey,Ezekiel	Roc- 18	Wm	Bft- 39
Wisener,Jesse	Sto-102	Witty,Andy	Glf-160	Wm	Bft- 25
John	Sto-103	Wlijah	Glf-160	Woller,Daniel	Rth-143
Michael	Sto-102	Wod,Jonathan	Bun- 96	Wollf,Daniel	Sto-129
Wisenhart,Michael	Bur-106	Wodhouse ----in	Cur- 85	Wom---,John	Jon-306
Wisenheart,John	Bur-131	Hezekiah	Cur- 85	Womack,Adison	Rth-140
Wishard,Mrs	Mec- 28	Wofford,Wm	Glf-181	Britain	Mor- 67
Wishart,Jonathan	Rob-220	Woldridge,Josiah	Roc- 11	David	Cas- 73
Wisher,Francis	Cur- 92	Wm	Roc- 11	George	Rth-140

Name	Ref	Name	Ref	Name	Ref	Name	Ref
Womack,Green	Per-146	Wood,James		Way-238	Wood,Simion	Nor- 81
Jacob	Ora-110	James		Pit-252	Sol	Glf-189
James	Ora-167	James		Nor- 81	Surrell	Glf-188
James	Rth-140	Jas		Ans- 26	Stephen Sr	Sur-173
Jesse	Cas- 74	Jesse		Cum-268	Thomas	Sur-192
John	Cha-195	Jesse		Brt- 55	Thomas	Wil-270
Josiah	Cas- 73	Jno L R		Ora-175	Thos	Glf-187
Merideth	Cha-214	John		Sur-195	Thos	Prq -229
Thomas	Roc- 12	John		Joh-290	Wiley	Glf-197
William	Rth-141	John		Ran-185	Will	Pas-209
William	Rth-140	John		Ran-184	William	Row- 80
Womble,John	Edg- 47	John		Ire-242	William	Row- 85
Saml	Cha-207	John		Row- 80	William	Pan-185
Wombles,Josiah	Hal-121	John		Row- 80	William	Ran-183
Wommack,Abner	Rth-139	John		Row- 81	William	Hal-121
Abram	Rth-140	John		Row- 84	William	Pas-208
David	Rth-141	John		Wil-270	William	Pas-208
Wommock,Brittain	Mor- 67	John		Pas-208	William	Per-146
Wons,David	Brt- 43	John		Per-228	William	Bun- 96
Wooard,David	Nsh- 72	John		Bun- 89	William	Bur-120
Woob,Peter	Grn-121	John		Rth-144	William	Rth-144
Wood,Aaron	Jon-306	John Junr		Nor- 80	William Junr	Sam-161
Alfred	Ans- 26	John Senr		Nor- 81	Willis	War-183
Brittain	Fra- 87	Jonathan		Sam-161	Wm	Ans- 6
Burgess	Glf-187	Jos		Ora-149	Zebedee	Ran-183
C	Ora-138	Jos Jr		Glf-165	Zebedee	Ran-183
Clement	Ran-183	Joseph		Rob-243	Wo d. l,Absalom	Joh-276
D	Glf-163	Joseph		Pas-209	James	Joh-277
Daniel	Edg- 68	Joseph		Jon-306	Wo ard,Aron	Nsh- 72
David	Ran-184	Joseph		Wil-270	Arthur	Hrt-211
Edward	Nor- 80	Joseph Jr		Wil-270	Briton	Nor- 80
Elizabeth	Sto- 95	Josiah		Edg- 72	Danl	Nsh- 72
Elizabeth	Grn-139	Judith		Nor- 81	David	War-170
Elizabeth	Sto-124	Livia		Ora-171	Isaac	Way-244
Esther	Prq-229	Lott		Rth-141	Isaiah	Bft- 27
Frame	Ans- 28	Lurance		Way-239	James	Joh-288
Francis W	Edg- 70	Martha		Wil-270	James	Joh-286
Frederick	Ons-106	Matthew		Dup- 24	James	Ran-185
Geo	Cha-214	Mark		Pas-209	Jessee	Nor- 80
Green	Sam-161	Moses		Jon-306	Jessey	Joh-286
H	Ora-138	Nancy		Rth-140	John	Nor- 80
Harry	Cum-266	Nathan		Prq-228	John	Way-244
Hennery	Jon-306	Patty		Ran-184	John	Joh-287
Henry	Fra- 86	Pennel		Ran-185	Kedar	Way-244
Henry	Row- 81	Peter		Sur-168	Lewis	Nor- 80
Henry	Bun- 75	Peyton D		Nor- 80	Luke	Way-245
Hugh	Per-146	Preter		Jon-305	Martin	Joh-277
Isaac	Pas-209	Rachal		Row- 81	Matthew	Joh-286
Isaac	War-175	Rebekah		Bur-122	Michael	Joh-286
Isaac	Ora-136	Reuben		Ran-186	Olliver	Nor- 80
Izral	Row- 71	Richard		Prq-228	Penny	Nor- 81
Jacob	Ons- 95	Richd		Tyr-210	Salley	Nsh- 72
James	Rth-144	Robert		Sur-193	Samuel	Way-232
James	Tyr-210	Robert		Row- 89	Sarah	Way-244
James	Row- 81	Robt		Ran-183	Sherad	Joh-286
James	Bft- 37	Robt		Ran-183	Stephen	Joh-283
James	Bur-124	Sampson		Ora-142	Thomas	Nor- 80
James	Mor- 58	Sarah		Row- 85	West	Joh-286
James	Prq-228	Siddy		Jon-306	William	Bun- 93

Woodard,Willm	Fra- 79	Woods,James		Ire-258	Woody,James	Wil-267
Willm	Fra- 93	James		Cas- 74	Jas	Ora-128
Woodas,Littleberry	Cum-256	James		Row- 71	Jas Jun	Ora-129
Woodbon,Arthur	Glf-179	Jas		Mec- 47	Jno	Ora-128
Wooddy,Namon	Sur-193	Jno		Ora-127	John	Ora-115
Woode,William	Grn-127	Jno	Shff	Ora-128	Jonathan	Wil-257
Woodel,C	Col- 18	John		Cas- 74	Ro	Ora-113
J	Col- 17	John		Sto-138	Ro	Ora-129
Jaimiah	Mon- 26	John		Lnc-342	Ro Senr	Ora-129
Woodey,T	Ash- 10	John		Grn-142	Robert	Bur-117
T	Ash- 10	Jonathan		Hay-201	Saml	Ora-128
T	Ash- 12	Jos		Ora-147	Saml	Ora-143
Woodfin,John	Bun- 89	Joseph		Ora-166	Tarleton	Hay-201
Thomas	Bun- 75	Joshua		Row- 71	Wiat	Bun- 76
Woodfur,Nicholas	Bun- 83	Micael		Grn-146	William	Wil-267
Woodhous,John	Glf-156	P		Mon- 39	Wm	Ora-114
Robt	Glf-155	Polly		Lnc-328	Woodzelyt,J	Glf-179
Thos	Glf-155	R		Ash- 9	Wooff,Elkaner	Sur-180
William	Cur- 87	Richard		Grn-142	Woolard,James	Edg- 51
Woodhouse,Linley	Cur- 85	Richd		Ora-116	Simeon	Edg- 51
Linley	Cur- 85	Robert		Ire-258	Woolever,John	Row- 77
Woodlen,David	Glf-153	Sam		Ora-157	Woolf,Daniel	Sto- 99
Woodley,John	Wsh-224	Sam		Ora-123	Frederick	Sto-120
Margt	Bft- 38	Saml		Ora-115	Lewis	Sto- 98
Samuel	Tyr-205	Sampson		Ora-169	Woolfolk,Joseph	Wil-259
Stephen	Tyr-212	Samuel		Cas- 74	Ritter	Sto-108
Woodlief,Peter	Nor- 81	Sarah		Lnc-342	Ritter	Sto-144
Woddliff,John	Fra- 92	Thomas		Ora-167	Woollard,Simon	Mar- 9
Littleberry	Fra- 91	Truth		Row- 71	Woollen,Edward	Roc- 10
Woodly,Ephraim	Per-228	William		Cas- 74	Isaac	Roc- 30
John	Per-228	William Jr		Row- 82	Leven	Roc- 29
Thos	Per-228	William Jr		Row- 70	Woollf,Lewis	Sto-129
William	Pas-208	William Sr		Row- 70	Woolling,Joshua	Roc- 11
Woodring,Daniel	Lnc-348	Wm		Mon- 39	Woolly (sic)	Mon- 51
Woodrough,James	Hal-122	Wm		Ora-149	Elisabeth	Mon- 25
Wilson	Mon- 40	Wm (WM)		Ora-118	James	Mon- 25
Woodruff,A	Ash- 13	Wm		Ora-113	Woolridge,Lydia	Cur- 91
Cornelius	Sur-174	Woodsedy,S		Bru-230	Wooten,Abner	Wil-263
Gedion	Sur-174	Woodside,Archabald	Row- 71	Absalom	Edg- 52
Moses	Sur-194	Jean		Cab-138	Amos	Edg- 52
Woodruffe,Richard	Nor- 81	Woodsides,Jane		Ire-248	Caleb	Len-317
W	Glf-162	John		Ire-262	Counsel	Pit-237
Wm	Nsh- 74	William		Ire-263	Edward	Hal-122
Francis	Nor- 81	Woodson,David		Row- 77	Fanny	Nor- 81
John	Nor- 81	David Senr		Row- 89	Henry	Edg- 69
Mary	Nor- 81	Woodward,Asa		Edg- 48	Icey	Wil-263
Woods,Widow	Lnc-338	Benj		Cho-227	James	Edg- 69
Abraham	Row- 71	Demsy		Ire-252	Jno	Len-319
Barton	Per-146	Elisha		Edg- 48	Jno	Len-313
Benj	Grn-138	Jethro		Cho-231	John	Grn-128
Charles Jr	Row- 82	John		Ire-258	Jonathan	Ire-268
Charles Sr	Row- 89	Jordan		Ans- 22	Josiah	Pit-252
Chas	Ora-176	P		Cam-159	Lucy	Len-319
David	Ora-115	Patty		Ran-184	Robert	Len-318
Ellen	Ora-169	Richd		Cho-231	S	Col- 20
Ezekael	Grn-142	Samuel		Roc- 15	Stephen	Edg- 68
H	Ora-146	Susan		Cho-231	T B	Bla- 3
Hugh	Ora-157	Woody,David		Per-134	William	Hal-122
Isaac	Ora-128	Hugh		Cha-212	William	War-182

-352-

Name	Ref	Name	Ref	Name	Ref	Name	Ref
Wooten,William	Edg- 51	Worley,Henry	Sto-113	Worthington,Jacob	Ran-185		
Wooters,Markland	Len-314	Jno	Ans- 7	Jacob	Ran-185		
Wooton,Aaron	Sur-195	Loftus	Dup- 29	Worthum,Benj	Grn-137		
George	Sur-170	N	Col- 18	James	Grn-141		
George Jr	Sur-171	Reddick	Dup- 29	Worthy,John	Mor- 58		
Isaac	Sur-171	Robert	Nsh- 82	Wortman,Daniel	Rth-139		
James	Sam-161	Rosser	Joh-280	Michael	Rth-139		
Jere	Sur-184	Sally	Grn-130	William	Rth-141		
Peter	Way-241	Stephen	Sur-186	William	Sto-148		
Thomas	Sur-165	Thomas	Brt- 43	Wosters,Lewis	Gat-116		
Thos	Sam-162	William	Brt- 47	Wray,Andrew	Roc- 29		
Thos	Sam-161	William	Joh-281	Pleasant	Roc- 32		
William	Way-242	William Sr	Joh-280	Robert	Roc- 29		
William	Pit-263	Worman,Meriam	Ons-102	Skipwith	Roc- 6		
Wootten,Nathan	Nor- 80	Wornum,John	Nor- 81	William	Roc- 32		
Word,Benjn	Ran-185	Joseph	Nor- 81	Wraye,Parham	Roc- 18		
Camiel	Cas- 74	Samuel	Nor- 81	Wren,Allan	War-167		
Francis	Nsh- 76	Worrel,Amos	Hal-122	Benjamin	Per-134		
Henry	Gat-108	Charles	Hal-123	Elias	Fra- 82		
John	Nsh- 76	Thos	Grn-141	Eliz	Ons-100		
Mark	Ons-102	Worrell,D	Col- 21	Joel	Row- 51		
Mary	Glf-155	Isaiah	Way-253	Joel	War-174		
Nathan	Gat-107	James	Way-252	Joseph	War-174		
Robin	Gat-111	Jesse	Way-252	Samuel	War-181		
Simon	Ons-102	John	Way-252	Sherick	Rth-138		
Thomas	Per-134	John	Way-232	Wricks,M	Glf-175		
Thomas A	Sur-164	Josiah	Edg- 61	Wright,A	Cam-156		
Willis	Nsh- 81	Levy	Edg- 66	A	Cam-153		
Worden,Elijah	Sur-186	Needham	Way-151	Aaron	Sur-180		
Polly	Sur-186	Richd	Way-253	Absolom	Mon- 26		
Wordin,Michael	Sur-171	William	Way-252	Alexr	Glf-188		
Wordle,Luke	Rch-205	Worren,John	Nsh- 76	Anderson	War-167		
Matthew Senr	Rch-205	Worsham,Aplin	Row- 78	Angus	Cha-213		
William	Rch-205	Berrymore	Cas- 73	Ann	Hyd-222		
William Junr	Rch-205	Elizabeth	Roc- 15	Anna	Sur-195		
Work,Alexr	Mec- 53	Susa	Cas- 73	B	Cam-163		
H	Glf-160	Worsley,Sampson	Pit-244	B	Cam-156		
Jas	Glf-160	Tho	Bft- 28	B	Cam-155		
John	Glf-159	William	Edg- 71	B	Glf-164		
Worke,Robert	Ire-257	Worsly,Wm	Bft- 38	C	Mon- 28		
Workman,Danl	Bur-105	Worth,Charles	Sur-196	C	Cam-156		
Henry	Row- 83	David	Glf-180	C	Cam-156		
Henry	Rth-139	J	Glf-176	Caleb	Cas- 73		
Jno	Ora-127	Jas	Glf-157	Cecilla	Wil-279		
John	Cab-139	Mary	Glf-186	Charles	Roc- 11		
P	Ash- 12	Silas	Sto-144	David	Dup- 5		
Richd	Ora-136	Thomas	Ran-182	David	Hyd-221		
Tho	Cha-216	Wm	Glf-165	Duncan	Cum-253		
Thomas	Row- 83	Wm	Glf-158	E	Cam-156		
William	Row- 83	Z	Glf-176	Edwd	Mon- 28		
Worldly,Jacob	Rth-140	Wortham,E	Ora-168	Elijah	Roc- 3		
Joseph	Bun- 75	Edward	War-170	Elizabeth	Ans- 31		
Nathan	Bun- 75	George	War-171	Ezekl	Cab-137		
Pleasant	Rth-138	John	War-174	Fenny	Mec- 53		
Silas	Rth-142	John	War-175	Fielding	Roc- 14		
Silas	Rth-144	John Senr	War-174	Fielding	Roc- 11		
William	Rth-142	Robert	Roc- 12	Francis	Roc- 10		
Worley,E	Col- 18	Thomas	Roc- 8	Gilbert	Ran-184		
Henry	Sto-155	Worthington,Ephraim	Ran-184	Francis	Per-139		

Wright,George	Rch-202	Wright,Richardson	Ran-184	Wright,William	Mar- 16
George	Ran-183	Robert	War-179	Wyatte,Jno	Mec- 33
Gideon	Grn-128	S	Cam-156	Silvester	Mec- 34
Griffin	Fra- 88	Saml B	Mec- 51	Wycoff,Isaac	Lnc-353
H	Cam-160	Samuel	Rth-141	Nicholas	Lnc-353
Isaac	Bla- 3	Solomon	Bur-114	Wyett,Richard	Rch-199
Isaac	Ran-183	T	Cam-156	Wyley,William	Bun- 87
Isaac	Cas- 73	Thomas	Roc- 9	Wylie,Jas	Mec- 34
J	Cam-157	Thomas	Sur-165	Jno	Mec- 25
J Jnr	Cam-160	Thomas	Dup- 4	Jno	Mec- 38
J Snr	Cam-160	Thomas	Glf-158	Robt	Mec- 38
Jacob	Cas- 74	W	Cam-156	Robt	Mec- 41
James	Hal-121	W	Cam-159	Wyndham,Isaac	Bla- 6
James	Roc- 5	William	Bur-115	Wynn,Benjn	Prq-228
James	Lnc-330	William	Sur-165	George	Brt- 61
James	Roc- 9	William	Rch-204	John	Hrt-209
James	Roc- 23	William	Roc- 6	Matthias	Hrt-207
James	Hyd-227	William	Roc- 29	Thos	Mon- 39
James	War-176	William	Roc- 33	Wynne,Ann Sr	Tyr-212
James	Cha-191	William	Prq-229	Jeremh	Tyr-208
James	Nor- 80	William	Mor- 69	Jesse	Wsh-225
James	Dup- 5	William	Nor- 81	John	Tyr-210
Jas	Ans- 22	William	Dup- 5	Robert	Tyr-210
Jas	Glf-181	William	War-183	Wynns,Charles	Fra- 77
Jeptha	Fra- 81	Wm	Hyd-221	David	Mar- 11
Jesse	War-176	Wm	Cab-144	John	Mar- 7
Jo	Lnc-364	Wm	Mor- 69	John	Bft- 50
John	Cum-252	Wm Jr	Nsh- 75	Daniel	Brt- 52
John	Hal-123	Wm Jr	Nsh- 75	Robert H	Fra- 82
John	Cha-211	Willis Jr	Glf-180	Thos	Hrt-216
John	Cha-209	Wrightell,John	Ora-139	Watkin Wm	Mar- 14
John	Sam-164	Wrightsell,Jno	Ora-172	William	Hrt-216
John J	Roc- 33	Wrightsman,Christen	Ran-186	Wyse,James	Jon-306
Johnson	Roc- 11	David	Ran-184	John	Jon-306
Jos	Mon- 27	Jno	Ora-135		
Joseph	Hal-122	Jno	Ora-129	Yales,Elizabeth	Sto- 94
Jourdin	Grn-139	P	Ora-152	Yallolay,Charlton	Nor- 81
Joshua	Ran-184	Wrink,Martin	Glf-183	Yalloley,Edward	Mar-445
Joshua	Mon- 27	Wristry,Ben	Cha-201	Yance,George	Row- 69
Kenan	Sam-164	Write,Polly	Joh-276	Yancey,Ann	Cas- 75
Kenan	Sam-156	Wruston,Thomas	Roc- 26	Bartlett	Cas- 75
L	Cam-160	Wry,John	Rch-209	George G	Grn-125
L	Cam-156	Wumble,Nancy	Cha-201	Henry	Grn-125
Lecky	Ran-184	Wyas,Selvey	Jon-305	Henry	Grn-125
Linder	Cha-211	Wyatt,Cornely	Row- 83	James	Cas- 75
M	Cam-155	Elisa	Ora-124	Jickonias	Grn-125
M	Cam-152	Esaw	Mar- 16	Joel	Grn-125
M P	Cam-157	Ezekiel	Mar-445	Lewis Sr	Grn-125
Martin	Roc- 29	Fred	Ora-124	Mary	Grn-125
Mary	Hyd-221	James	Prq-228	Oning	Grn-134
Mathias	Sto-137	John	Bun- 73	Sterling	Cum-239
N	Col- 19	John	Row- 66	Thomas	Grn-125
Nulon	Roc- 2	Jos	Ora-124	Thomas Sr	Grn-125
O	Cam-152	Parthena	Prq-228	Yancy,John	Ons- 99
P	Cam-157	Simmons	Mar- 9	Lea James	Per-147
Phineas	Roc- 8	Sollomon	Mar- 9	Strawbridge	Bur-115
Polley	Cas- 74	S̶o̶l̶o̶m̶o̶n̶	Mar- 10	Yandle,Alexr B	Mec- 50
Rebecca	Dup- 4	William	Prq-229	Jas	Mec- 50
Reuben	Roc- 14	William	Bun- 90	Saml	Mec- 50

Yandle,Saml	Mec- 30	Yates,Elizabeth	Sto-122	Yelvington,Shadrack	Joh-283
Saml Jnr	Mec- 30	George	Cas- 75	Yeoman,John	Cab-142
Wm	Mec- 41	Henry	Rch-195	Yeomans,Ann	Cho-222
Wm	Mec- 50	Hugh	Wil-281	Yerbery,Emond	Mec- 42
Wm	Mec- 30	Isaac	Rch-195	Shem	Mec- 42
Wm	Mec- 50	James	Jon-306	Yerborugh,Reubeon	Mec- 42
Yants,Peter	Row- 54	James	Rch-194	Yerby,Jas	Mec- 43
Rudolph	Row- 53	James	Ran-186	Wm	Mec- 43
William	Row- 53	John	Wil-281	Yergain,Mark	Ora-142
William	Row- 53	John	Rch-207	Yielding,Richard	Rth-145
Yarberry,Matthew	Rch-202	John	Wil-280	Yoder,Adam	Lnc-369
Yarborough,Abner	Cha-200	John B Junr	Jon-306	David	Lnc-329
Eli	Cha-200	John B Senr	Jon-306	Jacob	Lnc-368
Elisha B	Mor- 57	Joshua	Car-185	John	Lnc-337
Isaac	Cha-195	L	Col- 18	Yoemans,Joseph	Car-179
Jeremiah	Cha-192	Peter	Ran-186	Yokeley,M	Ora-146
John	Hal-124	Richard	Wil-283	W	Ora-152
Joel	War-174	Sarah	Cha-201	Yokely,Hugh	Row- 79
Joseph	Cum-253	Tho	Bft- 30	John	Row- 80
Lewis	Lnc-342	Thos	Mon- 19	Wm	Ran-187
Martha	Hal-124	W	Ash- 8	Yokley,John	Row- 84
Nathan	Cha-200	William	Jon-306	Yoll---,Thomas	Dup- 19
Peterson	Cha-213	William	Wil-280	Yong,J	Col- 20
Richard	Hal-124	Wm	Mon- 19	Yopp,Jeremiah	Ons- 97
Shedrick	Mec- 43	Wm	Cha-200	York,Aaron	Roc- 3
Wiatt	Lnc-335	Wm Jnr	Mon- 19	Charlotte	Ran-186
Wm Senr	Per-134	Yaunce,Philip	Row- 53	Crabtree	Ran-186
Yarbro,Micajah Jr	Fra- 85	Rudolph	Row- 43	Edward	Way-235
Micajah Senr	Fra- 85	Yeargan,Jarrett	Ora-170	Edward	Nsh- 83
Yarbrogh,John	Per-147	Thomas	Ran-186	Eli	Ran-186
Yarbrough,Archbd	Fra- 94	Yeargin,Ben	Ora-130	Eli	Ran-186
Charles	Fra-100	Henry	Ran-186	Henry	Wil-271
Charles	Mon- 27	Yearly,John	Rth-145	Isaiah	Roc- 18
David	Ora-111	Yearnist,Danl	Row- 66	Jabaz	Mor- 57
Henry	Fra- 92	Yearwood,Ephraim	Rth-145	James	Sur-173
Henry	Row- 37	Yeasley,Charles	Cas- 75	Jane	Nsh-643
J	Mon- 35	Yeates,Bennet	Ons-103	Jeremiah	Ran-186
Jacob	Row- 85	Burton	Ons-100	Jerremiah	Bun- 86
James	Fra- 77	Edward	Brt- 46	Jesse	Ran-186
James Senr	Fra- 95	Izma	Brt- 44	John	Rth-145
John	Mon- 30	James	Brt- 46	John	Sur-171
Jonathan	Ans- 22	James	Ons-104	John	Nsh- 84
M	Mon- 35	Jesse	Brt- 47	John	Ran-186
Mrs Milly	Fra- 94	Thomas	Ons-108	Jonathan	Sur-173
Peter	Cha-211	Wm	Brt- 46	Levi	Roc- 4
Samuel	Per-147	Yeats,Jesse	Hrt-212	Mark	Sur-173
Thomas	Fra- 92	Joseph	Cab-139	Nancy	Ran-186
Thomas	Row- 85	Yelton,James	Ire-242	Nathl	Ran-186
Wm Junr	Per-146	James	Ire-242	Saml	Ran-186
Yarrell,Matthew	Mar-445	John	Rth-145	Shubel	Ran-186
Thomas	Mar- 9	Yelventon,Elizabeth	Way-241	Thomas	Grn-128
William	Mar- 7	Elizabeth	Way-241	Thos Senr	Grn-130
Yates,Alexr	Cha-190	Etheldred	Way-241	Tobas	Ran-186
Betsy	Car-180	Hardy	Way-241	William	Rth-145
Charles	Car-185	Jaceath	Way-241	William	Ran-186
Clifford	Sto-141	James	Way-241	Yorke,Abner	Ire-270
Clifford	Sto-106	Yelvington,Asa	Joh-284	Yost,John	Row- 69
Daniel	Jon-306	Levi	Joh-283	Philip	Cab-138

Name	Ref	Name	Ref	Name	Ref
Yostin, Phillip	Cab-141	Young, John	Bun- 97	Younger, Jos	Ora-122
Yother, Danl	Lnc-369	John	Hal-124	Joseph	Wil-263
Elias	Lnc-369	John	Ora-111	Rebecka	Cha-202
Younce, F	Ash- 4	Joseph	Bur-116	Thos	Cha-190
J	Ash- 10	Joseph	Fra- 97	Yount, Ann	Lnc-369
Young, -----	Sto- 94	Joseph	Fra- 80	Peter	Hay-201
-----	Hal-124	Joseph	Sto-141	Susannah	Hay-201
Mrs	Cum-235	Joseph	Cab-137	Yours, Martha	Roc- 5
Alexander	Sam-152	Joseph	Hay-201	Yow, Andrew	Mor- 65
Alexr	Bur-118	Joseph	Roc- 29	Christopher	Mon- 46
Ann	Row- 74	Joseph	Bun- 98	Christopher	Mor- 59
Banister	Fra- 99	Joshua	Sto-106	Christopher	Mon- 48
Barney	Row- 52	Joshua	Wsh-220	Henry	Mor- 59
Benjamin	Sto-140	Joshua	Bur-116	John	Mor- 59
Benjamin	Ire-241	Martha	Roc- 4	Yunger, Henry	Ora-163
Christopher	Sto-151	Mary	Wsh-223		
Christopher	Sto-109	Mary	Roc- 19	Zachary, John	Sur-175
Daniel	Brt- 43	Mary	Roc- 21	Oliver	Pas-209
David	Bla- 7	Mary	Hal-124	William	Sur-175
Demetrius	Fra- 97	Molly	Fra- 97	William Jr	Sur-175
Dobbs	Sam-156	Moses	Bur-114	Zackary, John	Cas- 75
Elam	Len-322	Phillip	Lnc-361	Zigler, Abraham	Sto-137
Elick	Sam-159	Richd H	Hyd-228	Benjn	Sto-141
Elijah	Sto-123	Robert col	Fra-100	Benjamin	Sto-106
Elijah	Joh-275	Robert	Fra- 97	Christopher	Sto-110
Eliz	Bft- 37	Robert	Rth-145	Christopher	Sto-149
Elizabeth	Grn-121	Robert	Ire-239	James	Sto-141
Elizabeth	Ire-239	S	Len-322	James	Sto-106
Ellison	Roc- 6	Saml	Bft- 36	Leonard	Sto-121
Francis	Hal-124	Samuel	Fra- 91	Zimmerman, Chn	Row- 53
Francis	Ire-267	Samuel	Fra- 84	Joseph	Sto-127
Frederick	Row- 87	Samuel	Rth-145	Reuben	Sto-106
George	Sto-105	Samuel	Rth-145	Reubin	Sto-141
George	Sto-140	Samuel	Sto-140	Zliger, Leonard	Sto- 92
Giffin	Rth-145	Samuel	Roc- 29		
H	Bru-230	Samuel Esq	Rth-145		
Henry	Ran-186	Stephen	Lnc-330		
Isbel	Roc- 27	Stephen	Fra- 97		
Jacob	Roc- 19	Thomas	Bur-124		
Jacob	Row- 80	Thomas	Sto-123		
James	Dup- 21	Thomas	Sto- 94		
James	Bur-118	Thomas	Bla- 7		
James	Fra- 97	Thomas	Ire-269		
James	Rth-145	Thomas	Ire-266		
James	Rth-145	Thomas B	Hal-124		
James	Cab-138	Turner	Hal-124		
James	Sto-123	William	Sto-124		
James	Fra- 90	William	Row- 75		
James	Fra- 84	William	Roc- 33		
James	Bun- 88	William	Bun- 98		
Jas	Mec- 39	William	Bun- 84		
John	Ire-267	William	Sto- 95		
John	Grn-125	William	Bun- 80		
John	Bur-110	Wm	Cab-137		
John	Fra- 91	Wm Senr	Cab-136		
John	Brt- 56	Willis	Hal-124		
John	Lnc-337	Youngblood, Bud	Joh-290		
John	Row- 75	Wm	Lnc-336		
John	Roc- 23	Younger, Ellen	Bft- 23		

www.ingramcontent.com/pod-product-compliance
Lightning Source LLC
Chambersburg PA
CBHW021134230426
43667CB00005B/109